HISTORY

OF THE

IRISH BRIGADES

IN THE

SERVICE OF FRANCE.

JUSTIN MAC CARTHY,

(LORD MOUNTCASHEL.)

HISTORY OF THE IRISH BRIGADES IN THE SERVICE OF FRANCE

FROM THE REVOLUTION IN GREAT BRITAIN AND IRELAND UNDER JAMES II, TO THE REVOLUTION IN FRANCE UNDER LOUIS XVI

BY

JOHN CORNELIUS O'CALLAGHAN

The Naval & Military Press Ltd

published in association with

FIREPOWER
The Royal Artillery Museum
Woolwich

Published by
The Naval & Military Press Ltd
Unit 10 Ridgewood Industrial Park,
Uckfield, East Sussex,
TN22 5QE England
Tel: +44 (0) 1825 749494
Fax: +44 (0) 1825 765701
www.naval-military-press.com

in association with

FIREPOWER
The Royal Artillery Museum, Woolwich
www.firepower.org.uk

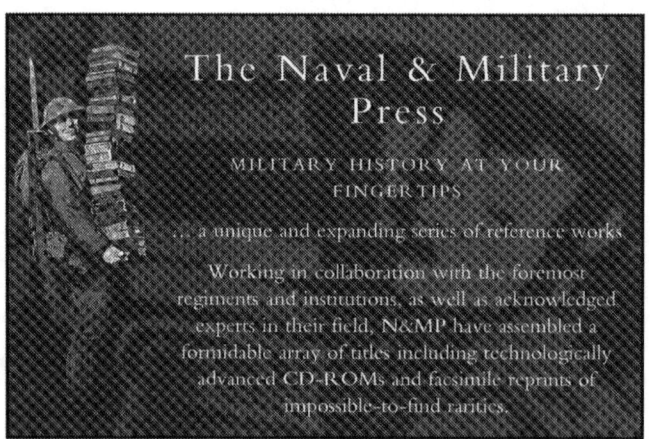

In reprinting in facsimile from the original, any imperfections are inevitably reproduced and the quality may fall short of modern type and cartographic standards.

PUBLISHERS' NOTE.

The Publishers consider it requisite to observe, that the earlier sheets of this important work are chiefly and *necessarily* occupied by what may be termed the Army-List portion of it; or accounts of the several Jacobite regiments, with corresponding notices of their successive commanding officers, of the most distinguished families of Ireland, engaged at first in the War of the Revolution there, and subsequently in the campaigns on the Continent. Such preliminary details, though as essential for an honest or correct treatment, as for a proper comprehension, of the subject, and very attractive for many connected with the families thus noticed, may *not* be so agreeable to the taste of the general reader. But *he* will be amply compensated, for the intervention of such introductory particulars, by the remaining narrative, respecting hostile dynasties and conflicting nations for a century, extending from Book III. to Book X. *There* he will find the

> "Battles, blood, and rage,
> Which princes and their people did engage;
> * * * * *
> A larger scene of action is display'd;
> And, rising hence, a greater work is weigh'd."
>
> Dryden's Virgil, Æneis, vii., 60–67.

Nor will those sheets, containing the indispensable regimental and family preliminaries referred to, be without interest, on several points, for the public at large. The campaign of Newtownbutler, for example, will be read by every one; and the author's clear, broad-minded, and liberal account of the great triumph of the men of Enniskillen will be duly appreciated by all parties.

To compress into ciphers, rather than spread into words, whatever the former appeared more specially designed to express, has been adhered to by the author as a general rule; and so, it may be thought, to an *extreme* extent, as in preferring, for example, to write even 1 or 2, rather in figures, than in letters. But this, even if objected to, will not, it is hoped, be reckoned anything beyond an excusable peculiarity by those, who judge a book in the fair or liberal spirit of the poet's remark, that

> "He, who expects a perfect work to see,
> Expects what never was, and ne'er will be."

PREFACE.

AMONG the deficiencies of information connected with the history of Ireland, none, perhaps, has been more regretted, than the absence of a satisfactory narrative of the services of the great numbers of Irish, who devoted themselves to a military life abroad; at first, as belonging to the army of James II., and, afterwards, on account of the many obstacles to employment at home, created by the hostile sectarian and commercial legislation that followed the Treaty of Limerick. During the century from the fall of the Stuart dynasty in these islands to the 1st Revolution in France, the Irish exile was to be found, in the various armies of the Continent, from Russia to Spain. But, as a "restoration of the Stuarts" was, for a long period, the only occurrence to which the oppressed majority of the Irish nation could look for a deliverance from the penal *régime* of the Revolution, and as the French cabinet, from the hostilities in which it was so much involved with England, had a greater interest, than other governments, to effect such a "restoration," or keep up an expectation of its being effected, there were far more Irish in the service of France, than of any other Continental power. The existence, in the French service, of a force so considerable in number, so distinguished in reputation, and so attached to the Stuart family, as the Irish Brigades, naturally gave an importance to the cause of that family, which it would not otherwise have possessed, either in these islands, or upon the Continent. An account of those Brigades consequently cannot be without *much* interest to a British reader, as associated with the claims of opposite dynasties to the government of *his* country. Indeed, without a due comprehension of the influence of the Irish element in the affairs of the ejected Royal Family, the history of Jacobitism, and, so far, that of Great Britain itself, *must* remain imperfect. To the feelings of an Irishman, (in the strict sense of the term,) an account of those gallant exiles in the service of France is a subject of higher and more peculiar interest, as constituting, for a century, (and too sad a century!) the bright, as contrasted with the dark side of the national story; Ormuzd abroad, to compensate for Ahriman at home. A general reader, too, cannot but be attracted by a series of military achievements from France, through Flanders, Italy, Germany, the Peninsula, besides Great Britain in

1745-6, to Sweden, Poland, the Crimea, and the East Indies in the Old World, and thence to the West India Islands and North America in the New. "If you would read truly great things," said a Spartan to Augustus Cæsar, "read the 7th book of Thucydides." And the spirit of the Spartan's observation to the Roman Emperor, with reference to the acts related by Thucydides, will be found fully applicable to others recorded in *this* work, with no inferiority to the Athenian in *one* respect, or a love of truth equal to his.

The history here submitted to the public consists of 10 books.* The 1st book, after such a view of the Revolution and War from 1688 to 1691, in Great Britain and Ireland, as to explain the origin of the Irish Brigades in France, is devoted to regimental accounts of the 3 earliest established Irish corps there, or those of Mountcashel, O'Brien, and Dillon, under their original and subsequent Colonels; and to the Continental campaigns of those corps till the arrival in France of the remains of King James's army from Ireland, after the Treaty of Limerick. The 2nd book proceeds with similar details respecting the regiments then organized from that army, as well as other subsequently-formed national regiments; such details, like those respecting Mountcashel's Brigade, comprising biographies of the Colonels of each regiment, from its commencement to its extinction. The 3rd book, having accounted for the long-continued emigration of so many Irish, as soldiers, to France, by legislative as well as dynastic causes, describes the military services of the Brigades from 1692 to 1697, or the Peace of Ryswick; continuing its narrative to the decease of King James II. in 1701, and the acknowledgment of his son as James III. by those Irish corps, as his most zealous and valuable subjects abroad. The 4th book, opening with the War of the Spanish Succession, contains the interesting campaigns in Italy, Flanders, Germany, and the Peninsula, from 1701 to 1707. The 5th book commences in 1708 with James III.'s expedition from France for Scotland, in consequence of the Union; gives an account of that measure, as productive of subsequent struggles having relation to the Irish Brigade; in mentioning the capture of some officers of that corps attached to the expedition, alludes to the excitement occasioned by it in Ireland; and, having brought the War of the Spanish Succession and prolonged hostilities in Germany and Catalonia to a close, relates the Tory ministerial plans, with corresponding apprehensions among the Whigs, that James III., instead of George I., might be Queen Anne's successor. The 6th book, having contrasted George and James, in 1714, as rivals for royalty, notices the general aversion to, and the insurrections against, the former in Scotland and England,

* "All classical histories are in books. Gibbon says, that, if he came to give a complete revision and new edition of his work, he would call his chapters books."—*Walpoliana.*

joined in Scotland by James and some Irish officers from France; shows the consequent alarm of the Whig-Hanoverian "ascendancy" in Ireland, and hostility towards the Catholics there; narrates the chivalrous adventures of the gallant Irish Jacobite, Charles Wogan, especially in delivering, along with some of his countrymen of the Brigade, the Princess Sobieski, subsequent Queen of James III., from her Austro-Hanoverian captivity; gives an outline of the war against France and England by Spain, under the administration of Cardinal Alberoni, and of the very strong Jacobite feeling in Great Britain and Ireland, favoured by the Cardinal, through invasions and risings planned against George I., under the Duke of Ormonde, and the last Sarsfield, Lord Lucan; then, having described the precautionary government measures, and opposite public feeling in Ireland favourable to Spain, presents a general review of the remarkable military career and obnoxious Jacobitism of the Irish Brigades, from a pamphlet, published in 1728, upon the necessity of the British Government's demanding an abolition of those corps in France and Spain; and, after a sketch of the war from 1733 to 1735 between France and Germany, and notices of eminent deceased officers of the Brigade, proceeds to the War of the Austrian Succession, and consequent engagement at Dettingen, in 1743, between the English and French, before any declaration of hostilities by either; and concludes with preparations, as regards the Brigade, for *that* declaration, in 1744. The 7th book, beginning with the French expedition designed in 1744 to land Prince Charles Stuart in England, glances at the state of Ireland with respect to that undertaking, refers to the baffling of England and her Allies in Flanders that year by the Marshal de Saxe, and gives, in connexion with the addition of a regiment to the Irish Brigade, a memoir of the Colonel, Count Thomas Arthur Lally. In 1745, it describes the battle of Fontenoy with the important part taken there by the Irish Brigade, the fortunate results for France during the rest of the campaign, and the consequent hostile legislation to the Brigade in Ireland by the colonial and sectarian "ascendancy" there. The enterprise of Prince Charles Stuart to Scotland, with which so many Irish of the Brigade, or others, were associated, follows, from his landing till his return from England at the close of 1745; when, after a notice of the death, &c., at Avignon, that year, of the old Duke of Ormonde, as head of the Jacobite party, a sketch is given of the effects of the Prince's enterprise in Britain upon political feeling in Ireland. The 8th book contains the sequel of the Prince's career in Scotland in 1746, till his escape, after the battle of Culloden, to the Continent; and resumes the narrative of the successful contest of France against England and her Allies in Flanders, from 1746 to the Peace of Aix-la-Chapelle in 1748, and conclusion of the most flourishing period of the history of the Irish Brigade. The 9th book, referring to the decline, from 1748, of the

Brigade as a national force, and after several memoirs of distinguished Irish officers deceased, more especially Field Marshal Count Peter Lacy, shows the hostility, as war with France approached, of the local "ascendancy" in Ireland to the Catholics, and to recruiting for the Brigade; and from the appointment, after the declaration of war between France and England in 1756, of Lieutenant-General Count Lally to command for France in the East Indies, continues his history till his most unjust execution at Paris in 1766, &c.; next, inclusive of the extensive naval and military plans by France for the invasion of Ireland in 1759, details the services of the Brigade on the Continent till the Peace of 1763; and terminates with an instance of the liberal feeling arising about that period in England as to a relaxation of the Penal Code in Ireland, and the consequent attempts made by George III. and the English cabinet for that purpose, though frustrated by the unrelenting "ascendancy" of sectarian and agrarian oppressors there. The 10th book, having shown the generally high opinion of the Irish as soldiers on the Continent, with a corresponding regret in England at their legal exclusion from her service, notices the death, in 1765, of James III., at Rome, and the long-enduring loyalty towards the Stuarts in England, as well as among the Irish; after a reference to the Brigade in Corsica in 1768-9, and elsewhere, adverts to the growing quarrel between England and her North American colonies since 1763, and to partial experiments she had made since 1757, and with satisfactory results, to recruit from Catholics in Ireland, and to the growing indispensability of such recruits, for the approaching contest in America, occasioning those of their faith to be officially acknowledged as subjects through an Oath of Allegiance to that effect; next mentions the birth of Daniel O'Connell in 1775, from its occurrence amidst various family and local circumstances relating to the Brigade; then refers to the avowed necessity in Parliament for recruiting against America in Ireland, with the parliamentary admission of Irish Catholics to hold landed property subsequent to the surrender of General Burgoyne, and the consequent dissatisfaction of France at this legislation, as calculated to undermine *her* military interest in Ireland; and, after an account of the services of Walsh's, Berwick's, and Dillon's corps with the French in Africa, the West Indies, and North America, during the war against England from 1778 to 1783, and a survey of the several events tending to the dissolution of Irish corps in France, or the prosperity of Ireland after 1782, the virtual extinction of the Stuarts by the death of Prince Charles, in 1788, the ensuing Revolution of 1789 in France and its effects upon the Brigade in 1791, ends the work, with notices of the 2 last eminent officers of that force deceased on the Continent, or General O'Connell in 1833, and the Count de Nugent in 1859.

Such, exclusive of the numerous military events to be found under the years in which they occurred, is a *general* synopsis of the subject here treated of, at an expense of more than 25 years' research and labour; often, from the difficulties of obtaining information, and other causes, attended by a painful despair of the task undertaken being *ever* completed, in a manner at all worthy of a portion of history, so " blending the rays of modern days with glories of the past," or honourable in itself, and interesting in its antecedents.

In anticipation of any superficial criticism of this work as *too* Jacobite, it may be observed here, that the work is *so* Jacobite, as a history of Jacobites. The Irish Catholics were Jacobites, or haters of the Williamite Revolution; and could not feel otherwise towards it, as the representative to *them* of foreign military invasion, landed confiscation, and breach of treaty by Penal Laws, to degrade them religiously, and pauperize them collectively; to which were added festivals and monuments to gall the feelings of the fallen, contrary to even the old maxim of *Pagan* morality, that, though it was lawful to raise a trophy for success, it should be of perishable materials, and be unlawful to repair it, as tending to keep alive bitter recollections, or a desire of revenge. In noticing the sad condition of the older Irish, or "children of the soil," as Catholics, or Jacobites, after the success of the Revolution, Lord Macaulay observes—" To *them* every festival, instituted by the state, was a day of mourning, and every public trophy, set up by the state, was a memorial of shame. We" in England "have never known, and can but faintly conceive, the feelings of a nation, doomed to see constantly, in all public places, the monuments of its subjugation. Such monuments everywhere met the eye of the Irish Roman Catholics. In front of the Senate House of their country, they saw the statue of their conqueror. If they entered, they saw the walls tapestried with the defeats of their fathers." Elsewhere, moreover, they were insulted yearly by several armed public processions, to commemorate the same events, with Orange colours, tunes, &c., too frequently attended with insolence and outrage involving a destruction of property and life, yet perpetrated with perfect impunity! Even in England, which was the gainer, by the way, at the expense of both Scotland and Ireland, by *both* revolutions in opposition to the Crown, or that under Oliver Cromwell, as well as that under William of Orange, the latter revolution and its results, however "glorious," were long the sources of very extensive dissatisfaction. The great leading journal of England, the *Times*, alluding, July 12th, 1862, to the Revolution of 1688, and its consequences for half a century, remarks— "As for the earlier Princes of the House of Hanover, the nation never could be induced to entertain any cordial feeling towards them, and, indeed, we do not know why it should. Faction, instead of being extinguished by our glorious Revolution, became more rife, and more rampant, than ever. A system of Parliamentary corruption was organized, which might lead a political purist to regret the days of naked and unblushing tyranny. We had our panics, our assassination-plots, our rebellions, our vast military expenditure, our bitter feuds between High and Low Church. Whoever looks back upon that period might form very plausible reasons for believing, that England was ruined by her glorious Revolution." If this view could be taken of the "glorious Revolution" in England, which profited so much by it, *how* could that revolution be anything but detested in Ireland by the mass of the population, who, in addition to the oppressive laws directed, through the Revolution, against them, as regards religion and property, were pronounced, from the judicial bench, to exist, as Papists, merely by a connivance of the ruling powers; and were even not admitted, until considerably within the reign of George III., or 1774, to the privilege of taking an Oath of Allegiance as subjects! It was consequently not till *then* that the House of Hanover could claim allegiance from a people, legally incapacitated or excluded from making any pledge of the kind. Under such circumstances, the Irish Brigades were necessarily Jacobites, and have accordingly been written of by their historian *only* as Jacobites.* Happily, the Irishman can *now* serve, and has *long* been entitled to serve, as well as the Englishman, and the Scotchman, beneath the standard of their common Sovereign; so that, in *this* respect, there is as much reason for satisfaction with the present state of things, as for regret at the past.

In conclusion, the author, for favours connected with the execution of his task, has to express his specially grateful acknowledgments to the kindness of several friends, now *all*, alas, no more!

> "Can storied urn, or animated bust,
>   Back to its mansion call the fleeting breath?
> Can Honour's voice provoke the silent dust,
>   Or Flattery soothe the dull cold, ear of death?"—GRAY.

To the late Daniel O'Connell, he is indebted for getting him an admission to the State Paper Office, London, in 1841, when such a privilege was rare, compared with what it has *since* become; to his son, the late John

---

* Lord Macaulay, writing October 24th, 1850, to the author, expresses himself more favourably of the Irish, than of the English, Jacobites. "To a considerable extent," he says, "our views coincide. I admit that the Irish Jacobites were not, like the English Jacobites, the defenders of arbitrary power. The cause of James presented itself, no doubt, to the Roman Catholics of Munster, as the cause of civil and spiritual liberty. Nevertheless, I think, that the dearest interests of the human race were staked on the success of the English in that struggle; and that, though the victory of William produced much evil, far greater evil would have been produced by the victory of James." This work, however, is merely connected with the "*much evil*" *admitted* to have been "produced" by that "victory;" of which "evil," so great a portion was the existence, for so long a period, of Irish Brigades in the service of France, &c.

O'Connell, who had contemplated writing a History of the Irish Brigades in France, he is also obliged for some useful French MSS. on that subject, procured at Paris; to the late Sir William Betham, Ulster King at Arms, for an introduction to M. de la Ponce, and consequently obtaining from that gentleman the use of his extensive collections on Irish families and officers in France; to the late eminent Irish scholars, Dr. John O'Donovan and Professor Eugene O'Curry, for such particulars as were needed on the Celtic portion of his work; and, " though last, not least," to the late Rev. J. H. Todd, of Trinity College, (the great promoter and cultivator of his country's literature,) for access to various sources of information, in manuscript and print, indispensable for the biographical notices of the leading officers of the Irish Brigades. The author, too, is thankful for the facilities at all times afforded to his researches, in the valuable libraries of Trinity College, Royal Irish Academy, and Royal Dublin Society. He now has only to hope, that the result of his long labour and anxiety, abroad and at home, or at London and Paris, as well as in his native city, *may* prove to be something, that posterity will "*not* willingly let die."

J. C. O'C.

1, UPPER RUTLAND STREET, DUBLIN,
January 15*th*, 1869.

HISTORY OF THE IRISH BRIGADES

IN

THE SERVICE OF FRANCE.

BOOK I.

The History of the Irish Brigades in the Service of France dates its origin from the war between Great Britain and Ireland occasioned by the change of dynasty in those islands, which commenced with the British Revolution of 1688, and was not accomplished till the acquiescence of Ireland in the results of that Revolution, by the Treaty of Limerick in 1691. In Great Britain, it was but natural that such a change of dynasty should have occurred. At a period when theological differences of opinion had such a considerable influence on the politics of Europe in general, and of Great Britain and Ireland in particular, the reigning Sovereign of the 2 Protestant kingdoms of England and Scotland, James II., had deserted the Protestant for the Catholic faith, and, through the birth of a male heir, was likely to establish a Catholic dynasty over those 2 Protestant nations; who could hardly be expected to acknowledge a Catholic Monarch, but for the expectation, existing previous to that birth, of his being succeeded, in the course of a few years, by a race of Protestant Princes. In an age when the boundaries between the monarchical and the other branches of the constitution had not been determined with sufficient accuracy, that Monarch had also considered himself justified in exercising powers, which, whatever may have been their defensibility on the score of precedent, were *felt* to be incompatible with the state of intellectual and political advancement at which Great Britain had then arrived. Under such circumstances, the applications of the disaffected English and Scotch for assistance against King James were addressed to William, Prince of Orange, and Stadtholder of the Dutch republic, who, besides being the nephew of James, was married to that Monarch's eldest daughter, the Princess Mary, and was thus the next Protestant Prince interested in the succession to the sceptre of these islands. William, who, in consequence of the birth of a son to James in June, 1688, would, if a revolution did not occur, be debarred of that share in the royal succession to which he had long looked forward, and who, as a Dutch patriot, wished to add the resources of James's dominions to the great League of Augsburg, privately entered into, some time before, by the principal states of the Continent against the overgrown power of Louis XIV., was necessarily glad to avail himself of the invitations he received to invade England. He accordingly equipped such a fleet and army in Holland as he judged to be sufficient for the success of his enterprise, when supported by such a state of religious and political feeling in his favour as he knew to exist in Great

Britain, and landed without opposition, November 15th, 1688,* at Torbay, in Devonshire. James, though too long deceived respecting the real destination of the Dutch armament, by the treachery of his minister, Robert Spencer, Earl of Sunderland, had, nevertheless, assembled a force, that, if well affected towards him, would have been much more than sufficient to overpower the invaders. But, incapacitated from defending his crown by a defection so general as even to include his own daughter Anne, afterwards Queen Anne, and not altogether without reasons to be mindful of the fate of his father, King Charles I., it was soon judged requisite for him to send off his Queen and infant son privately to France. After having been turned out of his own palace at Whitehall, and for some time a prisoner under a Dutch guard, the King likewise considered it necessary for him to escape from England, and seek in France the protection of his cousin-german, Louis XIV. Early in the following year, 1689, the flight of James, notwithstanding his proposal, in writing, from France, to return, summon a Parliament, and endeavour, in a regular way, to adjust matters between himself and his subjects, was voted in England by a Convention, assembled under William's auspices, to have been an "abdication" of the Crown. The royal dignity, thus pronounced to have been *abdicated* by James, against his public protest to the contrary, was conferred upon the Prince and Princess of Orange, with the executive power to be vested in the Prince. The Crown of Scotland, still a separate one from the Crown of England, was, in the spring of the same year, also transferred from James (as James VII.) to his son-in-law and daughter; so that, with the exception of a brave, though comparatively unimportant, opposition in favour of the deposed Monarch, maintained in a corner of Scotland amongst the Highlanders, the Dutch Prince became the *de facto* Sovereign of the 2 Protestant kingdoms of Great Britain.

But, while England and Scotland considered themselves justified in preferring William as *their* Sovereign to James, in Ireland, the great mass of the population, or those of Milesian, and Anglo-Norman, or Old English descent, thought that *they* were at least as well entitled to *retain* James for their Sovereign, as the English and Scotch had been to *reject* him. On strictly constitutional grounds, or, viewing the Monarchy, in the 3 kingdoms, not as elective, but hereditary, the Irish, in adhering to James, regarded themselves as *loyalists*, and looked upon the English and Scotch, for deposing him, as *rebels*. If, by a recognized axiom of British law, "the King can do *no* wrong"—anything deemed so being chargeable upon his Ministers, as evil counsellors, and to be visited with punishment, not of HIM, but of *them*, in order to deter others from acting similarly—ought not such a course of *ministerial* impeachment and chastisement have been adopted, with respect to whatever had been objectionable in the government of James, instead of expelling HIM from the throne?† to say nothing of his SON, the Prince of Wales,‡ who, as an

---

* The days of the month in this work are generally given according to the present or new style, in opposition to the old style, used by British writers at the time of the Revolution, and long after, or till 1752.

† "Whereas," observes Higgons, "the laws of England assert, that the King can do no wrong, and make his Ministers only accountable, in *this* case the King alone was punished, and the evil Counsellors rewarded."

‡ The unscrupulous and indecent sectarian fiction, as to James's alleged son not having been his actual son, was despised and discredited, as it *deserved* to be, by the Irish. See its confutation, at the end of Book III.

infant, had unquestionably done "*no* wrong!" If popular election, instead of hereditary right, were to decide the possession of the royal dignity, on *what* principle were the Irish, as a distinct nation, or with a distinct Parliament as well as the English and Scotch, to be precluded from electing James, when the English and Scotch claimed a right to elect William? If the English and the Scotch, as Protestants, objected to James for their King, as a Catholic, and adopted William, as a Protestant, the Irish, as Catholics, did not see *why* they should not prefer James for their King, as a Catholic, and reject William, as a Protestant. Finally, if, on account of the general faults of James's administration in Great Britain, the English and Scotch conferred the Sovereignty of their respective countries on William, as expecting to be better governed by him than they were, or could be, by his predecessor, the Irish, from a contrast of their improved political condition, under James's administration, with the previous oppression they had endured, under the "ascendancy" of the Cromwellian, Whig, or Revolution party of which William was the head, had every reason to anticipate, that *his* Sovereignty in Ireland would lead to a renewal, if not an increase, of the grievances they had so long and so recently felt; and were consequently so far justified in believing, that both the present and future hope of good government, for the Irish nation at large, would depend upon its support of James, and its rejection of William. James, during his short reign over the 3 kingdoms, or from February, 1685, to December, 1688, had laid the foundations for ruling Ireland in a manner more adapted to gain the affections, and improve the condition, of the nation at large, than any other British Sovereign had ever done. Indeed, a comparison of what James was able to do, with what his writings attest his intention of doing, for Ireland, shows his plans for its government to have been so much more suitable to the comprehensive views acted on in the 19th century, than the exclusive theories of his English and Anglo-Irish contemporaries, and the subsequent representatives of such exclusiveness, that the mass of the Irish nation, in his time, could have adopted no other course, consistent either with a sense of gratitude or self-interest, but that of espousing *his* cause, in opposition to the Revolution. The Catholic religion, previous to his reign, so persecuted or discountenanced in Ireland, met with that official protection and respect under his government, which the followers of every system of belief, forming the creed of a nation, consider it entitled to receive from the civil power. The Prelacy had access personally, or by letter, to the King, and had liberal pensions assigned them, from the Treasury of Ireland. Members of the Bar, of that religion, were placed in the highest judicial and other appointments, connected with their profession. Catholics were likewise elevated to the Privy Council of Ireland. The Corporations, of which the recently-planted Cromwellian oligarchy, and its partizans, would have made a mere sectarian monopoly, were so remodelled by the royal orders, that no member of the community, for whose benefit such institutions were originally intended, could be excluded from their privileges, by any mere theological test. The re-organization of the Army of Ireland, in which, under the same Cromwellian "ascendancy," during the preceding reign, there had been considerable jobbing or corruption, was committed to the political head, for many years, of the national religion, the celebrated Colonel Richard Talbot, who was elevated to the Peerage by the title of Earl of Tyrconnell, and likewise created a Lieutenant-General. Under his inspection, all Cromwellians, or the sons of Cromwellians, were dismissed, as persons, whose principles having occasioned the overthrow of the Monarchy, and brought King Charles I. to the block, were not to be trusted by his son, King James; and besides, as a class whom the King considered he had reason to suspect, of being tainted with the disaffection of Monmouth's and Argyle's late insurrections against himself, in England and Scotland. Such abuses, as those of men, physically inadequate to the service for which they were designed, having been enrolled among the privates, and even of certain Protestant Lords' servants having been provided for as officers, were exposed. Instead of the former, a superior or native Irish soldiery, remarkable for their stature, were introduced; instead of the latter, a more trustworthy and respectable class of officers, mostly drawn from the best old families in the country, that had suffered so much by the success of the Puritans in Great Britain and Ireland against the Crown. Notwithstanding the opposition to be expected in England, from the general hatred there of the Irish,* it was also the King's intention, from the year 1687, to at least considerably modify the injustice of the Acts of Settlement and Explanation; through which, after the restoration of Monarchy, in the person of his brother, King Charles II., several thousands of the Irish Catholic proprietary, of Milesian, Anglo-Norman, or Old English descent, who had fought for royalty, at home and abroad, against the Parliamentarian or Cromwellian rebels, were nevertheless ruined, by the transfer of their lands to those rebels. Previous, therefore, to the Revolution, these unjust Acts in Ireland were already, to use the words of a Williamite writer, "doomed in every coffee-house;" a sentence afterwards carried into effect, by their total repeal in 1689. In short, from the post of Viceroy of Ireland, conferred on the Earl of Tyrconnell, down to the lowest situation in the power of James to bestow, never were the Irish so favoured and promoted, in every capacity, by a British Sovereign, as they were by that Monarch. While, from the success of James's cause, they consequently had everything to *hope*, they were not less convinced, by their experience of the same spirit of national and religious hostility to them which afterwards violated the Treaty of Limerick, and enacted the Penal Code, that, from James's fall, they would also have everything to *fear*. These circumstances naturally rendered the Irish so unanimous in the King's favour, that he had more reason to rely for his "restoration" on *them*, than on all the rest of his subjects. Between the period of his escaping from England to France, in January, 1689, and that of his disembarking from Brest, at Kinsale, in March, the issuing of commissions by the Earl of Tyrconnell to the nobility and gentry of the island, for raising troops in the royal cause, was responded to, by no less than 100,000 men coming forward, to take arms in the King's defence. But this abundance of men, for the formation of an army in Ireland, was accompanied with a want of almost all the other means for equipping and maintaining a regular force. By the results of the long Parliamentarian or Cromwellian war from 1641 to 1653, Ireland, only about 35 years before the Prince of Orange's invasion of England, had been reduced to the most frightful state of misery and depopulation. By the transfer, after the Restoration, in 1660, of so much of the landed property of the older Irish or royalists to the Crom-

* The Irish, as Lord Macaulay correctly observes, were considered "foreigners" in England; "and of *all* foreigners," he adds, "they were *the most hated*."

wellians, and by other circumstances connected with that transfer, the Anglo-Protestant "ascendancy," thus established in Ireland, were rendered so superior in wealth—as well from the rent of land, and the emoluments of office, as from the profits of business—that when, on the prospect of a war in Ireland, in consequence of the Revolution in Great Britain, as many of the members of that "ascendancy" as could get away to England and Scotland removed there with their money and plate, Ireland was left almost entirely destitute of the circulating medium requisite for the payment of an army. Nor were the Irish loyalists less deficient in such other military necessaries as muskets, cannon, &c.; partly through the policy of the English government, that as few arms and as little ammunition as possible should be kept in Ireland; and partly owing to the unlucky circumstance, of some thousands of the best equipped portion of the Irish army, who were sent over to James in England previous to William's invasion, having been detained there by the latter, on the success of his enterprise; and thus lost to their country, when it stood in the greatest need of their assistance.

For the supply of so many discouraging wants, the Irish were therefore obliged to have recourse to their Sovereign's ally, Louis XIV. But, on account of the political and military situation of France with reference to its neighbours, the Irish were disappointed of anything like the assistance that was necessary to support the contest in which they engaged. From the commencement of Louis's reign, but particularly from his attack on the Dutch Republic, in 1672, that Monarch's general policy had been such, as to make the principal powers of the Continent finally consider him a common enemy; against whom it was necessary to combine, either for the purpose of avenging past injuries, or of averting future insults, and encroachments. With this view, under the pretext of making arrangements for a war upon the Turks, a great confederacy against France, called the League of Augsburg, was secretly entered upon there, by the representatives of several of those states, in 1686; and such was the general animosity of the Continental powers, of *all* religions, to Louis, that, from 1686 to 1688, the adhesions to this alliance continued to increase, till it embraced the Emperor of Germany, the Electors of Saxony, Bavaria, and Brandenburg, the Elector Palatine, the Circles of Suabia and Franconia, the Kings of Spain and Sweden, the Dutch Republic, the Duke of Savoy, and Pope Innocent XI. The political and military soul of this secret confederacy against the French Monarch was the Prince of Orange. As Stadtholder, or first magistrate of his native country, William was interested in the formation of such a League, on account of the injuries which Holland had suffered, and the dangers she had to apprehend, from the unscrupulous ambition and formidable power of France. On personal grounds, he could not forgive the sequestration of his Principality of Orange, in the south of France, and the insulting refusal of redress for that injury, by the French government. As a Protestant, he was naturally indignant at the Revocation of the Edict of Nantes, in 1685, and the violent persecution directed against the Protestants of France (including the inhabitants of his own Principality of Orange), for the extinction of Protestantism, in that kingdom.* Nor

---

* "The Revocation of the Edict of Nantz," says Mr. O'Conor, "was a proceeding even *more* oppressive than the Penal Code in Ireland. It suppressed all the privileges granted by Henry IV. and Louis XIII; inhibited the exercise of the Protestant religion; enjoined the banishment of all its Ministers within 15 days;

had the Prince and his countrymen, the Dutch, as members of a Protestant state, less cause to be alarmed, on the score of their religion; from the fact of those sweeping measures, for the destruction of the reformed faith in France, being accompanied, on the other side of the Channel, by the administrative changes of Louis's relative, friend, and brother-religionist, King James, to the weakening of the Protestant Established Church in England and Ireland; while James likewise deprived the League of Augsburg of its best expectation of success, the alliance of England, by signifying *his* determination to remain neuter, between the parties to that coalition, and the French Monarch. These circumstances, with the invitations William received from England to invade that country, and the necessity he himself was under, of effecting a revolution there to the prejudice of James and his son, or of resigning any hope of a share in the succession, at once suggested, and facilitated, the undertaking of such an enterprise; through the final triumph of which, the important object of adding England to the League of Augsburg being attained, France was exposed, everywhere but on the side of Switzerland, to hostilities by land or sea. While such an immense drain upon the resources of France was thus required for *her* defence against so many enemies, the Irish Jacobites could not be aided as they might otherwise have been, and they consequently found themselves abandoned, with comparatively little more than their own very inadequate means of defence, against the enormous superiority of every description of force directed against them by the Prince of Orange, as King of England and Scotland, Stadtholder of Holland, and Head of the League of Augsburg. The following particulars respecting the War of the Revolution in Ireland during the years 1689, 1690, and 1691, will give a sufficient idea *here* of the courage and perseverance, with which, under so many disadvantages, the Irish loyalists sustained the cause of James, for 3 campaigns, against the power of William. Consisting, at the most, of not above 1,200,000 men, women, and children—having to guard against *another* population in the country, able to furnish 25,000 hostile *Militia* or *Yeomanry*—with a national revenue, in its comparatively flourishing state, or from 1682 to 1685, amounting to only £266,209 a year, and which, after soon dwindling into a mere copper currency, finally left no resource for defence, in addition to the tardy and insufficient supplies from France, but that of bartering the butter, wool, tallow, and hides of the island, with the French merchants, for powder, ball, and arms—the Irish Jacobites had, in 1689, opposed to them, under the veteran Marshal Duke of Schonberg, a *regular* force of 30 regiments and 1 company of foot, 9 regiments and 3 troops of horse, and 4 regiments of dragoons, or 43 regiments, 1 company, and 3 troops of infantry and cavalry, that would make above 34,900 men and officers—in 1690, between what William himself and Marlborough brought over, 50 regi-

held out rewards for converts; and prohibited keeping schools, or bringing up children in any but the Catholic religion. Dragoons were sent into Languedoc, Dauphiné, and Provence, to enforce this decree," and "100,000 Protestants, the most industrious and peaceable subjects of the French Monarchy, fled from the sword of persecution, and brought with them to Germany, Holland, and England, their arts, manufactures, and resentments. In every field of battle in Europe, they displayed the same invincible valour against France, that was evinced by the Irish against England." But, in as much as the Huguenots were such a small minority of the nation in France, while the Catholics were the great majority of the nation in Ireland, was not the persecution of the latter the *less* defensible of the 2?

ments and 9 companies of foot, 21 regiments and 5 troops of horse, and 5 regiments of dragoons, or 76 regiments, 9 companies, and 5 troops of infantry and cavalry, that would make above 59,200 men and officers—and, in 1691, under Lieutenant-General, Baron de Ginkell, the Duke of Wirtemberg, Majors-General Ruvigny, Mac Kay, and Talmach, &c., 42 regiments and 1 company of foot, 20 regiments of horse, and 5 regiments of dragoons, or 67 regiments and 1 company of infantry and cavalry, that would make above 48,800 men and officers.* At length, amidst a desolated territory—blocked up by land and water in their last fortress of any consequence, Limerick—with a great portion of the town reduced to ruins, and a large breach made in the walls by nearly 90 pieces of artillery—and without any appearance of the relief expected from France—the Irish army found themselves obliged to enter into a negotiation, for the conclusion of hostilities. In this situation, they, by the Treaty of Limerick, obtained such terms for their countrymen who chose to remain at home, as, if not subsequently violated by the enactment of the Penal Code, would have saved Ireland from the innumerable evils produced by that Code for so long a period, and have rendered unnecessary the various efforts made for Catholic Emancipation, and other measures connected with it, down to the 19th century. Though offered by Baron de Ginkell, if they would lay down their arms and remain quietly at home, to have their properties restored, and the exercise of their religion guaranteed them as in the reign of Charles II., that army, rather than acknowledge William, whom *they* considered a "usurper," decided on following their exiled Sovereign abroad; and, in addition to the full military honours with which they were to be received on giving up Limerick, and the other places held by them in the Counties of Clare, Cork, and Kerry, they even stipulated, that not only they, but all of their countrymen, who might wish to follow their example, should have shipping, and every thing requisite for a free passage to France, for themselves, their horses, money, plate, equipages, moveables, or household goods, supplied at William's cost. Thus terminated this long-protracted, though, on the part of the Irish, very unequal, contest; in which, for their principles, they are stated to have forfeited 1,060,792 acres, and, by their resistance, to have occasioned an expense of above £18,000,000 sterling to their enemies.

It was in the spring of 1690, the 2nd year of the War of the Revolution in Ireland, that the formation of the force, styled "the Irish Brigade in the Service of France," was commenced, by the arrival there, of the first Irish regiments belonging to that corps. King James, who was then in Ireland, having repeatedly pressed upon the French government, the insufficiency of the means of that country for making a due resistance to the powerful resources of every description from

* In the statements respecting the numbers of the Williamite regular forces in Ireland in 1689, 1690, and 1691, derived from regimental *data* in Trinity College, Dublin, and the State Paper Office, and British Museum, London, as well as printed Williamite works, the complements of men and officers attached to the Williamite trains of artillery are *not* included, as I did not meet with due accounts on that point. It is certain, however, from the narratives on *both* sides in this war, that the Williamite superiority in artillery was *very* great. It is also to be borne in mind, that the Williamite regulars were powerfully aided by the colonial *Militia* or *Yeomanry*, referred to. On the diversity of *nations* in William's army, see, in Book III., the note under the petition of the Irish disbanded officers to Louis XIV., in 1698.

England, Scotland, Holland, Denmark, &c., with which he was to be attacked by the Prince of Orange, requested that a French force, and a supply of military necessaries, should be sent to Ireland. A body of Louis's troops, of the Regiments of Zurlauben, Merode, Famechon, Forest, La Marche, Tournaisis, and Courvassiez, consisting, according to the Marquis de Quincy, of above 6,000 *effective* men, were consequently ordered to sail for Ireland, with some of those supplies, which had been requested for the Irish. The passage of this land-force, under the Count de Lauzun, was to be secured by a squadron of 36 sail of the line, 4 fire-ships, and other vessels, commanded by the Marquis d'Amfreville, assisted by the Marquis de Nesmond, and the Chevalier de Flacour. The French fleet sailed from Brest, March 17th (St. Patrick's day) 1690; reached Cork and Kinsale by the 22nd and 23rd; against the 27th, landed the Count de Lauzun, and his men; and, early in April, had disembarked the military stores. From the difficult circumstances under which James and Louis were then placed, and the consequent arrangements between them,—James requiring the *prestige* and example of a corps of French soldiers in Ireland as *some* set-off against the numbers of Continental veterans in William's army, and Louis being so pressed near home by the League of Augsburg, that he required as many men from James, as might compensate, as far as possible, for the force forwarded to Ireland—the Irish had to send to France, on board the same fleet which had brought over Lauzun's contingent, the body of troops before referred to, as the origin of the Irish Brigades in the French service. After a delay of above 12 days on board by unfavourable weather, which prevented the French fleet setting sail for France till the 18th of April, and a similar interruption to their voyage between Ireland and France, the Irish reached Brest, and were landed there, early in May. Those troops, according to their 1st formation, or on their embarkation in Ireland and landing in France, consisted of 5 infantry regiments, whose Colonels were Lieutenant-General Justin Mac Carthy, Lord Viscount Mountcashel, the Honourable Colonel Daniel O'Brien, the Honourable Colonel Arthur Dillon, Colonel Richard Butler, and Colonel Robert Fielding. This organization was changed in France; the 5 regiments being formed into 3, under Lord Mountcashel, the Honourable Colonel Daniel O'Brien, and the Honourable Colonel Arthur Dillon. Each of the regiments contained 15 companies of 100 men, and its Colonel's company. Into the 3 Colonels' companies, besides Cadets, (of whom, in Mountcashel's, for instance, there were 20, at 10 pence each, a day, till 1714, and 16 Cadets, at the same pay, and till the same year, in Dillon's,) as many men as could be found were admitted; the Irish soldiers, on their landing in France, having been remarked, as "tous gens bien faits," or "all well-made men." According to the arrangement made for those regiments with the French government, by Lord Mountcashel, the officers and soldiers were to have strangers' or higher pay than that of France; the privates, by this agreement, getting a sol a day more than the French soldiery. The Colonels, in addition to their pay, were to have a sol in the livre, as well from the appointments of all officers, as from the funds for the general maintenance of their respective regiments; and Lord Mountcashel, besides the enjoyment of this privilege in his own regiment, had a sol in the livre, from the pay of the 2 other regiments; thereby securing a very beneficial establishment in France. These 3 Regiments of Mountcashel, O'Brien, and Dillon, named from his Lordship, "the Brigade of Mountcashel," each consisted of 2 battalions, and, according to Count Arthur Dillon, amounted altogether to 5371 officers and soldiers.

The Colonels of the 3 regiments of this Brigade were of some of the noblest families in Ireland. With respect to Justin Mac Carthy and Daniel O'Brien, this was more particularly the case. They represented in their persons the blood of the 2 old royal races of Desmond, or South Munster, and Thomond, or North Munster, descended from Heber, eldest son of Milidh, or Milesius; by which races, for 900 years previous to the Anglo-Norman invasion of Erin in the 12th century, Mumha, or Munster, is related to have been ruled; *each* race supreme in its own peculiar territory; and *both*, in turn, entitled to give an Arch-King, or Sovereign, to the entire province. From the will of their common ancestor, Olil-Olum, King of Munster, about the middle of the 3rd century,* this privilege was derived; that Prince partitioning his kingdom between his 2 sons, Eogan or Eugene More, and Cormac Cas; the former, the progenitor of the Mac Carthys, or the Eugenian Princes of Desmond, or South Munster; the latter the progenitor of the O'Briens, the Dalcassian Princes of Thomond, or North Munster; and the Sovereign, or King of *all* Munster, to be of the Eugenian and Dalcassian line, in alternate succession. If viewed with reference to primogeniture and the rights of seniority, the house of Mac Carthy should be accounted the 1st, according to a native authority, as being the leading branch of the eldest of the sons of Milesius, Heber, whose posterity, from the Milesian conquest of the island previous to the Christian era, are recorded to have given Kings to Munster, and several Monarchs to Ireland, until the supreme sceptre was fixed in the line of the younger of the sons of Milesius, Heremon, as represented by the descendants of Niall of the Nine Hostages, ancestor of the O'Neills, in the 5th century. Through the Anglo-Norman intrusion of the 12th century, the Mac Carthys, indeed, suffered much diminution of their territory by the "stranger," but especially by the ambition of the great feudal house of Desmond. Yet, during the middle ages, the heads of the old native regal tribe were Princes or Chiefs, who, though so much less powerful than their forefathers, could, when too far provoked, inflict severe blows in battle on the unscrupulous Geraldine; could hold the Sassenagh "settler" in various parts of the south under "black rent," or tribute;† and whose descendants finally survived, in the Peerage, the downfall, under Queen Elizabeth, of that proud Geraldine Earldom, the historian of which, regarding its ruin, in the light of a moral retribution for long injustice, bids his readers "ponder on all the cruel acts of rapacity and blood, committed against the Mac Carthys!" Of such ancestry, from royalty, chiefdom, or nobility, for so many centuries, was Justin Mac Carthy. He was the son of Donough Mac Carthy, Viscount Muskerry, and Earl of Clancarty, General of the Irish forces of Munster for Charles I. and Charles II. against the Parliamentarian or Crom-

* "He," as is observed, "must have been both a great and an able Prince, to have established the supremacy of his race upon such solid foundations, in times of such extreme convulsion." He was interred at the hill of Claire, near Duntryleague, County Limerick; where, adds Dr. O'Donovan, "a remarkable cromlech was raised over him, which *still* remains in good preservation."

† See the English admissions of the payments of such tributes during the 15th, and far into the 16th, century, in my Macariæ Excidium, Note 71.

wellian revolutionists. This nobleman, when resistance was no longer available at home, followed, with a large body of his countrymen, the fortunes of Charles II. to the Continent; and, surviving the Restoration, died in August, 1665, at London. He had, by the Lady Ellen Butler, eldest sister of James Butler, 1st Duke of Ormonde, 3 sons, Cormac or Charles, Callaghan, and Justin Mac Carthy. The eldest, Cormac, or Charles, Lord Muskerry, about 2 months previous to his father Donough's decease, or in June, 1665, fell in battle. He was slain on board the *Royal Charles*, by the same cannon-shot that killed the Honourable Richard Boyle, son of the Earl of Cork and Burlington, and Charles Berkely, Earl of Falmouth, next to James, Duke of York, (afterwards James II.) in the memorable sea-fight, where James, at the head of 98 ships of the line, and 4 fire-ships, against the Dutch Admiral, Opdam, and 113 ships of war, gained the most glorious victory that had ever been obtained by the English marine over the naval power of Holland. This Cormac, or Charles, Lord Muskerry, a particular favourite of James, and spoken of in his Memoirs as a brave and good officer of infantry, was only 31 at his death, universally regretted; and received a most honourable public funeral in Westminster Abbey, attended by the Archbishop of Canterbury, and the Lord Chancellor, with numbers of the nobility of the 3 kingdoms, &c. His Lordship having been married to Lady Margaret de Burgo, only daughter of the celebrated Ulick de Burgo, 5th Earl of Clanricarde, left 1 son, Charles-James, who died a minor. The titles and estates of Muskerry and Clancarty consequently devolving to the Honourable Callaghan Mac Carthy, he, who had betaken himself in France to an ecclesiastical life, quitted his monastery, became a Protestant, married Lady Elizabeth Fitz-Gerald, 6th daughter of George Fitz-Gerald, 16th Earl of Kildare, (ancestor of the ducal family of Leinster,) and by her, besides 4 daughters, left, on his decease in 1676, 1 son, Donough. Of the extensive landed possessions of his ancestors for so many centuries, this Donough was the last noble head of the Mac Carthys, who retained a remnant; *then* producing a rent of £9,000 per annum, and in our time estimated as yielding one of not less than £200,000 a year. He was educated a Protestant by the Archbishop of Canterbury, and bred up at Oxford. Through the influence of his uncle, Justin, (afterwards Lord Mountcashel) he was privately married, before he was 16, to the Lady Elizabeth Spencer, 2nd daughter of Robert Spencer, Earl of Sunderland, (the same who was Prime Minister to James II.) and sent over to Ireland. When James ascended the throne, Donough became a Catholic, and, with his uncle, who was of the same religion, warmly espoused that Monarch's cause, in opposition to the disturbances attempted against his government in Ireland by the Williamites of Munster, after the defection of England to the Prince of Orange, and the escape of the King to France. Justin, the Earl's uncle, had, as a younger son, entered the army, and was well connected in England; being married to the Lady Arabella Wentworth, 2nd daughter of the famous Thomas Wentworth, Earl of Strafford. In his profession, Justin had attained the rank of Lieutenant-General, and was possessed of such courage and talent, that, but for his being somewhat near-sighted, he was considered to have had every qualification for a complete officer. His moral character is described, in politically-hostile sources of intelligence, as that of a man of honour and liberality.

Early in March, 1689, the inhabitants of Bandon, an Anglo-Protestant town in the County Cork, (erected from English confiscations made in Ireland, at the beginning of that, and the conclusion of the previous century,) being from race, from creed, and from the success of the Prince of Orange in England, equally favourable to the Revolution, disaffected to King James, and hostile to the nation arming in his favour, fell by surprise upon their small Jacobite or Irish garrison of only 2 companies of foot, and 1 troop of horse, under Captain Daniel O'Neill, killed a Serjeant and 2 soldiers, seized all their arms, clothes, and horses, and shut the gates, before the Earl of Clancarty, who was advancing with a reinforcement of 6 companies to that detachment of his men which was thus overpowered, could reach the place. About the same time, Captain Henry Boyle, father of the 1st Earl of Shannon, and a descendant of the original English "settler" who founded Bandon, also attempted an insurrection, by standing on his defence at his residence of Castle-Martyr, in the same County, with 140 followers; while William O'Brien, 2nd Earl of Inchiquin, reared a Protestant in London, and who was an experienced officer, having fought in the war of Catalonia, lost an eye in a sea-fight against the Algerines, and been for several years British Governor and Vice-Admiral of Tangier in Morocco, and Colonel of the Tangier Regiment of Foot, headed, with similar intentions to those of Captain Boyle, a considerable number of Williamite insurgents. But Lieutenant-General Justin Mac Carthy prevented any effective co-operation with those movements in the city of Cork, and the adjacent villages, by taking up the arms and horses of the Anglo-Protestant inhabitants, or Revolution party there; and collected such a body of mounted men and 2 or 3 field-pieces, that the Williamites of Bandon found themselves compelled to seek pardon, by opening their gates, agreeing to pay £1000, and to level their walls, which have never since been re-built; Captain Boyle was likewise obliged to surrender; and the Earl of Inchiquin and his followers had to give up their arms. By these successes, and the consequent capitulation, to Captain Phelim Mac Carthy and a superior Irish force, of a party of English colonists, who, with their adherents, had fortified themselves at Kilowen house, in Kerry, under the expectation of assistance from England, every attempt at Williamite insurrection in Munster was put down, previous to King James's arrival from France, on the 22nd of March, 1689, at Kinsale. That Monarch, upon his landing, was received by the Lieutenant-General and his nephew, the Earl of Clancarty. By the Lieutenant-General, the King was informed in council of the state of the country, and was entertained by the Earl; whom he rewarded, for his loyalty, by making him a Lord of the Bedchamber, appointing him Clerk of the Crown and Peace for the Province by letters patent, and creating his infantry regiment a Royal Regiment of Guards. To the Lieutenant-General, James, in order to establish a regular force as soon as possible, gave directions, before leaving Kinsale, to regiment and weapon the levies designed there for infantry and dragoons; and then to despatch quickly for Dublin the remainder of the arms, landed from the French fleet. Previous, also, to his setting out for Cork, the King, inspecting Kinsale, left due orders for securing the place from any sudden attempt of the enemy; committed the execution of those orders to Lieutenant-General Mac Carthy; and appointed, to command under him, the gallant M. de Boisselot, Captain of Louis XIV.'s Guards, who was sent, with the rank of Maréchal de Camp, or Major-General, to Ireland; and who subsequently gained such celebrity for the successful defence of Limerick against the Prince of Orange. On James's return to Dublin from Derry early in May, in order to make arrangements for the meeting of the Irish Parliament then at hand, and to forward to his small and very badly-supplied force before the latter place, such means as could be collected for attacking it, Lieutenant-General Mac Carthy, as the best qualified officer for inspecting the preparation of arms, ordnance, and engineering tools, was made Master-General of Artillery in Ireland. In the Parliament, opened by the King in person on the 17th of the same month, the Lieutenant-General, who was Lord Lieutenant of the County of Cork, likewise sat as its representative along with the Attorney-General for Ireland, Sir Richard Nagle of Aghnakishy and Carrignaconny Castle, in that County, who framed the Bill for the Repeal of the Acts of Settlement and Explanation; or the restoring to the Irish royalists the properties lost by them in fighting against the Parliamentarian or Cromwellian revolutionists; and yet confirmed to these revolutionists, after the Restoration, by those Acts. The Bill for their Repeal, thus drawn by one of the representatives of that County, was brought up by the Lieutenant-General as the other, on the 2nd of June, from the Irish House of Commons to the Irish House of Lords. The next day, the Lieutenant-General was created by King James, Lord Viscount Mountcashel, and Baron of Castle-Inchy, in the County of Cork, and, on the 4th, was introduced, and took his seat, by these titles, amongst the Peers of Ireland. The attention of the King, in military matters, being, next to the blockade of Derry, directed towards the equipment of such a force as might, with what were already in the North, be sufficient to reduce Enniskillen, Lord Mountcashel was appointed to command the additional body of troops designed for that undertaking.

The Enniskilleners, a hardy and stubborn race, mostly Scotch by origin, and Presbyterians by creed, had commenced their insurrection against King James's government in December, 1688, by refusing to admit into Enniskillen 2 companies of Sir Thomas Newcomen's Regiment of Foot, sent to quarter there. Between the time of this outbreak and the end of January, 1689, they continued to arm, and sent 2 envoys to the Prince of Orange, for assistance from England; in March, proclaimed the Prince and Princess as Sovereigns of these islands; and, early in April, rejected the terms offered to them, from King James, by Brigadier Pierce Butler, 3rd Lord Galmoy. That officer, after trying what could be accomplished, rather by intimidation than by other means, against the castle of Crom, a frontier post of the enemy, about 16 miles from Enniskillen, found himself obliged by the determination of his opponents, the insufficiency of his force, and his want of artillery, to retire without effecting any thing. The Enniskilleners, being strengthened by numbers of the bravest of the Protestants of Sligo, Donegal, Cavan, Leitrim, and Monaghan, whom the defeats of their forces elsewhere by the Irish army could not frighten into submission, occasioned such a diversion to the Irish blockade of Derry, and extended their predatory excursions so widely, that, besides a force stationed under Brigadier Patrick Sarsfield on the Connaught side of Lough Erne to guard the country in that direction, and the detachment of another force, under the Duke of Berwick, from the Irish army before Derry towards Enniskillen, that 3rd body of troops, previously mentioned as more especially designed for reducing those insurgents, was to proceed against them, under Lord Mountcashel. From the scarcity and the difficulty of preparing military necessaries in Ireland, and the insufficiency with which such supplies had been furnished by France, Lord Mountcashel's troops could not be assembled for action at Belturbet, before the 6th of August. They consisted of 3 complete regiments of infantry, 2 regiments of dragoons, and some horse; the infantry 2418, the dragoons 1086, the horse 96; the total 3600 men; and they had 7 brass field-guns, with 1 heavy iron piece, for battery. These levies were the best-equipped portion of the King's army, and, with the aid that might be expected from Brigadier Patrick Sarsfield, and the Duke of Berwick, were judged sufficient for the reduction of the Enniskilleners; whose force then under command, besides irregulars, amounted to 30 companies of foot, 17 troops of horse, and 3 troops of dragoons; the foot 2216, the horse 950, the dragoons 180; the total 3346 men; and their artillery 6 field-pieces. But, as belonging to a class, who, having constituted both a political and religious " ascendancy " in Ireland, were before, as well as since, the Revolution, familiar with the use of fire-arms, and whose independent sort of creed, and comparatively easy circumstances, served to form an equally spirited and comfortable yeomanry, the Enniskillen soldiery were composed of an order of men much superior to the mass of Lord Mountcashel's troops; who, besides the moral, political, and military disadvantages under which they laboured, from the general inferiority of their condition previous to their entering the army, had not subsequently seen any service to raise them above raw levies.*

Lord Mountcashel, having collected his forces at Belturbet on the 6th of August, came on the 7th before Crom castle, and commenced raising a battery against it; of which an account was forwarded by the Governor, Creighton, to Enniskillen, and received there that night. By the morning of the 8th, this battery began to play upon the castle, while the Irish made their approaches very near it; and, though they suffered by the small shot of the garrison, and the fire of long fowling-pieces in the place, on rests, for killing game about the Lough, which served as a light artillery, yet the Governor was so alarmed at the effects of the besiegers' cannon, that he wrote pressingly to Enniskillen for relief. To this 2nd letter, which reached Enniskillen early the same day, or the 8th, Colonel William Wolseley, an able English officer who had arrived, by the way of Ballyshannon from England, at Enniskillen, only the night before, and upon whom, owing to the sickness of Colonel Gustavus Hamilton, the command of the town and its forces then devolved, replied, that, by the 10th, he would advance from Enniskillen, to endeavour to raise the siege of Crom. The Colonel, from the slight opinion he entertained of the strength of Enniskillen, having determined to march out and engage Lord Mountcashel alone, rather than wait to be besieged there both by his Lordship and Brigadier Sarsfield, accordingly despatched away orders, that all the Enniskillen troops who could be spared from Ballyshannon, as well as those quartered 2 or 3 miles beyond it, should, the following day, or the 9th, make a forced march, so as to be at Enniskillen that

* "I should be very sorry," said Napoleon, "to undertake a war with an army of recruits." The only portion of Lord Mountcashel's force, that would appear to have constituted an exception to the term "recruits," as having had any thing like due training, was his own regiment of infantry. The numbers on each side in this Enniskillen contest are either copied or deduced from data unobjectionable to either party.

night, and be ready, on the 10th, to go and fight Lieutenant-General Mac Carthy. The night of the same day, or the 8th, on which he issued these commands, Wolseley, likewise receiving a report of Lieutenant-General Mac Carthy's intending to send, next day, an Irish detachment to establish itself at the castle of Lisnaskea, within 10 miles of Enniskillen, directed Lieutenant-Colonel Berry, another English officer lately arrived at Enniskillen, to proceed the following morning, or the 9th, with 4 troops of horse, 1 of dragoons, and 2 companies of foot, or about 404 men, towards Lisnaskea, to garrison its castle, if tenable, and to learn all he could respecting the strength and position of the Irish; assuring him of being followed, in due course, by the whole of the Enniskillen forces, to raise the siege of Crom. Berry marched, on the morning of the 9th, to Lisnaskea, to anticipate the Irish in taking possession of its castle; which, however, he reached, without meeting any hostile party; and, finding the edifice too much out of order to be worth a garrison, he kept his men that night in the open fields, about 6 miles from the Irish. By the day of Berry's advance to Lisnaskea, or the 9th, Lord Mountcashel had already gained the entrenchments about Crom castle, with a facility so animating to his raw troops, that, contrary to *his* express orders to go no further, they had imprudently rushed on towards the very walls of the fortress; the loss being thus greater than it otherwise would, or from 75 to 80 killed or wounded, including the Lieutenant-Colonel and several other officers of his Lordship's regiment, and 3 of his cannoniers. Yet, through the formation of a battery under cover of the night, he calculated on being enabled to give a general assault, when he was informed 4000 men were coming from Enniskillen, in order to relieve Crom. In this state of things, his post there being very ineligible for giving battle, his Lordship withdrew 2 miles thence towards Newtown-Butler; that if the Enniskilleners approached, he might be in a better situation to receive them; or that, if they should not do so, he might still be sufficiently at hand to resume his operations against the castle. And, as an additional precaution with reference to the enemy's approach, the Clare or O'Brien's Regiment of Dragoons were to proceed early next morning, or the 10th, towards Lisnaskea, and after driving before them such a hostile advanced party as it might appear they would be able to dispose of, they were to halt at, and occupy a certain pass, where, it was said, that 100 men might stop 10,000! The officer to command the dragoons, with these instructions, was Brigadier Anthony Hamilton.

This accomplished gentleman, and elegant writer, known, in the light literature of France, as the "Comte Antoine Hamilton," author of the "Mémoires du Comte de Grammont," &c., was (by the Lady Mary Butler, sister of James Butler, 1st Duke of Ormonde) the 2nd surviving son of Sir George Hamilton, of the house of Abercorn, Receiver-General of Ireland, under King Charles I. Anthony had risen to military rank in France, like his 3 brothers—George, created a Count, and Maréchal de Camp or Major-General, for his services against the Germans, and 1st husband of the beautiful Frances Jennings, subsequently Duchess of Tyrconnell—Richard, also an officer of reputation in Louis the XIV.'s armies, banished the French Court for being in love with that Monarch's daughter, the Princess of Conti, to whom his conversation was *most* agreeable, and, in this war, as a Lieutenant-General in the Irish army, distinguished at Derry and the Boyne—and John, for his military experience abroad, made a Major-General in the same army, and eventually killed at Aughrim. After the accession of James II. to the throne, by which that preferment in their own country was opened to Irish Catholic officers, which they had been previously obliged to seek abroad, Anthony Hamilton was created a Privy Counsellor in Ireland, and Governor of Limerick, with a pension of £200 a year upon the Irish Establishment. On the revolt of England against the King in 1688, he retired, as his Sovereign did, to France, and was one of those officers who accompanied him from Brest to Ireland. He was then appointed Colonel to a Regiment of Infantry by the King, and finally Brigadier in the force, under Lord Mountcashel, designed to reduce Enniskillen.

Early in the morning of the 10th, as has been observed, the Clare Regiment of Dragoons, which might make about 543 men, advanced, under the Brigadier, towards Lisnaskea, and at 6 o'clock, when about 2 miles from that village, or near a place called Donough, they discerned the out-scouts of Lieutenant-Colonel Berry, who was then on his march from Lisnaskea, towards Lord Mountcashel's position. Berry, according to his design of not engaging any Irish corps till he could discover its strength, and be so reinforced and posted as to fight with advantage, ordered his men to retreat before the Irish, and sent off an express to Enniskillen, to represent, that the Irish, having raised the siege of Crom, were on the march towards Enniskillen in pursuit of him; and to impress the consequent necessity of his being joined, as speedily as possible, by Colonel Wolseley, with the rest of the Enniskillen troops. Wolseley, who was on the road from Enniskillen with those forces when he met the express, in order to give the more effectual assistance, despatched, in advance of himself and his main body, some troops of horse and dragoons to reinforce Berry. Meanwhile, Hamilton, when he had driven the Enniskillen detachment beyond the pass, where he might be secure with his dragoons, until rendered still *more* so by Lord Mountcashel, instead of halting, as he should have done, at that pass, transgressed his orders, by continuing to pursue Berry. In that officer's retreat from Donough to Lisnaskea, the Irish dragoons pressed so hard upon, and occasioned such disorder among a portion of the Enniskillen cavalry, that, but for *his* exertions, with 1 or 2 of the best troops, in several times facing about, and thereby bringing the Irish to a stand, in order to draw up, the whole of the retiring force would have been certainly routed to Enniskillen. Of 2 roads, an old one on the right, and a new one on the left, leading from Lisnaskea to Enniskillen, Berry, in retiring through Lisnaskea, determined to follow the latter and nearer one to Lough Erne; as running through boggy and fenny ground, and affording several passes, where a defensive stand might be much more easily made than on the old road. When he had retreated about a mile from Lisnaskea, he arrived at a spot, that was well calculated to be maintained by a force as numerous as his, against one much stronger than the regiment of dragoons by which he was followed. It was a very boggy, deep defile, where a river crossed the road, whose breadth, for a considerable space before reaching the river, was so small, that 2 horsemen could scarcely ride abreast; and this road, through the bog, was, as it led to the river, flanked with underwood, affording a convenient shelter for musketeers, by whose fire, those approaching the river would consequently be commanded. Here Berry determined to engage; if the Enniskillen horse, who, by his efforts, and by the necessary obstacles to their being quickly pursued along the difficult road he wisely selected for his retreat, had been hardly prevented from running away, could be gotten to stand. To accomplish this, the English Lieutenant-Colonel resorted to the influence of the Enniskillen officers. On crossing to the side of the stream farthest from the Irish, the horse, by the exertions of 1 of their best leaders, Captain Martin Armstrong, and the coming up of a brave and skilful infantry officer, Captain Malcolm Cathcart, with about 120 foot, were prevailed upon to rally there. Captain Cathcart then requested the horse-officers to let him know plainly, if the horse meant to abandon their foot, as in the recent action against the Duke of Berwick,* or would promise to stand?—which, if they would do, he would answer for the Irish being beaten from that pass. The horse-officers protested, that none of them would fly, but would do their duty; a promise the more likely to be kept, through the arrival of the reinforcement sent on by Wolseley, after the receipt of Berry's express. The strength of the latter, from but 2 companies of foot, 4 troops of horse, and 1 of dragoons, or only 404 men, was thus raised, by the Enniskillen writer Hamilton's account, to 7 or 8 troops of horse, about 3 foot companies, and 2 troops of dragoons; that, according to the variations in the numbers of those troops and companies, would form from 736 to 892 men. Under such combined advantages of numbers and position, arrangements were adopted to maintain the defile. Committing the disposition of the infantry and dismounted dragoons to Captain Cathcart, who so placed them in the bushes, on each side of the narrow causeway leading to the stream across the road, that the passage would be swept by their levelled muskets and carabines, Berry, for the support of the infantry and dragoons, ranged his horse to the rear of all, or beyond the stream, and gave the word, *Oxford.* By this time, or about 9 o'clock, the Irish (whom the difficulties of a pursuit through such a causeway would appear to have considerably delayed) came up; and Hamilton, not aware of the Enniskilleners being reinforced beyond the 5 troops of cavalry and 2 companies of infantry, at which the nature of the ground enabled him to estimate them in the earlier part of their confused retreat before him to that defile, determined on attacking them there. Dismounting, and causing the dragoons to do so likewise, he led them on gallantly. The dragoons, firing smartly and wounding 12 or 14 of the Enniskilleners, advanced without receiving a shot from them, till within about 40 yards of the stream. Then Captain Cathcart, who, with 18 or 20 ambushed marksmen, was to give the signal from one side of the causeway to the marksmen on the other, finding the assailants sufficiently close to him, let fly at one of their flanks, while a similar discharge was poured upon the other; killing or wounding about 20 of the Irish. Amongst the latter was Hamilton, who, being shot in the thigh, retired a little to the

* The particulars respecting the difficulty which the English Lieutenant-Colonel had in preventing the Enniskillen horse from abandoning their foot during this retreat, as they had recently done in the engagement near Enniskillen against the Duke of Berwick, and likewise respecting the little reliance the Enniskillen foot consequently had on their horse, are derived from the narrative of M'Carmick, who had so much to complain of, as having been an officer on duty with that party of the Enniskillen foot defeated by the Duke, after their horse, who should have supported them, ran away from an equal body of the Duke's, without even firing a shot! M'Carmick, on that unfortunate occasion, paid dearly for the cowardice of those horse; having been made prisoner by the Irish, after seeing his son killed beside him. The Enniskillen cavalry, indeed, were not worthy of being compared, as soldiers, with their infantry.

rear, to mount his horse; ordering another officer to lead on the men. That officer and more of the dragoons being slain by the close flanking volleys from Cathcart's ambushes, and no chief officer being present to lead on the men, Hamilton told a Captain Lavallin to order a "wheel to the left"—for the purpose of getting out of this double line of fire, and withdrawing, to rejoin Lord Mountcashel. But Lavallin gave the word as "to the left about," which was understood in a *worse* sense.* The Enniskilleners, on seeing this, huzzaed, and exclaiming that the Irish were running, advanced to attack them—the infantry and dismounted dragoons, previously in ambush, taking the bog on each side—the horse rushing through the water along the causeway. The Irish, at first quickening their retreat, soon broke, before the superior numbers of the enemy, into a disorderly flight, notwithstanding all Hamilton could say, or do, to stop it. He having, wounded as he was, a horse shot under him, with difficulty escaped. For about 3 miles, or from the scene of action, through Lisnaskea, to near Donough, the pursuit continued. The Enniskilleners, by *their* accounts, suffered to no greater extent, than the 12 or 14 men above mentioned as wounded. The Irish, according to the same accounts, had, from above 106 to about 230 men and officers killed or taken; so many horses and arms of the dragoons being (in any view of the matter) lost, that they were broken up as a regiment. Near Donough the pursuit was stopped by Berry's sounding a retreat to his former fastness, as Lord Mountcashel, who had marched that morning from Newtown-Butler after O'Brien's regiment, came up with the main body of his cavalry, to protect the beaten dragoons. This misfortune of the dragoons, which, besides its naturally depressing effects upon the remainder of Lord Mountcashel's newly-raised force, deprived him of nearly half his cavalry—the report, likewise, of the entire body of the Enniskilleners, represented as more numerous than they were, or as considerably reinforced from England, being upon their march to attack him—the certainty, in this case, of Sarsfield and Berwick *not* having advanced against Enniskillen, since their doing so would have prevented this march of the Enniskilleners—and the consequent expediency, under such circumstances, of being upon his guard—caused his Lordship to determine upon retreating immediately towards Belturbet.

But the enemy did not give him time to accomplish this. Lieutenant-Colonel Berry, from the pass to which, on perceiving the Irish army near Donough, he had a 2nd time retreated, was summoned, about 11 o'clock, by Colonel Wolseley, to meet him at the moat beyond Lisnaskea, where the Colonel had arrived, by the upper road, from Enniskillen.

* "After a short dispute," states my contemporary Irish Jacobite authority on this affair, "Brigadier Hamilton sent the word by Captain Lavallin to his men to wheel to the left, as if it were to rejoin Mountcashel. Lavallin delivered it to the left about, as he thought it was, though Hamilton maintain'd it afterwards, that it was as aforesaid. . . . In 3 weeks after the action, Brigadier Anthony Hamilton and Captain Lavallin were brought to a Tryal, before a Court Martial in Dublin, wherein General de Rosen sate President. The Brigadier was acquitted; and the Captain condemned to a military death; tho, at his execution, he protested, that he delivered the word as he had receiv'd it: and many believ'd his protestation. He was a gentleman of a good estate in the County of Cork, within 12 miles to that Citty: and was much regretted by his friends." Hamilton, it would seem, was too influentially connected at the Castle of Dublin to be condemned; or why was *he* not called to a special account for his complete breach of orders, in risking that pursuit, which led to the destruction of so many, as well as poor Lavallin?

The force, mustered by Wolseley and Berry at the moat, were, according to their own annalist Hamilton, 21 companies of foot, 16 troops of horse, and 3 troops of dragoons, "men under command," or regulars. Of these, the foot would be 1568, the horse 900, the dragoons 180—or both, as cavalry, 1080—the entire 2648. There were "besides," says Hamilton, "some that were not under command," otherwise volunteers, or irregulars, that appear, by the subsequent loss in action, to have borne, to the "men under command," the *considerable* proportion of 8 to 12.* In fine, the account from Major-General Kirke, published as official in the *London Gazette*, No. 2481, states Wolseley's and Berry's united troops as 2700, or 1500 foot, and 1200 horse. Lord Mountcashel, deducting, say 70, (exclusive of officers) for his killed and wounded at Crom, and 543 for the dragoon regiment subsequently put *hors de combat*, would still have 2348 infantry, and 543 dragoons, with 96 horse, or, between both, 639 cavalry, making altogether 2987 men.†

Wolseley, after congratulating Berry upon his good fortune, observed to the Enniskillen officers, that, as, in the haste made to relieve their friends, little or no food had been brought from Enniskillen, they should either at once push forward, and fight Lieutenant-General Mac Carthy, or return home. The Enniskillen officers were for going on; but, thinking it better to learn the opinion of their men on the matter, assembled them, in close order, and asked them, which course would they adopt? The soldiers, though many of them, only the day before, are related to have marched, in that warm season, between 20 and 23 miles, from Ballyshannon, or beyond it, to Enniskillen, and above 10 miles more that morning, were so animated, by what they considered the lucky presage of the late success, that they were all for pushing forward. Wolseley, thereupon arraying them in line of battle, selecting the due number of troopers for a forlorn hope, and giving the word, *No Popery!* as best suited to draw out all their political, religious, and military enthusiasm, commanded them to advance. Meantime, Lord Mountcashel had retreated from between Lisnaskea and Donough, in the direction of Newtown-Butler, with his army, still more morally than physically weakened by the result of the late unlucky affair against Berry, besides a general, though erroneous, belief, as to the forces, hastening after them from Enniskillen, having been rendered greatly superior in number, to what they originally were, by recent reinforcements from England. In this unfavourable aspect of affairs, his Lordship broke up the arrangements he had previously made for resuming the siege of Crom; and directed the troops and artillery, left before the castle, to be drawn off towards Newtown-Butler. When his van, arriving there, was about 2 miles from Donough, and his rear not advanced further than about half a mile from the latter place, the forlorn of the Enniskilleners appeared in

* The Enniskillen "men under command," and "not under command," are lumped by Hamilton, as only "something more than 2000." But assertion cannot stand before arithmetic. Besides the circumstance indicating the irregulars to have been to the regulars as 8 to 12, we know, from Enniskillen evidence, that, about 2 months before, "near 2000" Enniskillen troops, in marching from Enniskillen to Omagh, were swelled to "double the number," by the Protestant *sympathizers* on their route. Were there not, consequently, *more* of such Williamite irregulars, or Orange guerillas, opposed to Lord Mountcashel, than *we* have a satisfactory account of?

† The 70 foot and 543 dragoons, or 613 men, set down as lost, with 2987 estimated as remaining, or still effective, would form 3600, the total of Lord Mountcashel's *original* force.

view. As the Irish rear retired, the Enniskilleners continued to come on, until the ground, within about half a mile of Newtown-Butler, presented an opportunity for holding the enemy in check, which was not neglected by the Irish commander. On the way towards the town was a steep hill only accessible by a bog, and a causeway through it, capable of admitting no more than 2 mounted men side by side. Upon the declivity of this hill fronting the bog and the enemy, the Irish rear, after its passage of the causeway, was drawn out, to assume an imposing attitude; which the nature of the position enabled it to do, as Colonel Wolseley, on coming up, judged it necessary to have the ground inspected by his officers, and the dispositions made for a regular attack. To further occupy his attention, the houses of the adjacent country were committed to the flames; the semblance of a design to contest the hill being kept up by distant firings from it, till his van was within about musket-range. Then, preparations being made for delaying him still more by burning Newtown-Butler, the Irish were drawn off in good order towards it, after arresting his progress for half an hour. On passing through Newtown-Butler, they burned it, and continued, for a mile beyond it, to retreat; facing about and firing, so as to render Wolseley apprehensive of advancing, unless in an equally regular manner. Here, finding it no longer possible to retreat towards Belturbet without fighting, and having selected such a position, as, under existing circumstances, gave the best hopes from a battle, Lord Mountcashel determined to engage the Enniskilleners. At the foot of an eminence lay a bog, nearly half a mile across. To assail this eminence along its front, cavalry had no way to approach, but a narrow road, through the bog, admitting but 2 troopers, at most, to proceed abreast; while infantry should advance over the bog, on each side of the road. Along the slope of this eminence, Lord Mountcashel ranged his army. His horse and dragoons, reduced, by the morning's reverse, so much below the number of the enemy's cavalry, formed the centre, drawn up across the causeway leading out of the bog, with 7 pieces of cannon planted before them, to cover the narrow passage by which the Enniskillen cavalry should come on; and to the right and left of his horse and dragoons, his infantry, protected by thickets, were posted as wings.

Colonel Wolseley made the following dispositions for action. His centre, consisting of horse, was to assail the Irish horse and dragoons, ranged behind their artillery, at the opposite end of the causeway. His right and left wings, that were to proceed through the bog against the opposite divisions of the Irish infantry among the hedges, were formed out of the musketeers of his foot, composing between 700 and 800 of such excellent marksmen, that a hostile officer could hardly show himself without being picked down. Between those wings, the 3 troops of dragoons, dismounted, were equally divided. The right wing was placed under an English officer, Colonel Zachariah Tiffin; the left under an Irish officer, Colonel Thomas Lloyd. The centre of horse was led by Lieutenant-Colonel Berry; behind which Colonel Wolseley took his station, as that best calculated for surveying, and directing the progress of, the engagement. The horse of the Enniskillen centre first attempted to advance, but were obliged by the Irish cannon to desist. Wolseley then despatched through the bog his 2 wings of marksmen and dismounted dragoons, under Colonel Tiffin on the right, and Colonel Lloyd on the left, against the Irish left and right of foot stationed in the thickets; the

Enniskillen wings being principally directed to fight their way along the sides of the causeway towards the Irish artillery, so as to seize it; and thus enable their centre of horse to charge the horse and dragoons of Lord Mountcashel. The contest was proceeding in this manner, when some of the enemy, having gotten round unperceived through a wood at one end of the morass, took the Irish in the rear, with a surprise and consternation on the part of the latter proportionately favourable to the hostile advance against their cannon in front.* The artillery was reached, the cannoniers killed, the guns seized, and the causeway thus opened for the charge of the Enniskillen centre of horse upon that of the Irish. Discouraged by the reverse of that morning, panic-struck at the flight among their infantry who had been attacked in the rear, at the seizure of the artillery, and at the superior number of the enemy's cavalry advancing by the causeway, the Irish horse and dragoons of the centre wheeled about, and rode away towards Wattle-Bridge, in spite of all that Lord Mountcashel, and *some* of their officers, could do;† among whom was Sir Stephen Martin killed, Claud Hamilton, 5th Lord Strabane, and 4th Earl of Abercorn, wounded; besides Lord Drummond, and Mr. Plowden, acting as volunteers, who very narrowly escaped, with the loss of their horses and baggage, after behaving most bravely. The routed horse and dragoons were followed with due effect, by a portion of the Enniskillen cavalry, for several miles. On the Irish right, the slaughter would appear to have been less than elsewhere; that wing being nearest to the open country for an escape; the Enniskillen horse not being able to act out of the causeway; and the Enniskillen infantry, though as swift of foot as their opponents, having marched farther than they did that morning, or about 15 miles before engaging. On the Irish left being prevented from getting across the causeway to the open country by the Enniskillen horse, who secured the road as far as Wattle-Bridge, and being also pursued through the bog towards Lough Erne by the Enniskillen foot, almost all of the infantry, but some officers who received quarter, perished; about 500 in one spot, who were driven into a wood on a branch of the lake, and thus deprived of any prospect of escape but swimming across, being all shot or drowned, except 1 man, who saved himself from the volleys sent after him! In fine, the Enniskillen troops, continuing the pursuit and search for their enemies until about 10 the next morning, and the country-people, as irregulars, being similarly active for some days after, almost the whole of the Irish force, except such as had gotten off through the open country to their right, or with the horse and dragoons of the centre, were destroyed or taken. The Enniskilleners specify their loss as but 2 officers (a Captain and Cornet) and about 20 soldiers, of whom 12 were regulars, and 8 irregulars; and their wounded, at from 40 to 50 men. As to the Irish loss, no Jacobite detail of it being transmitted, we can only know what the Irish are *said* to have estimated it at, through the Enniskillen annalist Hamilton, who alleges, that those who returned to Dublin confessed a deficiency of 3000 men, between killed, taken, and *missing.* Under the *last* head, however, he

* Plunkett informs us, of the Enniskillen party, how they "passed thro' a wood that was at one end of the said morass, and march'd unperceiv'd against the rear of the Irish;" thus, as "the foe coming surprizeingly upon them in that posture," &c.

† "La terreur panique des troupes," says a French veteran historian, "est un mal, auquel la valeur, les prières, et les menaces d'un Général sont presque toûjours un remède inutile."

adds, that they, who admitted this, included many, who, from a fear of disgrace and punishment for their defeat, had availed themselves of the confusion that followed it, to desert the service. According to the most probable estimate deducible from English and Enniskillen authority, or allowing for the escape of about 600 cavalry of the centre, and for others that would appear to have gotten off on the right, the Irish loss, with artillery, colours, camp, baggage, &c., would be about 1500 slain, 500 drowned,* and from above 300 to 500 prisoners, including 48 or 50 officers.

Among the captured officers was Lord Mountcashel, under circumstances most honourable to himself, notwithstanding the overthrow of his army. On the defeat of his cavalry, with whom he might have easily escaped, he, with 5 or 6 officers, who would not abandon him, retired into a wood, near to where his cannon were planted; and resolved not to survive that day. Over those guns, the Enniskilleners had placed a guard of about 100 foot, under Captain George Cooper. Lord Mountcashel with his little party, after a short stay where he was, to the surprise of the Enniskillen guard, who did not suppose any enemy so near, rushed out of the wood, discharging his pistol at them. Upon this, 7 or 8 of the Enniskilleners, pointing a volley against him, shot his horse dead under him, and brought himself, severely wounded, to the ground. In addition to the balls by which he was struck, but from which he was protected by his armour, he received 2 through his right thigh, 1 in his left loin through the lower part of the back-bone, and a slighter hurt in the groin, from part of a bullet, that, had it met with no opposition, would certainly have been mortal; but, after beating his watch to pieces, is stated to have been broken by its wheels into fragments, of which only 1 inflicted an injury. An Enniskillen soldier then clubbed his musket, to put an end to the prostrate nobleman's life and sufferings by knocking out his brains, but 1 of the officers, who accompanied his Lordship, desired the soldier,—" Hold his hand, as he was about to kill General Mac Carthy!" Captain Cooper, being informed of this, came up, and gave quarter to the Irish commander, and to the officers who were with him. He was carried that night to Newtown-Butler; and being asked, " How he came so rashly to hazard his life, though he might have gone off with his horse, when they made their escape?" he replied,— " Finding the kingdom like to be lost, since *his* army was the best for their number King James had, unless those before Derry, then much broken, he had come with a design to lose his life; and was sorry that he missed his end, being unwilling to outlive that day!"† As our great national bard observes—

> "The soldier's hope, the patriot's zeal,
> For ever dimm'd, for ever crost—
> Oh! who shall say what heroes feel,
> When all but life and honour's lost!"—MOORE.

The wounded General, and some of his officers, (probably those most hurt) were removed from Newtown-Butler to Enniskillen by water, or

---

* Could *any* honour arising from this success compensate for the disgrace of the *extreme* destructiveness that followed it? But such is " civil war !"

† Of *these* interesting particulars of Lord Mountcashel's heroism in connexion with his fall and capture, we would be "in utter darkness," but for the Enniskillen writers, Hamilton and Mc Carmick.

along Lough Erne,* as the easiest mode of conveyance; the rest of the prisoners going there by land. At Enniskillen, bread being then extremely scarce, beer and ale very bad, wine not to be had, and surgeons and medicines for the wounded greatly wanted, his Lordship obtained permission to make known his condition there to King James. The King thereupon despatched, from Dublin to Enniskillen, 1 of the royal physicians, Doctor Connor, and 1 of the royal surgeons, Mr. Huben, accompanied by some hogsheads of wine, and such other provisions, as, though most requisite, were not at Enniskillen; to which was added a supply of money, both for his Lordship, and the officers taken with him.

About a fortnight subsequent to this disaster of Newtown-Butler, William III.'s General, the Marshal Duke of Schonberg, disembarking from England near Carrickfergus, with the 1st portion of his British, Dutch, and Huguenot army, commenced operations, in the course of some days, with the siege of that place, by land and water; and, having taken it, after a gallant defence and honourable capitulation by Colonel Charles Mac Carthy More, proceeded, about the middle of September, through Newry, towards Dundalk, on his intended advance to Dublin. In this interval, Lord Mountcashel was reduced to a very weak state of health, from the effects of his severe wounds, in such an unwholesome place as Enniskillen. Being consequently desirous, for his cure, to obtain leave, on parole, to go to Dublin, upon the condition of afterwards returning as a prisoner to Enniskillen, he wrote to his friend and brother representative for the County of Cork, Sir Richard Nagle, Attorney-General, and Secretary of State and War for Ireland, to apply, in his own name, by letter, to Marshal Schonberg, for this permission. Sir Richard having written to that effect, the Irish trumpeter, by whom the letter was forwarded for the Marshal, met the Williamite army on its march from Newry, and the communication was presented to the Marshal's Secretary; who soon after returned it with this message, that his master, the Duke, could not receive that letter, because it was not directed to him as the *Duke* of Schonberg; which rank he claimed as conferred upon him by *King* William. Besides this message to be brought back by the trumpeter along with the returned letter, the Duke's Secretary gave a letter from himself for Sir Richard Nagle; in which, having stated the same reason as that verbally assigned for the refusal of the letter, he added, that his master, the Duke, had renounced the title of Marshal, when, on account of the recent measures adopted for the extinction of the Protestant worship in France, by the Revocation of the Edict of Nantes, he had left that kingdom, for the sake of his religion. This application, to obtain for Lord Mountcashel the privilege of going on his parole to Dublin, in order to get cured, therefore failed. But, it having been the same month agreed by William III., in consequence of an application from the family of Lord Mountjoy, who was a prisoner in the Bastille at Paris, that a negociation should be attempted, through King James's government in Ireland, to obtain his Lordship's liberty by way of exchange, and Lord Mount-

* "I compared," states the English tourist Twiss in 1770, "the beauties of this with those of other lakes which I had seen, such as Loch-Lomond in Scotland; the Lake of Geneva, which receives much grandeur from the immense snow-clad mountains that bound it on the Savoy side, and much beauty from the vines on the opposite shore; the lakes near Naples, which are all classic scenes; and, though I afterwards saw the celebrated Lake of Killarney, Lough-Erne did *not* suffer by the comparison."

cashel, as the Jacobite officer of the highest rank and character in Williamite custody, being the most suitable for such an exchange, his Lordship, about the month of October, wrote from Enniskillen to one of Schonberg's officers in Ireland, Major-General Kirke, who had been kind to him since his captivity, to request an application on the subject in London, to the English Secretary of State, Charles Talbot, 12th Earl of Shrewsbury, Waterford, and Wexford. Major-General Kirke, early in November, complied with this solicitation, enclosing, in a letter of his own to the Earl of Shrewsbury, the letter of Lord Mountcashel. The Earl, who had known Lord Mountcashel in England, as the Honourable Justin Mac Carthy, previous to the war between England and Ireland occasioned by the Revolution, expressed, in his answer to Kirke, from Whitehall, about the middle of November, his great regard for Justin Mac Carthy; observing, "I am so well satisfyed of his being a man of honour, that, as to my owne particular, I should rely upon his word, for whatever he thought fit to engage it;" and, moreover, mentioning the solicitude he then, and, from the commencement of the negociation, had felt for his old friend's release; but remarking upon the political obstacles that delayed, and might continue to delay, its accomplishment. In consequence of this uncertainty as to *when* he might be restored to his liberty, (if, indeed, he would not be more likely to *die* should he be detained where he was!) Lord Mountcashel determined on effecting his deliverance, by a plan of his own. On his former representation, of the inconvenience of having a guard placed over him during his illness, his Lordship, by an application, through Major-General Kirke, to the Marshal Duke of Schonberg, had gotten the guard to be removed, and had been allowed the liberty of the town of Enniskillen, on his parole. While in the actual enjoyment of the liberty of the place, by virtue of such a pledge, he therefore could not endeavour to escape, without a breach of faith. In order to be freed from that pledge, he consequently caused a rumour to be circulated through Enniskillen, that, although he *had* been granted the liberty of the town on his parole, he intended to attempt getting away; which, in fact, he did, though only in such a manner as the necessary alteration of conduct towards him, in consequence of such a *discovery*, would supply him with a justification for doing. And so it happened; for this report reaching the Governor of Enniskillen, Colonel Gustavus Hamilton, that officer, in order to provide against such an event, placed Lord Mountcashel *again* under a guard. Being thus released from his parole, and consequently *not* precluded as a nobleman, a gentleman, or a soldier, from adopting any measures he could for escaping, his Lordship soon had the means arranged for the purpose.* To the house in Enniskillen, where he was confined, and which was on the border of Lough Erne, 2 little boats, called *cots*, or as many

---

* On the like *principle*, the famous French sea-captain, Jean Bart, and a brother officer, when prisoners this year in England at Plymouth, are represented in the Memoirs of Brigadier la Fontaine, as having acted, and *justifiably* acted, in managing to escape. "Upon their parole of honour, they had the liberty of the town granted them for some time. But, at last, under pretence that they had made themselves suspected, they had a guard of 4 soldiers placed upon them, to keep a watchful eye upon all their actions. This happened very *fortunately* for them, for, *being thereby discharged from their word*, they now began to contrive how to save themselves by flight." In that contrivance, they were successful; the point, however, of their *not* being considered to have broken faith, by escaping under *such* circumstances, being ALL that need be noted *here*.

as were sufficient for carrying away himself, and all he wished to remove with him, were to be brought in the night by the contrivance of a Serjeant, named Acheson, whom he had bribed, and who agreed to go off with him. The Serjeant, returning the same night, to deliver a letter, which, and his Lordship's pass, were found in the lining of his hat, was next day tried, and shot. But Lord Mountcashel effected his object, and towards the end of December, 1689, reached Dublin. His entrance there was preceded by several carriages, and from 200 to 300 horsemen, military or civilians. At the Castle, says the Jacobite official account, "his Lordship was very kindly received by the King with a hearty welcome, and carressed by all the great officers, and others, his friends, with all demonstrations of joy and gladness imaginable." The same evening, numbers of fires were lighted in the streets. The exultation of the metropolis was shared by the provinces; the greatest rejoicings, however, being at Cork, and throughout Munster, where they more especially regarded his Lordship as their countryman, and a descendant of their ancient Princes. The loss of a prisoner of such eminence was, on the other hand, a source of much vexation to the enemy, whose General, the Marshal Duke of Schonberg, alleged, (or has, more probably, been represented, on report, by the Williamite annalist, Story, to have alleged,) of Lord Mountcashel, that "he took Lieutenant-General Mac Carthy to be a man of honour, but would not expect *that*, in an Irishman, any more!" In reference to such an aspersion upon himself and his countrymen, or the hostile rumour on which it was based, Lord Mountcashel took no measures till previous to the active resumption of his military duties, after landing at Brest, the following May, with the regiments that commenced the formation of the Irish Brigades in the service of France. His Lordship then submitted himself to be tried by a French Court of Honour for the circumstances under which he got away from Enniskillen, adds the hostile or Orange historian Harris, and was acquitted by that tribunal, of having been guilty of any breach of his parole. Such was the career of the Colonel of the 1st regiment, and Commander-in-Chief of the 3 regiments, of this Brigade, up to the period of his entering the French service.*

The Colonel of the 2nd of those regiments, the Honourable Daniel O'Brien, was descended from the royal race or Dalcassian Princes of Thomond; between whom, and the Eugenian Princes of Desmond, the right, as has been said, existed, for so many centuries, of alternately appointing the supreme King of Munster. Of those 2 royal lines, that of the Dalcassians attained the higher eminence in the history of their country, by having produced the renowned Brien Boru, Ard-Righ or Monarch of Erin, and conqueror of the Danes at Clontarf, in 1014; from whom the name of O'Brien was henceforth transmitted to his descendants. In the warlike period of above a century and a half, which elapsed between the death of Brien Boru, at Clontarf, and the Anglo-Norman invasion of Erin, his descendants of the house of Thomond, but with a sway extending far beyond its limits, were among the greatest Princes of the island; as attested, independent of native authority, by

* This account of Lord Mountcashel has been carefully revised since 1854, and, in reference to the portion of it concerning Enniskillen, has been *particularly* improved, through the additional contemporary Jacobite information supplied by Plunkett's Light to the Blind, and the Correspondence from Ireland of the Comte d'Avaux; for access to which valuable original authorities, I am indebted to my kind friends, Sir R. W. Wilde and the late John Dalton, Esq.

foreign evidence to the connexion of *their* history with that of Britain and the Continent. On the expulsion from England, in 1051, of the famous Earl Godwin and his family by Edward *the Confessor*, for the opposition given by the Earl and his sons to the King's too great partiality for, and advancement of, Norman adventurers and intriguers in England, Godwin and some of his sons retired to Flanders, and the others, among whom was Harold, the future King of England, sought an asylum in Erin. There Harold was compensated for the hostility of *one* of his brothers-in-law—Edward *the Confessor* being married to his sister Edith—by the reception he met from the *other*, or the son of the great Brien Boru, Donough O'Brien, King of Munster, who, being married to Harold's other sister, Driella, (by whom he had a son, named Donald,) acknowledged the claim of the illustrious Saxon to protection and assistance, and accordingly supplied him with a body of troops, and 9 ships, for the liberation of his country, and the restoration of his family. With this aid from Munster, Harold, joining the fleet of his father and brothers from Flanders at the Isle of Wight, they, in 1052, were enabled, by the co-operation of their countrymen, to regain their former honours and estates, and effect the downfall of the Norman or foreign and antinational faction at the Court of Westminster.* Donough's successor in Munster, Turlough O'Brien, is addressed by the Norman Primate of England, Lanfranc, as "the magnificent King of Hibernia," and by the celebrated Pope Gregory VII., as "the illustrious King of Hibernia." Murkertagh O'Brien, successor to Turlough, is designated by Lanfranc's successor, St. Anselm, as "the glorious," and, "by the grace of God, King of Hibernia."† Connor O'Brien, another of their successors, in the records of the Abbey of Ratisbon in Germany, chiefly raised through *his* munificence, is also alluded to as if "King of Hibernia;" the same records adding of that Prince, in reference to the Crusades, how, by lords, or "Counts, of great power and nobility, wearing the badge of the cross, and on their way to Jerusalem, he forwarded large presents to Lotharius, King of the Romans,"‡ or Emperor of Germany. After the Anglo-Norman intrusion under Henry II., the de Clares, as its leading feudal representatives in Thomond, by availing themselves of that native division, which was but too favourable for the advancement of foreign power, endeavoured to establish themselves there. But, though successful to some extent for a time, they and their adherents were entirely defeated and expelled. The ambitious Earls of Desmond likewise, who would willingly have done what the defeated de Clares had left undone, were on several occasions taught, by "sad experience" in the field, to respect the O'Brien motto and war-cry, "Lamh laidir abu!" or *The strong hand for ever!*—and the "settlers" in Limerick, and districts far beyond it, had to pay "dubh cios," *black rent*, or tribute, to the old Dalcassian race, whose heads continued to be Kings or Princes of Thomond, until

* Compare Mac Geoghegan, Moore, and O'Mahony's Keating, with Thierry and Lingard, on this incident.

† Of King Murkertagh, or Murtogh, known at home as "More," or the *Great*, one daughter was married to the son of Magnus, King of Norway, the Hebrides, and Man; another to the Anglo-Norman nobleman, Arnulph de Montgomery, Earl of Pembroke; and, in reference to the friendship between the Irish King, and his royal brother of Albany, or Scotland, it is related that the latter sent him a camel "of wonderful magnitude."

‡ "Per magnæ nobilitatis ac potentiæ Comites, cruce signatos, et Hierosolyman petituros, ad Lotharium, Regem Romanorum, ingentia munera misit."

1543. Then, Murrough O'Brien, on surrendering his kingdom, or principality, to King Henry VIII., was created 1st Earl of Thomond for life, with the title of Baron of Inchiquin, to his male heirs; the whole of this Murrough's territorial and other possessions beyond the river Shannon, with their abbeys, and the right of presenting to all spiritual benefices, except bishoprics, being confirmed to him and his descendants. At the same time, Henry conferred on Murrough's nephew, Donough O'Brien, the dignity of Baron of Ibrackan, with the right of succession to the title of Earl of Thomond for life, after his uncle Murrough's decease; Murrough, as the *de facto* ruler of Thomond, at the period of his submission, being considered deserving to be created its Earl, though not to transmit that title to his posterity, as having, only through popular election, under the old Irish law of Tanistry, attained the principality of his name and territory, after the death of Conor O'Brien, King or Prince of Thomond, in 1540; to the exclusion of Conor's eldest son, the above-mentioned Donough, who, being then a minor, was set aside by the law of Tanistry, as less worthy to succeed, or *govern*, than his uncle Murrough. After this Murrough's death, his nephew, Donough, the Baron of Ibrackan,—to whom, as well as to his late uncle, Henry VIII., in 1542, had confirmed all his castles, lordships, manors, &c., beyond the Shannon, with a considerable grant of ecclesiastical property,—became 2nd Earl of Thomond, for life; which title, by a new patent of Edward VI. in 1552, was confirmed, in perpetuity, to the Baron and his heirs male, along with all the honours and lands that had fallen to the Crown, by Earl Murrough's decease. This Donough O'Brien, surnamed *the Fat*, and the 2nd Earl of Thomond, dying in 1553, was succeeded, as 3rd Earl of Thomond, by his son, Conor or Cornelius O'Brien. He had 3 sons, Donough, the 4th Earl of Thomond, Teige, whose posterity are extinct, and Daniel, of Moyarta and Carrigaholt,* in the County of Clare. Daniel, distinguishing himself and receiving many wounds, in the wars of Ireland, under Queen Elizabeth, was knighted as Sir Daniel O'Brien, and rewarded by the Crown with considerable grants of land in that County. He was its representative in the Irish Parliament of 1613, and, in consideration of his own and his children's services to the royal cause, both at home and abroad, during the subsequent convulsions and wars, was, after the Restoration of King Charles II., created 1st Viscount of Clare, in the County of Clare, in 1662; and had his estate of 84,339 acres in Clare, besides lands in Limerick, that had been lost during the Cromwellian usurpation, restored to him. He was succeeded, as 2nd Viscount of Clare, by his son Conor O'Brien; on whose death, about the year 1670, his son Daniel became the 3rd Viscount. Daniel had followed King Charles II. in his exile, and served him so zealously until the Restoration in 1660, that, after his return with the King to London, his

* Carrigaholt, in Gaelic, or Irish, *the rock of the fleet*, is a commanding cliff, overlooking a bay, so called from it. The Castle, situated on this cliff, and kept in order, as a residence, to our own times, belonged to Lord Clare till the War of the Revolution, when he forfeited it, with the rest of his estates, for his adherence to King James II. The popular legends concerning this Castle, according to a modern work, were blended with traditions of the Lord Clare, and the Regiment of Yellow Dragoons (so-called from the colour of their facings) which he levied for the service of King James. The ghost of that Lord, and those of his dragoons, were supposed to traverse the west, in the stormy nights of winter, and to disappear at dawn, into the surges, off Carrigaholt! How comparatively uninteresting is a Castle, without *some* story of the kind, attached to it.

merit is, in a great degree, supposed to have obtained the title of Viscount Clare for his grandfather. On the defection of England to the Prince of Orange in 1688, the loyalty of this noble Irish family was the same to King James II. against the Dutch Prince, as it had been to King Charles II. against Oliver Cromwell. Daniel, the 3rd Viscount Clare, was Lord-Lieutenant of that County for King James, a member of his Irish Privy Council, sat among the Peers of Ireland in the Parliament of 1689, and raised, for the royal service, a Regiment of Dragoons, called after himself, the Clare Dragoons, and 2 Regiments of Infantry. By his marriage with the Lady Philadelphia, eldest daughter of Francis Lennard, Lord Dacre of the South, and sister to Thomas, Earl of Sussex, his Lordship had 2 sons, for whom he levied those infantry regiments. The 1st was commanded by the elder son, the Honourable Daniel O'Brien; the 2nd by the younger son, the Honourable Charles O'Brien; to both of whom, as 4th and 5th Viscounts, the title of Lord Clare afterwards descended. The Infantry Regiment of the Honourable Daniel O'Brien was that selected by King James, to form a portion of the Brigade of Mountcashel.

The Colonel of the 3rd regiment of this Brigade, the Honourable Arthur Dillon, was likewise a member of one of the noblest houses in Ireland. The founder of it was a Chevalier Henry Delion of Aquitaine, sent, in 1185, by King Henry II. of England to Ireland, with his youngest son Johan, or John, Comte or Earl of Mortagne, as his First Gentleman, and one of his Secretaries. By the latter Prince (afterwards King John) Henry Delion was granted a large territory, reaching from the river Shannon to Cloghanenumora, east of Mullingar, to hold *per Baroniam in Capite*, and the service of several knights' fees; according to which grant, he and his heirs were entitled to a summons to Parliament, like the Anglo-Norman Barons on the other side of the Channel, who held their baronies by the same tenure. This extensive tract was, after its Lord, denominated *Dillon's Country*, and was held, as a kind of sovereignty, till reduced to shire-ground, under King Henry VIII. The Chevalier Henry Delion is entitled, "Sir Henry of Drumrany," from having fixed his residence there. "He," observes my authority, "built his mansion house, with a church in Drumrany, pretty much in the centre of his country, in the west of Meath; also a castle in Dunimony; and several abbies (as those of Athlone, Kilkenny-West, Ardnecrany, Holy-Island, Hare-Island, &c.), churches and castles were built and endowed by his descendants, Lords of the said territories. He," it is added, "was progenitor to all who bear the name of Dillon, a name of great note, in the Counties of Meath, Westmeath, Longford, Roscommon, Mayo, and other parts of the kingdom, where, and in many foreign countries, they have flourished in the highest departments of church and state." Of the several great families, sprung from this "Sir Henry of Drumrany," that of the Viscounts Dillon of Costello-Gallen, in the County of Mayo, was founded, in the reign of Queen Elizabeth, by Sir Theobald Dillon, Knight; who derived his origin, through the house of Dunimony, from that of Drumrany. Theobald, commanding an Independent Troop of Horse in 1559, was knighted, or created Sir Theobald Dillon, for his bravery, on the field of battle. In 1582, he was appointed, by the Queen, General Collector and Receiver of the Composition Money of Connaught and Thomond; and had this office not only renewed to him by King James I., but was granted, in 1604, that of General Cessor and Collector for the Counties of Galway, Mayo, Sligo, Leitrim, Roscommon, and Clare; and finally was, for his long services to the Crown, raised by James, in 1622, to the Peerage of Ireland, as Viscount Dillon of Costello-Gallen, in the County of Mayo. His Lordship died, in 1624, possessed of a very large landed property in Leinster and Connaught, and so advanced in years, that, says the account, "at one time he had the satisfaction of seeing above 100 of his descendants in his house at Killenfaghny," or Killenfeagh, in the County of Westmeath. During the subsequent Parliamentarian wars, and Cromwellian usurpation, the house of Costello-Gallen signalized itself in support of the royal cause; for which Thomas, the 4th Viscount, had his extensive estates seized, and was obliged to live, with his 4 sons, in exile upon the Continent; where several of his name, expatriated on a similar account, distinguished themselves in war. 1. Charles, his heir apparent, was a General Officer in the service of France, as well as Spain, and Governor of Tournay in Flanders. 2. Sir James Dillon, Knight, 8th son of the 1st Viscount Dillon, a Lieutenant-General, Governor of Connaught for the royal cause against the Parliamentarian and Cromwellian rebels, and proscribed as such, but finally rewarded by the Crown with a pension of £500 per annum, was a Major-General, both of France and Spain. 3. James Dillon, after the success of the Cromwellians in Ireland, was also a Major-General, or Maréchal de Camp, in the service of France, by brevet of March 26th, 1653; raised an Irish regiment of his name, by commission of June 20th following; until the Peace of the Pyrennees, commanded it in Flanders with distinction, particularly at the battle of Dunkirk; and kept it till his death; after which, or by order of February 29th, 1664, it was disbanded. Thomas, the 4th Viscount Dillon, remained, with his 4 sons, in banishment, until the Restoration. His Lordship then returned home, and, in 1663, was put into possession of his property, amounting to 64,195 plantation acres of profitable land in Mayo, Roscommon, and Westmeath. In the war of the Revolution, this ennobled line of Costello-Gallen adhered to the Stuart family, as it had *previously* done. Theobald Dillon, successor to the family title, in 1682, as 7th Viscount, and married to Mary, daughter of Sir Henry Talbot, of Temple-Oge, County of Dublin, and Mount-Talbot, County of Roscommon, was then head of the house of Costello-Gallen. His Lordship himself served, as Lieutenant-Colonel to the Earl of Clanricarde's Irish Regiment of Guards; and raised 2 Regiments of Infantry for King James. Of these, 1 regiment was commanded by his Lordship's eldest son, and subsequent successor in the title, the Honourable Henry Dillon, Lord-Lieutenant of the County Roscommon, Member for Westmeath in the Irish Parliament of 1689, and afterwards Governor of Galway. The Colonel of the other regiment, or that appointed to form part of the Brigade of Mountcashel, was Lord Theobald's 2nd son, the Honourable Arthur Dillon. He was, at the time of his landing with his regiment in France, *not* 20 years of age; afterwards rose to high rank in the French army; and was father to the Lords Charles and Henry Dillon, the 10th and 11th Viscounts of Costello-Gallen, also officers of distinction in the same service.

These 3 Regiments of Mountcashel, O'Brien, and Dillon, the first of King James's Irish army that entered the French service in the spring of 1690, were followed to France, after the conclusion of the Treaty of Limerick, in October, 1691, by the rest of the Irish army, that adhered to James's cause, rather than acknowledge the Prince of Orange, as *their* Sovereign. Between those who sailed in November, from the Shannon, with the Comte de Chateaurenaud's fleet of 18 men of war, 6 fire-ships, and 22 large vessels of burthen, &c., that, although too late for the relief of Limerick, served to convey to Brest a large body of the Irish with their wives and children, and the remainder who followed in as many as were required of the 14,000 tuns of shipping, stipulated, by the 7th and 8th of the Military Articles of the Treaty of Limerick, to be provided at William's expense for the same purpose, the landing in France, of all the Irish who chose to go there, was completed in January, 1692. From the returns of the French "Commissaires," obtained through the Lord Marshal of Thomond and Clare, the Irish officers and soldiers, who followed the King to France, are specified by Mac Geoghegan at 19,059; which number, added to the previously-arrived Brigade of Mountcashel of 5371 military of every rank, would make 24,430 officers and soldiers; and these, with others, who came over at different times not specified, would, according to the English and Irish authority of King James's Memoirs, and a letter of the Chevalier Charles Wogan, nephew of the Duke of Tyrconnell, amount, in all, to about 30,000 men. "Thus," add the royal Memoirs, "was Ireland after an obstinate resistance in 3 years campagns, by the power and riches of England and the revolt of almost all its own Protestant subjects, torn from its natural Sovereign; who, tho' he was divested of the country he was not wholly deprived of ye people, for the greatest part of those, who were then in armes for defence of his right, not content with the service already render'd, got leave (as was sayd) to come and loos their lives, after haveing lost their estates, in defence of his title, and brought by that means such a body of men into France, as *by their generous comportment in accepting the pay of the country, instead of that which is usually allowed there to strangers, and their unimitable valour and service during the whole cours of the war, might justly make their Prince pass for an ally rather than a pentioner or burthen to his Most Christian Majesty*, whose pay indeed they received, but acted by the King their master's commission, according to the common method of other auxilliary troops. As soon as the King heard of their arrival, (in France) he writ to the Commander to assure him, how well he was satisfyd with the behaviour and conduct of the officers, and the valour and fidelity of the soldiers, and how sencible he should ever be of their service, which he would not fail to reward when it should please God to put him in a capacity of doing it." The letter, which, on being informed of the arrival of the 1st body of Irish troops, December 3rd, at Brest, was despatched by the King from St. Germain to their commanding officer, Major-General Dominick Sheldon, was as follows:—

"JAMES *Rex*.

"Having been informed of the Capitulation and Surrender of Limerick, and of the other places which remained to us in our Kingdom of Ireland, and of the necessities which forced the Lords Justices and the General Officers of our Forces thereunto; we will not defer to let you know, and the rest of the officers that came along with you, that we are extreamly satisfied with your and their conduct, and of the valour of the souldiers during the siege, but, most particularly, of your and their declaration and resolution, to come and serve where we are. And we assure you, and order you, to assure both officers and souldiers that are come along with you, that we shall never forget this act of loyalty, nor fail, when in a capacity, to give them, above others, particular marks of our favour. In the mean time, you are to inform them, that they are to serve under our command, and by our commissions; and, if we find, that a considerable number is come with the fleet, it will induce us to go personally to see them, and regiment them. Our brother, the King of France, hath already given orders to cloath them, and furnish them with all necessaries, and to give them quarters of refreshment. So we bid you heartily farewell. Given at our Court at St. Germaine, the 27th of November,* 1691."

According to this promise, that, in case a considerable number of troops should come from Ireland, he would go to see and regiment them in person, the King set out from St. Germain for Bretagne, about the middle of December. Accompanied by his son, the Duke of Berwick, James reviewed and regimented at Vannes all the men that had arrived from Ireland, returned on the 11th of January, 1692, to St. Germain, and on the landing of another or the last division, under Major-General Patrick Sarsfield, Lord Lucan, at Brest, and the other ports of Bretagne, the King again left St. Germain, and reviewed and regimented that body, as he had done the rest. It was decided, that the Irish, who were to act under his commission as *his* army, should consist of 2 Troops of Horse Guards, 2 Regiments of Horse, 2 Regiments of Dragoons à *pied*, or *Dismounted* Dragoons that were to serve as Infantry, 8 Regiments of Foot, (containing altogether 15 battalions) and 3 Independent Companies. The extensive alterations connected with this new formation of the Irish army inflicted, like *all* great public changes, much hardship upon individuals; some, who had been Major-Generals, being reduced to Colonels, and so downwards to the Ensigns, several of whom had to become Serjeants, and even privates. The old or Milesian Irish, who had levied regiments for the War of the Revolution, suffered most. Of the O'Neills, for example, of whom several had been Colonels of Regiments in Ireland, Brigadier Gordon O'Neill alone obtained a regiment; and other regiments, or those of O'Donnell, Mac Donnell, Mac Guire, Mac Mahon, Mac Gennis, and O'Reilly, were dissolved as separate corps, and their officers proportionate sufferers. In the arrangements with the French Government concerning the rate of pay for the newly-formed regiments, the further sacrifice made by the Irish to their exiled Sovereign's interest—as previously alluded to in the extract from his own Memoirs respecting "their generous comportment in accepting the pay of the country, instead of that usually allowed there to strangers"—is thus related, with other affecting particulars, in a manuscript, written, after the King's death, by a contemporary Irish Jacobite, or loyalist. "Upon capitulating with the enemy," says this writer, of his countrymen, at Limerick, "they stipulated also with their own French Generals, that they should be put in France upon strangers' pay; but when they were modled at Rennes, it was regulated they should have but French pay, to which they acquiesc'd meerly to please their own King, and in hopes the over-plus of their just pay, amounting to 50,000 livres a month, retrench'd from them, might abate the obligations of their Master to the French Court. The world knows with what constancy and fidelity they stuck ever since to the service of France, not but that they might push their fortunes faster in other services, but because it was to his Most Christian Majesty their Master ow'd obligations most, and had from him sanctuary and protection; nay so wedded they were for these

* December 7th, N.S.

reasons to the French service, that many who were, some of them Field Officers, others Captains, and Subalterns, and who coud not be all provided for, pursuant to the methods taken for the modlement of their troops in France, had submitted to carry arms rather than quit the service their Master expected succour from: most of these poor gentlemen moulder'd away under the fatigues and miseries of the musket, before there was room to replace them as Officers. This vast stock of loialty was not appropriated to the officers alone, it ran in the blood of the very common soldiers; an instance whereof was seen in ye wonderful affection they bore to the service, and the confidence the Captains had in the fidelity as well as bravery of their men, who were so little acquainted and tainted with desertion, that, upon a day of march or action, the Commanders were not seen in any apprehension their maroders or straglers woud give them the slip; and it was frequently observed the officers were less in pain for the return of the men, than these were to rejoin their comrades." Of the effects of such conduct of the Irish troops upon King James, this writer then adds—" His late Majesty was so sensibly touch'd with all these particulars, and especially with the acquiesence of his troops to be reduc'd to the French pay, that, by an instrument under his hand and seal, he made a solemn promise he would pay them what their actual pay wanted, to make it full English, whenever God was pleas'd to restore him, and so made it his own and the Crown's debt."

Sir Walter Scott remarks, "whatever our opinion may be of the cause for which the followers of James abandoned their country and fortunes, there can be but one sentiment concerning the courage and self-devotion, with which they sacrificed their all to a sense of duty;" and the light, in which this conduct of the Irish was regarded by all ranks in France, is noticed, as follows, by Count Arthur Dillon. "Louis XIV. wrote with his own hand, in 1704, to the Civil-Lieutenant, Le Camus, ' that he had always treated the Irish Catholics, who had passed into his kingdom, as his own subjects; and that it was his wish that they should enjoy the same rights as natural-born Frenchmen, without being, on that account, obliged to take out letters of naturalization.' This letter of Louis XIV.," continues the Count, " only served to confirm the sentiments of the nation, and every one knows, that all orders of the state, by a sort of universal feeling, had already assigned to the Irish the right of citizenship; and then it was, that, in order to stamp with a name, for ever memorable, those strangers admitted to the honour of being French citizens, they were termed JACOBITES, that is to say, *faithful to King James.*" Forman, too, who was attached to the change of dynasty effected by the Revolution of 1688, and, consequently, of opposite political principles to those of the Irish Jacobites, after alluding to so many of the latter, as " unhappy gentlemen, who, by the loss of plentiful fortunes at home, had nothing left them but their swords, to procure a scanty, painful maintenance abroad," thus speaks, in the reign of George II., of the general sacrifices of the Irish military followers of James to his service—" Their inflexible steadiness to the interest of an unfortunate and declining King, whom they looked upon to be their lawful Sovereign, notwithstanding our Acts of Parliament to the contrary; their refusal of those advantageous terms which King William so generously offered them; their exposing themselves to inexpressible hardships, to perpetual dangers, and even to death itself, rather than acknowledge any other Prince than King James, at least while any farther resistance in his favour was practicable, first gained them that esteem in France, which their behaviour ever since has preserved for them even to this day." The right, it may be added, of French, citizenship, so conferred upon the expatriated Irish by Louis XIV., being contested, under Louis XV., by the Fermiers du Domain, on the pretext, that such a privilege granted to the Irish Jacobites was not formally legal, a decree issued the same year, or in March, 1736, to the Bureau du Domain, confirming to the Irish exiles in France the right attempted to be contested with them. Again, or in a letter of March 25th, 1741, to the Chapter of Lille, Louis XV. confirmed that right to the Irish. His letter on this occasion, and that of Louis XIV. to the Civil Lieutenant, Le Camus, above referred to, and cited by various French lawyers, were both deposited in the Bureau de la Guerre at Paris; and, on these documents and decisions, the various "arrêts" or decrees of the French Council of State, and the Parliament of Paris, in suits connected with Irish claims to property in France, were based, down to the period of the Revolution.

Of the origin, and successive changes amongst the commanding officers, of the 3 first Irish regiments in the French service, the following particulars are given in my authorities.

THE INFANTRY REGIMENT OF MOUNTCASHEL.

This regiment was formed in 1683, out of several Independent Companies of Irish, which King Charles II. withdrew from Tangier, in Africa, when he caused it to be demolished. The corps was composed of 2 battalions in 16 companies, variously stated, or, as it would appear, at different times, consisting of 80 or 100 men a company. Its 1st Colonel was James Butler, afterwards 2nd Duke of Ormonde, who, being made Colonel of a Regiment of Horse in the Irish army, resigned his previous post to the Honourable Justin Mac Carthy, subsequently Lord Mountcashel. After the destruction of this regiment at the unlucky affair of Newtown-Butler, in August, 1689, it was renewed with fresh recruits, and brought to France, in May, 1690, by his Lordship. Soon after landing there, or May 20th, Lord Mountcashel received a commission from Louis XIV.; entitling his Lordship to command all the Irish troops taken into the French service, or his own, with the other corps of O'Brien and Dillon. May 30th, he was empowered to act as a Lieutenant-General of France, as he already was of England and Ireland; and, June 1st, was specially commissioned to be Colonel of his regiment under Louis, as he had previously been under James. Employed by letters of July 26th, the same year, with M. de St. Ruth, in Savoy, he signalized himself, at the head of his regiment, in the reduction of that province; particularly at a defeat of the Piedmontese, September 12th; where he was wounded, though but slightly. Transferred by letters of June 13th, 1691, to serve under the Duke de Noailles, with the Army of Rousillon or Catalonia, he was present at the captures of Urgel, the castles of Valence and Boy, and the raising of the siege of Pratz-de-Mollo. He remained, in 1692, with the same army, which kept, however, merely upon the defensive. Despatched, by letters of April 27th, 1693, to the Army of Germany, as 1 of its Lieutenant-Generals, under the Marshals de Lorges and de Choiseul, he and his regiment contributed to the successes of that campaign; at which he shared in the reduction of the city and castle of Heidelburg, of Wingemburg, of Eppenheim, and of Darmstadt. He was to have continued with the Army of Germany, in 1694; but the injurious effects of his wounds obliged him to seek the benefit of the waters of Barrege, where he died that summer. His decease is thus announced, under the head of "Paris, 31st July, 1694," in the French official journal. "Mylord Montcassel, Lieutenant-General of the Armies of the King, Commander of 3 Irish Regiments, died the 1st of this month at Barrege, of the wounds that he has received on several occasions, in which he was always extremely distinguished."

Lord Mountcashel was succeeded in his regiment by Colonel Andrew Lee, or de Lee, according to the prefix given to his and other names by French writers. Lee was born in 1650, and first belonged to the infantry regiment of 1500 men, besides officers, permitted by King Charles II. to be levied in Ireland, in 1671, for the service of France, by Sir and Count George Hamilton, from whom, as its Colonel, it was called the "Régiment d' Hamilton."* After the Count's death in 1676, the Irish of his

* George Hamilton was the eldest surviving son of Sir George Hamilton of Dunnalong in the County of Tyrone, and Nenagh in the County of Tipperary, by Lady Mary Butler, 3rd daughter of Thomas Butler, Lord Thurles, and sister to James Butler, 12th Earl and 1st Duke of Ormonde. Sir George, who was a Catholic, served King Charles I. and Charles II. faithfully against the Parliamentarian and Cromwellian rebels in Ireland, where he was a Captain of Horse, and afterwards a Colonel of Foot, and Governor of the Castle of Nenagh, against those insurgents, as well as Receiver-General for the Crown. On the final prevalence of the Cromwellian invaders, he resolved to join the royal family in France; but, before leaving Ireland, "he staid," says Carte, "to pass his accounts, which he did to the satisfaction of all parties, notwithstanding much clamour had been raised against him." He then, or in 1651, went into exile with his family, when King Charles II., it is observed, "being sensible of his good and acceptable services, and willing to show him all reasonable favour for the same, created him a Baronet." As attached, however, only to a nominal or refugee King, such as Charles II. was till 1660, Sir George, like numbers of banished Irish loyalists, had to encounter much privation and distress on the Continent. In this interval, the young George Hamilton was made 1 of the Royal Pages; after the Restoration was enrolled in the Horse-Guards; and is named by his brother Anthony, in the Memoirs of their brother-in-law, the Comte de Grammont, among the brilliant intriguers of the English Court, as a lover of the pretty Mrs. Wettenhall. In 1667, on account of the jealousy of the English against "Popery," the King had to dismiss from his Horse-Guards such English, Irish, and Scotch officers, &c., as were Catholics; but was enabled to provide for them elsewhere by Louis XIV., who offered them employment, under young Hamilton. Having gotten due permission from King Charles to enter the service of France, and being considered, on their arrival there, as "tous bons hommes et bien faits," or, "all good and wellmade men," those who were natives of Scotland were incorporated with the ancient Compagnie de Gendarmes Ecossois of the Royal Guards; the rest were formed into another Compagnie, called Gendarmes Anglois, of which Louis (in order, it would seem, to compliment them the more,) named *himself* the Captain; and, November 28th, 1667, appointed Hamilton his Captain-Lieutenant. Sir George Hamilton (thus entitled, either as having been knighted, or as successor to his father's baronetcy in 1667, or for *both* reasons,) commanded this Compagnie de Gendarmes Anglois, at the conquest of Franche-Comté in 1668. In 1671, he raised, under an agreement made in April, "un Régiment d'Infanterie *Irlandoise* de 15 compagnies de 100 hommes chacune," exclusive of officers; "sa Majesté," it is added, "ayant satisfaction des services qu'elle a receus des régimens Irlandois qui ont esté cy-devant à sa solde," and this regiment, as "infanterie estrangère," to have "les hautes payes." Of this corps, of 2 battalions, Sir George was commissioned as Colonel, May 12th, and commanded it, in 1672, with the French Army of Holland, after its passage of the Rhine. He

D

regiment, being drafted into the German Regiment of Furstemberg, and then of Greider, or Greder, were accompanied by Lee. A Lieutenant in the corps, in 1678, under its appellation of Furstemberg, he fought against the Brandenburghers, near Minden, in 1679; and obtained a company by commission, May 7th, 1682. He served at the siege of Girona, in 1684; was made Lieutenant-Colonel, by commission of December 11th, 1687; was with the Army of Flanders, under the Marshal d'Humieres, in 1689, when he was engaged in the unsuccessful affair of Walcourt; and with better fortune, in 1690, under the illustrious Marshal de Luxembourg, at Fleurus; where the regiment, as that of Greider, was lauded by the Marshal, for its very good conduct, and its having taken 1 or 2 standards. Shortly before that battle, or June 18th, Lee received a commission of Lieutenant-Colonel, empowering him to hold rank as Colonel of Infantry to the new Regiment of O'Brien, (afterwards Clare) under which, see him noticed, till appointed, by commission of July 28th, 1694, to the Colonelship of the regiment previously Lord

then joined the Marshal de Turenne; shared in the successful operations against the Elector of Brandenburgh in 1673; "and," remarks Lodge, "being to recruit his regiment of foot in the service of the French King, his Majesty," King Charles II., "sent his directions to the Lord-Lieutenant, 12 January, 1673, to give license unto him and his officers to raise 600 foot soldiers of his *Irish* subjects by beat of drum." He was at the battles of Sintzheim, Einsheim, and Mulhausen, in 1674. At that of Einsheim, he was severely wounded, and is described, by my French authorities, as having "performed great acts of valour," or having "with a battalion of his regiment, cut to pieces a hostile battalion, and dispersed the dragoons who supported it." Continuing with the Army of Germany under Turenne, he distinguished himself at the battle of Turkheim, January 5th, 1675; and was made a Brigadier of Infantry, by brevet of March 12th. July 27th, at Salzbach, being near the battery which Turenne approached on horseback to inspect, he warned the Marshal to take a different direction, was, on his fall, soon after by a cannon-shot, the 1st, with presence of mind, to throw a cloak over the corpse; and, in the subsequent retreat of the French, he signalized himself, by protecting it at Wilstet and Altenheim. The leading French military historian of those times, relating the retreat of his countrymen, and the attack upon them by the Imperial General, Montecuculli, at Wilstet, states—"The Comte de Montecuculli followed them with all his army, and came up with their rear-guard at Wilstet. He attacked it with a large detachment, with which he had pushed forward; but he was repulsed by the Chevalier de Bouflers, and by the Comte d' Hamilton." And, elsewhere noticing this affair at Wilstet, and that at Altenheim, the same historian specifies Hamilton, to have "given the greatest proofs of valour" against the enemy; having "repulsed them after an action of the most animated kind," where "the Irish did wonders," as well as the English, who were then serving with the French. Created Maréchal de Camp, or Major-General, February 25th, 1676, and still being with the Army of Germany under Turenne's successor, the Marshal Duke de Luxembourg, Hamilton was present, when, in the retreat of the French on Saverne, their rear was attacked, and thrown into confusion by the enemy, under the Duke of Lorrain. This Luxembourg hastened in person to repair, at the head of his cavalry, "and seconded," according to the French historian, "by the Comte d' Hamilton, who had posted his regiment advantageously, he put a stop to the enemies by the great fire which he caused to be poured upon them, and compelled them, by means of the cavalry, to retire in disorder." But the affair, it is added, "cost his life to the Comte d' Hamilton, whom the King had made Maréchal de Camp." At his death, the Count possessed both his Irish Regiment of Infantry and the Compagnie de Gendarmes Anglois, or rather Anglois *et Irlandois*. He married, in 1665, the beautiful Frances Jennings, elder sister of the famous Sarah, Duchess of Marlborough, and daughter of Richard Jennings, Esq., of Sandridge in Hertfordshire. By her, he left 3 daughters, who were all nobly married in Ireland; the 1st, Elizabeth, in 1685, to Richard Parsons, 1st Viscount Rosse; the 2nd, Frances, in 1687, to Henry Dillon, 8th Viscount Dillon; the 3rd, Mary, in 1688, to Nicholas Barnewall, 3rd Viscount Kingsland.

Mountcashel's. He served that year with the Army of Italy; passed to that of Germany, in 1695; was with the Army of the Meuse, under the Marshal de Boufflers, in 1696; at the taking of Ath, by the Marshal de Catinat, in 1697; at the great encampment, and the grand review, by Louis in person, at Coudun, near Compiegne, by letters of August 13th, 1698; with the Army of Flanders, by letters of June 6th, 1701; with the Army of Germany, under the Marshal de Catinat, by letters of May 8th, 1702; and was created Maréchal de Camp, by brevet of December 23rd, that year. Employed with the Army of Bavaria, under the Marshal de Villars, in 1703, he was at the siege of Kehl; at the taking of the lines of Stolhoffen, and the retrenchments of the Valley of Hornberg; at the combat of Munderkingen; at the defeat of the Count de Stirum, in the 1st battle of Hochstedt, where he was wounded; and was also at the taking of Kempten. In June, 1704, he transferred the command of his regiment to his son. Then, attached to the Army of Bavaria, under the Marshal de Marcin, he commanded the French force, united with the Bavarian troops, at the glorious defence of the retrenchments of Schellemberg, in July; next fought at the 2nd or unfortunate battle of Hochstedt, (more generally called that of Blenheim) in August; and obtained the grade of Lieutenant-General of the Armies of the King, by a power of 26th October. In 1705, he served with the Army of the Moselle, under the Marshal de Villars; with the Army of the Rhine, under the same General, in 1706 and 1707; and, during the winter of the last-mentioned year, was employed in Alsace, by order of 31st October. In 1708, he was with the Army of the Rhine, under the Marshal Duke of Berwick; when, hearing of the enemy's design of besieging the important fortress of Lisle, in Flanders, he threw himself into that place; under the gallant and worthy Marshal de Boufflers, contributed nobly to its celebrated defence, at which he was wounded; and, by brevet of 12th November, was nominated by Louis XIV. to the next vacancy of a Grand Cross of the Order of St. Louis, with permission, meanwhile, to wear the insignia of that honour. In 1709, he served with the Army of Germany, under the Marshal d' Harcourt; in 1710, 1711, and 1712, with the Army of Flanders, under the Marshal de Villars. The campaign of 1712 was his last; in which, he was present at the captures of Douay, Quesnoy, and Bouchain. He obtained the post of a Grand Cross of the Order of St. Louis, by provision of July 3rd, 1719. His son Francis, on whom he had devolved the command of his regiment since June, 1704, having died, he resumed the Colonelship, by commission of December 13th, 1720. In 1733, he made an arrangement, through which he had the regiment granted, by commission of September 16th, to the Comte de Bulkeley; and died not long after, or February 16th, 1734, aged 84.

The Comte François de Bulkeley, as he was called in France, was of a noble British Jacobite family, derived from Robert de Bulkeley, Seigneur or Lord of the manor of Bulkeley, in the Palatinate of Chester, under the Anjou-Norman King of England, Johan, or John. In January, 1643, Thomas Bulkeley, Esq., of Baron Hall in the Isle of Anglesey, was, for his great merit and strict loyalty, created by King Charles I., at Oxford, Viscount Bulkeley of Cashel, in the Kingdom of Ireland. The Viscount's 4th son, the Honourable Henry Bulkeley, was made Master of the Household to Kings Charles II. and James II., and married Lady Sophia Stewart, by whom he had 2 sons, and 4 daughters; who all joined the 2nd exile of the royal race, or that under King

James II. and his family, in France. The names of the sons were James and Francis. Those of the daughters were Charlotte, Anne, Henrietta, and Laura. James established himself in France, and left issue there; Francis was the particular subject of this notice; Charlotte was married, 1st, to Charles O'Brien, 5th Viscount Clare, 2ndly, to Lieutenant-General Count Daniel O'Mahony; Anne to the illustrious James Fitz-James, Marshal Duke of Berwick; Henrietta and Laura, each the theme of the muse of our countryman, Count Anthony Hamilton, author of the Memoirs of Grammont, &c., both died unmarried. Francis Bulkeley, born in London, September 11th, 1686, passed into France, in 1700, the year of his sister's marriage to the Duke of Berwick. He commenced his military career as an Aide-de-Camp to that nobleman, with whom he was present at the defeat of the Dutch, about Nimeguen, in 1702. He was at the victory of Eckeren over the same enemy, in 1703; and obtained a Lieutenancy in the Duke's regiment. In 1704, he followed the Duke into Spain, and was at the reduction of 20 places in Portugal. He was made a reformed Captain of the Regiment of Berwick, by commission of January 1st, 1705. Still acting as Aide-de-Camp of the Duke, he accompanied him into Languedoc for the subjection of the Camisards, or revolted Huguenots there; thence in October, into the Comté of Nice, in order to besiege the strong fortress of that name, which surrendered January 4th, 1706; and, on the 13th, he was commissioned as a reformed Colonel of the Regiment of Berwick. Again passing with the Duke into Spain for the campaign of 1706, he shared in its very varied operations, concluded by the siege and capture of Carthagena, in November, at which he took part. In 1707, he fought, April 25th, at the famous battle of Almanza; obtained, by commission of May 11th, a regiment of infantry of his name, which was previously the Chevalier de Tessé's; and commanded that regiment at the taking of the town and castle of Lerida, the ensuing autumn. He acted, in the same capacity, at the reduction of Tortosa, in 1708. He quitted this corps, May 23rd, 1709; resumed, by commission of same date, his former grade of reformed Colonel to the Regiment of Berwick; and remained this year with the army of Spain, which kept on the defensive. The 3 following campaigns, or those of 1710, 1711, and 1712, he served under the Marshal Duke of Berwick, in the Army of Dauphiné. In 1713, he was with the Army of Germany, under the Marshal de Villars, and was present at the captures of Landau and Friburgh. In 1714, he accompanied the Marshal Duke of Berwick to the reduction of Barcelona. Brigadier by brevet of February 1st, 1719, and employed, under the same General, with the Army of Spain, he was at the siege and capture of Fontarabia, of the town and citadel of St. Sebastian, of the Castle of Urgel, and also at the siege of Roses. Attached, by letters of September 15th, 1733, to the Army of the Rhine, under his illustrious brother-in-law, and becoming, by commission of the 16th, Colonel of the Irish Regiment of Infantry previously Lee's, he was at the capture of Kehl; and was employed at Strasburgh, during the winter, by letters of December 1st. Maréchal de Camp, or Major-General, by brevet of February 20th, 1734, and continued with the Army of the Rhine, by letters of April 1st, he mounted several trenches at the siege of Philipsburgh; and, by order of November 1st, commanded during the winter in Flanders, under the Marshal de Puysegur. In 1735, he remained by letters of May 1st, with the same

Army, who undertook nothing, on account of the approaching peace, which was made in October. Lieutenant-General of the Armies of the King, by power of March 1st, 1738, he was employed, in 1742, with the Army of Bavaria, under the Marshal Duke d' Harcourt, and then under the Comte (afterwards Marshal) de Saxe, by letters of April 1st, and was with the 4th Division, at the Camp of Neideraltack; where they maintained themselves for 5 months, in spite of the enemy's superior numbers. He then marched to the frontiers of Bohemia, under the Marshal de Maillebois, and returned to France after the campaign. Attached to the Army of the Rhine, by letters of April 1st, 1743, he fought at the battle of Dettingen, in June. With the Army of Flanders, under the King, Louis XV., by letters of April 1st, 1744, he was at the siege and capture of Menin and Ypres; and then passing, by letters of July 1st, under the orders of the Marshal de Saxe, he terminated the campaign at the Camp of Courtray. He was by letters of April 1st, 1745, with the Army of the Lower Rhine, under the Prince de Conti; who made themselves masters of Guermsheim, July 15th, and crossed the Rhine, within sight of the enemy, the 19th; but continued on the defensive, till the end of the campaign. He was retained at Strasburgh, during the winter, by order of November 1st. Transferred to the Army of Flanders, under the Marshal de Saxe, by letters of May 1st, 1746, he fought at the victory of Rocoux, in October; commanded, during the winter, at Bruges, by letters of November 1st; and was not removed from that command till April 30th, 1748. That year, January 1st, he was named Chevalier of the Orders of the King, and was received as such February 2nd. He was made Governor of St. Jean-Pied-de-Port, by provision of January 29th, 1751; resigned his regiment, in favour of his son, in March, 1754; and died, January 14th, 1756, in his 70th year.

The Lieutenant-General had married a daughter of Philip de Cantillon, a gentleman of Norman-Irish origin, who had followed the fortunes of the exiled Stuarts to France, and, besides founding one of the principal banks in Europe at Paris, was distinguished by his writings, and correspondingly high position in society. Under the various spellings of Cantelou, Cantelupe, Cantillo, Cantello, and Cantillon, several members of this family established themselves in England under *one* Norman conquest, in the kingdom of Naples under *another*, and in Ireland, since the period of Strongbow's landing there. This last branch of the name acquired the Lordship of Ballyheigh, or Ballyheigue, in the County of Kerry, besides lands in the County of Limerick; and intermarried with an offshoot of the Stuart line itself, as well as with the Fitz-Geralds, O'Briens, Mac Mahons, O'Sullivans, Seymours, O'Connells, &c. Of the house of Ballyheigh, we are informed, that "its fidelity to the Catholic religion, and its attachment to its legitimate Kings, the victims of adversity, were the causes of its dispersion and its ruin. It suffered all the misfortunes of exile, and forfeiture. Many of its members were reduced, in a foreign land, to a condition next to destitution; but they never forgot, on the field of battle, this noble and glorious motto to their armorial bearings, *Fortis in bello*."* Long after the lords of Ballyheigh were dispossessed of their ancient inheritance, they were remembered there. Dr. Smith, the historian of Kerry, in 1756, when mentioning the bay of Ballyheigh, states,—"The neighbouring inhabitants shew

* French MS. account of Cantillon family presented by the "Baron de Ballyheigue" to Dr. R. R. Madden, and obligingly communicated to me.

some rocks, visible in this bay only at low tides, which, they say, are the remains of an island, that was formerly the burial-place of the family of Cantillon, who were the ancient proprietors of Ballyheigh." And when, in our day, or December, 1839, the most distinguished military representative of his line in France, Antoine Sylvaine de Cantillon, was granted a title by King Louis-Philippe, he took that of a Baron, in connexion with the name of the patrimony of his ancestors in Kerry. Of the marriage of Lieutenant-General Comte de Bulkeley with Mademoiselle de Cantillon, François Henri Comte de Bulkeley was born in 1739; succeeded to the Colonelship of his father's regiment, March 7th, 1754; was made Brigadier of the Armies of the King, July 25th, 1762; Maréchal de Camp, January 3rd, 1770; and Lieutenant-General, January 1st, 1784. He was Minister Plenipotentiary from France to the Diet of the German Empire, and was pensioned proportionably to his services, about the commencement of the Revolution, or in 1789. But, in June, 1775, by a new arrangement in the French army, under the Ministry of the Marshal du Muy, the Regiment of Bulkeley about 92 years from its 1st formation by Charles II., and 85 years from its entering the French service, under Louis XIV., was incorporated with the Regiment of Dillon.

THE INFANTRY REGIMENT OF O'BRIEN, OR CLARE.

This regiment was raised, clothed, and armed, for the service of King James II., by Daniel O'Brien, 3rd Viscount Clare, early in 1689. On passing into France, in 1690, with the other regiments of Mountcashel's Brigade, it was called O'Brien's regiment, from the eldest son of Lord Clare, the Honourable Daniel O'Brien, through whom it was levied, and who was re-appointed there its 1st Colonel. As a new corps, however, neither it nor its Colonel appearing in France to have had the knowledge requisite for immediate service; and the 1st Lieutenant-Colonel, Fitz-Maurice,* returning to Ireland to take possession of the property coming to him by the death of his father; Lieutenant-Colonel Andrew Lee, of the German Regiment of Greider, received, June 18th, a commission of

* The Fitz-Maurices of Kerry derive their origin from one of the most distinguished chevaliers of the early Anglo-Norman settlers in Erin, Raymond le Gros. Raymond, being invited by Dermod Mac Carthy, King of Desmond, or South Munster, to assist him against his rebellious son, Cormac, who had imprisoned, and cruelly treated him, enabled the King to succeed against, and put to death, the unnatural rebel; in consequence of which, the King rewarded Raymond, about the year 1177, with the territory of Lixnaw, in Kerry. There Raymond established his son, Maurice; whence the territory was designated as that of Clan-Maurice; and the descendants of its owner were known by the name of Fitz-Maurice. The heads of this family, though subordinate to the great Earls of Desmond, were remarkable for bravery, power, noble alliances, &c., and were styled Barons of Lixnaw and Lords of Kerry—the 21st of whom, Thomas Fitz-Maurice, was created, by George I., in January, 1722, Viscount Clan-Maurice, and Earl of Kerry. In France, the chief officers of the Irish Brigade, named Fitz-Maurice, were,—1. Thomas Mac Robert Fitz-Maurice, born in 1721, at Dingle, in Kerry. He joined the Irish Regiment of Roth (afterwards Roscommon) very young; retired with the rank of Lieutenant-Colonel in December, 1766; and was a Chevalier of St. Louis. 2. Thomas Fitz-Maurice, born in 1725, at Listowel in Kerry; entered the Regiment of Roth as a Cadet at 16, in which corps he continued to serve under its successive Colonels, Lord Roscommon and the Comte de Walsh-Serrant; was created a Chevalier of St. Louis in 1776; and was afterwards a Lieutenant-Colonel, and Governor of the Isle of St. Eustache. He received the retiring pension of his rank in 1789.

Lieutenant-Colonel to the Regiment of O'Brien, with power to hold rank as Colonel; and an order was likewise given, to withdraw, from Greider's corps, all the Irish veterans, nearly 200 in number, the remains of Count George Hamilton's levies; that, by such an incorporation of old officers and soldiers with O'Brien's regiment, it might be the sooner fitted for the field. Lee, whom the Marshal de Luxembourg noticed as an officer, that, from his professional merit, and the esteem in which he was generally held, would be well suited for the new post allotted to him, acted as Colonel to the Regiment of O'Brien, in Savoy, that summer, with much distinction; and, October 17th, was commissioned Inspector General of the Irish Troops. He was subsequently stationed with the regiment at Pignerol, and served with the Army of Piedmont, under the Marshal de Catinat, till 1693. Meantime, the Honourable Daniel O'Brien, by the decease of his father in 1691, becoming 4th Viscount Clare, the regiment was named that of Clare, instead of O'Brien. This Daniel, 4th Viscount Clare, dying at Pignerol, in 1693, of the wounds he received at the victory of Marsaglia, gained October 4th, by Catinat, over the Allies, and at which the Regiment of Clare was present, Lee was commissioned, November 18th, in his Lordship's place, as full Colonel, and served in Piedmont the remainder of that year, and during the next; when, on February 6th, he was created a Chevalier of St. Louis, and, on July 28th, he was made Colonel of the Regiment of Mountcashel.

The Colonelship vacated by Lee, in the regiment previously his and Lord Clare's, was next filled by a natural son of the celebrated Duke of Tyrconnell, and bearing a similar name, or Richard Talbot. This officer had served in France from his youth; had greatly distinguished himself at the decisive repulse of the Prince of Orange, September 6th, 1690, before Limerick; was Colonel of the Regiment of Limerick, on the passing of the Irish army into France; became there, (as he had previously been in Ireland during the Williamite war) a Brigadier, April 28th, 1694; and, August 25th following, Colonel in the place of Lee. Brigadier Talbot remained Colonel until April, 1696, when, from some observations or proposals offensive to Louis XIV., that Monarch ordered him to be committed to the Bastille, and deprived of his command. He never regained the regiment, lost by his imprudence; yet was, after a year's detention, released from confinement, restored to active service, and fell, at the battle of Luzzara, in Italy, August 15th, 1702.

After the disgrace and imprisonment of Talbot, the regiment was granted, by commission of April 8th, 1696, to Charles O'Brien, 5th Lord Clare, who, on his elder brother Daniel's decease, at Pignerol, in 1693, became his successor in the title. As the Honourable Charles O'Brien, he commanded, in 1689 and 1690, 1 of the regiments of foot in Ireland, raised by his family, for King James II., against the Revolutionists; and, in 1691, he was Colonel of a cavalry regiment, that served as late as the 2nd siege of Limerick. But, of this corps, after the Treaty, only a remnant existing to sail for the Continent (with similar portions of the cavalry regiments of Tyrconnell, Galmoy, Lucan, Sutherland, Luttrell, Abercorn, Westmeath, and Purcell) Charles O'Brien was made, before leaving Ireland, a Captain in the Gardes du Corps or Horse Guards of King James, with which rank he arrived in France. He was afterwards attached to the Queen of England's Regiment of Dragoons à *pied*, under Colonel Francis O'Carroll, with which he fought at the battle of Marsaglia, in Italy, October 4th, 1693; and, on the fall of that distinguished officer there, was appointed to his post. His Lordship, (for, about the same time, this Charles, as before observed, succeeded his brother, Daniel, in the title of Clare) was Colonel of the Queen of England's Dragoons *à pied*, until his transfer, by commission of April 8th, 1696, to the Colonelship of the corps originally raised by his family; and its title as the regiment of Clare was revived by him. He commanded it the same year at the siege of Valenza in Lombardy; and with the Army of the Meuse, in 1697, the year of the Treaty of Ryswick. On the renewal of hostilities, he was attached with his regiment to the Army of Germany, in 1701 and 1702. Created Brigadier of Infantry by brevet, April 2nd, 1703, he and his corps were at the 1st or successful battle of Hochstedt, September 20th, that year; at the 2nd or unsuccessful battle of Hochstedt, (better known as that of Blenheim) August 13th, 1704; and signalized themselves, in the latter day of adversity, as well as in the former of prosperity. His Lordship was made Maréchal de Camp, by brevet of October 26th following; was employed with the Army of the Moselle under the Marshal de Villars in 1705; and, having been present at the disastrous engagement of Ramillies, May 23rd, 1706, he died at Bruxelles, or Brussels, of the wounds he had received in the action, under circumstances of great glory to himself and his regiment. By his marriage with Charlotte Bulkeley, (eldest daughter of the Honourable Henry Bulkeley, Master of the Household to Kings Charles II. and James II.) his Lordship left (besides a daughter, Laura, married to the Comte de Breteuil) a son Charles, the 6th Viscount Clare, born at St. Germain-en-Laye, March 27th, 1699. He was consequently but a child at his father's death; and as Louis XIV. did not wish to let this regiment out of a family, that had abandoned all but their *honour* and their *swords* for the cause they embraced,* his Majesty reserved a right of succession to the Colonelship of the regiment for the minor; in the meantime appointing its Lieutenant-Colonel Murrough O'Brien, a very experienced and distinguished officer, to command by brevet; in consideration of paying to the young Lord Clare, out of the appointments of the corps, an annual pension of 6000 livres.

Murrough O'Brien of Carrigoginniol, or Carrigogunnell, in the County of Limerick, belonged to a branch of the O'Briens, derived from Conor O'Brien, King of Thomond in 1406, through his son Brian, surnamed "Dubh," or "Duff," otherwise *the dark*, who settled in that Barony of the County, yet styled "Pobble-ni-Brien," or "Pobble-Brien," that is, *the country of Brian*. This Brian *the dark*, established his residence at Carrigogunnell, where his castle, and that of his descendants, nobly situated upon the summit of a lofty hill, continued to be a place of

* The estate forfeited by Lord Clare, for his loyalty to his legitimate Sovereign, consisted of not less than 56,931 acres! This property, like the rest of the Irish forfeitures, was designed by Parliament to be sold, for paying the debt of the War of the Revolution. But William, instead of reserving such lands, as far as possible, for that purpose, made immense assignments of them to several of his favourites— the *Dutch* ones, of course, not being without ample shares of what was going!— and, among such Batavian grantees, Joost Van Keppel, besides being created Earl of Albemarle, had the *modest* transfer to him, by patent, in 1698, of the Clare property! The result of this transaction, between the royal, noble, and other parties concerned in it, was, that the 56,931 acres, when resumed by Parliament, and sold, brought, towards defraying the cost of the war, but the comparatively trifling sum of £10,161, 17s. 5¾d.! See Mr. O'Donoghue's learned Historical Memoir of the O'Briens; and, for further misappropriations of the Jacobite forfeited estates, the next Book of *this* history.

strength till after the War of the Revolution. Murrough O'Brien was a volunteer in the Irish regiment of his countryman Count George Hamilton, when it passed into France in 1671. He was present at the sieges of Orsoy and Rhimberg, at the passage of the Rhine, and the taking of Doesburgh, in 1672; at the siege of Maestricht, in 1673; and that year became an Ensign. He was at the battles of Sintzheim, Einsheim, and Mulhausen, in 1674; and of Turkheim and Altenheim, in 1675. He was at the combat of Kokesberg, in 1676; and, after the death of his Colonel, Count George Hamilton, that year, was involved in the changes by which the Irish of his regiment were transferred into the corps, successively entitled the Regiment of Furstemberg and of Greider. He was at the siege of Friburgh, in 1677; at the combat of Seckingen, and at the sieges of Kehl and Lichtemberg, in 1678. He served at the siege of Girona, in 1684; obtained a commission, as a reformed Captain, in 1688; and a company, in 1689. He commanded the company with the Army of Rousillon, or Spain, under the Duke de Noailles, in 1690 and 1691; and from this company, in the regiment of Greider, was removed, in the latter year, to a similar command in the Regiment of O'Brien, or Clare; preserving his rank of Captain, according to the date of his commission in the older regiment. He fought at the victory of Marsaglia, in October, 1693; was made Major by brevet of March 12th, 1694; and remained with the Army of Italy till the conclusion of the war there after the siege of Valenza, at which he took part. In 1697, he was attached to the Army of the Meuse. He made the campaigns of 1701 and 1702, in Germany. He was at the siege of Kehl, the combat of Munderkingen, and the victory of Hochstedt in 1703; and at the defeat of Hochstedt, (or Blenheim) in 1704. Lieutenant-Colonel of his regiment by commission of January 25th, 1705, he served that year on the Moselle; fought valiantly at the unsuccessful engagement of Ramillies, in May, 1706; and, to the Colonelship vacated by Lord Clare's fall there, was commissioned August 11th following. He commanded the regiment in Flanders during the 6 following campaigns; in which important interval, he was present at the battle of Oudenarde, in July, 1708; that of Malplaquet, in September, 1709; was made Brigadier of Infantry by brevet, March 29th, 1710; served at the attack of Arleux, in 1711; and at the sieges of Douay, Quesnoy, and Bouchain, the ensuing year. Transferred to the Army of the Rhine, in 1713, under the Marshal de Villars, he was engaged in the sieges of Landau and Friburgh. He was brevetted as Maréchal de Camp, or Major-General, February 1st, 1719; and held the regiment, again known under *his* Colonelship as the "Régiment d' O'Brien," until July 1720, when he died.

Murrough O'Brien is characterized as having been an officer both of bravery and ability; in proof of which, his gallantry at Ramillies, and the fine manœuvre at Palluë, by which he saved Cambray, are particularly cited; and it is added, on official authority,—"If M. le Maréchal de Montesquiou had done him the justice which was due to him for the affair of Palluë, he would have had a greater share of the royal favours than he attained"—or have been elevated, (as would seem from the context) to a higher rank, than that of Maréchal de Camp, or Major-General. "That brave old soldier, Major-General Morough O'Brien," observes a contemporary adherent to the House of Hanover, "has left a son behind him, that joins all the abilities of the statesman, with the politeness of the courtier, to the martial spirit of his father." This son,

Daniel O'Brien, was a Colonel of Infantry in the service of France; was made a Chevalier de St. Lazare, or Knight of St. Lazarus, in 1716; was, by the exiled son of King James II., whom *he* regarded as King James III., created a Peer of Ireland, in 1747, under the title of Earl of Lismore, and Viscount of Tallow; was appointed a Grand Cross Chevalier or Knight of St. Louis, in 1750; and was Secretary of State to, as well as Minister from, his Sovereign, at the Court of Rome, where he died, November 5th, 1759, aged 76. James III. writing, November 20th, to the gentleman who was to succeed, "in quality of Minister, but without the title of Secretary of State," thus expresses himself respecting his Lordship,—"You will, I am sure, be concerned for poor Lord Lismore's death. I am myself very much, and with reason; for I have lost in him a true friend, and an old and most faithful servant." His Lordship's son, James Daniel O'Brien, the 2nd and last representative of this Stuart title, was born in 1736; finally attained the grade of a reformed Lieutenant-Colonel to the Regiment of Clare, and the honour of a Chevalier of St. Louis; and died, some time previous to the year 1789.

Charles O'Brien, 6th Viscount Clare (usually styled in France Mylord Comte de Clare) as pensioned upon, and destined to the command of, the family regiment, was, when very young, enrolled among its officers as a reformed Captain, July 1st, 1703, as Captain-en-Second, October 24th, 1704, and was commissioned, as a reformed Colonel *à la suite*, October 14th, 1718. He commenced his active military career with the Army of Spain, under the Marshal Duke of Berwick, in 1719, at the sieges of Fontarabia, of St. Sebastian and its citadel, of Urgel, and of Roses. On the decease of the Maréchal de Camp and Colonel Murrough O'Brien, in July, 1720, he was commissioned, as full Colonel of the Regiment of Clare, August 3rd following. During the peace which prevailed between France and England, under the reign of George I., this young nobleman was invited, and came over several times, to England, to see his cousin Henry O'Brien, the 8th Earl of Thomond. On one of these occasions, he is related to have been presented to King George by the Earl, as the heir-at-law to his estates and honours, and to have been promised forgiveness for the opposition of his family to the alteration of dynasty effected by the Revolution of 1688, if he would conform to the Established Church of England and Ireland. But Lord Clare could not be induced, by considerations of mere dignity and emolument, to forsake a religion, which he had been reared to believe as the only true one. On the breaking out of the war between France and the Empire in 1733, his Lordship was attached to the Army of the Rhine, under the Marshal Duke of Berwick, and was present at the siege of Kehl, which capitulated October 28th. Made Brigadier of Infantry by brevet, February 20th, 1734, he served, by letters of April 1st, with the same army; was at the siege of Philipsburgh, taken July 18th; and received a contusion on the shoulder there, from the same cannon-shot which killed his uncle, the Marshal Duke of Berwick. He remained, by letters of May 1st, 1735, with the same army, which undertook no expedition. He was advanced to the grade of Maréchal de Camp by brevet of March 1st, 1738; became Inspector General of Infantry by order of May 22nd, 1741; and was employed with the Army of Bohemia by letters of July 20th. The same year, Henry O'Brien, the 8th Earl of Thomond, died in Dublin; willing his estates to Murrough, Lord O'Brien, eldest son and heir to the Earl of Inchiquin, as being a Protestant; yet not forgetting Lord Clare, as a

Catholic, but bequeathing him a legacy of £20,000. On his relative's decease, Lord Clare took the title in France of Comte or Earl of Thomond.* Intrusted, in 1742, with the defence of the town of Lintz, in Upper Austria, under the Comte de Segur, he displayed much resolution and bravery, until comprised in the capitulation of the place, signed February 23rd; by which the troops and General Officers who had been inclosed there were not to serve for a year. Employed with the Army of the Rhine, under the Marshal Duke de Noailles, by letters of May 1st, 1743, he fought, June 27th, at the battle of Dettingen. Employed with the Army of Flanders, under Louis XV. and the Marshal Duke de Noailles, by letters of April 1st, 1744, and created Lieutenant-General May 2nd following, he marched to the siege of Menin, which capitulated June 4th. Acting by letters of the 7th as Lieutenant-General, and serving at the siege of Ypres, he mainly contributed, by a successful attack, to the capitulation of the place on the 27th. He was at the siege of Furnes, surrendered July 11th; and remained with the army under the Marshal de Saxe, by letters of the 19th, when Louis XV. quitted Flanders for Alsace. Attached to the Army of Flanders by letters of April 1st, 1745, he was present, May 11th, at the victory of Fontenoy; the gaining of which was so much owing to the valour of the Irish under his command, in contributing to break the previously-successful English and Hanoverian forces. He received 2 musket-shots there, but luckily on his cuirass; and, a few days after, was wounded by the bursting of a bomb, at the siege of Tournay, which was entirely reduced, by the surrender of the citadel, June 20th. Continued in Flanders, under the Duke de Richelieu, by letters of December 18th, he was destined for an embarkation, and landing in England, to second the invasion of Prince Charles Edward Stuart; which plan of co-operation was, however, frustrated, by the superior maritime force of the English. Nominated Chevalier of the Orders of the King, January 1st, 1746, he obtained permission, February 2nd, to wear the insignia of that rank. Remaining with the Army of Flanders, by letters of April 1st, he took a leading part in the gaining of the battle of Rocoux, fought October 11th. He was received as Chevalier of the Orders of the King, January 1st, 1747; and, early in the same year, he signalized himself, by his defence of Malines, of the bridge of Valheim, and by other operations, through which the best intelligence was acquired respecting the enemy, for Louis XV. Acting with the Army of Flanders, by letters of May 1st, he fought, with the Irish, July 2nd, at the battle of Laffeldt; there, as at Fontenoy and Rocoux, had a principal share in the success of the day; and had 1 of his Aides-de-Camp shot next him. Employed with the Army of Flanders by letters of April 15th, 1748, he commanded at Bilsen a body of troops, which covered the right of the army, occupied with the siege of Maestricht. During the armistice, he was placed over the troops cantoned in the territory of Malines. He was, by letters of November 1st, 1756, Lieutenant-General in Normandy, under the Marshal de Belle-Isle. He was made Governor of Neuf-Brisac, by provision of the 5th. Created Marshal of France at Versailles, February 24th, 1757, he was nominated to command in Guienne, by order of

* Of "les illustres maisons des ô Briens," notes Abbé Mac Geoghegan in France, in 1758, "le *chef* aujourd'hui est Charles ô Brien, Lord Comte de Thomond, ci-devant appellé Lord Clare, Maréchal de France, Chevalier des Ordres du Roi très-Chrétien, et Colonel du Régiment Irlandois de Clare, au service de Sa Majesté."

March 1st. He took the oath, as Marshal of France, the 13th. He was named to command the troops on the coasts of the Mediterranean, by power of November 1st, 1757; and Commander-in-Chief in the Province of Languedoc, by order of the same day. He obtained the *entrées chez le Roi*, by brevet of May 7th, 1758. In 1759, he was specially consulted upon, and would have been engaged in, the great landing meditated from Bretagne in Munster by the French, but for the defeat of Conflans at sea by Hawke. The veteran nobleman's decease, at Montpellier, in his 63rd year, September 9th, 1761, is mentioned in a contemporary Continental periodical, with an enumeration of his dignities, as that of "Charles O'Brien, Earl of Thomond, Viscount of Clare, &c., in the Kingdom of Ireland, Marshal of France, Chevalier of the Order of the Holy Ghost, Commander for the King in the Province of Languedoc, Governor of Neuf-Brisac in Alsace, and Colonel of a Regiment of Irish Infantry." The "Maréchal de Thomond," as he was called, was much regretted, and, by his marriage, in 1755, with the Lady Marie Geneviève Louise Gauthier de Chiffreville, Marchioness of Chiffreville in Normandy, left, as his heir, Charles O'Brien, 7th Viscount Clare, and 10th Comte or Earl of Thomond.* That young nobleman was born at Paris, in 1757, and being therefore, at his father's decease, a minor, the Colonelship of the Regiment of Clare was reserved for him, on condition that, out of the 12,000 livres a year which it was then worth, 6000 livres should be allowed to whatever officer might be appointed to command it in his place, as Colonel-en-Second.

The officer appointed was Brigadier James Fitz-Gerald. He entered the Regiment of Dillon, as a reformed or supernumerary Lieutenant, in 1730. He served at the siege of Kehl in 1733; at the attack of the lines of Etlingen, and at the siege of Philipsburgh, in 1734; upon the Rhine, and at the affair of Clausen, in 1735. He obtained a full Lieutenancy in 1739; and served, in that grade, with the Army of Flanders, in 1742. Nominated a reformed Captain, in the same regiment, by commission of January 8th, 1743, he was at the battle of Dettingen in June; and finished the campaign on the banks of the Rhine. In 1744, he served at the sieges of Ypres and Furnes; was employed at the camp of Courtray; and obtained, October 6th, a company in the Irish Regiment of Lally, at its formation. He commanded this company at the battle of Fontenoy, at the sieges of the town and citadel of Tournay, of Dendermonde, of Oudenarde, and of Ath, in 1745. He was granted a commission, July 11th, that year, to hold rank as a Colonel of Infantry. He served on the coasts, in 1746; fought at the battle of Laffeldt, in 1747; was at the siege of Maestricht, in 1748; and was employed, at the camp of Dieppe, in 1756. The Regiment of Lally being designed for the East Indies in November, 1756, the Sieur de Fitz-Gerald was nominated, by order of the 10th of that month, to command the 2nd battalion; but, circumstances having prevented his embarkation, he quitted that regiment. He was attached, by order of

* Charles O'Brien, 6th Lord Clare, 9th Earl of Thomond, and Marshal of France, had, besides his heir, a son, born in 1761, deceased in 1764, and a daughter, Antoinette-Charlotte-Marie-Septimanie O'Brien, born at Paris in 1758, and married to the Duke de Choiseul-Praslin. The representative of that title, who murdered his Duchess in 1847, was their grandson. Besides O'Briens of the 2 ennobled branches in the French service, there were in the Irish Brigade, or French infantry, 5 officers of the name, from the rank of Captain to that of Lieutenant-Colonel, who were Chevaliers of St. Louis.

February 16th, 1757, as a reformed Colonel, to the Regiment of Clare, with which he remained, for the protection of the coasts, during several campaigns. He was created a Brigadier by brevet, May 1st, 1758. He made the campaigns of 1760 and 1761 in Germany; being engaged at the affairs of Corback and of Warburgh in 1760, and at that of Felinghausen in 1761. In consequence of the decease of the Lord Marshal of Clare or Thomond that year, and the minority of the young Earl his son, Fitz-Gerald was commissioned, September 20th, to be, during the minority, Colonel-en-Second in command of the Regiment of Clare. He obtained the grade of Maréchal de Camp by brevet, February 25th, 1762; was employed as Brigadier, at the camp of Dunkirk; and was declared full Maréchal de Camp, in the December of that year. He then resigned the command of the Regiment of Clare; and finally died, at the close of 1773.

The Sieur de Fitz-Gerald's successor in that command was the Chevalier de Betagh, or, as anciently spelled, Biatagh. This officer, belonging to a very respectable Irish family, (believed to have been originally of Danish extraction) was the grand-son of a gentleman, whose case has been specially recorded, as an instance of the frightful injustice with which so many of the Irish Catholic gentry, or royalists, were, after the Restoration, stripped, through legalized fraud and perjury, of their estates, for the benefit of Parliamentarian or Cromwellian revolutionists, and other English land-adventurers. Hugh O'Reilly, Esq. of Lara, Master-in-Chancery, Clerk of the Privy Council, Member of Parliament for the Borough of Cavan, during the reign of James in Ireland, and titular Lord Chancellor for Ireland to the King at St. Germain, after noting the iniquities connected with the proceedings of the tribunal called the Court of Claims in 1662 and 1663, as introductory to the general land-spoliation carried out by the Act of Settlement, and its tail-piece the Act of Explanation, thus refers to the case of Mr. Betagh in 1693, when he was still living at St. Germain. " Mr. Francis Betagh of Moynalty, whose ancestors, for 700 or 800 years together, were in the possession of a considerable estate in the County of Meath, was but 9 years of age in October, 1641; yet he was sworn, in the Court of Claims, to have been then in actual rebellion, at the head of a foot company, plundering and stripping the Protestants; and that by 2 of the meanest scoundrels of the whole kingdom, hired for that purpose ; whereof one was then and there proved, not to have been 3 years old, at the time of that insurrection; and the other, no way qualified to be believed, when the gentry of the whole country declared and testified the contrary. Nevertheless, upon the bare oaths of these fellows, the gentleman was adjudged nocent," or guilty, "by the Court; and, although the perjury was afterwards more fully detected; insomuch, that Sir Richard Rainsford, (Chief Commissioner or Judge of that Court) when the Marchioness of Antrim expostulated the matter with him, plainly acknowledged the injustice of it to herself, to the now Earl of Limerick, and to other persons of quality; yet no redress cou'd be had for the gentleman, nor any remedy to be expected, while the inchantment of the Act of Settlement was of force." The grand-son of this gentleman joined the Irish Brigades, was a Captain in Fitz-James's Regiment of Horse previous to the battle of Fontenoy, or in 1744; from 1749 to 1762, had been its Major and Commandant, or acting Colonel for the Colonel-Proprietor of the Fitz-James family; was wounded with the regiment at the battle of Rosbach, in November, 1757, when it was so much distinguished; and became a Chevalier of St. Louis. Succeeding, in 1763, as Colonel-en-Second of the Regiment of Clare,* he was created a Brigadier of Infantry, April 16th, 1767, and a Maréchal de Camp, January 3rd, 1770; resigned the Colonelship that year; and is mentioned as still living, with the title of Count, in 1775.

He was followed, as Colonel-en-Second, in 1770, by the Chevalier de Meade—the representative of a name, respectable in Munster to our own times. This gentleman, who had previously served in the Regiment of Lally, continued to be Colonel-en-Second to the Regiment of Clare as long as it was kept up, or until 1775. For the young Comte or Earl of Thomond and Lord Clare dying under age, and unmarried, at Paris, December 29th, 1774, and the united titles of Thomond and Clare ceasing in his person, according to the new arrangement of the French army, already spoken of as having occurred in June, 1775, the Regiment of Clare, about 86 years from its first formation in Ireland, and 85 years from its arrival in France, was incorporated with the Irish Infantry Regiment of Berwick.

THE INFANTRY REGIMENT OF DILLON.

This regiment was, as previously mentioned, 1 of the 2 infantry regiments levied by Theobald, the 7th Lord Viscount Dillon of Costello-Gallen, for the service of King James II., and that selected to be sent to France, in the spring of 1690, as part of Lord Mountcashel's Brigade. Lord Theobald conferred the Colonelship in Ireland upon his 2nd son, the Honourable Arthur Dillon, who was born in 1670, and, in 1690, consequently not of age. This grant was confirmed in France, by a commission, dated June 1st, 1690. On the young Colonel's cousin, James Lally of Tullaghnadaly, County of Galway, Sovereign, in 1687, of the Corporation, and Member of Parliament, in 1689, for the Borough, of Tuam, the rank of Colonel, as Commandant of the 2nd battalion, was likewise conferred; a considerable portion of the regiment having been made up from Independent Companies, raised through the exertions of Lord Theobald's nephews of the Lally family. The Honourable Arthur Dillon, Colonel-Proprietor of the corps, was first, or in 1691, attached to the Army of Rousillon commanded by the Duke de Noailles, under whom he served at the siege of Urgel, and the relief of Pratz-de-Mollo. In 1692, he continued with the same army, which kept on the defensive. In June, 1693, he was at the taking of Roses, the only acquisition of the campaign, owing to the weakening of the army of the Duke de Noailles, in order to reinforce Catinat in Italy. In 1694, he fought, May 27th, at the overthrow, by the Duke de Noailles, of the Spaniards, under the Duke of Escalona, on the river Ter; at the succeeding captures of Palamos and Girona in June, of Ostalric, or Hostalric, in July, of Castelfollit in September, and at the raising of the siege of Ostalric, attempted to be retaken, the same month, by the Spaniards. In 1695, being attached, in May, by the Duke de Noailles,

* There was a family connexion between the names of Betagh and O'Brien, which may not have been without its influence in the Chevalier de Betagh's advancement to the command of the Regiment of Clare. See the Transactions of the Iberno-Celtic Society, or O'Reilly's account of native Irish writers, under the year 1720.

to the force appointed, under the Marquis de St. Sylvestre, to revictual Ostalric, he distinguished himself, when returning from the place, in command of the rear-guard, by routing several thousand Miquelets, or guerillas. In June, 1696, he was at the raising of the siege of Palamos, by the Duke of Vendome, who was appointed to succeed the Duke de Noailles in Spain. In June, 1696, he was at the defeat of the Spanish cavalry under the Prince of Hesse-Darmstadt, by the Duke of Vendome, near Ostalric. In 1697, he served at the capture of Barcelona by the same illustrious General; the last operation of consequence preceding the Peace of Ryswick. On the commencement of the War of the Spanish Succession, he was under the command of the Marshal de Villeroy with the Army of Germany, which undertook no expedition. In 1702, he was removed to the Army of Italy, under the Duke of Vendome, then opposed to the Imperialists, under the famous Prince Eugene of Savoy; fought at the affair of Santa Vittoria in July, at the battle of Luzzara in August; was created Brigadier by brevet of October 1st; and employed, in that grade, by letters of the same date. He was present in 1703 at the defeat of the rear-guard of the Imperial General Count Stahremberg at Castelnuovo-de-Bormida in January; accompanied the Duke of Vendome on his invasion of the Trentin in July and August, where he signalized himself at Riva; was at the overthrow of General Visconti, the following October, in the combat of San-Sebastiano; and at the reduction of Asti and Villanova d'Asti, in November. In 1704, he was at the important capture of Vercelli, of Ivrea and its citadel, by the Duke of Vendome; and, being made Maréchal de Camp by brevet, October 26th, that year, marched to the difficult siege of Verue, or Verrua, in November; which was not terminated by the Duke, until April, 1705. Transferred to the force under the Duke's brother, Lieutenant-General and Grand Prior Philippe de Vendome, he served at the siege of Mirandola, taken in May; signalized himself at the very gallant defence of the Cassine of Moscolino against the Prince of Wirtemberg in June; and at the victory of Cassano, gained, August 16th, by the Duke, over Prince Eugene. He likewise signalized himself under the Duke, at the defeat of the Count de Reventlau, April 19th, 1706, in the battle of Calcinato; and September 9th following, under the Count de Medavi, at the defeat of the Prince of Hesse, in the battle of Castiglione. The 24th of that month, he was made a Lieutenant-General. Employed, by letters of April 20th, 1707, with the army on the frontiers of Piedmont, under the Marshal de Tessé, he eminently contributed to the disastrous result of the great expedition of the Allies against Toulon, under the Duke of Savoy and Prince Eugene, aided by Admiral Sir Cloudesly Shovel. He continued with the same army under Tessé's successor, the Marshal de Villars, in 1708; and under the Marshal Duke of Berwick, in 1709. While stationed that year in the vicinity of Briancon, he defeated 2 considerable bodies of the Allies; the former, August 28th, under General Count Rebender; and the latter soon after, under the Governor of Exilles. In 1710, 1711, and 1712, he remained in the south, under the orders of the same Marshal; and generally commanded at the camp of Briancon. On the expedition into Catalonia, undertaken in December, 1712, for the relief of Girona, then besieged by the Count de Stahremberg, he accompanied the Marshal Duke of Berwick, as 1 of his 5 Lieutenant-Generals; and, being ordered, in January 1713, to pursue Stahremberg who raised the siege, he routed the detachment left by that General at a defile, to cover his retreat. Removed to the Army of the Rhine in 1713, under the Marshal de Villars, he took Kaiserslautern and made its garrison prisoners of war, in June; also took the Castle of Verastein; mounted the trenches, on several occasions, at the siege of Landau, which defended itself from June till August; and, during the operations for the reduction of Friburgh, which occupied from September 30th to November 16th, was placed, by the Marshal de Villars, at the head of a separate force, to form a camp for the protection of the siege. His last campaign was that of 1714, when he served with much distinction, under the Marshal Duke of Berwick, at the conquest of Barcelona. Lieutenant-General, the Honourable Count Arthur Dillon, is represented to have been a gallant and able officer, universally esteemed by the great Generals of his time, and beloved by the soldiery. He was in person beautiful, and very fortunate, having never received a wound, notwithstanding all the dangers to which he was exposed, from 1691 to 1697, and from 1701 to 1714. Though led into some irregular amours during his campaigns, he is stated to have been a fond husband, as well as an attached father; and, in short, to have ranked, in an age of illustrious men, among its best and most estimable characters. It is consequently the more to be regretted, that the literary materials left by him for a history of his life, were destroyed, amidst the excesses of the 1st Revolution in France. Such materials, too, from the leading position which he occupied at Paris with reference to the affairs of *his* exiled Sovereign, or James III., would have been very valuable, as comprising so much information respecting the plans concocted, and the correspondence kept up, from "both sides of the water," by the restless Jacobites, in order to realize what they used to sing—

> " We'll root out usurpation
> Entirely from the nation,
> And cause the restoration
> Of James, our lawful King!"

By his marriage with Catherine Sheldon, daughter of Ralph Sheldon, Esq., niece of Lieutenant-General Dominick Sheldon, Lady of Honour to Mary, Queen of James II., and who died at Paris, in 1757, aged 77, Lieutenant-General Arthur Dillon, besides daughters, had 5 sons. In 1730, quitting the service, as he was then in his 60th year, he resigned his regiment to his eldest son; and died, February 5th, 1733, at the Palace of St. Germain-en-Laye, aged 63 years.

The Comte Charles de Dillon, born in 1701, was, so early as 1705, named on the rolls of his father's regiment as one of its intended officers; became a full Captain, November 10th, 1718; and Colonel, May 1st, 1730. He commanded the regiment on the Rhine against the Germans, in 1734; was advanced to be a Brigadier, January 1st, 1740; and retained his Colonelship till the following year. Having married his Irish cousin-german, Lady Frances Dillon, in January, 1735, he came over to Ireland, in September, 1736, to take possession of the property to which he was entitled; and, on the decease of her father, Richard, 9th Viscount Dillon, in 1737, succeeding to the family honours and estates as 10th Viscount, he did not return to France. He died in London, early in November, 1741, aged 40, without issue. He was succeeded, as 11th Viscount Dillon in Ireland, as well as in the command of the family regiment in France, by his next brother, the Comte Henri de Dillon. This nobleman was, when very young, or in 1716, Ensign to the Colonel, his father; became full Captain in May, 1730; in the war from 1733 to 1735, against the Germans, served at the sieges of Kehl and Philipsburgh, and the affairs at Etlingen and Clausen; between February, 1735, and November, 1738, obtained his Majority, and a commission to hold rank as Colonel; was appointed full Colonel, November 14th, 1741; and was made Brigadier by brevet, February 20th, 1743. But, after the battle of Dettingen, at which he was present, the English, from auxiliaries, becoming principals in the war against Louis XV.; and an Act of Parliament being then in preparation, to prevent British subjects from entering foreign service; by which his Lordship's remaining in the French army would have exposed him, as a Peer of Ireland, to the confiscation of his estates; he, by the *consent*, and even by the *advice*, of Louis, quitted France in the spring of 1744. He arrived in London in May; and not long afterwards married the Lady Charlotte Lee, eldest daughter of George Henry Lee, 2nd Earl of Litchfield; by whom, besides daughters, he left 3 sons, and died in October, 1787. When he was about to quit France, in 1744, he resigned his regiment there to his next brother, the Chevalier Jacques (or James) de Dillon, Knight of Malta, who was killed at its head, May 11th, 1745, at the victory of Fontenoy. The Colonelship was then given, on the field of battle, by the French Monarch, to the 4th brother, the Comte Edouard de Dillon, who, like the Chevalier, did not long survive his advancement; being mortally wounded at the victory of Laffeldt, July 2nd, 1747.

After the death of this Colonel Count Edward Dillon, no son of Lieutenant-General Count Arthur Dillon remained in France, but the 5th, or youngest, Arthur Richard. He had entered the Gallican Church, in which he became one of the most eminent Prelates of his time. He was successively Bishop of Evreux, Archbishop of Toulouse, then of Narbonne, Commander of the Order of the Holy Ghost, Primate of the Gauls, President of the States of Languedoc, twice a Member of the Assembly of Notables, and twice President of the Clergy of France. "To this Prelate," adds our learned Protestant countryman, the Revd. Mervyn Archdall, previous to the 1st French Revolution, "the literati of this country confess much obligation; he has manifested a liberality of principle, almost hitherto unknown; and, through his enquiries, and exertions, the antiquities of Ireland have lately been much elucidated." This only surviving son of Lieutenant-General Dillon in France being thus incapacitated for military employment, Louis XV. was earnestly solicited to give away the regiment, on the plea, that there was no Dillon to claim it. But the French Monarch good-naturedly replied, in allusion to the nobleman, whom he had kindly advised, in 1744, to leave the French service, for fear of forfeiting the family estates in Ireland—"Lord Henry Dillon is married; and I cannot consent to see, that a proprietorship, cemented by so many good services, and so much blood, should go out of a family, as long as I may entertain a hope of witnessing its renewal." From 1747, the proprietorship of the regiment was consequently allowed to remain with the Lord Henry Dillon referred to; who, though resident in England, drew the profits on the appointments; as far as circumstances admitted, took part in the affairs of the corps, and recommended those to be employed in it; the actual military duty, connected with the post he held, being performed by competent officers successively deputed for the purpose, during about 20 years, or until August, 1767.

By that time, the Lord Henry Dillon's eldest son, Charles, named Dillon-Lee, from his becoming heir to the Lee or Litchfield estates in England, as well as to those of Dillon in Ireland, and afterwards the 12th Viscount Dillon, was in his 22nd year, having been born in November, 1745; and the next son, Arthur, born in September, 1750, was in his 17th year;* or of an age deemed sufficient for entering upon the Colonel-Proprietorship of the regiment, which had been reserved for him in France. He accordingly obtained it by a brevet of August 25th, 1767, from Louis XV., referring, in suitable terms, to the Irish origin of the corps, and to the honourable military services of the several members of the family by whom it had been successively commanded. The young Colonel revived the name of his grandfather, Count Arthur Dillon, in France; under the same designation, distinguishing himself, with his regiment, against the English, during the War for the Independence of the United States of America. He powerfully contributed to the conquest of the islands of Grenada, St. Eustacia, Tobago, and St. Christopher, in the West Indies. He served under the Comte d'Estaing, at that officer's unsuccessful operations, in September and October, 1779, against Savannah, in Georgia. He was subsequently appointed Governor of the island of St. Christopher, and proved himself so well qualified for the post, that, upon the restoration of the island to the English by the Peace of 1783, they confirmed the regulations he had made there; and, on his visiting London, and being presented at the English Court, he was officially complimented for his display of such eminent administrative ability, as well as military talent. He was created a Brigadier of Infantry, March 1st, 1780; transferred the command of his regiment, the following month, to the Comte Theobald de Dillon; and was made Maréchal de Camp, or Major-General, January 1st, 1784. Some time after his return from England to France, he was nominated Governor of the island of Tobago; where he resided 3 years, when he was chosen Deputy to the Etats-Généraux or States-General of 1789; in which capacity, he was a steady defender of the colonial interests. When France was invaded by the Prussians and Austrians, in 1792, he was, from his military reputation, a General of Division; shared with Dumouriez the honour of the successful opposition made to the invaders in the plains of Champagne and the forest of Argone; and, pursuing the retreating enemies to Verdun, retook that town, which he entered in triumph, October 14th, at the head of his troops. November 18th following, he was at the "English civic feast, at White's Hotel, in Paris, to celebrate the triumph of liberty, in the victories, gained over their late invaders, by the armies of France." Though designed to be merely a British festival, it was attended, nevertheless, by the natives of various countries, as well as by Deputies of the National Convention, with

* The 2 elder sons of Henry, 11th Viscount Dillon, by the Lady Charlotte Lee, or *Charles*, subsequently 12th Viscount Dillon, and *Arthur*, Colonel-Proprietor of the Irish Regiment of Dillon in France, were born in England; the former at London, in November, 1745; the latter at Braywick in Berkshire, in September, 1750. The 3rd and only remaining son, *Henry*, a Colonel of 1 of the Regiments of the Irish Brigade in British pay after the French Revolution, and a Major-General in the same service, was also born in England, in June, 1759. Charles, the 12th Viscount Dillon, conformed to the Established Church of England and Ireland, in December, 1767.

General Officers and others of the different French armies. The apartments, ornamented with civic and military trophies, were greatly crowded, and the assembly was enlivened by the bands of the 1st Regiment of Cavalry, and of the German Legion. Among the proceedings, which were marked by the greatest revolutionary enthusiasm, "Sir Robert Smith and Lord Edward Fitzgerald renounced their titles;" the former giving the toast, "The abolition of hereditary titles in England." Then General Dillon rose, and "expressing the satisfaction which he felt at meeting so respectable an assembly on so happy an occasion, testified the joy he had felt in being one who had contributed to drive the horde of its invaders from France, and his willingness, when called on, to perform, if necessary, similar service to his own country." After which he proposed—"The people of Ireland; and may Government profit by the example of France, and Reform prevent Revolution." The political principles of the General were conformable to the toast thus proposed by him, in favour of Reform, as a means of averting Revolution. He was, in fact, the advocate of a limited or constitutional system of Monarchy in France, like that in England. He had consequently opposed the foreign invasion of France, in as much as the apparent results of that invasion, if it succeeded, would have been a restoration of the late absolute Monarchy, with the many abuses which had attended it. In his hostility to the invasion of France, he was, so far, united in opinion with her democracy. But, for advocating Monarchy in *any* shape, he became regarded, at first, in a suspicious, and finally, in a hostile, light by that maddened democracy, hurried into every crime, as it was, by its unscrupulous and sanguinary leaders. His services, and those of his family, to France, were consequently insufficient to save him, under the increasing domination of the mob, the demagogue, the accuser, and the guillotine. He was arrested, early in 1793, by the Mayor of Paris, upon an order of the so-called Committee of Public Safety, and confined in the Luxembourg. Subsequently arraigned, as having conspired to deliver the celebrated Danton and his accomplices detained in the same prison, and as being desirous of proclaiming for King the young Prince who should have been Louis XVII., he was delivered over to the Revolutionary Tribunal, and, as in such cases usual, condemned to death. He was executed, April 14th, 1794, in the Place de la Revolution, or that of the guillotine *en permanence!* It is related of 1 of the female victims who were to share his fate, that when, after getting out of the vehicle in which she and others were conveyed to the scaffold, she was touched on the shoulder by the executioner, and beckoned to ascend the ladder conducting to the guillotine, she shuddered, and turning to her companion, said—" Oh! M. Dillon, will *you* go first?" To which, with his customary politeness, he replied, smiling—"Any thing to oblige a lady!" and proceeded. His last words, "Vive le Roi!" or "God save the King!" are mentioned to have resounded from the scaffold through the Place de la Revolution; having been pronounced in as loud and firm a tone, as if he had been giving the word of command for a military evolution. General Arthur Dillon was married 1st to Mademoiselle Lucie de Roth, daughter of the Comte Charles Edouard de Roth, (of the Kilkenny family of that name) Lieutenant-General in the service of France, and Colonel-Proprietor of Roth's (previously Dorrington's) Irish Regiment of Infantry. By this lady, deceased in September, 1782, he had a son, who died young; and a daughter, married, in 1786, to a French nobleman of very high rank, the Comte de la Tour du Piu Gouvernet. General Dillon's 2nd wife, whom he married in 1784, was the widow of the Comte de la Touche. This lady was a native of the island of Martinique in the West Indies, where she had a considerable landed property; and she was first-cousin to the subsequent Empress of France, Josephine. She died at Paris in 1816, leaving, by General Dillon, a daughter, who was the wife of General Bertrand that accompanied the Emperor Napoleon I. to St. Helena, and remained with him there, till his death. From General Arthur Dillon, as a writer, we have a publication, entitled "*Compte rendu au Ministre de la Guerre, suivi de piéces justificatives, & contenant des détails militaires, dont la connaisance est nécessaire pour apprécier la partie la plus intéressante de la mémorable campagne de* 1792; *Paris, Migneret,* 1792, *in* 8*vo. de* 108 *pages.*" He was also author of the following tract, made due use of in the present work, and designated "*Observations historiques sur l'origine, les services, & l'état civil des officiers Irlandois au service de la France, adressées à l'Assemblée Nationale. Rédigées par M. A. D. Député à l'Assemblée Nationale.*"

The Comte Theobald de Dillon, to whom, as previously remarked, the regiment of his name had devolved, was generally known as "le beau," or *the handsome*, and commenced life, with great prospects, at the Court of Versailles. He was appointed Mestre-de-Camp-Propriétaire, or Colonel-Proprietor of the Regiment, April 13th, 1780; was made Brigadier of Infantry the same year; and Maréchal de Camp, or Major-General, June 13th, 1783. After the Revolution, serving under Dumouriez and Rochambeau in Flanders, the Count perished at Lille by assassination, under the following melancholy circumstances. He was ordered, April 28th, 1792, to advance towards the Austrians from Lille upon Tournay, at the head of 10 squadrons, 6 battalions, and 6 pieces of cannon; with directions, however, to avoid every sort of combat. At day-break, Sunday, the 29th, he discovered a body of Austrians, estimated at 3000, on the heights of Marquain, who made preparations to engage him. Upon this, he commanded a retreat, according to the directions he had received, to that effect, from his superior officers. The French soldiery, who, at this period, were filled with the strongest suspicions, that their officers, as members of the aristocracy, were privately confederated with the Austrians to restore the *ancien régime*, or former absolute monarchy, and feudal *noblesse* in France, immediately regarded themselves as betrayed. On the firing of some random cannon-shot by the Austrians without injury to man or horse, the squadrons appointed to cover the retreat, breaking through the infantry, and abandoning them and the artillery, amid such cries as, "*Let every one shift for himself! We are betrayed! Aristocrats to the lamp-post!*" galloped off towards Lille. The Count did all he could to halt and rally his men, till he was himself assailed with tumultuous shouts, and insulting exclamations, struck with a pistol-shot fired by an enraged soldier, and obliged to get into a cabriolet. Meanwhile, the infantry in this panic-struck and exasperated state, beginning to re-enter Lille, seized upon M. Berthois, an engineer officer, hung him up by the feet with cords, discharged several shots through his body, and inflicted other mutilations and indignities on it, as well as on the bodies of 4 unfortunate Austrian prisoners, who were trampled under foot, and run through. The fate of the unhappy Count, and other matters connected with it, are thus narrated by a gentleman, his intimate friend for 15 years, who dined with him the day before, and was present at his death. "About 4 o'clock, I went towards Fiffe gate. In the entrance of the street, the agitation was great, and the howling most terrible. At last I heard the cry of '*He's coming! He's coming! To the lantern!*' I asked, with a trembling voice, '*Who?*' '*Dillon,*' they answered, '*the traitor, the aristocrat! We are going to tear him to pieces, he and all that belong to him! Rochambeau must also perish, and all the nobility in the army! Dillon is coming in a cabriole; his thigh is already broken; let's go and finish him!*' The cabriole soon appeared; the General was in it, without a hat, *with a calm and firm look;* he was escorted by 4 horse-guards; he had hardly passed through the gate, when more than 100 bayonets were thrust into the cabriole, amidst the most horrible shouts. The horse-guards made use of their sabres, it is true; but, I don't know, whether it was to defend themselves, or to protect the General. The man who drove the cabriole disappeared, the horse plunged, and no bayonets had yet been fatal, when a shot was fired into the carriage, and I think *this* killed M. Dillon, for I never saw him move afterwards; he was taken from the carriage, and thrown into the street; when they trampled upon his body, and ran 1000 bayonets through it, I neither heard from him complaints or groans. Between 7 and 8 o'clock, I went to the market-place, where a great fire was lighted, in which his body was thrown. French soldiers danced round the burning body of their General. This barbarous scene was intermixed with the most savage howlings. Parties of Swiss were passing and repassing in good order during this atrocious scene, with the greatest indignation painted in their countenance." The National Assembly, when informed of this murder, and other atrocities with which it was accompanied, denounced the perpetrators for punishment, and settled pensions on the family of the unfortunate Count Theobald Dillon. The Count was the last Colonel-Proprietor of the Regiment of Dillon; which alone, of all the Irish Regiments in the French service, continued under the command of members of the same name during about 101 years, that elapsed, from the landing of Lord Mountcashel's Brigade in France, in 1690, till 1791, the period of the breaking up of the Irish Brigade. It was towards the close of the Colonelship of Theobald Dillon, or in the latter year, that, according to the regulation occasioned by the Revolution, the various regiments of the French Army, except the Swiss, instead of being named from any particular district, family, or nation, were numbered; when the *ci-devant* Regiment of Dillon was entitled, the 87th. A number, also, it may be observed, illustriously associated with Irish military fame, in the Army of the United Kingdom of Great Britain and Ireland, as represented by the 87th Regiment of Infantry, or Royal Irish Fusileers.

Of Lord Mountcashel's Brigade, as the 1st body of King James's troops who went to the Continent, it is now necessary to notice the services there during the 2 campaigns of 1690 and 1691; or down to the arrival of the remainder of their countrymen in France, after the ratification of the Treaty of Limerick, in the autumn of the latter year. In May, 1690, when Mountcashel's Brigade landed from Munster at Brest, the enemies of Louis XIV., though already so numerous, were increased, on the side of Italy, by Victor Amadeus II., the ducal Sovereign of Piedmont and Savoy. The French, by the 2 great fortresses of Pignerol and Casal, had a sort of bridle over his states;

and, whenever the garrisons of those places required any change or revictualling, Louis's imperious Minister of War, Louvois, was accustomed to send troops through the territory of the Duke, as if he were a mere vassal to France. This was naturally so irritating to the Duke, who was a Prince of equal courage and ability, that, although from a similar aversion to Protestantism as Louis XIV.'s, he had for some time united his forces with that Monarch's, to wage a war of extermination against the poor Waldenses, Vaudois, or Barbets of the Alps, he had long determined upon joining the Allies, in order to vindicate his independence. He had therefore been a secret party to the League or Augsburg from the time of its formation, and had more recently strengthened his connexions with the Allies, though privately; that he might not be overpowered by the French, before he could be joined by a sufficient aid, to enable him to set them at defiance. Louis, becoming aware of this, directed Lieutenant-General Catinat, with 12,000 men, to enter Piedmont in May, 1690, and to demand a satisfactory explanation from Victor Amadeus. Should the Duke not give it, he was to be attacked there; while another French force was to invade Savoy. The operations of the latter expedition alone belong to *our* subject.

The campaign in Savoy commenced later than in Piedmont; and, when it was decided upon by Louis XIV., he appointed Monsieur de St. Ruth to command. That officer had served from 1667, through the wars of Holland, Flanders, and Germany; became a Lieutenant-General in 1688; and was attached to the Army of the Moselle, when he received his commission of June 28th, to proceed to Dauphiné, in order to make the necessary arrangements there against Savoy. The troops were to consist of about 5000 French, and 3000 Irish belonging to the Regiments of Lord Mountcashel and the Honourable Daniel O'Brien. The royal order, for St. Ruth to leave the Army of the Moselle for Dauphiné, being dated so late in the season; the distance between such opposite destinations being so considerable; and the 3000 Irish, in addition to the remodelling which they (with the rest of their countrymen) underwent after landing in Bretagne, having to take such a long march as that to Savoy; the summer was necessarily far advanced, before every thing could be ready for action. When the preparations for invading that difficult, or rocky, mountainous, and precipitous country were completed, St. Ruth directed the Marquis de Varennes to march towards its capital, Chamberry, by the route of Les Echelles, (or *the ladders*) while he himself should approach it by Champarluen. The Count de Bernex, Governor of Chamberry for Victor Amadeus, on intelligence of those movements by the French, evacuated the place. St. Ruth reaching it, August 12th, garrisoned the town with 400 of the Irish, and the castle, or citadel, with as many more troops of the same nation, under the command of the Marquis de Thoüy, Brigadier. Annecy, following the example of Chamberry, was likewise secured by a garrison; Rumilly, attempting to defend itself, was carried by assault; and 2000 militia, and 500 fusileers, that were collected to defend the river Ruë, having retired before the French General, the noblesse and peasantry of that part of the country submitted to the King of France. St. Ruth then reduced the districts of the Chablais, of Fausilly, the Tarentaise and the Genevais, or territory as far as the borders of the little Calvinistic Republic of Geneva. His next object was to overtake, and defeat, 2 bodies of Victor Amadeus's troops, under the Baron,

Marquis, or Count, de Sales, or de Salles, (as he was variously entitled) and the Count de Bernex. Their superior knowledge of such an intricate country, and the facility for retreat amongst its mountains, assisted them to elude all pursuit, until they had chosen 2 such strong positions about the river Isere, as they judged would best enable them to defend the passes that led into Italy by the Little St. Bernard and Mount Cenis. St. Ruth, marching with 2 battalions of infantry, and a regiment of cavalry, for the banks of the Isere, directed the Brigadier Marquis de Thoüy, who had been left at Chamberry as its commandant with 800 Irish troops, to set out and join him with those troops; and the Marquis de Vins to do the same from Annecy, with the Bretagne regiment of dragoons, and a detachment of cavalry. They were all 3 to meet on the Isere; whence, after being joined by 2 pieces of light artillery, they were to proceed to action. Having entered the upper valley of the Isere, and gone to inspect the ways with 300 men, St. Ruth found De Sales in the lower valley, posted, with 1200 men, upon a rock, fronted by the river, and extending to the great mountain of the same name. At the foot of this mountain, he ordered the Brigadier Marquis de Thoüy, with the regiment of Bretagne, and 100 of the Irish, to watch during the night between the 11th and 12th of September, for the purpose of guarding against any design of De Sales to escape in that direction; who, however, was so far from making such an attempt, that he occupied himself in adding as much as possible to the strength of his position by an abbatis of felled trees, that embarrassed the whole way between the rock and the river. It was necessary to proceed by this way, although it constituted a defile so narrow, that it could only be passed 1 by 1. St. Ruth, after reconnoitring the ground, arranged his troops for attacking the rock, at 3 different points. The dragoons, under the Marquis de Vins, were to pass by the little way along the river, in order to ascend the rock. The cavalry were to clamber up in the centre. Lord Mountcashel, at the head of his own Irish regiment of infantry, with the Brigadier Marquis de Thoüy, was to march along the mountain, to gain the same rock, through a very rugged gorge. St. Ruth himself ascended among the first, at a very steep place. The assailants were received with a great fire. But the defenders of the rock were dislodged; vigorously pursued to the highest tops of the mountains; and about 150 of them slain. Their leader, De Sales, after his Lieutenant-Colonel had been killed beside him, took refuge amidst some vines, where he was, with difficulty, discovered, and made prisoner, by the Irish. Several other officers were also taken. St. Ruth is related to have had only from 10 to 15 men, and 3 or 4 horses, killed or wounded. There were, say the French accounts, "3 Irish killed, and 2 wounded, with Milord Moncassel slightly, by a musket-shot, in the left breast; having been very much distinguished, as well as those of his nation." And a hostile narrative observes of the same troops—" The Irish, commanded by Milord Moncassel, who were present at this encounter, fought exceedingly well, and having seen how their Chief was wounded, they refused to abandon the pursuit of their enemies, till they should have taken the Comte de Sales, who commanded them. They led him in triumph to Lord Moncassel, in order to console him for the wound which he had received." After this advantage, St. Ruth, being joined by more cavalry, and the Irish infantry of the Regiment of the Honourable Daniel O'Brien, proceeded towards the sources of the Isere in the High Alps, between the little St. Bernard and Mount Cenis; in order to dislodge the Count de Bernex from a still stronger position, where he was entrenched, with 400 men. It was situated in a very narrow defile, bounded, to the left, by mountains, regarded as inaccessible, and, to the right, by the Isere, which was no where fordable. Nevertheless, under Lieutenant-Colonel Andrew Lee, the officer then in command of the Regiment of O'Brien, "a mountain to the left was climbed up to the top, and gotten round by passes, which seemed so impracticable, that the imagination could with difficulty be brought to conceive the success of such an attempt!" By these means, Lieutenant-Colonel Lee "came right down upon the enemy's retrenchments, protected by several fosses, as wide as they were deep. As soon as the enemy saw this, they fled; abandoning those retrenchments, with their cannon and falconets," or lighter artillery. Then, descending the river to a bridge, leading, on the other side, to a mountain upon the right, the beaten troops escaped, in the direction of Italy, by the Valley of Aosta. After a pursuit for some time, the enemy's spoils were very fairly applied, by the French General, to reward those troops, to whom, on this occasion, his success was *most* attributable. "We found in their camp," says my contemporary French historian, "some bread and some wine, which Monsieur de St. Ruth caused to be given to the Irish; whom," it is likewise added, "he allowed to go into the mountains, to seize the flocks, that were known to be at pasture there." The French, in this affair, are said not to have had 1 man killed, and but 3 wounded. The same evening, St. Ruth received the Deputies of Montiers, and the 13th, in the morning, at a small distance from the town, had its keys brought to him by the Archbishop and Magistrates; upon which, making his entry, he caused *Te Deum* to be chanted there. Two days after, he marched to Morienne, whose keys were also brought to him; and, the 15th, reaching Brisansonnet, with his whole army, he encamped there, to rest. Lord Mountcashel, with the 3000 Irish, were appointed to garrison Chamberry; and no post remaining untaken in Savoy, but the town and strong citadel of Montmelian built on a lofty rock, St. Ruth blocked up the place, caused it to be bombarded, and was able to spare 3 of his French regiments, to reinforce Catinat in Piedmont. By these conquests, for which he was so much indebted to the Irish, the French General rendered a great service to his master; it being calculated, that, in addition to the quartering of troops, a considerable revenue could be realized from Savoy; while a country was secured, respecting which, it was alleged, on the side of the Allies, that 50,000 of their men could not be better employed than *there*, from the facility it would afford, of communicating with, and exciting an insurrection among, the oppressed Huguenot or Protestant population of Dauphiné, Provence, and Languedoc, against their government.

The next campaign, or that of 1691, the Irish of Lord Mountcashel's Brigade served partly in Savoy, and partly towards Catalonia. Lieutenant-General St. Ruth, being destined to command for King James II. in Ireland in 1691, was replaced in Savoy, in the autumn of 1690, by the Marquis de la Hoguette, Maréchal de Camp, who had returned, with the force of the Count de Lauzun, from Ireland. The blockade of the town and citadel of Montmelian was continued; the French and Irish troops being stationed in palisaded lines and redoubts at certain distances around the place, to reduce it, if possible, by famine; and it was attempted, early in February, to approach so near, as to subdue it, by a regular battering, and bombardment. The French bombs did considerable injury to a magazine of grain in the place; but the garrison could not be prevented making frequent sorties or forays, with considerable losses to both sides, of which the Irish had their share. The French cannon and mortars were also dismounted; so that close operations had to be given up, and the blockade resumed, until a regular attack could be undertaken, with a force both stronger as regarded the garrison within, and entirely secured against any interruption from without. To effect this security ere such a force could be assembled, M. de la Hoguette, leaving the Tarentaise, June 16th, with 7 battalions and 2 dragoon regiments made his way, in spite of the enemy's parties, across the rivers and through the difficult passes of those mountainous regions, as far as the valley and town of Aosta. On his approaching the town, the 22nd, it submitted; the valley furnishing a great abundance of cattle. After securing a general submission of the country, and mining or blowing up such bridges as might give a passage to any relief coming from Piedmont by Ivrea and the Little St. Bernard, through the Valley of Aosta, to Montmelian, the French commander had trenches opened before that town, the night between July 27th and 28th. It was finally agreed, August 4th, that the town of Montmelian should surrender the 5th; its reduction having cost the besiegers, in these last operations, but from 100 to 200 men killed or wounded. The citadel very advantageously situated, and still defended by the brave Marquis de Bagnasco, with 600 men, 30 or 40 guns, &c., was then blocked up, till further assistance to attack it could be obtained from the Marshal de Catinat, in Piedmont. There, meanwhile, the Allies, having collected a very fine and numerically superior army in order to arrest that Marshal's progress against Victor Amadeus, the first design of their Generals was, to relieve Montmelian with a detachment of 8 battalions of infantry and 5 regiments of cavalry, by the way Hoguette had foreseen. But that officer, in addition to his other precautions, having obtained a reinforcement from Catinat, so as to command the pass, by the Little St. Bernard, with 12 battalions of infantry and 3 regiments of cavalry, the intention of relieving Montmelian had to be abandoned. After the campaign in Piedmont was terminated, Catinat, to complete the reduction of Savoy, made such arrangements with Hoguette, as, by November 22nd, to assemble, for attacking the castle of Montmelian, a competent force, with 40 cannon, 25 mortars, and proportionable ammunition. The castle held out till December 22nd, when, of 600 troops that had composed its garrison, the gallant Governor (already named) having only 200 famished men, capitulated, on condition of marching out with military honours, arms, baggage, 3 cannon, and of being escorted, with sufficient provisions, carriages, &c., into Piedmont; where he was knighted, and pensioned, as he deserved to be, by Victor Amadeus. In the blockade of this place, the Regiment of O'Brien took part, being marked as stationed at Montcassel, under the title of the Regiment of "Clare;" its Colonel, the Honourable Daniel O'Brien, by the death of his father, Daniel, the 3rd Lord Clare, this year, in Ireland, having become the 4th Lord Clare; and a consequent change being made in the name of the regiment, from that of "O'Brien," to that of "Clare." At this blockade, also, was slain James O'Mullaly or Lally, Esq. of Tulachnadala, Tolenadally, or Tolendal, County of Galway, who, in Ireland had been, under King James II., in 1687,

Sovereign of the Corporation, and, in the Parliament of 1689, Member for the Borough, of Tuam, and who, through the several Independent Companies, raised by himself and his younger brothers, Gerard, William, and Mark, having mainly contributed to form the 2nd battalion of the regiment of his first-cousin, the Honourable Colonel Arthur Dillon, had, in that corps, by commission of June 1st, 1690, the rank of Colonel, too, as commandant of the battalion in question, hence called "Lally's battalion."

On the side of Catalonia, where its Viceroy, the Duke of Medina Sidonia, was expected to have a force of 10,000 foot, and 4000 horse, the Duke de Noailles was appointed, in April, to command for the campaign of 1691. The French army, besides the disadvantage of its being generally made up of new troops, consisted of but 6500 infantry, and 2340 cavalry. With these, Lord Mountcashel, Colonel Arthur Dillon, and a select body of 1000 of their countrymen, were to serve. Notwithstanding the adverse circumstances for offensive operations presented by broken-up roads and a rocky and mountainous country, through which, while favourable for native skirmishers, yet an invader's artillery, in many places, was only to be conveyed by clearing a passage for it with mines, the French General determined to advance against and besiege Urgel. The roads being repaired, and the Catalonian miquelets, militia, or guerillas, being repulsed by the detachments sent forward in May to open the march towards Urgel, the Duke secured his communications with France against the Duke of Medina Sidonia, by encamping and fortifying himself in the post of Belver, or Belvert, where he kept the 1000 Irish with him; and, meantime, caused his battering guns to be drawn across the mountains, and gotten through the rocks, with gunpowder. The management of the siege of Urgel was committed to M. de Quinson, Maréchal de Camp. Ground was broken before the place, June 5th; the artillery coming up the 10th, opened fire the 11th, and, with such effect, that, in the course of a few hours, the Spanish Governor had to surrender himself prisoner with his garrison, of between 900 and 1000 regulars of 2 regiments, among the best in Spain, and 1200 armed peasantry, or guerillas. The Duke, after some weeks, demolished the fortifications—while strengthening his head-quarters at Belver, sent out detachments that advanced, in the direction of Barcelona, 3 days' march beyond Urgel, and towards the frontiers of Aragon, foraging the country and capturing several castles, among which were those of Valence, Boy, and Soor—beat the hostile parties when they showed themselves—obliged the Spanish army, after retiring from before Belver, to abandon the siege of Pratz-de-Mollo—and, notwithstanding the considerable numerical inferiority of his force, closed the campaign with honour to himself, and such good care of his troops, that their loss, in every way, was no more than between 400 and 500 men. Of the Irish generally, it has been observed, that the 1000 men, of whom they consisted, were disposed of by the Duke, for the security of his head-quarters at Belver. Of the Irish officers, Lord Mountcashel is mentioned to have been at the taking of Urgel, the castles of Valence and Boy, and the relief of Pratz-de-Mollo; and Colonel Arthur Dillon to have been present at the first and last of these affairs. The loss suffered by Mountcashel's Brigade, in those 2 campaigns, was, on the whole, considerable; since, for the 3 regiments, 5371 strong, when organized in France before the campaign of 1690, and subsequently increased by nearly 200 veterans drafted from the Regiment of Greider, we find, by a letter of the French Minister of War, Louvois, to the Duke of Tyrconnell, that, even so early as the spring of 1691, there were 1200 recruits then required from Ireland. This loss mostly occurred in Savoy, owing to the hardships necessarily connected with a blockade and siege like that of Montmelian, which lasted, in those Alpine regions, from the autumn of 1690 till the latter end of December, 1691. Henceforward, the history of the Regiments of Mountcashel's Brigade unites with that of the rest of the Irish troops, who followed the fortunes of King James II. to the Continent.

HISTORY OF THE IRISH BRIGADES

IN

THE SERVICE OF FRANCE.

BOOK II.

OF the Irish forces, amounting to above 19,000 men and officers, who, from the conclusion of the Treaty of Limerick, in October, 1691, to the month of January, 1692, left their country in successive embarkations for France, it has already been stated, that those who were to act under King James's commission, as his army—or, so far, as a distinct force from Lord Mountcashel's Brigade, and others of their countrymen in the French service,—were to be divided into 2 Troops of Horse Guards, 2 Regiments of Horse, 2 Regiments of Dragoons, à *pied*, or dismounted, in order to serve as Infantry, 8 Regiments of Foot, (these last making between them 15 battalions) and, finally, 3 Independent Companies of Foot. The heads of the original capitulation, or agreement, between Louis XIV. and James II., with reference to those troops, specified, that they were to be, says the abbreviator of the document, "under the command of James, and of such General Officers as he should appoint. All the officers were to receive their commissions from him, and the troops were to be subject only to such rules and discipline of war, as he should appoint." For the government of those forces, he was to have a Secretary at War, a Judge Advocate General, a Provost Marischal General, a Chaplain General, with subordinate Priests, besides Physicians and Surgeons. The last article of this document, in which, from a previous statement, it appears, that the Brigade of Mountcashel, as well as the troops arrived from Limerick, were to be equally comprehended, should James choose to require the aid of *both* for his "restoration," is as follows,—"That the King of Great Britain be at liberty, at any time hereafter, to bring all, or such part of, the said forces, as he shall think fit, into any of his Majesty's dominions, or elsewhere, as he shall judge necessary, or convenient." The 3 Regiments of the Brigade of Mountcashel and their commanding officers having been duly treated of, the remaining corps of the Irish troops in France have now to be similarly noticed.

THE 2 TROOPS OF IRISH HORSE GUARDS.

The formation of these 2 Troops of Horse Guards, or *Gardes du Corps*, in Ireland, was commenced by King James II. in 1689, some time after his arrival from France. Previous to the encounter of the Boyne, or in April, 1690, each of the Troops of Guards is stated to have consisted of 200 privates; the 1st Troop, under Henry Jermyn, Lord Dover; the

2nd Troop, under the King's son, James Fitz-James, Duke of Berwick. To these, there is mentioned to have been a Troop of Mounted Grenadiers attached, commanded by Colonel Butler. According to the regulations of the service at that period, the privates of the Troops of Guards were gentlemen, and the officers stood higher, both in point of rank and pay, than the officers of other corps. The proportion of officers, &c., to each Troop of Guards, besides its commander or Captain, who ranked as a Colonel, consisted, by the same regulations, of 2 Lieutenants, 1 Cornet, 1 Guidon, 4 Exempts, 4 Brigadiers, 4 Sub-Brigadiers, 1 Chaplain, 1 Surgeon, 4 Trumpets, and 1 Kettle-drum. The officers, &c., of the Troop of Mounted Grenadiers attached, besides their Captain, or Colonel, were 2 Lieutenants, 2 Serjeants, 2 Corporals, 2 Drums, and 2 Hautbois. Thus each Troop of Guards would contain 224, both Troops 448, the Troop of Mounted Grenadiers attached 71, and the whole, 519 men and officers. These *Gardes du Corps*, as was to be expected from their composition, distinguished themselves during the war in Ireland, and suffered in proportion. On the remodelling of the Irish army, after its arrival in France, the Irish Life Guard, as it was called, was again formed into 2 Troops. The complements of these Troops of Guards are specified as 80 privates, (if this word can be applied to gentlemen) and 20 officers in each Troop; the total of *both* Troops consequently making 200 men. The 1st Troop was bestowed, by King James, on the Duke of Berwick; a memoir of whom will be given, in connexion with the Infantry Regiment of Berwick. The 2nd Troop was conferred on Major-General Patrick Sarsfield, Earl of Lucan.

This nobleman was descended from a sufficiently old and respectable race *paternally*, and from a most ancient and illustrious race *maternally*. The name of De Saresfeld, Sarsfield, &c., is related to have first appeared in Ireland with King Henry II.; it occurs among those of the Anglo-Norman gentry of the Pale, summoned for military attendance, on King Edward I. and King Edward III., into Scotland, in 1302 and 1335; and, between the reigns of King Henry VIII. and Queen Elizabeth, that name is to be found among those of the chief civic magistrates or Mayors of Dublin, distinguished for munificent hospitality in the city, and activity and gallantry in the field. Of the Sarsfields, in the reign of King James I., the head of one branch, Sir Dominick Sarsfield, was the 1st Baronet created in Ireland, and was likewise ennobled by the title of Viscount Kinsale, subsequently agreed to be changed to that of Viscount Kilmallock; another branch, represented by Sir William Sarsfield, held the manor of Lucan, in the County of Dublin. The origin of the race of O'Mordha, O'Morra, O'More, or O'Moore, is deduced from the most remarkable royal house of Erin, in the heroic times; that of the Kings of Uladh, or Ulster, of the line of Ir, who reigned at Eman, or Emania, till its destruction by the brother Princes, Colla, of the Heremonian line of Con of the Hundred Battles, A.D., 332. Of this Irian dynasty in Uladh, the most celebrated epoch at Emania (according to our best technical chronology, about the commencement of the Christian era,) was the period of King Conor Mac Nessa, and his Champions of the Red Branch, of whom the renowned Conall, or Connell, himself of the royal race, and known as "Cearnach," or *the Victorious*, was the most eminent hero. A descendant of this Achilles of Uladh, and, like him, a great warrior, was Lugad Laighis. The people of Mumha, or Munster, having attacked Laighin, or Leinster, and overrun the country almost as far as

the hill of Mullach-Maistean, now Mullagh-mast, the King of Laighin, Cuchorb, sought the aid of Lugad Laighis, who, in a series of encounters, destroyed the previously-successful invaders; in consideration of which, he was granted the district, called Laighis, or Laoighis, subsequently latinised into Lagisia, or Lisia, and anglicised into Leix, or Leax. Lugad's descendants, after the introduction of surnames, took that of O'Mordha, (otherwise O'Morra, O'More, or O'Moore,) from "Mordha," or *the Majestic*, the 25th in descent from Conall "Cearnach," or *the Victorious*. Over the territory of Leix, comprehending, at first, that portion of the modern Queen's County commensurate with the Baronies of East and West Maryborough, Stradbally, and Cullenagh, and subsequently all but the Baronies of Portnahinch, Tinnahinch, and Upper Ossory in that County, the posterity of Lugad Laighis, who for ages resided at Dun-Mask, now Dunamase, were the ruling race, with more or less power as Princes or Chiefs, according to the fortune of war, until about the middle of the 16th century; and, even when expelled, they recovered their country more than once by the strong hand, until the time of Calvagh O'Morra, or O'More, and the final plantation of his country by "the stranger." This Calvagh, called Charles in English, had 2 sons, Rory or Roger, and Lewis, both Colonels; the former of whom was, in 1641, so famed in song among his countrymen, whose general exclamation was, "God and our Lady be our assistance, and Rory O'More!"—or, as the idea has been well versified, in the ballad on the subject—

> "Do you ask why the beacon and banner of war,
> On the mountains of Ulster, are seen from afar?
> 'Tis the signal, our rights to regain, and secure,
> Through God, and our Lady, and Rory O'Moore!"

Colonel Rory O'More, or O'Moore, by his marriage with Jane, eldest daughter of Sir Patrick Barnewall, of Turvey, and Grace-Dieu, in the County of Dublin, had 1 son, Charles, (Colonel of Foot, under King James II., slain, at the battle of Aughrim, without issue,) and several daughters.* Of these, Anne O'More was married to the grandson of Sir William Sarsfield, head of the branch of Lucan, in the reign of James I., or Patrick Sarsfield, Esq., by whom she was the mother of 2 sons, William and Patrick. William Sarsfield, leaving no son by his marriage with Mary, sister of the unfortunate James, Duke of Monmouth, the family residence and estate of Sarsfield at Lucan, &c., were inherited by Patrick Sarsfield, with an income of about £2000 sterling a year.

Patrick first served in France as Ensign in the Regiment of Monmouth; then as Lieutenant in the Guards in England; whence, on the success of the Revolutionists supported by the Dutch invasion, he followed King

* The race of Colonel Rory O'More, of 1641 celebrity, ending in Colonel Charles O'More, the headship of the O'Mores, with the property of Ballynagh, or Ballyna, (a grant from Queen Elizabeth,) devolved to the line of his brother, Colonel Lewis O'More; from whom descended, in successive generations, Anthony, Lewis, and James. This James O'More, Esq., of Ballyna, (whose will is dated December 13th, 1778,) left no issue but a daughter, Letitia, who married Richard O'Ferrall, or O'Farrell, Esq.—also of old Irian descent. Their eldest son was Ambrose O'Ferrall, Esq., of Ballyna House; and that gentleman was father of the Right Honourable Richard More O'Ferrall, Member of Parliament for the County of Kildare, and Governor of Malta. A portrait (in his possession) of his famous maternal ancestor, Colonel Roger or Rory O'More of 1641, had, very properly, a place at the great Exhibition in Dublin, in 1853.

James II. into France. In March, 1689, he accompanied the King to Ireland; was created a Member of the Privy Council; made a Colonel of Horse, and Brigadier; and appointed to command the royal force for the protection of Connaught against the northern Revolutionists, whose head-quarters were at Iniskilling, or Enniskillen. With that force, he remained in north Connaught, until the effects of the unlucky affair at Newtown-Butler, and the raising of the blockade of Derry in August, by the landing of Major-General Kirke's relief from England and Scotland, compelled him to retire to Athlone. That autumn, however, he retook Sligo, and entirely expelled the Revolutionists from Connaught. In July, 1690, he was present at the affair of the Boyne; and, after the King's departure to France, he, by his vigorous exhortations to his countrymen to continue the war, and, by his surprise of the Williamite battering-artillery, ammunition, &c., in August, only 7 or 8 miles from the enemy's camp, mainly contributed to the successful defence of Limerick against William III. In December and January, 1690-91, he foiled the military efforts of the Williamites, though aided by treachery, to cross the Shannon into Connaught; and was, at the next promotion, made a Major-General, and ennobled by King James, as "Earl of Lucan, Viscount of Tully, and Baron of Rosberry." In June and July, he was at the defence of Athlone, and the battle of Aughrim, or Kilconnell. Soon after, he detected, denounced, and arrested, for corresponding with the enemy, his intimate friend and neighbour, Brigadier Henry Luttrell, of Luttrellstown, in the County of Dublin; though that officer was either too wary, or too powerful, to be condemned. After the Treaty of Limerick, in October, 1691, to which his Lordship was a chief contracting party, he used all his influence to make as many as possible of his countrymen adhere to the cause of King James, and accompany the national army to France; thus sacrificing to his loyalty his fine estate, and good prospects of advancement from William III. In 1692, he was appointed by James to the command of his 2nd Troop of Irish Horse Guards, after the grant of the 1st Troop to the Duke of Berwick. On the defeat at Steenkirk, in July, 1692, of the Allies, under William III., by the French, under the Marshal de Luxembourg, the Marshal complimented Lord Lucan, as having acted at the engagement, in a manner worthy of his previous military reputation in Ireland. In March, 1693, in addition to his rank of Major-General in the service of James II., his Lordship was created Maréchal de Camp, or Major-General, in that of France, by Louis XIV.; and, at the great overthrow, in July, of the Allies, under William III., by Luxembourg at the battle of Landen, (otherwise Neer-Winden, or Neer-Hespen,) he received his death-wound. The character of Patrick Sarsfield, Earl of Lucan, may be comprehended in the words, simplicity, disinterestedness, honour, loyalty, and bravery. In person, he was of a prodigious size. By his marriage with Lady Honor de Burgo, 2nd daughter to William, 7th Earl of Clanricarde, he had a son, who fought under his illustrious step-father, the Marshal Duke of Berwick, in Spain, and was honoured accordingly there by King Philip V., but left *no* family—the Sarsfields, *since* distinguished in the military services of France and Spain, being, consequently, of *other* branches of the name.

The successor appointed by King James, in October, 1693, to Lord Lucan, as commander of the 2nd Troop of Guards, was Donough Mac Carthy, Earl of Clancarty. The history of this nobleman has already been given previous to the capture of Cork by the Williamites in October, 1690, when, being made prisoner of war with the Jacobite garrison by the Earl (afterwards Duke) of Marlborough, he was conveyed to the Tower of London. He was still there, when named, by King James, successor to the command of the 2nd Troop of Horse Guards, recently Lord Lucan's; and he remained in confinement for about another year, or till the autumn of 1694. Then, as his uncle, Lord Mountcashel, had formerly done at Enniskillen, he managed to escape. Leaving, it is said, his perriwig-block dressed up in his bed, with this inscription, *The block must answer for me*, he got out of the Tower, and finally to France, where he commanded the Troop of Horse Guards assigned him, until after the Peace of Ryswick, in September, 1697. In January, 1698, it being intended in France, that King James's Horse Guards should be broken up; in England, such an Act of Parliament being designed against King James's adherents, as made the Earl think it most expedient for him, to endeavour to effect an accommodation with the existing government there; and his Lordship, at the same time, being naturally most anxious, after his long absence, to see his Lady, the daughter of the Earl of Sunderland, he left France, and came over to England. He was received with joy by his wife, but they were only 2 or 3 hours in bed, when he was arrested, and led away to prison, in consequence of information to the Williamite government, given by his *noble* brother-in-law, the Lord Spencer! When asked the reason for thus venturing into England? the Irish nobleman alleged,—"Having learned the Parliament proposed to pass an Act against those who should be in the service of, or correspond with, King James, he had resolved on coming over to England, to place himself again at the disposal of King William's clemency; and, that, before he was arrested, it had been his intention, to present himself to the Secretary of State." The Earl, nevertheless, was strictly guarded for some months, till King William sent him a pardon. With this, his Lordship was brought before the Court of King's Bench, in June, 1698; he presented the document for enrollment; and the Judges announced the necessity of his immediately leaving the kingdom. The purport of the agreement connected with the grant of this pardon to the Earl was —that he should reside abroad—that he should not attempt to disturb the political settlement of affairs, made in Great Britain and Ireland by the Revolution—and that, on these conditions, he was to receive an annuity of £300 a year. This pension was but an inadequate source of livelihood for the Earl, the representative of a race of Princes, Chiefs, or Nobles, for so many centuries! and whose estate, notwithstanding the colonial acquisitions which had continued so long at the expense of the Mac Carthys, and notwithstanding that the rent bore no proportion to the vast extent of the property, was still worth £9000 per annum. To the magnitude of that property, in fact, its owner's proscription was owing. For, not long after his conveyance from Cork to the Tower at London, or in 1691, an exertion was made in England, that, for a Dutch officer of rank, taken prisoner the year before by the French at the battle of Fleurus, the Earl might be exchanged as a prisoner of war, in order that, as a fair enemy, instead of "a rebel," he might, in a short time, be restored to his fine estate. And indeed, that the Earl should have been regarded as a fair enemy, and treated accordingly, it was the more natural to expect, if it were only on account of his extreme youth, at the period of the War of the Revolution in Ireland; he having been but about 19 years of age at the commencement of the troubles in 1688, and but about 22 at the termination of the contest in 1691! Such a restoration, however, as that of his Lordship's large landed property, was not suitable to the designs of that forfeiture-advocating party in Ireland, whose views, if carried out, would have condemned *all* the Catholics of Ireland with estates to confiscation or beggary; but more especially *all* those of the old Irish race—the chief of whom was the Earl of Clancarty.

As the unfortunate Earl of Desmond, with such a vast property in Elizabeth's time, was an "antler'd monarch of the herd" in too fine condition *not* to be hunted down, that land-seeking blood-hounds might divide so much noble territorial venison amongst them; so, in the War of the Revolution, Mac Donnell, Earl of Antrim in the North, and Mac Carthy, Earl of Clancarty in the South, were marked out, as 2 Hiberno-Popish deer, in the primest order for feasting a similar estate-hunting pack.* The Earl of Antrim was luckily placed beyond the fangs of the Williamite animals referred to, by being included in the Articles of Limerick. With respect to *him*, consequently, however great might be the irritation of famished disappointment, there could be no gratification of covetous gluttony.

> "So roams the nightly wolf about the fold:
> Wet with descending show'rs, and stiff with cold,
> He howls for hunger, and he grins for pain,
> (His gnashing teeth are exercis'd in vain);
> And, impotent of anger, finds no way,
> In his distended paws, to grasp the prey.
> The mothers listen; but the bleating lambs
> Securely swig the dug, beneath the dams."
> DRYDEN's Virgil, Æneis ix., 66-73.

The Earl of Clancarty, on the other hand, having, unluckily, been pounced upon the year before the Treaty of Limerick, or at the surrender of Cork, his merciless hunters were proportionally determined, that such a rich and keenly-anticipated banquet, as the partition of his Lordship's immense inheritance would furnish, should be secured, beyond doubt, by the ravening partizans of the "glorious Revolution." Their principle, with reference to what would afford such ample and savoury "cutting up," was—

> "This be the burden of *our* song,
> To day a stag *must* die!" †

In noticing how the opulent Duke of Bedford would fare at the hands of the French Jacobins—or rather how the French Jacobins would fare at the expense of the opulent Duke of Bedford—if, after effecting *one* "glorious Revolution" in France, they could have landed to effect *another* "glorious Revolution" in England—our great countryman, Edmund Burke, remarks, how, according to the maxims of such Revolutionists, "his Grace's landed possessions" would be "irresistibly inviting to an *agrarian* experiment" as "a downright insult upon the rights of man!"—while, as to any alleged claims of his Grace to those possessions, it was not to be imagined, that such "flimsy cobwebs" should "stand between the savages of the Revolution, and their natural prey!"

* Memoire donné par un homme du Comte O'Donnel à M. d'Avaux.
† The Clancarty arms display a stag on the shield, as if in allusion to the "days of old," when the heads of that race had such ample territory, in South Munster, "to hunt the deer, with hound and horn."

And so it was with unfortunate Lord Clancarty, other "savages of the Revolution," and what they, in *his* case, regarded as "*their* natural prey!" Burke adds of the Jacobin advocates for such a partition, at the cost of the English Duke—"the *sans culotte* carcase butchers, and the philosophers of the shambles, are pricking their dotted lines upon his hide, and, like the print of the poor ox that we see in the shop windows at Charing-Cross, alive as he is, and thinking no harm in the world, he is divided into rumps, and sirloins, and briskets, and into all sorts of pieces for roasting, boiling, and stewing!" Just, in fact, as the extensive possessions of the Irish Earl likewise caused *him* to be marked out for Williamite subdivision into several joints, on which *others* were to feed, to *his* ruin!

This confiscation-roaring party, as specially represented by the colonial, Cromwello-Williamite, "glorious-revolution," or Whig Grand Jury of the County of Cork, exerted itself but too successfully to frustrate any proposal in favour of the obnoxious, or Hiberno-Popish, Earl. Their leading advocate for this *meritorious* object was the Williamite Justice of the Court of Common Pleas in Ireland, Sir Richard Cox; who, having had the drawing up of the Declaration of William III. after his success at the Boyne, instead of endeavouring to end the war, *as William was inclined*, by offering an amnesty for the past, excluded all the Irish Jacobites, with estates, from *any* terms short of forfeiture, in order to make them persevere in resistance, until forced, as he hoped, to submit merely at discretion, or thus be *all* reduced to forfeit; who was consequently dissatisfied at the very different termination of the struggle, not by *any* submission at discretion, but by the regular Treaty, or Articles, at Limerick, that nullified *his* scheme for such a *general* forfeiture; and who, in fine, was under the influence of a two-fold, or national and sectarian animosity to the Irish, that cannot be better illustrated than by the reflection, which, in his work, called *Hibernia Anglicana*, he connects with the execution of King Charles I., in 1649. "And now how gladly would I draw a curtain over that dismal and unhappy 30th of January, when the royal Father of our Country suffered martyrdom. *Oh! that I could say they were Irish men that did that abominable fact, or that I could justly lay it at the door of the Papists!*"* Cox was successful in his application to the prejudice of the unfortunate Earl, whose enormous landed spoils in Williamite "appropriation *claws*," gave rise to due political and legal jobbing, at the expense of justice and humanity even to women; or to such a with-holding even of the fair pecuniary claims of the female members of the family, on the property, for their support, as reduced those unfortunate Ladies to great privation and suffering. The printed Case of the Ladies Margaret, Catherine, and Elizabeth Mac

* The pickings which this land-robbery-advocating gentleman had out of the estates of the Earl of Clancarty and of the Duke of York, or James II., in Ireland, are adduced by himself, in August, 1714, as due reasons for his attachment to the Hanoverian succession. "The part I have acted," he writes, "has been perfectly Hanoverian, as to the succession; *and £400 per annum I have of Lord Clancarty's forfeiture, and £150 per annum out of the Duke of York's private estate, are sufficient motives thereunto.*" Of this bitter enemy of the old Irish, alive and dead, it may be added here, how, according to Mr. Gilbert's History of Dublin, he "availed himself of his position, to imprison illegally, for a year, in Newgate, Hugh Mac Curtin, an Irish historiographer of the County of Clare, for having, in a treatise, published in 1717, exposed the unfounded statements, which were promulgated, in his Hibernia Anglicana, relative to the laws and customs of the Irish, previous to the English invasion."

Carthy, daughters of Callaghan, and sisters of Donough, Earl of Clancarty, addressed to the English Parliament, presents a melancholy picture of the state to which they were reduced, by this Williamite seizure of their brother's estate. Having, among other matters, set forth, how the Countess of Clancarty, their mother, was entitled to a sum of above £12,000, and each of themselves to a fortune of £4000, from their brother's property, and how William's Queen, Mary, pitying their condition under the detention of this money, gave the Countess, in July, 1693, a letter to receive by patent the larger sum from the forfeited estate, accompanied with assurances of the Countess's 3 daughters being likewise paid, the document adds of William III.'s grasping Dutch favourite, William Bentinck, whom he created Baron of Cirencester, Viscount Woodstock, and Earl of Portland,—" But before the said Countess, or her said daughters, could have *any* benefit of the said grants, or prevail to have the same pass the seals, the whole estate was granted to the Lord Woodstock, who had better success in passing patent, without any, the least provision, for the said Countess or daughters, or any notice taken of her said grants, or of several caveates entered against the said Lord's passing patent of the said estate. The said Countess, having lived some years in misery, and being quite spent and fatigued by her solicitation about this affair, and worried by creditors, who, upon the credit of this debt, advanced money for the managing and carrying on her said business, and for the support of herself and her daughters; and seeing, by these disappointments, all her credit failing, and no way left to pay what she owed, or to keep herself or her said daughters from the greatest distress and want, she died; leaving her said daughters in a most deplorable condition, without any, the least subsistence, and exposed to all the calamities, that can attend persons of their age, sex, and circumstances. Therefore, the said Ladies, Margaret, Elizabeth, and Catherine, being all Protestants, do humbly address themselves to the honor and justice of the great and wise Council, the Parliament of England, for relief, in their most deplorable condition;" &c. "And," concludes the document, "the parties in this case have this farther to say for themselves, that they are so many innocent persons, and miserably necessitous, to the highest degree of distress; to which may be added, the consideration of their sex and quality; in all which regards, over and above the equity of their pretentions, they hope to be found proper objects of Christian charity, humanity, and common justice." In the "Report made to the Honourable House of Commons, December 15th, 1699, by the Commissioners appointed to Enquire into the Forfeited Estates of Ireland," we find, among other extravagant grants of such lands, from William III. to his foreign favourites,—" To William Bentinck, Esq., commonly called Lord Woodstock, 135,820 acres of land." And how anxious this Dutch patentee was to wring all he could out of the property he had gotten into his possession, before such unjustifiable grants of William could be resumed, as they afterwards were, by Parliament, appears in another part of the Report, or that respecting the enormous waste perpetrated on the forfeited estates, by felling the woods, in order to turn the trees, as quickly as possible, into ready money. On this head, the Report observes, —" The waste on the woods of the late Earl of Clancarty's estate, now in grant to the Lord Woodstock, is computed at £27,000"—adding in illustration of such waste, how, "indeed so hasty have several of the Grantees, or their Agents, been in the disposition of the forfeited woods, that vast

numbers of trees have been cut and sold for not above 6 pence a piece!"*
Thus, they, who were so unfortunate as to have incumbrances on
such properties, were, like the Ladies Clancarty, kept out of their just
claims, or reduced to poverty; and we read of the forfeited estates in
Ireland having been so much deteriorated in value before they could be
resumed by Parliament, that, when finally sold, they realized nothing
like what was expected, towards defraying the great expense of the Irish
war! The audacious begging, by the above-mentioned Bentinck, Lord
Woodstock, Earl of Portland, &c., from William, in 1695, of the Lordships of Denbigh, Bromfield, and Yale, with other lands in the Principality of Wales, the ancient demesnes of its Princes, and William's
monstrous grant, *also*, of such a territory and revenue to his favourite,
until obliged, by the English Parliament, to recall that present, constitutes
a portion of *English* history. But the foreigner, though compelled to
disgorge in *England*, was left "ample room and verge enough," to fill his
pockets, from the devastation and misery of *Ireland!* At all events,

> " What a king ought not, that he cannot give,
> And what is more than meet for princes' bounty
> Is *plunder*, not *a grant*."—YOUNG.

Of the exiled Earl Donough, my English authority says,—" This
unfortunate nobleman retired to Hamburgh, on the Elbe; and, of the
citizens of Altena," or Altona, " on the same river, (which belongs to
Denmark, though but half a mile from Hamburgh,) purchased a little
island, in the mouth of the Elbe, which went by his own name. There
he built a convenient dwelling-house, with a range of store-houses, and
formed a convenient plan of an useful garden. In this place, he made
great profit by shipwrecks that drove on shore; *not like the robbers on
our coasts in England, that wish as much for a storm, as our farmers do
for a good harvest,*" and " *who will sooner murder the unfortunate wretches,
that they may plunder at pleasure, than assist them.* But this unfortunate
nobleman gave the distressed all the assistance in his power; saving the
lives of many; taking them from the arms of death; and, by proper
remedies, restoring them to life. With the same assiduous care, he
endeavoured to save their vessels from a wreck, when *the fore-mentioned
brutes will murder, to make one.* All this gentleman's profit arose from
those goods that were thrown upon the coast of his little island, which
he carefully placed in his store-house; and, if demanded by the true
owners within the year, he honestly returned them, receiving only 2 per
cent. for store-room; if not, he made use of them as his own. When my
brother and I were at Hamburgh, in our travels home last year," concludes this fair English writer, " our Consul there, Sir C——l W——h,
took us in his yacht to view this island; and, from that worthy gentleman, I had this account." † Under King George I., or in 1721, Earl

* As an additionally-flagrant instance of such "general waste committed on the
forfeited woods" in Ireland, the Report mentions *that*, on the Kenmare estate, in
Kerry, "where, to the value of £20,000 has," it says, "been cut down, and
destroyed!"

† A Tour through Ireland, in several Entertaining Letters, wherein the Present
State of that Kingdom is considered; and the most noted Cities, Towns, Seats,
Rivers, Buildings, &c., are described. Interspersed with Observations on the
Manners, Customs, Antiquities, Curiosities, and Natural History of that Country,"
&c., " by 2 English gentlemen. Dublin: Printed for Peter Wilson, Bookseller in
Dame-street. 1748.

Donough's attainder was reversed, and his honours restored. But he remained abroad till his death, which occurred at Prals-Hoff, in the territory of Hamburgh, September 19th, 1734. His titles and appointments under King James II., in Ireland and France, were "Earl of Clancarty, Viscount of Muskerry, and Baron of Blarney, Lord of the Bedchamber, Lord Lieutenant or Civil and Military Governor of the County of Cork, Clerk of the Crown and Peace for the Province of Munster, Colonel of a Royal Regiment of Foot Guards, Captain of the 2nd Troop of Horse Guards, and Brigadier-General of Infantry." The Earl's death was regretted abroad and at home by his countrymen of the race and religion to which he belonged. Of those abroad, James Mac Geoghegan, author of "*Oeuvres Melées en Latin, Anglois, et François sur Divers Sujets, en Prose et en Vers*," printed at Hamburgh, in 1730, and dedicated to his Lordship, composed an elegy on his patron's decease, soon after its occurrence, and published it the same year, 1734, at Hamburgh. Of those at home, Eoghan or Owen Mac Carthy, a gentleman of the Earl's own tribe and district, and a good Gaelic poet, in a song to the praise of the river Lee, which flows through Cork, does not conclude, without an appropriate allusion to the fall of the great head of his clan. After dwelling upon the beauties of the country along

> "That river, so shining, so smooth,
> So fam'd both for waters and shore,"

he adds—

> "And yet tho' the nobles, and priests,
> And Gaels, of both high and low ranks,
> Tell tales, and indulge in gay feasts,
> On its dark-green and flowery banks,
> I mourn for the great who are gone—
> And who met by the Lee long ago—
> But *most for the Church's true son,*
> *Who now in Altona lies low.*"

By his estimable English Lady, who accompanied him into banishment, and died abroad in June, 1704, the Earl's son Robert, Lord Muskerry, Commodore in the British navy, was his successor in the title of Clancarty, as he should also have been in the family estates. *These* had been so secured by Donough's marriage-settlement, that no alleged *rebellion* or *treason*, on his part, in supporting King James II. against the Revolutionists, even admitting the support of the King to have really been *rebellion* or *treason*, could legally affect more than Donough's life-interest in such estates; and his marriage having taken place in 1684, any children he might have had by that marriage down to any period of the War of the Revolution in Ireland, (from 1688 to 1691,) would necessarily be of such a "tender age" then, as to be quite incapable of *rebellion* or *treason;* and therefore equally incapable of being subjected to any forfeiture of property, for offences of which they could not be adjudged guilty. Robert, Lord Muskerry, who, on his succession, by his father's death, to the title of Earl of Clancarty, was in command of a ship of war off the coast of Newfoundland, consequently returned to Europe, to endeavour to recover his property in Ireland. The influence which existed for the purpose was very considerable. The Earl's sister, Lady Charlotte Mac Carthy, was married to John West, 1st Earl de la Warr, created, in 1725, Lord of the Bedchamber to King George I., and Knight of the Bath; and, in 1731, appointed Treasurer of the Household, and a Member of the Privy Council, to King George II. Sarah, Duchess of Marlborough, (widow of the celebrated John Churchill, Duke of Marlborough,) whose sister, the Duchess of Tyrconnell, suffered so much by the Revolution in Ireland, and who, through the common union of the Marlborough and Clancarty families by marriage with that of Sunderland, sympathized with the Earl of Clancarty as a connexion, or relative, likewise agreed to furnish him with money, for the attainment of his rights. Cardinal Fleury, too, Prime Minister of France, made use of such interest with Sir Robert Walpole's administration, that the British Cabinet were induced, in 1735, to countenance a measure, for the restoration of the Earl to his confiscated estates; at that time producing, according to the English Lord Primate of Ireland, Dr. Boulter, the noble income of £60,000 a year. But the landed spoils of the Earldom of Clancarty had fallen into so many hands, that the idea of any thing like a restoration of those spoils excited a great consternation and clamour in Ireland, not merely among such as were living upon the immediate spoils of the Earldom, but among the existing "ascendancy" there in general, owing to the injurious effects which such a precedent as *any* restoration of confiscated lands might have upon the recently-acquired fortunes of a colonial proprietary, "2-3ds" of whose estates, according to the remonstrance of *their* advocate, Primate Boulter, to the British Cabinet, "were Popish forfeitures originally." On this closer, or more "English-interest," view of the matter, the London Ministry became alarmed, and left Lord Clancarty to such redress as he could obtain by law from the dominant representatives of that "interest," or the so-called "glorious Revolution," in Ireland. "The law," says my legal authority, Mr. O'Conor, with respect to the Earl, "was clear in his favour. A minor at the Revolution, he was incapable of treason; and he claimed under a marriage settlement, which placed his title beyond the reach of attaint. With this incontestible title, he brought an ejectment; but met an insuperable obstacle, in the unconstitutional, unexampled interference of Parliament. By *a resolution of the Commons, all Barristers, Solicitors, Attorneys, or Proctors, that should be concerned for him, were voted* PUBLIC ENEMIES. His Lordship's cause was, in consequence, abandoned." His situation, on this occasion, was, in fact, no better than that of "one," as the national saying expresses it, "*going to law with the Devil, and the Court in Hell!*" It was only natural, that the splendid birth-right, which he had been deprived of by shameless robbery, should be detained from him by as shameless injustice.

"Crowns bought by blood must be by blood maintain'd!"—SHAKSPEARE.

The despoiled Earl, though feeling as we may so easily imagine he felt, yet remained, from expediency, in the English navy for some years, or till after the breaking out of the war in 1741, when he was promoted to the command of a 1st rate vessel. By this time, the rankling reflection of what he *only* was then, compared with what he had been born to—his attachment, as a Tory, to the House of Stuart, deprived of their kingdoms, as he was of his immense estate, for the loyalty of his father to their interest—and the prospect of the Stuarts making an attempt on England, during the existing contest, in order to effect their "restoration" to royalty, through which *alone* he could hope for a recovery of his birth-right — caused him to throw up his command under the Hanoverian *régime*, pass into France, and actively connect himself with the cause of the exiled Royal Family. There, during the enterprise of Prince Charles in Britain, or November 8th, 1745, we find his Lordship with the Prince's brother, Prince Henry, Duke, and subsequently Cardinal, of York, writing thus, from Paris, to their father, as King James III. of England and Ireland, and VIII. of Scotland. "In my opinion, things have a very favorable aspect. I hope, and believe, the French are in earnest. His Royal Highness, the Duke, dispatched (4 days since) the same person that was in England in May last, by whom I have, in concert with my Lord Marischal," Keith, "wrote to the people attached to your Majesty's cause, as was the desire of the French Ministry. We have sent for a person, who is a gentleman of estate and worth, and entirely devoted to your Majesty, and of great weight and interest with the party. I expect him in 3 weeks, and, so soon as he arrives, I hope we shall embark, and, by what I know of the dispositions of the people, I make no doubt, if it please God that we debarque the troops in safety, (of which, I think there is no great hazard,) but that his Royal Highness will carry his point. I most humbly beg leave to assure your Majesty, that nothing shall ever be wanting, on my part, to manifest how profoundly and zealously I shall ever be, Sir, your Majesty's most dutiful, most loyal, and most devoted subject, and servant." The year after Prince Charles's overthrow at Culloden, or March 26th, 1747, the Prince, notifying his design of being "absolutely in private" at Paris, while endeavouring to bring the French Ministers "to reason, iff possible," as regards a new invasion of Britain; and likewise observing, of himself and his adherents, how they "must leave no stone unturned, and leave the rest to Providence;" then adds, in writing to Lord Clancarty—"Iff you have anything to lett me know of, you have only to write to me under cover to young Waters, who will always know where to find me. At present, I have nothing more particular to add so remain, assuring you anew of my particular regarde and friendship." In the Hanoverian or Georgeite edict of proscription designated an "Act of *Indemnity*," passed in June, 1747, and purporting to pardon, with what are termed "certain exceptions," all persons engaged in the recent contest for the restoration of the Stuarts—but these exceptions being so numerous as to divest the Act in question of any pretension "to the character of grace or favour," since, in addition to so many already attainted by Act of Parliament, judgment, conviction, verdict, confession, or otherwise, above 80 persons were specially condemned by name—the 2nd of those denounced was "Robert Maccarty, styling himself Lord Clancarty."

According to a curious account of the Earl in Walker's Hibernian Magazine for 1796,* his situation in France, when considered as that of the adherent to a defeated cause, and of a disinherited exile, was, on the whole, as good as could be expected; including due military rank, a distinguished position at Court, and privileges of the higher class of nobility. He, nevertheless, was rendered unhappy by the recollection of his past misfortunes. Regretting, also, his banishment from England,

---

* The article referred to is in the number for July, and is commented on by another writer in the number for August. The paragraphs I take from the former are sometimes given by me in a different or what has seemed a better order, than that observed in the original. Several statements, too, have been corrected, abridged, or modified, where it appeared requisite, from other authorities, or *superior* information.

where, having been born, he would have preferred to reside; and, though unable to return there, yet being desirous, he said, "to live and die in sight of it," he removed from Versailles, to settle at Boulogne-sur-mer. A widower by the decease of his 1st Lady, a Miss Jane Plyer, daughter of Captain Plyer of Gosport, County of Southampton, he, at the advanced age of 63, married a young wife, who brought him 2 sons; and to whom he is stated to have been "very much attached, by every tie of affection and esteem." But, in this tie, a new and deep mortification, "the unkindest cut of all," awaited him. "Sarah, Duchess of Marlborough, on her death, left him a legacy of £20,000; and, as he could not go over in person to receive this legacy, he sent his *dearly-beloved wife*, with full powers to act for him. The executors of the Duchess fulfilled her Grace's request, and paid the money to Lady Clancarty. But, alas! under this temptation she fell. Such a sum offered independence, and pleasures," apart "from the controul of her Lord; and she was base enough to prefer those to her duty. In short, she remained in England; and, though letter after letter from the Earl entreated her to come back, and be forgiven, they never met afterwards. This was a finishing blow to his misfortunes; he felt more the loss of her affection than the money; and he proved it by his continued attachment to her children." The Earl resided in a chateau on the skirts of the town of Boulogne. His pension from the King of France amounted to £1000 *per annum*, "exempt from wine-duties, postage, &c; and, as the articles of life were then very reasonable, his income enabled him to live with splendour, and hospitality. Every Thursday was his open day for a select party of the inhabitants to dine with him; who generally were composed of as many English gentlemen, as were either resident, or passing through the town; and to them he paid particular compliment, except when English politics became the subject of conversation. Here he sometimes forgot the decencies of his rank, and situation as a host,—but, as the company generally knew the history of his misfortunes, they bore everything with good humour. To these days of meeting his friends and neighbours, he added another, which could not be positively fixed, but happened generally, once in 3 weeks, or a month; and that was a club dinner at his countryman O'Doherty's, who kept *Le Lion Rouge*, in that town. On these days, there was a large round of ox-beef, brought over from Leaden-Hall Market by one of the Boulogne packets, ready salted, and this was served up boiled, entirely in the English fashion. To this was added 2 courses in the French style; and, for this dinner, with as much Burgundy, Champagne, and other liquors, as the company could drink, (such *was* the cheapness of living in France) the reckoning amounted to no more than 6 livres per head. At these meetings, his Lordship always presided, and was particularly convivial. He enquired, with obliging attention, after the healths of the persons present, and their families; gave his eye, and ear, to everybody around him; told his stories very pleasantly; and generally finished the evening, in an oblivion of all his former cares and misfortunes." As for the Earl's disengaged evenings, he mostly passed them "at O'Doherty's Hotel, where he selected 1 or 2 of the townsmen to drink a bottle with him. In these lounges, he was fond of some *butt*, on whom he could let off his wit and sarcasms—and Monsieur Jacques, (a partner of O'Doherty's, and a shrewd, humorous fellow,) always undertook this character with great readiness. The Earl loved his bottle, as well as joke, and, as the latter generally encouraged a repetition of the former, Monsieur Jacques, at a certain hour of the night, did not lose sight of his knowledge of *multiplication*, in the reckoning. This the Earl knew very well, though he blinked at it, and sometimes used to say—'Well, Jacques, though I *joke upon your head*, you are even with me, for you *score upon mine* most damnably.' . . . In this simple, uniform life, his Lordship passed the remainder of his days, very vigorous, both in body and mind, to the last. He died, after a few days' illness, at his chateau, about the year 1770, in the 84th year of his age; leaving 2 sons, who were very little better provided for, than having commissions in the army."

The Earl "was, in his person, about the middle size; stout-made, long-visaged, pock-marked, and, until he softened in the civilities of conversation, had rather an austere and haughty look." He had lost the sight of 1 of his eyes, having, in the younger or wilder period of his career, one night given the lie direct to the infamous Duke of Wharton; who, in consequence, flung a bottle of claret at him, thereby occasioning the injury mentioned. It is asserted of the Earl in the Magazine, that "his Lordship always owned the justice of his punishment"—though, as an Irish Peer, and I may add, as a British naval officer, it will *not* be believed, that this was ALL he did, in connexion with the matter—but, at any rate, could obtain nothing in the way of "personal satisfaction" from such an unblushing compound of the bully and the poltroon—such a

"Monster, mix'd of insolence and fear,
A dog in forehead, but in heart a deer!"—
Pope's Homer, Iliad I., 297-298.

as Wharton. "He wanted personal courage," writes Dr. William King of Oxford respecting Wharton, which "would probably have been concealed, if he had been a sober man. But he drank immoderately, and was very *abusive*, and sometimes very *mischievous*, in his wine; so that *he drew on himself* FREQUENT *challenges, which he would* NEVER *answer!*" The Earl, "though not very highly educated, had a strong, observing mind, loved," as has been shown, "the pleasures of the table, and contributed very considerably to them himself, by his wit, and humour." In the early portion of his life, "he was a visiting member of the famous Saturday Club, established by Lord Oxford in Queen Anne's reign, consisting of most of the leading Tories of that time, and which Swift so much celebrated in his Journal, Letters, &c. . . . The Earl was likewise an acquaintance of Swift, and he always coincided with Lord Orrery, in thinking the Dean was not *wholly* entrusted with the *secrets* of Oxford's Ministry.[*] The Saturday Club, he said, as it appeared to him, was merely convivial and literary, and when politics were introduced, they were no more than the reports, or the published news, of the day. He acknowledged the Ministers paid great court to Swift, as likewise most men of the Club. . . . He discredited the assertions of Swift and Bolingbroke—'That Queen Anne's last Ministry had *no* thoughts of bringing in the Pretender, in bar to the Hanoverian succession.' He said, he KNEW to the contrary, and that the first of the quarrel between Oxford and Bolingbroke was upon *that* head—the latter wanting to push that matter forward with expedition, and the other wavering

[*] Or, it would seem, among these "secrets," *that* of the correspondence for continuing the royal succession, after Queen Anne's decease, in the person of her brother, as James III.

between the danger and the impracticability of it. Had the Queen lived a little longer, Bolingbroke would have attempted it alone.* . . . He always spoke on this point with warmth, and," remarks the Georgeite writer of this narrative, "in such terms as were not so pleasant for a British subject to hear. . . . The Duke of Ormond was another of his contemporary friends, of whom he always spoke, as a nobleman of the highest honour and integrity, and with whom he corresponded till the Duke's death, which happened at Avignon," in 1745. "He always spoke of Sarah, Duchess of Marlborough, with great respect, and professed his obligations to her, both for the share she had in her protection of him, and education. . . . He, however, totally disliked her politics—she was a WHIG—and the Earl, from principle, as well as the bias which his misfortunes gave him, was a *rank Tory*, or, in the language of that day, a JACOBITE." Through his grandmother, previous to her marriage, Lady Elizabeth Fitz-Gerald, the Earl "was allied to the Leinster family," and used to call James, 20th Earl of Kildare, and 1st Duke of Leinster, "when only Earl of Kildare, his cousin; but, no sooner did he hear of his being created a Duke, than he renounced the relationship in great contempt"—as, it appears, a connexion with one, who had dishonoured the antiquity, &c., of his race so much, in accepting a Dukedom from such a reprehensible or *Hanoverian* source. The "original estates in Ireland," of which, through the "*glorious* Revolution," or dominant Whiggery, the Earl of Clancarty was so scandalously robbed, "were, upon a loose calculation 20 years ago," concludes my authority in 1796, "supposed to be worth £150,000 per year; and, perhaps, now, what from the rise of lands, and the cultivation they may have undergone by the industry of so many different families, may be worth £200,000; whilst his 2 sons, if living, have, perhaps, little more than their commissions, in the French service, to support them." We know no more of those 2 sons than is here stated; so that, in the person of their father—additionally alluded to by his venerable contemporary, Charles O'Conor of Belanagare, as "a nobleman of the strictest probity, a sea-officer of the greatest valour and experience," and his unjust treatment as "the hard fate of one worthy of a better"—the Earldom of Clancarty, as a dignity denoting the head of the great sept, or name, of Mac Carthy, may be said to disappear from history. Of the Irish Brigade, in the national Regiments of Lee, Dorrington, Roth, Clare, Berwick, Walsh, there were Mac Carthys officers, including various Chevaliers of St. Louis, down to the Revolution under Louis XVI. The heads of the eminent branch of Mac Carthy "Reagh," from Spring-House, in the County of Tipperary, have also flourished in France with the honours of French nobility, heightened by those of literary taste and military rank, down to the present century. Nor have other Mac Carthys been without distinction in the services of the 2 kingdoms of the Iberian peninsula, and that of Austria.

The Duke of Berwick was Captain of the 1st Troop of Guards, as long as it was kept up in France. After the Peace of Ryswick in 1697, a great reform or reduction, among the Irish troops in France, being resolved upon, the remains of the Irish Life Guard, amounting to no more than 105 men, were broken up, as such, in February, 1698, and drafted into the corps, successively known as the Royal Irish Regiment,

---

* The magazine writer adds here, "though *not* with probable success." In refutation, however, of such an evident *tack* to what the Earl *really* said, see the concluding portion of Book V., connected with the Queen's death, &c.

or the King's Foot Guards, commanded by a veteran of the Irish wars and subsequent Continental campaigns, Colonel William Dorrington. In this regiment, those 105 survivors of the Horse Guards remained until 1701, when they were attached to the Duke of Berwick's Irish Infantry Regiment, as Cadets, with high pay, and thus continued, until they became extinct in 1710.

THE KING'S AND QUEEN'S REGIMENTS OF HORSE.

These 2 horse regiments were organized from the remains of 9 cavalry regiments of the Irish army—namely, Tyrconnell's, Galmoy's, Lucan's, Sutherland's, Luttrell's, Abercorn's, Westmeath's, Purcell's, and O'Brien's —that came over from Ireland to France. The 2 regiments each consisted of 2 squadrons; each squadron of 3 troops; each troop of 50 privates; each regiment, with its 2 squadrons, or 6 troops, consequently mustering 300 privates, and the 2 regiments 600. The officers to both corps were comparatively few down to the period of the list of them by Abbé MacGeoghegan, or 1695. In the King's, or "Régiment du Roi, Cavalerie," they were—"Dominick Sheldon, Colonel—Edmond Prendergast, Lieutenant-Colonel—Edmond Butler, Major—4 Captains—6 Lieutenants—6 Cornets." In the Queen's, or "Régiment de la Reine, Cavalerie," they were—"Lord Galmoy, Colonel—René de Carné, (a Frenchman,) Lieutenant-Colonel—James Tobin, Major—4 Captains—6 Lieutenants—6 Cornets."* Thus each of these regiments of 300 privates, having 19 officers, would, so far, consist of 319 men; and both regiments would be 638 strong. But the officers being subsequently increased to 72 per regiment,† each of these corps of 300 troopers and 72 officers was 372, and both 744 strong. The Colonel of the 1st, or King's Regiment, Dominick Sheldon, was an officer of experience; having first served in the army of Louis XIV. on the Continent, and afterwards in that of James II. through the whole of the War of the Revolution in Ireland. The Colonel of the 2nd, or Queen's Regiment, was Pierce Butler, (originally Le Botiler) 3rd Lord Galmoy, who also served with distinction through the whole of the latter war. The 2 corps were under the command of these Colonels during the contest terminated by the Peace of Ryswick, in September, 1697. In the extensive reduction which occurred among the Irish troops in France, early in 1698, the KING's and QUEEN's Regiments of Horse, or, as they were likewise styled from their Colonels, *Sheldon's* and *Galmoy's*, were broken into 1 Irish Regiment of Horse, to consist of 2 squadrons. Of this, Dominick Sheldon was made the Colonel, and Lord Galmoy was elsewhere provided for, as Colonel of an Irish Regiment of Infantry. Of Sheldon, an account will be found under the head of his new Regiment of Horse, next that of Nugent, and finally that of Fitz-James. Of Lord Galmoy, a similar notice will be given, in connexion with his Regiment of Infantry.

* It would seem that, in these 2 Regiments of Horse, the Colonel was without a special troop; the Lieutenant-Colonel and Major making 2 Captains, in addition to the 4 enumerated, in order that each of the 6 troops might have a Captain.

† The very considerable augmentation of officers here, as in the other Irish corps, from 1695, would appear to have arisen from an increased necessity to provide, in that capacity, for the number of unfortunate gentlemen, who became more and more the victims of the Revolution, and its various disastrous results for Ireland.

THE KING'S REGIMENT OF DISMOUNTED DRAGOONS.

This corps was a modification of one formed in Ireland, so early as 1685. It was called the Earl of Limerick's Dragoons, from William Dongan, (commonly, though erroneously, spelled Dungan,) Earl of Limerick, who was its Colonel, till the spring of 1689. The Earl, who, from his advanced period of life, and the bad state of his health, was unfitted for the active military exertion that would be required in the warm contest which was then approaching, about the middle of April that year, resigned his command; and the Colonelship of the regiment was transferred to his son, the Lord Walter Dongan. The family of Dongan, distinguished, in the 17th century, by its extensive landed property, high connexions, and honourable civil and military posts, was equally remarkable for its loyalty to the Crown in the Parliamentarian and Cromwellian wars, and its adherence to the Stuarts, during their exile on the Continent, after the execution of King Charles I. It was among the few Irish families who were restored to their estates, when Monarchy was re-established, under King Charles II. In 1685, its head, William Dongan, was created, by King James II., Viscount Dongan of Claine, in the County of Kildare, and Earl of Limerick. His Lordship was also made a Member of the Royal Privy Council for Ireland, Lord Lieutenant of the County of Kildare, and Governor of the Province of Munster; and, upon the breaking out of the Revolution, he adhered to King James, and sat in the House of Lords of the Parliament convened by that Monarch in Dublin, in 1689. After the loss of his only son, (hereafter more particularly noticed,) at the Boyne, the Earl proceeded, with the rest of the Irish Jacobites, to Limerick. He was, consequently, attainted by the Revolutionists, or Williamites, in April, 1691; but, continuing stedfast to the royal cause, retired to France. There, Captain Peter Drake, of Drakerath, in the County of Meath, his exiled relative, (and whose father, the Earl, before the Revolution, had appointed, at Limerick, 1 of the Commissioners of Customs, and Chief Comptroller of the Mint,) speaks warmly of his Lordship's good nature; mentioning him, in the year 1694, as " my best friend, William, Earl of Limerick, who took me to his house, and there supported me;" and, in 1696, it is added, sent him, with a recommendation for a military provision, to Lieutenant-Colonel Alexander Barnwell, of the Queen's Regiment of Dragoons, commanded by Colonel Oliver O'Gara; and then forming part of the French army of Catalonia, under the Duke of Vendome. By following his banished Sovereign to France, rather than acknowledge the revolutionary government by remaining in Ireland, the Earl of Limerick forfeited a noble estate, in the Counties of Kildare, Dublin, Carlow, Meath, Kilkenny, Longford, Tipperary, and Queen's County, containing 26,480 acres, beside house-property in the City of Dublin, and many tithes; all which, (and much *more*,) were granted, as a reward for his successes against the Irish, to the Dutch Lieutenant-General, Baron de Ginkell, created Earl of Athlone, and Baron of Aghrim, or Aughrim.

Under King James's administration in Ireland, the Earl of Limerick's son, Lord Walter Dongan, held by Deputy and Sub-Deputy, the civil situation of Clerk of the Common Pleas in the Irish Court of the Exchequer; was, with Charles White, Esq., of Leixlip Castle,* 1 of the

---

* "Among the different families of the Whites," in Ireland, alleges Abbé Mac Geoghegan, " that of Leixlip was the most celebrated, as well for its virtues, as its

Members for the Borough of Naas, in the County of Kildare, in the Parliament of 1689; and, in the national army, Colonel of the Regiment of Dragoons bearing his name. The regiment was part of the small Irish force, despatched early in 1689, by King James's government, against the Revolutionists of Ulster. With that force, it assisted to beat the superior numbers of the Williamites out of the field into Derry; was at the blockade of that place; and, after the disembarkation of the Prince of Orange's commander, the Marshal Duke of Schonberg, in Ulster, and his advance to Dundalk, is noticed, in the Irish official account, as one of the best cavalry regiments in the army, by which that campaign was brought to its miserable termination on the side of the invaders. Next year, 1690, the regiment were at the engagement of the Boyne, where the death of their Colonel, by a cannon-ball, as they were coming into action, produced such depressing effects upon them, that King James, in his account of the conduct of the Irish cavalry there, which, with the exception of these and the Clare dragoons, he describes as excellent, says —"Lord Dungan being slaine, at their first going on, by a great shot, his dragoons could not be got to doe anything." His Lordship's body was conveyed from the field to the family mansion of his father, the Earl of Limerick, at Castletown, near Celbridge, in the County of Kildare; where, on the retreat of the Jacobite troops from Dublin to Limerick, the day after the battle was devoted to the ceremony of the funeral; the troops, on the next, resuming their journey to the south. *

Lord Walter Dongan was succeeded, in command of the regiment, by his relative, Walter Nugent; descended from the old French or Norman race of the Nugents, through the respectable branch of Moyrath and Dardistown, in the County of Meath. The father of Walter Nugent, Francis Nugent, Esq., of Dardistown, was the 2nd son of Sir Thomas Nugent, Baronet; and his mother was the Lady Bridget Dongan, sister of William Dongan, Earl of Limerick. Of this marriage, 3 sons were

opulence, magnificence, and illustrious alliances." In the reign of James II., Charles White, Esq., of Leixlip, was a Member of the Royal Privy Council of Ireland—a Deputy Lieutenant to William Dongan, Earl of Limerick, as Lord-Lieutenant for the County Kildare—joint Member, with Lord Walter Dongan, the Earl's son, for the Borough of Naas, in the Irish Parliament of 1689—Clerk of the First Fruits and Twentieth Parts in the Irish Court of Exchequer—and Captain of an Independent Troop or Company, in the Irish army. Of the baronial residence of this family, or the Castle of Leixlip, an interesting notice, in 1840, alluding to that edifice as so "magnificently situated on a steep and richly-wooded bank over the Liffey," &c., states—"This Castle is supposed to have been erected, in the reign of Henry II., by Adam de Hereford, one of the chief followers of Earl Strongbow, from whom he received, as a gift, the tenement of the Salmon Leap, and other extensive possessions. It is said to have been the occasional residence of Prince John, during his governorship of Ireland," or rather of the Anglo-Norman settlements in Ireland, "in the reign of his father; and, in recent times, it was a favourite retreat of several of the Viceroys."

* According to legal documents connected with the family of Dongan, William Dongan, Earl of Limerick, died in 1698, without leaving issue; in consequence of the death of his son, Lord Walter Dongan, Colonel of Dragoons, at the Boyne, in 1690. The title of Earl of Limerick then came to Colonel Thomas Dongan, brother of Earl William. Thomas, under the will of his father, Sir John Dongan, Baronet, inherited an estate in the Queen's County, and served in the army of Louis XIV., till 1678, as Colonel of an Irish Regiment, "worth to him above £5000 per annum." He had from Charles II. a life-pension of £500 a year; was made Lieutenant-Governor of Tangier in Morocco; and subsequently Governor of New York in America. The title of Earl of Limerick ceased, in the Dongan family, in December, 1715.

officers of eminence; Christopher, attaining the rank of Lieutenant-Colonel of Horse under King James II., and of Major-General of Cavalry in France, of whom more, at large, farther on; Patrick, after serving as Captain in Lord Dongan's Dragoons, becoming Lieutenant-Colonel to the Duke of Berwick's Regiment in France; and Walter, (who was the elder brother of Patrick) succeeding, as Colonel, to his cousin, Lord Dongan. Colonel Walter Nugent being slain at the battle of Aughrim or Kilconnell, in July, 1691, the next Colonel was the Honourable Richard Bellew, 2nd son of John Bellew, 1st Lord Bellew.

The origin of the Bellews, (or, as the name is sometimes corruptly written, "Bedlow," and "Bedloe,") is traced to Normandy; whence a nobleman, called "Belew," and holding a high post in Duke William's army, appears enrolled in the lists of the French conquerors of England. It is uncertain, at *what* period, after the extension of the invasion of those conquerors from England to Ireland, the Bellews passed into the latter country, and commenced the acquisition of those large estates, owned by bearers of the name to this day. But from the latter end of the 14th century, the immediate ancestors of the ennobled representatives of the race appear, on the records of the English settlements in Ireland, among those of honourable rank; or with considerable landed possessions, and intermarried with the leading families of the Pale, such as the Fitz-Geralds, Nugents, Dillons, Talbots, Barnwells, Flemings, Plunkets, Fitz-Williams, Sarsfields. After the restoration of King Charles II., John Bellew, Esq. of Castletown, near Dundalk, in the County of Louth, was, by the Act of Settlement, reinstated in the lands belonging to his father, and which had been usurped by the Parliamentarian or Cromwellian rebels. In the reign of King James II., he was at first knighted; afterwards, or in 1686, was ennobled by the title of Baron Bellew of Duleek, in the County of East Meath; and was also made a Member of the Royal Privy Council for Ireland. At the Revolution, Lord Bellew adhered to the royal cause against the Prince of Orange; early in 1689 was appointed Lord Lieutenant and Governor of the County of Louth for King James, and Colonel of a Regiment of Infantry in the Irish army; and, in the Parliament of the same year, took his seat in the House of Peers. When, towards the latter end of that campaign, the Williamite forces, under the Marshal Duke of Schonberg, occupied Dundalk, Lord Bellew suffered a great loss upon his property; his castle, not far from that town, having been made a garrison-post by the invaders; about 2000 of his sheep having been killed by them; and his orchard-trees cut down, as wood for their camp. In the autumn of 1690, the 2nd year of the war in Ireland, his Lordship, for his continued services to King James, had all his estates sequestered by William III., for the benefit of 1 of his English favourites, Henry Sidney, created Viscount Sidney, and Earl of Romney, and enriched by grants of 49,517 acres of the forfeited lands of Ireland, intended by Parliament to have been appropriated towards defraying the large public debt incurred for the War of the Revolution there! In April, 1691, Lord Bellew was outlawed by the Revolutionists; and, the ensuing July, being present with his regiment of infantry in the Irish army at the battle of Aughrim or Kilconnell, he was severely wounded there, and made prisoner by the enemy. His Lordship only survived the effects of his wound until the following January, 1692, and with his Lady, who died in 1694, was, in the middle of the south aisle of Duleek

Church, interred in a large tomb, decorated with their coat armour, and thus inscribed—

"THIS TOMB HATH BEEN REPAIRED AND THE VAULT MADE BY DAME MARY BERMINGHAM OF DUNFERT, WIFE TO JOHN, LORD BELLEW, WHO WAS SHOT IN THE BELLY IN AUGHRIM FIGHT, THE 12TH OF JULY 1691. AS SOON AS HE FOUND HIMSELF ABLE TO UNDERTAKE A JOURNEY, HE WENT WITH HIS LADY TO LONDON, WHERE HE DIED THE 12TH OF JANUARY 1692. HE WAS LAID IN A VAULT IN WESTMINSTER, TILL THE APRIL FOLLOWING, HIS CORPSE WAS BROUGHT HITHER."

By his marriage, in 1663, to Mary Bermingham, who, with her younger sister Anne, (afterwards Lady Clanmalier,) was co-heiress of Walter Bermingham, Esq. of Dunfert, in the County of Kildare, to a property of about £1500 a year, Lord Bellew had 2 sons, the Honourable Walter and the Honourable Richard Bellew, both officers, like their father, in the Irish army. Walter, Captain of a troop of horse in the Regiment of Richard Talbot, Duke of Tyrconnell, fought throughout the war in Ireland, or till its conclusion by the Articles of Limerick. He then succeeded his father, as 2nd Lord Bellew; and, partly by being included in those Articles, and, partly by forgiving Lord Sydney £3400 received out of the Bellew property while in his possession, as well as remitting Lord Raby a debt of between £1700 and £1800 in order to secure the favourable influence of those 2 English Lords with King William, recovered the family estate, which still produced £1000 a year. This Walter, 2nd Lord Bellew, died in 1694, like his father, as it is said, or from the effects of a wound at Aughrim; leaving by his Lady, Frances Arabella, eldest daughter of Sir William Wentworth, of North-Gate-Head, Yorkshire, sister to the Earl of Strafford and Maid of Honour to Mary, Queen of King James II., only 2 daughters.

The other son of John, the 1st, and brother of this Walter, the 2nd, Lord Bellew, or the Honourable Richard Bellew, the immediate subject of our notice, was, early in the War of the Revolution in Ireland, Captain of a troop of dragoons in the Regiment of the Earl of Limerick. On the first insurrectionary disturbances by the Prince of Orange's partizans in Ireland, he was only a Lieutenant, and commenced his active military career with distinction, at the head of his troop, against a body of the enemy, double his number, under a Major Pooe; the circumstances of which affair are thus given in a Jacobite account. "Major Pooe, a Cromwellian officer, opened the scene, and began hostilities. He commanded 2 troops of horse, and desiring to put the country under contribution, he commenced his demands with the tenants of Lord Bellew. He required of them the sum of £500 sterling, on pain of military execution. The Lord Bellew, being informed of what was going on, despatched, to the assistance of his farmers, his 2nd son, aged 18 years, at the head of a troop of dragoons, of which he was Lieutenant. These 2 parties meeting one another, a brisk engagement took place; but young Bellew, having shot the Major through the head with his pistol, the 2 troops of the latter were defeated; some being slain, others made prisoners, and the rest saving themselves by flight." The same troop of dragoons, not long after, or in May 1689, are likewise mentioned as taking a distinguished part against the Williamites of the County of Down, at the overthrow, near Cumber, beside Lough Strangford, of Captain Henry Hunter, and his adherents, by King James's commander, Major-General Thomas Buchan. On this occasion, Hunter, and his insurgent force of some thousands, being broken and routed by the royal troops, the Captain himself with difficulty effected his escape, in a little boat, to the Isle of Man; while his defeated followers were chased as far as Donaghadee, and driven into the sea by young Bellew's troop of dragoons, until this pursuit was arrested by the fire from a vessel, armed with 4 cannon, under a Captain Agnew, then lying at anchor off the coast; by which interposition, 68 of the fugitives were saved from the Jacobite dragoons, and thence conveyed to Scotland. Of the further personal conduct of the Honourable Captain Richard Bellew, we are, from the want of sufficiently minute information, without any knowledge from this period, or May, 1689, to July, 1691; but may justly suppose his behaviour was very creditable, both from what has been related, and from his being, though only about 20 years of age, the successor of Colonel Walter Nugent, in the command of the regiment, after the fall of that officer at Aughrim. On the termination of the war in Ireland, by the Treaty of Limerick, in the autumn of 1691, the Honourable Colonel Richard Bellew brought the regiment to France, under the designation of the King of England's Dismounted Dragoons. There, however, notwithstanding *his* merit and that of his father and brother, it being found imperative to provide for an older officer, and one of a higher grade in the service, by giving that officer the Colonelship of the regiment, young Bellew regarding himself as thereby unjustly treated, returned to Ireland. On the decease of his elder brother, the Lord Walter, in 1694, he became 3rd Lord Bellew; in May, 1695, married Frances, youngest daughter of Francis, Lord Brudenell, and widow of Charles Livingston, 2nd Earl of Newburgh in Scotland, with a fortune of £17,000; conformed to the Established Church of England and Ireland, early in 1705; took his seat in the House of Peers there, in July, 1707; had a pension of £300 a year from Queen Anne; and, dying in March, 1714, left, as his successor, John, the 4th Lord Bellew, born in 1702; on whose decease at Lisle, in Flanders, in September, 1770, the title became extinct.*

The officer, through whose superior age, and political influence, as well as military rank, under King James's Government in Ireland, and the consequent possession of a similarly superior interest at the Court of St. Germain for his subsequent promotion in France, the Honourable Colonel Richard Bellew was necessarily supplanted in his command, was Thomas Maxwell. He was a Catholic gentleman of an ancient family in Scotland, and married in England to the handsome Jane, Duchess of Norfolk, widow of Henry Howard, 6th Duke of Norfolk. He was appointed by King James II., in November, 1688, Colonel of the regi-

* During the War of the Revolution in Ireland, the name of Bellew was represented by officers in the Duke of Tyrconnell's and Lord Abercorn's Regiments of Horse; in Lord Dongan's and Colonel Simon Luttrell's Regiments of Dragoons; and in the Lord Grand Prior's, Lord Louth's, and Colonels Oliver O'Gara's and Sir Michael Creagh's Regiments of Infantry, besides that of the chief of his name, Lord Duleek. There were, also, some Bellews officers of the Irish Brigade in France; the most distinguished of whom, as a Chevalier of St. Louis, was a Captain Bellew of the Regiment of Walsh, in 1787.

G

ment known at present as the 4th Dragoons, and, on the success of the Prince of Orange's invasion of England, left that country, as the King did, for France, and came over to serve in Ireland. He was made there, as he had been in England, Colonel of a Regiment of Dragoons, and, in the course of the Irish war, rose to be a Brigadier, and Major-General. After the 2nd year's campaign, or that of 1690, it being resolved by the discontented portion of the Irish, that a deputation, consisting of Dr. John Molony, Catholic Bishop of Cork, and Colonels Simon Luttrell, Henry Luttrell, and Nicholas Purcell, should be sent to King James, at St. Germain, to request the removal of the Duke of Tyrconnell, Brigadier Maxwell, who was in the confidence of Tyrconnell's representative in Ireland, the Duke of Berwick, was deputed, by the latter, to accompany those agents to the King, in order to give him private information of the circumstances by which permission for such an embassy to proceed to France was extorted, and to suggest the adoption of hostile measures there towards some of those envoys. This, being suspected by the embassy, was near costing the Scotch Brigadier his life; Colonels Henry Luttrell and Nicholas Purcell proposing, to cut short his errand, by throwing him into the sea; which would have been done, but for the influence of Colonel Simon Luttrell, and the Bishop of Cork. After his return to Ireland, or in 1691, Major-General Maxwell was taken prisoner, at the capture of Athlone by Lieutenant-General Baron de Ginkell, and, for the rest of that decisive campaign, remained so, either in Ireland, or at Chester, and London; during which time he was treated by the Williamites with the respect due to a man of high connexions, and honourable character. Till November, that year, he was in the Tower, as, with reference to him, and his wife, (probably ere taking their *last* farewell!) we find an "order" there, "by command of the King," or William III., "for the Duchess Dowager of Norfolk to have access to Mr. Maxwell, and to stay with him 3 days." On the subsequent remodelling of the Irish army in France, in 1692, it has been shown, how his interest was not forgotten at St. Germain. In July, 1693, he was, for his eminent services, created by Louis XIV. a Brigadier of Dragoons in the French army, in addition to his previous posts of Major-General and Colonel of Dragoons in that of King James; and was killed, fighting with great bravery, at the head of the 2 Irish Regiments of Dragoons *à pied* in the battle of Marsaglia, or Orbassan, between the Marshal de Catinat and the Duke of Savoy, October 4th following.

Major-General Maxwell's successor, as Colonel of the King's Regiment of Dragoons *à pied*, was Dominick Sarsfield, 4th Lord Viscount Kilmallock. His Lordship, of the same Anglo-Norman ancestry as the Earl of Lucan, and married to his sister,* was descended from Dominick Sarsfield, Chief Justice of the Irish Court of Common Pleas, in the reign of King James I. The Irish Chief Justice was made by his Majesty, in October, 1619, the 1st of the newly instituted order of Baronets in

* Captain Peter Drake, of Drakerath, County of Meath, who left Ireland, in the cause of James II., for France, and who served among the Irish forces on the Continent, after mentioning his arrival, in 1694, at Paris, says—"From Paris I went to St. Germain's, where I met with Mrs. Sarsfield, mother to Lord Lucan, and her 2 daughters, the Ladies Kilmallock and Mount-Leinster; the eldest of whom, Lady Kilmallock, was my god-mother. These Ladies, though supported by small pensions," adds the Captain, "received me with great generosity, and treated me with much good nature."

Ireland, as Sir Dominick Sarsfield; and, by King Charles I., was created, in May, 1625, Lord Viscount Kilmallock. His Lordship's descendants evinced the usual attachment of the Irish nobility to the Crown in the Parliamentarian and Cromwellian wars, and that of the Revolution of 1688. The representative of the title of Kilmallock at the Restoration was, with other Irish Peers, (or the Lords Westmeath, Mayo, Galmoy, Athenry, and Brittas,) ordered to be reinstated in the lands, usurped from them by the Cromwellians. That order, however, though acted upon in the other cases, would not seem to have been carried into effect as regards the Kilmallock property, by what the Comte d'Avaux, Louis XIV.'s Ambassador to James II. in Ireland, writes from Ardee, October 30th, 1689, to the French Minister, Louvois, regarding the Lord Kilmallock here treated of; who is mentioned by the Count, as having been obliged, by the deprivation of his estate, to conceal his rank, and serve, for several years, as a soldier in France, till enabled to return, with the King, to Ireland, resume his title, and regain his patrimony. "Estant Irlandois Catholique, et depouillé de tous ses biens, il changea de nom, et alla porter le mousquet dans le Régiment de ———. Son Capitaine, luy trouvant de la valeur, et de l'application, le fit Serjeant. Mylord Kilmaloc ne voulut pas dire qu'il estoit, et exerca cet employ pendant quelques années, jusques à ce qu'il soit revenu en Irlande avec le Roy d'Angleterre; et il a esté remis par le Parlement en possession de son bien, qui va, à ce qu'on dit, à plus de 50,000 francs par an." After King James's arrival from France in Dublin, in April, 1689, Dominick Sarsfield, Lord Kilmallock, was made a Member of the Royal Privy Council for Ireland; sat in the House of Peers of the Parliament soon after held by the King; and was Colonel of a Regiment of Infantry in the national army,* during the campaigns of 1689 and 1690; in the latter of which, he distinguished himself, at the successful defence of Limerick against the Prince of Orange. Next year, when his Lordship was outlawed by the Revolutionists for his loyalty to King James, he commanded a Regiment of Horse in that Monarch's service, with which he is mentioned to have been at the battle of Aughrim; though not killed there, as hostile or Williamite accounts pretend, since he accompanied the Jacobite troops who went to France, after the Treaty of Limerick. His Lordship's "broad acres" in the County of Cork with those of other Stuart loyalists there, became the prey of William III.'s Principal Secretary of State for Ireland, Sir Robert Southwell, a duly unscrupulous confiscation-clutcher from the Irish, and non-resident pensioner upon Ireland.† At the reorganization of King James's forces in Bretagne, in 1692, Lord Kilmallock was appointed 1st Lieutenant in the 2nd Troop of Horse Guards commanded by his brother-in-law, the

---

* As might be expected, from what D'Avaux tells us of his Lordship's antecedents, he proved an *excellent* Colonel. D'Avaux adds of him, "il a esté tres assidu et tres appliqué, et il ne s'est occupé qu'à maintenir son régiment en bon estat."

† Even the moderation of Mr. Dalton has not been "so good, or so cold," as to pass uncensured Sir Robert Southwell's estate-grabbings from unfortunate Irish families. See King James's Irish Army List, vol. I., pp. 444-5, and vol. II., p. 436. In 1690, William appointed Sir Robert "his Principal Secretary of State, and Keeper of the Signet and Privy Seal for the Kingdom of Ireland," says Harris, "with the sallary of £200 a year, and an augmentation of £100 a year, to hold during pleasure; which office his family have enjoyed ever since." Namely, till 1749, when Harris's work was published!—and how much *longer* I know not.

Earl of Lucan; and, in 1693, successor to Major-General Maxwell, as Colonel to the King's Regiment of Dragoons *à pied*. His Lordship continued to be Colonel of this corps until after the Peace of Ryswick. Then, or early in 1698, Lord Kilmallock's Dragoons were broken up, and incorporated with the Athlone, or Colonel Walter Bourke's, Regiment of Foot, and the 3 Independent Companies of Foot previously mentioned; and the new regiment, thus organized, was conferred upon James Fitz-James, Duke of Berwick. Lord Kilmallock is stated to have died abroad, about 12 years subsequent to the Peace of Ryswick.

According to the 1st formation of the Irish troops after their landing in France, in 1692, the King's Regiment of Dragoons *à pied* contained 6 companies of 100 privates. The officers to each company would be 5; namely, 1 Captain, 2 Lieutenants, and 2 Cornets or Ensigns; these 5 to each of the 6 companies would make 30 for the entire corps; so that, between soldiers and officers, the former 600, and the latter 30, the battalion would muster 630 men. In 1695, the officers to the "Régiment Du Roi, Dragons," were more, or—"The Viscount de Kilmallock, (Sarsfield) Colonel—Turenne O'Carrol, (the Marshal de Turenne's godson) Lieutenant-Colonel—De Salles, (a Frenchman) Major—5 Captains—14 Lieutenants—14 Cornets." The regiment being still further increased in officers, though lessened in soldiers, consisted, at its full complement, of 558 men; of whom 108 were officers, and 450 soldiers.

THE QUEEN'S REGIMENT OF DISMOUNTED DRAGOONS.

Of the 2nd of the 2 Regiments of Dragoons *à pied*, or the Queen's, the 1st Colonel was Francis Carroll, or rather O'Carroll, an officer of note during the war in Ireland. The great sept of O'Carroll of Eile, or Ely, deduced its origin from Olil Olum, King of Munster in the 3rd century, through his youngest son Kian; the hereditary surname of the sept being derived from Caerbhall, or Carroll; 21st in descent from Kian. The territory of Eile, so designated from Eile, the 7th in descent from Olil Olum, anciently comprehended the Baronies of Ikerrin and Eliogarty in the County of Tipperary, with those of Clonlisk and Ballybrit in the King's County. It was divided into 8 tuatha, or districts, under as many subordinate tribes and their chiefs, among whom the dominant or regal race was that of O'Carroll; whose head was poetically known, as "King of Eile of the gold," of "the land of cattle," of "the most hospitable mansion in Erin," and of "the host of yellow, curling hair, brave at gathering a prey." Donald O'Carroll, from whom the principal houses of the name have descended, was King of Ely O'Carroll in the 12th century, when the Anglo-Norman intrusion into Erin took place; after which period, the principality, chiefdom, lordship, or captainship, of Ely O'Carroll became limited to the Baronies of Clonlisk, and Ballybrit, in the King's County; but, with no diminution, during the middle ages, of the reputation of the O'Carrolls, as some of the stoutest and most formidable borderers to "the stranger," among the old races of Erin. Of the heads of "that celebrated tribe," the very learned native or Gaelic scholar and lexicographer, Edward O'Reilly, testifies,—"It is indisputable, that they were, in very early ages, the supreme Princes of the entire district; and, in more modern times, when sirnames became hereditary, gave their patronymic name to that part of the district which they then possessed; and which, from that circumstance, was called Ely O'Carroll. When they were Kings of the entire district, and even since they became Lords of Ely O'Carroll only, they had under them several very famous tribes;" and, adds O'Reilly, " of the patriotism, piety, and prowess of the Chiefs of the O'Carrolls of Ely, the annals of Ireland teem with abundant proofs." Hence, the popular Gaelic song in Munster, among the most renowned names in the national records and recollections, refers to

"The O'Carrolls, also, fam'd where Fame was only for the boldest,"

exclaiming—

"Who so great as they of yore in battle, or carouse?"

Various of the leading branches of the O'Carrolls were connected with the principal nobility of Ireland, as the Lords Athenry, Clanricarde, Antrim, Dillon, Mayo; and the race has been represented, to our day, by families of note in Galway, Clare, Mayo, Tipperary, King's County, Wicklow, Carlow, as well as in the United States of America.* In the " great rebellion" of the Puritans against King Charles I., several gentlemen of the O'Carrolls were remarkable for their devotion to the royal cause, as well as during the banishment of King Charles II. on the Continent;† and a similar adherence to the Crown, as that against the Parliamentarian insurgent and Cromwellian regicide, was subsequently displayed in support of King James II., against the Orange revolutionist and foreign invader.

In that Monarch's national Parliament of 1689, Owen O'Carroll, Esqr., was 1 of the Members for the King's County, of which he was likewise a Deputy-Lieutenant; Lieutenant-Colonel Owen O'Carroll was Chief Commissioner of Oyer and Terminer there, and King's Commissioner for seizing on Forfeited Estates and the Property of Absentees; and, during the 3 years' unequal contest against the British and colonial Williamites, and their numerous and veteran Continental auxiliaries, the O'Carroll motto, " In fide et in bello fortis," or " Strong in fidelity and in war," was verified by a number of O'Carrolls, or Carrolls, in the horse, dragoon, and infantry regiments of the Jacobite army, from the ranks of Brigadier, Colonel, and Lieutenant-Colonel, to those of Captain, Lieutenant, and Cornet, or Ensign. Towards the fall of the ancient or clan system of

* Of the name, in the great Transatlantic republic, the chief representative was the venerable Charles Carroll, of Carrollton; at his decease, in November, 1832, the *last* survivor of the signers of the American Declaration of Independence, and, through his descendants, connected with nobility in these islands.

† Of this devotion of O'Carrolls to Kings Charles I. and II., there is a most striking instance on the part of Donough O'Carroll, Esqr., (brother to the chief of the name,) possessed of the estates of Modereeny and Buolybrack, County of Tipperary, and married to Dorothy O'Kennedy; by whom, (besides a daughter, More, wife to Roger O'Carroll of Emly,) he had 30 sons, whom he presented, duly armed and mounted as a troop of horse, with all his interest, to the Marquis of Ormonde, for Charles I.; most of which gentlemen died in foreign service, having followed Charles II. in his exile. A contemporary Italian writer from Ireland, observing how "almost all the women who marry have large families," adds, "there are some who have as many as 30 children alive; and the number of those who have from 15 to 20 is immense!" In our own day, a most eminent authority, Dr. Collins, Master of the Rotunda Lying-in Hospital, mentions, that, in Ireland, "the proportional number of women, giving birth to twins, is nearly a 3rd greater, than in any other country, of which he had been able to obtain authentic records!"

society in Ireland, a respectable branch of this tribe was founded in Dublin by Thomas O'Carroll; who, in consequence of a disagreement with the head of his sept, removed thither, and was the father of James, that, under King James I., was knighted, granted 1000 acres of land in Wexford, appointed King's Remembrancer, and, between 1613 and 1634, was thrice Mayor. Francis, the officer here under consideration, who has been identified with the "Francis Carroll, Esquire," attainted by the Williamites, in May, 1691, at the Tholsel, in Dublin, as possessing property in the metropolis, was, most probably, of this family. In 1686, as Captain in the Colonel's company of Colonel Justin Mac Carthy's Regiment of Foot, we find Francis dispensed, along with other Catholic officers, by King James II., from taking such sectarian or English-concocted oaths contrary to their religion, as would have precluded them from serving their king and country. During the contest that ensued in Ireland, Francis became a Colonel of Dragoons and a Brigadier; was most engaged in the winter and spring warfare of outposts between 1690 and 1691, directed, by the Government of King James at Limerick, against the Williamites in the County of Cork; and to a later period, or August, 1691, acted, for King James, as "Governor and Commandant-in-Chief of his Majesty's Army in the Counties of Kerry and Cork." On the rearrangement of the Irish army in France in 1692, he was nominated Colonel (as has been said) to the Queen's Regiment of Dismounted Dragoons, and fell gloriously in Italy, in 1693, at the great victory of Marsaglia. Besides this gallant representative of his name, Turenne O'Carroll, after serving in Ireland, as Major, and Lieutenant-Colonel of Dragoons, was, in France, Lieutenant-Colonel to the King's Regiment of Dismounted Dragoons; 2 O'Carrolls have been Lieutenant-Colonels to the Regiment of Berwick; some have been Chevaliers of St. Louis; and, to our own day, O'Carrolls have been officers in the armies of France. Francis O'Carroll's successor in the Colonelship was Charles O'Brien, 5th Lord Clare; of whom a fuller notice has been already given, under the head of the Infantry Regiment of O'Brien, or Clare. His Lordship having been advanced to the Colonelship of his family regiment, in 1696 we find the Queen's Dragoons under the command of the chief of his name, Colonel Oliver O'Gara.

The O'Gadhras, or O'Garas, were another branch of the Clan-Kian, or race of Kian, youngest son of Olil Olum, King of Munster in the 3rd century. The original territory of the O'Garas consisted of the district, in the County of Mayo, yet known as "Sliabh Lugha," or *Looee's Mountain;* of which, it is noted, in the old account of the privileges " of the supreme King of Connacht of the red swords," that "one of his prerogatives" was "the hunting of Sliabh Lugha." This territory embraced the portion of the modern Diocese of Achonry, including the northern half of the Barony of Costello, or the Parishes of Kilkelly, Kilmovee, Kilbea, Kilcolman, and Castlemore-Costello. After the invasion of Erin by Henry II., the "Tighearnas" or *Lords* of Sliabh Lugha, as the heads of the O'Garas were styled, were driven, by the Anglo-Norman families of the Nangles and Jordans, (subsequently nationalized into Mac Costellos and Mac Jordans,) to seek another territory. This was acquired in the district, anciently known as "the Greagraidhe of the fine trees," and afterwards as the Barony of Coolavin, in the County of Sligo. The representatives of the former Lords of Sliabh Lugha, thus became Lords of Coolavin; and, in the locality called from them "Moy O'Gara," or

O'Gara's plain, on the north-east extremity of Lough Techet, which likewise changed its name to Lough *O'Gara*, they built their principal castle. To the head of this race in the early part of the 17th century, or Fergal O'Gara, then Lord of Coolavin, as well as 1 of the Members for the County of Sligo in the Irish Parliament, those venerable memorials of our old native or Celtic history, the *Annals of the Four Masters*, were dedicated; in gratitude for his patronage and support of the brothers O'Clery, and their assistants in the work, after the O'Clerys had been dispossessed of the castle and lands, with which they, as the local chroniclers of Tir-Connell, had been so liberally endowed, under its ancient Princes, or Chiefs, the O'Donnells. Another gentleman, and namesake of this distinguished patron of his country's literature, or the Rev. Fergal O'Gara, displayed a similarly creditable zeal for its preservation, by making abroad, or (as an exile from Cromwellism) in the Netherlands, in 1656, a most valuable collection of Irish historical poems, and transcribing them into a volume, yet extant. And it was to a lady of this race, famed among the native poets, or Celia O'Gara, that the air was composed, which Moore has incorporated with our national Melodies, to the beautiful words, beginning,

"Oh! had we some bright little isle of our own,
In a blue summer ocean, far off and alone."

In the Parliamentarian and Cromwellian wars, the O'Garas were involved in the ruin of their country; having been stripped of their property by *republican* rapacity, as the O'Clerys had been by *royal* injustice. Under King James II., however, Oliver O'Gara, the head of his race, was highly connected; being married to the Lady Mary Fleming, daughter of Randal Fleming, Lord Baron of Slane, and 21st Irish Peer of the family of Fleming, originally Le Fleming; derived from a chief of the Norman army, at the conquest of England, in the 11th century, whose grandson, in the 12th, settled in Ireland.* Oliver O'Gara, (as well as the representative of the noble family into which he had married,) adhered, at the Revolution, to the cause of King James; was 1 of the Members, in the Irish Parliament of 1689, for the County of Sligo; served with distinction against the Revolutionists, in the national army, as Colonel of a Regiment of Infantry, with which he was present, at the battle of Aughrim, or Kilconnell, in July, 1691; was accordingly attainted by the Williamites, with his wife, and others of his name; and was appointed, by his superior officers, Lord Lucan, and Major-General John Wauchop, the following October, to be 1 of the

* At the Revolution, Christopher Fleming, (whose father and uncle were particularly distinguished for their fidelity to the Crown in the Parliamentarian and Cromwellian wars,) was the 22nd Lord Baron of Slane. He sat in the House of Peers of the Irish Parliament under King James II. in 1689; was Colonel of a Regiment of Infantry in the Irish army; and was taken prisoner in the battle of Aughrim, or Kilconnell, July 22nd, 1691. After following his exiled Sovereign to France, his Lordship was restored, by an English Act of Parliament, under Queen Anne, to his Peerage, though not to his estates; and died in July, 1726, without male issue, in his 45th year. He had a pension of £500 per annum allowed him, and his nephew William Fleming, commonly called Lord Slane, also had a pension of £300 a year, till his decease, in 1747—from *some* shame, it would seem, at the Williamite, or "glorious-revolution" plunder of the family of its fine property, for the benefit of the Dutchman, Ginkell—already rewarded, for his services in Ireland, with the large estate of the Earl of Limerick.

hostages, on the part of the Irish, for the safe return, from France, of the Williamite ships, by which the Irish troops, &c., were to be conveyed there, pursuant to the Treaty of Limerick. After the satisfactory termination of every thing connected with this conveyance, and the consequent dismissal, in March, 1692, of Colonel O'Gara for France, he appears to have been involved, on the resumption of his military duties there, in the same reduction of rank as so many other Irish officers were; being made, instead of Colonel, a Lieutenant-Colonel, to which post he was appointed in the King's Regiment of Irish Foot Guards, under Colonel William Dorrington. As Colonel, however, of the Queen's Dragoons, with which he served in Spain under the Duke of Vendome, O'Gara eventually regained the rank he had possessed in the Irish wars. By his marriage with the Lady Mary Fleming, the Colonel had 4 sons. The 3 elder of these entered the Spanish service, in which, the 1st died with the rank of Brigadier; the 2nd was Colonel of the Regiment of Hibernia; the 3rd Lieutenant-Colonel of the Regiment of Irlandia, and signalized himself so much at the affair of Veletri in Italy, in 1743, that the King of Spain rewarded him with a Commandership in the Order of Calatrava. The 4th, born at St. Germain-en-Laye in 1699, was baptised, in the "Chapelle du Château Viel" there, as Charles, "par M. l'Abbé Ronehy, Aumônier du Roi et de la Reine, d'Angleterre" and having for "parrain," the "très-haut et très-puissant Prince Jacques II., Roi d'Angleterre," signing accordingly "JACQUES, *Roi*." Although reduced to live in France on but small means as a follower of James II., Colonel Oliver O'Gara managed to situate this, as well as his other sons, in such a manner, as was suitable to the respectability of their origin; obtaining, through his distinguished countryman and friend, Francis Taaffe, Count of the Empire, and Earl of Carlingford, an introduction, for young Charles, to Leopold, Duke of Lorrain. Charles was, by that Prince, appointed 1st Equerry to his 2 sons, and, when the elder became Emperor of Germany, was created by him an Imperial Councillor of State and Chamberlain, Grand Master of the Household to the Princess his sister, and Knight of the Golden Fleece. He was also made a Count, and died in opulent circumstances without issue, at Brussels, the latter end of the year 1775, or early in 1776. After the Peace of Ryswick, or in February, 1698, Colonel Oliver O'Gara's or the Queen's Regiment of Dragoons *à pied*, which had signalized itself upon several occasions, being subjected to the general change amongst the Irish troops in France, was broken up; and, along with the Charlemont Regiment of Infantry, or that of Colonel Gordon O'Neill, was formed into a Regiment of Foot, which was given to Brigadier Pierce Butler, 3rd Lord Galmoy, late Colonel of the Queen's Regiment of Horse, merged into Brigadier Dominick Sheldon's.

Like the King's Regiment of Dragoons *à pied*, the Queen's, by the earliest organization of the Irish force in France, when they came over after the Treaty of Limerick, contained 6 companies of 100 privates each, with a regimental complement of 30 officers; presenting a total, for the battalion, of 630 men. The list of the officers of the "Régiment de la Reine, Dragons," in 1695, shows the same increase in its officers, as in the King's. Those of the Queen's, by that list, were—"Charles, Viscount Clare, (O'Brien,) Colonel—Alexander Barnewal, Lieutenant-Colonel—Charles Maxwell, Major—5 Captains—14 Lieutenants—14 Cornets." At its complete amount, towards the end of the war, when the soldiers were so many less, while the officers were so many more, the Queen's Dragoons, like the King's, mustering 450 soldiers, and 108 officers, would be 558 strong.

THE KING'S ROYAL IRISH REGIMENT OF FOOT GUARDS.

This regiment was ordered by King Charles II., in the spring of 1662, to be raised in England, to the number of 1200 men, for his service in Ireland; James Butler, 1st Duke of Ormonde, and Viceroy of Ireland, being, by the royal patent, constituted its Colonel; and empowered, upon the conveyance of the men to that country, to name whoever he might think fit, as his subordinate officers. Partly, it appears, from the men thus levied, and partly from others, belonging to the old detached or Independent Companies at that time existing in Ireland, the new regiment was eventually formed. It consisted of 2 battalions; was first called the Royal Irish Regiment; and afterwards the King's Foot Guards. In the succeeding reign, or that of King James II., the loyalty of the corps was insured, by its being generally purified, or nationalized, like the rest of the army in Ireland, under the superintendence of Richard Talbot, Earl of Tyrconnell.* The Colonelship, however, remained in the Ormonde family; James, the 2nd Duke of Ormonde, filling that post at the time of the Revolution. The Duke going over to the Prince of Orange in 1688, the command of the regiment in Ireland was reserved, with other honours, for its Lieutenant-Colonel, William Dorrington. The day after King James's arrival, in April, 1689, from France, at the Castle of Dublin, that officer—with the Dukes of Powis and Berwick, the Earls of Clanricarde, Abercorn, Carlingford, and Melfort, the Lords Kilmallock, Clare, Meryon, and Kenmare, the English Lord Chief Justice, Sir Edward Herbert, (who followed the King's fortunes, and subsequently became his Lord Chancellor for England, at St. Germain,) Colonel Patrick Sarsfield, afterwards Earl of Lucan, and Sir Ignatius White of Limerick, Baronet of England, and Baron de Vicke, and Marquis d'Albeville, on the Continent,—was sworn before his Majesty, as a Member of the Royal Privy Council for Ireland. The Lieutenant-Colonel was then appointed Colonel of the Royal Irish Regiment of Foot Guards, instead of the Duke of Ormonde, who adhered to the cause of the Revolution, in opposition to that of the King. Dorrington, who was an Englishman, (but unaffected by Whiggery,) had belonged to the Regiment of Guards from its formation. During the War of the Revolution in Ireland, he signalized himself at the blockade of Derry in 1689, at the action of the Boyne in 1690, was Governor of the City and County of Limerick, and was taken prisoner at the battle of Aughrim, or Kilconnell, in 1691. He was successively transferred to Dublin, Chester, and the Tower of London,† but was so soon exchanged, or released, by the Revolutionists, as to be able to

* From the official correspondence with Ireland, in the State Paper Office, London, it appears, that the Earl of Tyrconnell wished to have as few as possible of any but natives of Ireland in the Irish army, and that he forwarded an intimation of that kind to the King.

† There was an order, in September, for Major-General Dorrington "to have the liberty of the Tower, and for his friends and relations to visit him." Yet, among other matters for which, in 1694, Lord Lucas, as "Governor of the Tower," was "several times called before the Council," is mentioned, "the ill usage of Major-General Dorrington."

resume, in France, his active adherence to the Jacobite cause, with the forces which came over from Ireland after the Treaty of Limerick. Retaining in France his Colonelship of the Royal Irish Foot Guards, he served with that regiment on the coasts of Normandy, as part of the army designed for the invasion of England, and restoration of King James, in 1692; and at the taking of Huy, the defeat of William III. at the battle of Landen, and the capture of Charleroy, by the Marshal de Luxembourg, in 1693. Brigadier by brevet in the service of France, (as previously in that of Great Britain and Ireland) April 28th, 1694, he was employed that year with the Army of Flanders. He was present at the bombardment of Bruxelles (or Brussels) by the Marshal de Villeroy in 1695; and was with the Army of Flanders, under the same Marshal, in 1696 and 1697. The Royal Irish Regiment of Foot Guards being broken up, after the Peace of Ryswick, by order of February 27th, 1698, and another regiment formed out of it, the Brigadier was named its Colonel, by commission of the same day. He served with the Army of Germany, under the Duke of Burgundy, by letters of June 21st, 1701; with the same Army, under the Marshal de Catinat, by letters of May 8th, 1702; and, the 23rd of December following, was made a Maréchal de Camp, or Major-General of France, by brevet. Employed with the Army of Bavaria, under the Marshal de Villars, in 1703, he was present at the siege of Kehl, at the capture of the lines of Stolhoffen, and of the retrenchments of the Valley of Hornberg, at the combat of Munderkingen, at the 1st battle, or victory, of Hochstedt, and at the taking of Kempten. Remaining with this army under the Marshal de Marcin in 1704, he fought at the 2nd battle, or defeat, of Hochstedt, famous, in English history, as the battle of Blenheim. He was made Lieutenant-General of the Armies of the King, by power of the 26th of October following. He was attached, with this rank, in 1705, to the Army of the Rhine, under the Marshal de Marcin; in 1706, under the Marshal de Villars; and to the Army of Germany, under the Marshal d'Harcourt, in 1709 and 1710. With the last of these campaigns, his active services terminated; though he kept the Colonelship of his regiment, hence known as that of Dorrington, till his death at Paris, December 11th, 1718. In a Dublin newspaper, the *Morning Register*, of March 27th, 1841, the following additional information respecting this English Jacobite officer and his family is cited from a contemporary French print, the Paris *Quotidienne;* in which, however, the mistake of an "English," instead of an "Irish," regiment must be noted and corrected, from what has been stated here. "At Abbeville, there have just died, within a few days of each other, the Comte and the Chevalier Macclesfield Dorrington, aged the one 85, the other 74, and descended from Lord William Dorrington, Colonel of an *English* regiment, which bore his name. He emigrated with James II., and was created, during his exile, a Peer of England, by the Monarch, whose melancholy fortunes he had served and followed, with the most courageous fidelity. In these 2 brothers, the branch of the Dorringtons, established in France since the expulsion of the Stuarts, has become extinct." When I was at Paris, in the summer of 1841, to collect materials for this work, and a History of the War of the Revolution in Ireland, I met an elderly French gentleman, who told me, he had been acquainted with those 2 brothers. He regretted, that I had not come to France previous to their decease, or in time to be introduced to them, from the interest they would naturally have felt in the 2 subjects of my researches, as *both* connected with the establishment of their distinguished ancestor in France.

The regiment was next transferred to the Comte Michael de Roth. The family of Roth (or, according to its earlier spelling, Rothe,) was among the oldest and most wealthy of the mercantile families of Kilkenny; where it was one of particular note in the reigns of Queen Elizabeth, King James I., and King Charles I.; and, in addition to its emoluments from commerce, was possessed of considerable property in houses and lands. The town residence of the head of the Rothes, which was built in the reign of Queen Elizabeth, has remained, to our own times, in Kilkenny; with the family arms carved in stone, over the archway conducting to the entrance. The edifice was raised by John Rothe *Fitz*-Piers—the use of *Fitz*, (then, and long after, so observable among the names of the higher burghers of others of our leading towns, as well as Kilkenny,) evidently pointing back to the times, when a Norman name or connexion was most honourable in England, and in the different settlements established from that country in Ireland. A learned antiquarian, the Rev[d]. James Graves, who, with a well written article in 1849, has given a lithographic representation of the "Entrance Arch to Rothe's House," says—"This building exhibits a most interesting and nearly perfect example of the urban architecture of the period; affording ample accommodation to the opulent merchant's family, his apprentices, and servants, together with storage for his goods." Of this family was Dr. David Rothe, Catholic Bishop of Ossory, during the reigns of James I. and Charles I.; author of various publications in Latin, connected with the history of Ireland; and of whom the great Archbishop Ussher speaks in high terms, for his extensive erudition upon that subject, or as "*patriarum antiquitatum indagator diligentissimus*." Another gentleman of the name of Rothe, a contemporary of the Bishop, or Robert Rothe, Esq., who was family-lawyer, and agent, to the Earls of Ormonde, compiled a pedigree of that renowned leading branch of the house of *Le Botiler*, or Butler, to the year 1616; which has been made use of by Carte, in his Life of the 1st Duke of Ormonde, and yet remains in manuscript, in the Library of Trinity College, Dublin. Under King James II., John Roth, Esq., was Mayor of Kilkenny in 1687, and also in 1689; as well as Member of Parliament, the same year, for that city. Of the 24 Aldermen of the remodelled, or reformed, Corporation of Kilkenny, headed by Richard Butler, 5th Viscount Mountgarret, there were 3 Aldermen of the name of Roth, or Edward, David, and Michael; the 1st, a merchant, and the 2 others, gentlemen. Among the 36 Burgesses of the same Corporation, we find Matthew Roth, merchant, and Robert Roth, gentleman. In other Corporations of the County Kilkenny, or those of Gowran and Knocktopher, there were also gentlemen of the name; and, for the neighbouring County of Wexford, Francis Roth, merchant, was 1 of the Members of Parliament in 1689. Michael Roth (our present subject) was born September 29th, 1665. Under Colonel Dorrington's predecessor in command, the Duke of Ormonde, he entered the Irish Foot Guards, as a Lieutenant, in 1686. After the breaking out of the Revolution in 1688, he was a Captain of the 1st or King's Company of the corps. He remained in it through the succeeding war in Ireland; on the termination of which, by the Treaty of Limerick, in the autumn of 1691, he passed into France. He served on the coasts of Normandy, with the French and Irish force designed for the invasion of England in 1692; at the capture of Huy, the victory of Landen, (or Neerwinden) and the reduction of Charleroy in 1693; with the Army of Germany in 1694; with the Army of the Moselle in 1695. He became Lieutenant-Colonel of his regiment in March, 1696; continued that campaign with the Army of the Moselle; and was attached, in 1697, to the Army of Flanders. King James's Regiment of Foot Guards being formed, by order of February 27th, 1698, into the Regiment of Dorrington, M. de Roth was made its Lieutenant-Colonel, by commission of April 27th following. Granted by commission of May 9th, 1701, the rank of Colonel, he served that year with the Army of Germany, under the Duke of Burgundy; and with the same army, the following year, under the Marshal de Catinat. Acting under the Marshal de Villars in 1703, he was at the capture of Kehl, at the storming of the retrenchments of Stolhoffen and Hornberg, at the combat of Munderkingen, at the 1st, or successful, battle of Hochstedt, and the reduction of Kempten and of Augsburg. Serving under the successor of Villars in Bavaria, the Marshal de Marcin, he fought, in 1704, at the 2nd, or unsuccessful, battle of Hochstedt, or Blenheim; and remained with the Army of the Rhine, under the same Marshal, in 1705. Created Brigadier by brevet, April 18th, 1706, and attached to the Army of the Rhine under the Marshal de Villars, he contributed to the reduction of Drusenheim, of Lauterburgh, and of the Isle de Marquisat. In 1707, also under that General, he was at the carrying of the lines of Stolhoffen, the reduction of Etlingen, of Pfortzheim, of Winhing, of Schorndorf, at the defeat and capture of General Janus, the surrender of Suabsgemund, the affair of Seckingen; and, by order of October 31st, he was employed, during the winter, in Alsace. He continued with the Army of the Rhine, under the Marshal Duke of Berwick, in 1708. Transferred to the Army of Flanders, by letters of June 8th, 1709, he highly signalized himself by his bravery at the great battle of Malplaquet. Appointed Maréchal de Camp, or Major-General, by brevet of March 29th, 1710, and being next in command to M. du Puy de Vauban in the remarkable defence of Bethune against the Duke of Marlborough and Prince Eugene of Savoy, he was so distinguished for professional ability as well as courage, that Louis XIV., by brevet of December 15th, named him for the 2nd Commandership of the Order of St. Louis, that should become vacant. He served with the Army of Flanders, in 1711; obtained, by provision of April 9th, 1712, the post of a Commander of the Order of St. Louis; was present, that campaign, at the taking of Douay, Quesnoy, and Bouchain, by the Marshal de Villars, in Flanders; and, in 1713, was at the reduction, by the same General, of Landau and Friburgh, in Germany. He was granted, by commission of December 12th, 1718, the Irish regiment of infantry of which he was so long Lieutenant-Colonel; and the Colonelship of which became vacant the preceding day, by the decease of Lieutenant-General Dorrington. Attached, in 1719, to the Army of Spain under the Marshal Duke of Berwick, he served at the capture of Fontarabia, of the town and castle of St. Sebastian, and at the siege of Roses. Created a Lieutenant-General of the Armies of the King by power of March 30th, 1720, he transferred his regiment, in May, 1733, to his son, next-mentioned; served no more; and died in his 76th year, May 2nd, 1741.

Charles Edward Comte de Roth, to whom his father resigned the regiment known, from the period of his becoming its Colonel, as the

Regiment of Roth, was born December 23rd, 1710. Having been designed from his childhood for the military profession, he was commissioned, May 28th, 1719, as a Capitaine-en-Second in the family regiment. He had a company, June 8th, 1729, and on the secession of his father, or May 28th, 1733, became Colonel. He acted in that rank, the same year, at the reduction of Kehl; at the forcing of the lines of Etlingen, and the capture of Philipsburgh, in 1734; and continued to serve with the Army of the Rhine, in 1735. He was attached to the Army of Flanders, which kept on the defensive, in 1742. Appointed Brigadier by brevet, February 20th, 1743, he was with his regiment at the battle of Dettingen; finished the campaign on the Lower Rhine, under the Marshal de Noailles; and commanded, during the winter, at St. Omer, by order of November 1st. Employed with the Army of the King (Louis XV.) in Flanders, by letters of April 1st, 1744, he was at the sieges of Menin, Ypres, and Furnes; then passed into the army commanded by the Marshal de Saxe; and finished the campaign at Courtray. Again employed, by letters of April 1st, 1745, with the Army of the King, and made Brigadier by brevet, May 1st, he fought, with the Irish Brigade, on the 11th, at the victory of Fontenoy; contributed to the reduction of Tournay, of Oudenarde, of Dendermonde, and Ath; and, during the winter, was stationed at Dunkirk, by letters of November 1st. Having embarked in 1746, to join Prince Charles Edward Stuart in Scotland, he was made prisoner by the English at sea; but, being exchanged in April, 1747, repaired to Bruxelles, or Brussels, the 15th. Included in the Army of Flanders, by letters of May 1st, and engaged at the battle of Laffeldt, July 2nd, he was distinguished along with the Irish Brigade, to whom the gaining of that victory, as well as Fontenoy, was so much owing. He also covered the siege of Bergen-op-Zoom; and was stationed, during the winter, at Ostend, by letters of November 1st. He served in 1748 at the siege of Maestricht; obtained the grade of Lieutenant-General of the Armies of the King, by power of May 10th; returned to command at Ostend, after the taking of Maestricht; and, having been declared Lieutenant-General in December, he quitted Ostend, and returned to France. He was created Lieutenant-General of the Irish and Scotch troops in the service of France, by commission of March 31st, 1759; was employed with the Army of Germany, by letters of May 1st, 1761; was present with it at various actions, in which he signalized himself; and died, in his 56th year, August 19th, 1766. He married an English lady of the noble house of Cary. Of the several branches of this race, connected with the Peerage, were, besides the representatives of the title of Falkland, the Barons, Viscounts, or Earls of Hunsdon, Rochfort, Dover, and Monmouth; and, of branches not ennobled, yet of eminent respectability, were the Carys of Torr Abbey and of Follaton, in Devonshire. The founder of the house of Falkland, Sir Henry Cary, Knight of the Bath, was the son of Sir Edward Cary of Berkhampstead, Master of the Jewel Office to Queen Elizabeth and King James I., by his marriage with Catherine, widow of Henry, Lord Paget. Sir Henry, who was elevated, in November, 1620, to the Peerage of Scotland, as Viscount Falkland of Fife, was, from 1622, for several years, Lord Deputy of Ireland; and his son Lucius, 2nd Viscount Falkland, was the accomplished nobleman, whose high character and lamented fall at Newbury, in September, 1643, during the war between King Charles I.

and the Parliament, are so celebrated in the Lord Chancellor Clarendon's history of that calamitous or revolutionary period. Of Lucius Henry Cary, 5th Viscount Falkland, by his 2nd marriage to Laura, daughter of the 1st Lieutenant-General Count Arthur Dillon, the issue was a daughter, who became the wife of Lieutenant-General Count Charles Edward de Roth. Their family, too, consisted of a daughter Lucie, or Lucy, married, as before related, to the 2nd Lieutenant-General Count Arthur Dillon, in the service of France. The Countess de Roth, or as she was called in England, the Honourable Mrs. Roth, had a pension from the French Government proportioned to the military rank of her husband, and survived him till February 9th, 1804; when, after an illness of nearly 3 years, borne with great fortitude, she died, at her house in Somerset-street, London, aged 76.

On the decease of Lieutenant-General Count de Roth, his regiment became that of Roscommon. It was so called from being transferred to the command of the representative of that Peerage; first conferred, in 1622, on Sir James Dillon of Moymet, and most honoured in the person of Wentworth Dillon, the 4th Earl, deceased in 1684; of whom, as a poet, Dryden says,

"The Muse's empire is restor'd again
In Charles's reign, and by Roscommon's pen;"—

and Pope, with more point, adds,

"To him the wit of Greece and Rome were known,
And ev'ry author's merit, but his own."

The successor, in the Colonelship, to the Count de Roth, Robert Dillon, son of Patrick Dillon, Esq., of Tuaghmore or Twomere, County of Roscommon, took the title, in France, of Earl of Roscommon, as he was, by right, the 9th Earl, and could have established his claim in form, had he attempted it. He was born at his father's residence above-mentioned, in November, 1712. Being, at first, only a younger son, he was attached, when a boy, as a Cadet, to the Regiment of Roth. He was a full Lieutenant in March, 1734; a reformed Captain in February, 1739; obtained his company, or was full Captain, in September, 1741; was a Chevalier of the Royal and Military order of St. Louis in 1745; was a Captain of Grenadiers, and entitled to rank as Colonel, in March, 1757; Brigadier by brevet, in February, 1759; Major, in May, 1761; and Lieutenant-Colonel, in February, 1764. In August, 1766, he became Colonel, and his regiment that of Roscommon, from his title; since the decease of his elder brother, and that of James Dillon, the 8th Earl, in August, 1746, at Harold's Cross, near Dublin. He was present at the attack of the lines of Etlingen, and the siege of Philipsburgh, in 1734; at the affair of Clausen, in 1735; at the battle of Dettingen, in 1743; at the victory of Fontenoy, and the reduction of Tournay, Oudenarde, Dendermonde, and Ath, in 1745; at the victory of Laffeldt, in 1747; at the taking of Maestricht, in 1748; and served with the Army of Germany, in 1760. He was made a Maréchal de Camp, or Major-General, in April, 1767; and died, in his 58th year, at Paris, in March, 1770.

The regiment was then given to the Comte Antoine Joseph Philippe de Walsh-Serrant. After having been attached to the Irish Horse Regiment of Fitz-James, the Count joined the Regiment of Roscommon; of which, from August, 1766, he was Colonel-Commandant under Lord

Roscommon, as Colonel-in-Chief; and, by becoming that nobleman's successor, altered the appellation of the corps to that of Walsh. The origin of the family of Walsh-Serrant has been generally deduced from the Walshes, or Welshes, of Ireland, styled by the natives, *Brannaghs*, *i. e.* old Britons, as having come over from Wales. The earliest representatives of the name of Walsh, in Ireland, were 2 noblemen, in the time of Henry II.—*viz.*: Philip Walsh, distinguished for his gallantry, in 1174, at a naval engagement against the Ostmen, or Danes, of Cork, by boarding the hostile Admiral, Turgesius, and killing his son, Gilbert —and David Walsh, who signalized himself, in 1175, at the crossing of the Shannon, when Raymond *le Gros* attacked Limerick. From this Philip and David sprang the Walshes of Castlehoel, in the County of Kilkenny, (where a range of mountains is called by their name); of Ballykilcavan, in the Queen's County; of Ballycarrickmore, in the County of Waterford; of Greaghlabeg, in the County of Tipperary; of Old Court and Old Connaught, about Bray, in the County of Wicklow; and of Carrickmaine, or Carrickmines, in the County of Dublin. Of these Walshes, upon the confines of the Counties of Wicklow and Dublin, Camden remarks, on their numbers having been equal to the nobility of their origin—"*quorum ut nobilitas antiqua, ita familia hoc tractu numerosa.*" And they required to be not less warlike than numerous on this southern, or most dangerous, frontier of the Pale, towards the high lands or mountains of Wicklow, the territory of those formidable border clans, the O'Tooles and the O'Byrnes; by 1 of whose leaders, so late as 1533, or in the reign of King Henry VIII., the Castle of Dublin itself was taken, and sacked; and who, down even to the latter end of the reign of Queen Elizabeth, were the dread of Dublin and its vicinity. In the War of the Revolution, the Walshes contributed their proportion of infantry, horse, and dragoon officers to the Irish army; and, in the privateering hostilities, which, after the conclusion of the contest in Ireland, by the Treaty of Limerick, the expatriated adherents of King James II. carried on with the French, from the ports of St. Malo, Brest, &c., against the English and Dutch, and along the coast of Ireland, as subject to the antinational *régime* established there by the detested Revolution, we find, among the Irish cruisers, the name of Walsh, or Welsh, several times connected with the annoyance of the enemy's commerce. Of representatives, in France, of the name of Walsh from Ireland, Abbé Mac Geoghegan adds, about the year 1762—" We behold, at the present day, 2 brothers, off-shoots of the noble family of the Walshes of Ireland, established in France, one of whom had conveyed, in 1745, Prince" Charles " Edward into Scotland; a service so signal, as to merit for him the title of Lord: the other, having purchased the fine estate of Seran," or Serrant, "in Anjou, was honoured with the title of Count by the King of France." Such is the origin of the family of Walsh-Serrant which I would *wish* to believe, if I did not meet with another and very different account of the matter. It is set forth in a pamphlet of 157 pages, thus entitled— "*Memoir of M. Macdonagh, a Native of Ireland, Lieutenant-Colonel of the 60th Regiment of Infantry,* (Royal Marine) *Chevalier of the Royal and Military Order of St. Louis, shut up, during 12 years and 7 months, in a Dungeon in the Isles of St. Margaret,* (the same in which was imprisoned the famous Man with the Iron Mask) *by virtue of a Lettre de Cachet granted by M. de Montbarrey, formerly Minister of War. Printed at Lyons, by Louis Cutty; and to be had in Paris at Desené's, Bookseller,*

Palais Royal; in Rochelle at Roy's & Company, 1792." This Lieutenant-Colonel André, or Andrew, Macdonagh—who supports his assertions by an appendix of "justificatory pieces," which, exclusive of those in notes to the text of his narrative, occupies from page 111 to page 157 of the pamphlet—belonged to the ancient sept of the Macdonaghs or Mac Donoughs of Sligo; and first served in the Regiment of Dillon, in which he shows, by a due certificate, that from 1690 to 1770, so many as 42 of the family of Macdonagh had been Captains or Lieutenants. The substance of the writer's case is, that he, having been the nearest or presumptive heir to the great wealth of old Count Charles O'Gara, (son of Colonel Oliver O'Gara already described) was intrigued out of this inheritance by a Randal Plunkett, styled Lord Dunsany, General Plunkett, Governor of Antwerp,* and Rose Plunkett, to whom he, the writer, was married; which intriguing was rendered successful by the influence of the old Count's valet Deuzan, with whom Rose did not scruple to commit adultery; and that then, to be ridded of the writer, a *lettre de cachet* was obtained from the French Minister of War, by a bribe to the Count de Walsh-Serrant; in consequence of which, the writer was imprisoned as related, until released by the Revolution; declared innocent of any crime; compensated by military advancement, proportioned to his standing in the army; and enabled to expose to the world the infamy of his persecutors; including Rose, who had meantime been enjoying her share of the spoil with another husband! The Irish Lieutenant-Colonel, in "unveiling," as he states, the "pretended Count de Walsh-Serrant, Colonel of a Regiment of the same name," says—"The rapid progress of this favourite of fortune is as extraordinary, as the sudden increase of his dignities. The Sieur Wash (for *that* is the true name of the pretended Count, and not Walsh, as he has been pleased to name himself,) is son of a Sieur Wash, trader at Cadiz. This trader was son of a ship-owner, and grandson of a private individual of Strasbourg, named Isaac Abraham Wash. Such is, according to the exact truth, the genealogy of the pretended Count de Serrant. Wash the ship-owner, no doubt wishing to make his origin be lost sight of, corrupted the name of his father; he added an *l*, transposed the letters, and, of an obscure Israelitish family, he formed all at once an illustrious Irish family. It is by the favour of this transposition, that the Sieur Wash has put himself forward under the proud title of Count; has driven in the carriages of the King, has married a lady of the house of Choiseul, without any other portion than her charms; and is at present Colonel of an Irish Regiment, and Maréchal de Camp. I have already made known to the public, through the medium of the newspapers, that the father and uncle of the *ci-devant* Count de Serrant were descended from a Sieur Wash, a Jew of Strasbourg; and I confidently reiterate, to the *ci-devant* Count, the most formal defiance, to produce any authentic and faithful certificate of baptism, or of marriage, contradictory of what I have just stated. I defy him also to produce a legal genealogy, establishing the slightest connexion between the existence of any of his ancestors, demonstrated as such, and the possession of any property in Ireland, in Scotland, or in England. So far, then, from belonging to any noble family of those 3 kingdoms, he is not even a gentleman; and it is merely by the riches

* Of the family of Castle-Plunkett, extinct by the deaths of the General's 3 elder sons in the Austrian service, in the Turkish, German, and Italian campaigns, and by that of the 4th son as a Dominican friar.

which his father, formerly in commerce, has left him, that he has acquired the superb estate of Serrant, situated on the confines of Anjou and of Bretagne," &c. "It is this *ci-devant* Count de Walsh-Serrant, who took upon himself to hunt out the *lettre de cachet* which has kept me during 12 years and 7 months in a dungeon, behind 6 gates, triply-grated, next to a privy, and deprived of the power of communicating with any body, either by conversation, or by writing. The interest of the *ci-devant* Count Serrant was not at the service of his friends for nothing, since he has accepted from my wife a sum of 1000 louis; for the purpose of delivering her from a man, by whom she dreaded to be prosecuted, and that her new husband might be permitted to enjoy, in peace, the fruit of her baseness." So far, Lieutenant-Colonel Macdonagh, whose public, contemporary statement, on this point, I could not conceal, without a violation of the laws of history. In 1775, the same year that the 2 other Irish Regiments of Bulkeley and Clare were dissolved, the Regiment of Walsh was likewise broken up, and incorporated with the Legion of Dauphiné. But it did not long continue so; being restored to its former composition and appellation by the Comte de St. Germain, Minister of War, in 1776; and it remained under the command of a representative of *this* family of Walsh, until the advance of the Revolution, and the consequent change of the titles of all, except the Swiss, regiments in France, from a family, feudal, or local, to a simply numerical, designation. According to this new arrangement, the corps previously known as the Regiment of Walsh, became the 92nd Regiment. The exile of the Bourbon family was anticipated, and so far as may be surmised from Lieutenant-Colonel Macdonagh's terrible *exposés*, and the guillotine-doom that menaced any *ci-devant* aristocrats at all concerned in the misdeeds of the *ancien régime*, was, with Jewish cunning, most seasonably anticipated, by Anthony Count Walsh de Serrant, and Charles Viscount Walsh de Serrant; who, with the same craft, turning *this* altered state of things to their own account, contrived to be provided for, in the light of "suffering loyalists," as Colonels of 2 of the Regiments of the Irish Brigade, formed in the British service, after the fall of the French Monarchy.

From 1692 to 1698, or from the year of the 1st Continental organization in Bretagne, as the King's Foot Guards, to that of the 1st great reform among the Irish troops in France, that regiment, which, like all the Irish infantry regiments of King James's army there, but 1, (to be hereafter noted) consisted of 2 battalions, differed considerably, at different times, in the proportions of its officers and privates. My earliest account of the number of privates and officers, after the Treaty of Limerick, specifies that there were in the regiment 2 battalions, these containing 16 companies between them, or 8 in both battalions; that, in each of the 16 companies, there were 100 soldiers, or 1600 in the entire regiment; that the officers to each company were 4, namely, 1 Captain, 2 Lieutenants, and 1 Ensign, who would form 64 officers; and thus, the total force of the regiment would be 1664. Mac Geoghegan's later list of officers to the Irish regiments in 1695 mentions those of this "Régiment des Gardes du Roi, Infanterie," as "William Dorrington, Colonel—Oliver O'Gara, Lieutenant-Colonel—John Rothe, Major—12 Captains—28 Lieutenants—28 Sub-Lieutenants—and 14 Ensigns." By other and contemporary documents, giving, to a more recent period of the war, the strength, both in men and officers, of every corps belonging to King James's Irish army in France, the proportion of officers is much greater, and of privates much less, in the regiment, than those above-stated; the 2 battalions of the Foot Guards being set down as 1342 men; or 1100 privates, and 242 officers.

THE QUEEN'S REGIMENT OF INFANTRY.

This regiment was one of those organized in France, from the Irish who came over after the Treaty of Limerick; there being no mention made of any foot regiment, called the Queen's Regiment of Infantry, among those of King James's army, during the 3 campaigns of the War of the Revolution in Ireland. Its Colonel was the Honourable Simon Luttrell, of Luttrell's-town, in the County of Dublin. This officer was sprung from the ancient Norman or French race of the Luttrells— otherwise written Loterel, Lottrell, Luterel, and Lutterell—several of whom are stated to have been, October 14th, 1066, amongst the chiefs of the army of the Duke of Normandy at the battle of Hastings, where England fell beneath its French invaders. Of the confiscated lands of the vanquished English, or Saxons, the Luttrells, like others of the dominant race, obtained their share. Under the Norman Conqueror's son, Henry I., or *Beauclerc*, as well as his royal successor, Estevene or Etienne de Blois, otherwise Stephen, we find the Chevalier Johan de Luterel, or according to the modern English mode of expression, Sir John Luttrell, Knight, holding *in capite* the manor of Hoton-Pagnel, in Yorkshire, by certain feudal services, as his descendants continued to do, until the 6th year of King Henry V. In the time of King Henry II. the Chevalier André de Luterel or Sir Andrew Luttrell, Knight, founded the Abbey of Croxton-Kyriel in Leicestershire, with a dependent cell at Hornby in Lancashire. The 1st of the name of Luttrell who acquired an establishment in Ireland was the Chevalier Geoffroi de Luterel, or Sir Jeoffry Luttrell, Knight. Jeoffry, having attached himself to the interest of King Richard I.'s brother, Johan, *sans-terre*, afterwards King John, the Luttrell estates in the Counties of Derby, Leicester, Nottingham, and York, were confiscated by Richard. On that Monarch's death, however, and the consequent accession of John to the throne, the confiscated estates of Jeoffry were not only restored to him, but some good additions were made to them. The Chevalier de Luterel attended his royal benefactor to Ireland; was much intrusted with public business there; and, upon the conditions of paying 20 ounces of gold, and of holding by military service, obtained, from the Crown, a grant of the castle, lands, and manor of Luttrell's-town, in the County of Dublin.* In the 16th year of the same reign, this Chevalier Geoffroi de Luterel was the King's representative at the Court of Rome; the next year was appointed his Embassador Extraordinary there along with the Archbishops of Bourdeaux and Dublin, and Johan, (or John) le Mareschal, to request assistance, from the Pope, against a hostile confederation of the

---

* The fine castle and noble demesne of Luttrell's-town, situated upon the right bank of the river Liffey, along the delightful Lower Road leading from Dublin to Lucan, and at a distance of about 6 miles from the Irish metropolis, were disposed of, by the last proprietor of the name of Luttrell, Henry Lawes Luttrell, 2nd Earl of Carhampton, to that excellent and liberal-minded citizen, Luke White, Esq., of Dublin, early in the present century. Since Mr. White's purchase of the castle and demesne of the Luttrells, the former name of *Luttrell's-town* has been changed, or attempted to be changed, for that of *Wood-lands;* an appellation, true, indeed, to Nature, but uninteresting to History.

Anglo-Norman Barons; and finally surviving his royal friend, died in the 3rd year of the ensuing reign, or that of King Henry III.; leaving issue by his wife, the daughter of Henry de Newmarche, whose ancestors were Barons as early as the Conquest. The next chief representative of the Luttrells, another Chevalier André de Luterel, or Sir Andrew Luttrell, Knight, proved his claim, before Henry III. at Westminster, in 1229, to certain estates, as heir to Maurice de Gant; the 1st settler of which name in England was the nephew of the great Duke-King, Guillaume *le Conquerant*, or William *the Conqueror*, and the son of Baudouin, or Baldwin V., Comte or Earl of Flanders, by a daughter of Robert, King of France, son of Hue Chapet, or Hugh Capet, the founder, in 988, of the Capetian line of the French Monarchs. This Chevalier André de Luterel, shortly after proving his claim to those estates of the De Gants, Comtes or Earls of Lincoln, Barons of Folkenham, &c., likewise made out his right, through the same Maurice De Gant, to the Barony of Yrneham, or Irnham, in the County of Lincoln, together with Quantock-head in Somersetshire, and more lands in the west. From other circumstances in this reign, or that of King Henry III., it appears, that the Chevalier André de Luterel, while thus nobly descended in the male line, was likewise so on the female side, through the great family of the Paganels or Paynels in Normandy, who became, by the conquest of England, Barons of Dudley, Lords of Newport-Pagnel, &c., in that country. From this period of the 13th, till the latter half of the 17th century, or during upwards of 400 years, the house of Luttrell continued to display, through various branches, an illustrious line of descent in England and Ireland—in the *former*, as Barons of Irnham, Lords of Hoton-Pagnel, Quantock, the Isle of Lundy in the Bristol Channel, Dunster Castle, Carhampton, &c., distinguished, likewise, in the wars of France, Scotland, and the 2 Roses—and, in the *latter*, as the ancient proprietors of Luttrell's-town, connected, in various capacities, with the English government of the country, and intermarried with the leading nobility and gentry of colonial origin. The great-grand-father of the Honourable Simon Luttrell, or Thomas Luttrell, Esq., of Luttrell's-town, was, early in the 17th century, 1 of the Members for the County of Dublin in the Irish Parliament, a Privy Councillor for Ireland, and a man of ability and high spirit; as evinced by his speeches in Parliament, and by his having had, in the reign of King James I., "the confidence," adds my Anglo-Irish authority, "to make comparisons, with the Earl of Thomond (chief of the O'Briens) even in the Lord Deputy's presence!" Simon Luttrell, Esq. of Luttrell's-town, the eldest son of the preceding Thomas, (by the Lady Eleanor Preston, 5th daughter of Christopher, 4th Lord Viscount Gormanstown,) having succeeded to the property of his father, adhered to the royal cause, in the Parliamentarian and Cromwellian wars. He shared the general fate of the Irish loyalists; his castle of Luttrell's-town being seized by the regicide Colonel Hewson, Cromwellian Governor of Dublin, and detained from its legitimate owner, while the military interregnum called a Commonwealth, and Protectorate, lasted. This Simon died in 1650; leaving, as heir to Luttrell's-town, his eldest son, Thomas; who, after the accession of King Charles II., was restored to his estates by the Act of Settlement; was made a Gentleman of the Bedchamber to the King; and dying, in 1674, left, by his lady, the daughter of William Segrave, Esq., of the County of Dublin, 4 sons; the 2 elder of whom were named Simon and Henry.

Simon, the eldest, and immediate subject of the present notice, succeeded to the estate of Luttrell's-town, and was, in the reign of King James II., placed in the public position to which it was considered that *he* was entitled, as well as the members of those *other* loyal Irish families of Milesian, Norman, and Old English blood, who, on account of their religion as Catholics, amongst a nation the vast majority of whom were of that belief, had, nevertheless, been, as far as possible, excluded from office in their native land, by the intolerant "ascendancy" of a recently-planted minority of British republican intruders. The owner of Luttrell's-town was consequently appointed by that Monarch to be Lord Lieutenant of the metropolitan county of Ireland, in which his ancient castle and estate were situated; his brother Henry, who had served for some campaigns in the French army, being likewise made Governor of Sligo. Of the 2 brothers, the Duke of Berwick, who knew them both, says, Simon was "of a mild disposition, and always appeared to him to be an honest man;" while Henry possessed "a great deal of talent, a great deal of intrigue, a great deal of courage, and was a good officer, capable of every thing in order to bring about his own ends." When Ireland, after the success of the Revolution in England and Scotland, declared in favour of maintaining King James as *her* Sovereign, the 2 brothers who were abroad in France came home, and zealously embraced that Monarch's cause; raising, arming, and equipping, between them, no less than 5 squadrons of cavalry, for the Irish army. Simon was made Colonel of a Regiment of Dragoons, and Henry Colonel of a Regiment of Horse, in the royal service; and the 2 brothers sat in the Irish Parliament of 1689; the former, for the County of Dublin, and the latter, for the County of Carlow. Simon was also appointed a Member of the Royal Privy Council for Ireland, and Governor of the City and Garrison of Dublin. This last post he continued, during the royal residence in Ireland, to fill, under the designation of the Honourable Simon Luttrell. When, after landing in August, 1689, near Carrickfergus, and capturing that place, the Prince of Orange's commander, the Marshal Duke de Schonberg, proceeded as far as Dundalk towards Dublin, and, by way of distracting the attention of King James, who was advancing from the Irish metropolis to oppose him, sent off, in September, 10 or 12 English vessels, with some troops, into the Bay of Dublin, to attempt a diversion there, such effectual measures were taken for the security of the capital, under the directions of its Governor, that the national army was not interrupted in its march after the King to Dundalk, and the English vessels were obliged to sail out of the Bay, without effecting any thing. The following November, the Governor's brother, Colonel Henry Luttrell, at the expedition under Brigadier Patrick Sarsfield, which terminated in the expulsion of the Williamites from Sligo, greatly distinguished himself, in a successful affair, near that place. Simon continued to be the Governor of Dublin till after the action of the Boyne, July 11th, 1690; during which he was stationed in the metropolis, with a body of militia, to keep down disaffection, and preserve order; and, late in the evening of the following day, when the Irish army had marched out, and the militia had followed, he was among the last who left the city, and retreated to Limerick with the rest of the "loyal party," or Jacobites. After the defeat of the Prince of Orange at Limerick, where Henry Luttrell was also distinguished, the 2 brothers, as opponents of the administration of the Duke of Tyrconnell in Ireland, were nominated, with Colonel Nicholas Purcell, Baron of Loughmoe, and Dr. John Molony, Catholic Bishop of Cork, to go, with charges against the Duke, to St. Germain. Simon, as has been seen, then justified the good character given of him, by being, during the voyage to France, the means, along with the Bishop of Cork, of saving the life of the Scotch Major-General, Thomas Maxwell; who was judged hostile to the embassy, from the circumstance of his being sent with it by the Duke of Berwick, to give *his* views on the matter to the King, and who, on that account, would have been thrown over board, but for the opposition of the Bishop, and the late Governor of Dublin. In the 3rd or succeeding campaign of 1691, which was decisive of the fate of Ireland, and towards the end of which, Henry Luttrell, being accused of a treasonable correspondence with the enemy's commander, Lieutenant-General Baron de Ginkell, was arrested, tried for it by Court Martial, and committed to the Castle of Limerick, we hear nothing important of Simon, until the conclusion of the Treaty of Limerick, when it was stipulated, in the 4th of the Civil Articles, that, in case he, and other Irish officers then in France with him, should choose to return within 8 months, and take the Oath of Allegiance to King William III. and Queen Mary, he and his companions should have the benefit of the 2nd of those articles, or, in other words, be restored to the possession of their estates, &c.

Henceforth, as well as for some time previous, or from the commencement of Henry Luttrell's correspondence with the invaders of his country, and the enemies of his king and religion, the fate of the 2 brothers was very different. Simon, unwilling to abandon what *he* considered to be equally the cause of his country, his king, and his religion, would not return from France, to avail himself of the advantageous stipulation made for him in the Treaty. Henry, with the popular odium on his character of being a traitor, had, in case his brother did not return, the promise, from Lieutenant-General Baron de Ginkell, of being put into possession of the family property of Luttrell's-town, &c.; and in consideration of bringing over, after the Treaty, his fine horse regiment of 12 troops, the horses and arms of which were worth £10,000, was to be under King William, as previously under King James, a Brigadier-General, and Colonel of a Regiment of Horse. From this period, Henry Luttrell was admitted to the confidence of King William's government at home;* attended his Majesty abroad in Flanders; had, in lieu of his Regiment of Horse, which was disbanded, a royal pension of £500 a year; and, when the next war after the Peace of Ryswick, or that of the Spanish Succession, was at hand, he was appointed by the King to be a Major-General in the Dutch Army; and was likewise to have been created a Colonel of Horse in the service of the States, but for that

* From official documents of 1692 and 1693 in the State Paper Office, London, and other official sources of information, we find Colonel Henry Luttrell employed, under King William's administration in Ireland, as the agent to enlist for the service of the Republic of Venice, then engaged in a war against the Turks, (and into which service Irish refugees had previously gone as early as after the Cromwellian war,) a body of 1500 or 2000 Irish Catholics. In a French official journal of May 2nd, 1693, under a paragraph from Venice in April, after an enumeration of the aids received against the Turks, from the Pope, the Knights of Malta, the Archbishop of Saltzburgh in Germany, &c., it is added—"The republic has decided on a negotiation for procuring 2600 Irish, who are to be conducted by the noble Berengani as far as Zante, in order to pass from that into the Morea, where each of them shall receive a present of 50 ducats."

Prince's death.* After William's decease, Henry Luttrell retired to Luttrell's-town, and mostly resided there, till November 2nd, 1717; when, being waylaid between 10 and 11 o'clock at night, in Dublin, as he was proceeding from Lucas's Coffee-House, situated where the Royal Exchange now stands, to his town-house in Stafford-street, he was fired at, and mortally wounded, in his sedan-chair. He lingered until the next day, and then died, in the 63rd year of his age. A Proclamation on the subject was issued by the Duke of Bolton, Lord Lieutenant, and the Privy Council in Ireland, 2 days after, premising how, on Tuesday, &c., "between the hours of 10 and 11 at night, a tall man, with long, lank hair, in a short, light-coloured coat, did, in Stafford-street, in the City of Dublin, in a most barbarous and inhuman manner, murther and assassinate Colonel Henry Lutterell, as he was going in a hackney-chair, from a coffee-house on Cork-hill, to his own house in Stafford-street aforesaid, by firing a pistol, or gun, loaden with ball, into the said chair, and thereby so dangerously wounding the said Henry Lutterell, that he was since dead, of his said wounds; and that the said assassin found means to make his escape, and the authors and contrivers of such an horrid murther were still undiscovered." In consequence of which, continued the document, "We, the Lord Lieutenant and Council, having a just abhorrence of all such barbarous and horrid practices, and thinking it absolutely necessary, that all due encouragement should be given for the discovery and apprehension of the said assassin, and the authors and contrivers of the murther of the said Colonel Henry Lutterell, do, by this, our Proclamation, publish and declare, that we will give the necessary orders for payment of the sum of £300 to such person, or persons, as shall discover, take, and apprehend the person who fired the said pistol, or gun, or any of the authors, or contrivers, of the said horrid murther, so as he, they, or any of them, may be convicted thereof; and, in case any of the persons concerned therein, (other than and except the person who fired the said pistol, or gun,) shall make a full discovery of his accomplices, so as one or more of them may be apprehended, and thereof convicted, such discoverer shall, besides the said reward, have and receive his Majesty's most gracious pardon for the same." The same month, it was moved in the colonial and sectarian House of Commons, Dublin, that there being reason to suspect, the late barbarous murder of Colonel Henry Luttrell was *done by Papists*, on account of *his services to the Protestant interest of the Kingdom*, the House should address the Lord-Lieutenant, to offer by Proclamation a suitable reward, or £1000, for such as should cause the guilty to be convicted. This motion, unanimously passed, was as expe-

* Colonel Henry Luttrell, being a Catholic, was to be provided for in the Dutch service by William III., as Stadtholder of Holland; the Dutch Republic, although a Protestant state, admitting, unlike England, Catholics, as well as Protestants, into the national land and sea forces. As to any exclusion of the former from such employment in Holland, the famous Pensionary Fagel, in his letter of November, 1687, to Mr. Stewart, says—"*That* had indeed been hard, since, in the first formation of our State, they joined with us in defending our public liberty, and did divers eminent services during the wars"—or those against Spain, &c. The zealous English Williamite, Oldmixon, also remarks of the government of the Seven United Provinces—"They *had* Generals of their Armies, and Admirals of their Fleets, who were Papists. Witness," he adds, "a saying of one of their Admirals, *My conscience is my God's, but my sword is their High-Mightinesses*"—or, in other words, was at the disposal of the government of his country, whatever might be the difference between *his* religion, and that of the government. See, likewise, Note 22 of my edition of Macariæ Excidium.

ditiously acted on, and the Proclamation issued accordingly. Some arrests on suspicion soon after took place. But nothing of more consequence was the result, than what tended to cast additional reproach upon the blood of Luttrell; when, in 1719, for *wilful perjury* against Caddel and Wilson, charged with the murder, a nephew of the Colonel was tried, and convicted in the Court of King's Bench, Dublin, and sentenced "to stand 3 hours in the pillory, with *his ears nail'd to it*, then *to have them cut off*, and to remain 8 months in prison!" Mr. O'Conor of Mount-Druid, in his unfinished work on the military history of Ireland, intimates, of the Colonel's untimely death by the hand of an assassin, that the latter was "an enthusiast, probably, who sought to avenge the wrongs of his country, in the blood of the traitor"—a surmise, not unlikely, from the state of political feeling at the time. Yet, according to a tradition which I heard about 1839, from an intelligent peasant, between 45 and 50, whose information was derived from his grandmother, who lived to be extremely old, and who, having been born, and a constant resident, in the vicinity of Luttrell's-town, remembered Colonel Henry Luttrell well, it is probable the Colonel's death was not less connected with his addiction to illicit amours, than with political animosity towards him. The statement of the old woman, as to the Colonel's conduct with respect to her sex, being, that, even when at mass, at the old straw-roofed parish chapel, nearest to Luttrell's-town, where he was accustomed to kneel only upon 1 knee—which, though he was lame, the poor people considered a serious irreverence—he used to employ himself in gazing at, or ogling, every well-looking female of the lower orders, whether other men's wives, or not; and would even sometimes take a dexterous opportunity to cast little pebbles, of which he kept some for the purpose, at their caps, or bonnets, in order to attract their attention. The old woman's account of "*Harry* Luttrell" is, in this respect, sufficiently countenanced by the satirical Jacobite elegy on his death. It exclaims—

" Ring Luttrell's knell with wofull harmony!
* * * * * *
Come whores, come pimps, come harlots, all in one,
His dismal end, with one accēnt, bemoan!
He was the spark lov'd best your Venus games,
Tho' now laments, I fear, in fiery flames.
* * * * * *
He serv'd 3 mighty Lords most faithfully,
And with their humours firmly did comply.
The 1st, and chief, was SATAN, black of hue;
The WORLD, the next, that's like *himself*, untrue;
The 3rd, the FLESH, *he serv'd with might and main,*
And did, with zeal, its lustful sports sustain."

By his wife, Elizabeth, daughter of Charles Jones, Esq., of Halkin, in Flintshire, the Colonel had 2 sons, Robert and Simon; through the 2nd of whom, successively ennobled as Baron Irnham, Viscount and Earl of Carhampton, and most unenviably notorious, in prose and verse, for lewdness, &c., he was the grandfather of a man, infamous for combining the unscrupulous military bravo, and hard-hearted despot in power, with the outrageous wencher and adulterer, and consequently marked out, in 1797, for assassination—Henry Lawes Luttrell, 2nd Earl of Carhampton. The memory of Colonel Henry Luttrell was held up, after his death, to national hatred, in the following epigram, cited by Hardiman, and unsurpassed for comprehensive bitterness :—

> "If HEAV'N be pleas'd, when mortals cease to sin—
> And HELL be pleas'd, when villains enter in—
> If EARTH be pleas'd, when it entombs a knave—
> ALL must be pleas'd—now Luttrell's in his grave!"

The peasant, who supplied the local traditionary information above noticed as so well founded, likewise told me, that, towards the end of the last century, Henry Luttrell's tomb, near Luttrell's-town, was broken open at night by some of the peasantry of the neighbourhood, and his skull taken out, and smashed with a pick-axe, and suitable execrations, by the labourer, named Carty, who was afterwards hanged, for being concerned in the plan to cut off Lord Carhampton, in 1797, on his way to Luttrell's-town, as a character not less detested living, than his grandfather dead!

Henry's elder brother Simon, on the other hand,—in every sense, the HONOURABLE Simon Luttrell, as having given up everything, rather than in any way submit to the Sovereign and the cause he did not consider to be legitimate,—was appointed Colonel of the Queen's Regiment of Infantry in King James's army, after its new formation in France. He served with distinction on the Continent; first, or until 1696, in Italy, under the Marshal de Catinat, where we find him acting at the siege of Valenza, with the rank of Brigadier, among the forces, with which Catinat, and the ducal Sovereign of Savoy, Victor Amadeus II., terminated the contest in Italy, by the Treaty of Vigevano; and next, or the following campaign, which concluded the war of the League of Augsburg with great glory to the French arms in Spain, he was attached, with his regiment, to the army of the Duke of Vendome in Catalonia. The date of Brigadier Simon Luttrell's decease is mentioned as follows in an inscription in gilt letters, on a slab of black marble; which, on account of the remarkable contrast presented by that officer to his brother and others of the name, I copied, in 1841, with great interest, and no less veneration, from the wall, near the holy-water font of the Chapel of the Irish College in Paris.

D. O. M.
PIÆ MEMORIÆ

CLARISSIMI NOBILISSIMIQUE VIRI SIMONIS LUTTREL SUB LUDOUICO MAGNO REGE XTIANISSIMO MILITUM TRIBUNI, CIVITATIS DUBLINIENSIS HIBERNIÆ METROPOLIS SUB JACOBO 2° MAGNÆ BRITANNIÆ REGE PREFECTI. QUI CUM REGE CATHOLICO PRO FIDE CATHOLICA EXULARE MALUIT ET MILITANDO VICTITARE QUAM DOMI PACATAM VITAM AGERE, ET AMPLISSIMIS POSSESSIONIBUS GAUDERE.

OBIIT 6. CAL. 7-BRIS A.R.S.H. M.DC.XCVIII. EIUSQUE PIAM MEMORIAM NON INGRATA DOMUS HUIC INSCRIPTAM MARMORI SERVARI VOLUIT, CUJUS IPSE MORIENDO NON IMMEMOR FUIT.
Requiescat in pace.

By his wife, Catherine, daughter of Sir Thomas Newcomen, Baronet, of Sutton, in the County of Dublin, whom he married in August, 1672, the HONOURABLE Simon Luttrell had no issue.

The Queen's Regiment of Infantry, of which he was Colonel, shared in the reduction to which so many other regiments of King James's Irish army in France were subjected in 1698, after the Peace of Ryswick. According to my manuscript and other authorities, this regiment consisted at first, in France, of 2 battalions; each battalion containing 8 companies, each company 100 privates, making a total of 1600 soldiers; and these, with their officers, who, like Dorrington's, were 64, consequently formed a corps of 1664 strong. Subsequent to this organization of 1692, or in 1695, the officers of the "Régiment de la Reine, Infanterie," as Mac Geoghegan calls it, are thus given by him—"Simon Luttrell, Colonel—Francis Wachop, Lieutenant-Colonel—James O'Brien, Major—12 Captains—28 Lieutenants—28 Sub-Lieutenants—14 Ensigns." By documents, coming down to a later period of the contest between Louis XIV. and the League of Augsburg, the Queen's Regiment of Infantry, or that of Luttrell, in 2 battalions, appears with a less number of privates, and an increased amount of officers, or 1100 of the former, and 242 of the latter; making 1342 men, of every description.

THE INFANTRY REGIMENT OF THE MARINE.

This regiment was originally levied in Ireland for the War of the Revolution, and finally established as that of the Lord Henry Fitz-James, otherwise the Lord Grand Prior of England. Its Colonel, then very young, owed this post to his being of royal blood, or the offspring of 1 of the various intrigues, which his father, King James, both as Duke of York and King of England, though twice married to young and handsome women, carried on with married and unmarried females of the Court, or the Ladies Southesk, Chesterfield, Robarts, Denham, and Darlington, as well as the more immediate subject of this narrative, Miss Arabella Churchill. This lady, born in March, 1648, was the sister of the famous John Churchill, afterwards Duke of Marlborough, and the daughter of Sir Winstan Churchill—descended from the Courcils of Anjou, Poictou, and Normandy, through Roger de Courcil,* who, coming over from France to England in 1066, with Duke William of Normandy, received his portion of the forfeited estates of the conquered Saxons, or English, in Dorsetshire, Somersetshire, and Devonshire. Sir Winstan Churchill, having adhered to the cause of Kings Charles I. and Charles II. against the Parliamentarians and Cromwellians, and having been proportionably punished under the usurpation, and fined above £4400 for his loyalty, was rewarded with suitable appointments by the Crown after the Restoration; and had his daughter, Arabella, created Maid of Honour to the 1st wife of James, Duke of York, Anne Hyde, daughter of the Lord Chancellor Clarendon. Miss Churchill, though described by our countryman, Colonel Count Anthony Hamilton, in no better terms than "a tall creature, pale-faced, and nothing but skin and bone," was, however, sufficiently attractive not to escape the attentions of the Duke of York; who, as one of the greatest "oglers" of his time, looked upon his wife's Maids of Honour, as "*his* property." The discovery of those hidden charms, which led to the mistress of them likewise becoming the mistress of his Royal Highness, occurred during a summer

* "Courcil" became gradually altered into Curichil, Chirchil, Cherchile, Churchile, *Churchill*, as the surnames of others of the Norman conquerors, taken, for instance, from "Rochefort, La Rochelle, Cahors," in France, have, in England, says Thierry, "become, by corruption, *Rochford, Rokeby, Chaworth.*" And thus, it may be observed, Marlborough was not of *Anglo-Saxon*, but *French*, origin.

excursion to Yorkshire, in 1665, for the amusement of the Duchess, at a coursing-match, where the Maids of Honour had to be present on horseback. "The Duke," says Count Hamilton, "attended Miss Churchill, not for the sake of besieging her with soft, flattering tales of love, but, on the contrary, to chide her for sitting so ill on horse-back. She was one of the most indolent creatures in the world; and, although the Maids of Honour are generally the worst mounted of the whole Court, yet, in order to distinguish *her*, on account of the favour *she* enjoyed, they had given her a very pretty, though rather a high-spirited, horse; a distinction she would very willingly have excused them. The embarrassment and fear she was under had added to her natural paleness. In this situation, her countenance had almost completed the Duke's disgust, when her horse, desirous of keeping pace with the others, set off in a gallop, notwithstanding her greatest efforts to prevent it; and her endeavours to hold him in, firing his mettle, he at length set off at full speed, as if he was running a race against the Duke's horse. Miss Churchill lost her seat, screamed out, and fell from her horse. A fall, in so quick a pace, must have been violent; and yet it proved favourable to her in every respect; for, without receiving any hurt, she gave the lie to all the unfavourable suppositions that had been formed of her person, in judging from her face. The Duke alighted, in order to help her. She was so greatly stunned, that her thoughts were otherwise employed, than about decency on the present occasion; and those, who first crowded around her, found her rather in a negligent posture. They could hardly believe, that limbs of such exquisite beauty could belong to Miss Churchill's face. After this accident, it was remarked, that the Duke's tenderness and affection for her increased every day; and, towards the end of the winter, it appeared, that she had *not* tyrannized over his passion, nor made him languish with impatience." Of this illicit connexion of the Duke and Miss Churchill, the following were the offspring, who came to maturity. 1st, James Fitz-James, born in August, 1670, created, during his father's reign in England, Duke of Berwick, Earl of Tinmouth, and Baron of Bosworth, Knight of the Garter, Lord Lieutenant of Hampshire, Ranger of the New Forest, Governor of Portsmouth, successively Colonel of the Infantry Regiment, now the 8th Foot, of the Cavalry Regiment, now the Blues, and Captain of the 3rd Troop of Life-Guards; besides, by commission from Leopold I. of Austria, a Serjeant General of Battle, or Major-General, Colonel Commandant *ad interim* of the Imperial Regiment of Cuirassiers, likewise known from its Irish Colonel, as that of Taaffe; and, after the Revolution, or in Ireland and on the Continent, Captain of a Troop of the Irish Horse-Guards, and Colonel of the Irish Infantry Regiment of Berwick, Marshal, Duke of Fitz-James, Member of the Council of Regency, Governor of the Limousin and Strasbourg, Chevalier of the Order of the Holy Ghost, and of the Orders of the King, in France; and Captain-General, Duke of Liria and Xerica, Grandee of the 1st Class, and Knight of the Golden Fleece in Spain. 2nd, Henrietta Fitz-James, born in 1671, first, Lady Waldegrave, next, (though too late to preserve her character,) Lady Wilmot, and deceased in April, 1730. 3rd, * * * Fitz-James, born in 1672, and a nun in France, where she died in February, 1762, aged about 90. 4th, Henry Fitz-James, born in 1673, and Lord Grand Prior of England. The Duke of York having granted to Miss Churchill, in January, 1668, £1000 a year, from a rent-charge on the manor of Newcastle, in the

County of Limerick, she was married, when her concubinage with him ceased, by Charles Godfrey, Clerk Comptroller of the Green Cloth, Master of the Jewel Office, and Colonel, for some years, of the 1st Regiment of Horse—since 1788, the 4th or Royal Irish Regiment of Dragoon Guards. By this union, she had 2 daughters, Charlotte and Elizabeth, highly married in England; and died in May, 1730, aged about 82; having long survived her husband, deceased in 1715.

When King James, on account of the general defection of the English to the Prince of Orange in 1688, had to retire to France, the Lord Grand Prior shared his father's exile there, and thence accompanied him to Ireland, in the spring of 1689. His Lordship was present at the royal entry into Dublin, on Palm-Sunday that year; on which occasion, he, says the contemporary Williamite account, "rid alone, in 1 of the Earl of Tyrconnel's coaches, with 6 horses." He was subsequently appointed Colonel of an Infantry Regiment in the Irish army, thenceforward known as the Lord Henry Fitz-James's, or the Lord Grand Prior. According, however, to the letter of the Comte d'Avaux to Louis XIV. from Dublin, February 11th, 1690, this "graceless scion of royalty" was so sunk in dissipation as to be a mere *nominal* Colonel. "C'est un jeune homme fort debauché, qui se creve tous les jours d'eau de vie, et qui a esté, tout cet esté, par ses debauches, hors d'estat de monter à cheval." But his regiment served at the blockade of Derry, and being afterwards stationed at Drogheda, and recruited to oppose the Williamite invasion under the Marshal Duke of Schonberg, it formed part of the national force, with which the Marshal's progress, farther south than Dundalk, was arrested by the King. Next campaign, or that of 1690, it was present at the action of the Boyne, and the defence of Limerick, where, along with the Munster Regiment of Major-General Boisselot, the French Governor, it is mentioned, as having highly signalized itself at the defeat of the great assault of September 6th, which led to the raising of the siege by the Prince of Orange. The Lord Grand Prior, as well as the King, returning to France after the affair of the Boyne, his Lordship's regiment in Ireland was left under the orders of Nicholas Fitz-Gerald. That officer, who was of an old and respectable branch of his name, had entered the service, as a Cadet, in 1675; and successively rose to be Lieutenant, Captain, Major, and Lieutenant-Colonel, acting as Colonel in command, of this corps. After the 2nd defence of Limerick in 1691, where he took a leading part, as 1 of the "Lieutenants of the King," he passed, with his regiment, into France.

From the Lord Grand Prior's being originally destined for the British navy, and his having, on account of his father's dethronement in Great Britain and Ireland, entered the French sea-service, this regiment of the Irish army on the Continent, of which he was the Colonel, was styled in France, the "Régiment de *la Marine;*" and, owing to his necessary absence in the French navy, and the command in the field consequently devolving on the 1st, or most experienced, of its 2 Lieutenant-Colonels, Nicholas Fitz-Gerald, the corps is sometimes mentioned, as if that officer had been its Colonel. While the Lord Grand Prior distinguished himself on sea—particularly at the severe blows, inflicted, off the coasts of the Peninsula, in 1693, upon the English, Dutch, and Spanish shipping, by the celebrated Chevalier Comte de Tourville—the Irish Regiment of the Marine had its due share in the campaigns on the Continent, under Lieutenant-Colonel Fitz-Gerald. With him, it served on the coast of

Normandy, in 1692, as a portion of the Irish and French force, intended to effect the "restoration" of King James—with the French army of Germany in 1693, 1694, and 1695—with that of the Meuse in 1696—and with that of the Moselle in 1697—when the War of the League of Augsburg was terminated in autumn, by the Peace of Ryswick. In the extensive reform, among King James's troops in France, in February, 1698, the Regiment of the Marine was, by an order of the 26th of that month, included; yet, not that it might be broken up, or disbanded, like several others of the Irish corps, but remodelled under the designation of the "Régiment d'Albemarle," from the additional title of Duke of Albemarle conferred by King James in France upon his son, the Lord Grand Prior; and Nicholas Fitz-Gerald was still the acting officer in command, as Colonel-Lieutenant. After the breaking out of the War of the Spanish Succession, he commanded the regiment in Germany, in 1701; in 1702, in Italy, at the battle of Luzzara; and, for his distinguished conduct there, was made, October 1st, that year, Brigadier of Infantry. After having been long in bad health, the Colonel Proprietor of the Regiment, Henry Fitz-James, Lord Grand Prior of England, and Duke of Albemarle, died, December 17th, aged only between 29 and 30, at Bagnols, in Languedoc. A Chef d'Escadre towards the end of 1695, he was 1 of the 4 officers, of that rank, placed, in January, 1696, over the Toulon fleet, to consist of 50 sail of the line, &c.; and, about that period, appears to have been created, by his father King James, Duke of Albemarle. In December, 1702, shortly before his death, he had been nominated a Lieutenant-General of the Marine by Louis XIV.; who put the Court of France into mourning for him. He had married the only daughter of Jean d'Audibert Comte de Lussan, Baron de Valrose, Chevalier des Ordres du Roi, &c., or Marie Gabrielle d'Audibert de Lussan, a lady whose fortune was among the largest in France, but left no children by her.

The proprietorship of the "Régiment d'Albemarle" was not filled up till February 10th, 1703; when, by a commission of that date, appointing the late Colonel-Lieutenant to the command of the corps, it became the "Régiment de Fitz-Gerald." From 1703 to 1706, the Brigadier was employed in the campaigns of Italy, where, besides other important operations in which he was engaged, he served at the sieges of Vercelli, of Ivrea, of Verrua, and at the battle of Turin. In 1707, he was transferred to the Army of Flanders. Created, by brevet of March 3rd, 1708, Maréchal de Camp, or Major-General, he was attached, that month, to the service of King James II.'s son, for the expedition, designed, under the Chevalier de Forbin, to effect a landing in Scotland. After the frustration of the attempt, by the greater naval strength of the English, the Major-General rejoined the Army of Flanders. He was wounded, and taken prisoner there, July 11th, at the battle of Oudenarde; and died at Gand, or Ghent, August 1st, with the character, from all the Generals under whom he had served, of being as good an officer as any of his rank in France.

His successor in the Colonelship was Lieutenant-Colonel Daniel O'Donnell; from whom the corps was accordingly named the "Régiment d' O'Donnell." He was a member of the illustrious family of the O'Domhnalls, or O'Donnells, (or, as they generally write, " O'Donell,") Princes or Chiefs of Tir-Connell, sprung from Conall, or Connell, son of Niall the Great, of the Nine Hostages, Ard-Righ of Erin, or Monarch of Ireland, at the end of the 4th, and beginning of the 5th, century. From this Connell, deceased A.D. 464, the territory of his descendants, who formed various tribes, comprehended under the general term of "Kinel-Connell," or the *race of Connell*, was designated "Tir-Connell," or the *land of Connell*, which nearly corresponded with the present County of Donegal. Of the Tir-Connell branch of the posterity of the royal "Hero of the Nine Hostages," there were 10 Ard-Righs of Erin, or Monarchs of Ireland, previous to the Anglo-Norman invasion of the island, in the 12th century. The O'Donnells, however, until a comparatively recent period, did not acquire that supremacy in Tir-Connell, by which every Prince or Chief of that territory was an O'Donnell. With the 2 exceptions of Dalach, deceased in 868, (from whom the O'Donnells were sometimes called the Clan Dalach, as from his grandson, Domhnall, O'Donnells,) and of Eignechan, who died in 901, *both* Princes of Tir-Connell, none of the line of O'Donnell reigned over that country, till about 30 years after the coming of the Anglo-Normans into Erin. The O'Muldorys and O'Canannans were the septs of the race of Connell, whose heads, according as either clan happened to be the more powerful, had previously been the supreme rulers of Tir-Connell.* The original country of the O'Donnells was confined to a mountainous district of Donegal, between the waters of the Suileach, or Swilly, and the Dobhar, or Simmy; the latter of which falls into the sea, near the present village of Glenties. About the centre, however, of this district,—and as if prefigurative of the final pre-eminence to be acquired by the clan who possessed it,—stood the Hill of Doon and the Church of Kilmacrenan, the locality appointed, from the earliest times, for the inauguration of the chiefs, designed for the supreme rulers of Tir-Connell. "The ceremony of inaugurating the Kings of Tyrconnell," according to the native account in Keating, "was this. The King, being seated on an eminence, surrounded by the nobility and gentry of his own country, 1 of the chief of his nobles stood before him, with a straight, white wand in his hand; and, on presenting it to the King of Tyrconnell, used to desire him—' To receive the sovereignty of his country, and to preserve equal and impartial justice in every part of his dominions.' The reason that the wand was straight and white was, to put him in mind, that he should be unbiassed in his judgement, and pure and upright in all his actions." Eignechan O'Donnell, Prince of Tir-Connell from 1200 to 1207, was the 1st of the O'Donnells, from whose accession to power Tir-Connell may be considered the country of "*the* O'Donnell;" or of the heads of that name, during the 403 years which elapsed, until the *land of Connell* ceased to be a Principality, or Chiefdom, at the commencement of the reign of King James I. During those 4 stormy centuries, the O'Donnells proved how well they were entitled to be the rulers of Tir-Connell, by the bravery with which, in ages when bravery was every thing, they not only defended their territory against foreign and native foes, but extended their sway far beyond the limits of that territory. The O'Donnells were celebrated for their attachment to the literature of their country as well as for their bravery. The O'Clerys, as Ollaves, or Professors of History, Antiquities, and

* The Chief Poet of O'Kelly of Hy-Many, Shane O'Dugan, who died in 1372, alludes, in his topographical poem, to the original pre-eminence of the O'Muldorys, and O'Canannans, among the Kinel-Connell, and yet to their entire disappearance, before *his* time, from Tir-Connell. He adds, how, to the O'Donnells, "by a sway, which has *not* decayed. *now* belongs the hereditary Chieftainship!" This reads strangely at present.

Poetry, in Tir-Connell, were endowed with the castle of Kilbarron, near Ballyshannon, in the County of Donegal, and lands, worth, in our times, nearly £2000 a year; and, independent of this endowment, several of the O'Donnells are particularized, in the chronicles, as eminent, in their day, for their powers of mind, or information, for their acquisition of valuable books, (some still preserved) and for their generosity to the "sons of song." The heads of this great name, as the leading representatives of their race, and the first native potentates of the north-west of Erin, were regarded with suitable consideration in other countries, as well as their own; being entitled, and treated according to the designation of, Princes, Chiefs, and Lords of Tir-Connell, by the Kings of England, Scotland, France, and Spain, to the 17th century.

In England, Henry III., requiring assistance from Tir-Connell against Scotland, writes from Stannford, in July, 1244, "*Rex*, Donnaldo, *Regi* de Terchenull." Edward II., upon a like requisition, writes from Westminster, in March, 1314, "*Rex*, dilecto sibi Eth. O'Donnuld, *Duci* Hibernicorum de Tyrconil"—this designation of *Duci* (or *Dux*) answering to that of Chief. In 1512, Aodh or Hugh O'Donnell, Chief of Tir-Connell, during 16 weeks which he remained in London after a pilgrimage to Rome, (as well as 16 weeks which he likewise remained previous to his going there,) "received," say the native annalists, "great honour and respect from the Saxon Monarch, King Harry"—or Henry VIII. In the same reign, or the latter period of the sway of the O'Donnells in Tir-Connell, its Chief, Manus O'Donnell (without reference to any of his race having ever been ennobled in the *English* manner) is entitled, in the indenture, ratified, August, 1541, with Henry's representative, Sir Anthony Sentleger, "*Dominus* Odonell"—on which occasion, the appearance of the Irish potentate is thus described by Sir Anthony. "He was in a cote of crymoisin velvet, with agglettes of gold, 20 or 30 payer; over that, a greate doble cloke of right crymoisin saten, garded with blacke velvet; a bonette, with a fether, sette full of agglettes of gold." In the reign of Queen Elizabeth, or in 1564, the same title of "*Dominus* O'Donnell" (likewise irrespective of any rank but that which had been derived from a *native* source) is given by her Lord Deputy, Sir Henry Sydney, to Calvagh O'Donnell, Chief of Tir-Connell, and to Aodh or Hugh O'Donnell, in 1574, that of "*Capitaneus* nationis suæ de Tyrconnell." In Scotland, Hugh O'Donnell, Chief of Tir-Connell, is recorded to have met with such distinction from the gallant James IV. on a visit to his Court, in 1494-5, as was suited to the general designation of the Chief as "great Odonell;" with whom a league, for mutual aid, was concluded by James.* In 1513, the namesake and successor of this

* Under James I. of Scotland, who reigned from 1406 to 1437, the Scotch statute-book alludes to the "gude auld friendship" with "Irishrie in Ireland." On which, a commentator in the Scot's Magazine, May, 1768, observes—"'Irishrie in Ireland' means that part of Ireland under the dominion of the Irish Princes, in opposition to 'Irishrie subject to the King of England,' which is mentioned in the same statute." And, after repeating of such "gude auld friendship" in Scotland, that it was "with the native Irish, who were *not* subject to the government of England," the commentator notes, how, in speaking of those times, Æneas Sylvius also (afterwards Pope Pius II.) has thus adverted to these circumstances. "Hibernia, partim libera, *Scotorum amicitia & societate gaudet*, partim Anglicano paret imperio." Tytler, the Scotch historian, who cites, from the accounts of the Treasurer of James IV., the items "for the receving of great Odonnel," which, he adds, was done "by the King with great state and distinction," assigns 1494 for the date of the occurrence, while the Ulster Annals and Four Masters assign 1495.

Hugh went over to Scotland with a select band, at the solicitation of James, and "on his arrival there," it is added, "received great honours and gifts from the King," and "remained with him a quarter of a year." In France, it is related, how Francis I., in 1544, "despatched to Ireland, Theobald de Bois, a French nobleman, in the rank of Ambassador to O'Donnell, with an offer, to that *Prince,* of arms and of money, should he wish to declare war against the English." In 1550, Henry II. of France is also stated to have sent, through Scotland, into Ireland, as his Envoys, Raimond de Beccarie de Pavie, Marquis de Fourquevaux, and Jean de Montesquiou de Lasseran-Massencomme, then Protonotaire de Montluc, and Chancellor in Scotland, and afterwards Bishop of Valence and Die in Dauphiné, accompanied by the Capitaine d'Auvroy, Sieur du Bosc, to "negociate with the Princes of Ulster," for the purpose of "engaging them to enter into a confederation with France against the English." These French noblemen, after reaching that part of Ulster, in which they were to land, "as the most remote from the district possessed by the English," were "to address themselves first to the Seigneur *Audonnel,*" i. e., O'Donnell, "chief Seigneur and Prince of the said country, whose ancestors were regarded of old as Kings of the whole island," &c. On this occasion, Manus O'Donnell, by a letter in Latin from his castle of Donegal, February 23rd, 1550, to Henry II., and intrusted for delivery to the Capitaine d'Auvroy, Sieur du Bosc, promised, on the part of himself and other Irish Princes, to unite with a French force, if landed in Ireland, and to transfer the sovereignty of the island to Henry; provided, says the writer, with reference to himself and his brother Princes, "*that your Majesty shall treat us all in a benign, humane and Christian manner—shall not permit that there should be any curtailment of our holy religion—shall not diminish, in any respect, the rights of the nobility—shall maintain the clergy, and ecclesiastical persons, and the holy churches in their privileges and franchises.*" Which negociation, however, had no further results with respect to Ireland, on account of the peace that occurred shortly after, between England and France. In Spain, at the commencement of the next century, or after the unfortunate battle of Kinsale in January, 1602, when the famous Hugh O'Donnell *the red* went to solicit succour against Queen Elizabeth from King Philip III., and arrived at Corunna, the light in which the exiled Chief was viewed appears from the conduct of the Marquis de Carazena, Governor of Gallicia, and the Spaniards, in general, at the time, as well as from that of their Sovereign—the head of the greatest empire *then* in the world. By a contemporary letter from Corunna—in which that place is called, after the English manner, "the Groyne," and the Marquis de Carazena is termed in like manner, the "Earle of *Caraçena*"—it is noted, how the Chief, after his arrival there, "was nobly received by the Earle of *Caraçena,* who invited *Odonnell* to lodge in his house; but hee, being sea-sicke, in good manner refused his curtesie; wherefore the Earle lodged him in a very faire house, not farre from his; but, when his sea-sicknesse was past, he lodged in the Earle's house; and upon the 27th of Ianuary, *Odonnell* departed from the Groyne, accompanied by the Earle (and many Captaines and Gentlemen of quality) *who evermore gaue Odonnell the right hand,* WHICH, WITHIN HIS GOVERNMENT, HEE WOULD NOT HAUE DONE TO THE GREATEST DUKE IN SPAINE; and, at his departure, hee presented *Odonnell* with 1000 duckets, and that night hee lay at *Santa Lucia:* the Earle of *Caraçena* being returned, the next day hee went to *Saint Iames* of *Compostella*, where he was received with magnificence by the Prelats, citizens, and religious persons, and his lodging was made ready for him at *Saint Martin's*, but before hee saw it, hee visited the Archbishop, who instantly prayed him to lodge in his house; but *Odonnell* excused it. The 29th, the Archbishop, saying masse with pontificall solemnity, did minister the sacrament to *Odonnell*, which done, hee feasted him at dinner in his house; and, at his departure, hee gaue him 1000 duckets." Of the Chieftain's further progress, and interview with Philip III., the Donegal chroniclers inform us, "he proceeded to the place where the King was, in Castile, for it was there he happened to be at this time, (after making a visitation of his kingdom) in the city which is called Samora," or Zamora. "And, as soon as O'Donnell arrived in the presence of the King, he knelt down before him; and he made submission and obeisance to him as was due to his dignity, and did not consent to rise, until the King promised to grant him his 3 requests. The 1st of these was, *to send an army with him to Erin, with suitable engines and necessary arms, whatever time they should be prepared.* The 2nd, that, *should the King's Majesty obtain power and sway over Erin, he would never place any of the nobles of his blood in power or authority over him, or his successors.* The 3rd request was, *not to lessen, or diminish, on himself, or his successors for ever, the right of his ancestors, in any place where his ancestors had power and sway before that time in Erin.** All these were promised him to be complied with by the King; and he received respect from him; and it is not probable, that any Gael ever received, in latter times, so great an honour from any other King." Of the honours paid to the Chieftain's remains, on his premature decease, in the royal Palace of Simancas, not long after —an event respecting which contemporary bards sang, that it was "a cause of grief to Erin from sea to sea," and that "Erin died in Spain"— the following account is given by the chroniclers previously cited. "His body was conveyed to the King's Palace at Valladolid, in a four-wheeled hearse, surrounded by countless numbers of the King's State Officers, Council, and Guards, with luminous torches, and bright flambeaux, of beautiful wax-light, burning on each side of him. He was afterwards interred in the Monastery of St. Francis, in the chapter precisely, with veneration and honour, and in the most solemn manner that any of the Gaels had ever been interred before. Masses, and many hymns, chaunts, and melodious canticles, were celebrated for the welfare of his soul; and his requiem was sung with becoming solemnity."

But a stronger and more recent instance of the honour paid to a branch of this old race abroad, however reduced in circumstances at home, was shown in 1754, to 1 of the O'Donnells, when only about 26—or Henry, afterwards Lieutenant-General and Count,—by the marriage of this Henry, with the consent of the Empress-Queen of Austria and Hungary, Maria Theresa, to her own cousin, of another royal house, or one that

---

* Compare the requests made to Philip III. of Spain by the exiled Chief of Tir-Connell, with the stipulations previously quoted from the letter of his predecessor to Henry II. of France, in February, 1550. The claims of "dauntless red Hugh," with respect to his own principality and that of his ancestors, as elsewhere explained by another candidate for the Chiefdom of Tir-Connell, implied, that "wheresoever *any* of the O'Donnells *had*, at that time, extended their power, *hee* made accompte *all* was his." This extension of the power of Tir-Connell was more particularly towards the south, or in the direction of Connaught; where the O'Donnells held a high hand, after the great diminution and division of the power of the house of O'Conor, which followed the Anglo-Norman invasion of Erin.

formerly held the sceptre of Constantinople in the person of John Cantacuzeno, the famous Emperor and Historian, who reigned from 1347 to 1355. This matrimonial alliance has not been the only one formed by the O'Donnells with the Cantacuzenos in Germany, and, through them, with the House of Austria; and it is a sufficient evidence of the high consideration with which the members of old or Milesian Irish families of rank were regarded in the haughtiest Court on the Continent, that has claimed for itself a succession to the ancient majesty of the Cæsars, and has been so supercilious towards all who could not produce a pedigree, indicative of what was deemed "noble blood."

After the junction of the Crowns of England, Ireland, and Scotland, in the 1st English and Irish Monarch of the House of Stuart, Rory or Roderic O'Donnell, the last Prince or Chief of his name, was created, in September, 1603, Earl of Tyrconnell, with the title, during his own lifetime, for his eldest son, of Baron of Donegal; till the flight of both to the Continent, in 1607, led to that fall and dispersion of the O'Donnells in their own country, which has been succeeded, to *our* times, by the existence of the name of O'Donnell in the highest posts, that military merit could attain, abroad. Of the several gallant officers so distinguished, all, however, acquired their honours in the services of Spain and Austria,* except the immediate object of this narrative, Daniel O'Donnell. On the commencement of the revolutionary disturbances in Ireland, excited by the successful landing and progress of the Prince of Orange in England against King James, Daniel O'Donnell was appointed Captain of a company for the royal service, December 7th, 1688, and, in 1689, was authorized to act as a Colonel; in which capacity, there were several officers of merit attached during this war to various regiments, raised by, and, as such, bearing the names of, other Colonels. Passing, after the Treaty of Limerick, into France, Daniel O'Donnell appears to have suffered much by the new arrangements of the Irish troops there; under which he did not obtain a higher post, than that of a Captain in the Regiment of the Marine, by commission of February 4th, 1692. He served, in this grade, on the coasts of Normandy, with the Irish and French forces designed for the invasion of England, and "restoration" of King James, that year; with the Army of Germany from 1693 to 1695; and with the Army of the Meuse till 1697, or the Peace of Ryswick. On the remodelling of his regiment into that of Albemarle in 1698, he was retained as Captain, by commission of April 27th, that year. Next war, he served with the Army of Germany in 1701, and, from 1702 to 1706, in the Army of Italy; during which 5 campaigns, he was at the battle of Luzzara, the reduction of Borgoforte, of Nago, of Arco, of Vercelli, of Ivrea, of Verrua, of Chivasso, at the battle of Cassano, and the siege and battle of Turin. He was Lieutenant-Colonel of his regiment, at the last-mentioned siege and battle; having attained that rank the preceding year, or October 20th, 1705. Transferred to the Army of Flanders in 1707, he fought at the battle of Oudenarde, in July, 1708; and was appointed successor to Nicholas Fitz-Gerald as Colonel, by commission of August 7th following. He commanded the regiment, as that of O'Donnell, in Flanders, from 1708 to 1712; being with it, at the battle of Malplaquet, the attack of Arleux, the affair of Denain, and the sieges of Douay, Quesnoy, and Bouchain. Removed to the Army of Germany, under the Marshal de

* See, with respect to *them*, Dr O'Donovan's Topographical Poems of O'Dugan and O'Heerin, introduction, pp. 31-35: Dublin, 1862.

I

Villars, in 1713, he was at the reduction of Landau and Friburgh, and the forcing of the retrenchments of General Vaubonne, which led to the Peace between France and Austria, at Rastadt, in March, 1714. The regiment of O'Donnell was reformed 11 months after, or by order of February 6th, 1715; half of it being incorporated with the Regiment of Colonel Francis Lee, and half with the Regiment of Major-General Murrough O'Brien. To the latter corps, O'Donnell was then attached, as a reformed or supernumerary Colonel. He was made a Brigadier by brevet, February 1st, 1719; and finally retired to St. Germain-en-Laye, where he died, without issue, in his 70th year, July 7th, 1735.*

Brigadier Daniel O'Donnell was descended from Aodh Dubh, or Hugh *the dark*, known as "the Achilles of the Gaels of Erin," and younger brother to Manus O'Donnell, Chief of Tir-Connell, deceased in 1563. The Brigadier's father was Terence O'Donnell, and his mother Johanna O'Donnell, both of the County of Donegal; and, as *their* son, being thus, on *each* side, an O'Donnell, he retained through life the feelings of the old name and territory with which his origin was associated. From the early ages of Christianity in Erin, there were handed down, among her leading races, certain memorials of the Saints whom they most venerated; respecting which memorials, there were predictions, that connected the future destinies of those tribes, for good, or for evil, with the preservation, or loss, by them, of such local palladiums. That of the Kinel-Connell, or descendants of Connell, consisted of a portable square box, of several metals, variously ornamented, and gemmed, and containing, in a small wooden case, a Latin Psalter, believed to have been written by the hand of him, who was the most eminent ecclesiastic, and great religious patron, of their race—the famous St. Columba, or Columb-kille, who flourished from A.D. 521 to 597, was the Apostle of the northern Picts, and the founder of the celebrated monastery in Hy or Iona through which it became "that illustrious island," in the language of Doctor Johnson, "once the luminary of the Caledonian regions, whence savage clans, and roving barbarians, derived the benefits of knowledge, and the blessings of religion." † The consecrated reliquary above-mentioned was styled the *cathach*—pronounced *caagh* or *caah*—of St. Columb-kille, from the persuasion entertained and handed down by tradition, that it was a sort of spiritual talisman, which would procure victory for the forces of Tir-Connel, if conveyed with, and accompanied by, a certain ceremonial among them, previous to their giving battle.‡ Accordingly, the custody of it

* Other O'Donnells, besides the Brigadier, were officers in the Regiments of O'Donnell, Berwick, Clare, and Dillon. Of these, Michael O'Donnell was Captain in the Regiment of Berwick, in June, 1770, and a Chevalier of St. Louis, in May, 1777. Yet some of those officers were *not* of the great O'Donnells of Ulster, but of the less noted sept of the O'Donnells of Munster; or originally of the district of Corcobaskin, County of Clare, until dispossessed by the Mac Mahons (a branch of the O'Briens) early in the 14th century.

† Doctor Johnson might likewise have described Iona, through St. Columba's great monastic and missionary foundation there, as not merely the "luminary of the *Caledonian* regions," but of the "*Anglo-Saxon* regions," too; the *far* greater portion of the Saxon Heptarchy having been indebted to the Columban or Irish preachers from that island, but more especially to St. Aidan, and St Finan, for being reclaimed from Paganism and ignorance to Christianity and letters.

‡ Manus O'Donnell, Prince of Tir-Connell, in his life of St. Columb-kille, written about the year 1532, says of the mystical box alluded to—"Et *Cathach*, id est *præliator*, vulgo appellatur, fertque traditio, quod si circa illius exercitum, antequam hostem adoriantur, tertio cum debita reverentia circumducatur, eveniat ut victoriam

was committed to a member of a particular family, named Magroarty of Ballymagroarty, near the town of Donegal; and it was usually borne to the field, with the banner of the Kinel-Connell. It was once, or in 1497, lost by the O'Donnells, when they were defeated by a superior force under Tiege Mac Dermot, Chief of Moylurg, (or the old Barony of Boyle, County of Roscommon,) but was regained in 1499, when Cormac Mac Dermot was obliged to submit to the Chief of Tir-Connell, to pay tribute, and to restore the prisoners previously taken, as well as the *caagh*. It was afterwards carefully preserved by the O'Donnells, with reference, as it would seem, to that warning, attributed to St. Caillen, in the Book of Fenagh. "He doth admonish the sept of *Conall Gulban*, which is the *O'Donells*, to look well to the *Caagh*, that it should not come to the handes of *Englishmen*, which yf yt did, it should be to the overthrowe and confusion of the sept of *Conall Gulban*, and to the great honnor of the *English*." Of the Jacobite possessor, and conveyer to the Continent, of that remarkable relic, as a sort of "household god" of his race, Sir William Betham adds—"Colonel O'Donell, in 1723, to preserve the box, had a silver case made, and placed round it, open at the top and bottom, so as to show them, but which totally hid the sides. On this case, he caused to be engraved the following inscription.—'JACOBO 3° M. B. REGE EXULANTE, DANIEL O'DONEL, IN XTIANISS⁰ IMP⁰ PRÆFECTUS REI BELLICÆ, HUJUSCE HÆREDITARII SANCTI COLUMBANI PIGNORIS, VULGO CAAH DICTI, TEGMEN ARGENTEUM, VETUSTATE CONSUMPTUM, RESTAURAVIT ANNO SALUTIS, 1723.'" This hereditary pledge of St. Columba, always considered by the O'Donnells as containing reliques of the great Saint of their race and principality, after its being repaired by Brigadier Daniel O'Donnell, was deposited in a monastery of Belgium—a country most friendly to Irish exiles, as well from community of religion in modern times, as from its inhabitants having been anciently so much indebted to Ireland for their conversion to Christianity *—and the Brigadier directed, by his will, that this old family memorial should be given to whoever could prove himself to be the head of the O'Donnells. The *caagh* was discovered at that monastery in our own times, and the purport of the Brigadier's will likewise ascertained by an Abbot of Cong, County of Mayo; who, on his return to Ireland, acquainting Sir Neal O'Donnell, Baronet, of Newport in that County, with the circumstance, Sir Neal, as believing himself to be "the O'Donnell," applied for, and obtained, the relic. Sir William Betham was thus enabled to get the access to it, to which we owe the earliest published details respecting its form, workmanship, and contents. It was subsequently intrusted, by Sir Richard O'Donnell, to the care of the Royal Irish Academy, to be placed in their valuable Museum of National Antiquities, for the inspection of the public; and, among that "unrivalled collection," it appeared, at the great Dublin Exhibition, in 1853, along with other interesting remains of ancient art, mentioned as having been objects of religious veneration to the North Hy-Niall.

The Regiment of the Marine, like the Irish infantry regiments in reportet." In Scotland, too, we find, in the 10th century, the crozier of the Irish Saint, as her Apostle, borne for a standard, under the designation of the "cath-bhuaidh," or *battle-victory*, against the Heathen Norsemen.

* On the great extent which Belgium *admits* its conversion from Paganism to have been owing to Irish missionaries, see the publication, in 1639, of the learned Professor of Louvain, Nicolaus Vernulæus—"*De Propagatione Fidei Christianæ in Belgio, per Sanctos ex Hiberniâ Viros,*"—or Notes 4 and 5 of my edition of *Macariæ Excidium* for the Irish Archæological Society.

France already mentioned, or Dorrington's and Luttrell's, consisted, at first, or in 1692, of 2 battalions, of 8 companies each; 100 soldiers in every company; and consequently 1600 between the 2 battalions; that, with 64 officers, would make the whole 1664 men. According to Mac-Geoghegan, the officers of the "Régiment de la Marine, Infanterie," in 1695, were—"The Lord Grand Prior, Colonel—Nicholas Fitz-Gerald, 1st Lieutenant-Colonel—Richard Nugent, 2nd Lieutenant-Colonel—Edmond O'Maddin, Major—11 Captains—28 Lieutenants—28 Sub-Lieutenants—14 Ensigns." By later accounts of the numerical strength of the corps, it, as well as the 2 preceding Irish infantry regiments, had, in its 2 battalions, a smaller complement of soldiers, and a larger complement of officers, or 1100 of the one, and 242 of the other; forming 1342 men altogether.

THE INFANTRY REGIMENT OF LIMERICK.

Of the 1st Colonel of this corps, Brigadier Talbot, an account has been given, under the Infantry Regiment of O'Brien, or Clare. The next officer that I find Colonel of the "Régiment de Limerick, Infanterie," was Sir John Fitz-Gerald, Baronet, or, according to his French designation, the "Chevalier Jean Fitz-Gerald." Sir John, who bore the character of "a person of known worth and honour," had suffered under the unscrupulous sectarian machinations of the Whigs, in the reign of King Charles II.; having been 1 of the Irish Catholic gentlemen arrested and conveyed to England, "on account of the pretended Popish plot, in the year 1680." After the accession of King James II. he was appointed Lieutenant-Colonel to the Infantry Regiment of the Honourable Justin Mac Carthy, (subsequently Lord Mountcashel) and, in 1689, was Colonel of 1 of the regiments of the national army, raised for the defence of the King, against the colonial partizans of the Revolution in Ulster, and their British and Continental supporters. In that year's campaign, Sir John's regiment of foot appears as one of those which served at the blockade of Derry, where he lost his brother, Captain Maurice Fitz-Gerald; and it is likewise to be found in the later lists of the Irish army. Sir John, in addition to his military post during the War of the Revolution in Ireland, was Member for the County of Limerick, in the national Parliament of 1689, along with Gerald Fitz-Gerald, "Knight of the Glin, or Valley." Next to the old or Milesian Irish families of rank, these gentlemen were of the most esteemed origin in their native country; being descended from that brave nobleman of mixed Continental and ancient British or Welsh lineage, *Morice le fiz Gerout—Moriz le fiz Geroud* —or MAURICE FITZ-GERALD, who was 1 of the first chevaliers, or knights, that, at the solicitation of the exiled King of Laighin, or Leinster, Diarmaid Mac Murchadha, or Dermod Mac Murrough, in the 12th century came over from Wales, to restore him to his dominions; and, through the considerable aid received by the King from his *native* adherents, and the consequent success, and still further important results, of the enterprise, was enabled to lay the foundation for immense acquisitions by those of the race of FITZ-GERALD in Ireland.

The great-grand-father of Maurice Fitz-Gerald was a nobleman named Otho, who, even *before* the Norman Conquest, or, in the 16th year of the reign of King Edward *the Confessor*, appears as a powerful Baron in England, possessing no less than 35 lordships there. Of these lordships,

1 was in Somerset, 2 were in Berkshire, 3 in Surrey, 3 in Bucks, 3 in Dorsetshire, 4 in Middlesex, 9 in Wiltshire, and 10 in the County of Southampton. The origin of Otho himself has been referred to an Italian stock, and his race connected with England by a removal first from Italy to Normandy, and afterwards from Normandy across the Channel. From Otho's having been such a flourishing potentate in England in King Edward *the Confessor's* time, he was, most likely, one of those Continental cavaliers, among whom Edward, during his exile, was reared; and of whom, on his restoration to the crown of his ancestors, after the cessation of the Danish line of Kings, he is mentioned to have brought or invited over several from Normandy; and to have so much favoured them, as to excite a great jealousy, and even an insurrection, on the part of the native Saxons, or English, under the famous Earl Godwin, father of Harold, the last Saxon King of England. The probability of this is countenanced, by the fact of the Lord Otho's son, Gaultier, or Walter, (hence named Gaultier or Walter *Fitz*-Otho,) being treated as a fellow-countryman by the Normans after their subjugation of England; when, or at the general survey of that kingdom made under those French conquerors, we find him Castellan of Windsor, Warden of the Forests of Berkshire, and in possession of all his father Otho's above-mentioned extensive estates; instead of being used like the *mere* Saxons, or deprived, as such, both of lands and office. This Gaultier or Walter Fitz-Otho, by his wife of Welsh blood, or Gladys, the daughter of Rywall ap Conan, had 3 sons. Of these *Gerout, Geroud, Gerard, Girauld*, or GERALD, (as the name is variously written,) and who was called from his father *Fitz-Gaultier*, or FITZ-WALTER, had a grant, from King Henry I., of Molesford in Berkshire; and serving against the Welsh, was made the Norman Constable of Pembroke Castle, in their country. This fortress he strengthened and defended with success; slew the Welsh Lord or Chieftain of Cardiganshire; was appointed President of the County of Pembroke; and rewarded with the grant of many lands in Wales. There he settled, and, like his father Walter Fitz-Otho, married a native of that country, Nesta, daughter of the Prince of South Wales, who had been the mistress of King Henry. Among his family by this marriage, *Gerald* Fitz-Walter had that Moriz, Morice, or Maurice, accordingly designated *son of Gerald*—which Maurice, through the King of Leinster's invitation, became, as has been said, the founder of the race of FITZ-GERALD in Ireland, where he died in September, 1177.

Of the posterity of Maurice, the 2 principal houses were that of Offaley, or Kildare, in Leinster, and that of Desmond, in Munster. The former, or that established in Leinster, sprang from Maurice by his descendants the Barons of Offaley, the 3rd of whom, John Fitz-Thomas, was created, in 1316, by Edward II., for great services in Ireland and Scotland, 1st *Earl of* KILDARE—whose line, through 20 Earls so entitled, and, since 1766, through several *Dukes of* LEINSTER, have transmitted their honours, for above 5 centuries, with a landed revenue, consisting, in our days, of many thousand pounds a year. The latter branch of the Fitz-Geralds, or that established in Munster, sprang from Maurice Fitz-Thomas, 4th Lord of Decies and Desmond, whom Edward III. ennobled in 1329, creating him Earl of Desmond by patent; according to which, the Earl and his male heirs were to hold from the Crown the County of Kerry, as a County Palatine, or one under a separate jurisdiction; rendering him, in whom it was vested, a kind of sovereign prince, within the territory thus granted. The Lord Palatine had the power of exercising capital punishments, of erecting his own tribunals for civil and criminal causes, and of appointing his own Judges, Sheriffs, Seneschals, Coroners, &c. He had likewise Courts for the payment of his feudal revenues, which would appear to have included so many sources of emolument as to constitute a very large increase to the income derived from his own immediate lands, or estate. Finally, like other great Anglo-Norman potentates of a similar rank in Ireland, the Lords Palatine of Kerry had the power of making tenures *in capite*, and were the heads of a subordinate local aristocracy, or noblesse, of their own; respecting which, we are told, that, of the kindred and surname of the house of Desmond alone, there were above 500 gentlemen. From Maurice, appointed 1st Earl of Desmond in 1329, by Edward III., to the unfortunate Gerald, attainted in 1582, under Queen Elizabeth, 16 Earls of this race ruled over their numerous followers, or in the language of an eminent English writer, their "*Commons, who,*" he observes, "*in this land haue euer bin more deuoted to their immediate Lords heer whom they saw euery day, then unto their Soueraigne Lord and King, whom they neuer sawe.*" Hence Francis I., King of France, in a treaty of alliance against Henry VIII. with Earl James III. of Desmond, June 20th, 1523, the original of which was deposited in the Chambre des Comptes at Paris, in addition to the designation of Comte or Earl of Munster, entitles that nobleman, "*Prince in Ireland.*" But the vast extent of power and wealth, to which the heads of this great southern branch of the race of Fitz-Gerald arose, may be more clearly estimated from the facts—that, about the middle of the 14th century, when we read of the salary of the Viceroy of the Pale, as having been but £500 a year, the Earl of Desmond is alleged, to have been able to expend, in every way, £10,000 per annum—that the great Earl of Kildare, writing, in 1507, from Castle-dermot, to the Gherardini family of Florence, (who *claimed* an affinity with the Irish Fitz-Geralds) describes his kinsman, the Earl of Desmond, as having then "under his Lordship 100 miles in length of country"—that the Earl of Desmond, before-mentioned, as attainted, in 1582, under Queen Elizabeth, is asserted to have been able to raise, at a call, 2000 foot and 600 horse, but, with more preparation, to have been able to bring 4000 foot and 750 horse into the field—that the number of acres directly acquired by the Crown, through the Earl's attainder, was 574,628 independent of those in the territory over which he claimed jurisdiction, and which were above double as many more—that, at a period, when the Queen's revenue in Ireland was not so much as £23,600 per annum, the Earl's rents *alone*, consisting, as a hostile authority observes, of "a prodigious revenue for those times, and perhaps greater than any other subject's in her Majesty's dominions," amounted to more than £7039 a year—and yet, that this very large annual sum, for those days, would appear, from information derived through the son of 1 of the most trusty of the unfortunate nobleman's followers, to have been but a portion of the yearly emoluments of the head of the house of Desmond from his spacious domains. "Alas! the noble tree of the Geraldines, Earls of Desmond,"—exclaims Dr. Dominick O'Daly, Bishop of Coimbra in Portugal, and son of Cornelius O'Daly, a faithful adherent of the ruined Earl, and commander of a body of his troops,—" 450 years had its branches extended over the 4 provinces of Ireland; no less than 50 Lords and Barons paid their tribute, and were ever ready to march under their banners. Besides the Palatinate of Kerry, the country, for 120 miles in length, and 50 in breadth, was theirs. The people paid submission to them throughout all their holdings; they had, moreover, 100 castles and strong-holds—numerous sea-ports—lands that were charming to the eye, and rich in fruits—the mountains were theirs, together with the woods—theirs were the rocky coasts, and the sweet, blue lakes, which teemed with fish. Yea, the fairest of lands did they win with the sword, and govern by their laws; loved by their own, dreaded by their enemies, they were the delight of Princes, and patrons of gifted youth. . . Alas! alas! the mighty tree was doomed to perish, when scathed by the lightning of England's hate. . . Desmond's possessions were forfeited to the Crown, and all those, of every age or sex, who honoured his memory, were maltreated and outraged. The entire property was parcelled out amongst *adventurers*, and they were put in possession of those great domains, which used to pay the Geraldines more than 40,000 golden pieces per annum."

Of the various families of the name of Fitz-Gerald,—a name eminently identified with bravery, at home and abroad, in our military annals,—there were a number of infantry, horse, and dragoon officers in the national army during the War of the Revolution, as well as the subsequent Colonel, in France, of the "Régiment de Limerick, Infanterie." Sir John Fitz-Gerald, Baronet, called among the Irish, from the seat of his property, the *Lord of Clonglas*—at present *Clonlish*, on the frontiers of the Counties of Cork, Kerry, and Limerick—belonged to the previously-described great southern branch of the race of Fitz-Gerald; being descended, though illegitimately, from the celebrated John Fitz-Thomas Fitz-Gerald, ancestor of the house of Desmond; who, from his death, at the severe defeat given by Fineen Mac Carthy to the Fitz-Geralds and their confederates in 1261, is known in history as John of Callan, the place of the engagement in Kerry. Sir John Fitz-Gerald, as disbelieving that good faith would be observed to his countrymen by their enemies, attached *no* value to the Treaty of Limerick. In Ireland, indeed, writes an English Protestant clergyman, "the English had been, though a superior people, yet not sufficiently so, to warrant the attempt at dominion by mere force; they had been obliged, therefore, to affect an unity of interests, and equality of rights, with their victims, which their illiberality forbade them really to intend, and their insufficient refinement incapacitated them to effect. They had, in consequence, continually violated the most solemn compacts, to which their want of brute power compelled them to have recourse." * *The better, in short, the Treaty was for the Irish, the less likely it was, that the English would observe it.*

"And hissing Infamy proclaims the rest!"—Dr. Johnson.

Sir John, accordingly, influenced as many of his retainers as he could, to

* Vindiciæ Hibernicæ, &c., Dedicated by Permission to His Royal Highness, the Duke of Sussex, by a Clergyman of the Church of England, as cited in Macariæ Excidium, Note 144. Of 3 great instances, in European history, of breach of treaty between parties of opposite religions—or that of the treaty of Granada by Spain with the Moors—that of the Edict of Nantes by France with the Huguenots—and that of the Treaty of Limerick by England with the Irish Catholics—were the results, in any case, so *beneficial* as to compensate the violators of public faith, for the dishonour incurred by such conduct? History says they were *not*, but of quite a *contrary* nature.

'Discite justitiam moniti, et non temnere divos!'"—Virgil.

emigrate with him, and "went," says his native Irish pedigree, "to France, with the Chiefs of the *Gaels* in November, 1691"—where he finally died.* His regiment, or that of Limerick, formed, with the majority of the Irish troops in France, a portion of the land force, designed, in 1692, but for the defeat of the French at sea, to land in England, for the purpose of restoring King James to his throne. From 1693 until 1696, when, in consequence of the treaty between Louis XIV. and Victor Amadeus II., Duke of Savoy, peace was restored to Italy, the regiment shared in the successes of the French army in that country, under the Marshal de Catinat. In 1697, the regiment served with the French army of the Rhine, under the Marshal de Choiseul; and was eventually broken up with other regiments, by the extensive reform, or reduction, which, early in 1698, was ordered among the Irish troops, in consequence of the Peace of Ryswick, the preceding autumn.

Like Dorrington's, Luttrell's, and the Lord Grand Prior's regiments of infantry, the 16 companies, or 2 battalions, of Brigadier Talbot's, afterwards Sir John Fitz-Gerald's, regiment would muster originally, or in 1692, 1600 privates, and 64 officers. The officers, by the list of 1695, were—"The Chevalier John Fitz-Gerald, Colonel—Jeremiah O'Mahony, Lieutenant-Colonel—William Therry, Major—12 Captains—28 Lieutenants—28 Sub-Lieutenants—14 Ensigns." The subsequent statements, showing, in the 2 battalions of the regiment, an augmentation in the officers, and a diminution in the soldiers, make the former 242, and the latter 1100; or 1342 on the whole.

THE INFANTRY REGIMENT OF CHARLEMONT.

The first establishment of this corps, as the Regiment of Colonel Gordon O'Neill, was at the commencement of the War of the Revolution in Ireland. During that contest, it was, like other Irish regiments, known by the name of its Colonel; and it was probably designated in France the "Régiment de Charlemont," from its Colonel having been Governor of Charlemont Fort at the beginning of the revolutionary disturbances in Ulster, and from its subsequent connexion with the long and honourable defence, amidst the Williamite quarters, of that fort,† under Major Teague O'Regan, for which that brave old officer was so deservedly knighted by King James. Of the royal houses of Heber, Heremon, Ir, and Ith, to which, from the conquest of Erin by the sons of Milidh, or Milesius, her Ard-Righs, or Monarchs, are recorded to

* The leading officers of the name of Fitz-Gerald, belonging to the Irish Brigade in France, have *now* been noticed. Of minor officers of the Brigade, there were several Fitz-Geralds, Captains and Lieutenants in the Regiments of Dillon, Clare, Berwick, O'Donnell, Bulkeley, and Walsh; the principal of whom was a Captain Fitz-Gerald of the Regiment of Dillon in 1777, who was a Chevalier of St. Louis. Under the other modification of the name, or that of *Geraldine*, there was likewise a noble house in France, derived from Raymond Geraldine, Esq., a native of Waterford, deceased at St. Malo, in June, 1657. His descendants in France were Seigneurs de Lapenti, de St. Symphorien, de Corsine, &c.; and an officer named Geraldine, born in 1714, was Lieutenant-Colonel of Fitz-James's Regiment of Horse, and Brigadier of the Armies of the King, in July, 1762.

† After the defeat of Lord Mountcashel, King James, writing from Dublin Castle, August 3rd, O. S., 1689, to Lieutenant-General Richard Hamilton in Ulster, directs that, among the troops to be left at Charlemont, should be Colonel Gordon O'Neill's Regiment of Foot; for which many recruits were to be made, as it had been amongst those engaged in the harassing blockade of Derry.

have belonged, the house of Heremon—from the number of its Princes, or great families—from the multitude of its distinguished characters, as laymen, or churchmen—and from the extensive territories acquired by those belonging to it, at home and abroad, or in Alba,* as well as in Erin —was regarded as by far the most illustrious. So much so, says the best native authority, that it would be as reasonable to affirm, 1 pound is equal in value to 100 pounds, as it would be to compare any other line with that of Heremon. Towards the "decline and fall" of Druidism, and the rise of Christianity in Erin, or from A.D. 379 to A.D. 406, the head of the line of Heremon was the Ard-Righ Niall, styled "More," or *the Great*, and "Naighiallach," or *of the Nine Hostages*—in reference to the principal hostile powers overcome by him, and compelled to render so many pledges of their submission. Niall was chiefly renowned for his transmarine expeditions against the Roman empire in Britain, as well as in Gaul; where he finally fell, on the river Liane, not far from Boulogne, by the poisoned arrow of an assassin. In one of those expeditions, Niall carried off, among his numerous captives, the youth Succat, afterwards so famous as St. Patrick. And when, many years subsequently, that liberated captive, entering, in a maturity of manhood and experience, upon his mission, was summoned before the supreme assembly at Tara, to show *why* he presumed to interfere with the old religion of the country, by endeavouring to introduce a new creed?—it was Laogaire, the son of his former captor, Niall, who presided as Sovereign there. In the posterity of the "Hero of the Nine Hostages"—4 of whose sons, that settled in Midhe, or Meath, and its vicinity, were styled South Hy-Niall, the other 4, established in Uladh, or Ulster, being called North Hy-Niall—the dignity of Ard-Righ, as represented sometimes by the head of one branch, and sometimes by that of another, was maintained, with an interval of but 20 years, (or the reign of Olil Molt,) down to the year 1002. During this period, making, from the reign of Laogaire inclusive, to the deposition of Maelseachlain or Malachy II. by the celebrated Brian "Boru," in the year last specified, about 554 years,† the Monarchs of the race of Niall amounted to 46. Of the 4 sons of the hero Niall who established them-

* Alba is the original Irish or Gaelic name for Scotland, whose Kings were derived from the race of the Ard-Righs of Erin, of the Heremonian line. The 1st Prince of the House of Stuart who reigned over the 3 Kingdoms of the British Isles, or James VI. of Scotland and I. of England and Ireland, observed, of the latter Kingdom, to the Irish Agents, in 1614,—"I have an old claim as King of Scotland—for the ancient Kings of Scotland are descended from the Kings of Ireland." The Hanoverian dynasty, through its connexion with the Stuarts, has succeeded *them* upon the throne. And hence, says a writer of the last century, Forman, respecting the *earliest* origin of that dynasty's claim to the government of the 3 nations—"Even the greatest antiquity, the august House of Hanover itself can boast, is deduced from the royal stem of Ireland"—as the origin of the "royal stem" of Scotland. Accordingly, it is related, adds the learned Hardiman, of King George IV., that his Majesty, "during his visit to Ireland, passing in view of the hill of Tarah, declared himself proud of *his* descent from the ancient Monarchs of the land."

† Niall's son, Laogaire, having reigned 35 years, or from 428 to 463, after the next or exceptional reign of Olil Molt for 20 years, or from 463 to 483, Laogaire's son, Lugad, in 483, restored the succession in Niall's line, which, as generally uninterrupted from 483 to 1002, would include 519 years, and, with the 35 of Laogaire, 554 years. Niall's own reign, from 379 to 406, or 27 years, with the above-mentioned 554, would constitute a supreme royalty, in the hero and his descendants, until 1002, of 581 years; and, for the *legitimate* resumption of power, after Brian's death, by Maelseachlain, or Malachy, from 1014 to 1022, an addition of 8 more gives a connected total of 589 years.

selves in Uladh, or Ulster, Eoghan, not long before the arrival of the great Apostle of Christianity in Erin, acquired the territory hence styled Tir-Eoghain, or the *land of Eoghan*, or Owen, (otherwise Tir-Owen, or Tirone,) and its inhabitants *Kinel*-Eoghain, or *Kinel*-Owen, as being of his *race*, or *kindred*.* Eoghan, who is celebrated, in poetic eulogy, for " the strength of a hero from the size of a child, and an aspect that glowed with hospitality," settled in the nearly water-surrounded territory of Inis-Eoghain, or Inish-Owen, which—according to the double application of the word *inis* to mean either an *island*, or a *peninsula* as almost so—has received its appellation of *island* or *peninsula of Eoghan* from him. † In the southern and narrower part of that district, upon the summit of an eminence above 800 feet high, and commanding one of the best and most diversified prospects, was a great Cyclopean strong-hold, called Grianan Aileach, now Greenan Ely. The erection of this fortress, the most remarkable monument of the kind in the north-west of the island, and revered, as the abode of Princes or Chiefs of the country, for ages previous to its acquisition by Eoghan, was referred, in tradition and song, to the wonderful times of the Tuatha-de-Danans, whose mysterious memory is yet preserved in written story, as *sidhe, i. e.*, fairies, or little local deities, haunting the forts and hills where they formerly dwelt; and the mention of whom is still proverbially associated, in the mind of the native Irish peasant, with the idea of a race that possessed supernatural knowledge and power.

At Aileach, Eoghan, (in Latin Eugenius,) is related to have resided A.D. 442, when he was converted to Christianity by St. Patrick. "The man of God," says the old biographer of the Apostle, "accompanied Prince Eugenius to his court, which he then held in the most ancient and celebrated seat of kings, called Aileach, and which the holy Bishop consecrated by his blessing." Eoghan, the father of the great *Tir-Owen*, as his twin-brother, Conall, or Connell, was the father of the great *Tir-Connell*, line of the race of Niall of the Nine Hostages, died of grief, A.D. 465, for the loss of the latter the year before, as the Bard notes—

"Eoghan, son of Niall, died
Of tears—good his nature!—
In consequence of the death of Conall, of hard feats"—

and he was buried, it is added, in Inis-Eoghain, at Uisce-chaoin, or the *handsome water*, a name modernized into Eskaheen, as that of the townland in which the origin of both appellations, a *beautiful well*, is situated, near an old chapel, which occupies the site of a monastery, still older. The power of the race of Eoghan continued to increase in Uladh, until, assuming, among her Princes, the supremacy of the famous Kings of Emania of the heroic times, the O'Neill took, for *his* heraldic emblem, the ancient "red hand of Ulster," designated, by an English writer, in Elizabeth's reign, "the bloody hand, a terrible cognizance!"—and, in allusion to that "terrible cognizance," the battle-cry of "Lamh dearg abu!"

* It is an interesting feature of the intimacy which existed, in the 4th and 5th centuries, between the Gael and the Saxon, as united in hostility to the Romans in Britain, &c., that the mother of the renowned Niall was Carinna, a Saxon princess, and that the wife of his son Eoghan, the founder of the great Tirone race, was likewise a Saxon princess, named Indorba.

† Thus, too, in classic antiquity, another *peninsula* was, from King Pelops, designated PELOPONNESUS, or the *island of Pelops*.

or, as it would be shouted at present, *The red hand for ever!* Of the Ard-Righs of Erin of the Hy-Niall race to the year 1002, there were 16 Princes of Tir-Eoghain; which territory, before the Anglo-Norman invasion, included the modern Counties of Tirone, Londonderry, the Baronies of Rapho and Inishowen, in the County of Donegal, and parts of the County of Armagh. In 1088, Domhnall Mac Loughlin, (O'Neill,) Prince of Aileach, as the Princes of Tir-Eoghain were then styled—or, in the language of the Bard,

"Domhnall, of the lion fury,
Chief of the generous race of Eoghan"—*

having marched against Murkertagh O'Brien, King of Mumha, or Munster, and destroyed his famous family-residence of Kincora, the latter, in 1101, revenged this injury upon "Aileach, among the oak forests immeasurable"—ordering, that, for every sack of provisions in his army, a stone, from this great northern edifice, should be carried away to the south. Such, after an existence extending beyond the dawn of history, was the fate of Aileach; from which its possessor, in old writings, is designated, "King of Aileach of the spacious house—of the vast tribute—of the high decisions—of the ready ships—of the armed battalions—of grand bridles—the Prince of Aileach who protects all—the mighty-deeded, noble King of Aileach." After the destruction of Aileach, the Princes of the North Hy-Niall for some time retained, and for a longer time were given, the title of "King of Aileach," although they fixed their residence in the south of the present County of Tirone, at Enis-Enaigh, now Inchenny, in the Parish of Urney; and the green eminence, and the stone-chair upon which each of those Princes was proclaimed, were at Tullaghoge, or *the hill of the youths,* now Tullyhawk, in the Parish of Desertcreaght, and Barony of Dungannon; the tribe, in whose immediate territory this district lay, or the O'Hagans, otherwise known as "the Kinel-Owen of Tullaghoge," not having to pay any tribute—

"Because in it's proud land was assumed
The Sovereignty over the men of Erin." †

* The Mac Loughlins or O'Loughlins of the north were, from the latter half of the 10th century, a leading offshoot of the Hy-Niall or O'Neill race there. Of this offshoot, the head, as well as an O'Neill, was sometimes Prince in Tir-Owen, until 1241; when Donnell O'Loughlin, with 10 of his family, and all the chiefs of his party, were cut off by his rival, Brien O'Neill, in "the battle of Caim-Eirge of red spears," and the supreme power thenceforth remained with the O'Neills. I have designated the Domhnall in the text, O'Neill, in a parenthesis, as *virtually* or by *origin* such, though not so named.

† The "Leac-na-Riogh," or *Flag-stone of the Kings* on which the old Princes or Chiefs of Tir-Owen were "inaugurated," say the native chroniclers, "and called O'Neill after the lawful manner," was demolished by Lord Mountjoy in 1602. "The Lord Deputie," writes his Secretary, "spent some 5 dayes about Tullough Oge, where the Oneales were of old custome created, and there he spoiled the corne of all the countrie, and Tyrone's," i. e., O'Neill's, "owne corne, and brake downe the chaire wherein the Oneales were wont to be created, being of stone, planted in the open field." Dr. O'Donovan informs us, "that pieces of Leac-na-Riogh were to be seen in the orchard, belonging to the glebe-house of Desertcreaght, till the year 1776, when the last fragment of it was carried away." And he adds, "the site of the ancient residence of O'Hagan is to be seen on a gentle eminence, a short distance to the east of the village of Tullaghoge. It is a large circular encampment, surrounded by deep trenches and earthen work. Within these stood the residence of O'Hagan, the Rechtaire, or Lawgiver, of Tullaghoge; and here, too, was placed the stone, on which the 'O'Neale was made,' till it was destroyed, as above men-

A sovereignty, to which, even when *not* possessing it, the Chiefs of the race of Eoghan considered themselves best entitled, and are often referred to, in the subsequent native annalists, as really best entitled, had not the existence of so many conflicting potentates in the country prevented the formation of such a royal centre of union, for the general welfare.

When Henry *Plantagenet,* or *Fiz-Emperiz*—authorized by a bull from the Pope, and an emerald ring of investiture, to take possession of Hibernia, as his great-grandfather, William *the Bastard* of Normandy, had been, a century before, empowered by a similar document, and a diamond ring from Rome, to conquer Anglia—came to Athcliath, or Dublin, and was acknowledged by the Prelacy, and by the Princes of the South and East, as Sovereign or Lord of Hibernia, under the Pope—at the court of the Plantagenet intruder, there were *no* representatives from the North Hy-Niall—among whose Princes it was not forgotten, that *their* predecessors in the legitimate or native Monarchy of Erin, although great benefactors to their national Church, yet were so, without having admitted of *any* superior to themselves in temporals. In the "confusion worse confounded," that, un il the reign of King James I., or for above 4 centuries, was the result of this half Anglo-Norman, half Anglo-Papal, settlement in Ireland,—during which what has been so absurdly styled a *conquest* would be better represented by the text of the Hebrew annals, " in those days, there was no King in Israel, every man did that which was right in his own eyes"—the O'Neills continued to hold a leading position in the history of their country. " O'Neil, Prince of Ulster," says an old treatise on the Statute of Kilkenny, " would *never* acknowledge obedience to King Henry II." During the century that followed the Anglo-Norman settlement in Erin, the rulers of the North Hy-Niall in Tir-Owen are styled " Kings" in the historical documents of the invaders, as well as in the native writings. In 1174, when the Monarch Ruaidhri, or Roderic, (O'Conor) overran the enemy's principal plantation of Midhe, or Meath, prostrated the castles of the Anglo-

tioned. According to the tradition in the country, O'Hagan inaugurated O'Neill, by putting on his golden slipper, or sandal; and hence the sandal always appears in the armorial bearings of the O'Hagans." With reference to this observance, in Erin, of a superior Prince, or Chief, when inaugurated, having his shoe, slipper, or sandal, put on him by an inferior potentate, but still one of consideration, we find that, at the inauguration of the O'Conor in Connaught, the same office was performed for him by the powerful Chief of Moylurg, Mac Dermot, as that performed by O'Hagan for the O'Neill in Uladh, or Ulster. There is a resemblance between this custom at the inauguration of the old Princes of Erin, and that connected with the ceremonial of the later Roman Emperors, or those of Constantinople, on their creation as such. Under the head of " honours and titles of the Imperial family," Gibbon notes, that " the Emperor alone could assume the purple or red buskins." And subsequently relating, how the celebrated John Cantacuzene assumed, in 1341, the Imperial dignity, he mentions John being accordingly "invested with the purple buskins;" adding, " his right leg was clothed by his noble kinsmen, the left, by the Latin chiefs, on whom he conferred the order of knighthood"—this office of putting on the buskins being thus one of honour in the *east,* like that of putting on the shoe, or sandal, in the *west.* The O'Hagans were distinguished among the septs of Uladh, or Ulster, in the final struggle for Celtic independence under the great Aodh or Hugh O'Neill. O'Hagan's country furnished, for that contest, to the army of O'Neill, 100 infantry and 30 cavalry; Henry O'Hagan was Constable to O'Neill; and 7 O'Hagans are named among his Captains of Foot, as commanding, between them, 500 men. The family of O'Hagan was one of eminence, and seated at Tullaghoge, down to Cromwell's time; and, in our day, the name is most worthily represented by the Right Honourable Thomas O'Hagan, Lord Chancellor of Ireland.

Norman colonists, and devastated the territory of the "stranger" as far as Ath-cliath, or Dublin, the forces of the Kinel-Owen, in Roderic's army, are thus noticed by the hostile French rhyming chronicler—

" De Kinelogin, O'Nel, li Reis,
Od sei menad trei mil Yrreis."*

In 1244, King Henry III. writes to the famous Brian O'Neill, for aid against Scotland, as to "Bren O'Nell, Regi de Kinelun." In 1275, the colonial municipality of Cragfergus, or Carrigfergus, mention Aodh or Hugh (Boy) O'Neill, to King Edward I., as "Od O'Neill, Regem de Kinelyon." From 1177, when the Anglo-Normans invaded Ulster under De Courcy, the Kinel-Owen, though having thenceforward so often to resist the GALL, or *foreign* enemy, as well as the GAEL, or *native* foe, maintained their independence, under several Princes, until the death, in 1230, of the brave Aodh O'Neill, " Lord of Tir-Owen—King of the Kinel-Eoghain—King of Aileach—King of the North of Erin—Roy damna, or he who should be King of all Erin—a King, the most hospitable and defensive that had come of the Gaels for a long period, inferior to none in renown and goodness—a King, who had never rendered hostages, pledges, or tribute, to Galls, or Gaels—a King, who had been the greatest plunderer of the Galls, and demolisher of castles—who had gained many victories over the Galls, and had cut them off with great and frequent slaughter—a man, who, though he died a natural death, it was never supposed that he would die in any other way, than to fall by the hands of the Galls."

From the decease of this able Prince in 1230 to 1315, or for about 85 years, the fortunes of the Kinel-Owen, as well as the Kinel-Connell, very much declined, owing to impolitic wars with each other, and to frequent contests for the supreme power in both principalities, which led to applications for aid to the "stranger," and a consequent extortion of hostages and tribute by him, from *both* territories. The great feudal representative of this foreign supremacy, towards the close of the 13th and at the beginning of the 14th century, was Richard de Burgo, the 2nd of the powerful Anglo-Norman Earls of Ulster of his name, generally styled "Iarla ruadh," or the *red Earl*. But this encroachment was interrupted, through the victory of Bannockburn, in June, 1314, by the illustrious Robert de Brus, (or Bruce) which caused his gallant brother, Edward, to be invited into Erin, as her Ard-Righ, or Monarch; in whose favour, the Prince of Tir-Owen, Donald O'Neill, resigned his claim. By the results of the Scotch invasion, from May, 1315, to October, 1318, the power of the *red Earl* was greatly shattered; and, on the assassination (in a family feud) of his successor, "Iarla don," or the *brown Earl*, near Carrickfergus, in June, 1333, the proud Earldom of Ulster fell to pieces. The old Princes of the north, O'Neill, O'Donnell, &c., with "upspringing vigour," again became independent; and "the race of Eoghan of red weapons" even extended their immediate possessions farther than ever.

* The Norman versifier's couplet may be thus translated—
" Of Kinelogin, O'Nel, the *King*,
With him 3000 Yrreis did bring."

The native Irish were called *Yrreis, Irreys,* or *Irrois,* in the idiom of the dominant race from France in England, and the settlements from the latter country in Ireland.

The warlike clan of Aodh Buidhe, or Hugh Boy, O'Neill, Prince of Tir-Owen from 1260 to 1283, passed the Ban into Ulidia, eastern Ulster, or Antrim and Down, and, between 1333 and 1353, with what colonial antipathy terms "persevering *virulence*," wrested, from the mixed population of old natives, and descendants of Anglo-Normans planted there by De Courcy, &c., the territory, hence designated Clannaboy. It was divided into North and South—the former situated between the rivers Ravel and Lagan, embracing the modern Baronies of the 2 Antrims, 2 Toomes, 2 Belfasts, Lower Massereene, and County of Carrickfergus—the latter, south of the Lagan, including the present Baronies of Upper and Lower Castlereagh. Upon the hill of Castlereagh, about 2 miles from Belfast, was the stone-chair, on which the rulers of the country were inaugurated;* and, from the chieftain-line of this 2nd Hy-Niall, or Clannaboy, principality, has sprung the last *ennobled* representative of the race of O'Neill in Ireland.† On King Richard II.'s arrival in Ireland, in 1394, with 34,000 men, the Prince of Tir-Owen, Niall "More," or "le *grand* O'Nell," did homage, at Dundalk, as "Prince of the Irish in Ulster," to the King, though without being really less independent than before; since, notwithstanding the vast expense of this expedition to Richard, "yet," says Sir John Davies, "did he not encrease his reuennue thereby 1 sterling pound, nor enlarged the English border the bredth of 1 acre of land; neither did he extend the iurisdiction of his Courtes of Justice 1 foote further then the English colonies"—in which that narrow "iurisdiction" was previously established. From the ruin of the Earldom of Ulster, the chief external contest of the O'Neills, till

* In 1832, Mr. subsequently Dr. Petrie published an engraving of, and article on, the "coronation chair" of the O'Neills of Clannaboy at Castlereagh. Having remarked, that "the curious piece of antiquity represented was, for a long period, the chair, on which the O'Neils of Castlereagh were inaugurated, and originally stood on the hill of that name, within 2 miles of Belfast," he says—"After the ruin of Con O'Neil, the last Chief of Castlereagh, and the downfall of the family, in the reign of James I., the chair was thrown down and neglected, till about the year 1750, when Stewart Banks, Esq., Sovereign of Belfast, caused it to be removed to that town, and had it built into the wall of the Butter-Market, where it was used as a seat, until the taking down of the market-place, a few years ago. It was then mixed with the other stones and rubbish, and was about to be broken, when Thomas Fitzmorris took possession of it, and removed it to a little garden, in front of his house, in Lancaster Street, Belfast, where it remained till the present year, when it was purchased from him, for a young gentleman of cultivated mind and elegant tastes, R. C. Walker, Esq., of Granby Row, Dublin, and Rathcarrick, in the County of Sligo, who has had it removed to the latter place, where it will be preserved, with the care due to so interesting a monument. This chair, which," it is added, "is very rudely constructed, is made of common whin-stone—the seat is lower than that of an ordinary chair, and the back higher and narrower." It is considered, by the learned archaeologist, to have probably belonged to chiefs of the country previous to the O'Neills, from its resemblance to seats of the kind to be seen in other parts of the island, and from the mode of inauguration, connected with such seats, having been of very remote antiquity in Erin; or "said to have been introduced, even before the arrival of the Milesians, by the Tuatha-de-Danan colony."

† The Right Honourable John Bruce Richard O'Neill, 3rd Viscount and Baron O'Neill of Shane's Castle, County of Antrim, a Representative Peer of Ireland, General in the Army, Vice-Admiral of the Coast of Ulster, and Constable of Dublin Castle, born at Shane's Castle, December, 1780, and deceased, February, 1855, in his 75th year. The O'Neill estates devolved to the Rev[d]. William Chichester, Prebendary of St. Michael's, Dublin, who hence took the name of O'Neill, and has since, or in 1868, been created Baron O'Neill of Shane's Castle, County of Antrim, in the Peerage of Great Britain and Ireland.

the 16th century, was with their neighbours, the O'Donnells, who, in Inish-Owen—the original seat in Ulster of the Kinel-Owen—encroaching, about the middle of the 14th century, upon the border-territory there of the race of Owen, which corresponded with the modern Barony of Rapho, and in which the old royal residence of Aileach stood, early in the 15th century supplanted the older O'Gormleys, of the race of Owen, by the O'Doghertys, of the race of Connell. This being naturally resented by the O'Neills, as a usurpation of the very cradle of their race in Ulster, occasioned a long and bloody war with the O'Donnells, which was not completely terminated, till O'Neill's final confirmation, by charters, in 1514, of Inish-Owen to O'Donnell. Yet the power of the Kinel-Owen, though thus contracted towards Tir-Connell, or on the west, extended as usual, to the sea on the north, and was undiminished towards Uriel and Lecale, or Louth and Down, on the south and east; where, to the 16th century, the foreign borderer, or Saxon settler, continued to pay them "black rents," or tribute.*

Until the reign of Con O'Neill, surnamed "Bacach," or *the Lame*, in Tir-Owen, the heads of the race of Niall there "despised," observes an English writer, "the titles of Earles, Marquises, Dukes, or Princes, in regard of that of *Oneale*." But, in 1542, inasmuch as, "of all the Irish Princes, none was then comparable to *Oneale* for antiquity and noblenesse of bloud,"† Con was created, by King Henry VIII., Earl of Tir-Owen. In 1559, however, Con's celebrated son and successor, Shane, or John, known as "an Diomais," or *the Proud*, set no value on the title of Earl granted to his father, but, after the ancient manner, was inaugurated "O'Neill," and styled "King of Ulster." As a national poet writes of that venerated ceremony, and the feelings of HIM, with whose "pride of place"‡ it was associated—

> "His Brehon's around him—the blue heavens o'er him—
> His true clan behind, and his broad lands before him;
> While, group'd far below him, on moor, and on heather,
> His tanists, and chiefs, are assembled together;
> They give him a sword, and he swears to protect them;
> A slender white wand, and he vows to direct them;
> And then, in God's sunshine, O'NEILL they all hail him,
> Through life, unto death, ne'er to flinch from, or fail him;
> And earth hath no spell that can shatter or sever
> That bond from *their* true hearts—*the* RED HAND *for ever!*"§

---

* After the fall of the intrusive Earldom of Ulster in 1333, the O'Neills, says Dr. O'Donovan, "were not only free from all Anglo-Irish exactions, but they compelled the English of the Pale to pay them *black rent*." Which tributary state of the English of the Pale to the O'Neills in the direction of Lecale and Uriel, or of the *settlers* in Down and Louth, is shown, independent of *any* native Irish evidence, by the English records respecting Ireland, in the 15th and 16th centuries.

† Moryson. A few years before, it was alleged, "O'Neill's mind is to be King of Ireland, and to proclaim himself King, at the hill of Tara."

‡ "An eagle towering in his pride of place."—*Shakspeare*.

§ In accounting for the failure of all his devices to cut off the great Ulster potentate in 1602, Queen Elizabeth's Lord Deputy, Mountjoy, mentions how he did not find "any subiects haue a more dreadfull awe to lay violent hands on their sacred Prince, then these people haue to touch the person of their O'Neales." With reference to the different fate, in the south, of the Earl of Desmond, by the hand of a native assassin, the Secretary of Mountjoy also observes—"wherein the Vlster men challenge an honour of faithfulnesse to their Lords aboue those of Mounster; for, in the following warres, none of them could be induced, by feare, or reward, to lay handes on their renerenced Oneale." And again he notes—"The

"Proud Lords of Tir-Owen! high chiefs of Lough Neagh!
How broad stretch'd the lands that were rul'd by your sway!
What eagle would venture to wing them right through,
But would droop on his pinion, o'er half ere he flew!
From the hills of Mac Cartan, and waters that ran,
Like steeds down Glen Swilly, to soft-flowing Ban—
From Clannaboy's heather to Carrick's sea shore,
And high Armagh of Saints to the wild Innismore—
From the cave of the hunter on Tir-Connell hills
To the dells of Glenarm, all gushing with rills—
From Antrim's bleak rocks to the woods of Rosstrevor—
All echo'd *your* war-shout—*the* RED HAND *for ever!*"

Then, "greatlie it was feared," remarks a hostile contemporary, "that his intent was to haue made a conquest over the whole land. He pretended to be King of Vlster, euen as he said his ancestors were, and, affecting the manner of the great Turke, was continuallie garded with 600 armed men, as it were, his Ianisaries about him, and had in readinesse to bring into the fields 1000 horssemen and 4000 footmen. He furnished all the pesants and husbandmen of his countrie with armour and weapons, and trained them vp in the knowledge of the wars. . . . He cared not for so *meane* an honour as to be an Earle, except he might be better and higher than an Earle. ' For *I am* (saith he) *in bloud and power better than the best, and I will giue place to none of them; for mine ancestors were Kings of Vlster. And as Vlster was their's, so now Vlster is mine, and shall be mine: with the sword I wan it, and with the sword I will keep it.*'" The title of Earl was, in fact, of no account in Tir-Owen to that of O'Neill, "compared with which," says Camden, "even the title of Cæsar is contemptible in Hibernia." After a sanguinary war against the English and his neighbours, but especially the O'Donnells, this John *the Proud* being assassinated in 1567, the revival of an O'Neill in Ulster was made, in 1569, "high treason," by the Parliament of the Pale—"forasmuch," it remarked, "as *the name of O'Neyle, in the judgments of the uncivill people of this realm, doth carrie in it selfe so great a Sovereigntie, as they suppose that all the Lords and people of Ulster should rather live in servitude to that name, than in subjection to the Crown of England.*" Nevertheless, Turlough, John's cousin, "whom, *after his decease, the country had elected to be O'Neyle,*" continued to be so in Tir-Owen; avenged his predecessor's murder upon the Scots, by killing their leader in battle; and was exhorted by the Bards to attempt *greater* things, as descended from ancestors, who had been Ard-Righs of Erin. But his advanced years, and the complicated circumstances of his position, rendered peace with the English most expedient, until his decease, in 1595.

Meanwhile, as Turlough's destined successor, and "to suppress the name and authority of O'Neal,"* the famous Aodh, or Hugh, was, in 1585, designated, and, in 1587, confirmed, as *Earl* of Tirone, by Queen Elizabeth. But that this foreign or antinational, and comparatively modern, title should supersede in Tir-Owen the time-honoured distinction

name of Oneale was so reuerenced in the North, as none could bee induced to betray him, vpon the large reward set vpon his head." This fidelity arose from the system of *clanship*, unknown among the English.

* Or, in the words of the contemporary Life of Sir John Perrott, "to abolish the title and power of O-Neale in Ulster, who, because they had byn Princes of that province, as longe as the name remayned, they thought the dignitie and prerogative must ever follow."

of the "O'Neill," as head of the old royal and martial race of Eoghan, was so intolerable in *their* eyes, that, according to the popular and traditional belief, the Benshee, or guardian spirit of the house of Niall, night after night, in the Castle of Dungannon, upbraided the so-called *Earl;* and conjured him to cast away such an odious designation, as no better than a brand of slavery, stamped upon him by the enemies of his country; at the same time, summoning HIM, to draw the sword, for HER deliverance. And, at *this* period, indeed, the general condition of Ireland was such, that she but too much needed a deliverer. Hence the Earl " did afterwards," adds my Anglo-Irish annalist, "assume the name of O'Neal, and therewith he was so elevated, that he would often boast, that *he would rather be O'Neal of Ulster, than King of Spain!"* * Under this " illustrissimus Princeps Hugo O'Nellus"—to use his designation on the Continent, where he was ranked among the greatest Generals of the day—occurred the final struggle for Celtic independence against Queen Elizabeth—which, from 1595 to 1603, cost the Queen such an enormous amount of blood and treasure—which was so long unfavourable, and at one time confessedly almost fatal, to her arms in Ireland—which did not terminate by *his* capitulation until after *her* decease—and, in reference to which, as concluding a contest of 434 years, from the 1st Anglo-Norman landing in 1169, King James I.'s Attorney-General for Ireland, Sir John Davies, has observed—" *The truth is, the conquest of Ireland was made peece and peece, by slow steppes and degrees, and by seuerall attempts, in seuerall ages; there were sundry reuolutions, as well of the English fortunes, as of the Irish, some-whiles one preuailing, some-whiles the other; and it was neuer brought to a full period, till his Maiestie, that now is, came to the Crowne.*" The Earl of Tirone, whose title and estates were confirmed to him by Elizabeth's successor, James I., in 1603, having subsequently, or in 1607, to retire, from the machinations of his enemies,† to the Continent, died there, at Rome, in 1616. He has been called "the Irish Hannibal;" and, as long as he survived his departure from Ireland, although old and finally blind, he was, to his foes, as Hannibal indeed banished, but as Hannibal feared; a rumour of " *Tirone is coming!*" was one of alarm to the despoilers of his race; and, in connexion with the site of the ancient regal residence of Aileach, from which the O'Neill, down to 1283, was styled " King of Aileach," a curious local reminiscence of the great opponent of Elizabeth has existed, in the popular imagination, to recent times. " A troop of Hugh O'Neill's horse," it was said, "lies, in magic sleep, in a cave, under the hill of Aileach. These bold troopers only wait, to have the spell removed, to rush to the aid of their country; and a man," continues the legend, " who wandered

* The celebrated Ulster Bard, Rory O'Cahan, surnamed "Dall," or *the Blind*, having made an excursion to Scotland not long before the succession of King James VI. to Queen Elizabeth, and having gained great admiration there by his musical skill, is related to have been sent for by the King, to play on the harp before him. " O'Cahan accordingly attended at the Scottish court, and so delighted the royal circle with his performance, that James walked towards him, and laid his hand familiarly on his shoulder. One of the courtiers present remarking on the honour *this* conferred on him, Rory observed, 'A *greater* than King James has laid his hand on my shoulder.' ' Who is that man?' cried the King. ' O'NEILL, Sire,' replied Rory, standing up."

† On those machinations of the land-coveting description, (likewise employed, as has been shown, for the ruin of the Earl of Clancarty,) see the Revd. C. P. Meehan's learned and interesting " Fate and Fortunes of Hugh O'Neill, Earl of Tyrone, and Rory O'Donel, Earl of Tyrconnell," &c.

accidentally into the cave, found them lying beside their horses, fully armed, and holding the bridles in their hands. One of them," it is added, "lifted his head, and asked, '*Is the time come?*'—but, receiving no answer, dropped back into his lethargy!" This suggestive story very naturally became, in Ulster, the subject of a suitable poem, on "the awakening of Hugh O'Neill's horsemen."* The great Hugh was succeeded abroad, in the title of Earl of Tirone, by his sons, Don Henry and Don John O'Neill, Colonels, &c., in the Spanish service; of whom the latter, dying in Catalonia, in 1641, the chief of the O'Neills then in Ireland was Sir Phelim O'Neill of Kinard, or Caledon, in the County of Tirone. In the civil war of 1641-53, Sir Phelim headed the rising of Ulster; and, during that contest, the name of O'Neill was likewise represented by the illustrious Major-General Owen Roe O'Neill, the defender of Arras against 3 Marshals of France, and the router of the Puritans at Benburb, considered, but for his inopportune death, in 1649, to have been the fittest opponent for Cromwell; and by Major-General Hugh Duff O'Neill, the subsequent gallant defender of Clonmel and Limerick.

The father of Gordon O'Neill was Sir Phelim above-mentioned, and his mother, the Baroness of Strabane, originally Lady Jean Gordon, and daughter of George Gordon, 1st Marquis of Huntly in Scotland; whence the name of Gordon, borne by her son. Under King James II., Gordon O'Neill was Lord Lieutenant of, and Member of Parliament for, the County of Tirone. He was Captain of Grenadiers in the infantry regiment of William Stewart, Lord Mountjoy, before the Revolution; and, after it broke out, he raised, for the royal cause, mostly in Tirone, the Regiment of Foot, which bore his name, as its Colonel. He served, in 1689, at the successful operations against the Williamites in Ulster, previous to the blockade of Derry; then at that blockade, where he was wounded in the thigh; in 1690, was at the Boyne; and was present, as Brigadier, July 22nd, 1691, at the battle of Aughrim, or Kilconnell. There he was stationed on the Urrachree side of the position, with the Irish right wing, composed of some of the best corps of the army, which wing was victorious that day, but for what happened in other quarters; and he duly signalized himself, at the head of his regiment, capturing, after the 3rd great repulse of the enemy, some pieces of their artillery; till, having been so severely wounded, as to be apparently lifeless, he was stripped, and left upon the field, among the slain. But, being recognized by some Scotch Williamite officers, connected with him, through his mother, as a Gordon, they had him attended to. He was removed to Dublin, recovered, and, being released under the Treaty of Limerick, he followed his Sovereign to France. No officer had stronger military claims upon the exiled Court of St. Germain, through his own services, and as the head of a race, among whom, besides so many gentlemen of subordinate rank that fought for the royal cause in Ireland, Sir Neal O'Neill, Colonel of a Regiment of Dragoons, died, after being wounded

---

* This legend, about O'Neill's sleeping horsemen at Aileach, is like another, in Continental literature. "The German," too, we are told, "goes back to the Hohenstaufens, to the great Barbarossa, the ideal Emperor, who, according to popular tradition, is not dead, but asleep, in the Hartz mountain! And he *will* awake some day, *will* reappear in his strength, to uphold justice, vex evil-doers, and establish the Empire in its glory! Why does he tarry so long?"

at the Boyne,* Sir Donald or Daniel O'Neill was also Colonel of a Regiment of Dragoons, Henry O'Neill was a Brigadier of Infantry, and Cormac, Felix, and Brian were all Colonels of Infantry; Brigadier Henry and Colonel Felix having fallen at Aughrim. Brigadier Gordon O'Neill was therefore made Colonel in France of the Irish Infantry Regiment of Charlemont. From the frustrated invasion of England in 1692 to the Peace of Ryswick in 1697, this regiment served against the Germans; and, in February, 1698, its remains, with those of the Queen's Dragoons à pied, were formed into the infantry Regiment of Galmoy; to which Gordon O'Neill was attached, as a supernumerary or reformed Colonel. By his lady, Mildred, (a Protestant of the Established Church, deceased, in December, 1686, at Derry, where he used to reside before the Revolution,) Gordon O'Neill had a daughter, Catherine, married to John Bourke, 4th Lord Brittas and 9th Lord Castle-Connell, also exiled in France, as a Jacobite loyalist. Of this marriage, there were 2 sons—John, 5th Lord Brittas, and 10th Lord Castle-Connell, variously mentioned as Captain and Colonel in the French service—the Honourable Thomas Bourke, Lieutenant-General in that of Sardinia.† Brigadier-General Gordon O'Neill died in 1704. In the various corps of his countrymen serving in France, numbers of O'Neills have since been officers, from the Cadet and Ensign, to the Colonel, Chef-de-Brigade, and Maréchal de Camp, and several of them Chevaliers of St. Louis; among the most eminent of whom was the late Colonel Charles O'Neill, (of the branch of Derrynoose, County Armagh,) Chef du Bureau de l'Infanterie au Ministre de la Guerre, Officier de la Legion d'Honneur, &c.‡ To Spain, also, the O'Neills have supplied officers of distinction

* In September, 1791, at Madrid, the decease is mentioned of Don Carlos Felix O'Neill, a great favourite of the King, an old Lieutenant-General, formerly Governor of the Havannah, and the son of Sir Neal O'Neill of the Province of Ulster, &c.

† "He," relates Ferrar, in 1787, "is a most disinterested friend to his countrymen; so much so, that the King has said to him, 'Bourke, you have solicited many favours for your Irish friends, but never asked one for yourself.'"

‡ To an abstract of this officer's career, I prefix a *fuller* notice of his father's, as *more* a portion of my subject—the Brigade in France previous to the Revolution. John O'Neill was born January 20th, 1737, at Derrynoose, County of Armagh. He left Ireland when young for Paris, where his brother was Principal in the College des Irlandais. After completing his studies at the College of Plessis, he entered the Regiment of Clare, in December, 1753, as a Cadet; passed, with the same rank, to the Regiment of Roth, in 1759; became, April 26th, 1761, a 2nd Lieutenant; March 1st, 1763, Ensign; March 24th, 1769, (when the corps was, for some years, that of Roscommon) a 1st Lieutenant; February 13th, 1774, (when the regiment was that of Walsh) was made Captain Commandant of the Lieutenant-Colonel's company; and, under the renewed formation as Walsh's, after being merged in the Legion of Dauphiné, or in 1776, was likewise a Captain commandant. January 22nd, 1779, he was created a Chevalier of St. Louis; July 6th, 1788, he was appointed Major; July 25th, 1791, Lieutenant-Colonel of the regiment, then the 92nd; and January 8th, 1792, Colonel of the corps, which he continued to be till 1794; having previously, or May 15th, 1793, been nominated General of Brigade and Maréchal de Camp. He had gone through the campaigns in Germany from 1759 to 1762; those of 1769 and 1770 in Corsica; and, during the war for the emancipation of the United States of America from England, had fought at 3 naval engagements in the *Victoire* against Admiral Rodney, and at the reduction of the 3 West India Islands of Tobago, St. Eustache, and St. Christophe between 1781 and 1783. He was stationed in the Isle of France and St. Domingo from 1788 to 1792, and finally served in 6 campaigns from 1793 to 1798. Authorized July 9th, 1799, to retire, he was granted, March 28th, 1801, a pension of 3000 francs; and, at Paris, where he fixed his residence, died, in his 75th year, about March, 1811. Colonel Miles Byrne, who mentions the veteran, in 1803, as then *en retraite* with

down to the war against Napoleon I.; and the name has been connected with nobility there to our days, in the person of Don Juan Antonio Luis O'Neill y Castilla; whose titles, dating from 1679 to 1695, are Marqués de la Granja, de Valdeosera, de Caltojar, and Conde de Benajiar.

Like the preceding Irish infantry regiments of King James in France, that of Charlemont, or O'Neill, in 1692, had 2 battalions, 16 companies, 1600 privates, and 64 officers. By Mac Geoghegan's subsequent list of the officers, they were—"Gordon O'Neill, Colonel—Hugh Mac Mahon, Lieutenant-Colonel—Edmond Murphy, Major—12 Captains—28 Lieutenants—28 Sub-Lieutenants—14 Ensigns." The more recent strength of the corps was the same as that of the others referred to, or 2 battalions, 1100 privates, and 242 officers.

THE INFANTRY REGIMENT OF DUBLIN.

The "Régiment de Dublin, Infanterie," appears to have been so called in France, from having been first levied, on the breaking out of the War of the Revolution in Ireland, by Sir Michael Creagh, Knight, Lord Mayor of Dublin for 1688-9, Member, also, for Dublin in the Parliament of the latter year, and Pay-Master-General of the Forces in Ireland to King James II. The corps was all raised in Dublin, where the Colonel had much property. The name of Creagh, anglicized from an old Irish word meaning a *branch-bearer*, was, according to family tradition, originally O'Neill—of the North Munster or Dalcassian sept of Tradraidhe or Tradry, County of Clare*—until connected with the annals of Limerick,

the rank of General of Brigade, adds—"He was a small man, rather handsome, with fine features," and, "having been born and brought up in Ireland, he spoke English. He had the reputation of being a just chief, though a severe disciplinarian, and a strict observer of military rules and honours. Though proud and haughty as one of the descendants of the great O'Neill of the North, still he was much liked by his officers," who "used to call their Colonel, 'the Monarch,' in their chat among themselves."—His son, *Charles* O'Neill, born in France, September 29th, 1770, became, April 22nd, 1788, a Sous-Lieutenant in the Regiment of Walsh; and in the course of the wars under the Republic, the Empire, and subsequent to the Restoration of the Bourbons, rose to be a Colonel, an officer of the Legion of Honour, and Chevalier of St. Louis, &c. He was wounded, and made prisoner, November 4th, 1799, at the battle of Fossano. He served at sea in the *Jupiter*, the *Valeureuse*, and the *Courageux*, from June, 1804, to November, 1807. In the Peninsular contest, which he passed through from 1808 to 1812, he received a contusion on the left arm, at the 1st siege of Saragossa; and, at the battle of Salamanca, in command with his battalion of Voltigeurs, was disabled in the left foot, from a gunshot wound, and made prisoner by the English. Though sent back to France, in April, 1813, as so seriously injured, and notwithstanding his consequent severe suffering, he headed a battalion of National Guards in the decisive campaign of 1814, where he was engaged at the affairs of Meaux, of Claye, and in the defence of Paris. Afterwards, or in 1823, at the head of the 27th Regiment in Spain he was distinguished, July 16th, before the Isle of Leon. He held the appointment of Chief of the Bureau of Infantry till the Revolution of July, 1830, and died at Paris, in July, 1844. He appears to have been an honour even to the honourable name he bore; a good comrade and friend; ever willing, while employed in the War Office, to oblige his father's countrymen. He was very fond of music, and both sang well, and played on several instruments.

* These southern or Clare O'Neills, of the line of Heber, must not be confounded, as they have been by some, with the greater northern or Tirone O'Neill's, of the line of Heremon. The fertile and beautiful territory of Tradry, the best in the County of Clare, and co-extensive with the present Deanery of Tradry, was, after the Anglo-Norman invasion, usurped by the De Clares; and, on their overthrow, passed into the possession of the Mac Namaras. But numbers of the O'Neills have remained

by some of those O'Neills having assisted its inhabitants to expel the Danes. On this occasion, the O'Neills, who acted gallantly, were additionally distinguished by wearing green branches on their caps or helmets; "whence," alleges the local historian, "they took the name of Creagh; and the action happening near Creagh Gate, that and the Lane received their names from them." The race of Creagh were of eminent respectability, during several successive centuries, in Limerick. Notwithstanding the many gaps in the rolls of its Mayors, and of other civic officers corresponding to Sheriffs at present, the name of Creagh, from 1216 to 1651, the year when the city fell into the hands of the Cromwellians, is to be seen, among those who bore the former dignity there, 34 times, and, among those who filled the latter office there, 60 times. After the capture of the city, by Cromwell's brother-in-law, Ireton, in the autumn of 1651, when Pierce Creagh Fitz-Pierce was Mayor, and William Creagh 1 of the Sheriffs, many Creaghs, with others of the old families, retired, from the yoke of the usurpers, in various directions. Of those Creaghs, "several," we are told, "went to Rochelle in France, where they obtained patents of nobility." Another branch of the Creaghs, established, about the reign of Edward III., in Cork, became wealthy merchants there, and intermarried with the leading families until about 1644, or during the same civil war which was so disastrous to those of the name in Limerick, when the representatives of the race in Cork were plundered, and expelled the city, as belonging to its "ancient Irish inhabitants." In 1541, Christopher Creagh, a man of great influence and power, both with the English government and the old natives, was Mayor of Cork, the 4th in descent from whom, Michael Creagh, by his marriage with a Miss O'Driscoll, was the father of Sir Michael Creagh, Lord Mayor of Dublin. The Regiment of Sir Michael Creagh was among the best equipped, most efficient, and healthy in the Irish army. The command of it was sometimes devolved by Sir Michael upon Colonel Lacy. It served in the campaigns from 1689 to 1691; at the blockade of Derry; under King James against Marshal Schonberg; at the action of the Boyne; on the frontier at Ballyclough, against the Williamites in the County of Cork, &c.* There were Creaghs officers of the Irish

in the territory of their ancestors till our time; among whom the tradition relative to the Creaghs has been preserved. Under too many circumstances long unfavourable to the retention of the name of O'Neill, in its old form, some of this Clare race modified it into Nihell, or Nihill. My Limerick authority in 1787 writes—"Of this family" of Nihell "is Baron Harrold, a native of Limerick, and Colonel of the Regiment of Koeningsfeldt, in the German service. Several of them have served honourably in the Irish Brigades on the Continent. Lieutenant-Colonel Nihell of Dillon's regiment particularly distinguished himself at the battles of Fontenoy and Lafeldt; and the present Sir Balthasar Nihell, now a Brigadier-General in the King of Naples' service, and Colonel of the regiment, formerly called the Regiment of Limerick. This gentleman was 1 of the gallant Irish officers, who disengaged the King's person at Villetri, when he was surprised by the Imperial General Count Browne," also of Limerick origin. Of such of the Tradry sept, as did *not* modify their old name, seems to have been the Lieutenant-Colonel O'Neill of the Regiment of *Clare*, who fell at the battle of Fontenoy.

* The circumstance of Sir Michael Creagh, as a Protestant, having also been a Jacobite loyalist, appears to have rendered his memory proportionably obnoxious to Williamite prejudice in Dublin. Accordingly, in the annual processions of its Williamite corporation during the following century, headed by the Lord Mayor of the day, it was a custom to halt at Essex Gate, and summon Sir Michael to return as a fugitive, if he would not be outlawed, for having absconded, as Lord Mayor, with the official gold collar of S.S., granted to the Corporation by Charles

Brigade in France till the 1st Revolution, the principal of whom was a Maréchal de Camp, or Major-General; the name occurs with high military rank in Spain, as late as the contest against Napoleon I.; and the late Sir Michael Creagh, who was 58 years in the army of Great Britain and Ireland, and received the thanks of Parliament, was a Major-General, and Colonel of the 73rd Regiment of Foot, on his decease, aged 80, in September, 1860, at Boulogne.

The Colonel of the "Régiment de Dublin" in France was John Power, apparently the same gentleman who had been Lieutenant-Colonel to Sir Michael Creagh in Ireland; another John Power was Lieutenant-Colonel to his namesake in France; and the Major, in *both* countries, is mentioned as Tobias or Theobald Burke. The Powers, or Poers, passed from France into England with William the Conqueror in the 11th century, and were among the earliest and most distinguished Anglo-Norman settlers in Ireland in the 12th. The head of the Powers in Ireland at the Revolution, Richard Power, Lord Baron of Curraghmore, Viscount Decies, Earl of Tyrone, Lord Lieutenant of the County of Waterford, &c., adhered to King James II., sat in his Parliament of 1689, and levied a Regiment of Foot, of which he was Colonel in 1690, at the Williamite capture of Cork. Being conveyed as a prisoner to the Tower of London, he died there the same year, leaving 2 sons, John and James, successively Earls; through the only surviving issue of the last of whom, Lady Catherine Power, the Barony was conveyed by marriage, in 1717, into the Beresford family, whose chief is the Marquis of Waterford. Of Powers, there were, besides the noble head of their name, in the Irish army during the War of the Revolution, a Colonel, several Lieutenant-Colonels, Captains, Lieutenants, &c.; and afterwards various officers in France in the Regiments of Dublin, Dillon, Berwick and Bulkeley. But the most distinguished of the name abroad, as uniting the honours of the pen with those of the sword, was " Colonel Power, an Irishman by birth, in the Spanish service," who having been Adjutant-

II.! But Sir Michael's mayoralty for 1688 having expired, according to old style, in March, 1689, he was succeeded, until 1690, by so many as 2 Aldermen, Terence Dermot, and Walter Motley, and so had *not* the gold collar to abscond with, when the Jacobite, or, what *he* considered, the legitimate, government, was obliged to quit Dublin for Limerick by the reverse at the Boyne; till which time, he, as a leading official of that government, was at Dublin. And, independent of what he suffered through his consequent attainder, and the sale of his property by the Williamites, he was no small loser by their getting possession of Dublin. The Report, in December, 1699, to the English Parliament, of the Commissioners for Forfeited Estates in Ireland, thus refers to the spoliation in Dublin, with which even William's Lords Justices, Coningesby and Sydney, were connected. "Indeed, the plunder at that time was so general, that some men in considerable employments were not free from it, which seems to us a very great reason why this matter has not been more narrowly search't into; particularly the Lord C—n—ngsby seized a great many black cattle, to the number of 300 or thereabouts, besides horses that were left in the Park after the battle of the Boyne, and which we do not find ever were accounted for to his Majesty; he also *seized all the plate and goods in the house of Sir Michael Creagh*, (Lord Mayor of the City of Dublin for the year 1689,) *which are generally thought to amount to great value,* but this last is *said* to be by grant from his Majesty; there were several rich goods and other household stuff," it is added, " delivered by the Commissioners of the Revenue to the then Lords Justices, the Lord S—dn—y & Lord C—n—ngsby, which we do not find were ever returned accounted for to his Majesty, or left at the Castle, at their departure from the government." Thus, it was *not* sufficient for Sir Michael Creagh to be plundered, when living, by Williamite rapacity, without being libelled, when dead, by Williamite mendacity.

General to the Infante Don Philip in the War of the Austrian Succession in Italy, published, in 2 volumes, at Berne, in 1785, "*Tableau de la Guerre de la Pragmatique Sanction en Allemagne & en Italie, avec une Rélation Originale de l'Expédition du Prince Charles Edouard en Ecosse & en Angleterre*"—the details of the latter interesting enterprise, having been communicated, as the Colonel states, either by the Prince himself, or by some of his companions.

The Regiment of Dublin, like that of Charlemont, was employed in the campaigns against the Germans from 1692 to 1697, and was dissolved by the general reform in 1698. It likewise comprised, at first, 2 battalions in 16 companies, or 1600 soldiers, and 64 officers. Its officers afterwards, according to Mac Geoghegan, were—"John Power, Colonel—John Power, Lieutenant-Colonel—Theobald Burke, Major—12 Captains—28 Lieutenants—28 Sub-Lieutenants—14 Ensigns." More recently, its 2 battalions mustered 242 officers, and 1100 soldiers.

THE INFANTRY REGIMENT OF ATHLONE.

This regiment was commanded, on the Continent, until 1693, by Sir Maurice Eustace, Baronet, of Castlemartin, in the County of Kildare. The race of Eustace or Fitz-Eustace is of French or Norman origin. From 1326 to 1496, the Fitz-Eustaces were several times Lord Treasurers, Lord Chancellors, and Lord Deputies of the Pale; the most celebrated of whom was Sir Roland Fitz-Eustace of Harristown, in the County of Kildare, who, having filled *all* those posts, was created Lord Portlester, by Edward IV.; and the family was further ennobled, with the title of Viscount Baltinglass, by Henry VIII. The subject of our immediate notice, Sir Maurice Eustace, was grandson of William Fitz-John Eustace of Castlemartin, and son of Sir Maurice Eustace, Lord Chancellor of Ireland from 1660 to 1665. Previous to the Revolution, Sir Maurice Eustace was Captain, first, in the Infantry Regiment of Sir Thomas Newcomen, Baronet, &c., whose 4th daughter, Margaret, he married; afterwards commanded a troop in Colonel Theodore Russell's Regiment of Horse; became a Catholic; and when the Orange invasion took place, and the Revolution broke out, he, with proportionable attachment to King James II., levied, for his service, a Regiment of Foot, in Kildare. The name of Sir Maurice, or of his regiment, was among the most prominent in the campaigns from 1689 to 1691; being mentioned at the blockade of Derry; at the routing of Hunter's insurgents in the County of Down; at the 1st siege of Limerick; at the guerilla or frontier war in Kildare, and the Queen's County; at the defence of Ballymore; at the battle of Aughrim, where Sir Maurice was severely wounded; at the subsequent contest in Kerry; and among those corps, the remains of which left Limerick, after the 2nd siege, to embark for France. The name of Eustace had displayed, among King James's supporters against the Revolutionists in Ireland, 2 Members of Parliament, a Colonel and Lieutenant-Colonel, with several Captains, Lieutenants and Ensigns; including various estated gentlemen attainted for their loyalty, and subjected to Williamite confiscation, in the Counties of Kildare, Carlow, Wicklow and Dublin. Sir Maurice, as the head of his name in rank and services, was, accordingly, not overlooked at the Court of St. Germain, on the remodification of the Irish forces in Brittany. He was made Colonel of the "Régiment d'Athlone, Infanterie," which was appointed to serve in Italy; and he held that command until the latter end of 1693, when the Colonelcy was conferred by King James on its previous Lieutenant-Colonel, Walter Bourke, Esq., of Turlough, in the County of Mayo.

This gentleman belonged to a race, which ranks, with those of Fitz-Gerald and Le Botiler, or Butler, as among the 3 most illustrious of French, or Norman, origin in Ireland. The name has been variously written in France, England, and Ireland, as De or Du Bourg, or Burgh, De Burgo or Burgho, Bourke, and Burke. The founder of the race in Ireland, in the 12th century, was Guillaume Fitz-Aldelm, or William Fitz-Adelm, de Burgo. That nobleman, accompanying Henry II. to Ireland, in 1171, as his Steward, was made Governor of Wexford; on the King's return to England, in 1172, was intrusted with the management of his Irish affairs; was named Chief Governor of the Anglo-Norman settlements in 1178; obtained large possessions, particularly in Connaught, by the civil war between the rival O'Conors * during the latter portion of that, and the earlier years of the next, century; and died in 1204-5. The eminence of the house of De Burgo increased, until, through its matrimonial connexion with Maud de Lacie, or Lacy, it acquired, in addition to its own possessions, the Earldom of Ulster, and became the greatest Anglo-Norman family in Ireland; its head, Richard, the famous *red Earl*, having sat as the 1st nobleman in the Parliament of the Pale at Dublin in 1295, and, in all Commissions and Parliament Rolls, being named, even *before* the Lords Justices themselves. But upon the murder near Carrickfergus, in June, 1333, of this Richard's successor and grandson, William, or the *brown Earl*, leaving only an infant daughter, a great revolution occurred in Connaught, as well as in Ulster. That in Ulster has been duly noticed under the Regiment of O'Neill, or Charlemont. In Connaught, Sir William de Burgo's 2 elder sons, the leading male representatives of the house of De Burgo, from whom and those of the name in general, according to Anglo-Norman law, or if the late Earl's daughter were to be his heir, all his lands might be conveyed, in marriage, to a *stranger*, preferred the Irish or Brehon law, which provided that, by a male succession, the territory of a race should be preserved in *that* race; and they accordingly seized upon, and divided into 2 distinct lordships, the large possessions, from which the preceding heads of the De Burgos had, among their titles, "Lords of Connaught." Then, renouncing Anglo-Norman, for Irish, laws and customs, and causing nearly all those of the same colonial origin in that province to do so likewise, these 2 noblemen henceforth proclaimed themselves Irish Chiefs, as Mac William "Eighter," and Mac William "Oughter;" determining to keep by force what they had gotten. And, in this, they succeeded, although the rights of the former "Lords of Connaught" and "Earls of Ulster" devolved by the marriage of the last Earl's daughter, in 1352, to no less a personage than Lionel Plantagenet,

---

* Through the insane and sanguinary divisions for supremacy amongst the O'Conors, their power declined, and that of the Anglo-Norman feudalist, invited by the contending parties to assist them, increased in Connaught, till Turlough Don, slain in December 1406, was the last of his old royal house, called *King* in Connaught. "Because," says my authority, "they were not themselves steady to each other, they were crushed by lawless power, and the usurpation of foreigners. May God forgive them their sins!"

Duke of Clarence, 3rd son of Edward III., King of England; which nobleman in vain came over twice, or in 1361, and 1367, as Chief Governor of the Anglo-Norman settlements in Ireland, with the hope of recovering what *he* regarded as *his* property.* The territory of Mac William "Eighter," or *the Lower*, comprehended the 6 Baronies of Loughreagh, Dunkellin, Killtartan, or Killtaraght, Clare, Athenry, and Leitrim, in the County of Galway; whose chief, Ulick de Burgh, was first ennobled, in the English manner, by King Henry VIII., in July, 1543, as Earl of Clanricarde, and Baron of Dunkellin. The territory of Mac William "Oughter," or *the Upper*, comprehending, in general, the County of Mayo, was far more extensive, as observed by the Lord Deputy, Sir Henry Sidney, writing of its Chief, Sir Richard Fitz-David Bourke, in 1576. "He is a great man; his lande lyeth a longe the west, northwest coast of this realme, wherein he hathe maney goodly havens, and he is a Lorde of 3 tymes so moche lande as the Earll of Clanricarde is." Of this Chief, or Mac William "Oughter"—by his wife, Grace, daughter of Eoghan or Owen O'Mailley (or O'Malley) Chief of the district called the Owles, or 2 Baronies of Murresk and Burrishoole, in Mayo, and a heroine, that, under the popular designation of *Grauna Weale*, is so generally known for exploits, suitable to a race, of which the native proverb says, "there never was a genuine O'Mailley who was not a mariner"†—the eldest son, Sir Theobald Bourke, surnamed "ny long," or *of the ship*, from being born at sea, and who was also a distinguished captain in the Elizabethan wars, was the 1st of the line of Mac William "Oughter" created a Peer, as Viscount Bourke of Mayo, by King Charles I., in 1627.

The family of Turlough, a branch from the above chieftain and ennobled line, and possessed of a considerable property, was represented, at the Revolution, by Walter Bourke, as eldest son of Richard Bourke, Esqr., of Turlough, by his marriage with Celia O'Shaughnessy, of the ancient dynastic house of Kinelea, and subsequently of Gort, in the County of Galway. Like so many of the name of Bourke—who, including 5 noblemen, or the Lords Clanricarde, Castleconnell, Brittas, Galway, and Boffin, amounted to not less than between 70 and 80 commissioned officers in the Irish army during the war of the Revolution—Walter Bourke early embarked in the contest; as Member for the County of Mayo, sat in the national Parliament of 1689; and, the same year, undertook to raise a Regiment of Foot, of which he appears on the muster-rolls, in April, 1690, as Colonel, and which was subsequently attached to the army, that fought at the Boyne. At the battle of Aughrim, July 22nd, 1691, he was stationed, with his regiment, on the Irish left, in and about the Castle of Aughrim, to arrest an ascent from the adjoining

---

* The circumstance of the De Burgos having been *able* to set at defiance the claims of a son of the renowned Edward III., *twice* acting as the representative of his royal father in Ireland, is explained by the very great weakening of the power of the colonial government there, that was a result of the Scotch or Bruce's invasion; and by the utter inability of Edward, from the employment of his forces in so many wars, to spare anything like a sufficiency of troops for a defence even of the diminished territory *left* him, which was but precariously held through payments of black-rents, tributes, or pensions, to some of the old natives, for peace, or protection against others!

† This ancient sept likewise appear, in Bardic panegyric, as "the clan of the sea-sent treasures, the prophets of the weather, and the Mananuans, or sea-gods, of the western ocean."

defile, or old broken causeway, which was the key to the Irish position on that side, as the sole access for hostile cavalry there. The defile being but a narrow, boggy trench, 60 yards in length, through which 2 horsemen at most, or with difficulty, could attempt to proceed abreast, and *that* exposed to musketry from the Castle and its environs at between 30 and 40 yards' distance, if not even less, the Colonel might have baffled such an apparently hopeless undertaking, had he been supplied with proper ammunition. But the barrels of bullets sent him were unfortunately found to consist of balls that had been cast for English guns, or too big for the bore of his men's French muskets.* The Williamite cavalry consequently passed beyond the Castle, and, through a 2nd piece of good fortune, in the fall of St. Ruth by a cannon shot, (when about to charge them with a superior body of horse before they could form,) were enabled to change the fortune of the day; while the Colonel, assailed by 2 infantry regiments, had to retire into, or more immediately about, the Castle. This edifice, though dilapidated, or of little strength, except as commanding the defile, and though the Colonel was without available bullets, he continued to hold, till nothing more was to be hoped from maintaining it. Then sallying, in order to effect his escape, over the adjacent great bog, towards Galway, by breaking through the investing force, he, notwithstanding that they were double his number, and had been duly provided with ball, so roughly handled them, that he would probably have succeeded in his attempt, but for the arrival of some fresh squadrons of Williamite horse and dragoons, to the aid of their infantry; by whose junction the sortie was repulsed, and the Castle taken; the Colonel himself, and 52 more, being all who survived of his regiment, as prisoners.† On the Colonel's release by the Treaty of Limerick, and his subsequent passage into France, he suffered a similar reduction of rank to that of so many other officers there; being made only a Lieutenant-Colonel to the Regiment of Athlone. This regiment was not attached, in 1692, to the Irish and French Force prevented landing in England by the naval reverse of La Hogue; but commenced its active services on the Continent, in the Army of Italy under the Marshal de Catinat, whom it joined May 15th, at Fenestrelles. At the overthrow of the Allies in the battle of Marsaglia, or Orbassan, October 4th, 1693, the Lieutenant-Colonel was distinguished, and he was commissioned by King James, at St. Germain, November 13th, to succeed Sir Maurice Eustace, as Colonel. Till after the siege of Valenza that led to the pacification of Italy in 1696, Walter Bourke commanded the regiment there; and the next campaign, or that of 1697, he did so on the Rhine. By the general reform among the Irish troops in 1698, the remains of the Regiment of Athlone, united

* "The men," says the contemporary Jacobite, Plunkett, "had French pieces, the bore of which was small; and had English ball, which was too large!" He then naturally exclaims, at that "miscarriage, thro' heedlessness—*why* was not this foreseen, and the damage prevented?" With Plunkett before Lord Macaulay, *why*, too, it may be fairly asked, has his Lordship been entirely silent upon such an important point, as this respecting the unsuitable bullets, in *his* version of the battle? The Williamites were *confessedly* unsuccessful in the contest, up to their attempt, as a *last* resource, to get through the pass of Aughrim, the strongest or most defensible portion of the Jacobite position—and should the *cause* of their having gotten through be left *untold?*

† In addition to the other more generally known authorities concerning Bourke's regiment here, I am indebted to that of the Scotch Williamite veteran, Major General Mackay, who acted at the battle, in the immediate direction of the pass of Aughrim.

with those of the King's Dismounted Dragoons, and the 3 Independent Companies, were formed into a Regiment of Foot, for the Duke of Berwick; the late Colonel of the Regiment of Athlone being attached, as a supernumerary or reformed Colonel, to the new corps, until, (as hereafter shown,) more fully provided for.

The Regiment of Athlone, (seemingly named so from some connexion with the defences of that place in 1690 and 1691,) was the last of the larger infantry corps of King James's army in France, which consisted of 2 battalions, and 16 companies of 100 soldiers, with 64 officers. The officers, as specified by Mac Geoghegan, were—"Walter Burke, Colonel —Owen Maccarty, Lieutenant-Colonel—Edmond Cantwel, Major—12 Captains—28 Lieutenants—28 Sub-Lieutenants—14 Ensigns." Afterwards the officers of its 2 battalions were 242, and the soldiers 1100.

THE INFANTRY REGIMENT OF CLANCARTY.

Among the earliest of the additional infantry regiments, ordered to be established, in 1688, by King James II., previous to the Revolution, was a Regiment for Colonel Roger Mac Elligot; the formation of which was commenced in the spring of that year. The Colonel was an experienced officer, who had served, on the Continent, with 1 of the 6 regiments, permitted, by King Charles II., to remain in the pay of the Dutch republic; on condition that, if those corps should be wanted at home, they should be sent back by the republic to England, upon a requisition from the Crown, to that effect. When, after having applied, without success, both to the Prince of Orange, and to the Dutch government, for the fulfilment of this agreement, King James II., by his Proclamation from Whitehall, in March, 1688, finally ordered those regiments to return home, Colonel Mac Elligot, and such as were Catholics in the regiments, naturally obeyed the Proclamation; while the Protestant officers and soldiers as naturally preferred staying in Holland, in order to form part of the expedition under the Prince of Orange, invited over by the Revolutionists of England, to aid them against the King. Roger Mac Elligot was of an ancient Munster race, the Mac Elligots or Mac Elligods, whose territory consisted of Bally-Mac-Elligod, and other possessions, in the Barony of Truchanacmy, in Kerry; a County, that supplied, during the War of the Revolution, several other eminent officers to the Irish army—such as Colonel Charles Mac Carthy More, who raised a Regiment of Foot, and so gallantly defended Carrickfergus in the summer of 1689 against the land and sea force of the Marshal Duke of Schonberg—Colonel Daniel Mac Carthy, also commander of a Regiment of Foot, with which he signalized himself, and fell, at the battle of Aughrim, in July, 1691—Brigadier Dennis Mac Gillicuddy, likewise Colonel of a Regiment of Foot, slain, shortly before, at the 2nd siege of Athlone—Maurice O'Connell of Ibrahagh, or Iveragh, and of Ash-Tower, County Dublin, Brigadier, and Colonel of Foot, killed at Aughrim—Sir Valentine Browne, 1st, and his son Nicholas 2nd, Lord Kenmare, both of whom were Colonels of Foot, and behaved well, at Aughrim, Limerick, &c. After the breaking out of the Revolution in Ireland, Colonel Mac Elligot was elected, with Cornelius Mac Gillicuddy, Esqr., to represent the Borough of Ardfert in Kerry, in the national Parliament of 1689; his Regiment of Infantry appears upon the muster-rolls of King James's army for that year; and the Comte

D'Avaux, Louis XIV.'s Ambassador to King James in Ireland, in a letter from Dublin of May 6th, referring to "M. Mac Elligott," as then "Gouverneur de Kinsal," or Kinsale, adds of him, " c'est un fort honneste homme de mes amis." In July, 1690, the Regiment of Mac Elligot was among those present at the Boyne.

In the succeeding autumn, the Colonel was stationed in Cork as its Governor, when the Earl of Marlborough (afterwards the famous Duke) landed from Portsmouth, near the town, with 9 regiments of infantry, 2 detachments of marines, and a due supply of cannon, mortars, and every thing requisite for a siege, besides ships of war, to second, by battery and bombardment from the water's edge, the operations of the army on shore. Colonel Mac Elligot had a garrison of, perhaps, 4500 men. But the town was quite unfitted for enduring a siege, from its completely commanded position in a hollow; it was inadequately supplied with ammunition; and no relief of it could be undertaken by the Duke of Berwick, in opposition to the very superior numbers, &c., of Marlborough, as reinforced and covered by Ginkell; so that nothing better was expected, on the prospect of such a siege, than that the place should be set on fire, and the garrison withdrawn. The Colonel, nevertheless, defended it from the 4th to the 8th of October; when, a breach, effected from the 7th, being about to be stormed; a bombardment going on from the sea; and only 2 small barrels of powder being left, he had to capitulate; and was conveyed, as a prisoner of war, to the Tower of London. Next year, also, or early in September, 1691, on the advance of the Williamites under Brigadier Levison to Listowell in Kerry, it is noticed, in their accounts, that among 20 Catholic or Jacobite ladies captured at Lord Kerry's, including Lady Westmeath, Lord Merrion's sister, &c., there was " the wife of Mac-Elicut, formerly Governour of Cork, and who was taken prisoner there, when the town submitted to the Earl of Marlborough." In his captivity at London, which lasted till after the Treaty of Ryswick in 1697, Colonel Mac Elligot, for nearly 4 years, or to the period of Lord Clancarty's escape from the Tower, was treated with liberality; having been allowed the range of the Tower at large, and even to go occasionally into town, for his health. But henceforth, although without having given, as *he* says, any additional cause for offence, he was kept so close a prisoner, that his constitution suffered "to the last extremity." Meantime, he was not forgotten by King James, who, at the remodelling of the Irish army on the Continent, made him Colonel to the "Régiment de *Clancarty* Infanterie." That appellation seems to have been given to the regiment from the various circumstances of its connexion with South Munster, or Desmond; *of* which the Mac Carthys, whose head was the Earl of Clancarty, were the royal tribe; *from* which nobleman's regiment some men were originally detached, to make up a regiment for Colonel Mac Elligot; and *to* which part of Ireland the Colonel himself belonged by race. This regiment, after the battle of La Hogue, in 1692, was attached to the Marshal de Catinat's army in Italy; served against the Barbets of the Alps; and was finally transferred to the Duke de Vendome's army in Catalonia, with which it assisted at the reduction of Barcelona, in 1697. Among the Irish corps broken up, by the reform of King James's troops in France, early in 1698, was the regiment of Mac Elligot. The name of Mac Elligot, besides supplying a Major-General and Baron to the military service of Austria under the Empress Maria Theresa, has been represented, to more recent times, in the service of

France, where, including a Maréchal de Camp, it contributed several officers to the Regiments of Clare, Berwick, Roscommon, &c.

The Regiment of Clancarty, or Mac Elligot, was the smallest of King James's "infantry" regiments in France. It made, in 1692, but 1 battalion, in 8 companies of 100 privates each; the officers, according to the previously mentioned infantry scale of 4 to each company, would be 32; and the whole, therefore, 832. Mac Geoghegan's later list of the officers increases them thus—"Roger Mac Elligot, Colonel—Edward Scott, Lieutenant-Colonel—Cornelius Murphy, Major—6 Captains—16 Lieutenants—16 Sub-Lieutenants—8 Ensigns." The soldiers were afterwards many less, or but 550; the officers were many more, or 121. The battalion, or regiment, consequently, as complete at first, would be 832, and, as complete at last, would be 671, strong.

THE 3 INDEPENDENT COMPANIES, &c.

The "Trois Compagnies Franches," or "3 Independent Companies" of Sutherland, Browne, and Hay, by the organization of 1692, consisted *each* of 104 soldiers, and 4 officers—viz., a Captain, Lieutenant, Sub-Lieutenant, and Ensign—the whole 3 therefore including 324 men of all ranks. By their more recent formation, the full complement of these Companies in soldiers was but 60 to each, or 180 between the 3, while their officers were altogether 21; the entire 3 thus containing 201 men of every kind. By the general reform, in 1698, among the Irish troops in France, those 3 Independent Companies, as already observed, were merged into the infantry Regiment of Berwick. When the Irish, conveyed into France after the Treaty of Limerick, were formed anew into an army for James II., those in Louis XIV.'s service, or the Brigade of Mountcashel, also underwent a change in their organization, by which the Regiments of the Lords Mountcashel and Clare were to have 3 battalions each, while the Honourable Arthur Dillon's had but 2. According to these arrangements of 1692, there were, of Irish infantry in France, counting the 2 corps of Dragoons *à pied* as such, 13 Regiments, or 25 battalions, and 3 Independent Companies, making, in round numbers, above 19,000 men; of Irish Cavalry, 2 Regiments, or 4 squadrons, and 2 Troops of Horse Guards, forming, in like manner, above 800 men; and the total of Irish infantry and cavalry consequently being upwards of 19,800 men. Of these, Louis's force, or the Brigade of Mountcashel, would be about 5000 men; so that the army of James would be more than 14,000 foot, and 800 horse. Besides these Irish military, we are informed of "une quantité prodigieuse," either attached, as volunteers, or reformed officers, to the regiments of their own nation, or serving, in the like capacity of supernumeraries, along with different *French* corps.

By the latest table I have found of the Irish troops in France, previous to the dissolution of James II.'s army there after the Peace of Ryswick, and from which table the Irish battalions appear to have been increased from 25 to 26 subsequent to 1692, by the addition of a 3rd battalion to Dillon's Regiment, the full strength of the various corps was as follows:—

INFANTRY.

	Regiments.	Battalions.	Officers and Soldiers.	
In Louis XIV.'s service.	1. Lee's	3	2013	Louis's 3 Regiments of Foot, in 9 battalions, being 6039 strong.
	2. Clare's	3	2013	
	3. Dillon's	3	2013	
In James II.'s service.	4. Guards	2	1342	James's 10 Regiments of Foot or Dismounted Dragoons, in 17 battalions, making, with 3 Independent Companies, 11,382 Infantry; his 2 Troops of Horse Guards, and 2 Regiments of Horse, of 2 squadrons each, making 944 Cavalry; and the whole being 12,326 strong.
	5. Queen's	2	1342	
	6. Marine	2	1342	
	7. Limerick	2	1342	
	8. Charlemont	2	1342	
	9. Dublin	2	1342	
	10. Athlone	2	1342	
	11. Clancarty	1	671	
	12. King's Dismounted Dragoons	1	558	
	13. Queen's Dismounted Dragoons	1	558	
		26	17,220	
	The 3 Independent Companies		201	
	Total of Infantry		17,421	

CAVALRY.

	Troops.			
	1st Troop of Horse Guards		100	
	2nd Troop of Horse Guards		100	
	Regiments.	Squadrons.		
	1. King's	2	372	
	2. Queen's	2	372	
	Total of Cavalry		944	

SUMMARY OF INFANTRY AND CAVALRY.

In *both* services.	*Infantry*, 13 Regiments (or 26 battalions) and 3 Independent Companies		17,421	Louis's force 6,039
	Cavalry, 2 Regiments (or 4 squadrons) and 2 Troops of Horse Guards		944	James's force 12,326
	Grand Total		18,365	18,365

By the extensive reform among the Irish troops in 1698, the 3 regiments, originally of Lord Mountcashel's Brigade, and the infantry, or dismounted dragoons, and detached companies of King James's army, were reduced, from 26, to but 8 battalions; each of these battalions constituting a regiment of 14 companies of 50 men per company, instead of 100 as formerly. These 8 Regiments of Foot of 1 battalion consequently mustered 700 soldiers each; giving a general total of 5600 men, besides officers. The 8 were Lee's, Clare's, Dillon's, Dorrington's, Albemarle's, Berwick's, Galmoy's, and Bourke's. The 2 Troops of Horse Guards were, as already shown, disbanded; and, instead of the 2 Regiments of Horse, but 1 regiment, of 2 squadrons, was kept up, as the Regiment of Sheldon. From what has been related of the 5 first of those infantry corps, it now only remains to give corresponding notices of Berwick's, Galmoy's, and Bourke's Regiments of Foot, and Sheldon's Regiment of Horse.

THE INFANTRY REGIMENT OF BERWICK.

This regiment, organized from what remained of the Regiment of Athlone, the King's Dismounted Dragoons, and the 3 Independent Companies of King James's army after the Peace of Ryswick, was granted, February 27th, 1698, to James Fitz-James, Duke of Berwick, natural son of James, Duke of York, subsequently King James II., by Arabella Churchill, sister of the famous John Churchill, Duke of

Marlborough. James Fitz-James was born August 21st, 1670, and educated as a Catholic in France, at the Colleges of Jully, Du Plessis, and La Fleche. In 1686, his father, then King of England, placed him under the care of an Irish officer of eminence in the Imperial service, Lieutenant-General, the Honourable Count Francis Taaffe, (brother of the Earl of Carlingford,) in order to commence his military career, against the Turks, with the Austrian army, under the Duke of Lorrain, in Hungary. He was present there, and distinguished, at the capture of Buda. Returning for the winter to England, he was created, in March, 1687, Duke of Berwick, Earl of Tinmonth, and Baron of Bosworth. He rejoined the Austrians that spring in Hungary; was commissioned, by the Emperor Leopold I., a Colonel Commandant of Taaffe's Regiment of Cuirassiers; was at the defeat of the Turks, in the battle of Mohatz; and was also made a Serjeant-General of Battle, or Major-General, by the Emperor, who gave him his picture, set in diamonds. Between this period and the Revolution in England, he was appointed Governor of Portsmouth, Lord Lieutenant of Hampshire, Colonel of the present 8th Regiment of Foot, and of the Cavalry Regiment of Oxford Blues, Captain of the 3rd Troop of Life Guards, and Knight of the Garter. On the success of the Revolution, he accompanied the King, his father, in his escape to France, in January, 1689; and thence came with him to Ireland, in March. In the campaign that followed against the Revolutionists of Ulster, he served, as Major-General, at the routing of their superior forces into Derry; signalized himself there repelling the sallies, in 1 of which he was wounded; beat a hostile party at Donegal, burning their magazines, and taking a good booty of cattle; defeated another Orange party before Enniskillen; was made Lieutenant-General; and commanded, with ability, a detachment to delay Marshal Schonberg's advance by Newry towards Dundalk, against the Irish main army, under the King. Despatched, in February, 1690, from Dublin to Cavan, with a force designed to dislodge the Revolutionists from Belturbet, he was anticipated, by their attacking him, with greater numbers, at Cavan. He repulsed them at first, but had his horse shot under him, and was afterwards compelled to retire, with his infantry, into the fort; the Revolutionists, with the smaller loss on their side, firing the town, and its magazines, yet having to return, without taking the fort, to Belturbet. In July, as Lieutenant-General, and Captain of a Troop of Horse Guards, he commanded the cavalry of the Irish right wing at the Boyne; charged and recharged the Williamite cavalry 10 times; though it was more numerous, broke it, unless when it was supported by infantry; had his horse killed, was trampled down and bruised, only rescued in the *mêlée* by a trooper; and, with the other General Officers, conducted the retreat to Dublin. In August and September, he was at the successful defence of Limerick against William III. On the Duke of Tyrconnell's departure for France in September, being left Deputy-Governor of the Jacobite territory in Ireland, he, with a body of infantry and cavalry, and 4 guns, attacked Birr Castle; but, on the advance of a very superior Williamite force against him, had to retire into Connaught. A like Williamite superiority of numbers, &c., prevented his attempting to interrupt the subsequent siege and capture of Cork and Kinsale, in October. He, nevertheless, preserved the Jacobite territory during the remainder of 1690, and till February, 1691; constantly harassing the enemy, from beyond the Shannon, with a guerilla warfare; and, in

January especially, when they collected their forces to cross that river, obliged them to retire with loss.

In February, 1691, quitting Ireland for France, he joined, as a Volunteer, the army, under Louis XIV., at the siege of Mons; signalized himself greatly in the 2 assaults upon the horn-work of that fortress; after it was taken, remained with the Marshal de Luxembourg; and likewise signalized himself at the surprise and cutting up, September 19th, of the Allied cavalry at Leuze; where he is stated to have killed an English officer who attacked him. In 1692, created Captain of the 1st Troop of Irish Horse Guards, he was to have accompanied his father, King James, with the Irish forces, to England, but for the battle of La Hogue; after which, he rejoined the French army in Flanders, and was among its most distinguished officers, in the defeat of the Allies, August 3rd, at the battle of Steinkirk. Serving as Lieutenant-General in 1693 under Luxembourg, he, at the overthrow, July 29th, of William III., in the battle of Landen, headed the attack upon the village of Nerwinden, and carried all before him, until, not being duly supported, he was overpowered, made prisoner by his uncle, Brigadier Charles Churchill, (brother of the Duke of Marlborough,) and presented to William III. Released, not long after, for the Duke of Ormonde, he, during the reduction of Charleroy by Luxembourg in September and October, sometimes mounted the trenches, and sometimes commanded the covering detachment of 17 battalions and some horse, about Mons. Employed, in 1694, under the Dauphin in Flanders, he led a column in the famous forced march from Vignamont to Pont d'Espieres, which secured French Flanders from William III. Acting, in 1695, with the same army under Marshal de Villeroy, he took several castles garrisoned by 400 men, and was at the bombardment of Bruxelles. In 1696, nominated by King James Captain-General of his Armies, he went over in disguise to London respecting a projected rising in England, to be supported by an expedition from France, for the "restoration" of the King; but had to return, without success, in the object of that hazardous journey. This, and next year, 1697, he also served in Flanders, though without being engaged in any operation of consequence. In 1698, his Troop of Irish Horse Guards being broken up, he obtained the Irish Infantry Regiment named from his English title. In 1701, he went to Rome, on the part of King James and Louis XIV., to compliment the new Pope, Clement XI., on his accession; and to offer Irish troops, under his own command, to the Pope, should he, as Louis advised, levy an army against the approaching war in Italy. Clement declined to do so, but received the Duke favourably; giving him 2000 pistoles for the expenses of his journey, 4000 pistoles for the distressed Irish Catholics or Jacobite exiles in France, and several presents for King James, his Queen, and the young Prince of Wales. In 1702, acting as Lieutenant-General under the Duke of Burgundy in Flanders, he led the pursuit of the Dutch General Ginkell from the vicinity of Cleves to Nimeguen, which cost the enemy several hundred men and horses, artillery and other carriages, besides a pillaging of their territory, to the amount of some hundred thousand crowns, and of many thousand cattle. In 1703, having served with the same army under the Marshal de Villeroy, he was named, in December, to command 18 battalions and 19 squadrons to be sent into Spain; and, the same month, after permission obtained from King James II.'s son as James III., was naturalized a Frenchman. Received in state, February 15th, 1704, at Madrid, he, as Captain-General of Spain, proceeded, March 4th, with King Philip V., to the camp. From his entering Portugal early in May, till obliged by the excessive heats to retire into quarters early in July, he made a most successful campaign, reducing above 30 of the enemy's towns; capturing 8 English, 2 German, 2 Dutch, 4 Portuguese battalions, and 18 independent companies; besides taking a very large spoil of bombs, grenades, powder, ball, small arms, saddles, &c., sent from England, 300,000 piastres in coin, and a great quantity of plate and tents; including those of the King of Portugal, and the Archduke Charles of Austria, *Pretender* to the Crown of Spain. On the renewal of active operations in September and October, the Duke's army, reduced by drafts elsewhere, was but 10,000 men. That of the King of Portugal and Austrian Archduke was above 21,400 men. With this superiority, accompanied by the figure of St. Anthony of Padua as spiritual Generalissimo of Portugal, the King and Archduke advanced from Almeida towards the Duke, defensively posted, about Ciudad Rodrigo, behind the river Agueda. There, while by various movements, and the fire of their artillery, the Allies endeavoured to dislodge the Duke, they likewise attempted to bring over his troops to the Pretender; and, at Madrid, the disadvantages under which the Duke laboured appeared to be such, that he was even ordered, not to attempt maintaining his ground. Yet he repulsed the enemy everywhere, silenced their artillery, harassed them with parties, and having smashed St. Anthony's image with a random cannon-shot, thereby rendered the superstitious Portuguese so indisposed for further active service, that, before the middle of October, their main force retreated, covered by the English and Dutch, into winter quarters; the rest, that had laid siege to Valencia d'Alcantara, being also subsequently compelled to retire.

Receiving, in November, from Philip V., at Madrid, the insignia of the Order of the Golden Fleece, the Duke returned to France; in February, 1705, was made Commander in Languedoc, to appease the troubles, renewed there, among the Camisards, or revolted Huguenots, by emissaries from the Allies; and, having suppressed those disturbances, he was, in October, selected to reduce Nice. It ranked among the first fortresses in Europe; was situated on a lofty rock, accessible only on 1 side; there and elsewhere strengthened by works, which cost a vast sum; was furnished with an experienced Governor, and garrison of 2000 men; and supplied with about 100 cannon, and other requisites in proportion. To attack the place, secure his rear, and work 86 cannon or mortars, the Duke had only about 5000 men, and the operations consumed above 60,000 cannon-shot, 8000 bombs, and 700,000 pounds weight of powder, until January 5th, 1706, when the fort capitulated. February 15th, created Marshal of France, he, on the 20th, was named to command in Spain, against the Portuguese, English, and Dutch, and, March 12th, reached Madrid. The Allies having assembled their army of 45 battalions and 56 squadrons, he arrived at Badajos, the 27th, to oppose them. But, after throwing 8 battalions into Alcantara, which was betrayed to the enemy, the Marshal was left only 30 squadrons, subsequently reinforced by 8 battalions!—or too small a force to attempt anything beyond manœuvring, to delay, as long as possible, the Allies' advance to Madrid. They entered it, June 25th, under Lord Galway and the Marquis de Lasminas; and were to be joined there by the Austrian Archduke, as Charles III., and by Lord Peterborough, with more troops. But the Marshal, previously joined by King Philip, was supplied from the Castiles, Andalusia, &c., with a force, whose operations, aided by the loyal peasantry, or guerillas, rendered Madrid and the surrounding country so untenable, that, before the Archduke could arrive, or early in August, that metropolis was recovered; the enemy during their stay, and in their subsequent retreat out of Castile, having numbers of their troops cut off or taken, with quantities of baggage, and several convoys intercepted, including 1 with Lord Peterborough's plate, &c., and 100,000 pieces of 8. The reduction of above 200 cities, burghs, or villages, in Valencia and Murcia, among which was that of Carthagena on November 18th, completed the Marshal's achievements in this campaign, that, without a battle, cost the enemy a loss, in prisoners alone, of 10,000 men. Continuing to command the French and Spanish armies against the Allies, under Lord Galway, the Marshal gained his greatest victory at the battle of Almanza, April 25th, 1707, where, with only about 2000 men killed or wounded, he destroyed, or made prisoners, not less than 13,000 English, Dutch, and Portuguese; taking 120 military ensigns, all the hostile artillery, &c. For this signal success, which led to the recovery of almost the whole of Valencia and Aragon, the Marshal was rewarded, soon after the action, by King Philip; who conferred upon him the former appenages of the 2nd sons of the Kings of Aragon, or the cities of Liria and Xerica in Valencia, with their dependencies, accompanied by the title, from those places, of Duke, and the dignity of Grandee of the First Class, for himself and his descendants. After further conquests in Valencia, including, May 6th, that of its capital, the Marshal was to join the Duke of Orleans, for the siege of the strong fortress of Lerida; which, from various causes, could not be commenced until October 2nd, but was successfully terminated, November 11th. The 24th, the Marshal was made Governor of the Limousin by Louis XIV. Appointed in May, 1708, to command the Army of the Rhine under the Elector of Bavaria, he supplied Fort Louis with additional artillery, rendered the lines along the river secure, and was transferred, for the rest of the campaign, to Flanders.

From 1709 to 1712, except while for some time, and not as General-in-Chief, in Flanders, he commanded the Army of Dauphiné, or that on the frontiers of Piedmont, for the protection of the southern provinces of France against the Piedmontese and Germans, under the Duke of Savoy and the Imperial Generals. The Marshal's arrangements for this purpose were so excellent, that, while he spared for other services so many as 20 battalions from the force considered requisite for him, he was able to baffle all the designs of enemies, much superior in number. Hence, in France, these campaigns were esteemed masterpieces of defensive tactics, while the Marshal's opponent, the Duke of Savoy, observed of him, in reference to them, that "He had never beheld any one manœuvre so well, or make war so skilfully, or so nobly." In the winter of 1709, the Marshal was granted by Louis XIV. the lordship of Warty, the name being changed to that of Fitz-James, and was further nominated a Peer of France, under the title of Duke of Fitz-James; the royal letters patent, to that effect, being dated in May, 1710. In 1712, Girona having been so blocked up by the Count de Stahremberg, as to be reduced to great extremities, the Marshal was commissioned, in November, to relieve it from France; which he accomplished, early in January, 1713. In September, 1714, his services to the Crown of Spain were completed by the reduction of Barcelona, after a resistance so obstinate, that, between besiegers and besieged, the loss amounted to about 16,000 killed or wounded. For this achievement, Philip V. granted him a pension of 100,000 livres a year, and sent him a sword, adorned with diamonds of very great value. In April, 1716, the Marshal was nominated Commander in Guyenne. War having broken out with Spain in 1719, he reduced Fontarabia in June, St. Sebastian in August, Urgel in October; and, peace occurring in 1720, he was elected, for his services, a Member of the Council of Regency, under Louis XV.'s minority. In 1721, he was intrusted with the command over Guyenne, Bearn, Navarre, the Limousin, Auvergne, Bourbonnais, Forez, Rousillon, and part of Vivarais, in order to arrest the progress of the plague beyond the southern provinces of France, and most ably achieved that very important object. He was made Chevalier of the Order of the Holy Ghost, and of the Orders of the King, in June, 1724, and Governor of Strasburgh, in April, 1730. Chosen to command upon the Rhine, in 1733, when hostilities broke out between France and Austria, he crossed that river about the middle of October; from the 14th invested Fort Kehl, and occupied it, the 29th. In May, 1734, he passed the lines of Etlingen, considered so impregnable by the minor German powers, as to have mainly influenced them to take part with the Emperor Charles VI. against France. Early in June, he opened trenches before Philipsburgh, and, the 12th, visiting the works, about 7 in the morning, he ascended a portion of them, best situated for judging what was fittest to be done, though most dangerous, as exposed to the cannon of *both* sides, when a French and German battery, firing at the same time, a ball, it is uncertain from which, swept off his head, in his 64th year.

The Marshal Duke of Berwick was 1 of those commanders of whom it is the highest eulogium to say, that to such, in periods of adversity, it is safest to intrust the defence of a state. Of the great military leaders of whose parentage England can boast, he may be ranked, with his uncle, Marlborough, among the first. But, to his uncle, as well as to most public characters, he was very superior, as a man of principle. The Regent Duke of Orleans, whose extensive acquaintance with human nature attaches a suitable value to his opinion, observed—"*If* ever there was a perfectly honest man in the world, it was the Marshal Duke of Berwick." In France, he was compared for his virtues, his abilities, and the manner of his death, to the illustrious Marshal de Turenne. In Spain, his name, with the triumphs of Almanza and Barcelona, was stamped upon her military annals for ever. In England, his loss was felt, in proportion to the value of his achievements to her enemies. "He left, indeed, behind him," writes Lord Mahon, "a most brillian military reputation; and, though his whole career was passed in the service of France, yet may England, as his birth-place, and as his father's kingdom, claim some share of his glory as her's; and, while she deplores the defeat of her arms at Almanza, proudly remember, that the blow was struck by an English hand." In Ireland, with which he was variously connected, through his early services, his marriage, and his regiment, he was always remembered with respect, and regarded with hope, by the old population of the country, suffering under the oppression of the Revolution; and was celebrated, in Gaelic verse, as the "victorious hand of the battles," and "cause of joy to Inisfail." He was an excellent husband, father, and friend, an enemy to vanity or ostentation, a lover of truth, and very generous, indeed too much so for his means, to those in need, especially the exiled Jacobites. He was fond of gardening, and of reading, and was the friend of learned men—among whom were Lord Bolingbroke, the President de Montesquieu, and our accomplished countryman, Count Anthony Hamilton*—and he left Memoirs of his life in French, down to 1716, in a clear, concise, unaffected style. In person, his figure was noble, and his stature and air commanding. "I," adds Montesquieu, "have seen, at a distance, in the works of Plutarch, what great men *were;* in Marshal Berwick, I have seen what they *are!*"

The Duke was 1st married, at St. Germain, in 1695, to the widow of Patrick Sarsfield, Earl of Lucan, originally Lady Honor de Burgo, 2nd daughter of William, 7th Earl of Clanricarde. She died, January 16th, 1698, at Pezenas, in Languedoc, to the great grief of her husband; who had her heart preserved in a silver box, and her remains suitably interred, the next month, at Pontoise, with the following epitaph by Father Gelasius Mac Mahon, head of the old chieftain-race of Mac Mahon of Monaghan, and brother of Colonel Art Mac Mahon, killed at the last siege of Athlone.

> "*Perspice quisquis ades, memorique ex Marmore disce,*
> *Gemma sub hoc Tumulo quam pretiosa jacet,*
> *Inclyta Stirpe Ducum, Regalis Sanguinis Auctrix,*
> *Lecta Ducis Conjux, Principe digna Parens.*
> Clanrickard *Natam,* Ormond, *& Clancartiæ Neptem,*
> Berwici *Dominam,* plorat Jerna *Nurum.*
> *Integritas, Virtus, florensque Modestia Morum,*
> *Gaudia sunt Cœlo, cætera Luctus habet.*
> Pontis *Sacra Domus commissum Pignus honora,*
> *Mortua demeritas poscit* Honora *Vices.*"

By this lady, the Duke had, October 21st, 1696, 1 son, James Francis Fitz-James, Marquis of Tinmouth, to whom, after having served 2 campaigns with him, he transferred his regiment, in May, 1713. The young Marquis was at the reduction of Barcelona in 1714, and held the regiment until 1716. Then, for having accompanied King James II.'s son to Scotland against George I., with whom France was at peace, the regiment was taken from the Marquis. It was given back to his father, who established him that year in Spain, by a marriage with Dona Catarina de Portugal, heiress to the Duke de Varaguas, and by settling upon him the Duchies of Liria and Xerica. There, in addition to his titles of Duke of Berwick, Liria, and Xerica, Earl of Tinmouth, Baron of Bosworth, and Grandee of the 1st Class, he was a Chamberlain to his Catholic Majesty, a Knight of the Golden Fleece, and of the Russian Orders of St. Andrew, and St. Alexander, Colonel of the Irish Regiment of Limerick, a Lieutenant-General; and, after having been Ambassador to Russia, where he obtained the 2 Orders of Knighthood last-mentioned, he was likewise appointed Ambassador to Naples, where he died, June 1st, 1738; leaving 2 sons, the succeeding Duke of Berwick and Liria, &c., and Don Pedro Fitz-James, an Admiral in the Spanish service. The Marshal next gave his regiment to the eldest son of his 2nd marriage with Anne, daughter of the Honourable Henry Bulkeley, in 1700—the Duke of Fitz-James, born in 1702. The Duke was Colonel till his death in 1721, with the rank of Mestre de Camp d'Infanterie. His brother, the Lord Henri de Fitz-James, succeeded in command of the corps till December, 1729; when he, too, was followed, as Colonel, by his brother, the Comte Edouard de Fitz-James; who, after serving, first in the

---

* Author of the Memoirs of Grammont, &c.

wars of Germany, then of Flanders, and finally of Germany again, from 1733 to 1758, died in May, that year, at Cologne, a Lieutenant-General. The regiment devolved, the same month, to Charles, Duke of Fitz-James, born in 1712; enrolled in the Mousquetaires in 1730; distinguished in the Continental wars last referred to; Marshal of France in 1775; and deceased in 1787. In 1783, his son, Jean Charles de Fitz-James, subsequently Duke, and Maréchal de Camp, from Lieutenant-Colonel became Colonel-Proprietor of the corps, and was so until the Revolution, by which he was obliged to quit France; and, in 1791, the old appellation, from 1698, of the "Regiment of Berwick," was changed for that of the 88th Regiment of Infantry—the number, also, it may be remarked, of another Irish Regiment of Infantry, or the Connaught Rangers, 1 of the most celebrated in the army of Great Britain and Ireland.

THE INFANTRY REGIMENT OF GALMOY.

Of the Irish descended from the Norman conquerors of England, no name ranks higher than that of Le Botiler, or Butler. A learned writer on "Feudal Dignities in Ireland," notes—"That 25 patents, ennobling various branches of the house, have issued from the Crown, amongst which may be enumerated, not only Peerages of England and Ireland, but also of Wales and Scotland; and that, of no other family, do so many ancient baronial and castellated mansions still remain, as of the house of Butler in Ireland." It has been represented, in the Peerage of Ireland, by the titles of Ormonde, Dunboyne, Cahir, Mountgarret, Ikerrin, and Galmoy. The heads of all these ennobled houses, except that of Ormonde, as well as various untitled, though distinguished, branches of the Butlers, fought for King James, in the War of the Revolution; among whom were several Colonels. Of those officers, the most eminent was Lord Galmoy. Pierce Butler, 3rd Viscount Galmoy, in the County of Kilkenny, and Earl of Newcastle, was born, March 21st, 1652. He was the son of Edward, 2nd Viscount Galmoy, by Ellinor, daughter of Charles White, Esq. of Leixlip Castle,* in the County of Kildare, and widow of Sir Arthur Ashton, Governor of Drogheda, slain, in the massacre there, under Oliver Cromwell, in 1649. The house of Galmoy suffered much, in those calamitous times, for its adherence to the Crown against the Parliamentarian and Cromwellian revolutionists. The heir to the title, taken prisoner, in 1650, as a Captain of horse in the royal army, was killed, after quarter, and the family-property was seized by the rebels, until the extinction of their usurpation, by the re-establishment of the Monarchy. In August, 1677, Pierce, the representative of the title here treated of, was created a Doctor of Laws of the University of Oxford, under the Chancellorship of the great head of his name, the Duke of Ormonde. In the reign of King James II., his Lordship was a Privy Counsellor of Ireland, Lord Lieutenant of the County of Kilkenny, and Colonel of the 2nd Regiment of Horse in the Irish army. He served with distinction, especially at the Boyne and Aughrim, through the War of the Revolution, in the course of which he was a Brigadier, and Major-General of Horse; was 1 of the Commissioners to the Treaty of Limerick, on behalf of his Catholic countrymen in 1691; and, though he had been

* See the note on this family under the King's Regiment of Dismounted Dragoons.

attainted for his loyalty by the Revolutionists, might have gotten back his estate of several thousand plantation acres in the Counties of Kilkenny and Wexford, (or nearly 10,000 in the former, and about 5000 in the latter,) had he consented to remain at home, instead of following King James to France, and inducing others to do so likewise. On the re-arrangement there of the Irish troops in 1692, he was made Colonel of the 2nd or Queen's Regiment of Horse. He served with it that year on the coasts of Normandy, for the proposed invasion of England, to restore the King; and at the siege of Roses, in 1693. Created Brigadier by brevet (in the service of France), April 28th, 1694, he was attached that year to the Army of Germany; to the Army of the Moselle, under the Marquis d'Harcourt in 1695; to the Army of the Meuse, under the Marshal de Boufflers in 1696; and again to the Army of the Moselle, under the Marquis d'Harcourt in 1697. His Lordship's horse regiment being broken up by the general reduction among the Irish forces in 1698, he was compensated by orders of February 27th-28th; according to which the remains of the Infantry Regiment of Charlemont and the Queen's Dismounted Dragoons were formed into a Regiment of Foot, as that of Galmoy. Employed with the Army of Italy in 1701, he was present at the combats of Carpi and Chiari. In 1702, he fought at the affair of Santa-Vittoria and at the battle of Luzzara; and was made Maréchal de Camp or Major-General (in the service of France) by brevet of December 3rd, that year. Attached, with this rank, to the Army of Germany in 1703, he was at the sieges of Brisach and Landau, and at the battle of Spire.

Detained by sickness from taking the field in 1704, and not having been made a Lieutenant-General in France, he passed into Spain, where he obtained that grade from Philip V., in March, 1705, served that campaign in Italy, and signalized himself greatly at the battle of Cassano. In 1706, he likewise signalized himself at the battle of Calcinato, and was present at the unfortunate siege and battle of Turin. He was attached to the Army of the Rhine in 1708; to the Army of Dauphiné in 1709; and, from 1710 to 1712, to the Army of Flanders; serving, the last-mentioned year, at the sieges of Douay, Quesnoy, and Bouchain. He was employed in Spain in 1713, and was at the reduction of Barcelona in 1714. After the general peace, the "Régiment de Galmoy" was dissolved, and incorporated with that of Dillon, by order of January 30th, 1715. In 1722, Lord Galmoy, returning from Spain to France, obtained, May 10th, the rank of Lieutenant-General there also; to date from March 1st, 1705, the period of his appointment to the same grade in Spain. His Lordship died in his 89th year, at Paris, June 18th, 1740. He had been 1st Lord of the Bedchamber to King James II. at St. Germain, and had married a daughter of Toby Matthew, Esq. of Thomastown, County of Tipperary; but survived his son, who was slain, without issue, in 1709, at the battle of Malplaquet. The successive claimants of the title of Galmoy were, down to the Revolution, officers in France; in whose armies, as well as in others, various gentlemen have honourably represented a name, of which the illustrious General Lafayette is related to have said, in the war for the Independence of the United States of America, that "whenever he wanted anything well done, he got a BUTLER to do it."

THE INFANTRY REGIMENT OF BOURKE, &c.

By the general reform among King James's troops in 1698, the remains of the Infantry Regiment of Athlone, or that of Bourke, having been united with those of other corps, to make a Regiment of Infantry for the Duke of Berwick, Colonel Walter Bourke was only attached, as a secondary or reformed Colonel, to the new corps, until June 18th, 1699, when he was commissioned, as Colonel of another Irish Regiment of Infantry, to be called by his name. He joined the Army of Italy with it in 1701, and fought at Chiari. He was at the battle of Luzzara in 1702, and at the invasion of the Trentin, and the combats of Santa Vittoria and San Benedetto, in 1703. Brigadier by brevet, February 10th, 1704, he served that and the ensuing year at the sieges of Vercelli, of Ivrea, of Verrua, and at the battle of Cassano. In 1706, he was at the siege and battle of Turin. Removed from Italy to Spain, he contributed to the reduction of Lerida in 1707, and of Tortosa, and several other places, in 1708. Maréchal de Camp by brevet, March 20th, 1709, he remained that year in Spain, under the Marshal de Besons, who kept on the defensive. He passed, in 1710, into Dauphiné, where, and in Provence, he served, under the Duke of Berwick, until 1712; upon the frontiers of Spain in 1713; and at the capture of Barcelona in 1714. After the general peace, apprehending, from the changes which were to occur among the Irish troops in France, that his regiment would be disbanded, and himself and his corps being so well known in Spain where they had made several campaigns, he, with the permission of Louis XIV., proposed to Philip V., to pass into his service. The offer was favourably received by the Spanish Monarch; but, before the matter could be concluded, Major-General Count Walter Bourke (or, as he signed himself in France, "De Bourke,") died at Barcelona, in March, 1715. By his marriage with Catherine, daughter of John Nolan, Esq. of Iniscrowen, he had a son, Rickard, or Richard, a Captain in France,* besides daughters; 1 of whom was wife there to the son of Sir Richard Nagle, King James II.'s Attorney-General, and Secretary of State and War, for Ireland.

In March, 1715, the late Regiment of Bourke was granted to its Lieutenant-Colonel, Francis Wauchop. This Scotch veteran had held the like grade, during the War of the Revolution in Ireland, in the Ulster Infantry Regiment of Brian Macgennis, Lord Iveagh, as well as, after the Treaty of Limerick, in the Queen's (or Luttrell's) Regiment of Infantry, when he was appointed Lieutenant-Colonel to the Regiment of Bourke. Having commanded, and been wounded with it, at the

---

* Of the old Norman Irish name of the deceased Major-General and Colonel of the Regiment of Bourke, there were, among the Irish troops in France, various officers in the Regiments of Dublin, Albemarle, Dillon, Berwick, Lally, and Walsh. Next to *Walter*, the most eminent, in Louis XIV.'s wars, was *Michael*. Having been a reformed Lieutenant-Colonel attached to the Regiment of Albemarle, (subsequently that of Fitz-Gerald and O'Donnell) he was made Lieutenant-Colonel by commission, September 3rd, 1702. He was that year at the battle of Luzzara, and thenceforward till 1706 served in the Trentin, at the sieges of Nago, Arco, Vercelli, Ivrea, Verrua, and the battles of Cassano and Turin. In Flanders, from 1707 to 1712, he was at the battles of Oudenarde and Malplaquet, the attack of Arleux, obtaining, by brevet of July 20th, 1711, the grade of Brigadier, and acted as such, at the successful affair of Denain, and sieges of Douay and Quesnoy. Transferred in 1713 to Germany, he took part in the reduction of Landau and Friburgh; and, after the reform of the Regiment of O'Donnell, in 1715, served no more.

famous affair of Cremona, in February, 1702, he was granted the brevet-rank of Colonel; and, as such, he is mentioned among the officers of the Irish Brigade, captured at sea by the English, in March, 1708, on board 1 of the vessels accompanying the son of King James II. to Scotland. The proposal made by Bourke being finally accepted of under his Scotch successor, that officer passed, in June, 1715, with the regiment, into Spain. There, apparently in reference to its late Colonel, and to its composition, through a corresponding connexion with Connaught, it was entitled the Regiment of Connacia. Having fought with distinction in Sicily, in Africa, and finally in Italy, in the war of 1733, it was given by the King of Spain to his son, the King of Naples; was there variously styled the King's Regiment, and the King's Irish Regiment; its published strength, in 1741, being 2 battalions, each 650 strong, and subsequently 4 battalions. Into this service, as previously intimated, another Irish corps in Spain, or the Regiment of Limerick, commanded by the Marshal Duke of Berwick's eldest son, the Duke of Berwick and Liria, &c., was likewise transferred; and, from some of the officers of these regiments, it would seem, that the illustrious Corsican patriot, Pascal Paoli, when an officer, too, at Naples, attained his 1st knowledge of English. "I asked him," says Mr. Boswell in 1765, "if he understood English? He immediately began, and spoke it, which he did tolerably well. When at Naples, he had known several Irish gentlemen, who were officers in that service. Having a great facility in acquiring languages, he learned English from *them*."

THE HORSE REGIMENT OF SHELDON, &c.

The Colonel of this corps, Dominick Sheldon, an English Catholic gentleman, was of an ancient family, whose earliest progenitor, Anselme de Sheldon, so called from Sheldon in Warwickshire, is mentioned in the reign of King Henry III. In later times, the name was distinguished for fidelity to King Charles II. against Oliver Cromwell, and to King James II. against the Prince of Orange. Dominick Sheldon first served abroad, among the troops sent by King Charles II. to aid Louis XIV. against the Dutch. With these, a Lieutenant, February 1st, 1673, in the Regiment of James, Duke of Monmouth, he was, that year, at the siege of Maestricht. Removed, in 1674, to Germany, he fought at Sintzheim, Einsheim, and Mulhausen; at Turkheim, and Consarbrick, in 1675; and in Flanders, at the sieges of Condé, Bouchain, and Aire, in 1676. His regiment being reformed in 1678, he returned to England. Shortly after the accession of King James II., he appears in the Irish army, as a Captain in the King's Regiment of Infantry, or Royal Irish Foot Guards under the Duke of Ormonde; then, or in 1685-6, as having exchanged into, and become Lieutenant-Colonel of, the Horse Regiment of Richard Talbot, Earl of Tyrconnell; and, in 1687, he obtained, through the Earl's interest with the King, a pension of £200 per annum from the Irish Concordatum Fund. A Brigadier at the commencement of the War of the Revolution in Ireland, he served with credit throughout that contest, in which he became Major-General of Cavalry; particularly distinguished himself at the Boyne, where he had 2 horses killed under him; on the Duke of Tyrconnell's departure for France after William III.'s defeat at Limerick, was 1 of the 12 Counsellors of

State left to assist the Duke of Berwick in the government and defence of the Jacobite territory; and, after the Treaty of Limerick in 1691, commanded the 1st body of the Irish troops who went to France. On the new formation of the Irish army there in 1692, he was created Colonel of the 1st or King's Regiment of Horse. He had a commission February 11th, 1693, from Louis XIV. to rank as Mestre de Camp de Cavalerie. Brigadier, also, by brevet, March 3rd, 1694, he served that year with the Army of Germany; with the Army of the Meuse in 1696; with the Army of the Moselle in 1697.

After the Peace of Ryswick, or early in 1698, the 2 Irish, or King's and Queen's, Regiments of Horse, in France, were formed into 1, as that of Sheldon; the Colonel's commission being dated February 15th, that year. His name and regiment are mentioned, 1st with the Army of Germany, and afterwards with the Army of Italy, in 1701; towards the close of which, or in December, the corps was distinguished against the Imperialists, between Mantua and Cremona. Maréchal de Camp by brevet, January 29th, 1702, and attached, by letters of February 21st, to the same Army, he was wounded, cutting up the Austrian cuirassiers, in July, at Santa Vittoria. From this period I do not find him regularly employed; probably from his being chiefly engaged in the service of *his* Sovereign, the son of King James II. But he was made, October 26th, 1704, a Lieutenant-General; parted with his regiment, in January, 1706; appears to have been among the General Officers to accompany his Sovereign to Scotland in 1708; to have been taken prisoner, previous to the battle of Malplaquet in 1709; and to have been soon released. He went with James to Scotland in 1715; after the failure of the Jacobite rising there, returned, with him, to France, in 1716; and died, in 1721. The name of Sheldon—or, as it was sometimes written in France, "Scheldon"—is to be found in the Regiment of Dillon down to the Revolution, as well as in the ranks of Maréchal de Camp, or Major-General, and Lieutenant-General.

The successor to Dominick Sheldon, in the Colonelship of his regiment, was Christopher Nugent, Esq. of Dardistown, County of Meath. The origin of the Nugents is traced to 1 of the leading French or Norman conquerors of England; whose descendant, in the following century, was the Chevalier Gilbert de Nogent, or Nugent. He came over, under Henry II., to Ireland, with the famous Chevalier Hugue de Lacie, or Lacy; married his sister Rose; and was granted, by that powerful feudal intruder in Midhe, or Meath, the country of Dealbhna, or Delvin, the ancient territory of the O'Finnallans,* as a Barony, to be held, with the exception of certain ecclesiastical property, by a service of 5 knights' fees. In this considerable territory, Gilbert provided for his brothers and other followers; from which period, the race of the Nugents has extended into several honourable branches; the principal being that of the Barons of Delvin, additionally ennobled, since 1621, as Earls of Westmeath. The head of the next greatest branch, that of Moyrath and Dardistown, County of Meath, or Thomas Nugent, Esq., was, the same

---

* The O'Finnallans were of remote Munster or Dalcassian origin. Their last Chief in Delvin was Ceallach, or Kellagh, mentioned in 1174. Since then, those of the race, under the oddly-modernized name of *Fenelon*, have been "in a state of obscurity and poverty;" and Dr. O'Donovan adds, that, when he "examined the Barony of Delvin in 1837, he did not find many of this family in their original locality."

year, created a Baronet; whose 2 sons were Sir Robert, as next Baronet, and Francis of Dardistown. The latter, by Lady Bridget Dongan, sister of William, Earl of Limerick, had 3 sons, officers in Ireland and France; the 2 younger already noticed, under the King's Regiment of Dismounted Dragoons, and the eldest, Christopher of Dardistown, our present subject. Among the distinguished representatives of the name of Nugent in the War of the Revolution—of whom may be mentioned Thomas Nugent, 4th Earl of Westmeath, first Colonel of Foot, next of Horse—his brother, the Honourable John Nugent, afterwards Major-General of Cavalry, and Earl—their uncle, the Honourable William Nugent, Member for Westmeath, Lord Lieutenant of the County of Longford, Colonel, and Brigadier of Infantry—Sir Thomas Nugent, 3rd Baronet, of Moyrath, and Richard Nugent, Esq., both Colonels of Infantry—Walter Nugent, Colonel of Dragoons, &c.—was the head of the house of Dardistown. He was member for the Borough of Fore in the Parliament of 1689; attained the rank of Lieutenant-Colonel of Cavalry; was attached to the 1st Troop of the Irish Horse Guards in 1691; after the Treaty of Limerick, refused, on condition of remaining in Ireland, the offer of his estate, though it was a very considerable one; and went to France.

He was appointed there to be the officer in command of the 2 Troops of Irish Horse Guards; served on the coasts or in Flanders in 1692, and in 1693, when he was wounded at Landen; acted with the Army of Germany in 1694; and with the Army of the Moselle in 1695. He was commissioned May 25th, that year, to hold rank, as a Mestre de Camp de Cavalerie, among the troops of France; and was employed with the Army of the Moselle, in 1696 and 1697. The 2 Troops of King James's Horse Guards being disbanded, February 27th, 1698, he was attached, as a reformed Mestre de Camp, to the new Regiment of Sheldon, by order of March. He joined the Army of Italy, with this regiment, in July, 1701, and was present at the combat of Chiari, in September. He fought at the battle of Luzzara, in August, 1702; was with the Army of Germany, and very distinguished, and wounded, at the battle of Spire, in November, 1703; and was with the Army of Flanders, in 1704 and 1705. By the retirement of Colonel Sheldon, he obtained his regiment, June 16th, 1706; changed its name to that of Nugent; and commanded it in Flanders till 1711; during which 6 campaigns, he fought at the battles of Ramillies, Oudenarde, and Malplaquet. Employed, by order of October 29th, 1711, at Calais, during the winter of 1711-12, he was present, the latter year, at the attack of Denain and the siege of Douay. Transferred to the Army of Germany, he was at the sieges of Friburgh and Landau, and the defeat of General Vaubonne in 1713, and at the camp of the Lower Meuse in 1714. Having, without permission from the French Government, accompanied King James II.'s son into Scotland in 1715-16 against the Elector of Hanover as George I., he was, on the remonstrance of the British Ambassador in Paris, deprived of his regiment; though only in such a manner as to save appearances. He was made by brevet of September 13th, 1718, Maréchal de Camp or Major-General of Horse, to take rank from the promotion of March 8th preceding. He did not serve afterwards, and died June 4th, 1731. Major-General Christopher Nugent was 1 of the most eminent officers of a name, which, besides himself, and several gallant gentlemen of inferior rank, gave, to the service of France, a Major-General of Cavalry in the

Honourable John Nugent, finally 5th Earl of Westmeath—a Lieutenant-General of Cavalry in the Chevalier and Baronet Peter de Nugent—a Major-General to the service of Venice in Christopher Nugent of Upper Killasonna, County of Longford—and, to Austria, furnished, with other distinguished officers, a companion to her Field-Marshals of Irish parentage, in Laval, Count and Prince Nugent, of the house of Bracklyn and Balnacarrow,* derived, through the branch of Dromeng, from the 15th Baron of Delvin, and 1st Earl of Westmeath. Major-General and Colonel Christopher Nugent of Dardistown, by his marriage with the Lady Bridget Barnewall, 2nd daughter of Robert, 9th Lord Trimleston, had a son, the Comte de Nugent, to whom, in 1716, when only between 16 and 17 years of age, his father's fine regiment was transferred.

It remained under that son's command, and continued to bear his family name, until 1733, when he resigned it to the Comte Charles de Fitz-James, who was commissioned, March 16th, as Colonel of the corps, henceforth known as that of Fitz-James; was finally Marshal of France, and, as already mentioned, was also Colonel of the Regiment of Berwick. By this nobleman, the Regiment of Fitz-James was granted, February 10th, 1759, to his son Jean Charles de Fitz-James, afterwards Marechal de Camp, Duke of Fitz-James, and likewise Colonel of the Regiment of Berwick. Under the Colonelship of this nobleman, the Regiment of Fitz-James was disbanded, December 21st, 1762, after, says the account, "it had served very gloriously, on all occasions." †

* This illustrious officer, born in Ireland in 1777, entered the Austrian service in 1794, and died on his estate in Croatia in 1863, or his 86th year. Besides being a Field-Marshal and Proprietor of the 30th Regiment of Infantry in Austria, he was a Count, Imperial Chamberlain, Counsellor of State, and Knight of the Golden Fleece; he was likewise a Roman Prince, a Magnate of Hungary, a Croatian Stelnick; and held the rank, in the British service, of a Lieutenant-General. I had the honour of an introduction to him, when he was last in Ireland.

† By *far* the most difficult portion of this work to write has been that, commenced in the *preceding*, and generally concluded in the *present*, Book—or the portion devoted to the history of the several regiments, and the family particulars respecting their commanding officers. The wide extent of Irish, British, and Continental information, printed and manuscript, which that portion involved, histories, memoirs, peerages, magazines, pamphlets, gazettes, state-papers, or letters, squibs of the day, traditions, have been so generally referred to in my volume of 1854 on the Brigade, as to dispense with the cost of a reprinting or rehashing of them, on the present occasion.

HISTORY OF THE IRISH BRIGADES

IN

THE SERVICE OF FRANCE.

BOOK III.

FROM the foregoing details respecting the different Irish corps in France, except that of Colonel Lally, to be more particularly noticed hereafter along with the account of his services, it appears, that there were, in French pay, from 1690 to 1692, 3 Regiments of Infantry—from 1692 to 1698, including Mountcashel's Brigade, King James's army from Limerick, &c., and counting Dismounted Dragoons as Infantry, there were 13 Regiments of Infantry, (in 25 or 26 battalions,) and 3 Independent Companies, 2 Regiments of Horse, and 2 Troops of Horse Guards—from 1698 to about the middle of 1699, there were 7 Regiments of Infantry, and 1 Regiment of Cavalry, and, from the remainder of that year to 1714, 8 Regiments of Infantry, and 1 Regiment of Cavalry—from 1714 to 1744, 5 Regiments of Infantry and 1 Regiment of Cavalry—from 1744 to 1762, 6 Regiments of Infantry and 1 Regiment of Cavalry—from 1762 to 1775, 5 Regiments of Infantry—and from 1775 to 1791, 3 Regiments of Infantry. The existence of so considerable an Irish force in France, for a century after the Treaty of Limerick, proceeded, at first, from the attachment of the mass of the Irish people, as Catholics, to the representative of the Stuart dynasty, as deriving his origin from the old Monarchs of Erin,* as also a Catholic, as excluded on *that* account, from the Crown, and as the only source from which, through a recovery of that Crown, anything better was to be expected, than a continuance of the Cromwel-

* Consult, on this point, among other authorities which might be referred to, the following curious work, by a County Limerick gentleman of ancient native origin, who, after he had held office under King James II.'s government in Ireland, retired with that Monarch to France. "A Chronological, Genealogical, and Historical Dissertation of the Royal Family of the Stuarts, beginning with Milesius, the Stock of those they call the Milesian Irish, and of the old Scotish Race; and ending with his present Majesty K. James the 3rd of England and Ireland, and of Scotland the 8th. By Mathew Kennedy, Doctor of Laws, Master of the High Court of Chancery, and Judge of the Admiralty of all Ireland. Printed in Paris by Lewis Coignard, Printer and Bookseller in St. James-street at the Eagle d'Or, 1705. With Privilege." The Irish Jacobite Doctor's work, in which the pedigree of King James II.'s son is traced not only to the Ard-Righs or Monarchs of Erin, but to the Kings of Ulster, Leinster, Connaught, and Munster, concludes thus—"And here I end this young Prince's genealogy, as well preserv'd and prov'd as any that can be found in profane history or records; with a hearty prayer to the Holy Trinity, on whose festivity he was born, that he may be speedily establish'd in the safe possession of his Crowns, and all the rights of his Royal Predecessors, to the satisfaction of his loyal subjects, and the confusion of his obstinate enemys; and that from his loins may spring as long a train of Kings and Princes, as this, from which he derives his most noble bloud and extraction."

lian system of legalized land-usurpation and upstart sectarian "ascendancy," imposed, after the Restoration, upon Ireland, by the odious Acts of Settlement and Explanation,* and rendered *worse* by the results of the subsequent Williamite revolution. But the resort of so many Irish to the French service, so long after the great emigration from Limerick, though *partly* owing to the feelings which occasioned that emigration, was still *more* owing to such oppressive religious and commercial legislation, as left multitudes in Ireland no better means of escaping the fate of unemployed poverty at home, than emigration to obtain a livelihood by military service abroad. Thus, to an English writer, denouncing, in 1730, the idea of any countenance being given in Ireland to recruiting there by the Kings of France or Spain, Swift replied—"Supposing that these 2 potentates will only desire leave to carry off 6,000 men, between them, to France and Spain, then, by computing the maintenance of a tall, hungry Irishman, in food and clothes, to be only at £5 a head, here will be £30,000 per annum *saved* clear to the nation; for they *can find no other employment at home, beside begging, robbing, and stealing!*" Consequently, adds the Dean, in the same vein of bitter sarcasm, justified by the miserable condition to which his country was reduced—"If 30, 40, or 50,000, which we would gladly spare, were sent on the same errand, what an immense *profit* it must be to us!" The general position of the Catholics and Protestants in Ireland, from the termination of the Jacobite and Williamite contest, till towards the commencement of the American War of Independence, has been sketched as follows by the late learned Dr. William Cooke Taylor. "Time has *now* set the broad seal of prescription on the Cromwellian and Williamite settlements of Ireland; but, in the last century, the descendants, or reputed descendants, of those whose estates had been forfeited, were accustomed to point out the broad lands of their ancestors to their children, and to impress upon their minds the cruelty and injustice of those by whom they had been confiscated. Like Roderick Dhu, the pauperized descendant of a line of kings could point to

'Deep-waving fields, and pastures green,
  With gentle groves, and slopes between;'

and, with *more* truth than the Highland chieftain, he might add,

'These fertile plains, that soften'd vale,
  Were once the birthright of the Gael;
The stranger came with iron hand,
  And, from *our* fathers, reft the land.'

The Penal Laws were then in full force; priest-hunting was as favourite a sport, with the ultra-Protestant gentry, as fox-hunting, and hare-hunting, at a later period; the ritual and services of the Catholic church, proscribed by law, were celebrated in the rocky ravines and remote recesses of the mountains; any Protestant could compel his Catholic neighbour to give him up his best horse for £5, 5s. 0d., and this law was absolutely enforced by a Protestant squire, whose horse was worsted in a race by the steed of a Catholic gentleman. He consoled himself for his defeat, by the compulsory purchase of the winning horse. The peasants of Ireland, goaded to agrarian insurrections by intolerable oppression, were

* On the monstrous injustice of the Acts of Settlement and Explanation, see Irish Archæological Society's Macariæ Excidium, Note 28, and the general references, under "Settlement, Act of" at Index, p. 539, of that work.

coerced by laws, which Arthur Young declared to be 'fit only for the *meridian* of Barbary;' and the great bulk of the Protestant clergy neglected almost every clerical duty, save the levying of tithes."*

The system of religious oppression alluded to arose from the Penal Code, by which the Treaty of Limerick was violated—the Treaty of Limerick guaranteeing to the Catholics of Ireland, on taking a simple oath of allegiance to the Sovereigns established by the Revolution, and "no other oath," those rights, as subjects, which the possessors of their religion had by *law* under King Charles II., or substantially the same as at present †—the Penal Code setting all this aside, by imposing such additional oaths, and disqualifications, as excluded the members of that faith from both Houses of Parliament, from the legal professions, from the corporations, from acquiring any beneficial interest in land, from military and naval employment; and, in short, reducing the proscribed majority of the Irish nation so low, that, in 1759, it was decided, from the Bench in Dublin, by the Lord Chancellor of the day,—"That *the laws did not presume an Irish Papist to exist in the kingdom, where they were only supposed to breathe, through the connivance of Government!*" ‡ The system of commercial oppression, to which Ireland was simultaneously subjected, proceeded from the mercantile jealousy in England, which, leaving only the linen manufacture in Ulster, because, at the time, of comparatively little importance, put down the Irish woollen manufacture, worth upwards of £1,000,000 a year, to the ruin and dispersion of those it employed, or 20,000 persons of *both* religions! § and prevented, as far as possible, either the establishment of other branches of industry, in the island, or such a mercantile intercourse as was natural with foreign nations—no commerce being judged suitable for Ireland by this shameless spirit of monopoly, but such as might enable its insatiable representatives to drain away from the comparatively scanty population that struggled to exist there, even what little profits they could derive from pasturage and the linen trade.|| This mercantile tyranny was, indeed, abolished, several years previous to the French Revolution, through the acquisition of Free Trade and Legislative Independence by the Volunteers from

* "Reminiscences of Daniel O'Connell," &c., "by a Munster Farmer," *i.e.*, Dr. Taylor; a native of Munster, a Protestant, a Whig, and, on the whole, a fair Irish, as well as a good foreign, historian. I correct him, however, in substituting "meridian" for "regions," the former being the word used by Young; and in changing £5, 0s. 0d. into £5, 5s. 0d., as the sum legally payable to a Papist for his horse, according to Meriton's Abridgment of the Irish Statutes, pp. 388-9: Dublin, 1700.

† Irish Archæological Society's Macariæ Excidium, Note 278.

‡ The case, in reference to which that remarkable declaration was made, is mentioned by Dr. O'Conor, in his Memoirs of his uncle, Charles O'Conor of Belanagare, pp. 376-9.

§ "In acting upon these commercial restrictions," alleges Sir Walter Scott in his life of Swift, " wrong was heaped upon wrong, and insult was added to injury, with this advantage, on the side of the aggressors, that they could intimidate the injured people of Ireland into silence, by raising, to drown every complaint, the cry of *rebel* and *Jacobite*. These evils Swift beheld, with all the natural ardour of a disposition which rose in opposition to tyranny. 'Do not,' said he to Delany, 'the corruptions and villanies of men eat your flesh, and exhaust your spirits?'"

|| From the many ruinous effects of the *double* yoke of sectarian and anti-commercial legislation under which Ireland groaned for the greater part of the century after the Treaty of Limerick, "it can afford no matter of surprise," says the learned Newenham, "that, notwithstanding the extraordinary physical advantages of that country, it was distinguished, above *all* others, by immense emigrations of people." The truth of which *assertion* he demonstrates by *facts*.

1779 to 1782; and, from 1774, when the political existence of Catholics was first acknowledged, by a parliamentary *"permission to express allegiance to the Sovereign which before they had not,"* the severity of the Penal Code was considerably lessened, in 1778, and 1782. These improvements, however, in the state of Ireland, were not sufficient to affect the existence, in France, of regiments entirely officered by the descendants of Irishmen, or Irishmen by birth, who still came there, in greater numbers than there were posts for them. That military connexion with France was not severed, till the progress of revolutionary opinion there to republicanism, from 1789 to 1791, occasioned a break-up in the existing organization of those corps, on account of the attachment among them to monarchy; at the same time that the contest then approaching, between monarchy in England, and republicanism in France, impressed upon the English cabinet the necessity of uniting the interests of the Catholics, or great body of the Irish nation, more closely with England, in opposition to France, by a fuller relaxation of the Penal Code. With this view, that Act was passed through the Irish Parliament, early in 1793, by which the prospect of military as well as other professional advancement being opened to the higher classes of the Catholics, they, no less than the lower orders, might hope for better employment, in war and peace, under the existing government of their country, than what they had been so long obliged to seek elsewhere. In addition to this prudent measure, an Irish Brigade was subsequently formed in the British service, to provide for the emigrant officers, of Irish origin or birth, from France, as well as for others of their religion; and thus, about a century after the Revolution in Great Britain and Ireland, which was the origin of the Irish Brigades in the service of France, *their* history ceased, except as a portion of information respecting the past, for the instruction of the future.

Before giving an account of the *general* exploits of the corps above described, it remains to show, in what manner, and to what amount, the armies of France were strengthened, during that century, by exiles from Ireland. Notwithstanding the danger of recruiting there for the Brigades —the penalty for doing so being DEATH, and that to be *decided by a Jury on which* NO *Catholic could sit*—so extensively did such recruiting exist, that, through agents and vessels, employed by France, as well as by Spain, for her Irish regiments, men were engaged, and brought away, even from Dublin, and its vicinity. By an abstract, from the Stuart Papers, of a " Mémoire touchant des Moyens pour avoir des Recrues d'Irlande, 1693," we are informed—" An Agent was to be established at Dublin, who was to have Agents, to act, according to his directions, in the several Counties. They were to enlist recruits, and to facilitate their escape from Ireland." Of recruits from the Irish metropolis, or its vicinity, successfully enlisted for France, (even at a period when a very great alarm was raised by the ruling " ascendancy " against any attempt of the kind,) the Protestant Lord Primate Boulter, writing from Dublin, in January, 1730, mentions how, on information that some officers in the French service* had men engaged to sail with them from Bullock, the Commander-in-Chief of the Forces in Ireland, General Pearce, " ordered 50 foot and 4 dragoons to march to Bullock, and either seize or disperse those people. When they came there on Wednesday," continues the Primate, " they found there had been about 40 men listed for abroad,

---

* Irish ones, of course, as sent to recruit in Ireland, for the Irish corps in France. Native French officers would not do for *that* business.

and 4 or 5 French officers with them; but that they went on board a sloop, about 11 o'clock, the night before." Of Irish for the service of Spain, Captain Moses Nowland—or rather O'Nowlan, of the ancient sept whose original territory was in the modern County of Carlow,*— before his trial, in the Court of King's Bench, in June, 1726, and subsequent hanging at Stephen's Green, Dublin, in July, for enlisting men, had, according to the evidence on the trial, "shipp'd off 200 men those 2 months past for the said service, and had 100 more to go off that night," respecting which the fatal information was given. In the published version of this unfortunate gentleman's last speech and dying words, (so coloured, under the Penal-Code administration of that day, as to make the sufferer appear as *criminal* as possible, though otherwise useful for its information,) he is represented as saying—" I believe there are very few here who are not sensible, that some foreign Potentates entertain natives of this Kingdom as soldiers in their service, and that the Kings of France and Spain have several Regiments, composed solely of Irish ; and, as it is next to an impossibility, but that these Regiments must, from time to time, be deficient in their number, so, whenever a compleating is necessary, they send here, for that purpose. About February last, I was ignorantly employed by an unknown gentleman, well dress'd, to carry some of these recruits, under the notion of passengers, aboard a ship, then at anchor in the Bay; where, dreadful time and place, which with horror I reflect on! I was made privy to the fatal secret, and, for a few pieces of gold, and the promise of a capital commission to satisfy my ambitious spirit, not only bribed to secrecy, but employ'd as an Agent, to seduce more to enter themselves in the King of Spain's service, under the notion it was for the Pretender; a bait, which the ignorant readily swallow, and by which they are easily deluded." He concludes thus respecting his death. " Nothing troubles me more, than the thoughts of the grief it will give my poor parents at Carlow, whose grey hairs will come with sorrow to the ground."

Owing, however, to the Catholic religion having been more peculiarly that of Munster and Connaught; to their situation having been more distant from the seat of government, as well as more favourable for a communication with France, than the rest of Ireland; and to a considerable contraband, or "*free* trade" having existed between those provinces and France; the great majority of the soldiers of the Brigades were Munster and Connaught men. The maritime intercourse of France and Ireland had been increased beyond what it ever was by the War of the Revolution. After the termination of the contest, the French privateers from the ports of Bretagne, or Brest and St. Malo, that were very active on the look-out for the rich English merchant-men making for the Munster harbours of Cork, Kinsale, &c., were not without aid in these enterprises,

* The old Leinster clan of O'Nuallain, O'Nowlan, or O'Nolan (a name sometimes anglicized, or corrupted, as above, into Nowland, or Noland) are descended, according to the ancient Celtic genealogies of their country, from a brother of the renowned " Con of the 100 Battles," Ard-Righ or Monarch of Erin in the 2nd century. The last of the Chieftain line of O'Nolan, of the Barony of Forth, in the County of Carlow, died in the time of O'Flaherty, author of Ogygia. But the race, in various subordinate branches, has been respectable to our days. There were several among the officers of the Jacobite or national army in Ireland during the War of the Revolution, as well as among the consequent victims of Williamite proscription or spoliation; and, down to the French Revolution, the name is to be found in the Irish Brigade, with the distinction of Chevalier of St. Louis.

through a communication with the native population of the sea-coast; sympathizing with those belonging to a nation, so recently the ally of theirs, and the enemy of their enemies, the Williamites. Privateers likewise from France, manned with Irish and Scotch exiles, the adherents of King James, and acting by his commission from St. Germain, were so animated by the successes obtained against the Williamite trade, that they extended their operations into the Bay of Dublin; and Irish Jacobite officers, commanding French vessels, are mentioned as very injurious to the same commerce in their cruises. Hence the communication went on between Ireland and France, where there were many Irish, besides the flower of the nation engaged in the service of *their* exiled King and Louis XIV. But, through the arbitrary suppression by England of the Irish woollen manufacture, her other legislation for the injury or ruin of Irish commerce, and the continued limitations to employment in Ireland by the constant additions to the Penal Code, the causes for such intercourse with France were necessarily increased. Of the productions of Ireland, the wool and the men, rendered equally incapable by law of becoming the great sources of wealth they might have been at home, were in request for the manufactures and the armies of France abroad. Well-equipped smuggling vessels, freighted with brandy, claret, laces, and silks, consequently plied to the coasts of Kerry, Clare, and Connaught, having Irish officers, and occasionally friars, on board, speaking the old language, which was still that of *far* the greater part of the country, and possessing a proportionable influence with their countrymen.* For these arrivals from France, cargoes of *wool* were returned, accompanied by suitable numbers of hardy *recruits*, whose periodical emigrations were fancifully styled, "the flights of the wild geese." † These enlistments for the Brigades in France were most extensive to about 1748, or the Peace of Aix-la-Chapelle. Then, on account of the serious injury so long experienced from the valour of the exiled Irish by the Allies in general, added to the more recent and immediate experience of that valour by England herself in particular at the defeat of Fontenoy, such prohibitory measures were adopted in Ireland by the government—who, to a certain degree, had hitherto connived at the levies in question as a sort of safety-valve for the relief of the country under the unfortu-

---

* The old Milesian or Gaelic population of Erin were naturally as much attached to their own language, as they were averse to that of the Sassenaghs, or English. In the middle ages, when a native or independent territory was menaced with invasion from the settlements of "the stranger," it was customary for one clan, or sept, to claim aid from another, "for the sake of the language of the Gaels;" since, though "as septs, they might be distinct as the billows, as to the language, they were one as the sea." Among the Irish Brigades in France, during the most celebrated period of their existence, or down to the war of Dettingen, Fontenoy, &c., the Gaelic was so general, that an officer, not knowing it on entering those corps, subsequently learned it; and the exclamation of vengeance from the Brigade, in charging their opponents at the famous battle last-mentioned, is related to have been expressed in the ancient national tongue.

† The celebrated English commercial writer, Dr. Josiah Tucker, Dean of Gloucester, mentions, in 1753, how, in the west of Ireland, wool-smugglers "got upwards of 50 per cent. by the wool they sold to the French;" adding, "as long as this is the case, laws, and restrictions, will signify *nothing.*" And, with that injurious transmission, for England, of the Irish wool abroad, since it enabled France to rival her "in that most essential article of foreign commerce," a contemporary English pamphleteer connects the necessity there was, to "take off those numbers from the Irish Brigades, who annually enlist themselves into the French or Spanish service, to the inconceivable detriment of Great Britain."

nate circumstances in which it was *legally* placed—that those recruitings may henceforth be said to have comparatively ceased. Yet, until long after, they did not do so altogether. For several years within the present century, the numbers of those, who, during the latter half of the preceding one, were in the habit of emigrating to serve in France, especially from the remote and rocky coasts of Kerry and Clare, were a subject of familiar recollection and conversation, in the south of Ireland, with the fathers of men still living. As to the Irish of the rank in society for officers, their emigration to France, from the facilities for going there which their superior means afforded them, could not be prevented; so that, during the continuance, under the Bourbon monarchy, of regiments known as Irish, those corps, to the last, were generally officered either by the descendants of Irish settlers in France, or by natives of Ireland.

According to estimates, stated to be deduced from the Bureau de la Guerre, or War Office of France, between the troops of the Irish regiments in her service, and the Irish in other corps of the French army, from October, 1691, to May, 1745, or, from the Treaty of Limerick, to the battle of Fontenoy, those military exiles amounted to above 450,000, and, from 1745 to 1791—or the breaking-up of the Irish Brigade, through the fall of the Bourbon monarchy by the 1st French Revolution,—the rest of those exiles are alleged to have been so many more, as made up, for the century, a grand total of 480,000 men.* The existence of such a large number of refugees, during the former period, will appear the less surprising from this circumstance,—that, during the earlier, and more generally celebrated, days of the services of the Irish in France, as well as in Spain, their strength was, to a very great extent, kept up by deserters from the British army. These, though, as Catholics, legally excluded from the British service, yet, having been without any better resource, from their misery, than to enlist in that service, pretended to do so as Protestants; but only acted thus, to get a free passage to the Continent, and there join, as soon as possible, those famous corps of their countrymen, with whom they might enjoy the exercise of their religion, *then* interdicted in the British army; might rejoin beloved relatives, or friends, "not lost, but gone before;" † might obtain, in

* "Par des calculs et des recherches faites au Bureau de la Guerre," observes the Abbé Mac Geoghegan, "on a trouvé, qu'il y avoit eu, depuis l'arrivée des troupes Irlandoises en France en 1691, jusqu'en 1745, que se donna la bataille de Fontenoy, plus de 450,000 Irlandois, morts au service de la France." After sifting this statement of the Abbé by other and hostile, yet corroborative, evidence (which might be considerably augmented) the industrious Protestant statistician, Newenham, remarks—" Upon the whole, I am inclined to think that we are *not* sufficiently warranted in considering the Abbé Mac Geoghegan's statement as an exaggeration." That statement, however, must be understood, as including all the Irish who served in France, instead of those who belonged to Irish regiments *only*. One of my French MSS., entitled, " Souvenirs des Brigades Irlandaises," in treating of the Irish belonging to the armies of the principal Continental powers, from the War of the Revolution in Ireland to the first Revolution in France, says, " 480,000 sont morts au service *seul* de la France." The MS. adds—"Ce résultat est basé sur des recherches faites aux Archives du Ministre de la Guerre à Paris." M. de la Ponce alleges, from *his* authorities, "que par suite de calculs et de recherches exécutés dans les Archives du Département de la Guerre, il a été constaté, qu'entre les années 1650 et 1800, plus de 750,000 Irlandais avaient été moissonnés par le fer ou le boulet sur les divers champs de bataille," for the honour of *his* country, or "l'éclat du nom Français."

† An example of such desertions, as those above alluded to, occurs, among the records of the O'Keeffe family, in France. Arthur O'Keeffe, Esq., J.P. for the

battle, some of the vengeance *then* due for the many oppressions, and insults, so long inflicted upon their race, and creed; and even might, as they anticipated, return, one day or another, to Ireland, to overthrow the detested state of things established there by the Revolution.* Of those numerous desertions from levies made in Ireland, almost to the close of the war ended by the Peace of Utrecht, a well-informed or war-office writer notes—" Entire regiments were rais'd in that kingdom, of which I can *name* several, until the experience we had, of their frequent desertions to the French and Spaniards, shew'd us, that, to list men in Ireland was only to recruit for the Irish troops in the service of France and Spain; and, consequently, to raise forces, at that time, for the Chevalier." Hence, too, the hopes thus expressed in the versification of the native Jacobite song—

> " O ! the French and Spanish
> Soon our foes will banish;
> Then at once will vanish
> All our grief and dread;
> City, town, and village,
> Shall no more know pillage,
> Music, feasting, tillage
> Shall abound instead;
>
> " Poetry, romances,
> Races, and long dances,
> Shouts, and songs, and glances,
> From eyes bright with smiles!—
> *Our* King's feasts shall Fame hymn,
> *Though I may not name him,*
> Victory will proclaim him
> *Monarch of the Isles!"*

Under such circumstances, " let no one asperse the character of the Irish," exclaims an Irish Protestant writer, respecting his Catholic countrymen in the foreign military services, " they lent their valour to the states which supported their dethroned kings, their outlawed religion, their denationalized country, their vow of vengeance, or their hopes of freedom." These regimental and other particulars, connected with the formation of the Irish Brigades, will suffice, as an introduction to the more attractive portion of their history, on which we *now* enter—or the general narrative of their achievements.

County of Cork in King James's reign, raised, for the royal service, a company of foot, which he commanded, as Captain, in the Regiment of Lord Kenmare, till the end of the War of the Revolution. Then, obliged by his numerous family to remain at home, he sent his company to France, whither 2 of his sons had previously gone; one as Captain, the other as Lieutenant, with 60 men, whom they had raised for the Regiment of O'Brien, or Clare. Some time after, a 3rd son, desirous of following his brothers abroad, got himself into the English army, after the manner noticed in the text; and succeeded in joining the French, "bringing over," says the account, " 14 men of the army commanded by Milord Marlborough." By these means the 3 brothers "all met together," as officers in the same regiment. The name of O'Keeffe has been one of military distinction in France to our time, or represented among her General Officers down to 1852. For *Huguenot* desertion, on the other hand, from the French to the English army, see a note to Book IV., under battle of Almanza, in 1707.

* The Protestant Lord Primate for Ireland, Dr. Boulter, writing from Dublin, in 1730, to the Duke of Newcastle, in England, remarks—" All recruits, raised here for France or Spain, are generally considered as persons, that may, some time or other, pay a visit to this country, as enemies. That all, who are listed here, in those services, hope and wish to do so, there is *no* doubt."

The first service appointed for the greater portion of the Irish troops, after their reorganization in France in 1692, was an expedition to England. That invasion was concerted between James II. and Louis XIV., as equally for the interest of *both;* of the former, as the means of effecting his "restoration;" of the latter, as his best resource against the League of Augsburg; since, unless William, its chief, could be dethroned, that great confederacy would be stronger than ever, from *his* being enabled, by the Treaty of Limerick, to employ, on the Continent against France, so many of the regular force of 67 regiments, absorbed, by the last year's war, in Ireland. The "Armée de Normandie," for James's service, was, including his household and officers, to consist of 30,000 men, with 50 guns. Of these, the Irish—as exclusive of the 3 Regiments of Mountcashel's Brigade, and the Regiment of Athlone, appointed to serve elsewhere—would amount, in round numbers, to 12,400 infantry, and 800 cavalry, or above 13,200 men and officers. The whole were to be commanded, under the King, by the veteran Marshal de Bellefonds, to whom Patrick Sarsfield, Earl of Lucan, was Maréchal de Camp, or Major-General. From the great discontent against the Williamite government in England, the correspondence of William's own Ministers with James, and the Jacobite arrangements made, that, if a landing could only be effected, "the King should enjoy his own again," nothing seemed requisite for success, but that the French fleet should be ready in time, to protect the proposed disembarkation, before the English and Dutch fleets could unite, to oppose it. Early in April, the French and Irish troops, destined for the expedition, were assembled, between Cherbourg and La Hogue, in Normandy; and James, with his son the Duke of Berwick, the Marshal de Bellefonds, &c., arrived the 24th at Caen. The embarkation of the troops might *then* have been commenced. But, *for several weeks, the " Protestant winds,"* as they were styled in England, *prevented the attempt,* by damaging the French transports, and by preventing the junction of the Toulon fleet, and other vessels, with the Brest fleet under the famous Chevalier Comte de Tourville; while the several English squadrons *thus* had time to unite under Admiral Russell, with the Dutch fleet under Admiral Van Allemonde.* Louis, informed that there would be a great Jacobite defection in the English fleet on meeting his, and that the Dutch were *not* ready to join the English, at length ordered Tourville to enter the Channel, and give battle. Tourville sailed accordingly. But, the Dutch meanwhile joining the English, the Jacobites despatched intelligence of the fact to France, whence 10 light vessels were sent after Tourville with the news, and a counter-order, that he was *not* to fight, till strengthened by the Toulon fleet. None, however, of the 10 (strange to say!) reached

---

* "I am sorry, from my heart, for our good King James," writes Charlotte Elizabeth, Duchess of Orleans, from Paris, May 11th, 1692. "Hitherto *Heaven,* or, to speak more strictly, the *wind*, fights on the Prince of Orange's side; for King James has not been able to embark." And Francis Annesley, writing to Sir Arthur Rawdon, from London, May 29th, O. S., 1692, on the defeat of the French, observes —"It is concluded their design was, to have taken the advantage of Admirals Carter and Delavalle's squadron, which consisted but of 36, and to have managed them, so as to have made way for the safe conduct of their transport-ships, with their army, to have poured in upon us here; and we may thank our *Protestant* winds for the escape." How remarkable was the favour from the *same* quarter experienced by William himself in 1688, through which he was enabled to reach, and disembark unmolested, in England, is shown by Lord Macaulay.

him, when, May 29th, between Barfleur and La Hogue, he met the combined fleets. They, according to their published "line of battle," consisted of 99 sail of the line, 40,675 men, and 6994 cannon, besides nearly 30 frigates, or fire-ships. Of these, there were, for action, 88 sail of the line, including 36 three-deckers, besides minor vessels, or fire-ships. The French, by their accounts, had but 44 sail of the line, 22,451 men, and 3216 cannon, with no more than 13 fire-ships—the strength of the Allied armament, between men-of-war and minor vessels, consequently being, as compared with that of the French, in the proportion of *more than 2 to 1!* Nevertheless, from 10 in the morning till 10 at night, (except while interrupted by a fog,) Tourville maintained a noble engagement, against such enormous odds; not losing a single vessel himself, and disabling several of the enemy's; so that never was the glory of the French marine higher than that day! The result, however, from May 30th, to June 3rd, was, that, obliged to retire towards his own coasts, where there was not due harbourage for his fleet, which he would otherwise have saved, 15 of his principal men-of-war went aground at Cherbourg, Fort Lisset, and La Hogue, and, with some small craft, were burned by the enemy.* This action, though honourable to the French, was a fatal blow to their navy. "The defeat of La Hogue," remarks an English contemporary of Louis XIV., "was such a shock to his naval power, that he was never after able to put out a fleet, to meet the English and Dutch fleet in the Channel. He had been 30 years making up a navy, at as much expence as would have maintain'd all his garrisons; it has been computed at 20,000,000 sterling. He had form'd to himself the project of making himself master in *both* seas, and, then, of giving laws to ALL Christendom. He cou'd not do this without a fleet, superior in strength to *both* English and Dutch; *his own was so in Beachy fight 2 years ago;* and now *wou'd have been so again, had it come up before the junctions already mention'd.* But this blow put an end to his dream, of of being the NEPTUNE, as well as the MARS, of Europe." The expedition against England was consequently given up; King James returned to St. Germain; and the Irish troops were ordered, to join the Armies of Flanders, Germany, Spain, and Italy.

The campaign of 1692 in Flanders commenced with the reduction of Namur by Louis XIV. in the presence of William III., as Mons had been reduced the preceding campaign. The fall, under those mortifying circumstances, of 2 Allied fortresses of such importance, gave rise to sharp reflections and sarcastic songs, or squibs, on *both* sides of the Channel, to the glorification of Louis, at William's expense.

"Il est facheux, on le sait bien,
  Pour des guerriers habiles,
De voir, sans entreprendre rien,
  Forcer de telles villes.
Mais, Nassau, du moins tu sauras
  Comment il les faut prendre;
Si Mons ne te suffisoit pas,
  Namur doit te l'apprendre!"

* On this engagement, and circumstances connected with it, I have availed myself of French official sources of information; besides more generally-known authorities. There can be little, if any, doubt, from the very gallant contest maintained by Tourville under such disadvantages, that, if joined by his entire force, or the Toulon fleet, he would have beaten the English and Dutch, as formerly; and a disembarkation, and 2nd Stuart "restoration," in England, would then have been *certain.*

> "The author sure must take great pains,
> Who fairly writes his story,
> In which of these two last campaigns,
> He gain'd the greatest glory.
> For, while that he march'd on to fight,
> Like hero, nothing fearing,
> *Namur was taken in his sight,*
> *And Mons within his hearing!*"

Louis, after the capture of Namur, returned to France, early in July; leaving the command of his forces in Flanders to the Marshal Duke de Luxembourg. William, to obtain some satisfaction for this affront, collected his utmost strength, or, according to his own accounts, between 95,000 and 100,000 men, and, August 3rd, advanced against Luxembourg. From the diminution of the French army at the siege of Namur, and by a detachment to Germany, Luxembourg would appear, as inferior in number, to have betaken himself to the strong position of the hedged and wooded country between Enghein and Steinkirk. A very warm engagement of infantry took place; the "firing, muzzle to muzzle, through the hedges," being compared to "continued claps of thunder." William's main attack was that of his left, under the Duke of Wirtemberg, upon the French right towards Steinkirk. There the Allies,—having had a great advantage in the way of a surprise of the French, through the medium of a detected and double-dealing spy,—at first carried all before them, and won 7 pieces of cannon; until Luxembourg, ordering up the French and Swiss Guards, accompanied by several princes and noblemen, to charge the assailants sword in hand, the 7 guns were recovered, others taken, and Wirtemberg repulsed with great slaughter. After a close contest, from about midday to 7 in the evening, Luxembourg remained master of the field, by the retreat of William—but in good order. "The King," we are told, "tho' he dissembled the matter very much, yet could not but discover his regret for the disappointment; he being observed, the night after the action, while he sate at supper, frequently to frown, and bite his lips." In alluding to a popular English statement of the day, attributing the loss of the battle "to Count Solmes, the *Dutch* General, who refused to obey the King's orders, in supporting the *English*," the British historian, Salmon, remarks—"But, there is no doubt, if the Dutch General had refused to obey the King's orders, he would have lost his head; whereas, I don't find he was so much as turned out, or even tried for breach of orders. I'm afraid Monsieur Luxembourg, was the best General in the field; and, though King William was sensible there was very little hopes of forcing the French camp, yet he was, in a manner, compelled to fight, to silence the clamour of the Allies, who expected something extraordinary from a King, who had been cried up for the greatest hero and General of the age. And, indeed, we had so high an opinion of the King at *that* time, that we were ready to impute the misfortune to any thing, rather than to *his* want of courage or conduct." This victory of the French was, as a defeat of William, publicly rejoiced at in England, by the Jacobites, notes a Williamite author, "particularly at Bath, and at Windsor. As to Bath," he continues, "no better could be expected from that rendezvous of sharpers and prodigals. But Windsor was taken more notice of, because some of the offenders were said to be the Princess's" Anne's "servants."* The French acknowledged 6966 killed and wounded, and claimed the capture of 1350 men of all ranks, 8 colours and 10 guns. The Allies published their killed and wounded as 6653; that, with the above-mentioned prisoners, would make a total loss of 8003. Among Luxembourg's officers, who "gave proofs of a great valour, and a rare capacity," the Marquis de Quincy names "the Duke of Berwick, and the Earl of Lucan." And the Marshal himself, in his despatch to Louis XIV., the day after the victory, writes—"Monsieur, the Duke of Berwick, was present from the commencement, when we proceeded to reconnoitre the enemy; and behaved, during the entire combat, as bravely as I have rendered an account to your Majesty, that he had done the last campaign. The Earl of Lucan was with him; in whom we have particularly noticed the valour, and the intrepidity, of which he had given proofs in Ireland. I can assure your Majesty, that he is a very good, and a very able officer."†

The Marquis d'Harcourt was detached, in September, by Luxembourg, with a flying camp, towards Namur, and proceeded to encamp, the 8th, at Roumont, with the Ourte before him, when 4000 Germans, despatched, without baggage, to surprise him, appeared, in 30 squadrons, on the opposite side of the stream. Their advanced party of dismounted dragoons was held in check, among the hedges, by a similar party of the Marquis's forces and piquet, till he drew together his cavalry in 26 squadrons. The Marquis placed at their head King James's 2 Troops of Irish Horse Guards, or the Duke of Berwick's, and Lord Lucan's; next the 2 French dragoon regiments of Asfeld and De Rannes; and, leading the 1st Troop of those Horse Guards himself, while M. de St. Fremont led the 2nd Troop, crossed the stream, to attack the enemy. The charge was then made with such vigour, that the German cavalry were broken at the 1st shock, put to a precipitate rout, and pursued above 2 leagues. From 300 to 500 were slain, among whom were their leader, a Danish Major-General, 2 Mestres-de-Camp, and several more officers. From 100 to 200 were taken prisoners, including the Count de Wheten, commander of the troops of Neubourg, 2 Captains of Dragoons, and other subaltern officers. From 700 or 800 to 1000 of their dragoon-horses are variously stated to have been captured. The Marquis d'Harcourt's loss is alleged to have been but 1 Irish officer killed, and only 13 private men killed or wounded. Of the conduct of the Irish in this dashing affair, the French account says—"The Guards of the King of England, and the Irish regiments, have very much signalized themselves there."‡ And a

* The *Princess*, subsequently *Queen* Anne, from High-Church influences, &c., was no lover of her ungracious brother-in-law, William; and her "upper servants," the Marlboroughs, husband and wife, for revenge against William at *this* time, not improbably caused the "under servants" of the Princess, at Windsor, to rejoice the more publicly at the King's defeat. Such satisfaction, at an overthrow of William, would be very generally felt, even where not actually displayed, in England. According to Lord Macaulay, "9 clergymen, out of 10, were Jacobites at heart, and had sworn allegiance to the new dynasty, only in order to save their benefices. A large proportion of the country gentlemen belonged to the same party. The whole body of agricultural proprietors was hostile to that interest, which the creation of the national debt had brought into notice, and which was believed to be peculiarly favoured by the Court, the monied interest."

† "Berwick" is, in the French, metamorphosed into "*Barvick;*" and "Lucan" into "*Livan,*" and even "*Livau.*"

‡ "Les Gardes du Roi d'Angleterre, et les régiments Irlandois, s'y sont fort signalez." The "régiments Irlandois," apparently the 2 Irish Regiments of Horse.

hostile Continental narrative observes—" It is testified of the Guards of King James, that they have performed their duty perfectly well, as did likewise the Irish regiments who were present there." The Irish officer, who fell on this occasion, in the first onset, was Matthias Barnewall, 10th Lord Trimleston.* The family name, written in old documents, De Berneval, Bernevale, and Barnevale, first appears, as of feudal distinction in Basse Bretagne, connected with the Dukes of Bretagne, and was of high repute there, down to the Revolution in France. The earliest representative of the race in England is to be found upon the rolls of her French conquerors, under the Duke of Normandy. After the subjugation and planting of England from France, and the extension of the Norman arms to Ireland under Henry II., the 1st of the De Bernevals who emigrated there acquired large possessions, from whom sprang several eminent houses, under the anglicized designation of Barnewalls, or Barnwells. The 1st of the Barnewalls, created a Peer in Ireland, was Robert, 2nd son of Sir Christopher Barnewall of Crickston, County of Meath; which Robert was ennobled, in March, 1461, by Edward IV., as Lord Baron of *Trymleston*, in that County. The 2nd of the Barnewalls similarly honoured was Nicholas Barnewall, Esq. of Turvey, County of Dublin, made Viscount *Kingsland*, in said County, and Baron of Turvey in 1645-6 by Charles I. The representatives of both these noble houses, with others of their name, adhered to King James II. against the Prince of Orange, as previously to Kings Charles I. and Charles II. against the Parliamentarian and Cromwellian revolutionists; the Barnewalls having been officers of the Jacobite or national army in the Duke of Tyrconnell's, Lord Galmoy's, and Colonel Henry Luttrell's Regiments of Horse, in Lord Dongan's and Colonel Simon Luttrell's Regiments of Dragoons, in Colonel William Dorrington's, Lord Gormanstown's, Lord Slane's, Lord Westmeath's and Colonel Charles O'More's Regiments of Foot. During the century, also, from the British and Irish Revolution under James II., to the French Revolution under Louis XVI., there were Barnewalls officers in the Irish Brigade. Matthias, 10th Lord Trimleston,—eldest son of Robert, 9th Lord Trimleston, by Margaret, daughter of Sir John Dongan, Baronet, and sister of William, Earl of Limerick—had fought for King James in Ireland, and was a Lieutenant in the Duke of Berwick's Troop of Guards, when slain, as above mentioned, in action against the Germans, being then not more than 20 years of age.

The Irish appointed, in 1692, to reinforce the Marshal Duke de Lorges in Germany, did not join him, till late in the summer. The French and German armies then, or in September, were separated by the Spirebach, which flowed through Spire. The Germans raised a battery near the tower of Spire, as if meditating an attack in that quarter; but, meanwhile, marching troops, on their right, through a wood, to seize upon the village of Dudenhoven, where there was a passage over the river. They established 4 battalions of Swedes there, with 3 pieces of cannon. To cut off the main body of the French troops, and that, under the Marquis de Feuquieres, stationed amidst the ruins of Spire, the enemy only required to gain the tower of Dudenhoven, which was but a carabine-shot from that village, and where there was a bridge over a branch of

* "Il n'y a eu aucun officier tué de nôtre part, sinon Mylord Tremblestown Irlandois, qui fut tué à la prémiere charge."

the stream, otherwise impassable. There, however, they were prevented crossing by an Irish battalion, which kept their superior numbers at skirmishing distance. This gave time for the whole of the French to come up,* and range their infantry in a well-covered position, extending from Spire beyond Dudenhoven; a brisk cannonade and musketry taking place between both armies. Half an hour before night, the Allies advanced towards the post of the Marquis de Feuquieres on the right, where the firing became so lively, that the Marshal de Lorges, with most of his General Officers, hastened there; while the Marquis de Villars was sent to the left, to guard against an attack on that side. There the Irish battalions, that had come up from Brisach a little before the action, advanced most opportunely; bore, with such bravery, the fire to which they were exposed, as to signalize themselves greatly; before troops, destined for their support, reached them, silenced the hostile musketry; and compelled the enemy, after a considerable resistance, to quit the church and castle of Dudenhoven, abandoning their dead.† There were 2 Swedish battalions, in particular, (though the Swedes *still* ranked among the best troops in Europe,) so bewildered by the fire they had to encounter, that they flung down their arms, and ran away in great disorder, as testified by the prisoners taken, and by the number of drums, chevaux-de-frise, &c., left behind. Next day, the Germans retreated, with a loss variously reported, but certainly much larger than that of the French; among whose killed and wounded, likewise variously reported, were " 2 Irish officers." The British historian Ralph notices, how " a part of the Irish troops, by the Articles of Limerick so liberally made over to the service of France, behav'd extremely well, on this occasion." And, from the important portion of the position, occupied by the Irish, and their defence of that position, it is sufficiently evident by *inference*, though not directly affirmed in the French accounts, that to those Irish, in all probability, the preservation of the French army was owing.

On the side of Italy, or Piedmont, the campaign of 1692 was one of defence with the French under Catinat, whose army, (as *not* duly reinforced, in order to strengthen that of Flanders,) was but 16,000 men; the Duke of Savoy, between his own Piedmontese and Vaudois troops, and his Spanish, Austrian, and other confederates, having, on the contrary, above 50,000. As Louis XIV., moreover, preferred risking even a hostile invasion of France to a loss of Pignerol or Susa, Catinat could only intrench himself between those fortresses; while the Allies, leaving a sufficient corps to watch him, and a smaller corps to blockade Casal, were able, under the Duke of Savoy himself, the famous Prince Eugene,

* "Il y avoit un pont sur le bras du même ruisseau, qui étoit impraticable par tout: mais M. de la Breteche y arriva assez heureusement, avec 5 or 6 officiers, pour sauver ce poste, où il établit un bataillon Irlandois, ce qui ne se passa pas sans escarmouche. Cela donna le tems aux troupes, que conduisoit M. d'Uxelles, d'arriver, et enfin à toute l'armée."

† "Les bataillons Irlandois, qui avoient em embarquez à Brisac, et qui arriverent un peu avant l'action, essuierent, avec beaucoup de bravoure, le feu des ennemis, et s'y signalerent."—"Les bataillons Irlandois, qui venoient d'arriver, firent un grand feu. On marcha pour les soûtenir, et on trouva que le prémier feu étoit fini. Les ennemis abandonnerent l'eglise et le château de Dudenhoven avec précipitation, n'aiant pas retiré leurs morts," &c.—"Les bataillons Irlandois, qui arriverent à propos dans ce tems, firent un très-grand feu, et obligerent les ennemis, après une assez longue resistance, d'abandonner l'eglise et le château de Dudenhoüen."

Charles, Duke of Schonberg, (son of the old Marshal, slain at the Boyne,) and other leaders of eminence, to penetrate into Dauphiné, with above 28,000 men, through unsuspected passes, pointed out by the Vaudois. The 1st place, which ventured to resist the invaders, was a little town, named Guillestre, having, indeed, a wall, but neither a fosse, nor outworks, and apparently so inadequate to oppose the force brought against it, that Prince Eugene accompanied his summons to surrender with a threat of no quarter, if the least resistance should be attempted. This menace not being attended to, Eugene ordered an immediate assault; by way of carrying such a place sword in hand, as a matter of course. But, says that Prince's historian, "M. de Chalandreu, a gentleman of the country, commanded there 200 Irish, and 600 men of the militia of Dauphiné;" and this "Chalandreu, who was a brave man, animated his band so well, and the Irish defended themselves with so much bravery, that the troops commanded to escalade the wall were repulsed." The assailants had from 60 to 90 men killed or wounded; no loss being mentioned on the side of the defenders. The place, whose only chance of being maintained, for any considerable time, would have arisen from an impossibility of conveying a sufficient battering-train across the mountains from Coni, was held for 3 days against the enemy, (when, to delay him was so important,) and did not surrender, until the arrival of such a siege-train, as rendered any further resistance unavailable. The Allies next proceeded to attack Embrun, into which the Marquis de Larré threw himself with 3000 men, a portion of them Irish of the Regiment of Clare; and, though the town was not regularly fortified, the Marquis defended it from the 5th to the 15th of August; quitting it only on most honourable terms, after occasioning a loss to the besiegers, differently reported at from 600 or 700 to 1300 or 1400 men; of whom there was a very unusual proportion of great officers wounded; Prince Eugene himself included. This much will suffice for the defence of Embrun, since, although a gallant feat of arms, in which Irish troops were concerned, yet I find no particulars of what *they* did there, as distinguished from their *French* fellow-soldiers. The Allies retired into Italy at the end of September, after extensively ravaging and plundering the French territory; which would, however, have suffered to a still greater extent, but for the interruptions to their advance, given at Guillestre and Embrun.

The principal event, in 1693, of the war in Flanders, was the battle of Landen, otherwise Neerwinden, or Neerhespen, fought, July 29th, between the Marshal Duke of Luxembourg and William III. The force of the Marshal amounted to 96 battalions, 210 squadrons, and 70 pieces of cannon. The force of the King amounted to 65 battalions, 150 squadrons, and 80 pieces of cannon, besides mortars, or howitzers. William compensated himself for his numerical inferiority in men by the superiority of his position. It had the well-secured villages of Neerwinden and Neerlanden on the right and left; the intervening ground was generally a commanding eminence, which afforded great advantage for the play of his artillery upon the French; and this eminence was, moreover, intrenched in front of his infantry, so as to place an enemy, marching up to attack, under a very considerable disadvantage. The contest lasted from 4 in the morning till 3 in the afternoon, or 11 hours. The generally determined and destructive resistance of the Allies, to the greater numbers and fiery perseverance of the French, was well exemplified at the time by a commemorative medal, having, on one side, William's bust and name; on the other side, a porcupine, keeping, with his prickly quills erected, 2 bull-dogs at bay; the motto being, "*Never provoked unrevenged.*" A contemporary letter, in the Rawdon Papers, asserts of this battle—"While the stress of the business lay on the foot, and the Spanish horse, we lost not 1 foot of ground; but, as soon as the Dutch horse came to be pushed, they gave way in less than 2 minutes, and put all in confusion. . . . . I am sorry to tell you, *some of the English horse made as much haste to preserve their dear persons, as any body there.*" The letter then indignantly attributes the loss of the day to "the damned misfortune of those devils giving way;" and the Williamite historian Oldmixon adds, that, " of *the English Life Guards, the 1st Troop were so scar'd with the fury of a pursuing enemy, that they did not think themselves secure, till they reach'd Breda.*" * The Allies were driven, from their entire position, across the Geete; suffering severely ere they could pass it, though subsequently able to effect their retreat, for the most part, respectably, or in a body. Among the confused and terrified multitude, who, to escape the French, had rushed into the river, where above 2000 of them were drowned, was William's late Commander in Ireland, Ginkell, created for his success (through such very superior means) there, Earl of Athlone, and enriched with a due share of confiscated Jacobite estates; but who, in this less fortunate situation at Landen, was only so far lucky, as to narrowly extricate himself from a watery grave. Luxembourg's loss was estimated, by the Duke of Berwick, as at least 8000 men; William's loss was finally owned in the London Gazette, No. 2897, as 10,473 men of all ranks, killed, wounded, or taken; though other accounts, by General Officers in the action, say several thousands more; and the French published, that they captured 84 pieces of Allied artillery, with 82 colours or standards, besides drums and pontoons.

The leading corps of Irish infantry, that of Dorrington, or the Royal Regiment of Foot Guards, was with the French at this victory. Its station is marked, in the 2nd line of the centre of Luxembourg's "ordre de bataille," as with the Brigade of Harbouville, consisting of 5 battalions; 3 French, or those of La Marche, Charolois, and Harbouville, and the "Gardes du Roi Jaques" forming the remaining 2.† To these Guards, a gentleman of high respectability in the County of Cork, Colonel John Barrett, was attached, in the capacity of a 2nd officer of that rank. His family name, as spelled "Baret" and "Barret," is to be seen in 2 lists of the original French conquerors of England, under the Duke of Normandy; and, after the descendants of those subjugators of the Anglo-Saxons effected settlements further west at the expense of the Gaels of Erin, a district was acquired, yet known, in the County of Cork,

---

Concerning the cowardice among the Allied cavalry here, a Dutch periodical further informs us—"The King of Great Britain, after having caused the conduct of the troops that have fought at Neerwinden to be carefully examined, and having found *that 4 regiments of cavalry had not done their duty, caused the troopers to draw lots, and the lot having fallen upon 3 of each regiment, they were shot to death.*"

† In Quincy's sheet of Luxembourg's army, the printer having had to contract "Gardes du Roi Jaques" into "Gardes du R. J.," a misprint occurred of "D" for "J." This has occasioned Mr. O'Conor, who did not read *behind* Quincy, to allege, "there was *no* Irish corps in Luxembourg's army." I correct these errors from 2 contemporary Continental documents, an "Ordre" and a "Liste" of Luxembourg's army in July, 1693. *both* of which give the words "Gardes du Roi Jaques," &c.

as the Barony of *Barrets*, consisting of above 26,280 acres. When the great Aodh or Hugh O'Neill, marching to the siege of Kinsale in 1600, as he passed by Castlemore, near Mallow, asked, "Who lives in that castle?" he was answered, "Barrett, a good Catholic, whose family has possessed that estate above 400 years." Colonel John Barrett, as the chief representative of his name, sat, after the breaking out of the War of the Revolution in Ireland, as 1 of the Members for the Borough of Mallow, in the national Parliament of 1689; and raised a Regiment of foot for King James II., which he commanded during that contest. He was, in 1690, Military Governor of Waterford, with his own and another regiment of foot, when, in consequence of the advance of the Williamites thither after their success at the Boyne, he had to surrender the town; stipulating, however, to march away with his garrison, their arms, baggage, and a military escort, to the County of Cork. His regiment being subsequently a portion of the Jacobite garrison of Cork, on its reduction by Marlborough, he was 1 of a number of prisoners placed on board the Breda man-of-war, in the harbour there, to be conveyed to England. At the destruction of that vessel, by the accidental igniting of its powder-magazine, he had the good fortune to be among some who escaped, by being merely blown into the shallow water, near the shore. Upon the conclusion, in 1691, of the war in Ireland, by the Treaty of Limerick, the Colonel was among the principal estated gentlemen who decided on going to France, * where, as has been observed, he was appointed to serve, in his former rank, along with the Royal Regiment of Foot Guards. On this occasion at Landen, the Brigade of Harbouville suffered much from the fire of troops, so well intrenched, and so obstinate in defence, as its Allied opponents were. Indeed, it is admitted, that, to a comparatively late period of the day, Luxembourg "repented, more than once, for having engaged in a combat, the success of which appeared so doubtful!" At last, in that part of the field where the Brigade of Harbouville was appointed to act, the Irish "Gardes du Roi Jaques," distinguished as in their own country against Ginkell and his *Allied* force at Aughrim, † and duly animated by the signal intrepidity of Colonel Barrett as a leader, obtained a glorious revenge for the reverses of the Boyne and Limerick, by being the 1st corps to make an opening into the Williamite intrenchment, through which their French companions-in-arms followed —this honourable success, however, having been purchased by the death of the brave Colonel Barrett.‡ The gallant Lieutenant-Colonel of the

* The Williamite "attainders of 1691," according to Mr. Dalton, "include this officer, described as John Barrett of Dublin, Esq., as also of Castlemore, County of Cork, with 12 others," in that county, for confiscation, as Jacobite loyalists.

† The *Allied* or mixed national composition of the Williamite army in Ireland, for the War of the Revolution, is regimentally shown further on, in a note under the year 1698. Adverting to this mixed composition of it, a Jacobite rhymer boasts of his countrymen, that, but for Luttrell's treachery,

"All the *Allies* could not them subdue!"

And, in mentioning "the English" at Aughrim, the contemporary Jacobite historian, Plunkett, adds—"I mean, under the word English, the Forraigners also, who were the better moyety of the army"—alluding to the Dutch, Danes, and Huguenots, as contrasted with the English and Anglo-Irish, of Ginkell's 50 regiments there. On the Jacobite right wing, the *last* obliged to yield, and only through the result of events *elsewhere*, even the Dublin Williamite account refers to "the opposition made by the Royal Regiment of Foot so called," or, in other words, the King's Foot Guards.

‡ The Light to the Blind states, respecting the Irish Foot Guards, and Colonel

Irish Horse Regiment of Sheldon, or Christopher Nugent of Dardistown, was likewise at, and received 4 wounds in, this battle, although his regiment does not seem to have been there. In connexion with the high distinction of these Irish Catholic exiles on the side of France, as opposed to England and her Allies, it is interesting to observe, how a corps of French Protestant refugees, or Huguenots, the cavalry Regiment of Ruvigny, Lord Galway, (originally the Marshal Duke of Schonberg's) noted, in Ireland, for its bravery at the Boyne, and still more so for its share in gaining the battle of Aughrim, was headed by William himself in charging here at Landen, where it was among the most remarkable for bravery, on the side of England and her Allies, against France!

Of the General Officers of King James, the Duke of Berwick and Lord Lucan were employed on Luxembourg's left wing, to force the strongly-guarded village of Neerwinden on the Allied right. Of the 3 Lieutenant-Generals appointed for that difficult service, each at the head of 2 *French* brigades, the Duke of Berwick was to lead in the centre; M. de Rubantel, to whom Lord Lucan was Maréchal de Camp, on the right; and M. de Montchevreuil on the left. "This village," says the Duke of Berwick, "extended, like a belly, into the plain, so that, as we all 3 marched in 1 front, and as I was in the centre, I attacked 1st. I pushed the enemy, chasing them, from hedge to hedge, as far as the plain; on the border of which I again formed, in line of battle. The troops, who should have attacked on my right, and my left, instead of doing so, judged that they would be exposed to less fire, by throwing themselves into the village; thus, all of a sudden, they found themselves behind me. The enemy, perceiving this bad manœuvre, re-entered the village, on the right, and the left: the firing then became terrible; confusion took place among the 4 brigades under the command of De Rubantel and De Montchevreuil to such an extent, that they were driven out; and I consequently found myself attacked on all sides. After the loss of a vast number, my troops, in like manner, abandoned the head of the village; and, as I strove to maintain myself in it, under the hope, that M. de Luxembourg, to whom I had sent for assistance, would forward some to me, I found myself at last entirely cut off. I then became desirous of attempting to save myself in the direction of the plain, and, having removed my white cockade, I was mistaken for 1 of the enemy's officers; unluckily, Brigadier Churchill, brother of Lord Churchill, at present Duke of Marlborough, and my uncle, was passing near me, and recognized my only remaining Aide-de-Camp; upon which, instantly suspecting the probability of my being there, he came up to me, and made me his prisoner. After having embraced one another, he told me, that he was obliged to conduct me to the Prince of Orange. We

Barrett—"It was the Irish Royal Regiment of Foot which first open'd the enemy's retrenchment; whereby the Gallick troops immediately reaped advantage, after suffering much, for awhile before, in fighting against an intrenched army. In this action, Coll. Barret of Cork, by his bould leadeing of the said Irish Regiment signalized himself, and slept in the bed of honour." Hence, likewise, the allusion of Forman to "the Irish" here, where he asserts of France—"It is not apt to forget, how gallantly Sarsfield, Earl of Lucan, and the *Irish*, behav'd at Landen." Fieffé, in his "Histoire des Troupes Etrangères au Service de France," mistaking the 2 appellations, and 2 battalions, of James's Guards, for 2 *different* regiments, nevertheless acquaints us, how "les Régiments des Gardes Irlandaises, et des Gardes du Roi d'Angleterre, y vengèrent glorieusement l'affront de la Boyne et de Limerik."

galloped off for a long time, without being able to find him; at last, we met him very far away from the action, in a hollow, where neither friends nor enemies were to be seen.* That Prince made me a very polite compliment, to which I only replied by a very low bow: after having gazed at me for a moment, he put on his hat, and I mine; then he ordered, that I should be conducted to Lewe." The young Duke was subsequently sent to Antwerp, in order to be transferred to the Tower of London and imprisoned there, under the pretext of his having been, as an Englishman, the subject of William, and, consequently, or for being taken in arms against *him*, a rebel! But Luxembourg soon put down this *Dutch* impudence, by threatening reprisals with respect to several Allied officers, and, among others, the Duke of Ormonde;† so that the Duke of Berwick was, in due course, sent back to the Marshal, instead of being lodged in the Tower of London. As for Lord Lucan, in that attack upon the village of Neerwinden, (which the French took twice, and were driven from as often, ere they could master it,) his Lordship, behaving gallantly, was severely wounded, and, being removed to Huy, shortly after died there, of a fever ‡—" but gained," says a Williamite writer, "as much honour by his generosity and humanity to the English in that fatal battle, as by his bravery and conduct in the field." Mr. O'Conor adds of his Lordship—"Arminius was never more popular among the Germans, than Sarsfield among the Irish—to this day his name is venerated—*canitur adhuc*. No man was ever more attached to his country, or more devoted to his king, and religion."§ In a manuscript volume, written in the reign of William's successor, Queen Anne, and containing a copy of Dean Lynch's Latin version of Keating's History of Ireland, &c., (for a knowledge of which I am indebted to Mr.

* William, up to this period of the engagement, having been successful, there was *no* necessity for his incurring any unusual personal risk. But, when it became requisite, that his troops should be encouraged as much as possible, he acted, at the head of artillery, infantry, and cavalry, to the admiration of friends and foes.

† James Butler, 13th Earl and 2nd Duke of Ormonde, heading a charge of British cavalry, received 2 sword-wounds; had his horse shot under him; and, when on the point of being killed, was rescued, as a prisoner, by 1 of the French Guards, who judged him to be a person of distinction, from the rich diamond ring on his finger. At Namur, to which the Duke was conveyed, "the misfortune of his Grace," says his biographer, "was a blessing to a great many of the poor prisoners of the Allied troops, who were confined in the same town, as he distributed among them a considerable sum of money." He also amply rewarded the French Guardsman, to whom he owed his life. This illustrious Irish Protestant nobleman had, from *very natural apprehensions for the safety of his Church*, deserted King James II. in 1688, and afterwards voted for the Prince of Orange as *King*; but only as "*fearing a Regent might pave the way to a Republick.*" He finally sacrificed everything for the Stuart cause, of which more hereafter.

‡ Those particulars respecting Lord Lucan's death are derived from the Lettres Historiques for September, 1693, and from his Lordship's countryman and contemporary, Plunkett. The editor of the Continental periodical writes—'Le Lord Lucan, Sarsfield, celébre par la derniere guerre d'Irlande, et que je mis au nombre des morts, n'étoit alors que blessé; mais on a apris depuis, qu'il est mort de ses blessures à Huy, où il avoit été transporté." Plunkett states—"The Earl of Lucan, after doeing actions worthy of himself, was desperately wounded, and thereby fell into a feaver, of which he dyed soon after." Such is what we know from History, as contrasted with Romance, on the subject.

§ If compared, however, with such commanders, of the old native race, as Hugh O'Neill, in Elizabeth's, and Owen Roe O'Neill, in Cromwell's time, Sarsfield was no better than a puffed Palesman. "In the science of war," Mr. O'Conor elsewhere justly remarks, "Hugh, the famous Earl of Tyrone, and Owen Roe O'Nial, far surpassed him. He had neither their skill, experience, or capacity."

Gilbert,) I find, with Father Gelasius Mac Mahon's lines on the Duchess of Berwick, previously cited, the following :—

"EPITAPHIUM ILL^{MI} D^{NI} SARSFIELD, COMITIS DE LUCAN, &c.

"Ingens exiguâ Sarsfield hic conditur urnâ,
Inclyta sed virtus cuncta per ora volat.
Stemma, fides, Patriæ pietas, constantia Regi
Invictum Pugilis vexit ad astra Decus.
Heu gratum Auriacis! Heu flebile funus Hibernis!
Terror ut Auriacis, his jacet unus Amor."

The Duke of Berwick was employed in operations connected with the reduction of Charleroy, which, after a creditable resistance of 27 days' open trenches, was surrendered, October 13th, to the French; the gallant M. de Boisselot, so famous for the successful defence of Limerick against William in 1690, being made Governor of this important acquisition from the Allies.

The French Army of Germany, in 1693, was at first commanded by the Marshal Duke de Lorges, and afterwards by Monseigneur. Among its Lieutenant-Generals was Lord Mountcashel; and the Irish troops attached to it were the Regiments of Mountcashel, Dublin, Charlemont, and the Marine; forming altogether 9 battalions. But, by the ability of the Imperial General, Prince Louis of Baden, that army was prevented effecting any thing in proportion to its considerable numerical superiority. Hostilities, indeed, commenced in May, with a quick reduction of Heidelberg by De Lorges; but, owing to the incapacity or cowardice of its miserable Governor, who was duly degraded by the Prince of Baden. At Heidelberg, and elsewhere, Lord Mountcashel, or his men, are noticed, yet not in any case worth detailing; the campaign, on the French side, having been 1 of plunder, rather than glory.* In Spain, the conquests of the French, in 1693, under the Marshal Duke de Noailles, supported by the Comte d'Etrées at sea, were confined to the reduction, June 1st—10th, of Rosas, or Roses, in Catalonia, and the adjacent Fort of the Trinity. Brigadier John Wauchop mounted the trenches before the town twice, and the Honourable Arthur Dillon, and the grenadiers of his regiment, were among the troops who carried the counterscarp.

In Italy, the Allies were so strong, in 1693, that the Marshal de Catinat was obliged to remain upon the defensive till autumn, when, being well reinforced, he marched against and engaged them, October 4th, in the battle of Marsaglia, or Orbassan. The Allies, under the Duke of Savoy, the famous Prince Eugene, and other distinguished Generals, including Charles, Duke of Schonberg, on the part of William III., consisted of Italian, Imperial, Spanish, Huguenot or Vaudois troops, to the amount of 38 or 39 battalions, and 79 squadrons,† with 31 pieces of cannon. The French army, in which Catinat had some eminent officers of the War of the Revolution in Ireland, or his own countryman, Lieutenant-General the Marquis de la Hoguette, and Major-General D'Usson, besides Major-General Thomas Maxwell, Brigadiers

* Henceforth, to the end of this war, *no* mention is made of the Irish corps serving in Germany, since nothing has been found related, to *distinguish* them from their French fellow-soldiers there. What were the national corps acting with the French in *that* quarter may be collected from the histories of the several regiments previously given.

† Lines of battle, in Quincy, and St. Gervais, compared, and retotted.

John Wauchop, Francis O'Carroll, &c., consisted generally of French troops, and several Irish corps; making, altogether, 47 battalions, and 78 squadrons, with 30 pieces of cannon. After a warm contest of between 4 and 5 hours, Catinat was victorious, with only about 2000 men, killed or wounded; having taken about 2000 prisoners, including 215 officers, besides 103 colours or standards, and all the artillery of the enemy; who acknowledged their loss in killed, wounded, and prisoners, to have been about 5500 men; though it was *far* greater, according to the French.

The Irish troops, marked in the line of battle as present, were the King's and Queen's Dismounted Dragoons, each composing 1 battalion, and both brigaded together in the 1st line of the centre under Thomas Maxwell; the Regiment of Daniel O'Brien, 4th Viscount Clare, forming 3 battalions, brigaded with a French regiment in the 2nd line of the centre; and the Queen's Regiment of Infantry, or Luttrell's, in 2 battalions, with 1 battalion of the Regiment of Limerick, or Talbot's, brigaded together in the same line under John Wauchop. To these Irish, the victory was, in a great degree, attributable. The French official narrative refers to the Irish regiments, as having "fought with an extreme valour," and as having "in the space of half a league," or a mile and a half, "despatched more than 1000 of the enemy with sword-thrusts, and clubbed muskets." Another notice in French, by Lieutenant-General Count Arthur Dillon the younger, relates, how "the Irish distinguished themselves by a remarkable stratagem. Finding themselves very much incommoded by a redoubt, situated on the right of the enemy, they advanced towards him, holding their arms with the butt-ends upwards. It being supposed, that they were coming forward to desert, they were allowed to approach. They then jumped into the redoubt, of which they made themselves masters, and turned its cannon against the enemies. M. de Catinat, who had granted permission for this manœuvre, availed himself of the enemy's surprise, and put them to the rout. He gave," it is added, "the most advantageous account of the conduct of the Irish, and of the share which they had in his victory." Of the King's and Queen's Dismounted Dragoons, more especially, the Marshal, writing, October 7th, to Louis XIV., states—"These 2 regiments of dragoons, Sire, which were in the centre of the line, have done surprising things, in the way of valour and good order, during the combat. They have overthrown squadrons sword in hand, charging them face to face, and overthrowing them."* Plunkett, referring to the Duke of Savoy, alleges— "The Duke broake the 1st line of the French. Then he came up, to charge the 2nd; not doubting, but to have the like success. In this line were several battalions of Irish, mixed with French. The Duke of Savoy, having perceiv'd great numbers of Irish to be in the line, ordered his men, to attack them, with sword in hand. In this attempt, his Royal Highness committed an important errour. For, by that method of fighting, the Irish generally prevayl. The attack being given, the Confederates were soon forc'd to ply," *i. e.*, give way, "and take their flight. The line pursued. The Irish overran their orders, and Cattinat, seeing there was no recalleing of them, commanded the whole army to follow.

* Of these 2 Irish corps of Dismounted Dragoons, it is also reported, in connexion with a very distinguished French officer—"Le Comte de Medavy, a fait des actions extraordinaires à la teste des Dragons du Roy et de la Reyne de l'Angleterre, où il a toûjours esté," until wounded, as particularized.

Great was the slaughter of the Confederats. The Irish pursued so swiftly, that their foot overtook some of the hostile cavalry. The Duke of Savoy narrowly escaped with 10 horsemen, into his capital citty of Turin."* Of the Jacobite officers who fell, alluded to as "having fought with an extraordinary valour at the head of the Irish regiments," and as having "signalized themselves by the actions which they had performed on that day of battle," were the Major-General and Brigadier Thomas Maxwell, Colonel of the King of England's Dismounted Dragoons, Brigadier John Wauchop, also Colonel of Dragoons, "both Scots;" Brigadier Francis O'Carroll, Colonel of the Queen of England's Dismounted Dragoons, "and others, worthy of lasting memory." Daniel O'Brien, 4th Viscount Clare, acting as Colonel of his family regiment, was so severely wounded, that he subsequently died at Pignerol. James de Lacy, of the family of Ballingarry-Lacy, County of Limerick, Brigadier, Quarter-Master-General, Colonel and Commandant of the Prince of Wales's Regiment of Infantry in Ireland, was likewise mortally wounded. His young nephew, Peter de Lacy, who had been an Ensign under him in Ireland when only 13, and whom, after the Treaty of Limerick, he brought into France, was, at the time of this battle, a Lieutenant in the Regiment of Athlone, and was ultimately the famous Field-Marshal de Lacy, in the service of Russia, and father of the celebrated Field-Marshal in the service of Austria.†

The greatest officer, who fell on the side of the Allies, was Charles Duke of Schonberg, son of the veteran Marshal-Duke, slain at the Boyne. He was the commander of those regiments, mostly of French and the rest of Swiss Protestants, or Vaudois, maintained, for the Duke of Savoy's service, by William III. Having disapproved of giving battle, he declined to act in any higher rank than that of Colonel, at the head of his own regiment. In that capacity, he behaved most gallantly, as did his Huguenot or Vaudois forces in general, who suffered in proportion; above 2-3rds of them having been destroyed. He was brought to the ground by a wound in the thigh, and was about to be immediately despatched by the hostile soldiery, (probably Irish,) who knew him, when his faithful valet De Sale, crying out "Quarter!" threw himself between his master and them, thereby sacrificing his own life. An Irish officer, then coming up, saved the Duke for the time, by ordering him to be made a prisoner; and the Marshal de Catinat allowed him to be conveyed to Turin, for his recovery. But the Duke died there, October 17th, generally and deservedly regretted; and was interred, according to his wish, at Lausanne.‡ Sir Paul Rycaut, the English Resident for William III. at Hamburg, after noting how very sad this overthrow of the Allies was according to the accounts from Paris, though he hoped the next letters from Turin

* Fieffé says—"La victoire fut decidée en faveur des Français par une charge de 20 bataillons, qui s'avancèrent, en croisant la baïonnette. C'était la première fois qu'on employait cette manœuvre, dont s'acquaittèrent fort bien les Régiments Etrangers," or those, with others, of "Talbot, *Athlone*, Dragons à Pied de la Reine d'Angleterre, et Clare." Yet, neither in the "ordre de bataille" given by Quincy, nor in those given by St. Gervais, is the Regiment of *Athlone* mentioned as present there, though certainly 1 of those attached to the army of Catinat in Italy.

† Copy of the Marshal's journal and other family papers.

‡ Compare the self-devotion of De Sale with that of Coteron farther on, or at the battle of Cassano, in 1705. The particulars respecting the Duke of Schonberg are taken from the contemporary accounts published in Holland; including the narrative of the Allied defeat from Vander Meer, the Resident of the Dutch Republic at Turin.

would show the loss of the Confederates to have been less, concludes thus—"Nothing, however, in this battle, can repaie the loss of so great a man as the Duke of Schomberg, which is too glorious a triumph for our enemies to boast of." Such are the most interesting particulars connected with the battle of Marsaglia, or Orbassan, where the Irish appear to have gained the highest honour which they acquired since their landing in France. In the account given of this engagement by Lord Macaulay—in which he certainly ought *not* to have been silent respecting the above-recorded circumstances of the death of Charles, Duke of Schonberg, as well from the nature of the circumstances themselves, as from the Duke being the chief officer of the Williamite Huguenot contingent there, and son of the veteran Marshal, who bore such a remarkable share in the events, which secured to William the triple royalty of the British Isles—his Lordship adverts, as follows, to the creditable conduct of the Irish, in Catinat's army: "This battle is memorable as the *first* of a long series of battles, in which the Irish troops retrieved the honour, lost, by misfortunes, and misconduct, in domestic war. Some of the exiles of Limerick showed, on that day, under the standard of France, a valour, that distinguished them, among many thousands of brave men." But, on *several* occasions, previous to this famous day, or *wherever* the Irish were brought into immediate or direct contact with an enemy since their landing on the Continent, it is sufficiently evident, from *this* work, that they were duly noticed as remarkable for their bravery.

In 1694, the Marshal Duke de Noailles, with 15,000 foot, and 6000 horse, entered Catalonia in May, and, by the 27th, reached the river Ter. It was dangerous to pass in presence of an enemy, from its considerable width, the uncertainty of footing occasioned by its moving sands, and a depth of water up to one's waist. The Spanish army under the Duke of Escalona, variously represented as somewhat less, and as considerably more in number, than the French, but certainly inferior in point of artillery, were posted along the banks, in order to defend the fords, from Verges, on their left, to Montgry, on their right; those fords being well intrenched. The passage was first attempted by Noailles at Montgry, where the Spaniards had three battalions, protected by good works, and supported by 10 squadrons. The assailants were received with a warm fire, accompanied with a loud defiance from drums, trumpets, and hautbois. But, states the Marshal, writing to Louis XIV., the same day—"The Carabiniers, headed by M. de Chazeron, the grenadiers of the army, with the Regiment of the Queen of England's Dragoons, which is an excellent corps that M. de St. Silvestre was desirous to lead as *he* commanded the infantry, dashed into the water with an extraordinary vigour, and forced the enemy to abandon their retrenchments. An action of greater vigour, or better conducted than on the part of these gentlemen, could not be witnessed." The Spanish infantry there were either slain, or captured, their cavalry put to flight; and, higher up the stream, another party of infantry, stationed at a wood about the Duke of Escalona's quarters to defend the ford of Ouilla, "wishing to make a stand," says a French contemporary, "on the approach of the Dragoons of La Salle, and of the Carabiniers, to whom were joined the Dismounted Dragoons of the Queen of England, was defeated; such as were not killed being made prisoners of war." In this engagement, which, including a pursuit, mixed with cavalry-charges, for 12 miles, lasted from between 3 and 4 in the morning to about 11 o'clock, the French did not lose above 500 men. The

Spaniards admit their loss, in killed and taken, to have been 3000 or 4000 men, though the French make it many more; and, among the spoils of the vanquished, were their tents and baggage, with the Duke of Escalona's equipage and papers, 16, colours, &c. Of officers praised by the Marshal, for having been "several times distinguished" during the day, was Charles O'Brien, 5th Viscount Clare, as "Milord Clare, at the head of a regiment of dragoons," or that of the Queen of England above mentioned. Among the important results of this victory, were the reduction of Palamos, Girona, Ostalric, or Hostalrich, and Castelfollit.

In Italy, the Marshal de Catinat, assembling, in May, 1694, a portion of his army near Pignerol, "despatched, in the mean time," observes my French authority, "8 Irish battalions into the Valley of La Perouse, in order to oppose the Vaudois, and to put a stop to their incursions. On arriving there, they killed a great number of those who were taken off their guard; which obliged the Duke of Savoy, who had an interest in protecting them, to send them 600 men of his regular troops, and the Marquis de Parelle to command there." King William's historian, Harris, refers to some "small successes of the Vaudois in the Valley of Pragelas," and "their routing some Irish detachments in the Valley of St. Martin," as not "worthy the reader's notice." On the other hand, according to Mr. O'Conor, between the number of the Alpine mountaineers cut off, and the extent of devastation and pillage committed among them, by the Irish, Catinat's commission was executed with a terrible fidelity; the memory of which "has rendered the Irish name and nation odious to the Vaudois. Six generations," he remarks, "have since passed away, but neither time, nor subsequent calamities, have obliterated the impression made by the waste and desolation of this military incursion."

This year, we, in reference to the Irish of Catinat's army, renew our acquaintance with Brigadier Don Hugh O'Donnell, known on the Continent as Earl of Tyrconnell; so celebrated during the War of the Revolution in Ireland, from the alleged prophecies, and consequent popularity, associated with him as "Ball-dearg," or of the "red mark;" and subsequently still more talked of, as, like another Jacobite Brigadier, Henry Luttrell, having finally passed over to the side of William III., receiving a similar government pension, or 1 of £500 per annum. After the conclusion of the war in Ireland, or in 1692, O'Donnell, having proceeded by Dublin to London, was offered there the command of that body of his countrymen in Ireland, who, not having chosen to accompany the majority of the Jacobite or national army to France, were formed, as Catholics, into a corps for the service of William III.'s Catholic ally, the Emperor Leopold I. of Austria, to be employed against the Turks in Hungary. Desirous, however, of returning to the service of Spain, O'Donnell refused this command; which was, in consequence, conferred upon a nobleman of the most anciently-renowned or Irian race of Uladh or Ulster, Brian Macgennis, Lord Iveagh; who accordingly led those Irish destined for the Imperial service into Germany, and thence into Hungary.* O'Donnell, after being detained by illness till 1693 in

* These Irish, about 2200 in number, were long delayed in Munster by contrary winds; landed from Cork at Hamburg, early in the summer of 1692; and, being mustered by the Imperial Commissary near Bergersdorf, were marched thence into Hungary; where they suffered so much against the Ottomans, that the remnant had, by November, 1693, to be drafted into other corps of the Imperial army.

London, first went to Flanders, and then into Spain. By the State Papers, abstracted in Thorpe's Catalogue for 1834 of the Southwell MSS., we find the Brigadier, in May, 1694, corresponding, from Madrid, with the English Secretary at War, William Blathwayt, upon "a design for forming Irish Regiments in Spain for the service of that state, in order to draw off the malcontents against the government of King William III." The next letter, mentioned as directed to Secretary Blathwayt by O'Donnell, is dated from Turin, in September; the writer noting how, through the assistance given him at the Allied quarters by the Duke of Savoy, and the Spanish Viceroy of the Milanese, he, in order to induce the Jacobite Irish in Catinat's army to desert, had "officers, on all the passes in the neighbourhood of their encampments, to receive 'em, and invite 'em." But, he complains of those Irish corps, how watchful the officers were of their men; as "having no other livelihood but their companies, and no way of recruiting the desertions." As a Brigadier in the service of Charles II. of Spain, and pensioned by William III., as likewise a Brigadier in James II.'s service when abandoning it, O'Donnell, by thus seeking to gain over the Irish from the French, was aiming to be equally useful to his Catholic and Protestant patrons, Charles and William; *both* members of the same great alliance, or that of the League of Augsburg, against Louis XIV., and James II., as confederated with Louis.

In 1695, the Spaniards attempted, early in the campaign, to recover some of the places lost in 1694, and, among them, Ostalric, or Hostalrich, which was accordingly blocked up. The Marshal Duke de Noailles, being ill himself, ordered Lieutenant-General de St. Silvestre, accompanied by the Honourable Colonel Arthur Dillon, with a portion of the army, including the Irish troops, to relieve the town in May; which was effected, the enemy retiring at the Lieutenant-General's approach. "On his return," writes the Marshal, "the rear-guard was attacked, with an insolent audaciousness, by the miquelets, to the number of about 4000, and by 5 squadrons of cavalry. Dillon commanded it. This Irish Colonel made such a good disposition of the troops, that the enemy, far from being able to break in upon them, was put to flight." Quincy, who describes the rear-guard as "composée de troupes Irlandoises," adds, that the enemy had about 50 men killed, besides a Colonel of Dragoons, and that some, also, were taken prisoners. On the French advance, in July, under the Duke of Vendome, to raise the blockade of Castelfollit, after descending a mountain, "and observing another which the enemies occupied, and which commanded the road to Castelfollit," says the official journal, "he sent forward to it Mylord Clare, with the Dismounted Dragoons of the Queen of England, and the grenadiers of the army, who made themselves masters of this height." In August, the Marquis of Gastanaga, Viceroy of Catalonia, with a considerable Spanish force, and a very fine corps of 3000 British and 500 Dutch troops, disembarked by Admiral Russell from his fleet, invested Palamos by land; while the Admiral himself bombarded the town and castle so severely from the sea, that they were, in a manner, demolished; having been set on fire in several places, and continued burning for a whole night. The enemy, however, had finally to retire, without attaining their object, before the Duke of Vendome. "During the siege," observes the contemporary Paris account, "150 Irish threw themselves into the place, where they distinguished themselves by their valour."

On the side of Italy, or Piedmont, the Irish of Catinat's army were still employed against the Vaudois, or Barbets. A French correspondence on this head, dated "Pignerol, January 16th, 1695," states—"The snows have fallen in these quarters this winter in such great abundance, that, for several years, we have not witnessed a similar quantity. . . . The Barbets have always been repulsed with loss, by the troops, which have been posted in different places. Yesterday, notwithstanding the care that is taken to have good intelligence between the several quarters, 100 Barbets placed themselves in ambush between Villar and Diblon. They, nevertheless, did not venture to attack a convoy of meal proceeding from La Perouse to Villar; and contented themselves with seizing upon 6 mules, laden with merchandise, that passed 2 hours afterwards, without an escort. But the news of this having been brought to Villar, where the Irish Regiment of Clancarty was quartered, the enemy were pursued so closely, that the booty was recovered, with a loss, to the Barbets, of 7 or 8 killed or wounded, and of 3 prisoners. We destroyed, moreover, 1 of their *corps de garde*." On another occasion, after mentioning the despatch of a detachment, under a French Captain, from the garrison of Pignerol, and the narrow escape of that officer and his men from 500 of the Barbets, aided by 500 Germans, who burned a large mass of wood provided for the fortress, the same correspondence from "Pignerol, March 6th, 1695," adds—"An Irish officer, who is quartered in the Valley of Pragelas, has made a foray into the mountains of the Barbets, where he has burned many houses, made some prisoners, and brought away a quantity of cattle." In treating of this mountain-war, Mr. O'Conor naturally expatiates on the vigour of his countrymen, at "the pursuit of the Vaudois, in the unknown and lonely defiles of the Alpine hills, where deep chasms, and narrow pathways, fit only to afford a footing to the chamois, and the wild-goat, led to the retreats of brave and desperate men; where every rock afforded cover for a deadly aim; where the repercussion and echo of distant discharges of musquetry from concealed enemies magnified their numbers; where deep caverns and hollows, concealed by treacherous snows or frail glaciers, swallowed the unwary adventurers in fathomless abysses." In such perilous service, "they displayed their wonted bravery, agility, perseverance, and endurance of privations. They scaled the highest rocks, plunged into the mountain streams, evaded the avalanches of stones and trees which the Vaudois rolled down, beat them from their intrenchments, pursued them into the wildest recesses, and carried terror and dismay into the heart of the mountains; plundered, pillaged, destroyed, and burned what they could not carry off, and returned to the camp, driving before them herds and flocks, the only wealth of the foe." The intelligence from "Pignerol, October 16th, 1695," after a remark, of the campaign having been, to all appearance, over, and the enemy only thinking of getting into winter-quarters, gives this anecdote, as the most interesting exception to that state of things. "The 12th of this month, 6 Irish soldiers, and 1 of the Regiment of Bearn, crossed the Cluson, without arms, to go in quest of some forage. They were surprised by an equal number of Barbets, well armed, under a Captain, who made them prisoners, and conducted them to the top of a mountain, in order to strip them of their clothes. For this purpose, they laid down their arms; but the Irish giving the word in *their* language, each seized upon 1 of them, the soldier of the Regiment of Bearn killed 2 of them; and the 6 Irish soldiers treated, in like manner, the Captain, and the rest, except 1, who asked for quarter, and whom they conducted to the camp at Diblon; where the Marshal de Catinat caused some money to be distributed among them."

On February 19th, this year, Brigadier Don Hugh O'Donnell addressed, from Turin, to William III., a letter, described, in Thorpe's Catalogue, as "long and interesting," with respect to the enlistment of Irish fugitives on the side of the Allies, or that of the League of Augsburg; such refugees to be employed in Catalonia, where William's confederates in that League, the Spaniards, were so pressed by the French. During this campaign, O'Donnell, who, since 1693, had served as a volunteer, obtained a regiment of foot—how far through desertions from Irish in the French army, or from other sources, I cannot say—which regiment he carried into Catalonia, and continued there to the conclusion of the war by the fall of Barcelona, where he was present. Having, by this time, recovered the favour he had lost at the Court of Madrid, by leaving its army, in order to espouse the cause of King James in Ireland, O'Donnell, soon after, became a Major-General in Spain, and is mentioned, in that rank, with its forces in Flanders, in August, 1701.* His Williamite pension of £500 per annum was still payable in 1703, or the reign of William's successor, Queen Anne. It is the 6th on the list of those Irish pensions, to the yearly amount of £17,634, 17s. 0½d., voted unnecessary by the colonial Parliament in Dublin, under the Lord Lieutenancy of James Butler, 2nd Duke of Ormonde. But, of the general representation based upon this vote, a contemporary English historian says, that it, "when it was perfected, and presented to his Grace, met with a cold reception;" Mr. Secretary Southwell merely informing the House, "that the Lord Lieutenant would take such care of it, as might most conduce to the service of the nation." How much longer O'Donnell's pension continued to be paid, and consequently when he *died*, I have not discovered.

The earliest enterprise of the campaign of 1696 was one for the "restoration" of King James in England, with the aid of a French veteran force of about 16,000 men, under the Marquis d'Harcourt as Captain-General, and the gallant Richard Hamilton of the War of the Revolution in Ireland, as Lieutenant-General. "King James," writes the Duke of Berwick, "had privately concerted a rising in England, to which he had sent over a number of officers. His friends there had found means to raise 2000 horse well-equipped, and even regimented, ready to take the field at the earliest notice. Many persons of the first distinction were also engaged in the affair. But all had unanimously resolved, not to throw off the mask, until a body of troops should have first landed in the island. The Most Christian King," Louis XIV., "had readily consented to supply these; but he insisted, that, before they should be embarked, the English should take up arms; as he was not willing to risk his troops, without being sure of finding there a party to receive them. Neither side being desirous of relaxing from what it had resolved upon, such fair dispositions could not lead to any thing; which determined the King of England to send me over, as his envoy on the spot, to endeavour to convince the English of the sincerity of the intentions of the Court of France,

* So far our information respecting O'Donnell is brought down by Dr. O'Donovan, in his learned papers, entitled "The O'Donnells in Exile;" but without being aware of the correspondence, from the Continent, of O'Donnell with the Williamite government, mentioned in Thorpe's Catalogue.

and to engage them to take up arms, without waiting for the descent; promising, that, as soon as they should do so, the Marquis d'Harcourt, who was nominated General of this expedition, would cause the troops to embark. I then passed over in disguise to England. I proceeded to London, where I had several conversations with some of the principal Lords. But, it was to no purpose, that I said to them whatever I could most strongly conceive, and represented to them the necessity of not allowing so fine an opportunity to escape. They continued firm to their desire, that, previous to their rising, the King of England should land with an army. To tell the truth, their reasons were good; for it was certain, that, as soon as the Prince of Orange would have witnessed the revolt, or would have had information of the project, which could not long remain concealed, on account of the preparations which it was necessary to make for the landing, he would have immediately ordered a fleet to sea, and would have blockaded the ports of France; by which means, those who might revolt, finding themselves driven, with their hastily-raised troops, to fight against a good army, composed of veteran and disciplined soldiers, it was certain, that they would have been very soon crushed." The Duke, although disguised, could not remain so generally unknown, as he necessarily wished to be, while in England. "I recollect to have heard him say," observes Montesquieu, "that a man had recognized him by a certain family air, and, particularly, by the length of his fingers; and that, fortunately, this man was a Jacobite, who said to him—'*May God bless you, in all your undertakings!*' which recovered him from the embarrassment he was in." Unable to accomplish the object of the very unpromising commission with which he was intrusted—or that of endeavouring to make those to whom he was sent act against the dictates of good sense—and being likewise apprised of the formation of a conspiracy against William's person with which *he* did not wish to be mixed up, the Duke left London, as soon as possible, by the way he had come, and reached the house, near the coast, where he was to hear of his vessel. There, lying down upon a bench, he fell asleep, until roused, in a couple of hours, by a loud noise at the door, when, on getting up, he beheld a number of men entering, armed with guns. His first natural surprise and alarm were soon dissipated, at recognizing, by the glimmering light of a lamp, the master of his vessel; who, to be the better provided against any accident, had taken the precaution of bringing with him a trusty guard of 12 well-armed sailors. The Duke then embarked, and reached Calais in 3 hours. The general results of this enterprise against William were, that, on the discovery of the Jacobite plot, to be supported by an invasion from France, he obtained forces from Flanders, in addition to the troops he had already in England, and likewise sent a fleet to sea sufficient to oppose the designed invasion; so that the French corps intended for that undertaking were finally ordered elsewhere; King James, after remaining for some time at Calais and Boulogne, returned to St. Germain; and the Duke of Berwick, who had rejoined his father, went to serve that year's campaign in Flanders, where nothing of consequence occurred. According to the Irish Jacobite Plunkett, the frustration of the plan, for effecting King James's "restoration" on this occasion, was owing, among other causes, to the obstruction offered by the weather to an invasion of England, at a period when a landing there might otherwise have been effected, with every prospect of subsequent success. "There was," alleges that writer, "*no opposition by sea*, nor any, at that nick of time, on the land of England. Yett this most excellent opportunity miscarryed also. For *the wind remained contrary for a fortnight: in which space 1 of the English fleets came home:* and so his Maiesty was forced to return to St. Germains." A similar observation is made by a contemporary Williamite annalist of this war, in reference to the disappointment of the French. "God," he says, "caused *the winds to blow directly against them, till the whole was discovered, and the English and Dutch fleet upon their coasts.*"

The Duke of Vendome, in 1696, commanded the French in Catalonia against the Spaniards under Prince George of Hesse Darmstadt, who had fought for William III. in Ireland. At the beating of the Spanish cavalry, June 1st, in the combat near Ostalric, or Hostalrich, the Duke, states my authority, "posted so advantageously, upon the heights, the grenadiers, and the Dismounted Dragoons of the Queen of England, that they equally overlooked the plain where the combat was to take place, and the retrenchments of Ostalric, so that they covered the flanks of our troops." On the 16th, having advanced to Tordera, in order to cut off the communication of the Spanish army with Barcelona, the Duke, upon the 22nd, despatched the "Lieutenant-Colonel of the Regiment of Dillon,* with 600 men," add the French accounts, "to fortify himself at Calella, a little town on the sea-shore, beyond Pineda. He was attacked there, the 23rd, by 2000 men of the regular troops, and by 3000 miquelets, or peasants, who were repulsed with the loss of 25 or 30 men killed, without our having had more than 3 soldiers wounded. He was again attacked, the 24th; which obliged the Duke de Vendome to send there a detachment of cavalry, at whose appearance the enemy took to flight; though they had some brigantines to second them, with the protection of their cannon." This Lieutenant-Colonel, by the time the Spaniards assailed him, would seem to have been sufficiently fortified or covered in his post, from the little *he* suffered, compared with what the very superior force of the enemy did.

The Duke of Savoy, having finally decided on seceding from the League of Augsburg, and restoring tranquillity to his own dominions, as well as to Italy in general, by a treaty of peace and alliance with Louis XIV., united his forces, in 1696, with those of France under the Marshal de Catinat, to compel the Allies to consent to the neutrality of Italy. The Duke and the Marshal, for this purpose, September 18th, invested Valenza, in the Milanese. It was under an experienced Governor, Don Francisco Colmenero, with a garrison of between 6000 and 7000 men, Germans, Spaniards, and Huguenots in William III.'s pay. All the preparations for reducing the place being completed, the trenches were opened, September 24th, and the operations lasted till October 8th, when the siege terminated, in consequence of the submission of the powers confederated against France, on the 7th, at Vigevano, to ratify the terms dictated to them for the pacification of Italy. At this siege, the Honourable Brigadier Simon Luttrell of Luttrell's-town, County of Dublin, mounted the

---

* The Honourable Arthur Dillon, having been so young, or not 20, when he brought to France the corps levied in Ireland by the interest of his family, and of which he should consequently be Colonel, it was necessary, that his inexperience should be compensated by the experience of a competent Lieutenant-Colonel, the officer referred to in the text, who was a Frenchman. The Lieutenant-Colonel's family name, long connected with this regiment, was Manery, or Mannery, which I, more than once, find misprinted, and correct accordingly.

trenches, September 28th, and the 2 battalions of his corps, the Queen's Regiment of Infantry, as well as the 2 of Sir John Fitz-Gerald, Baronet, of Clonlish, or the infantry Regiment of Limerick, did so, the night between September 30th and October 1st. The most considerable affair was during the night between the 29th and 30th, when, among several regiments upon duty in the trenches, there were 100 of the King of England's Dismounted Dragoons, or the corps of Dominick Sarsfield, 4th Viscount Kilmallock, and the 3 battalions of the infantry Regiment of Charles O'Brien, 5th Viscount Clare. "About 10 o'clock at night," according to the French narratives, "the besieged made a sortie with 200 grenadiers, sustained by 400 fusileers, who had orders not to fire, but to descend into the boyau," a portion of the trenches, "and sword in hand, and with fixed bayonets, to surprise, and kill, all that were to be found there. This was to avoid drawing upon them the French cavalry; from which there were, every night, 200 on the right and left of the palisades and trenches. The Allies advanced very silently as far as the head of the trench, without being perceived on our part, until the instant they were upon the workmen, who, falling back upon the trench, spread much disorder there. The alarm having been given, the Allies, on perceiving they were discovered, fired a severe volley, inflicting much injury upon the companies of Netancourt and of Condé. But, as soon as these were reassembled, rallied, and sustained by a detachment of the Irish Regiment of Clare, the Allies were obliged to retire, and were pursued even to their palisades. In this smart encounter, the besiegers had 25 soldiers, 2 Captains, and some other officers killed, with 35 soldiers, and several officers wounded."

In 1697, Louis XIV., strengthened by his peace with the Duke of Savoy, assembled 3 armies in Flanders; the 1st under the Marshal de Villeroy; the 2nd, under the Marshal de Boufflers; the 3rd under the Marshal de Catinat. The 2 former were to hold the Allies, under William III., and the Elector of Bavaria, in check, while the 3rd was to attack the important fortress of Ath. Before this town, defended by the Comte de Rœux, with above 3800 men, Catinat, aided by the great military engineer Vauban, broke ground, May 22nd, with about 40,000 men, and a powerful artillery. It held out till June 5th, when the capitulation was regulated, and the garrison marched out, the 7th. At the reduction of this fortress, Colonel Andrew Lee, or the 3 battalions of his regiment, are mentioned, as having, on different nights, mounted the trenches, sometimes accompanied by the illustrious Vauban, and Catinat himself.

In Spain, the great object of France, for 1697, was the reduction of Barcelona. This was a very difficult undertaking—from the strength of the fortifications—from the ample supply of artillery, above 240 pieces, with munitions of war in proportion—from the amount of the garrison, under Prince George of Hesse-Darmstadt, consisting of 11,000 regular infantry, and 1500 cavalry, besides 4000 civic militia—from the compass of the walls, and of the adjacent Fort of Montjuich, preventing an entire investment, and thus facilitating an introduction of external supplies— while the Count de Velasco, Viceroy of Catalonia, lay encamped about 6 miles from the town, with a body of 3000 regular cavalry, forming, with militia, irregulars, or guerillas, not less than 20,000 men, to interrupt the progress of a besieging army! That army, under the Duke of Vendome, consisted of 42 battalions, and 55 squadrons, besides marines, from its attendant fleet under the Comte d'Etrées; the whole, however, represented as considerably under 30,000 men,* and consequently appearing rather inadequate for the capture of a place, situated, and supplied as Barcelona was. The French battering-train of 84 pieces of artillery, or 60 heavy cannon and 24 mortars, with ammunition and provisions, being landed from the fleet, June 10th, the troops encamped before the town the 12th, and the trenches were opened the night between the 15th and 16th. The siege, in the course of which, or July 12th, Velasco was ably surprised and routed, at St. Filieu, by Vendome, lasted to August 5th, or for about 52 days' open trenches; the negociations respecting the terms of capitulation occupying till the 10th; and the garrison marching away the 11th. This very important conquest, which cost the French above 400 officers, with from 8000 to 9000 soldiers, and the Spaniards in proportion, reflected corresponding honour upon the Duke of Vendome, who was duly rewarded by Louis XIV.

Among the Irish attached to the Duke's army there, was the Honourable Simon Luttrell of Luttrell's-town, in whose Brigade were the 2 battalions of his own corps, or the Queen's Regiment of Infantry, the single battalion of the infantry Regiment of Clancarty, or that of Colonel Roger Mac Elligot, and a battalion of Vendome's own regiment. The Honourable Arthur Dillon likewise served with a battalion of his regiment; and Colonel Oliver O'Gara with his battalion of the Queen's Dismounted Dragoons. On the approaches to the town, June 13th, says the contemporary French narrative, "the besieged, having abandoned the Convent of the Capuchins, 350 toises from the covered way of the place, the Duke de Vendome caused it to be occupied, that evening, by Colonel Dillon, with 600 men." On the night of June 16th-17th, when, notwithstanding "a violent tempest," and "the besieged having lined the rampart, fronting the attack, with 40 pieces of cannon very well served," the battalions in the trenches acted so well that their progress was but "little retarded," 1 of those corps was the Regiment of Clancarty. Finally, or August 4th, the enemy, on the side of the Llobregat, having "sent out all their cavalry, to cover the entrance of a convoy into the town," while, "to cause a diversion, a very large body of infantry, sustained by some cavalry, came down from a mountain to assail the French posts, the Regiments of Dillon and of Solre, that were encamped conveniently to defend them, flew to arms, and, the Colonels having headed them, attacked the foes so vigorously, charging amidst them sword in hand, that they pursued them even to the tops of their mountains, after having slain a very great quantity of them."—Which overthrow of this very large body of Spaniards, with the routing elsewhere of the main force of their cavalry, prevented the intended entrance of the convoy into Barcelona, and the negociations for a surrender were commenced the following day. To these French statements respecting the Irish there, the Whig writer, Forman, adds—"That, in the siege of Barcelona, in the year 1697, the great Vendosme was so charmed with their courage, and so amazed at the intrepidity of their behaviour, that the particular esteem and notice with which he distinguish'd them, even to the day of his death, is yet very well remembered in France. If what I say here," he concludes, "is not literally true, there are Frenchmen enough, still living, to contradict me."—And this assertion, concerning

* Bellerive says of Vendome—" Il avoit tout au plus 26,000 hommes, en comptant les troupes de la Marine, et les Milicos qui lui étoient venuës du Languedoc." See, likewise, Quincy, and the Continental publications of the time, on this siege.

the high opinion of the Irish as soldiers by Vendome, is corroborated by the testimony of the Chevalier de Bellerive, who afterwards fought under that great commander with the Irish in Spain, and who, noticing their gallantry there, under him, in 1710, says—" M. de Vendosme, who had a particular esteem for this warlike nation, at whose head he had delivered so many combats, and gained so many victories, confessed, that he was surprised at the terrible enterprises which those *butchers of the army* (it is thus that he named them) achieved in his presence."*—Among the garrison of 10,000 men, placed in Barcelona by Vendome, was the Regiment of Dillon; in connexion with which, the veteran Peter Drake of Drakerath, in the County of Meath, observes—" And here I cannot omit the mention of a very extraordinary event. The centinels placed on the breach confidently affirmed, that they saw, in the night, numbers of dreadful apparitions, who were wont to engage one another as in an attack; furiously crying, *kill, advance,* and such like expressions, commonly used on those occasions; and what added the greater authority to these assertions was, that several centinels on that post were found dead without any visible marks of violence, and so supposed to have died of their fears. This occasioned orders for doubling the centinels, and, being sometimes of the number, imagined I both heard and saw the like." The War of the League of Augsburg against Louis XIV. was soon after terminated by the general Treaty of Peace with France, signed at Ryswick by Holland, Spain, and England, in September, and by the German Emperor, and the Empire, in October following.

Early in 1698, Louis XIV., after such a long and burthensome war, was obliged to relieve France, by lessening, as much as possible, the vast and expensive military establishment he had maintained against the Allies; and since his acknowledgment, by the late treaty, of William, as King of England, was incompatible with a continuation, in France, of the Irish forces, hitherto kept up there as James II.'s army, a great reform was ordered to be made among the Irish troops in general. The extent of that reform, or reduction, as already sufficiently shown, in connexion with the special histories of the Irish regiments, need only be referred to here. But the disbanding of so many soldiers, as had belonged to the several broken corps, was productive of the very bad consequences, that might be expected from the long-accustomed avocation of such a number of men being at an end; while it was so very difficult, if not, in the great majority of cases, so impossible, on their part, to obtain *other* regular employment, or means of subsistence, in the strange country which France was to *them*, that they had, on the whole, but too just cause to sympathize with the purport of the noble Moorish veteran's exclamation in the play—

> " Farewell content!
> Farewell the plumed troop, and the big wars,
> That made ambition virtue! O, farewell!
> Farewell the neighing steed, and the shrill trump,
> The spirit-stirring drum, the ear-piercing fife,
> The royal banner; and all quality,
> Pride, pomp, and circumstance of glorious war!—
> And, O you mortal engines, whose rude throats
> The immortal Jove's dread clamours counterfeit,
> Farewell! *Othello's occupation's gone!*"—SHAKSPEARE.

---

* See a further commendation of the Irish by Vendome, in Book iv., under battle of Cassano, in 1705.

Accordingly, "the route between St. Germains and Paris," writes Dr. Doran, "was not safe, because of them; and they added murder to robbery, when they met with resistance. One Irish Jacobite trooper, named Francis O'Neil, was broken alive upon the wheel, for the double crime of plunder, and assassination. Two other ex-soldiers in James's service, *Englishmen*, lacked nerve to take their chance against stout travellers on the road; but they practised the double profession above named, in a quieter and more cowardly way. On pretence of being ill, they sent for a physician, and, when the latter entered their apartment, they fell upon, stabbed, and robbed him. The law was stringently applied to these Jacobite ruffians, whose desperate crimes testify at once to their own utter destitution, and the fallen condition of their Sovereign." In fine, "the town of St. Germains became almost uninhabitable, through the sanguinary violence of the Jacobite brigands. No sober citizen dared venture abroad at night, even in the summer-time; and, to what extent, pillage and murder were carried, by the fierce and hungry partisans who had followed the standard of James, may be seen in the fact, that, on one and the same day, 5 Irish soldiers were 'broken alive,' in St. Germains, for the crime of robbery and assassination, by night, in the town, or its vicinity." As to the Irish Jacobite officers, the hardships, which the reform in question inflicted upon the multitude of unfortunate gentlemen subjected to it, appear, from the consequent representation of their case to Louis in April. "The Irish officers, who have been reformed in France," says my authority, in May, 1698, "have presented a Petition to the King, to inform him of the state they are in, and to entreat assistance from him. They represented to him, that they have remained silent until now, in expectation of what it might be his Majesty's pleasure to order respecting them; but that the extreme necessity, to which they have been reduced, has constrained them to break that silence, in order to lay before his Majesty the pitiable condition of their affairs. That they had fought, during 10 years, in defence of their religion, and of their legitimate Sovereign, with all the zeal, and all the fidelity, that could be required of them, and with a devotion, unparalleled, except among those of their unhappy nation. That, for this cause, they had made a sacrifice of those who were the authors of their birth, of their relatives, their properties, their country, and their lives. That they had the happiness of rendering some important services to his Majesty, by a diversion of 3 years, during which they had sustained, in Ireland, the brunt of the choicest troops of his enemies.* That they had subsequently served in

* The "choicest troops" of Louis XIV.'s enemies, or "the Allies," against which the Irish Jacobites, though so very inadequately supplied with military necessaries, contended for 3 campaigns, were, reckoned by nations, and without including some odd troops, or companies, as follows. In 1689, 28 British, 9 Hiberno-Williamite, 4 Huguenot, and 2 Dutch regiments. In 1690, 34 British, 9 Hiberno-Williamite, 4 Huguenot, 11 Danish, and 18 Dutch regiments—1 of these last, or William III.'s famous Blue Guards, being counted as 3, since containing 3 battalions, and considerably *more* men, than 3 British infantry regiments. In 1691, 29 British, 8 Hiberno-Williamite, 4 Huguenot, 11 Danish, and 15 Dutch regiments. And this formidable array of British, Hiberno-Williamite, and Continental *regulars*, was backed by an active colonial *militia* of many thousand men; the expense of which was, of course, an additional drain upon William III.'s finances. To the diversion, for 3 years, of such a great amount of men and money from the service of "the Allies" on the Continent, the Irish Jacobite officers might well refer, as most beneficial for France, and as consequently entitling *them* to the gratitude of *Louis*. On this "Allied" formation of William's army in Ireland, see, also, a note, under the battle of Landen, in 1693.

France, with a zeal scarcely differing from that of the King's natural subjects; as his Generals, under whose commands they were placed, had borne testimony to his Majesty. That, by the Peace, they not only found themselves deprived of the properties to which they had legitimate claims, but were likewise prohibited returning to their country under pain of *death*.* That they could not look for an asylum among the other Christian Princes, to whom they could assign no other reason for their unhappiness, but that of having served his Majesty, and their own Sovereign, against them. That those Princes would have no regard for them under existing circumstances, since, during the war, they had refused to enter their service, when, after the loss of Ireland, they decided on passing into France. That neither could they any longer remain in the service of their Master, since he had not been mentioned in the Peace, and he was not in a condition to help them.† That they therefore entirely placed their hopes in the goodness and in the compassion of his Majesty, from whom alone they had some right to expect some relief. That they would not represent to him, that the Huguenots, who had quitted the service of his Majesty, were advantageously supported, and put into possession of the inheritances of his suppliants, because his Majesty was in a position, rather to give, than to receive, examples of charity, and of compassion. That they were satisfied with representing to him, that they had no way of making out a subsistence, in a foreign country, except by casting themselves at the feet of his Majesty. That such of them, as would be fit for other occupations than those of war, had neither the means, nor the friends, necessary to enable them so to apply themselves. That it had pleased his Majesty to promise the reformed allowance to Captains and Lieutenants who chose to remain attached to their regiments; but that this reformed allowance was so trifling, that scarcely could it supply them with indifferent food, without leaving them anything for clothing. That the condition of the Sub-Lieutenants and of the Ensigns was much more lamentable still, since they had only been promised the pay of common soldiers; a very small recompense, for a service of 10 years, to persons, most of them with a wife and children.

* In the Declaration from the Williamite "Camp, by Lymerick, the 5th of October, 1691," to "the officers and soldiers of the Irish army," William's Commander-in-Chief, Baron de Ginkell, after instituting a distinction between such as "had rather promote the British and Irish interest, than the designs of France against both," mentions the Irish military, as "being at full and entire liberty to chuse what part they will take; but, if once they go into France, they," he adds, "must not expect to return into this kingdom again." Of the penalty, on being found guilty of doing so, without a special permission from King William, we have, at Cork, under the date of 1699-1700, or even *after* the termination of the war between France and England by the Treaty of Ryswick, an instance, in the Memoirs of Captain Peter Drake, of Drakerath, in the County Meath. "There was," he says, "at that time, in the prison, one Captain Barrett, under sentence of *death*, for returning from France, without the King's sign manual, which the laws then required."

† Yet, writes Sir David Nairne of James—"He was very charitable; and, as there were a great many of his poor, faithful subjects at St. Germains, who had lost their fortunes to follow him, he was touched with their condition, and *retrenched, as much as he could, to assist them.* He used to call, from time to time, into his cabinet, some of these bashful, indigent persons, of all ranks; to whom he distributed, folded up in small pieces of paper, 5, 10, 15, or 20 pistoles, more or less, according to the merit, the quality, and the exigency of each." Sir David was with the King at St. Germain, and passed "upwards of 46 years" in his service, or that of his son.

That an exclusion from every mode of earning their bread had been the result of the disposal of their own time allowed by his Majesty to the Sub-Lieutenants of his troops, whose service had not been so long as theirs. That they could not avail themselves of the dismissal which his Majesty had ordered to be granted to those who should wish for it, unless he might have the goodness to obtain for them the permission to return to their own country, which they were prohibited doing, under pain of *death*. That they most humbly prayed his Majesty to cause some of the effects of his accustomed goodness and charity to be experienced by men, whose misfortunes had proceeded from their attachment to the service of their King, the ally of his Majesty, and to that of his Majesty himself. That they prayed him, to afford them the means of continuing in his service, with the same attachment which they had hitherto displayed. Or, if his Majesty's affairs afforded no occasion for retaining them in his service, they prayed him most humbly, to recommend them to some other Prince, or State, that might employ them."

This appeal of the Irish officers, which appears to have been drawn up for presentation to the King, with the understanding that it would be agreeable to his Majesty, was received as it deserved to be. The petitioners obtained their request from Louis, to be formed into a distinct corps of officers, to serve wherever he might be desirous of employing them; and they are referred to, in connexion with an abstract of their subsequent conduct, as "an invincible phalanx, that, if owing much to the munificence of the French Monarch, was, upon all occasions, deserving of the honourable treatment experienced from him." Some of those officers passed into Spain with Louis's grandson, Philip V., in December, 1700. Others, after acting very effectively, under the Marshals de Montrevel, Villars, and Berwick, against the Huguenots of the Cevennes, were attached to the expedition of Prince James Francis Edward Stuart, (or, in Jacobite language, King James III.) when he sailed from Dunkirk, in March, 1708, with the Chevalier de Forbin, to endeavour to land in Scotland. After returning to France, they were at the famous defence of Lille, under the Marshal de Boufflers, at that of Tournay in 1709, and at those of Douay, Bethune, and Aire, in 1710. Of such as survived those campaigns, the majority entered the service of Philip V., in 1711. After the reduction, also, among the Irish regiments in France, in 1715, (on account of the general peace in 1714,) Philip V., besides the Regiment of Major-General Walter Bourke, which he took altogether into his pay, engaged so many reformed officers, that he raised the strength of 3 of the Irish regiments, which he previously had, from 3 to 6 battalions. These, we are told, "served at Oran, in Sicily, in Italy, in 1733 and 1734, with the highest distinction;" and "4 of them had the honour, in 1743, with the Gardes Wallonnes, to repulse the enemy at Veletry, and to save Don Philippe, when he was in danger of being made prisoner."

In the course of the measures adopted, in 1698, by the English Parliament, for the diminution of their army to but 7000 men for England, and 12,000 for Ireland, against the opinion of King William, (who advocated the maintenance of a regular or standing force worthy of England as a nation, instead of one below that of several petty Princes of Germany,) the supporters of the King, in opposition to the popular notions of the *sufficiency* of a Militia for the defence of the country, pointed to the danger which might arise from such a regular Irish force as that which King James had in France, and circulated a specification of its different corps, to the same effect as already given in this history. The paper thus circulated in England was headed—"*A List of King James's Irish and Popish Forces in France, ready when called for: in Answer to an Argument against a Land Force, writ by A, B, C, D, E, F, G, or to whatever has been, or ever shall be, writ upon that Subject.*" In Holland, the like accounts of the Irish army in France were printed, and commented upon, in a corresponding spirit. If, argued an eminent periodical at the Hague, King James, with such an army, above 18,000 in number, were to make another attempt upon England, what could such a small regular force, as the previously-mentioned 7,000 men, avail against him? "They," it adds, "would be cut to pieces, along with all the Militia of the kingdom, if they came to an engagement." On this reduction of their army by the English Parliament, it may be noted, (after the affecting case of the Irish Jacobite officers reformed in *France*,) that William III. felt particularly aggrieved at the legislation, which likewise pressed so hard upon the poor French or Huguenot officers, in the service of *England*. Writing from Kensington, in January, 1699, to his Huguenot Lord Justice in Ireland, Ruvigny, Earl of Galway, William, after referring to his "vexation of what passed in Parliament," affirms—"It is not possible to be more sensibly touched than I am, at my not being able to do more for the poor refugee officers, who have served me with so much zeal and fidelity. I am afraid the good God will punish the ingratitude of this nation." At the great encampment and review, in the ensuing summer, by Louis XIV., of a picked force of 33 battalions, 132 squadrons, and 70 guns, at Compiegne and Coudun, where all the movements of actual warfare were performed for the instruction of the King's grandson, the Duke of Burgundy, then in his 16th year, the Irish Brigade were represented by the veteran Colonel and Chevalier Andrew Lee, with the surviving battalion of his regiment. And it was an honour to be a portion of such a force as that then assembled; since, it was observed, "a finer army, or more beautiful troops, were never seen together." The King testified his pleasure at their excellent discipline, and magnificent appearance, by giving 100 crowns to every Captain of Infantry, 200 crowns to every Captain of Cavalry, &c.

On the death of King James II., at the Palace of St. Germain-en-Laye, September 16th, 1701, his only legitimate son, James Francis Edward Stuart, born Prince of Wales, at St. James's Palace, London, June 20th, 1688, was considered by the numerous adherents of his family, of the Protestant as well as Catholic religion, to be the Sovereign *de jure*, though not *de facto*, of the British Isles, as James III. of England and Ireland, and James VIII. of Scotland. This rank he assumed, and was acknowledged as such by the Kings of France and Spain. The nickname of "the *Pretender*," under which, as if not the real son of King James II., he was proscribed, and excluded from reigning, by the party opposed to him, or that of the Revolution, is thus disposed of by a respectable English Protestant writer, Mr. Jesse, in his Memoirs of the Court of England under the Stuarts. "Besides the necessary attendants, there were present, at the Queen's delivery, 42 persons of rank, 18 of the Privy Council, 4 other noblemen, and 20 ladies, all of whom, as far as circumstances and modesty would allow, were witnesses of the birth of the Prince of Wales. By the desire of James, the depositions of these persons were taken down, and may *still* be seen, with the autographs of the deponents, in the Council Office. . . . No person, indeed, who was ever introduced to the *Pretender*,—as he was afterwards invidiously styled,—who had previously been acquainted with the features and character of his misguided father, ever, for a moment, questioned, that he was the genuine offspring of King James." Whence, also, the contemporary lines of Dryden, in his Britannia Rediviva, or poem on the Prince's nativity—

> "Born in broad day-light, that th' ungrateful rout
> May find no room for a remaining doubt;
> Truth, which itself is light, does darkness shun,
> And the true eaglet safely dares the sun."

To the cause of the banished Stuart Prince, as previously to that of his uncle and father, Kings Charles II. and James II., the mass of the Irish nation as Catholics were naturally devoted, in opposition to the revolutionary principle, so ruinous to *them* under Oliver Cromwell and William of Orange. And, from the still further ruin of the Irish, as Catholics, meditated by Cromwello-Williamitism in its substitution of a shameless Penal Code for a fulfilment of the Articles of Limerick, there appeared to be no chance of *any* escape, except through a "restoration" of the hereditary representative of that dynasty, who, as a Catholic himself, should, at the very least, cause the Articles of Limerick to be observed towards his fellow-religionists in Ireland; if he would not consider himself bound, as he certainly would be, in honour, to do a great deal more for them. The late Daniel O'Connell, in noting, how "every right, that hereditary descent could give, the royal race of Stuart possessed," and how "all the enthusiastic sympathies of the Irish heart were roused for them," remarked, "and all the powerful motives of personal interest bore in the *same* channel. The restoration of their rights, the triumph of their religion, the restitution of their ancient inheritances, would have been the certain consequences of the success of the Stuart family, in their pretensions to the throne." Hence, with reference to the disinherited Prince, nevertheless designated as "his present Majesty, K. James the 3rd of England and Ireland, and of Scotland the 8th," we find the Irish, in 1705, congratulated by their countryman, Dr. Kennedy, in France, for "*their loyal firmity to their true Monarch's interest; to which,*" he adds, "*they have postpon'd their bloud, their fortunes, and their country.*" And, concludes the Doctor—"*God grant that his Majesty may soon reap the fruits of their bloud, and of their labour, and see all the rest of his subjects rival, or outdo, if possible, the Irish, in faithfulness and duty!*" Of these "subjects," the most important abroad were the Irish Brigade; so that a noble Spaniard observed in Paris—"*Were it not for the great actions of the Irish on the Continent, the cause of King James III. would be quite forgotten in Europe!*" This high reputation of the Irish military abroad had a due influence on their enslaved countrymen of the same creed at home; especially those of the ancient Milesian or Gaelic population, who longed, in the translated words of 1 of their songs, that

> "The Prince, then an exile, should come for his own,
> The isles of his father, his rights, and his throne,"

with sufficient aid, from Louis the Great, for that purpose; but, still more, for the emancipation of the oppressed Catholic loyalists of Erin.

> "Oh! where art thou, Louis? our eyes are on thee—
> Are thy lofty ships walking in strength o'er the sea?
> In Freedom's last strife, if you linger, or quail,
> No morn e'er shall break on the night of the Gael!"*

That "night," however, was destined to grow darker and darker, and "no morn" was to "break" upon its starless gloom of religious and political thraldom, till above half a century after the remains of the great Louis were deposited, with those of his ancestors, at St. Denis; and till his *protegé*, the exiled son of James II., had found an appropriate sepulchre at ROME, for whose religion the Stuart family forfeited the triple royalty of the BRITISH ISLANDS.

* See the "Jacobite relic," commencing, "O say, my brown Drimin, thou silk of the kine," as versified by J. J. Callanan.

HISTORY OF THE IRISH BRIGADES

IN

THE SERVICE OF FRANCE.

BOOK IV.

CHARLES II., the last King of Spain of the Austrian line, deceased in November, 1700, having, by his will, nominated, as heir to his dominions, Philip, Duke of Anjou, grandson of Louis XIV., in order that, through the aid of France, the Spanish monarchy might be preserved from the dismemberment with which it was menaced, Louis, by accepting this will, gave rise to the confederacy against him, between the House of Austria, England, Holland, and other powers, which occasioned the long and sanguinary contest, known as the "War of the Spanish Succession." The 1st hostilities occurred in Italy, in 1701, between the Imperialists, under the illustrious Prince Eugene, and the French, Spanish, and Piedmontese forces, under Victor Amadeus II., Duke of Savoy, (then allied with France) and the Marshal de Catinat. Through the talents of Eugene, a considerable disposition of the Italians in his favour, and the treachery of the Duke of Savoy, (who corresponded with him) the armies of the 2 crowns, though superior in number, were so outmanœuvred, that Louis XIV., annoyed at Catinat's want of success, sent the Marshal Duke de Villeroy to act in his place, and bring the Imperialists to a battle. The day after Villeroy's arrival at the camp of Antignato, or August 24th, he reviewed the united forces there, consisting of 64 battalions and 73 squadrons. Of these, there were 4 battalions Irish, or the Duke of Berwick's, Lord Galmoy's, Colonel Walter Bourke's, and the Honourable Colonel Arthur Dillon's, and 2 squadrons, or Colonel Dominick Sheldon's. Writing to Louis XIV. next day, the Marshal represents the Irish battalions as better, or stronger, than others. Having specified "the 40 first battalions as from 360 to 400 men," he says, "except the Irish, who are numerous, with a great number of reformed officers." The combined forces marched, September 1st, to attack Prince Eugene, who, duly aware of their design, had made such preparations to receive them, at Chiari, that they could not have dislodged him, even if their very considerable superiority of numbers had been much beyond what it actually was. His position was protected by the town, by fosses and rivulets, and by intrenchments; from behind which, his infantry, with the tops of their hats only visible along the parapet, might securely direct their musketry, seconded by a raking fire from 50 pieces of cannon, loaded with cartridge-shot; and, in advance of those formidable obstacles, he had country-houses, and mills, occupied by some of his troops. The approaches to his position were likewise so difficult, as to prevent the confederates bringing up more than a few cannon. After a massacre, rather than a battle, of between 1 and 2 hours, Villeroy had consequently to draw off, with not less, if not *many* more, than between 1000 and 2000 killed and wounded, including several eminent officers, and, among the former, " 2 Irish Colonels" (not named)—while Eugene's acknowledged loss was but 117 men in all, or only 36 killed, and 81 wounded!* The Irish, who were engaged in support of the 2 first French brigades which attacked, formed, with other regiments, the right of that supporting attack. There were, writes Villeroy to Louis the following day, " Auvergne, Medoc, Dillon, and Galmoi on the right. They made a new attack, with some pieces of cannon, which we contrived to push forward, amidst extreme difficulties." Then, after stating, how " all the brigade of Auvergne advanced, and carried some portion of the enemies' retrenchments," or " the 1st entrenchment," the Marshal adds—" The Irish and Medoc, who attacked upon the right, performed *all* that could be expected from the bravest troops." In describing the repulse of the first brigades which attacked, and occupied for a time, the houses and wind-mills, the Austrian account, indeed, that supposes the latter to have been first taken by, and then recovered from, the *Irish,* says—" The enemy lost 4 standards of the Regiment of Normandy on this occasion, and a musketeer of the Regiment of Guttenstein captured a standard of an *Irish* regiment; but, in the hope of making a greater booty, he threw it into the water, and has not been able to recover it, to the present time"—namely, to the 2nd day after the action, or September 3rd. But, besides the improbability of an Austrian soldier, under the circumstances, throwing away a standard for other booty, it does not appear *how* he could have gotten an *Irish* standard among the first of Villeroy's brigades that attacked, since the only Irish, whom the Marshal describes as engaged, were *not* with those first brigades, but with, as he alleges, " the 2 brigades who sustained the first;" and, moreover, he makes *no* mention to Louis, of the Irish having lost *any* standard. On the Marshal's breaking up, in November, of his encampment in front of the Imperialists, to retire into winter-quarters, among the 3 select brigades of " the little camp, forming the rearguard," to cover his retreat, was the brigade of Lord Galmoy. By the hostile cannonading and musketry, connected with this service, numbers were killed and wounded; and, among the latter, was the illustrious Marshal de Catinat, though slightly, by 2 shots.

The Comte de Tessé, (afterwards Marshal, and elder brother of the Chevalier and Maréchal de Camp, who served in the last campaign of the War of the Revolution in Ireland,) having his head-quarters at Mantua in December, marched, on the 10th, from that place towards Borgoforte, with 800 horse, including the Regiment of Sheldon, and 400 grenadiers, mounted behind. Towards this force, Prince Eugene had detached the Baron de Mercy with one more numerous, or 1200 horse, and 200 dismounted dragoons. After stationing 800 men at Fossa Mantucena to secure a retreat, Mercy, with the rest, or 600 horse, advanced to within 3 leagues of Mantua. Tessé, meanwhile, prepared to entrap him. Posting the great body of his men in a defile, he caused only 4 troops to march beyond it, for the purpose of presenting themselves before the

* The advantage, in point of a protecting position, under which Eugene fought against Villeroy at Chiari, like that of General Jackson against the British at New Orleans, *may* account for the great difference observable between the losses of the defending and attacking forces, in *both* cases.

enemy, and drawing him on. Mercy, supposing he had only to deal with the 4 troops who presented themselves, briskly advanced against them. These troops hastily retired towards the defile, and re-entered it, followed by Mercy and his 600 horse without any apprehension, until they all found themselves taken between 2 fires. From 100 to 200 of them, including 20 officers, were killed upon the spot; their commander, 8 other officers, and 50 men, were made prisoners; and the rest defeated. As to the conduct of the Irish horse in this affair—"The King," says my French manuscript, "to signify to the Regiment of Sheldon the satisfaction that he experienced, from the distinguished manner in which it had acted upon this occasion, granted to the reformed officers, who were attached to this corps, the same appointments as those of the commissioned officers."

The first great military occurrence in Italy, in 1702, was the celebrated enterprise against Cremona by Prince Eugene, which I notice more fully than other events, in proportion to the very high distinction acquired there by the Irish. That ancient city, then belonging to the Spanish dominions in northern Italy, and furnished with a good citadel, ramparts, fosses, &c., was under the government of a loyal, active, and gallant Spanish officer, Don Diego de la Concha. The Marshal de Villeroy, as commander of the French and Spanish troops during the winter, had made it his head-quarters. The principal officers of the garrison, under the Marshal, were, the Lieutenants-General Count de Revel and Marquis de Crenan, the Maréchal de Camp, Count de Montgon, the Marquis de Praslin, acting as Commandant of Cavalry, the Brigadier d'Arene, acting as Commandant of Infantry and the Etat-Major, and M. Desgrigny, Intendant of the French Forces in Italy. The garrison consisted of 12 battalions, and 12 squadrons; all French, except the 2 battalions of Colonels Arthur Dillon and Walter Bourke. The whole, however, made, according to the French official journal, only "about 4000 men." Of these, the 2 Irish battalions are elsewhere stated to have formed no more than 600 men; a circumstance requisite to be noted, in order to duly estimate the extent of *their* merit, at the defence of the place. As the capture of such an important city, with its garrison, military stores, and so many of the principal officers of the confederate forces, would enable Prince Eugene to drive the French and Spaniards out of Italy, by putting him in a position to fall upon and conquer their various detachments in detail, he directed his particular attention, during the winter, to the surprise of the town; and the intelligence he received, respecting the state of things there, inspired him with the liveliest hopes of accomplishing his design. The Marshal de Villeroy, indeed, was most attentive to his military duties; but his subordinate officers, upon whom the maintenance of proper discipline among the garrison devolved, allowed a shameful neglect of the details of the service to prevail. The guards, stationed at the gates and upon the works, had no communications with each other at night, by rounds. No sentinels were placed on the ramparts, over the gates, to give notice of any approaches that might be made towards the town. No outposts were obliged to traverse or scour the different roads, leading from the surrounding country towards those gates. No patrols of horse or foot were ordered to parade the streets. In short, the heedlessness was such, as to be most favourable for Eugene's design.

At this time, there was in his army a native of Cremona, Antonio

Cozzoli, who had been obliged to leave it for debt. He was brother of the Rev? Gianantonio Cozzoli, Rector of the Parish of Santa Maria Nueva; whose church and private residence, but particularly the latter, stood near a sewer for carrying off the foul water and other impurities of the city into the trenches surrounding the walls. At the entrance of the sewer was an iron grating. If this were removed, and other measures taken, troops might be introduced, by the subterraneous passage, into the Priest's wine-cellar, and might thence ascend into the town. The Cozzoli were partizans of the house of Austria; and in consideration, it is said, of a sum in hand to the Priest, and a promise of his being suitably promoted in the Church, by the Imperial interest, he agreed to support Eugene's project. He accordingly applied to the Governor, Don Diego de la Concha, to have the grating removed, and the sewer cleaned out, as being, he alleged, so choked with filth, that it was a great nuisance, particularly to himself, since his wine-cellar was injured by the water, that could not find a due vent elsewhere. The Spaniard, little suspecting the treacherous object of this modern Sinon, ordered some soldiers to do what the Priest desired. A passage from the sewer into the Priest's cellar next remained to be opened; for which purpose Eugene despatched to his reverend friend 8 able miners; who, being introduced into the cellar, completed their task, covering the aperture which was required, merely with such a thin coat of masonry as could be easily removed. Eugene then, or from January 20th, commenced slipping by degrees into the town, in different disguises, several experienced officers, and, as variously stated, from 300 to 600 picked men or grenadiers, who, till the time for action, were to remain concealed with Father Cozzoli, and other partizans of the Emperor. The Prince likewise obtained from Cremona a plan of the town representing everything necessary to be known, especially with respect to the fortifications and barracks, the number and disposition of the troops of the garrison, the particular quarters intrusted to, and the lodgings occupied by, the principal officers, &c. After these arrangements for the surprise of the place, Eugene formed 2 bodies of his best troops. The 1st body was to march from Ostiano on the Oglio to Cremona, in order to enter it on that side of the river Po, where the measures for doing so had been specially concerted with Father Cozzoli. The 2nd body was to proceed through the Parmesan territory, on the other side of the Po; to profit by the admission of the 1st body into the place, so as to master a redoubt which guarded a bridge of boats, leading over the river to that gate of Cremona, hence called the Po gate, and then, getting by it into the town, was to effect a junction there with the other body of troops from Ostiano. Against such a junction within the place, resistance by the garrison would have been unavailing. The 1st body of troops drafted from the infantry Regiments of Geschwind, Herberstein, Bagni, and Lorrain, and the cavalry Regiments of Neuburgh, Taaffe, Lorrain, and Diak, was to be under Eugene himself. The infantry amounted to 3000 picked men, or grenadiers, and the cavalry to 1500 men; or 1395 cuirassiers, and 105 hussars. Thus, on entering Cremona, Eugene would have 4500 men; and, according to his being reinforced by 300 or 600 more in waiting for him there, he would be at the head of from 4800 to 5100 men. The 2nd body of his troops, or that intended to proceed through the Parmesan territory against Cremona, was to be under the young Prince de Vaudemont. Its infantry, selected from the Regiments of

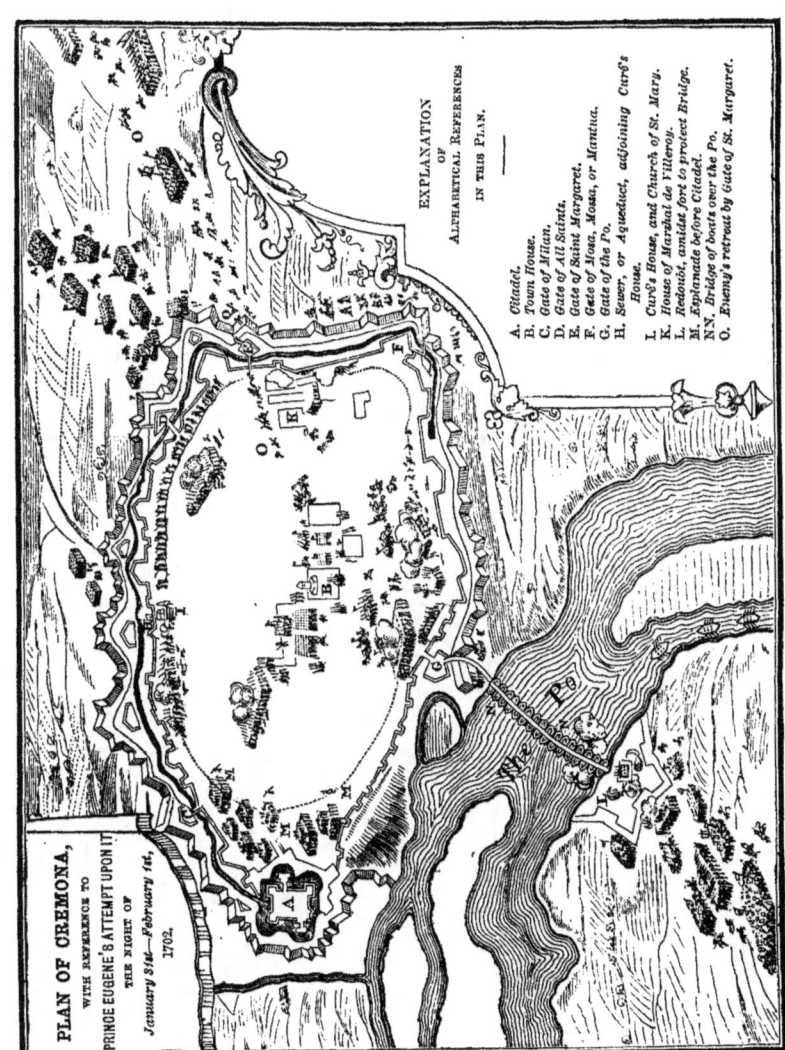

Stahremberg and Daun, consisted of 2000 men; its cavalry, composed of the young Prince's own regiment, with those of Darmstadt and Deidrichstein, made 3000 men; and both consequently 5000 men. The united forces of Eugene and Vaudemont, (according to the foregoing particulars, deduced from German, as well as French, sources of information,) would form from 9800 to 10,100 men; or more than sufficient, within Cremona, to overpower a surprised garrison of only about 4000 men—if there was not even reason to believe, that garrison would be much diminished by the absence of a considerable detachment, designed for service elsewhere.*

Eugene commenced his march January 31st, at an hour before midnight, from Ostiano. Having to travel about 6 leagues, or 18 miles, over roads in bad order from heavy rains, and being accompanied by a number of carpenters, masons, smiths, &c., with everything necessary for passing over ditches, breaking through walls, and opening gates, he could not collect all his troops before Cremona, till it was nearer morning than he wished. The Germans, however, *worked*, and the French *slept*, so well, that not only the gate of All Saints, nearest to Father Cozzoli's wine-cellar and to the passage into it from the sewer, was surprised, but the gate of St. Margaret, which had been walled up, was reopened in good time. The one served for the entrance of the Imperial foot, the other for that of the horse; and the Prince himself was by day-light in the town, with from 3,000 to 3,600 grenadiers, and 3 divisions of heavy cavalry, or 1016 cuirassiers; leaving about the gate of St. Margaret, and to patrol the roads by which aid might come to, or fugitives escape from, the place, a reserve of 379 of Dupré's cuirassiers, and 105 of Diak's hussars.† Before any alarm of consequence occurred, the Germans, besides the 2 gates of All Saints and St. Margaret, and the Priest's house and Church of Santa Maria Nueva, were masters of the leading squares, and the adjacent streets, the great street which separated half the garrison of the town from the other half, the Podesta, or Hotel de Ville, the Cathedral, the Round Chapel, and, in short, the principal portion of Cremona! Eugene established himself, with the Prince de Commercy and General Stahremberg, at the Podesta, or Hotel de Ville; many officers were captured in their lodgings, pointed out to the Germans by a native of Cremona who had come from Ostiano, and by Father Cozzoli; and, as the consternation spread, several of the garrison whose quarters were so situated towards the gates, or ramparts, that an escape seemed possible by getting out of the town, attempted to do so; but there, too, they were intercepted by Dupré's cuirassiers and Diak's hussars. In the words of my Italian historian—"Confusion, terror, violence, rage, flight and slaughter were everywhere! Dreadful for all was the awakening! Still more dreadful what they saw when awake! The citizens believed, that their last hour was come! The French, between fury and surprise, arming themselves hastily and irregularly, seized their muskets, sabres, and bayonets, and sallied out from their

* It *had* been intended, that 800 foot and 500 horse should be detached from the garrison of Cremona; an intention fortunately not acted on; yet attended with preparations, of which the Austrian partizans and spies did not fail to take note there, and transmit information to the Prince.

† These and the previous calculations of Eugene's and Vaudemont's forces are given, as the closest estimates I could form, from a minute comparison and analysis of the *various* statements on the subject, in the writings on *both* sides.

lodgings or posts, naked and bare-footed, or covered only with a shirt, ignorant of where they were rushing, what enemy they were going to engage, or what had reduced ill-fated Cremona to such extremities, during that horrible night. The Austrians believed," adds the historian, " that victory was already within their grasp!" Like the Greeks of old, under similar circumstances,

> "To sev'ral posts, their parties they divide;
> Some block the narrow streets, some scour the wide;
> The bold they kill, th' unwary they surprise;
> Who fights finds death, and death finds him who flies!"
> DRYDEN'S Virgil, Æneis ii., 447-450.

Meantime, the Marshal de Villeroy, whose quarters lay in that part of the city towards the gate of St. Margaret, was aroused. As watchful, as others were careless, he had inquired several times, during the night, " Was there any news from the enemy?" and was always answered, "*None!*"* It was about 7 o'clock when he was awoken by 3 or 4 musket-shots to the left of his residence, followed by his valet's running into his chamber, crying—"The Germans are in the town!" The Marshal hurried out of bed, had his horse saddled and bridled, dressed himself as rapidly as possible, and, from the continuing increase and approach of the musketry no longer doubting that he was betrayed, and would soon be visited by the enemy, he directed his papers and cypher of correspondence to be burned, flung on his military cloak, mounted, and galloped off alone for the principal square, in order to head some troops there, and first endeavour, with them, to set matters to rights. His situation on this occasion, at Cremona, reminds us of that of Æneas at Troy, as also betrayed and surprised.

> "Now peals of shouts came thund'ring from afar,
> Cries, threats, and loud laments, and mingled war!
> The noise approaches! * * * *
> Louder, and yet more loud, I hear th' alarms
> Of human cries distinct, and clashing arms!
> Fear broke my slumbers; I no longer stay—
> * * * * * * *
> New clamours, and new clangors, now arise,
> The sound of trumpets, mix'd with fighting cries!
> With frenzy seiz'd, I run to meet th' alarms,
> Resolv'd on death, resolv'd to die in arms;
> But first to gather friends, with them t' oppose,
> (If Fortune favour'd) and repel the foes."
> DRYDEN'S Virgil, Æneis ii., 397-426.

When about 300 paces from his house, the Marshal was fired at by a hostile detachment, but escaped uninjured, took a round to avoid being intercepted, reached the square, and was doing all he could to encourage his men assailed there by the Germans, when more of their horse and foot, rushing from 2 neighbouring streets, surrounded all attempting to resist. In the *mêlée*, 12 grenadiers fell upon the Marshal, seized the bridle of his horse, pulled himself to the ground, wounded him (though but slightly) in the side and hand, were dragging hat, péruke, cloak, coat,

---

* Eugene's surprise of Cremona would have been rendered impossible, had but 1 order of the Marshal been executed—that 50 horse of the garrison should patrol all that night, and until the evening of the following day, on the road to Ostiano, in quest of intelligence respecting the enemy. What a heavy penalty was the result of this neglect!

cravat, &c., from him, and would probably have killed him, when, fortunately, an Imperial officer, in a red uniform, and armed with a halbert, hastened up to rescue him, and did so, though not without much difficulty. This officer, an Irishman, Francis Mac Donnell, belonged to a name, of which he was not the last who attained distinction in the service of Austria.* He appears to have been of the old *galloglass*, or heavy-infantry, sept of the Clan Donnells, subsequently Mac Donnells, of Mayo; whom the English Lord Deputy, Sir Henry Sydney, in 1576, refers to as so powerful, in mentioning the reduction of the great Mayo Chief, Sir Richard Fitz-David Bourke, or the Mac William Eighter. "Out of the Countye of Maio," writes Sir Henry, "came to me to Galway, first 7 principall men of the Clandonells, for everye of theire 7 linagies 1 of that surname, and enhabiting that Countye, all, by profession, mercenarie soldiers, by the name of *Galloglas;* they are verie stronge, and moche of the wealth of the countrie is under theim," &c. Then Sir Henry adds of Mac William Eighter,—"I wan his chiefe force from hym, in getting theise Clandonells." † Francis Mac Donnell himself was connected with the best of the old native races of Connaught—with the O'Rourkes, whose heads were Princes or Chiefs of Brefny-O'Rourke, or Leitrim, from the 10th to the 17th century, some of them anciently Kings of Connaught, several of them distinguished officers in various Continental services, their name being represented, to our days, among the nobility of the ranks of Prince and of Count in Russia—with the O'Conors, so long Kings of Connaught, in some instances, Monarchs of Ireland, in modern times, among the leading gentry of their province, and still *more* respectable for theirs ervices to the literature of their country. His uncle, Captain Tiernan O'Rourke, who had accompanied the Irish army from Limerick in 1691, and had signalized himself upon various occasions, was then in the French service. His first-cousin, the Captain's son, Doctor O'Rourke, had been Chaplain and Domestic Secretary to Prince Eugene, till invited by his countrymen to become Bishop of Killala, and thereby doomed to a miserable end, in those intolerant days. His second-cousin was the venerable Charles O'Conor of Belanagare, the eminent antiquarian and patriot. Mac Donnell, who had long been in the Imperial service, was then a Captain in the infantry Regiment of Bagni, and had an important part assigned him in effecting the passage into the town. Without knowing the rank of his captive, the Marshal, he conveyed him

* James Mac Donnell, of the Mayo race, died in the Austrian service, October 4th, 1766, a Count, a General, Imperial Chamberlain, and Inspector-General of the Guard in Camp; and was succeeded, from Ireland, in his Countship, by his nephew, Francis MacDonnell. This Count James was very generous to his relatives in Ireland, during his life; and their descendants derived pecuniary advantages from Vienna, under his will, as late as 1841-2.

† Cox, in noticing this submission, introduces a circumstance, indicative of the education of an Irish Chief, or gentleman, of those times. "To Galway came 7 of the family of the Clandonells, and, after them came Mac William Eighter, who *could* speak Latin, though he could *not* speak English. He submitted, by oath and indenture, and agreed to pay 250 marks per annum for his country, besides contribution of men, on risings out, and consented the Clandonells should hold their lands of the Queen," &c. Sir William Betham, too, observes—"The Irish Chiefs, not understanding the English language, their correspondence with the English was carried on in Latin." During the great civil war under Charles I., we find the stout Catholic Bishop of Clogher, Heber Mac Mahon, in the General Assembly of the Confederates at Kilkenny, while he "addressed them in Latin," admitting his equal "ignorance of the French and *Sassenagh* languages."

to a guard-house in the square, showed him into an upper room, helped him as far as possible to arrange his dress, and treated him with every attention. Soon after the Germans in the square were so warmly assailed by some of the Régiment des Vaisseaux, that, at one time, the Marshal thought he would be released. Meanwhile, he made different attempts to procure his liberty by tampering with Mac Donnell; offering, upon condition of being allowed to escape, a cavalry regiment in the French service, along with a large pension; and, in fine, as he himself relates, more than Mac Donnell could hope to realize by the military profession, or, in other words, to make that officer's fortune. But, to these efforts to corrupt him, Mac Donnell replied—"He had, for a long time, served the Emperor with fidelity. It had not yet fallen to his lot to commit an act of perfidy to the prejudice of that service, and he therefore thought, he ought not to commence with one. He preferred his honour to making his fortune; and it was useless to endeavour to tempt him by the prospect of a post, a little higher than what he already possessed; since he felt himself assured of attaining, among the Imperial forces, by his services, what it was thought to induce him to purchase, among those of France, by an act of treachery or treason." Then suspecting, from the magnitude of Villeroy's offers, *who* he was, he questioned him to that effect. Villeroy would not admit his rank, being desirous of remaining *incognito*, lest the Germans, on learning it, should place him beyond the possibility of being recaptured; and, if they delayed doing so, he entertained hopes of being liberated, on account of the increasing resistance made by his troops to the enemy. This state of things, on the other hand, rendered Mac Donnell proportionably solicitous to secure such an evidently important prize; the more especially as he had been promised some thing by the Marshal, (apparently for having rescued, and been so kind to him,) which might be lost, should he be released. Mac Donnell accordingly informed an officer of superior rank then in the square, of the prisoner of distinction who was in the adjoining guard-house. The officer galloped off to the Count de Stahremberg, with whom he soon returned; upon which, Villeroy, finding any hope of saving himself, by a further attempt at concealment, to be useless, confessed who he was to Mac Donnell. The Irish officer then introduced the Count by name to the Marshal, who was effectually secured, consistent with the respect due to his rank.

The reverses of the garrison did not cease with the taking of the Marshal. The Count de Montgon, Maréchal de Camp, who attempted, with some horse and foot, to join the Marshal, was defeated, dismounted, and made prisoner. The Chevalier d'Entragues, Colonel of the Régiment des Vaisseaux, who, having assembled a battalion of his regiment for review by day-break near the Po gate, was the 1st *French* officer ready, with any considerable body of men, to meet the enemy, was, after a temporary success against them in the great square, overpowered and slain there. The Marquis de Crenan, Lieutenant-General, with another party of troops, after a similar success in the little square, was mortally wounded, made prisoner, and his men also driven out of that square. The brave Spanish Governor, Don Diego de la Concha, heading a detachment, was likewise mortally wounded. Desgrigny, too, the Intendant of the French Forces in Italy, was captured, with several more officers and soldiers. In short, by this time, the communications between the different portions of the garrison became so intercepted, that of its 12 battalions only 6 and a few fragments of the others could assemble; and of its 12 squadrons only 5 could be extricated for action.

The Irish presented the 1st insurmountable obstacle to the enemy's success. Though the barracks of the 2 battalions of Bourke and Dillon were situated in streets not far from the Po gate, and Major Daniel O'Mahony, who commanded the latter battalion in the absence of Colonel Lally, had directed it to be up for reviewing near that gate, at the same early hour that the Chevalier d'Entragues had ordered his men to be ready, none of the Irish were prepared for action when the Austrians surprised the town, except a Captain and 35 men, who were stationed at a barrier before the Po gate. Upon the 1st alarm of the Germans being in the city, Entragues, as having had the only considerable corps (or one of about 200 men) equipped for action, hastened, from the scene of his intended review, towards the principal square, to meet the enemy; thus leaving the 36 Irish at the barrier to themselves. The Baron de Mercy, on the opening of St. Margaret's gate for the admission of his cavalry, lost no time in attending to the special order he had received from Prince Eugene to master the Po gate; since, without the possession of it, for the introduction of the Prince de Vaudemont's corps, the fall of Cremona could not be looked upon as certain. With above 250 cuirassiers, sword in hand, the Baron galloped towards that gate. But the Irish Captain there (whose name I regret not to find mentioned) was too quick for the cuirassiers; ordering the barrier to be shut in time—by which he was the 1st saviour of the place. Mercy, foiled in his attempt to carry that Irish post by a dash, was brought to a stand before it, and had still further to defer assailing it, owing to the non-arrival of Lieutenant-Colonel Baron de Scherzer with 400 infantry designed to aid in the attack, but whose advance was delayed through the death of his guide, by a shot from a window. These infantry coming up after some time, and the cavalry under Mercy's orders being increased to 800 cuirassiers, he blocked up, with his horse and foot, all the space between the Po gate and the gate of Mossa or Mantua to his left, and to the right of the 36 Irish at the barrier; thereby confining to their barracks, between his own and another Austrian force to his rear and left, the greater portion of the French cavalry, whose quarters lay towards the gate of Mossa; but omitting to shut up the passages from those streets towards his right, in which were the barracks of Bourke's and Dillon's battalions. However, no aid from those battalions having yet reached the Irish Captain and his 35 men at the barrier before the Po gate, Mercy ordered that post to be assailed by a body of his best infantry or grenadiers. The barrier was constructed in the form of a palisade, and the German grenadiers had orders to march up, and, thrusting their bayonets through the openings, to overpower the Irish, by the combined superiority of fire and numbers. The Irish Captain, causing his men to remain as much as possible out of bullet-reach, made them keep their muskets and bayonets steadily fixed between the intervals of the palisades, and not give *out* their fire till they could give it *in* with the best effect. The Austrian grenadiers, directing a tempest of musketry against the barrier, were accordingly allowed to come so near, as about a halbert's length of it. But they then found the openings assigned for *their* weapons to be most fatally preoccupied; being saluted with such a destructive volley, that they had to fall back amidst loss and disorder. Mercy again endeavoured to make his grenadiers close upon the barrier and carry it by the bayonet. But the Irish availed themselves so well of the protection afforded by their post, that, even without being seen by their enemies, they marked them out, and picked them down, at pleasure; so that the German infantry could effect nothing against the "line of bayonets, and of musket-mouths vomiting fire and death." The enemy were only able to take possession of an adjacent battery of 8 twenty-four pounders, called the battery of St. Peter, which had been left without a guard.

By this time, the 2 Irish battalions of Bourke and Dillon, at their barracks in the streets not far from the Po gate, were alarmed at the noise of the attack upon their countrymen at the barrier. The greater part of the officers of those battalions were either away on leave from their regiments, or were lodged in various parts of the city, more or less remote from their men. Nevertheless, the soldiers, with such officers as they had, prepared to rush, in their shirts, from their barracks, to the aid of their countrymen against the Germans. Among those officers quartered away from their men in the town, was Major Daniel O'Mahony. He was of a respectable branch of one of the best Milesian names of Desmond, or South Munster, as deriving its origin both from the blood of the old Princes of Desmond, and that of the Princes of Thomond, or North Munster; the immediate founder of the race Mahoon or Mahon —whence the name, in its modern or general form, of O'Mahony—having been the son of Cian, Prince of Desmond, and of Sabia, daughter of the illustrious Brian "Boru," head of the line of Thomond, or North Munster. This Cian was famous for his generosity to the Bards, as well as his stature and beauty; for which, at the battle of Clontarf, where he had a high command in the army of his renowned father-in-law, he is noted as excelling all the other men of Erin, or as "altissimus et pulcherrimus Hibernorum." The O'Mahonys survived the convulsions of the middle ages with various lands and castles, belonging to representatives of the name, in those districts comprised within the ancient Kingdom of Desmond, or the Counties of Cork and Kerry. Among the officers of King James, during the War of the Revolution in Ireland, were several gentlemen of the O'Mahonys, including 2 brothers, Dermod and Daniel. Dermod, as a Colonel, was distinguished at the Boyne, Aughrim, and Limerick. Daniel, having attained the rank of Captain in the Royal Irish Foot Guards, accompanied the national army to the Continent; where, after being Major in the Regiment of Limerick, he obtained the like post, as a reformed officer, in the Regiment of Dillon. He was honourably connected in England, as well as in Ireland,—being 1st married to Cecilia Weld, daughter of George Weld, Esq., of the ancient Catholic family of Weld, represented in chief at present by the Welds of Lulworth Castle, Dorsetshire, of whom was the late Cardinal Weld— being 2dly married to the eldest daughter of the Honourable Henry Bulkeley, or Charlotte, widow of Charles O'Brien, 5th Viscount Clare, and thus brother-in-law of the Marshal Duke of Berwick. Appointed, for his very distinguished conduct at this affair of Cremona, to convey the intelligence of it to Paris, Daniel received the rank of Colonel from Louis XIV., next that of Brigadier, and was subsequently recommended by Louis to his grandson, Philip V. of Spain; where he was granted a Regiment of Irish Dragoons, and, at his decease, at Ocana, in January, 1714, was a Lieutenant-General, Count of Castile, and Commander of the Military Order of St. Jago. He had, by his 1st marriage, 2 sons, neither of whom left male descendants. 1. James, a Lieutenant-General, Governor of Fort St. Elmo, Commander of the Order of St. Januarius, and Inspector-General of Cavalry in the service of Naples. 2. Demetrius, (or Dermod) Lieutenant-General, Count, Commander of several Orders, and Ambassador from Spain to Austria, where he died at Vienna, in 1776. Of the "fameux Mahoni," as Daniel was styled in France,—where the name of O'Mahony has been eminent in military service to our own times,*—his contemporary and acquaintance, the Chevalier de Bellerive, has observed—" He has always been not only brave, but indefatigable, and very pains-taking; his life is, as it were, a continued chain of dangerous combats, of bold attacks, of honourable retreats. . . . If he has mounted to the first dignities of th army, he has raised himself to them by degrees; he has passed through all the military grades so as to make himself master of their respective duties; he has learned to obey before commanding, without having been precipitately elevated to these glorious employments, which he has exercised, during this war, with so much applause." This gallant officer, as Major in command of Dillon's battalion, having ordered that it should be up early for exercise near the Po gate like the battalion of the Régiment des Vaisseaux, before he threw himself upon his bed for the night, charged his valet and landlord to call him next morning, as soon as day should appear. He, however, was first aroused from his slumbers neither by his valet nor by his landlord, but by the galloping of heavy cavalry under his windows, when it was full day-light; or so much later than the time when he should have been called. This caused him to rise immediately, and bring his landlord to an account for such neglect; upon which, the latter informed him—" The cuirassiers of the Emperor were in the streets, as the enemy had surprised the place!" The Major, consequently perceiving that it was more necessary for him to attend to the Germans than to his landlord, seized his arms, kept a sharp look-out, for some time, at what was going on in the street, and chose such a good opportunity for endeavouring to reach his men, that he luckily effected his purpose. Then heading his own, or Dillon's battalion, while Lieutenant-Colonel Francis Wauchop led on that of Bourke, those 2 Irish corps advanced towards the Po gate.

The Baron de Mercy had just gained the battery of St. Peter, and the adjacent parts of the rampart on the left of the 36 Irish guarding the barrier to the gate, and had stationed a troop of his cuirassiers near the battery, when the 2 Irish battalions, under the command of Wauchop, suddenly presented themselves upon the flank of the Germans, in the direction of the rampart and the streets bordering upon the Po gate. The Baron, on recovering from his first surprise, commanded his infantry to advance against the Irish; causing a detachment of his cuirassiers, at the same time, to support the attack of the infantry. But Bourke's and Dillon's battalions received those infantry and cuirassiers with such a galling fire, and charged them with such fury, that they were defeated;

* Of the several O'Mahonys who were officers in France, may be mentioned 2 of distinction *within* the present century. 1. Barthelemy O'Mahony, Chevalier of St. Louis in 1781; Colonel en Seconde to Regiment of Berwick from 1788 to 1791; Count, Lieutenant-General, Commander of the Order of St. Louis, after restoration of the Bourbons in 1814; and living in 1819. 2. The Chevalier Jean Francois O'Mahony, Colonel of the 3rd Régiment Etranger in 1813; Colonel of the 41st Regiment of the Line in 1819; Maréchal de Camp from 1823 to 1833; and a Commandant of the Legion of Honour.

the Baron himself, in attempting to rally his men, being wounded. The Po gate, the adjoining rampart, battery, and Place of St. Peter were thus freed from the enemy, except such of their infantry as availed themselves of the protection of the opposite houses; and, in addition to the good service done by the preservation of the contested gate, the recovery of the battery &c., such of the French cavalry, as Mercy had previously blocked up in their barracks, were enabled to get out to the assistance of their infantry. The Austrians kept up a fire from the houses where they had sheltered themselves; but it was answered so effectively from St. Peter's battery by the Irish, that they were able, at the same time, to set about barricading themselves with barrels, carts, &c., in the position they had won. Brigadier d'Arene, who joined the Irish just as they had chased the cuirassiers from the battery, stationed the 2 battalions at the different posts about the Po gate in which they were to intrench themselves; then directed the battalion of Beaujolois, which happened to come up, to place themselves beside the battery; also caused the Church of St. Salvador, on the left of it, to be occupied; and next sent to the Citadel for ammunition, which was beginning to be wanted, and at a most critical juncture. For the young Prince de Vaudemont's corps of 5000 men—whose arrival, too late by several hours, should have been simultaneous with that of Eugene's force—was *now* to be seen advancing, on the opposite side of the river, towards the redoubt and bridge of boats, conducting to the Po gate; so that the artillery had to be turned round, from playing upon the Austrians *within* the place, in order to be fired upon those approaching it from *without*. The Irish, in this emergency, perceived what was best to be done would be, to withdraw, at once, the small number of men, or only about 50, who were in the redoubt on the other side of the river; and to break the bridge, by removing every boat of which it consisted to their own side; through which simple remedy any danger from Vaudemont would be obviated, since he could not then cross the stream; while the garrison, so far from being weakened, by having to detach men from itself to oppose him, might be strengthened by the party withdrawn from the redoubt. Such a suggestion respecting the bridge was accordingly made to D'Arene by the Irish. But he, not venturing to adopt it, without permission from his superior officer the Count de Revel, preferred, meantime, to endeavour to defend the redoubt; dispatching 100 of the battalion of Beaujolois, to strengthen the little outpost there, of about 50 men, under Captain Stuart of Dillon's battalion. And this arrangement of D'Arene, aided by the misconception under which the approaching enemy appear to have laboured as to the obstacles they would have to deal with at the redoubt, answered the temporary object for which it was intended. For Vaudemont, to whom a friendly signal was to have been made from the ramparts of the town, finding from the very different salute, or the fire of hostile artillery, with which he was hailed, that the garrison had the superiority there, and the 100 men being seen passing over the bridge of boats to the redoubt, the Austrian troops were ordered to halt, preparatory to a distribution of fascines among them for a *regular* attack upon that outpost, as if it had been much stronger than it really was, or not to be carried by a *coup-de-main*. Such was D'Arene's conduct on this point, answering, indeed, his purpose, on account of the ignorance, and consequent timidity, of the Austrians. But, as to owe our safety to our own foresight is better, than to be indebted for that safety merely to the incapacity or error of an enemy, the advice of the Irish was far the better counsel to have acted on, even were it not eventually found necessary to be followed, as the *only* mode of preserving the place—for, had Vaudemont's Austrians been better informed or more adventurous than they were, they could not, as 5000 in number, have been long prevented crossing the river by a force so inadequate to oppose them as the 150 men in the redoubt, and, the river once crossed, Cremona *should* fall.

While these events were occurring about the Po gate, Prince Eugene was informed of the defeat of his troops there by the Irish. He was greatly mortified at this, and, knowing how indispensable it was for him to gain that gate, if he would not be driven from the town, he directed the Prince de Commercy to go and inspect the Irish position, in order to judge how it was most likely to be mastered; an object the more necessary to accomplish, on account of the approach of Vaudemont's corps. Commercy, on returning, stated, that he thought the Irish were too well posted at the gate to be forced from it. Then Eugene, says the Italian historian, " took it into his head, to try, if the Irish were as proof against gold, as against steel." He accordingly despatched to them, as *his* best deputy for a proposal of that nature, Captain Francis Mac Donnell, both as their countryman, and as the very officer who had captured the Marshal de Villeroy. Mac Donnell, on arriving opposite the Po gate, where he found his 400 countrymen obstinately defending their post against 1200 Germans, advanced from the ranks of the latter towards the former, with a white handkerchief in his hand as a sign of truce, and demanded, if he might make them some propositions? The Irish replying, that he was welcome to do so, and the combat ceasing, Mac Donnell thus addressed himself to the Irish officers. " My fellow-countrymen, his Serene Highness, Monsieur, the Prince Eugene of Savoy, sends me here to tell you, that, if you wish to change sides, and to pass over to that of the Emperor, he promises you higher pay, and rewards more considerable, than you have in France. The affection which I have for all persons of my nation in general, and for you besides, gentlemen, in particular, compels me to exhort you, to accept the offers which the General of the Emperor makes to you; for, should you reject them, I do not see how you can escape inevitable destruction. We are masters of the city, with the exception of your post. It is, on this account, his Highness only waits for my return, to attack you with the greatest part of his forces, and to cut you to pieces, should you not accept of his offers." Mac Donnell added, as an instance, among others, of the bad situation in which the garrison were, that he himself had made the Marshal de Villeroy prisoner; he likewise specified, that the pay which the Irish should receive from the Emperor Leopold would be equal to the highest in France, or that of the Swiss regiments, besides a special gratuity in money, proportioned to the service rendered his Imperial Majesty, by joining him on this occasion; and finally stated, that such as accepted of those terms might also have their peace made with the King of England, (William III.) through the influence of Prince Eugene—this last proviso referring to the penal regulations, by which such Irish as entered the service of France after the Treaty of Limerick were capitally interdicted ever to revisit their native soil, unless with an express or written permission from the revolutionary Sovereign of Great Britain and Ireland. To these offers of Mac Donnell, O'Mahony, as the Commandant of Dillon's battalion, acutely replied—" Prince Eugene seems to fear us more than he esteems us, since he causes such propositions to be made to us." A Lieutenant of Grenadiers bluntly added—" Though your Prince Eugene should send us all the Emperor's cuirassiers, I would not believe that he could drive us out of this." Then, addressing himself to O'Mahony, he observed— "Let us send back that man, to convey our answer." Upon which, O'Mahony, resuming the conversation, said to Mac Donnell—" Monsieur, if his Highness only waits for your return to attack us and cut us to pieces, there is a likelihood, that it will be long before he will do so; for we are going to take measures against your returning in sufficient time. With this view," continued the Major, " I arrest you as a prisoner, not looking upon you any longer as the envoy of a great General, but as a suborner; and it is by such conduct we wish to earn the esteem of the Prince who has sent you here, and not by an act of cowardice and treason, unworthy of men of honour."* O'Mahony then had Mac Donnell arrested, amidst the exclamations of the Irish officers, that " they would die to a man, in the service of the King of France, and never serve any other Prince but him"—whilst the Irish soldiers, if not prevented, would, in a rage of fidelity, have killed the prisoner on the spot. Mac Donnell was next transferred to the commander of the 2 Irish battalions, Lieutenant-Colonel Wauchop of the Regiment of Bourke. By this officer, and 2 or 3 others of that battalion, he was conducted and presented to Brigadier d'Arene, then occupied with the arrangement of the battalion of Beaujolois. The Brigadier, on hearing from Mac Donnell, and from the officers who accompanied him, the circumstances of his detention, told him, that "he deserved rather to be treated as a suborner, than a hostage;" and, after causing him to be disarmed by the Irish themselves, had him conveyed to the Citadel, along with other prisoners whom they had taken. Carried away by the force of this last accusation against Mac Donnell—and one, natural enough, indeed, on the part of those who made it—the Italian historian, Botta, has joined in aspersing that officer, on the ground of his having engaged to corrupt others, although incorruptible himself. But, in thus censuring Mac Donnell, has Botta duly considered, that the Irish Captain, in making the proposals he did to his countrymen, was acting in obedience to his General, and this *not* in any underhand manner, (like the British Adjutant-General John André, with the American traitor Major-General Benedict Arnold,) but openly and fairly, or in presence of the forces of *both* parties—from which circumstances, it does not appear *why* any stigma should be attached to Mac Donnell's character. That his conduct, in refusing the tempting offers made him, was approved of in Austria, and admired throughout Europe at the time, and long after, is certain. Being soon exchanged as a prisoner, he was made a Major by the Emperor; but fell, the following August, at the battle of Luzzara. And an English periodical, under the date of October, 1772, in noting how " old Macdonnel, the Irish officer, who lately died, at the age of 118, at Madrutz, in Croatia," or the Austrian dominions, " was father to the brave officer of that name, who, in 1702, in the war about the Spanish Succession, made prisoner the

* The liveliest or most dramatic accounts of the interview between Mac Donnell and his countrymen at the Po gate are given in the Histoire du Prince Eugène de Savoye, and the valuable French Letter from Milan, or "Rélation exacte de l'Entreprise faite sur Crémone par le Prince Eugène. Copie d'une Lettre écrite de Milan, le 12 Fèvrier, 1702." To what I have selected from those accounts, I have made suitable additions from the correspondence of the Depôt de la Guerre, &c.

Marshal de Villeroi," and showed such integrity there, adds—"Such greatness of soul so well established his reputation, that his father, interrogated by his friends, 'How he managed to look so fresh and well, in his old age?' used commonly to reply—'That the remembrance of the disinterestedness and fidelity of his son contributed greatly to prolong his days!'"* Upon Mac Donnell's arrest, the firing recommenced, and the preservation of the place became even *more* attributable than before to the Irish. For the cannonade from St. Peter's battery, which *they* had wrested from the enemy, among others of Vaudemont's troops mortally wounded Count de Deidrichstein, the officer intrusted with the arrangements for attacking the redoubt; owing to which fortunate shot, the attack that, if made as proposed, *must* have succeeded, was postponed, until time was given, by the delay, to evacuate the redoubt, and remove the bridge of boats, at last, according to the suggestion of the Irish, at first.

Prince Eugene, now suspecting, from seeing no more of Mac Donnell, that he was detained by those to whom he was sent, resorted to another stratagem, to make the Irish lay down their arms. He proceeded with the Prince de Commercy, to the captive Marshal de Villeroy, to induce him, if possible, to issue such an order as would cause the resistance of the Irish to cease. "You have, Monsieur," said the Prince to the Marshal, "traversed the entire city, and you must have observed that we are masters of it. You have still some musketeers upon the rampart. If they continue there, they will at last oblige me to put them all to the sword." But the Marshal, comprehending sufficiently, that those very Irish musketeers, whom the Prince affected to despise, were the special cause of his embarrassment, replied—"Having the misfortune to be your prisoner, I have no longer any orders to give in the town, and those who are upon the rampart must be left to act as they have done." Eugene, baffled in this attempt upon Villeroy, bethought himself of another expedient for effecting his object. This was to procure the municipality of Cremona to embrace his party, and to excite their fellow-citizens to aid his forces against the garrison, which, in that case, would undoubtedly be overpowered. He accordingly summoned those magistrates, by the sound of the tocsin or alarm bell, to meet him at the Hotel de Ville, where he was with the Prince de Commercy. There he addressed them with great ability, omitting nothing that could be most likely to persuade or terrify them into the course he wished them to adopt. Those wise Italians, however, very properly resolving to incur no additional danger for the sake of a mere change of masters, could not be gotten to make Eugene any more satisfactory answer than this—"That they were not in a condition, under existing circumstances, to act in the manner he required them; but that the Imperialists, when entirely masters of the city, should meet with such a reception as had been granted to the French." Eugene, in fine, could obtain nothing more from the meeting, than what, to avoid the imprudence of refusing him *all* he demanded, was granted, a supply

---

* To this interesting notice of the Annual Register may be joined another from Collet's Relics of Literature, under the year 1772. "Died, at Madrutz, in Croatia, in the 118th year of his age, Henry Magdonel. To that place he had retired, with a property sufficient to support him decently. He had been in the service of different Sovereigns. He was father to the brave officer of that name, who, in 1702, in the War about the Spanish Succession, made prisoner, at Cremona, the Marshal de Villeroi," &c.

P

of bread for his troops; which, evidently for the purpose of making those troops be thought many more than they really were, he fixed at *twelve thousand* rations!

Meanwhile, the Count de Revel, by the cry of "Frenchmen to the ramparts!" got together a considerable number of infantry, and arrayed them near the Citadel; the Marquis de Praslin likewise collecting as many cavalry there, as, through the facilities afforded by the success of the Irish against Mercy, or other opportunities, had been able to escape from the blockade of the Austrians. The plan adopted by the Count de Revel for the expulsion of the enemy was, after securing a connexion with the Marquis de Praslin at the Citadel, to march, by the ramparts on his left, to recover the gates of Milan, All Saints, and St. Margaret. Having reached the 1st, he found it possessed by some of his own men; but, before advancing against the 2nd, it was requisite to guard his rear at an avenue, through which it was assailable by the enemy's horse and foot. For this service, 40 French infantry were placed under Captain Mac Donough of Dillon's battalion, who, like so many of his brother-officers, was separated from his own corps. And, scarcely had Mac Donough caused his little guard to barricade or intrench themselves, when the Austrian infantry and cavalry came down upon him. But he obliged them to retire; and, though they renewed their attempts upon his position throughout the day, they could not force it.* Thus covered by Mac Donough, the Count recovered from the enemy the Church of Santa Maria Nueva, or that of Father Cozzoli, as well as his residence, through which they had surprised the town; the reverend traitor, however, escaping, by the sewer, to his Austrian friends beyond the walls, in time to avoid the gallows, which awaited him, if he were caught. † An intrenchment, and bastion, on the way to the gate of All Saints, were likewise regained by the Count de Revel. Nevertheless, before the Count proceeded to attack that gate, he sent word to the Irish at the Po gate, that, while *he* advanced on his left, *they*, after leaving 100 men at their intrenchment, or barricade, and St. Peter's battery, should endeavour to push forward to the gate of Mantua, or Mossa, upon their right; on arriving at which, they should get fresh orders.

When Major O'Mahony received these commands, (for Lieutenant-Colonel Wauchop now appears to have been prevented acting in chief as wounded,) the Major manned the intrenchment and battery as directed, and marched into the open ground, towards the gate of Mantua, with the rest of the Irish. They first encountered, and drove before them, 200 Austrian grenadiers, as far as a guard-house, where there were above 200 more. From this post, the Austrians "poured a fire so terrible," says my French authority, "that it was capable of disheartening any troops, except such as resolved to conquer, or to die." Nevertheless, this superior force was beaten out of the guard-house, and put to flight. In the meantime, Prince Eugene, finding that nothing was to be gained by negociation, determined to avail himself of the advance of the Irish from the

* Besides the above Captain, there were, of the old Sligo sept, in the Regiment of Dillon, at Cremona, 3 brothers, of whom Andrew, the youngest, was appointed Lieutenant-Colonel to that corps in 1735, and died, with the rank of Colonel, in 1745. Other noted officers of the name are mentioned elsewhere, or in connexion with the Regiment of Walsh, and the battle of Fontenoy.

† His house was levelled with the ground, as that of a traitor. He is reported to have been concerned, in 1705, in a 2nd Austrian design to surprise Cremona. But it came to nothing.

protection of their intrenchment, as well as of their lessened and harassed state, to overpower them, and so reach the Po gate. For this service, he appointed, as successor to Baron de Mercy, the Baron de Freiberg, Lieutenant-Colonel of the Regiment of Taaffe.* Freiberg was furnished with such a body of cuirassiers, as, with the infantry and other cuirassiers by whom he was to be joined, were supposed capable of overcoming any opposition they could meet with. The ground occupied by the Irish was so open, owing to the distance of any houses from the ramparts, that cavalry could march in squadrons. The Baron de Freiberg, on surveying how very favourable the place was for the design he meditated, commanded his men to advance—in order, as he supposed, to trample to the earth such a comparatively small and feeble force as that of the Irish— and, by way of shortening the work, he caused them to be charged at once, with the greatest fury, in front, flank, and rear. But O'Mahony, arraying the Irish so as to face their assailants on every side, received the onset of the Imperialists with an intrepidity that astonished them. The fire of the Irish battalions strewed the ground with men and horses; compelling the cuirassiers to fly with such precipitation, that the infantry, advancing to support them, was obliged to open, in order to give them a passage through its ranks. It was in vain that the officers of those panic-struck horsemen attempted to rally them for another effort. They continued their flight to the main body of cavalry in the Sabatine square. Another corps of cuirassiers, however, came to the aid of Freiberg, who, enraged at this reverse, put himself at their head, and, with the assistance of the infantry, resolved, "to perish, or to crush the Irish." And he accordingly broke through, and penetrated even into the midst of, Dillon's battalion. O'Mahony, rushing up to arrest the Baron's career, seized the bridle of his horse, and desirous to preserve, if possible, the life of such a gallant young man, exclaimed—"Good quarter for Monsieur de Freiberg!" But the Baron fiercely replying—"This is no day for clemency, only do your duty, I'll do mine!"—and endeavouring to push forward, was fired at, and killed; to the regret of his enemies, as well as his friends, and particularly of Prince Eugene. The cuirassiers, dismayed at their brave leader's fall, wavered, and suffered so much by the bullet and bayonet, that they were routed by the Irish, who took a pair of their kettle-drums, and made a number of their officers prisoners. The remains of those beaten cuirassiers (whose fate their infantry appears to have shared) fled towards that body of their troops engaged in blocking up the French about the gate of Mantua, or Mossa.† The slaughter of the

* This corps, previously the Duke of Lorrain's Regiment of Cuirassiers, and at its full complement 1000 strong, was called that of Taaffe, from its Colonel, the celebrated Francis, 4th Viscount Taaffe, and 3rd Earl of Carlingford in Ireland, Count, Imperial Chamberlain, Counsellor of State and Cabinet, Lieutenant-General of the Horse, and Veldt-Marshal in Austria, and Knight of the Golden Fleece in Spain, deceased in 1704. Among the Imperial officers who fell at Cremona was a nephew of that distinguished nobleman, or the Honourable Lambart Taaffe, son of the Honourable Major John Taaffe, slain in King James II.'s army before Derry in 1689, and whose other son, Theobald, succeeded to the family titles. The name of Taaffe has continued to our times connected with Irish and Austrian nobility.

† The Abbé de Vairac, in his "History of the Revolutions in Spain," (as translated and printed at London in 1724,) observes—"It must be said, to the honour of the Irish, that this day was appointed by Providence to signalize their fidelity and undauntedness. The 2 regiments of that nation, which were in garrison, at Cremona, made a most terrible fire upon those who offer'd to approach near the post they had taken; and what is most singular in it is, that the officer, who had taken the

Germans, in this attack, was great; but, as the Irish likewise suffered severely; as, in *their* fatigued and diminished condition, they would have to encounter new and increased opposition, should they continue their march towards the last-mentioned gate; and, as the battery of St. Peter would be infallibly retaken during their absence, O'Mahony judged it better, for the present, to return to his intrenchment, at the Po gate. And he judged correctly. For, as he returned, his retreat was harassed by the musketry of fresh troops sent against him; and, on his resuming his post at the gate, the enemy likewise opened fire upon it, from a house which they had seized for the purpose. But O'Mahony, stationing himself near the battery, drove the Austrians out of the house by playing the artillery upon it; and, with cartridge-shot, swept the enemy's troops away, wherever they attempted to show themselves. The Austrians, on the other hand, did not cease to answer this fire from such eminences, angles of bastions, or other places, as they could do so, under cover. So various were the conflicts now raging through the city, that the most voluminous French historian of Louis XIV.'s wars observes on this occasion—"I do not pretend to enter into a detail of each particular action, or to report in full all that happened there, since those actions would be sufficient to fill an entire volume." And the biographer of Prince Eugene, after expressing his inability to record so many combats, adds—"Nothing was to be seen upon the pavement but blood, and slaughtered men and horses, in every direction. The cries of the wounded, and of the dying, joined with the lamentations of the townspeople who witnessed this frightful spectacle, increased the horrors of the struggle."

During the stubborn contest of the Irish with the enemy about the Po gate, the Count de Revel, whose force was augmented by different parties of his countrymen, stormed the gate of All Saints, and other posts beyond it, or in the direction of St. Margaret's gate. Then preparing to clear his way towards, and attack, the latter gate,—which Prince Eugene had particularly strengthened to retreat by in case of necessity,—the Count despatched a distinguished cavalry officer, Captain de Langeais, to the Irish, with orders, to secure their intrenchment, as before, at the Po gate, and renew the attempt to penetrate to the gate of Mantua, or Mossa. And, as the Irish, by this time, had suffered extremely, and *no* cavalry were to support them in such a discouraging enterprise against infantry and cavalry,* the Captain brought some money to distribute among the wearied soldiery. Leaving 100 men in the intrenchment, Captain Dillon of the grenadiers of that battalion marched out at the head of the rest of his countrymen; and they advanced at first with success, driving the Austrians from several houses to the left, and from

Marshal de Villeroy, going to them, from Prince Eugene, to persuade them to surrender, they secur'd him; which so exasperated the Prince, that he sent Baron Frieberg, at the head of a great body of Cuirassiers, with orders to put them all to the sword, if they did not immediately surrender. That officer, having beheld many of his men kill'd about him, resolv'd rather to lose his own life in a fresh attack, than to yield himself up to the Irish. His death daunted the Cuirassiers, who instantly turn'd their backs and fled; and their defeat snatch'd the victory out of the hands of the Imperialists."

* The latest and fullest account, or "Rélation de ce qui s'est passé a Crémone le 1er Février, envoyée par M. le Duc de Vendôme le 3 Mars, 1702," reports—"Les Irlandais, après avoir laissé 100 hommes dans leur retranchement, marchèrent aux ennemis, *sans* avoir de cavalerie pour les soutenir."

several posts upon the ramparts to the right. But, on reaching a spot of ground very open, and where the streets, bordering upon the rampart, were very wide, the Irish were attacked, in front, flank, and rear, by the enemy's horse and foot. A most obstinate combat ensued; both parties being, for a very long time, mixed up in close conflict. Finding, however, from the superior force opposed to them, that it would be impossible either to maintain themselves where they were, or to advance any farther, the overpowered remains of the 2 battalions retired to and re-entered their retrenchment, through the aid of the 100 men left to guard it. In this attack, the Count de Leiningen, 1 of the enemy's chief and bravest officers, was killed, and the Baron de Mercy was wounded a 2nd time, and made prisoner. The Commandant, and Captain of Grenadiers, Dillon, although wounded on this occasion, would not withdraw till he had placed his regiment within the intrenchment, and had caused that position to be so additionally fortified, as to prevent a recapture of the cannon by the enemy, which there was reason to apprehend.

It was not till this late period of the day, or till the attack of the posts leading to the enemy's last gate, of St. Margaret, that the long and dangerous delay which occurred between Brigadier d'Arene, the Count de Revel, and the Marquis de Praslin, with respect to the affair of the redoubt and bridge of boats, was terminated. The Marquis then proceeding to the bridge, sent orders to the officers that defended the approach to it on the other side of the Po, or Captain Stuart of Dillon's battalion, and Captains de Châteauperrs and Caussade of the battalion of Beaujolois, to retire with their men, after destroying the redoubt and works connected with it. This was effected, notwithstanding the superior numbers and fire of Vaudemont's corps; and a brave Serjeant, with a party of soldiers, completed the removal of the bridge, by burning some of the boats, and by pulling away the remainder, to the Cremona side of the river. The 150 men withdrawn, of whom Captain Stuart's proportion, or 50, appear to have been Irish, were placed under Major O'Mahony, to reinforce the posts about the Po gate. Thus, towards 3 o'clock, was Cremona finally secured on this side, after its safety had been too long endangered, by *not* adopting the counsel of the Irish. And now those bodies of Eugene's infantry and cuirassiers that had hitherto occupied the ramparts and streets towards the Po gate, seeing any further attempt upon it to be hopeless, and being affected by the successes of the garrison elsewhere, fell back towards the gate of Mantua, or Mossa.

In the division of the city called "the New Town," and to which that gate belonged, a noble resistance had been made to the enemy, since morning. That quarter of the town had been so filled by the Imperialists, that the greater portion of the French cavalry were at first blocked up in it; afterwards, the 2 Irish battalions, ordered to force their way to the gate there, were *twice* obliged to desist; and, in fine, so completely occupied by the enemy was the district supposed to be, that the gates of All Saints and St. Margaret were not believed to have been more certainly gained by the Germans, than that of Mantua, or Mossa. Such, however, was *not* the case. For, when the Austrians poured into this part of the city, Captain Lynch, of Dillon's battalion, was stationed at that gate. Like his countryman, the Captain, with the 35 men at the Po gate, Lynch was not to be surprised. Collecting what men he could from the vicinity, and being lucky enough to find powder and ball at the guard-house to his gate, he intrenched himself there; maintaining it the whole day against the Imperialists, whose commander, Count de Kuffstein, Lieutenant-Colonel of the Regiment of Herberstein, was wounded at the attack. Lynch did more. For, the Germans occupying the adjacent Church of St. Mary of Bethlehem, and placing musketeers in the steeple as a post from which *their* fire would completely command *his* intrenchment at the gate, he dislodged the enemy from the Church, and kept possession of it, as well as the gate. The achievements of the Irish this memorable day, on which, in the words of a French General Officer, they "performed incomprehensible things," * were concluded, by the remains of the troops at the Po gate at last fulfilling the orders they had received, to penetrate to the gate of Mantua, or Mossa. Although so much weakened by fatigue, cold, fasting, and wounds, as well as diminished by those killed or taken in such a long struggle against superior numbers, the comparatively few effective survivors of Bourke's and Dillon's battalions did not allow the enemy to "depart in peace," but followed his retiring infantry and cuirassiers *beyond* the gate last-mentioned, charging both with great effect, especially the cuirassiers, from whom they wrested a 2nd pair of kettle-drums, and some standards.

Eugene's contest with the French, at St. Margaret's gate, was well maintained, his assailants being repeatedly repulsed, and successfully kept at bay there, until it was late, or dark; when, after a conflict of about 11 hours, (or from 7 in the morning, to a little before 6 in the evening,) the fate of Cremona was decided, by his having to abandon that city, "taken by a miracle," as was said, "and lost by a still greater one!" He retired in good order, bringing away, as companions for the Marshal de Villeroy, who had been sent off to Ostiano, 80 or 90 officers, of whom 38 were Irish, besides about 400 soldiers, including 29 Irish, and above 500 horses captured from the garrison. According to the most probable accounts on the Prince's side, his loss was from 1500 to 1600 men, of whom about 1200 were killed or wounded, and the rest prisoners. The official table of the killed, wounded, and prisoners of the French and Irish *infantry*—for I have seen no such return of the *cavalry* of the garrison—presents a total of 1429 men and officers; of whom the French were 1079, and the Irish 350; the last number a large proportion out of 600 men! The details of the loss of the 2 Irish battalions, counting serjeants among the privates, were thus:—

BOURKE'S.

	Killed.	Wounded.	Taken.	Total.
Officers,	1	13	2	16
Soldiers,	53	78	3	134
	54	91	5	150

DILLON'S.

	Killed.	Wounded.	Taken.	Total.
Officers,	6	29	36	71
Soldiers,	37	66	26	129
	43	95	62	200

* The Brigadier Count de Vaudrey, above alluded to, writes thus—"Les Irlandais, qui avaient l'attaque de la droite, du côté du Pô, *ont fait des choses incompréhensibles.* . . . Ils ont arraché les, étendards des cuirassiers de l'Empereur, et se sont emparés de 2 paires de timbales qu'ils avaient à leur tête."

The officers distinguished in Bourke's battalion were Lieutenant-Colonel Wauchop, Plunkett, Captain of Grenadiers, Captains Donnellan and Mac Auliffe, and the Lieutenant of Grenadiers, Mac Auliffe, besides the reformed officers, Lieutenant-Colonel Connock, and the Lieutenants Corrin, Power, Nugent, and Ivers.* Those distinguished in Dillon's battalion were its 2 successive Commandants, Major O'Mahony and Dillon, Captain of Grenadiers, Captains Lynch, Mac Donough, and Macgee, Lieutenants Dillon and Gibbons, and 2 gentlemen, mentioned, without any rank attached, as John Bourke and Thomas Dillon. The Count de Revel, who, though his countrymen, the French, did wonders where they fought, yet acknowledged (as well as the enemy) that it was to the obstinate courage of the Irish in defence of the Po gate the preservation of Cremona was principally owing,† appointed, as *their* most distinguished representative, Major O'Mahony, to carry the despatch to Paris. The Major, for his excellent character in the service, previously known to Louis, was, on the day of his reaching Versailles, received by his Majesty, according to the Duke de Saint Simon, in a manner proportioned to the importance of the intelligence from Italy. The King, on rising from dinner, proceeded to his private cabinet accompanied by the Irish officer *only*, and continued there, with shut doors, for about an hour; while the numerous courtiers, including, to the general surprise, Chamillart, the Minister of War himself, had to remain in the apartment outside, where the deliverance of Cremona was the topic of universal curiosity; as Chamillart sufficiently experienced, from the incessant questions to which he was exposed respecting such a remarkable event. After quitting his cabinet, the King, while changing his dress in order to walk in the palace garden, expressed himself with great approbation on the affair of Cremona, and especially on the conduct of his principal officers there; at the same time evincing how gratified he was with O'Mahony in particular, by the length at which he spoke of him; alleging that he had never heard anybody give so good an account of everything that occurred; or a narrative displaying such clearness of perception and exactness, united with an agreeable manner of communication. From another contemporary, the Chevalier de Bellerive, we are informed of Louis and the Major on this occasion, how his Majesty, having listened to the description of what happened at Cremona with pleasure, intimated that he was only dissatisfied with the deficiency of the narrator's details respecting the acts of his own countrymen. The King observed, on that point, to the Major—" *Vous ne me parlez que*

* Printed, in French, "Yvert." The old name of O'Hiomhair, famous for valour in the wars of Thomond, was anglicized into "Ivers."

† The historian of Prince Eugene observes of the garrison of Cremona—"Il faut rendre justice aux François; ils y firent des merveilles. Les Irlandois s'y distinguerent aussi beaucoup; et *leur obstination à la défense sauva la place.*" In fact, of the 4 gates fought for, or those of the Po, Mantua, All Saints, and St. Margaret, the Irish, though but 600 men, preserved the 1st, and, through it, the town, as their countryman, Lynch, held the 2nd, till they forced their way to, and drove the Imperialists from, it; while the French, though 3400 men, only regained the 2 remaining gates. It was, likewise, in connexion with the contests for the Po and Mantua gates, that the chief Imperial officers were put *hors de combat*, or Mercy, Deidrichstein, Freiberg, Leiningen, and Kuffstein. The illustrious Lieutenant-General Pelet, Directeur Général du Bureau de la Guerre, writing how "chacun fit des prodiges de valeur," adds, "*surtout* les 2 régiments Irlandais." In other words, they were,

"Where all were brave, the bravest of the brave!"

des François, hè! qu' auront donc fait mes braves Irlandois?"—"Sire," rejoined the Major, merely paying back as an Irishman, to the French, the compliment which Louis, as a Frenchman, had paid to the Irish—"*Nous avons suivi leur rapidité guerrière.*" A reply, presenting, says Mr. O'Conor, "a memorable instance of the modesty of merit, or of pride, conscious of merit, and disdainful of vain-glory." Louis rewarded the Major with a brevet as Colonel, and a pension of 1000 livres, besides a present of 1000 louis d'ors, by way (as it were) of defraying the expense of his journey.* Lieutenants-Colonel Wauchop and Connock were likewise brevetted as Colonels. And, as a general testimony of the French Monarch's satisfaction at the conduct of the Irish on this occasion, not merely Bourke's, but the other 4 Irish Infantry Regiments of Dorrington, Albemarle, Berwick, and Galmoy, like it only on French pay, *all* had their pay raised to the higher scale of the 3 corps originally comprised in the Brigade of Mountcashel, and, at this period, or 1702, consisting of the Regiments of Lee, Clare, and Dillon. The last, as 1 of those already enjoying that pay, only received a special gratuity in money, for its bravery at Cremona. After his interview with Louis XIV., "Coll. Mahoni," notes the contemporary Irish Jacobite loyalist, Plunkett, "went from Versaills to St. Germains, for to pay his respects to his own King: who knighted him for his late service, reputeing what was don to his great friend to be don to himself. And 'tis so in the event. For the greater progress is made by France and her Allyes in the warr, the sooner will *the Restoration of James III.* be effected."

The Whig writer, Forman, remarking of the affair of Cremona, "that the Irish perform'd there the most important piece of service for Louis XIV., that, perhaps, any King of France ever received, from so small a body of men, since the foundation of that monarchy," adds—"This action of the Irish, by an impartial way of reasoning, saved the whole French army in Italy; the destruction of which, according to the account itself, as well as the opinion of all military men, *must* have been the infallible consequence of the loss of Cremona. It was also thought, in England, to have so much influence over the affairs of Europe, as they stood at that time, that, as I have been informed, a Member of the House of Commons, upon the arrival of the news, said, in Parliament, that those 2 regiments had done more mischief to the High Allies, than all the Irish abroad could have done, had they been kept at home, and left in the entire possession of their estates. . . . Had they done nothing else," concludes Forman, "this 1 action would alone be sufficient to eternize them." In Ireland, the older natives, though groaning under the many oppressions of the Orange revolution,† might naturally exult,

* "Mahoni, an Irish gentleman, a reform'd Major in a regiment of his nation," says the Abbé de Vairac, "was appointed to carry to his Most Christian Majesty an account of that memorable transaction, and perform'd that commission so much to his Majesty's satisfaction, that he granted him a breviate for Colonel, and gave him a pension of 1000 livres, besides 1000 louis-d'ors to defray the expenses of his journey to the Court."

† M. Picot d'Orleans, in his Memoirs for the Ecclesiastical History of the 18th Century, (or from 1700 to 1800,) after observing, that "all the documents of the times present a deplorable picture of how religion was situated in Ireland" previous to and *at* the commencement of that century, says—"The Catholics were marked out for all sorts of vexations, and the Protestants, although inferior in number, or because they were inferior in number, made their yoke press most severely upon them." Thus, in the Dutch Lettres Historiques for January, 1702, we read, under head of Ireland, an exact search proclaimed for all Priests, Monks, and Jesuits,

on this memorable occasion, at such a gratifying realization, in representatives of their race, of all that the highest eulogium of poetic patriotism could associate with the character of an Irishman—

> "By honour bound in woe or weal,
> Whate'er *she* bids, *he* dares to do;
> Tempt him with bribes, he will not fail,
> Try him in fire, you'll find him true.
> He seeks not safety; let his post
> Be where it ought, in danger's van,
> And, if the field of fame be lost,
> 'Twill *not* be by an Irishman."—ORR.

The feeling of a just national pride, at being the countrymen of such heroes, found a popular expression in music; and, to our times, the piper in Munster has performed the air of—"*The day we beat the Germans at Cremona.*"* A late patriotic writer, Thomas Davis, has well observed —"We would not like to meet the Irishman, who, knowing these facts, would pass the north of Italy, and *not* track the steps of the Irish regiments, through the streets, and gates, and ramparts, of Cremona." †

The celebrated Duke of Vendome was appointed to succeed Villeroy in Italy, with a sufficient army to oblige Prince Eugene to raise the blockade of Mantua, and to force him to an engagement. The Irish troops, under the Duke's orders, were the 5 battalions of Bourke, Dillon, Albemarle, Berwick, and Galmoy, and Sheldon's 2 squadrons. Of Colonels present, from May 27th to June 1st, at the reduction of Castiglione delle Stiviere, were Bourke and O'Mahony; the latter of whom, and an officer named O'Carroll, appear as distinguished, July 26th, at Vendome's surprise and cutting up of 4 of Eugene's cavalry regiments under General Annibal Visconti at Santa Vittoria. Sheldon, who volunteered there acting as Aide-de-Camp to Vendome, was severely wounded; behaving so very well, that he was 1 of 3 officers (2 of them French) specially recommended, for such good service, to Louis XIV.'s consideration, by his grandson, the King of Spain. These movements were followed, August 15th, by the battle of Luzzara. Eugene's force

with the offer of £100 reward for a Popish Archbishop, £50 for a Bishop, and £40 for a Vicar-General, and every Jesuit or Monk. Yet how much *worse* penal legislation was to come!

* I allude to the famous Gansey, deceased in February, 1857. "He passed away calmly and peacefully," says the account, "at Killarney, in the 90th year of his age," and, by his performances, left a name "associated, for over half a century, with the talismanic recollections of Killarney, in the breast of millions, at home, and abroad." The late Maurice O'Connell mentioned to me, his having often heard the air, on the combat at Cremona, from Gansey; to whom it had been transmitted by his Munster predecessors in "the tuneful art."

† For this narrative of the affair of Cremona (which has cost me an amount of time and trouble *painful* to think of) I have made use of the French contemporary journals, the various publications, on the Bourbon and the Imperial side, in the Mercure Historique and the Lettres Historiques for 1702, the original documents on the subject in the great work on the War of the Spanish Succession from the Dépôt de la Guerre at Paris, the large history of the Marquis de Quincy, the accounts of the Marquises de Feuquieres and Dangeau, the Chevalier de Folard, the Histoire du Prince Eugène de Savoye, and the Italian writer Botta, with subordinate matter from the Duc de St. Simon, the Chevalier de Bellerive, the Abbé de Vairac, the pamphleteer Forman, the Abbé Mac Geoghegan, the Memoirs of Charles O'Conor of Belanagare, his grandson's unfinished Military Memoirs of the Irish Nation, Plunkett's Light to the Blind, the MS. History of Kerry, and Ponce MSS., in the Royal Irish Academy, &c.

has been differently represented at from 24,000 to 26,000 men, with 57 cannon. Vendome's force has been computed at 35,000 men; of whom, however, *not* so many as 2-3rds, could engage, or be up for action; and they had but 37 cannon. The contest, which, from the broken nature of the country, was one chiefly of musketry and cannon, lasted from 5 in the evening till 1 in the morning. Vendome acknowledged about 2500, and Eugene 2695, killed and wounded. Both remained intrenched in presence of one another; and the engagement was, so far, a drawn battle. The main attack of Eugene having been against Vendome's left wing, the latter posted there " the flower of his troops," including the " Brigade des Irlandois," or Bourke's, Dillon's, Berwick's and Galmoy's battalions; that of Albemarle being upon the French and Spanish right. The French accounts thus notice the several assaults of the Imperialists upon Vendome's left wing. At their 1st onset, that wing " received them with so much vigour, that they were repulsed; leaving the ground covered with dead. Half an hour after, they returned to the charge, and they were again repulsed. Then they made fresh troops advance, and charged a 3rd time, with as little success. At last, the 4th time, they caused the Irish, and the Regiments of Perche and of Sault, that had suffered severely, to lose a little ground. But the Comte de Besons caused the cavalry Regiments of the Colonel-General, of Dourches, of Montperoux, and of Bourbon, to march, leading them several times to the charge against the enemy, which arrested his progress." After admitting the repulse of those 3 furious charges of the Imperialists, and mentioning their reinforcement by 3 battalions of Danes for a 4th effort, —" At last," says Prince Eugene's historian, " the Brigade of the Irish, being no longer able to sustain the fire of the Imperialists, and having lost a quantity of soldiers, and its best officers, was obliged to fall back above 500 paces. The majority of the French regiments, when they saw this, fell back also, and the Imperialists made themselves masters of their ground." Thus, " the Imperialists penetrated the left wing of the army of the 2 crowns, but they did not dare to pursue the Irish, nor the *other* brigades which had turned their backs "—this caution proceeding from " the apprehension of encountering a 2nd line, and of being surrounded." The same hostile writer subsequently refers to " the disorder of the Irish," and the necessity, on the part of M. de Besons, " to make some squadrons advance to sustain them, and gain time for them to rally." How very hard it was to make *them* give way is thus attested by the accounts of *both* sides. The French admit the confusion to have been so great on this wing from its heavy loss, especially of officers, that Vendome himself was obliged to rally it; and it was not until after aid obtained from the right, and 6 attacks, that the enemy could be repulsed. Meanwhile, the battalion of Albemarle, under its Lieutenant-Colonel, Nicholas Fitz-Gerald, signalized itself very much upon the right. It is described, in the letters of 3 French General Officers, as " having, though with a great loss, performed wonders—delivering the very distinguished corps of the Carabiniers, towards the close of the action, at a most critical period, or when they were flanked, and on the point of being overpowered by the enemy—the charge, by which this deliverance was effected, having been the most vigorous possible—trampling down all before it, though those who made it were inferior in number—so that," it is added, " they could not be too highly praised." Of the general conduct of the Irish, from the deliverance of Cremona, to the end of this campaign of 1702,

Fieffé says—"Dans toutes ces actions, les Irlandais déploient encore la plus grande bravoure."

Among the 52 battalions and 90 squadrons, which, as "le plus en état de servir," Vendome still kept at hand in November, lest Eugene should attempt any offensive movement instead of retiring to winter-quarters, the 5 battalions of the Irish Brigade were included; the number of men in each of those battalions being thus officially returned—Dillon's, 350—Bourke's, 397—Galmoy's, 397—Berwick's, 460—Albemarle's, 327 —in all, 1931. Among the cavalry regiments of the Duke, detached for garrison duty, Sheldon's Irish, as 2 squadrons, are marked, as stationed at Cesoli. In a Stuart document of 1693, concerning the fittest methods of obtaining recruits for the Irish Jacobite army on the Continent, it is specified, how "Irish officers were to be established on the frontiers of Flanders; and 2 louis d'ors were to be given to every soldier, they could engage to desert from the Allied army." Accordingly, from *that* remote quarter, we find arrangements on foot in 1702, to reinforce the Irish Brigade in Italy for the campaign of 1703. Our adventurous countryman, Peter Drake of Drakerath, County of Meath, informs us, how several Irish officers, of whom he names the Captains O'Driscoll and Mac Carthy Reagh, were employed in Flanders, so early as the spring of 1702, to engage 600 deserters from Marlborough's army; which number, and a few over, were obtained in the course of the summer; Drake himself having procured so many as 156.* With all these, he left Brussels, in August, 1702, and reached Pavia, in February, 1703; *minus*, indeed, 257 men from desertion on "the long, laborious march by land;" but with about 343 remaining, that "were divided among the several officers of the Irish Brigade, who waited there to receive them." The official "Mémoire de M. de Chamlay" to Louis XIV., dated October 20th, 1702, likewise shows the solicitude of the French Government, to have as many Irish troops as possible, for 1703. "Il faudrait faire passer avec soin en France les Irlandais qui sont en Espagne, et qui ont déserté de la flotte d'Angleterre et de Hollande, quand elle était auprès de Cadix.† Je ne doute pas que le Roi n'ait déjà pourvu à ce qui est contenu dans cet article. Je crois que si on s'y prenait bien, on pourrait *tirer des Irlandais d'Irlande*. Si cela était possible, il serait très-important de le faire au plus tôt, *ces troupes étant excellentes;* et d'ailleurs cela soulagerait d'autant le royaume. On dit qu'il y a beaucoup d'Irlandais répandus en Bretagne. On pourrait les ramasser, et les mettre dans le service."

This year, 1702, began the insurrection of the Camisards, or Protestants of the Cevennes, in Languedoc, on account of the persecution to which they were subjected, through the measures, connected with the Revocation of the Edict of Nantes, to compel all those of *their* religion in France to become Catholics. This struggle between the Camisards and their government was, as a *religious* war, attended with the peculiar cruelty, for which such *holy* contests have been infamous in every age. "Nowhere," says the learned and liberal American historian, Prescott, "do we find such a free range given to the worst passions of our nature, as in the wars of religion—where each party considers itself as arrayed against the enemies of God, and where the sanctity of the cause throws a

* Drake got in all 159, but 3 gave him the slip.
† The English might obtain sailors, as they did soldiers, from Ireland, in those times; but, it appears by the text, with *desertion* in view, on the part of the former, as well as the latter.

veil over the foulest transgressions, that hides their enormity from the eye of the transgressor." The contest in the Cevennes continued unabated until 1704, towards the close of which, the Marshal de Villars seemed to be entirely successful; and, on the renewal of the disturbances, in 1705, they were extinguished by the Duke of Berwick. But, since the encounters, in the course of this insurrection, though honourable to the courage of the Camisards, and proportionably so to that of *their* opponents, were, amidst a great European war, not of such a nature, as to confer any distinction upon the Irish worthy of more than a passing notice, it will suffice to observe *here*, that, on several occasions, Irish appear to have signalized themselves, especially officers; and, no doubt, with a greater portion of zeal, from the miserable condition to which those of their own race and creed were reduced at home, by the violation of *their* Edict of Nantes—the Treaty of Limerick. It has been well remarked, that "intolerance is the vice of *all* religionists, when the philosophy of the FEW has not yet instructed and humanized the *many*." For

"Philosophy consists not
In airy schemes, or idle speculations:
The rule and conduct of all social life
Is her great province. Not, in lonely cells,
Obscure she lurks, but holds her heav'nly light
To senates, and to kings, to guide their councils,
And teach them to reform and bless mankind."—THOMSON.

In 1703, the Duke of Vendome continued to command in Italy; having the Irish battalions of Berwick, Bourke, Dillon, Galmoy, and Fitz-Gerald, (late Albemarle,) in his army. At the assault and capture, January 13th, of the intrenched post of Bondanello, in an angle at the junction of the Parmeggiana and the Secchia, Lieutenant-Colonel Alexander Barnewall of the Regiment of Galmoy, with a detachment from Reggiolo, took a leading part. The Imperialists, under General Stahremberg, were so weakened at the opening of this campaign, that Vendome, while leaving a force to hold them in check along the Secchia, was able to march, during the summer, with 32 battalions, and 29 squadrons, into the Tyrol, in order to reduce that territory, through a junction with the Elector of Bavaria from Germany. Among the battalions engaged in this expedition were those of Dillon, Galmoy, Bourke, and Fitz-Gerald. Notwithstanding the many difficulties of invading a country of such great natural strength, defended by a peasantry of hardy and active mountaineers, ranking among the best sharp-shooters in the world, and aided by Austrian engineers, the French penetrated to the city of Trent; when, from the failure of the Elector of Bavaria to advance far enough to effect a junction, and, from the meditated treachery of a secession to the Allies, on the part of the Duke of Savoy, against which it was necessary to take precautions, Vendome had to retire into Italy. Of Irish officers, in this expedition, the Honourable Arthur Dillon, as Brigadier, with 1500 men, signalized himself, at the end of July, in dislodging from a mountain-pass, deemed impregnable in front, and considered inaccessible elsewhere, 500 of the enemy; by which he was able to reach and take the town and castle of Riva, without even the loss of a man! The Comte de Medavi writes, July 31st, on this affair, to Vendome, "que M. Dillon s'y est tout à fait distingué." On the surrender, July 28th, (during Vendome's absence in the Tyrol,) of the important fortified town of Brescello, Colonel Daniel

O'Mahony was appointed its Governor. At the pursuit, and cutting up, by Vendome, in October, of the select corps of Imperial cavalry, despatched, under General Visconti, to assist the Duke of Savoy, as well as at the similar operations, in December, and January, (1704) against the larger force that marched, under General Stahremberg, to join the Duke, the Regiment of Dillon, and its Colonel, are mentioned, as sharing in Vendome's successes, at San-Sebastiano, and Castel-Novo-de-Bormida.

In Germany, where France was most successful in 1703, the Irish were employed in the Army of the Rhine, first, under the Duke of Burgundy, next, under the Marshal de Tallard; and in the army of the Danube, or Bavaria, under the Marshal de Villars. In the former force, were Lord Galmoy, as Major-General, and the 2 squadrons of Sheldon's horse. In the latter force, were the Major-Generals Andrew Lee, and William Dorrington; Charles O'Brien, 5th Viscount Clare, as Brigadier of Infantry, and the 2 battalions of Dorrington and Clare. The principal achievement of the Army of the Rhine, under the Duke of Burgundy, was the siege and reduction of Brisach, in the summer. But this acquisition was much surpassed by the Marshal de Tallard's conquest of Landau, invested October 11th, and surrendered November 18th, in consequence of the Marshal's overthrow, on the 15th, of the Prince of Hesse Cassel's army, at the battle of Spire, with a loss stated at above 6000 men, between killed and prisoners, from 50, to upwards of 60, colours or standards, 30 pieces of cannon, tents, &c.; the French having, it is said, only 600 men, but, more probably, a *far* greater number, killed and wounded. In this battle, the French, at first, are alleged to have had several of their standards and kettle-drums captured by the German cavalry; and several cannon taken from, and turned against, them. But the Regiment of Sheldon, although its 2 squadrons did not muster, exclusive of officers, above 180 men, "charged," says an Allied writer, "and routed 2 regiments of Imperial cuirassiers, recovered the fortune of the day, and thus led the way to the victory." Its Lieutenant-Colonel, with rank as Colonel, Christopher Nugent of Dardistown, County of Meath, showing himself here, as at Landen in 1693, and on so many other occasions, a gallant man, and a good officer, received 7 wounds;* and, among the Irish killed, was a brave officer, of a name deducing its origin from the heroic ages of Erin, Colonel Bernard Macgennis. He was the father of 4 sons, who all died in the service of France; as did various other representatives of the same ancient Irian race, in the Irish Regiments of Galmoy, Lee, Bulkeley, Roth, Dillon; of whom several were Chevaliers of St. Louis. In noting of the Regiment of Sheldon "s'étant distingué à la bataille de Spire," Mac Geoghegan adds, "il fut accordé une augmentation de traitement aux Capitaines et Lieutenans réformés qui servirent à la suite de ce corps."

* The circumstance of Christopher Nugent having been so distinguished, and receiving, "au combat de Spire, 7 blessures," is given in a copy of an official Memorial, endorsed, "Promotion d'Officiers Généraux Irlandois, Mai, 1705," and described as marginally noted, "in pencil, apparently by Louis XIV." This document belonged to a collection of materials for an intended History of the Irish Brigade, obtained at Paris by the late John O'Connell, Esq., and kindly transferred to me, in 1842. The Memorial, though emanating apparently from a French source, dwells much, in justice to the Irish, on the manner in which such *Irish* officers as Lord Galmoy, Lord Clare, Nicholas Fitz-Gerald, and Christopher Nugent, were passed over in the way of promotion, compared with several *French* officers, of inferior claims to advancement in the service.

At the reduction, early in the year, of the important Fort of Kehl, by the Marshal de Villars, Major-General Andrew Lee was among his most distinguished officers, as well as a young Irishman, named Mac Sheehy, acting as an Engineer; who, reconnoitring the breach, correctly pronounced it, in opposition to the other Engineers, to be practicable; and the operations against that fort cost the Regiment of Clare 1 Captain, and nearly 90 men. The engagement, called "the 1st battle of Hochstedt," was fought, September 20th, by the Marshal de Villars, and the Elector of Bavaria, against the Imperial General, Count de Stirum. At the commencement of this action, the Count, having a much inferior force to deal with, under Lieutenant-General D'Usson, (the same who formerly commanded in Ireland,) gave that force a very rough handling. But the Marshal, and the Elector, after a long and harassing march, coming up, and falling to work with their cavalry, while their artillery and infantry advanced as quickly as possible to second them, the Count was then so outnumbered, that he endeavoured to retreat, fighting, towards Nordlingen. And he continued to do so most creditably, until, after a combat altogether of 9 hours, his army were broken, and routed; having between 7000 and 8000, (if not more,) killed, or made prisoners, and their entire artillery, consisting of 33 pieces, taken, with 22 colours or standards, tents, baggage, &c.; the French and Bavarian loss not amounting to 1000 men. The reputation of the Irish Brigade was much increased at this victory. According to the official letters, or those of D'Usson and Villars, Major-General Dorrington always led on his infantry, with great regularity, and valour. Major-General Lee, in command of a French corps broken by the enemy, displayed his usual resolution, by the manner in which he exposed his person, to remedy the disorder that occurred; and, in doing so, received 5 or 6 wounds. In hastening up to gain a village in the centre, which it was requisite to possess, in order to advance in front with effect against the enemy, the Irish, under Lord Clare, occupied that post, with an ardour for fighting that could not be sufficiently praised; and they continued to manifest their usual good-will and corresponding ardour, being the 1st body of infantry, (*followed* by the brigade of Artois, and some companies of grenadiers,) to which was due the final or decisive breaking and dispersion of the German infantry, attended by a great slaughter of that infantry, during the night, in the woods, through which they endeavoured to escape.* Count Arthur Dillon adds respecting this battle—"The Regiment of Clare highly distinguished itself there. Having lost, at the commencement of the action, 1 of its colours, it precipitated itself, *à l'arme blanche*, upon the enemy, recovered that, and took 2 other colours from the enemy." † *This* was being "double and quit" with the Germans.

* Villars, mentioning to Louis XIV. how "l'on attendit que l'infanterie eût gagné un village, qui était dans le centre, pour marcher de front aux ennemis," states, "les Irlandais, commandés par milord Clare, l'avaient occupé, avec une ardeur de combattre que l'on ne peut assez louer." And again, or in reference to their *general* conduct in the action, he alleges, "les Irlandais ont marqué leur bonne volonté et leur ardeur ordinaires." As to the infantry, whose coming up, &c., with that of the enemy, *decided* the event of the contest, the Marshal writes, "la brigade des Irlandais, celle d'Artois, et quelques compagnies de grenadiers, ayant joint leurs derniers rangs, le désordre s'y mit; elle fut entièrement rompue; nos troupes en tuèrent beaucoup dans les bois, où le massacre fut très-grand, et dura même toute la nuit."

† Le Régiment de Clare s'y distingua beaucoup. Ayant perdu, au commence-

The greatest efforts of the Allies, in 1704, were made in Germany, to save the House of Austria, attacked by the Bavarians and French on one side, and by the Hungarians on another. For this purpose, in June, the Anglo-Dutch and Imperial armies joined in Swabia, under the Duke of Marlborough and Prince Lewis of Baden. Each was to command day about, and they proceeded in July to enter Bavaria. To oppose them, the Bavarian Field-Marshal, Count d'Arco, was stationed on the hill of Schellenberg, extending from Donawert on his left, towards a wood on his right. That eminence, very steep, rough, and difficult to ascend, had been, some time before, ordered to be intrenched along the summit. But, according to an Italian officer there, the Marquis Scipio Maffei, Lieutenant-General in the *Bavarian* and subsequently in the *Imperial* service, the works commenced were on a scale that would have accommodated 15,000 men, and yet were so little advanced, that they could not be completed before they were to be attacked; while the Bavarian and French force for the defence were no more, at most, than 8000 men, and 14 guns. July 2nd, Marlborough, whose day it was to command, cannonaded the imperfectly-intrenched eminence, with a corresponding advantage on his side, from 5 to 6 o'clock in the afternoon, and then ordered the post to be attacked in form. In artillery, from the Allied train being previously mentioned as having included 44 field-guns, he appears to have been much superior. His infantry, by Allied accounts, consisted of 5580 select British and Dutch, 3000 Imperial grenadiers, 30 additional battalions, half on the right and half on the left, that, at 500 men per battalion, would be 15,000, or, with the 8580 British, Dutch, and grenadier Imperialists, 23,580; his cavalry amounted to 30 British and Dutch squadrons, that, at 150 men each, would make 4500; and his entire force would thus be (exclusive of officers) 28,080 strong. The assault was commenced, on the side of the hill towards the wood, by the British and the Dutch; the former headed by a party of their Guards, under Lord Mordaunt, with shouts of *"God save the Queen!"* and both being seconded by the rest of the troops present. But the assailants, for an hour or more, were repulsed, and with such a smashing, especially of the British, that, it is said, the survivors could not be gotten to make another effort, when the remainder of the Allies opportunely came up, to attack the hill towards Donawert. This they did gallantly, under Prince Lewis of Baden, who was wounded, and had a horse shot under him; and the works having been most imperfect there, and the orders respecting the most effective mode of defending them not having been followed by the French officer at Donawert, Brigadier Dubordet and the 2 battalions of Toulouse and Nettancourt, the lines on that side were forced, in about half an hour, by the infantry of the Imperialists; the general assault upon the position, from its commencement by Marlborough at 6 o'clock, having occupied from an hour and a half to an hour and 3 quarters. Exposed, on the storming of their imperfect intrenchments, to such "a world of enemies"—or, by line of battle, 71 battalions and 152 squadrons against but 19 battalions and 6 squadrons!—the Gallo-Bavarians were obliged to abandon their artillery, (but first spiked or rendered useless,) their tents, their baggage, and 13 standards; yet had not, according to Maffei, in or after the action, 2500 slain or taken. The killed and wounded of the Allies are recorded, on their side,

ment de l'action, 1 de ses drapeaux, il fondit, à l'arme blanche, sur l'ennemi, et le reprit, avec 2 autres drapeaux ennemis.

by Serjeant Millner of "the Honourable Royal Regiment of Foot of Ireland,"* as 1536 British, of other nations 3772, of whom 1331 were Dutch, and 2441 Germans, making a general total of 5308 men, including 360 officers!† Such was the famous combat at the lines of Schellenberg, where Marlborough, at the head of a much superior force, was *beaten*, till aided by the Prince of Baden, with still greater numbers;‡ and where, considered apart from the mere circumstance of ultimate success, which, in war, as well as in peace, is too often *not* the reward of the greatest merit, the very vigorous defence, and unparalleled slaughter of their enemies, by the Gallo-Bavarians, with every advantage against them but that of position, unquestionably entitled *them* to the principal glory of the day. At this action, there were no Irish troops. But Major-General Andrew Lee commanded upon the Gallo-Bavarian right, where the British were so roughly handled previous to the entrance of the lines by the Imperialists, on the left, or towards Donawert. Being thus cut off from retiring by Donawert, Lee proceeded to withdraw his men, in the direction of the wood, to Neuburgh. And this, he, says a French contemporary, "executed with so much prudence, by availing himself of some squadrons of dragoons, that he suffered no loss, although closely followed by the enemy as far as the wood, where, having totally despaired of being able to break in upon him, they retired."

The next and most famous engagement of the campaign of 1704 was "the 2nd battle of Hochstedt," or Blenheim, fought, August 13th, between the Allies under the Duke of Marlborough and Prince Eugene of Savoy, and the French and Bavarians under the Marshals de Tallard and Marcin, and the Elector of Bavaria. Of the Gallo-Bavarians, the army of the Marshal de Tallard formed the right; the army of the Marshal de Marcin and the Elector formed the left. The former force extended from the village of Blenheim, which it occupied on its right, to the vicinity of the village of Oberglau, on its left. The latter force extended from the village of Oberglau, which it occupied on its right, to beyond the village of Lutzingen, which it held on its left. The general position of the 2 armies was along a sloping eminence, with the Nebel, a marshy rivulet, before them; a hostile passage of which was, however, much facilitated by the dryness of the season. The army of the Marshal de Tallard was opposed, on the Allied left, by the British, Dutch, German, and Danish troops, under the Duke of Marlborough. The army of the Marshal de Marcin and the Elector was opposed, on the Allied right, by the Prussians, Danes, Imperialists, and other German troops, under Prince Eugene of Savoy. The following were the proportions of men and artillery on both sides, by the best contemporary accounts of each, respecting its own strength.

* The 18th Royal Irish Regiment of Foot, a most distinguished corps, from the capture of Namur under King William III., to the *half*-capture of Sebastopol under Queen Victoria.

† The Dutch, as 378 killed and 953 wounded in Millner's table, would have 1331 killed and wounded; which last number is also consistent with his general total of the Allied loss as 5308. I have therefore corrected into 1331 an evident misprint of the Dutch total killed and wounded as but 1311. Of the 1536 British *hors de combat*, 115 were *officers*, and 1421 *soldiers*.

‡ The medal, struck by the Dutch, on this occasion, had Prince Lewis of Baden's bust on one side, and, on the other, the intrenchments of Schellenberg, a plan of Donawert, with the Genius of the city, represented by an old man leaning upon an urn, and an inscription in Latin, thus translated—"*The enemy vanquished, put to flight, and their camp taken, at Schellenberg, near Donawert, 1704.*"

	Battalions.	Squadrons.		Battalions.	Squadrons.
Tallard's,	36	44	Marlborough's,	48	89
Marcin's,	42	83	Eugene's,	18	92
	78	127		66	181
	Infantry.	Cavalry.		Infantry.	Cavalry.
Tallard's,	14,400	4,400	Marlborough's,	24,000	13,350
Marcin's,	16,800	8,300	Eugene's,	9,000	13,800
	31,200	12,700		33,000	27,150
		Men.			Men.
Gallo-Bavarian infantry,		31,200	Allied infantry,		33,000
——— cavalry,		12,700	——— cavalry,		27,150
Grand Total,		43,900	Grand Total,		60,150

Cannon, 90.   Cannon, 66.*

From about 9 o'clock in the morning, the cannonading was kept up till near 1, when the charging began; and the contest was not entirely terminated till after sunset. By that time, the army of Tallard, from its great disparity in number to its opponents, from the very inferior condition of its horses, owing to long marches and a vast mortality among them, from the sun and wind having been against it during the most difficult and critical portion of the engagement, and from some defects in its arrangement, and some faults in its conduct, was routed, destroyed, or surrounded. The Marshal himself was taken, with upwards of 90 colours, 25 standards, and 34 pieces of cannon; and so many as 27 of his battalions and 12 of his squadrons, cut off from the rest, had finally, or about 8 o'clock, to surrender *en masse* as prisoners at Blenheim. But Marcin and the Elector, being differently situated from what Tallard was with reference to Marlborough, or not having to contend, like Tallard, against a force so superior in number, were proportionably fortunate, on their side of the field. They maintained their position, and repulsed Eugene's attacks until about 7 o'clock, when, obliged *not* by him, but by Tallard's overthrow, to retire, they retreated honourably; abandoning, indeed, along with Eugene's artillery, which they had captured, 13 pieces of their own cannon, but carrying off the rest, or 43 guns, accompanied by 36 Allied colours or standards, 4 pairs of kettle-drums, and 2084 prisoners. On this disastrous day, the Gallo-Bavarians admitted a diminution of nearly 22,100 men; of whom the killed and wounded, by the Paris account of the action, were 12,000 at most, and the prisoners, by the Archives of the Dépôt de la Guerre, were 1076 officers and 9019 soldiers, or, 10,095 of both ranks;† and, with these, there fell into the hands of the Allies,

* The Allied battalions are *admitted* to have averaged 500 men, the Allied squadrons 150 horses, each; those of the Gallo-Bavarians but 400 and 100 respectively. The proportion of the confederates of Marlborough to *his* insular contingent, (in *both* cases, exclusive of officers,) would be—

Continentals,	47,611
British,	12,539
Total,	60,150

† The Allies claim many more; but *must* not this have been by including supernumeraries, or mere camp followers, as *military?*

according to Marlborough's and Eugene's bulletin, a total of military ensigns and guns, amounting to above 115 colours or standards, and 47 pieces of cannon. Many men also perished in the subsequent retreat, under Marcin and the Elector, towards the Rhine; all the French, that were found straggling, being knocked on the head by the German boors. The Allies enumerated their killed and wounded, as in Millner's tables, at 2234 British, and 10,250 other Confederates, of whom 2196 were Dutch, and 8054 Germans and Danes, making, in all, 12,484 slain or hurt; that, with the 2084 men, previously referred to as captured, would form a general loss of 14,568 men.*

The Irish, at this celebrated battle, consisted of the 3 battalions of Majors-General Andrew Lee, and William Dorrington, and Brigadier Charles O'Brien, 5th Lord Clare. Those battalions had been recruited from France, in May, with 300 of their countrymen. By the "Instruction du Roi à M. le Comte de Marcin, 14 Octobre, 1703," &c., it would seem that Louis was particularly desirous to fill up, with their own countrymen, the "Régiments Irlandais dans l'Armée d'Allemagne," from the excellent opinion he entertained of those national corps— "Sa Majesté etant *persuadée*, que *ce qu'ils pourront, ils le feront*, et que *ce qu'ils promettront, ils le tiendront!*"—an eulogium of the Irish regiments, by the French Monarch, the more valuable, as expressed in a document, *not* intended for the public eye. The 3 Irish corps, as attached to the army of the Marshal de Marcin, formed a portion of the infantry, stationed, under the gallant Marquis de Blainville, (son of the great Minister, Colbert,) about the centre of the Gallo-Bavarian position, or at the village of Oberglau. Partly by the road, passing, on the Allied side of the Nebel, immediately through Underglau, and then, on the Gallo-Bavarian side of the stream, leading, in a curving direction, to Oberglau, and partly by a fordable place to the right of Underglau, the Duke of Marlborough had to advance against, and cause Oberglau to be assailed on its right. Still farther away to the Allied right, or beyond Wilheim, with such of the Dutch infantry (or German and Swiss infantry in Dutch pay) as were nearest to Prince Eugene's army, and were accordingly designed to be aided by some Imperial cavalry, another attack was to be made, under the Prince of Holstein-Beek, or Holstein-Beck, on Oberglau in front; an almost straight road conducting to it there, on both sides of the water.

The troops of Marlborough, to act against Oberglau on its right, were Danes, Hanoverians, and English. Of these, the Danes and

* The small difference between the Gallo-Bavarians and the Allies in killed and wounded *may* be explained by the very severe execution of the superior and well-served artillery of the former against the latter, for several hours before both sides could actually charge or engage; so that, if the Gallo-Bavarians lost most men towards the end of the day, the Allies seem to have lost most in the earlier part of it. From about 9 to 1 o'clock, during which the Gallo-Bavarian artillery played uninterruptedly upon the Allied masses, they were supposed to have suffered to the amount of about 2000 men. Eugene, too, was right well mauled, by Marcin and the Elector, *throughout* the day. If Marlborough was so very successful against Tallard on the Gallo-Bavarian right, "cependant," alleges the Paris narrative of September 6th, "l'aîle gauche de l'infanterie, commandée par le Marquis de Blainville, avoient, en 5 differentes charges, toûjours enfoncé et rompu la droite des ennemis avec un grand carnage, gagné l'artillerie, et pris beaucoup d'etendarts et de drapeaux, de manière que l'Electeur crut la victoire certaine. . . . On leur a pris 36 etendarts et drapeaux, et 4 paires de timbales." The numerical details of the *accompanying* 2084 prisoners are given by Lieutenant-General Pelet.

Hanoverians, who were cavalry, having first gotten over the stream at Underglau and on its right, were so warmly received, that they were immediately driven back to their own side. They renewed the attempt to cross, sustained by infantry, but with no better result. A 3rd attempt, however, supported by Marlborough in person, with some British squadrons, some Imperial squadrons of the *corps de reserve*, more battalions, and a battery from Wilheim, effected the passage, and made the Gallo-Bavarian outposts of horse commence retiring towards Oberglau. At this time, the Duke, according to the London Gazette, "very narrowly escaped being shot by a cannon-bullet, which grazed under his horse's belly, and covered him all over with dirt, insomuch that all that saw it concluded him to be dashed to pieces." The fire from Oberglau now flanking Marlborough on the right, and so protecting Marcin's cavalry, as to enable them, when repulsed, to form again, and return to the charge, the Duke, who, after establishing his men beyond the rivulet here, was obliged to proceed elsewhere, or to act with vigour against Tallard on the left, ordered, ere he departed, that the obnoxious village should be stormed by fresh English and Dutch troops. This order respecting Oberglau appeared the more likely to be carried into effect, as *all* the hedges about that village had been levelled by the Marquis de Blainville, to admit of infantry-charges from it. "But," says Prince Eugene's historian, "it could not be forced, in spite of all the intrepidity of the English, who encountered such a furious tempest of musket-balls, of grenades, and of cartridge-shot from the artillery, that the ground was very soon covered with their dead." Nevertheless, these attacks from Marlborough's side of the field on Oberglau, although insufficient to carry that stoutly-defended post, were most serviceable to *him*, as constituting such a diversion, that he was finally able to overpower Tallard elsewhere.

Meantime, the Prince of Holstein-Beek, in the Dutch service, had proceeded, as ordered by Marlborough, to assail Oberglau in front. The Prince, from the 1st line where he commanded, drew the 2 infantry brigades of Marlborough's army nearest to Eugene's, or Wulwen's and Heidenbregh's. Of Wulwen's brigade, the battalions or regiments were 5, or Beinheim's, Swerin's, Wulwen's, Varen's, and the Prince of Prussia's. Those of Heidenbregh's brigade were also 5, or Heidenbregh's, Rechteren's, Hirsel's, Sturler's, and Goor's. With these 10 battalions, and calculating on the co-operation of some Imperial cavalry not above a couple of musket-shots from where he was to array his infantry on the other side of the stream that ran across the road conducting directly up to Oberglau, the Prince advanced towards the termination of the road on his side of the water. But, finding, it seems, Marcin's outguards (unlike Tallard's elsewhere) too closely stationed at and about the pass there, he left some of his battalions to engage the enemy's attention in that quarter. Then, turning off the road, on his right, to where there was a marshy winding of the stream unguarded, (apparently as supposed so difficult to pass, that, ere any considerable corps could get over, it might be duly interrupted by a detachment from Oberglau) he managed to cross the rivulet with 3 or 4 of his battalions, including Beinheim's and Goor's, and began to put them in order.* But, before he could accomplish this, or be assisted by the

* This movement of the German Prince upon Oberglau has been involved in a wretched hotch-potch of blunders by preceding writers; to expose the extent of whose misconceptions on the subject would occupy too much space here.

Imperial cavalry, the Marquis de Blainville caused him to be charged from Oberglau by (according to Allied computation) from 7 to 9 battalions there, headed by the Irish Brigade. This charge was most vigorously executed. The Prince, wounded in several places, was made prisoner. Of his regiments, 2 suffered terribly by the Irish. Goor's, a fine corps, most to the right, is stated to have been destroyed, with the exception of its Colonel, a few more officers, and 50 or 60 privates. Beinheim's, noticed by Marlborough as always distinguished, and particularly so on this occasion, is mentioned by him to have lost so many officers as to be incapacitated from future service, or virtually annihilated, till they could be replaced. The rest of the Prince's troops were put to the sword, or routed.* Oberglau, in short, was not only unapproachable, through the fiery hail of musketry and the crushing thunder of artillery by which it was guarded, but, in 5 several charges made by its brave defender, the Marquis de Blainville, and his choice corps of infantry, including the Irish, 6 other battalions, and the brigades of Champagne and Bourbonnois, the Allies were uniformly overthrown, and very severely handled. The English and Dutch had the 2084 men (or 201 officers and 1883 soldiers) taken prisoners, previously referred to as such, and specified in the French archives as "Anglois et Hollandois." Neither were the Imperialists, from what *they* suffered, in any better condition to penetrate to Oberglau, until the order for retreat was given by Marcin and the Elector in the evening, when the place was evacuated, after being set on fire.† "The battle being lost," observes 1 of my

* Under *such* circumstances, what is to be thought of *all* that Marlborough's Chaplain, Dr. Hare, (afterwards Bishop of Chichester,) has thought fit to communicate respecting the Irish, and the 2 *demolished* Dutch regiments? It is as follows. "The Irish regiments in the French service attacked those of Goore and Beinheim, but they were so warmly received, that, after a sharp dispute, they were forced to retire." *Suppressio veri suggestio falsi!* Of the 3 or 4 battalions under the Prince of Holstein-Beek, of which Goor's and Beinheim's were 2, the French historian, the Marquis de Quincy, speaks, as "entièrement défaits"—Prince Eugene's biographer, as "taillés en pièces," adding of "celui de Goor," that "il ne revint pas 50 hommes"—and the Dutch Lieutenant-General Baron Hompesch, among the Allied battalions which suffered most by the engagement, specifies "surtout ceux de Goor et de Beinheim." The latter regiment is thus referred to by Marlborough, in writing to the Dutch government, about a fortnight after the battle. "Ce régiment a toujours servi avec distinction, et particuliérement dans la dernière bataille." Of the condition to which it was reduced by that engagement, the Duke adds—"Le régiment de Beinheim se trouvait tellement degarni d'officiers, que, sans y en placer incessamment, le corps ne serait plus en état de servir, et courrait risque d'être entièrement perdu."

† In Alison's "Life of John, Duke of Marlborough," (2 vols., 1852,) the Irish Brigade, *after* the discomfiture of "Prince Holstein!" is represented as driven back in confusion, by Marlborough in person, to that village. But, it will be manifest, how utterly untenable such a statement is, by a reference, in the Lettres Historiques for 1704, to the excellent Dutch official relation of the battle, with an annexed plan of the action, taken upon the spot, by M. Ivoy, Colonel, and Quarter-Master-General at the Camp, under Marlborough. The difference of the locality of Marlborough's movement towards Oberglau as marked I, and that of the Prince of Holstein-Beek's as marked K, in this plan by M. Ivoy, shows how very distant, and proportionally distinct, the 2 movements were from each other; so much so, as, along with the Dutch account, &c., to *utterly* discountenance the notion of Marlborough's having been in a part of the field to bring him into such an immediate and successful conflict, as that *supposed*, with the Irish Brigade. The complete separation between the respective sites of the English General's and the German Prince's operations in person against Oberglau may be seen, even in Tindal's continuation of Rapin, (vol. iv., pp. 656-7, London,

accounts in French respecting the Irish, "they forced a passage for themselves through the enemy, who took no prisoners from them; and they did not lose any colours, which may be regarded as a creditable circumstance, upon that fatal day." Another remarks—"It was the Regiment of Clare that sustained the retreat of the French army, and thus covered itself with glory." Forman, after referring to "the behaviour of Clare's regiment, commanded by the Lord Clare in person at Blenheim, where they cut a Dutch or German regiment to pieces, consisting of 500 men, and commanded by Colonel Goore,"* adds the following anecdotes and reflections—"The Colonel himself, with a few of his officers, and about 60 men, were all that escaped. The melancholly, dejected Goore went the next morning to the Duke of Marlborough's levee, where, as he was giving his Grace an account of the action, an English Colonel says pertly to him—'I wish I had been in your place:'—'I wish, with all my heart, you had,' replies Goore very gravely to him, 'I should have had a very good regiment to-day, and you would have been without one.' The Duke smiled, and everybody applauded the justness of the repartee. If every regiment in the French army had behaved that day like the Irish, England, instead of a trifling expence in building a house to preserve the memory of so great a victory as the Duke of Marlborough gained at Blenheim, would have found herself incumbred with a fugitive Emperor, a numerous Imperial family, which she must, at a heavy charge, have been obliged to maintain, if a visit from the Chevalier had not brought a worse remedy to prevent it."†

The Allies, after their success at Blenheim, having advanced to the fortress of Landau, before which they were detained, by the stubborn defence of the French, from September 9th to November 23rd, Prince Eugene, during the tedious progress of this siege, concerted measures for surprising the 2 Brisachs. The former, on the German bank of the Rhine, was known as the *Old*, the latter, on the French bank, as the *New*, and there was a bridge-communication between them. The French garrison was but 4 battalions and 6 independent companies. The comparative disorder, necessarily resulting from 1200 labourers being then employed in strengthening the works of the old town, was a favourable circumstance for the Prince's design, in connexion with a frequent entrance of carts of hay for a magazine there; and the German Governor of Friburgh, who was to command the force for the intended surprise, had

1745,) from these items in its engraved plan of the battle. "3. The D. of Marlborough assists and rallies the Danish and Hanoverian horse."—"4. Goor's regiment routed, and the Pr. of Holstein-Beck desperately wounded." So much for the *imaginary* repulse of the Irish Brigade by Marlborough in person!

* I correct into "500" the apparent error, or misprint, in Forman, of Goore's, or Goor's, regiment, as "1500."

† Since Forman tells us, (and *truly* tells us) that he "had the honour to serve in the War-Office of Great Britain," he could learn many particulars of the Continental campaigns, not generally known. In my extract from him, I omit, as irrelevant *here*, his controversial allusions to Arnall, a contemporary Whig government-libeller, writing under the signature of "Francis Walsingham," and a proportionate defamer of the Irish; who is reported to have received from Sir Robert Walpole "about £10,000 for his ignominious labours, and to have retired from them with a pension." He is thus apostrophized by Pope—

"Spirit of *Arnall!* aid me while I *lie!*"—

and consigned to additional infamy, in the Dunciad, as a shameless politico-literary hireling.

obtained a knowledge of the interior of the place through his valet, who had gotten a passport to go in and out, on the pretext of purchasing wines for his master. On the night of November 9th, which was previous to a day when a quantity of hay was expected to reach the town, the Governor of Friburgh, with 4000 select German and Swiss infantry and 100 cavalry, set out to effect his object. His van was preceded by 50 waggons, apparently of hay, but containing men and arms concealed; and those waggons were accompanied by a number of the most determined officers or grenadiers, disguised as drivers or peasants. The vehicles and their immediate escort reached 1 of the gates of the town about 8 o'clock in the morning, favoured by a very thick fog, and 3, containing men and arms, actually entered the town. But, at this critical juncture, the "Sieur de Bierne, Irlandois,"* a Mr. O'Beirne or O'Byrne, an Irishman, overseer of the labourers on the fortifications, remarked near the gate about 40 men, who, though disguised as peasants, could not pass with *him* as such. Upon which, he demanded, "Who they were? why they were not at their labour, like the rest?"—and addressing himself more particularly to 1, who was the Lieutenant-Colonel of the Regiment of Bareuth, he asked him, "Where he came from? what was the meaning of all those faces, that were never there before?" Obtaining no answer to these puzzling questions, the uncompromising Hibernian proceeded, "more patrio," to extract a reply by a more summary process, or by a rapid and unsparing application of the "argumentum baculinum" to the German's wincing back. The Lieutenant-Colonel, not relishing this kind of *cross*-examination, and so smarting under the Irishman's cane, as to forget, that to take revenge *then* for the pain he was in might ruin the enterprise in which he was engaged, rushed to the nearest waggon, and, snatching a musket from the hay, discharged it, but ineffectually, at his tormentor. Between 15 and 20 of the Lieutenant-Colonel's companions likewise fired, and, though at only 5 or 6 paces' distance, missed their mark. Unarmed against so many armed opponents, the Irishman betook himself to the fosse amidst the reeds; in which direction, too, they aimed several shots at him, (the whole, from first to last, about 40!) but still without even wounding *him;* while he gave the alarm on *them* by shouting "to arms!" with all his strength, and they justified this alarm by their shots at him! The consequence of this "1st alarm" occasioned by the Irishman was, that the garrison and citizens were apprised of their danger in due time to save the place, in doing which they had but 20 men killed or wounded. The Germans and Swiss, on the other hand, according to Prince Eugene's biographer, lost about 200 men; including the Lieutenant-Colonel of the Regiment of Osnabruck, who was to be Governor of the town if taken; the Lieutenant-Colonel of the Regiment of Bareuth, whose premature resort to musketry, under the stimulus of the cudgel, ruined the undertaking; a Major, and many Captains and Lieutenants. There were likewise left behind several carts, 500 muskets, a quantity of hatchets, &c. The defeat of this attempt by land on Old Brisach caused the enemy to abandon another meditated by water against New Brisach. Thus was a single Irishman, furnished with no better weapon than a

* This vigilant Hibernian, "minding his business, just as he ought to be," is fairly acknowledged as "Irlandois," in the *original* French account of the attempt on Brisach, dated, from that place, November 11th, 1704. But that acknowledgment has been uncopied by succeeding writers, and thus "the cold chain of silence hath lain o'er it long," or until here assigned a little niche in the temple of history.

stick, the medium of frustrating at Brisach (as his better-armed countrymen had done at Cremona) an enterprise of Eugene, that, if attended with success, would have been very injurious to France. The importance of Brisach to the French will be best conceived, from Louis XIV. having employed 40,000 chosen men, 120 cannon and 40 mortars, the year before, for its reduction, under the heir to his crown, the Duke of Burgundy, aided by the famous engineer, the Marshal de Vauban, and from the irritation of the Emperor Leopold I. having been very great at its loss.

The leading operations in Italy in 1704 were the difficult sieges, by the Duke of Vendôme, of Vercelli, of Ivrea, and Verrua, the last not terminated till April, 1705. The Irish battalions, acting more immediately under the Duke, were Dillon's, Galmoy's and Berwick's. Those of Bourke and Fitz-Gerald served elsewhere. At Verrua was killed, by a bomb-shell, the veteran Colonel William Connock. As Major, he had accompanied or followed King James II., early in 1689, from France to Ireland, to oppose the Revolutionists; and was then appointed there Lieutenant-Colonel to Lord Boffin's Regiment of Infantry. After the war in Ireland, he continued to serve with the national army on the Continent; and, in 1702, was a reformed or supernumerary Lieutenant-Colonel, as previously mentioned, to the Regiment of Bourke, when brevetted, for his distinguished conduct at Cremona, to the rank of Colonel.

The successful campaign of the Duke of Berwick in the Peninsula in 1704 has been already noticed in the history of his regiment. Brigadier Daniel O'Mahony, who was also sent to serve there, soon signalized himself. The Portuguese having had Monsanto delivered up to them, except the Castle, in which a French Captain held out with 50 men, M. de Jeoffreville and Don Francisco Ronquillo resolved, in June, if possible, to relieve the Captain, when they learned, that the Portuguese General-in-Chief and the greatest part of his forces were in battle array, only a mile and a half off. Upon this, Jeoffreville and Ronquillo decided, that their infantry should remain about Idanha Velha, while the cavalry should proceed to reconnoitre the enemy, and endeavour to succour the Captain in Monsanto. "The Sieur de Mahoni," observe the contemporary accounts, "commanded on the right, when, towards evening, 20 Portuguese squadrons were seen, that, after remaining some time drawn up for action, opened, to make room in the centre for their infantry, apparently amounting to 16 battalions. They advanced with much confidence, as calculating, from the superiority of their numbers, on surrounding the Spanish troops, and cutting them to pieces. They even took in flank and rear the dragoons, and the Regiments of the Queen, of Milan, and of Orders, which the Sieur de Mahoni, the Irish Brigadier, commanded. But he received them with such firmness, and repulsed them with so much vigour, that he stopped them, until he gained time for the rest of his troops to reach a defile on their left. When this was passed, he caused the Regiment of the Queen to turn upon them, and charged them so effectively, that 1 of their regiments of dragoons, in a yellow uniform, which had likewise passed, was driven back again in confusion, leaving 200 dead upon the place. This brought the enemy to a halt, till they could be joined by their infantry, and artillery. Then the Spanish troops retired in good order behind a ravine; the Sieur de Mahoni," on the renewal of the pursuit, "repeatedly facing the enemy with his rear-guard, and arresting their progress, with the almost unceasing fire which he kept up. Thus this retreat was accomplished, without any greater loss than about 50 men, in the presence of a force 3 times more numerous." And that retreat was the more honourable to the Irish Brigadier, since, on reaching Idanha Velha, he met *no* infantry there; they having left that place in disorder, on a report, that their cavalry had been defeated.

In 1705, I do not find the Irish distinguished by their achievements from the French in Germany and Flanders.* In Italy, where Louis XIV. made every effort to crush the Duke of Savoy in Piedmont, and prevent his being assisted through Lombardy, by the Imperialists under Prince Eugene, the Irish battalions of Berwick, Bourke, Dillon, Fitz-Gerald, and Galmoy, served under the Duke of Vendome. May 20th, 2 French regiments of cavalry, attacked in the night by 500 of the enemy's cavalry at the village of Castel Alfero in Piedmont, had a Colonel, other officers, and several horses captured, and would have suffered more but for Colonel Walter Bourke, who, being in the castle with 2 companies of his regiment, sallied out, and made such a good disposition of his men in different directions, as, partly by imposing upon the enemy, and partly by a well-served fire of musketry, to oblige the assailants to retire. July 20th, the Duke of Vendome, with 500 horse and 6 companies of grenadiers, including those of the Regiments of Berwick and Galmoy, and Lieutenant-Colonel Daniel O'Carroll of the former corps, marched from Soresina towards a strong post of Prince Eugene's near Genivolta, fortified for a battalion of 400 Croats, and 200 horse. The Duke's intention was, merely to approach the place, in order to reconnoitre. It was surrounded by deep ditches only traversible by a bridge, and then 3 intrenchments should be successively forced, the last secured by pointed stakes, and palisaded. Nevertheless, such spirit was shown by the grenadiers in beating the enemy's outposts into the intrenchments, that, on reaching them, an assault was ventured, and the place taken in less than a quarter of an hour; but 7 of the grenadiers being killed or wounded, while, besides those of the enemy slain, 130, including a Lieutenant-Colonel, 2 Captains, and 2 Lieutenants were captured, with the standard, and all belonging to the Croatian battalion. The Chevalier de Forbin, who was present, writes—"The grenadiers of Auvergne, of Berwick, and Galmoy, entered the first. A more daring feat has never been achieved. M. de Carolles commanded the grenadiers, and was always at their head." The Duke of Vendome observes to Louis XIV.—"This event has surpassed my hopes, and nothing could occur, at the present conjuncture, more important for your Majesty's service." The Duke then highly eulogizes O'Carroll, as well for his past services, as for having "done wonders" on this occasion; and accordingly requests for him "a brevet as Colonel;" adding, "the action which he has just performed is so brilliant, that it deserves the grant of a distinguished reward from your Majesty." August 2nd, at a similar reconnoitring affair, ending in a *coup de main* upon a fortified work to protect a bridge of the enemy on the Oglio, O'Carroll again signalized himself. "The grenadiers, having at their head MM. de Muret and de Carolles," says my author, "attacked it with so much vivacity, that they carried it in an instant; the troops of the enemy scarcely having time to repass the river, in order to reach Ostiano."

* This year, says Mr. O'Conor, "great desertion prevailed in Marlborough's army whilst on the Moselle; and, it is presumed, the Irish Brigade was recruited by this desertion."

After much skilful marching and countermarching between Eugene and Vendome, they came, August 16th, to the general engagement, known as the battle of Cassano. It took place among the canals beyond the river Adda, and the town of Cassano; the French and Spaniards having been both inferior in number, and so situated, with the Adda behind them, that, if beaten, they *must* have been utterly ruined. They were, moreover, assailed there by Eugene, when they were in a state of disorder, quite unsuited for action, through the very scandalous misconduct of Vendome's brother, the Grand Prior; out of which alarming position, it required the utmost exertions of Vendome himself to rescue them. Conspicuous, (like his great progenitor, Henry IV., at the battle of Ivry,) from the fine white plume which he wore, 12 or 13 of his officers or attendants were killed beside him by the Imperial musketry and cannon; his famous bay horse, a present from Louis XIV., and, like Marshal Turenne's formerly, remarkable for its sagacity, fell under him, pierced by numerous bullets; while he himself was hit, in various portions of his dress, from his hat to his boots, by 5 bullets, though without being injured. And he would certainly have perished there, but for the noble self-devotion of 1 of his officers to save him. Not waiting to be remounted, the Duke headed on foot a bayonet-charge with the grenadiers of the Brigades of Grancey and Bourke, to repel the Imperialists, when, says my French contemporary historian, "1 of their soldiers having recognized M. de Vendome in the midst of the fire, detached himself from his troop, and took aim at him, in order to kill him. M. de Coteron, Captain of his Guard, having perceived the soldier, placed himself before him, received the shot in his own body, and thus preserved the life of his master. *A remarkable action, deserving of everlasting remembrance, and a fine proof of the strong attachment which he felt for a Prince, so useful to his country, so beloved by his troops, and so worthy of being beloved.*" * Vendome's illustrious opponent Eugene likewise exposed himself in the thick of fight, till obliged by 2 shots, one on the neck, and the other below the knee, to retire from the field. The contest was maintained for about 4 hours with a terrible fire of artillery, or of musketry at about a pike's length, and with furious infantry charges, in the course of which, besides those slain or disabled, multitudes were drowned. Vendome's acknowledged killed and wounded were 2728; Eugene's acknowledged killed and wounded were 3966. The French and Spaniards claimed the capture of 9 Imperial colours or standards, with 7 cannon, and 1942 prisoners; the Imperialists also claimed the capture of several colours or standards, but without specifying how many, and with only 530 prisoners.† The greater amount of killed and wounded, on the side of the Imperialists, was attributed to their muskets and powder having been wetted, in crossing the canals, to dislodge opponents, firing from the banks. By losing less men, by keeping possession of the field, and by thus preventing Eugene from effecting a junction with the Duke of Savoy, Vendome was, so far, the conqueror. By retiring, in generally good order, to his camp, but 3 miles from Cassano, and by then so long maintaining his position, as he likewise did, 3 years before, after the

* Compare this heroic death with that of De Sale, in Book III., at the battle of Marsaglia, in 1693.

† Vendome's loss, in killed and wounded, 2728; in prisoners, 530; in toto, 3258. Eugene's loss, in killed and wounded, 3966; in prisoners, 1942; in toto, 5908. Both totals, 9166.

battle of Luzzara, Eugene could scarcely be deemed conquered. For both engagements, both sides had *Te Deum* chanted, as both claiming to be victorious! Yet, on both occasions, how great soever were Eugene's merits, (and they *were* great,) Vendome, as results attested, had the better claim to be styled *the* conqueror.

The Irish acquired *very* high honour at Cassano. Eugene, according to the French reports, having "directed his chief efforts against Vendome's centre, opposite to the Brigades of the Marquis de Grancey, of (Walter) Bourke, and of the Marine, the Imperialists* broke through a battalion of the last-mentioned brigade, and forced their way to the artillery in the rear. But Du Heron's and Verac's Regiments of Dragoons, and the Regiment of (the Honourable Arthur) Dillon, belonging to the Brigade of the Marine, then so bravely attacked the Imperialists, that they were overthrown, and the brigades rejoining, nearly all, who had pierced through, were killed. Others of the enemy, who, in a different direction, had penetrated between the Brigades of Grancey and of Perche, were vigorously assailed by the Marquis de Grancey and the Sieur (Walter) de Bourke, who, uniting to the right and left, charged so furiously with fixed bayonets, that all who had passed the canal there were destroyed, or driven back into it, and numbers of them drowned. The Sieur (Daniel) de Carol, Lieutenant-Colonel of the Regiment of Berwick, signalized himself very much, in this part of the action." It is added—"The Sieur Dillon, Mylord Galmoy, and the officers of the Irish Regiments, sustained the greatest efforts of the enemy, with an extreme bravery," and that "the Irish suffered considerably." The Regiment of Galmoy alone is said to have had so many as 40 officers killed or wounded. In addition to the preceding particulars, it is stated, by Quincy, of the battalions of Dillon, Galmoy, and *Fitz-Gerald*—"The regiments of Dillon, of Galmoy, and of *Figueral*, being incapacitated from acting in the same manner as many of the other brigades, posted themselves in fosses, with water up to their waists, and holding the branches of trees and bushes between their teeth in order to raise themselves up, and get a better view of the enemy, by this means opened such a flanking fire upon him, as annoyed him much." Count Dillon, too, after relating how the Irish, on being galled by some Imperial batteries from the opposite bank of the Adda, swam across and captured the batteries, observes of those troops—"Their happy audacity very much contributed to the gaining of the battle, and M. de Vendome wrote to Louis XIV.—That the Irish had fought in this affair with an exemplary valour and intrepidity, and that they formed a band, whose zeal and devotion might be relied upon, in the most difficult emergencies of war."† In recompense for this good conduct, as well as for their services at the 2 battles of Hochstedt, Louis augmented each company of the troops of that nation by 2 officers; and attached several more, as supernumeraries, to each of the regiments, with full pay. The campaign between Vendome and Eugene terminated, by the latter being obliged to retire, for the winter, towards the Alps, about the Lake of Garda, whence he had taken the field for the summer.

In Spain, several plots were concerted, and still more were rumoured

* A substitution here, and elsewhere, for the less *distinctive* term of "enemy," or "enemies."

† Lieutenant-General Count Arthur Dillon, the younger. See, likewise, the commendation of the Irish by Vendome, in Book III., under reduction of Barcelona, in 1697.

to have been concerted, in 1705, against Philip V., by emissaries of the Allies in favour of the Archduke Charles of Austria, as Charles III.; which plots, though frustrated for the time, were but too sure indications of the formidable footing the latter Prince was about to acquire, and long maintain, in the Peninsula. One of those plots was against Cadiz, but it was discovered, and the safety of that city duly provided for by a strong garrison, including the "Régiment de Mahoni Irlandois," at this period one of infantry, and stationed in the Isle of Leon. In June, (according to the Abbé de Vairac, then in the Spanish metropolis) the number of French in each house at Madrid was found marked on the door, in figures of red lead, on the eve of the great festival of Corpus Christi; it was given out, that next day every native of France was to be massacred, and their Majesties to be carried off from the Palace of Buen Retiro to Portugal, and even slain on the road, in case of resistance; all which, according to the report, was to be effected by certain foreigners, at that time in the city as pretended deserters, but engaged, it was said, for those designs, by no less a personage than the Marquis de Leganez, Grandee of Spain, Governor of the Palace, Grand Master of Artillery, and Vicar General of Andalusia. The Marquis, when proceeding at 8 o'clock in the morning towards the King's apartment, was consequently arrested by the Prince de Tilly, Captain of one of the Troops of Life Guards, and then committed to the custody of a Kilkenny gentleman, Don Patricio or Patrick Lawless, commanding a detachment of the Guards, who had orders to convey the prisoner to the Castle of Pampeluna. The Marquis, on the way there, made many advantageous offers to the Irishman, to be allowed to escape; but Lawless (who was no more to be tempted than his countryman Mac Donnell by Villeroy at Cremona) duly fulfilled the commission with which he was intrusted. After the capture of Barcelona by the Allies for the Archduke Charles, and the revolt, to his party, of nearly all Catalonia and parts of Aragon and Valencia, the Prince de Tilly was despatched, by Philip V., from Madrid, with a force for the defence of Aragon; and, says a British writer, "he had under him the famous Colonel Mahoni, who had distinguished himself, in so extraordinary a manner, in driving the Germans out of Cremona." In the sharp and continual struggle which Tilly had to maintain against the Austro-Carlist miquelets, the Irish officer's name occurs with credit. Thus, an account from Madrid, of December 18th, 1705, after noting how the frontier was assailed by various parties of miquelets, and, in some instances, with success, adds—"One advanced on the side of Mequinença, which was put to flight by Colonel Mahoni; and 40 of them, who had rushed into a boat, to save themselves on the opposite side of the river, were all drowned."

The campaign of 1706 in Flanders opened on Whitsunday, May 23rd, with the battle of Ramillies, between the Duke of Marlborough and the Marshal de Villeroy. Marlborough had 73 battalions, and 123 squadrons; Villeroy had 74 battalions, and 128 squadrons. In artillery, the Allies were superior by 48 pieces; they having had 120 guns, or 100 cannon and 20 howitzers; while the French had only 72 guns, or 60 cannon, and 12 mortars. The arrangements of the French General, for the action of that day, have been as severely censured, as the ability with which the English General achieved, and the vigour with which he followed up, success, have been highly commended. After the usual cannonade, the French, having been generally attacked at from 2, to half-past 2, in the afternoon, were beaten, by between 6 and 7 in the evening. The Allied pursuit did not cease until about 2 next morning. Villeroy was utterly defeated; losing 54 cannon, besides mortars, 87 colours or standards, about 2000 waggons, with a quantity of baggage; perhaps 10,000 men, between killed, wounded, and missing;* and, in consequence of this overthrow, all Spanish Flanders. The Allied killed and wounded were officially published as 3633; but, according to Kane, Parker, and Milner, *all* present there, were *many* more, or from above 5000 to 6000 men. It was remarked in France, alleges my British contemporary historian of Marlborough and Eugene, respecting the French Marshal's preparations for this unfortunate battle, that Villeroy "made the worst disposition imaginable, notwithstanding he had the greatest advantages in point of ground; and he would never alter his disposition, notwithstanding several General Officers, and particularly M. de Gassion, took pains to shew him his errors; and though the enemy gave him 5 hours' time, while they altered the whole disposition of their troops, in order to take advantage of his mistakes. He neglected even the common precaution of sending away his baggage, suffering it to remain, during the engagement, between his lines, in such a manner, that it hindred any reinforcement from going to his right, and afterwards proved the ruin of the troops by hindring their retreat; which could never have been so unhappy as it was, but for this blunder of his, since the left wing never engaged at all, but marched off leisurely, and in good order, till night came on, and, by the breaking of the waggons, the rout became general." Thus, in proportion as Villeroy here was but *little* of a General, Marlborough was *great* as a General, or, it would seem, "not so great after all"—for, can mere success really glorify, apart from any consideration of the merit, or demerit, of the adversary, with whom one has to contend? But, for an officer of the ennobled branch of the Molesworths in Ireland, Marlborough, moreover, *would have been taken prisoner, or slain instead of being victorious!* For, having, in the engagement, been ridden over, left almost senseless on the ground, and his horse having run away, he was only enabled to escape, or rejoin his own troops, in consequence of being remounted by the gallant officer referred to, his Aide-de-Camp, the Honourable Richard Molesworth, Captain of Cavalry, subsequently 3rd Viscount Molesworth of Swords, County Dublin, Baron of Philipstown, King's County, and Field-Marshal. At the hazard of his own life, the Captain thus, as observed, "certainly, under God, preserved *that* of the General"—respecting whom, "this remarkable fact," it is added, "was very industriously hushed up in the army," and the more easily, since the Aide-de-Camp, equally modest and brave, "was quite silent upon it!"

At the village of Ramillies, only quitted when Marlborough's sweeping success to its right rendered a further defence impossible, and *last* maintained, in that quarter of the field, previous to the commencement of Villeroy's retreat, the Regiment of Clare was stationed, under its Colonel, Charles O'Brien, 5th Lord Clare, and Maréchal de Camp, or Major-

* It is noted, by Lieutenant-General Pelet, of the Comte de Saillant, who commanded at Namur, (which fortress, by the way, was *not* reduced by the Allies during this war,) how the Count sent some detachments from his garrison, 2 days after the action, towards the field of battle, where, and in the adjacent villages, 34 pieces of the cannon, with about 800 of the wounded, that had fallen into the enemy's hands, were left by them. These were brought away to Namur, and the Count also collected, and sent back to Villeroy's army, about 1500 fugitives from the battle.

General. "Lord Clare himself," says an Allied writer, "was noted in the French army for his intrepidity in action," and, "at Ramillies, we see Clare's regiment shining with trophies, and cover'd with laurels again, even in the midst of a discomfited, routed army." According to Captain Peter Drake of Drakerath, County of Meath, who was at the battle, with Villeroy's army, in De Couriere's regiment, "Lord Clare's ingaged with a Scotch regiment in the Dutch service, between whom there was a great slaughter; that nobleman having lost 289 private centinels, 22 commissioned Officers, and 14 Serjeants; yet they not only saved their colours, but gained a pair from the enemy." This "Scotch regiment in the Dutch service" was, by my French account, "almost entirely destroyed;" and, by the same account, Clare's engaged with *equal* honour the "English Regiment of Churchill," or that of the Duke of Marlborough's brother, Lieutenant-General Charles Churchill, and then commanded by its Colonel's son, Lieutenant-Colonel Charles Churchill. This fine corps, at present the 3rd Regiment of Foot, or the Buffs, signalized itself very much in the action with another, or Lord Mordaunt's, "by driving 3 *French* regiments into a morass, where most of them were either destroyed, or taken prisoners." But the "Régiment Anglois de Churchill," according to the French narrative, fared very differently in encountering the Regiment of Clare, by which its colours were captured, as well as those of the "Régiment Hollandois," or "Scotch regiment in the Dutch service." Following up the advantages thus obtained, observes my Allied authority, Forman, respecting the Regiment of Clare, "their courage precipitated them so far in pursuit of their enemy, that they found themselves engaged at last in the throng of our army, where they braved their fate with incredible resolution, till an Italian regiment, in the service of France, and a regiment, vulgarly called the Cravats, generously pushed up to their relief, and as bravely favour'd their retreat." Then, alluding to, though unwilling to be precise regarding. the capture of English colours, or those of the Regiment of Churchill, the same writer adds—"I could be much more particular in relating this action, but *some reasons oblige me, in prudence, to say no more of it.* However, if you are desirous to know *what* regiment it was they engaged that day, the colours in the cloister of the Irish nuns at Ipres, which, I thought, had been taken by another Irish regiment, will satisfy your curiosity." Of this religious establishment—respecting which Mac Geoghegan likewise notes, that the "*two* colours, taken from the enemy at the battle of Ramillies, were deposited in the house of the Irish Benedictine nuns at Ypres," by the Lieutenant-Colonel of the Regiment of Clare, Murrough O'Brien—an English tourist, in 1724, erroneously speaks, as *founded*, instead, more correctly, as *endowed*, "by the late King James's Queen, for the daughters of such as followed her husband's fortunes," in Ireland, and France.* A recent, or contemporary Irish visitor of this interesting nunnery at Ypres, mentioning "the little chapel as a perfect gem in its way, richly ornamented in the chastest style of Christian art," and refer-

* The well-informed writer of "Glimpses d'outre Mer, No. 1, Ypres," in Duffy's Hibernian Magazine, July, 1860, says of this once Irish nunnery at Ypres—"We looked up, and beheld the *date of its erection*, 1612, set, in raised characters, over the narrow, arched doorway." Harris, in mentioning the foundation of a convent for Irish Dominican nuns near Lisbon, "in the same century," adds,—"This is the only nunnery for Irish ladies abroad, except one at Brussels for Dominicans, and another for Benedictines at Ipres."

ring to the nuns "screened from view, doing homage before the tabernacle," remarks—" *We* thought of *other* adorers, too, long since passed away; many of whom often gazed with joy, and, it may be, with sadness betimes, on the conquered flags, hung up, in that very chapel, by Murrough O'Brien, as an offering to God, and fatherland." Those "colours and worshippers are *now* no longer to be seen. We were unconsciously treading on the graves of the latter; for the floor, on which we stood, was but the roof of a necropolis. And, on that roof, we could read the names of sleepers, whose hearts once throbbed but for the glory of God, and the welfare of Ireland—of Dame Margaret Arthur, who died in 1715 —of Madame Butler, who died in London, in 1719—of Dame Marie Benedicte Dalton, deceased in 1783—of Dame Marie Scholastique Lynch, in 1799—of Dame Marie Bernard Lynch, who departed life in 1830— and of Marie Benedicte Byrne—born in Dublin, 1775, deceased in Ypres, 1840. She was the last of the long line of Irish Abbesses that governed the Benedictine Convent of Ypres; and, by a strange permission of Providence, there is not *now*—at least there was not at the period of *our* visit —a single Irish nun amongst a sisterhood, once exclusively Irish. The words of the Psalmist arose to our memory—'*Adorabimus in loco ubi steterunt pedes ejus*'—and, applying them, for the moment, to the last Irish Abbess of Ypres, we knelt upon *her* grave, and gave God thanks, for having afforded such a calm retreat, such a cheering home, to many a sorrowing daughter of Ireland, who had seen the bravest and last of her kindred perish in the battle-field—'*semper et ubique fideles*' to the cause of King Louis, and the hapless Stuarts." The capture of the Scotch an English colours at Ramillies—the *only* 2 lost by the Allies that day!— cost the Irish Regiment its brave Colonel, Lord Clare, who received " 9 wounds," of which he died, a few days after, at Brussels; and, besides his Lordship, there fell 38 officers, and 326 soldiers, out of 800 men.

Among these officers was 1 of the respectable Munster or Clare branch of the great Ulster name of O'Cahan, O'Kean, or O'Kane, also anglicized, or written without the O', as Kean, or Kane. That branch contributed (according to its pedigree in French) several gallant gentlemen, some of them Chevaliers of St. Louis, to the Regiment of Clare. Eugene O'Kean, on the 1st formation of the corps, raised an entire company for it, at whose head he fell in Italy, in 1693, at the battle of Marsaglia. His brother Charles, who accompanied him to France, commanded the grenadiers of the regiment in the village of Ramillies, when a cannon-ball carried away his legs, and he was despatched there, with 22 more wounds, by the English soldiers. Just as this occurred, he was recognized by an Ulster officer of his name, but, as a Protestant, then in the English army, in the very distinguished corps at present known as the 18th Royal Irish Regiment of Foot. This officer was Richard Kane, subsequently Brigadier-General in the British service, and Governor of Minorca, to whom a monument has been deservedly raised in Westminster Abbey. He had the unfortunate Charles interred the day after the engagement, with due military honours, in the village of Ramillies.* On the "horrid necessity" by which Irishmen, as in opposite armies, were too frequently

---

* Brigadier-General Kane was born in December, 1661; obtained his 1st commission in the army in 1689; and died in December, 1736. He was one of the best officers of his time, as well as a gentleman of the greatest humanity and generosity, particularly kind to his relations; so that his death was very generally lamented. In a word, a noble character.

exposed, in those times, to act against their own countrymen in battle, the celebrated Lord Charlemont, who deplored the circumstance with an illustrious Irish officer in Austria, remarks—" My most particular friend, the brave, and truly amiable, General O'Donnell, when speaking on the subject, has often wept."

The following epitaphs of the gallant Colonel and Major of the Regiment of Clare, both mortally wounded on the same day, both survivors of their wounds to the same day, and both interred in the same receptacle for the dead, have been preserved, as copied by Dr. de Burgo, among the sepulchral monuments of the Church of the Holy Cross at Louvain, in 1769.

D. O. M.
Hic jacet
Illmus D. D. Carolus O-Brien,
Ex stirpe Regum Hiberniæ,
Par, Comes de Clare, & Maigh-airty, &c.
Campi Marischallus,
Legionis Hibernicæ Colonellus,
Qui plurimis heroicis,
Pro Deo, Rege, & Patria,
Peractis Facinoribus,
In Prælio Ramiliensi
XXIII Maij MDCCVI vulneratus,
Triduo post Bruxellis obijt,
Ætatis suæ XXXVI.
R. I. P.
Posuit pia ejus Conjux,
Illma Dom. Carola Bulkeley.

D. O. M.
Hic, ubi voluit, jacet,
Prænobilis Dominus,
D. Joannes O-Carroll,
Major Hibernicæ Legionis
De Clare,
Vulneratus in Ramilie,
XXIII. Maij MDCCVI.
Obijt Lovanij XXVI. ejusdem.
R. I. P.*

The Irish Horse Regiment of Colonel Christopher Nugent of Dardistown, consisting of 2 squadrons, likewise suffered much at Ramillies; so that, it is marked, above 2 months after the battle, or July 29th, as still unfitted for service. But, with any details of the rough handling of *this* corps in the engagement, I am unacquainted. The other leading events of the campaign of 1706 in Flanders were the sieges of Ostend,

* The late Thomas Davis has celebrated, in prose and verse, as at Blenheim and *Ramillies*, a regiment he calls "Clare's *Dragoons!*" But, during *all* this war, there was, in the French service, *no* Regiment of Clare, except one of *Infantry;* and no Irish Cavalry Regiment, but that which was first Sheldon's, and next Nugent's, Regiment of Horse.

Menin, Dendermonde, and Ath, by the Allies; the reduction of which cost them (by accounts on their side) above 4400 men, killed or wounded. No Irish troops, however, were engaged in the defences of those places.

In Italy, the Duke of Vendome took the field, early in 1706, against the Imperialists, (in Prince Eugene's absence) under the Danish Count de Reventlau. The Duke had 23,000 men, and the Count had only 12,000; but fortified, about Calcinato, by good retrenchments, besides canals, eminences, and fosses, which rendered an access to his position very difficult. The Duke, having marched all night to surprise the Count, appeared in front of his position, April 19th, about daybreak, and attacked him, before he could bring up his artillery. The Count, nevertheless, opposed the assailants with resolution, and, for some time, with considerable success, but was finally defeated; losing about 6000 men, between killed, wounded, and prisoners, 6 cannon, above 1000 horses, several colours or standards, and the greater part of his baggage; the Duke having no more than 700 or 800 men, killed or wounded. The principal Irish officers belonging to Vendome's army were the Lieutenant-General Lord Galmoy, Major-General the Honourable Arthur Dillon, Brigadiers Nicholas Fitz-Gerald and Walter Bourke; its Irish battalions were Galmoy's, Dillon's, Fitz-Gerald's, and Bourke's—Berwick's not being in this engagement. Among the General Officers in the 1st line, of whom Vendome wrote to Louis XIV., as having "done wonders there," was Dillon; and Fitz-Gerald and Bourke performed important parts with the brigades of Piedmont and the Marine, which they led in the action. The conduct of the infantry altogether, or Irish as well as French, was, according to the Duke, "far beyond anything he could say of it, every individual of the battalions engaged, as well as those who commanded them, being entitled to marks of his Majesty's satisfaction."

This victory at Calcinato was the last where the Irish were *generally* distinguished in Italy. Prince Eugene, soon after Reventlau's defeat, took the command of the Imperial army, largely reinforced; and the road to his subsequent decisive triumph over the French at Turin, which led to their final evacuation of Italy, was opened by the removal of Vendome to Flanders, after the battle of Ramillies, in order to succeed Villeroy, and recover the army there from the discouragement of that great overthrow. The only success of the French in Italy, after Vendome's recall, was at the battle of Castiglione, gained, September 9th, with very small loss, by the Count de Medavi, over the Prince of Hesse, who had about 4500 men killed, wounded, or taken, with 33 colours or standards, all his cannon, and all his baggage. The Honourable Arthur Dillon, who commanded the French left there, routed the enemy's right. For having "acted in such a manner as few General Officers had acted for a long time past," so that to his, and M. de St. Pater's, "good conduct and resolution, the greater portion of the gaining of the battle was due," Dillon was recommended by the Count de Medavi, to be made a Lieutenant-General. The Count adds of him, in writing to Louis XIV., —"He is a foreigner of merit, and of valour, who, on every occasion, has always served your Majesty well."

In Spain, where the Allies, in 1705, acting for the Austrian Archduke Charles as claimant of that Monarchy, had gotten possession of all Catalonia except Roses, and of many places in Valencia, and Aragon, the famous Charles Mordaunt, Earl of Peterborough, proceeded, early in 1706, to relieve the city of Valencia, then threatened to be recovered for Philip V. by the Duke of Arcos. Before Peterborough could reach Valencia, he should pass by Murviedro, (the ancient Saguntum,) where Brigadier Daniel O'Mahony, with his own Regiment of Dragoons, some other troops, and a river in his front, was stationed; and if O'Mahony were dislodged from that post, there was next a plain of about 2 leagues, where a junction of the Duke with him would present a superiority of cavalry too great for the Englishman to encounter. Despairing of success by force, Peterborough did not scruple to attempt accomplishing his object by " means *unworthy of an honourable foe.*" He despatched a flag of truce to O'Mahony to solicit an interview, which was the more readily granted, as there was a connexion between the parties by marriage, through the Lady Penelope O'Brien of the Thomond family, who was Countess of Peterborough. The Englishman and Irishman met at the place appointed, each accompanied only by a few horsemen. "In their conversation," says my English authority, Lord Mahon, "Peterborough made every exertion to gain over his adversary to the cause of Charles; offering him high rank, and every other advantage, in the Austrian or English service. Failing in his attempt, he determined to impute the treachery, which he could not produce. In the interview, he had so far misused the open-hearted confidence of the honest Irishman, as to draw from him an avowal of his intention to advise Arcos, to march across the plain to his assistance; and he also found means, by pretending an equal frankness and a kinsman's regard, to impress Mahoni with the conviction, that an overwhelming force, both in men and artillery, lay before him. Peterborough then made choice of 2 dragoons, who, upon the promise of promotion, undertook to go over to Arcos, as pretended deserters. Being admitted to the Duke's presence, they reported, that, while drinking wine together behind a rock, they had witnessed the conference between Peterborough and Mahoni; had seen the former hand over to the latter a bag of 5000 pistoles; and had heard him promise Mahoni the rank of a Major-General on the English establishment, and the command of 10,000 Irish Catholics, to be raised for the service of Charles. On the other hand, they declared, that Mahoni had undertaken, not only to betray his post at Murviedro, but to induce the Duke of Arcos to march across the plain, and thus entrap him into a position, where the English army might find it easy to overpower him.* The Duke was confounded with this intelligence, and still doubted its truth; but, shortly afterwards, he saw Mahoni's Aide-de-Camp arrive with the

* Dr. Freind, in his account of the Earl of Peterborough in Spain, says of the Earl—"He chose 2 Irish dragoons out of Zinzendorf's regiment, which he well instructed, and well paid, and sent immediately as deserters to the Duke of Arcos. He promised to make them officers, if they succeeded: which was punctually made good to 1, who well had deserved it; the other dying soon after his return." If we disapprove of the conduct of those 2 Irish dragoons, in *consenting, for gain, to destroy their countryman, by becoming false witnesses against him,* what are we to think of the *honour* of the English nobleman, who *could suborn them to act thus against a gentleman with whom he was connected, and for whom, as such, he affected a corresponding friendship?* Such a specimen of honour, on his Lordship's part, too strongly countenances the damning purport of the statement in Biographiana, as to the praise Lady Peterborough deserved, after his Lordship's death, "by preventing the publication of his manuscript 'Memoirs,' in which *he had* CONFESSED, *he had been* GUILTY OF 3 CAPITAL CRIMES, *before he was* 21!"

very proposal of which the spies had forewarned him, and of which Lord Peterborough had become apprised by his enemy's incautious frankness. No doubt could now remain on the mind of Arcos, as to Mahoni's treason: he had him immediately arrested, and sent off a prisoner to Madrid; while, so far from marching across the plain as Mahoni had suggested, and as good policy required, he broke up his camp, and retreated with precipitation to the mountains." Peterborough was *thus* enabled to pass by Murviedro, and the plain beyond it, to Valencia, which he entered early in February.

On O'Mahony's explanation, at Madrid, of the circumstances of his arrest, he was created by Philip V. a Maréchal de Camp, or Major-General, and, before the end of the month, was again sent to the province of Valencia, to endeavour to preserve the places there still faithful to the King, with such troops as were collected, which were mostly new levies, or country militia. In April, having vainly summoned Enguera, he stormed and sacked it, by way of example, which caused many other places to return to their duty. He was at Alicant in the summer, when it was attacked by the Allied land and sea forces, under Brigadier Richard Gorges and Vice-Admiral Sir John Leake. The town was breached and entered, August 8th, by the Allies, and he retired into the Castle, after receiving 3 dangerous wounds; for which, being without a Surgeon, and requesting Brigadier Gorges for 1, that officer generously granted the request. The Castle was next invested, and Sir John Leake menaced the Major-General, that, if he attempted to hold out to the last, himself and his garrison should receive no quarter. O'Mahony, however, defended himself for 27 days, or till his provisions failed; not surrendering the place till September 4th, on honourable terms; by which he and his men were to be conveyed, in English vessels, to Cadiz, with 4 cannon, and 2 mortars. His garrison then consisted of but 62 Neapolitans, 36 Frenchmen, and as many dragoons of his own regiment, or no more than 134 men; the rest having been killed! These "honourable terms" were concluded with the Earl of Peterborough, who arrived at Alicant to take the command of the besiegers, after the garrison had retired into the Castle. And a Captain of the Earl's escort makes this creditable allusion *en passant* to another Irish officer, Colonel O'Gara. "We marched next morning by Monteza; which gives name to the famous title of Knights of Monteza. It was at the time that Colonel *O'Guaza*, an Irishman, was Governor, besieged by the people of the country, in favour of King Charles; but very ineffectually, so it never changed its Sovereign." *

In November, the Chevalier Don Miguel Pons, with 500 men of his own regiment, and that of a distinguished Irish officer, Colonel Henry Crofton, having appeared before Daroca, which was defended by a larger force, consisting of 8 companies of the Archduke Charles's regular troops, and the armed inhabitants under their ecclesiastics, summoned the place to resume its allegiance to Philip V. The summons not being complied with, the town was ordered to be attacked; and, as there was nothing but its fire to prevent the assailants reaching the foot of the

---

* Memoirs of Captain George Carleton. The historical authority of this work is, in opposition to some cavillers, as judiciously admitted, as satisfactorily proved, by Lord Mahon; whose proof can be strengthened by a Petition and Memorial from the worthy Captain himself to the Duke of Ormonde, as Lord Lieutenant of Ireland in 1703.

wall, the Irish rushed forwards to a place least exposed to the hostile musketry; and, "with extraordinary bravery," says the gazette account, "set themselves to open a breach by the pick-axe." When 1 was effected, sufficient to admit a single man, a gallant Spaniard, Captain Raimond Escallart; of the Regiment of Pons, and Captain Daniel O'Carroll of the Regiment of Crofton, led in their troops; who, putting to the sword those they met, or compelling them to throw down their arms, became masters of the place, with a loss stated at but 27 killed, besides wounded. Captains Escallart and O'Carroll were appointed to convey 4 standards captured there to Madrid; and, among the other officers "wounded," or "extremely distinguished," were the Sieur Gibbons, the Lieutenant-Colonel of the Regiment of Crofton, and the Sieur O'Beirne, Captain of Irish Dragoons. Soon after this, the Aragonese Count de Sastago, with a detachment of the Archduke Charles's regular troops, and a great number of his insurgent adherents, proceeded to recover Daroca. Although the Chevalier de Pons had taken the place in 3 hours, he, with only 500 or 600 harassed dragoons, maintained it for 5 days; slew (as reported) in a sally 400 or 500 of the enemy, from whom he likewise gained 4 colours; and, when at last obliged to abandon the town, he did so by night, bringing away to Molina 500 mules loaded with booty; his killed and wounded being very few. The enemy's colours were sent to Madrid by an Irish Captain of Dragoons, the Sieur Henry O'Beirne; the Chevalier de Pons was made a Camp-Marshal, or Major-General, by Philip V.; and the Sieur Henry Crofton, Colonel of Dragoons, a Brigadier, "for having seconded, with so much valour, the Chevalier de Pons, in this enterprise." The same month, King Philip, in consideration of the services of Major-General Daniel O'Mahony, created him a Count of Castile, and also appointed him Governor of Carthagena. But, in December, the Chevalier de Pons, who was sometimes too deficient in caution, was surprised, and defeated, at Calamoche, in Aragon, with a loss of 300 or 400 men, and Brigadier Henry Crofton was taken prisoner. He, however, was subsequently exchanged. At the siege of Barcelona, by Philip V., in the spring of this year, among the prisoners taken from the enemy, were a number of Irish; and the larger or Catholic portion of them, that had been driven by misery to enter the English service as pretended Protestants, gladly availed themselves of the opportunity, afforded by their capture, to join the regiments of their own nation, and religion, in Spain.

On the Rhine, in 1706, Lieutenant-General Andrew Lee and Brigadier Michael Roth, with Lee's and Dorrington's battalions, served under the Marshal de Villars. At the successful attack, in July, upon the Isle du Marquisat, which, although not attended with a great loss of life, presented a fine military spectacle, and was honourable to the troops engaged in it, Roth, with a detachment of grenadiers, displayed his "usual valour," and the Regiment of Lee had its Captain and Lieutenant of Grenadiers, and 5 or 6 other subalterns, killed or wounded.

The French campaign of 1707 in Flanders, under the Duke of Vendome, consisted of a judicious system of tactics, by which the Duke of Marlborough was completely foiled, without fighting. "After so disastrous a campaign as that of 1706," says my contemporary British historian of Marlborough, "it was generally supposed, that France would be able to make no stand at all on the side of Flanders; but that the same great genius, which had destroyed so fine an army as that of

Marshal Villeroy's at Ramellies, would force the French army either to another disadvantageous battle, or go on, in reducing towns, till it would be easy for him to make an irruption into France itself." But, continues this writer, " the Duke de Vendome, having consumed the forage in the neighbourhood of his lines, did not, like his predecessor, provoke the Allies by gasconades, or pretend to dare them to a battle, but he made such movements, and chose such camps, as did *all* that could be expected; for it constrained the Duke of Marlborough, 1st, to lay aside all thoughts of fighting, and 2ndly, of making any important siege." Moreover, though lessened in number, by 2 deductions, in June, and August, amounting to 16 battalions and 21 squadrons, the French army in Flanders drew subsistence from the Allied territory; and Marlborough, much lowered in reputation, had to retire for the winter, "that he might concert measures for making the *next* campaign more effectual than this, which had been spent in marching and countermarching, and in which *none but the Duke de Vendome had gained any honour.*" On Marlborough's return to England, "nothing of importance having been done in the last campaign, his Grace did *not* receive the thanks of either Houses of Parliament. On the contrary, a very warm spirit began to discover itself, especially in the House of Lords, against his Grace, and the Ministry, on account of the management of the war." In short, concludes the same British authority, "the French were as much *pleased* with the situation of things in Flanders, as the Allies were *disgusted.*" The game, on the whole, between the Frenchman and the Englishman, may be illustrated by that between Marius, and the Italian commander Pompedius Silo, during the Social War or that of the Allies, in Roman story. "If you are a great General, Marius," said Pompedius Silo, "come down, and fight us!"—"If you are a great General, Silo," answered Marius, "*make me* come down, and fight!" In the "Ordre de Bataille" of Vendome's army, the Irish infantry Regiments of O'Brien and Fitz-Gerald were in the 1st line with the Brigade of Piedmont commanded by Brigadier Nicholas Fitz-Gerald, and the Irish horse Regiment of Nugent was in the 2nd line with another cavalry regiment, both commanded by Brigadier Christopher Nugent. The campaign, however, as unattended by battles or sieges, did not admit of the Irish acquiring any more distinction than resulted from such of them as were in the Brigade of Piedmont, under Fitz-Gerald, having been united with the Brigade of Vendome, 20 companies of grenadiers, 2 regiments of dragoons, and 100 Gardes du Roy, in forming, August 13th, a rear-guard under Lieutenant-General Albergotti, which kept at bay a very considerable detachment from a large Allied corps under the Count de Tilly, Lord Albemarle, and the Prince d'Auvergne, during a long retreat made "à la demie-portée du mousquet;" wherein it is noted, of the retiring force, "les ennemis firent plusieurs tentatives pour l'entamer sans oser l'entreprendre, à cause du bon ordre dans lequel les troupes marchoient." My military authority adds, "cette retraite fut des plus belles."

From Italy, above 38,000 Piedmontese and Germans, under the Duke of Savoy and the famous Prince Eugene, attended by Sir Cloudesley Shovel with 48 English and Dutch ships of war, and about 60 transports conveying 100 heavy cannon, 40 mortars, above 72,000 ball, 35,000 bombs, &c., proceeded, in July, 1707, to attack Toulon, the great naval port of France in the Mediterranean. The capture of this place was so much desired by the English, from the very deep wound it would inflict upon France as a maritime power, that their government went to an immense expense for its reduction. And what France would have suffered by losing it appears from the number of vessels there, with an arsenal worth several millions, prodigious magazines, and above 5000 pieces of cannon. The Allies came before the town, July 26th; but, after various operations against the outworks, and a bombardment of the place itself, they found themselves obliged to raise the siege, August 21st—22nd, at night, and, with proportionate disappointment and loss, to retrace their steps for Piedmont.* Among the Lieutenant-Generals prominently mentioned as serving under the Marshal de Tessé, in this important defeat of an enterprise, planned by Marlborough, and conducted by Eugene, was the Honourable Arthur Dillon. At the grand assault, more especially, on the Allied position before the place, in the middle of August, which saved the town, and, most probably, France with it, "the Sieur de Dillon, who commanded on the left," says the French official journal, "attacked the height of the Croix Faron, where all those who defended that post were killed or taken." Another officer, named Dillon, Captain of Grenadiers in the French Regiment of Vexin, signalized himself, by his defence, with 100 men, of Fort St. Louis, 1 of those situated on the shore, to guard against a hostile entrance to Toulon by sea, through the "Grande Rade" into the "Petite Rade." From August the 9th to the 17th, the Allied fire upon the fort, by land and sea, having effected such a breach as was very practicable, the Duke of Savoy, on the 18th, directed General Rebinder, with a suitable body of grenadiers, to advance to the assault. "But," states my French historian, "M. Dillon, Captain of the Grenadiers of Vexin, who had orders from the Maréchal de Tessé to evacuate it in the evening at 10 o'clock, managed to withdraw his garrison by sea into the city; so that, when the enemy marched to attack the place, they found it abandoned altogether." Dillon, it is observed, "acquired a great deal of reputation by this defence, it having been 3 days since he had received orders from the Maréchal de Tessé, to retire with his garrison." Prince Eugene's biographer takes a like creditable notice of the defender of Fort St. Louis. "It was," remarks that writer, "3 days since M. Dillon, who commanded in this Fort, had received an order of the Maréchal de Tessé to abandon it; but he had not judged it would be yet time to do so."

In Spain, Count Daniel O'Mahony quitted Madrid, February 10th, 1707, for his command in Valencia, and the Duke of Berwick set out, on the 15th, to prepare for the leading operations of the campaign. April 1st, the month destined to be subsequently memorable for greater success, was auspiciously commenced by Captain Daniel O'Carroll, with 100 Irish dragoons, at the Castle of Seron, on the frontier of Aragon; where, having been assailed by 1000 of the enemy's regular troops, or militia, "he received them with so much bravery, that, after a combat of 6 hours, he obliged them to retire." Meanwhile, Count O'Mahony, from Elche, extended his forays even to the gates of Alicant; spreading consternation through the territory of the disaffected. The opponent of the Duke of Berwick, as Commander-in-Chief of the Allied, or British, Dutch, and Portuguese forces, was a French nobleman, Henri de Massue, originally

* The concluding data in Quincy, respecting the numerical strength, and general loss, of the Allies, would, (by a correction of his miscalculated totals of each,) make the former 38,760 infantry and cavalry, and the latter on both elements, or land and sea, so many as 15,485 men.

Marquis de Ruvigny. Banished from France as a Protestant, in consequence of the violation of the Edict of Nantes, he served William III. bravely, in his Irish and Continental campaigns; was made by him Earl of Galway, and Lord-Justice in Ireland from 1696 to 1699; was granted above 36,140 acres of the Jacobite forfeited estates there; and, in the country, whose revolutionary spoliation he thus so largely shared, was distinguished for his Calvinistic intolerance to the majority of its inhabitants, as Catholics.* The British, Dutch, and Portuguese, under this nobleman, are stated by him at 42 battalions, and 53 squadrons. The French, Spaniards, and Irish, under the Duke, were, by their line of battle, 51 battalions, and 76 squadrons. The Duke would thus be considerably superior in number, taking the battalions and squadrons on each side as complete. But this would not seem to have been the case in either army, since the Earl, while referring to his own battalions and squadrons as very imperfect, appears to have considered those of his opponents so much *worse* in that respect,† that, notwithstanding their having *more* battalions and squadrons than he had, yet, by his Council of War, he says, "'twas thought reasonable to run the hazard of a battel, wherein we had an *equal* chance to come off victors." The comparative strength of the 2 armies in artillery is uncertain; nor was it much used. "To bring the Lord Galway to a battle, in a place most commodious for his purpose, the Duke," we are told, "made use of this stratagem. He ordered 2 Irishmen, both officers, to make their way over to the enemy, as deserters; putting this story in their mouths, that the Duke of Orleans was in full march, to join the Duke of Berwick, with 12,000 men; that this would be done in 2 days; and that *then* they would find out the Lord Galway, and force him to fight, wherever they found him. Lord Galway, who, at this time, lay before Villena, receiving this intelligence from those well-instructed deserters, immediately raised the siege; with a resolution, by a hasty march, to force the enemy to battle, before the Duke of Orleans should be able to join the Duke of Berwick. To effect this, after a hard march of 3 long Spanish leagues, in the heat of the day, he appears, a little after noon, in the face of the enemy, with his fatigued forces." ‡ The Duke, "rejoiced at the sight, for he found his plot had

* King James's Memoirs note, with reference to Ireland, under the year 1698,— "The Prince of Orange, notwithstanding all his fair pretences to the Confederate Princes" or Catholic powers allied with him against Louis XIV., "even during the Congress at Riswick passed a new law in that kingdom, for *the rooting out Popery,* which, amongst other articles, order'd the banishment of all regular Priests, which Monsr Ruvigny, who commanded there, fail'd not to put in execution; so that they came flocking over into France, and above 400 arrived there, in some months after." According to the Anglo-Protestant evidence on this point given by Newenham, there were, in 1698, in Ireland, 495 of those regular clergy, of whom the number "*shipped, for foreign parts, by Act of Parliament, was* 424."

† Consult, on this head, as regards the French, the very important passage of Voltaire referred to in Book V., note to citation from Captain Parker, at battle of Malplaquet, in 1709.

‡ This anecdote, of the remarkable share of the 2 Irishmen in bringing about the engagement, I copy from Captain Carleton, who relates it, as communicated to him by an officer in the Duke of Berwick's army. "The day after this fatal battle," adds the Captain, "the Duke of Orleans *did* arrive in the camp" of the Duke of Berwick, "but with an army of only 14 *attendants*," a very different *force* from that of "12,000 men!" Tindal, by the way, mentions Lord Galway as having also gotten information respecting the French, through 2 deserters, "young French gentlemen of a good Protestant family, who had been educated in the principles of the reformed religion by the care of their parents; a practice very common in France after the

taken," was duly prepared for the decisive engagement at Almanza. The combat commenced April 25th, Easter Monday, about 3 o'clock in the afternoon; Lord Galway displaying very great intrepidity, and receiving, in the *mêlée*, 2 cuts in the face, so as to lose an eye; yet heroically returning to the fight, and being gallantly supported by his men, especially the British—the Duke of Berwick, on the other hand, acting as a consummate General, and being also gallantly supported by his French, Spanish, and Irish troops, until they gained a victory, "the most fatal blow," says an English contemporary, "that ever the English received, during the whole war with Spain;" and, adds another, "as fatal in itself, and its consequences, to the Allies in Spain, as the battle of Blenheim, or that of Turin, was, to the French, in Germany, and Italy." The conquerors mention their loss as only about 2,000 slain, or hurt. The conquered left upon the field not less, if not considerably more, than 3000 killed, or mortally wounded, and had nearly 10,000 made prisoners; of whom about 800 were officers, including 6 Major-Generals, 6 Brigadiers, and 20 Colonels; the British officers alone, killed, or taken, being *acknowledged* as 374.* All the Allied cannon, 24 in number, were likewise captured, with 120 colours, or standards, and other spoil, constituting a very large military booty.

The Irish, in this action, consisted of a battalion of the Regiment of Berwick (a 2nd battalion, of deserters from Marlborough's army, having been added since 1702-3,) and those of the 4 squadrons of Count O'Mahony's Regiment of Dragoons. All were in the Duke of Berwick's 2nd line; the infantry, in that line of his centre; the cavalry, in that line of his right wing. The battalion of Berwick, posted between the 2 battalions of the French Regiment of Maine, and another French battalion, or that of Bresse, acted with those 3 battalions, under the general designation of "the brigade of Maine." Opposed to "5 English battalions," that brigade of 4, led on by the Duke of Berwick's brother-in-law, and countryman, the Honourable Francis Bulkeley, received the hostile fire at about 30 paces, made no reply until almost touching the English, then blazed into them, and, says Quincy, "charged them with fixed bayonets, and threw them into such disorder, that they gave way, without being able to rally; and as, in flying before this brigade, those battalions were obliged to repass a ravine, a great carnage of them then took place." In describing the general routing of the Allies, that writer also observes,— "The Brigade of the Spanish Guards, and that of Maine, always following up their success, drove the enemy even into the mountains"—a distance of 2 leagues, or 6 miles. In addition to 6 Allied battalions captured in the action, the remains of 13 more, or 5 British, 5 Dutch, and 3 Portuguese, had to seek refuge in the woods on those mountains, where, "next morning," continues the English annalist Boyer, "being surrounded by 2 lines of foot, the commanding officers agreed to the same capitulation that was granted to the French at Blenheim, and surrendered themselves prisoners." Of the conduct of the battalion of

persecution;" and who "told him, they had entered, as volunteers, into the French service, in a regiment that was coming to Spain, in hopes of meeting with an opportunity to come over to the English."

* Of the rank of Major-General 1, Brigadier 2, Colonel 12, Lieutenant-Colonel 17, Major 9, Captain 100, Lieutenant 127, Ensign 90, Cornet 6, Adjutant 2, Quarter-Master 4, Chirurgeon or Surgeon 3, Mate 1, or in all 374—of whom 88 were *killed*, and 286 *taken*. Their *names* are generally preserved.

Berwick, it is noted, by Lieutenant-General Count Arthur Dillon, how, when ordered, with other regiments, by the Duke, "to turn the division of the English who were on the left of the Portuguese," that Irish corps advancing against the English, "attacked them, à l'arme blanche, and contributed much, by their defeat, to the gaining of the battle." Count O'Mahony is named, by my previously cited French military historian, with the "General Officers distinguished there, as having each contributed to that victory, by movements duly executed." And, of the Count and his regiment more particularly, "at the battle of Almansa," relates the Chevalier de Bellerive, "he performed, at the head of his Irish Regiment of Dragoons, astonishing actions."

On the side of the Allies in this battle, there was a corps of refugee French Protestants, or Huguenots, fighting as exiles for their religion, or under similar circumstances to those of the Irish Catholics of the Regiment of Berwick, and the rest of the Irish, on the side of France and Spain. That Huguenot corps was the Regiment of Cavalier* in the Dutch service, which, being opposed to a regiment of their own countrymen, consisting of Catholics, the hostile religionists as *such*, or Protestants and Papists, rushed at each other, when a most furious conflict took place, without firing, or only with the bayonet, until, between the 2 regiments, not 300 men were left! "Le Maréchal de Berwick," says Voltaire, "contait souvent avec étonnement cette aventure." Here was 1 of the *blessed* results of the violation of the Edict of Nantes, or the Huguenot "Treaty of Limerick," and of the other measures of persecution, or "Penal Laws," against Protestantism in France, connected with the violation of that Edict! But for such intolerant legislation, those 2 regiments of gallant Frenchmen, though of different creeds, would have served their common country, France, instead of destroying one another, in opposite armies. The intolerance of those times, on *both* sides of the Channel, as further represented in the anomalous Generalship of *both* armies, is cleverly glanced at by a French writer, in doing justice to the courage of the English, although unfortunate on this occasion. "The English," he alleges, "certainly fought like lions, and perfectly maintained their reputation for bravery. They might, also, have the satisfaction of saying, that they were *commanded by a Frenchman*, and *beaten by an Englishman*."

Among the Irish officers, who fell in this engagement, was the Aid-Major of the Regiment of Berwick, Philip O'Dwyer, of the old Milesian sept of Kilnamanagh, County of Tipperary; a race represented in the service of France by several Chevaliers of St. Louis, of the rank of Lieutenant-Colonel and Captain, down to the Revolution, and, to our own days, or 1846, by Joseph Abel O'Dwyer, Colonel of Artillery, and officer of the Legion of Honour; in the service of Austria, by a Major-

* This was the famous leader of his Huguenot countrymen, the Camisards, in the war of the Cevennes, referred to under the year 1702. Alluding to the Regiment of Cavalier at Almanza, as 1 of those that "suffered most," Oldmixon asserts— "Colonel Cavalier himself gave repeated proofs of that courage, by which he had before acquir'd great reputation in the Cevennes. He receiv'd several wounds, and, having lain some time among the slain, made his escape, by the favour of an horse, given him by an English officer." His "Memoirs of the Wars of the Cevennes," written in French, but translated into English, and dedicated to Lord Carteret, as Lord-Lieutenant of Ireland, were published at Dublin, in 1726. Having attained the rank of Major-General in the British service, and been Governor in the Channel Islands, he died, May, 1740, at Chelsea, in his 61st year.

General, and Count, Governor of Belgrade, under the Emperor Charles VI.; in the service of Russia, by an Admiral O'Dwyer, under the Empress Catherine II.* After the rejoicings, at Madrid, for the victory, another officer, of the ancient race of his country, Captain Miles Mac Swiny, or Mac Sweeny, of O'Mahony's Regiment of Dragoons, was granted, by Philip V., the Cross of the Military Order of St. Jago—as, it may be added, several other gentlemen of the old galloglass name of that brave Captain have likewise entitled themselves, during the same century, in France, to the Cross of the Military Order of St. Louis. And, from the Irish Catholics, among the so-called English prisoners taken at this battle, Philip V. commenced the formation, in 1708, of 3 Irish battalions, and 2 dragoon regiments; to complete which corps, he obtained a due proportion of the supernumerary or reformed officers, attached to the Irish regiments in the service of France.

Captain Daniel O'Carroll of Crofton's Regiment of Dragoons, who continued to occupy the Castle of Seron, sallied out, May 11th, with Captains O'Neill and Fitz-Harris, and 70 dragoons, to surprise Monteagudo, garrisoned by 150 of the enemy. They abandoned that place, betaking themselves to Ariza, where they mustered 150 foot and 60 horse. There, too, O'Carroll followed them, and forced them to leave behind them, in their flight, a quantity of munitions of war, with which he returned to Monteagudo. In Valenica, after 5 days' open trenches, Alcyra, with an English garrison, under Colonel Stewart, was reduced, June 5th, by Count O'Mahony. From June 5th till July 7th, the Count next besieged Denia, when a breach being made, and an assault given, that proved unsuccessful, he "received orders, some days after, not to persist, with reference to that place, and he raised the siege, from the want of sufficient troops, to go on with that enterprise." This want appears to have been owing, to the Count having been likewise obliged to keep the citadel of Xativa blockaded; which he finally took July 12th. He was then enabled to blockade Denia, with 7 battalions, and 9 squadrons.

In Catalonia, the leading design of Philip V., against the Allies and Austro-Carlist insurgents, was to reduce Lerida, for which the French, Spanish, and Irish troops, the last consisting of Dillon's and Bourke's battalions, and Berwick's 2 battalions, were quartered in the adjacent country. There they were not allowed to rest by the hostile miquelets, or Carlist guerillas, who particularly attended to surprising the horses at pasture. Thus, about the middle of August, 200 miquelets made an attempt of that kind near Lerida; thinking to take the grenadier-company of the Regiment of Dillon off their guard. But Captain O'Heffernan (or the "Sieur d'Yffernan," as my French document styles him,) was on the alert, protected his charge at pasture well, and after sustaining the enemies fire for an hour, obliged them to retire. The Dukes of Orleans and Berwick, with King Philip's army, broke ground, October 2nd—3rd, before the strongly-fortified town of Lerida, garrisoned

* Of this name, (likewise written "Dwyre,") Abbé Mac Geoghegan notices a family, highly connected in France, whose founder, John, son of Edmond, emigrated to that country from Ireland, about 1537. By the French, O'Dwyer was at first changed to ó Doyer, and finally into *Haudoire!* During the War of the Revolution, the name contributed officers to the Jacobite or national army in the cavalry Regiments of Lords Abercorn and Galmoy, and the infantry Regiments of Colonels Charles O'Brien and Dudley Bagnall.

with 5 English, Dutch, or Portuguese battalions of regulars, and 2 of miquelets, or irregulars, under the Prince of Hesse-Darmstadt, and, by November 11th, both the town and the citadel were taken. In the long and troublesome operations against this important fortress, Bourke's, Berwick's, and Dillon's battalions had their share. In Valenica, Count O'Mahony, finding Denia too numerously garrisoned to be effectually besieged by the complement of troops that he commanded, marched against Alcoy, with 1400 regulars and 400 miquelets, and reduced it to such straits, that its garrison agreed, if not relieved in 4 days, to surrender. To prevent this, the English Governor of Alicant, Sir Charles Hotham, took the field with 800 of his garrison, and 50 mules laden with stores for Alcoy; and this body was to be joined by 3000 miquelets, conveying further supplies of ammunition and food. O'Mahony routed the greater part of those miquelets, and took the stores they escorted. But 1200 who remained, and the detachment from the garrison of Alicant, being too strong for the Count, from the dispersion of his forces in different posts about the place, he could not prevent the relief entering the town, and had, in consequence, to retire. He lost, at this siege, Major O'Rourke of his own Regiment of Dragoons—"this Major O'Roirk, or O'Roork," writes Captain Carleton, "being much lamented; for he was esteemed, both for his courage and conduct, one of the best of the Irish officers in the Spanish service. I was likewise informed, that he was descended from one of the ancient Kings of Ireland. The mother of the Honourable Colonel Paget, one of the Grooms of the Bedchamber to his present Majesty,* was nearly related to this gallant gentleman."

The Austro-Carlist Governors of Denia and Denisa mustered, October 4th, at Molinete, 1000 regulars, about 2000 miquelets, and 90 horse, to make themselves masters of Pego. About 300 English, and 800 miquelets, were detached to take possession of the suburbs; which were so well defended by a Spanish Colonel, that the assailants suffered a considerable loss, before he withdrew into the town. Intelligence of this attack reaching Lieutenant-Colonel Cornelius O'Driscoll of O'Mahony's Regiment of Dragoons,† at Oliva, he hastened, with 100 dragoons, 200 French infantry, and 100 loyal Valencian militia, to make a diversion against the main body of the foreigners, and Austro-Carlists, at Ondara. "They," says my French narrative, "retired in confusion, and they were pursued even to the gates of Denia. Then the Sieur

---

* George II.

† The old Ithian sept of the O'Driscolls in Munster duly figure, as Stuart loyalists, in the confiscation-records of Cromwellian and Williamite rebellion and revolution, at the expense of the plundered Irish. Several officers of the sept fought for King James II. against the Prince of Orange in Ireland; of whom a Colonel, Governor of the Old Fort of Kinsale, fell, at its defence, in October, 1690, against the Williamites from England, under Marlborough. To Colonel Daniel O'Donovan's Regiment of Foot in that war, Cornelius O'Driscoll, an old cavalier, who, during the Cromwellian usurpation, had adhered abroad to King Charles II., and accordingly received, after the Restoration, the royal thanks "for services beyond the sea," was Lieutenant-Colonel; and, by the eventual success of Williamitism, was attainted as a *rebel!* The Lieutenant-Colonel of O'Mahony's Regiment of Dragoons in Spain was, probably, a Cornelius *junior*, similarly attainted, and Captain, in France, in 1693, to the 2nd battalion of the corps of Henry Fitz-James, Lord Grand Prior, or the "Régiment de la Marine d'Irlande." Down to the French Revolution under Louis XVI., the name of O'Driscoll, with the distinction of Chevalier of St. Louis, is to be found among the officers of the Irish Brigade.

Odriscol marched diligently towards Pego, and, without giving the enemy, who had occupied the suburbs, time to recollect themselves, he charged them sword in hand; in the 1st shock, slaying above 300 of them upon the spot. The others intrenched, and defended themselves for some time, in the houses, which had consequently to be set on fire. The dragoons cut to pieces all those, who, in striving to save themselves from the flames, fell into their hands; the greater part of the rest, especially of the miquelets, were burned there; so that scarcely any of them got off." In this "vigorous action" of O'Driscoll, his loss was comparatively trifling, being stated at but 22 killed, or wounded; his dragoons making 14 of the number, and having 10 of their horses slain. In November, Count O'Mahony, levying contributions upon the disaffected Valencians, demanded 1000 pistoles from the little town of Muchemiel. But, it was so strengthened with troops, and 4 pieces of artillery, by Brigadier Charles Sibourg, British Governor of the Castle of Alicant, that the Count had to retire towards Gaudia. In his march, he burned down 7 villages in the valley of Gallinar, that there might be no shelter for the hostile Carlists, or miquelets. He likewise committed to the flames, another village, and a Church, to which 11 insurgent or Austro-Carlist Priests, with 26 of their followers, betook themselves; the whole of whom were put to the sword.

The campaign of 1707 in Germany, under the Marshal de Villars, was commenced by the passage, in May, with little or no loss, of the famous lines of Stolhoffen, or Bihel, previously the bulwark of the Empire; and this success was followed by the overrunning of Baden, Wirtemberg, Swabia, Franconia, and the Palatinate. From the countries he overran, and a number of Imperial towns, a vast sum, at the rate, it is said, of not less than 10,000 crowns a day for 3 months, was levied by the Marshal. He thus enriched himself, as well as supported his army, while in the field; so that it was no cost, for that campaign, to Louis XIV., who observed—"*There is no one can do these things but Villars!*" The Marshal was unchecked, in his prosperous career, till the summer was considerably advanced; when, his army having been very much diminished in order to strengthen other quarters against the Allies, while that of the Germans was very much increased, he had to retire towards the Rhine; yet, without any greater reverse, than a surprise, September 24th, by much superior numbers, in a morning fog, of 14 *detached* squadrons of his troops, under the Marquis de Vivans, and their consequent defeat, with the admitted loss of 400 or 500 men, besides horses, tents, and baggage. Among the Irish officers serving under Villars were Lieutenant-General Andrew Lee, noticed in connexion with the operations against the lines of Stolhoffen, and Brigadier Michael Roth, who was present at several successful affairs, already mentioned in the biographical account of him given with the history of his regiment. Of Lee, more especially, in reference to the measures of Villars, for assailing the lines of Stolhoffen, my contemporary British historian notes—"Lieutenant-General Lee also executed *his* commission very exactly; for he thundered on the Isle of Dalunde with 10 pieces of heavy cannon, and drew together several boats about Drusenheim; which gave the Germans to apprehend that he intended to pass, with a considerable corps of troops, *there;* upon which, expresses were immediately despatched from one place to another, and they," the Germans, "were everywhere put into confusion."

HISTORY OF THE IRISH BRIGADES

IN

THE SERVICE OF FRANCE.

BOOK V.

THE warlike operations for 1708 were commenced by Louis XIV. with the equipment of an expedition to place Prince James Francis Edward Stuart on the throne of his ancestors as King James VIII. of Scotland, and James III. of England and Ireland. The Prince was to be landed in Scotland, where his presence was most desired, partly from the attachment of that nation to the *true* or only legitimate *male* representative of its ancient Sovereigns, and partly from the general indignation there at what was deemed the unprincipled sale of the country, the preceding year, to England, by the so-called Act of Union. On that measure, as here, and subsequently, so connected with the subject of this work, some observations are requisite. King James II. of England and Ireland and James VII. of Scotland, in his Advice to his Son, as Prince of Wales, written in 1692, remarks it to have been the true interest of the Crown (meaning in the *direct* Stuart line) to keep Scotland separate from England, or governed by its own laws, and constitution; and he likewise lays it down, that any specious pretence of uniting the 2 Kingdoms should be regarded, as emanating, either from weak men bribed by some private concern in the matter, or from enemies to the Monarchy; Scotland, as she was, being, in his opinion, a great support to the Crown, which, he considered she could not be, if united to, or swallowed up by, England, as in Cromwell's time. And this view of the matter seems to have been well-founded, with reference to the interest of *his* family. For, notwithstanding the success of the Whig-Orange Revolution in Scotland, to the prejudice of James himself, and his son, from the reign of William and Mary to that of Anne—or, in other words, notwithstanding that Anne, as a Protestant, was accepted as a Sovereign, after William's decease, in preference to her brother, the Prince of Wales, nicknamed a "*Pretender!*"—still the Scotch were too much attached to the House of Stuart, to think of excluding it altogether from *their* Crown, after *her* decease, for the sake of the completely foreign family, or that of Hanover, advocated, as rulers for others, as well as themselves, by the English Whigs, and their partizans. And this, although, upon the final trial of strength, in 1702, in the English House of Commons, as to securing the royal succession *there* to the House of Hanover, the measure proposed only passed by the narrowest possible escape, or, "in a division for the affirmative, *yeas* 118," to "*noes* 117; so that," remarks my English Whig annalist, under George I., "to this happy majority, tho' but of 1 vote, we owe our present glorious condition, under his most excellent

Majesty!"—the earlier observations, or those at the time of this "escape," having been "*the Prince of Wales has lost it in the House by 1 vote*, or *the House of Hanover has carried it but by 1 vote!*" * Hence, in the next year of Anne's reign, or 1703, "the Earl of Marchmont," writes Lockhart of Carnwath, respecting the Scotch Parliament, "having one day presented an Act for Settling the Succession on the House of Hanover, it was treated with such contempt, that some propos'd, it might be burnt, and others, that he might be sent to the Castle, and was at last thrown out of the House, by a plurality of 57 voices!"—a majority, it may be added, strangely enough amounting to the exact number of claimants nearer by blood to the Crowns of Great Britain and Ireland than George I.! To hunt, therefore, the House of Stuart out of its old Kingdom of Scotland, as well as to exclude that House from its 2 more recently-acquired Kingdoms of England and Ireland; or, to prevent, in case of Anne's death, a Scotch Parliament adhering to the direct line of their ancient Sovereigns, by calling to the Throne the son of James II. of England and Ireland, and James VII. of Scotland, as James VIII. of Scotland; the English Whigs and their tools elsewhere decided, "per fas aut nefas," to get passed, through the Scotch Parliament, an Act, at once ousting the House of Stuart in Scotland, as it had been ousted in England, for the House of Hanover, and decreeing a Union between Scotland and England—since what should be *thus* decreed in Scotland, however unjus, twould be beyond any future reversal there, as, after a Union, no Scotch Parliament would exist, to undo what had been done.

The so-called Act of Union was nothing more deserving of respect, in Scotland, than an act of bribery and sale to the amount of £50,000, backed by the aid of such Government terrorism, and military force, as were naturally required to secure the job against interruption, from the general and just indignation of those who were to be denationalized by the jobbers.† The bribe to the Scotch Parliamentary Commissioners to treat of the terms was £30,000, for which they sacrificed the rights of their country as follows—

Scotch Peers.	Disfranchised.	Retained.	English Peers.
160.	144.	16.	180.
Scotch Members.	Disfranchised.	Retained.	English Members.
155.	110.	45.	513.

This Anglo-Whig arrangement of but 16 Peers for Scotland against not less than 180 Peers for England, and of but 45 Members for Scotland

---

* The Annals of King George, Year the First: containing not only the Affairs of Great Britain, but the General History of Europe during that Time, &c., p. 17: London, 1716.—The *names* of the 117 and 118 voters are given by Oldmixon, in his History of England during the Reign of Queen Anne, pp. 283-4, who further observes, in reference to the Hanoverian succession—"About the same time, one Fitzgerald was prosecuted, for writing a pamphlet against that succession, and, being found guilty, had this mild sentence past upon him; to appear near the Courts in Westminster-hall, with a paper pinn'd to his hat, specifying his crime; which was thought to be a very moderate punishment, and what a zealous Irish Jacobite would rather have gloried in, than been asham'd of." Is not the mildness, or moderation, here alluded to, likewise clearly indicative of the great strength of the Jacobite party *then?*

† The corrupt Scotch Members, who voted for the Union, are described as "having horses laid, and always ready, to carry them off from the danger they had reason to dread, and justly deserved."

against so many as 513 Members for England, was more particularly complained of under the latter head, or inasmuch as, on the score of revenue, Scotland should have gotten 60, and on that of population, 66, Members—the paramount objection, however, of Scotch nationalists, to the measure, being, that it was altogether objectionable, as nothing better than a legislative or national subjection of Scotland to England. The additional bribe of £20,000, given to the party of Scotch Members called the "Flying Squadron," completed the sale of Scottish independence. Never, perhaps, was there viler corruption displayed. "One noble Lord," writes Sir Walter Scott, in reference to Lord Bamf, "accepted of so low a sum as 11 guineas; and," adds Sir Walter, "he threw his religion into the bargain, and, from Catholic, turned Protestant, to make his vote a good one!" In allusion to such baseness, the English Secretary, Harley, subsequently said, in reply to some Scotch *Union* Members —"Have we not bought the Scots, and do we not acquire a right to tax them?—or, for what other purpose did we give the equivalent?" The unprincipled Scotch Members of Parliament were, indeed bought. But the Scotch people could, neither morally, nor constitutionally, be thus disposed of. The general indignation, therefore, in Scotland, at the shameless corruption, with which her people's inalienable rights, as those of a nation, and the hereditary claims of her royal family, as a dynasty, were equally bargained away, in opposition to the will of *both*, by a set of venal wretches, for foreign objects, strengthened the cause of the Stuarts in their ancient realm, so far as such circumstances led to the inference, that, as the blow aimed to exclude the true heir to the *Crown* of Scotland was also one to destroy the *Parliament* of Scotland, so that Parliament could only be restored, by restoring the true heir to the Crown. Indeed, this reasoning was countenanced by precedent; since, on the restoration of the true heir to the Crown, in the person of King Charles II., after Cromwell's death, Charles restored to Scotland, as well as to Ireland, the Parliaments, which had been *both* extinguished in a United or London Legislature, under the Cromwellian usurpation.

Nor was the conduct of the Presbyterian clergy such, with reference to the Union, as to give them any considerable influence, in opposition to this mode of thinking among their flocks; that reverend body having afforded too much cause for a general belief, of their being actuated by no higher principle, in connexion with the measure, than that of maintaining themselves as "the established clergy" of the land, and proportionable recipients of "the loaves and fishes;" on being guaranteed which, against such invasion as was feared from a Union, *their* object was gained, though the independence of the *nation* might be lost! At first, we are informed, "the Ministers were every where apprehensive of," i. e., for, "the Kirk government, and roar'd against the wicked Union from their pulpits, made resolves, and sent addresses against it from several Presbyteries, and the Commission of the Assembly. . . . But, no sooner did the Parliament pass an *Act for the Security of the Kirk*, than most of their zeal was cool'd, and many of them quite chang'd their notes, and preach'd up what, not long before, they had declar'd anathemas against; yet with no effect, for their auditories stood firm, and *the Clergy lost much of their reputation, by shewing so much selfishness, and little regard to the interest and honour of the country*." Consequently, it is remarked, of the uncorrupted laity, "the Presbyterians appear'd most zealously *against* the Union." And, in the general exasperation of the Scotch against that measure, we are told, with reference to the young representative of the House of Stuart, or James VIII., that even "the Presbyterians, and Cameronians, were ready to pass over the objection of his being *Papist;* for, said they, (according to their predestinating principles,) *God may convert him, or he may have Protestant children, but the Union can never be good!*" The Scotch patriotic song, also, in lamenting, how there should be "such a parcel of rogues in a nation," that Scotland, under the pretext of a Union, should be "bought and sold," as "England's province," feelingly notes—

> "What force, or guile, could not subdue,
> Through many warlike ages,
> Is wrought now by a coward few,
> For hireling traitors' wages.
> The English *steel* we could disdain,
> Secure in valour's station;
> But English *gold* has been our bane—
> *Such a parcel of rogues in a nation!*"

Another song, known as "*The Curses,*" indignantly deplores that—

> "Scotland and England must benow
> United in a nation,
> And we must all perjūre, and vow,
> And take the abjuration!
> The Stuarts' ancient freeborn race
> Now we must all give over,
> And we must take into their place
> The bastards of Hanōver!"

Then "*curs'd,*" it says, be those

> ——————————"traitors, who,
> By their perfidious knavery,
> Have brought our nation now into
> An everlasting slavery!
> *Curs'd* be the Parliament that day,
> Who gave their confirmation!
> And *curs'd* be every whining Whig,
> For *they* have damn'd *the nation!*"

Under these circumstances, the Scotch Jacobites and Anti-Unionists having solicited Louis XIV. to send over James VIII., accompanied by so many troops, as, with the patriots ready to co-operate, would enable James to recover his THRONE, and Scotland to re-establish her PARLIAMENT, the French Monarch made corresponding naval and military arrangements.

The disembarkation in Scotland was to be effected at or near Dunbar by a squadron from Dunkirk, under the famous Chevalier de Forbin, which was to convey a land force of 12 French battalions, or above 6000 men, with a supply of fire-arms, cavalry-equipments, &c., for the rising of the Scotch against the English. Among the subjects of James, appointed to sail with him, were several Irish or British veterans of the campaigns in Ireland and on the Continent, or the Lieutenants-General Richard Hamilton, Dominick Sheldon, William Dorrington and Lord Galmoy, Major-General Nicholas Fitz-Gerald, Colonel Francis Wauchop, and a number of subordinate officers of the corps of Lee, Dorrington, Galmoy, Berwick, O'Brien, &c., whose names generally display their connexion with the best races of Ireland, or those of Milesian, and Norman, or French, origin. From an unlucky illness of James, and other causes, the French fleet did not leave Dunkirk till March 17th, could not reach the mouth of the Firth of Edinburgh till the evening of the 23rd, and, when about to enter it next morning, beheld Sir George Byng's very superior armament. It thus became necessary to avoid an unseasonable engagement, and, finally, to return to Dunkirk. This was effected by the French Admiral with the loss of only 1 heavy-sailing ship, the *Salisbury*, that had been formerly taken from the English. On board the recaptured vessel, with Colonel Francis Wauchop of the Irish Brigade, were 15 other officers, Lieutenants of the Regiment of O'Brien, (late Lord Clare's,) 10 Serjeants, 10 Corporals, 10 Lanspessades, and a French Commissary of War. The 15 officers of the Regiment of O'Brien were of the families of O'Donovan, O'Keeffe, O'Sullivan, O'Clery, Mac Carthy, Mac Mahon, Fitz-Gerald, Fitz-Maurice, Prendergast, &c. These Irish gentlemen were sent up to London, committed to Newgate, with irons to their legs like felons, and were then removed, by order of Government, to the Press-Yard, preparatory to being tried for their lives, and executed. But the French taking 2 ships conveying supplies to the Allied forces in Spain, as well as several French Protestant officers in the English service, these Huguenots would have been executed in France, had the Jacobite officers been executed in England; so that *both* were saved, by being exchanged. All the time the Irish officers were imprisoned in London, they met with much kindness, from the sympathy of some worthy Tory or Jacobite loyalist. "There was a dinner of several dishes, with a small hamper of wine, sent from a tavern near Newgate; and they never knew, to *whom* they were obliged, for that benefaction." Thus well supplied, it is added, they every day had "good company; for they never were without 2, 3, or more gentlemen from abroad, to dine with them; and seldom missed a day, of having a visit from one Mr. Heffernan, famous for the harp, which he never failed to bring with him, to divert the gentlemen; and sometimes would leave it there for 3 weeks, to avoid the trouble of fetching it." The stout Peter Drake of Drakerath, who furnishes these interesting particulars respecting the imprisoned Irish officers, was also, at this time in Newgate, along with an English sea-captain, named Smith; and, by the orders left with the dinner, and wine, at the prison, *both* shared the mess sent to the officers. Drake and Smith were imprisoned, as charged with "high treason," for having been taken on board French vessels, fighting against the English—a charge *justly* made against Smith, as a native-born Englishman—but *not* so against Drake, as an Irishman, privileged to enter the service of France, according to the Treaty of Limerick, ratified by William III. Of the consequent Trial at the Old Bailey, in June, 1708, Drake writes—"I shall not trouble the reader with many of the particulars of this Tryal, which lasted above 2 hours and a half; and shall only say, that my Councel pleaded strongly, my being under the Articles of Limerick; and therefore hoped the Court would grant me the benefit of them Articles, which they were ready to prove I was intitled to; and then called my witnesses, which were sworn; the chief of which was my Lady Tyrone, who knew me in Limerick, at the time of the surrender, and after that in France, at our landing at Brest. *This, and all my defence, was overruled, and the Jury brought in their Verdict,* GUILTY. At this, my poor brother, who was close to the Bar, sounded"—*i. e.,* swooned—"away, and fell down motionless. This Verdict made a greater impression on him, than it did on me; and I here solemnly declare, that, seeing him in that condition for near a quarter of an hour, gave me more concern, than the dread of any sentence that should pass upon me. . . . One of the learned Judges, whose name was Powel, made a long harangue to Captain Smith, and to me; which he concluded, telling us, that *good subjects should chuse rather to lie down in a ditch, and starve, than take up arms against their lawful Prince.* To which I took the liberty to answer, that *they must be good subjects, indeed;* that, *if that doctrine had been preached and adhered to at the Revolution, I should not be now hampered as I was.* . . . Then Sir Charles Hedges proceeded to pass sentence on us, as is usual in cases of High Treason." Smith was executed; but Drake, through interest made by his worthy brother, was, after some time, released. The cutting pertinency of Drake's reply to Judge Powell needs no comment. His shameless condemnation to death by an English Court of *Justice*, in contempt of the Articles of Limerick, was of a piece with England's *general* conduct to Ireland, as regards the Treaty of Limerick.

The alarm, at this expedition from France for Scotland, was great in London. It is related, that, notwithstanding the interposition of the House of Commons in favour of the Bank of England, the run upon it was such, that it was only on intelligence of the retreat of the French squadron the panic was arrested, and the concern thus preserved from shutting up, when within but 12 hours of having to do so. In Scotland, it would appear, that James had only to land, in order to succeed. And his success there would not have been without active results in Ireland, whose " disposition," says my contemporary Stuart document, " is constant, and always the same, founded on interest, on liberty, and on religion. It is notorious, from the great number of Bishops, of Priests, and of Monks, who have been obliged to seek an asylum in France, how much religion is oppressed in Ireland; almost all the ancient families despoiled of their properties; not 1 Catholic admissible to any civil or military office; and all disarmed. Yet, it is certain, that there are, in that kingdom, at least 6 Catholics, for 1 Protestant;[*] and it may be easily judged, by the valour and irreproachable conduct of the Irish regiments that served in France, of what their countrymen would be capable at home, if they had arms. In fine, it may be confidently affirmed, there are no motives in nature to induce a man to adopt a party, which do not exist to make the Irish Catholics adopt that of their legitimate King." The fate, then, of the Cromwello-Williamite or Whig settlers in Ireland—whose hated "ascendancy" there was based upon the landed spoliation, and religious and political oppression, of the older people of the country—may be easily conceived, had events been such, as to embolden the suffering majority of the nation to rise in favour of HIM, to whom alone *they* could look to *any* relief from their tyrants. That the contemplation of such a fate was, for a time, a cause for apprehension among the latter, may also be sufficiently inferred, from the subsequent admission by *their* Legislature in Dublin, with respect to the Catholics. "We," it observed, "with abhorrence call to mind the satis-

---

[*] The Catholics are likewise represented, in an important Presbyterian petition to the colonial House of Commons in Dublin, in 1705, as having been in the proportion of 6 to 1 of the entire Protestant population in Ireland!—on which assertion, the Jacobite statement, in the text, seems to have been based.

faction, which too visibly appeared in the faces, and the insolent behaviour, of the generality of them, when the late attempt was made, by the Pretender, on the north part of Great Britain." The most ancient or Milesian portion of the population were especially eager for "the Avenger," to use the expression of 1 of their Gaelic songs; which added, with a due perception of the connexion of their cause, as a despoiled Catholic race, with that of their disinherited Catholic Prince—

> "Ten thousand huzzas shall ascend to high heav'n,
> When *our Prince is restor'd*, and *our fetters are riv'n!*"

Besides, as is remarked by the translator of that song, they sympathized with the Prince's misfortune, inasmuch as they regarded "the Stuarts as of the Milesian line, fondly deducing them from Fergus, and the Celts of Ireland."*

In Flanders, Prince Eugene of Savoy and the Duke of Marlborough obtained a victory, July 11th, 1708, at Oudenarde, or Audenarde, owing to the Duke of Vendome having been so hampered with, and opposed by, the Duke of Burgundy, heir presumptive to the Crown of France, and his ill advisers, or flatterers,† that little, if *any*, honour could be fairly claimed from the advantage gained over the French under such circumstances, and *no* honour at the expense of Vendome, who, when unfettered in command, had shown himself to be an opponent worthy of each of those famous Allied Generals. Had *his* judgment been permitted to direct the movements of the French army, it is *certain* the French would *not* have been defeated at Oudenarde; and when, from the unwise contradiction he experienced, that disaster occurred, which he predicted would occur, he preserved his country from results, still more disastrous. On the disorder becoming general among the troops, he dismounted, and ran from regiment to regiment sword in hand, doing everything he could to bring back the officers and soldiers to their duty, until it became no longer possible to arrest a torrent, which was the more overwhelming, from the intervention of the night. Then, with a select rear-guard of 25 squadrons, and about as many battalions, he protected the retreat; giving a chosen corps of 40 squadrons, and 12 battalions, sent forward, next morning, by Marlborough to *complete* the victory, such an unexpected or disagreeable reception, on the road from Oudenarde to Ghent, that they had to retire; numbers of the cavalry being destroyed, particularly 1 Continental regiment, which is *named* as almost annihilated; and, among the infantry, Major Irwin's grenadiers being repulsed, with the loss of half the men, and a quantity of their officers, besides Major-General Meredith, wounded. "Who could have believed," exclaims my Allied authority, "that, after so glorious and so complete a victory, the victors themselves should receive, the next day, a check, from an enemy,

---

* The acknowledgment of the origin of the Kings of Scotland from the old Kings of Ireland, by the 1st Scotch or Stuart Sovereign of England and Ireland, has been already cited. Upon the earliest intelligence received, by the "ascendancy" Government in Ireland, of the sailing of King James II.'s son for Scotland from France, several of the chief Catholic laity and clergy were committed to prison, and required to take the Oath of Abjuration, but they would *not* do so.

† It is very displeasing to see the Duke of Burgundy, the excellent pupil of the exemplary and accomplished Fenelon, so much astray, on this occasion, as to disagree with the veteran Vendome. The writers on the side of the Allies are the loudest in Vendome's praise.

beaten, flying, and astonished? But, indeed, it was *not* so—those, who repulsed the Allies, were troops under the Duke de Vendome, who were *never* broken." Subsequently, by the position, which, against the opinion of *all* the other Generals, he had the firmness to take at Lovendeghem, Vendome, according to the admission of friends and enemies, saved the French army, and France itself. Hence, Eugene's and Marlborough's historian refers to Oudenarde, as "a battle which, but for the Duke of Vendome's retreat, would have been much more fatal to the French than that of Ramillies," though it, "as it was, overturned all that prudent General's schemes, and gave the Allies an opportunity of besieging Lisle, which otherwise perhaps they would not have found." And, on the impolicy of trusting a Villeroy, whereby the battle of Ramillies was lost, and of not relying upon a Vendome, whereby the battle of Oudenarde was lost, the same writer remarks—"We may say, that it was the peculiar felicity of the Duke of Marlborough, that the weakness of the French councils contributed no less to his glory, than his own wisdom." At this " untoward event"—which should merely be termed, *the defeat of the Duke of Burgundy by Prince Eugene and the Duke of Marlborough*—I find, as regards the Irish, that Fitz-Gerald's and O'Brien's Regiments of Foot, and Nugent's Regiment of Horse were present; and that the Colonel of the 1st, or Major-General Nicholas Fitz-Gerald, was among the leading officers of the French army, who were disabled, made prisoners, and died, of injuries received in the action. According to the best historian of these wars on the side of the French, they had about 7000 soldiers, and 685 officers, slain, or made prisoners. The enemy, of course, reported the French loss to have been several thousands more. The killed and wounded of every rank, on the side of the Allies, as published, at the time, by themselves, present the following aggregates, for the various nations engaged. Dutch, 1503; Danes, 606; Hanoverians, 466; Prussians, 209; British, 173; the small proportion of these last, to the other Allies, and the general amount, having consequently been—

British,	173
Others,	2784
Total,	2957

Thus, adds my British author, as he might *specially* do with reference to the little that *his* countrymen suffered, "all things considered, this victory was as cheap, as it was considerable; and it would certainly have been much more so, if, as the Duke of Burgundy and his party designed, the French had quitted the neighbourhood of Ghent, and retired towards Ypres"—as they *would* have done, but for Vendome's decision to encamp at Lovendeghem.

The most important consequence of the Allied success at Oudenarde was the famous siege and reduction of the skilfully-fortified and strongly-garrisoned city and citadel of Lisle by Eugene and Marlborough, whose military reputation was very much increased by the ability with which they conducted the enterprise; they having to guard, on the one hand, against the French army of above 100,000 men endeavouring to raise the siege; and having, on the other, to overcome such a fine defence of the place, as that under the Marshal de Boufflers, from August until December; a defence, which cost him, in every way, above 5000, and the besieging force from 15,000 to 20,000, men! The Irish noted in this defence were a veteran Lieutenant-General and Chevalier Andrew Lee, those seemingly of a provisional battalion, styled, from the Queen of King James II., "Fuseliers de la Reine d'Angleterre,"* and the supernumerary or reformed officers, who, after returning from the late unsuccessful expedition to Scotland, were attached to the several corps of the garrison of Lisle. Lee, who was wounded in the head by a bomb, received a pension of 6000 livres, with permission to wear the Cordon Rouge of the Order of St. Louis until a vacancy should occur to a Grand Cross, or Commandership, which he then obtained. At the Camp of Saulsoy on the Scheld, there were Irish also, or the 5 battalions of Lee, O'Brien, Dorrington, O'Donnell, and Galmoy, who increased their strength, at the expense of Marlborough's army. "I can," says a writer connected with the English War Office, "name a regiment or 2, or, perhaps, more, in Flanders, in the year 1708, which we generally call the campaign of Lisle, that lost considerably by desertion; one of them no less than 130 men, as well as I can remember. They all went off to the Irish, and fought against us at Malplaquet"—the following year. "They were esteemed brave fellows in our regiments; and I can hardly think, that changing sides abated anything of their courage." The youthful representative of the *legitimate* as distinguished from the *revolutionary* royalty of Great Britain and Ireland served this campaign with the French army as *incognito*, or under the designation of the Chevalier de St. George, from the popular or legendary tutelar Saint of England. He, relates the Duke of Berwick of the Chevalier, "was present at the combat of Oudenarde, where he displayed a great deal of valour and presence of mind; and he acquired, by his affability, the friendship of every one; for *we are naturally prepossessed in favour of the unfortunate, when they have not been so through their own fault, and when, moreover, their conduct is good.*" It may be added, that the young Hanoverian Prince, afterwards George II., was at the same combat, in the opposite or Allied army, and likewise behaved himself gallantly.

In Spain, Count O'Mahony, with 6000 regular troops, among whom were the Irish corps of Berwick, Bourke, and Dillon, besides some militia, and 1000 workmen, appeared before Alcoy in Valencia, January 2nd, 1708. The place being breached by his battering train of 6 guns on the 4th, was twice, or on the 5th and 7th, assaulted with much loss, and without success; but on the 9th, was obliged to surrender—the few English there as prisoners of war—the inhabitants as rebels at discretion—and the town having to pay a fine of 48,000 piastres. At this siege, repulsing a sally on the 2nd, the Count's brave Lieutenant-Colonel, Cornelius O'Driscoll, was wounded in the foot dangerously. The Count then reduced a long list of places towards the sea-coast, causing his troops to observe the strictest discipline; which was the more gratifying

* Connect this with what appears farther on, about the Irish deserters, at the defence of Tournay, in 1709. King James II.'s Queen survived her husband nearly 17 years, or until May, 1718, when she died, at St. Germain, in her 60th year, or the 30th of her exile from England. "In England," writes Mr. Hardiman, "she was never popular, in consequence of her being a Catholic, and warmly attached to her religion; but, for the same reason, she was an especial favourite with the Irish." See, in that learned and patriotic collector's "Irish Minstrelsy," among the "Jacobite Relics," the native Milesian or Gaelic poet's "Lament for the Queen of King James II.," in the original Irish, with a spirited versification into English, by Henry Grattan Curran, Esq.

to the people of the country, as they had been made to believe, that nothing was to be expected, but massacre and pillage.

In March, 1708, the Count was appointed to command in Sicily, to which he was to proceed with 3000 Spanish troops, and his 500 Irish dragoons. He reached Messina in April; soon acquired, by his polished and generous manners, the friendship of the Sicilians; and inspired them with feelings of confidence, the stronger, in proportion to the great superiority of *his* abilities and reputation to those of their Viceroy, the Marquis de los Balbases. The Imperialists, in the kingdom of Naples, conquered by them in 1707 from Philip V., were designing to add Sicily to that acquisition; and the naval power of their Allies, the English, in the Mediterranean, was very serviceable to the cause of the Emperor's brother, the Archduke Charles of Austria, as claiming to be King of Spain, in opposition to Philip V. In August, writes a British historian respecting Sir John Leake, " the Admiral reduced the Island of Sardinia, of which the Conde de Cifuentes was declared Viceroy by King Charles; and, soon after, by the assistance of Lieutenant-General Stanhope, he reduced Minorca also, excepting Port Mahon, and 2 other ports, which were afterwards reduc'd by Sir Edward Whitaker; who likewise cruis'd in the Mediterranean, and struck such terror into Italy, that the Pope acknowledg'd King Charles, and did every other thing that the Emperor desir'd, tho' with a very ill grace." Such effective precautions, however, were adopted by Count O'Mahony for the preservation of Sicily, that no Allied landing took place *there;* while the Neapolitans, on the other hand, were, adds my British authority, " harassed by a fleet from Sicily, with a body of land forces on board, which had the hardiness to appear in the very Port of Naples, and to exact contributions all along the coasts."

In the Peninsula, the chief army of Philip V., in 1708, was that of Catalonia, under the Duke of Orleans, consisting of 36 battalions, and 55 squadrons. The leading Irish corps employed there, or in Valencia, were the 2 battalions of Berwick, and the battalions of Bourke, and Dillon, in the French service, and Brigadier Henry Crofton's Regiment (or 4 squadrons) of Dragoons, in the Spanish service. The strong fortress of Tortosa, garrisoned by 8 Allied battalions of regulars, 2 battalions of miquelets, and 300 horse, assisted by the armed inhabitants, was invested, June 12th, by the Duke, and, after a laborious siege, was compelled to capitulate, August 11th. Of Irish officers there, William Talbot of Haggardstown, County Louth, nephew and successor to the Earldom of Richard Talbot, Earl and Duke of Tyrconnell, and attainted in Ireland by the Revolutionists as William Talbot of Dundalk, served as Aide-de-Camp to the Duke of Orleans; in which capacity he is erroneously noticed by the French historian, as *Duke,* instead of *Earl,* of Tyrconnell. Berwick's battalions several times mounted the trenches. In December, the battalions of Berwick, Bourke, and Dillon are mentioned, as constituting part of the force with which the Chevalier d'Asfeld reduced the town of Alicant, defended by Colonel Richards, to surrender—the Castle holding out till the ensuing spring, or April, 1709.

In 1709, France was reduced to such terrible distress, from the effects of a most ruinous season, combined with the immense taxation requisite for the maintenance of hostilities against so many nations, that Louis XIV. spared no efforts to obtain peace, though he was unable to do so, notwithstanding the fairest offers on his part. In this melancholy state of things, the greatest sacrifices had to be made in France, in order to continue the war. "All the people of quality, without distinction, and all the people who had any plate in Paris, sent it immediately to the mint. The King sent all his own gold plate, and particularly some tables at Versailles, the workmanship of which came to 4 times the value of the metal." Yet, by every means that could be resorted to, such a military force as was raised for the public defence could only be kept on foot in much privation and misery.* The Duke of Marlborough and Prince Eugene, on the other hand, assembled, in June, for the campaign in Flanders, a very fine, and more numerous army, referred to by an Allied writer, as "*all choice troops, all eager to engage, and all flushed with the hopes of penetrating into and of plundering France, which was the general discourse in Germany, England, and Holland, at the opening of this campaign!*" The French, nevertheless, were so skilfully posted, by the Marshal de Villars, from Pont-à-Vendin to Bethune, that the enemy could only commence active operations by investing Tournay, on the 27th. That town was well fortified, had likewise a fine citadel, and was peculiarly formidable to attack, from the number of mines connected with the works. The Governor was the Marquis de Surville, distinguished, in 1708, at the defence of Lisle; and he was well aided by M. de Megrigny, the able engineer who had planned the citadel. But the garrison was not proportioned to the fortifications, having been diminished to but 6400 men, in order to increase the French army; and there was an insufficiency of provisions and money, though ammunition was abundant. The Allies, from the night of July 7th-8th, when the trenches were opened, till September 3rd, when the citadel surrendered, suffered severely, especially by the sallies and mines; their admitted loss having been 5340 men. That of the garrison was returned as 3191 killed and wounded, including 125 officers. At this siege, the Irish reformed officers signalized themselves, as they had done the year before at Lisle; and a corps of Irish formed by M. de Parpaille for the occasion out of deserters from the English army (under those circumstances already explained) are described, as in a sally, on the night of July 21st-22nd, "having achieved wonders, and having ruined a great deal of the enemy's works."

Soon after the conquest of Tournay, the Allies invested Mons; but could not besiege it, without first giving battle to the French. The Marshal de Villars, assisted by the worthy Marshal de Boufflers, the gallant defender of Namur and Lisle, (who, although an older officer, agreed to act under his junior for the public good,) took up a strong position in the territory about the village of Malplaquet, with woods to the right and left, and an open country between, and to the rear of, those woods. Along the woods as his wings, and over the intermediate ground as his centre, the Marshal placed his infantry behind triple intrenchments, trees cut down, and fastened together, &c. The whole of those arrangements were such, that an advancing enemy, while struggling with the difficulties of attacking the intrenchments, might be well torn and mashed by a crossing fire from the musketry and cannon of the defenders; and the remaining space, to the rear of those works manned by the infantry, the Marshal occupied with his cavalry; having had every obstacle cleared away, which could interfere with their movements to support the infantry. The French army, according to its official authori-

* Louis XIV. was undergoing the punishment, in his old age, for that *fault*, or rather CRIME, which he himself condemned on his death-bed, of having been too fond of war, for so many years of his life; and France was involved in *his* punishment.

ties, consisted of 120 battalions, and 260 squadrons; being, in the number of *both*, as well as the complements of *each*, generally inferior to the enemy. Of those troops, too, but a comparatively small proportion were old soldiers; the relics of so many destroyed at Blenheim, Ramillies, Turin, Oudenarde, &c. The great remaining majority were merely new levies; and *all* were naturally under the dispiriting influence of that series of misfortunes to their arms for several years, which, as the Marshal de Boufflers wrote to Louis XIV., "had so humbled the French nation, that one hardly dared to own one's-self a Frenchman!" They were likewise inferior in artillery; having, according to their above-mentioned accounts, but 80 pieces of cannon. Nevertheless, they were resolved to recover their former character, if possible, under Villars; whose past achievements, and present dispositions, inspired them with as much confidence, as the recent Allied insolence, which refused their Sovereign any tolerable terms of peace, was calculated to fire them with loyal and patriotic indignation. The Allied army, according to Marlborough's historian, Archdeacon Coxe, amounted to 129 battalions, and 252 squadrons; but, according to Serjeant Millner, who fought under Marlborough in the action, and whose enumeration is not discountenanced by other Allied statements, it consisted of 152 battalions, and 271 squadrons.[*] Prince Eugene, contrasting the composition of this army with that of France, thus described the Allied troops—"They are all men accustomed to fire and slaughter; of whom there is scarcely 1, that has not been present at some battle, or at sieges. Besides, with what daring are they not animated, by the recollection of such a long series of victories?" They had also, according to the Histoire du Prince Eugène, the Marquis de Quincy, and Drake's Memoirs, a much more powerful artillery than the French. It was divided into heavy and light guns. Of the heavy guns, to level the French intrenchments, there were, in the 3 chief batteries, 103; and the rest appear to have made up 120. The light guns, to accompany the respective brigades in their advance, have not been enumerated, but included a number of field-mortars, to dislodge the French from the woods, by discharging such a quantity of shells and stones, as to dash down, or shatter to fragments, the trees upon those about them, and spread destruction, and confusion, in every direction. With so many circumstances in favour of the Allies, may be noted the generally superior "condition" of their troops to those of France, owing to the vast misery there, already mentioned. The Marshal de Villars, among his heavy apprehensions respecting the campaign he had to make against an enemy so superior in numbers, artillery, &c., particularly refers to his "perpetual fear each day of being without bread" —adding how, as he passed through the ranks of his army, the poor soldier, struggling to subsist on a half or a quarter ration, would address him, in the words of the Lord's Prayer—"*Give us this day our daily bread!*" And, for a day previous to the battle of Malplaquet,

---

[*] Marlborough's and Eugene's *published* line of battle, June 23rd, about Lisle, at the opening of the campaign, presents a total of 170 battalions and 271 squadrons. The Allies had likewise a *corps-de-reserve*, to cover Brabant, under Lieutenant-General Dompré, quartered about Alost; from which, and other sources, the French computed that their opponents could be swelled, in the field, to 180 battalions and 289 squadrons. Subsequently, or August 6th, at Orchies, Marlborough's and Eugene's *published* line of battle is given as 164 battalions and 270 squadrons—exclusive, of course, of such as were *then* absent, or detached.

according to one account, and, even for 2 days, according to another, there had not been a distribution, sufficient to extend to the whole of the army. "On Wednesday, the 11th, early in the morning," alleges Drake, "our army received a day's bread, which we stood in great need of, *not having had any for 2 days before!*" Of this bread, the last which so many of them were ever to eat! these brave fellows having taken some, threw away a part, that they might be the less encumbered, or more alert, for the approaching engagement.

Prince Eugene, and the Duke of Marlborough, perceiving that, to attack the Marshal de Villars, as he was posted, would require the presence of every man they could muster, and, not being able to have all in hand until the 11th, deferred the decisive contest to that day. A dense summer mist, very favourable to the Allies, as enabling them to make their various dispositions for the action unseen by the French, did not uncurtain the landscape before the increasing brightness of the morning sun, till between half-past 7 and 8 o'clock. The stage then being clear for the bloody drama in preparation, the firing of the artillery commenced, and, from 8 to half-past 8, the entire of the French line in front was assailed by the Allied infantry; who, duly encouraged by their leaders, well primed with brandy, animated to the utmost with military music, and most formidably pioneered by the destructive discharges of their cannon and mortar batteries, "advanced," as described, "not like men, but devils," against the "infernal gulph" of the French intrenchments. The combat raged with great obstinacy, varied fortune, and a frightful carnage, particularly of the Allies, until past 3 o'clock in the afternoon; when the Marshal de Villars having been carried off senseless from a wound received in repelling an attack towards the left; and the intrenchments of the left and centre having been completely penetrated, so that those on the right, which were the last held, had to be evacuated; the Marshal de Boufflers, after several gallant and effective cavalry-charges, made an excellent retreat towards Quesnoy and Valenciennes. The French appear to have left behind them 14 or 15 pieces of their artillery as dismounted, with 29 colours or standards, but to have carried off the rest of their 80 cannon, along with 32 Allied colours and standards;* and they had 7837 slain, or hurt, besides, according to Millner, 1369 irremovably wounded, or made prisoners; forming, so far, a loss of 9206 men. The Allied official list of slain or disabled infantry, distinguishing the proportion of every nation, makes them 18,353; and a similarly minute list, by Millner, of the casualties of the Allied cavalry, makes them 1963. By these accounts, there were killed and wounded, of *British* infantry and cavalry, but 2040; of those of the *other* Confederate nations, 18,276; of whom the Dutch, who suffered *most*, as opposed to the French right under the Marshal de Boufflers, were 10,496,† and the *rest* 7780, making, of the Allies altogether,

---

* The 32 captured Allied banners, which are particularized as "24 colours and 8 standards," were forwarded to Louis through the Marquis de Nangis, an officer of the highest character, most distinguished in the battle along with the Irish Brigade; and were solemnly presented, as trophies, September 21st, at l'Eglise de Nôtre Dame, in Paris.

† The fine Regiment of Dutch Blue Guards, of 3 battalions, which had been such a favourite corps with William III., and contained so many Dutch Catholics, suffered extremely here. Its choice Company of Cadets, especially, a body of "young heroes," exclusively of Huguenot families, and which, since its institution, under William, supplied so many excellent officers to the Dutch

20,3 6; and the French having had 9206, and the Allies 20,316, *hors de combat*, the loss, or suffering, of BOTH armies would consequently extend to not less than 29,522 men! Such was the famous battle of Malplaquet, which I notice so fully, as the most sanguinary of any fought during this war. It was won, indeed, by the Allies, as having every advantage on their side, except an intrenched position; and even *that* single advantage of the French was, to a considerable extent, neutralized, by the circumstance of a marsh, on their left, thought impassable, proving passable, and thus opening a way for the 1st success of their assailants. Yet so high was the price at which victory was attained, that Prince Eugene's historian doubts, whether it would not have been as well, if not better, for the conquerors (like Pyrrhus of old after 1 of his encounters with the Romans,) had they *never* achieved such a disastrous triumph. As to the Duke of Marlborough's connexion with it, our gallant countryman, Brigadier General Richard Kane, observes—"It was the only rash thing the Duke of Marlborough was ever guilty of; and it was generally believ'd, that he was press'd to it by Prince Eugene; and this very battle gave the Duke's enemies a handle to exclaim against him, in saying, he was a man delighted in war, and valued not the lives of men." Which serious charge—the more serious, as Marlborough was insatiably avaricious, and profited proportionably by the war,—continued to gain more and more credit in England, till it contributed, in a great degree, to his final deposition from command.

The Irish, in the French army, that remarkable day, were Lee's, O'Brien's, Dorrington's, O'Donnell's, and Galmoy's infantry regiments, and Nugent's cavalry regiment. "They," says Lieutenant-General Count Arthur Dillon concerning those infantry, "were posted towards the centre, in the opening of the wood of Sart, having the Swiss Guards on their right, and the Brigade of Champagne on their left. It was towards this point, that the enemy directed their greatest efforts. These 3 brigades, after having sustained, for upwards of 3 hours, the murderous fire of a battery of 20 pieces of cannon, repulsed so many as 3 of the most furious attacks, in which the enemy suffered a considerable loss. They were at last obliged to retire, because 4 battalions, who secured their flank, having abandoned their post, the enemy were about to turn them. They returned, notwithstanding this, to the charge, and, after having gained some advantages, they received orders to retreat altogether, which they executed with the left of the army, after the wounding of the Marshal de Villars." Of 1 of those repulses of the enemy by the Irish Brigade, the leading French historian of Louis XIV.'s wars, after observing how Lieutenant-General Albergotti having "marched against the enemy, attacked them so well as to drive them from the ground they had gained, and to force them to betake themselves to the extremity of service, was annihilated. "This Company," says my British authority, "distinguished itself on every occasion which offered during the war, till the battle of Malplaquet in 1709, wherein they were entirely cut to pieces, in forcing the retrenchment on the left of our army." Prince Eugene's Continental biographer, too, in relating how, on the Allied left, the ground " was covered with the dead bodies of the Dutch," and how "their Foot Guards were reduced to a lamentable state," adds, "of 200 Cadets of French refugee families, there were 195 left upon the field." Of the Scotch Brigade in the Dutch service, the British historian previously cited likewise remarks—"The unfortunate Marquis of Tullibardine, with the rest of the Scotch officers in the service of the States, did wonders, though to little better purpose, than barely to shew with how much bravery they could die."

the wood," adds—" The Irish Brigade, at whose head were the Comte de Villars and the Marquis de Nangis, overturned all that came in their way." The Allied troops, "who," according to Marlborough's biographer, Archdeacon Coxe, " recoiled a considerable way before the impetuous onset of the Irish," were " British and Prussians."

The following passage respecting this battle occurs in the Memoirs of Captain Robert Parker of Kilkenny, then serving with the 18th, or Royal Irish Regiment of Foot, in Marlborough's army. "We happened to be the last of the regiments that had been left at Tournay to level our approaches, and therefore could not come up till the lines were all formed and closed, so that there was no place for us to fall into. We were ordered therefore to draw up by ourselves, on the right of the whole army, opposite to a skirt of the wood of *Sart*; and when the army advanced to attack the enemy, we also advanced into that part of the wood, which was in our front. We continued marching slowly on, till we came to an open in the wood. It was a small plain, on the opposite side of which we perceived a battalion of the enemy drawn up, a skirt of the wood being in the rear of them. Upon this, Colonel *Kane*, who was then at the head of the regiment, having drawn us up, and formed our plattoons, advanced gently toward them, with the 6 plattoons of our 1st fire made ready. When we had advanced within 100 paces of them, they gave us a fire of 1 of their ranks: whereupon we halted, and returned them the fire of our 6 plattoons at once; and immediately made ready the 6 plattoons of our 2nd fire, and advanced upon them again. They then gave us the fire of another rank, and we returned them a 2nd fire, which made them shrink; however, they gave us the fire of a 3rd rank after a scattering manner, and then retired into the wood in great disorder: on which we sent our 3rd fire after them, and saw them no more. We advanced cautiously up to the ground which they had quitted, and found several of them killed and wounded; among the latter was one Lieutenant *O-Sullivan*, who told us the battalion we had engaged was the Royal Regiment of *Ireland*. Here, therefore, there was a fair trial of skill between the 2 Royal Regiments of *Ireland*, one in the *British*, the other in the *French* service; for we met each other upon equal terms, and there was none else to interpose. We had but 4 men killed, and 6 wounded; and found near 40 of them on the spot, killed and wounded. The advantage on our side," adds the Captain, " will be easily accounted for, 1st, from the weight of our ball; for the *French* arms carry bullets of 24 to the pound: whereas our *British* firelocks carry ball of 16 only to the pound, which will make a considerable difference in the execution. Again, the manner of our firing was different from theirs; the French at that time fired all by ranks, which can never do equal execution with our plattoon-firing, especially when 6 plattoons are fired together. This is undoubtedly the best method that has yet been discovered for fighting a battalion; especially when 2 battalions only engage each other." These remarks of the Captain are deserving of much attention, for more reasons than one; or 1stly, as showing the serious disadvantages, in point of weapons and discipline, under which the French infantry, as contrasted with the British, laboured in Marlborough's time, to which disadvantages, no doubt, as well as others, so many defeats of the French were, in a very great degree, attributable;* and 2ndly, as demonstrating that, even if the whole, instead of

* The successes of the Allies, in this final war respecting the Spanish succession,

(as it will appear) merely a detachment from, the *French* Royal Regiment of Ireland, was really engaged with the *British* Royal Regiment of Ireland, still the meeting mentioned by the Captain should not be considered as one upon anything like equal terms, since the corps which fired by 6 platoons or ranks at once, opposed to a corps of which only 1 rank fired at a time, may be regarded, as having the advantage of 6 men or bullets to every 1 against it. Besides, even if the whole of both regiments had been arrayed there, the fight would not have been a fair one, unless it could likewise be shown, that there was no superiority of numbers in the British over the French Royal Regiment of Ireland. That the affair mentioned by Parker was nothing more than one against a detached party or outpost of the French Royal Regiment of Ireland on the outskirt of a wood is made still more obvious, even without appealing to any French evidence, by the circumstance of Colonel Kane and Serjeant Millner, both in Parker's regiment, having *each* left a description of the battle of Malplaquet, yet without *either* of them at all noticing the matter so dwelt upon by Parker; which is rather *irreconcilable* with an actual occurrence of what would have been such *a remarkable feat, as their regiment having beaten the entire regiment of the like name and nation in the French army!* Neither have I found any allusion whatever to anything of the kind, in any contemporary British historian.

But, according to the French documents, the French Royal Regiment of Ireland, or Dorrington's, was mainly engaged, *not* in such a mere outpost affair at the wood as that last noticed, but in the hottest portion of the battle, under its Lieutenant-Colonel, ranking as Colonel, Brigadier Michael Roth, and a Kilkenny man, as well as Parker ——, the Brigadier, in the absence of the Colonel-Proprietor, Major-General William Dorrington in Germany, having commanded the regiment in Flanders, where he is specially noticed, as having "combated with the greatest valour at Malplaquet." In connexion with the Regiment of Dorrington forming a portion of the Irish Brigade *en masse* in repelling the English, I translate the following interesting passage in a letter to John O'Connell, Esq., from "Le Baron Cantillon de Ballyheigue," County of Kerry, Lieutenant-Colonel of the 3rd Regiment of Hussars in France, and President of the Council of War at Paris, in 1843—a nobleman, the representative of the old Norman or French race of the De Cantillons, so long established in Ireland, and still, or after the re-establishment of his branch of the name in France, honourably cherishing recollections of the land, in which his ancestors were so long eminent. "A celebrated painter," writes the Baron from Paris, December 8th, 1843, to Mr. O'Connell, "has reproduced in a picture, which is at present my property, an historical subject, concerning my family and yours. It treats of my great-grandfather, who was likewise the uncle of Mary O'Connell, the wife of Maurice, your grand-uncle. The subject is drawn from the Archives of the Minister of War at Paris. This picture represents Captain James Cantillon, at the battle of Malplaquet in 1709, charging,

against Louis XIV., will *not* be wondered at by any reader of Voltaire's description, in his "Siécle de Louis XIV." chap. xviii., of the *vast* degeneracy in the military administration of France, under Chamillart. Indeed, if a reader combines, with that powerful description, the pernicious jobbing connected with the carrying out of the King's decree of January 26th, 1701, respecting the levies for his infantry, the wonder will rather be, how the French could have made such a stand, as they *did*, in the ensuing contest. See the "History of the French Army," in Colburne's New Monthly Magazine for December, 1861.

at the head of the grenadiers of the Irish Regiment of Dorrington, the English troops, commanded by the Duke of Marlborough. The official documents explain the subject of it in this manner:—'When the left of the French army, taken in flank by the right wing of the enemy's army under the orders of the Duke of Marlborough, began to recoil, the Maréchal de Villars brought up as quickly as possible the Irish Brigade, which was in the centre. It attacked with fury the English troops, whom it repulsed. Cantillon, at the head of the grenadiers of the Regiment of Dorrington, first approached the enemy's line, exclaiming to his men—*Forward, brave Irishmen! Long live King James III., and the King of France!* He had his sword broken in the combat, and fell, covered with wounds, in the midst of the ranks of the English infantry, after having killed, with his own hand, an officer, and several soldiers. There remained, after the charge, only 15 men of the company of Cantillon; the others were stretched dead, or wounded, around their brave Captain, whose glorious example they had followed!' The painter," concludes the Baron, "has represented Cantillon, sword in hand, pointing out the enemy's troops to the Irish, and holding up his hat in his left hand, while exclaiming, *Forward, brave Irishmen*," &c.

Prince James Francis Edward Stuart, (or, in Jacobite language, King James III.,) highly signalized himself at Malplaquet, as the Chevalier de St. George. Though ill with a fever at Quesnoy, he requested the Marshal de Villars, to let him know when the engagement was to take place, in order to be present at it; and, notwithstanding his illness, arriving by post as the action was commencing, he placed himself at the head of the famous Maison du Roi, or Horse Guards of Louis XIV., whose behaviour that day was, says the Marshal de Boufflers, "*indeed beyond human nature, and above all expression!*" After an exposure to the cross-fire of 50 pieces of cannon for several hours, that fine corps gave or received so many as 12 charges; penetrated, sword in hand, the 1st, 2nd, 3rd, and even to the 4th line of the comparatively fresh Allied cavalry; and was only at last obliged to retire, through the combined strength of the Allied horse and foot, supported by the fire from a flanking battery of 30 pieces of artillery. In the last of these charges, the Prince received a sabre-wound on his right arm. "*The Chevalier de St. George,*" writes the Marshal de Boufflers to Louis XIV., "*behaved himself, during the whole action, with all possible bravery and vivacity!*" * According to the contemporary unpublished Irish Jacobite historian, Plunkett—"The King of England was *remarked for his valour and zeal, when several persons were killed and wounded about him*; and his subjects, the Irish Brigade, under his gallant countenance, exhibited uncommon bravery in 4 occasions." In the words of our native Jacobite song,

"He *was* as fit to wear the Crown,
As any *whelp* in London town;
But of his right they cut him down,
A noble Stuart born!" †

* The *details* respecting the very gallant conduct of the Maison du Roi, and the Prince at its head, are taken from the contemporary French and British authorities of the Marquis de Quincy, and the honest compiler of the Military History of Prince Eugene of Savoy, and the Duke of Marlborough, in 4 volumes.

† The song, of which the above is a fragment, and the air "of the right sort," continued to be sung about in Munster, till late in the last century. It began thus—

"I wish that day would come to pass,
With all the Catholics going to mass!"

The adventurous Peter Drake of Drakerath, who fought most gallantly in the Chevalier de Janson's Company of Gendarmerie, and was very severely wounded, observes, in relating his arrival at Quesnoy 2 days after the battle, and his then going to the Prince's quarters there— "Being acquainted with one M°Carty, who was Master of his Wine-cellars, I got myself conducted thither, in hopes to get some comfortable refreshment, which I stood much in need of. In this I succeeded, as well as I could wish. Mr. M°Carty came to me, brought me into the hall, went and brought me a silver cup of excellent wine, and some French bread; I drank some of the wine, but could not touch the bread, though I was very hungry. He went and got me a porringer of good soup, with bread well soaked in it, which I sucked in as well as I could, and it was great comfort to me. At this time, General Sheldon came in, and being informed who I was, immediately called for one of the Pretender's Surgeons, and ordered him, to examine and dress my wounds. . . . There came a good number of gentleman on horse-back to the door, belonging to the Pretender, and it was said, he was going to the camp; he soon came down, which was lucky for me, for, as he was going by, he saw me, and General Sheldon told him, I was the gentleman that came from England, and had waited on him about a fortnight ago: he stopt a little, and looked towards me, and went off; in 2 or 3 minutes, one Captain Booth, who belonged to the Duke of Berwick's Regiment, and was one of the Pretender's Aid-de-Camps, came to me, and gave me 20 French louis d'ors, amounting then to 400 livers; a strong and timely supply."

The 3 leading English and Irish Jacobite prisoners, connected with the operations preceding this engagement, or the engagement itself, were Sheldon, acting as Brigadier, who was "taken near Bossu, doing his duty with valour, at the head of 400 horse;" an Irish veteran of the War of the Revolution, belonging to the Regiment of Nugent, Matthew Cooke, Brigadier of Cavalry; and the Lord Macguire,* Lieutenant-Colonel of the Regiment of Dillon, which corps, however, was *not* serving in Flanders. The French state the killed and wounded officers of the 5 Irish Regiments of Foot thus—Lee's, 17—O'Brien's, 9—Dorrington's, 30—O'Donnell's, 16—Galmoy's, 11—in all 83, or, with 2 of Dorrington's *alone* mentioned as taken, 85. Yet, of captured officers of the Regiments of Dorrington, Lee, Galmoy, and O'Donnell, I find 1 Aid-Major, 4 Captains, and 7 Lieutenants in a Dutch list of prisoners from the French, printed at the Hague. In this, I am able to make out the names of Condon, Cantillon, Mandeville, Walker, Comerford, Ryan, Fitz-Gerald, Murphy, O'Neill. A letter of September 13th, on the battle, from the camp at Ruesne, near Quesnoy, by M. de Contades of the Etat-Major, after observing, " all the infantry in general have done wonders," adds, " the Regiment of Navarre, that of Royal Champagne, and the Irish have been very distinguished."

I derive my knowledge of it from my venerable mother, who heard it when a child. The italicized word "*whelp*," was a contemptuous term, among the Jacobites, for Guelph, the family name of the House of Hanover.

* "Of the Macguires," says the introduction to Dr. O'Donovan's edition of O'Dugan and O'Heerin, "the noble representatives of the title of Baron of Enniskillen were officers in France, from the reign of Louis XIV. to that of Louis XVI.; and during the same period, gentlemen of that old sept were to be found there in the national Brigade, or the Regiments of Lee, Dorrington, Dillon, O'Donnell, Fitz-James, Bulkeley, and Lally."

The active operations of 1709 in Flanders terminated in October, with the reduction of Mons by the Allies, after a creditable defence of between 6 and 7 weeks. Its garrison, though neither numerous enough, nor sufficiently supplied, for duly maintaining such a fortress, killed or wounded above 2200 of the besiegers; who, with their fellow-sufferers at Tournay, and Malplaquet, and, with those lost by minor warfare, desertion, and disease, would amount to considerably more than 30,000, if not, as the French said, above 35,000 men! Rather a dear price, in *either* case, for the successes of *this* campaign! Maubeuge, was the next post exposed to attack by the Allies, when the French, under the Duke of Berwick, provided against any further conquests, by the construction of an intrenched camp, where the 5 battalions of Lee, O'Brien, Dorrington, O'Donnell, Galmoy, with the 2 squadrons of Nugent, were stationed; and Eugene and Marlborough, having gotten quite enough of fighting for *this* year, dismissed their troops into winter-quarters.

Of Irish, with the French forces in Spain, Rousillon, or Dauphiné, in 1709, or Major-General Walter Bourke, Lieutenant-Generals Arthur Dillon, and Lord Galmoy, and the battalions of Bourke, Dillon, and Berwick; and Irish in the service of Spain, or Brigadier Henry Crofton and his Regiment of Dragoons acting there, and Count Daniel O'Mahony in Sicily; the following are the principal circumstances recorded.

May 7th, 1709, was fought the battle of the Guadinna, or La Gudina, near Badajos, between the Spanish army of Estremadura, under King Philip V.'s General, the Marquis de Bay, and the Portuguese and British, under the Marquis de Fronteira, and Queen Anne's General, the Huguenot Earl of Galway. The Allies, according to the Portuguese account, were 49 regiments of infantry and cavalry, against but 40 on the side of their Spanish opponents; according to the London Gazette, No. 4538, about 17,000 foot and 5000 horse in very good order, and, by the reports from deserters, *much* superior in number to the enemy. The Spanish army were, by their published line of battle, but 24 battalions and 47 squadrons. The artillery of each party was stated as equal, or 20 pieces of cannon. The Portuguese and English were defeated, with the loss, in every way, of about 4000 men, 17 cannon, 15 colours or standards, as well as tents, and baggage; the Spaniards having had, it is alleged, only about 400 men, and 100 horses, killed or wounded. Of the British contingent, the brigade of Pearce, consisting of the 2 English regiments of Barrymore and Stanwix, and a 3rd, or that of Galway, composed of recently-levied Carlist Spaniards, after some resistance, were, owing to their total abandonment by the Portuguese horse, compelled to surrender *en masse*. The Allies had about 1700 men killed and wounded; those captured were altogether about 2300; of whom the greater number, or 1500, were Queen Anne's troops, and the remainder, or 800, were Portuguese. The chief British (besides Portuguese) officers, made prisoners, were Major-General James Barry, 4th Earl of Barrymore, and Nicholas Sankey; Brigadier-General Thomas Pearce; the 2nd Colonel of the Regiment of Galway, with Major Thomas Gordon of that corps; Lieutenant-Colonel Henry Meredith of the Regiment of Colonel Thomas Stanwix, and Lord Henry Pawlet, Aide-de-Camp to the Earl of Galway; the latter nobleman, (unfortunate *here* as at *Almanza*,) after having a horse shot under him, only escaping with difficulty. The Allies were thus disappointed in the calculation they had made, of being able, through their superior numbers, to reduce

Badajos, and had the additional mortification to witness above 30 leagues of the Portuguese territory placed under contribution by the Marquis de Bay, who subsisted his army at the expense of his adversaries, to the end of this campaign. In short, so generally discreditable to the Confederates did their intelligence from Portugal appear, that, says a contemporary London annalist—"For my part, I think the stories, and excuses, sent us from thence, are as mean, and poor, as our fighting, and conduct, seem to be." At the victory, which led to such satisfactory results for Philip V., Brigadier Henry Crofton, with his Regiment of Dragoons of 4 squadrons, was in the 1st line of the Spanish right wing of cavalry, by whose impetuous charge, upon their Portuguese opponents, it is stated, that " all the cavalry of the 2 lines of the enemy's left was, in less than half an hour, broken, overthrown, and put to flight." And Crofton is elsewhere specified, as having "performed wonders, in his capacity of Brigadier, at the head of his Regiment of Dragoons, in the famous battle of Guadinna." He was created, December 15th following, a Maréchal de Camp, or Major-General, by Philip V. Elsewhere in the Peninsula, the brave Don Miguel Pons, Maréchal de Camp, with 3 horse-regiments and 2 battalions, surprised, August 6th, near the river Noguera, about the bridge of Montannana, 6 regiments of Austro-Carlist infantry and cavalry so successfully, that he routed them at the 1st volley, only 4 of his men being mentioned as killed, and some of his horses slain, or disabled; while the enemy had about 700 men killed, wounded or taken, with their baggage, and 6 standards. One of the 2 battalions, engaged, under the gallant Pons, in this well-managed affair, was Dillon's.

August 28th, 1709, Lieutenant-General Arthur Dillon, attached to the Army of Dauphiné under the Marshal Duke of Berwick, gave a sharp repulse to one of the enemy's Generals, at the head of a detachment estimated as superior in number, or 3000 foot and 200 horse. The Marshal Duke thus relates the affair. "General Rebender, desirous of performing some striking achievement, marched, for that purpose, from his camp about Exilles, and traversed Mont-Genevre with the design of placing under contribution the Val-Després, and, more especially, the market-town of La Vachette, which was no more than half a league from Briançon. M. Dillon, who commanded in these parts, perceiving that Rebender had descended from Mont-Genevre upon La Vachette, marched thither with 2 battalions and 6 companies of grenadiers, whom he stationed behind the town. As soon as the enemy, (after being arrayed for engaging,) approached to assail a weak palisaded intrenchment that had been constructed there, M. Dillon sallied out upon them, from the right and left of the town, and charged them with so much bravery, that he beat them; killing 700 or 800 of them upon the spot, and making 400 prisoners. Rebender retired, as expeditiously as possible, towards Exilles, and did not show his nose any more, for the rest of the campaign." Nevertheless, not long after this sharp repulse, the hostile Governor of Exilles, with 3000 men, came down from a mountain, in sight of the French guarding Briançon, and twice retired, in order to entice them after him. Dillon, expecting the Governor would return a 3rd time, caused the mountaineers to intrench themselves so secretly, and supported them so well with infantry ambushed behind the mountain, that the enemy, on their reappearance, had 300 men slain, 70 taken, and the remainder put to the rout. In making his arrangements for this campaign, the Duke of Berwick had written from Grenoble, May 4th, to Louis XIV., respecting Dillon—"His activity and his vigilance cannot be surpassed; and your Majesty scarcely has an officer more capable of serving you well." And, when the campaign was over, Lieutenant-General Comte de Medavi "rendered justice to the care which M. Dillon had taken, during the campaign, to place the intrenched camp and works in the environs of Briançon in such a state of defence, that everything was in the best order there, for excluding the enemy from that leading pass into Dauphiné; as well as facilitating the transmission, to other parts of the frontier, of detachments, able to resist such enterprises, as might be directed against them."

In Sicily, in 1709, the deficiencies of its Spanish Viceroy, the Marquis de los Balbases, alluded to as "a poor creature," were so well compensated by the ability of Count O'Mahony's arrangements, with the native militia, and regular troops from Spain, for the defence of the island, that it had nothing to fear from invasion. "The Neapolitans," says an Allied letter in June, "who are the chief promoters of it, and who used to represent it as a slight matter, to be undertaken with 3000 or 4000 men, and 6 ships, do now, when one comes to talk in detail of the execution, insist, that there should be 10,000 men sent, with a good battering train, and they all agree, that it will be necessary to besiege Messina, by sea and land. The enemies have, in the island, at least 4000 regular foot, and 1500 horse, commanded by Mahoni, under the Viceroy, who is a poor creature." The naval strength of the English and the Dutch this year in the Mediterranean was such, that they took very considerable prizes; and these advantages led, as might be expected, to an attempt in the direction of Sicily, though not with such a result as its contrivers would have wished. For, alleges my account from "Madrid, July 30th," on the authority of a courier expressly despatched from Sicily, "a squadron of English vessels appeared off the coasts of the kingdom, from which 2 landings were effected; one between Trapani and Castellamare, and the other near Melazzo. But the Sicilians, sustained by some veteran corps of Spanish troops, received their enemies with such vigour, that they were forced to re-embark with precipitation, after having lost about 600 men, including those who were drowned, ere they could regain their shipping." These unsuccessful landings in Sicily seem to have been predatory attempts, from the Neapolitan territory, through the maritime aid of the English, to retaliate the successful hostile visits from Sicily, the year before, to the Bay, &c., of Naples.

On the side of Germany, in 1709, the Allies under the Elector of Hanover, had formed a design, the accomplishment of which, by rendering them masters of Franche-Comté and Lorrain, by cutting off all communication between France and Alsace, and by *other* results, would have been a very severe, if not a fatal, blow to Louis. But, by a defeat of the Imperial General, Count de Mercy, at Rumersheim, the contemplated design was rendered impracticable, and the Elector of Hanover was prevented undertaking anything further; the French army under the Marshal d'Harcourt recovering Hagembach, encamping on the ground where the Germans had previously posted themselves, and levying contributions in Baden, and all the country about Landau. In the list of the Marshal d'Harcourt's Lieutenant-Generals were Lee and Dorrington; but neither accompanied by any Irish troops, nor having been so situated, during the campaign, as to gain any particular distinction.

T

Among the General Officers serving under the Marshal de Villars, in Flanders, in 1710, were Major-General Michael Roth, Brigadiers Murrough O'Brien and Christopher Nugent; and there were, in the Marshal's army, the 5 Irish battalions of Lee, Dorrington, O'Brien, Galmoy, O'Donnell, and the 2 squadrons (or cavalry regiment) of Nugent. The Allies, under Eugene and Marlborough, though baulked in their leading object of investing Arras, yet were so superior in strength to the French, as to hold them in check during this campaign, and reduce Douay, Bethune, St. Venant, and Aire; those 4 sieges, however, costing the Confederates, by their own admission, upwards of 19,200 men, killed and wounded; but far more, according to the French.* In the very able defence of Bethune, which, says an Allied writer, "held out much longer than any body expected, and longer than any place of the same force was ever held before,"—the loss of the Allies in taking it having been above 3360 men, killed and wounded—the Governor, Lieutenant-General Vauban, a worthy nephew of the great engineer, had, as next-in-command, or Maréchal de Camp, the Kilkenny veteran, Michael Roth. And, remarks my French contemporary historian,—" M. de Vauban was usefully seconded by M. Rhot, Maréchal de Camp, who availed himself of the opportunity of frequently signalizing his zeal for the service of the King, his capacity for, and his great devotion to, the military profession, and of giving similar proofs of valour to those he had manifested in numerous encounters." Another French authority states of Roth at Bethune—"Commanding under M. du Puy Vauban, besieged in this place, he gave the most decisive evidences of valour, of prudence, and of firmness, and very much contributed to the fine defence which M. du Puy Vauban made, during 35 days of open trenches. M. de Rothe," it is added, "headed numbers of the sorties there." For this, Louis XIV. rewarded Roth with a Commandership of the Order of St. Louis, as his countryman, Lee, was rewarded, in 1708, for similar conduct, under the Marshal de Boufflers at Lisle. In Flanders, this year, "2 brigades d'officiers Irlandois" are officially mentioned; and the supernumerary or reformed officers, who were distinguished at the great sieges of Lisle and Tournay, also took part, with much honour to themselves, in the gallant defences of Douay, Bethune, and Aire. Those, especially, belonging to the Regiments of Dorrington, Galmoy, O'Donnell, Bourke, and Berwick, for their services this campaign, and henceforward to the end of the war in Flanders, were, as a mark of Louis's favour, allowed the same subsistence in winter-quarters as officers *en pied.* In the Duke of Berwick's campaign for 1710 against the Imperialists and Piedmontese, General Rebender advanced by Mount Genevre to dislodge some of the French posts; but Lieutenant-General Arthur Dillon, from his camp at Briançon, so harassed the invader by detachments, that he had very soon to retire to Sesanne.

The Irish, in 1710, signalized themselves most effectively in Spain,

* "This campaign," alleges the English historian, Salmon, "tho' not so bloody as some others, did not cost the Allies less than 25,000 men, upon a modest computation; and, if I should say, it cost them 10,000,000 of money, I might speak within compass. At this expense, we added, to the dominions of the Dutch and the Imperialists, the towns of Douay and Aire, Bethune and St. Venant . . . . But the principal design of the Allies against Arras miscarried; that town being so covered by the French army, that they had no opportunity of investing it." To losses by killed and wounded, a very considerable addition must, of course, be made, on the score of those who die by *sickness,* especially in a war of *sieges.*

where Philip V., and his Austrian competitor, the Archduke Charles, were early in the field. Among the General Officers of King Philip, were Lieutenant-General Count Daniel O'Mahony, (returned with honour from Sicily) and Major-General Don Henry Crofton. Among the royal regiments were 2 of Irish infantry, newly formed of deserters from the enemy, in Catalonia, and Portugal. These regiments were commanded by Colonel Don Demetrio (or Dermod) Mac Auliffe, and Colonel Don John de Comerford; the former, head, or chief, of the ancient sept of the Mac Auliffes, or Clan-Auliffe, of the Barony of Duhallow, in the north-east of the County of Cork; the latter, whose name was established since the time of the Anjou-Norman King Johan, or John, in Erin, was long of baronial eminence, at Danganmore, in the County of Kilkenny; and, in France, as well as in Spain, has been distinguished by its gallant officers, including several Chevaliers of St. Louis.* With those 2 Irish regiments, there was a 3rd brigaded under Colonel Mac Donnell. In May, some of the Irish were engaged with success against the miquelets; and, in June, Count O'Mahony, with 2600 men, seized at Cervera, a hostile magazine of articles of clothing for 4500 men; at the Castle of Calaf, which he subsequently reduced, and levelled, destroyed a great quantity of the enemy's provisions; and, according to the Jacobite historian Plunkett, "still advanced towards the sea, takeing of little houlds, and obligeing the country to submission, until he came within 4 leagues of Barcelona." After 2 cavalry-encounters, with varied success, at Almenara and Penalva, in July and August, the hostile main armies came to a general engagement on the 20th of the latter month, near Saragossa. The Archduke Charles's army, commanded by the famous Count de Stahremberg, was superior both in numbers and condition to that of King Philip, commanded by the Marquis de Bay, or from 23,000 to 24,000, against but 15,000, combatants; the latter being reduced to that number from 17,000, by having been obliged to live, for several days, without bread, or only upon such fruit as they could pick up, and un-wholesome water. A warm cannonade from about day-break was the prelude to a closer contest between 12 and 3 o'clock; in which King Philip's army was defeated, with the loss of most of its artillery, colours and standards, and between 3000 and 4000 men; the enemy stating their loss at but 2000. In this engagement, Count O'Mahony commanded on the right of the royal army, at the head of the cavalry. With the King's Guards and Spanish dragoons, he charged so furiously the Portuguese

* An Irish writer, in 1723, referring to the finding at Barnanely, or the Devil's Bit, County Tipperary, in 1692, by some labourers digging turf, of an enchased gold cap, or provincial crown, resembling the close, half-crown, half-helmet, diadem of the Eastern Empire, notices the family of Comerford, in relating, that such an interesting relic of Irish antiquity would have been melted down, but for "a curious gentleman," Joseph Comerford, Esq. "This gentleman," it is added, "being *render'd incapable, by reason of his religion, to purchase lands in his own country*, has bought the Marquisate of Anglure, with a good estate, upon the river Aule, in Champaigne, which he has settled, in default of issue from himself, upon his brother Captain Luke Comerford, (an officer of great esteem in the French service) and his heirs male; and, in default of such issue, upon his kinsman, Sir John Comerford (a Major-General and Colonel of a Regiment of Foot in the service of the King of Spain) and his male issue." The last-named gentleman is the officer mentioned in the text. My French MS. specifies 7 Comerfords of the same branch, inclusive of Luke previously alluded to, as having been officers of the Irish Brigade, in the Regiments of Dillon, Lee, and Bulkeley; of whom 6 were Captains, 1 Lieutenant, and 4 of the 7 were Chevaliers of St. Louis.

horse of the enemy's left under General Hamilton, that they were broken, routed, and driven into the Ebro, where a multitude of them were drowned. The Count next fell upon the hostile cannon; although they were most bravely defended by Colonel Bourgard, (who received several wounds) took those guns; but, not being able to carry them off, hamstringed 400 mules attached to the train; and then, although assailed upon all sides by Stanhope's cavalry, and some corps of infantry, he cut his way back to his own army, with 5 standards won from the enemy, and escorted the King on his retreat.* The conduct of the Count, in this engagement, was censured by some, as having contributed to the loss of the day, owing, it was objected, to his having pushed his 1st success too far; to which it was answered, that, notwithstanding the very inferior number and condition of the royal army, if the behaviour of the King's Guards, and dragoons, under the Count, had been equalled by the rest of the royal cavalry, the battle would have been gained, instead of lost. The 3 battalions of Mac Auliffe, Comerford, and Mac Donnell, or "Brigade of Irish infantry of Castelar," were likewise much distinguished.

Philip V. reached Madrid on the 24th, but being unable to remain there, had, by September 9th, to quit it, with his Queen, and little Heir to the Crown, or Prince of Asturias, for Valladolid, the ancient residence of the Kings of Castile. Ere he left Madrid, he "summoned all the Councils, wherein he told them, that his affairs were in a very bad condition; that he did not pretend to constrain any body to follow him; and that, in his desperate situation, his sole resource was in the hearts of his subjects. This did not hinder, however, great numbers of persons of quality from following him; insomuch that, when he quitted Madrid, he had 1000 coaches in his train; *almost all the inhabitants followed for 3 leagues, wishing their Majesties a happy return; and obliging them to stop several times, that they might weep over the Prince of Asturias, who sate in his mother's lap, sick of an ague!*" The King arrived, the 16th, at Valladolid, where he was joined, the 20th, by the illustrious Duke of Vendome from France, to act as Generalissimo against the Archduke's army, which had penetrated to Madrid. The 28th, that city was entered in state by the Archduke, who, however, in reference to his chief supporters, the *Protestant* English and Dutch, met with no better reception, than as "CHARLES III., BY THE GRACE OF THE HERETICS, THE CATHOLIC KING!"—and, from September till November, while his mixed English, Dutch, Huguenot, German, Catalonian, Portuguese, and Italian army occupied the metropolis and the adjacent parts of Castile, the conduct of those intruders was a compound of insults to national feeling, oppressive exactions, and outrageous sacrileges. Meantime Philip, as really the King of the people's choice, and the Duke of Vendome as "*the Liberator, the man of the right hand of God, destined from on high to restore the Monarchy,*" obtained, from the loyal, patriotic, and religious enthusiasm of the nation, abundant supplies of every kind; so that the royal army, re-established, increased in number, and zealously aided by the honest peasantry as irregulars, or guerillas, con-

---

* O'Mahony, known as the "fameux Mahoni," has likewise been termed, "the *Murat* of his day." Here and elsewhere, I make use, among my authorities, of Targe's Histoire de l'Avénement de la Maison de Bourbon au Trône d'Espagne, published at Paris in 1772. But the Chevalier de Bellerive, as a "témoin oculaire" in this important campaign under Vendome, is most satisfactory, from the justice he does to the Irish.

tinually narrowed the quarters, diminished the subsistence, and cut off the detachments, of the detested invaders, till they had to abandon Madrid, in despair, for Catalonia. The King, and the Duke, entering that capital in triumph, December 3rd, quitted it, on the 6th, to pursue the retreating enemy; whose van, or main body, the more advanced upon the retreat under the Count de Stahremberg, was considerably separated from the rear under Lieutenant-General Stanhope, owing to the difficulty of subsisting such numbers together, in a devastated country. Stanhope had 7 battalions, and 8 squadrons, all English but 1 Portuguese battalion, and making about 5500 men. The King, and the Duke, coming by surprise upon Stanhope, the 8th, at Brihuega, breached, and entered it, the 9th, and compelled the Englishman, after a brave resistance, in which he spent nearly all his ammunition, and lost about 600 men, to surrender, with the rest, in the evening, as prisoners of war; even while Stahremberg's 9 signal-guns, from Campo de las Vinnas, announced his encampment for the night there, or but 2 leagues off, on his approach to the rescue! The 2 armies—Stahremberg's experienced troops, about 12,500, Vendome's in great part new levies, about 17,000, and the artillery on each side equal, or 22 pieces,—met, on the 10th, at Villaviciosa, and, from about 1 o'clock in the afternoon, manœuvred, cannonaded, or more closely and decisively engaged, until about 6 in the evening, when the conflict terminated, amidst the darkness of December. After acting in every way worthy of his designation as "a 2nd Eugene," and being so vigorously sustained by his veteran forces that they are stated to have "performed such actions as might almost pass for supernatural," Stahremberg was defeated, with the loss of several thousands killed or taken there, all his artillery, so many colours and standards, as, with those captured at Brihuega, made 68, his own equipage, his military chest, containing 30,000 doubloons, (each worth 15 livres, 5 sols, French money,) a quantity of muskets, horses, mules, &c.; and was subsequently pursued through Aragon into Catalonia, suffering so much *en route*, that he reached Barcelona, in January, 1711, with only from 4000 to 5000 men. The successes of Brihuega and Villaviciosa are alleged to have cost King Philip but between 2000 and 3000 men, killed or wounded; while the Allies, by their advance to Madrid, are reported to have lost, in addition to their slain, ere the close of December, above 11,250 men, as prisoners of war.

From the battle of Saragossa, to the termination of this very important and glorious campaign—which was *a mortal wound to the cause of the Allies, and their Austrian candidate for royalty in the Peninsula,*— the Irish proved themselves "good men and true" to King Philip V. In the operations that led to the recovery of Madrid, Count O'Mahony was active at the head of the dragoons of the royal army, including the Irish regiment recently Crofton's, but transferred to David Sarsfield, 5th Lord Viscount Kilmallock, Governor of Badajos, and brother, and successor in the title, to the Lord Dominick, previously noticed in this history. On the left wing at Villaviciosa under Vendome, the Maison du Roy, or King's Horse Guards, and the dragoons, were, as at Saragossa, with the Count, who flanked the right of the enemy, upon which were the Archduke's Guards. And the Count had a terrible contest to maintain against Stahremberg, who fought there, with a square body of above 6000 of his choicest German infantry, supported by cavalry and artillery. In fact, the battle was in Stahremberg's favour, there, and in the centre, until he was finally taken in the rear, with a reserve of 15 squadrons of King Philip's cavalry, under the Marquis de Val-de-Canas, and Count O'Mahony. "M. de Vendome," writes King Philip the day after the action, "seeing that our centre gave ground, and that our left of cavalry did not make an impression upon the right," *i. e.*, of Stahremberg, "believed it was necessary to think of retiring towards Torrija, and gave the order for that purpose; but, as we were going there with a considerable portion of the troops, we were informed, that the Marquis de Val-de-Canas, and Mahoni, had charged the enemy's infantry with the cavalry which they had under their orders, and had handled it very roughly. . . . Which caused us immediately to adopt the resolution of marching back, with the rest of the army"—that is, the rest, except the 15 squadrons under Val-de-Canas, and O'Mahony, and also except the right wing under the King himself; which wing alone had fought successfully, but, as is evident, *should* have retired, as well as the rest, if the enemy were victorious in the other 2 portions of the battle, as the King shows they *would* have been, from the order given to retreat, even by such an experienced commander as Vendome; and which order was actually in process of execution, till the cause for countermanding it, afforded by the conduct of the 15 squadrons, under Val-de-Canas, and O'Mahony. Indeed, it was only to the intervention of a night, the more obscure from a great mist, to a want of some artillery by O'Mahony, and to his pursuing dragoon-horses being exhausted, without any forage for them, that even Stahremberg himself, and the troops he still retained about him, would seem to have been indebted, through a stratagem on his part, for escaping at all! Ere the night "had entirely set in," says my French authority, "the brave Comte de Mahoni, having no cannon to fire upon those troops, invested them on one side, and then sent a drummer to M. de Staremberg, to summon him to surrender. This General, who had gotten into very advantageous ground with what remained of his infantry and the fragments of several regiments who had retired thither, having perceived how the advantage of this position, the night, and a very thick fog would render it the more easy for him to effect an honourable retreat, kept the drummer with him until the following day, and exerted his utmost possible speed, all that night, to leave the field behind him, by making off in the direction of Cifuentes." Nevertheless, the Irish officer intercepted 700 of the enemy's most valuably-loaded mules, referred to by a British historian, in noting how "M. Mahoni took some hundred mules, laden with all the plunder of Castile!" It is added elsewhere of him— "The Comte de Mahoni acquired a great deal of glory on the battle-day of Villaviciosa, at the head of the dragoons. The King was so satisfied with him, that he conferred upon him a Commandership of the Order of St. Jacques," *i. e.*, Jago, "producing a rent of 15,000 livres." Of Major-General Henry Crofton, in this engagement, and at Brihuega, it is stated, that "he was very much distinguished in the 2 actions, where he did every thing that could be expected from so valiant a man; he charged, with an incredible ardour, the English and the Germans." Of the 3 Irish infantry Regiments of Mac Donnell, Mac Auliffe, and Comerford, it is observed—"The Sieurs de Magdonel, Makaoli, Combefort, Colonels of the Brigade of Irish Infantry of Castelar, each acted at the head of his battalion with a great deal of courage and conduct, as they had already done at Saragossa."

The Chevalier de Bellerive supplies these particulars, with respect to Lord Kilmallock's Regiment of Dragoons, his Lordship's death, and that of the Marquis d'Albeville, (son of King James II.'s Ambassador in Holland,) the Chevalier O'Healy, &c. When the 2 armies were so near, (or within carabine-shot) that almost every movement of each was perceptible, "M. de Staremberg caused to be brought to his right wing, a battery commanded by an officer wearing a red mantle, and mounted upon a white horse, who let fly from the van into the Regiment of Irish Dragoons of Mylord Kilmaloc, which was upon our left, and which nearly closed it up. This regiment was not long without feeling the fire of that battery; the 1st ball killing a horse, and then 2 dragoons. Mylord Kilmaloc, its Colonel, being struck by a cannon-shot, 1 of his sons caused him to be carried to the rear of the regiment. The father, fixing his eyes upon him, said to him,—'My dear son, let me at least expire within your arms, since I have so short a time to live.'—'Father,' he replied to him, 'it is necessary for me to go, where my duty, and the service of Philip V., summon me.'—'What! my dear son, you refuse me that consolation, and you abandon me, at the hour of my death!'—'My dear father, I go to avenge it, or to find my own, with the regiment!'—The cannon-shot fell there like hail; the enemy themselves were surprised to see men so firm, as immoveable and insensible to the terrible discharges of their artillery, and they knew by that what was the courage and the intrepidity of those brave dragoons. . . . Although this regiment had been very much weakened during the cannonade from the right wing of M. de Staremberg, it did not cease to charge the enemy's troops with such an impetuous ardour, that they could not resist it. . . . The Lieutenant-Colonel of this regiment received a musket-shot through his body while charging the enemy, and the Marquis d'Ableville, 1 of its brave Captains, sabre in hand, lost his life there, all covered with wounds, after having won admiration by many brave and intrepid actions. The Chevalier de Heli, Captain in the same regiment, distinguished himself in it, having had 2 horses killed under him by the enemy's cannon; and his brother, a Cadet in his company, was slain there." Their Colonel, Lord Kilmallock, is described to have been 1 of those officers, whose rare merit, and sincere devotion to the service of King Philip, caused their deaths to be very much regretted by his Catholic Majesty, who testified his sensibility, on that account, to their relatives. Of the old Milesian name of O'Callaghan—which has been successively connected with royalty, chiefdom, and nobility, at home, and represented by several officers in the service of France, as well as Spain, abroad, but most distinguished in that of Great Britain and Ireland—my gallant authority, last cited, in alluding to the conduct of the Spanish cavalry Regiment of Milan, and its Colonel, at Villaviciosa, observes—"The Sieur Ockalagan, being, for the 3rd time, in the thick of the fight, where he defended the standards of Milan with a proud intrepidity, received a sword-thrust through his body, and many wounds, by which he was, for some time disfigured." * The Major, likewise, of the very

* Of O'Callaghans in the service of Spain, besides the valiant Colonel of the Regiment of Milan, wounded at Villaviciosa, there were various subordinate officers. In France, several O'Callaghans were Captains in the Regiments of Dillon, of Dorrington or Roth, of O'Brien or Clare, and of Fitz-James. The chief modern military representative of the O'Callaghans, referred to as in the service of Great Britain and Ireland, was of the titled or "Lismore" branch, Lieutenant-General the Honour

fine Spanish cavalry Regiment of Vallejo, "an Irishman by nation, rendered himself remarkable by his courage at Villaviciosa, where he received a musket-shot in the arm, while charging the enemy."

Stahremberg, as he hastened towards Catalonia, was continually harassed by Count O'Mahony, who completed his important services this campaign, by capturing, after a short resistance, at the Castle of Illueca, (or Illuesca) a Spanish Lieutenant-General, "who had gone over to the party of the Archduke," and the detachment which that Lieutenant-General had with him in the Castle—"consisting," according to the Marquis de Quincy, "of 660 men, among whom there were 150 reformed officers, who had lost their companies, either in the battle of Villaviciosa, or in the retreat of the Comte Staremberg." At Saragossa, too, which was entered by King Philip's troops on the night of December 31st, 1710, an Irish officer ended "this wonderful year" well. The dismounted dragoons of the royal force were ordered to occupy the Castle of the Inquisition, in which, as containing a considerable magazine that could not be removed, Stahremberg, on retiring, had left several thousand pounds of powder; with a train lighted, so as to blow up the building, and all who might enter it. "And," to use the words of the account, "the match, which was in a very forward state, would have effected its purpose, but for the precaution of an Irish Lieutenant-Colonel, who had been despatched there to command those dragoons, and who, having soon detected this stratagem, rendered it useless." The Irish, in King Philip's army, were increased, after the victory of Villaviciosa, by numbers of their countrymen, who, as having been made prisoners, and being Catholics, agreed to pass into his service. Such were the very remarkable and most decisive results of the contest of 1710, in the Peninsula; by which, after having been a defeated fugitive, driven from his capital, Philip V. found himself, writes Lord Macaulay, "*much safer at Madrid than his grandfather at Paris*," and "*all hope of conquering Spain, in Spain, was at an end!*"

The Whig Cabinet in England, by its impolitic prosecution of the High-Church Doctor Sacheverell, in 1710, having elevated him to an importance in public opinion, which led to the eventual downfal of that Cabinet, and proportionately raised the hopes of the Stuarts and their friends at home and abroad, it was suggested to Louis XIV., that there could not be a more favourable opportunity for another expedition by King James to Scotland, to recover his dominions, even with no larger force to accompany him, than the Irish troops in France. The Stuart Memorial to Louis's Minister, the Marquis de Torcy, dated August 29th, having noted of the attempt on Scotland in 1708, "that both friends and enemies acknowledged, that, *if his Britannic Majesty had landed then, all Scotland would have declared for him, the Bank of England would have been shut up, and consequently the Government of England overturned, and the League dissolved*" against France, remarks—"If his Most Christian Majesty will find this expedition of importance enough to consider it as a capital object; in that case, money, arms, and ammunition, as well as ships and troops, will be found, without any difficulty; and he

able Sir Robert William O'Callaghan, G.C.B., born in October, 1777, deceased in June, 1840, Commander-in-Chief of the Forces in Scotland and India, 46 years in the army, and specially decorated for his bravery, during the war against Napoleon I., at the battles of Maida, Vittoria, the Pyrenees, the Nivelle, the Nive, and Orthez. I am of a totally different or *Ulster* race of that name.

will likewise find sea-officers, who will undertake it, and who, with God's assistance, will accomplish it. . . . His Britannic Majesty, considering how difficult it would be to transport a greater number, has limited his demand to *the Irish troops, his own subjects;* who, at the end of the campaign, will be scarce 3000 effective men. What absolutely determines his Majesty to ask the Irish is, that they speak the same language, and are accustomed to the hardy manner of living of the country; and that, of each Irish regiment 2 or 3 may be formed, by incorporating with them the new levies of the country; besides, that *it will be impossible to keep the Irish in France, after they know that the King is landed in Scotland.* . . . The port of Dunkirk has its advantages for the embarkation, on account of the neighbourhood of the troops, and the shortness of the passage. But the secret can never be kept: for every thing that is done there is known the next day at Ostend; and, when once the English and the Dutch have discovered the design, they will be always in a condition to thwart it. It appears then, that Brest would be more suitable, because the enemies could not easily hinder the vessels from sailing from that port, *as was seen by experience, during the war in Ireland.* In case the preference is given to that port, the Irish troops should be put into winter-quarters in the neighbouring provinces. It might be likewise examined, whether Portpassage, near Fontarabia, was fit for embarkation. In that case, the Irish regiments might be sent to that quarter, as if they were to go to serve in Spain; and his Britannic Majesty might repair thither, under the same pretext; and his removing, at a distance from his kingdoms, would conceal the design. In case the troops embark at Brest, or at Portpassage, they may land any where on the west coast of Scotland, from Kirkcudbright to the mouth of the river Clyde. . . . The squadron, sailing from Brest or from Portpassage, may steer their course through St. George's Channel, or round the west of Ireland; the 1st is the shortest course; but is esteemed the most dangerous. Yet the English merchant-ships daily pass through that Channel, at all seasons. *In sailing along the coast of Ireland, some Irish officers may be landed, with arms, &c., in order to put the inhabitants in a condition to rise.* . . . It may be added, that *the Catholics, who are at least 6 to 1 Protestant, are reduced to such despair, by the last persecution of the English Government, that they are more disposed than ever to hazard all, and to undertake every thing, in order to free themselves from the oppression they suffer.*"*

The proposed expedition, however, did not take place; it appearing better in France, on maturer consideration, *not* to interrupt, by the "disturbing force" of such an enterprise, the favourable consequences to be expected from the numerous politico-religious gatherings of Doctor Sacheverell's High-Church followers, with "white ribbons in their hats," &c., when, after that damaging termination of *his* trial for the Whigs, which led to *their* ejection from power, "he made a triumphal progress

* The editor of the collection of native Irish or Gaelic Jacobite songs, entitled "The Poets and Poetry of Munster," likewise notes, on "the frequent allusions to France and Spain throughout these popular songs," how, in consequence of the various tyrannical enactments of the Penal Code in Ireland, "the old Irish longed for an appeal to arms, and earnestly desired the co-operation of their expatriated kinsman, whose military achievements, in foreign countries, had won the admiration of Europe."

through England; and was received in college-halls, town-halls, and private mansions, with the pomp of a Sovereign, and the reverence of a Saint." The Marshal de Villars, as a Frenchman and a Jacobite, spoke in "raptures" of the Doctor's "monster meetings," (to use a more modern designation) sagaciously terming those assemblages, "*our* people." For the dissolution of the Whig Parliament, and the ensuing elections, that were owing to those "monster meetings," established in office the Tories, or that party which was as favourable to peace, instead of war, with France, as it was attached to the House of Stuart, in preference to the House of Hanover. "Although the Whigs left no stone unturned to promote their interest," says the contemporary Scotch Jacobite loyalist, and Tory nationalist, Lockhart, "the Tories got the better of them by far, in most of the elections in England. Neither were they less diligent, on all sides, in Scotland. The Whigs *there*, to the fears of Popery and the Pretender, added the danger that Presbytery was in"— as the "Established Church" in that country, through Whig-Revolutionism. "The Tories spoke little above board, but underhand represented, that now or never was the time to do something effectually for the King, and, *by restoring him, dissolve the Union.*" In Ireland, too, while still undelivered from the viceregal yoke of that infamous Whig stimulator of Penal-Code persecution and spoliation, the Earl of Wharton, (whose character has been duly damned, in the prose of Swift, and the verse of Pope,) the spirit of Tory hostility to the Whigs, which preceded the ejection of the latter from power there, evinced itself, among other ways, by a nocturnal mutilation, in which 2 students of Trinity College were concerned, of the obnoxious statue of William III., the great Whig idol in College Green, Dublin. "On Sunday, the 25th of June [O. S.] at night," complains an exasperated Anglo-Whig authority, "the Tories very much defac'd the statue of King William, out of spite to the present Government, which paid so profound a respect to his *glorious memory*. The statue was erected by the City of Dublin, after the battle of the Boyne; and these ruffians twisted the sword it had in one hand, wrested the truncheon out of the other, daub'd the face with dirt, and offer'd it other such indignities"—as, it may be added, nothing better, in *their* eyes, than the representation of another *Cromwell!* The Tory successor to the Viceroyalty of Ireland was the great Duke of Ormonde, accompanied by the recent legal defender of Dr. Sacheverell, Sir Constantine Phipps, as Lord Chancellor; who may be noticed here, for endeavouring, though unsuccessfully, to put an end to those insulting anniversary displays of domineering Cromwello-Williamitism, or Whiggery, connected with the Dutchman's statue, which have been unfortunately continued, under the factions and sectarian modification of Orangeism, to the present century, till at length abolished, as equally opposed to correct national feeling, religious propriety, and public tranquillity. The Duke likewise gratified the popular or Jacobite sentiment amongst his countrymen, by wearing the white rose himself on the anniversary of the birth of the so-called "Pretender," or James III., in June, and by ornamenting the collars of his dogs with rosettes of white satin; as thus alluded to in the song—

"Our noble Ormond he is drest,
A rose is glancing on his breast,
His famous hounds have doff'd his crest,
White roses deck them over."

JAMES BUTLER,
(DUKE OF ORMONDE.)

To the proportionable apprehension and vexation of the Whig or Revolution "ascendancy," whose territorial and political position was so incompatible with the justice to its victims, expected from a Stuart "restoration."

In 1711, the 5 battalions of Lee, O'Brien, Dorrington, Galmoy, O'Donnell, and the 2 squadrons of Nugent, with Major-General Michael Roth, and Brigadiers Murrough O'Brien and Christopher Nugent, were attached to the army, opposed, in Flanders, under the Marshal de Villars, to the Duke of Marlborough; and the battalion of Dillon, that of Bourke, and the 2 battalions of Berwick, with Lieutenant-General Arthur Dillon and Major-General Walter Bourke, were attached to the army of Dauphiné, opposed, under the Marshal Duke of Berwick, to the Duke of Savoy. But, in the published accounts of the general operations of either Marshal, no fuller notice occurs of any immediate connexion of the Irish with such operations, than has been previously given in my biographies of the Colonels of the Irish regiments. In the sketch of the military career of Murrough O'Brien, an allusion has been made to an excellent manœuvre of his at Pallué, through which, after the passing of Villars's lines in August, by Marlborough, the important city of Cambray was covered, or saved, "until Villars came up with his whole army, and forced Marlborough to confine his operations to the siege of the small town of Bouchain," the reduction of which was his *last* achievement. In Spain, Count Daniel O'Mahony was engaged in the movements by which Philip V.'s forces, in February, narrowed the enemy's territory in Catalonia by 2-3rds; and the Count continued to act, during that campaign, under the Duke of Vendome. In March, Major-General Henry Crofton, beating the famous miquelet leader, Chover, out of several mountain-passes, in the Viguerie of Cervera, occupied Solsona, where that chief had his quarters, and likewise seized upon the advantageous post of Ingualada. There, during his stay, Crofton brought in quantities of provisions from the surrounding country, notwithstanding the constant opposition of the armed inhabitants; and, finally, when a force of regular and irregular troops, to which his was but a handful, were despatched by Stahremberg to surprise him, he baffled the design, and effected a judicious retreat, in spite of such a superior enemy.*
From the scarcity of provisions on the side of Vendome, and the delay in the arrival of reinforcements to Stahremberg, this campaign was passed merely in irregular warfare, mutual cannonading, and attacks on some places, such as Venasque, Castel-Leon, Tortosa and Cardona, with results mostly in favour of Vendome. In these occurrences, the Irish, of course, had their share; though those of their nation (except O'Mahony and Crofton as above-mentioned) are only referred to in the account of the winter-quarters, as "the Brigade of the Irish at Tervel," or rather "Teruel," enumerated of old among the conquests of the Cid.

By the close of 1711, and the earlier portion of 1712, the Tory, or Jacobite Cabinet in England—partly anxious to terminate a contest with

* Crofton (with whom this is *our* final meeting on active military duty) died a Lieutenant-General in Spain in 1722, to the last a Jacobite loyalist; and, as such, considered "a great loss," particularly by his countryman, the Duke of Ormonde, in the various measures with which that exiled nobleman was occupied abroad, to bring "the auld Stuarts back again." Lieutenant-General Crofton left, as his heir, James Talbot, an Irish Catholic gentleman, much distinguished in the English Jacobite rising against George I. in 1715, and who, after surviving the dangers connected with that movement and its suppression, was an officer in Spain.

France, which they considered to have become as unnecessary, as it was ruinously expensive, to their country, and partly desirous for peace, the better to concert measures for retaining the Stuart line on the throne, after Queen Anne's decease, in opposition to the family of Hanover, favoured by the Whigs, or Revolutionists—decided upon dismissing from the command of the British forces the celebrated John Duke of Marlborough, as an obstinate advocate, from selfish or pecuniary motives, for a continuance of the war. Lord Mahon states the yearly income of the Duke of Marlborough so high as £54,825, and that of his Duchess as £9500, making for *both* £64,325 per annum!—to say nothing "of Blenheim, of parliamentary grants, of gifts of marriage-portions from the Queen for *their* daughters." This £64,325 a year Lord Mahon designates as a sum, "infinitely greater than could *now* be awarded to the highest favour, or the most eminent achievements;" since, in Queen Anne's reign, "the rate of salaries, even when nominally no larger than at present, was, in fact, 2 or 3 times more considerable, from the intermediate depreciation of money." It appears, likewise, according to the able continuation of Sir James Macintosh's history of England, that the peace finally concluded with France, in spite of Marlborough, and his friends, the Whigs, reduced taxation from £7,000,000 a year to but £2,000,000 at most, and that the war cost England £48,500,000; of which sum, *owing to the neglect of the Dutch, and other so-called Allies, to defray their due proportions of the expense England had been obliged to contribute* £19,000,000 *more than her just share!* There, says Dr. Johnson, "the people, who had been amused with bonfires, and triumphal processions, and looked with idolatry on the General and his friends, who, as they thought, had made England the arbitress of nations, were confounded, between shame and rage, when they found that 'mines had been exhausted, and millions destroyed,' to secure the Dutch, or aggrandize the Emperor, without any advantage to ourselves; that we had been bribing our neighbours to fight their own quarrel; and that, amongst our enemies, we might number our Allies." In short, alleges the Doctor, "the war was unnecessarily protracted to fill the pockets of Marlborough, and it would have been continued without end, if he could have continued his annual plunder." The Whigs, on the other hand, did their utmost, to frustrate, if possible, this peace-policy of the Tories; hoping, if by no other means, to effect their object, through a great public appeal, in London, to *sectarian* prejudices. They, writes Salmon, "had recourse to their old expedient of spiriting up the mob, and raising an insurrection, in order to compel their Sovereign to comply with their demands. To this purpose, they provided themselves with the effigies of the Devil, the Pope, and the Pretender, to be carried in solemn procession, on the 17th of November, being the anniversary of Queen Elizabeth's accession. But their design was unluckily discover'd, and their poppets seiz'd, on the evening before they were to have been exposed; and the Trained Bands were order'd to be under arms, to prevent any disturbance." Marlborough's Tory and Jacobite successor in command was the gallant and generous James Butler, 13th Earl and 2nd Duke of Ormonde; of whom, as contrasted with his predecessor, it was remarked, in the English House of Lords—" Nobody could doubt the Duke of Ormonde's bravery; but he was not like a certain Lord, who led troops to the slaughter, that a great number of officers might be knocked on the head in a battle, or against stone walls, in order to fill his pockets, by disposing of their commissions!"* This observation of Earl Powlet was such a severe cut at the blood-soaked money-bags of Marlborough, that a challenge from the latter was the consequence; which, however, through the interposition of friends, and her Majesty's authority, came to nothing. And no wonder that such *was* the case, as, relates a London contemporary,—"I remember the town was very merry, that our intrepid General should pitch upon a man, who could not see to the point of his sword, to wreak his vengeance on!"

The French army of Flanders in 1712, under the Marshal de Villars, and containing the same Irish corps as in 1711, was estimated at 90,000 men. The Allied army, under Prince Eugene of Savoy, though diminished by the secession of the British under the Duke of Ormonde, as ordered *not* to act any longer against France, was still, through the great efforts of the Dutch, 110,000 strong, or the more numerous by 20,000 men. Eugene, having taken Quesnoy in July, proceeded to besiege Landrecy, after the reduction of which, he calculated upon prostrating France at his feet; the line of communication he made for his supplies, from Marchiennes by Denain, being presumptuously designated, in his camp, "the high road to Paris!" But Villars, by a series of successful operations, commencing with the well-contrived attack at Denain in July, and followed up, till October, by the capture of several military posts, and fortified towns, including Marchiennes, Douay, Quesnoy, and Bouchain, signally chastised Eugene, as the adversary of peace in Europe; having weakened the opposing Allied forces this campaign by not less than 45 battalions, and several squadrons, and having taken considerably more than 400 pieces of Allied artillery, besides an enormous amount of ammunition, provisions, &c. And all this he achieved at a comparatively trifling loss; thereby rescuing his country from such a depressed condition, that he was styled "the saviour of France!" The Irish were not without sharing in the success at Denain, and were present at the reduction of Marchiennes. Major-General Michael Roth mounted the trenches against the Fort of Scarpe connected with the siege of Douay, in August; and the Lieutenant-General Pierce Butler, Lord Galmoy, also mounted the trenches, and was several times smartly and successfully engaged, before Quesnoy, in September.

In Spain, the Austro-Carlists—strengthened by the decease of the great Duke of Vendome,† though weakened by the withdrawal of English

* Dr. King of Oxford, in his "Anecdotes of his Own Times," says of Marlborough,—"The Duke left, at his death, more than £1,500,000 sterling!"—or a sum double or treble in value *then* to the like amount *now*. Yet he, "when he was in the last stage of life, and very infirm, would walk, from the public rooms in Bath, to his lodgings, in a cold, dark night, to *save 6 pence in chair-hire!*" Could Swift's powerful pen therefore have been better employed than it was in advocating a peace, or exploding the war-dodge for filling the Marlborough coffers?

† A contemporary British military historian, after reviewing the earlier services of the Duke of Vendome, and then particularly noting, how, in Flanders, in 1707, "he hindred the Allies from making any conquest," and, in 1708, "he made a glorious retreat at Audenarde, after the Duke of Burgundy had forced him to lose the battle," adds respecting the deceased General—"To sum up his character in a few words, he always deserved victory, and almost always atchieved it. The French owe all their reputation in Italy to him. To him Spain owes her safety, and the Most Catholic King his Crown. The King of Spain ordered his corpse to be interred in the Monastery of the Escurial; for, as he revered him living, he was desirous of shewing the utmost regard to his memory, after his death." The Irish might justly be proud of this renowned Commander's high estimation and repeated eulogies of them, as soldiers.

assistance,—maintained the contest against Philip V. in Catalonia under Stahremberg; who, in addition to his other enterprises, blocked up Girona so closely, that he calculated on famishing it into a surrender. In the irregular warfare of this campaign, the name of an Irish officer, who attained to high diplomatic as well as military rank, or Sir Patrick Lawless, occurs under the disguise of Don Patricio Laulés. His grandfather, Richard Lawless, Esq., of Kilkenny, in 1648, or during the great civil war under King Charles I., was Procurator of the Supreme Council of the Confederate Catholics of Ireland. His father was Walter Lawless, Esq., of Talbot's-Inch, near Kilkenny, and High-Sheriff of the County; his mother, Anne Bryan, sister of James Bryan of Jenkinstown in that County, Alderman, and Member for the city of Kilkenny in King James II.'s Parliament of 1689. Patrick entered the national army under that Monarch, and attained, in the war against the Revolutionists, the rank of Major, when he was taken prisoner at the battle of Aughrim, in July, 1691. After the Treaty of Limerick, he followed King James II. into France, became Gentleman of the Bedchamber there to Prince James Francis Edward Stuart, (or, in Jacobite language, King James III.,) by whom he was selected as his Envoy to Philip V. He was appointed by Philip to the command of his Irish Guard with rank as Colonel, (in which capacity, he was intrusted with the custody and conveyance of the Marquis de Leganez to Pampeluna in 1705, and of the Duke of Medina-Celi to Segovia in 1710,) was also created a Knight of the Military Order of St. Jago, and a Camp-Marshal or Major-General. Acting as Commandant (this campaign of 1712) at Benavarri, 800 miquelets occupied Venasque, in order to surprise him. But, instead of their surprising him at Benavarri, he surprised them at Venasque. They were beaten, in great disorder, out of the town, and chased into the mountains; upwards of 400 of them being slain, others made prisoners, and most of their horses, abandoned by them in their flight, being captured. In 1713-14, after the peace of Utrecht, Sir Patrick Lawless was Ambassador from Philip V. to Queen Anne, and was, at the same time, deputed by her brother, Prince James Francis Edward Stuart, as *his* representative to *her*, in order to make an arrangement with her Majesty, for a continuation, after her decease, of the Crowns of Great Britain and Ireland in *her* family, or the Stuart dynasty, as represented by the Prince, instead of permitting those Crowns to be transferred, on revolutionary principles, to the House of Hanover. The reception of Sir Patrick Lawless in state, at the English Court, as the Spanish Ambassador, and his admission to the most confidential or private intercourse with the Queen, as the agent for her brother,* excited great

* Baron de Schutz, the Hanoverian Envoy in London, writing to Hanover, "February 6th, 1714," how, "the Queen was in a dangerous situation," adds, that "Sir Patrick Lawless saw her Majesty last night, having returned from her about midnight," &c. And, complains a contemporary Georgeite annalist—"The Pretender's Envoy, Sir Patrick Lawless, was publickly entertain'd at Court, while the Elector's," or Hanoverian, "Minister was disgrac'd, for demanding a Writ, that the Electoral Prince might come, and take his place in the House of Lords." Or rather "might come," to be, in hunting phraseology, "in at the death" of the poor Queen. Dr. de Burgo, in his valuable Hibernia Dominicana, makes a useful reference to Sir Patrick Lawless, as well as to other eminent Irish exiles of the same century, serving on the Continent. With *that* reference to Sir Patrick, I have connected the substance of the several contemporary allusions to him in British and Continental publications.

exasperation, and proportionable clamour, outside and inside Parliament, among the Whigs, previous to the Queen's death. And this violent Whig feeling continued after the accession of the Elector of Hanover as George I., or in 1715, when "receiving Patrick Lawless, an Irish Papist, as a Foreign Minister, and causing several sums of money to be paid to him," was 1 of the Articles of Impeachment against the Earl of Oxford, as head of the Queen's Ministry. Sir Patrick Lawless was subsequently Ambassador to France from Spain, where he likewise attained the rank of Lieutenant-General, and was Governor of the Island of Majorca.

The Duke of Berwick—in whose army were the 2 battalions of his own regiment, and the battalions of Dillon and Bourke—terminated, in October, 1712, a campaign of successful manœuvres against the Piedmontese and Imperialists. At its conclusion, he and his regiment were deprived by death of a very gallant officer, Daniel O'Carroll, previously mentioned as so distinguished under the Duke of Vendome in Italy. O'Carroll came to France with the Irish troops of King James's army, that arrived there after the Treaty of Limerick, in 1691, and served thenceforward, with the national corps to which he was attached, in all its campaigns on the Continent till the Peace of Ryswick in 1697, when he was a Lieutenant-Colonel of the Queen's Regiment of Dismounted Dragoons. He was appointed Lieutenant-Colonel of the Regiment of Berwick, May 4th, 1698. Employed with the French army of Italy in 1701, he was at the combats of Carpi and Chiari; in 1702, at the battle of Luzzara, and reduction of Borgoforte; in 1703, at the affairs of Stradella, Castel-Nova-de-Bormida, with the force that invaded the Trentin, and at the sieges of Nago and Arco; in 1704 and 1705, he was engaged at the sieges of Vercelli, Ivrea, Verrua, Chivasso, and August 16th, of the latter year, at the memorable battle of Cassano; for his very creditable conduct on which occasion, he was made, on the 30th of the same month, a Brigadier. He was present at the unfortunate siege and battle of Turin in 1706. Removed to Spain, he served there at the victory of Almanza, and capture of Lerida in 1707; and at that of Tortosa in 1708. From 1710 to 1712, he was attached to the army of Dauphiné, where he ended his honourable career with the last-mentioned campaign; being still Lieutenant-Colonel to the Regiment of Berwick. After the close of hostilities for the season between the Duke of Berwick and his Piedmontese and Imperial opponents, the Duke was ordered to raise Stahremberg's blockade of Girona; which he ably did "in the nick of time," just when the place could hold out no longer, or early in January, 1713; Stahremberg being obliged to retire precipitately from before the town, leaving in his intrenchments several cannon, with much provisions, tools, &c. Lieutenant-General Arthur Dillon, despatched, by the Duke, with some grenadiers and a good body of horse, to fall, if possible, upon the enemy's rear, picked up several stragglers as prisoners; and then attacking, at a defile, 250 men, posted there to favour the retreat of their army towards Ostalric or Hostalric, he killed, captured, or put to flight, the whole detachment, and rejoined the Duke. A French biographer of the Duke, terming this relief of Girona, "an enterprise which had appeared the more difficult, as Count Staremberg had taken all possible precaution to render impracticable the avenues of a town which he expected to reduce by famine," adds—"But all these obstacles, and all the difficulties which arose from the situation of the place, and the rigorous season of the year, were surmounted by Marshal Berwick; who, by saving a town of so great importance, did as signal a service, as he ever rendered, to the King of Spain, or the King of France." Having duly provisioned, garrisoned, and ammunitioned Girona, the Duke "set out from Catalonia, and came post to Versailles, where he arrived on the 5th of February, and was received by the King, and the whole Court, with deserved esteem, and applause."

The last affair of arms in this war between Spain and Portugal occurred in the campaign of 1712, under circumstances so creditable to an Irish officer as to deserve notice here, though that gentleman was not in the Irish Brigade. Notwithstanding the negociations for peace at Utrecht, no truce having taken place by September between the 2 Peninsular kingdoms, the Marquis de Bay, (styled "the scourge of the Portuguese,') appeared, on the 28th, with nearly 20,000 men before Campo Mayor in Portugal, and broke ground, October 4th-5th; the place being then in anything but a condition to make a suitable resistance. As, however, it was of the utmost consequence to preserve it, the Count de Ribeira, and a gallant French Protestant engineer officer, Brigadier de Massé, contrived, a day or 2 after, to make their way into the town with 200 or 300 Portuguese grenadiers, and 400 or 500 more Portuguese subsequently succeeded in doing so likewise, under an Irish officer, Major-General Hogan—apparently the same "M. Hogan, Irlandois," Lieutenant-Colonel in the Bavarian Guards, tried by Court Martial in 1706 at Mons, for killing a Captain and countryman of his own in a duel,* and hence, most probably, obliged to enter another service. Having assumed the command of the garrison, the Major-General took due measures for the defence. After battering and bombing the place from October 14th with 33 cannon or mortars, the Marquis de Bay ordered a grand assault to be made on the 27th, in the morning, by 15 battalions, 32 companies of grenadiers, and a regiment of dismounted dragoons, under Lieutenant-General Zuniga. "By the help of a prodigious fire from their cannon and small arms," observes my English narrative of the "Compleat History of Europe" for 1712, with respect to the enemy, "they made a descent into a part of the ditch that was dry, and gave 3 assaults with a great deal of fury; but they were as bravely repulsed by the Portuguese under Major-General Hogan, and forced to retire after an obstinate fight that lasted 2 hours, though the breach was very practicable, and so wide, that 30 men might stand abreast in it. Their disorder was so great, that they left most of their arms and 6 ladders behind. This action cost them 700 men killed and wounded, whereas the Portuguese loss did not amount to above 100 men killed, and 187 wounded; and such was their ardour, that they pursued the enemy into their very trenches without any manner of order, notwithstanding the endeavours used by Major-General Hogan to put a stop to them, which might have proved very fatal to them, if the enemy had had courage to improve the opportunity." The Spaniards next day

* Maffei's Memoirs. The O'Hogans were a sept located about Ballyhogan, County of Tipperary; and the name was respectable in the County of Clare, &c. During the War of the Revolution in Ireland, they supplied officers of the ranks of Captain, Lieutenant, and Ensign, or Cornet, to the Jacobite regular army, in the infantry Regiments of Dorrington, Mountcashel, Bagnall, Grace, and in Lord Clare's Dragoons. But the most remarkable representative of the race, in that contest, was the famous Captain of mounted irregulars, guerilas, or rapparees, known as "galloping Hogan."

raised this siege, stated to have cost them altogether 3000 killed and wounded, to only about 400 Portuguese; a cessation of hostilities took place a few days after; and for such an honourable conclusion of this war was Portugal indebted to the gallantry of a Hogan, as, a century after, for the successful termination of a greater contest, to the discipline of a Beresford, and the generalship of a Wellington.

The Emperor Charles VI. of Austria not having acceded to the general peace concluded with France at Utrecht, in April, 1713, and having collected his forces along the Rhine under Prince Eugene of Savoy, to continue the war, Louis XIV. placed under the Marshal de Villars, assisted by the Marshal de Besons, such a powerful army as might reduce the Teutonic Kaiser of the so-called Holy Roman Empire to reason.

> "Still, Cæsar, wilt thou tread the paths of blood?
> Wilt thou, thou *singly*, hate thy country's good?
> * * * * * * *
> Give o'er at length, and let thy labours cease,
> Nor vex the world, but learn to suffer peace!"
> ROWE'S LUCAN'S Pharsalia, v., 446-7, 450-1.

Holding Eugene in check, at the lines of Etlingen, and about Muhlberg, Villars, in June, laid siege to the strong and well-garrisoned fortress of Landau, which, after 56 days of open trenches, he compelled to capitulate, in August. Meantime, Eugene, though unable to attempt the relief of Landau, and obliged to remain about the lines of Etlingen, caused General Vaubonne to occupy, with 17,000 or 18,000 men, and a sufficient artillery, 2 lines of such well-constructed intrenchments in the difficult country leading to the fortress of Friburgh, that, it was considered, Villars, if not repulsed before them, could only carry them with a loss of half his infantry; the 2nd line, in particular, of those intrenchments having been so strong by nature and by art, that, we are told, 4000 determined men behind them might have arrested the progress of 50,000 opponents. But Vaubonne's troops, on being attacked, September 20th, about 7 in the evening, by Villars, behaved so disgracefully, that the Marshal captured the whole of their works, with a loss mentioned as no more than 60 men of all ranks, killed, or wounded! The French, by the end of the month, broke ground before Friburgh; which, having had a Governor, garrison, &c., suited to its importance, made a very stubborn and sanguinary defence, until forced to surrender, about the middle of November. These conquests of Villars, which opened the way for more extensive acquisitions by the French arms in Germany, obliged the Austrian Court, and its deservedly-humiliated General, Eugene of Savoy,* to desist from their unfeeling prolongation of human misery and bloodshed after a war of so many years, and to enter upon negociations for a peace with France, which was concluded the following year.

The chief Irish officers, who served under the Marshal de Villars, in 1713, were Lieutenant-General Andrew Lee, (accompanied by his son,

---

* For the *amiable* object of preventing, if possible, the conclusion of the Peace of Utrecht, Eugene had been over in England; and his presence at London was proportionably welcome to the Whigs, who were, like himself and Marlborough, for going on with a war, which had *certainly* become unnecessary. So his mortified Highness met with no more success, as a negociator there, than, as a commander, against Villars, elsewhere.

Colonel Francis Lee,) Lieutenant-General Arthur Dillon, Major-General Michael Roth, and Brigadiers Murrough O'Brien and Christopher Nugent. The Irish corps were Dorrington's, Galmoy's, and O'Donnell's 3 battalions, Berwick's 2, and Nugent's 2 squadrons. In the reduction of Landau, which cost the French 2980 men, killed or wounded, Lee, Dillon, and Roth were employed in their respective ranks, and all the above-mentioned Irish battalions, but Berwick's, were attached to the like service. Prince Eugene, with a view to passing the Rhine, having placed above 740 men, and 10 pieces of artillery in the town and castle of Kaiserslautern, Lieutenant-General Dillon was detached, in June, with a body of troops, to reduce that place, which he did the same day, sending the garrison, as prisoners, into France. He likewise took the Castle of Verastein, in which were 80 men; whereby the enemy were deprived of every post between Coblentz and Mayence. The Lieutenant-General subsequently mounted the trenches at Landau, as well as his regiment; and Major-General Roth did so too. The sharpest affair, in the trenches before that fortress, at which the Irish were engaged, was, on the night of July 4th-5th, in assailing a work called the Pâté. The attack was made by 4 companies of grenadiers, 1 of the Swiss Regiment of Villars, and 1 of each of the 3 Irish Regiments of Dorrington, O'Donnell, and Galmoy. "Although this work," says the account, "was defended by the fire from the redoubt of the demi-lune, and from the works overlooking it, it was carried, nevertheless, with a great deal of valour. It was occupied by 100 men, a Captain, who was made prisoner, and the rest killed, or drowned. There were killed, or wounded, at the taking of this post, a Major, a Captain, and 150 grenadiers, or workmen."

For the operations against Friburgh, there were present Nugent's horse, and Galmoy's, O'Donnell's, Berwick's, and O'Brien's infantry. At this harassing siege, in the night of October 6th-7th, by the splinter of a rock from a cannon-shot, near the Marshal de Villars in the trenches, was wounded the Captain of his Guards, Colonel Skiddy, Chevalier of St. Louis, of a family long respectable in Munster, where, besides such as were the possessors of estates, there were 35 of the name Mayors of Cork, between 1364 and 1621; in which city, also, a charitable foundation, or "Skiddy's Alms-House," has preserved their memory to the present century.* On the night of the 14th-15th, Francis Lee, son of the Lieutenant-General, headed 2 battalions of the Regiment of Rousillon, in the grand assault, and storming of the covered way, and of an advanced lunette, under the eye of Villars; which cost the French 1500 men, killed, and wounded, including 183 officers. About the same time,

* The name of "Skiddy," usually Frenchified "Squiddy," is metamorphosed by the Marquis de Quincy, or his printer, into "Esquiddy," on this occasion. In 1703, a Skiddy was Lieutenant-Colonel of the Regiment of Clare. In 1723, a "Sir George Skiddy" is alluded to, by an Irish contemporary, as having "acquired a good estate in France," as being "a Knight of the Military Order of St. Louis, and a Colonel of Foot;" and as "great-grandson to Sir George Skiddy, formerly of Waterford, and also of Skiddy's Castle, in the County of Cork." The name is likewise to be seen, among the records of Williamite landed proscription, or Jacobite forfeiture, in Munster. In the Mémoires de Villars, "le Sieur de Squiddy" is twice named as Captain of the Guards to the Marshal during the campaigns of 1712 and 1713; or first, as sent, after the reduction of Marchiennes, "porter les drapeaux" to Louis XIV.; and next, or at Friburgh, as "blessé près de moi," or wounded near the Marshal, there.

or on the 14th, Prince Eugene, advancing at the head of 6000 men, to within 9 miles of Friburgh, and it being given out, that he would succour it, the Marshal de Villars, among his measures to prevent this, detached Lieutenant-General Dillon with 1200 infantry and 6 troops of cavalry, to the head of the Valley of Kinderstral, to mark out a camp for 12 battalions there; and no attempt was made by the enemy to save the besieged fortress.

Peace was signed, March 6th, 1714, at Rastadt, between France and Germany. Yet Catalonia, though abandoned, since the year before, by the Allied troops, through whose aid it had supported Charles of Austria against Philip V., still refused to submit to, and maintained a very obstinate and bloody contest against, Philip, notwithstanding his being every where else the acknowledged King of Spain! Philip's domineering Ministers required the Catalonians to submit to him at discretion, merely on condition of a general amnesty for the past. The Catalonians would *not* submit, unless the several rights, immunities, and privileges, which they had enjoyed under the former or Austrian dynasty in Spain, should be specially guaranteed to them; and, for a confirmation of those ancient liberties, they offered, besides submitting, to pay a very large sum, to the King; but otherwise added, that they would oppose him to the last. The great focus of this resistance was the strong fortress and metropolis of the province, Barcelona, where all possible means, political, military, and ecclesiastical, were adopted, in order to make a most vigorous defence. All property there, church-plate included, was voted applicable for that object; all above 14 years old, not excepting priests and monks, were to bear arms at the sound of the tocsin; and the garrison amounted to 16,000 men, with about 215 pieces of artillery. The stubborn valour of the Catalonians, and the exhaustion of Spain by so long a war, rendering it impossible for Philip to reduce Catalonia merely by his own resources, he was obliged to seek assistance, for that purpose, from his grandfather, Louis XIV.; and he requested the Duke of Berwick might accompany that assistance, as General-in-Chief of the forces of both Crowns. With an army of the best of those forces, considerably above 40,000 in number, an artillery of 120 pieces, and a profusion of every thing requisite for a siege, the Duke opened the trenches, July 12th, before Barcelona. The Barcelonese, under the significant ensign of a death's-head, made a defence worthy of the country of a Saguntum, a Numantia, a Saragossa, and a Girona; holding out until their provisions were exhausted, and the town was stormed through 7 breaches! Then, or September 12th, they had to surrender, after a total loss, on their part, of about 6000 killed or wounded, including upwards of 540 ecclesiastics; and on the Duke's side, 10,000 men.

Of the Irish Brigade, at this remarkable siege, there were the battalions of Lee, Dillon, Berwick, and Bourke. Among the most noted British and Irish officers there, after the Duke of Berwick, were Lieutenant-General Arthur Dillon, and Major-General Walter Bourke; the Duke's eldest son by his 1st wife, widow of Patrick Sarsfield, 1st Earl of Lucan, or James Francis Fitz-James, Marquis of Tinmouth, and Colonel of the Regiment of Berwick; and the Duke's step-son, James Francis Edward Sarsfield, 2nd Earl of Lucan. The Duke, after having effected such a breach, by a fire of several days from 30 pieces of cannon, that he resolved, July 30th, to assault the covered way, repaired in person to the trenches, to inspect the attack, which was committed to Lieutenant-General Dillon. On the appointed signal, at 9 in the evening, 4 companies of grenadiers on the right, and 4 on the left, advanced against the covered way, extending from the bastion of the Porta Nova to that of Santa Clara. Without wasting time at firing, the grenadiers dashed at the work they were to master, carried it, and put all they met there to the sword. The workmen, at hand to avail themselves of this success, and protected by the fire kept up from the trenches, then made good the lodgement; and Dillon's troops were so well disposed there, that, although the Barcelonese sallied out, in great force, the same night, to recover the counterscarp, they became discouraged, and were repulsed with a very severe loss; while that of the Lieutenant-General's party amounted only to 60 men. Dillon was also prominently engaged in the last great assault upon the place, September 11th, when 44 companies of grenadiers, and 49 battalions had to be employed against the Barcelonese, who, from half-past 4 in the morning, defended themselves so long as 11 or 12 hours; 1 portion of the works, in particular, where the besiegers suffered most, not becoming finally theirs, until after it had been taken, and retaken, on both sides, 11 times! At this assault, Dillon, as Lieutenant-General, having, under his orders, a French and Spanish Major-General, and 3 Brigadiers, (2 French and 1 Spanish,) with 20 companies of grenadiers, 20 battalions, and 500 workmen, was intrusted with the attacks to be made, from the right to the centre. He reserved the great breach of the centre for himself and 7 battalions, while 1 of his Major-Generals, M. de Guerchois, ascended that, at an angle flanking the bastion of Santa Clara; and the 2 officers made themselves masters of the whole of an intrenchment behind the Monastery of St. Augustin, and of a portion of that edifice; killing all whom they encountered. Nevertheless, the Barcelonese, renewing the combat, with desperation, and increased numbers, at 8 in the morning, retook, among other posts, part of the Monastery of St. Augustin, and maintained a long and terrible fire against Dillon's troops, as well as the rest of the Duke's army. This fire continued, until every post was recovered by the final overpowering and driving of the besieged into the New Town, at between 3 and 4 in the afternoon; when signals were displayed for a cessation of hostilities, that led to the surrender of the place, the following day. Of the Duke of Berwick, at this equally important and difficult siege, it will suffice to state, that the ability he manifested was worthy of his previous reputation, and his high position, as the General-in-Chief for 2 Monarchs. How he was recompensed by Philip V. has been elsewhere mentioned. Lieutenant-General Dillon's conduct there is described, by the Duke, as "everything that was to be expected from an officer of courage and capacity." The Duke's son, the Marquis of Tinmouth, who was appointed to deliver the standards of the Barcelonese to Philip V., was rewarded with the Order of the Golden Fleece. The Duke's step-son, the Earl of Lucan, who was wounded in the last assault, received from the King the Collar of the Golden Fleece, and a company of his Guardes du Corps. The eulogium of the Irish battalions engaged in this trying contest was comprehended in that of the army to which they belonged; generally referred to, as having displayed "numberless proofs of extraordinary intrepidity." *

* On this struggle in Catalonia, and siege of Barcelona, I have made use of the Duke of Berwick's Memoirs, the great history of Quincy, the contemporary Mercure

Such were the services of the Irish to the House of Bourbon during the War of the Spanish Succession, when, from the intimate nature of the alliance between France and Spain, the Irish in the pay of Louis XIV., and of his grandson Philip V., might be regarded as virtually belonging to 1 army; numbers of them, including Count O'Mahony, Lord Galmoy, Sir Patrick Lawless, &c., having passed, with permission, from the service of one Monarch into that of the other; and those, in both services, having continually fought together. I have consequently noticed the acts of the Irish in the Spanish service during *this* war, as fully as those of their countrymen in the French service, my more immediate subject. On the consideration in which the exiled Irish were held in Spain and other Continental countries, as well as in France, 1 of my French manuscripts observes—" France was not the only power which granted the rights of citizenship to the Irish. Philip V., King of Spain, by a Declaration of June 28th, 1721, placed the Irish, who were Catholics by birth, and resident in Spain, upon a footing with all the other subjects of his kingdom; and this favour was, as in France, the recompense for the services of the officers of this nation. In all the states to which the Irish emigrated," adds this document, " they found a country to adopt them; *and every where their important services have proved, that they deserved the rank of citizenship which was conferred upon them.*" As regards Spain, the Irish Brigade, that was kept up there, still consisted, in 1782, of 2400 men; and, of the regiments continued to the present century, were the 3 of Irlandia, Hibernia, and Ultonia. The 1st, or that of Irlandia, was formed, in 1638, from levies made in Ireland, by permission of King Charles I. The 2nd, or that of Hibernia, was created by Philip V., in 1703, from soldiers and reformed officers, obtained through France. The 3rd, or that of Ultonia, was established the same year, and from similar sources, by Philip. But, to return.

In England, the conclusion, by the Tories, in 1713, of the Peace of Utrecht with France, was hailed with delight by the Jacobites, as an event, which *they* considered so likely to make way for the succession of the exiled son of James II. to the throne.

"Too long *he*'s been excluded;
Too long *we*'ve been deluded;
Let's with one voice, sing and rejoice,
The peace is now concluded.
The Dutch are disappointed;
Their Whiggish plots disjointed;
The sun displays his glorious rays,
To crown the Lord's anointed!"

From the termination of the war, indeed, to the decease of the Queen, the prospects of the Whig party, or that in favour of the House of Hanover, were very discouraging. The Whig writer, in 1716, of the annals of the 1st year of George I., having premised how in England the friends of the preceding Tory Ministry "were in all the chief posts of the nation," and that Ministry "had a Parliament which they led as they pleased," says—" They had corrupted great numbers of the Clergy, and of our University-men, so as they zealously maintained, and dispersed

Historique, and Lettres Historiques, the respectable British historian of Eugene and Marlborough, and Fieffé.

through the nation, those doctrines which were calculated to bring in the Pretender. By their Occasional Act, and other methods, they had so modelled the greatest part of our Corporations, as to get in Magistrates, that went along with all their measures. Our metropolis, the City of London, formerly an impregnable bulwark against Popery and Slavery, was so corrupted by a few hot-headed Priests, encouraged by the Court, and so poysoned by a Tory Common-Council, imposed upon them *Viis et Modis*, that it became the principal scene of rebellious tumults, and all Elections there were carried by Jacobite mobs. The Commissions of Lieutenancy and Peace, through the nation, were, generally, in the hands of persons disaffected to the Hanover Succession; and the meaner sort of people, through the Kingdom, were so much debauched by the influence of such men, of the High-Church Clergy, and of the Officers belonging to the Excise and Customs, that the Pretender, and his friends, thought their game sure. This he tells us himself, in his Declaration after the Queen's death, and gives it *as the only reason of his continuing quiet for some years, that he reckoned himself sure of the friendship of the Queen;** *by which we must understand her Ministry, and depended upon their promises.* The only body of people in England, that stood then united in his Majesty's interest, was the moderate Church-men and Dissenters; but the former were put out of all power, and the latter were, by law, excluded from it, and put under a new and unnatural hardship by the Schism Act, which was to take place the very day that her Majesty died." After noticing the state of Scotland, where the Tory Ministry, "to strengthen their interest, kept the Popish and Jacobite Highlanders in pay," &c., this Whig writer remarks, how circumstances did not seem more favourable for his party in Ireland, from the very superior amount of the Roman Catholic population, Jacobites to a man, in connexion with the dominant power of the Tory or High-Church Protestant party there, also averse to a Hanoverian Succession, and proportionably severe upon such as were not so, or Protestants of Whig and Dissenting opinions. "Their Dissenters," he remarks, "who are by much the greatest body of Protestants in that nation, were, by the influence of the High-Church party, brought under an incapacity to bear any civil or military commission for the defence of themselves, or their country. This was not only highly impolitick, as it weakened the English and Protestant interest in that Kingdom, but highly ungrateful to the Irish Dissenters, and particularly to those of the Province of Ulster, who had been twice, under God, the principal instruments of saving that Kingdom to the Crown of England, as well as the Established Church of Ireland. Yet, such was the rancour of the High-Church party, that they did all they could to persecute and oppress, not only their Dissenting brethren in that nation, but even the moderate Church-men; and the Government there was put into such hands, and administered in such a manner, as plainly discovered, that *the designs of the Ministry were so laid and carried on, in all the 3 Nations, as to pave the Pretender's way to the Throne.* . . . In short, *there was nothing wanting to have entirely delivered up that Kingdom into the hands of the Pretender, but to have modell'd the Troops there to their purpose, by putting out all the honest Officers, and placing Jacobites in their stead.*"

* Queen Anne, "in dying," says Klose, "*confirmed* the belief, that had long prevailed, of her partiality for the exiled Prince, by exclaiming—'Oh, my dear brother, how I pity you!'"

The accounts of the Queen's illness were accompanied by information from Ireland, as to what efforts were on foot there, to strengthen the Brigade in France—" Great numbers of lusty, young fellows, all Papists, having gone, since last Michaelmas, into France, on assurances given them, that they should soon return home, with their lawful *King*, James III.—many recruiting officers being alleged to have arrived from France in various parts of the island, Dublin not excepted, where James Roche, a considerable Popish merchant, expended large sums of money in listing ——— and vessels, sailing for France, bringing from 20 to 60 of the lower order of Irish on board, under the pretence, it was affirmed, of emigrating merely as agricultural labourers, but, in reality, as so many recruits for the Irish regiments abroad, in the interest of the Pretender. Hence, the proceedings of the House of Commons in Dublin on the subject, the declaration of the Grand Jury of the County of Dublin, for the adoption of immediate measures to stop the transporting of such great numbers of Popish youth into the service of the Pretender, and the consequent issuing of a Proclamation, against such recruiting, from the Lord Lieutenant and Council of Ireland." From the commencement of the Queen's indisposition, the advocates for the accession of the House of Hanover to the Sovereignty of Great Britain and Ireland likewise referred, with much uneasiness, to the Irish troops in France, as being quartered too near the coasts opposite to England; with a view, it was believed, of being *ready to come over, in support of her brother's claim to the Crown, as King James III.* " Upon the first news of the Queen's sickness," writes the Hanoverian Envoy, Baron de Schutz, from London, January 25th, 1714, " several French battalions had orders to march towards the sea, under pretext of changing the garrisons; and they remain there, *viz.*, at Graveling, Calais, Berg, St. Winnox, St. Omers, and Boulogne. Most of the Irish regiments in the French service, who made the campaign on the Upper Rhine, are arrived likewise in the Low Countries. Clare's regiment is at Douay, Galmoy's at Valenciennes, and Dorrington's, which was the late King James's Regiment of Guards, at Avesnes." February 6th, the Baron notes, of men of rank of the Hanoverian party in England, how, under such circumstances, " many of them expected to be sent to the Tower, as soon as the French designs were ripe;" and how, consequently, 1 of them " gave £100 to an officer, for going to France, to learn, with certainty, if the Irish troops were assembled in the neighbourhood of Boulogne?" The alarm at such intelligence from Ireland, and the Continent, *caused public credit to suffer very much, for several weeks, in London; the funds falling, and a severe run taking place upon the Bank of England.* With respect to the Jacobite recruiting in Ireland, we likewise read, how information being given, in May, to the authorities in Dublin, of about 150 men being at the Hill of Howth, in order to sail thence to France for the service of James III., some constables, with a file of musketeers, were despatched against the Jacobite party. Of the 150, but 24 were taken; who were imprisoned, tried, and, by one-sided, hostile Juries, of course condemned for what was called "high treason;" and, some time after, 3 of the number, " John Reilly, Alexander Bourke, and Martin Carrol, were executed for it, at Stephens's-Green"—or where poor Captain Nowlan subsequently met the like fate. What became of the other 21 captured Jacobites *we* do not know, but may not unreasonably suspect, that the Dublin *hangman* could tell. In Harris's Williamite account of the notorious Lord Chief-Justice, Sir Richard Cox, author of Hibernia Anglicana—already noticed in connexion with the virulent proscription, after the battle of the Boyne, of all the older Irish having lands in general, and of the unfortunate young Earl of Clancarty in particular—we have additional circumstances respecting the prosecutions, here referred to, of those enlisting for the Brigade in France. Having premised, how much the Irish regiments there required recruits after such a long war on the Continent, Harris states—"Therefore as soon as the Peace was made, several of the officers came to Ireland to recruit. They, and those whom they employed, the sooner to complete their business, and well knowing that the inclinations of the Papists were all in the interest of the Pretender, made use of his name to inveigle them into his service. This powerful argument soon inlisted great numbers, who were firmly persuaded they were to return in a year to extirpate all the English. In February, 1713, William Lehy, 1 of the persons so inlisted, gave an information of the treason to the Lord Mayor, who laid it before the Government, and the informant and Michael Lehy were examined before the Council. Upon this examination, a Proclamation was immediately issued, to encourage the apprehending the inlisters and the inlisted, and several were taken, in different parts of the Kingdom, but most about Dublin. In the Spring Circuit in Munster, Lord Chief-Justice Cox received 2 letters from the Lord Lieutenant," much approving his care to punish persons who inlisted men for the Pretender's, or for foreign, service; "and, when he returned to Dublin, his time was chiefly employed in taking Informations, sending out Warrants, Guards, and Constables to apprehend, and in examining the inlisted persons, when apprehended. So zealous and active were he, and others lawfully authorized, that the Goals of Newgate and Kilmainham were soon full of these traytors; so that the Government thought it necessary, to send a Special Commission to Kilmainham, to try the criminals in custody there. Accordingly, Commissioners of Oyer and Terminer sat at Kilmainham, the 2nd of July, 1714, and Lord Chief-Justice Cox gave the Charge to the Grand Jury." This charge was, of course, such as might be expected from him, who, in addition to so much land, the spoil of Irish Jacobite loyalists, possessed a portion of what was King James II.'s property, and, in case of a "restoration," would be King James III.'s; * and, as an address to a jury of opinions corresponding with those of the addresser, was duly effective, to the prejudice of the accused. Consequently, we are told, "*many* were condemned, and *executed*, by virtue of this Commission, and 3 in the Queen's Bench, where Sir Richard presided."

The great apprehension among the Whigs in England, with respect to the Irish military abroad, was the more natural, from Lord Bolingbroke's reported design, with regard to the army at home; which, if not arrested by the Queen's premature death, *must* have placed her brother, as James III. of England and Ireland, and James VIII. of Scotland upon the thrones of his ancestors. On this design of his Lordship, Ibberville, the French Agent in London, writing to Louis XIV. the day following the

* "Besides," says Harris, of Cox, "he was attainted by King James's Irish Parliament, held every foot of his estate under the Act of Settlement, (which stands repealed by the same Parliament,) or under the Trustee Act, (which must have the same fate with the Protestant Succession,) so that his religion, his property, and his life, all depended on the House of Hanover."

Queen's decease, and after expressing how penetrated with grief Lord Bolingbroke was at that fatal circumstance, observes of his Lordship—"He has assured me, *measures were so well taken, that, in 6 weeks' time, things would have been put into such a condition, as there would have been nothing to fear from what has just occurred.*"* Of the same design, Oldmixon informs us—"That the army, in both England and Ireland, was to be modell'd, is most certain. Major-General Devenport, (Lieutenant of the 1st Troop of Life-Guards, who was ordered to sell,) shew'd myself, and others, the next day after the Queen dy'd, a list of 60 or 70 officers, most of them of the Guards, that were to be cashier'd, with the names of those that were to have their commissions," &c. Another Anglo-Whig contemporary alleges—" The army was to be new modell'd, in such a manner, that *all* the troops in Great Britain might be blindly devoted to the Ministry. One branch of this scheme was, to *break 9 of the battalions in Ireland;* entirely to lay aside 72 officers, that were thought improper instruments for the designs in hand; and to raise 15 *other* battalions, that should be *sure to obey all commands,*" &c. And we are informed, how the "other branch of his scheme was, to remove such officers of the Guards as were eminently well effected to the most Serene House of Hanover;" among whom were the names of 3 Major-Generals, 3 Brigadiers, and 21 Colonels, as men who would not consent "*to serve the Queen, without asking questions!*"†—while, of those who were to be commissioned instead of them, it was given out, that "some were Irish Papists," besides "a Popish Lord!" Even as matters stood *at* the Queen's death, or although it occurred before those military precautions could be taken, the moment she expired, Dr. Francis Atterbury, the famous High-Church Bishop of Rochester, proposed "*to go, in his lawn-sleeves, and proclaim James III., &c., at Charing Cross!*" On which, "Bolinbroke's heart failing him," writes Horace Walpole, "Atterbury swore—*There was the best cause in Europe lost, for want of spirit!*" With reference to such Tory plans in favour of the accession of the Queen's brother, as *King* James, and to the particular apprehension, by Whiggism, of the Irish

---

* Of Louis XIV.'s sincere attachment to the cause of James II.'s son, Lord Bolingbroke, in noticing the circumstances of his own flight to France after Queen Anne's death, and his taking office there under James, alleges—"If the late King," Louis XIV., "had lived 6 months longer, I verily believe, there had been war again, between England and France." But, continues his Lordship, "when I arrived at Paris, the King was already gone to Marly, where the indisposition which he had begun to feel at Versailles, increased upon him. He was *the best friend the Chevalier had;* and, when I engaged in this business, my principal dependence was upon his personal character; this failed me, in a great degree—he was not in a condition to exert the same vigour as formerly." In short, concludes his Lordship, "all I had to negociate—by myself first, and, in conjunction with the Duke of Ormond, soon afterwards,—languished with the King. *My hopes sunk as he declined, and died when he expired.*" Of Ibberville, it is amusing to read, under the head of "St. James's, November 16," this paragraph, with reference to King George I., instead of King James III., in the London Gazette for 1714, No. 5277. "Yesterday, Monsieur d'Ibberville, Envoy Extraordinary from his Most Christian Majesty, had a private audience of the King, to congratulate his Majesty's happy accession to the throne." Such are politics and politicians!

† With such a *large* majority of the population of Great Britain opposed to a Hanoverian succession, as will be seen in the next Book, *must* not James have succeeded his sister, had she only lived till such a remodelling of the army, as Lord Bolingbroke planned, should have been completed, to render any Whig opposition *hopeless?*

Brigade, as the especial champions of *that* succession, the zealous Irish Whig, Captain Parker, adds in his Memoirs—" It is most certain, that, was it not for the brave defence the Catalans made at Barcelona, (for they still held out) *the Duke of Berwick, with his Irish regiments, would have landed among us, before the Queen's death;* and then, *what a scene of blood must have followed!* Surely *the hand of Providence appeared visibly, at that very critical juncture, in favour of the religion, laws, and liberty of England!*"

HISTORY OF THE IRISH BRIGADES

IN

THE SERVICE OF FRANCE.

BOOK VI.

GEORGE GUELPH, Elector of Hanover, being, as George I., made King of Great Britain and Ireland, in August, 1714, on Whig or Revolution principles; according to which King James II.'s son, James Francis Edward Stuart, born Prince of Wales at St. James's Palace, London, in June, 1688, was styled a *Pretender*, and his claim to the throne, upon legitimate or hereditary grounds, was, on account of his religion as a Catholic, passed over, and set aside; that Prince, who, nevertheless, regarded himself, and was also regarded by far the larger portion of the population of Great Britain and Ireland, as, by right, King James III., ordered his adherents in Great Britain, in 1715, to rise against the Hanoverian, as a usurper.* Nor, while George appeared to so many, as

---

* The popular feeling in Great Britain respecting the rival dynasties is expressed in the verse of the Jacobite song—

"God prosper King James, and the German confound,
And *may none but true Britons e'er rule British ground!*"

The Marshal Duke of Berwick, in 1715, from the intelligence he had, asserts, that, beyond dispute, 5 out of 6 persons in England were for James III. "Le gros de la nation Angloise est si bien disposé, qu'on peut avancer hardiment que, de 6, il y en a 5, pour le Roi Jacques." And this he might safely write, since he tells us, he was informed by the Duke of Ormonde, the Earl of Mar, &c., how the English were never better disposed towards the Stuart cause, 9 out of 10 being for James against George. "Ormond, Marr, &c., nous assûroaent, que jamais les peuples n'avoient été si bien disposés; que, de 10, il y en avoit 9, contré George, et par conséquent pour Jacques." Dr. Johnson, likewise, who was born previous to the accession of the House of Hanover, observed to Mr. Boswell, on the subject, in the reign of George III., or 1773—"The present family on the throne came to the crown against the will of 9-10ths of the people. Whether these 9-10ths were right, or wrong, it is not our business now to inquire." In fact, with the great Country, Church, or Tory party, a vast majority of the population of England, generally in favour of the Stuarts, as well as the Episcopalians and Highlanders in Scotland, and the Catholics in Ireland, similarly inclined, how *small* a numerical minority of the population of these islands *must* the supporters of a change of dynasty have been, consisting, as they almost universally did, merely of the Whigs in England, the Presbyterians in Scotland, and the comparatively few Protestants in Ireland—these last, too, not being without *some* Jacobites among them! It was only in the least-peopled of the 3 kingdoms, or in Scotland, that Whiggery could *pretend* to claim a majority, and even *there*, that majority was weakened by the disaffection of many, who were Whigs, indeed, by party inclination, but, as nationalists, were altogether opposed to the Union, and, so far, friendly to the cause of the Stuarts, since their "*restoration*" would have been attended by that of the Parliament of Scotland. Writing as an English historian, Lord Mahon says—"We, on our part, should do well to remember, that the Revolution of 1688 was not *sought*, but *forced* upon us." But, in whatever light the cause of the Stuarts may be viewed as

no better than a usurper, did he seem entitled to any more respect, from a view of his moral character, mental attainments, and personal endowments. "He," says Mr. Jesse, "was indebted for his aggrandizement merely to the accidental circumstance of his having been educated in the Protestant faith; there being, at the period of his accession, so many as 57 individuals of the blood royal, who possessed superior hereditary claims." Married, in 1682, to his young, beautiful, and accomplished cousin, Sophia Dorothea, Duchess of Zell, who, by bringing him that Sovereign Duchy as her dowry, so much enlarged his Hanoverian dominions, he, nevertheless, only "a few months after, attached himself to undeserving mistresses, and even insulted his young wife, by constantly introducing them into her presence." In short, "he was himself the most notorious adulterer, and the most unscrupulous libertine, in his dominions." Yet, though claiming such a wide and shameless range of animal indulgence for himself, he, on a single charge of matrimonial infidelity,* shut up in the Castle of Alden, in the river Aller, in Zell, his unfortunate wife; keeping her there, under the name of Duchess of Halle, until her death; after "a long captivity of 32 years, deprived of the society of her children, and snatched from the pleasures of life, when she was best qualified to enjoy them." While thus debauched and cruel, he was likewise "ignorant and illiterate, inelegant in his person, and ungraceful in his manners;" and, though in his 55th year, when he came over to rule these islands, he was encumbered with "a seraglio of hideous German prostitutes, who rendered him equally ludicrous by their absurdities, and unpopular by their rapacity." To this sufficiently repulsive specimen of Whig-Hanoverian royalty, the Tories, or Jacobites, preferred the young representative of the House of Stuart, although a Catholic.†

" Let our great James come over,
And baffle Prince Hanover,
With hearts and hands, in loyal bands,
We'll welcome him at Dover.

regards England, in Scotland, as involving, if successful, a Repeal of the hated Union, and in Ireland, a dissolution of the perjury-enacted Penal Code, by a fulfilment of the violated Treaty of Limerick, that cause *was* the representative of nationality, in opposition to provincialism, and of religious emancipation in opposition to sectarian oppression, and, *so far*, was the cause of JUSTICE *versus* INJUSTICE. Great historic events have *various* aspects, from which they *must* be contemplated, and studied, in order to be duly understood.

* The object of George's jealousy was the famous Swedish Count Konigsmark, who, in despot-fashion, was *privately* made away with. When George II., after his accession, "first visited Hanover, he ordered some alterations in the Palace, and, while repairing the dressing-room which belonged to his mother, the Princess Dorothea, the body of Konigsmark was discovered under the pavement, where he is supposed to have been strangled, and buried."

† Lord Mahon justly considers the Jacobites to have been wrong, "in seeking to impose a Roman Catholic head upon the Protestant Church of England." In *that* objection to the Stuart family, *the* strength of the party for the Revolution *unquestionably* lay. Yet political measures, like the Revolution, however desirable in *one* point of view, may seem most objectionable from *others;* and men *will* act accordingly. Hence, though the Stuarts were driven out, as has been observed, "to *keep* them out required a standing army, many campaigns and battles, the decapitation of many honourable heads, the confiscation of estates, the imposition of taxes on almost every useful commodity, and the borrowing of millions of money, which laid the foundation of the present enormous national debt; which swallowed up, year after year, wealth as it was made; and prevented much of the best capital, and the most skilful hands, from engaging in the production of wealth."

> Of royal birth and breeding,
> In ev'ry grace exceeding,
> Our hearts will mourn, till *his* return,
> O'er lands that lie a-bleeding."

And again, after exclaiming, that

> " England *must* surrender
> To him, they call PRETENDER,"

it was alleged—

> " The royal youth deserveth
> To fill the sacred place;
> 'Tis he *alone* preserveth
> The Stuarts' ancient race.
> Since 'tis our inclination,
> To call him to the nation,
> Let each man, in his station,
> Receive his KING in peace!"

As the Stuarts, previous to the junction of the 2 British Crowns, in 1603, had been the national Sovereigns of Scotland, and, as the so-called Act of Union, recently imposed upon the Scotch by corruption and terrorism, for the special purpose of excluding their ancient dynasty from the throne,* was to be repealed, if that dynasty could be restored, the Stuart interest was proportionably powerful there, and its policy duly directed, to excite a popular insurrection against the Hanoverian. "We," says the Declaration of James to the Scotch, as James VIII., "are come to relieve our subjects of Scotland from the hardships they groan under, on account of the late unhappy Union; and to restore the Kingdom to its ancient free and independent state." And subsequently, " We hope," adds the document, "to see Our just rights, and those of the Church, and People of Scotland, once more settled, in a free and independent *Scots* Parliament, on their ancient foundation. To such a Parliament, (which we will immediately call,) shall we entirely refer both our and their interests; being sensible that *these interests, rightly understood, are always the same.*" The 1st movement against the German consequently occurred in Scotland, where the Earl of Mar, (late Secretary of State under Queen Anne,) with other noblemen, assembled, in September, 1715, a Jacobite force in the Highlands, and proclaimed the Stuart Prince, at Brae-Mar, and elsewhere, as *King* James. The national and Tory feeling, against the English and Whigs, for supplanting the old native royal line by a "foreign brood," was suitably expressed in the songs of the day:—

> "*Our* King they do despise, boys,
> Because of Scottish blood;
> But, for all their *oaths*, and *lies*, boys,
> *His* title still is *good*."

> "How lang shall our old, and once brave, warlike nation,
> Thus tamely submit to *a base usurpation?*
> * * * * *
> How lang shall the Whigs, *perverting all reason*,
> Call honest men knaves, *and loyalty treason?*"

---

* See, under the year 1708, the account already given of the passing of the Act of Union for Scotland, denounced at the time, or February, 1707, by Sir Charles Packington, in the English Parliament, as "a Union, that was carried by corruption and bribery within doors, by force and violence without."

The general hostility to the Union, noticed in the same powerful effusions of popular opinion,—

> "All UNIONS we'll *o'erturn*, boys,
> Like Bruce at Bannockburn, boys,
> The English home we'll chase!"—

likewise appeared upon the Stuart standard at Brae-Mar; of which, says the description, "the colour was blue, having, on the one side, the Scottish arms, wrought in gold, and, on the other, the Scottish thistle, with these words beneath, *No Union.*" Mar, soon after he took the field, was to have been joined by James from the Continent; but that Prince's arrival was prevented, by various unfavourable circumstances, until January, 1716. Meanwhile George's Commander in Scotland, the Duke of Argyle, engaged Mar at the battle of Sheriff-Muir, or Dumblain, in November, with such a result, as to arrest any progress of the main Stuart force southwards; and subsequent reinforcements, with an importation of several thousand Dutch troops (as in 1688, &c.) so strengthened the side of the foreign Prince, against the English Prince and his British supporters,* that the latter was obliged to retire northwards, until, in February, 1716, he had to embark by night with Mar, and other noblemen, for the Continent, and the Jacobite force had to disperse.

During the short stay he was able to make in Scotland against his Georgeite opponents and their Dutch supporters, James expressed how solicitous he was to obtain the Irish Brigade from France; which, however, after a peace, so very recently concluded, and so very necessary to be maintained, with England, could *not* be sent to him. From "Kinnaird, Jan. 2, 1716," he wrote to his Minister, Lord Bolingbroke, at Paris—"What is absolutely necessary for us, and that without loss of time, is, a competent number of arms, with all that belongs to them;" and "our 5 Irish regiments, with all the officers of the D." of "Berwick at their head." Then, alluding to the Regent of France, he states of the Duke of Ormonde and the veteran Lieutenant-Generals Michael Roth,† and Arthur Dillon—"Could the Regent send him," Ormonde, "with troops into England, at the same time that our Irish regiments

---

* Among the circumstances, which Lord Macaulay reckons the least "glorious" connected with the Revolution of 1688, was that of James II. having only been dethroned through the aid of a foreign or Dutch army. Again, or in 1715-16, we see the foreign occupant of James's throne excluding that Monarch's son from it, through a treaty for obtaining 6000 foreigners from Holland, "who," says a contemporary English historian of the Hanoverian party, "did very good service in North Britain, and were *more* terrible to the rebels, than the native Britons in the King's army." Finally, or in 1745, George II. also claimed Dutch aid, which he obtained, even to a *more* considerable amount. And, though such aid was afterwards withdrawn, and though the army with which his son, the Duke of Cumberland, decided the contest against Prince Charles Stuart at Culloden, in 1746, was *not* composed of foreigners, yet this army was enabled to advance and fight that decisive battle in Scotland, by having had about 6000 foreign auxiliaries, or Hessians, to serve elsewhere in the country. Hence, the offer of Prince Charles, acting as Regent for his father in Scotland, in opposition to the Elector of Hanover, as George II.—"Let him, if he pleases, try the experiment; let him send off his foreign hirelings, and put all upon the issue of a battle, and I will trust only to the King my father's subjects!" But the largest amount of *foreigners* was employed to *force* the Revolution upon Ireland, under William III., as shown in Book III., under the year 1698.

† As *also* spelled "Rothe," mistaken, by Lord Mahon, for "Roche."

come here, it would *end* the dispute very soon. . . . I should have mentioned before, that Rothe, or Dillon, I must have. One I can spare you, but not both; and may be Dillon would be useful in Ireland," &c. Several other Irish officers evinced their loyalty to James, as *their* King, although they were not able to arrive, from France in Scotland, soon enough to be of service in any combat. "They," observes a contemporary, "were seen abandoning *all* engagements, and certainties, to follow him, without the least hesitation, into Scotland, as fast as they could ship off, notwithstanding the rigours of a most hard and rigid season, and the many dangers they were to run, by sea, and land, as well as the hardships, and hard shifts, they might guess they should meet with in the service"—which, it will be noted, exposed those engaged in it, if taken prisoners, to the savage mode of execution, (or half-hanging and disembowelling alive!) appointed, by the law of England, for "high treason." Among the officers of King James II. with his son, as *King*, in Scotland, were Lieutenant-General Dominick Sheldon, and Brigadier Christopher Nugent of Dardistown. The Marquis of Tinmouth, son of the Marshal Duke of Berwick, and then Colonel of the Regiment of Berwick, and the Marquis's kinsman, the Honourable Francis Bulkeley, reformed Colonel of the same Irish regiment, likewise came to serve there. Sheldon was 1 of those who departed, along with James himself, for the Continent. The Marquis of Tinmouth, and Colonel Bulkeley, had sailed together for Scotland, *with* 100,000 *crowns in gold*, contributed by Philip V. of Spain; but were unluckily shipwrecked by night off the Scotch coast, and *lost all the money*, as they only had time, to make for land, in a boat.* The Marquis, and the Colonel, being finally left behind with the Jacobite force when it was obliged to disperse, ventured, instead of seeking a concealment in the Highlands, or Western Isles, to proceed from the north to Edinburgh; passed undiscovered, though 8 days there; embarked for Holland; and thence reached France. They, and the rest of the officers, who were with James in Scotland, upon the complaint of George's Ambassador at Paris, were deprived, by the French Government, of their employments, but only to save appearances; the Regiment of Berwick, for instance, though taken from the Marquis of Tinmouth, being given back to his father, the Duke of Berwick, who made another of his sons its Colonel; and the Regiment of Nugent being taken from the Brigadier, but transferred to his son, though then a mere youth.

Some of this regiment had gone over with their countryman, James Butler, 2nd Duke of Ormonde, to England. This Irish nobleman, from the antiquity of his family, from the magnitude of his rent-roll, among the largest in Great Britain and Ireland, besides the emoluments of several high civil and military appointments, from his public spirit, his personal bravery, affability, magnificence, benevolence, and hospitality, was the head and idol of the great Tory or Jacobite party in England,† whose cry was, we are told, "*an Ormond!* in opposition to *King* George,"

* The Duke of Berwick is the authority for Philip V.'s contribution, thus, as regards James, and Scotland, destined to be "neither good for king nor country," or "in the deep bosom of the ocean buried!" James's son, Prince Charles, was likewise very *unlucky*, with reference to remittances for him, in Scotland, from Spain, as will be seen farther on.

† On the Whig or Georgeite attainder of the Duke, his friend, Dean Swift, writes

or "*High Church and Ormond!*" Their feelings of hostility to Hanoverianism, and of proportionable attachment to the exiled and attainted Duke, were particularly displayed this year, 1715, in London, with reference to the 1st celebration there of George's birth-day as *King*— the Hanoverian's entrance into this world happening, awkwardly enough, to date from the day immediately previous to that appointed for commemorating the re-establishment of the House of Stuart on the thrones of Great Britain and Ireland, in the person of King Charles II. "The 28th of May being the *King's* birth-day," says an Anglo-Whig annalist with respect to George I., "the great Officers of State, the Foreign Ministers, and Nobility, waited on his Majesty at St. James's, the guns were fired, and the flags displayed, &c." But "the Jacobites reserved the demonstrations both of their *joy* and *insolence* for the next day, (29th) which, being the Anniversary of the *Restoration* of the Royal Family, they celebrated in a most extraordinary manner; not so much out of compliment to the *former*, as in hopes of what they call a *future*, Restoration. Their mobbs in the city broke the windows of such houses as were *not* illuminated, and, among 'em, those of the Lord Mayor. Their cry was, *High Church and the Duke of Ormond!* In Smithfield, there was 1 of the greatest mobbs that has been known since Sacheverell's Trial, where *they burnt a print of King William*, &c." Another Georgite writer of the day, after noting of the Jacobites on this occasion, how "they made *greater* illuminations and *more* bonfires than were seen the day before, especially in the City of London," adds, "they insulted 4 Life-Guards who were patrolling, and oblig'd them to cry out, as *they* did, *High Church and Ormond!*" Although the Duke (as above intimated) had found it necessary, soon after the Hanoverian accession, to retire to France, where he was at the time of those manifestations, and others of the kind, by his party, he was confidently expected, by that party, to return before long, in spite of his enemies, the Whigs, to get the better of them, and to send their odious foreign importation, George the Elector, packing home again to Hanover! As the Jacobite ballad exclaimed—

"What tho' th' *Usurper's* cause prevail?
Renew your constitution!—
Expel that race, the curst entail
Of Whiggish revolution!—
Be bought and sold no more
By a sordid German power,
Is it like our old proud-hearted nation?
Let KING JAMES *then be the toast*,
May he bless our longing coast
With a speedy and a just RESTORATION!"

In James's court, "over the water," to which, as well as the Duke, Lord Bolingbroke had fled from England, the accounts of such public

—"Now it is done, it looks like a dream to those, who consider the nobleness of his birth, the great merits of his ancestors, and his own; his long unspotted loyalty, his affability, generosity, and sweetness of nature. I knew him long and well, and, excepting the frailties of his youth, which had been for some years over, and that easiness of temper which did sometimes lead him to follow the judgment of those, who had, by many degrees, less understanding than himself, I have not conversed with a more faultless person; of great justice and charity; a true sense of religion, without ostentation; of undoubted valour, thoroughly skilled in his trade of a soldier; a quick and ready apprehension, with a good share of understanding, and a general knowledge in men and history; although under some disadvantage by an invincible modesty, which, however, could not but render him yet more amiable

displays of sympathy in England with the "true King," excited duly favourable anticipations amongst his exiled followers. At that court, writes Lord Bolingbroke, " the Jacobites had wrought one another up, to look upon the success of the present designs as infallible; every meeting-house which the populace demolished,* every drunken riot which happened, served to confirm them in these sanguine expectations; and there was hardly one amongst them, who would lose the air of contributing, by his intrigues, to the restoration, which, he took for granted, would be brought about, without him, in a very few weeks. Care and hope sat on every busy *Irish* face." Accordingly, in autumn, the Duke of Ormonde, accompanied by 20 officers, and 25 select troopers, of the Regiment of Nugent, from their quarters in Normandy, sailed for the opposite coast of England, in order to act upon the extensive arrangements which he had made there, for a rising against the new dynasty. On reaching his destination, however, he found nothing could be attempted in the west against the Elector of Hanover, owing to the various measures that Prince had been enabled to take for his defence, principally through the aid of a Colonel Mac Lean. That officer (of a Highland name, most illustrious in the annals of loyalty to the Stuarts,) had been the confidant of the Duke with respect to all his plans and dispositions for the rising in question, but turned out such a villain, as to become an *informer!*

> " Oh for a tongue to curse the slave,
> Whose treason, like a deadly blight,
> Comes o'er the councils of the brave,
> And blasts them, in their hour of might! "—MOORE.

In consequence of this baseness, " the principal friends of Ormond," says Lord Mahon, " were arrested; the others dispersed; and when the Duke came to the appointed place, he found no signs of a rising—not a single man to meet him, instead of the thousands he expected; and he was compelled to steer again towards France!" After a conference there, at St. Malo, with his young Sovereign, the Duke re-embarked, it is added, " with the daring and indeed desperate project of throwing himself upon the English coast, and taking the chance of some favourable circumstances; but a violent tempest forced him back a second time." The Duke eventually retired to Avignon, with his young Sovereign; and, when that Prince left France, continued to reside at Avignon under the appellation of Colonel Comerford, until invited by Philip V. into Spain, for the purpose to be soon related.

Not long after the Earl of Mar had risen in Scotland, the English Jacobites of Northumberland, and Cumberland, under Thomas Forster, Esq., Member for the former County, the Earl of Derwentwater and others, joined by a body of Scotch, under the stout Brigadier William

---

to those, who had the honour and happiness of being thoroughly acquainted with him. This is a short, imperfect character of that great person, the Duke of Ormond, who is now attainted for high treason."

* Of the Anti-Hanoverian Toryism, or High-Church Jacobitism, displayed at such demolitions, the following specimen occurs, in a letter, of July, 1715, from Mr. Baily of Staffordshire. "When the mobb pull'd down the Meeting-House at Wolverhampton, one of their Leaders, getting on the top of the same, flourish'd his hat round his head, and cry'd, ' G—— d—— King G——ge, and the Duke of *Marlborough!*' A fellow, at the same place, standing by as an idle spectator, was charg'd by the rioters, with being a spy; and, to attone for his supposed offence, they made him go down on his knees, and cry, ' *God bless King James III.!*'"

Mac Intosh of Borlum, took up arms in the name of *King* James; and, having caused a much more numerous gathering of Cumberland and Westmoreland Militia, &c., to disperse with disgrace,* advanced, proclaiming James, as far as Preston, in Lancashire. They, however, were finally reduced to surrender at that place in November, by a superior corps of regular troops, under Lieutenant-General George Carpenter and Major-General Charles Wills. With this captured Jacobite force, there was an Irish gentleman of a most honourable name, Charles Wogan, of the house of Rathcoffy, in the County of Kildare. By this name, that County was represented in the Supreme Council of the Confederate Catholics of Ireland, at Kilkenny, during the great civil war under King Charles I., as well as in the Parliament of King James II. during the subsequent War of the Revolution in Ireland. Against the Cromwellians, the name of Wogan was distinguished in the annals of cavalier gallantry by the defence of Duncannon in 1649, which compelled those revolutionists, or rebels, to raise the siege with loss; and, in 1650, that name was still more distinguished by the unparalleled courage and devotedness of the hero who, having undertaken "the desperate task of marching through England with a party of royalist cavalry," in order to join a body of King Charles II.'s adherents in the Highlands of Scotland, "made good his romantic undertaking, though *all* England had then submitted to the Parliament;" and who afterwards "saved the King's life, at the battle, or rather flight, of Worcester, by the desperate stand he made, at the head of 300 horse, against Cromwell's whole army," (consisting of 30,000 men,) "in the suburbs of that town, till the King and Colonel Careless were out of sight!" † With such glorious family recollections before him, and, to use his own words, "as a good subject, who despised dangers, and death itself, when he had to execute the orders, or to avenge the honour, of his Prince," Charles Wogan did not hesitate to join the Jacobite rising in the north of England; considering Prince James Francis Edward Stuart, as, by hereditary right, *King* James III., to be denounced, with no more justice, by George of Hanover, and *one* Parliament, than Prince Charles Stuart, or King Charles II., had been denounced by Oliver Cromwell, and *another* Parliament; both of the Princes, so denounced, having the like title to the Crown by birth, as both Princes of Wales; and the denunciation, in the case of Charles, being afterwards reversed, as illegal, by his "Restoration." Upon the forming, early in 1715, of the extensive secret confederacy in England, in favour of James III., with London as its head-quarters, "from which metropolitan and central site, a correspondence was conducted with the Jacobites who dwelt in different parts of the kingdom," Charles Wogan, his brother, Captain Nicholas Wogan, Colonel Henry Oxburgh, who had long served in King James II.'s army, and James Talbot, Esq., were the Irish Catholic gentlemen delegated to Northumberland, to arrange for

*The Cumberland and Westmoreland Militia behaved no better, in 1745, at Carlisle.

† Charles Wogan, commenting, (as the Chevalier, or Sir Charles, Wogan,) in his letter to Dean Swift, on the historical unfairness of Clarendon towards Colonel Wogan, remarks, how Clarendon sinks all mention of the Colonel's country, and "omits giving him the honour of having saved the King's life," as above recited. Abbé Mac Geoghegan, under "le Comté de Kildare," notices "la noble famille des Wogans de Rathcoffy;" and, for additional information on this old name, see Dalton's Irish Army List of King James II., under Lieutenant-Colonel John Wogan of the Infantry Regiment of Sir Maurice Eustace.

the insurrection there. Of those 4 Irish Catholics, and 3 English gentlemen, of whom 1 was a Protestant clergyman,* despatched on the same design in that quarter, we are told—"These gentlemen, under the pretence of being tourists, anxious to examine objects of nature and art, dispersed themselves in every direction. For the alleged protection of their equipments as scientific travellers, yet with the view of preventing surprise from their political opponents, they armed themselves with swords and pistols. In thus riding from place to place, they contrived to visit the various sites of their Jacobite partizans, in order to stimulate them to a general and simultaneous rising." The English movement, however, for a 2nd "Restoration," in favour of the nephew of King Charles II., and the son of King James II., being put down by superior force at Preston, Charles Wogan, with the principal prisoners, was brought pinioned on horseback, to London, under a military escort, and committed to Newgate. He was cast into irons there with the veteran Brigadier Mac Intosh (who, having served in King James II.'s Guards and in Holland, had been for fighting, instead of surrendering, at Preston,) his son James Mac Intosh, Robert and William Dalmahoy, (sons of Sir Alexander Dalmahoy) Hepburne of Keith, &c. The Grand Jury of Westminster, in April, 1716, found Bills of Indictment against Wogan and the Brigadier; and the latter, and some of his companions in arms, were appointed to be tried for their lives, at Westminster Hall, in May. But, between 11 and 12 o'clock, the night before those trials were to have taken place, Wogan, and the 2 Mac Intoshes, the 2 Dalmahoys, Hepburne, James Talbot, and a gallant servant, John Tasker, in all 8, mastered the Keeper and Turnkey, and in spite of 9 armed grenadiers through whom it was necessary to effect a passage out of the prison, succeeded in doing so, and regained their liberty. Six other "imprisoned rebels" in Hanoverian, but "suffering loyalists" in Jacobite language, seized the opportunity of getting out at the same time. But, unacquainted with the streets, and running into Warwick Court, beyond which they could not pass, they were obliged to return by Warwick Lane, and were consequently recaptured. James Talbot, 1 of the gallant 8, who commenced the work against the Keeper, Turnkey, and grenadiers, and got off, was unfortunately taken, 2 days after, at a house in Windmill Street, near

* The Rev. Mr. Buxton. "This is not very strange," says the zealous contemporary Whig-Hanoverian writer, Oldmixon; "for who of *all* the Episcopal Clergy in the North of England, except the reverend and worthy Mr. Peploe, Minister of Preston, distinguish'd themselves by the least opposition the rebels met with from them, in deed, or in word? If there were *some* that did so, I should have been glad to have known it, and would, with pleasure, have done as much justice to their loyalty, as the giving it place in my History could do it." Of the Scotch Episcopal Church, he alleges, "there were but 2 Episcopal Clergymen who behav'd with loyalty to King George, and who thereby made themselves odious to their whole party." Hence, on the *general* Jacobitism, or aversion to the House of Hanover, which existed, at its accession to the Crown, among the Protestant Episcopal Clergy in Britain, Dr. Johnson has remarked—"The Church was all against this family." Of the 2 classes of religionists to whom they were opposed, the Catholics, and the Dissenters, those Jacobite Churchmen feared the Catholics *less* than the Dissenters, and sympathized with them *more*, as supporters of monarchy, than they could sympathize with the latter, as representatives of the Puritan, democratic, or republican principles, whose triumph, under the Parliamentarian and Cromwellian *régime*, was attended by the subversion of the Established Church, as well as the execution of one Monarch, and proscription of another; whereas, in the great contest connected with these events, the members of the Established and Catholic churches were equally royalists, and sufferers for having been so.

Piccadilly, and again lodged in Newgate.* This, however, was all the success obtained against the Jacobite fugitives. As for Wogan, £500 being offered for apprehending him, the asylum which he made out, in what he calls "the thick forest of the city of London," in some days became known to the Hanoverian "detectives;" so that "he found himself driven to take refuge, at noon-day, upon the roof of the house where he lodged; whence, (in spite of the rage of his persecutors, and of an innumerable crowd of people,) Providence enabled him to escape, as well as from other crosses by sea and land, until he reached, towards the end of June, a country where he had no longer any thing to fear, or France."

The outbreak, in 1715, of the Jacobite insurrections in Great Britain was productive of suitable apprehensions on the part of the colonial and sectarian "ascendancy" in Ireland; whose existence there depended on the maintenance of the unnatural order of things, established in the country, by Oliver Cromwell, and William of Orange, upon the landed spoliation, religious persecution, and legalized depression, of the nation at large. "The Government, conscious of its own harshness, and dreading the workings of revenge or despair," says Mr. O'Conor, the learned historian of the Irish Catholics, "took the precaution of arresting the principal leaders of the Catholics, and holding them in confinement, until the storm of rebellion subsided. The Commons addressed the Lords Justices, praying that 'they would give directions for apprehending the persons of all suspected Papists;' and the Justices accordingly issued orders, for the rigid execution of the laws against the priests, and for the apprehension of the Earls of Antrim and Westmeath, the Lords Netterville, Cahir, and Dillon, and most of the principal Catholics. This measure, however arbitrary or illegal, might derive some justification, or at least palliation, from the instability of the Government, and the provocation given to the Catholics; but the wanton persecution of priests, and the base and detestable artifices resorted to for their detection and expulsion, admit of no apology, or extenuation. . . . The Popery Code was not only rigidly enforced, but a race of men, hostile to the very name of Christianity, were employed, to hunt Catholic priests out of their hiding-places, and drag them from their lurking-holes. These agents of persecution, mostly foreign Jews, whose love of money, and hatred of Christianity, animated them to the darkest deeds of treachery, assumed the character of clergymen,† and performed the ceremonies of the Catholic religion. Under this mask of dissimulation, they insinuated themselves into the confidence of the unwary and unsuspicious, through whom they were introduced to the concealed priests; and, as soon as they had fully ascertained their haunts, and devised means for their caption, they threw off the mask, and proceeded, at the head of a licentious soldiery, to complete the work of their detestable treachery. Priests were thus dragged from their altars whilst celebrating the most solemn ceremony of their religion, and exposed, in their vestments, to derision and insult, shut up in dungeons, and condemned to perpetual exile."

The proscribed Stuart claimant of the Crowns of Great Britain and Ireland, having resolved to marry among the Catholic Princesses in

* Talbot's subsequent career has been referred to in Book V., under the year 1711, as an officer in Spain.
† I substitute "clergymen," for the more doubtful term "ministers," in Mr. O'Conor's text—not improbably by a misprint.

Germany, intrusted the selection of his future bride there to his dashing Irish cavalier, Charles Wogan, who, in 1718, fixed, with excellent taste, upon the Princess Maria Clementina Sobieski, daughter of Prince James Louis Sobieski, son of John Sobieski, King of Poland, so famous for his wars against the Turks, but, especially, for the great victory, by which, having saved Vienna in 1683, he was designated, in the language of Scripture, "a man sent from God, whose name was John." The match *privately* agreed to, was, for political reasons, to be similarly carried into effect. But the completion of the arrangements for that purpose being taken, by a Scotch political intrigue in the Stuart court, out of the hands of Wogan, and transferred to 2 Scotch Protestants, the Honourable James Murray, and the Honourable John Hay, (subsequently created by James Earls of Dunbar and Inverness,) the Elector of Hanover got intelligence of the contemplated match. Alarmed at the great additional prestige which his injured competitor for the Crowns of Great Britain and Ireland would derive from such a connexion with the race of Sobieski, as well as at the dangerous relationship which that connexion would establish between the excluded Prince and the Houses of Austria, Spain, Bavaria, &c., the Elector, whom the power and purse of England enabled to bully and bribe upon the Continent,* resolved, by his influence there, to prevent the match, if possible. The Anglo-Hanoverian Ministers, on the one hand, frightened the Emperor Charles VI. with the prospect of losing his extensive dominions in southern Italy and Sicily, then, or in 1718, principally defended against Spain by the maritime aid of England, unless he would undertake to stop the accomplishment of that match with his relative by force; and, on the other hand, the large sum of £100,000 (English money, of course,) was offered as an increase to the Princess Sobieski's dowry, if she would agree to marry the Prince of Baden-Baden, or any other Prince, than the Head of the House of Stuart, to whom she was affianced. The Emperor, under this "pressure from without," had his cousin-german and aunt, the Princess and her mother, arrested, in September, 1718, and detained, under the guard of General Heister, at Inspruck, in the Tyrol; with no more right than Elizabeth Tudor of England had to shut up Mary Stuart, Queen of Scotland; though with sufficient for the satisfaction of the Hanoverian, who had provided for his own unhappy cousin and wife, in a similar manner! No course now remained to be adopted in the Stuart Court, but to apologize to Wogan, for not having left *him* to conclude the business which he had commenced so well; and to induce *him*, if possible, to extricate the Princess from *her* confinement. Though such an attempt, on his part, seemed so little likely to succeed, as to be deemed, by the *wisest* heads to whom it was mentioned, an affair of mere Don Quixotism; and though, if he should fail, and be arrested in striving to liberate the Princess, his own doom

* The subsidies, accompanying treaties with Continental powers, for *Hanoverian* interests, speak for themselves. At home, it will suffice to cite from Walpoliana, under "secret services," with respect to the Hanoverian family. "Some have confidently asserted, that Sir Robert Walpole's *large secret service money* went to newspapers; while, in fact, *it was necessary, in order to fix this family on the throne. Lord Orrery, Secretary to the Pretender, had a pension, from Sir Robert Walpole, of £2000 a year.*" This was Charles Boyle, 4th Earl of Orrery; and thus was the cause of James in England *sold* to George! That the unscrupulous newspaper supporter of Hanoverianism was *also* well remembered is apparent from the case of Arnall, already mentioned, in a note, under the battle of Blenheim, in 1704.

might be *death*, either upon an Austrian scaffold, or by his being handed over to the Elector of Hanover for execution in England, on the plea of having been "guilty of high treason" there; Wogan, nevertheless, agreed to take the matter in hands, if his Sovereign would give him such a letter to the Prince Sobieski, as might induce that Prince to write to his daughter, that, with the bearer of the communication, as equally the envoy of her father and her intended husband, she should escape, if possible, from Inspruck. Wogan, after having had, under a due disguise, a personal communication with the Princess Sobieski, and her mother, at Inspruck, to whom he delivered suitable letters from his young Sovereign, proceeded, towards the end of the year 1718, to the Prince Sobieski, at Ohlau in Silesia, to obtain the requisite orders from the Prince to his daughter. But, from the utter disbelief of the Prince in the possibility of his daughter being ever rescued under the circumstances, it was, with much difficulty, he could be gotten to put pen to paper on the matter, although he did so at last, in the most satisfactory manner; presenting, as a testimony of his special regard, to Wogan, a unique and beautiful snuff-box, formed of a single turquois, so admirably enchased in gold as to be pronounced by jewellers of an inestimable value; particularly as having formed a portion of the spoil of the Grand Vizier's splendid scarlet pavilion, in which it was taken, by the great John Sobieski, the day of his famous triumph at Vienna.

Having obtained the documents requested by March, 1719, and likewise gotten fictitious passports, Wogan selected, for his enterprise, from the officers of the regiment of his near relative, Lieutenant-General Count Arthur Dillon, 3 kinsmen of his own, namely, Richard Gaydon of Irishtown, its Major, and a Knight of St. Louis, and Captains Luke O'Toole of Victoria, and John Misset of Kildare. These, with Wogan himself, and a trusty Florentine valet of his young Sovereign, named Michel Vezzosi, were to form the men of the party. They were to be accompanied by 2 women, Madame Misset, the Captain's wife, then several months gone with child,* and her maid, Jannetton; the former,

---

* I subjoin, as containing various characteristic circumstances, this extract from "Female Fortitude Exemplify'd, in an Impartial Narrative of the Seizure, Escape, and Marriage of the Princess Sobiesky," &c., having merely "London: Printed in the Year 1722," at the bottom of the title-page, since it might be the *ruin* of a publisher, who should venture to put his name there. "General Dillon's regiment lay then in garrison at Scelestat, within 9 leagues of Strasbourgh. Mr. Wogan went thither, not doubting but that he should find some of his," Dillon's, "officers, who should assist him in the undertaking. Upon his arrival, he communicated his design to Major Gaydon, Captain Tool, and Captain Missett, all 3 his relations, and persons who had given several sufficient proofs of their conduct and resolution. They readily embraced the proposal, and *warmly engaged to serve him with their lives and fortunes in so worthy an enterprize, notwithstanding an order prohibiting all Irish officers to leave their posts upon pain of being cashier'd;* there being then a report, that preparations were making in Spain, to enable the Chevalier," as James III., "to make a descent on England. They all spoke French very well, and Tool was master of High Dutch, which proved of great use. Missett was married to a gentlewoman of Irish birth and extraction, but bred in France. She was young, had a sprightly turn of wit, and a conversation so engaging, as could not fail to make her an acceptable companion to the Princess. But as she was, on the other hand, *timorous in her nature, of a very tender constitution, and 4 months gone with child*, the greatest difficulty was, how to break so nice an affair to *her*. This the husband undertook; laying before her the glory of the enterprize, with this prevailing inducement, that he himself was engaged in it. Mr. Wogan and the Major back'd what he said, with all that was proper to be urged on such an occasion.

designed to attend upon the Princess Sobieski, during her journey into Italy, after leaving Inspruck; the latter, to change clothes with the Princess at Inspruck, and occupy her bed for some time after her flight, in order to make the Austrian *keepers* think, till the substitution should be discovered, that they had her still; and thus postpone the commencement of a pursuit. But Jannetton, not being made aware of the real object of the journey, accompanied the party merely under an impression, that it was an arrangement to enable her friend, Captain Luke O'Toole, (nearly 6 feet high, and the finest man in his regiment!) to rescue a rich heiress, to whom he was engaged, from her relatives who detained her by force; and, for aiding in which meritorious design, she, Jannetton, was, of course, not to be a loser. The equipage prepared at Strasburgh for the undertaking was to consist of a travelling-carriage of strong construction to stand the wear and tear of such a long and rough journey, and provided with double braces and spare tackle of all sorts in case of accidents; it was to be drawn by 6 post-horses, and attended by 3 outriders well-armed. In this vehicle were to be Major Gaydon and Madame Misset, with Wogan and Jannetton. The Major and Madame had passports, procured by Wogan at Rome, as for the Count and Countess de Cernes, of a noble house in Flanders, travelling, with their family, to visit the Santa Casa of Our Lady of Loretto; Wogan being included as a brother to the so-called Countess; the Princess Sobieski, after taking Jannetton's place (as "the girl she'd leave behind her!") being intended to pass for the Countess's sister; while Captains O'Toole and Misset, with the valet Vezzosi, were to act as the 3 mounted and armed attendants, or outriders.

Wogan, and his adventurous little party, set out, April 16th, from Strasburgh, where, in passing the bridge, and taking leave of their veteran friend, Lieutenant-Colonel Lally of the Regiment of Dillon, (father of the subsequently famous and unfortunate Count Lally) the Lieutenant-Colonel, "brave as he was," they remarked, "could not refrain from tears in bidding farewell to those, whom, from the rashness of their enterprise, there seemed to be no likelihood of his ever beholding again!" Proceeding on their apparent "road to ruin," or "journey," as the Intendant of Strasburgh said, "to *make a hole in the moon!*" they reached, in about a week, the vicinity of Inspruck. There, after a due correspondence with the 2 Princesses, it was arranged that, the 27th, at night, Jannetton, having been privately admitted into their apartment, in a shabby riding-hood or female surtout of the English fashion, the Princess Maria Clementina should put it on, and slip down with her Polish Page, Konska, to the door leading into the street, near which Wogan, in waiting to receive them, was to bring them to the inn, and the carriage there; that, the better to deceive General Heister, and the Magistrates of Inspruck, if possible for 24 hours, the Princess, 2 days previous to her elopement, should keep her bed as very unwell, and, from the time of her departure, Jannetton should occupy the bed, having the curtains closed the ensuing day, under the pretext of the patient being so much worse, as to render this necessary; and, in fine, that, the Princess, the better to protect her mother against the imputation of having connived at the escape, should leave a letter on her toilet asking

She heard them all very attentively, and, after pausing some time, briskly rose up, and said, *What would she not do for a* King *and* Queen, *and a* Husband, *she loved so well?"*

pardon for her flight, on the plea of being obliged by all laws, human and divine, to follow her husband, rather than remain with her parents. April 27th-28th, about 1 o'clock in the morning, amidst a tempest of wind, hail, and snow, so severe, that the sentinel on the Princess's residence at Inspruck, being without a sentry-box, was obliged by the wet and cold to seek shelter, for *inside* and *outside* warmth, in a little tavern opposite, the grand-daughter of John Sobieski made her way out in the dark to a corner of the street, where the Irish cavalier (or her "Papa Warner," as she used to call him in Germany,) was waiting, beyond the time appointed, in such uneasiness as may be easily supposed, to receive her; and, followed by her Page carrying a parcel of some articles of dress, with jewels to the value of 150,000 pistoles, she proceeded with her deliverer to his inn. There she put on a dry suit, which Madam Misset had for her; all were on the road by about 2 o'clock; and they were 15 miles from Inspruck at sun-rise. By the following night, they were beyond the danger of any arrest, except what was to be apprehended, should they be overtaken by a special courier from Inspruck, to alarm the Governors of Trent and Roveredo. The Chevalier provided against this, by directing O'Toole and Misset, to keep at a considerable distance in the rear of the carriage, to intercept any such courier. If necessary, they, after stripping him of his papers, were to kill his horse, and leave himself securely tied, at some place off the road, with ropes, of which they had a supply for the purpose; but they were not to take his life, if they could avoid doing so. The courier from Inspruck was, however, more easily disposed of by the Irish Captains, 2 posts from Trent, at a village named Wellishmile. There, having ordered supper, about 2 o'clock in the morning, they fell in with the very man, greatly knocked up by the road; invited him to supper with them; and amused and plied him so well with liquor, that he blabbed out the object of his journey, *viz.*, to have the *banditti* who carried off the Princess Sobieski intercepted; and produced to them his despatch to that effect. This, they, after making him still more drunk, purloined from him, tore to pieces, and left him in bed in such a state, the wine they gave him having been well mixed with *eau-de-vie*, that he was incapable of travelling farther for 24 hours!

Thus, notwithstanding several mischances, or breakings-down, and delays for horses, which might have been fatal to the undertaking, the Princess was able to proceed on her journey, during which she charmed her companions by her affability and cheerfulness. "They offer'd," it is observed, "to place a cushion under the Princess's head, in hopes she might take a little rest; but she seem'd to take pleasure in nothing so much as to inform herself in everything relating to England, their manners, the most considerable families, the dress and beauty of the ladies; at the same time learning some English words. Thus she diverted herself all the journey, and, as she had a very happy memory, she retain'd everything they had told her, to every one's admiration. She made Mr. Wogan relate the adventure at Preston (he having acted a principal part in that affair,) and tell her the names of all those who suffered upon that occasion, whose misfortunes touched her very sensibly; but, more particularly, the Chevalier's," her intended husband's, "voyage into Scotland, what passed whilst he was there, and the many dangers he ran through, during the time of that adventurous expedition. After this, the Major," Gaydon, "entertain'd her with the many sieges and battles General

Dillon's regiment had been engaged in, particularly the battle of Cremona," and "the pleasure she took in hearing those martial stories showed her to be the genuine offspring of the great Sobiesky." By April 30th, she was safe out of the Imperial, or in the Venetian, territory; May 15th, entered Rome in great state, amidst the acclamations of all there, except those of the Austrian or Hanoverian party; and was married, September 2nd, to the Stuart Prince, as King James III. By him, at her decease, in January, 1735, (when only in her 33rd year, as born in July, 1702,) she was the mother of the 2 last direct, legitimate, male representatives of the royal House of Stuart—Charles-Edward-Louis-Philip-Casimir, born at Rome, in December, 1720, named, at his birth, Prince of Wales, afterwards, or in 1745-6, so famous in Scotland, and deceased at Albano, in January, 1788—Henry-Benedict-Edward-Alfred-Louis-Thomas, born at Rome, in March, 1725, Duke and Cardinal of York, Bishop of Ostia and Velletri, &c., and deceased at Rome, in July, 1807.

The Emperor Charles VI., lest he should be suspected by his Hanoverian confederate at London, not to have acted with good faith as the bailiff and jailer of his own cousin-german at Inspruck, proceeded to vindicate his Imperial honour on that point, by conduct most worthy of *such* honour. The 2 Duchies of Ohlau and Brieg in Silesia, which his own uncle and the fugitive Princess's father, Prince James Louis Sobieski, held, in consideration of a large sum of money advanced to the Emperor Leopold by King John Sobieski in 1683 for the war against the Turks— in which, as has been observed, that hero *likewise* delivered Vienna!— were sequestered, without any repayment of the capital advanced. The Prince himself was exiled to Passau. His wife, the aunt of the despicable Austrian despot, was, moreover, treated so tyrannically by him, that the harassing of body and mind which she endured threw her into a violent fever. And then, we are told, authentic testimonials of all these proceedings were forwarded, with due punctuality, to the Court at London, "as a proof of the sincerity with which the Emperor sacrificed the most sacred ties of nature to his politics!" Verily, as Achilles observes in Homer,

——————"Kings of such a kind
Stand but as slaves before a noble mind."
POPE'S Homer, Iliad ix., 494-495.

At Rome, on the contrary, Pope Clement XI., in order to mark *his* admiration of such a bold and singular enterprise as the liberation of the Princess to whom he himself was god-father,* ordered a patent to be made out, for the gallant Wogan, as a Roman Senator. Wogan, however, being unwilling to receive any title, unless the same should be conferred upon his brave countrymen, who had left their employments and risked their lives to share the hazard and glory of his undertaking,

* John Francis Albani was born in July, 1649, at Pesaro, in the Duchy of Urbino. Having embraced the ecclesiastical state, he was made Secretary of the Briefs by Pope Innocent XI.; Cardinal by Alexander VIII.; on the decease of Innocent XII., in 1700, became Pope, as Clement XI.; and died, March, 1721, in his 72nd year, after a reign of above 20 years. He was a warm friend to James III., whom, in his last illness, having sent for to his bed-chamber, he recommended the Cardinals there; that James should be allowed to reside in the Palace, which had been assigned him; that the pension, which had been granted him, to maintain the royal dignity, till restored to his kingdoms, should be continued; and that he might be supported in all things, against his enemies, by the succeeding Pope.

petitioned the Pope to reward *them* in like manner. Wogan, with his companions, Major Gaydon and Captains O'Toole and Misset, were accordingly received, June 15th, by the Senate assembled in state at the Capitol, amidst the sound of ancient Roman *litui* and *tubœ;* and, in the presence of an immense multitude, were honoured by the Count Hippolito Albani, Prince of the Senate, with a suitable oration, in praise of the Princess Sobieski, and of themselves as her liberators. This title of Roman Senator, though so much lessened in importance from what it was of old, was still that of the highest civic distinction at Rome; was never venal, nor granted to any but Kings, Princes, nephews of Sovereign Pontiffs, or persons eminent for bravery, or other merit; and each Senator was addressed throughout Italy as "Your Excellency." On the return of his young Sovereign from Spain, Wogan was also received by him as he deserved to be. That Prince, after meeting, and saluting with transports of joy, his bride, on the road to Montefiascone, where the nuptials were to take place, turned to her deliverer who accompanied her, and said to him, in the kindest and most impressive manner—"Wogan, you have behaved yourself in such a way as I expected from your zeal, from your address, and from your courage; and you may feel assured, that, if I desire to occupy the throne which is my right, it is partly that I may likewise render you, if possible, contented and happy in proportion to my power, and to what you so well deserve from me." The Prince made Wogan a Knight-Baronet, and he knighted Gaydon, O'Toole, and Misset; expressing his gratitude to them in the handsomest terms. All, too, were granted brevets of military advancement, which were to be made good in Great Britain or Ireland in case of a "Restoration;" and, should a dismission from the French army be pronounced the penalty for being absent to liberate the Princess, such brevets would be available for obtaining employment in the services of other Catholic powers on the Continent, who acknowledged the Prince as *de jure,* though not *de facto,* King of England. Gaydon was created a Brigadier, and O'Toole and Misset Colonels, as well as Madame Misset's father, who was a Captain, likewise, in the Regiment of Dillon. Gaydon and O'Toole, however, considered themselves sufficiently fortunate, under the hostile political circumstances of the times in France, to be able to resume the posts they had in their regiment, before their adventure to Inspruck. The former, from Major, became Lieutenant-Colonel, and died, very old, about 1745. The latter, serving as Captain of Grenadiers, fell, in the last action between the troops of France and those of the Emperor Charles VI. under General Seckendorf, on the Moselle. The Chevalier de Misset, the companion of those officers in rescuing the Princess, instead of returning with them to his regiment in France, decided on seeking service with the Chevalier de Wogan in Spain; for which they proceeded to embark, at Genoa, in November, 1719. While detained there some days waiting for a favourable wind, the Anglo-Hanoverian Envoy Davenant, in order to have the Chevalier de Wogan given up to him, presented to the Senate of the Republic a memorial against the Chevalier, based upon *falsehood;* or representing him as no better than *an assassin, who had to answer for the lives of 5 or 6 couriers between Inspruck and Trent!* * The Genoese Senate, however, treated this memorial with the contempt which its

---

* A due exemplification, at Genoa, of what had been said by a similar English official at Venice, that "an ambassador was one sent to foreign courts, to tell lies in the cause of his country!"

calumnies deserved, and consequently refused to withdraw their protection from the Chevalier; who thus managed there, as elsewhere, to "confound the politics," and "frustrate the knavish tricks," of his enemies.

In Spain, Wogan met with the kindest reception from Philip V., who made him and his brother Chevalier both Colonels. Misset died Governor of Oran, in Barbary, in 1733; and his widow retired to Barcelona, where she was still living in 1741; having been long rejoined by Jannetton, who died in her service there, about 1739. Wogan signalized himself against the Infidels of Barbary, especially in 1733, when heading, (according to the contemporary Spanish official account,) a detachment of 1300 Spaniards from Oran, to relieve the fortress of Santa Cruz, in opposition to 15,000 Moors, he, although 544 of his party were killed or wounded, *himself* being among the latter, defeated the efforts made to cut him off, with a loss to the enemy, estimated at not less than 2000 men, slain or disabled; including 19 Agas of Janissaries, and the son of their General, the ferocious Bey Bigotillos. The Chevalier was rewarded for his bravery with a Government; and, as he united a love of literary with military pursuits, he corresponded with the illustrious Dr. Jonathan Swift, Dean of St. Patrick's, whom he admired, as the sharpest scourge of the antinational oppression, then imposed upon Ireland, as government. The Chevalier sent from Spain a present of Cassala wine to the Dean, and a green velvet bag, with strings of silk and gold, containing various compositions in prose and verse, for the perusal and criticism of the Dean; who, when he opened the bag, "little expecting a history, a dedication, poetical translations of the seven penitential psalms, Latin poems, and the like, and all from a soldier!" observed in his reply—"In *these* kingdoms, you would be a most unfortunate military man, among troops, where *the least pretension to learning, or piety, or common morals, would endanger the owner to be cashiered.* Although I have *no* regard for your trade from the judgment I make of those who profess it in *these* kingdoms, yet *I cannot but highly esteem those gentlemen of Ireland, who, with all the disadvantages of being exiles and strangers, have been able to distinguish themselves, by their valour and conduct, in so many parts of Europe, I think, above all other nations.*"* The Dean sent Dublin editions of his own works, and those of Pope, Gay, &c., to the Chevalier, for his camp-library. This correspondence took place from 1732 to 1735. The Chevalier printed "Mémoires sur l'Entreprise d'Inspruck en 1719," dated from St. Clement de la Manche, March 4th, 1745—a well-timed publication, with reference to the design *then* medi-

* Wogan remarks of his brave brother refugees from slavery in their native country—"They have shewn a great deal of gallantry in the defence of foreign States and Princes, with very little advantage to themselves, but that of being free; and without half the outward marks of distinction they deserved. These southern Governments are very slow, in advancing foreigners to considerable or gainful preferments. Their chief attention is reserved for their own subjects, to make them some amends for the heavy yoke they have laid over them." In France particularly, I find the obstacles to a due promotion of the Irish officers as *strangers* were very great, from the superior interest of the numerous *noblesse*, who looked for a suitable provision in life to the army. So that, whatever was the distinction the Irish acquired in that service, (and the other services referred to) such distinction is to be set down, as much inferior to that of their actual merit; or to such merit as, in a *native*, would have been far sooner or far higher advanced. English intrigue, too, in France, was exerted to *prevent* the promotion of Irish officers; on which point, see farther on, or under the year 1744, the account of Sir Gerard Lally.

tated, by Prince Charles in France, for a landing in Great Britain—and most appositely dedicated to the Queen of France, who was a Polish Princess, as well as the heroine, rescued from captivity by the writer. I have not ascertained, how long the Chevalier Wogan lived after giving to the world this narrative of his excursion to Inspruck, of necessity only abridged here. I find him last noticed in a letter of Prince Charles, from "Guadalaxara, March 12th, 1747," to his father at Rome; in which the Prince mentions, on his arrival at Madrid on the 2nd, "Sir Charles Wogan being at his Government"—or *not* then in the Spanish metropolis. Thus, he survived the fatal blow given to the Stuart cause at Culloden, under the offspring of that remarkable marriage, which, but for him, could not have been effected.

The measures of Cardinal Alberoni, from 1717 to 1719, as Prime Minister of Spain, to recover Sardinia, Sicily, &c., which Spain had been forced to resign by the Treaty of Utrecht, and his intrigues against the existing governments of France and England, united *both* those powers against him. The French and English—the former, acting principally under the Marshal Duke of Berwick by land, and the latter, under several officers, chiefly by sea—pushed on hostilities so vigorously, that, in 1719, Port Passage, Castel-Leon, Fontarabia, St. Sebastian, Santona, Urgel, Vigo, were reduced, and Spain was obliged to make peace, in January, 1720. Of the Irish, during this short war of sieges, I meet nothing beyond the passing allusions to them in the regimental notices of some of their leading officers already given, and in the general glance at their services by M. de la Ponce. But, at Madrid, Philip V., in February, 1719, published a manifesto, in favour of the "male and Catholic line of the House of Stuart," whose representative landed, by invitation, in March, from Italy, in Catalonia. He entered the Spanish metropolis the same month in the royal coach, accompanied by the Gardes du Corps, and the Officers usually present on such occasions, as well as by a number of Grandees, who went out several miles to meet him. He was conducted to the Palace of Buen Retiro, which had been prepared for his residence. King Philip, the Queen, and the Prince of Asturias, visited him in state, to congratulate him upon his happy arrival; the King presented him with 25,000 pistoles, and a service of silver plate to the value of 60,000 crowns; the Queen gave him a magnificent diamond; all dined together nearly every day; the English Prince, in fine, meeting with a reception, similar to that of his father King James II. at St. Germain, from Louis XIV.* In addition to every honour thus paid the Prince as *King* James III. of Great Britain and Ireland, a considerable military force, "most of them Irish," were announced to be designed for his service; to the great joy of the Spaniards, as anticipating, that the emancipation of their brother-religionists, throughout the British Isles, was consequently at hand. The plans laid for the English Prince's "restoration" extended to Scotland, and to Ireland, as well as to England. A select detachment of Spanish infantry, with several Scotch noblemen and Irish officers, 2000 stand of arms, &c., in a couple of frigates, sailed, early in March, from Port Passage, and landed, early in April, in Scotland, at

* Continental and British publications of the day. James's grandfather, ere he was Charles I., or as Prince of Wales, had entered Madrid in March, 96 years previous to 1719, or in 1623, respecting a match with the Infanta, which did not take place.

Kintail, in Ross-shire; where, with such native or Highland assistance as they expected, they were merely to keep their ground, till informed of the arrival of the Duke of Ormonde, with the leading armament from Spain, in England.

There, the suppression of the rising of 1715 in favour of the old dynasty, and the subsequent executions of the Jacobite loyalists, having increased the popular hostility to the dominant Whig party, and Hanoverian royalty, that party, and its German importation, had so little prospect of anything but defeat and expulsion by the Tories, or Jacobites, from the next Parliament to be elected under the Triennial Act of William III., that, in order to retain place and power, "by hook or by crook," the measure called the Septennial Act was introduced; whereby the duration of the existing and every future Parliament was to be for 7 instead of 3 years; or, in other words, the voters for this Act, *elected* but for 3 years, were, by *self-appointment*, to be Members for 4 years beyond the period for which they had been *legally* chosen to sit!* Such an arbitrary alteration of the Constitution by the Whigs—even at the expense of the much-lauded Triennial Act of their own glorified William! —rendered the Hanoverian *régime*, for whose maintenance it was perpetrated, still more obnoxious in England, where Jacobite hostility to George was displayed with proportionate virulence. Thus, James Shepherd, a young English Jacobite, under 20, condemned to death, for having designed "to smite the *Usurper* in his Palace!" persevered, to the last, in avowing, "that he meant it, intended it, and did not think there was any harm in it, or any guilt in the fact, if committed!"— the Rev. Mr. Orme, a Nonjuring or Jacobite Protestant clergyman, who attended him at Newgate, extolling him, as a pious, sensible youth, excited by zeal for a good cause; and administering the sacrament to him several times, as well as absolving him at the gallows!† An equestrian statue of George, erected in Grosvenor Square, Westminster, was also defaced; and other striking instances, in London, of this violent animosity to the Hanoverian Prince, as a *usurper*, might be given. "In the eyes of the high Tories," remarks Lord Macaulay, "*the* ELECTOR

---

* The *Whig* historian, Smollett, having noted, with reference to this repeal of the Triennial Act in 1716, how, "though the rebellion was extinguished, the flame of national disaffection still continued to rage," and how "the severities exercised against the rebels increased the general discontent," adds—" *The courage and fortitude with which the condemned persons encountered the pains of death, in its most dreadful form, prepossessed many spectators in favour of the cause, by which these unhappy victims were animated. In a word, persecution, as usual, extended the heresy.* The Ministry, perceiving this universal dissatisfaction, and dreading the revolution of a new Parliament, which might wrest the power from their faction, and retort upon them the violence of their own measures, formed a resolution, equally odious and effectual, to establish their administration. This was no other than a scheme to repeal the Triennial Act; and by a new law, to extend the term of Parliament to 7 years." According to Sir Edward Bulwer Lytton, in his Caxtoniana, had not public opinion in England been prevented speaking out (in a new election) by this Whig violation of the constitution, "There would have been a cry loud enough to have rent the land in twain, of ' God save the King—at the *other* side of the water!'"

† Thus, too, we are informed, of the famous high Tory or Jacobite Parson and writer, the Rev. Jeremy Collier, that, when "Sir John Friend and Sir William Parkins were tried and convicted of high treason for planning the murder of King William, Collier administered spiritual consolation to them, attended them to Tyburn, and, just before they were turned off, laid his hands on their heads, and, by the authority which he derived from Christ, solemnly absolved them."

was the most hateful of ROBBERS *and* TYRANTS. THE CROWN OF ANOTHER WAS ON HIS HEAD; THE BLOOD OF THE BRAVE AND LOYAL WAS ON HIS HANDS!" Hence, such bitter effusions as the following:—

> "When Israel first provok'd the living Lord,
> HE punish'd them with famine, plague, and sword;
> Still they sinn'd on—HE, in his wrath, did fling
> No thunderbolt amongst them, but a King;
> A George-like King was Heav'n's severest rod—
> The utmost vengeance of an angry God:
> *God, in his wrath, sent Saul to punish Jewry,*
> AND GEORGE, TO ENGLAND, IN A GREATER FURY!"

On the state of dynastic feeling, in so many of the provincial parts of England, when the Duke of Ormonde's landing was expected, Lockhart of Carnwath gives, from "Colonel Guest," as "a very discreet gentleman, and well disposed towards the King," or James III., an incident, showing at once the fear and ferocity of the German on the throne, and the very delicate circumstances in which officers were placed, as commanding for *his* government in such districts. In the shire, where the Colonel was quartered with 2 or 3 troops of dragoons, he "received orders, sign'd by King George himself, directing him, that, if there happen'd any riots, or disorders, to burn, shoot, or destroy, without asking questions; for which, and all that he, in execution of these orders, should doe, *contrary to law*, he thereby previously indemnifyd him. The Colonel was thunderstruck with these orders; they were what, on no account, he would execute, neither durst he, for *the people, in that country, were all well-affected to the King*," James III., "*and would have torn him and his men to peices;* and if Ormond had landed, *he*," the Colonel, "*must either have surrendered, or joynd them with his men*. Having seriously reflected on these orders, he thought it best to communicate them to some of the leading gentry of the place; telling them, that he did not know, whither they were design'd as a snare to him, or them; that, for all their sakes, he wisht they would keep the peace; for, as he would not perform what was required, he hoped they would, at the same time, prevent his being brought to trouble. This method was kindly taken, and they assured him, he should be safe, and free from all insults, unless there was a general insurrection, when they would be glad to have him with them. There was accordingly no disturbance in that place, tho, at the same time, *the people were prepared, and resolved, to take the fields, as soon as Ormond landed*. This passage I take notice of," adds Lockhart, "as it seems somewhat a kin to the affair of Glencoe, and 'tis probable the like orders were given to other officers." That is, "the like orders," in the way of burning, shooting, and destroying, "*contrary to law*," with a proportionable indemnification for doing so, from the Hanoverian!

In Ireland, about the time that the English Tories, or Jacobites, mutilated George's statue at Westminster, some of the same party in Dublin cut in pieces the picture of George, which he had given to the Corporation, and which was set up in the Tholsel. Nor were 2 Proclamations, one, from the Castle, offering £1000, and another, from the Corporation, offering £500, for a discovery on this matter, of any effect. "Such," exclaims a furious Whig, "was the hellish rage and spite of the Irish Tories!" Meanwhile, James Francis Edward Sarsfield, 2nd Earl of Lucan—already noticed, as distinguished at the reduction of Barcelona, under his stepfather, the Marshal Duke of Berwick,—was despatched, with several officers, into Ireland, to excite and organize due insurrections, among the oppressed Catholics, in favour of the old royal family; through whose "restoration" alone *any* relief was expected, from the Cromwello-Williamite yoke of colonial and sectarian oppression, established there by the so-called "glorious Revolution." A Jacobite song of the day in Irish, still preserved, accordingly refers to the *true* King, or James, son of James, and his troops, coming, with the Duke,* over the ocean; the priests, as one man, imploring Christ; the bards songful, and their gloom dispelled; while the poor Gaels of *Inis Eilge—i. e.,* native or Milesian population of the *noble island*—were anticipating the arrival of those who were on the sea.

The main Spanish fleet of 5 select men-of-war, and about 20 transports, with 5000 soldiers, "partly Irish," and arms for 30,000 more, horses for cavalry, &c., designed to disembark near Bristol, where the Stuart cause was more popular than the Hanoverian, sailed in March from Cadiz, under Admiral Don Balthazar de Guevara and the Duke of Ormonde; but, when 50 leagues off Cape Finisterre, towards 1 o'clock in the morning, encountered a storm, which blew with such violence, for 48 hours, that *the ships were shattered, and dispersed, and a quantity of cannon, horses, &c., had to be thrown over board.* Instead of proceeding for England, it *therefore was necessary, to make for such ports of the Peninsula, as it was possible to reach.* This great disaster to Ormonde, on the ocean, was followed, in Scotland, after a skirmish at the Pass of Strachells, near the Valley of Glenshiel, by the dispersion of the armed Jacobite loyalists, and the capitulation of the Spaniards there; since they had nothing to hope for, unless through a co-operation with his movements, subsequent to landing.

In Ireland, the Earl of Lucan arrived in Connaught, where he was allied, by his mother, to the great family of Clanricarde; and he, with other officers, would appear to have laid several trains of insurrection, which, upon Ormonde's reaching the English coast, were to explode throughout the island, as useful distractions to the power of the enemy. But these designs were rendered altogether useless by the failure of Ormonde's enterprise, and became known to the Anglo-Hanoverian administration in Dublin; where, after an alarmed assemblage, in April, of the Whig Privy Council at the Castle, which did not break up till 2 o'clock in the morning, the adoption of hostile measures towards Catholic ecclesiastics, and the stationing guards of the colonial Militia through the streets by night, a Proclamation was issued to this effect—"That the Government having certain intelligence, that *Sarsfield, otherwise called Earl of Lucan, and several officers, who had lately landed and dispersed themselves in several parts of the kingdom, had held conferences with divers Papists of distinction, with design to foment a rebellion in favour of the Pretender;* and that they had certainly *concerted a general insurrection, which was to be in all parts of the kingdom the same night and hour, having, to this end, their emissaries in each province;* therefore it was thought fit, to give notice thereof to all the inhabitants, that they might take the necessary measures to *apprehend the said Sarsfield, and all the*

* A Proclamation, from the Georgeite Lords Justices in Ireland, offered, for an apprehension of the Duke of Ormonde there, alive or dead, £10,000; a like document against him being issued in England, where, adds my authority, "the expectation of his landing was so great among the Jacobites, that they cou'd not help discovering it, in the insolence of their looks and expressions."

officers who were come into the kingdom with that design; and a reward of £1000 sterling was promised for securing any 1 of the said persons, within the space of 3 months. And, inasmuch as there was reason to believe, that this traitorous design could not have been formed and fomented except by Papists, and other persons disaffected to the Government, excited by the Popish Priests of the kingdom, all officials were required to *apprehend all Popish Archbishops, Bishops, Jesuits, Monks, &c.,* in order that the laws against the Papists, especially those of Limerick and Galway, might be put into execution; all seditious meetings, or assemblies of Papists and other ill-designing persons, were likewise to be prevented, and *all strangers, travellers, and others, were to be carefully examined, who should be suspected of disaffection to the person and government of King George,"* &c. Those who were connected with the proposed Jacobite risings for a "restoration" and emancipation in Ireland had consequently to provide for their safety, as well as they could; and, (to the honour of the country!) none of them are recorded to have been betrayed. The Earl of Lucan took shipping from Kilcolgan, in the County of Galway, for the Continent, which he reached; and he died, not long after, or in May, at St. Omers, in Flanders; being the last Earl of Lucan of the Sarsfield family.*
Such were the circumstances, by which the Irish, engaged in those undertakings of the Court of Madrid, were disappointed in their hopes of contributing to the "restoration" of the Prince, whom *they* regarded as their lawful Sovereign. But their countrymen, who were appointed to serve, with the Spanish army in Sicily, against the Germans, and who thus had a better field for distinction, duly availed themselves of it; particularly at the affair of Melazzo, where they behaved with similar valour, to that displayed at Cremona against the same enemy—" 1 single brigade of them," writes the gallant Wogan to Swift, " having driven the whole German army into the town, or the sea, after they had been deserted, by the Spanish troops, and Generals, to a man!" On this occasion, when 6000 Imperial infantry, and 800 cavalry are mentioned to have sur-

---

* According to a published letter of Lady Clanricarde in July, 1717, to her grandson, the Duke of Liria, his step-brother, the Earl of Lucan, was in such narrow circumstances notwithstanding his post in the Spanish service, the pension of 3000 livres a year attached to it having been reduced to 2000, and, from 1714, or about 3 years, left totally in arrear, that he was above 8000 livres in debt; was consequently obliged to request the writer for pecuniary assistance, and to quit the service of Spain for that of France; where he was made a supernumerary or reformed Colonel in the Irish Horse Regiment of Nugent; the pay of which appointment was, however, but 2000 livres a year. Lady Clanricarde likewise mentioning, that "he had a most dangerous fit of sickness soone after he left Spaine," adds, she intended assisting him against Christmas that year with what she could, "being £200, though it be very insufficient." The good Lady finally suggests to the Duke of Liria, that his father, the Marshal Duke of Berwick, having so many considerable commands at his disposal, something better might be gotten for poor Lord Lucan, than the small post which he was "left to live and subsist on." Lord Lucan's decease is noticed in the London Gazette, May, 1719, No. 5747, under a paragraph from "Paris," thus—" M. Sarsfield, called Lord Lucan, who had lately been in Ireland, died, at St. Omers, on the 12th instant." The facts of this nobleman having been an officer of the Irish Brigade in France for *some* time, and of his having been employed as related in Ireland, have, through *his* person, connected the Spanish designs in favour of the Stuarts with the history of *that* Brigade; though his Lordship, by acting as he did in Ireland, must have returned to the service of Spain, against whom France was *then* allied with England.

prised the Spanish camp before day-break, they are stated to have had about 2200 men, including General Veterani, and 37 officers, killed, wounded, and taken, and the Hiberno-Spaniards not more than 600 killed, or wounded, with 2 Colonels, and some other officers. Hence, alleges a hostile contemporary, respecting the Irish military in Spain—"they consist, at present, of 8 regiments, at least, and are in as great esteem there, upon account of their eminent services to that Crown, especially in the late War of Sicily, as their countrymen are in France."

In a Stuart state paper of the following year, 1720, from the pen of the celebrated Irish Protestant Jacobite, Dr. Charles Leslie, being an application to the Duke of Orleans, Regent of France, to espouse the cause of James III., considerable light is thrown on the feelings of the partizans of the Stuart family, connected with the preceding expedition from Spain under the Duke of Ormonde, &c. Having noted, how "the great discontents of all ranks of men, in England, Scotland, and Ireland, have been so visible for these last 5 years," (or since the Hanoverian accession,) as to be unnecessary to detail, though there was "1 thing to be accounted for, how the Government in England have been hitherto able to support themselves *against 9 parts in 10 of the people,** who not only wish, but would most willingly and vigorously concur, to remove them," the Doctor says—" The security of the Government is reducible to 1 point, that the people have hitherto been *utterly destitute of a small body of regular troops, to give a beginning to the design, and to make head at first, and of arms, and other military stores, to put into the hands of the majority of the nation, who are most ready and impatient, to receive and use them, for the recovery of their liberties.* There are a greater number of officers, of all ranks, and degrees, discarded, and dispersed in the country, than are at present in the armies of the *usurper.* These men are equally desirous to appear in the rescue of their country, and only want the means of doing it. And *no* man in England, of *either* party, doubts, but that, *if the Duke of Ormond could have landed from Spain last year, with the forces and arms designed for the expedition, it would have restored King James, probably without a war, but certainly with a war of 2 or 3 months at most.* And, it is evident, that the attempt miscarried, *only* from the great distance, and situation, of Spain." Should his Royal Highness, the Regent of France, consent to undertake the expedition to England, for another " restoration," in which, it is alleged, he would easily succeed, then, continues the Doctor, "*at least 20 of the most considerable men in England, of opulent fortune, are willing to come over into France, and return with the troops his Royal Highness will lend them, and take their fate with them;* and his Royal Highness' discernment

* This estimate, by Dr. Leslie, of the extent of Jacobite principles, combined with those estimates cited in the 1st note to this Book, will further show what very little chance the House of Hanover would have had to reign in Great Britain and Ireland, were the contest between that family and the Stuarts to have been submitted for determination to "universal suffrage," or " *Vox Populi, vox Dei.*" Indeed, the year previous to Dr. Leslie's writing his above-cited state-paper, or in the autumn of 1719, a Jacobite tract, to the effect of this remark, being entitled "*Ex ore tuo te judico,* VOX POPULI, VOX DEI," cost its printer, John Matthews, a trial, and condemnation to DEATH, at London; pursuant to which, though only an apprentice, having 3 years still to serve, and aged but 19, he was *hanged,* at Tyburn, in November! Here was a Whig-Hanoverian or "glorious-revolution" illustration of *liberty* of the press—with a *vengeance!* If the will of the people be represented by "universal suffrage," was George I. as *justly* King of Great Britain and Ireland, as Napoleon III. is Emperor of France?

Y

must see clearly, that *mere disgust against the present Government would not induce them to put their whole fortunes upon 1 stake, if they were not infallibly assured of its success.* And, as they would not desire his Royal Highness to undertake it without such *infallibility of success,* tho' perhaps a smaller number might do, they desire 10,000 foot, and 2000 horse and dragoons, with 20, or 30,000 arms, as a force which their adversaries cannot possibly make head against, nor so much as dispute the game. And here, they beg leave to lay before his Royal Highness, that they conceive, that no 1 circumstance can contribute so much to make the English nation press to take up those arms, in the quarrel of their own country, and of France, as *the Duke of Ormond being at the head of those troops.* This would entirely remove the only possible objection against such an invasion, as if France proposed the conquest of the kingdom. And whereas possibly an army of 12,000 men, under any other General, might continue only the same number, at least for some time; *under the Duke of Ormond, the most beloved and esteemed man ever England had, whatever arms they had would be as many men in* 10 *days;* and, *on their approach to London, swell to* 40, *or* 50,000 *men.* But this is most certain, that, in this cause, *the Duke of Ormond is, in his own person, very many thousand men; and is alone more than all the other heads of the party put together, in the affections, and expectations, of the English nation."* Of the Tories of England, it is further remarked, "they would *now* throw off the yoak which crushes them, if his Royal Highness will enable them, by his generous assistance, &c." Of Scotland and Ireland, it is added—" Tho' there cannot be the least doubt of the unquestionable success of an attempt made in England with the forces and armies mentioned, yet so small an additional number could *infallibly light the flames in Scotland and Ireland,* that, if his Royal Highness pleases to embrace the design, it shall be made very clear to him, that *less* than 5000 would be sufficient for *both* those nations." How very disaffected Scotland was, as well on dynastic as on national or Anti-Union grounds, is sufficiently known; and the not less discontented condition of Ireland was marked in the deep disappointment and grief felt there by the enslaved Catholics, or great majority of her population, more especially those of the older or Milesian race, at the recent peace which Spain had been obliged to make, accompanied by a renunciation of the cause of James III. At this peace, a contemporary native poet alleges of his brother Gaels in Erin, how

———————————— "despairing they shriek,
For Spain's flag in defeat and defection is furl'd!"

and in reference to the Penal Code "ascendancy," or race of upstart sectarian "settlers," from whose obnoxious domination *no* deliverance was to be hoped, except through another "restoration of the Stuarts," he passionately exclaims to Heaven—

"Just Power! that for Moses the wave didst divide,
Look down on the land, where *thy* followers pine!—
Look down upon Erin! and crush the dark pride,
Of the scourge of *thy* people—the foes of *thy* shrine."

In 1721, died 1 of the leading officers of the Irish Brigade, "Jean de Gaydon, Maréchal de Camp," or Major-General John Gaydon, brother of the Chevalier Richard Gaydon of Irishtown, Major of the Regiment of Dillon, whose honourable share in the liberation of the Princess Sobieski has been narrated. The name of Gayden, or Gaydon, is to be found, several times, between the years 1333 and 1589, among the chief civic magistrates of Dublin, under their different designations of Provosts, or Mayors; and it was connected, in the 16th and 17th centuries, with the possession of the Castles, &c., of Irishtown, Straffan, and other property in the County of Kildare, until divested of those estates by British revolutionary confiscation. After the accession of King James II., among the promotions of Irish Catholic gentlemen, in the army of their own country, was John Gaydon, to a commission, in 1687, as Cornet of Horse. In 1689, or at the beginning of the War of the Revolution in Ireland, he was a Lieutenant in Colonel Patrick Sarsfield's Regiment of Horse. He accompanied the Irish army to France, after the Treaty of Limerick, as a Cornet in the Gardes du Corps. In 1692, and 1693, he served in Normandy, and Flanders; in 1694, on the Moselle; in 1695, on the Meuse; and in 1696, and 1697, again on the Moselle. After the disbanding of the Irish Horse Guards in 1698, he was commissioned, March 25th, to hold rank as a Mestre-de-Camp-de-Cavalerie, attached to the Irish Regiment of Sheldon. In 1701, with this regiment in Italy, he was at the combat of Chiari; and, in 1702, at the battle of Luzzara. Removed, in 1703, to Germany, he was at the captures of Brisach and Landau, and the victory of Spire. From 1704 to 1707, he served in Flanders, where he fought at the battle of Ramillies, in 1706. Brigadier, by brevet, March 3rd, 1708, he was at the battle of Oudenarde, that year, and the next, at the battle of Malplaquet. Continued in Flanders till 1712, he was particularly distinguished, in 1711, under the Comte de Gassion, at the surprise, and overthrow, of a considerable corps of the enemy, under Lieutenant-General Hompesch, near Bouchain; and fought at the successful action of Denain, and the subsequent reductions of Douay, Quesnoy, and Bouchain. Transferred to Germany in 1713, he was at the taking of Landau, and Friburgh, and the defeat of General Vaubonne. He was attached to the camp of the Lower Meuse, in 1714; obtained the grade of Maréchal de Camp, by brevet, February 1st, 1719; and died, September 11th, 1721, aged 62 years.

In 1725, a veteran of, I believe, the Clannaboy branch of his ancient name, or Lieutenant-Colonel and Brigadier Gordon O'Neill (the younger) was "gathered to his fathers." He came to France, with Lord Mountcashel's, or the 1st Irish Brigade, in 1690, as an Ensign in the Regiment of the Honourable Daniel O'Brien, subsequently that of Clare; and remained, under Catinat, with the Army of Italy, till, obtaining a company, or being made Captain, August 7th, 1694, in the Regiment of Lee, he was attached, in 1695, to the Army of Germany; in 1696, to that of the Meuse; and, in 1697, was at the taking of Ath. In 1698, he was at the brilliant encampment, and review, under Louis XIV. in person, near Compiegne. He was with the Army of Flanders in 1701; and with that of Germany, from 1702 to 1704. During this period, he was, from 1702 to 1703, at the reduction of Kehl, the successful affairs of Hornberg and Munderkingen, the 1st battle, or victory of Hochstedt, and the captures of Augsburg and Ulm. Major of his regiment, by brevet of January 30th, 1704, he fought at the 2nd battle, or defeat, of Hochstedt, otherwise Blenheim, in August; and was, September 14th, appointed Lieutenant-Colonel. He was employed in the army of the Moselle in 1705 and 1706; and at all the successful expeditions of the Marshal de

Villars in Franconia and Swabia, in 1707. He served, from 1708 to 1712, on the Rhine, or in Flanders; and, in the latter quarter, was engaged at Arleux, Denain, Douay, Quesnoy, and Bouchain. In the next or concluding campaign of the war against the Imperialists, he was at the reductions of Landau and Friburgh. Brigadier, by brevet of April 3rd, 1721, he was still Lieutenant-Colonel of the Regiment of Lee, at his decease, in January, 1725.

The high reputation which the Irish Brigades abroad by this period attained, and the proportionable apprehension with which, as attached to the House of Stuart, they were regarded by the supporters of the Revolution and Hanoverian dynasty in England, are forcibly expressed by a writer of the latter opinions, Mr. Forman, in a pamphlet, dated from "Amsterdam, 8th of August, 1727," and entitled, "*A Letter to the Right Honourable Sir Robert Sutton, for Disbanding the Irish Regiments in the Service of France and Spain.*" From this pamphlet I give the following extracts:—

"Amongst several things, which, I think, have been hitherto omitted, for the future safety of Great Britain, I cannot comprehend, by what honest policy it is, that the Irish regiments are still permitted to remain in the service of France. If that nation is sincerely resolved to keep her treaties with Britain, she has no great occasion for their service : but, if she is only wheedling us to gain time to re-establish her former power, which we can still give a check to, we shall be very much wanting to ourselves, if we suffer those regiments to continue any longer on foot. As long as there is a body of Irish Roman Catholick troops abroad, the Chevalier will always make some figure in Europe, by the credit they give him; and be consider'd as a Prince, that has a brave and well-disciplined army of veterans at his service; tho' he wants that opportunity to employ them at present, which he expects time, and fortune, will favour him with. Should France, when grown wanton with power, forget her engagements, and obligations, to Britain, can she anywhere find such proper instruments as the Irish regiments to execute such enterprizes as she may then undertake, in favour of the Chevalier's pretensions, when they square with her own interest, and private views? They are British subjects, they speak the same language with us, and are consequently the fittest troops to invade us with. They are season'd to dangers, and so perfected in the art of war, that, not only the Serjeants and Corporals, but even the private men, can make very good officers, upon occasion. *In what part of the army soever they have been placed, they have always met with success, and, upon several occasions, won honour, where the French themselves, warlike as they are, have received an affront.* To their valour, in a great measure, France owes, not only most of what trophies she gain'd in the late war, but even her own preservation. And, in King William's reign, the Duke of Savoy had a fatal proof of their courage, under the conduct of the brave Lord Mountcashel, so well known, in the Court of King Charles II., by the name of Justin Maccarty. They wrested Cremona out of the hands of the great Eugene, when, by surprise, he had made himself master of all the town, except the Irish quarters, and saw the Marshal Duke de Villeroy his prisoner, who was taken by Colonel Mac Donnall,* an Irishman in the

---

* Not *Colonel*, but *Captain*, as mentioned in my narrative of the affair of Cremona. In the pamphlet of Forman, from which I give the extracts in the text, he makes

Emperor's service. By that action, hardly to be parallel'd in history, they saved the whole French army on that side of the Alps. At Spireback, if my memory does not fail me, Major-General Nugent's Regiment of Horse, by a brave charge upon 2 Regiments of Cuirassiers, brought a compleat victory to an army, upon which Fortune was just turning her back. At Ramillies, the Allies lost but 1 pair of colours, which the Royal Irish in the service of France took from a German regiment. At Toulon, Lieutenant-General Dillon distinguished himself, and chiefly contributed to the preservation of that important place. To the Irish Regiments, also, under the conduct of that intrepid and experienced officer, Count Medavi himself very generously attributed his victory over the Imperialists in Italy. And the poor Catalans will for ever have reason to remember the name of Mr. Dillon, for the great share he had in the famous siege of Barcelona, so fatal to their nation. Sir Andrew Lee, Lieutenant-General, and one of the Great Crosses of the Order of St. Louis, shewed likewise how consummate a soldier he was, when he defended Lisle, under the Marshal Duke de Bouffleurs, against those thunderbolts of war, the Prince of Savoy, and our own invincible Duke of Marlborough. And Lieutenant-General Rothe has, by several memorable actions, particularly his conduct under the Marshal Duke de Berwick, in the late war between France and Spain, acquir'd an immortal reputation, and shown himself not inferior to any of the best of the Irish Generals abroad. In short, Sir, the Irish troops did the Allies the most considerable damage which they received in the last war, and will do so again, if another war should happen, while they continue regimented.

"I have mention'd a few of the actions of the Irish, to let Britons see what sort of an enemy is still reserv'd *in petto* against them. And, when you call to mind the late great Earl Cadogan, and several of his countrymen, who, at the Revolution, took the right side of the question, and served their late Majesties, King William, and Queen Anne, you will the more readily believe, that I have not been too extravagant, in representing the courage of those of the same nation abroad. They consist, at present, of a Regiment of Horse, and 5 Regiments of Foot, in France; all double or treble officer'd; so that, including the Reform'd Officers, placed *a la suite* of the garrisons, they can, by advancing some of the private men to be Serjeants and Corporals, and the present Serjeants and Corporals to be Lieutenants and Ensigns, furnish, amongst themselves, a sufficient number of experienced officers for 40, or 50,000 men upon occasion. And I believe their number in Spain is equal, if not superior, to that in France, provided they have not suffer'd extremely by the siege of Gibraltar. *

"This is as impartial and as full an account of the Irish abroad as the subject requires. Some of them by inclination, but most of them by interest, as the case stands, are entirely devoted to the Chevalier; and the hopes of being restored to their estates make the Irish officers

some mistakes, requiring no more notice here, than to remark, that he either corrected them in his subsequent pamphlet concerning the Irish, or that they will be found corrected in *my* accounts of the several occurrences to which *he* refers.

* At the siege of Gibraltar in 1727, alluded to by Forman, we see, in the Spanish army, the Regiments of Irlandia and Limerick, with the Colonels and Dons Raymond Bourke, Charles Cusack, William Lacy, James Leland, Lewis O'Mahony, and Peter Sherlock.

daily wish for an occasion of exercising their aversion to the present establishment. In the year 1715, as many of them as found an opportunity slipp'd over to Scotland; amongst whom were some General, and several Field, Officers; but they could not arrive time enough to be at the battle of Dumblain. And the French Court, far from shewing any displeasure at their thus abandoning their colours without leave, seem'd rather to wink at it. . . . You are sensible, Sir, and so will every honest Briton be, when he seriously considers the case, that, while the Irish regiments are suffer'd to continue in the service of France and Spain, they will always furnish those nations with instruments to carry on their designs against us, and prove a nursery of inveterate enemies to Britain as long as she continues under the government of the august House of Hanover, which, I hope, will be to the end of time. They daily make recruits in London and several parts of Ireland, tho' surrounded with difficulties, which, one would think, ought to be insuperable, under a Ministry, so celebrated for its vigilance and ability."

"His late Majesty* (of glorious and immortal memory) was suddenly called from the British throne, to take possession of a better. If, then, through any fatal accident, we should fall under a minority (which God forbid!) would not such an unhappy change afford an ample opportunity to ill-designing men for carrying on their wicked schemes against their country? If, in such a conjuncture, a Ministry, or Juncto, should start up, with secret inclinations for the Chevalier, cou'd such people have better engines to set to work, than the Irish troops abroad? Or, in the mean time, could his friends, were they in power, take a more politick step in his favour, than to intail Pretendership upon Britain, of which those troops are the very vitals? Pretendership, you know, will always propagate plots and conspiracies. For tho' the Chevalier should remain indolent and inactive, yet such men would never want a pretext to coin them, as long as those regiments recruit, as they must necessarily do, in his Majesty's dominions."

"But here 2 objections may, perhaps, be brought against what I propose. First, that the Irish troops abroad are no more, at present, than soldiers of fortune; and that it would be a great pity to reduce so many brave men to a starving condition. Secondly, that France and Spain, being independent in themselves, will *not* consent to disband those regiments."

"As to the 1st objection. If the Irish officers abroad are no more than soldiers of fortune, they can continue so in French and Spanish regiments, as well as in Irish regiments; and several of them may merit a provision in his Majesty's German troops, and also in the troops of Prussia and Hesse-Cassel. But, if they are still friends, followers, devotees of the Pretender, and tools of France, my arguments stand good against them. When King Charles II. was in exile, the Irish officers then abroad were very kind to him; *most of them privately contributing a good part of their pay to help to support him in his distress;* yet *they were nothing consider'd for it, after the Restoration.* Tho' there was then no Pretender to fear, they were, nevertheless, disbanded. And shall the present Irish have more favour shewn them, when they publickly acknowledge themselves servants and subjects to his Majesty's *Competitor*, who is perpetually allarming Great Britain with his motions?

* George I.

The braver the present Irish are, the more dangerous they are; and the greater strength my proposal carries with it, for disbanding them. But, by the word disbanding, I don't mean entirely cashiering, and sending them to seek their bread, after so long a service. No, Sir, I only mean to abolish the name of Irish forces abroad, by incorporating them into French and Spanish regiments. By such means, that military nursery of inveterate enemies to his Majesty's title, and the British constitution, will be entirely broken, and dispersed. Except General Lee's, Lord Clare's, and General Dillon's Regiments, (which are a part of the Lord Mountcashell's Brigade,) very few will suffer by the change. Those Regiments, indeed, are upon foreign pay, which is higher than that of France. But what have Britons to say to that? Is it the interest of their enemies, or their own safety, that they are to consult, upon this occasion? The Royal Irish, commanded by General Rothe, are upon French pay; so is General Nugent's Horse, and the Duke of Berwick's Regiment of Foot; yet the officers have all along lived, as well as those of the other Regiments; and what should hinder them from doing so under French, as well as under Irish, Colonels?"

"Some men of good sense, but little knowledge of Courts, may wonder why France and Spain have not taken notice of this, and, by incorporating those regiments long ago," have "saved those of their own communion in Ireland from what they call *a daily persecution?* But this riddle is easily solved. The Irish regiments were, and will always be, of too great consequence to their designs to be parted with, *upon such frivolous reasons as religion and humanity dictate to some sort of politicians.* They have as great an interest in keeping them up, as we have in insisting upon the breaking of them. When they are once broke, or incorporated, the officers will be too much dispersed to be brought together upon occasion, without giving too great an allarm. They will not so readily obtain the connivance of French or Irish Colonels for deserting their colours, when the Chevalier may have occasion for their service, as in the year 1715. And there will then be no more nurseries, as I have already observ'd, for training up young officers in the principles and inveteracy of the old ones. The private men will, also, for want of recruits, dwindle, in a very few years, to too inconsiderable a numbers to be any ways serviceable to the Chevalier, or formidable to us."

"I come now to the 2nd objection, that France and Spain will not consent to disband those troops. But why not? Are they not British subjects, and has not Britain a right to demand it? Does not her security require it? Yes, certainly, if the author of the *Enquiry* has been ingenuous, in the view he has given us, of the late designs and inclinations of the Court of Madrid. Should France refuse it, we ought, from that moment, to suspect her, and insist the more strenuously upon it, and apprehend *a snake in the grass.*"

The Emperor Charles VI. of Austria, by conspiring, in 1733, with Russia, to thrust a foreign or *Saxon* Prince upon Poland as her King, instead of the native and duly-elected candidate for that Crown, Stanislas Leszczynski, father-in-law of Louis XV., provoked hostilities with France. The Marshal Duke of Berwick was consequently ordered, October 12th, to cross the Rhine, with 52 battalions and 78 squadrons; including 5 of the Irish battalions of Berwick, Bulkeley, Clare, Dillon, and Roth, that made about 3300 men and officers. The passage of the troops, artillery, and ammunition occupied till the 18th. But Fort Kehl was invested the

14th, the trenches were opened the night of the 19th-20th, and by the 28th, the Governor, General Pfuhl, beat the chamade, and subsequently surrendered, on terms suitable to his honourable resistance under the circumstances; in testimony of which, he was presented by the Marshal with 2 pieces of cannon, besides those mentioned in the capitulation. This conquest terminated the campaign in Germany; nothing else more remarkable having taken place than the following incident connected with the Irish there. In consequence of some irregularities which occurred in 1 of the regiments of the Brigade, its Lieutenant-Colonel was despatched from Kehl, with a serious communication on the subject, from the Duke of Berwick to Louis XV. The King, on the delivery of the Duke's message by the officer, observed, with emotion—"The Irish troops give me more uneasiness than all the rest of my forces." To which the Lieutenant-Colonel replied—"All your Majesty's enemies make the same complaint!" In Italy, a French force under the veteran Marshal Duke de Villars, acting with the Piedmontese, or Sardinians, under their gallant King, Charles Emanuel III., between October and January, conquered the Imperial Duchy of Milan. As there were *no* Irish troops with Villars, it will suffice to remark *en passant* of these operations, that the stoutest defence opposed to the King and the Marshal was, in November, at Pizzigitone, by its Governor, Langton, an Irish officer in the Imperial service, who obtained a proportionably creditable capitulation.

In 1734, the Marshal Duke of Berwick, passing the Rhine in April, with the Regiments of Bulkeley, Dillon, Berwick and Fitz-James in his army, and dislodging, with little loss, about 12,000 Germans from the lines of Etlingen in May, proceeded to invest the important fortress of Philipsburgh; well supplied with artillery, ammunition and provisions, and garrisoned by between 4000 and 5000 men, under an experienced officer, the Count de Wutgenau. The Marshal broke ground the night of June 3rd-4th, and was killed (as elsewhere more fully noticed) on the 12th. But the operations were carried on by his able successor-in-command, the veteran Marquis d'Asfeld, who, though obliged to protect himself with immense lines against Prince Eugene desirous to raise the siege, and though having, at the same time, to suffer much from hardships and disease, as well as from the resistance of the garrison of Philipsburgh, reduced that fortress to capitulate, July 18th. At this siege, stated to have cost the Germans about 1200 men and the French above 3000, the trenches were mounted by the Irish battalions of Berwick, Bulkeley, Clare, Dillon, and Roth; among which, those of Clare and Dillon are specially referred to as distinguished. The rest of this campaign consisted in movements of no general interest.

The campaign of 1735 in Germany, the last of this short war, was one of manœuvres between the Imperial forces and those of France. Of the Irish Brigade, however, Bulkeley's, Roth's, and Berwick's battalions were stationed in Flanders, and only Clare's and Dillon's were employed in Germany. "The Irish regiments," says a contemporary, in reference to these 2 last-named corps there, "bravely secured the retreat of the French army out of the Empire, altho' closely follow'd by the brave Count Seckendorff, who did his utmost to cut off their rear, but was as bravely disappointed, by the intrepid behaviour of the Irish."

The year 1736 was marked by the decease of a veteran survivor of the War of the Revolution in Ireland, and of the subsequent campaigns of the Brigade on the Continent during Louis XIV.'s reign—the Comte Charles de Skelton, Maréchal de Camp de Cavalerie, or Major-General of Horse. He belonged to a race, distinguished, in several branches, abroad and at home, for loyalty to the House of Stuart. Its principal representative, Sir Bevil Skelton, having been Envoy Extraordinary for King Charles II. at various Courts in Germany, filled the like post for King James II. in Holland and France. After suffering a temporary discredit owing to the *Orange* treason which surrounded the throne, he was restored to the favour he had so well merited; was rewarded, for his zealous attachment to his master's interest, by being appointed Governor of the Tower of London, and Colonel of a Regiment of Foot; and, retiring to France with the royal family, he was Comptroller of the Household to the exiled Court at St. Germain, till his death, in 1696. In 1689, among the persons of consideration who came over with the King from France to Ireland, or followed him soon after, was Lieutenant-Colonel John Skelton, who obtained the same rank in the Infantry Regiment of Donough Mac Carthy, Earl of Clancarty. James Skelton was mortally wounded, as Colonel, in the last combat before Thomond Bridge at Limerick, in October, 1691. Thomas Skelton was a Lieutenant in the King's or Royal Irish Regiment of Foot Guards. Charles Skelton, the subject of this notice, entered the French army in 1688. In 1689, passing into Ireland to defend the royal cause, he became a Lieutenant in Colonel John Parker's Regiment of Horse; served through the whole of the Irish war, during which he was at the battles of the Boyne and Aughrim, and siege of Limerick; and returned to France in 1691. Aide-de-Camp, from this time, to the Duke of Vendome, he accompanied that renowned commander through *all* his campaigns, till his death. He was commissioned, March 4th, 1703, as a reformed Mestre-de-Camp to the Irish Horse Regiment of Sheldon. He was made a Brigadier, by brevet, March 29th, 1710, and Maréchal de Camp, by brevet, February 1st, 1719. He then served no longer, and died at Paris, with "the character of an excellent officer, and a very gallant man," May 24th, 1736, aged 62 years.

In 1738, died an Irish Jacobite officer, much trusted in Stuart and Bourbon politics, Nathaniel Hooke; by creation of James II., in France, Baron de Hooke of Hooke Castle, County Waterford. The name, originally La Hougue, from the lordship so-called in Normandy, was represented among the French conquerors of England under Duke William; and afterwards among the early settlers from that country in Ireland under Henry II. in the southern locality above-mentioned, as finally, or by Anglican corruption, Hooke. Nathaniel was the 2nd son of an offshoot of the old line of Hooke Castle, (expelled by the Cromwellians,) or John Hooke of the County Westmeath. Having served in King James's Guards, with whom he came to France, and been attached there, as a reformed Colonel, to the Irish Regiment of Galmoy, he was transferred, with the like grade, to the Regiment of Sparre, by order of January 8th, 1703. In this regiment, he served that year with the army of Flanders; in 1704, and, except while in Scotland, in 1705, on the Moselle; and, in 1706, at the battle of Ramillies. In 1707, he was sent again from Louis XIV., and the Stuart Court at St. Germain, to Scotland, in order to turn to account the national exasperation there at the Union, by making arrangements for the Jacobite invasion from France, undertaken the following year. Created Brigadier by brevet,

March 3rd, 1708, he was 1 of the General Officers to accompany his young Sovereign, as James III. of England and Ireland and James VIII. of Scotland, in the expedition referred to. On the frustration of the proposed landing in Scotland, he returned to France, and was present, that campaign, at the battle of Oudenarde. In 1709, he was at the battle or Malplaquet. In 1710, after having been Agent for the House of Stuart with the French Plenipotentiaries at the negociations in Holland for a general peace, he served with the Army of Flanders. He was Envoy to the Princes and States of the Empire and of the North, in 1711 and 1712; and, during the Regency, was nominated to the Embassy to Prussia. He was created, March 15th, 1718, a Maréchal de Camp; was appointed, April 27th, 1721, a Commander of the Order of St. Louis; and died at Paris, October 25th, 1738, aged 75. By his marriage with Eleonor Susan Mac Carthy Reagh, of the direct line of the old Princes or Chiefs of Carbery, the Baron had 1 son, James Nathaniel, slain, *sine prole*, with the Army of Bohemia, in 1741. Another branch of those Hiberno-Norman Hookes, that retired from the Cromwellian *régime* to the French West Indian islands, after having held the position of noblesse there, and having given officers of the ranks of Captain and Colonel to the Irish Brigade in the national regiments of Fitz-James, Dillon and Berwick, finally *re*-settled in Normandy; where a Baron de Hooke was established, in 1814, at Gatteville, as a barony belonging to his house. Of those Irish and Catholic Hookes likewise were Nathaniel Hooke, author of the well-known History of Rome, (1 of the most honest books that *ever* was written) and other works, born in Dublin about 1690, deceased in England in 1763; and his son, the learned Abbé Hooke, Doctor of Sorbonne, editor of the Duke of Berwick's Mémoires, &c., born in Dublin in 1716, and deceased in France, in 1796.

Of the ancient family of Plunkett, of Danish origin in Ireland, distinguished by various branches, especially in the Counties of Louth, Meath, and Dublin, and dignified by "almost every honour which the Crown could bestow," including several Peerages, Robert Plunkett, 15th Lord Baron of Killeen, and 6th Earl of Fingal, Captain of the Infantry Regiment of Berwick in the Irish Brigade, also died this year, 1738, at Paris, where he was interred. By his marriage with Mary, daughter of Roger Macgennis, Esq., of the branch of Deriveagh, County of Down, and likewise an officer in the service of France, his Lordship was grandfather of Arthur James, 17th Lord Baron of Killeen, and 8th Earl of Fingal, deceased in 1836; who duly estimated his consequent participation in the most illustrious or old Irian blood of Uladh, or Ulster, through that of its leading name Macgennis, (or Mac Guinness,) compared with which, as sprung from the line, for so many ages, of the celebrated Kings of Emania, and thus best entitled, in that province, to bear the heroic ensign of the "red hand," other races there, Clan-Colla, or Hy-Niall, were but of yesterday, or no better, in Bardic language, than "adventurers, strange tribes, and foreigners."* In reference to

* The race of Ir are related to have reigned for ages at Emania over Uladh, or Ulster, with greater fame, in song and story, than any other dynasty of the Bardic annals of Erin, till a century previous to the coming of St. Patrick as the national Apostle, or A. D. 332. Then, by the Clan-Colla invasion, this older Irian race of Uladh were conquered, and their royal residence of Emania destroyed; the survivors retiring into the separate island, as it were, of the Counties of Antrim and

Lord Fingal's just feeling on this point, my friend, Mr. O'Farrell Doran, writes—"A few gentlemen, of whom my father was 1, passing a day, in the neighbourhood of Killeen Castle, in the summer of 1820, or 1821, went to see the castle and demesne. They were fortunate enough to find the late Earl of Fingal at home, who very politely accompanied them through the various apartments, with the exception of the drawing-

Down, situated between the waters of the northern Ban, and Lough Neagh, and the southern Ban, and the sea, with the Newry river to the south; the only, and comparatively small, space, unoccupied by a watery barrier on the west, or the frontier from the southern Ban to the Newry river, being secured by a fortified rampart, on the principle of that raised by the Romans, against the incursions of the Picts and Scots, in Britain. Eoghan, son of Niall, the progenitor of the Hy-Niall, or O'Neill sept, who, in turn, or at the expense of the Clan-Colla, were to attain a subsequent political ascendancy in Uladh, did not *begin* to establish himself in that province till shortly previous to St. Patrick's arrival, A. D. 432, in Erin, or nearly 100 years *after* the fall of the Irian supremacy, and destruction of Emania. By the descendants of the old Irians, in their little Uladh, or *Ulidia*, of Antrim and Down, the Clan-Colla and Hy-Niall races, who held all the rest of Uladh, were naturally regarded in no better light, than the remains of the ancient Britons, driven into Cambria, or Wales, regarded the Saxons and Normans in England; or as the unjust possessors of the better and larger portion of a country, wrested, by the intrusion of the stranger, from its rightful, or original owners. Hence, in Ulidia, "the land of hospitality and spears," *the* Macgennis, as eldest in descent from the royal line of Ir, or the Red Branch, looked upon the more modern Heremonian, or Clan-Colla and Hy-Niall *settlers* in Uladh, as comparative "*novi homines;*" *his* Bards maintaining, "that the red hand of Ulster was derived from the Heroes of the Red Branch, and that, therefore, it belonged by right to MACGENNIS, the senior representative of Conall Cearnagh," or *the Victorious*, "the most distinguished of those heroes, and *not* to O'Neill; whose ancestors, although they had *no* connexion with those heroes by descent, had *usurped* the sovereignty of Ulster!" The Macgennis territory of Iveagh originally included the modern Baronies of Upper and Lower Iveagh, and half the Barony of Mourne, in the County of Down. The 1st of the name, ennobled after the English manner, was Sir Art or Arthur Macgennis, married to Sarah, daughter of the great Aodh or Hugh O'Neill, Earl of Tyrone, and created, by King James I., in 1623, Lord Viscount Iveagh. By the results of the civil war of 1641-53, the Macgennises were greatly shattered in their fortunes, like the old Irish families in general. Had King James II. been able to maintain himself in Ireland, the Macgennises, through the repeal, in 1689, of the Acts of Settlement and Explanation, by the Irish Parliament of that Monarch, would have recovered what had been their considerable landed possessions, at the commencement of the troubles in 1641. In the War of the Revolution, James was served with proportionate zeal by those of the name; the head of whom, Brian Macgennis, Viscount Iveagh (married to Lady Margaret de Burgo, eldest daughter of William, 7th Earl of Clanricarde,) was Colonel of a Regiment of Foot in the Irish army. On the unfavourable conclusion of that contest, which left very few of the Macgennises with estates, his Lordship went into the Austrian service with an Irish corps to fight the Turks in Hungary, and, in 1693, died abroad, without issue. Of Macgennises in the service of France, —besides Bernard the Colonel of Dragoons, and his 4 sons, already mentioned, under the battle of Spire, in 1703,—there were several born in Ireland, who, from the rank of Captain to that of Chef-de-Bataillon, were in the Regiments of Bulkeley, Roth, and Dillon, and Chevaliers of St. Louis. In addition to the honourable family alliances of the higher members of the name of Macgennis at home, it was connected abroad with the great house of Justiniani—ennobled by various branches in Venice, Genoa, Naples, the Greek Empire, and France— Prince Francis Justiniani, its head in France, being married, September 1st, 1746, at the Church of St. Sulpice, in Paris, says my authority, "à Demoiselle Marie Françoise Roze Magenis, d'une des plus anciennes Maisons d'Irlande." In our own times, A. C. Macgennis, Esq., has been Minister for Great Britain and Ireland at the Courts of Stockholm, Naples, and Lisbon; and, under another form of the name as Guinness, instead of *Mac* Guinness, the spirit of an Emanian Prince has been displayed by the late magnificent restorer and preserver of the venerable Cathedral of our national Apostle, St. Patrick.

room, which he apologized for *not* showing, as the ladies were there. In the principal dining-room, of which the furniture was all Irish oak, he directed their attention to where the family-arms were quartered; and, in doing so, he observed, evidently with peculiar pride, that his grandmother was a Macgennis; at the same time, particularly pointing out the arms of Macgennis, as connected with that circumstance." And, indeed, what more honourable recollections could be excited by any connexion than by this, as constituting a family link, between the remote storied celebrity of the Heroes of the Red Branch, and the modern military renown of the Irish Brigade?

The decease of Charles VI., last Emperor of Germany of the House of Hapsburgh, in October, 1740, without sons, and the consequent hostilities by Prussia, Bavaria, and Saxony, against Charles's daughter, the celebrated Maria Theresa, Queen of Hungary, gave rise to the War of the Austrian Succession, which first extended from Germany to France, and afterwards to England and Holland. But, among the Irish troops in France, the only event of any note this year was the death of Lieutenant-General "Matthieu de Coock," or Matthew Cooke—1 of the representatives of a name settled in Ireland within the century following the Anglo-Norman invasion—variously employed, in civil and military service, by King James II., in Ireland, in its Catholic branches—and, as such, proportionately marked out for Williamite proscription, or land-spoliation, there. After the termination of the War of the Revolution in Ireland, in 1691, this gentleman came to France, as an Ensign in the King's or Royal Irish Regiment of Foot Guards. He served, in 1692, on the coasts of Normandy; fought at the battle of Landen in 1693; and continued with the Army of Flanders till the peace in 1697. He was commissioned, March 25th, 1698, as a reformed Mestre-de-Camp to the Irish Horse Regiment of Sheldon. Passing with this corps to the Army of Italy, in July, 1701, he was at the combat of Chiari, in September. He served, in 1702, at the battle of Luzzara; and, in Germany, in 1703, at the successful sieges of Brisach and Landau, and the victory of Spire. He was attached to the Army of Flanders from 1704 to 1707; having been at the battle of Ramillies, in 1706. Brigadier, by brevet, March 3rd, 1708, he was at the battle of Oudenarde, that year; and, in 1709, at the battle of Malplaquet. In 1713, acting with the Army of Germany, he was at the reductions of Landau and Friburgh. He was made Maréchal de Camp, by brevet, February 1st, 1719; a Lieutenant-General, by power of February 20th, 1734; but did not serve in either of these grades; and died, August 16th, 1740, aged 82 years.

It was some time before the Irish regiments in France were generally and actively engaged in this contest, respecting the Austrian succession. In 1741, all the fusilier companies of the several Irish battalions were increased by 10 men each, or from 30 to 40 men per company; all the grenadier companies by 15 men each, or from 30 to 45 men per company; and there was likewise an addition made of 2 officers to every company. In 1742, a British force of 16,000 men having landed in the Austrian Netherlands, for the purpose of joining a much larger German force, with whom the Dutch were solicited to unite, the French, to oppose any invasion on that side, assembled a suitable army along their northern frontier, from Dunkirk to Givet. Against such an infall as the English from Ostend might make upon the French territory towards Dunkirk, the Irish battalions were posted, so as to be specially on the alert there;

that town, from its port, being then such an eye-sore to English commercial jealousy, that its avowed aim was to reduce the place, if possible, to a mere "hamlet for fishermen," * But no hostilities occurred in this quarter. The single Irish Horse Regiment of Fitz-James, consisting of 3 squadrons, (raised to 4 next campaign) served this year, 1742, under the Marshal de Maillebois, in Germany.

In 1743, ere the French or the English had yet made any official declaration of hostilities—the French professing to act only as auxiliaries to the Bavarian Emperor of Germany, Charles VII.—the English only in the same capacity to that Emperor's Austrian opponent, Maria Theresa—the 1st engagement, in this war, between the armies of France and England, took place, June 27th, at Dettingen. The Anglo-German force there under the Earl of Stair, accompanied by George II., and his son, the Duke of Cumberland, were so outmanœuvred, and cut off from provisions, by the French under the Marshal de Noailles, that the

* The English, since their acquisition of Dunkirk from Spain in Cromwell's time, and its unpopular sale to France under Charles II., always regarded that place with a very hostile feeling, on account of the great facilities which its maritime situation afforded to France in war, for the annoyance of *their* trade. With the history of the Irish Brigade, (although *after* the breaking up of that force by the Revolution,) Dunkirk is remarkably associated, through its defence, against the English, and their Allies, under the Duke of York, in 1793. Its French garrison was then commanded by the General of Brigade, O'Meara, who had entered the service early in the Irish Regiment of Roth, and was 1 of the sons of a veteran Captain of the Regiment of Clare, and a native of Ireland, then aged 76. "He," says a contemporary Allied notice of the defender of Dunkirk, "is a very fine, lusty man, full 6 feet high, and was always beloved as a good officer, and esteemed as a man of general knowledge. He married a young lady of Dunkirk, with a fortune of 80,000 livres. He is about 40 years of age. He has 4 brothers, all officers, and fine men." The Duke of York summoned Dunkirk, as being, he said, "destitute of any real defence," against his force, then above 35,000 men; and, by another Allied or British account, "the works of the place were in a most deplorable state, and the garrison, consisting of only 3000 men, was totally insufficient to defend the town." However, O'Meara replied, "I shall defend it, with the brave republicans, whom I have the honour to command." And he *did* so, until relieved; the Duke having finally to raise the siege; abandoning 52 pieces of heavy artillery, with a great quantity of ammunition and baggage. "In the engagement which relieved Dunkirk from siege," writes Mr. O'Conor, "O'Moran, another Irish officer, commanded the right wing of the French army . . . O'Moran was the son of a shoemaker of Elphin, in the County of Roscommon. He had risen from the ranks in Dillon's regiment, and, by his conduct and courage, had obtained the Government of Conde; but he fell a victim to the revolutionary spirit of the times, upon a false charge, of having received British gold, to favour the escape of the British army." The O'Mearas, or O'Maras, of Tipperary, deduce their origin from Cormac Cas, King of North Munster, in the 3rd century, by Samhair, daughter of the famous warrior-bard, Oisin, or Ossian. Previous to the Revolution in France, various O'Mearas were officers there in the Irish Brigade, from the rank of Sous-Lieutenant to that of Colonel, several of whom were Chevaliers of St. Louis, and M. de la Ponce specifies 4 as born at Dunkirk, from 1752 to 1763. Of the defender of Dunkirk, who was still living there in 1814, there were 2 brothers, Daniel, and William, both Colonels under Napoleon I.; the former having been an officer of the old Irish Brigade, in the Regiment of Berwick; and the latter rose to be a General of Brigade, and Baron of the Empire. The O'Morans were an ancient Connaught sept, whose territory was situated between Belanagare and Elphin, in the County of Roscommon. The unfortunate James O'Moran, above referred to as put to death unjustly, (like so many of every rank, age, and sex, by the Jacobin hellhounds,) was born at Elphin, May 1st, 1739. Before the Revolution, or in 1784, he had attained the rank of Maréchal de Camp, or Major-General, and was likewise a Chevalier of St. Louis, and of the American Order of Cincinnatus. From October, 1792, he was a Lieutenant-General.

approaching capture or destruction of opponents thus situated was looked upon as certain in the French camp; when, unluckily, the Marshal's nephew, the Duke de Grammont, rashly quitted a secure position, to make an attack, under such circumstances, as frustrated all the able arrangements of his uncle, after a conflict of some hours, ending in success, and a consequent "escape," on the part of the Confederates.* The Duke, in fact, instead of having to deal, as he thought, only with a rear-guard, exposed himself to a struggle against the entire Allied army, and that force having, besides its superior numbers to his, the fullest use of its powerful artillery; while 2 of the French batteries, which had been planted so skilfully as to play with the most destructive effect upon the Allies, were rendered useless, by the Duke having placed himself, through his misconduct, *between* those batteries and the enemy! The French cavalry, among whom were the choice Horse Guards of the Royal Household, or Maison du Roi à Cheval, and other picked corps, at first carried all before them;† but their infantry being inadequate to sustain them, the Allies were finally victorious, or able to effect their object of a retreat; acknowledging in killed, wounded, and missing, 1530 Germans —of whom 977 were Austrians, 553 Hanoverians—and of British, 821; or, in all, 2351 men; the French loss not being thus explicitly acknowledged, since probably much greater.

Of Irish, in the French army that day, there were Charles O'Brien, 6th Lord Clare, and 9th Earl of Thomond, as Maréchal de Camp, or Major-General, the Honourable Count Henry Dillon, subsequently 11th Lord Dillon, and Count Charles Edward Roth, *both* as Brigadiers, and the battalions of Clare, Dillon, Roth, and Berwick. These the Marshal de Noailles had designed to be "the 1st Brigade to attack"—although it turned out, that they were not engaged at all. An Irish officer, who wrote from the French camp, July 14th, after observing of the Allies, how, "instead of pursuing the advantage they had gain'd, they retir'd from the field of battle into the woods, and disappear'd before we," the Irish, "arriv'd," adds, on this point,—"As our Brigade found the impossibility of arriving time enough at the action, from the distance we were at, my Lord Clare, who commanded as Major-General, sent 3 Aid-de-Camps, to beg the Marshal would let us pass the bridge at Shaffenburgh to which we were convenient, and to give us leave, with 2 other Brigades with us, to attack them in the rear. But, in the hurry and confusion, this disobedience" of his nephew, the Duke de Grammont, "had thrown the Marshal into, he could not be met with. *The poor Household*," or Maison du Roi à Cheval, "*during the whole action, were crying out for us, as were all the Princes of the Blood, because, in the 1st disposition, or order of battle, we were to have sustain'd each other; and several compliments had pass'd between us, of the mutual joy it caus'd in each of us, to be supported by each other.* We had been posted at the right, because it was thought the enemy would defile that way, rather than return to the left; and it was the Marshal's intention

* An English periodical writer, in May, 1745, when referring to "the *victory* of Dettingen," adds, "which most people rather call an *escape!*"

† Of the English cavalry, Horace Walpole says—"It is allowed, that *our fine horse did us no honour:* the victory was gained by the foot." And he subsequently alludes to that cavalry, as "*the horse, who behaved wretchedly.*" See, however, a remarkable exception to this conduct in that of Ligonier's Regiment of Horse, consisting of Irish Protestants, as noticed in next Book, at conclusion of battle of Fontenoy.

we should be the 1st Brigade to attack. Providence, perhaps, had us that day in peculiar care; for, had we been of the number that attack'd, we might have retriev'd the affair, by inspiring *other* troops with an equal intrepidity, and thus the action might have been continued, till the whole army arrived. But *we should have been infallibly cut to pieces, to the last officer and soldier, before either Frenchman or Englishman should have had it in their power to reproach us with turning our backs, notwithstanding any inequality, till a retreat should be commanded.** As I was early at the field of battle, *I had every Irish and English soldier transported to the hospital, before I suffered an Austrian or an Hanoverian to be moved, and did them every kind office in my power,*" &c. This last-cited portion of the Irish officer's letter refers to about 600 disabled men left by the Allies on the field, with a letter from Lord Stair, recommending them to the French Marshal's protection; and whom, accordingly, writes Smollett, "the French General treated with great care and tenderness." Such treatment, indeed, was only what was to have been expected. Captain Parker observes, on an incident of the kind, between officers, in 1711, or during Marlborough's wars in Flanders—"This humane and generous treatment is, for the most part, the practice of all European nations, when once the heat of action is over. But, it must be allowed, to their honour, that none are so remarkable for it as the English and French; insomuch that, with them, it prevails, even among the common soldiers." In 1794, also, when the infamous Jacobin decree, forbidding any quarter to be given by the French troops to the English, was passed by the National Convention, the reply of the Duke of York to that ferocious enactment was an order of the day, commanding that *his* army should act as previously towards the French. "Humanity and kindness," alleged his Royal Highness, "have at all times taken place, the instant that opposition ceased; and the same cloak has been frequently seen covering those who were wounded, friends and enemies, while indiscriminately conveyed to the hospitals of the conquerors." The honourable sentiments and creditable conduct of the Duke on this point "were seconded by the corresponding feelings of the French officers; and the prisoners, on *both* sides, were treated with the same humanity, as before the issuing of the bloody decree." Our illustrious military historian, Napier, in relating the entry of the French into Talavera in 1809, after the retreat of the British under Sir Arthur Wellesley (subsequently Duke of Wellington) likewise remarks of the French commander, Marshal Victor, Duke of Belluno— "Thus, the English wounded, left there, fell into his hands, and their treatment was such as might be expected from a gallant and courteous nation; for, between the British soldiers and the French, there was no rancour, and the generous usages of a civilized and honourable warfare

---

* He glances sarcastically *here* at the French Foot Guards, of whom he had previously written—"The Foot Guards were the 1st to run away, and lost a 3rd of their officers, mostly of the highest quality." The officers had killed numbers of the soldiers, to endeavour to make the rest rally, and stand their ground, but in vain. Connect with this point, and the Irish officer's assertion of himself and his countrymen in reference to it, the following passage from Forman's refutation of Arnall, Sir Robert Walpole's lying *Whig* libeller of the Irish, as *cowards.* "Wherever they serv'd, whether they had courage or not, they *always had the good fortune to distinguish themselves:* and it may be said, to their eternal honour, that, from the time they enter'd into the service of France, to this hour, they *have never made the least false step, or have had the least blot in their scutcheon.*"

were cherished." The Allied forces, soon after the affair of Dettingen, were increased by several thousand Hanoverians and Hessians, and, later in the season, by a still larger number of Dutch auxiliaries; but, "in October, were distributed into winter quarters," complains one of their writers, "after an inactive campaign, that redounded very little to the honour of those by whom the motions of the army were conducted."

The year 1744 opened with the decease of the oldest Irish officer in France of the rank of Maréchal de Camp, or Major-General, whose services in Ireland dated from the War of the Revolution there, and whose arrival in France, from the landing of the 1st Irish Brigade, under Lord Mountcashel. This gentleman, "Guillaume d'Oshagnussi," or William O'Shaughnessy, son of Roger O'Shaughnessy, Esq., and Helen, daughter of Conor Mac Donogh O'Brien, Esq. of Ballynue, was, on his father's death, in July, 1690, the representative of the Chieftain branch of his name in the County of Galway—which is referred to, from its principal residence there, by a learned local authority, as the "præclarissima familia de *Gort*, cujus nobilitatem, antiquitatem, et integritatem, qui non novit, *Hiberniam* non novit"—and which, like so many other ancient houses, was, for its loyalty to King James II., stripped of its estates, by revolutionary vengeance and rapacity. Of the heads of this old sept, likewise "ever remarkable for their munificence and liberality, a writer, who travelled through Ireland and the Continent, in the times of Charles I., tells us, that the O'Shaughnessys then excelled, in elegant hospitality, all the nobility of Connacht, with the sole exception of the Marquis of Clanricard." In 1689, or on the commencement of the war in Ireland, William O'Shaughnessy, then only about 15, was Captain of a company of 100 men, with which he served there, till sent to France, in the spring of 1690, in the Regiment of the Honourable Daniel O'Brien, (afterwards that of Clare) and July 10th, 1691, was commissioned by Louis XIV., as a Captain in that corps. In this grade, he was, the same year, at the siege of Montmelian; in 1692, with the Army of Italy; in 1693, at the victory of Marsaglia in Piedmont; in 1696, witnessed the conclusion of military operations beyond the Alps by the siege of Valenza, at which he became Commandant of the 3rd battalion of his regiment; and, in 1697, was attached to the Army of the Meuse. On the reform, in 1698, of the 2nd and 3rd battalions of his regiment, he was made, April 1st, Captain of Grenadiers, in the battalion which was kept on foot. After the breaking out of the War of the Spanish Succession, or in 1701 and 1702, he was employed with the Army of Germany; in 1703, was at the reduction of Kehl, the combat of Munderkingen, the 1st battle of Hochstedt; and, in 1704, was at the 2nd battle there, otherwise known as that of Blenheim. In 1705, he was with the Army of the Moselle; and, in 1706, at the battle of Ramillies. By the death, from wounds there, of his Major, John O'Carroll, he became, July 4th, successor to that gallant officer, and September 12th, Lieutenant-Colonel. He was with the Army of Flanders in 1707; at the battle of Oudenarde in 1708; at that of Malplaquet in 1709; at the attack of Arleux in 1711; at the action of Denain, and the sieges of Douay, Quesnoy, and Bouchain, in 1712; and, in Germany, the following campaign, at those of Landau and Friburgh. Brigadier by brevet, April 3rd, 1721, he was, by letters of September 15th, 1733, employed with the Army of the Rhine, and at the successful siege of Kehl, in October. In the same army, by letters of April 1st, 1734, he was at the attack of the lines of Etlingen, and the siege of

Philipsburgh; was made Maréchal de Camp by brevet, August 1st; and finished the campaign in that capacity. Continued as Maréchal de Camp with the Army of the Rhine by letters of May 1st, 1735, he was present at the affair of Clausen. Attached to the Army of Flanders by letters of August 21st, 1742, he commanded at Cambray during the winter; remained there during the campaign of 1743; and having been appointed, November 1st, to command at Gravelines, died, without issue, January 2nd, 1744, aged 70.

"The lands of the O'Shaughnessys, forfeited in consequence of their attachment to the cause of King James II.," says Mr. Gilbert, "were granted, for a term of years, by William III., to Sir Thomas Prendergast, whose character has been depicted, by Swift, in the darkest colours, as a sordid betrayer of his friends, and a relentless persecutor of the clergy of the Established Church." By this loss of his property in Ireland, William O'Shaughnessy was necessarily obliged to remain in the service of France, as his only source of subsistence. "On his death, his cousin, Colman O'Shaughnessy," Catholic "Bishop of Ossory, essayed at law to recover the property of his ancestors. The suit was continued by his brother Robuck, whose son, Joseph, assisted by his relatives, took forcible possession of the mansion-house of Gort; on which occasion the bells of Athenry and of Galway were rung for joy. The whole clan believed, that the *strangers* were defeated; and the Irish poets of the locality sung, that the rightful heir was restored, and that the old splendour of the O'Shaughnessys was about to be renewed in the halls of their fathers. This triumph was, however, but of short duration. All the efforts of the O'Shaughnessys were rendered abortive by the influence of Prendergast's representatives, who re-obtained possession; and are said, for carrying on their suit, to have borrowed £8000 from Lord Chancellor Mansfield; which sum was charged on, and paid by, the estate. Having been thus stripped of their inheritance, the old clan of O'Shaughnessy sunk into obscurity." In the Indian and Australian portions of the British empire, this ancient name, however, has not of late years, been without distinction; and, from those who derived their possession of the Gort property through the Williamite or "glorious-revolution" spoliation of the O'Shaughnessys, *we* have seen *that* property wrested by the Nemesis of the Encumbered Estates Court—which tribunal, in so many instances, added Mr. Gilbert at the time, "is effectually fulfilling the predictions of the Irish Jacobite poets, who never ceased to sing, 'that *Providence would only suffer the foreign churls, who had usurped the lands of the old English, and of the noble Gaels, of Erin, to hold their white mansions transiently.*'"*

Early in 1744, previous to the declaration of war in form by France against England, the French Court resolved on measures to strengthen the Irish Regiments in Flanders, at the expense of the British army there; for which purpose the Comte d'Argenson wrote as follows from Versailles, in February, to the Marquis de Ceberet, commanding in Flanders. "The King, having been informed that several Irishmen present themselves on the frontier, with the intention of serving in the regiments of their nation actually in his service, and that most of these regiments being complete, the supernumeraries could only find their means of subsistence at the expense of the Captains, if it were not otherwise provided for; his Majesty,

* Essay on "The Historic Literature of Ireland."

in consideration of the useful services which he has received in the preceding wars, and of those which his Irish troops continue to render him daily, commands me to acquaint you, that the Commissioners of War, appointed to the direction of the 5 Irish Regiments which are in his service, are to comprise, in their returns, all the supernumeraries, capable of serving, who may present themselves; taking care to hold a separate register of those who shall exceed the full number of each regiment, in whatever number they may come; and shall see that their pay be remitted to them at the rate of 6 sols, 6 decimes per day each, until his Majesty shall come to a determination of raising the regiments of this nation, which he maintains, by 1 or more battalions." The letter concludes by requiring that the Prefect of Flanders should be directed to make the necessary financial arrangements for this object.

HISTORY OF THE IRISH BRIGADES

IN

THE SERVICE OF FRANCE.

BOOK VII.

THE French cabinet, through the influence of Cardinal de Tencin, who owed his Cardinalate to the Stuart interest at Rome, having decided, in 1743, on undertaking an invasion of England, in 1744, for the "restoration" of the exiled royal family, communicated this intention to the son of King James II., known as King James III. at Rome. There, or elsewhere within the Papal territory, that Prince had resided, since his marriage with the Princess Sobieski, in 1719; and had kept up a due correspondence with the numerous friends of his house in Great Britain and Ireland, but, more particularly, in Scotland. Partly, however, from the habits of body connected with his advanced time of life, he being then about 56, and partly from the depressing effects of the past on his mind, James was unfitted to act in person, at this important juncture, as the head of his family.* He accordingly devolved that task upon his eldest son, the gallant and attractive Prince Charles, who, from his boyhood, was a source of as much hope to the adherents of the House of Stuart, as of natural apprehension to the partizans, and of restless *espionage* to the government-agents, of the House of Hanover. In 1734, the Duke of Berwick and Liria, (son of the illustrious Marshal-Duke, by his 1st marriage with the widow of Patrick Sarsfield, Lord Lucan,) thus writes of the young Prince, when but 14, at the siege of Gaeta.† "Immediately on his arrival, he accompanied me into the trenches, where he appeared quite regardless of the bullets, that were whistling about us. The next day, I commanded in the trenches. I was in a house, that stood somewhat detached, into which the besieged fired 5 cannon-balls, so that I was obliged to leave it. Immediately afterwards, the Prince came to me, and no representation of the danger, to which he exposed himself, could deter him from entering the house. He remained there, for some time, perfectly cool, though the walls were riddled by bullets. The Prince, in a word, shows that, in men born to be heroes, valour does not wait on years. From all these causes of uneasiness, I am now relieved," by the surrender of the place, "and

---

* Lord Macaulay correctly enough refers to James, as "born the most unfortunate of Princes, destined to 77 years of exile and wandering, of vain projects, of honours more galling than insults, and of hopes such as make the heart sick."

† That connected with the conquest, from Austria, of the Kingdom of Naples, by Spain, and the placing of Don Carlos on the Neapolitan throne. "In consequence of this war," says Heeren, "Alberoni's formerly unsuccessful plans on Italy were, for the *most* part, carried into execution."

enjoy the gratification of seeing the Prince adored by officers and soldiers. His manner is charming; and, be assured, if it were otherwise, I would tell you so, in confidence. The day after to-morrow, we start for Naples, where, I have no doubt, his Royal Highness will captivate the people, as well as the soldiers. The King of Naples thinks him extremely pleasing. He never requires to be prompted, as to what he ought to say, or do. Would to God the bitterest enemies of the House of Stuart had been witnesses of the Prince's conduct during this siege! —it would, I believe, have changed the minds of many of them. I remark in him, particularly, a happy physiognomy, that is full of good promises." About 8 years after, or in 1742, Prince "Charles Edward," says his future Secretary, Murray of Broughton, in a letter to a lady, "is tall, above the common stature; his limbs are cast in the most exact mould; his complexion has in it somewhat of uncommon delicacy; all his features are perfectly regular, and well-turn'd; and his eyes the finest I ever saw. But that which shines most in him, and renders him, without exception, the most surprizingly handsome person of the age, is the dignity that accompanies every gesture. There is, indeed, such an unspeakable majesty diffus'd through his whole mien and air, as it is impossible to have any idea of without seeing; and strikes those that have, with such an awe, as will not suffer them to look upon him for any time, unless he emboldens them to it, by his excessive affability.* . . . His mind, by all I can judge of it, is no less worthy of admiration. He seems to *me*, and, I find, to *all* who know him, to have all the good nature of the Stuart family, blended with the spirit of the Sobieskys. He is, at least, as far as I am capable of seeing into men, equally qualified to preside in peace and war." Then, referring to the Prince's learning, as "extensive beyond what cou'd be expected from double the number of his years," including a power of conversation with ease and fluency, in several European languages, a masterdom of the different kinds of Latin, a good knowledge of Greek, and even some acquaintance with Hebrew, the writer adds—"History and philosophy are his darling entertainments, in both which he is well vers'd. The one, he says, will instruct him how to govern others, and the other how to govern himself, whether in prosperous, or adverse, fortune."† Charles, who, on setting out from Rome, *viâ* France, for England, was in his 24th year, received, in the capacity of Prince of Wales, and Regent, from his father, the requisite Proclamations for England and Scotland; for the former, in the name of James III., and, in that of James VIII., for the latter; as *not* acknowledging the validity, and promising a dissolution, of the so-called *Act of Union*, by which, to exclude the Stuart family from *all* royalty within the British Islands, Scotland, against her will, had been specially extinguished, through such very indefensible means, as a distinct *Kingdom*. These

---

* Captain Malcolm Macleod, 1 of Charles's friends and companions in his miseries and concealments after the fatal day of Culloden, has asserted—"There is not a person, that knows what the air of a noble or great man is, but, upon seeing the Prince, in any disguise he could put on, would see something about him that was not ordinary, something of the stately, and the grand."

† The Whig Edinburgh Review admits of Charles, that he "spoke Latin, Italian, French, and English, and was well versed in ancient and modern history." Lord Mahon, indeed, refers to "Charles's letters," as "written in a large, rude, rambling hand like a schoolboy's," and, "in spelling, still more deficient." But, Klose justly notes, how these were deficiencies of other eminent men, as well as of Charles—Frederick the Great, and Napoleon the Great, included.

documents are described, as "Given from our Court in Rome, on the 23rd of December, 1743, and in the 43rd year of our reign"—thus ignoring the idea of any reign, *de jure*, in Great Britain and Ireland, from 1688 to 1701, but that of James II., and treating the entire period, from *his* decease in 1701, to 1743, as the reign only of his *son* —William, Anne, and the 2 Georges being thereby snuffed out, as no better than the mere representatives of revolutionary usurpation—or so many Cromwells, in the place of the *hereditary* representative of the *true* royal line.

An English panegyrist of Charles, on this occasion, admiringly notes—

> " How, at an age, when Pleasure's charms
> Allure the stripling to her arms,
> *He* form'd the great design,
> T' assert his injur'd father's cause,
> Restore his suff'ring country's laws,
> And *prove his right divine!*"

And, at this period, the state of public feeling in Great Britain and Ireland was indeed such, as, with reference to the Prince's enterprise, says Mr. Jesse, " certainly held out a fair prospect of success. An influential portion of the English nobility and gentry, at the head of whom was the Premier Duke, the Duke of Norfolk, were known to be thoroughly disgusted with the reigning dynasty; and, though reluctant to risk their lives and fortunes without a tolerable certainty of success, were, nevertheless, secretly prepossessed in favour of the Stuarts. The great majority of the Highland Chieftains were enthusiastically devoted to their cause; several of the most influential of the Lowland gentry were known to be well-inclined towards the exiled family; while Ireland was certain to embark in a cause, of which the watchwords were Papal supremacy and legitimate right"—including, it should be more fairly or unequivocally added, *a repeal of the Anglo-Protestant violation of the Treaty of Limerick, and consequent abolition of the infamous Penal Code.* Then, alluding to the other sources of strength for Jacobitism, arising from the circumstances of England, that was at war with Spain, being likewise on the eve of a war with France, where such a great Stuart churchman, as the Cardinal de Tencin, was in power, Mr. Jesse alleges—" George II., moreover, was, at this period, in the zenith of his unpopularity; and not only did there prevail throughout England a vast amount of distress and misery, which was ingeniously exaggerated by party writers, but the undue preference which had long been shown, both by the King and his father, to the interests of their native and petty Electorate over those of England, had long excited universal indignation and disgust. 'No *Hanoverian* King!' had become the frequent toast, not only of the Jacobites, but of many who had formerly been well-affected towards the existing government; and the very term of '*Hanoverian*' is said to have become a bye-word of insult and reproach." Nor were such sentiments unexpressed in another form.

> " Britons, now retrieve your glory,
> And your ancient rights maintain;
> Drive th' usurping race before you,
> And restore a Stuart's reign.
> Load the Brunswick prancer double,
> Heap on all your care and trouble,
> Drive him hence, with all his rabble,
> Never to return again.

> "Call your injur'd King to save you,
> Ere you further are oppress'd;
> He's so good, he will forgive you,
> And receive you to his breast.
> Think on all the wrongs you've done him,
> Bow your rebel necks, and own him,
> Quickly make amends, and crown him,
> Or you never can be blest."

"The English," concludes the great Protestant Continental historian, Sismondi, with respect to Prince Charles's effort for the "restoration" of his family to the Crown, "had no attachment to the House of Hanover; they found it covetous, brutal, ignorant of their manners, entirely engrossed by German interests, entirely devoted to Austria, and always desirous to drag them into Continental wars, in which they were called upon to expend their money, still more than their blood. With these causes for discontent were combined, in favour of the Stuarts, the interest which misfortune inspires, the chivalrous enthusiasm of fidelity to an ancient royal race;" in fine, "the irritation of the Scotch, who, since the Union of their country with England, believed they had lost their independence, and flattered themselves, by replacing upon the throne the heir of their ancient Kings, to bring back to their country her ancient glory, and to re-establish her once more as a nation."

Prince Charles, whose movements it was so essential to disguise from the Whig-Hanoverian spies at Rome and elsewhere, pretended to leave that city, January 9th, 1744, merely for a boar-hunt, as was his custom in winter. Then, under the feigned name of the Marquis Spinelli, with only a single attendant, he rapidly traversed Tuscany for a Genoese port, where he embarked on the 13th; sailing through a squadron of British ships, landed in France at Antibes;* and after an interview at Avignon, with the venerable Duke of Ormonde, aged nearly 80, and other Jacobites, he reached Paris on the 20th. The military force with which he was to sail for England consisted of 15,000, (if not, according to Voltaire, 24,000,) men, including the Irish and Scotch troops in the service of France; with these were many thousand supernumerary fire-arms, swords, saddles, and bridles, for such Jacobite loyalists as might join after the landing; and the whole were to be under the command of the veteran Count Maurice Arminius de Saxe, subsequently so celebrated as Marshal. The passage of the transports, with the troops from Dunkirk, to the shores of Kent, was ordered to be protected by an able and experienced naval officer, M. de Roquefeuille, with a suitable armament from Brest and Rochefort. The intelligence, in February, of these hostile preparations, occasioned proportionable apprehensions and counter-preparations in England. The danger from France and "the *Pretender*" was announced by the Hanoverian occupant of the throne to his Parliament; orders were issued to assemble as many native regulars and militia as possible, besides the 6000 foreigners stipulated by treaty with Holland to be furnished in support of the revolutionary succession to the Crown;†

---

* "Not far," it is remarked, "from the spot, destined, in the 19th century, to acquire an historical celebrity, by the landing of Napoleon from Elba."

† The effective native force, that *could* be assembled, for the protection of London, seems to have been rather *small* in amount. Horace Walpole, writing from the House of Commons in February, asserts—"*All* the troops have been sent for, in the greatest haste, to London. We shall *not* have above 8000 men together, *at most*. An express is gone to Holland, and General Wentworth followed it last night, to demand 6000 men," &c.

the Habeas Corpus Act was suspended; James Barry, 4th Earl of Barrymore, as an intended General for the House of Stuart, the octogenarian Colonel Cecil, as its local Secretary of State, and several other Jacobite loyalists, were taken up; Captains O'Brien and O'Hara of the Irish Brigade, about to return (no doubt with serviceable news!) to the Continent, *viâ* Harwich, were arrested there; and Sir John Norris was despatched, with a due naval force, to oppose the landing from Dunkirk, by endeavouring to defeat M. de Roquefeuille, who was to cover the transports "over the water with Charlie." But, early in March, when the Prince, and the Count de Saxe, having shipped 7000 men at Dunkirk, were actually *at sea with a fair breeze, for the English coast,* and *protected by their men-of-war,* the wind shifted to an adverse point in the evening, and a violent tempest of several days' duration commenced, which dispersed the fleets of both nations that had been in sight of each other about Dungeness, and sank, drove back, or shattered the French transports in such a manner, that the proposed invasion had to be abandoned. A contemporary French historian has observed, Louis XV. might have exclaimed, on this occasion, like Philip II. formerly, with reference to his Armada—"I did not send my fleet to war with the elements!" The Whig historian Home, then living, after noting the position, as regards Dunkirk, of the 2 fleets, before their separation by the storm, has remarked—"Both the fleets were far enough from Dunkirk; and, if the weather had been moderate, *Marshal Saxe might have reached England, before Sir John Norris could have returned to the Downs.* But, when the storm arose, it stopped the embarkation; several transports were wrecked; a good many soldiers and seamen perished; a great quantity of warlike stores was lost;" and "the English fleet returned to the Downs." Had this expedition from France effected a disembarkation in England, we are informed of Scotland, that "the whole of the disaffected clans, who were able to bring to the field 12,000 men, were prepared to rise," as "the Chiefs were *all* then united"—instead of *not* being so, as subsequently, or in 1745. By such prospects, the English Jacobites, according to their song, "Come, here's to the knights of the true royal oak!" appear to have been proportionably elated—

"God bless Charlie Stuart, the pride of our land,
And send him safe o'er to his own native strand!
My noble companions, be patient awhile,
And we'll soon see him back to our brave British isle;
And he, that for Stuart and right will not stand,
May smart for the wrong, by the Highlander's brand!"

The song, too, of the same party, entitled "the Restoration," in announcing, how, to curb *usurpation* by the assistance of France, Charlie, with love to his country, was coming, observed of the Prince—

"In his train, see sweet Peace, fairest queen of the sky,
Ev'ry bliss in her look, ev'ry charm in her eye,
Whilst oppression, corruption, vile slav'ry, and fear,
At his wish'd-for return, never more shall appear.
Your glasses charge high, 'tis in great Charles' praise!" &c.

"Ye brave clans, on whom we just honour bestow,
O think on the source whence our dire evils flow!
Commanded by Charles, advance to Whitehall,
And fix them in chains, who would Britons enthral!
Your glasses charge high, 'tis in great Charles' praise!" &c.

In answer to a naturally querulous note of March 11th from Prince Charles, the Count de Saxe, on the 13th, wrote—"*Vous ne pouvez, Monseigneur, accuser que les vents et la fortune des contretemps qui nous arrivent.*" Hence, also, in referring to the danger escaped by Hanoverianism in England, through the frustration of the intended landing from France by the interposition of the elements, the Speaker of the British House of Lords having stated, how "great preparations were made and ready at Dunkirk," added, "but *the Providence of God disappointed them!*" Prince Charles left Dunkirk, with such feelings as may be easily imagined; and the faithful old Duke of Ormonde, who, as "his name and popularity in England had long been a tower of strength," had been summoned from his retreat at Avignon to join the expedition, and was on his way to do so, learning, upon the road, how the enterprise was foiled, went back to his residence—thus, in 1744, as in 1719, with a French as with a Spanish armament, prevented returning to England, by the hostility of the winds!*

In Ireland, those preparations of France to support Prince Charles with so considerable an invading force, including the famous Brigade under Charles O'Brien, Lord Clare, and Earl of Thomond, were, of course, not without exciting a due interest among the Catholic or oppressed majority of the nation; but particularly among the Milesian or Gaelic portion of the population, in 1 of whose songs it is observed—

> "To wage the fierce battle for Erin,
>   Comes the fiery Brigade of Lord Clare,
> 'Tis oft from their pikes, keen and daring,
>   The Saxon fled back to his lair.
> And favour—not now shall he get it,
>   Save from lances on every hand—
> Oh, short are their days, who abetted
>   The murderous deeds in our land!

> " May Charles have but courage to hasten,
>   With troops and with arms, to our shore,
> We'll scorch, from their tyranny wasting,
>   Our treacherous foemen once more.
> We pray to the just Lord to shatter
>   Their hosts and their hopes to the ground,
> To raise our green island, and scatter
>   The blessings of Freedom around!" †

And there *was* good reason for such a prayer, the Whig Penal Code government, issuing, says the History of the Irish Catholics, "a Proclamation for the suppression of convents and monasteries, for the detection and apprehension of ecclesiastics, the punishment of magistrates remiss in the execution of the laws, and for the encouragement of spies and informers, by an increase of the rewards already held out under the existing laws." In consequence of which, "the Catholics were everywhere disarmed, domiciliary visits were made in quest of priests and friars, the chapels were shut up, and a cruel persecution commenced in every quarter of the kingdom."

* On this projected French and Stuart invasion of England in 1744, I have consulted contemporary English and Continental periodicals, Voltaire, Home, Johnstone (the Chevalier) Lord Mahon, Jesse, Klose, Dr. Browne (the historian of the Highlands,) Chambers, &c.
† See, in "The Poets and Poetry of Munster," 2nd Series, the Gaelic song to Philip V. of Spain, versified into English.

Before the end of March, war was at last officially declared both by France and England; and the Count de Saxe was made a Marshal, to command in Flanders, under Louis XV. in person—poetically eulogized or sung of in Ireland, as

"The torch-tossing Louis, a lion in danger,
Sagacious, unshaken, to terror a stranger!"—

with whom Charles O'Brien, Lord Clare and Earl of Thomond, Lieutenant-General, and the Irish troops were to serve. The French, after levying contributions and sweeping away cattle nearly as far as Ghent, between May 18th and July 11th, reduced Menin, Ypres, Fort Knock, and Furnes. In these operations, Lord Clare is mentioned as mounting the trenches, with due distinction, at Menin, as well as at Ypres, and Furnes. The King, departing in July from Flanders for Germany, thereby diminished so considerably the force left with the Marshal de Saxe at Courtray, that he had but 45,000 men at most, to oppose 70,000 Dutch, British, Hanoverians, and Austrians. Yet, under this disadvantage in point of numbers, the Marshal showed himself so superior in tactics to his opponents till the conclusion of this campaign, that, says a British contemporary historian, "the conduct of the Allied Generals was severely censured in England, and ridiculed in France, not only in private conversation, but also on their public theatres, where it became the subject of farces and pantomimes." The Irish are elsewhere alluded to this year, but not in connexion with achievements specially detailed. October 1st, the pay of the non-commissioned officers and privates of each of the national corps of infantry was increased by 2 sols, or French pence, a day; and every regiment was reduced from 685 to 645 privates, besides 16 cadets, each at 16 sols a day. From the supernumerary officers and 200 men obtained by this retrenchment, and 245 men subsequently levied, the formation of a new Irish Infantry Regiment of 445 men, besides officers, was commenced, and, by April, 1745, completed; which, from the name of the gentleman for whom it was raised, was known as the REGIMENT OF LALLY.

The ancient territory of Moenmagh, or "Moen's plain," in Connaught, comprehended the fertile district around Loughrea, in the modern County of Galway; including the townland of Moyode to the north; the country as far as the mountain of Slieve Aughtee on the south; that extending to the barony of Longford on the east; and that to the diocese of Kilmacduagh on the west. Previous to the Anglo-Norman intrusion of the 12th century, the chieftainship of this rich plain was possessed in turn by 2 families, according to the preponderating power of each. Both were of the royal Heremonian stock of the famous Clan-Colla subjugators of the greater portion of Uladh, or Ulster, in the 4th century, through Maine the Great, conqueror of Hy-Mainy, in Connaught, in the 5th century. Those 2 ruling families were that of O'Neachtain, subsequently spelled Naghtan, Naghten, Naghton, or Naughton,* and that of O'Maoilalaidh, or O'Mullally, finally shortened

* The family of O'Neachtain removed from Moenmagh into the Faes, or Fews, of Athlone, in the County of Roscommon. The last "Chief of the Feas" was Shane O'Naghten, who died in Queen Elizabeth's reign, or in May, 1587; and, in 1843, E. H. Naughton, Esq. of Thomastown Park, held a very respectable portion of the territory of his forefathers. A branch of the O'Naghtons was settled at Lisle, in Flanders, at the close of the last century; and a Baron O'Naghten attended the Prince of Hesse-Homberg, when he married the Princess Elizabeth.

into LALLY. From the fertile territory, where, for so long, says the old native poet, "their fight was heavy in the battles," the latter family, when obliged to recede before the invader, retired to and settled in the parish of Tuam; their residence being the Castle of Tulach-na-dala, or *the hill of the meeting*, otherwise Tullaghnadaly, Tullenadally, or Tolendal, 4 miles north of the town of Tuam. In the civil wars of the 17th century, the Lallys fought for the Crown, against the Parliamentarian, and Cromwellian, as well as the Williamite, revolutionists, and suffered accordingly. At the breaking out of the War of the Revolution in Ireland, the 5 brothers of this family, sons of Thomas O'Mullally or Lally, Esq. of Tullenadally or Tolendal, by the Honourable Jane Dillon, sister of Theobald, 7th Lord Viscount Dillon, were James, Gerard, William, Mark, and Michael. 1. James, the eldest, Member for the Borough of Tuam in King James's Parliament of 1689, and consequently outlawed and subjected to confiscation by the Williamites, went to France, in 1690, with his cousin, the Honourable Colonel Arthur Dillon; in whose regiment, as Colonel-Commandant of the 2nd battalion, he fell, unmarried, at Montmelian in 1691. 2. Gerard, of whom more presently. 3. William, a Captain in the Regiment of Dillon, was slain at Barcelona in 1697. 4. Mark was an officer in the same corps. 5. Michael, by marriage with Helen O'Carroll, had a son, also named Michael, deceased a Brigadier-General, at Rouen, in 1773. Gerard, above referred to, and styled Sir Gerard Lally, as a Baronet by Stuart creation, died in France in 1737, a Brigadier-General, and intended Maréchal de Camp, or with the promise of the latter rank on the next promotion; and, by his marriage with Marie Anne de Bressac, was father of the object of our immediate notice, COUNT THOMAS ARTHUR LALLY.

This heroic man was born at Romans, in Dauphiné, and baptized January 15th, 1702. Designed, from his infancy, for a soldier, he was commissioned, from January 1st, 1709, as a reformed Captain in the Irish regiment, of which his father, Sir Gerard Lally, was Colonel-Commandant, and his uncle, the Honourable Arthur Dillon, was Colonel-Proprietor. When not 8 years old, he was brought to the camp before Girona, in September, 1709, by his father, who "wished," as he said, "that he should at least smell powder, in order to gain his 1st step in the service." When hardly 12, his father also caused him to mount his earliest trenches at Barcelona in 1714, and, after this "amusement for the vacation," sent him back to College. This sort of education very soon developed in young Lally an extreme taste for the military profession; which, however, did not prevent him devoting himself ardently to the study of the classics, and acquiring a familiar knowledge of several of the living languages of Europe, as well as of history, and the manners and interests of the different nations. Gifted with a good memory, a quick discernment, a great strength of body, and an astonishing activity of soul, everything became easy to him, and he was as successful in the exercises of the body, as in those of the mind. He would have been very rapidly advanced in the army by the Regent Duke of Orleans, who would have made him a Colonel at 18, but for the unaccountable opposition, or caprice, of his father, Sir Gerard Lally. Deprived of his patron the Regent in 1723, young Lally had only to look for advancement to his own immediate services, and no peculiar opportunity for such occurred, during the long pacific *régime* that succeeded the Regency. He employed this period in an increased application to the theory and practice of the several branches of his profession, to evolutions, to encampments, and, above all, to become familiar with the various duties of the *état major*, for which he was subsequently so noted, as to be, according to Frederic the Great's appreciation of such knowledge, *the soul of an army.* Provided with a company, or made full Captain, February 15th, 1728, in the Regiment of Dillon, he was appointed, January 26th, 1732, its Aid-Major. He served, in 1733, at the reduction of Kehl, and "was as much distinguished by his brilliant valour there, as by his uncommon military knowledge." In 1734, he acted very differently towards his father, from the manner in which his father had acted towards him. During the long peace between France and England under the government of the Cardinal de Fleury in the former, and the Whig-Hanoverian administration of Sir Robert Walpole in the latter country, Walpole, from his natural hostility to the Irish Brigade in France, as entirely attached to the House of Stuart, used his influence with his friend, the Cardinal, to keep back, as much as possible, the promotion of Irish officers of eminence, particularly such as were most remarkable for loyalty to the Stuarts. Sir Charles Wogan, about this time, or February, 1733, noting of the Irish military in France, how "the arms of Whiggism are extremely long, and reach them to their remotest haunts," adds on that point—"Their principal officers, who have signalized themselves equally upon *all* occasions, have been advanced to no higher preferment than that of Lieutenant-General; whereas Scots, Germans, Livonians, Italians, have been promoted to the dignity of Mareschals of France. . . . Some of the Irish had been Mareschals of France before now: the whole voice of that nation was for them; but the fear of disobliging the present government of England gave a check to their promotion." One of those officers most devoted to the House of Stuart, as acknowledged on its part by his Baronetcy, was Sir Gerard Lally; and his promotion to the rank of Brigadier, although amply due to his long and distinguished services, as well as actually promised 13 years before by the Regent Duke of Orleans, was retarded, through the intrigues of Whig-Hanoverian hostility to the Irish in France.* His son, however, availed himself so well of his alliance, by his mother, with many French families of consideration, and of his connexion with others by education and society, to impress upon the government the great injustice done to his father, that such a "filial remonstrance" was found irresistible, and Sir Gerard was brevetted, February 26th, 1734, a Brigadier, with the promise of being made, on the next promotion, a Maréchal de Camp, taking rank from 1719. In May, 1734, accompanied by his son, Sir Gerard, acting as Brigadier, was engaged in the attack on the lines of Etlingen, and being "grievously wounded, was upon the point of falling into the enemies' hands, when his son threw himself between them and his father,

---

* Mr. O'Conor, in his "History of the Irish Catholics," referring to the Jacobitism of the Tories, and the Hanoverianism of the Whigs, remarks—"Of the 2 parties, the Whigs were the most implacable enemies of the Catholics. The enmity of the Irish Whigs proceeded from a consciousness of injustice, and a dread of retaliation; that of the English was the result of a spirit of freedom, and ill-judged patriotism. They cherished liberty, as the first of blessings, and the exaltation and glory of England, as paramount to the laws of nations, to all moral or religious obligations. They abhorred Popery, as the parent of servile and passive obedience, and viewed Ireland, as the rival and competitor of England. To extirpate the one, and keep down the other, became a principal object of the policy of the Whig administration," &c.

covered him with his own body, and, by prodigies of valour, succeeded in disengaging him; thus preserving at once the life and the liberty of the author of his existence!" In like manner, Alexander of Macedon, subsequently *the Great*, when his father, King Philip, was disabled, and about to be slain, or taken, in a combat amongst the Triballi, personally rescued him from the enemy; Scipio, afterwards the conqueror of Zama, also saved his father, the Consul, when wounded, and in danger of being made prisoner, at the engagement against the Carthaginians on the Ticinus; and the good taste of Virgil has adorned his epic with a similar circumstance, of young Lausus interposing, to defend his wounded father, Mezentius. "The pious youth," to cite Dryden's version,

———————— " springs forth to face the foe;
Protects his parent, and prevents the blow.
Shouts of applause ran ringing through the field,
To see the son the vanquish'd father shield!"
ÆNEIS, x., 1131-1135.

Sir Gerard Lally was next at the siege of Philipsburgh "with his son by his side, whom he styled *his protector*," for having both achieved his promotion, and rescued him in battle. The last affair in this short war, at which the younger Lally fought, was that of Clausen, in 1735. Then, impatient of repose, and an ardent Jacobite like his father, he applied himself closely to the advancement of projects, which he had long since sketched out, for the re-establishment in England of the exiled royal family.

In 1737, the year of his father's decease, he decided on going over himself to England, in order to ascertain personally, what was *still* the strength of the Jacobite party there? Nor did he confine his travels to England. He traversed the 3 kingdoms, making observations on the coasts, the points at which to effect a landing, the various lines of march, and the posts for occupation in the interior of the country; and, after having established connexions and correspondences with the most considerable and most discreet partizans of the son of James II., he returned to France. Following up these projects in favour of the Stuarts, he next aimed to establish a party in their favour in the north of Europe, or Russia, where the veteran Peter Lacy, of the family of Ballingarry-Lacy in the County of Limerick, who had served James II. both in Ireland and France ere he went into Peter the Great's army, and who was a warm Jacobite, then held the highest military rank of any of his countrymen on the Continent, or that of Field-Marshal. Having obtained full powers for this important object from the son of James II., and due recommendations to the Sobieskys and their connexions in Poland, as favourable to the Stuart cause, from the marriage between the 2 families,* Lally gave out, that he was going to Russia, in order to make a campaign, as a volunteer, against the Turks and Tartars of the Crimea, with the Russian force, under the command of his countryman, Lacy. At this time, the Cardinal de Fleury was looking out, among the foreigners in the service of France, for some officer, whose

* The gallant Lord George Murray, so distinguished for the Stuart cause in 1745-6, writing in his exile, or from Cleves, September, 1748, as having been "lately in Poland," to James III. at Rome, alleges—"All the Polish nobility in general are much attached to your Majesty, and your Royal House."

name, intelligence, and courage would at once qualify and embolden him to undertake a secret and hazardous negociation in Russia; with the double aim of detaching that power from its alliance with England, and of causing it to contract one with France. Lally, then, or by creation of February 6th, 1738, Captain of Grenadiers, was recommended for this delicate mission to the Cardinal. At Petersburgh, he fully justified this recommendation, having so insinuated himself into the good graces of the Empress Anne, and her favourite, Biron, Duke of Courland, that the adherence of Russia to France, in opposition to England, required only due definitive measures, on the part of the French government; nor were the interests of the Stuarts less attended to with the Duke of Courland, Field-Marshal Lacy, and the Sobieskys. But the timid indecision or obliquity of the Cardinal's policy, in not following up, or completing, what had been so auspiciously commenced, left his envoy so unsupported, and thus so disagreeably situated, in Russia, that, after having entered that country as a lion, to use his own observation, he considered himself fortunate in leaving it as a fox! The only fruits of this negociation, successful so far as it depended upon Lally, were his despatches, and 2 Mémoires connected with it, which were preserved in the Depôt des Affaires Etrangères, and always referred to, by the best judges of such compositions, as masterpieces. The 1st of those Mémoires was devoted to the internal statistics of Russia. The 2nd Mémoire treated of the foreign relations of Russia; pointing out such arrangements, as, while terminating her war with the Turks, might unite her with France against England, and also transfer to France, instead of England and Holland, the extensive commerce with the great northern empire, which occupied above 630 English and Dutch vessels a year. But this bold policy—like Napoleon's *afterwards*—of aiming to empty the purse, as well as to reduce the power, of England, was too vigorous for the old Cardinal; and Russia, whose friendship might have been secured had the iron been struck while hot, was left to be subsequently gained over to the cause of England and the Allies, and to consequently furnish them with 35,000 men against France! Nominated Major of the Regiment of Dillon, November 15th, 1741, Lally served, as such, with the force for the defence of Flanders, in 1742; and the capacity he displayed there caused the Marshal de Noailles to demand him as his Aid-Major, for the campaign of 1743. In that grade, Lally was present at the unfortunate business of Dettingen; and, writes the Marshal de Noailles, "he there rallied the army several times in its disorder, and saved it in its retreat, through the advice which he laid before the Council of War after the action." Empowered, February 19th, 1744, to hold rank as Colonel of Infantry, he was again employed by the Marshal de Noailles as Aid-Major in Flanders, where he was engaged in the reduction of Menin, Ypres, and Furnes. Then, proceeding to Alsace, he was at the affair of Haguenau, against the Germans. October 1st, he was commissioned as Colonel of the new Irish Regiment of Infantry which was to bear his name; and, indeed, says an English notice of him, in connexion with this appointment, "he seemed perfectly fitted for military affairs; his courage was unquestioned, his constitution vigorous, and his person very fine; but, to these qualifications, he added a still more useful talent, he was a person of excellent understanding." To the formation and instruction of his new corps, he applied himself with such attention, and corresponding success, during the autumn, winter, and spring of 1744-5, that it was in perfect order for the next campaign, or that of the memorable battle of Fontenoy.

The Allied force, assembled about Bruxelles, or Brussels, in April, for the campaign of 1745 in Flanders, under the Duke of Cumberland, son of George II., consisted, at the Duke's arrival, according to the English contemporary historian Rolt, of 21,000 British, and 32,000 troops of other nations; of whom 22,000 were Dutch, 8000 Hanoverians, and 2000 Austrians; making a general total of 53,000 men. But, after being reviewed, and reinforced for action, early in May, at Soignies, the Confederates were estimated, on their own side, or in Holland, as perhaps 55,000, if not 56,000, "of the finest troops in Europe, and all their corps complete."* The French army, accompanied by Louis XV., and the Dauphin, and commanded by the Marshal de Saxe, according to the contemporary French writers, Voltaire, and Dumortous, and the other French authorities consulted by Sismondi, was thus divided—about 18,000 invested the very strongly-fortified and numerously-garrisoned Dutch barrier-town of Tournay—6000 were employed to guard the bridges over the Scheld, and the other communications—and 40,000 remained, to protect the siege, and give the Allies battle.† With these 40,000 men, including the best corps in the service, were the whole of the Irish, or the infantry Regiments of Clare, Dillon, Bulkeley, Roth, Berwick and Lally, and the cavalry Regiment of Fitz-James; for "the Irish," observed an able French Minister, alluding to their national and dynastic feelings, "are excellent troops, especially when they march against the English, and the Hanoverians." The Regiment of Fitz-James, as horse, being necessarily detached from the others, to act along with the cavalry of the army, the Irish Brigade, properly speaking, was composed of the 6 Regiments of Infantry, appointed to act under Charles O'Brien, 6th Viscount Clare and 9th Earl of Thomond, then Lieutenant-General, and subsequently Marshal of France, under the designation of the "Maréchal de *Thomond*," from that Earldom which was his by lineal right, though he had neither the title nor the possessions annexed to it in Ireland and England, on account of his adherence to the Stuart dynasty, and the Catholic religion. And, could there have been a more appropriate leader of those gallant exiles, in the cause of their disinherited princes, oppressed country, and proscribed faith, than *such* a descendant of the royal conqueror of the Danish invaders of old at Clontarf?

"Remember the glories of Brien the brave,
Tho' the days of the hero are o'er;
Tho' lost to Mononia, and cold in the grave,
He returns to Kinkora no more!
The star of the field, which so often has pour'd
Its beam on the battle, is set;

---

* On this last enumeration, see a "Journal of the Proceedings of the Army of the Allies, in the Low Countries, to the 8th of May, 1745," in "The Dublin Courant, No. 110," compared with the paragraph, headed "Hague, May 8."

† Dumortous, in his "Histoire des Conquêtes de Louis XV.," expensively published with plates and plans, and dedicated to Louis *himself*, calculates the French army at Fontenoy as not above 40,000 men, owing to the considerable number about Tournay, and otherwise detached. Sismondi also refers to the French main army as only 40,000, from the deductions in question. These deductions, Voltaire, who had official information, specifies as about 18,000 for Tournay, and 6000 for maintaining the Scheld-bridges, &c., or as 24,000 men in all.

From Dumortous' Histoire des Conquêtes de Louis XV.

PLAN
De la Bataille de **FONTENOY**,
Gagnée par les François,
sur les Alliés le 11. Mai 1745.

But enough of its glory remains on each sword,
To light us to victory yet! "*—MOORE.

The position selected by the Marshal de Saxe, to fight the Allies who approached to raise the siege of Tournay, was on the north side of the Scheld, along an advantageous slope. That portion of his troops, who were to oppose the British and Germans, extended behind the wood of Barry or Vezon to the village of Ramecroix on the left, and as far as the village of Fontenoy on the right; the space from the termination of the wood to the latter village being the most assailable. The other portion of his troops, who were to oppose the Dutch, extended from Fontenoy on the north to Antoin on the south. The entire position was protected in front by redoubts supplied with artillery, so as to form numerous crossing lines of fire, especially in the direction of the Dutch; the number of cannon employed being officially stated as 110 pieces. In the space between the wood of Barry, or Vezon, and the village of Fontenoy, previously referred to as most assailable, this position was alone found penetrable; owing, as confessed by the Marshal de Saxe, after the action, to his having omitted to place 1 redoubt more between the wood and the village, from his not having believed there were commanders daring enough to risk a passage even in that quarter, such was the raking fire through which it was to be approached, independent of any *extra* redoubt! And if, when the English and Hanoverians *did* pass so bravely and so successfully there, the Dutch had been able to pass elsewhere, it is allowed, that the Allies would unquestionably have been victorious. That the Dutch were not able to effect their object was attributed to the indefatigable Lally. "The evening before the day of the battle of Fontenoi," relates his French biographer, "having been desirous of inspecting, with his own eyes, the field of battle, which was about to be the theatre of such a great action, he discovered a way from Antoin to Fontenoi, which had been falsely considered impracticable, and *by which the French army would be infallibly turned.*" Accordingly, "this way was completely secured by 3 redoubts and 16 cannon, *to which, beyond dispute, the success of the battle was due*, says a narrative printed in the Correspondence of the Maréchal de Saxe."

May 11th, after a severe fire of artillery, on both sides, from about 5 to 9 o'clock in the morning, the Allies prepared to bring the contest to a decision. Brigadier-General Richard Ingoldsby, on their right, was to assault the redoubt, on the edge of the wood of Barry, or Vezon. The Dutch General, Prince de Waldeck, with their left, was to break in from Fontenoy to Antoin. The Duke of Cumberland, with the Anglo-German troops, was to attack in the centre. On their right, Ingoldsby could not be gotten to obey his orders; having, in the words of a contemporary, "smelt too long at the physic, to have any inclination to swallow it"—for which he was subsequently tried by Court-martial, and expelled the service. On their left, Waldeck, though aided with 2 English battalions, found such a line of volcanoes opened by the French batteries from Fontenoy to Antoin and the southern bank of the Scheld, that his

* In M. de la Ponce's valuable papers on Irish families, there is signed London, September 16th, 1731, by the British Heraldic Officials, and further signed at Paris, August 18th, 1732, by James, Earl of Waldegrave, Ambassador from George II. to Louis XV., "Genealogia antiquissimæ et olim regiæ O'Brienorum familiæ et domus," setting forth, in detail, the descent of Charles O'Brien, Lord Clare, from the renowned victor of Clontarf.

Dutch, after some efforts to advance, showed no greater taste for this "hot work," than Ingoldsby did for the "physic" of the redoubt. But, in the centre, matters proceeded very differently. The Duke of Cumberland, whose bravery that day merited the highest eulogium, at the head of a great column of 14,000 or 15,000 British and Hanoverian infantry, accompanied by 20 pieces of cannon, notwithstanding the difficulties of the ground, and the destructive cross-fire from the guns of the village of Fontenoy, and of the redoubt unassaulted by Ingoldsby, forced his way, beyond *both*, into the French centre. "There was 1 dreadful hour," alleges the Marquis d'Argenson, a looker-on with Louis XV., "in which we expected nothing less than a renewal of the affair at Dettingen; our Frenchmen being awed by the steadiness of the English, and by their rolling fire, which is really infernal, and, I confess to you, is enough to stupify the most unconcerned spectators. Then it was, that we began to *despair of our cause.*" * And no wonder they "began to despair!" Of their infantry, battalion after battalion of the Régiments des Gardes Françaises, Gardes Suisses, d'Aubeterre, du Roi, de Hainault, des Vaisseaux, de Normandie, &c., of their cavalry, squadron after squadron, including those of the Gardes du Corps, Gensdarmerie, Carabiniers, Régiment de Fitz-James, &c., gave way, shattered by the musketry, or smashed by the cannon, of that moving citadel of gallant men; from whose ranks, as having penetrated above 300 paces beyond the redoubt and village in spite of all that had *yet* crossed their path, the shouts of anticipated victory resounded over the plain! But, by this time, though its depth seemed undiminished, the column had suffered much; it looked as if astonished, at finding itself in the middle of the French, and without cavalry; it appeared motionless, as if without further orders; yet maintaining a fierce countenance, as so far master of the field of battle. Like a noble bull, faced by none with impunity, and wounded only at a distance by those still venturing to wound, *there* it stood, in the midst of a hostile amphitheatre, triumphant, and bellowing defiance, though weakened by past exertions, and loss of blood. Had the Dutch now burst through the redoubts from Fontenoy to Antoin in support of the Anglo-German column, the French would have been not only beaten, but ruined; since there would certainly have been no escape for the mass of their army, and, perhaps, no retreat even for the King, and the Dauphin. An attempt, indeed, to penetrate that part of the French line, in spite of the murderous artillery-fire from its redoubts, and from a flanking battery of 6 guns, or upwards, on the other side of the Scheld,† was made, at this alarming juncture, with much firmness by the Dutch infantry in column, similarly aided by their cavalry; while, from Tournay, a sally was also directed by its still numerous Dutch garrison (originally 9000 strong) against the French investing force of 27 battalions, and 17 squadrons, or about 18,000 men, under Lieutenant-General, the Marquis de Brezé. "When we picture to ourselves," ex-

---

* The letter of the Marquis d'Argenson, Minister for Foreign Affairs, from Fontenoy, is given as No. 1 in the Appendix to the 2nd volume of "The Private Life of Louis XV.," in 4 volumes, "translated from the French by J. O. Justamond, F.R.S.," 1781. This curious work has been otherwise useful for the description of the battle.

† The guns of this flanking battery are stated as 6 by Voltaire, who specifies them as 16-pounders. According to Dumortous' "plan" of the action, the guns there were *more* than 6.

claims my French authority, "the animosity, the blows, the cries, the reciprocal menaces of above 100,000 combatants armed for mutual destruction between Tournai and Fontenoy, the flashes and reports of 100,000 muskets, and of 200 pieces of cannon, the terrible thunder of which was 1000 and 1000 times reverberated along the Escaut," or Scheld, "as well as by all the forests about it, we may well conceive, that never has the air, or the sea, been agitated by a more horrible tempest, than that from Tournai to the field of Fontenoy." This attack of the Dutch from Fontenoy to Antoin, and the sally of their garrison from Tournay, were both fortunately repulsed; but the Duke of Cumberland was *still* triumphant.

Meanwhile, the Duke de Richelieu, having proceeded to reconnoitre the formidable column, met with Colonel Lally, "*impatient, that the devotion of the Irish Brigade was not turned to account;*"* and who, with due presence of mind to perceive, *unlike others*, that the unchecked progress of the column, since it had gotten beyond the artillery of the redoubt and village into the midst of the French, was greatly owing to its employment of 20 pieces of cannon, as well as musketry, against musketry *alone*, made such a suggestion on that point to Richelieu, as contributed, a *second* time, to the gaining of the day. This battle, "so celebrated," says the learned historian, Michelet, "*was lost without remedy, if the Irishman, Lally, animated by his hatred against the English, had not proposed, to break their column, with 4 pieces of cannon.*" As "an adroit courtier," continues Michelet, thus honourably exposing his own countryman's dishonesty, "*the Duke appropriated to himself the idea, and the glory of its success.*"† Hurrying away with such a useful hint, he came to where Louis XV. was stationed with the Dauphin, the Marshal de Saxe, &c., and the 4 cannon referred to, that were at hand in reserve for a retreat. "A rather tumultuous council," writes Voltaire, "was going on around the King, who was pressed, on the part of the General, and for the sake of France, not to expose himself further. The Duke de Richelieu, Lieutenant-General, and acting in the rank of Aide-de-Camp to the King, arrived at this moment. He

---

* This extract from the French memoir of Lally is important, as showing, along with the *other* or Irish and English evidence hereafter adduced *in opposition to Voltaire*, that the Irish Brigade were kept altogether in reserve, or unemployed, until the final charge that "carried the day."

† The passage above translated from Michelet is in his "Précis de l'Histoire de France jusqu'à la Révolution Française," 1 volume, 3rd edition, Paris, 1838; where, after noting of the French, "Aux Pays Bas, sous le Maréchal de Saxe, ils gagnent les batailles de Fontenoi (1745) et de Raucoux, (1746)" it is added—"La première, tant célébrée, était perdue sans remède, si l'Irlandais, Lally, inspiré par sa haine contre les Anglais, n'eût proposé de rompre leur colonne avec 4 pièces de canon. Un courtisan adroit, le Duc de Richelieu, s'appropria l'idée, et la gloire du succès." The 110 French guns, except 4 in the rear with the reserve, having been planted in the redoubts and village of Fontenoy, &c., constituting the fortified *outward* line of the French position round from the wood of Barry or Vezon to Antoin—the Anglo-Hanoverian column, with 20 cannon, having gotten *within* or *behind* that outward line, where, as originally placed, the mass of the French guns still remained, in order to prevent any further breach of the line in question—and the circumstance of cannon being so much required, while 4 pieces were *idle* in the rear, being unheeded by the French, in the excitement of the conflict with the formidable column—that column had possessed the great advantage alluded to, of artillery *on* their side, and none *against* them, until Lally, by his remark with respect to the 4 pieces, proved himself *then*, as well as *previously*, to be "the right man, in the right place."

was after reconnoitring the column near Fontenoi. Having thus galloped about in every direction without being wounded, he appears before them, out of breath, sword in hand, and covered with dust. 'What news do you bring?' said the Marshal to him, 'What is your opinion?' 'My news,' replied the Duke de Richelieu, 'is, that the battle is gained, if we will it; and *my* opinion is, *that* 4 *cannon should be immediately advanced against the front of the column;* while *this artillery will stagger it*, the Maison du Roi and the other troops will surround it; we must fall upon it as foragers.'" That is, as elsewhere explained, "like chasseurs, with the hand lowered, and the arm shortened, pell-mell, masters, footmen, officers, cavalry and infantry, all together." Louis at once approved of the counsel of his favourite, Richelieu; and 20 officers of distinction were detached to make the corresponding arrangements. The Duke de Pequigni, to whom the use for the cannon was explained, hastened them forward, crying out—"*No retreat, the King orders that these* 4 *pieces of cannon should gain the victory!*" Richelieu himself set off at full speed to bring up the Maison du Roi, and others advanced with the several corps of Gendarmerie, Chevaux Legers, Grenadiers à Cheval, Mousquetaires. The Marshal de Saxe likewise departed, to take general measures for the final effort to recover the day. Amidst the prevalent hopelessness of success, he had sent 3 several orders for withdrawing the troops at Antoin to Calonne; to secure, at all events, the retreat of the King and the Dauphin there. These repeated orders, only suspended on the personal responsibility of the officers at Antoin, would, if acted on, have rendered Fontenoy another Crécy in the military annals of France, by opening such an inlet for the Dutch to co-operate with the successful British and Hanoverians, as *had* certainly been found elsewhere, *but for the fortunate foresight, and suggestion of additional redoubts and artillery there, by Colonel Lally.* The Marshal first hurried to Antoin on the right, to countermand its evacuation, if possible; and he was, most luckily in time to stop it, when it was about to take place. He then quickly traversed the field in an opposite direction; ordering that the various regiments should not, as hitherto, make "false charges"—or each attacking on its own account, rather than connected with others—but that they should re-arrange themselves for a united assault upon the consolidated discipline, order, and numbers of the enemy's column, so as in front, and on both flanks, to close upon and break that column, by a great simultaneous rush of "each for all, and all for each." In this excursion, the Marshal, ere he rejoined Louis XV., proceeded as far round the hostile column to the left, as towards the position of the Irish Brigade.

The 6 regiments of infantry, of which this corps consisted, were stationed behind the wood of Barry, or Vezon, and a redoubt, with the Gardes Suisses on their right, ranged, in like manner, behind another redoubt, or that which stopped Ingoldsby—neither, however, of these redoubts having been manned by Irish, or Swiss, but French troops. Next in line, beyond the Gardes Suisses, were the Gardes Françaises; so that the Allied column, under the Duke of Cumberland, in penetrating the French centre, by breaking the Gardes Françaises, had the Gardes Suisses on its right flank.* Though the Irish, as still farther away to

* I take the respective positions, &c., of the several corps of the French army at Fontenoy from the large plan of the action in Dumortous.

the French left than the Gardes Suisses, were consequently not so posted as to be at all in contact with the hostile column when it made its was into the centre, they were disordered by the results of the column's success. Of the 4 battalions of which the Régiment des Gardes Françaises was composed, the effects of a continued residence in Paris were so injurious to the soldiery of 3, that these 3 battalions gave way sooner than they ought, in spite of the utmost endeavours of the officers to rally their men; the 4th battalion of the regiment alone behaving well. The Gardes Suisses, which formed the brigade between the Gardes Françaises and the Irish, being likewise repulsed in such a manner that cavalry had to interpose,* so many defeated Guards retired, or were driven back, upon the Irish Regiments of Clare and Roth, that their Brigade was necessarily put into confusion; and required to be proportionably reformed, or restored to order, ere it should be summoned to join in the engagement. The ranks of the Irish Brigade—thanks to the colonial, sectarian, and commercial misrule, which beggared, starved to death, or drove abroad, for bread, so many thousands of *their* race and creed!—then presented a fine military spectacle of young men, in high spirits, and discipline, and "eager for the fray."† Their natural indignation, at what *they* considered the shameless perjury through which their country was reduced to slavery in spite of a solemn Treaty, was attested by the stimulating cry, in their ancient language, of "*Remember Limerick and Saxon perfidy!*"‡ re-echoing from man to man, as "watchword and reply." Their feelings of loyalty—*doubly* hostile to those of their foe, from uniting devotion to the House of Stuart, and to the House of Bourbon, as its ally—were also excited to suitable ardour by the favourite or popular Jacobite air of "*The White Cockade.*" This animating tune, whose allusion to the common colour of the Stuarts and Bourbons was associated with words in favour both of the Stuart dynasty, and of enlisting to recruit the Brigade, was consequently then,

* On the misbehaviour of the Gardes Françaises, and its alleged cause, see Barbier's "Journal Historique et Anecdotique du Règne de Louis XV.," and Voltaire, for the heavy *punishment* of the Gardes Françaises, Suisses, &c., by the Allied column, in its successful advance.

† Mr. O'Conor, in his "History of the Irish Catholics," remarking, with reference to the reigns of George I. and George II. in Ireland, how "the Catholic youth sought shelter, from the miseries of famine, in the armies of the Continent," mentions—"The Irish Brigade recruited for the space of 20 years, from 1725 to 1746, by the wretchedness of the people, by the avarice of the proprietors, and the severities of the Popery Code;" adding—"Thus *the miseries of Ireland became a military resource to the hereditary and implacable enemies of Great Britain.*" And hence the allusion to the Brigade, at Fontenoy, by the Marquis de Tressan—

"Exilés d'une île cherie,
Victimes d'un sort inhumain,
Venez defendre la patrie,
Qui vous a reçu dans son sein!"

‡ Mr. C. H. Teeling, in his "Personal Narrative of the Irish Rebellion of 1798," gives, as from a journal of his maternal granduncle, who was *at* Fontenoy, "the stimulating cry," in *Irish*, to which the Brigade charged the British; the words of which Dr. O'Donovan, (whom I consulted on the matter,) would, more correctly, write thus, "Cuimhnigidh ar Luimnech agus feall na Sassonach!" and translate as above. The late learned James Roche, Esq. of Limerick, who was born in 1770, or but 25 years after the battle of Fontenoy, in his "Critical and Miscellaneous Essays by an Octogenarian," shows, from the testimony of officers of the Brigade, whose services were "contemporaneous with the battles of Dettingen and Fontenoy," and whom he himself *knew*, that "Irish was generally spoken in the regiments."

and long after, interdicted as treason by the Cromwello-Williamite or Whig-Hanoverian representatives of Revolution "ascendancy" in Ireland.* But its treason, or its loyalty, was, at Fontenoy, before a fairer tribunal, or that of *the oppressed, armed as well as, and face to face with, the oppressor!*

The general plan of action against the Anglo-Hanoverian column was, that, after the 4 cannon should breach it in front, the cavalry, headed by the Maison du Roi, Gendarmerie, and Carabiniers, should dash in upon it there. The reformed infantry Brigades du Roi and d'Aubeterre, reinforced and connected for their line of attack with the previously *unengaged* Brigade de la Couronne, were to fall upon the enemy's left, or Hanoverian flank. The other infantry Brigades, de Normandie, and des Vaisseaux, likewise formed anew after what they had suffered, and, drawn up in 1 line with the 6 Irish regiments, were to fall upon the enemy's right, or British flank—the Irish Brigade here the *freshest* troops, and thus, as it would appear, selected to *head* this movement,† having in consequence, (it will be necessary to observe,) the Carabiniers nearest to them of the 3 cavalry corps which were to attack in front. Mere firing was to be limited, as much as possible, to the artillery; the sabres of the horse, and the bayonets of the foot, being ordered to conclude the business. The gallant Lally, now that the Brigade *were* to act, as "an Irishman all in his glory was there;" and, filled, as he was, with every cause for animosity to the English, on national, family, religious, and dynastic grounds, he made a speech of corresponding vigour to the soldiers of his regiment—"*March against the enemies of France and of yourselves, without firing, until you have the points of your bayonets upon their bellies!*" ‡ Words, not less, if not more, worthy of remembrance, for their martial energy, than those, at Bunker's Hill, of the American General Putnam, to his men, against the same foe—"*Reserve your fire, till you see the whites of their eyes!*" §

The Duke of Cumberland's column hitherto presenting the appearance of a great oblong square, keeping up in front, and from both flanks, a terrible fire of musketry, as well as of cannon loaded with cartridge-shot, but, by this time, so unluckily circumstanced, that it could not make use of its cannon without injury to itself, was now within due range of the 4 pieces of French artillery, pointed in the best manner to make an

* The circumstances of "*The White Cockade*" having been played by the Irish Brigade at Fontenoy, and of the tune having been prohibited in Ireland by the dominant oligarchy of the day, are known to us by contemporary tradition from our grandfathers; and the popular or native words to the air, with reference to the Brigade and the Stuarts, speak for themselves.

† The Brigade des Irlandois, with the Brigade de la Couronne immediately to the rear, were *both* originally posted away to the left, behind the wood of Barry, or Vezon; and, as *not* having been brought, like the corps de Normandie, des Vaisseaux, d'Aubeterre, du Roi, &c., into conflict with Cumberland's column in its breach of the French centre, were thus the 2 fittest Brigades to give due vigour, the one on the right, the other on the left, to the respective infantry flank-charges upon that column.

‡ For this speech of Lally, we are indebted to Voltaire, though *not* in his immediate narrative of the battle of Fontenoy. He gives it thus—"Marchez contre les ennemis de la France et les vôtres; ne tirez que quand vous aurez la pointe de vos bayonnettes sur leur ventre."

§ Lord Macaulay alludes to America and Ireland, as the "*two* important dependencies of the Crown," in which *wrong* was followed by "*just retribution*"—and Fontenoy was a portion of the "just retribution" due for the "wrong" to Ireland, as Bunker's Hill was for the "wrong" to America.

opening for cavalry through the van of that as yet impervious and invincible mass, while the infantry should assault it on each side. The well-served discharges of the 4 cannon having raked rapid chasms through the opposing "wall of men," Richelieu, like a Bayard on this occasion, at the head of the Maison du Roi, gave the word to charge—

> "Now shall their serried column
>   Beneath our sabres reel—
> Through their ranks, then, with the war-horse—
>   Through their bosoms with the steel!"

The Maison du Roi, Gendarmerie, and Carabiniers galloped down upon the hostile van, unrecovered from the crushing fire of the artillery. The infantry Brigades du Roi, de la Couronne, d'Aubeterre marched against the enemy's left flank; while the other reformed infantry Brigades, de Normandie and des Vaisseaux, headed by the 6 *fresh* regiments of the Irish Brigade, under the Lord Clare and Earl of Thomond, advanced against the right flank. In the language of the national ballad,—

> "How fierce the look these exiles wear, who're wont to be so gay,
> The treasur'd wrongs of 50 years are in their hearts to-day!
> The treaty broken, ere the ink wherewith 'twas writ could dry,
> Their plunder'd homes, their ruin'd shrines, their women's parting cry,
> Their priesthood hunted down like wolves, their country overthrown,—
> Each looks, as if revenge for ALL were stak'd on *him* alone.
> On Fontenoy, on Fontenoy, nor ever yet elsewhere,
> Rush'd on to fight a nobler band, than *these* proud exiles were!"—DAVIS.

"Soon," adds an English letter from France, "as the English troops beheld the scarlet uniform, and the well-known fair complexions of the Irish; soon as they saw the Brigade advancing against them with fixed bayonets, and crying out to one another, in English, *Steady, boys! forward! charge!* too late they began to curse their cruelty, which forced so brave a people from the bosom of their native country, to seek their fortunes, like the wandering Jews, all over the world, and now brought them forward in the field of battle, to wrest from them both victory and life!" That portion of the British, immediately opposed to the Irish, were, though the worse for their morning's work, a choice body of men, containing, among other corps, the 1st battalion of the 2nd or Coldstream Regiment of Foot Guards, with 2 pieces of cannon in front; and they had the advantage of being upon a rising ground, the ascent to which they were to sweep with their musketry; while the Brigade had to ascend, and charge the occupants of the eminence, without pulling a trigger. As the Irish approached the British, an officer of the Brigade, Anthony Mac Donough, younger brother of Nicholas Mac Donough, Esq. of Birchfield, in the County of Clare, (an offshoot from the old sept of the Mac Donoughs of Sligo,) being in advance of his men, was singled out, and attacked, by a British officer. But the spirit of the gallant Briton was above his strength. Mac Donough, as the fresher man, soon disabled his adversary in the sword-arm, and making him prisoner, sent him to the rear; fortunately for him, as he was so fatigued, that, in all human probability, he must have fallen in the charge or retreat; and, it is pleasing to add, that these gentlemen afterwards became great friends. This rencontre, in the presence of both forces, occasioned a momentary pause, followed by a tremendous shout from the Brigade at the success of their own officer, the effect of which could only be felt by a spectator; and, at such a critical juncture, that startling shout, and the event of ill omen to the British with which it was connected, were remarked to have had a proportionable influence upon them.* The Brigade being now sufficiently near, the British prepared to give them that formidable tempest of bullets, which was reserved for the last moment, in order to be discharged with the more deadly effect. "Whether," observes our illustrious military historian, Napier, "from the peculiar construction of the muskets, the physical strength and coolness of the men, or all combined, the English fire is the most destructive known." And, by that fire, the Irish suffered accordingly. Their brave commander, the Lord Clare and Earl of Thomond, struck by 2 bullets, most probably owed his life only to the cuirass which he wore, according to the royal army-regulation of the previous year; the Colonel and Chevalier de Dillon (3rd son of the late Lieutenant-General Count Arthur Dillon, and brother of the 2 last Lords Viscount Dillon in Ireland,) was slain at the head of the family regiment; and a large number of officers and soldiers were likewise killed or wounded. But this did not arrest the impetuous determination with which their more fortunate comrades pushed forward, to the cry, in the old Celtic or Gaelic tongue, of "*Remember Limerick, and Saxon perfidy!*" and "à l'arme blanche," or "with the cold steel," to do business more effectually, in Vendome's language, as "bouchers de l'armée," or "butchers of the army." Like their stout countryman in the song, represented, in opposition to an English foot-pad with fire-arms, as relying only on coming to close quarters with his honest stick, and as finally exclaiming of the discomfited knight of the trigger,

"His pistol it flash'd,
But his head I smash'd,
Oh! shillelah, *you never miss'd fire!*"

without *any* volley in reply to the blaze of shot from the column, the Brigade ran in upon the British with fixed bayonets, thrusting them into their faces!† And, although the Carabiniers, in the confusion of the

* At the battle of Castalla, in Spain, in April, 1813, between the Allies under Sir John Murray, and the French under Marshal Suchet, a like encounter occurred between an Irish officer of the 27th Enniskillen Foot, and one of the enemy's officers, though with a more fatal result to the officer defeated there, than at Fontenoy. While the French, says Napier, "were unfolding their masses, a grenadier officer, advancing alone, challenged the Captain of the 27th grenadiers to single combat. Waldron, an agile, vigorous Irishman, and of boiling courage, instantly sprung forward, the hostile lines looked on without firing a shot, the swords of the champions glittered in the sun, the Frenchman's head was cleft in twain, and, the next instant, the 27th, jumping up with a deafening shout, fired a deadly volley, at half pistol-shot distance, and then charged, with such a shock, that, maugre their bravery and numbers, the enemy's soldiers were overthrown, and the side of the Sierra was covered with the killed and wounded."

† "The victory of the French at Fontenoy," says an annotator of Forman in 1751, or but 6 years after the battle, "is chiefly attributable to the Irish; for, when the Allies, in all appearance, had the advantage by the bravery of their troops, the French King order'd the Irish to attack the right wing of the Allies; which they did, with so much resolution and bravery, not firing a shot till they *push'd their bayonets into the faces of their enemies*, that, in spight of the intrepid behaviour of the English, they were obliged to retreat." The alleged conduct of the 6 regiments of the Irish Brigade here, with respect to the "faces of their enemies," resembled that of Cæsar's 6 picked cohorts of 3000 men at Pharsalia, by which the victory there is stated to have been decided against Pompey. See Plutarch's lives of Cæsar and Pompey.

mêlée, and from the similarity of uniform between the Brigade and the British, unluckily charged, and even killed, some of the Irish, ere the error could be arrested by the cry of "*Vive la France!*" or "*France for ever!*"* this temporary "mistake among friends" was soon rectified, and avenged, in the proper quarter. While the Carabiniers turned their steeds and sabres with due effect elsewhere, or from their brother Celts and fellow-soldiers against the common Teutonic foe, down went, or away along the far slope of the hill went, the immediate opponents of the Irish, before their crimsoned or flashing bayonets. Of the 20 cannon belonging to the late formidable Allied column, 15 pieces, with 2 colours, were among the recorded trophies of the Brigade; the 1st battalion of the 2nd or Coldstream Regiment of British Foot Guards being specially noticed, as losing a pair of colours and 2 horsed guns to the Irish infantry regiment of the exiled English Jacobite, and brother-in-law of the late Marshal Duke of Berwick, Lieutenant-General Count Francis Bulkeley.†
In a word, the enemy, pressed, on one side, by the irresistible vigour of "la furia Francese," and, on the other, where "the wrath of the Gael in its red vengeance found him," was, with great loss, so rapidly broken, and driven from the field, that his forces disappeared, as it were, by magic!—

"On Fontenoy, on Fontenoy, like eagles in the sun,
With bloody plumes the Irish stand—the field is fought, and won!"—
DAVIS.

"It seemed," to use the words of Louis XV.'s contemporary biographer, "as if we had been fighting against those enchanted legions which were visible and invisible at pleasure; it was," says he, "an affair of 7 or 8 minutes"—or, as the French Minister, who was present, affirms of the time in which victory was achieved by this final attack, "in 10 minutes the battle was won!" Then, we are informed, "the French, astonished to meet with Frenchmen everywhere, at length took breath; they felt the joy of a victory, so long disputed." Of the Irish, 1 of their poets, in a ballad, "The Brigade at Fontenoy, May 11th, 1745," having noted, how

"There were stains to wash away,
There were memories to destroy,
In the best blood of the Briton,
That day at Fontenoy,"

* "The bayonet and the sword now came in use," relates the Private Life of Lewis XV., of the last general charge upon the Allied column; "the fray was dreadful; and the confusion such, that the Carabineers, taking one moment the Irish, who were cloathed nearly the same, for English, obliged them to call out, *France for ever!* but, unfortunately, after some of them had been killed."

† My French War-Office memoir of the Marshal de Saxe makes the number of cannon abandoned upon "le champ de bataille," by the Allies, "20 piéces," as does also Dumortous. My memoir, on similar official authority, of the Lord Clare and Earl of Thomond, as Marshal of France, having premised, how, as Lieutenant-General at Fontenoy, "à la tête des Brigades Irlandoises, il tomba sur le flanc de la colonne d'Anglois et d'Hanovriens, qui s'étoit fait jour au milieu de l'armée Françoise," adds, how "il la culbuta, l'enfonça, la mit en fuite, *prit 2 drapeaux, et 15 piéces de canon*." The 1st battalion of the 2nd or Coldstream Regiment of Foot Guards is marked in the official "List of all the Regiments in the British Service," in March, 1745, as in Flanders; and as consisting, according to its due complement, of 639 privates, and 99 officers, or 738 men in all. The full French relation of the battle of Fontenoy published by authority at Paris, May 24th, 1745, (as translated in Exshaw's Magazine for that year,) says—"The 2nd Regiment of English Foot Guards, who had Bulkeley's Irish Regiment to deal with, must be almost destroyed. The latter took from them a pair of colours, and 2 pieces of cannon, with the horses belonging to them, which were before the battalions."

adds—

"As priz'd as is the blessing
  From an aged father's lip—
As welcome as the haven
  To the tempest-driven ship—
As dear as to the lover
  The smile of gentle maid—
Is this day of long-sought vengeance
  To the swords of the Brigade.

"See their shatter'd forces flying,
  A broken, routed line!—
See, England, what brave laurels,
  For *your* brow, to-day *we* twine!—
Oh! thrice bless'd the hour, that witness'd
  The Briton turn'd to flee,
From the chivalry of Erin
  And France's '*fleur de lis!*'

"As we lay beside our camp-fires,
  When the sun had pass'd away,
And thought upon our brethren,
  That had perish'd in the fray—
We pray'd to God, to grant us,
  And then we'd die with joy,
One day, upon our own dear land,
  Like *this* of Fontenoy!"—DOWLING.

Such was the conduct of the Irish at Fontenoy, where, including, of course, that of the able and gallant Lally, it is evident, as at Cremona 43 years before, what *they* did to gain the day was of such consequence, that, *but for them, it would have been lost.* The learned Dr. Maty, Principal Librarian of the British Museum, and Secretary to the Royal Society, in his contemporary Memoirs of the Life of Lord Chesterfield, referring to the very creditable behaviour of the British at Fontenoy, speaks of them, as owing their defeat there to the Irish Brigade, or as "retiring with this consolation, if it could be one, that they yielded the palm to their own countrymen." To which assertion the Doctor appends this note. "The great share which the Irish Brigade had in the success of the day was fully ascertained by one of their most respectable countrymen, Colonel Dromgold.* He published two letters in French, on purpose to expose the fallacious account, given by Voltaire, in his poem on the battle of Fontenoy; a poem, which Lord Chesterfield, notwithstanding his partiality to the author, very wittily ridiculed, in one of his French letters." And there could not have been a more respectable authority, in opposition to Voltaire, than this Irish officer, named by Dr. Maty. He is thus noticed by Dr. Johnson, when at Paris, about 30 years after the battle, or October 30th, 1775—"I dined with Colonel Dromgold; had a pleasing afternoon"—and was subsequently spoken of, to Mr. Boswell, by the Doctor, as "Colonel Dromgold, a very high man, Sir, head of *L'Ecole Militaire*, a most complete character; for he had first been a Professor of Rhetoric, and then became a soldier." The Colonel was also a friend of the celebrated Edmund Burke, and the virtuous and accom-

* Abbé Mac Geoghegan mentions, "dans le Comté de Louth, une famille des Dromgolds." The name, otherwise written with an u, instead of an o, in the 1st syllable, is now generally printed Dromgoole. Its most remarkable representative, after the Colonel, was the learned Doctor of the Catholic Board, who once made so much noise, in the struggle for Emancipation. The family are said to be "of Danish descent."

plished Lord Lyttelton; who, in some verses addressed to him, and eulogizing his literary abilities, observes—

"Tho' now thy valour, to thy country lost,
Shines in the foremost ranks of Gallia's host."

All Voltaire's niggardly mention of the Irish at Fontenoy, in his poem on that engagement, is as follows:—

"Clare and the Irish learn from us t'avenge
Their king's, their country's, and their church's wrongs."

His description of the battle in his Siècle de Louis XV., though in prose, and though, as such, it should have been more *true* than that in verse, is not better, if it is not worse, as regards the Irish. In opposition to other narratives, Irish, English, and French, which discountenance the notion of *any* attack having been made by the Irish until the last that was attended with decisive success, he says, speaking of the victorious advance of the Anglo-Hanoverian column, in the earlier part of the day—"Some Irish battalions rushed upon the flank of this column; Colonel Dillon falls dead: thus no corps, no attack, had been able to break in upon the column," &c.* Finally, having stated how the Marshal de Saxe proceeded, "from the right to the left, towards the Brigade of the Irish,"

* The following Irish and English authorities sufficiently refute this groundless assertion with respect to the Irish. "At the battle of Fontenoy," according to the County Clare gentleman previously noticed as distinguished there with the Irish Brigade, "*they* were a part of the *reserve* of the French army. The English were engaged all the morning with the French, and had the advantage, owing to their batteries, which were well served; and the English having advanced too far, the Irish Brigade was ordered to advance to sustain the French, and at a moment when the English batteries could not act against them, without endangering the British army. The orders to the Brigade were, to advance, and charge, without firing a shot. A wing of the British army was drawn up, on a rising ground, prepared to receive them; a fine body of men, *but fatigued, after the work of the morning*. The Brigade were very young men, in a high state of discipline, and *fresh*. They charged up the hill, in a quick pace, with fixed bayonets, until they came to close quarters, when the English army gave way, and fell back with great loss, and were driven off the field of battle," &c. The English contemporary writer Rolt, after describing the British soldiery, as so animated by the Duke of Cumberland, and encouraged by the other Generals, that, on the side of the French, "great part of their infantry was broke, several of their squadrons routed, and the French Monarch shuddered for the fate of the day," adds, without mentioning *any* previous encounter between the British and the Brigade—"Such was the furious bravery of the British infantry, that Marshal Saxe was now reduced to his last, sole, and principal effort, to retrieve the honour of the day. This was in bringing up the Irish Brigade; a corps, on whose courage, and behaviour, he entirely depended for a favourable decision of so great, so dubious, so well-contested a battle. The Irish Brigade," proceeds Rolt, after naming the regiments, "being drawn up, were sustained by the Regiments of Normandy and Vaisseaux, and marched up to the British line without firing. The British ranks were now prodigiously thinned, the men wearied, and, wherever they trod, obliged to fight over the mangled carcases of their dying countrymen, while their *new* and bravest opponents were *fresh for engagement*," &c. See, likewise, in further refutation of Voltaire, the statement previously given from the *French* biographical account of Lally, as to *his* impatience, at the Irish Brigade *not* having been called into action *before* the charge which decided the victory. And, in fine, the large French official account of the battle, compared with the engraved plan of the ground and disposition of the troops published by Dumortous, gives *no* sanction to Voltaire's *supposition*, or *invention*, of a repulsed attack of Irish battalions, or of those battalions having been engaged at all, until the encounter which terminated the contest.

he thus entirely disguises, in reference to the Brigade, the actual circumstances of the last charge. "The Régiment de Normandie, the Carabiniers, enter into the first ranks of the column, and avenge their comrades, slain in their former charge. The Irish *second* them." But in the French official account of the engagement, the Irish are thus named 1st, as *heading* the line of attack on their side of the field. "*The 6 Irish regiments*, sustained by those of Normandie and des Vaisseaux, being drawn up in 1 line, marched close up to the enemy without firing, and put them in confusion, by their bayonets fixed at the end of their muskets." And, independent of any further authority that might be adduced on this point, of the Irish having *headed* that attack, the fact of their having done so is placed beyond doubt, by what Louis XV.'s biographer informs us, of the unlucky mistake of the Carabiniers; from which mistake, the Irish could not have suffered at all, except as *heading* the attack on the right flank of the column, and as consequently being the *nearest* infantry to the Carabiniers, who were on the left flank of the 3 horse-corps, that constituted the van of the cavalry, appointed, with the 4 pieces of artillery, to break the column in front.

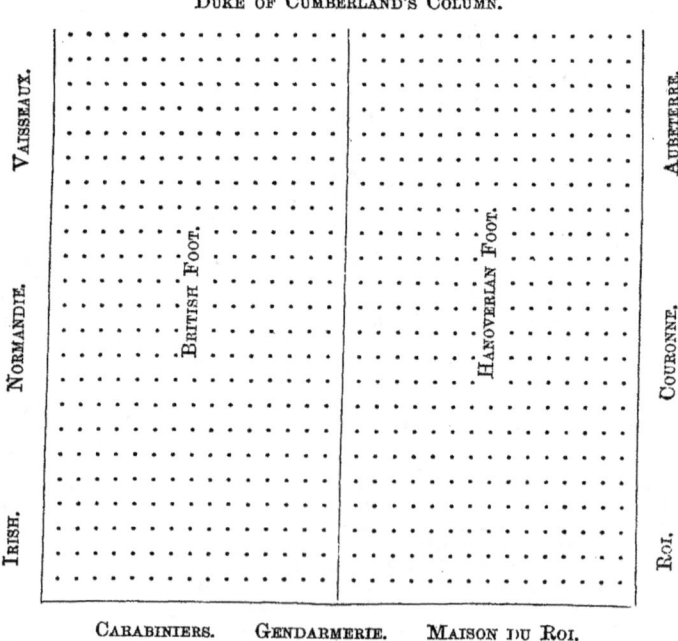

DUKE OF CUMBERLAND'S COLUMN.

CARABINIERS.   GENDARMERIE.   MAISON DU ROI.
DUKE DE RICHELIEU'S CAVALRY.

But, if Voltaire could write so, at first, to the prejudice of the Irish, though, even *then*, having such evidence in their favour, as hardly to admit the supposition of mere *error* on his part, what are we to think of his subsequent conduct, in allowing his original mis-statement of facts to remain unaltered in all the future impressions of his work, notwithstanding the additional and most unimpeachable means for ascertaining and writing the truth, afforded him by the 2 letters of a gentleman, a scholar, and a soldier, like Colonel Dromgold?—to say nothing of the number of *other* officers, Irish and French, whom he could have consulted. Thus, about 9 years after Voltaire's death, and 42 years after the battle, or in August, 1787, Mr. St. John, in his "Letters from France to a Gentleman in the South of Ireland," after referring to his having, at Paris, "frequently seen, particularly in the Luxembourg Gardens, many of the ancient officers of the Irish Brigade," says—"I met a group of these veteran soldiers, the other day, in the Luxembourg Gardens. They talked in raptures of the various battles and sieges they had fought; and, in a manner, having shaken off the burthen of old age, would delineate the plans of their encampments and encounters on the sand, and fight their battles o'er again; imagining themselves in all the vigour of youth, and ready to weep on finding it but a dream. I have often heard them recount the whole affair of Fontenoy, where the English army attacked the French, though posted in the most advantageous situation, with forts to defend them, on every side; and the rashness of the Duke of Cumberland was on the point of gaining, I may say, *already had gained*, the victory, when the Irish Brigades, with the French King's Household Troops, were ordered down to stop the Britons; and they absolutely turned the day in favour of France." And Lieutenant-General Count Arthur Dillon, some years later addressing the National Assembly respecting the Irish in the French service, makes such an observation on the many officers of rank then existing who were at Fontenoy, as would include French, rather than Irish, officers. Having remarked on Fontenoy, how "the Irish covered themselves with glory there," he adds, "a large number of General Officers, who were at this battle, *are still living*, and can *attest* that." Our indignation, therefore, at such unfairness of Voltaire towards the Irish, would be great indeed, if it were not entirely superseded by contempt, at his shabby ingratitude towards the brave men, but for whom, among the battles fought by the French in Flanders, the day of Fontenoy under Louis XV. would have resembled in disaster that of Waterloo * under Napoleon *le Grand*, instead of ranking in success with that of Bouvines under Philippe-*Auguste*.

The British and Hanoverians, after the dispersion of such of their troops as were thus engaged, having, with their reserve, and those who rallied, made an orderly retreat,† Louis caused his army to be re-arrayed after the confusion of the last charge, and leading it about 700 yards beyond the ground occupied by the enemy during the engagement, had it drawn out for review, in honour of the victory. The shouts of *Vive le Roi!* the hats waving in the air at the tops of the bayonets, the standards

---

* "Since St. Louis," remarks Dumortous of Louis XV.'s triumph at Fontenoy, "*no* King of France had beaten the English, in person, in a pitched battle." With which French admission respecting the English in *prose* may be cited the Irish statement respecting the Brigade in *verse*—

"And Fontenoy, fam'd Fontenoy, had been a Waterloo,
Were not these exiles ready *then*, fresh, vehement, and true!"—DAVIS.

† "That they did not push their success," alleges an English contemporary respecting the French, "and endeavour to destroy us in our retreat, may seem an oversight in them; but it was *not* their business to gain a complete victory over us; the taking of Tournay was *their* point; and they wanted no more, than *to prevent our molesting them.*"

riddled with shot, the felicitations of the officers embracing one another for joy, &c., formed a most exciting scene. The King rode, with the Dauphin, through the ranks, bestowing on the several corps the praises which they merited. As the royal *cortège* approached the Irish Brigade, the Dauphin ran forward to the brave Lally, who, having been the 1st to enter, sword in hand, the enemy's column* on its right, was wounded, though slightly, and was sitting on a drum in front of the shattered remains of his regiment; having, on each side of him, several English officers, whom he had himself disabled and made prisoners, but afterwards had taken due care of, since his animosity to England, for her villainy to Ireland, did not extend to individual Englishmen. The Dauphin, announcing to Lally the favours intended for his regiment by the King, Lally observed—" Monseigneur, they are like those of the Gospel, they descend upon the blind and the lame!"—at the same time pointing to his Lieutenant-Colonel, O'Hegarty, wounded by a bayonet in the eye, and his Major, Glascock,† whose knee was pierced by bullets. The King then, ordering Lally to advance in front of the army, nominated him Brigadier on the field. In addition to these particulars derived from Lally's biographer, Lieutenant-General Count Arthur Dillon relates, that "*Louis XV. came, the day after the battle, to the camp of the Irish, and thanked each corps, one after the other, for the service they had rendered him.*" As to their loss in the action—some of which, it will be recollected, was unfortunately owing to *friends*, as well as to *foes*—they, we are told, "left 98 officers and 400 men bleeding on the battle field." My French War-Office document, having noted how, "*at the battle of Fontenoy, fought May 11th, 1745, the Irish Brigade distinguished itself, in the most remarkable manner, in the presence of the King and of the Dauphin,*" and having also observed, "*it* WAS THIS BRIGADE THAT PRINCIPALLY CONTRIBUTED TO RESTORE THE BATTLE, *which had commenced in a most unfavourable manner, and* TO ACHIEVE THE COMPLETE VICTORY, THAT WAS ULTIMATELY GAINED," adds—" The King conferred numerous marks of favour on the Brigade. M. Stapleton, Lieutenant-Colonel in Berwick's Regiment, was made Brigadier. MM. de Lee and Cusack, Lieutenant-Colonels of Bulkeley's and Rothe's, got pensions of 1000 and 600 francs. . . . . . Commissions of Colonel and Lieutenant-Colonel were given to some of the officers of the different Regiments of the Brigade; gratuities to the Majors and Aides-Majors; the Cross of St. Louis to those at the heads of the several corps; gratuities of 600 and 400 francs to the wounded Captains, and of 300 and 200 to the Lieutenants."

According to 2 lists, published at the time, one in London, and the other in Dublin—the former premising, how " letters from Flanders say, that *the Irish troops in the French service, who signalized themselves, recovered the day in the late battle, when the French Guards ran,*" &c.—the

* After the passage, already quoted, on Richelieu's unfair *appropriation* of Lally's suggestion, Michelet says of the latter—" L'Irlandais entra le premier dans la colonne Anglaise, l'épée à la main."

† The respectable family name of the Major of Lally's regiment has been subjected to various British and French misspellings, or corruptions from its *correct* form of GLASCOCK. Thus the learned Walter Harris mentions, in 1746, as 1 of his literary correspondents in France, " Sir Christopher *Glascock*, Knight of the Order of St. Louis," as "compiling a history of Ireland in the French language." Other alterations or disfigurings of the Irish officers' names, as presented to the public in the contemporary printed lists, I correct from my own knowledge, without further remarks, which would only give rise to several tiresome notes.

following were the family names of the officers killed and wounded at Fontenoy in the Brigade—*all* Christian names, as only *sometimes* given in those documents, being *here* omitted, for uniformity's sake—and the errors, or obvious misprints, of each list being amended from the other, and personal information.—CLARE'S REGIMENT. Lieutenant-Colonel O'Neill, Captains Shortall, Mac Elligot, Kennedy, Fitz-Gerald, and Macnamara, *killed;* Major Shortall, Captains Creagh,* Grant, Macguire, Plunkett, Preston, O'Brien, Daniel, Mac Carthy, and Lieutenants O'Neill, Davoren, and 2 O'Briens, *wounded.*—BULKELEY'S REGIMENT. None *killed;* Major Mac Sweeny, Captain Morgan, and Lieutenant Burke, *wounded.* —DILLON'S REGIMENT. Colonel Dillon, Lieutenant-Colonel Mannery, Captains Kearney, Manning, Nihill, *killed;* Captains Wogan, Hagarty, Cusack, and Lieutenants Glascock, Barry, Moriarty, Flanagan, and 2 Burkes, *wounded.*—ROTH'S REGIMENT. Captains Windham, St. Leger, Grace, and Christian, *killed;* Colonel Roth, and Captains Healy, Delany, O'Hanlon, Osborne, Byrne, 2 O'Briens, and 2 O'Sullivans, *wounded.*—BERWICK'S REGIMENT. Captains Bourke, Anthony, and Cooke, *killed;* Captains Hickey, Colclough, and Lieutenants Plunkett, Carroll, Mac Carthy, Dease, and Nangle, *wounded.*—LALLY'S REGIMENT. Lieutenants Byrne, Kelly, and Fitz-Gerald, *killed;* Colonel Lally, Lieutenant-Colonel O'Hegarty, Major Glascock, Captains Butler, Warren, Wogan, and Lieutenants Creagh, Hennessy, Stack, and Mackey, *wounded.* —Of FITZ-JAMES'S REGIMENT OF HORSE, as acting in the centre with the cavalry opposed to and repulsed by the Allied column, in its successful advance, and, as thus suffering severely, especially by the hostile cannon, I merely find, that the Irish officers, killed and wounded, were 25, without any specification of names. And, consequently, those gentlemen in Clare's having been 19, in Bulkeley's 3, in Dillon's 14, in Roth's 14, in Berwick's 10, in Lally's 13, and in Fitz-James's 25, the whole, (as already stated without these details,) would amount to 98.

In this battle, which, from the commencement of the artillery-firing to that of the retreat, lasted about 8 hours, or from about 5 o'clock in the morning to about 1 in the afternoon, the French acknowledged a loss of 5339 infantry, and, in round numbers, 1800 cavalry, killed or wounded; forming a consequent total of about 7139 men. The Allies published their slain, hurt, or missing, as 4041 British, and 3726 men of other nations; or 1762 Hanoverians, 1544 Dutch, and 420 Austrians, being altogether 7767 men; but considerably *more*, it would seem, by contemporary English complaint, in the press, of the "printed accounts" of British casualties that day having, according to "private accounts," from "officers on the spot," been "too alleviating." † Of prisoners, the French claimed to have made about 2500, while they alleged, that scarcely any

---

* This Captain James Creagh was so severely "wounded," as to be published amongst the "killed;" which error I accordingly correct. The Captain, we are elsewhere informed, "received a ball in the breast, which shattered his Cross of St. Louis, and passed completely through his body." He was a native of the County of Cork, born in 1701. Having finally, or in 1771, become a Maréchal de Camp, he retired from the service on a pension, which he still enjoyed in 1789.

† See a letter in the Westminster Journal of "June 22nd, 1745." A like disagreement, between the accounts published as official in the London Gazette of July 18th, 1815, and those of the regimental records, with respect to the amount of the British loss at Waterloo, is *detected* by Captain Siborne, in his "History of the War in France and Belgium in 1815."

were taken from them; and 182 of the Allied munition and provision waggons are also claimed to have been intercepted, the night after the action, by a corps of 4000 men, sent, under the Lieutenant-General Comte d'Estrees, to follow the retiring army. The artillery lost by the Allies—either with the Duke of Cumberland's column, or unhorsed and abandoned on the subsequent line of retreat—is stated, on their side, as about 40 cannon, and is represented as almost all they had by the French, who refer to the captured pieces as between 40 and 50, or near 50, admitting their own cannon, in the engagement, to have been 110; so that, in guns, the French were much superior, although, in number of men, considerably inferior, or only 40,000 against 55,000. The Allies affirmed, that they took 1 standard from the French; yet, says an English historian, "it is extremely remarkable, the French did not take a single pair of colours, to wave, as a trophy, through the gates of Paris." But this, as has been shown from the French official accounts, was incorrect; "a pair of colours," as well as 2 cannon, of those 15 pieces won by the Brigade from the Allied column, being particularly mentioned as wrested from the Coldstream Guards by the Irish regiment, originally Mountcashel's, and, since 1733, that of Bulkeley. Thus, in the day of success at Fontenoy, as in that of defeat, about 39 years before, at Ramillies, the only hostile colours to show in the French army were gained by Irish valour—at Ramillies by the Regiment of Clare, as at Fontenoy by the Regiment of Bulkeley—and, on *both* these occasions, the colours captured were *British* colours. Yet if each of those memorable days was a day of glory, it was likewise one of sorrow, to those gallant exiles—apart from the grief naturally felt for such as fell among their own immediate "brothers in arms, and partners of the war." In the account given of the battle of Ramillies under the year 1706, an instance has been related, of the painful situation in which the Irish Brigade were placed when fighting against the British, from the number of Irish in the British army—a circumstance imparting to such a contest the lamentable features of a civil war. And of such a situation, and the feelings it excited at Fontenoy, the following description has been derived from the brave Mac Donough, previously mentioned as distinguished there. "When the British had retired," he said, "the Brigade was ordered to rest; and, when the officers came to mix with the men, they found several of them in tears. Being asked, 'What was the reason of this, when they so nobly did their duty?' they replied that, 'They did, and would do so again, when necessary; but it was hard they should have to fight against their own countrymen, and, perhaps, some of them even relatives!'" To divert attention, therefore, from this sad topic of consideration, the band," he added, "were ordered to play up '*Patrick's Day*,' when the men instantly started up, shouted an '*Hurrah for old Ireland!*' and were as alert, and ready for a row, as ever!"* This meeting between the Irish Brigade and the British troops at Fontenoy is referred to in the

---

* The gallant Anthony Mac Donough was sent over, after the affair of Fontenoy, to recruit, with an assistant, in Clare, for the Irish Brigade. This, according to a letter of the Lord Clare and Earl of Thomond, was done successfully; and his Lordship pressed Mac Donough to rejoin the Brigade, as in very fine condition. But Mac Donough, having meantime married in Clare, naturally declined going back to France. He lived to be some years above 80, and was the maternal grandfather of the late Anthony Hogan, Esq., Solicitor, of No. 18, Kildare Street, Dublin. This gentleman fortunately committed to writing the substance of what, as a boy, he had

same melancholy light by English writers. One of them designates suc a contest "an encounter like that on the plains of Pharsalia, where brothers might embrue their lands in fraternal blood, relations sluice out the tide of consanguinity, friends murder friends, countrymen countrymen; and where every dreadful act of war was dressed in more formidable, more awful horrors!" Another remarks—"It was horrible to see Irish fighting against English and Irish: I may say, countrymen and relations, in a foreign country, slaughtering one another!" When Cæsar beheld the plains of Pharsalia (above alluded to) heaped with so many Romans slain by each other, he laid the blame of that scene upon his enemies, as political persecutors, who forced him, for self-preservation, into the position, which occasioned such a deplorable spectacle of civic slaughter; and he is recorded to have said—"This they would have; to this cruel necessity they reduced me." But, whatever may have been the justice or injustice of that assertion on Cæsar's part at Pharsalia, the Irish Brigade at Fontenoy might, with perfect truth, allege, of the authors of the legislation which drove them to arms there—"This they would have; to this cruel necessity they reduced us." Hence, in arguing for the Emancipation of his Catholic countrymen, the illustrious Irish Protestant, Henry Grattan—

"With all which Demosthenes wanted endued,
And his rival, or victor, in all he possess'd"—BYRON.

so justly observed—"We met our own laws at Fontenoy. The victorious troops of England were stopped, in their career of triumph, by the Irish Brigade, which the folly of the Penal Laws had shut out from the ranks of the British army." Hence, too, George II., when informed of the details of that battle, and of the troops to whose gallantry his son's defeat there, when almost victorious, was chiefly attributed, is reported, on English authority, to have exclaimed, with unusual emotion,—"*Cursed be the laws, which deprive me of such subjects!*" * So much for the famous day of Fontenoy, and the various recollections of vengeance, of glory, of triumph, and of sorrow, with which it was connected.

The result, to the French, of this important victory, was an unvarying course of success in Flanders, during the rest of the campaign. That success comprised the reduction of the city and citadel of Tournay, the

been often told by his grandfather about the battle of Fontenoy; and, like his grandfather, he attained a fine old age; being, at his death, in 1845, (100 years after the battle of Fontenoy) about 85. For a copy of the narrative resting on such good authority, I am indebted to Mr. Hogan's nephew, Michael Richard O'Farrell, Esq., Barrister, 28, Upper Pembroke Street, Dublin.

* Plowden. George II., as a brave man himself, could proportionably value bravery in others; and seems to have had a *double* reason to wish, that he might have the Irish of *both* religions in *his* service. For while, on one hand, he had to lament, that victory was turned against his son, the Duke of Cumberland, at Fontenoy, by Irish *Catholics*; on the other hand, he is related to have been indebted for his own immediate preservation at Dettingen, from the French cavalry, to the gallantry of an Irish *Protestant* regiment, Ligonier's 4th, or old Black Horse, the predecessors of the present 7th Dragoon Guards. "This service," writes a gentleman, who belonged to the regiment at a later period, "was ever remembered by the Princes of the House of Brunswick; and, when a proposition was once made to good old George III., to reduce the 7th, he replied with energy, in his usual abrupt style, —'No! no! never, never; *saved my grandfather at Dettingen.* No! no! never hear of it—never!'" A regimental trophy, alleged to have been captured from their French opponents on this memorable occasion, has been preserved, to our times, by the victorious corps.

overthrow of an Allied or British detached corps of several thousand men at Melle, the surprise of Gand, or Ghent, the occupation of Bruges, and the captures of Oudenarde, Dendermonde, Ostend, Nieuport, and Ath. Louis returned to France in September, and, on the 7th, "made his triumphant entry into Paris, with the utmost magnificence. All the streets through which he passed were spread with tapestry; the shops were kept shut, by an edict of Parliament, for 3 days; and the fronts of the houses were illuminated, and fountains ran with wine in the streets." Nor were these public rejoicings disproportioned to the advantages they were designed to celebrate. "If Louis XIV.," writes Frederick the Great of Prussia, "subjugated a greater space of ground in the year 1672, he lost it, as fast as it had been conquered; but Louis XV. secured his possessions, and lost nothing of what he had gained." At the operations against Tournay, the Lord Clare and Earl of Thomond was wounded by a bomb; and the Irish were more or less engaged in the several sieges down to that of Ath. When Ghent was taken, in which an immense Allied magazine had been established, a quantity of new clothing and equipments for the English regiments being found among the spoil, Louis XV., the Comte d'Argenson (Minister of War) and the Marshal de Saxe complimented the Brigade, by deciding, "that these goods should be distributed *gratis* to the 6 Irish regiments." The notice taken of those brave fellows in their own country, by its ruling sectarian oligarchy, was very different.

> "The peasant here grew pale for fear
> He'd suffer for our glory,
> While France sang joy for Fontenoy,
> And Europe hymn'd our story!"—DAVIS.

In Dublin, the anti-national representatives of the Penal-Code *régime*, mistermed an "Irish" Parliament, evinced a suitable spirit of animosity to the Irish Brigade, for its mortifying triumph at Fontenoy. "It was impossible," observes the historian of the Irish Catholics, "to detach these gallant troops from the French armies. By way of retaliation, an Act passed, that all Irish officers and soldiers, that had been in the service of France and Spain since the 8th of October, 1745, should be disabled from holding any real or personal property; and that any real or personal property, in possession, reversion, or expectancy, should belong to the 1st Protestant discoverer." This new enactment, which became "part and parcel of the law of the land" in 1746, was, however, no more heeded, than other hostile edicts of the "ascendancy," by the Irish military abroad; whose services there so contributed to decide the general event of the war, as "left Great Britain no alternative, but ruin, or an inglorious peace."

The year 1745, memorable for the battle of Fontenoy, was also remarkable for the chivalrous attempt of Prince Charles Edward Stuart, to recover, with "native swords and native ranks," the Crowns of his forefathers, from the foreign or German dynasty, whom he, and his adherents, looked upon as *usurping* the government of Great Britain and Ireland. Through various sources, including the Irish influence of the Lieutenant-General Lord Clare and Earl of Thomond, and of Mr. Rutledge, a capitalist in France, the Prince, having realized the means for effecting his passage to Scotland, reached that country at the latter end of July. His principal companions in the enterprise, henceforth famous as "the 7 men of Moidart," were 3 of British, and 4 of Irish, birth or origin. The 3 British companions of Charles, were the illustrious old Marquis of Tullibardine, but for his Hanoverian attainder, as a Stuart loyalist, in 1715-16, lineally, or by right, Duke of Athol—Mr. Æneas Mac Donald, a banker, in Paris, Mac Donald of Kinlochmoidart's younger brother, and an honest man to his Prince and party—Francis Strickland, an *English* gentleman, but of such a character, that it was found, his absence would be more desirable than his company.* The 4 Irish companions of Charles were, Sir Thomas Sheridan—Colonel John O'Sullivan—Sir John Mac Donnell, or Mac Donald—Mr. George Kelly. Previous to the fuller details connected with the history of the 2 former, I subjoin the shorter particulars known of the 2 latter.

George Kelly was a Protestant clergyman of the Nonjuring branch of the Church of England; which, as believing in an indefeasible hereditary right of the House of Stuart to the royalty of Great Britain and Ireland, rejected, as no better than *usurpers*, the Sovereigns, who, in consequence of the Revolution of 1688, reigned in these islands, to the exclusion of the eldest representatives, or heads, of that exiled House. Preferring, however, the exciting path of politics to the comparatively monotonous course of the clerical profession, Mr. Kelly became 1 of the most active agents of his party, for the purpose of bringing about a "restoration" in the person of "James III.;" on which point, he kept up, from England, with the Continent, a regular correspondence, disguised in one form or another, to evade the penalty attached by the Whig-Hanoverian government to such intercourse, as "high treason." Mr. Kelly was most distinguished in 1722-3, when, for the detected "restoration" plot that brought him within the grasp of the ruling powers, he, with the famous Dr. Francis Atterbury, Lord Bishop of Rochester, the Earl of Orrery,† Lord North and Grey, the Duke of Norfolk, Captain Denis O'Kelly, (son of the author of *Macariæ Excidium*) &c., was committed to the Tower of London. It was Mr. Kelly whom the Bishop of Rochester was asserted to have employed as his most confidential Secretary for the correspondence with the Continent, that caused the proceedings to be taken against his Lordship, which terminated in deposition from his See, and banishment from England. In the spring of 1722, Mr. Kelly "was apprehended," says my contemporary Whig account, "at his lodgings in Bury-street, by 3 Messengers, for treasonable correspondences; and having delivered his sword and papers to the Messengers, they plac'd them in a window, and went in search of other things. Their negligence gave Kelly an opportunity of recovering his sword, which he drew, and swore he would run the first man through that disturb'd him in what he was doing; which was burning his papers in a candle with his left hand, whilst he held the drawn sword in the other. When the papers were burnt, he surrender'd himself!" This destruction of documents contributed much to disappoint the Minister of George, of the knowledge for which he was on the scent, in order to run down his game. "We are in trace of several things very material," he writes to his brother, "but we foxhunters know, that we do not always find every fox that we cross upon!" Mr. Kelly's defence before the House of Lords, in 1723, was "a

* Stuart correspondence, in Lord Mahon's History of England, and Dr. Brown's History of the Highlands.
† Mentioned in Book VI., as the *secretly-pensioned* betrayer of the cause of James to George—or the Leonard Mac Nally of Jacobitism!

very good one," according to a hostile historian, who adds—"After his Council had been heard, he made a very long speech, and a much better one, for style and method, than Bishop Atterbury's, tho' that Bishop spoke and wrote as well, till then, as any one of his contemporaries." Mr. Kelly was sentenced to be imprisoned in Great Britain, at the pleasure of George I. and his successors; and, in case of attempting to escape, was to suffer *death*, with any who might assist him, in such an attempt. His captivity in the Tower lasted till the autumn of 1736, when he, in this manner, regained his liberty. From the injurious effects of the confinement there on his health, he was frequently allowed, for change of air, to drive out in a coach to any place within 10 miles of London, but always in the custody of a government officer, or Warder. On the evening of November 5th, returning from Epsom, thus guarded, he was set down within the Traitor's Gate of the Tower, where, it appearing that he could only proceed, as usual, to his lodgings, and consequently that "all was right," the Warder took leave of him. But, instead of going merely to his lodgings for the night, he, it seems, made for the Sallyport Stairs which led to the Mint, and, meeting the same coach which had set him down at the Traitor's Gate, managed, in some disguise, or change of habit, to pass undetected out of the gates, between 7 and 8 o'clock. In effecting this escape, he was aided by a Catholic Priest, his relative, the Rev. Myles Macdonnell, who, writing from St. Germain, May 4th, 1747, to James III. at Rome, mentions Kelly, as "not only my very near kinsman, but a person for whom I exposed my life, to release him out of the Tower of London, and for whose sake I am actually in exile." A reward of £300—or £200 from Government and £100 from the Earl of Leicester as Constable of the Tower—was offered for a recapture of the Jacobite refugee; accompanied by a description of him, as about 48 years of age, and 5 feet 10 inches high, rather slender for his stature, fair complexion, good teeth, large blue eyes, broad and flat face, rather thin than fat, and his hair, except where he was very bald, rather grayish. Soon after this evasion, he wrote 2 letters; the 1st to the Duke of Newcastle as Secretary of State, duly thanking George II. for his goodness to the writer as a prisoner, yet excusing the endeavour naturally made to escape; the 2nd to a gentleman in the Tower, making him a present of all the books, &c., left there. From London he got to the Isle of Thanet; where, agreeing with 2 fishermen to convey him to France for £5, he sailed from Broadstairs in that island, and was disembarked at Calais. When set ashore, he gave the fishermen 5 *guineas*, observing—"If any one inquires for George Kelly, you may say, he is safe, landed in France!" The fishermen were not aware of the valuable passenger they had on board, till after their return home; when, 1 of them, hearing in an ale-house the advertisement read for the capture of George Kelly, cried out— "Lord, this is the man we landed in France!" Persevering in the same course of Jacobite loyalty, Mr. Kelly subsequently appears, as an Envoy from Prince Charles to Scotland, in the spring preceding the Prince's arrival there; then, as going back to the Continent, and, next, returning with the Prince, as 1 of "the 7 men of Moidart." After the war in Scotland, he became, and was, for some years, Secretary to Charles, who, in a letter from Paris, December 19th, 1746, to his father at Rome, thus expresses himself, in refutation of some aspersions directed against the Secretary's character—"It is my humble opinion, it would be very wrong in me to disgrace G. K.," *i. e.*, George Kelly, "unless your Majesty positively ordered me to do it. I must do him the justice, to assure you, I was surprised to find your Majesty have a bad opinion of him; and hitherto I have had no reason to be dissatisfied with him; for this was the first I heard of his honesty and probity to be in question. I shall take the liberty to represent, that, if what he has been accused of to you be wrote from hence, there is all reason to believe, *id est*, in my weak way of thinking, that such that have writ so to you mistake, because of my never having heard any body accuse him to me here of such things; and my having declared, that my ears were open to every body, so as to be the better able to judge the characters of people." * As Secretary to the Prince, Mr. Kelly was proportionably envied, and was accused of being too partial to his own countrymen; so that he, according to the exiled Scotch nobleman, Lord Strathallan, "never was a friend to any Scotsman." But this complaint must be received with a considerable allowance, as the complaint of a Scotchman—for, how few, if any, natives of any other country than Scotland, would a Scotchman promote? Hence, finally, or in November, 1749, the Irishman had to resign his Secretary-ship, through Scotch influence, represented by the famous Keith, Earl Marischal; although apparently undeserving of blame, in reference to the immediate allegation which led to such retirement from office; that retirement, too, not being attended by any breach between him and the Prince, with whom he still corresponded in 1750. After this, the stout and faithful Parson "fades from my view!" † Sir John Mac Donnell, or Mac Donald, who is alluded to as having belonged to the principal Irish or Antrim branch of the name, was attached, in the French service, with the rank of Colonel, to the Irish Horse Regiment of Fitz-James; acted, as 1 of the Prince's Aide-de-Camps, in Scotland and England; and was included among the Irish officers made prisoners, after the battle of Culloden.

Sir Thomas Sheridan was of old Irish or Milesian origin, the family name being noticed in the national annals as early as 1087, at the battle of Conachail, now Cunghill, in the County of Sligo, between Rory O'Conor, King of Connaught, and Aodh O'Rourke, Prince or Chief of West Brefny, or Leitrim; on which occasion, among the leaders slain with O'Rourke, was "the son of Godfrey O'Sheridan." The O'Sheridans were a sub-sept to the O'Reillys, Princes or Chiefs of East Brefny, or Cavan, down to the commencement of the 17th century. Since that time, several of the Sheridans (a race still numerous, especially in the Barony of Clonmahon, in Cavan) have been connected with high positions in church and state, as well as respectable for the utility, or eminent for the brilliancy, of their contributions to the literature of these islands. The Prince's companion, Sir Thomas, would appear to have been the son of the Honourable Thomas Sheridan, Secretary of State, Privy Counsellor,

* This Rev. George, or *Parson*, Kelly must *not* be (though he *has* been) confounded with another Kelly, a *Monk*, alluded to, in the Stuart papers, as, from his too great addiction to wine, a very bad companion for the Prince. The Parson, and Sir Thomas Sheridan, as Protestants, appear to have been united in opinion, that measures for a "restoration" should be conducted, as far as possible, by Charles, instead of his father,—by the former as the *rising* rather than by the latter as the *setting* sun—and hence would seem the statements made against Kelly to James, referred to in Charles's above-cited reply.

† This account of the adventurous George Kelly is collected from the state-trials, and publications of the day, as well as regular histories of the period, and the Stuart correspondence. He was a credit to his name.

and Commissioner of Customs in Ireland, under King James II., and who, adhering to the King in opposition to the Revolution, followed him to France. Young Sheridan, of whom the King is mentioned to have been "very fond," and not without reason, from the promise given by the boy of future eminence as a man, was at first appointed to be a Page, or to some post of the kind, in the royal household, at St. Germain. Under that Monarch, and his son, as James III., he continued to be attached to the Stuart Court, removing with it to Italy; and, having had much leisure at his disposal, he devoted himself to study, particularly in mathematics and moral philosophy; his general "literary accomplishments, join'd to his great sobriety, good sense, and fine behaviour," raising him so high in James's favour, as to be made by him *Governor* to his eldest son, Prince Charles.* This appointment was judicious, proving not less satisfactory to the father, than agreeable to the son; who had such an esteem for his Governor, that "he chose never to be without him;" and consequently could not be prevailed on to leave him behind, when undertaking the expedition to Scotland; though James, in regard to Sir Thomas's "declining age, and growing infirmities, would have had him remain at Rome. But Charles, who had been used to consult him on all occasions, and could not think of entering upon any action of consequence without his advice, foreseeing the many occasions he should have for him, during the prosecution of his approaching enterprize, resolved to carry him with him; nor was the latter, who tenderly lov'd his pupil, at all adverse to accompany him, and sharing his fate, let it prove never so adverse." During the subsequent contest in Great Britain, Sir Thomas retained his influence as Charles's Governor, in the capacity of his chief Privy Counsellor; and, after the battle of Culloden, he was fortunately able to effect such an early escape to France, as the bad state of his health, aggravated by the hardships of campaigning in Scotland, rendered most necessary. Thence he proceeded to Rome, where he died, November 25th, 1746, "greatly lamented by all his acquaintance."† In religion, Sir Thomas was a Protestant, like so many other adherents to the Stuart

* Lord Elcho, 1 of the Prince's Privy Council in Scotland with Sir Thomas Sheridan, the Chevalier de Johnstone in his Memoirs, Norman Mac Leod corresponding with the Lord President Forbes, and the contemporary London announcement of Sir Thomas's death at Rome, ALL mention Sir Thomas, as having been "Governor" to Charles. This post of "Governor" should *not* be confounded, or identified, as it has been by some, with that of "Preceptor," or "Tutor." So *many* had been intrusted with the education of Charles, that, as Klose notes, "it is impossible to say *what* share *each* had in educating the Prince." Among them, Sir Thomas is named *last*—evidently as *Governor*, rather than *Tutor* or *Preceptor*—yet not, it is possible, without his having also aided to complete the course of instruction, commenced and continued by so *many* predecessors.

† As Sir Thomas Sheridan's death was immediately attributable to the injurious effects, on his constitution, of what he had suffered campaigning in Scotland, it is rather strange that Lord Mahon and Mr. Chambers could give *any* countenance to the untenable assertion, how "Sir Thomas, having waited on Prince Charles's father at Rome, was so sharply reprimanded by the latter, for *persuading* his son to undertake the expedition in Scotland on no better grounds than he did, that the severity of the reproof caused Sir Thomas to fall ill, and die of grief!" But, it was *not* at Rome that Sir Thomas "*fell* ill;" and, if he ever received any such "reproof" as that asserted, it was undeserved. Prince Charles's Secretary in Britain, Murray of Broughton, in his Examination, March, 1746-7, before the British House of Lords, relates how he was told by Charles in Paris in 1744, that, even independent of any expedition from France, "he was determined to come into Scotland"—and, when strongly represented, that, to come thus, would be a desperate undertaking, "notwithstanding which, he insisted upon coming." Then, continues Murray of this

cause, who did not allow their creed to interfere with their loyalty; and he was doubly connected with the exiled royal family, as Charles's Governor, and by his wife having nursed that Prince's younger brother, the Duke, and future Cardinal, of York. The anxiety of Charles, after his return from Scotland to France, to be rejoined by his old "guide, philosopher, and friend," appears in the Stuart correspondence. Writing from Clichy, November 6th, 1746, to his father's Secretary, Mr. Edgar, the Prince observes—"I say nothing to Sir Thomas, because I am in hopes he is already set out, for to join me. My waiting on him gives me a great deal of trouble; for, though I have a very good opinion of Kelly, and must do him the justice to say I am very well pleased with him, yet neither he, or anybody else much less, I would absolutely trust in my secrets, as I would Sir Thomas, which occasions in me a great deal of toil and labour." Sir Thomas, 3 days before, had written from Albano, near Rome, to Charles, congratulating him upon his reaching France, and saying—"I shall not trouble your Royal Highness with representing to you the cruel anxieties under which I have laboured, ever since the unfortunate day that tore me from your presence." Secretary Edgar, in a letter of December 2nd, announced to Charles the death of Sir Thomas; forwarding, at the same time, all the papers found in Sir Thomas's repositories, having relation to the Prince and his affairs; among which was a *sketch of a dying speech, which Sir Thomas had prepared, in case of being taken, and to be executed !* Referring, in fine, to the difficulties occasioned by the demise of his lamented Governor and confidant, Charles thus expressed himself to Mr. Edgar, from Paris, January 16th, 1747— "Now that my old friend, Sir Thomas, is dead, I am at a vast deal of trouble; being obliged to write everything of consequence with my own hand." Sir Thomas left a son, the Chevalier Michel de Sheridan, or Sir Michael Sheridan, who was an officer in the Irish Brigade, and also engaged in this expedition to Scotland. Born in 1715, he entered the Regiment of Dillon in 1742, with which he made the campaign of Germany, or that of the battle of Dettingen in 1743; and the campaign of Flanders in 1744; when he was appointed a Captain. In 1745, he sailed with Prince Charles Edward for Scotland in the larger of the 2 vessels accompanying the Prince, or the *Elizabeth*, of between 60 and 70 guns; but, ere he could reach that country, he had to return to France with several wounds, received in the shattering combat maintained by that vessel for 5 or 6 hours against the English ship, the *Lion*, of 58 guns, which had also to retire shattered to port. As soon as his wounds woul'

obstinate resolution of Charles—"I was so much against it, that I spoke to Sir Thomas Sheridan, a person who lived with him for so many years, and told him of the danger of such an attempt; and that it would be the ruin of many families, and the destruction of the country. Sir Thomas Sheridan said, *he would endeavour to persuade him against it;* and, upon his arrival in Scotland, told me *he had ; but to no purpose.*" We learn, also, from the original testimony in the Jacobite Memoirs, how, on Sir Alexander Mac Donald's and the Laird of Mac Leod's refusals to join Charles after his arrival in Scotland, Charles was generally importuned to sail back to France—"insomuch that the few who had come along with the Prince (*Sir Thomas Sheridan not excepted*) joined in urging him to return. The Prince," it is added, "was *single* in the resolution of landing." How, then, could Sir Thomas Sheridan have merited *any* such "reproof" as that referred to?—and, consequently, has not his death been otherwise more naturally, or rationally, accounted for? Lord Mahon, too, should not have *singled* out Sir Thomas for censure, on account of some deficiencies in the Prince's education, with which, as shown in the preceding note, so *many* persons were connected.

permit, he joined the Prince in Scotland; who, conferring on him a brevet of Lieutenant-Colonel, retained him as his First Equerry, and Aide-de-Camp, during the war there. After the fatal affair of Culloden, he fought against the English, off the Scotch coast, in *La Bellone*, accompanied by *Le Mars*, despatched from Nantes; and he was among the Irish officers, who finally succeeded in bringing away the Prince, with a number of his adherents, from Scotland to France. He obtained, in connexion with this enterprise, a "gratification" of 2000 livres; and was 1 of the household of the Prince to the period of his removal, after the Peace of Aix-la-Chapelle, from the French, into the Papal, territory of Avignon. William Murray, by Stuart creation, "Lord Dunbar," writing from "Avignon, December 31st, 1748," says—" H. R. H. the Prince arrived here, in perfect health, on Friday morning, at 7 o'clock. I never was more surprised than to see him at my bed-side, after they had told me, that an Irish officer wanted to speak to me. He arrived, disguised in ane uniform of Ireland's regiment, accompanyed only by Mr. Sheridan, and 1 officer of the same regiment, of which H. R. H. wore the uniform," &c. The regiment here referred to, belonging to the Irish Brigade in the service of Spain, was the Regiment of Irlandia, then quartered at Chamberry in Savoy, and the "1 officer" was Lieutenant O'Donnell—the Prince, in return for the honourable and loyal reception which he met with, in his adversity, from its officers, as "*the hero who had lately made England tremble, and the son of him, whom they still recognized as their King,*" having, "in compliment to his hosts, assumed the Irish uniform." After Sheridan's return with the Prince from Scotland to France in 1746, he was nominated a Captain of Horse in the Regiment of Fitz-James; and, in 1760, was brevetted as a Maréchal-de-Camp-de-Cavalerie attached to that regiment, with which he served in Germany, to the close of the Seven Years' War. Included in the reform or dissolution of this corps at the ensuing peace, he received the Cross of a Chevalier of St. Louis in 1770, and resided at the Château d'Estiau, near Beaufort, in Anjou.* I do not know when he died.

Colonel John O'Sullivan, the most distinguished of the Irish companions of the Prince in Scotland, was likewise of Milesian origin, and of 1 of the best of the ancient southern septs of Erin. The O'Sullivans, descended from the old royal line of Munster, were seated, until the year 1192, along the river Suir, in the present County of Tipperary, in the fertile territory about Clonmel and Knockgraffon; on which last-mentioned eminence was their principal fort, or rath, particularly celebrated as the residence, in the 3rd century, of their famous progenitor, King Fiacha *of the broad head*, conqueror of the renowned Ard-Righ or Monarch, Cormac, son of the Art, who was consequently obliged to send hostages there from Tara. Compelled by the southward progress of the Anglo-Norman invasion to "forsake the pleasant regions once their own" for the mountainous districts of Desmond, or Cork and Kerry, the O'Sullivans acquired new possessions in the Baronies of Beare and Bantry in the former, and those of Iveragh, Dunkerron, and Glanarough, in the latter County; and became more famous than ever under 2 branches, or those of O'Sullivan More and O'Sullivan Beare, till the general submission of Great Britain and Ireland to the sceptre of the House of Stuart in 1603. Although, by the results of the long preceding

* French military notice of the Chevalier de Sheridan in MSS. on Irish Brigade, given to me by the late John O'Connell, &c.

struggle then terminated in Ireland, and by the subsequent Puritanic and Williamite contests during the same century, those of the name of O'Sullivan were subjected to great territorial losses, that name was still not without various respectable landed representatives at home. It has been honoured abroad, or in Spain, Belgium, and Germany, with the titles of Count and Baron. It contributed its proportion of officers to the national Regiments of Clare, Dillon, Bulkeley, &c., in France. It was one of note in the service of Naples. It has also attained high military, administrative, and diplomatic positions in the services of the United States of America, and the United Kingdoms of Great Britain and Ireland. In the annals of martyred Jacobite loyalty in 1715, after the mention of the arrest, at London, of Colonel Paul of the 1st Regiment of Foot Guards, as "charg'd" in Whig-Hanoverian language, "with listing men for the *Pretender's* service," we find Serjeant Joseph O'Sullivan, a native of Munster, of that Colonel's company, and who had previously served in the Irish Brigade, named, as imprisoned upon the same account; and after a due trial by a hostile London jury, as condemned to be "hang'd, drawn, and quarter'd," and to have his head "fix'd to a pole, on Temple Bar!" The companion of Prince Charles in Scotland was a native of Kerry,* of, it appears, a good, though, in point of fortune, a much reduced, branch of the O'Sullivans. "His parents," says the contemporary account of him printed in London in 1748,† "being very desirous of his making a figure in the world, for which his forward genius soon discover'd that he was naturally well qualified, but yet unable themselves to introduce him upon the great stage, on any other footing than that of an extraordinary education, they spared no expence their small estate would admit of to make him a compleat gentleman, in every respect, but that of a large fortune; which, they thought, it would be his business to acquire, after they had furnished him with such ample means. Accordingly, being Roman Catholicks, they sent this, their only son, at the age of 9 years, to Paris, the best place in the world for the education of youth, not only for the sake of cheapness, and the excellent methods the French have, of teaching children every thing that can be taught, but, on account of the great sobriety of manners, the strictness of morals, and the early notions of religion and piety, which the tutors are remarkably careful to inculcate. At 15 years of age, Mr. Sullivan went to Rome, where his education received a different turn," or towards a preparation for the Priesthood. The death of his father, who had survived his mother, rendering it necessary for him to return to Ireland, he did so; but, having no relations living, or any inducement as a Catholic to settle under the yoke of the Penal Code, he only remained there, until he sold his estate.‡ He then "went again into France, where, soon after his arrival, he had the good fortune to be recommended to Marshal Maille-

* The Colonel, with a brief general glance at his military career in Corsica, on the Rhine, and in Scotland, is mentioned, among the distinguished *Kerry* gentlemen in foreign service, by the contemporary writer of the unpublished History of Kerry, forming a portion of the Chevalier O'Gorman's MSS., in the valuable library of the Royal Irish Academy.
† The memoir alluded to is to be found, with I, likewise, on Sir Thomas Sheridan, in the Supplement to "Young Juba, or the History of the Young Chevalier." I have used *both* memoirs, checking, or correcting them, where able, from *other* information.
‡ In those "dark and evil days" of the Penal Code, Mr. O'Sullivan could only have had this estate, as a Papist, through its having been held for him by some

bois, by whom he was retained as a domestick Tutor to his son. It was not long ere the Marshal, perceiving in him some symptoms of a genius better adapted to the sword than the gown, encouraged him rather to apply himself to the former than the latter profession. This advice was well relished by our young *Reverend;* he followed it, and that with such success, that, attending the Marshal to Corsica, when the French attempted to deprive the poor, but brave, inhabitants of that little island of their liberties,* he acted as Secretary to that General. Maillebois, who was a *bon vivant*, and used constantly to get drunk every day after dinner, was almost incapable of business the greater part of the 24 hours; so that, during the whole time of this General's stay on the isle of Corsica, all the weight of the war, and the whole power, devolv'd on Mr. Sullivan, who executed it in such a manner, as deriv'd great honour both to himself and his patron. In short, here he gain'd a very high reputation for his military accomplishments in general; but, more particularly, for his knowledge in what is called the art of making *irregular* war. After finishing the conquest of Corsica, Marshal Maillebois returning to France, carried Mr. Sullivan with him into that kingdom; in which, however, he did not tarry long, but going into Italy, made 1 campaign there, and, the next year, he served the King of France, in another, upon the Rhine. Here he acquir'd so much fame among his Most Christian Majesty's Generals, that 1 of them, mentioning him in a letter to M. de Argenson, says, 'That he (Mr. Sullivan) understood the IRREGULAR art of war better than any man in Europe; nor was his knowledge in the REGULAR much inferior to that of the best General then living.'" He next entered the Stuart service, and James III. writes thus, respecting him, from "Rome, March 23rd, 1745," to Prince Charles, in France—"I am glad to find O'Sullivan is now with you. When a gentleman is capable of such detail and drudgery as that of family expenses, you will find it both of ease and advantage to you, because you can depend upon him, and he can act either with more *franchezza*, and less *soggezione*, than one of an inferior rank; and, on all accounts, it behoves you much, not to outrun your small income." The London narrative proceeds to inform us of O'Sullivan and the Prince, how "Charles soon contracted such an esteem for him, that he was never easy, but when this agreeable Irishman was with him. Indeed, no one who knows Mr. Sullivan can deny his being one of the best-bred, genteelest, complaisant, engaging officer in all the French troops, which, in these respects, are certainly inferior to none in Europe. To these external accomplishments were added (and Charles soon perceiv'd them in Mr. Sullivan) a sincerity of heart, and an honest freedom of both sentiment and speech, temper'd with so much good nature and politeness, as made his conversation and friendship equally useful and agreeable. But, if Charles was highly pleased with Mr. Sullivan, the latter thought himself no less happy in the regard paid him by the former; to whom,

worthy Protestant friend in his own name, or as apparently owned by a Protestant; otherwise the Popish proprietor would have been divested of his *illegal* possession by the privileged land-robbers of the time, at Papists' expense, known, to the ruin of so many, as "Protestant discoverers!"

* Those shameless republican oppressors of Corsica, the Genoese, unable, by their own strength, to put down the Corsican insurgents, or patriots, had negociated with the French, to restore, by *their* very superior military power, the broken connexion between Genoa and Corsica. As an *island*, Corsica should *belong only to herself*, or be *independent*.

in return, he passionately desir'd to render all the service his abilities, strengthened by the favour of the Grand Monarch, were possibly capable of rendering. Of this Charles was well satisfied; and he, on the other hand, expected no small things from the good sense, the solid judgment, the political knowledge, and the military skill of Mr. Sullivan. Nor was he deceiv'd, either in the prosecution, or the end, of his famous expedition. For, to the abilities of this gentleman we are chiefly to attribute the success with which the unexperienc'd Charles, with a handful of raw Highlanders, so long maintain'd a sharp, and, for some time, doubtful, dispute with the whole force of his Britannick Majesty, in which he so surprizingly over-run, and (as far as he pleased) plunder'd, not only the major part of the Kingdom of Scotland, but also a great part of the rich and powerful nation of England itself. A nation which is, or might be, the terror and arbitress of all Europe! But this *great spring*, and *first* or *chief mover* of all the Stuart army's motions, like that of a clock, or watch, (which animates and moves the whole machine) was unseen, and all its operations unperceiv'd by the gross of Charles's followers. Mr. Sullivan's authority and influence over Charles, as the *automical* spring in its box, was so closely conceal'd from the eye of the world, that none but the most prying, curious, artful of the Highland Chiefs, and those that were the most entrusted, and, as it were, let into the mystery, knew how greatly this gentleman was favoured and confided in both by Charles and the French Government. Though, in fact, he was the * * * * * General,* he never openly acted as such; all his advice was given in secret, and his orders never came directly from himself. While HE did all, CHARLES appeared as the principal, and, in his NAME, was every thing transacted." The *ostensible* posts of Colonel O'Sullivan under the Prince were those of Adjutant-General, and Quarter-Master-General. It was the decision of the battle of Fontenoy in favour of France, so attributable to the valour of the Irish Brigade, that determined the Prince to attempt, at this period, as the best opportunity, the vindication, in Great Britain, of the royal claims of his family. And, in this daring enterprise, to be commenced with disadvantages, under which it would be necessary to "strive with things impossible, nay get the better of them," he not unnaturally looked, from O'Sullivan's character, for such capabilities of service in *him*, as his chivalrous countryman Wogan had formerly displayed, in the apparently hopeless, though finally successful, achievement of Inspruck; but for the accomplishment of which, Maria Clementina Sobieski would never have been the mother of Charles Edward Stuart. The decision of fortune in the 2 undertakings was dissimilar, yet the Kerryman deserved as well of the *younger*, as the Kildareman did of the *elder*, Stuart; and Ireland, which had the honour of producing the hero, who so gallantly freed the *mother* from the Austrian in the Tyrol, was likewise honoured by furnishing the chief military adviser to the *son*, in his brave effort to recover the dominions of his ancestors from the Hanoverian in Britain. As an Irishman, so situated in Scotland, O'Sullivan was necessarily exposed to the narrow criticisms of personal envy, and the peevish reflections of national jealousy. But in what *high* estimation he was, for his conduct, both then and afterwards, with James as well as Charles, is attested by their family papers.

* Evidently *chief*, or *first*, General; the 5 asterisks corresponding in number with the 5 letters of those words.

The Prince, corresponding from Paris, December 19th, 1746, (or when the expedition to Scotland was all over,) with his father at Rome, remarks—"O'Sullivan showed me the letter your Majesty did him the honour to write to him. I cannot let slip this occasion to do him justice, by saying, I really think he deserves your Majesty's favour." Writing to his son in France from Rome, April 17th, 1747, James observing, "I am glad to find O'Sullivan is now with you," adds—"I have made him a Knight, since you desire it, and he *deserves* it, tho' it be against my present rule; but I have desired him not to say when he was knighted, so that that small mark of favour will be of no inconvenience. I must do him the justice to say, that by all I have heard, or marked of him myself, I am glad you have him about you; and I am persuaded he will serve you with diligence and fidelity, and never give you reason to be dissatisfied with him." By an allusion of James at Rome, January 2nd, 1748, to a document to be forwarded in successive portions by his Secretary, Mr. Edgar, to the Prince in France, it would likewise seem, that an outline or abstract of the memorable campaigns of 1745-6 in Great Britain was drawn out by O'Sullivan; who, as having so contributed to conduct them for Charles, was proportionately capable of supplying information to posterity for a regular history of the subject,

"When many a deed *might* wake in praise,
That long had slept in blame."—MOORE.

The King alleges—"Edgar will send you by degrees O'Sullivan's paper. It were a pity that an account of your unfortunate expedition should not be put in writing, and that by a good hand. But such a paper should be composed with nice regard to truth and prudence, so as to give you honour, and, at the same time, not to disgust, much less wrong, particular persons, who appeared for you, on that unhappy occasion." I am not aware, how long Sir John O'Sullivan lived beyond 1748. By his wife, a Miss Fitz-Gerald, daughter of Thomas Fitz-Gerald and Louisa O'Connor (most probably of the line of O'Connor-*Kerry*) he left a son, Thomas Herbert O'Sullivan, an officer in the Irish Brigade at the period of the American War of Independence, who, in consequence of a quarrel with, and a personal assault, against the rules of discipline, upon the famous Paul Jones, under whose command he then was for a proposed expedition to the coast of Ireland, had to fly from France to America, where he entered the British army under Sir Henry Clinton, at New York; and afterwards left it for the Dutch service, in which he died a Major, at the Hague, about the year 1824, much respected; having had, for instance, among his intimate friends, the celebrated Prince de Ligne. The Major, noted as "an extraordinary handsome and elegant person," had a son, similarly distinguished, John William Thomas Gerald O'Sullivan, born in Ireland, who, "after a romantic career of successful adventure," in the course of which "he was at one time the American Consul at the Canary Islands, and at Mogador in Morocco," terminated his existence very honourably by shipwreck, in 1825; when, as owner of the vessel in which he was, he perished "in an attempt to carry a rope ashore, for the safety of the rest." He was father of the Honourable John Louis O'Sullivan, Minister of the United States of America to the Court of Portugal, from 1854 to 1858, and a most amiable and accomplished gentleman and scholar. He writes, at Lisbon, August 26th,

1861,—" Of our name, in this line, I am now the last"—adding, in allusion to the unfortunate deaths of an elder brother, and 2 fine nephews, by accidents—" A fatality has seemed to pursue us. By what sudden end the name is to expire with me, time has *yet* to show." Among his family memorials, he mentions the watch of his celebrated great-grandfather of 1745-6, and his seal, containing his coat-of-arms, besides the still more interesting relic of a beautiful medallion portrait of the General, set in gold, representing him as advanced in years, as not unlike the illustrious Washington, and in a uniform of scarlet, faced with blue and gold.* Having premised so much with respect to the leading *Irish* associates of Prince Charles in commencing his memorable enterprise to regain the triple royalty of his forefathers, I now enter upon such a narrative of that enterprise as has hitherto been a *desideratum*— 1st, in reference to the Irish of the Brigade, &c., connected with the struggle, to the extent of whose participation in it justice has *not* been done; 2ndly, in reference to the *old* feelings of Scotch nationality, so intimately associated with the contest at the time, yet, to the glaring perversion of historic truth! comparatively ignored, in works, *since* compiled on the subject.

Prince Charles, having touched, July 29th, at the small Isle of Erisca,† anchored, the 30th, off the mainland of Scotland, in the Bay of Lochnanuagh, on the coast of Inverness-shire. Thence he proceeded to notify, to his most trusty Highland adherents in those parts, his arrival from France, as Prince Regent for his father King James at Rome; and observed, with reference to being unaccompanied to Scotland by *any* military force from the Continent, that "He did not choose to owe the restoration of his father to *foreigners,* but to his own friends; to whom he was now come, to put it in their power to have the glory of that event." ‡. The various discussions and arrangements which necessarily took place with the Highland leaders, ere they decided on committing themselves to an enterprise so hazardous under such circumstances, postponed the landing of the Prince till August 5th, when he disembarked, with his 7 previously-mentioned followers, at Borodale, on the southern

---

* According to the coloured representations of the "uniformes des 7 Régiments Irlandais en 1745," or those of "Bulkeley, Clare, Dillon, Roth, Berwick, Lally," and "Fitzjames Cavalerie" among the French MSS. given to me by the late John O'Connell, the *red* or *scarlet* coats of 2 of the regiments, namely, those of "Roth" and "Fitz-James," were faced, or turned up, with *blue.* The portrait of "Prince Charlie's" Irish General and favourite is certainly 1 of too much historical interest, as regards Ireland and Scotland, to be kept unphotographed, or unpublished. For my correspondence with his last living representative, the American Minister in Portugal, I am indebted to an introduction to the Very Rev. Dr. Russell, President of the College of Corpo Santo, Lisbon, from my learned and patriotic friend, Dr. R. R. Madden.

† "There," at Erisca, relates Æneas Mac Donald, of the Prince and his party, "they were all refreshed as well as the place could afford, and they had some beds, but not sufficient for the whole company; on which account, the Prince, being less fatigued than the others, insisted upon such to go to bed as most wanted it. Particularly he took care of Sir Thomas Sheridan, and went to examine his bed, and to see that the sheets were well aired." This superiority to self-indulgence, for the accommodation of others, does Charles much credit; more especially his solicitude for the comfort of his elderly companion, Sir Thomas Sheridan. It reminds us of the care of Achilles for old Phœnix in the Iliad.

‡ The comparatively *inglorious* dependence of the "glorious revolution," and its dynastic representatives, upon *foreign* military support or succour for success, has been already shown, and commented on, in Book VI.

shore of Lochnanuagh. The 1st gathering of the clansmen, and unfurling of the Stuart standard—"of red silk, with a white space in the centre, on which the celebrated motto, 'TANDEM TRIUMPHANS,' was, a few weeks afterwards, inscribed"—occurred, August 30th, in presence of Charles, at the valley of Glenfinnan, where, with about 2 companies of the Elector of Hanover's or George II.'s infantry, disarmed and made prisoners some days before, the Highland loyalists, from 1100 to 1200 in number, principally Camerons and Mac Donalds, under their Chieftains Lochiel and Keppoch, mustered in martial array.

"'Then loudly let the pibroch sound,
And bauld advance each true heart;
The word be, '*Scotland's King and Law!*'
And '*Death, or Charlie Stuart!*'"

That is, our word be, "The restoration of the national Dynasty, and the national Legislature!" Mr. Lockhart, writing from Scotland to the Prince's father at Rome, in 1725, remarked—"Aversion to the Union daily increases, and *that* is the handle by which Scotsmen will be incited to make a general and zealous appearance." Hence, in consideration of due assistance to reinstate his family in their ancient dominions, Charles, we are informed, "promised many things agreeable to the Scots, and, among others, the dissolution of the Union with England," since, it is added, "the Scots generally, but the Highlanders in particular, looked upon the Union with England, as a slavish subjugation." In fine, as Sir Walter Scott notes—"The words, 'Prosperity to Scotland, and no Union,' is the favourite inscription to be found on Scottish sword-blades, betwixt 1707 and 1746."

Of the army, thus commenced for this "noble attempt," as it has been designated by Dr. Johnson, Colonel John O'Sullivan was made Adjutant-General, and Quartermaster-General. From the 31st, when they marched forwards, till September 7th, when they reached Letterfinlay, their strength, by other Mac Donalds, with Stuarts, and Grants, was raised to several hundreds more. Meanwhile, the Anglo-Hanoverian Commander in Scotland, Lieutenant-General Sir John Cope, in order to confine the war to the Highlands, set out, August 30th, from Edinburgh; proceeding, with about 1400 infantry, and a train of artillery, towards the important mountain-pass of Corriearrack, popularly styled, *the Devil's staircase*. But Charles preoccupied it, September 7th, by a rapid march. Still, in order to keep the Highland force northwards, or away from the Lowlands, by the dread of a hostile advance into their own country, Cope, on finding himself obliged to retire from before Corriearrack, turned aside towards Inverness; calculating on being followed, and fought with, in that direction. But, by this movement, having left the way to the Lowlands and Edinburgh open, through the mountain-defiles of Badenoch into the fertile valley of Athol, &c.—or the best districts for maintaining a force, only to be kept together from the resources of the country it could occupy—Cope showed himself to be no match for the Prince, and his Kerry head-piece, O'Sullivan. Charles, passing through the glens of Badenoch, where he was continually reinforced, descended into the "pleasant vale of Athol," and entered Perth, the 15th; when, of 4000 louis d'ors, or guineas, he had brought from France, but 1 remained, which he showed Mr. Kelly; observing, he would soon get more. Dundee was seized the same evening, and 2 vessels there, with some arms and ammunition.* Besides refreshing, recruiting, and (as he had anticipated) raising funds for his army, at Perth, the Prince was joined there by several noblemen and gentlemen, including the Lords Strathallan, Nairn, Ogilvy, the Duke of Perth, Lord George Murray, &c. Lord George, a younger son of the Duke of Athol, had fought for the Stuart cause in 1715, again in 1719, and had consequently to retire to the Continent, where he passed some years in the Sardinian service; but, obtaining leave to return to Scotland, resided there, till he joined Charles. According to a fellow-soldier of his Lordship, "he was tall and robust, and brave in the highest degree; conducting the Highlanders in the most heroic manner, and always the 1st to rush, sword in hand, into the midst of the enemy. He used to say, when we advanced to the charge—'I do not ask you, my lads, to go before, but merely to follow, me.' A very energetic harangue, admirably calculated to excite the ardour of the Highlanders." He was immediately nominated a Lieutenant-General by Charles, who, on the 22nd, after an interesting visit to "the ancient Palace of his ancestors, the Kings of Scotland," at Scoon, or Scone, quitted Perth, and, strengthened *en route* by some Mac Donalds of Glencoe, and Mac Gregors of Glengyle, advanced the more eagerly to reach Edinburgh, as Cope, in order to repair the miscalculation through which he had been so outmanœuvred, was preparing to embark his forces at Aberdeen, for the metropolis; while, the Highland army, instead of being able to march by the most direct road, should take a longer one thither.

Driving before him Gardiner's and Hamilton's 2 scampering dragoon-regiments,† and equally frightening the miserable Whig Volunteers and Trained Bands at Edinburgh, the Prince approached and summoned that city on the 27th, and, by stratagem, soon effected his admission there; which it was so important to do, ere Cope's expected arrival with his troops by sea, to preserve the place. From 800 to 900 Highlanders, under several leaders, including Lochiel and O'Sullivan, were detached by night towards the walls, and 1 of the gates being opened for a coach, Captain Evan Mac Gregor of Glencairnaig, and "the foremost Highlanders," says Klose, "rushed in, seized the guards, secured the guard-house, while Colonel O'Sullivan sent small parties round to the other gates, which were likewise secured, without blood-shed, or disturbance." The Scotch metropolis, at night, under the House of Hanover, was, at morning, under the House of Stuart! Charles, the 28th, entered Holyrood House, the Palace of his forefathers, and, as coming to reinstate, in the person of his father, as "King James VIII.," the old dynasty of the country, and to raise that country to its former rank of a distinct *Kingdom*, by annulling the so-called *Act of Union*, he was welcomed by the acclamations of all, who preferred loyalty, chivalry, and nationality, to Whiggism, sectarianism, and provincialism. Of the connexion of Anti-

* But "the 2 vessels must have been poorly laden," it has been remarked, "as the insurgents continued only *half-armed*, till *after* the battle of Preston."

† These 2 regiments, so unenviably conspicuous, in this war, as "scarlet runners" from the Highlanders, were the predecessors of the present 13th and 14th Light Dragoons. They are thus, as keenly, as deservedly, ridiculed, by the contemporary songster, Skirving—

"The bluff dragoons swore, 'Blood and oons!
They'd make the rebels run, man;'
And yet they flee, when them they see,
And winna fire a gun, man!"

Unionism with Jacobitism, a remarkable instance occurred, at the Prince's entrance into Holyrood House. "When he," writes Home, "was near the door, which stood open to receive him, a gentleman stepped out of the crowd, drew his sword, and, raising his arm aloft, walked up stairs before Charles. The person, who enlisted himself in this manner, was James Hepburn of Keith. . . . He had been engaged, when a very young man, in the rebellion of 1715; and, from that time, (learned and intelligent as he was,) had continued a Jacobite. But he had compounded the spirit of Jacobitism with another spirit; for he disclaimed the hereditary indefeasible right of Kings, and condemned the government of James II.; but he also condemned the Union between England and Scotland, as injurious and humiliating to his country; saying, (to use his own words,) that the Union had made a Scotch gentleman of small fortune nobody; and that he would die 1000 times, rather than submit to it! Wrapped up in these notions, he kept himself for 30 years in constant readiness to take arms, and was the 1st person who joined Charles at Edinburgh!"* In the festivities which took place soon after at Holyrood, 1 of the able minstrels, that were *still·* numerous in Ireland as successors of the old Bards, was present as a performer—the famous Dennis O'Hampsey, otherwise Hampson, or Hempson, of Craigmore, County of Londonderry, born in 1695, deceased in 1807, aged 112, and whose harp was celebrated as "Queen of Music" by his hearers. "In his 2nd trip to Scotland, in the year 1745," says the Rev. George Sampson, the historian of Londonderry, of this venerable minstrel, who was, at that time, by his own account, above 50 years of age, "being in Edinburgh, when *Charley*, the Pretender, was there, he was called into the great hall, to play. At first, he was alone. Afterwards 4 fiddlers joined. The tune, called for, was, '*The King shall enjoy his own again.*' He sung here part of the words following—

'I hope to see the day,
When the Whigs shall run away,
And the King shall enjoy his own again!'

I asked him," adds Mr. Sampson, "if he heard the Pretender speak? He replied, I only heard him ask '*Is Sylvan* there?' On which some one answered, 'He is not here, please your Royal Highness, but he shall be sent for.' 'He meant to say *Sullivan*,' continued Hampson, 'for that was the way he called the name.'" For this introduction to the Prince's presence, the Ulster harper was indebted to his countrymen, Sir Thomas Sheridan, and Mr. Kelly.†

By the 29th, the day after his entering Edinburgh, Charles had gained more adherents of consequence, or the Lord Kellie, and others from the Lowlands—"many," we are told, "induced to join him, less by personal devotion, than by an unconquerable aversion to the Union." He was likewise reinforced by other Highlanders; he obtained several requisites for his troops, among which were some, yet comparatively few, muskets,

---

* Like Hepburn, as the annotator of the Scotch Jacobite Minstrelsy informs us,—"Many intelligent, well-educated men were known to have favoured the insurrection of 1745, *less* from attachment to the family of the Stuarts, than from a hope, that their restoration would lead to a repeal of what was called the *detested* Union." See, also, the letter of Burns to Mrs. Dunlop, April 10th, 1790.

† Not, as Mr. Sampson says, a "*Colonel* Kelly of Roscommon." Who the Kelly was is obvious. But the mention of "Roscommon" is useful.

owing to the previous conveyance of such articles into the Castle; and, notwithstanding that many of his men were consequently still most incompletely armed, he reviewed the whole, in order to march, on the 30th, against Sir John Cope, who, by that time, had landed at, and was advancing from, Dunbar, towards the Scotch metropolis. Cope was joined by his regular cavalry, besides a number of Edinburgh or other Lowland Volunteers, including some armed clerical zealots, or Presbyterian Ministers; and he had written from Banff, on the 20th, in due anticipation of victory,—" Though damage may be done by the quickness of the march, which the Highlanders are much more able to make than we are, yet a solid body, like ours, must effectually get the better of them, in the end." With similar confidence, in writing from Perth, on the 21st, how Cope, instead of fighting at Corriearrack, "escaped to the north, to the great disappointment of the Highlanders," the Prince had added, of that movement of the English force—" But I am not at all sorry for it— I shall have the greater glory in beating them, when they are more numerous, and supported by their dragoons." The 2 armies were in sight of, and arrayed against, each other, October 1st, about 7 miles from Edinburgh, for the engagement, variously styled the battle of Preston-Pans, or Gladsmuir. Cope's force had such comparative advantages on its side as to be seemingly invincible: the infantry were about 2100; the cavalry, 2 dragoon-regiments, 1 on the right, the other on the left, were 700 strong;* and these 2800 men, generally disciplined and equipped as English regulars, had 6 field-cannon, besides mortars; and were only approachable through a morass, and narrow pass. The Prince's followers, on the contrary, a rural militia, collected within 5 weeks, and, in part, very imperfectly weaponed—some having merely a sword, or a dirk, or a pistol, or a bludgeon, or a scythe-blade fastened straight to a pitch-fork handle—were, besides, inferior in number, or, even by the hostile computation of Home, *not* 2400 men;† their cavalry, as only about 50, having to be necessarily but a party detached, or in reserve; and the artillery, as but 1 iron gun, only adapted for firing a marching-signal, had to be left behind; while, to reach the English, it was necessary "to pass before their noses, in a defile and bog." Nevertheless, Charles, through good local intelligence, having effected this passage by day-break on the 2nd, his 1st line *alone*, of but 1456 combatants, mastered with a rush the enemy's artillery, ere it gave more than 5 shots; next put the 2 dragoon-regiments to a rapid and disgraceful flight, compared with that of "rabbits one by one;" and, having discharged and thrown down their muskets, with a most tremendous shout, closed, target and claymore in hand, upon the hostile infantry. "The English officers in Cope's army," says my contemporary London publication, "behav'd very gallantly, and did all in their power to oblige their men to perform their duty; but the terrible figure of the Highlanders, and the irresistible fury with which they charg'd them, baffled their utmost efforts, and struck such a dread into

* In March, 1745, the regular complement of every dragoon-regiment quartered in Great Britain was published, as 354 "effective private men"—*i. e.*, 6 troops of 59 each—and 81 "officers, &c.," or 435 for both. By this statement, 2 dragoon-regiments would contain 870 men of all ranks. A letter, in the Culloden Papers, from General Wightman, who was with Cope's force at Preston-Pans, refers to Cope's cavalry *there* as "the 700 dragoons."

† Home's numerical estimate of the Prince's army at Preston-Pans seems trustworthy, as deduced from a comparison of his own inquiries with the statement of Mr. Patullo, Muster-Master to that army.

the soldiers, that they soon gave way to the impetuous onset of their enemies." The Chevalier de Johnstone, who was with the Prince, in the 2nd line of his army, not above 50 paces behind the 1st, running, as fast as possible, to overtake that line, and near enough never to lose sight of it, asserts, "in less than 5 minutes, we obtained a complete victory!" The Prince himself, in his letter to his father, after noting, "only our 1st line had occasion to engage," adds, "for, actually in 5 minutes, the field was cleared of the enemies!" General Wightman, who was with Cope's army, not serving, but as a looker on, and who says, he "saw all the dragoons quite out of the field, and the foot surrounded on all sides," alleges, that the *entire* affair "lasted about 4 minutes, and *no longer!*" Hence the boast, and with so much truth, by the Jacobites, that "*their* young Prince could win a battle in 5 minutes!" Charles had, at most, 115 *hors de combat*, or but 35, including 5 officers, killed, and 70 or 80 men wounded. Of Cope's infantry, who were *the* sufferers on this occasion, as his dragoons fled at once, only 170 escaped, about 300 were slain, 450 wounded,* and between 1600 and 1700, including 70 officers, were returned, by their own Serjeants and Corporals, as prisoners; so that the Anglo-Hanoverians, or Georgeites, were diminished between 1900 and 2000 men by this routing.† Their colours and standards, among which were 7 that had belonged to the runaway dragoons, their artillery, consisting of 6 guns and 2 mortars, their camp, their baggage, and their military chest, containing some thousand pounds, were captured by the Highlanders; whose victorious loyalty, renewing that day the glories of their forefathers under Montrose and Dundee, was rewarded by "a fine plunder." The last triumph of Scotch nationality, in the national metropolis, under the representative of the ancient national dynasty of Scotland, and over the forces of her old national enemy, followed this dashing Celtic discomfiture of the Saxon, and the Southron. "The Camerons," says my authority, "entered Edinburgh scarcely 3 hours after the battle, playing their pipes with might and main, and exhibiting, with many marks of triumph, the colours they had taken from Cope's dragoons. But the return of the main body of the army was reserved for the succeeding day, Sunday. . . . . The clans marched, in one, long, extended line, into the lower gate of the city, with bag-pipes exultingly playing the cavalier air, '*The King shall enjoy his own again.*' They bore, besides their own standards, those which they had taken from the royal army; and they displayed, with equally ostentatious pride, the

* Of Cope's infantry, abandoned, from the very commencement, by the dastardly dragoons, Lord Mahon and Mr. Chambers specify those who escaped as but 170; and the contemporary London compilation, "Young Juba," makes their slain 300, and wounded 450—the latter, to be reckoned, of course, as *among* those taken prisoners. "For 1 that was killed by a bullet, 20 fell by the sword."

† Lord George Murray, the Prince's Lieutenant-General, relates that, by the lists he caused the English Serjeants and Corporals to take of their commissioned and non-commissioned fellow-captives after the engagement, the whole "made between 1600 and 1700 men," or say 1650; who, with the 170 escaped, and 300 slain, would make Cope's infantry 2120, or, in round numbers, 2100; and, adding to these his 700 cavalry, his entire army would be 2820, or, in round numbers, 2800 men. This computation moreover agrees with the contemporary estimate of Cope's force for the action by the English Whig Ray, who asserts, "of the King's troops, there were about 2800, who should have fought." He names (so far as I can make them out) 78 of Cope's officers as "killed, wounded, and prisoners." In the best Jacobite and Georgeite publications of the day, those officers are summed up as 83 or 84 in number.

vast accession of dress, and personal ornament, which they had derived from the vanquished. In the rear of their own body, came the prisoners, at least half as numerous as themselves, and then followed the wounded in carts. At the end of all, came the baggage, and cannon, under a strong guard."

This important victory rendered the Prince master of nearly all Scotland, except the forts held by the English in the Highlands, and the Castles of Edinburgh and Stirling, still garrisoned by them. His father was consequently proclaimed, in almost every town, under his national title (as in 1715) of "King James VIII.," and the public money was levied for *his* service; the previous Anglo-Hanoverian authorities having generally to skulk into privacy, or fly into England. "There is nothing to be seen, in town, and country, but people with *white cockades*," exclaims a contemporary, "and even the ladies have fixed them on their head-dress!" In short, "the *rebels* were now absolutely masters of Scotland," writes a howling Whig there, "and they might, when they pleased, have cut all our throats!"—the designation of "*rebel* foe," on the other hand, being already applied to the Whigs, in the exultation of Jacobite minstrelsy.

> "Now Charles asserts his father's right,
>   And thus establishes his own;
> Braving the dangers of the fight,
>   To cleave a passage to the THRONE.
> The Scots regain their ancient fame,
>   And well their faith and valour show;
> Supporting their young hero's claim,
>   Against a powerful *rebel* foe!"

The day after Cope's overthrow, Charles forwarded, to the northern English Jacobites, intelligence of his "wonderful success" for their deliverance, and of his intention soon "to move towards them," when "*they would be inexcusable, before God and man, if they did not all in their power, to assist and support him, in such an undertaking;*" adding, as to the imperative necessity then for an honest or uncompromising co-operation on their part—"*There is no more time for deliberation—now or never is the word!*" * Mr. Kelly, too, was sent to France, to represent to the Ministers there the expediency of assisting the Jacobites in Scotland; which commission, after a narrow escape of that gentleman from arrest by the Anglo-Hanoverian consular agent at Camp-Veer in Holland, was executed; and Sir James Steuart, (the distinguished writer on political economy,) was subsequently despatched to France, to second the application of Mr. Kelly. In the course of the month of October, 2 ships from France and 1 from Spain—where, as in France, the brightest hopes were excited among the Irish exiles by the Prince's success—reached the northern Scotch ports, conveying the Marquis d'Eguilles with a letter from Louis XV. to the Prince, £6000, some thousand stand of arms, 6 field-pieces, a detachment of French artillery-men, and several Irish officers in the services of France and Spain. Of the "Irish officers in the service of France," the principal was a gentleman of the Regiment of

---

* Charles, in corresponding, the year before, with the adherents to his family in Great Britain, "soon perceived his Scotch partizans," says Lord Mahon, "to be greatly superior, in zeal and determination, to his English." And, more recently, or in February, 1745, the Prince, writing to his father, remarks—"The truth of the matter is, that our *friends* in England are *afraid of their own shadow*," &c.

Lally, "Mr. Grant,* an able mathematician, who had been employed for many years with M. Cassini, in the Observatory at Paris."

As "the Act of Union was," observes the German biographer of Charles, "an object of general aversion in Scotland, and the re-establishment of Scotland, as a separate Kingdom, was, with a large portion of his adherents, a matter quite as important as the re-establishment of the Stuart dynasty" —so that, remarks a noble English historian, "no saying was more common, among the Jacobites, than that they were bound to restore, not merely the *King* but the KINGDOM of Scotland"—the 1st thought of the Prince was "to summon a Scottish Parliament at Edinburgh"—to which design, however, there were *then* such obstacles, that, as his better policy for the time, he had to relinquish it. But, in his Declaration of October 9th, O. S. (or 20th N. S.) from the Scottish metropolis, as Prince Regent, warning all "liege subjects, whether Peers, or Commoners," from attending the Parliament, which "the Elector of Hanover had taken upon him to summon to meet at Westminster" that month, Charles more especially prohibited any subjects of his father's "antient Kingdom of *Scotland*, whether Peers, or Commoners," to sit and act in "such an unlawful assembly," on pain of being "proceeded against as traitors and rebels to *their* King and Country;" adding, "*the pretended Union of the Kingdoms being now at an end.*" And, in another Declaration, from Holyrood House, next day, to all his father's subjects—a document of greater length and importance, drawn up by Sir Thomas Sheridan and Sir James Steuart, aided, not improbably, by Mr. Kelly—the so-called Union was denounced, as, on the part of James, it so well deserved to be, and its repeal was accordingly promised. "With respect to *the pretended Union of the 2 nations,*" says the document, "*the King cannot possibly ratify it*, since he has had repeated remonstrances against it, from each Kingdom; and since it is incontestable, that the principal point then in view was the *exclusion of the Royal Family from their undoubted right to the Crown;* for which purpose, the *grossest corruptions were openly used, to bring it about.*" Among others of the Scotch aristocracy by this time attached to the Prince were Alexander Forbes, Lord Pitsligo, an elderly nobleman, from his general amiability and prudence "the oracle of the Lowland gentry;" and the Honourable Arthur Elphinston, soon

* The name of Grant—in its Norman form, "le Graunt," or "Graunte"—has been respectable, during the middle ages and subsequently, in Ireland, or in Kilkenny, Waterford, and Cork. In the War of the Revolution, Jasper Grant, Esq. of Kilmurry, County Cork, and Grantstown, County Waterford, was a Captain of Dragoons in King James's service; and Walter Grant of Curlody, County Kilkenny, was, as a Stuart loyalist, attainted by the Williamites. The gentleman of this name, in the Regiment of Lally, sent from France to serve under Prince Charles in Scotland, appears, by his Stuart title of "Baron of Iverk," or, as Frenchified, "Iverque," to have been from the County of Kilkenny, in which "Iverk" is a Barony. He published in France a magnificent map of the British Isles, and a portion of the coasts of France, surmounted by the royal arms of Great Britain and Ireland, with the motto "Dieu et mon Droit" underneath on a scroll; the object of the document being thus set forth. "CARTE où sont tracées toutes les differentes routes que S. A. R. CHARLES EDWARD, PRINCE DE GALLES, a suivies dans la Grande Bretagne, et les marches, tant de son armée, que de celle de l'Ennemi. On y trouve, aussi les Siéges qui ont été faits, et les Batailles qui ont été données dans son entreprise. *Cette Carte sera très utile pour l'Histoire, les dates des principaux événemens y étant marquées avec exactitude.* Dressée et présentée à SON ALTESSE ROYALE, par son très humble et très obeïssant Serviteur, J. A. Grante, Baron d'Iverque et Colonel de l'Artillerie du Prince en Ecosse." Were this map republished, *many* copies of it ought to sell in the Highlands of Scotland.

after Lord Balmerino, who had been in arms against the Hanoverian intruder in 1715; consequently many years in exile on the Continent; and who finally became so illustrious for his intrepid death. "I might easily have excused myself taking arms on account of my age," he observed, being 57 when he joined Charles, "but I never could have had peace of conscience," he added, "if I had staid at home, when that brave Prince was exposing himself to all manner of dangers and fatigue, both night and day." Having, by November 11th, organized his utmost disposable strength, and overruled the argument of his Scotch Privy Counsellors, that "He should, for the present, merely aim, to secure himself in the possession of Scotland, and to defend that Kingdom, by a national war, against its ancient enemy,"* Charles quitted Edinburgh, to march for England; where he calculated on being supported by due risings of the Jacobites, as well as seconded by an invasion from France, in opposition to the Whig-Hanoverian government. That government, on the other hand, since Cope's defeat, had, to their several regular corps quartered at home, and levies of Militia and Volunteers, added 2 regiments of infantry from Ireland, and had sent over to Flanders for all but 2 battalions, and 4 cavalry regiments of the British army there, besides above 7200 foreign or Dutch mercenaries, for the greater security of the German sovereignty, or "Protestant succession," in England; while any transmission of assistance to Charles, from the Continent, was to be guarded against, at sea, by Admiral Vernon, Rear-Admiral Byng, and Commodore Knowles. Of those troops, there were to be 3 armies: that of the north, under the Irish Protestant veteran, Field-Marshal George Wade;† that of the centre, under the Duke of Cumberland; and the last, or that for the preservation of London, under the Elector-King, George himself; the whole well armed, equipped, and artilleried, and making considerably above 36,000 men.

The Scotch force, with which Charles, by the 19th, prepared to pass the frontier of the 2 nations into Cumberland, was below 5000 effective men. In noting the rank of the principal officers, as native Scots and noblemen—the Duke of Perth General, Lord George Murray Lieutenant-General, who, soon after, obtained the former post, &c.,—a contemporary Anglo-Whig writer, Ray, observes—"But tho', in regard of their interest, these people were honoured with such high commands, yet it was known, that the Pretender confided most in a few, that came over with him. At the head of his Council, was Sir Thomas Sheridan, an Irish gentleman, of a middle age, and reputed a man of capacity, who has long been about him." Then, alluding to Colonel O'Sullivan, as an Engineer, and his countryman, Sir John Mac Donnell, or Mac Donald, as an Aide-de-Camp to Charles, this writer adds—"Mr. Sullivan was a person the most concerned of any in the rebellion, and whose councils the Pretender chiefly relied on." Another hostile contemporary, Captain Bradstreet, an Irish Protestant spy, for the Anglo-Hanoverian government, in Charles's camp, informs us—"Colonel

---

* "Some of the Chiefs even told him," according to the Chevalier de Johnstone, "that they had taken arms, and risked their fortunes, and their lives, merely to seat him on the throne of Scotland; but that they wished to have *nothing to do with England!*" The old Wallace and Bruce feeling!

† Of this gentleman, a native of Westmeath, and of his countryman, Arthur Wellesley, Duke of Wellington, it is worth noting, that *both* were Colonels of the same corps, or the 33rd Regiment of Foot, as well as Field-Marshals.

Sullivan was a fat, well-faced man; Sir Thomas Sheridan was a drooping, old man; the rebel Prince reposed his greatest confidence in those 2, and Secretary Murray." It was to the court he paid to the *Irish* favourites of Charles, including the brave and faithful O'Neill hereafter mentioned, that Murray is elsewhere alleged to have been mainly indebted, for the regard shown him by Charles. Hence, too, when Murray, " desirous of a military as well as a civil command, made some progress in levying a Regiment of Hussars, designed for the light cavalry duties," they " were commanded under him by an *Irish* officer in the French service, named Lieutenant-Colonel Bagot." The brave Gaels of Alba* crossed the border into England on the 19th, with a loud shout of exultation, and flourish of their drawn claymores in the air—though the glow of this outburst of martial enthusiasm was checked, when it was remarked, among the clans, as an unpropitious omen, at which some grew pale, that Highland blood was *first* shed there; Lochiel, in unsheathing his weapon, having unluckily cut his hand! The 20th, the Prince marched against Carlisle, remarkable among the old northern strongholds of England, in her wars with Scotland. By the 22nd, he invested and summoned the place; at the same time, preparing to oppose the rumoured advance of Marshal Wade, with 10 English and 8 Dutch† battalions of foot, 2 regiments of horse, and 1 of dragoons, in order to raise the siege. Furnished with a castle or citadel, also surrounded by a wall planted with cannon, and so thick that 3 persons could walk abreast upon it within the parapet, having a ditch about 4 feet broad, and a garrison of 80 Invalids, and some hundreds of Cumberland and Westmoreland Militia, with a population of 4000 inhabitants, of whom 400 could have aided the Militia, Carlisle would have been defended by Lieutenant-Colonel James Durand, at least until something *like* honourable terms of capitulation might be obtained from an enemy, unprovided, as the Scots were, with heavy artillery. The latter, on the night of the 21st, opened trenches " 80 yards from the walls," alleges 1 of their narratives, when " Mr. Grant, an Irish officer of Lally's regiment, our principal Engineer, ably availed himself of the ditches of enclosures, by which we were able to approach close to the town, sheltered from the fire of the enemy. Our artillery consisted of the 6 Swedish field-pieces received from France with Mr. Grant, and the 6 other pieces of smaller calibre, which we had taken at the battle of Gladsmuir," or Preston-Pans. But the reduction of the place proceeded, continues this account, " rather from our *threatening* to fire red-hot balls upon the town, and reduce it to ashes, than from the *force* of our artillery, as we did not discharge a single shot, lest the garrison should become acquainted with the smallness of their calibre; which might have encouraged them to defend themselves!" In short, when no more than 2 of the Scots

---

* At the famous "Battle of the Standard," in 1138, between the Anglo-Norman and Scotch forces, "*Scottorum* exercitus," writes Brompton, of the onset, "exclamant *Albani! Albani!*"—that is, "*Albanach! Albanach!*" or men of ALBA, the Gaelic name for Scotland.

† A letter, dated "Berwick, September 25th, 1745," states—" Col. Herchet is landed here from Holland with 7220 Dutch forces; they seem mostly Papists, use the Romish ceremonies, and ask, Where they may have Mass?" The Dutch were, by treaty, to furnish but 6000 men, though *here* we have so many *more*, or 7220! On the non-exclusion of Catholics from the military and naval services in Holland, though a Protestant state, see the note in Book II., under the Queen's Regiment of Infantry, or that of Luttrell.

had been killed, or wounded, the *shameless* Militia, who should have supported Lieutenant-Colonel Durand at least to the extent above noted, shrank from their duty; submitting, on the 26th, not only to surrender the town and citadel to Charles, but to walk away without arms, horses, or honours of war; and even agreed, not to serve against him for a year! "The conduct of that city," complains my Whig-Hanoverian letter from Kendal, "fell much short of what was expected from a place of so much strength, and reputed loyalty. . . . The rebels have taken above 200 good horses, and all the arms, from the Militia, besides 1000 stand lodged in the Castle!"—to which, from other Georgeite authority, or that of Henderson, may be added, a quantity of powder, military stores, "and the money, plate, and most valuable effects of the country, for several miles round!" The Prince, having received the keys from the Mayor and Aldermen on their knees, and having caused his father to be proclaimed in form, as James III. of England and Ireland, &c., and himself as Regent, entered Carlisle on the 28th, mounted upon a white charger, and preceded by a great number of pipers. Leaving a garrison of 200 men there, by which the army was reduced to about 4500, Charles, as the result of a Council which he held, resumed his advance, December 2nd, into England; still reckoning upon a proportionable native and foreign, or Jacobite and French, co-operation.

Proceeding through Penrith, Shap, Kendal, Lancaster, and Garstang, he arrived, the 8th, at Preston, where he was first welcomed in England, by cheers, and ringing of bells, and obtained, *en passant*, some, though not many, recruits. Among these, was his most eminent English adherent in arms, Francis Townley, Esq., who, to literary attainments, united military knowledge, acquired in France, and belonged to a Catholic family of very high antiquity in Lancashire, and remarkable for its attachment to the Stuarts. "In this County," says a Whig writer, alluding to the female feelings and fashions there in favour of Charles, "the women are generally very handsome, by which they have acquired the name of *Lancashire witches*, which appellation they really deserve, being very agreeable. But some of the pretty *Jacobite* witches chuse to distinguish themselves, by wearing plaid breast-knots, ribbons, and garters, tied *above* the knee," &c. By another English account, "if the Lancashire witches could have carried the day for Prince Charles, his success would, indeed, have been certain."* From the 9th to the 10th, the Prince advanced by Wigan for Manchester, amidst crowds flocking to see him, and wish him success; but who, when offered arms, declined them, on the plea, that "they did not *understand* fighting!" At Manchester, the Georgeite Militia "were all discharged, and sent home, before the Highlanders came," according to the local or Byrom diary, that remarks *this* was "well contrived." To which its editor adds—" Well contrived indeed; it was just so in Carlisle. *The country gentlemen were very valiant, before the arrival of the rebels; but, as soon as they heard of their approach, they petitioned to be disbanded, on the plea of fatigue; and disbanded they were, being clearly useless!*" The sentiments of the Highland army on reaching Manchester, the most commercial town in

---

* With the attachment of so many of the fair sex to the Stuart cause in England, compare the very great and influential enthusiasm of the same sex in Scotland, for "Prince Charlie," so pointedly referred to by the Lord President Forbes, and duly noticed by other authorities.

England noted for Jacobitism, and the sympathy which existed with their appearance there, have been best conveyed in verse.

"Here's a health to all brave English lads,
 Both Lords and Squires of high renown,
Who *will* put to a helping hand,
 To put the vile *Usurper* * down!
For our brave Scots are all on foot,
 Proclaiming loud, where'er they go,
With sound of trumpet, pipe, and drum,
 The Clans are coming, oho! oho! &c.

"To set *our* King upon the throne,
 Not Church nor State to overthrow,
As wicked Preachers falsely tell,
 The Clans are coming, oho! oho!
Therefore forbear, ye canting crew,
 Your bugbear tales are a' for show;
The want of *stipend* is your fear.
 The Clans are coming, oho! oho! &c.

"Rous'd, like a lion from his den,
 When *he* thought on his country's woe,
Our brave protector, Charles, did come,
 With all his Clans, oho! oho!
These lions, for their country's cause,
 And *natural* Prince,† were never slow:
So now they come, with their brave Prince;
 The Clans advance, oho! oho! &c.

"And now the Clans have drawn their swords,
 And vow revenge against them a',
That arm for the *Usurper's* cause,
 To fight against our King and Law.
Then God preserve *our* royal King,
 And his dear sons, the lovely twa, ‡
And set him on his father's throne,
 And bless his subjects, great and sma'!
 The Clans are coming, &c."

The Prince's entrance was attended with pealing of bells, popular acclamations, an illumination, bonfires, a wearing of the *white cockade*, the presence of numbers to kiss his hand, and even a celebration, at the

---

* According to the English epigram on the 4 Georges, the 2nd was not less, if not *more*, unpopular than the 1st. Of George II., Lord Macaulay says—"The interests of his kingdom were as nothing to him, when compared with the interests of his electorate. As to the rest, he had neither the qualities which make dulness respectable, nor the qualities which make libertinism attractive. He had been a bad son, and a worse father, an unfaithful husband, and an ungraceful lover. Not one magnanimous or humane action is recorded of him; but many instances of meanness, and of a harshness, which, but for the strong constitutional restraints under which he was placed, might have made the misery of his people."

† "The patriarchal system of laws upon which Highland society was constituted," says Mr. Chambers, on the attachment of the Highlanders to the Stuarts, "disposed *them* to look upon those unfortunate Princes as the general fathers or *Chiefs* of the nation, whose natural and unquestionable power had been rebelliously disputed by their children"—and, in opposition to the English and Lowland Whigs, that writer adds of the Highlanders, how *they* 'could perceive no reasons for preferring a Sovereign, on account of *any* peculiarity in his religion."

‡ Prince Charles, and his brother, Prince Henry, Duke, and subsequently Cardinal, of York.

Collegiate Church, of his arrival, by the Rev. Mr. Clayton, in an eloquent address, which caused that gentleman to be subsequently degraded by the Hanoverian ruler of England. No more, however, than between 200 and 300 men had the courage to enlist, who, with their predecessors, were embodied as the "Regiment of Manchester," under Mr. Townley for their Colonel. On the 12th, the Jacobites left Manchester in 2 divisions, which joined at Macclesfield, and, after marching by Congleton, Leek, and Ashbourn, and dexterously gaining the start, towards London, of the Duke of Cumberland's much superior force, entered Derby, on the 15th, with colours flying and bagpipes playing. Shortly after 11 o'clock, says a hostile narrative from that place, "the van-guard rode into town, consisting of about 30 men, cloath'd in blue, fac'd with red. Most of them had on scarlet waistcoats, with gold lace; and, being likely men, made a good appearance. They were drawn up in the market-place; and sat on horseback 2 or 3 hours. At the same time, the bells were rung, and several bon-fires made, to prevent any resentment from them, that might ensue, on our shewing a dislike of their coming among us. About 3 in the afternoon, Lord Elcho, with the Life-Guards, and many of their Chiefs, also arriv'd, on horseback, to the number of about 150, most of them cloathed as above. These made a fine show, being the flower of their army. Soon after, their main body also march'd into town, in tolerable order, 6 or 8 abreast, with about 8 standards, most of them white flags and a red cross. They had several bag-pipers, who play'd as they march'd along." Then, having alluded to their Highland or plaid dress, &c., the narrative alleges of Charles— "Their Prince (as they call'd him) did not arrive till the dusk of the evening. He walk'd on foot, being attended by a great body of his men, who conducted him to his lodgings (the Lord Exeter's), where he had guards placed all around the house."

During this progress of the Scots, "we," notes a contemporary in England, "had alarms, every hour, that the Duke's army and the rebels were engaged; those dealers in news sometimes giving the victory to one, sometimes to another. 'Tis incredible to think, how all cares and business subsided, and attention was only given to the marches and motions of these 2 hostile armies. All other subjects were disregarded, but what related to battles, victories, or defeats, and their consequences." Another eye-witness adds of the English, in these circumstances—"*The least scrap of good news exalts them most absurdly, and the smallest reverse of fortune depresses them meanly.*" This was the more natural in England, from the final dissipation, by the "*Pretender*" in person, of the swaggering delusion too long practised on the public, more especially throughout the country parts, by a dishonest press, merely pandering to, or trading on, national vanity, at the expense of truth. An honest writer in the Old England Journal (November 9th, O. S., or 20th, N. S.,) under the signature of "Agricola," having premised, how "the first accounts they had by authority mentioned the landing of the young man only as probability," &c., then informs us—"For many weeks, the thing was laugh'd at in all companies; General Cope's march was looked upon as a parade of triumph, rather than an enterprize of danger; and the public, in idea, again saw the roads crowded with rebellious chains, and the gibbets loaded with Highlanders. Their march southward was the first step of theirs which transpir'd; and we rather laugh'd, than were alarm'd at, their seizing Perth. Nay, so very wise, or so mighty sanguine, were our coffee-house politicians, that Sir John Cope's passing them was extoll'd as a master-piece of military stratagem; since the small handful of desperate rebels were now betwixt 2 fires, that of his army, and that of the valiant Captain R. Tennant, who had taken upon him the command of the troops which were to defend Edinburgh. We then flatter'd ourselves, that not a single rebel could escape; and all the difficulty was, where to find prisons sufficient for stowing them, when they should throw themselves upon the mercy of the Government. Those pleasing ideas were heightened and encouraged by the loyal Address of the City of Edinburgh, which was presented, in a manner, in the very teeth of rebellion, and [by] the dutiful flourishes of the gallant Volunteers, who were to cock up the Pretender's beaver. But chiefly we were animated by the accounts published by authority, a few days before the fatal action of Gladsmuir, that the rebels were not above 3000 naked, needy, miserable wretches, and that their numbers were rather diminishing than increasing. After such assurances, it was look'd upon to be the height of folly and madness, not without a small spice of disloyalty, to doubt of their utter ruin in a very few days. Every post brought accounts of their cowardice, their desertions, their unruliness; nay, the very mention of the King's troops had made them scamper. All this made me laugh at their vain, giddy, distant efforts. I encourag'd my neighbours to do the same; and, tho' we were astonished at the unparallel'd defeat of the King's forces, yet the fresh accounts we had, in the papers, of the dissentions and mutinies of the rebels, kept us from being dismay'd. His Majesty's Speech from the Throne was the first thing that rous'd us from this security. It was then but too plain, that our dangers had been, from foolish or worse views, conceal'd or diminish'd, and I soon found, how fatally I had deluded myself and others." Indeed, "the terror of of the English," asserts an officer of Prince Charles, with reference to the Highlanders, "was truly inconceivable; and, in many cases, they seemed quite bereft of their senses. One evening, as " Mr. Cameron of " Lochiel entered the lodgings assigned to him, his landlady, an old woman, threw herself at his feet, and, with uplifted hands, and tears in her eyes, supplicated him, to take her life, but to spare her 2 little children! He asked her, If she was in her senses? and told her, to explain herself; when she answered, that everybody said the Highlanders ate children, and made them their common food! Mr. Cameron, having assured her, that they would not injure her, or her little children, or any person whatever, she looked at him, for some moments, with an air of surprise, and then opened a press, calling out, with a loud voice, 'Come out, children; the gentleman will *not* eat you!' The children immediately left the press, where she had concealed them, and threw themselves at his feet.* They affirmed, in the newspapers of London, that we had dogs in our army, trained to fight; and that we were indebted, for our victory at Gladsmuir, to those dogs, who darted with fury on the English army. They represented the Highlanders, as monsters with claws, instead of hands. In a word, they never ceased to circulate, every day, the most extravagant and ridiculous stories with respect to the Highlanders." Among the English, as among the Romans, in a period of civil war, it might be remarked,

---

* This anecdote of the Chevalier de Johnstone, as to the supposed *cannibalism* of the Highlanders, is supported by a like account of another gentleman in Prince Charles's army, Mr. Halkston of Rathillet.

> "*Cowards* thus their own misfortunes frame;
> By their own feigning fancies are betray'd,
> And groan beneath those ills *themselves* have made."
> ROWE'S LUCAN'S Pharsalia, I., 847-9.

In this manner did such a comparatively small body of Scots, only between 4000 and 5000 fighting men, and the loyal Irish gentlemen who had the honour to accompany them, advance, at a most inclement period of the year, through the 6 Shires of Cumberland, Westmoreland, Lancaster, Chester, Stafford, and Derby, or above 180 miles into England, and to within 127 miles of her metropolis; proclaiming their Prince as they went along; and levying the public money in HIS name! And this, in spite of 2 English armies, each above double as numerous, or Marshal Wade's, *owned* as about 10,000 men, and the Duke of Cumberland's *listed* as 12,700, of whom 2400 were cavalry, with 30 pieces of cannon—while the Hanoverian occupant of the throne at London could, it was *announced*, assemble, at Finchley Common, 14,000 infantry and cavalry, (including the Guards,) with 32 pieces of cannon—those 3 armies consequently forming about 36,700 men.* Such a bold and well-conducted movement, on the part of this handful of Jacobite loyalists,—the lowest number of Scotch invaders known to have successfully penetrated so far into the "land of the Southron!"—was now, however, found to have been undertaken without any appearance of receiving from English Jacobitism, or French invasion, that aid, on the prospect of which the movement was based. The Scotch ballad states—

> "Had English might stood by the right,
> As *they did vaunt full vain*, joe;
> Or play'd the parts of Highland hearts,
> The day was a' our ain, joe."

Nor is this assertion in verse unsupported by due evidence in prose. The editor of the Chevalier de Johnstone's Memoirs in 1820, from a perusal of the Stuart archives in the possession of George IV., alleges, that Prince Charles "was *first invited into Great Britain, and then abandoned to his fate, by a great part of the English aristocracy.* This fact cannot be denied, as *there is evidence of it, in their own handwriting.*" From "these archives, which consist of more than 500,000 documents, equally curious and instructive," we learn, "that the project of the *Pretender* was not so wild, as, since the result, it has usually been pronounced; and that the conduct of the Highland Chiefs, who staked their lives and properties upon the issue, though certainly bold, was not so imprudent, as it might, at first sight, appear to be." For, when those Chiefs had, continues this writer, "surmounted the greatest danger, to which every enterprise of that nature is exposed, namely, the *danger of being crushed in the outset*, they could hardly anticipate, when they advanced into England, that the powerful party, which had *promised* to join them, would, *when the risk was so much less, be so much more regardless of their word, than they themselves had been.*" But the English High-Church Jacobites of the country so chivalrously traversed by Charles, in reliance on *their* professions and promises, were generally mere braggarts and cowards. On the boastful assurances of many thousand recruits from their party, when constituting

---

* I give the numerical strength of the 3 armies from Georgeite authorities. But, that the "grand total" of troops in Great Britain was much *higher* in amount, will be seen farther on.

by far the majority of the population, such High-Church caballers in 1715 had drawn the Scots and the Catholics in arms to Preston, and then left them unassisted against the forces of the Whig-Hanoverian Government! The Catholics, who had honestly taken the field for the Stuart cause along with the Scots, and who suffered accordingly, (especially in the case of poor Lord Derwentwater,) were naturally so indignant at this treacherous poltroonery *then,* that they resolved not to be deceived, and sacrificed *again.* In consequence of which, and the subsequent lenity of the existing Government towards them, only 2 persons of any note belonging to their religion, or Colonel Townley, and a Mr. Andrew Blood of Yorkshire, as Captain in the Regiment of Manchester, now joined the Prince; * while the representatives of High-Church Jacobitism, though acting somewhat better at this juncture than in 1715, by supplying the Prince with, *perhaps,* 300 men at most,† yet, on the whole, were found wanting, as doing nothing like what they had given him reason to expect from them. Hence, with reference to the wretched contrast between the acts and the boasts of those High-Church Jacobite countrymen of his in 1745, the contemporary English writer, Ray, remarks—"The case was much the same in 1715; for, although a great many Lancashire gentlemen, with their servants and friends, had joined the rebels, yet they were most of them *Papists,* which made the Scots gentlemen and Highlanders mighty uneasy, very much suspecting the cause; for *they expected all the High-Church party to have join'd them;* ‡ who, according to Patten's History of that Rebellion, are never right hearty for the cause, till *they are mellow over a bottle,* and then *they do not care for venturing their carcases any further than the tavern.* There, indeed, (says he) with 'HIGH-CHURCH *and* ORMOND,' they would make men believe, who do not know them, that they would encounter the greatest opposition in the world. But, *after having consulted their pillows, and the fume a little evaporated,* it is to be observed of them, that *they generally become mighty tame, and, like the snail, if you touch their houses, they hide their heads, shrink back, and pull in their horns.* Upon the whole, it may be said, of the English Jacobites, *no people in the universe know better the difference between drinking and fighting.* It is true, the latter they know not practically; and, I believe, they are so well satisfied of the truth of what they have by relation, that they *never* will." Hence, too, in alluding to "the Jacobites," *his* countrymen, Horace Walpole sarcastically notes, "of which stamp, great part of England was, till—*the Pretender* came." And another contemporary, the Rev. Mr. Owen of Rochdale, adds of such swaggerers and skulkers—"The young Chevalier complained bitterly, during the course of his English expedition, of some political rats, *that*

* I have derived much "useful light," on English Jacobite politics, from the "Lancashire Memorials of 1715," &c., contributed to the publications of the Chetham Society by the learned and liberal Dr. Samuel Hibbert Ware.

† According to the Chevalier de Johnstone, the Regiment of Manchester "never exceeded 300 men;" and if it *ever* included so many, (as Voltaire, too, reports,) the greater number would appear to have soon deserted; since the total, at the surrender of Carlisle, presented only 114 men of *every* rank.

‡ After the arrival of George I. from Hanover, the High-Church mobs made great noise in England, rough-handling Dissenters, destroying Dissenting places of worship, to such cries as "*God damn King George! God bless King James III.!*" and indulging in other tumultuary outbreaks, expressive of aversion to the *former* and attachment to the *latter* Prince. But, in England, as elsewhere, it turned out, that such as were prominent at rows would be, by no means, proportionably so, in the genuine "tug of war."

had long drank and sworn in his service, and that had fought many campaigns for him over the bottle; but that, *when he invited them to join his standard, and make the campaign of danger, they all fled, and forsook him.*" Under these circumstances, the little work on the Prince, entitled "Ascanius, or the Young Adventurer," has, with reference to the English Jacobites, deservedly animadverted upon "*the treachery, or remissness, or want of sincerity in those, who made great professions of zeal for his interest,* and who, *after having drawn him into a vain dependance upon them, remained idle spectators of the danger they had run him into.*" From England *no* correspondence should have been held with, and *no* promises of assistance should have been made to, the Stuart family; or when held with, and made to, that family, should unquestionably have been found of *more* value, than they *were*, by Prince Charles, and the Scotch Jacobites. "The conduct of *cowards*, who join a movement to gratify their petty vanity," says an Irish writer, "and then, in the day of danger, shrink into concealment, tends to lead brave men to destruction, by giving them false notions of the support they may reckon on, in a bold enterprise. *The blood of the brave, who perish so deceived, is on the head of the recreants, who deceive them.*"

While *thus* unaided by the worthlessness of his English friends on land, the Prince too fatally experienced the efficiency of his English enemies, in depriving him of assistance from the Continent by sea;* *the winds also, in this, as on other emergencies, being prejudicial to the Stuart cause!* From Spain, where, as early as August, the Irish refugees had such intelligence concerning Charles, that they hoped for a speedy return to their own country, 4 vessels were despatched, with due supplies for Scotland. Only 1 of these, however, (as previously noticed) arrived there. In October, the *Trial* privateer of Bristol, of 16 guns and 120 men, took, and brought into that port, the *San Zirioco*, from Corunna, of 16 guns and 60 men, with 2500 muskets, as many bayonets, 100 barrels of powder, 150 quintals of musket-balls, several boxes of horse-shoes and flints, and about 24,000 dollars in gold and silver; this ship having an Irish Captain of Horse, and an Irish pilot on board, and being bound for Scotland; but sufficient information respecting it being withheld, by committing a box of papers to the deep; and the Irish Captain, having been brought up to London, was sent to Newgate. Of the 3rd and 4th of those vessels from Corunna, 1 was wrecked off the coast of Ireland, and the other not heard of. Another (or 5th) Spanish ship, the *San Pedro* brigantine of Corunna, under Don Gaspar Guiral, sailed for Scotland, with 2500 new muskets and bayonets, 110 barrels of powder, 70 cases of ball, each of 400 pounds weight, a great number of flints, and, of money, 60,000 pistoles in bags. But she encountered such terrible, contrary winds, that, after flinging her guns overboard, she was endeavouring to get back to Spain, when she was taken, in December, by the *Ambuscade* privateer of London under Captain Cooke, and brought to Crookhaven in Ireland; not, however, till she had disappointed the English, by sending her papers, and all but about 1217 of her 60,000 pistoles, in the same unremunerative direction as her

* The Marquis of Tweeddale, writing, as Secretary of State for Scotland, from "Whitehall, 17th September, 1745," alleges—"The Channel is now so well guarded by different squadrons, that we are under no apprehensions of a visit either from the French or Spaniards, should that ever have been their intention, though nothing can prevent a single ship passing in the night."

cannon. "There was aboard," states a contemporary Irish journal, "a young gentleman who speaks the English language perfectly well, and who says his name is Loftus; that he was born in France, but that his father was born in the County of Limerick; and was, for many years, an eminent Banker in Paris. . . . He acknowledges himself to be a Captain of Horse in the King of Spain's service." There was likewise on board a Catholic clergyman, the Rev. James Corbett, a native of Dublin, who, with Captain Loftus, was sent up for imprisonment in the Castle there; and George II. rewarded the Captain of the *Ambuscade*, for intercepting so much "warlike stores for Scotland, for the use of the rebels," by a present of "500 guineas."* From France, where the exciting accounts of Charles's progress, the presence of his brother, Prince Henry, Duke of York, and the general devotion of the Irish military to the Stuarts, led, especially through the zealous importunity of the gallant Lally, to preparations in her northern ports for landing 10,000 men, including the Irish and Scotch regiments, in Britain, of which expedition the Duke de Richelieu was to be General, and Lally himself Quarter-Master-General†—such detachments as were soonest ready to sail, or those of the Royal Scots under their Colonel, Lord John Drummond, of the infantry Regiments of the Irish Brigade, and the Irish cavalry Regiment of Fitz-James, under Brigadier Walter Stapleton, a Munster veteran distinguished at Fontenoy, on December 2nd, left Dunkirk for Scotland. But, on the 3rd, the *Sheerness* of 20 guns, under Captain Bully, took off the Doggerbank, the *Espérance*, and the following portion of the Irish Brigade, &c., with a great quantity of arms:—DILLON'S REGIMENT. Captains, Charles Ratcliffe, brother to the late lamented Jacobite Earl of Derwentwater, and, as such, taking the title, his son, the Honourable Bartholomew Ratcliffe, Murdoch Macgennis, and Edmund Reilly.—BERWICK'S REGIMENT. Captain, James O'Hanlon.—BULKELEY'S REGIMENT. Captain, Patrick Fitz-Gerald; Lieutenant, John Reilly; 2nd Lieutenant, William Fitz-Gerald; Ensign, Cornelius Mac Carthy.—ROTH'S REGIMENT. Captains, Lewis Shee and James Seaton; reformed Captain, Robert Cameron; Lieutenant, Edward Dunne. —LALLY'S REGIMENT. Reformed Captain, Robert Grace; Lieutenant, Thomas Renally. Equerry to Lord Derwentwater, Clement Mac Dermott. —DRUMMOND'S REGIMENT. Captains, Alexander Baillie, and Alexander Mac Donald; 1st Lieutenant, the Honourable Thomas Nairn, son of Lord Nairn; Lieutenant, Adam Urquhart; 2nd Lieutenant, Samuel Cameron. M. Devant, Lieutenant in a French regiment. Of which 22 prisoners, 13 noblemen or gentlemen, some of them English and Scotch, belonged to the Irish Brigade—exclusive of the Equerry; 5 to Drummond's Scotch corps; the remaining officer was a Frenchman; and 60 privates accompanied them, making, in all, 82 men, besides the ship's crew. About the same time, the *Milford*, of 40 guns, under Captain Hanway, took, off Montrose, the *Louis XV.* of Dunkirk, manned by 27 sailors, and having on board 330 stands of arms, with bayonets, broad-swords,

* George II. showed the importance he attached to this service; and, from what we are informed of the contents of those Spanish vessels lost to Charles, how very unfortunate it was for *him*, that (like the money, forwarded from the same quarter, for his father, in Scotland, in 1715,) so many valuably-laden ships could not reach their destination!

† Voltaire informs us, how much those arrangements to aid Charles were owing to the ardent Jacobitism of Lally, and his proportionate applications to the French Ministers on the subject.

horse-furniture, and a 2nd portion of the Irish Brigade, thus particularized:—BULKELEY'S REGIMENT. Captains, Nicholas Morris and Richard Nagle; 1st Lieutenant, Patrick Meagher; 2nd Lieutenants, John Ryan, Denis and Darby Mahony; Cadets, George and Francis Mathews; 2 Serjeants, 3 Corporals, 1 drummer, and 46 privates.—CLARE'S REGIMENT. Captains, James Conway and Valentine Mervyn; 1st Lieutenant, Bernard O'Brien; 2nd Lieutenant, John Egar; 2 Serjeants, 3 Corporals, 1 drummer, and 46 privates.—BERWICK'S REGIMENT. Captains, James Macraith, and Stephen Cullen; 1st Lieutenant, Christopher Plunkett; 2nd Lieutenant, George Barnwell; 3 Serjeants, 3 Corporals, 1 drummer, and 47 privates. Surgeons, John Dwyer* and Thomas Hogan, and 4 servants. Of which latter prisoners belonging to the Irish Brigade, the officers, reckoning the 2 Surgeons as such, were 18; the other military (excluding the 2 servants) 158; and the total of officers and soldiers, 176. Of about 150 of those conquerors of Fontenoy, thus intercepted at sea, and subsequently prisoners at Hull, a contemporary letter from that place states—"The men are all cloathed in red, and the officers have mostly gold-laced hats. To speak impartially, the officers are as proper men as ever I saw in my life, being most of them 5 feet 10, or 6 feet high, and between 40 and 50 years of age; and the common soldiers are very good-like men, and, if they had landed, might have done a great deal of mischief." But some hundreds of the Irish and Scotch military (the former the more numerous,) were destined to sail, from the French ports, with better success. Of these troops, the 1st portion from Fitz-James's Regiment of Horse, and from Dillon's, Roth's, and Lally's Regiments of Foot, belonging to the Brigade, with Brigadier Stapleton, and from the Royal Scots, with Lord John Drummond, effected their landing in the north of Scotland, where, remarks a historian of Prince Charles, "all that vast tract of land, from the Forth to the Spey, was possess'd by his friends," and "the very boys appear'd in his interest, by wearing *white cockades*, and martialing themselves in companies, under some young, sprightly leaders!" After cantoning in parties along the coast about Montrose, &c., the main body of those Irish and Scotch regulars from France were to march for Perth, to join Lord Strathallan, stationed there, with the most considerable corps of the Jacobite levies, designed to oppose the Anglo-Whig forces, which, since the Prince's march to the south, had re-occupied Edinburgh, and were endeavouring, in various quarters, to regain possession of the country. About the time of Lord John's and the Irish Brigadier's landing, the Jacobites also made an important acquisition at Montrose in the capture of an English war-sloop, the *Hazard*, of 16 guns, 24 swivels, and about 80 men, commanded by Captain Hill. That officer, after firing upon the town, and seizing 3 vessels laden with arms and stores, of which he burned 2, removing their cargoes into and manning the 3rd, was reduced to surrender with his booty, partly by some Highlanders who boarded him in boats, and partly by the skill with which a battery was raised against him on shore by an able Jacobite partizan, David Ferrier, and Major Nicholas Glascock, of the Regiment of Ogilvy, and previously of Dillon's, in the Irish Brigade. On Hill's surrender, (for which he and his Lieutenant were finally cashiered by Court-martial,) the name of his vessel was changed to the *Prince Charles*; the command of which was

---

* Misprinted, in the *English* list, "Divier." That a Dwyer and a Hogan should be together would not be wondered at in Tipperary.

given to 1 of the officers whose ship had been burned, and who had likewise been very instrumental in effecting the capture; and this prize became most useful from its several subsequent passages between Scotland and the Continent, notwithstanding the very superior strength and numbers of the Anglo-Hanoverian cruisers. Soon after the disembarkation of the previously-mentioned Jacobite auxiliaries from the Continent at Montrose, Peterhead, &c., and the capture of the *Hazard*—besides the arrival of another large ship from Dunkirk at Montrose, which compelled the *Ludlow Castle*, as overmatched, to cut her cables at the mouth of the river there, and make off to sea—Rear-Admiral Byng, " with 4 men of war," says an English account, " came before that harbour; but the rebels," it is added, " had planted their cannon so advantageously upon the beach, that it was impossible to get at them. The *Milford* lost her bowsprit, and received considerable damage in her rigging, in attempting it." The veteran regulars from France, at Montrose, seem to have understood gunnery too well for the English Rear-Admiral. Such, with reference to English and Continental aid, was the state of the Prince's affairs, when he reached Derby.

The conversation of Charles at supper, on the evening of December 15th, the day of his entering Derby, was about his approaching final success, and whether he should enter the English metropolis on foot, or on horseback, in a Highland, or an English dress? But the very natural uneasiness, which had already manifested itself at Manchester among the Scotch leaders, at finding themselves so very far advanced into England, with *no* visible likelihood of either such Jacobite or French aid as they had been led to expect, and exposed to 3 armies each above twice as numerous as their own, rendered it imperative that a Council should be held by the Prince at Derby, the following day, or the 16th. There, in opposition to Charles, who vehemently argued for pushing forward, to make way, through the Elector's army, at Finchley Common, into London —in which view, he is stated to have been at first supported by some of the Irish officers—the general opinion ultimately was—that, surrounded, in a manner, as the Highland force were, by so many more than their own number—deceived with respect to English and French assistance— even if victorious at Finchley, too small in amount, especially if diminished by loss, to hold such a metropolis as London, which Cumberland's and Wade's armies would still be on foot to relieve—if defeated at Finchley, exposed to be totally cut off—but, if desirous to retreat, being still able to retire to Scotland, where Lord Strathallan had from 3000 to 4000 men, with a portion of the Royal Scotch and of the Irish Brigade—under such circumstances, the best course would be, a return to Scotland. In addition to this decision, the "dissatisfaction among the Highland Chiefs," we are told, "renewed in them the belief, that it was of less importance to make conquests in England, than to take measures to secure the independence of Scotland," where, too, they would be recruited. With the utmost reluctance, therefore, or though passionately exclaiming, "*Rather than go back, I would wish to be 20 feet under ground!*" Charles had to acquiesce in retiring to Scotland;* the more so, as Sir Thomas

* "I believe," concludes Lord Mahon, with the best documentary sources at command for forming *his* belief, "that, had Charles marched onward from Derby, he would have gained the British throne." Charles, indeed, *would* have "marched onward." Yet, were *we* circumstanced as his Council were at Derby, or with such a generally alarming aspect of affairs about us, can we say, that we, *too*, would not

Sheridan, General O'Sullivan, and Secretary Murray finally concurred in representing to him, how the army could not be expected to fight well, if all the Chiefs should be acting with unwillingness, as they would be, if *he* ventured to oppose *their* previously-expressed conviction. The retreat was accordingly to take place early the ensuing morning, or that of the 17th. Meanwhile, during the 16th, on which this decision was embraced by their leaders, the soldiery under the influence of very different notions, or those of "a battle, and London!" occupied themselves in corresponding preparations, or putting their weapons into the best fighting order, and receiving the sacrament at Derby. On the 16th, too, partial intelligence of the Scots having occupied Derby reached London. But, on the 17th, when it was universally known there, that the Highlanders had done so; having thus gained the start of the Duke of Cumberland's army towards the metropolis; the panic excited by the news was so great, that it caused the day (the 6th O. S. as then used in England) to be long remembered as "*Black* Friday." According to a satiric, yet not the less credible, rhymer of the period,

"Poor London, alas! was scar'd out of its wits,
With arms, and alarms, as sad soldiers as cits!"—

most of the inhabitants being filled with anxiety for themselves, their money, their connexions, or their friends; numbers fleeing to the country with their valuables; so extensive a run being made upon the Bank of England, that it is said to have only escaped insolvency, by paying its notes in sixpences, to gain time; the greater portion of the shops being closed, and public business generally at a stand. "The trading part of the city, and those concerned in the money corporations," observes Smollett, "were overwhelmed with fear and dejection. They reposed very little confidence in the courage or discipline of their Militia and Volunteers; they had received intelligence, that the French were employed in making preparations, at Dunkirk and Calais, for a descent upon England; they dreaded an insurrection of the Roman Catholics, and other friends of the House of Stuart; and they reflected, that the Highlanders, of whom, by this time, they had conceived a most terrible idea, were within 4 days' march of the capital. Alarmed by these considerations, they prognosticated their own ruin in the approaching revolution; and their countenances exhibited the plainest marks of horror and despair. On the other hand, the Jacobites were elevated to an insolence of hope, which they were at no pains to conceal; while many people, who had no private property to lose, and thought no change would be for the worse, waited the issue of this crisis, with the most calm indifference." Such was the state of the public feeling in London on the very day when the *cause* for so much apprehension there was already removed, by the Jacobite evacuation of Derby.

The retreat of the Highlanders commencing early, or while it was still dark, on the 17th, they did not generally perceive, until daylight, that they were retracing their steps; upon which, their feelings corresponded in bitterness with those of their Prince. "If we had been beaten,"

have voted to retreat, especially as doing so implied a junction with reinforcements, or the considerable corps under Lord Strathallan? When England "was tried, and found wanting," would it not seem the best policy to return to Scotland? Besides, some of the troops from France having landed in Scotland, might not still *more*, if not *all* the rest, be expected to do so there?

exclaims a Scotch officer, "the grief could not have been greater." Another, in reference to their situation at Derby, states—"One thing is certain, never was our Highlanders in higher spirits, notwithstanding their long and fatiguing march; they had, indeed, got good quarters, and plenty of provisions, in their march, and were well paid; so that we judged we were able to fight double our numbers of any troops that could oppose us; and would to God we had pushed on tho' we had been all cutt to pieces, when we were in a condition for fighting, and doing honour to our noble Prince, and the glorious cause we had taken in hand, rather than to have survived, and seen that fatall day of Culloden, when, in want of provisions, money, and rest, we were obligded to turn our backs, and lose all our glory."* The English, also, who had joined the Prince, "*now* saw nothing before them, but the melancholy alternative of exile from their native land, or an unqualified submission to the vengeance of the House of Hanover." The country, moreover, which had been peaceful as the Scots advanced, became hostile as they retired; so much so, in the subsequent course of their march, that a village, for shooting at a Highland patrol, had to be set on fire; the armed inhabitants attempting, in turn, to revenge themselves on the sick, and on the stragglers, "who," as was complained, "could not be kept from going into houses, and committing abuses." The army passed that night at Ashbourn, and, next morning, the 18th, marched, "drums beating, colours flying, and pipers playing," for Leek, where they slept, the entertainment they experienced being generally little to their liking; and when, after entering Macclesfield in the usual military parade, and quartering there on the 19th, they approached Manchester on the 20th, they met with a reception so very different from what it had recently been, that "the Devil had been among the people, they were so altered!" was the common exclamation at such ill-treatment. "The party that came in first, to the number of 40," relates a contemporary, "were pelted by the mob with stones, as they came thro' *Hanging Ditch.* They sat on their horses, with their guns and pistols ready cock'd, and threaten'd to fire, but did not. The Bellman, by order of the Magistrates, had been about the town, the day before, to order all persons to provide pick-axes, &c., to spoil the roads, and then to arm themselves with such weapons as they could get; upon which, 10,000 of the country and town's folks were got together, ready to give the Jacobites an unwelcome reception. However, upon *second* thoughts, the Bellman was again order'd about town, to bid them disperse; and, the same day, Charles and his army came in, and billetted themselves at their old quarters." Bradstreet, the spy, in noticing the treatment of himself, and the Jacobite officers with whom he was associated, mentions an interesting exception to the change of conduct displayed here towards Charles. At "my quarters, near Manchester, this night we were all magnificently entertained by a beautiful lady, whose husband was abroad for some time before. She had the greatest desire to kiss the rebel Prince's hand, and had been promised by 1 of

---

* But, under the great disparity, as regards numbers and condition, between the 2 armies at Culloden, could the vanquished be justly considered to have *lost* glory by their defeat, or the victors to have *gained* glory by their success? Mere success, irrespective of the circumstances under which it has been attained, cannot constitute glory. The forcing of the pass of Thermopylæ by Xerxes was a success on his part, but nothing more than a success; the *glory* being attached to the memory of those, whom he overpowered and killed there.

the gentlemen, that he would introduce her to him next morning. I was of opinion, no Prince, or man, could refuse her his hand, or lips." For such disaffection, however, as had been manifested, the Prince imposed a contribution of £2500, ere he quitted the place, on the 21st; the rabble, as danger disappeared, venturing to annoy his rear by a desultory fire. Ahead, not only of the Duke of Cumberland with his cavalry and 1000 select mounted foot, followed by Sir John Ligonier, and a Brigade or Guards, &c., but likewise so many days in advance of Marshal Wade, that, hopeless of effecting anything with his infantry, he only detached his horse, under Major-General James Oglethorpe, to aid the Duke by forced marches in the pursuit, the Jacobites, whose rear did not leave Manchester till towards 3 in the afternoon, were, notwithstanding frost, snow, and the badness of the road, *all* at Wigan by midnight. The 22nd, as they were quitting Wigan, a Whig zealot, in wait to murder the Prince, fired by mistake at General O'Sullivan, but, fortunately, without effect.

Proceeding, the same day, to Preston, the Scots rested there all the next, or until the 24th; in connexion with which halt, a lady, corresponding from the place, about Prince Charles, his mistress, the famous Jenny Cameron, Sir Thomas Sheridan, and General O'Sullivan, writes— "O'Sullivan, one of the young Pretender's Council, and a very likely fellow, made free with our house, and we were under a necessity to treat him civilly. He returned it obligingly enough. From him, we learned some little anecdotes relating to Jenny Cameron. She is, it seems, the niece of a person of some fashion in the Highlands; and was sent by her uncle, to pay his compliments to the young Pretender," with the troops of that branch of the Camerons, a considerable number of cattle, and other contributions to the Stuart cause. "When," continues the letter, "she appeared before the young Pretender's tent, who received her very gallantly, she jump'd off her horse, and told him, with great frankness, that 'She came, like the Queen of Sheba, to partake of the wisdom of Solomon.' He answered, 'And thou shalt, my dear, partake of all that Solomon is master of.' He took her in his arms, and retired with her into his tent; and they were there some time alone. 'The rest,' Mr. Sullivan says, 'we are to guess!'"* Another English notice, at this time of O'Sullivan, or "a further account (from the *True Patriot*) of the aforesaid Mr. Sullivan, whom the *London Gazette* of the 19th mentions to have care of the artillery,"† after observing, how "the principal person, upon whom the Pretender's son hath depended in this expedition, is Mr. Sullivan, by birth an Irishman, and educated in a Romish College abroad, where he entered into Priest's orders,"‡ concludes a sketch of his life (similar to that previously given) thus—"To the abilities of this man, we may justly attribute the success, with which a handful of banditti have so long been able to overrun and plunder a large part of this opulent and powerful nation." The 24th, about 9 in the morning, the Scots left Preston, for Lancaster, where, (the interven-

* Jenny Cameron, having accompanied the Prince in his march through England, and back again to Scotland, was taken by the enemy, and subsequently retiring to the Continent, died at Ghent, in 1767.

† A mistake, however, for Mr. Grant of the Irish Regiment of Lally.

‡ Such a combination, as this, of a Popish Priest with a Popish Pretender, was "just the thing," to excite the strongest Protestant prejudice in Great Britain, against Prince Charles, among the masses there. But the notion of O'Sullivan's *priesthood* has been already disposed of.

ing distance being about 20 miles) the rear did not arrive till very late. The same day, about 1, Major-General Oglethorpe, with his cavalry despatched from Marshal Wade's army, joined the Duke of Cumberland at Preston, after a march of above 100 miles, in 3 days, over snow and ice! The 25th, Charles halted for the day at Lancaster, appearing to contemplate fighting the enemy; General O'Sullivan, with Lord George Murray, who commanded the rear-guard since the army left Derby, Lochiel, and other Highland officers, going out to reconnoitre the country for a good field of battle, or 1 best suited for the Highlanders as irregulars; a locality of which kind was found, and 2 or 3 of the enemy's mounted Rangers picked up as prisoners, who mentioned the large body of their cavalry that was collected at Preston; so, it being the obvious aim of the Duke of Cumberland to come up with his horse, and detain the Scots, till, by the junction of his infantry to his cavalry, he would possess an overwhelming superiority of force, Charles resumed his retreat, at 8 in the evening, towards Kendal. The 26th, at 8 in the morning, as the last of the Highlanders were quitting Lancaster at one end, Major-General Oglethorpe and his horse entered at the other, with orders, to refresh in the streets, and then pursue. But the receipt of an express from London to the Duke of Cumberland to arrest his advance, also caused Oglethorpe to fall back about 10 miles, to Gartstang. This was owing to "a report," says my authority, "that the French were actually landed in the south; which gain'd such credit, that the Ministry thought proper to advise the Duke of it by an express; who thereupon halted a day, in expectation of further notice. General Oglethorpe was likewise order'd to halt, till he should hear from the Duke. . . . But the coasts of England were so well watch'd and guarded by Admiral Vernon's fleet, that there was no possibility for the French to stir out of their harbours, without a manifest hazard of perishing, or being taken in the attempt. And, therefore, the report of their being landed was current only for a day; of which the Duke had soon notice by another express, and immediately resum'd his pursuit." Of these 2 expresses to the Duke, the one "to halt," the other "to pursue," a contemporary "letter from London" informs us—"The 1st express was owing to an account sent to St. James's, that the French *had* landed in Essex; upon which, the Privy Council was summoned, and agreed to send the above express. But, the next day, the Government had an account, that they were *not* Frenchmen who had landed, but a party of armed smugglers, who were conveying their goods into the country;* upon which, the 2nd express was sent, to pursue the rebels." In doing so from the commencement, or since, as was said, "Fortune turned her face with a smile," the Duke had the great advantage, that "the country people voluntarily supplied *his* army with horses, carriages, provisions, and all other necessaries; while the adventurers could get nothing but what violence forced from the grumbling English, who took *all* methods to distress *them*."

Meanwhile, or on the 26th, Charles, with his troops, artillery, &c., entered Kendal. Here, writes Lord George Murray, "Mr. O'Sullivan

* "The great number of smugglers in England," observes Dr. Tucker, Dean of Gloucester in 1753, "are of infinite detriment to trade. They carry nothing but bullion, or wool, out of the kingdom, and return mostly with the commodities of France. They are the necessary cause of creating many offices, maintaining sloops, smacks, &c., to guard against them."

was at supper with the Prince. He had got some mountain Malaga, which he seemed very fond of, and gave me a glass or 2 of it. There was always a Major, or principal officer of each regiment, for the orders, which were to be copied, for the different corps. It was 11 at night before I left the quarters, and Mr. O'Sullivan had not then wrote them out." That Charles and his agreeable Irish companion should enjoy themselves, whenever they could, between their winter-marches, was but natural.

"To-night, at least, to-night be gay,
Whate'er to-morrow brings."—MOORE.

Nor was their rest long. Between 4 and 5 o'clock next morning, the 27th, the drums beat, and the men, in the order they had entered, marched out* from day-break till near 10, for Penrith, but had to stop for the night at Shap; Major-General Oglethorpe, on the report about the French being contradicted, having continued, during the day, his cavalry pursuit. The 28th, Charles, after several hours' hard marching, came to Penrith; the rear, nevertheless, under Lord George Murray being greatly delayed by the breaking-down of baggage-carts, by the repairing of them, and even by the necessity of having sometimes to go a couple of miles off the road to procure others, as the country-people had put everything they could out of the way. This day Major-General Oglethorpe, the Duke of Cumberland, and their van-guard, entered Kendal, with increased hopes, from the circumstances above-mentioned, of overtaking the Jacobite rear. The 29th, Charles and his main force had still to halt at Penrith for the coming up of the rear; which, having with difficulty reached, and stopped the previous night so far behind as Shap, quitted that place at day-break. The column was headed by Mr. Brown, Colonel *en suite* to the Irish Regiment of Lally, with the 2 companies appointed to precede the artillery; then came the artillery, under the command of Mr. Grant of the same Irish corps, again referred to here as selected to act in that capacity, and as Engineer, from his "great talents;" next came the waggons, with 2 other companies attached to the artillery; the whole being brought up by Lord George Murray in person, with the Highland Regiment of the Macdonalds of Glengarry. The march scarcely commenced when it appeared how much the enemy had been able to gain ground, by a large number of their light horse hovering about, though at a sufficiently cautious distance, or beyond musket-range. On the van of the column reaching, at noon, writes an eye-witness, "the foot of an eminence, which it was necessary to cross in our march to Penrith, about half-way between that town and Shap, the moment we began to ascend, we instantly discovered cavalry, marching 2 and 2 abreast on the top of the hill, who disappeared soon after, as if to form themselves in order of battle, behind the eminence which concealed their numbers from us, with the intention of disputing the passage. We heard, at the same time, a prodigious number of trumpets and kettle-drums. . . . We stopt a moment at the foot of the hill; everybody believing it was the English army, from the great number of trumpets and kettle-drums. In this seemingly desperate conjuncture, we immediately adopted the opinion of Mr. Brown, and

* Does not the circumstance, of the Jacobite troops having evidently been designed to march out of Kendal in the same order they had entered it, sufficiently defend O'Sullivan from the *censure*, in reference to the issuing of orders, apparently aimed at him by Lord George Murray?

resolved to rush upon the enemy sword in hand, and open a passage to our army at Penrith, or perish in the attempt. Thus, without informing Lord George Murray of our resolution, we darted forward, with great swiftness; running up the hill, as fast as our legs could carry us. Lord George, who was in the rear, seeing our manœuvre at the head of the column, and, being unable to pass the waggons, in the deep roads, confined by hedges, in which we then were, immediately ordered the Highlanders to proceed across the inclosure, and ascend the hill from another quarter. They ran so fast, that they reached the summit of the hill, almost as soon as those who were at the head of the column. We were agreeably surprised, when we reached the top, to find, instead of the English army, only 300 light-horse and chasseurs, who immediately fled in disorder. . . . From the great number of trumpets and kettle-drums which the light-horse had with them, there is every reason for supposing, that it was their design, to endeavour to induce us to turn aside from the road to Penrith, by making us believe, that the whole English army was on the hill before us; and, if we had fallen into the snare which was laid for us, in a few hours every man of our detachment would either have been killed, or taken prisoner." This opinion was strengthened by the intelligence subsequently derived from a captured footman of the Duke of Cumberland, who stated, that the Duke, "having given all his trumpeters and kettle-drummers to the light-horse, had hoped, to retard the march of our detachment with the artillery; and, if we had been, in any manner, the dupes of this artifice, we should have been all destroyed; for, in half an hour, the Duke would have got between us and our army, and our communication would thus have been cut off." The detachment of light horse here routed were, in fact, precursors to the great body, or main force, of the English cavalry, about 4000, that emerging (though too late) from the side-road by which they were to have separated Lord George Murray's corps from that of Charles,* as night came on appeared before the village of Clifton.

The Duke of Cumberland, from the mass, whom he kept drawn up in 2 lines at a due distance, ordered 320 of Bland's, Kerr's, and Cobham's dragoons, to dismount, under Lieutenant-Colonel Philip Honeywood, as an attacking party; making a short address to the men ere they advanced, in which he referred to the honourable intrepidity of the English at Dettingen and Fontenoy, and intimated, that he had no doubt of similar conduct being displayed *here*. The detachment of dismounted dragoons, so exhorted and complimented by the Duke, and with such further aid as to appear 500 strong, proceeded to dislodge from its post the Highland rear, then consisting of about 1000 men, under Lord George Murray. But Lord George, with broad-sword and target in hand, shouting the old Highland war-cry, "*Claymore!*" and leading on gallantly, compelled the assailants to betake themselves to their *corps-de-reserve;* he having 17 or 18 men, and his opponents, as they alleged, 40, though probably a much more considerable number, killed and wounded,† including Lieutenant-

* See, in the Chevalier de Johnstone's Memoirs, the engraved plan, entitled, "Skirmish at Clifton Hall, 18th December, 1745. O.S."

† The loss of the dismounted dragoons of the English at Clifton has been published, for their *total* there, as 11 killed, and 29 wounded, or 40 men, including *both*. But, without going beyond English evidence, it is certain the Duke of Cumberland's loss was *not* limited to his dragoons. Thus, in a list of deaths, for July, 1746, I find that of "James Baily of Preston, Lancashire, a Voluntier under the Duke of Cumberland, of wounds received *in the action at Clifton.*" Macpherson of Cluny,

Colonel Honeywood, severely gashed, among the latter. Lord George remarks—" It was lucky I made that stand at Clifton; for, otherwise, the enemy would have been at our heels, and come straight to Penrith; where, after refreshing 2 or 3 hours, they might have come up with us, before we got to Carlisle. I am persuaded, that night and next morning, when the van entered Carlisle, there was above 8 miles from our van to our rear, and mostly an open country, full of commons. I have been the more particular about this little skirmish, because I observed it was very differently related in the English newspapers, as if *we* had been beat from *our* post, at Clifton; whereas I was there, about half an hour after the enemy was gone." And again, affirms his Lordship—" It was half an hour after the skirmish, before we went off. I was the last man *myself.*" Thus, through the resolution of Mr. Brown of the Regiment of Lally and of Lord George Murray, the meditated separation, by the enemy, of the Prince's rear-guard from the rest of his force, was prevented; and his army, in consequence, preserved from the general destruction, which *must* have been the result of the cutting off of 1 portion of it from the other. The Duke of Cumberland slept at Clifton; evincing his uneasiness there, by keeping his troops under arms upon a moor *all* night, although it was very rainy, and although they had marched that day so far, in such weather, and over such roads. For "orders had been communicated by the Duke to the country-people, to break down bridges, destroy the roads, and attempt, by all means in their power, to retard the insurgent army." Yet "while the hardy mountaineers found little inconvenience from either storm in the air, or ruts in the ground, these very circumstances served materially to impede the English dragoons." The Highland rear, after that check given to the enemy at Clifton which secured an unmolested retreat, joined the Prince, at Penrith, whence the entire Scotch force, by about 8 that evening, proceeded for Carlisle, and, after a very wearisome march, arrived there, about 7 next morning, or the 30th. The Duke of Cumberland, on the 30th, did not advance 3 miles, or only from Clifton to Penrith, and he continued there on the 31st; as well to rest his harassed cavalry, as, before venturing on any further operations, to wait for the coming up of his infantry, the last of whom joined him by the morning of the 31st, and were halted for that day and night. The Jacobites stopped from the 30th to the 31st at Carlisle, where, after leaving a garrison of about 400 men, and 10 out of the train of 13 field-pieces, Charles very late on the 31st, marched for the Esk, which separated Scotland from England; his route thither being 7 long miles, as, by the nearer road, the winter had rendered the stream unfordable. In passing the river, says my noble Scotch narrator, "we were 100 men abreast, and it was a very fine show. The water was high, and took most of the men breast-high. When I was near cross the river, I believe there were 2000 men in the water at once. There was nothing seen but their heads and shoulders; but there was no danger, for we had caused try the water, and the ford was good; and Highlanders will pass a water where horses will not, which I have often seen. . . . All the bridges that were thrown down in England, to prevent their advancing in their march forwards, never retarded them a moment." Another Jacobite officer adds—" Fires

in his letter, soon after, from Carlisle, makes the Highland slain or hurt 17 or 18, and, in his Memoirs, computes, that, of the English, "besides those who went off wounded, upwards of 100, at least, were left on the spot." He was present, with his regiment.

were kindled to dry our people as soon as they quitted the water, and the bagpipers having commenced playing, the Highlanders began all to dance, expressing the utmost joy, on seeing their country again!"

Such was the Jacobite march from Scotland to Derby, and from Derby back to Scotland; of which, from the participation of *some* of my countrymen in it, as well as of *others* in support of the cause with which that march was connected, I have given this outline; one, I hope, not among the worst of that remarkable event. It was "an expedition," observes its able Scotch historian, Mr. Chambers, "which, for boldness and address, is entitled to rank with the most celebrated, in either ancient or modern times. It lasted 6 weeks, and was directed through a country decidedly hostile to the adventurers; it was done in the face of 2 armies, each capable of utterly annihilating it; and the weather was such, as to add 1000 personal miseries to the general evils of the campaign. Yet such was the success which will sometimes attend the most desperate case, if conducted with resolution, that, from the moment the inimical country was entered, to that in which it was abandoned, only 40 men were lost out of nearly 5000, by sickness, marauding, or the sword of the enemy. A magnanimity was preserved even in retreat, beyond that of ordinary soldiers; and, instead of flying in wild disorder, a prey to their pursuers, these desultory bands had turned against and smitten the superior army of the enemy, with a vigour which effectually checked it." * The great English historian Gibbon notices the conduct of the English, with respect to this expedition, as, on the contrary, very inglorious. "In the year 1745," says he, "the throne and constitution were attacked by a rebellion, which does not reflect much honour on the national spirit; since *the English friends of the Pretender wanted courage to join his standard, and his enemies, (the bulk of the people,) allowed him to advance into the heart of the kingdom.*" Nay, *worse*, Gibbon might have added of the Whig-Hanoverian mass of his countrymen, since *they*, with such a vast superiority of military numbers on their side, did not prevent the Stuart Prince, and his little Scotch force, getting *out* of the kingdom, after having marched so far *into* it. A published "letter from Chester" in December, 1745, referring to the successful retreat of the Scots, alleges— "'Tis a pity, and, I think, a *disgrace* to us, that they should get away." Which opinion is but too strongly justified by facts. The printed official table, in March, 1745, of every corps of the British army, including officers, specifies the "total in Great Britain, 30,502," the "total in Flanders, 27,998," or *both* as making 58,500 regular troops. The far greater portion of those in Flanders, or as previously stated from Home, all but 2 battalions of infantry, and 4 regiments of cavalry, were ordered over to England, to oppose Prince Charles; and to these regulars, besides 2 foot regiments from the army in Ireland, landed at Chester in October, and above 7200 Dutch, are to be added Militia and Volunteers; so that the Scots, who marched into England with the Prince, did it in opposition to a much larger "grand total" of hostile force, than *historians* have hitherto sought to ascertain, and sum up, with anything like due clearness, for their readers. A London paper, the *Old England Journal*, in November, 1745, notes, of the advance of the Scots into England—"At

* "Many things," remarks Polybius, "which appear to be beyond measure daring, and full of danger, are not less safe in the execution, than admirable in the attempt; and the design itself, as well when frustrated, as when attended with success, will draw after it immortal honour, if it be only conducted with ability, and skill."

present, we are alarm'd, more than ever, by the news of their daring to enter England, at a time, when there are upwards of 60,000 men in arms, within the island, to oppose them!" And another London paper, the *True Patriot*, in December, 1745, referring to the Scotch invasion, specifies it, as occurring "at a time, too, when there are above 60,000 regular troops spread thro' the several parts of this United Kingdom," or England and Scotland, "in defence of the present establishment!" Had not, then, a very great deficiency of military energy been displayed by the English with respect to *this* invasion, surely the mere handful of Scots, who penetrated so far into England unaided, should have been ALL slain or made prisoners *there*, as the comparatively few thousand Greeks, with whom Xenophon, under that *real* "Pretender," the younger Cyrus, marched against Artaxerxes,* should, when they were unsupported by native assistance in the country they invaded, have ALL been destroyed or captured by the Persians. Referring to the dissatisfactory light in which his countrymen too often appeared during *this* war, both abroad and at home, Horace Walpole exclaims—"In short, we are a wretched people, and have seen our best days!" But as Xenophon's fellow-soldiers, victorious where *they* fought at Cunaxa, and so distinguished by their successful march through an enemy's country back again to their own, will ever be glorious to Greece, the memory of Prince Charles Stuart's Highlanders, who

—————————————"fam'd Gladsmuir gain'd,
And circled Derby's cross," &c.,

will always be most honourable to Scotland.

During the rest of the month in which the Prince retreated from Derby, or to the end of December, the apprehension, by the Whig-Hanoverian Government, of a French and Irish landing in England, was undiminished owing to the information received of the preparations carried on in the French ports, aided, as was stated, by constant intelligence there, of what was done in England, conveyed by English smugglers, who were likewise most capable of serving an invasion as pilots. "It is a pity," growls an exasperated Whig-Hanoverian agent, "such pernicious villains cannot be destroyed; their villainous trade is the least thing I think of at this time, for it keeps up, to my certain knowledge, a daily correspondence between England and France; so that, there is not the least thing done or ordered, but the enemy immediately knows it by their means."† When the necessity ceased for an extensive encampment at Finchley Common, the troops not required there were marched away to defend the coasts. Numbers of privateers and small vessels in the Thames were engaged and manned by the Admiralty, to be additionally on the alert against hostile designs from Ostend and Dunkirk. A Proclamation was issued from St. James's, "commanding all Officers,

* See Plutarch's Life of Artaxerxes.
† Down to the present century, the smugglers of England were as injurious to their own Government, as serviceable to that of France. The Emperor Napoleon I. said, at St. Helena, to Dr. O'Meara—"During the war with you, all the intelligence I received from England came through the smugglers. They are terrible people, and have courage and ability to do anything for money. . . . At one time, there were upwards of 500 of them at Dunkerque. I had every information I wanted through them. They brought over newspapers and despatches from the spies that we had in London. They took over spies from France, landed and kept them in their houses for some days, then dispersed them over the country, and brought them back, when wanted."

Civil and Military, to cause the coasts to be carefully watched; and, upon the first approach of the enemy, to direct all horses, oxen, cattle, and other provisions, to be driven and removed 20 miles from the place where the enemy should attempt to land. . . . Signals were ordered to be placed on the Sussex, Kentish and Essex coasts, by hoisting flags in the day, and firing guns in the night; by which means, notice of an invasion would be at the Tower and St. James's Park, in a few hours. All the Life-Guards and Horse-Grenadiers were ordered to be ready at the firing of some guns, which were to be as a signal. Orders were sent by the Lords of the Admiralty to all Commanders of Ships in the river (Thames) not to fire a gun upon any account, that the signal guns might be the more plainly heard, in case of any invasion or insurrection; 3000 foot and 1000 horse were ordered for the coasts of Essex and Suffolk; and 4000 foot and 1500 horse for the coasts of Kent and Sussex, to be ready to oppose any foreign invasion." The state of alarm and vigilance throughout the metropolis corresponded with the extent of the precautionary measures elsewhere. "The Court of Lieutenancy of London resolved, that 2 Regiments of the Trained Bands should be out every night, and 1 in the day-time. The Court of Aldermen ordered an additional number of Constables and Watchmen, to preserve the peace of the city." The Lord Mayor and Court of Lieutenancy likewise announced, that " his Majesty, having directed alarm-posts to be appointed with proper signals for the several guards to march on the first notice of any tumult, or insurrection, in the Cities of London and Westminster, the said signals were to be 7 cannon, 1 fired every half minute from the Tower, to be answered from St. James's Park, and *vice versa;* upon which, every officer and soldier of 6 Regiments of Militia, without waiting for beat of drum, or any further signal, should, immediately on hearing said signals, repair, with arms powder and ball, to their respective places of rendezvous; the Red Regiment on Tower Hill, the Green Regiment in Guildhall Yard, the Yellow Regiment in St. Paul's Churchyard, the White Regiment at the Royal Exchange, the Blue Regiment in Old Fish Street, the Orange Regiment in West-Smithfield. Of the 2 Regiments of the Tower Hamlets under orders, the 1st was to meet on Tower Hill, the 2nd in Sun-Tavern Fields, Shadwell." The money-market was duly affected by these measures. "The stocks," says a Whig letter of the last day of the year, "have been exceedingly low this week, and the Bank itself in danger;" then observing of "the public distress" which existed, "the dread of the French invasion has occasioned this;" and adding, "our political distresses, I assure you, have reduced the town to a state of Presbyterian dulness." The same day, Admiral Vernon, who was in command of 11 ships-of-war mounting 384 guns, besides 15 minor vessels, wrote over to Deal, to warn the people of Kent, to be upon their guard, "the Irish troops being march'd out of Dunkirk towards Calais," so that, he apprehended there might be "a descent from the ports of Calais and Boulogne, and which," he concluded, "I suspect may be attempted at Dungeness," &c. The superiority of naval force on the side of the English preserved their country, indeed, from any such "descent," yet *not* from a considerable commercial loss; for the concentration of their shipping, to prevent the menaced invasion, enabled the French privateers, in the course of November and December, to capture "160 British vessels, valued at £660,000."

In the autumn of 1745, at Avignon, where he had long resided on a pension from the Court of Spain, died the great Irish Tory or High-Church loyalist, and Protestant Jacobite cavalier, James Butler, 13th Earl and 2nd Duke of Ormonde, while success still shone in Britain on the last attempt to restore that dynasty, for which he, like so many of his countrymen of a different faith, had abandoned everything but honour. The Life of the Duke, published in London in 1748, after mentioning this selection of "Avignon for his retreat, where he lived, as if he was no longer one of this world," adds—"His Grace was here, as throughout the whole course of his life, remarkable for his hospitality and beneficence. His doors were open to *all*; but, to an Englishman, his heart, also, without distinction of parties. His charity was so extensive, that he would have *himself* wanted, had not his servants concealed, from his knowledge, numbers, who continually applied to him, for relief. Tho' he was unalterable in his religion, yet he did not think the difference of tenets ought to make him distinguish in his charities. He had Divine Service perform'd in his house, according to the Liturgy of the Church of England, twice every Sunday, and on every Wednesday and Friday morning throughout the year; at which all his Protestant servants were obliged to be present. The Sacrament was administer'd to the family once a quarter, and, for a week before he receiv'd, the late Duke wou'd see nobody, his Chaplain excepted, who was his constant attendant, for that space of time. He never prepared for bed, or went abroad in a morning, till he had withdrawn for an hour to his closet; and, tho' he had publick assemblies twice a week, to divert such melancholy thoughts as must naturally have occurr'd to him, when he reflected on his then situation, and the ingratitude of men, who had risen, even from obscurity, by his countenance and bounty, notwithstanding his complaisance for the company, at these meetings, made him assume a chearful countenance, and endeavour to enliven the conversation, yet was it not difficult to discover, that this was an outside only, owing to his good nature and politeness, as he was sometimes absent; and, from the opinion of a good judge of men, who had the honour to be conversant with the late Duke of Ormonde sometime before his death, I may venture to say, his thoughts, even at *these* times, were more upon heaven than on earth. In October, 1745, he complain'd of a want of appetite; every thing at his table was distasteful to him, and the only thing he seem'd to relish was mutton-broth, after the English manner. He, at length, grew too weak to walk. The Physician who attended him, seeing him in this declining way, propos'd sending for 2 others from Montpelier, which was accordingly done; they arriv'd on a Sunday, the 14th of November, N.S., and, after a consultation of these 3, they concluded on taking some blood from him; and, on the Tuesday following, (the 16th) about 7 o'clock in the evening, the late Duke left this world, 'tis hoped, for a better. On the 18th, his body was embalm'd by 4 Surgeons and the 3 Physicians, and, in the following May, as a bale of goods, brought thro' France to England, lodged in the Jerusalem Chamber, and soon after decently enterr'd in the vault of his ancestors, in King Henry VII.th's Chapel; the Bishop of Rochester, attended by a full Choir, performing the ceremony. He died in the 81st year of his age, after having suffered an exile of upwards of 30 years." The Duke, when about 40, has been described as "of a low stature, but well-shaped, a good mien and address, a fair complexion, and very beautiful face;" and, it is added, "loves, and is beloved by, the ladies;" being considered "the *best*-bred man of his age." He attended William

III. (one of the *worst*-bred men of his age) in all his campaigns;* to whom he was Gentleman of the Bedchamber, Captain of Horse-Guards, and a Lieutenant-General; and, in those campaigns, "his expenses were so great abroad, that, it may be said, he gained more reputation by his generosity, than many Generals have by their armies." His generosity to those taken prisoners with him at the battle of Landen, in 1693, has been previously noticed, with his personal gallantry there. Appointed, after Queen Anne's accession, or in 1702, to command in the Allied expedition against Cadiz, which failed not through his fault, he, on his return, effected, with Sir George Rooke, the important destruction of the French and Spanish plate fleet, at Vigo; and, consequently accompanying the Queen to St. Paul's, for the solemn *Te Deum* to be chanted there, it then "appeared; how much he was the darling of the people, who neglected their Sovereign, and applauded him more, perhaps, than any subject was, on any occasion." Soon after, he was Lord-Lieutenant of Ireland, where, it was observed, "his Court is in greater splendour than ever was known in that kingdom." In 1712, he maintained, (as successor to Marlborough,) the dignity of Commander-in-Chief of the British Forces in Flanders with such unprecedented grandeur, that, when the Flemings went, we are told, to "see the Duke at dinner, they were wonderfully pleased with the sight." One of them "declared, he never saw any thing to come up to it; he had often seen Marshals of France at dinner, but never in half that pomp." The Duke's Deputy-Quarter-Master-General, after relating his having pitched upon a Priest's house, in its owner's absence, for his Grace's quarters, states—"At our return, the Priest was amazed, to see the Duke's kitchen-tents already pitched in his orchard; 30 or 40 cooks, scullions, turnspits, and other servants, busy at their several employments; some spitting all sorts of flesh and fowl in season; others making pies, and tarts; and others making fires, and fixing boilers, and ovens. In short, in less than 3 hours, there was as grand a dinner served up, as if it had come from the markets of London, or Paris. The Priest declared, that, if he had not seen it, he could never have believed, that such a dinner *could* be had in a camp, even for the great *Louis Quatorze*. . . . Then we went to see the dining-tents, in the largest of which was a table of 24 covers, in another a table of 18, and in a third one of 12, all looking into each other, with a fourth for the musick to play, while his Grace was at dinner. The Priest was as much charmed, as surprized, at what he saw. I ask'd him, if he did not think, I had got a good lodger for him? He thank'd me. . . . We staid here about 10 days, his Grace shewing a great deal of respect to the Priest; for he dined and supped with him every day, and often sat with him, when at leisure. The night before the army marched, the Duke made him a handsome present." Of the Duke's principal family residence in his native country, or the Castle of Kilkenny, and his style of living there, an English tourist writes in 1698—"This Castle may properly be called the Elysium of Ireland, and, were not the Duke and Dutchess better principled than to forget Heaven for a perishing glory, they'd little think of mansions hereafter, who have such a Paradise at present to live in."

* A Whig writer, recording William's embarkation, at Gravesand, in May, 1695, for the campaign on the Continent, "attended by the Duke of Ormond, the Earls of Essex and Portland," adds, "and so few others of the nobility, that it reflects on the British name, to have no more of them to mention in history, attending their Sovereign, in the pursuit of true glory," &c.

Respecting that Castle, &c., we learn, by another English tour in Ireland, soon after the Duke's death—" The many offices here shew, what the older inhabitants of the city assured us, that, while this was the residence of that illustrious family, there was no officer wanting here, that is to be met within the Palaces of Sovereign Princes."* The Duke's English town-residence, in St. James's Square, London, (after his Whig-Hanoverian impeachment, and consequent retirement to France,) was sold to Mr. Hacket, an Irish gentleman, for £7,500. His English country-residence, at Richmond, where "il vivoit avec grande magnificence, tenoit table ouverte, et sembloit y avoir levé l'étendard contre le Roi George," was bought, for £6000, for the *Hanoverian* Prince of Wales. The Duke's Irish and English rental, at a period when the greatest estates of the British aristocracy very little exceeded £20,000 a year, was, after his forfeiture, *officially* returned (omitting shillings and pence) as £21,163 per annum. And, how very considerable was the revenue from his public posts, or independent of that from his extensive estates, may be inferred from the terms of his Attainder in 1715, as "*the Most High, Puissant and Noble* Prince,† *James Butler, Duke of Ormonde, Earl of Brecknock, and Baron of Lanthony and Moore-Park, in England—Duke, Marquis and Earl of Ormonde, Earl of Ossory and Carrick, Viscount Thurles, Baron of Dingle and Arklow, in Ireland—Baron of Dingwall in Scotland— Hereditary Lord of Regalities, and Governor of the County Palatine of Tipperary, and of the City, Town, and County of Kilkenny, Hereditary Lord Chief Butler of Ireland—Lord High Constable of England, Lord-Warden and Admiral of the Cinque Ports, and Constable of Dover Castle —Lord-Lieutenant of the County of Somerset—Lord-Lieutenant and Custos Rotulorum of the County of Norfolk, High-Steward of the Cities of Exeter, Bristol, and Westminster, Chancellor of the Universities of Oxford and*

---

* The following anecdote, as illustrating the vast benefit to Kilkenny and its vicinity from the Duke of Ormonde's presence, is given from the authority above-cited, "A Tour through Ireland by 2 English Gentlemen," published in 1748. In mentioning Bennet's-Bridge on the Nore, as 3 miles from Kilkenny, "Near this place," states the work, of the former locality, "the late Duke of Ormond reviewed the army in the year 1704, which will be remembered here, and at Kilkenny, as a particular æra; for I have heard several people say, *I have not seen or done such a thing, since the review at Bennet's-Bridge;* which made me curious in my enquiry. By all accounts, this was one of the finest sights ever seen in the kingdom. The late Duke commanded not only the Military but Civil Power to attend him, with all the ensigns of his high office as Lord Lieutenant of the Kingdom. These preparations drew together the whole nobility and gentry of the nation. Kilkenny and all the neighbouring towns were so crouded, that an old Officer told me, he was obliged to give an English crown nightly for a truss of straw, to lie in the stable of an inn, in the town. The fields were overspread with tents; not meaning those of the army, but for convenience of lodging the multitude, that repaired, from all parts, to be witness of this glorious sight; and, by attendance, added to the splendour. By a moderate judgment, a 5th part of the whole nation were assembled at this meeting. The master of an inn told me, he gained more, those few days of this review, by his beds only, than cleared his rent for 7 years. This very affair," conclude the tourists in reference to Kilkenny, "makes the memory of that great unfortunate man dear to many of the people of this city; and *who* can blame their revering such a benefactor, who made their trade flourish?"

† "Dukes and Marquisses of England," says Higgons, "are styled *Princes.*" In a document of 1712, among the Records of the Ulster King at Arms, Dublin Castle, (for access to which I am indebted to the kindness of Sir Bernard Burke,) the Duke of Ormonde is designated as "*Prince* Palatin of Tipperary." A native Irish Jacobite song, referring, with regret, some years later, to the exile of the Duke, terms him "*Prionnsa* na n-Gaoidheal," that is, "*Prince* of the Gaels," or Irish.

Dublin—Colonel of the 1st Regiment of Foot-Guards and the 1st Regiment of Horse-Guards, Captain-General and Commander-in-Chief of all her Majesty's Forces by Sea and Land throughout the British Dominions, or acting in conjunction with the Allied Powers—one of her Majesty's Most Honourable Privy Council in England and Ireland, Knight Companion of the Most Noble Order of the Garter, and Lord-Lieutenant-General, and General Governor of Ireland." At the time of the Duke's impeachment, with other noblemen of his party, by the Whig-Hanoverian faction in Parliament, even the bitter political animosity of *that* faction was not unmixed with sorrow for the Duke, as such "a noble, generous, and courageous Peer." As Sir Walter Scott justly notes—"*His* fate was peculiarly regretted, for the general voice exculpated *him* from taking any step with a view of selfish aggrandizement. Several of the Whigs themselves, who were disposed to prosecute to the uttermost the mysterious Oxford, and the intriguing Bolingbroke, were inclined to sympathize with the gallant and generous cavalier, who had always professed openly the principles on which he acted." And a writer of opposite politics to those of the Duke, after expressing a like regret for his fall, alleges of him— "He is an Irishman, if there is any such thing in the world; he has been Captain-General of Britain; and the greatest of his enemies will allow, that, as to personal bravery, Cæsar, or Alexander, never had more." Such was the illustrious head of the Jacobite aristocracy of these islands, like another illustrious aristocrat of Athens in her best days, the brave and munificent Cimon; of whose riches, Gorgias, the Leontine, asserted, that "he used them, so as to be honoured on their account;" and whom the poet Cratinus celebrated, as

"Cimon, the best and noblest of the Greeks!
Whose wide-spread bounty vied with that of Heaven!"

The contemporary Continental notice of the Duke's death in the Mercure Historique informs us, that the courier despatched from Avignon to Rome with that intelligence, also brought several documents of the utmost importance, which the Duke had ordered to be delivered, after his decease, to *his* banished Sovereign there. "True to the last!" No one sacrificed so much for the unfortunate House of Stuart, as the lamented James Butler, 13th Earl, and 2nd Duke of Ormonde.*

While, in this eventful year of the overthrow of England and her Allies at Fontenoy, and of the invasion of Britain by Prince Charles Stuart, the expatriated Irish signalized themselves in each field of action, their countrymen, the descendants of the old natives or Gaels of Erin, and the representatives of the later colonial population of Norman or English origin, who, as both Catholics, were subjected to 1 common yoke of religious persecution and political slavery under the last Protestant intruders from Britain, felt, in such a manner as it was but *natural* they should feel, at the reverses which afflicted, and the dangers which alarmed, the Hanoverian dynasty and its supporters, from the advance of French conquest on one side of the Channel, and of Jacobite insurrection on the other. Hence the dread of the local "ascendancy" in Ireland, based on Cromwello-Williamite land-spoliation, Limerick treaty-breaking, and Penal-Code intolerance, that "the Catholics," as their

* My chief authorities, besides those above-named, for the several particulars respecting the Duke of Ormonde, have been Mackey, Dr. King, Drake, Dunton, the Duke of Berwick, Oldmixon, Forman, and Lord Macaulay.

historian observes, "would eagerly seize the opportunity to burst their chains, and retaliate on their persecutors the cruelty and injustice with which they had been treated for half a century." This, however, it would have been too hopeless for the Catholics to attempt, without any weapons for insurrection, in opposition to the dominant Anglo-Protestant oligarchy, by whose law, since the reign of William III., none but Protestants were permitted to possess arms. For the enforcement of that regulation, severe penalties were allotted; information, if not to be procured by the inducement of gain, or reward, might be extorted by fining, imprisonment, the pillory, and whipping; general and periodical, as well as discretionary and occasional, searches were prescribed; and, under these despotic provisions, the largest powers were vested in the lowest magistrates.* The regular troops in Ireland, in the spring of this year, were, indeed, no more than 9,261 infantry and cavalry, officers included; and, even of these, there were 2 regiments of foot despatched to England, not long after the routing of Sir John Cope by Prince Charles. But, so apprehensive were the existing "ascendancy" of Ireland of the fate which menaced them if the House of Hanover should be dethroned and the Stuarts restored, that the regular troops in the country were a mere handful of men, when compared with the large number of colonial Militia, Yeomanry, or Volunteers, that armed in defence of the order of succession derived from the Revolution. Soon after intelligence of the Jacobite insurrection in Scotland arrived in Ireland, a great Protestant Association was formed, and signed throughout the island, in favour of the reigning dynasty. "A Proclamation," says an English contemporary, Ray, "was issued by the Lord Mayor of Dublin, offering a reward of £50,000 for apprehending the *Pretender* and his Eldest Son, or either of them that shall attempt to land in Ireland. Measures were concerted for raising several independent regiments of horse and foot, to be as well train'd and disciplin'd as the regular forces; so that there was quickly rais'd an army of 65,000 men, who were well cloth'd, arm'd, and disciplin'd, and many of them march'd to such places as it was judged they might be of the most service in." The military organization of the Protestants of Ireland was the more extended at this juncture, since, to the quantity of weapons already in their possession as the exclusively-armed class of the country, *their* Parliament voted an addition of 30,000 firelocks and 10,000 broad-swords; and these were augmented by several thousand muskets, sent over from England. The muster, in October, before Lord Chesterfield, of the City of Dublin Militia, will give an idea of the troops thus raised. A metropolitan journal, having premised how "the Militia of this City were reviewed, in St. Stephen's-Green, by his Excellency, the Lord-Lieutenant," adds—"The horse were all very well mounted, made a most noble appearance, and were upwards of 300. The foot, for the

* The Penal Code statute law of Ireland with reference to the possession of arms was, in brief, according to my legal Protestant authority, the Honourable Simon Butler, (son of Lord Mountgarret) a prohibition to *all* persons, *not* Protestants, to use or keep any kind of weapons whatever. And, adds a learned Irish Catholic writer, Dr. Nary, early in the last century, with reference to respectable members of his Church, thus exposed to the insolence of cowardly sectarian upstarts and ruffians—"Many gentlemen, who formerly made a considerable figure in the kingdom, are now-a-days, when they walk with canes, or sticks only, in their hands, insulted by men armed with swords and pistols, who, of late, rose from the very dregs of the people!"

most part cloathed in the uniform of their respective regiments, could not be less than 4000 men, all well armed, and, amongst them, a great number of the most eminent citizens. Such a sight could not fail of inspiring universal joy; and his Excellency was so pleased with it, that he walked on foot from one end of the line to the other; expressing, to the nobility and gentry about him, the highest satisfaction." On the comparative merits of this armed organization of the Protestants in Ireland, and that of a Militia in England under its less military squirearchy, a Mr. Lutwidge of Whitehaven, writing to Hill Wilson, Esq. of Purdy's-Burn in Ireland, from the Duke of Cumberland's camp, in January, 1746, after the recapture of Carlisle, while stigmatizing the previous loss of that place as "shameless," and "the result of fear and faintheartedness" on the part of "the country gentlemen" of the Militia there, observes—"I believe *our* country squires are *not* extraordinary fighters, and it were to be wished, when there is a necessity of raising the Militia, that more care was taken, in considering of proper officers to head them; without which precaution, there is little to be expected from them, as *the course of this rebellion has everywhere shewn*. You, gentlemen in Ireland, are more frequently conversant in the use of arms, and are almost all soldiers by practice; and, were there occasion, I doubt not you would, many of you, do notable service."

Among such of the old or native Irish and Catholics, who, as having retained *any* landed property, had something to lose in a time of public commotion, this period was necessarily one of very great alarm. "During that memorable enterprise," observe the Memoirs of the venerable Charles O'Conor of Belanagare,* with reference to Prince Charles's progress in Great Britain, "Mr. O'Conor, and his friends, thought it advisable, to see each other but seldom. Frequent meetings might give rise to frequent calumny; and suspicion was so much awake, that every thing, but perfect solitude, might be construed into combination. . . . Such, to Mr. O'Conor, the year of the rebellion was. 'Over us,' says he, in a letter to Dr. Dignan, 'there is a storm gathering, which is likely to involve us all indiscriminately in one common calamity. God help us, when it bursts! For my part, I am endeavouring to prepare myself for the worst, and cautioning my friends to do the same. *I have not seen the face of a clergyman these 3 weeks, and I know not what is become of our Bishop.*' . . . It was apprehended, at this time, that the flames of civil war would spread themselves throughout England and *Ireland*, as well as Scotland," and "when our interests and prejudices are deeply concerned, and our passions involved in a contest, it is not easy to be a frigid spectator." But the mass of the old natives of the country, left, as well by landed spoliation, as by religious and political oppression, with too little interest in the existing order of society to modify or restrain their feelings of hatred against it, longed for nothing more ardently than for such a change as might overturn the

* Charles, or to use his Irish name, *Cathal*, O'Conor was the son of Donchadh, or Denis, O'Conor, Esq. of Belanagare, County of Roscommon, 22nd in descent from Teige, surnamed *of the Three Towers*, King of Connaught, deceased in 954, through Turlough O'Conor *the Great*, King of Connaught, and Ard-Righ of Erin, or Monarch of Ireland, for 20 years, deceased in 1156, and through Turlough O'Conor Don, the last inaugurated King of the Irish of Connaught, slain in 1406. But Charles's services to his country, as a patriot, and a scholar, "when all around was drear and dark," reflect more honour upon him, than any line of descent, however ancient, or any property, however ample, could confer.

Cromwello-Williamite monopoly of land and power founded upon the ruin of the plundered and enslaved Catholics; might enable them to take due vengeance on the Whigs, as the establishers of such an unjust system through the Orange Revolution; and might, in fine, reverse that Revolution and all its detested results, by the success of Prince Charles, and consequent acknowledgment of his father as James III. These wishes of the naturally-disaffected majority of the population of Ireland were vigorously expressed by their song-writers, more especially such as wrote in the ancient national, Celtic, or Gaelic tongue; those successors of the Bards keeping a watchful eye on public occurrences at home and abroad, and consoling themselves and their fellow-sufferers with prospects of a 2nd Restoration of the Stuarts'; to be followed by a sort of millennium of enjoyment to the Catholic loyalists of Erin, in recompense for their long-enduring fidelity to the exiled royal family.* The obnoxious ruling race of the upstart "settler," at the expense of the old lords of the soil, was thus denounced:—

> "It makes my grief, my bitter woe,
> To think how lie our nobles low,
> Without sweet music, bards, or lays,
> Without esteem, regard, or praise.
> Oh! my peace of soul is fled,
> I lie outstretch'd, like one half-dead,
> To see our chieftains, old and young,
> Thus trod by *the churls of the dismal tongue!* †
> Oh! who can well refrain from tears,
> Who sees the hosts of a thousand years
> Expell'd from this, their own green isle,
> And bondsmen to the base and vile!"

Again—

> "But oh! my wound, my woe, my grief,
> It is not for myself, or mine—
> My pain, my pang without relief,
> Is noting how our nobles pine.
> Alas for them, and not for me!
> They wander without wealth or fame,
> While clowns and churls of low degree
> Usurp their gold, their lands, their name."

The following lines are a portion of "*A Whack at the Whigs*," to the soul-stirring piper's air known as "*Leather the Wig*." ‡ That is, "Thrash, with all your might, the *Wig*," which, in Irish, is synonymous with *Whig*.

> "Oh heroes of ancient renown!
> Good tidings we gladly bring to you—
> Let not your high courage sink down,
> For Erin has friends who'll cling to you!

---

* For the Jacobitism of the Milesian or Gaelic population of Ireland in the last century, as shown by their popular poets or song-writers, see Mr. O'Daly's 2 interesting collections, "Reliques of Irish Jacobite Poetry," Dublin, 1844, and "Poets and Poetry of Munster," Dublin, 1850-1860. From the able versifications by Mangan of the Gaelic songs in the 1st series of the latter work, *my* extracts are taken.

† The breed of the "settlers" that spoke the English language, and that, in the version of another Gaelic song, are similarly designated, as "*the sullen tribe of the dreary tongue*."

‡ I make a selection and arrangement of the words, and a modification of the chorus, to this tune in Mr. O'Daly's publication, suitable to the mode in which I have heard it played. According to *that* mode, every 4 lines of the words, including the chorus, should be repeated, or given twice, in singing the air.

Those insolent Sassenach bands
　Shall hold their white mansions transiently;
Ours shall again be those lands,
　Long till'd by our fathers anciently!
　　Chorus.—Let us be thrashing, thrashing;
　　　Let us be thrashing the perriwig!
　　Let us be thrashing, thrashing,
　　　Let us be thrashing the perriwig'

" We'll muster our clans, and their lords,
　And with energy great and thunderous,
With lances, and axes, and swords,
　We'll trample the Saxon under us.
We'll have bonfires from Derry to Lene,*
　And the foe shall in flames be weltering—
All Limerick hasn't a green,
　Nor a ship that shall give them sheltering! †
　　Chorus.—Let us be thrashing, &c.

" Up! arm now, young men, for our isle!
　We have here, at hand, the whole crew of 'em,
Let us charge them in haste and in style,
　And we'll dash out the brains of a few of 'em!
A tribe, who can laugh at the jail,
　Have found, on the banks of the Shannon, aid—
Oh! how the blue Whigs will grow pale,
　When they hear our Limerick cannonade! ‡
　　Chorus.—Let us be thrashing, &c.

" Oh! pity the vagabonds' case!
　We'll slaughter, and crush, and batter them—
They'll die of affright in the chase,
　When our valorous Prince shall scatter them!
Coming over the ocean to-day
　Is Charles, that hero dear to us—
His troops will not loiter or stay,
　Till to Inis-Loirc § they come here to us!
　　Chorus.—Let us be thrashing, &c.

" Our camp is protected by Mars,
　And the mighty Fion of the olden time, ‖
These will prosper our troops in the wars,
　And bring back to our isle the golden time!

* From the Lough of Derry in Ulster, or the North, to Lough Lene, or, the Lake of Killarney in Munster, or the South. O'Connell's expression, " from the Giant's Causeway to Cape Clear," was better.
† The author of this song was a native of the County of Limerick.
‡ An allusion to the defeat, at the 1st siege of Limerick, in 1690, of the great champion of the Whig Revolution of 1688, William of Orange.
§ A bardic appellation for Ireland.
‖ Fion, or Fin, son of Cumhal, known as Fin of " the golden hair," that " popular Irish hero," as Moore remarks, has had " a long course of traditional renown in his country, where his fame still lives, not only in legends and songs, but in the yet more indelible record of scenery connected with his memory." He is related to have flourished in the 3rd century, having been son-in-law of the famous Ard-Righ, or Monarch, Cormac, and commander of a standing force, styled the Fians, or Finians, of Erin, " still," notes Dr. O'Donovan, " so vividly remembered in the traditions of the people." In the fine Gaelic poem of " The Chace," so spiritedly versified into English by Miss Brooke, the poet Oisin, or Ossian, as 1 of that celebrated body of warriors, says,

　　　———" to the Finian race
　　A falsehood was unknown;
　No lie, no imputation base,
　　On our clear fame was thrown;

　　But, by firm truth, and manly might
　　　That fame establish'd grew,
　　Where oft, in honourable fight,
　　　Our foes before us flew."

The Finians would appear to have been modelled after the Roman legions, then, and long subsequently, occupying South Britain, which it was the custom of the Gaels of Erin to invade. Of Fion, or Fin, and this force organized by him, the Scotch historian, Pinkerton, observes—" He seems to

> Our cowardly foes will drop dead,
> When the French only point their guns on 'em—
> And Famine, and Slaughter, and Dread,
> Will together come down at once on 'em!
> *Chorus.*—Let us be thrashing, &c."

The sympathy of the Gaels of Erin with their brother Gaels of Alba, or Scotland, for the cause of Prince Charles, is still more vividly expressed in another song, which, after stating—

> "We'll chase from the island the hosts of the Stranger,
> Led on by the conquering Prince of the Gael!"

adds—

> "And you, my poor countrymen, trampled for ages,
> Grasp each of you now his sharp sword in his hand!
> *The war that Prince Charlie so valiantly wages*
> *Is one that will shatter the chains of our land.*
> Hurrah for our Leader! Hurrah for Prince Charlie!
> Give praise to his efforts with music and song;
> Our nobles will now, in the juice of the barley,
> Carouse to his victories all the day long!"*

> "The lads with the dirks, from the hills of the Highlands,
> Are marching with pibroch and shout to the field,
> And Charlie, Prince Charlie, the King of the Islands,
> Will force the usurping old German to yield! . . . .
> We will drive out the Stranger from green-valley'd Erin—
> King George and his crew shall be scarce in the land,
> And the Crown of Three Kingdoms shall HE alone wear in
> The Islands—OUR Prince—the man *born* to command!"

With these extracts before us, (which might be augmented by so many more), what then are we to think of this passage about Ireland, in connexion with Prince Charles's expedition, by a Continental historian of the Prince?—even if the passage did not embody, as it does, such an erroneous notions as that Ireland was "favoured," and that her "agriculture and manufactures flourished" in those times, when, and long after, English jealousy was so mischievously careful that they should *not* flourish! † "There was no part of the British islands," says this writer, "where there was less prospect for the Stuarts than in Ireland. That

---

have been a man of great talents for the age, and of celebrity in arms. His formation of a regular standing army, trained to war, in which all the Irish accounts agree, seems to have been a rude imitation of the Roman legions in Britain. The idea, though simple enough, shews prudence; for such a force alone could have coped with the Romans, had they invaded Ireland." Honest Dr. Keating, from the native authorities, states, how, whenever it was requisite to dispatch forces to Alba, or Caledonia, in order to support the Dalriadic settlement from Erin there against the Almhuraigh, i. e., *foreigners*, (or Romans,) 7 catha, containing 21,000 men, were under the hero's command; and, it is added, the Finians must have been frequently in Alba, since their names are hardly less associated with recollections of the "olden time" there, than in Erin. The death of Fin, "superior to all warriors in war," is recorded to have occurred in Midhe, or Meath, A.D. 284. It was *he* whom *Ossian* Macpherson has metamorphosed into Fingal.

* "On sait," observes Voltaire, "de quelle importance il est en Angleterre de boire à la santé d'un Prince qui prétend au trône; c'est se déclarer son partisan. Il en a coûté cher à plus d'un Écossais et d'un Irlandais pour avoir bu à la santé des Stuarts."

† To the admissions already cited on this point, I need only add *here* that of Mr. Pitt, addressing the British Parliament, February 22nd, 1785. "The species of policy, which had been exercised by the government of England, in regard to Ireland, had, for its object, to debar the latter from the enjoyment of its own resources, and to make her completely subservient to the opulence and interests of England. She had not been suffered to share in the bounties of nature, or the industry of her citizens; and she was shut out from every species of commerce, and restrained from sending the produce of her soil to foreign markets."

2 E

fertile land had been much more favoured than Scotland. Agriculture and manufactures flourished; and the general wish which seemed to prevail among all classes, that tranquillity might be maintained, overbore any friendly feeling that still might linger among the people for the descendants of James II. In Ireland, therefore, Charles had no prospect of active support." This last statement is only so far true, that, owing to the existence of such a large amount of hostile or Whig-Hanoverian armed force in Ireland, and to the Catholics having been all disarmed, as well as destitute of any *Highland* advantage for organizing without being immediately overpowered, the Prince, under such circumstances, certainly could not have landed, or hoped to land, in Ireland, with the effect that attended his landing in Scotland. But it appears by no means true, that, had he disembarked in Ireland with anything like due supplies for standing his ground at first, he would have "had *no* prospect of active support." The contrary, by the specimens I have given of the popular sentiment in his favour, has been sufficiently *shown*, and, I may add, the existence and general prevalence of that sentiment was, in Rome, well *known*. The dominant Orange authority in Ireland, at this period, might impose, within the immediate sphere of its observation, an "outward and visible" appearance of submission to the anti-national order of things which it represented. But, to that order of things, from its radical rottenness, or foundation upon injustice and persecution towards the nation at large, there could be no real, or "inward and spiritual," obedience on the part of the MANY, as enslaved by the *few*. The feeling of the country internally, however disguised externally, cannot be better typified than by the contemporary anecdote told of the accomplished Whig-Hanoverian Viceroy of the day, Lord Chesterfield, and a celebrated Irish Catholic, or Tory and Jacobite, beauty. This lady, Miss Ambrose, subsequently Lady Palmer, who, from her charms, was designated the "dangerous Papist," having appeared at the Castle, wearing orange, which was then the necessary etiquette, his Lordship, as he approached her, exclaimed—

"Tell me, Ambrose, where's the jest
Of wearing orange on the breast,
When, underneath, that bosom shows
The whiteness of the rebel rose?" *

An allusion to the flower, which, on every anniversary of the birth of James II.'s son, as Prince of Wales, at St. James's Palace, London, in June, 1688, the Tories or Jacobites used to wear in honour of that Prince, as *de jure*, though not *de facto* KING James III. of England and Ireland, and James VIII. of Scotland. Throughout Ireland, the Orange lily, indeed, might be presented to the eye; but the white rose bloomed, with the shamrock, in the heart of the country.

* Early in this century, my father residing at No. 38, (now No. 39) Upper Gloucester Street, Dublin, where I was born, had, for his neighbours, 2 worthy old ladies, the Misses Archbold. They were of the respectable Catholic family in the County of Kildare, whose head, in the Penal Code times, owned the Paudreen mare, so famous upon the Curragh; but which he was obliged to run there in the name of an honourable Protestant friend, lest, as the law then stood, the valuable animal, if acknowledged to be a Papist's, might, by some scoundrel, calling himself a Protestant, be made *his* property for £5 5s. 0d.! By the Misses Archbold, who were cousins-german to Lady Palmer, my mother was introduced to that once "dangerous Papist," then extremely advanced in life, and was subsequently visited by her. On *such* authority, the Viceregal compliment in verse is correctly given here, instead of incorrectly as elsewhere.

HISTORY OF THE IRISH BRIGADES

IN

THE SERVICE OF FRANCE.

BOOK VIII.

EARLY in January, 1746, the Duke of Cumberland, having united and rested his troops, proceeded to reduce Carlisle. Against such a considerable force and overwhelming artillery as his, the Jacobites there could only make such a defence as was sufficiently creditable to them, when contrasted with the conduct of the previous Anglo-Whig garrison, so much stronger, yet surrendering, as they did, to an enemy without *any* siege-train. "The Duke," notes a Whig contemporary respecting Carlisle, "was long enough before it, to prove *how basely, or cowardly, it was yielded to the rebel.*" By the 10th, the besieging cannon and mortars had such an effect upon the place, that the Scotch Jacobite Governor, John Hamilton, lest his little band should "be all massacred, as they certainly would, if they stood the storming of the town," surrendered, on the terms, for himself and his men, of not being put to the sword, but reserved for George's *pleasure;* at the same time, requesting from the *clemency* of the Duke, that he would be pleased to interpose for them with his father. But the veteran English Colonel, Townley, who had volunteered, with his Manchester Jacobites, to form a portion of the garrison, was, in opposition to Hamilton, for holding out to the last; or for perishing, sword in hand, rather than trust to the *pleasure* of the Hanoverian, or the *clemency* of his son. And the doom to which the Colonel, and the officers taken with him, were consigned the following August—that of being "hanged, drawn, and quartered," on Kennington Common —too well justified his repugnance to submit to such *pleasure* and *clemency.* With the Jacobite garrison of Carlisle—consisting, at its surrender, of but 396 of *all* ranks, or 274 Scotch, 114 English, and 8 natives of different places in the service of France—was a gentleman of Toulouse of old Irish origin, the Chevalier François de Geoghegan, (or Sir Francis Mac Geoghegan,) Captain in the Irish Regiment of Lally, and commander of artillery in the town. While the place still held out, this officer of the Irish Brigade sent 2 letters, 1 to the Duke of Cumberland, and the other for the officer in command of the Dutch troops, to demand, that, since these troops were bound, by their recent capitulations at Tournay and Dendermonde, to abstain from "any military function of what nature soever," until January 1st, 1747, they should serve no longer with the English. To that application with reference to the "perjured Dutch"—as I elsewhere find them designated, for coming over to fight for George II., under *such* circumstances,—the Duke sent this reply, in writing, by his Aide-de-Camp, Lord Bury. "To let the French officer know, if there is one in the town, that there are no Dutch troops here, but enough of the King's, to chastise the rebels, and those who dare to give them any assistance." On which swaggering reply, in connexion with its affected ignoring of Dutch aid, the Carlisle historian, Mr. Mounsey, observes—"This message contains a denial very unworthy of the Duke—*viz.*, that there *were* Dutch troops"—it "being a notorious fact, that, although there might be none at his quarters, nor yet in the army which he had brought with him, yet 1000 Dutch *had* arrived from Wade's army, and were actually shelling the town, from their works at Stanwix Bank, which the Duke had visited and inspected, 4 days before!" Shortly after the Duke had taken possession of Carlisle, "an express arriv'd, that was dispatch'd to him from Court, intimating, that the French were making vast preparations, and that a prodigious number of transports were lying in their harbours, ready to take on board the troops destin'd for the invasion; and therefore it was judg'd necessary to send for his Highness, in order to head the forces that were to oppose the French, in case they should think fit to proceed in their intended enterprise." The Duke, by the 15th, was consequently on the road for London, after appointing, as at once "his favourite General and Executioner" for Scotland, that most brutal, self-sufficient, and cruel specimen of an English military ruffian, Lieutenant-General Henry Hawley. Of this fellow, according to my authorities, "one of the first measures, on arriving at Edinburgh to take the chief command, was, to order 2 gibbets to be erected, ready for the rebels, who, he hoped, might fall into his hands; and, with a similar view, he bid several executioners attend his army on its march," against those whom he spoke of as "Highland rabble." In fine, we are likewise informed, that the common sarcastic saying, among his own soldiers, was—"He confers more frequently with his *hangmen* than with any *other* of his *Aides-de-Camp!*"

The leading ports whence the hostile embarkations for England were designed to take place were Boulogne and Calais, about which the forces for the invasion, including the Irish and Scotch regiments in Louis's service, were encamped; Prince Charles's brother, Prince Henry, Duke of York, with several noblemen and cavaliers exiled for their loyalty to the old royal family, being prepared to accompany the troops. The Irish Brigade, under the Lieutenant-General Lord Clare, and Earl of Thomond, were particularly animated by the prospect of getting over to Kent, and of the English being so rich, that every man of the corps might make his fortune by plunder. The run across the Channel was to be attempted by moonlight, but was frustrated, partly by the unfavourable state of the wind, and partly by Admiral Vernon's lying off Dungeness, with such a number of men-of-war as to prevent a landing. The notice of such an attempt from France, accompanied by the intelligence which the English Admiral received and communicated as to the march of the Irish towards Calais, occasioned, in the beginning of January, measures of precaution in Kent on the part of the Deputy-Lieutenants of the County; all who would defend their country being summoned to appear, on the 2nd, as well mounted and armed as possible with 2 days' provision, at Swinfield-Minnis, about 3 miles from Dover. The vigilant apprehension and superior naval strength with which the coast of England continued to be guarded by Vernon's successor, Admiral Martin, and the retreat of Prince Charles into Scotland, rendering it necessary that landings should be attempted for the future *there*, Dunkirk and Ostend, instead of Boulogne and Calais, became the sites for arrangements to succour the Prince, corresponding with the change of his position. Annoyed, however, at the unprogressive nature of his command, and likewise in ill health, the Duke de Richelieu demanded his recall, leaving subsequent measures for the aid of Prince Charles to be carried out principally by the devotion of the Irish, but more especially by the spirit of the gallant and indefatigable Lally, who is alluded to as distinguished by a zeal and a boldness suited to the achievement of the greatest enterprises. With a view to landing in Scotland, upon the earliest opportunity that might arise, the remainder, or by far the larger portion of the Irish Horse Regiment of Fitz-James and several great officers of the Brigade, of the houses of Fitz-James, Tyrconnell, Roth, Nugent, &c., were, with Lally's own Regiment of Infantry, to be kept in special readiness to sail. Meanwhile, to try whether something favourable to the Prince might not be effected in England itself, Lally, in spite of the numerous and watchful vessels of the enemy, managed to cross from Boulogne to Sussex in disguise; though not without the circumstance becoming known to the Anglo-Hanoverian officials, it being thus announced in a letter from on board the *Weasel* sloop, in the Downs —"Col. Lalley went over to England in a smuggling boat, dress'd in a sailor's habit, where I hope he will meet with his deserts." His plans for creating a diversion there were based on the connexion kept up from France with the smugglers, who, notwithstanding the war, and their calling being made so great an offence by Parliament, were both numerous and daring; 1 body of them, for example, about Hastings, estimated at above 300, domineering at the expense of the farmers in those parts. Among these bold "free-traders" contrary to law, Lally exerted himself to form a corps, entitled " Prince Charles's Volunteers," till a regular force was despatched against them, which caused them to disperse at the time; several of them, nevertheless, openly appearing, as late as the following March, under the Jacobite designation which they had previously assumed. "You," complains a letter from Hastings in that month, "will be surprised at the violences of some of the principal smugglers who appear sometimes in these parts, but live near London. They have the assurance to wear a uniform—*viz.*, the coat and breeches red, lined with the same colour, buttons and holes of gold; the waist-coat blue, buttons and holes of silver; and insolently call themselves *Prince Charles's Volunteers."* From the scene of this organization, Lally proceeded to London. There a price was placed upon his head, and the government-agents having discovered his place of abode, were actually approaching to arrest him, when he had the good luck to escape them, disguised as a sailor. Meeting, in his flight, some smugglers, to whom he was personally unknown, and who were in want of a sailor, they enrolled him among their crew by force. He had not gone far with this gang, when 1 of them suggested, what a good thing it would be, to keep on the look-out for that Brigadier-General Lally, for whom, if caught, they would be so well rewarded! From this, Lally, with due presence of mind, dissented; alleging how much more they were likely to realize on the coasts of France; with which, he added, how perfectly he was acquainted. They embarked accordingly with him as their guide, and he so directed the vessel that it might fall as soon as possible into the hands of the French, and be conveyed to Boulogne; where the Marquis d'Avary, and the Marquis de Crillon, commanding in the province, and then in the town, joyfully released their adventurous friend and comrade-in-arms from the strange enrolment to which he had been subjected. So much for Lally's adventures in England;* which country, although so extensively alarmed at the end of December and commencement of January by the preparations that menaced her coasts from France, had less and less cause, as January advanced, to be apprehensive of a French landing. For, as Horace Walpole observed, "we have a vast fleet at sea; and the main body of the Duke's army is coming down to the coast to prevent their landing, if they should slip our ships. Indeed, I can't believe they will attempt coming, as they must hear of the destruction of the rebels in England; but they will, probably, dribble away to Scotland, where the war may last considerably." And the result justified Walpole's anticipation, as he was able to add, with reference to England, ere the conclusion of January, "the French invasion is laid aside"—Fitz-James's horse at Ostend, and Lally's infantry at Dunkirk, being only embarked, with reference, as already noted, to a landing in Scotland.

Meantime, or after recrossing the border into Scotland on the last day of 1745, Prince Charles proceeded, in the direction of Dumfries, towards Glasgow. January 3rd he passed the night at Drumlanrig, the seat of that James Douglas, 2nd Duke of Queensbury, of execrated memory among the Jacobite or old national party in Scotland; since, though his family owed its Dukedom and a large fortune to the Stuarts, yet he was the first to go over to the Prince of Orange at the Revolution; was thenceforward among the most inveterate enemies of the exiled royal race; and finally rendered himself even still more obnoxious, by taking the leading part he did, in carrying the Union. The portraits of William, Mary, and Anne, presented to him for his "Union" services, were placed on the grand staircase at Drumlanrig; the sight of which, as no better, in Jacobite eyes, than the likenesses of so many *usurpers*, or infringers upon the direct line of succession, and the cause for the presentation of such gifts to him, were *both* so offensive to the Highlanders, that, ere they departed, they displayed the irritation of their dynastic and national feeling, by slashing those paintings with their swords—"an outrage," yet "*not*," as remarked, "one of a very serious nature, when the popular indignation against the Duke is taken into consideration."† The Prince entered Glasgow, with his rear-guard, on the 6th, and he remained there about 8 days, having, in the course of his westward march, and particularly during his stay in that city, refitted his harassed troops for new exertions, by proportionable requisitions from those Whig districts, which had evinced an inveterate spirit of Hanoverian hostility to his cause; a spirit connected, in some localities, with insulting provocations or acts of violence, and, even at Glasgow, with the aggravating circumstances, of a regiment (then

* Lally, amongst *other* adventures apocryphally or traditionally attributed to him, is said to have been at the head of the Irish piquets in the battle of Falkirk, an assertion, simply refuted by the circumstance, of Brigadier Stapleton having commanded those piquets there and elsewhere in Scotland, or from first to last, in that country. Klose has fallen into *this* error with respect to Lally, whom I have tracked, in England, through the magazine and newspaper press.

† Lockhart of Carnwath, after referring to this Duke, as altogether void of honour, loyalty, justice, religion, terms him, "an ungrateful deserter and rebel to his Prince, the ruin and bane of his country, and the aversion of all loyal and true Scotsmen."

absent) having been raised against him, and of an attempt being made there, as previously at Wigan, in England, to assassinate him. Yet here, as elsewhere, the magnanimity of Charles appears to have left the guilty altogether unpunished!* This last effort of a murderous fanatic to pistol him was, no doubt, more or less owing to the fact at Glasgow, that "the Presbyterian clergy, one and all, declaimed against him, from their pulpits, with indomitable zeal," alleges his German biographer, " one of them going so far as to declare, that all the marks of the Beast, mentioned in the Revelations, might be traced in the mild and amiable features of the Prince!"† The Presbyterian clergy of Scotland were generally hostile to Charles in 1745-6; so much so, that some of them did not confine their Hanoverianism merely to the "moral force" of preaching, but resorted to "physical force," in the capacity of armed Georgeite Volunteers. In thus opposing the Prince, they had, as previously at the Union, a due professional eye to self-interest, under the designation of, says a Scotch writer, "*Christ's* cause, the epithet they gave their *own!*"

On the 14th, Charles quitted Glasgow, in order to reduce Stirling, which, as fortified and garrisoned by his opponents, to command the chief pass from the Highlands to the Lowlands, prevented a suitable communication between the 2 main or southern and northern divisions of the Jacobite forces, and, if taken, would thus be a very useful as well as creditable conquest. The Governor of Stirling Castle, with a garrison of 600 men, was an Irish Protestant officer, Major-General William Blakeney. He was a County-Limerick gentleman; the place of his birth and family-seat being Mount Blakeney, about a mile from the Borough of Kilmallock, which he, for many years, represented in Parliament. A veteran survivor of William's and Marlborough's wars in Flanders, he was now above 75; but in that period of "a green old age," united with such a knowledge of the military profession, especially as a garrison-commander, that, even 10 years later, or when above 85, his conduct in the defence of Fort St. Philip, at Minorca, against the French, gained him the highest

* With Prince Charles's conduct on these occasions, contrast that with respect to the Duke of Cumberland, mentioned in this extract of a letter from Kilmarnock, in February, 1746—"One John Riddle, horse-hirer at Edinburgh, was taken at Stirling. He had offered 3 guineas to see the Duke of Cumberland, in order to shoot him, and he was *hanged immediately!*" Or, although he is *not* stated to have actually *fired* at the Duke.

† There was *no* act of Charles, during his expedition in Great Britain, indicative of *any* religious illiberality, or intolerance, on his part. Nor has his private correspondence been found to evince any feelings of the kind, but the contrary. Thus, in writing to his father, from Perth, in September, 1745, and alluding to the efforts that would be made to frighten several against a "restoration," on the plea that the old church and abbey lands in their possession would then be resumed, he repudiates such policy, observing—"You have lived too long in a Catholic country, and read the history of England too carefully, not to have observed the many melancholy monuments to be seen there of the folly of those pious Princes, who, thinking to honour religion, have lessened it, by keeping superstitious rites in the Church, whereby they have insensibly raised up a power, which has, too often, proved an overmatch for their successors." And he adds—"I cannot close this letter without doing justice to your Majesty's Protestant subjects, who, I find, are as zealous in your cause as the Roman Catholics," &c. But, in reference to the vile outcry of *vulgar* sectarianism against Charles, I may remark, that a bigot cannot conceive an existence without bigotry; the pole-cat of religious prejudice cannot imagine *how* others can be without a rankness and a rancour equal to his own.

renown at home and abroad, and elevated him to the Peerage. A remarkable circumstance, at such a very advanced time of life!—and his behaviour at Stirling was worthy of that elsewhere. Between the 15th and 21st, Charles, having intimidated the burgher garrison of the town of Stirling, (then containing from 4000 to 5000 inhabitants,) to give up the place without fighting, and being joined by the native northern levies under Lords Strathallan and Lewis Gordon, as well as by Brigadier Walter Stapleton's and Lord John Drummond's piquets of Irish and Scotch regulars in the French service, with battering-guns, &c., from the Continent, the entire Stuart force consisted of about 9200 men, and operations to reduce Stirling Castle were undertaken, after summoning the veteran Irish Governor to surrender. His reply was, "he would defend his post to the last, determined to die, as he had lived, a man of honour;" and his defence was such as to prevent any effective progress by the Jacobites towards a reduction of the Castle, ere what was considered a sufficient Anglo-Whig army to raise the siege, having been collected about Edinburgh, was on its march for that purpose, under Lieutenant-General Hawley. Upon this, Charles, leaving the Duke of Perth and Gordon of Glenbucket, with about 1200 men, to watch the Castle, advanced to meet and engage the English Commander.

The Prince's fighting force—of whom the Highland clansmen, and the Irish and Scotch from France, were, as contrasted with the Lowlanders, the choicer portion—amounted to about 8000 men. Hawley's army—whose infantry included 12 old regiments of the line, most of which had served abroad, and 2 of newly-levied local or Argyleshire and Glasgow Militia, with several English and other Volunteers, and whose cavalry consisted of 3 regiments of dragoons, were above 8000, if not about 9000, in number.* The 27th, Charles advanced to Bannockburn, to give the English, if they wished, a meeting there, as on "a field," he observed, "of happy augury to *his* arms!" But, finding they did not stir, from their camp near Falkirk, to fight him, he proceeded, the 28th, to bring them to action. His march was so directed, that he had, at the back of his troops, a violent storm of wind and rain, which, by blowing and splashing in the faces of his opponents, would proportionably confuse their sight, and render their musketry mostly useless, from the effects of the wet on their powder; and the locality of the combat was also such, that, although the movement he made, to bring it on, obliged him to leave *his* artillery behind him, the enemy had to do the same with *theirs*. Hawley, "who had boasted, that with 2 regiments of dragoons, he would drive the rebel army from one end of the kingdom to the other!" began the battle on his left, by ordering that Colonel Francis Ligonier, commanding there with 3 regiments of dragoons, or his own, (late Gardiner's,) Hamilton's, and Cobham's, should charge the Highlanders of the Prince's right, under Lord George Murray. "As we came within pistol-shot," relates 1 of the Mac Donald officers there, "the dragoons made up to us at full trot, thinking to bear us down by their weight, and break us at once; and, indeed, being well mounted and accouterd, they made a glorious show, sufficient to have struck other hearts than ours with a pannick." But this "glorious show" too soon became a very inglorious

* Hawley, according to 1 of the contemporary Georgeite accounts of the action at Falkirk in the Marchmont Papers, had 12 regiments of foot, 3 of dragoons, 1200 Campbells, 1000 other Volunteers—"in all about 9000."

one. For, with the creditable exception of a single troop, under Lieutenant-Colonel Shuckburgh Whitney, who was speedily shot dead, and his followers put *hors de combat*, Ligonier's and Hamilton's heroes, after their manner of signalizing themselves at Preston-Pans, wheeled about, and galloped off, amidst cries of "We shall all be massacred this day!" as they partly ran over, and partly suffered from the avenging musketry of, their maltreated and indignant reserve of foot,* that were thrown into irretrievable disorder. Cobham's dragoons, who behaved better, likewise fled; to betake themselves, however, to another part of the field, where they might be more useful, acting with *soldiers* than with such *poltroons;* some of whom did not pull bridle until they got near Linlithgow, about 8 miles from the engagement; while others prolonged their flight by a ride of about 24 miles in 5 hours; or until towards 9, that wet and stormy night, they reached Edinburgh, with alarming statements of what they *had* seen, and sundry additions with respect to what they had *not* seen, as usual on such miserable occasions. The infantry of the centre, under Hawley himself, consequently uncovered on its left flank, and unable in front, from the wind and rain, to make such a fire as could avert the dreaded close of the Highland broad-sword, was next, for the most part, rapidly broken, and driven away in confusion. But Major-General John Huske, who commanded Hawley's right, having his own infantry protected by a ravine, and being supported by some of Hawley's infantry and Cobham's dragoons, checked by a flanking fire the Highland pursuit of the mass of the beaten centre, and was, moreover, so successful in front, with his musketry across the ravine, against the Camerons and Stuarts on the Jacobite left, which he outwinged, that those clans had to give ground; while, of the Lowlanders with them, (the majority there being Lowlanders,) numbers ran off, as believing the battle lost on their side. †
At that critical juncture, Charles, from the rear of his centre, where, for the best view of the field, he was posted with his own mounted Guards, and the contingent from Fitz-James's Regiment of Irish Horse, and where he had the foot, as well as horse, of the regulars from France sufficiently at hand for action, hastened forward to the left, in order to regain the fortune of the day. These regulars, under Brigadier Walter Stapleton, consisted of the piquets from the Irish Brigade, or between horse and foot, about 350 men, that united with about 150 men, of Lord John Drummond's Royal Scots in the same service, would form, in all, about 500 men; whose gallant and orderly advance here, described by Haddock, an Irish soldier present, as that of those "who *only* kept in a body," contributed so much to rectify what was previously amiss, by reinforcing the Camerons and Stuarts in front, and, with other battalions from the 2nd

---

* Hamilton's regiment was more particularly noticed, to its disgrace, by the publications of the day. A letter on the battle says—"Hamilton's dragoons, to retrieve the honour they lost at Preston-Pans, went on like furies. But their courage soon cooled, and they, as usual, *turned tail;* wherefore their horses *suffered most in their buttocks from the balls.* By their confused retreat, the Royal Scotch Regiment of Foot suffered not a little," and, in consequence, "having received orders, fired after them!" Another account informs us, how, when Hamilton's cravens bore back upon the Glasgow Regiment of Militia, it made such an effectual discharge upon the mounted cowards, as "brought several from their horses!" A newspaper paragraph from London in February also states—"We hear the Court Martial at Edinburgh has already *sentenced* 2 *Captains,* 1 *Lieutenant, and* 6 *private men of Hamilton's regiment to be shot, for cowardice, in the late action.*"

"Part of the King's army, much the greater part," remarks Home, "was flying to the eastward; and part of the rebel army was flying to the westward."

line, extending the front, till then outlined by the enemy, that this movement, adds my English writer, Mr. Jesse, "turned the scale in favour of the Highlanders." A Scotch authority, the Chevalier de Johnstone, referring, in terms of especial admiration, to the conduct of "the Irish piquets" on this occasion, mentions them, as "these piquets, who *behaved with the most distinguished bravery and intrepidity at the battle of Falkirk, preserving always the best order, when the whole of the rest of our army was dispersed, and keeping the enemy in check by the bold countenance which they displayed!*" * The change, in short, effected by the coming up of Charles with this reserve was such, that Huske, too, quitted the field; yet, with his men, on the whole, in good order. The beaten Georgeites, fearful of being cut off from Edinburgh, abandoned their camp at Falkirk, retiring that night to Linlithgow; and they continued their dreary and mortifying retreat until about 4 o'clock next day, when they re-entered the Scottish metropolis, in a plight very different from the state in which they had so recently quitted it! There, "at no time from the beginning to the end of the rebellion," says the Scotch Whig, Home, "were the real friends of the constitution of their country more dejected, or more apprehensive, than they were, when they saw the troops return from Falkirk, who had marched against the rebels, a few days before, as *they* thought, to *certain victory!*" Which reflection, he remarks, was the sadder, as the men defeated there were, not "raw soldiers," but "the veteran troops of Britain, who had fought the battles of Dettingen and Fontenoy!" The English Whig, Horace Walpole, having alleged of Hawley's force of 17 regiments at Falkirk, "*we had scarce 3 regiments that behaved well,*" exclaims, "with many other glories, *the English courage seems gone too!*"—and he then observes, "the ill behaviour of the soldiers lays a double obligation on the officers, to set them examples of running on danger."

By this affair at Falkirk, of not above 20 minutes' duration, the Georgeites lost 10 pieces of artillery, or 7 cannon and 3 mortars,† 2 pair of colours, 3 standards, 1 pair of kettle-drums, 25 waggons of all sorts of

---

* Haddock, the Irish soldier referred to as *at* the battle of Falkirk, was born in Dublin, where his father was 1 of the Clerks in the Court of Chancery. Made prisoner at Fontenoy by the French, he joined the Regiment of Lally, with the detachment from which to Scotland, in the autumn of '45, he arrived there. After the affair of Falkirk, getting back to Ireland, *viâ* Belfast, and being taken up, he gave useful information to Government. It is more creditable to Mr. Jesse to have *admitted* the honourable share of the piquets from France in gaining the battle, than for Sir Walter Scott, Lord Mahon, and Mr. Chambers *not* to have duly noticed a fact so evident from Smollet, Voltaire, Home, Johnstone,—to say nothing of Haddock's statement, and the allusion, *not to be mistaken*, in the passage hereafter cited, from Lord George Murray.

† Captain Cunningham of Hawley's artillery "was tried for deserting the train in the action at Falkirk," says my English authority, and "he was sentenc'd to have his sword broke over his head by the Provost, his sash thrown on the ground, and himself turn'd out of the army; which was executed accordingly, at the head of the artillery." After remarking, how, the day following the action, the storm and rain continued, so as to keep all under cover, the Chevalier de Johnstone writes, in connexion with the captured Georgeite artillery,—"Having repaired to the Prince's quarters, about 7 o'clock in the evening, I found no one in his anti-chamber; but, when I was about to withdraw, Mr. Sullivan issued from the Prince's closet, and informed me, that, from the badness of the weather, the cannon, taken from the enemy, had to be left on the field of battle, without any guard; and he requested me, to go instantly, with a guard of a Sergeant and 20 men, and pass the night beside them. He added, that I should find the guard below, ready to march. I set out with this detachment."

military stores, 600 muskets, 4000 pounds' weight of gunpowder, all the baggage, and the tents they could not burn, the latter enumerated as sufficient for 4700 men; and, instead of but 280 of every rank, for killed, wounded, and missing, as officially alleged, are more credibly referred to by other authority, on their own side, as having had 16 officers, including 1 Colonel and 3 Lieutenant-Colonels killed, and from 300 to 400 privates; besides 500 made prisoners. The Prince's loss was acknowledged as but 193 killed or wounded; no more than 7 of his officers, or 3 Captains and 4 Subalterns, having been slain; and 1 officer, a Major, having, by ill luck, or a mistake, become a prisoner. Among the Irish piquets, fell Alexander Comerford, Captain in the Regiment of Bulkeley, a gentleman of a name eminent in the service of Spain, as well as of creditable record in that of France, from the campaigns of Flanders, during the War of the Spanish Succession, to those for the Independence of the United States of America.' Of this battle, according to the contemporary history of Charles, entitled, " Young Juba," it was complained, in *his* army, that "the clans, and the French picquets, were the only people that stood the brunt in the late action, when the Angus battalions, and those who join'd them at Edinburgh, *took to their heels, almost as soon as the fight began!*"*
As to the officers of the Irish Brigade in the reserve, whose opportune appearance on the left, under the Prince, decided the victory, the Jacobite official account of the engagement, written by Sir Thomas Sheridan, for "valour and prudence," notices "particularly Mr. Stapleton, Brigadier in his Most Christian Majesty's Army, and Commander of the Irish Pickets; Mr. Sullivan, Quarter-Master-General of the Army, who rallied part of the left wing; and Mr. Brown, Colonel of the Guards, and 1 of the Aid-de-Camps, formerly Major of Lally's regiment." This gentleman was appointed to convey the intelligence of the combat to Versailles, and was made a Chevalier of the Order of St. Louis by the King of France. The Mac Donald journal, too, in the Lockhart Papers, after mentioning of the Highlanders, " both our officers and men behaved with the greatest bravery, and our order in marching and attacking were allowed to be far beyond expectation, in the judgement of officers who had been in the wars abroad," has this further admission to the credit of the Irish from France—" It must be acknowledged indeed, that *the Irish officers were of great use to us, in going through the different posts, and assisting in the severall dispositions that were made.*"

Voltaire, in his sketch of this encounter, having duly specified, how, when the Scotch were broken, the "6 piquets of French troops covered them, sustained the combat, and gave them time to rally," adds, how the Prince "always affirmed, that, if he had only 3000 men, regular troops, he would have made himself entirely master of England." And this assertion of Voltaire, with respect to the Prince, is quite correct. In the Mémoire presented to Louis XV. by Charles, a month after his return from Scotland to France, or in November, 1746, he says—" With 3000 men, regular troops, I would have penetrated into England immediately after having defeated Mr. Cope, and there was nothing then to oppose my reaching London, since the Elector was absent, and the English troops had not yet come back"—from Flanders. Charles, indeed, is here so far

* By *all* accounts of this war, the Edinburghers and Lowlanders were contemptible as soldier, compared with the Highlanders; and, as regards the Angus men, at Sheriff-Muir in 1715, as well as here at Falkirk in 1746, we find their courage popularly impugned.

mistaken, that the Elector, as he calls George II., *had* returned from Hanover to London, about 3 weeks previous to Cope's defeat. But, if we consider that, with such a body of regulars, (which the Irish Brigade could furnish,) and with a corresponding sum of money, Charles would certainly have been joined by several thousands, who held back, from his not having brought *any* troops with him from the Continent—and if, with those regulars, and the additional strength and confidence that would be connected with their presence, he might have "struck the iron while hot," by advancing immediately after his victory into England, instead of having to stop, above 5 weeks, to organize an army for that march—*does* his assertion, as to what he could have effected, through the support of such a small regular force, appear improbable? The zealous English Georgeite, Ray, after exclaiming, of the delay of the Jacobites in Scotland subsequent to their success at Preston-Pans, "happy was it for *us*, that they stayed so long with their friends at Edinburgh!" expresses himself to the same effect as Charles—" For, had the rebels, flush'd with victory, follow'd their blow, whilst the hearts of his Majesty's subjects were dismay'd by General Cope's defeat, and very few disciplin'd troops in England, it is hard to say what would have been the consequence; by which it appears, that an overruling Providence retarded them!" The Marquis of Tweeddale, Secretary of State for Scotland at London, in corresponding thence, notices, even some weeks previous to Charles's reduction of Edinburgh, the alarm in England, as "the panic, that seems to have seized this nation to such a degree, that it is almost impudence to pray for success, in such a state of trepidation!" Mr. Henry Fox, likewise, a member of the Georgeite administration, whose opinion, as a civilian, was countenanced, it will be observed, by that of old Marshal Wade as a military man, writes thus confidentially *before* Charles's victory at Preston-Pans—" England, Wade says, and I believe, is for the first comer; and, if you can tell, whether the 6000 Dutch, and the 10 battalions of English, or 5000 French, or Spaniards, will be here first, you know our fate. . . . The French are not come, God be thanked! But, had 5000 landed in any part of this island a week ago, I verily believe the entire conquest would not have cost them a battle!" So much for the civil and military opinions of those Anglo-Hanoverian authorities. And, would not the difference between 5000 and 3000 men be far more than compensated by the very considerable addition of home aid which Charles would *unquestionably* have obtained, had he brought over 3000 regulars with him, especially if belonging to the Irish and Scotch corps in France, instead of his *not* having been accompanied, on his landing, by *any* force of the kind? Lord Mahon alleges on this point —" Had Charles really been able to push onwards, with a body of 2 or 3000 men, there is strong reason to believe, from the state of things I have described in England—the previous apathy—and the recent terror —the want of troops—and the distraction of councils—that he might have reached the capital with but little opposition, and succeeded in, at least, a temporary restoration." At all events, the Highlanders, as *irregulars*, having been unable, in this affair at Falkirk, to turn their 1st success to such account, as, if better disciplined, or *regulars*, they might have done, the result of the action was such, as to convince the more reflective portion of the Highland officers, remarks Lord George Murray, "that a body of regular troops was absolutely necessary to support them, when they should at any time go in, sword in hand; for they were sensible, that, without more leisure and time than they could expect to have to discipline their own men, it would not be possible to make them keep their ranks, or rally soon enough, upon any sudden emergency; so that any small body of the enemy, either keeping in a body when they," the Highlanders, "were in confusion, or rallying soon, would deprive them of a victory, even after they had done their best." The allusion here to the necessity there was for a larger number of regulars from France, on account of *the great benefit derived from the small number at the battle*, is obvious, especially when combined with the conviction expressed by Sir Thomas Sheridan, in his French correspondence from the "Château de Blair d'Athol," February 8th, 1746—"*Si nous avions eu 2000 hommes de troupes reglées à la dernière bataille, l'ennemi n'auroit jamais pu se retirer avec l'apparence d'une armée.*" A foreign historian of the Prince, having noted, how, in the line of battle, the "troops, recently arrived from France, formed the reserve," states—"*They* would willingly have occupied a more prominent position; but Charles could not venture to deprive the more important of the Clans of the honour of marching in the van." And how well it was, that, even the small number of regular troops from France *were* forthcoming from the *rear*, when disaster, menacing defeat, had taken place in the *van!*

According to a letter, in the Culloden Papers, from a General Officer, that *saw* Hawley and Cope after their respective defeats, "Hawley looked *most wretchedly*, even *worse* than Cope did;" and, while the countenance of the English savage thus so strongly attested his deep mortification at the unexpected overthrow he had received, he sought to compensate himself at Edinburgh, in the absence of captured Highlanders for the gibbet, by indulging his "passion for executions," at the expense of his own unfortunate men. Some of them, on his gallows there, known as *Hawley's shambles*, were consigned to the halter; and others subjected to the lash, to skelp them out of such *cowardice* as that of the past into more *courage* for the future—this last plan of slashing due soldiership, against the Highlanders, into his miserable runaways, reminding one of the shameful discipline inflicted upon the Asiatic slaves of Xerxes at Thermopylæ, to *make* them fight the Greeks there. "Behind each troop," says Herodotus, of the army of Xerxes, "officers were stationed, with whips in their hands; compelling, with blows, their men to advance." Meantime, Charles, after appropriately issuing, from Bannockburn, the site of the most glorious Scotch victory over the English, *his* gazette of the last defeat of the *same* enemy, and their adherents, at Falkirk, returned to Stirling, to resume the siege of the Castle. There, though the food and fuel of the garrison had so decreased when its relief was prevented by Hawley's defeat, old Major-General Blakeney was *not* discouraged, but replied as before to the summons he received to surrender; and continued his defence, in the manner best calculated to gain time for his Government to re-organize their strength, for another effort to save the place. Yet, however well defended by *one* Irishman, it would, most probably, have been taken by *another*, Mr. Grant of the Regiment of Lally, had *his* counsel been followed. "Mr. Grant," writes the Chevalier de Johnstone, "had already communicated to the Prince a plan of attack of the Castle, which was, to open the trenches, and establish batteries in the burying-ground, on that side of the town which is opposite to the Castle-gate. He assured the Prince, that this was the only place where they could find a parallel, almost on a level with the batteries of the enemy; and that, if a breach were effected, in the half-moon which defends the entry of the Castle, from a battery in the burying-ground, the rubbish of the work would fill the ditch, and render an assault practicable through the breach, and the works would be ruined near the gate. He added, that it was entirely useless to think of making an attack in any other place, from the impossibility of succeeding; that the hills, in the neighbourhood of the Castle, being 40 or 50 feet lower than the Castle itself, our batteries could produce little or no effect, whilst their batteries would command ours. Besides, supposing it even possible to effect a breach on that side, we could never mount to the assault; the rock, on which the Castle is built, being everywhere very high, and almost perpendicular, except towards that part of the town opposite to the burying-ground." Such was the evidently just advice of the Irish officer. But the inhabitants of Stirling remonstrating to Charles against its execution, on the plea that the erection of besieging batteries in the burying-ground would cause the town to be laid in ashes by the fire from the Castle, the Prince applied elsewhere, or to M. Mirabelle de Gordon, a French Engineer and Chevalier of St. Louis, to learn, if the Castle might not be reduced from some *other* point of attack, than that laid down by Mr. Grant? "It was supposed," continues my authority, "that a French Engineer of a certain age, and decorated with an Order, *must* necessarily be a person of experience, talents, and capacity; but it was unfortunately discovered, when too late, that his knowledge, as an Engineer, was extremely limited; and that he was totally destitute of judgment, discernment, and common sense. His figure being as whimsical as his mind, the Highlanders, instead of *M. Mirabelle*, called him always MR. ADMIRABLE. . . . As it is always the distinctive mark of ignorance to find nothing difficult, not even the things that are impossible, M. Mirabelle, without hesitation, immediately undertook to open the trenches on a hill, to the north of the Castle, where there were not 15 inches depth of earth above the solid rock; and it became necessary to supply the want of earth with bags of wool, and sacks filled with earth, brought from a distance. Thus, the trenches were so bad, that we lost a great many men, sometimes 25 in 1 day." By other accounts, it appears, that the Highlanders, as irregulars, being equally ignorant of, and averse to, the siege-service here required, the piquets of regulars from France, "perhaps," states a Scotch historian, "the best soldiers in their army," had to be specially ordered upon that laborious, harassing, and destructive duty—such a necessity was there on this occasion, as in the previous engagement, for those regulars! Hence, too, the severe loss incurred was, alleges the Chevalier, "particularly of the Irish piquets," of whom he justly exclaims—"What a pity, that these brave men should have been sacrificed, to no purpose, by the ignorance and folly of Mirabelle!"

At last, or February 10th, Mirabelle unmasked his battery, when only, proceeds the Chevalier, "3 embrasures of the 6, of which it was to have been composed, were finished, and immediately began a very brisk fire, with his 3 pieces of cannon; but it was of very short duration, and produced very little effect on the batteries of the Castle, which, being more elevated than ours, the enemy could see even the buckles of the shoes of our artillery-men. As their fire commanded ours, our guns were immediately dismounted; and, in less than half an hour, we were obliged to abandon our battery altogether, as no one could approach it without meeting with certain destruction; while our guns, being pointed upwards, could do no execution whatever. Thus, a work of 3 weeks, which prevented us from deriving any advantage from our victory at Falkirk, and which had cost us the lives of a great number of brave men, was demolished, in an instant, like a castle of cards, and rased as level as a ponton, and all our guns were dismounted. Justice ought to be done to the merit and good conduct of General Blakeney, who perceived our ignorance from the position of our battery, and did not disturb us while constructing it. Convinced that we could do him no injury from that quarter, he remained quiet, like a skilful General, and allowed us to go on, that we might lose those precious moments which we ought to have employed in pursuing the enemy; well knowing, that he could destroy our battery whenever he pleased, and level it, in an instant, with the ground." My contemporary memoir of the Limerick veteran, after noting how "his conduct in this service was very singular," adds—" He suffered the rebels to raise their works unmolested, and forbid his cannon to fire, till he saw they were ready to begin the assault. The inferior officers, in the meantime, suspected, that as he made no opposition, he intended to give up the fort. Upon which they held a private consultation, and were just on the point of putting him under an arrest,* when he suddenly ordered all the works to be manned, and the cannon to be charged, not with their proper shot, but with bags of musket-balls. When the rebels were within 10 paces of his battlement, he ordered a general discharge, which brought down whole ranks, that fell at once, like grass under a scythe." Thus successful was the defence until February 12th, when Charles's army, unable to effect anything against the place, pinched by a scarcity of provisions, harassed by their prolonged winter-campaigning, reduced by stragglers after the battle, into the Highlands with their booty, and elsewhere, to not above 5000 immediately-disposable or effective men, and consequently too weak to maintain their ground before Stirling against such superior numbers as were then advancing to attack them, had to blow up their magazines, abandon their heavy artillery, and retire over the Forth on the approach of the Anglo-Hanoverian force of about 10,000 men; which, during the siege, had been put into the best order at Edinburgh, and placed, instead of Hawley, under the Duke of Cumberland, when the presence of the Duke was no longer required in England, with reference to a French invasion.

On the 13th, about 1 in the afternoon, the Duke entered Stirling, where, being suitably complimented by the Governor of the Castle and the officers of the garrison, his Grace in reply expressed a satisfaction, proportioned to the success with which the Castle, as a post of such consequence, had been defended. The London Gazette extraordinary announced—" His Royal Highness is pleased to commend extremely the behaviour of Major-General Blakeney, who, by his conduct, as well as courage, has saved the Castle of Stirling, which is a place of the greatest importance, from falling into the hands of the rebels." When

* This undeserved suspicion of the Limerick veteran's integrity is further explained by the statement, in the London sketch of his life, how he was "misrepresented, as a disaffected person, for not complying with the views of a certain Lord-Lieutenant" in Ireland; and consequently "kept, upwards of 20 years, without a regiment, which he at length gained, merely by merit, without Parliamentary interest." That is, without the aid of such a combined system of legislative and administrative corruption, as, in those days particularly, was most prejudicial to the army and navy.

relieved, it is added, "the provision and firing were almost consumed." In Edinburgh, too, where the Anglo-Hanoverian party were so naturally alarmed at the defeat of Falkirk, the subsequent baffling of the conquerors by the Irish Major-General was the subject of due acknowledgment. "The gallant defence," it was published, "which General Blakeney has made of Stirling Castle, reflects the highest honour on that gentleman, as it was so important a service to this country, and tended to weaken and discourage the rebels." A Georgeite contemporary observes, on the motives of the Jacobites for undertaking that siege,—"What advantages they proposed to themselves by becoming masters of this place (though they were many) might be reduced under these 3: 1st, it would have given them reputation at home and abroad, as Stirling Castle is famous, and reputed a place of greater importance than it really is: 2ndly, if they could have got this place, and fortified Perth," *then* on their possession, "they might have secured the country behind them for the winter: 3rdly, it would have afforded them means of maintaining themselves along the coasts, on *both* sides of the island, which would have facilitated their receiving supplies from abroad." In keeping the Jacobites engaged, and baffling them at Stirling, after their success at Falkirk, until the army they had defeated was so reorganized as to be able to raise the siege, and oblige its previous conquerors to retreat, a diversion was effected by Blakeney, similar in value to that by the brave Dubreton at Burgos in 1812; when, by detaining the British before his post there, and foiling their efforts to reduce it, after their victory at Salamanca, he gained time for his countrymen, the French, to reassemble a force sufficiently strong to relieve him, and compel their former victors to retire. On the whole, the recollections associated with the attack and defence of Stirling, and Irishmen, as represented by Grant, Blakeney, and the gallant piquets from the Brigade, are such as to make us regret, that any differences between forms of Christianity—the religion common to ALL—should have prevented *such* men being united in arms, under *one* Sovereign and *one* standard.

In the consultations and arrangements for the retreat of Charles from Stirling over the Forth towards the Highlands, it appears how much O'Sullivan was "envied, for having his master's ear in preference to others;" and how Sir Thomas Sheridan's "having, seemingly, the pre-eminence in Charles's friendship and counsels was another cause of disgust to the Highland Chiefs." These discontents the Prince strove to dissipate, in various ways. "However," it is added, "the 2 Irish politicians had still the ascendant in the cabinet." On receiving a Memorial, in which the principal Highland leaders represented the necessity there was for retiring to the north, the Prince "sent Sir Thomas Sheridan to argue the matter with the Chiefs," in whose views it was finally requisite to acquiesce. For the manner that movement commenced, which was "extremely discreditable," says Mr. Chambers, "Lord George Murray seems inclined, in his narrative, to throw the blame of the transaction on O'Sullivan, but without showing any grounds for his surmise." *—The circumstance, referred to as so discreditable,

* In connexion with Mr. Chambers's just disapproval of Lord George Murray on *this* occasion, I may remark, that his Lordship seems, *throughout* what he has written, to have had too great an itch to censure O'Sullivan. It is evident that, as regards the Prince's attachment for O'Sullivan, Lord George could "bear, like the Turk, no brother near the throne." A Georgeite contemporary, noticing the

was, that, though it had been resolved, at the Prince's head-quarters, on the night of February 11th, the army should muster on the 12th, at 9 in the morning, and then proceed, with due regularity, across the Forth, the men were so discouraged at their situation about Stirling, and alarmed at the very superior hostile force approaching to attack them, that, without waiting for orders, and in a straggling manner, they presumed to set out at day-break; thus leaving the Prince and other leaders behind, or exposed, it might be, to a sally from the Castle, as well as to other hazards. On the Jacobites, indeed, the general effects of their failure before Stirling were such, that their strength, which had recently mustered there to its highest amount, may, from the period of that failure, be regarded as but comparatively flickering in the socket, to expire at Drummossie Muir, or Culloden. Besides the obvious necessity there now was for a force like that of Charles, so harassed, diminished, and in want of subsistence, to retire to the Highlands before an army like the Duke's, so much stronger, fresher, and better provided in every respect, as well as soon to be aided by several thousand veteran foreign mercenaries, or Hessians, it was in the Highlands better quarters and reinforcements were to be looked for by Charles; and it was there an irregular war of defence against the Duke might be most efficiently managed for the rest of the winter; at the same time, that a minor hostile force of about 2000 men under Lord Loudoun, and Forts George, Augustus, and William, should be reduced *there*, if the main contest, by the help of what supplies might arrive from abroad, were to be supported, with any prospect of success, in spring, against the Duke advancing from the south. The Jacobites retired from Stirling, in the direction of Crieff; whence, on the 14th, it was decided, that, for the sake of subsistence, the Highland corps should generally proceed northwards, under Charles himself, by the usual military road; and the Lowland infantry and horse, under Lord George Murray, by the roads along the coasts of Angus and Aberdeenshire; the point for reunion to be Inverness. With the latter troops were Brigadier Walter Stapleton, and the piquets from the Irish Brigade.

The Duke of Cumberland did not reach Perth till the 17th, where he quartered his main force, for several days, to rest his infantry; it being, says an English writer, "to no purpose to fatigue our men with forced marches." Here, observe the Georgeite announcements of the day respecting the Duke, "he has been graciously pleased to *pardon the private men who ran away at the late battle; but the officers are to await the King's pleasure*." And, it is added—"the Duke has given the soldiers permission to plunder the rebels' houses in and about this town." While the Duke was still at Perth, or on the 21st, the 6000 foreigners in English pay, whom he had expected to reinforce him,

paramount influence of O'Sullivan with Charles, speaks of "the Chevalier, ever observant of Sullivan's counsels, which he looked upon as *so many oracles*"—and, in the little work on Charles's campaigns of 1745-6, entitled, "Ascanius, or the Young Adventurer," Lord George is represented as *complaining*, "that Sullivan used to carry everything, in councils of war, against him." Yet, when O'Sullivan *might* subsequently have injured Lord George Murray, he did *not* do so. James III. writes thus from Rome, April 25th, 1747, to his son, the Prince, in France, "I am truly sorry to find you in the way of thinking you are to Lord George Murray. I spoke very fully about him to O'Sullivan, who should be with you before you get this; and, by all he said to me, I really cannot see any just reason to suspect his loyalty and fidelity."

2 F

landed at Edinburgh. These "Hessian soldiers," according to the Scotch accounts, "were remarkably handsome, good-looking men." Nor was their moral character inferior to their external appearance and military efficiency. "They acquired the affection and esteem of the people, who had occasion to mix in their society during the ensuing campaign;" and " their *good nature and pure manners, were favourably compared with the coarse conversation, and dissolute conduct, of the British soldiery.*" *
They were subsequently so stationed, as to guard against another Jacobite descent from the Highlands into the Lowlands. Leaving Perth on the 26th, the Duke proceeded to Dundee; whence he set out, March 3rd, advancing through Angus and Aberdeenshire, till, by 7 or 8 days more, he established himself at Aberdeen. In those districts, he found his presence to be detested, in proportion to the old national, or Jacobite and Anti-Union, feelings of the population. Hence, of some officers from the piquets of the Irish Brigade, detached to recruit for Prince Charles, the London Gazette states—"At Forfar, where each of our 4 divisions lay a night, 3 French-Irish officers were conceal'd in the town the whole time; and, after all our troops were pass'd thro', they were permitted to beat up for volunteers there. This," adds the Anglo-Hanoverian scribe, "shews the affection of that part of the country for the rebels!" The Duke determined upon remaining at Aberdeen, until the improving weather in spring would permit him to take the field, in full strength, for the final decision of the contest. Meantime, finding himself so situated at that place, from the want of intelligence, &c., as to be "*more* in an enemy's country than when warring with the French in Flanders," he, in the districts subjected to his power, visited with the rigours of military execution, the crime of Jacobitism, or loyalty to the ancient dynasty of the nation; the pillage and conflagration *here*, as subsequently *elsewhere*, including even a destruction of Protestant houses of worship, or those of the Episcopal Church of Scotland, on account of the attachment of the Episcopalians, as well as the Highlanders, to the Stuarts.†

During those occurrences, Prince Charles, on his route for Inverness, reduced upon honourable conditions, and blew up, February 22nd, the English barracks at Ruthven—held, since the preceding summer, with a few men, against very superior numbers, by a stout Irish Protestant officer, Lieutenant Molloy—and, March 1st, on the Prince's approach, Lord Loudoun and his forces evacuated Inverness, with the exception of

* Chambers.—The Hessians, employed by the Georgite Government in Scotland against Prince Charles, have been variously enumerated by writers, at from 5000 to 6000 men. In an official or parliamentary document, I find this item respecting those foreign mercenaries. "Jan. 22, 1746. For the charge of 6172 Hessian troops, being 1264 horse, and 4908 foot, from Dec. 25, 1745, to Dec. 24, 1746, together with the Subsidy, pursuant to Treaty, . . . £161,607 17s. 1½d."

† *After* the war, or according to a "Letter from Inverary," in June, 1746, the Catholic, and the Protestant Episcopalian, forms of religion were *tolerated* as follows in Scotland. "Several Mass-houses, which were publickly resorted to in the very face of the law, have been pulled down. The Nonjuring Meetings are generally shut up through the kingdom." But of Protestant Episcopalian churches, alluded to here, under the obnoxious designation of "Nonjuring Meetings," we know, how few, if any, on the Duke of Cumberland's northern line of march, would *remain*, to be shut up. Such a career of disgusting sacrilege was but a due prelude to the wholesale barbarities perpetrated in the Highlands after the battle of Culloden—diversified, according to Lord Mahon, by "*races of naked women on horseback, for the amusement of the camp, at Fort Augustus!*"

its Castle, called Fort George; in which Major Grant of Rothiemurchus was left as Governor, with a garrison of 3 companies, 1 of regulars, the other 2 brave and well-affected, 16 cannon, as many barrels of powder and ball, 100 barrels of beef, &c. But Grant behaved so badly, that, on the 3rd, he gave up the Fort, with its garrison, save his precious *self!* as prisoners of war; for which he was subsequently tried, and broken by Court Martial. From the extreme aversion of the Highlanders to have any English garrisons among them, this Fort, which cost £50,000, had likewise to be demolished by gunpowder. Previous to the surrender of Fort George, the Prince was rejoined at Inverness, by Lord George Murray, and the more advanced portion of his division of the army; the rest, with whom were the French piquets, or the Irish and Scotch regulars from France, under Brigadier Walter Stapleton, and Lord John Drummond, having yet to come up. The Irish, on their march, were reinforced, the 5th, by a detachment of their fellow-soldiers from the Continent, that, in a French brigantine, the *Sophie,* putting to sea, at night, from Ostend, were at once so lucky as to elude the numerous hostile cruisers, and to land at Aberdeen in good time, or but the day before it was evacuated by the Jacobites. This detachment, described as consisting of about 130 men and officers of the Regiment of Fitz-James, " cloath'd with red, turn'd up with blue," with horse-furniture, arms, breast-plates, and baggage, was received, by the national enthusiasm of the country-people, with joyful acclamations; the very women running out to welcome the strangers, and conducting the officers' horses by the reins!* With the Irish of the detachment, were incorporated some English troopers, that had deserted from their own army to the French, in Flanders; an Englishman, in those times, who, from Jacobite or other motives, might wish to desert to the French, having an additional inducement to do so, in the prospect of finding himself quite at home, in point of language, &c., among some of the regiments of the Irish Brigade, which he would *not* be in a purely *French* corps; whence, or so far as tending to promote desertion from her enemies, it was an advantage to France, to have those Irish regiments in her service.† The vessel, that brought this reinforcement to Aberdeen,

---

* "Trois compagnies du Régiment de Fitz-James," writes Voltaire, "abordèrent heureusement. Lorsque quelque petit vaisseau abordait, il était reçu avec des acclamations de joie; les femmes couraient au-devant; elles menaient par la bride les chevaux des officiers."

† That gallant Englishman, Lieutenant John Shipp, who fought his way up from the ranks, and was in several British regiments, expresses himself, in his Memoirs, as *most* gratified in serving with an *Irish* corps, the 87th Regiment of Foot, otherwise "Fogaboloughs," or "clear-the-way" boys. "I must confess," he says, "I do love to be on duty, on any kind of service, with the Irish. There is a promptness to obey, an hilarity, a cheerful obedience, and willingness to act, which I have rarely met with in any other body of men; but whether, in this particular case, those qualifications had been instilled into them by the rigid discipline of their corps, I know not, or whether these are characteristics of the Irish nation; but I have also observed in that corps, (I mean the 87th Regiment, or Prince's Own Irish,) a degree of liberality amongst the men, I have never seen in any other corps,—a willingness to share their crust and drop on service with their comrades; an indescribable cheerfulness in obliging and accommodating each other; and an anxiety to serve each other, and to hide each other's faults. In that corps, there was a unity, I have never seen in any other; and, as for fighting, they were very devils. During the Peninsular War, some General Officer observed, to the Duke of Wellington, how unsteadily that corps marched. The noble Duke replied,—'Yes, General, they do, indeed; but they fight like devils.' So they always will, while they are Irish. In some situations, they are, perhaps, too impetuous; but, if I know anything of the

had formed a part of the embarkations, at Ostend, and Dunkirk, of what remained of the Regiments of Fitz-James and Lally, with other military and pecuniary supplies; respecting which, in proportion to Prince Charles's increasing need of assistance, the French Court sent most pressing orders, that no effort should be spared to get over to Scotland; and the Duke of Cumberland's apprehensions became so great, concerning the Irish ready to sail from those harbours, that his uneasiness, on this score, contributed to his relinquishing the intention, which he had previously announced, of re-embarking his Hessians for the Continent.

But the remainder of the Regiment of Fitz-James, with some of the most distinguished officers of the Irish Brigade, cavalry-equipments, arms, artillery, ammunition, and several thousand pounds, dashing out from Ostend in the *Bourbon* and the *Charité* transports, amidst a hard gale, and by night, the better to escape hostile recognition, were, notwithstanding the darkness, perceived off that port by the enemy through a glass of recent invention, had to strike to his superior force, and were, on the 4th, brought by the *Hastings, Triton, Salamander,* and *Vulcan,* under Commodore Knowles, into the harbour of Deal. On board the *Bourbon* were—the Comte Edouard de Fitz-James, (son of the late Marshal Duke of Berwick) Colonel of the Irish Regiment of Berwick, Maréchal de Camp, or Major-General, and Commandant—Captain Patrick Darcy of Condé's Regiment of Horse, acting as Aide-de-Camp to the Comte de Fitz-James—the Comte Charles Edward Roth (son of the late Lieutenant-General and Chevalier Michael Roth of Kilkenny) Colonel of the Irish Regiment of Roth, and Maréchal de Camp, or Major-General—Brigadiers-General Richard Francis Talbot, 3rd Earl of Tyrconnell,* Sir Peter Nugent, Baronet, and Matthew Cooke—M. Nugent, Colonel of Horse—M. Betagh, Major of the Regiment of Fitz-James—Captain Nugent—Lieutenants Nugent, Fahy, and Dowdall—Cornets Nugent and Stapleton—Quarter-Masters Wolferston, Coghlan, Wickham, O'Brien, Cassidy, Mac Dermott, Betagh, and Rockly—a Chaplain, and 4 *French* officials, viz., a Commissary of Artillery, a Treasurer of the Extraordinaries of War, a Chief Commissary of Provisions, and a Surgeon-Major, besides 6 Gunners, 1 Corporal, 1 Miner, and 1 Labourer—of the Regiment of Fitz-James, 5 companies, making together 199 men. In other words, Officers 22, Privates 199, *both* 221, or with Gunners, Corporal, and Miner 229 military effectives—Chaplain, Officials, and Labourer, 6 non-combatants —total of prisoners, 235. On board the *Charité* were—M. le Baron de Butler, Captain of the Regiment of Fitz-James—M. Cooke, ditto—Lieutenants Barnwell, Coulaghan, and Butler—Cornets Byrne, Morris, and O'Farrell—Quarter-Masters Martin, Moore, Gernon, and 2 Farrells— a French Captain of Foot in the Regiment of Monaco, serving here as a Lieutenant-Colonel—of the Regiment of Fitz-James, 4 companies, making together about 160 men. In other words, Officers 14, Privates 160— total combatants prisoners 174. The list of the 36 officers, connected

service, this is a fault on the right side; and what, at the moment, was thought rashness and madness, has gained Old England many a glorious victory."

* Of this Irish nobleman, James III.'s Scotch Agent at Paris, Lord Sempill, writing to him the preceding autumn, or "22nd November, 1745," says—"Lord Tyreconnel is returned from the army, by the permission of the Court. There is a very advantageous marriage proposed to him; but, he assures me, nothing shall retard his going, where he can be of any use to your Majesty's service. The Minister of the War intends to employ him in the English expedition." See the memoir of Lord Tyrconnell farther on, or under the year 1752.

with the main portion of the Regiment of Fitz-James here captured, presents several names, that sufficiently show what a loss Charles suffered, by the interception of this convoy. Among the 359 troopers of the corps, there were 34 English, who, having deserted to, or been made prisoners by, the French, and having, in an evil hour, agreed to take service in this regiment which suffered considerably at Fontenoy, were, after reaching Deal, recognized there as deserters, separated from their companions, as specially disentitled to be considered regular prisoners of war, and marched away under a strong guard, to London, to be tried there.* The military chest on board, containing £5000, or upwards, and the other supplies, were of much less value to the captors, than they would have been to Charles; to whom money, more especially, even when a comparatively small sum, was a desideratum, in proportion as, to use Lord Lovat's words, "siller would go far in the Highlands." Nor was the Prince more fortunate, with respect to the remainder of the Regiment of Lally, that sailed, in several transports, from Dunkirk, when the other embarkation took place from Ostend; but, being chased by an English man-of-war were only so far lucky as to avoid the fate of the *Bourbon* and the *Charité*, in contriving to get back to port. According to the communication of Captain Shea, or Shee,† of the Regiment of Fitz-James to Charles, the entire Irish convoy destined for him would have been about 800 men (Fontenoy boys!) besides the money they were to bring—an additional or distinct sum from that with Fitz-James's corps being, of course, embarked with the Regiment of Lally, which had to return to Dunkirk. Yet, about the time of the landing, at Aberdeen, of the detachment of Fitz-James's men from the *Sophie*, 2000 louis-d'ors reached Charles from the Continent by Peterhead, and a piquet of the Irish Infantry Regiment of Berwick is likewise alleged to have managed to arrive safe at Portsoy. On the whole, however, Sir Walter Scott, alluding to the last capture of men and money by Commodore Knowles, notes how "unpitiably rigorous was Fortune, from beginning to end, in all that might be considered the *chances* from which Prince Charles might receive advantage. The miscarriage of the reinforcements was the greater, as the supplies of treasure were become almost indispensable. His money now began to run short, so that he was compelled to pay his soldiers partly in meal, which caused great discontent. Many threatened to abandon the enterprise; some actually deserted."

Immediately after the fall of Fort George, the reduction of Fort

* The first executions ordered in England, after the battle of Culloden, in connexion with the civil war, were those of 5 of the Foot Guards, who, having been made prisoners at Fontenoy, then listing into the Regiment of Fitz-James, and finally, being with the detachment of that corps intercepted by Commodore Knowles, were condemned to be shot, as deserters, in Hyde Park. Of the 5 thus executed, 2 appear to have been Catholics.

† The clan of O'Seagha, O'Shea, or O'Shee,—otherwise modernized or anglicized into "Shea," or "Shee" without the "O"—are related to have been of very old royal origin, and to have possessed the Barony of Iveragh, in the County of Kerry, down to that general disturbance of the ancient order of things in Munster, at the latter end of the 12th century, which was a result of the Anglo-Norman invasion. Since then, the race has flourished elsewhere in Ireland, and other countries; displaying, through several of its representatives, respectability or distinction in various stations, or pursuits, including some of the most honourable. For adherence to King James II. in the War of the Revolution, 8 cavaliers alone, of the branch long established in Kilkenny, are mentioned as attainted in 1691, or proscribed for Williamite spoliation; and, to the different corps of the Irish Brigade, as well

Augustus was assigned by Charles to Brigadier Walter Stapleton and 300 of his "French Irish," or "Irish picquets," as they are variously designated—in *either* case, more correctly, than as, in other instances, merely "French troops," and "French piquets." They executed their task in a few days; an outwork or barrack, in an old tower, occupied by a Serjeant and 12 men, being soon mastered; and artillery, laboriously brought from a distance of 32 miles through the snow, being so directed against the Fort itself, that its magazine being fired, Major Wentworth, the Georgeite Governor, and his garrison of 3 companies of the Regiment of Guise, had, on March 16th, to surrender. Brigadier Stapleton, with his 390 men, and a corps of Highlanders, was next ordered to besiege Fort William. That Fort, scientifically-constructed, and garrisoned by 600 Georgeite troops, could not be invested, as situated on the shore, and open to aid by sea; 2 war-sloops lying close to the place. "The resolution of besieging Fort William," writes Lord George Murray, "I did not approve, as I always had heard it was a strong place, and regularly fortified. But Lochiel, Keppoch, and other Highlanders, who had their houses anywhere in that neighbourhood, were very keen," on the matter, "as that garrison had already begun their burning orders: so I did not oppose it, though Brigadier Stapleton and I had *no* hopes of success, by what had happened at Stirling Castle, which was *not* so strong." While a body of Highlanders remained before the place, to keep the Georgeite garrison from devastating the country, the troublesome conveyance of the siege artillery, &c., was committed to the Irish. "The distance," says Home, "from Inverness to Fort William was 61 miles, and the intervening hilly road, in great part a continuation of steep paths and passes, so retarded the Irish troops with their cannon, that they took many days to reach the Fort." The batteries could not be raised and fire opened till March 31st; from which time, "by the Irish and Highlanders united," adds Chambers, "the most vigorous attempts were made to obtain possession of the place, but without avail." These operations, attended with the endurance of much fatigue and hardship, continued till April 14th, when the necessity for uniting all the Jacobite forces, against the advance of the Duke of Cumberland, caused the siege to be terminated; Brigadier Stapleton spiking his heavy guns, bringing away his field-pieces, and marching off to join the Prince at Inverness; "leaving the Highlanders and their Chiefs, to follow when they pleased." During this siege, other officers connected with Ireland and France, as well as Spain, were active in the Prince's cause.

March 29th, an advanced detachment of Georgeites, consisting of a Captain of Argyleshire Militia with 70 foot, and a Cornet with 30 of Kingston's Light Horse, were despatched, in the evening, from a considerable corps of their army, at Strathbogie, towards Keith. After halting in the dark, at a cautious or half-way distance from the latter place, for a considerable time, or until assured by a Presbyterian Minister, acting as their guide and spy, that *none* of the Prince's troops were there, the Georgeites, with a due flourish from their Captain in the shape of orders, that, if an action should occur, they should neither give nor take quarter, about daylight, on the 30th, entered the defenceless village, making themselves suitably unwelcome there by breaking open shops, and plundering.

as to French regiments, down to our own days, the O'Sheas, or Shees, have supplied officers, some of high rank, and several of them Chevaliers of St. Louis. The name, too, has been of note in the Austrian service.

But Major Nicholas Glascock of Ogilvie's regiment, previously of Dillon's in the Irish Brigade, and already noticed at the capture of the *Hazard* sloop, taking from Fochabers a select party of Jacobite foot, consisting of 16 of the piquet-men from France, 50 of Roy Stuart's regiment under a Captain Stuart, a detachment from Ogilvie's regiment, and 20 or 30 horse of different corps under a Lieutenant Simpson, in all 200 men, about midnight entered Keith, surprised the sentinel, and attacking with cries of "God save Prince Charles!—ye *rebels*, yield or die!" in less than an hour, so disposed of the Georgeite pillagers, that, between the loss they suffered in slain, and in prisoners, the number of whom was about 80, no more than 7 remained, to scamper back to Strathbogie; of whom 1 was obliged to have his shattered arm cut off there. In this enterprise, considered equally bold and dangerous, as directed against a post almost in the centre of the places occupied by the enemy's forces, Major Glascock, who gained much credit by it for prudence and skill, had Captain Stuart, and a good many, especially of Ogilvie's detachment, wounded, but only 1 man belonging to the piquets, who led the attack, killed. It was an affair, which, says a Scotch Jacobite officer, "had a very good effect, and made such an impression on the English, that, conceiving themselves insecure everywhere, they were obliged to redouble their service in" a severe season,* "in that cold and mountainous country; the fatigues of which occasioned so much disease, that the hospitals of Aberdeen, the head-quarters of the Duke of Cumberland, were continually filled with their sick."

Towards the end of March, an expedition against Lord Loudoun, and his Georgeite forces in Sutherland, was undertaken by General O'Sullivan, with the Duke of Perth, Lord Cromarty, and a chosen body of nearly 2000 men. Availing themselves of a dense mist of several days' duration, as well to collect a sufficient number of fishing-craft for crossing the Moray Frith, as to elude the hostile vessels there, the Jacobites, on March 31st, at 8 in the morning, landed about 2 miles west of Dornoch in Sutherland; to the proportionate surprise of Lord Loudoun, who conceived that all boats were withdrawn to *his* side of the water, and that the English shipping were an additional security to him against any attempt from the *other* side! The result of this well-effected passage was such a discomfiture and dispersion of his Lordship's followers, attended by a loss of 3 vessels in the Frith of Tain with arms, military stores, provisions, and valuables put on board at the evacuation of Inverness, that his Lordship, and his very busy and intriguing Georgeite coadjutor, President Forbes of Culloden, were obliged to take refuge, with 800 men, in the Isle of Skye.† But O'Sullivan, and the Duke of Perth,

* I correct the Chevalier de Johnstone's oversight, in writing "the midst of winter." But, what is such a venial lapse of memory to the comparative "mortal sin" of Sir Walter Scott's incorrectness, with respect to this matter at Keith. "A party," he states, "of 100 *regulars* were surprised at the village of Keith, and entirely slain, or made prisoners, by *John Roy Stuart!*" The foot, who formed above 2-3rds of the Georgeites at Keith, were *not* regulars, and John Roy Stuart did not command *there* at all.

† But for 2 hours' time, which the Jacobites, after their landing in Sutherland, lost, in parleying with the 1st outpost of Lord Loudoun's force ere they obliged it to surrender, Lord George Murray considers, that Lord Loudoun, and most of his men, could have been captured. Lord George here, as usual, *nibbles* at O'Sullivan, alleging, "I was told the Duke of Perth was advised in this by Mr. O'Sullivan." But Mr. Chambers more *justly* remarks of the impolitic delay of the Jacobites on this occasion—"It is not improbable, that this procedure was in consequence of an

having to return to Inverness, and the prosecution of the recent success, a comparatively easy task, devolving upon Lord Cromarty, that nobleman was unfortunately so far from being " the right man in the right place," that all previously gained in this quarter was lost, and himself finally, or April 26th, made prisoner,* after the occurrence, through his remissness, of another loss, *more* fatal, or irreparable.

From the comparative narrowness and poverty of the territory, to which, since the raising of the siege of Stirling, the Jacobites had been confined, and the increased facility thereby afforded to the numerous and active English cruisers for intercepting vessels attempting to reach that territory with assistance from the Continent, Charles was at last reduced to such straits for money, that his troops had not received any for several weeks. He expected, however, a supply, from Dunkirk, of between £12,000 and £13,000, which was to be accompanied by a number, also much required, of experienced engineers and veteran officers, mostly Irish, others Scotch, &c., in the French and Spanish services, together with a detachment from the Irish Regiment of Berwick, several chests of arms, and some barrels of powder. This cargo, so invaluable under the circumstances, was to be conveyed in the vessel already mentioned as called the *Hazard*, when captured at Montrose from the English, and under its subsequent change of name to the *Prince Charles*, also referred to as having proved so useful to the Prince by its repeated passages between Scotland and the Continent, notwithstanding the many odds, almost amounting to a certainty, that it would be recovered, on some of those passages, by its former masters. Such dangerous odds being now greater than ever, at the same time that the importance of the vessel reaching its destination was equally great, the command was confided to a gentleman highly and deservedly in favour with the Lieutenant General, Charles O'Brien, Lord Clare, and Earl of Thomond, whose zeal for the Stuarts could not have made a better recommendation for their service on this occasion. The gentleman so selected, Captain Talbot, an Irishman, was of distinguished reputation among the naval officers of France as a privateerer; having been intrusted with several vessels fitted out for that line of action, in which he made many expeditions against the enemy, with so much intelligence, valour, and success, that no one appeared more worthy of commanding the *Prince Charles*, in this very difficult emergency. The orders for sailing were so pressing, and the execution of them was of such consequence, that, notwithstanding the number of the English ships of various sizes, or men-of-war and privateers, on the watch, under Commodore Mitchell, along the French and Flemish coasts, 5 different attempts were made by the Irish Captain to leave Dunkirk, and, as might be expected, all without success. On the 6th effort, baffling the British Commodore in a thick fog, Talbot *did* get out; yet with no better luck than to be soon after discovered, encountered off Ostend by the enemy's superior force, and driven ashore there, apparently so damaged, that it was published in London, "the anxiety, entertained by individuals in the" Jacobite "detachment, to avoid, if at all possible, a hostile collision with" the Georgeite "troops, amongst which were some of their own nearest relatives. The Chevalier Johnstone informs us, that at least Macdonald of Scothouse, the first cadet of the house of Clanranald, was under feelings of this kind, having a son, an officer, under Lord Loudoun."

* The Earl was surprised and taken, by improperly staying behind his forces, with some of his officers, at Dunrobin Castle; delaying, we are told, "to see a few bottles out," and "witnessing, it is said, the tricks of a juggler."

Hazard sloop, which has been so useful to the Pretender's affairs, in passing and repassing from Dunkirk to Scotland, is drove on shore near Ostend, by 1 of our men-of-war, and destroyed." But, though driven on shore, the Irish Captain managed to get off again, and into Ostend, by the same tide, where he repaired the damage he had received. He then hoisted sail, with Fortune, however, still against him, being attacked, in sight of that port, by 2 English privateers, and suffering so much, as to be obliged to put back in order to refit; the enemy, meantime, increasing the strength of their naval blockade. Nevertheless, his vessel was such an excellent sailer, that she escaped the vigilance and pursuit of 6 or 7 English ships, cruising off Ostend to intercept her. Having thus, at last, gained the open sea, the indefatigable Talbot proceeded on his voyage, until, off Troopshead, where 4 British ships of war, the *Eltham* of 40, *Hound* of 16, *Shark* of 16, and *Sheerness* of 20 guns, with the *Mary*, a tender, were at anchor, he was descried, and duly bore away to avoid them. The *Eltham* giving the signal for a course, the *Sheerness*, which, under its previous commander, Captain Bully, had, last year, captured some of the Irish Brigade, was, under his successor, an Irish Protestant gentleman, Captain O'Brien,* ready to start in less than 5 minutes; when, a more exciting chase, than that between Achilles and Hector on another element, ensued between the 2 Irish Captains. It continued for above 150 miles, quite through the Pentland Frith; a running fight, against O'Brien's less encumbered or more manageable strength, being kept up, with great skill and courage, for 5 hours, by Talbot, while making signals of distress, to which there was no response from the land; until, after suffering a considerable loss in killed and wounded, he drove the *Prince Charles* aground, among the shallows of Tongue Bay, in such a manner as to avoid being followed or captured by O'Brien, and yet without sacrificing the vessel and her cargo, in order to escape.

On reaching the shore, April 5th, late in the evening, the harassed officers and men of the *Prince Charles*, (leaving, as in *their* situation of comparative unimportance to remove, 14 chests of pistols and sabres, and 13 barrels of powder aboard,) landed the boxes of money, the delivery of which was the main object of the voyage; securing the treasure for the night in the house of one William MacKay of Melness, who was thought to be rather favourable than otherwise to the Stuart cause; and whose son George engaged to do his best as a guide next morning, for a march to reach Lord Cromarty. But the MacKays were unfortunately a hostile or Georgeite clan, and had not been reduced to a submission, or neutrality, as they might have been, by that nobleman. The Chief of his name, George MacKay, 3rd Lord Reay, resided so near the Jacobite landing-place, that he soon obtained sufficient information respecting the stranded vessel, and its crew, &c., whom he accordingly resolved to intercept. His Lordship, though, from his advanced age of above 70, incapable of heading the enterprise himself, was able, by day-break, on

* O'Brien was a name of note at this period, in the British navy, in the person of another Captain O'Brien, since 1742, of the *Princess Royal* of 90 guns, after having, as Vice-Admiral in Russia, in 1740, disciplined the Cronstadt squadron for the Empress Anne. As *he* had a son in command of a British ship-of-war, the Captain of the *Sheerness* may have been that son. Several Irishmen, it may be here observed *en passant*, attained, during this century, high rank in the sea as well as the land service of France, Spain, and Russia.

the 6th, to despatch in pursuit 50 of his own MacKay vassals, headed by the active and courageous factor or agent of his estates, Mr. Daniel Forbes; to be followed by his Lordship's own son, a Captain, and by other officers of the Regiment of Loudoun, with about 80 of that corps, who had taken refuge in this quarter, after Lord Loudoun's recent surprise and defeat; and, in aid of those pursuing parties, expresses were sent through the country, to summon every fighting man to rise. Meantime the officers and men of the Prince Charles had set out early on their march, but were forsaken by their double-dealing guide, George MacKay, and were thus left at a loss how to proceed along the sands, with a mountain before them, when, at about 2 hours after day-break, they received a summons to surrender; adding that, if they did not, none of them could pass the mountain before them, as they would be all slain, or made prisoners. This summons was from the indefatigable Forbes, who with 11 of the most active of the MacKays had come up; concealing the smallness of their number behind a hill. The Jacobites refusing to surrender, Forbes and his men fired upon them, and being pursued to their hill, ran from it, with the speed of Highlanders, to another hill, repeating their fire. The contest was maintained in this manner for some time, while the number of the Georgeites continued to increase, till "at length 2 drums were heard from the lofty and steep pass of Duag, at the west shoulder of Ben-Lyall, the loud echoes of which, from the hollows of the mountain, exceeded the noise of 20 drums," and Captain George MacKay appearing with a fresh company, the harassed and betrayed Jacobites, without a guide, in a strange country, about to be closed on in front, flank, and rear, and hampered with what they had to guard against opponents in their own country, fresh for action, and entirely unfettered in their movements, under such a discouraging state of things, naturally considered a further resistance would be as hopeless as it would be useless, and thus found themselves "compell'd by too severe a fate" to surrender with the treasure, which they had made such praiseworthy exertions to convey to its proper destination. My MacKay authority admits, in reference to their surrender, "they could not at any rate have joined the *rebels*," alluding to Lord Cromarty; "for the country people from Durness and Edderachillis would have soon come up, and some of Loudon's troops were before them in Sutherland and Ross." But such would *not* have been the case, if Lord Cromarty did his duty; since, had he, or any other leader in his place, advanced, observes Lord George Murray, "with 6 or 700 men through Seaforth's country, the way Lord Loudon fled, they would have been joined by many more; and" had "the same number gone to Lord Rea's country to take security from them," the MacKays, "that they would no more carry arms against us, we *would have had the good fortune to have saved the money, &c.*" For, even after the success in capturing that money, an attack from Lord Cromarty was so much dreaded by the MacKays, that, says my Georgeite account, "Lord Reay and his friends, being apprehensive of a visit from the rebels, embarked with their treasure and prisoners" for Aberdeen—or *abandoned their country by sea, as unable on land to resist an invasion of it, if undertaken by Lord Cromarty!*

The following were the officers from France, taken with the money. Colonel Brown of the Irish Regiment of Lally, previously distinguished in the retreat from Derby, afterwards successful in escaping from Carlisle, then, as having signalized himself at Falkirk, despatched with the account of that success to Louis XV., by whom he was made a Chevalier of St. Louis, and finally appointed to command of all the military from France in the *Prince Charles*—Captain Talbot of that vessel *—Captain MacMahon, commandant of the piquet from the Irish Regiment of Berwick—Captain Rogers, and Lieutenants Nugent, Morris, and 2 Barnewalls of the same Irish corps—Lieutenants O'Brien and Birmingham, and a gentleman named O'Byrne (rank unspecified) of the Irish Regiment of Clare—Captain MacMahon of the Regiment of Hainault in the French service—Lieutenant Wyer, and Basil Barnewall (rank unspecified) both of the Royal Scotch Regiment in same service—Captain Gould and Lieutenant Hynes of the Irish Regiment of Ultonia, or Ulster, in the Spanish service—Captain MacPherson of the Irish Regiment of Hibernia in same service—Captain St. Clair (or Sinclair) of the Regiment of Virst in that service—Captains O'Farrell and Hay of Spanish corps not particularized—M. Chabellard of the Gens d'Armes of the Guard of Louis XV. Of these 21 officers, not less than 16 were Irish, 4 *perhaps* Scotch, and 1 French, by birth or origin. The soldiers of the piquet from the Irish Regiment of Berwick were about 80. The whole of the captured detachment, or landsmen and seamen of every rank, amounted to 156, of whom but a few were Scotch, and nearly all Irish; scarcely any French being on board, except sailors. The general total originally, or before sailing from the Continent, was greater; the officers at Ostend, instead of but 21, being referred to as 30, and the soldiers of Berwick's piquet, instead of but 80, being noticed as 90 or 100. And, from between 30 and 40, to above 40, being variously stated as killed in the sea and land combats, the proportion of wounded would be *many* more in amount; which proportion, as including such a number of those who remained, would not be without its effect in causing the final surrender. Some days previous to this most "untoward event" for the Jacobites, we likewise read, in the newspapers, under the head of "Hague, April 1st, N. S.," the frustration of a further effort, by a body of the Irish Brigade, to get away, by night, from the Continent for Scotland; the announcement stating, according to "letters from Zealand and Dutch Flanders, that the returned transports, with the Irish troops on board, made a fresh attempt, last Saturday night, to stretch over to Scotland; but, falling in with some of his Brittannick Majesty's ships of war, were chased, and driven back the next day into Ostend." If Prince Charles failed in his enterprise, it was certainly *not* from any deficiency of zeal for his interest, on the part of the Irish military in the service of France.

The Duke of Cumberland, since the establishment of his head-quarters, from the earlier portion of March, at Aberdeen, or during the severe season, which prevented a general prosecution of hostilities, had directed his attention to the remodelling of his army, and the collection, by land

* The gallant Talbot, after being long prisoner-of-war in England, and at much expense for the subsistence of his crew and attendants there, met with some obstacles to his reimbursement by the Government in France, till he was at last repaid, through the interest of the Lord Clare and Earl of Thomond with M. Rouillé, Secrétaire d'Etat de la Marine, as I find by that Minister's letter of September 27th, 1749. In addition to the information derived from the publications of the day respecting the Irish Captain's voyage, &c., with the money, I have consulted the "History of the House and Clan of MacKay," Edinburgh, 1829, by a gentleman of that name.

and sea, of every essential for taking the field in the best condition. "His Royal Highness," writes a contemporary, "hath applied himself, with diligence, to reform all abuses in the army; particularly he hath lately *broke* 50 *officers*, some of them for *cowardice* at the late battle of Falkirk, and some others because they were but *boys*, and such as he looked on to be very unfit for the command of brave men, and too soft to endure the severities of such a campaign.* And he has, in order to fill their vacant commissions, advanced such Serjeants and others, who, by their good behaviour, have proved themselves worthy of that honour, and from whose experience, in military affairs, his Royal Highness expects better conduct, especially that now they find *merit alone brings preferment.*" By these and other corresponding measures, the Duke was able, April 19th, to leave Aberdeen, with everything in the fittest order for bringing the war to a conclusion. His army, by most trustworthy estimates on its own side, could muster, for the day of battle, in round numbers, thus: regular infantry, 15 battalions, with those attached to artillery, 7560—militia infantry, 1 battalion, 500—or total of foot, 8060—cavalry, 2 regiments of dragoons, and 1 of horse, 900—total infantry, artillery, and cavalry, for battle, 8960—besides a militia reserve of nearly 1000, constituting a general aggregate of above 9960 men. His field train consisted of 16 pieces, managed by skilful gunners;† and a well-stored provision-fleet, with ships of war, advanced by sea, so as to insure the troops against any want of subsistence on shore, in their march for Inverness, the Jacobite metropolis and head-quarters. Meanwhile Prince Charles's resources, for the support of his adherents in a contest against an enemy supplied with everything, were dwindling away to nothing. In addition to the absence of the detachment with Lord Cromarty, the cessation of all pay in money, even for a considerable time preceding the unfortunate capture of the treasure with Captain Talbot, had caused a dispersion of many of the Highlanders, for subsistence, to places too distant from Inverness, to admit of their reaching it soon enough to encounter the approaching Georgeites; and such a force as Charles could draw together there, for that purpose, were sadly inferior to the enemy in number, and still worse off in other respects. The whole—including, among others, Brigadier Stapleton's and Lord George Murray's previously-detached corps—the latter obliged to raise the blockade of Blair Castle upon the advance of a body of Hessians, &c.‡—are alleged, on their side, to have

* "To observe some officers, both in the army and fleet," complains an English metropolitan journal in 1746, "one would be tempted to take regiments and ships not only for *schools*, in the literal sense, but even for *nurseries.*" The indignant journalist then descants on how "those who give commissions *can* be so mistaken, or *are* so dishonest, as to think they can answer to their country the disposal of them in such a manner," &c.

† My 2 leading Georgeite authorities, for enumerating the Duke's *infantry*, are the following:—1. "Return of the Number of Officers and Men in each Battalion of the King's Army the Day of the Battle of Culloden"—with an annexed general computation, or one, in round numbers, of the strength of its militia and cavalry. 2. "Account of the Distribution of the sum of £4000 amongst the Regiments engaged at Culloden, the Number on the Spot, and the Sums allowed to Each, according to the Apportionment transmitted by His Royal Highness, the Duke." Each of these documents supplies *some* defect of the other; yet *both* leave us in the dark, as to the *full* amount of the commissioned officers. The Duke's *cavalry* are taken from Lord Mahon as 900; and, according to the London printed "Plan of the Battle near Culloden House," the Duke's *guns* there were 16.

‡ I merely *allude* here to Lord George Murray's force, as there were *no* Irish with it.

been finally in action not at farthest above 5000—if, indeed, they were so many, since Charles himself estimated them to Louis XV. as but 4000. Of these, the horse, consisting one-half of Fitz-James's men, were no more than 150, and worn out with the hard day and night duty which necessarily devolved upon them, as the *only* cavalry remaining. The artillery for the field amounted to 12 pieces; but, as the result showed, with very inefficient gunners; mostly, if not altogether, mere native or Highland substitutes, it would seem, for the trained Frenchmen, killed off at the recent destructive sieges. As regards food, all were on the verge of starvation; even officers of rank being reported as glad to get cabbage-leaves from farmers' gardens; and the soldiers receiving only supplies, and those not regularly, of meal, or what was called meal, which they had to convert into money, at a rate that went but too short a way to maintain them; so that the poor fellows grumbled very much, as suspecting, though unjustly, that their pay was detained by the officers, and the obnoxious meal substituted. Of this so-called meal, when the army was drawn out in a bleak and proportionably hunger-exciting position, the day previous to that on which they were engaged, all the provision received was a small loaf, biscuit, or bannock a man, "and *some not even that!*" Upon such a wretched allowance, Mr. Chambers, who tasted a piece, " carefully preserved for 81 years by the successive members of a Jacobite family," remarks—" It is impossible to imagine a composition of greater coarseness, or less likely either to please, or satisfy, the appetite; and, perhaps, no recital, however eloquent, of the miseries to which Charles's army was reduced, could have impressed the reader with so strong an idea of the real extent of that misery, as the sight of this singular relic. Its ingredients appeared to be *merely the husks of oats, and a coarse, unclean species of dust, similar to what is found upon the floors of a mill!*" In a word, the Prince was ultimately so situated, that he should either order his adherents to disperse, and, at the same time, proceed to provide for his own safety, or, with such as were still in a body, should give battle immediately, whatever might be the disadvantages on his side, since *he had neither money nor provisions left, to admit of a middle course of action, by any attempt to defer an engagement.** And *this*, though, as

* In the "Particular Account of the Battle of Culloden," by "an Officer of the Highland Army," &c., dated from Lochaber, in May, 1746, published at London in 1749, and republished, under another heading, or title, in the Lockhart Papers, the writer affirms—" I am positively inform'd, that the whole Highland army did not consist of above 5000 fighting men "—*misprinted*, by the way, as " 7000 " in the republication—and he states, "there were not above 150 horse, of which one half," i. e., 75, " was of the Regiment of Fitz-James." Of this handful of cavalry, immediately previous to the action, he adds—" The horse of the Prince's army had been all on so hard duty, for several days and nights before, that none of them were fit for patrolling at that time "—of Cumberland's advance to engage. In the description we have of the contemporary print of the battle, it is alleged of the Prince's artillery-men, " *all* of whom appear to wear kilts like the rest "—that is, were no better than native or very inferior substitutes for his former French gunners, as intimated in the text. The number of the Prince's cannon in the engagement is given from the published line of battle. Mr. Chambers and Lord Mahon *agree*, as to the Prince not having had above 5000 combatants there. According, however, to the memorial to Louis XV., of November 10th, 1746, from Charles *himself*, he fought at Culloden with only "quatre mille hommes," or but " 4000 men." Smollett likewise makes the Prince's force no higher. In fine, remarks the " Highland officer," above-mentioned, of his countrymen there—" Another misfortune they lay under was, a total want of provisions, so that *they were reduced to the necessity, either of fighting an army a third stronger, starve, or disperse.*" But the Georgeite army was, as has been shown, *more* than " a third stronger."

Lord George Murray notes, but a day's delay, for that object, would have made the Jacobite force nearly 2000 stronger!

The Georgeite army, in its march northwards, April 23rd-24th, reached and crossed the river Spey, partly about Fochabers, "where," writes an English Volunteer, "I observed several good houses, and people of fashion standing, looking at us, but," he significantly adds, "not one person to wish us good success!" Before the enemy's superior force, the Prince's outposts withdrew, to join his other troops, concentrating towards Inverness. On this retreat, the Irish, as "French piquets, Fitz-James's horse, French horse," are thus noticed by the Mac Donald journal. "Clanranald's battalion had the rear, together with the French piquets and Fitz-James's horse, to cover us from the enemy's strong advanced guard, our French horse and they often exchanging shots, and once we thought they were to have actually engaged; upon which, our regiment, and the Stewarts of Appin, under Ardshiels, were ordered back, to support the French. Upon our advanceing, Fitz-James's horse formed themselves into the wings of our right and left, upon which, their," the enemy's, "advanced guard of 200 horse, and the Argyleshire Campbells as militia, immediatly halted, and drew up in order also, but we, perceiving their whole army advanceing, retreated again." In the continuation of the Duke's march, on the 25th, from Alves to Nairn, some of the Irish piquets are mentioned by Home, as, from one end of the bridge of the latter place, exchanging shots with the British grenadiers at the other; and the Jacobite retreat thence is also referred to by that writer, as covered by a troop of the Irish, or Fitz-James's, Regiment of Horse, with the 2nd Troop of the Prince's Horse Guards, till 5 or 6 miles farther on, or at the Lough of the Clans, Charles himself, riding up unexpectedly from Inverness, with his 1st Troop of Horse Guards, followed by the Regiment of Mac Intosh, ordered a halt and formation of the entire body to receive the attack of the Georgeite pursuers, who were very near. Upon which, the latter, as then outnumbered, fell back, retiring to their army, encamped about Nairn; while the united Jacobite corps proceeded unmolested to form a like junction with their main force. Ere evening, the whole were led by Charles out of Inverness, to bivouack around Culloden House, where he and his chief officers quartered that night. Next morning, the 26th, about 6 o'clock, they were marched farther off, or between 4 and 5 miles, from Inverness, to Drummossie Muir, and posted in order of battle, to meet the Duke of Cumberland, expected that day from Nairn. The Duke, however, not appearing, since, that being his birth-day, he and his troops were spending it in corresponding festivity, a night-attack upon the English, after their carouse, was, as most likely to succeed, proposed by Lord George Murray to Charles; who consented to it, as a measure already contemplated by himself—not improbably at the suggestion of his military Mentor, O'Sullivan*—and the design was accordingly under-

* By an extract, in the newspapers, of a "Letter from Edinburgh," respecting the action at Culloden, we are told, of the Highland force—"Early on Wednesday morning Mr. Sullivan advised, that they should fall upon the Duke, as his army would be overwhelmed with sleep and wine, the day before being his Royal Highness's birth-day." It is not unworthy of observation, that 1663 years before, or A. D. 83, on the advance of the Roman General, Agricola, against the Caledonians, under similarly advantageous circumstances to those of the Duke of Cumberland against the Highlanders, or with superior strength by sea as well as by land, a nocturnal surprise was considered by the Caledonians the best mode of opposing the invader, previous to the more general and decisive engagement at the Grampian

taken by Lord George, with O'Sullivan, and the Prince, to the watchword of his father's *national* title, as "KING JAMES VIII." But, from various obstacles to the success of the enterprise, the result of the attempt was nothing better than a long march, to Kilravock and back to Culloden; necessarily reducing, by proportionate fatigue, hunger, and weakness, the physical efficiency of the unfortunate Jacobite force, that, as if its previous privation and suffering were not enough, had thus, under an *aggravation* of those evils, to encounter the Duke of Cumberland.

> "Strength is derived from spirits and from blood,
> And those augment by gen'rous wine and food:
> What boastful son of war, without that stay,
> Can last a hero through a single day?
> Courage may prompt; but, ebbing out his strength,
> Mere unsupported man must yield at length;
> Shrunk with dry famine, and with toils declin'd,
> The drooping body will desert the mind."
> POPE'S HOMER, Iliad, xix., 159-166.

About 5 in the morning of the 27th, the disappointed, harassed, and famished troops returned from Kilravock to Culloden Moor, and some threw themselves down to rest, and others dispersed several miles round as far as Inverness for food or drink, when, in less than 3 hours, or between 7 and 8, Charles, who, after obtaining with difficulty some bread and whisky, had likewise retired to take some repose at Culloden House, was aroused by intelligence of the van of the enemy being not above 2, and the rest not above 4, miles off. He consequently mounted for the field with his General Officers, and the scattered men were signalled by cannon shot, and the trumpet, drum, and pipes, to return for the engagement that was approaching; a summons with which though numbers complied, yet too many were unable to do so. O'Sullivan, as Adjutant-General and Quarter-Master-General, drew up the army in a position as suitable as circumstances permitted; or upon ground less eligible, indeed, than some not far off on the south side of the Nairn, where the Highlanders would be most favourably situated, as comparatively inaccessible to the hostile cavalry and cannon; but a spot, the occupation of which implied "utter ruin," as uncovering or abandoning the last or only depôt-town of Inverness to the enemy; while the locality selected, in order to cover *that* town, and the corresponding military arrangements of the Irish officer, were admitted to be "very good," on the natural supposition, that the Georgeites, from their very superior numbers, would endeavour to dislodge their opponents by assault. That, however, was *not* to be the case; almost everything seeming to co-operate, on this occasion, for the final ruin of the Stuart cause. Each army was arrayed in 2 lines, with a reserve. The cannonade, commenced shortly after 1

Hills. "The fleet, now acting for the first time in concert with the land-forces," writes Agricola's biographer, "proceeded in sight of the army, forming a magnificent spectacle, and adding terror to the war. . . . In this distress, the Caledonians resolved to try the issue of a battle," but afterwards "changed their plan, and, in the dead of night, fell, with their united force, upon the 9th legion, then the weakest of the Roman army. They surprised the advanced guard, and having, in the confusion of sleep and terror, put the sentinels to the sword, they forced their way through the intrenchments. The conflict was in the very camp"—so that had not Agricola appeared, by "break of day," for the "relief of the legion" in its "distress," it would probably have been destroyed. See Murphy's Tacitus, Life of Agricola.

o'clock by the Prince's artillery, was of little effect; the fire of the Duke's, on the contrary, being so insupportably galling, that, in about 20 minutes, the Highland force were obliged to forfeit their *only* advantage, or that of their position, by quitting it, in order to become, though the weaker, the attacking party; at the same time, that a strong northeast wind, attended with a thick shower of snow and sleet, made what was bad worse, by blowing the smoke of the artillery and small arms into their faces. Nevertheless,

> "As near extinct, the torch new light acquires,
> Revives its flame, and in a blaze expires;
> So they, when scarce the blood maintain'd its course,
> With kindled ire recruit its dying force;
> Resolve their last of days with fame to spend,
> And crown their actions with a glorious end!"
> HOOLE'S TASSO, Jerusalem Delivered, xix., 143-148.*

Led on, by the heroic Lord George Murray, sword in hand, the right, consisting of the Athol men, the Camerons, Stewarts of Appin, &c., rushed, with a loud shout, to engage the English left. So destructive was the combined fire of the English musketry, and field-pieces loaded with grape-shot, that the brigade of Athol, by the loss of at least half its officers and men, was too cruelly shattered to be able to come to the charge, and had consequently to desist, or stop short. But the other clans closed with, and broke, the 1st line of the English; the 2 most forward regiments there of Barrell and Dejean (late Monro's) being very severely handled. In Barrell's, overpowered by the brave Camerons under Lochiel, among the Georgeite officers duly disposed of, was its Lieutenant-Colonel, Rich, who not long after died of a claymore-gash received on his head, and the loss of his hand, hewn away in vainly attempting to save his colours here; of which 1 stand and 2 pieces of cannon were taken, 125 men being killed or wounded, and the rest seeking refuge behind other corps of their 2nd line. Dejean's likewise repulsed, (apparently by the Stewarts,) had 82 men *hors de combat*, making, with the 125 men previously mentioned, an admitted total of 207 slain or hurt for *both* regiments.† In the centre, the 1st line of the English had also to yield, especially to the impetuosity of the Mac Intoshes, never before in action; who, anticipating even their right, under Lord George Murray, in dashing to the charge, penetrated far beyond the enemy's cannon; the Major of the clan, John Mor Macgilvra, a powerful swordsman, having brought down 12 men there with his trusty claymore, ere he was despatched by the reinforcements sent against him, and his

---

* An adaptation of a passage in the last noble combat of Tancred and Argantes.

† The above particulars respecting the Regiments of Barrell and Dejean, with the exception of the loss of the colours, are taken from Georgeite published authorities, combined with the account of the gallant Deputy-Paymaster of the Prince's army, Robert Nairn, communicated to Home. The loss of its colours by Barrell's regiment, hitherto, I believe, unacknowledged in print, is given from a letter, dated Inverness, April 22nd, O. S., 1746, of Thomas Ashe Lee, Captain-Lieutenant in Wolfe's regiment at the battle—for a copy of which document, I am indebted to my friend, W. J. Fitz-Patrick, Esq., of Kilmacud Manor, Stillorgan, so well known by his various writings. The Georgeite officer's words are—" Poor Barrell's regiment were sorely pressed by those desperadoes, and outflanked. *One stand of their colours was taken;* Collonel Riche's hand cutt off in their defence." Another Georgeite officer's letter from Scotland, to the Honourable Colonel Thomas Butler in Dublin, likewise states, how "Lieut. Col. Rich had his hand cut off, and a cut on his head with a broadsword," &c. He died in the ensuing month of May.

gallant corps, of whom no more than 3 officers survived the action.*
Had this conduct of the Prince's right and centre been simultaneously
supported by similar ardour on the part of his left, the result would,
perhaps, have added another triumph to those of Preston-Pans and Falkirk; particularly as the regiments of the Clan-Colla, or Mac Donalds, †
who were on that wing, were among the most distinguished of the
Highlanders for bravery. But here they behaved in such a manner, as
to occasion the immediate ruin of the cause in which they were engaged,
and to cover themselves with a disgrace proportioned to the general
indignation of the Jacobites, and, indeed, of all reasonable men. Partly
irritated, and partly regarding it as an evil omen, that *they* should be
placed on the left instead of the right, which, as "the post of honour,"
they had occupied on, and claimed ever since, the memorable day of
Bannockburn, they could merely be induced to advance a little, and fire
their muskets, but by no means to make an onset, to the accustomed
charging-cry of "Claymore!" In vain the Duke of Perth, endeavouring
to appease them, alleged, that, if they displayed their usual courage here,
they would make the left a right wing, and that he himself would ever
after take the honourable surname of Mac Donald. They refused to
proceed, sullenly enduring the fire of the English, and doing nothing
better than expressing their dissatisfaction by cutting up the heath with
their broadswords, until the other clans were compelled to give way.
Of those 3 Mac Donald regiments, however, 1 gentleman, a Protestant,
Alexander, "Chieftain of Keppoch, of chivalrous character, and noted
for great private worth," acted in a manner suitable to the *former* reputation of the name he bore. "When the rest of his clan retreated," we are
informed, "Keppoch exclaimed, with feelings not to be appreciated in
modern society, '*My God, have the children of my tribe forsaken me!*' ‡

* With the Chevalier de Johnstone's 2 assertions, "our centre had already
broken the enemy's 1st line, and attacked the 2nd," and "if our centre, which
had pierced the 1st line, had been properly supported, it is highly probable, that
the English would have been soon put to flight," compare the circumstances of the
fall of the brave Major of the Mac Intoshes, &c., in Mr. Chambers's history.

† The Mac Donalds, or Mac Donnells, were called "Clan-Colla," as descendants
of 1 of the 3 brothers Colla, of the royal Heremonian line of Erin, or the eldest
Colla, surnamed "Uais," that is, *the Noble*, as having been, from A.D. 327 to 331,
Ard Righ, or Monarch, at Tara. These 3 warlike brothers, in a long and bloody
engagement, about Fincarn, in the present County of Monaghan, popularly styled,
from them, "the battle of the 3 Collas," overthrew the dominion of the old Irian
Kings of Uladh, or Ulster, and destroyed, A.D. 332, their remarkable residence at
Emania, so renowned in Bardic tale and lay, for its connexion with the heroic times
of King Conor Mac Nessa, the Champions of the Red Branch, &c. By that important success, a large territory was acquired; in the next and subsequent ages
indeed diminished; yet, of which a very considerable portion, comprehended within
the present Counties of Louth, Monaghan, Fermanagh, and Armagh, as Oirgial, or
Orgiel, was, for the most part, held by the Clan-Colla, likewise called Oirghialla, or
Orgiallans, upwards of 1200 years, or until the 16th century; even the Primacy of
Armagh, "the Rome of Erin," having been a "vested interest" in 1 family of the
race, between the 10th and 12th centuries, for nearly 200 years. In Connaught,
too, the Clan-Colla conquered extensive possessions, as early as the 5th century.
The branch of the line of Colla "Uais," or *the Noble*, which established itself from
Erin in Alba, or Scotland, and became so powerful there in the western isles, and
on the mainland, was, in the person of Donald, Lord of the Hebrides, and Kintyre
in the reign of James III., the stock of *our* Earls of Antrim.

‡ "The Irish word *Clann*," writes Dr. J. H. Todd, "signifies *children*, or
descendants. The tribe, being all descended from some common ancestor, the
Chieftain, as the representative of that ancestor, was regarded as the common
father of the Clann, and they as his *children.*"

He then advanced, with a pistol in one hand, and a drawn sword in the other, resolved apparently to sacrifice his life to the offended genius of his name. He had got but a little way from his regiment, when a musket-shot brought him to the ground. A clansman, of more than ordinary devotedness, who followed him, and, with tears and prayers, conjured him, not to throw his life away, raised him, with the cheering assurance, that his wound was not mortal, and that he might still quit the field with life. Keppoch desired his faithful follower to take care of himself, and, again rushing forward, received another shot, and fell, to rise no more!" A death, not unworthy to be compared with some of the noblest of ancient story—with that of Æmilius Paullus at Cannæ—with that of Asdrubal Barca at the Metaurus *—and, in the elevated spirit of the Homeric exclamation,—

"Let future ages hear it, and admire!"
POPE'S HOMER, Iliad, xxii., 388.

Meanwhile, on the 2nd line of the English left, the infantry-regiments of Sempill and Bligh—the 1st rank kneeling with bayonets presented, the 2nd stooping, and the 3rd upright, so as to give a double line of fire—received the flushed van of the previously-successful Highlanders with a palisado of steel, and point-blank tempests of lead, insurmountable by men, who, after 1 discharge, having, as usual, dropped their muskets, to come to close quarters, had only swords and pistols remaining; the regiments of Barrell and Dejean, recently repulsed, also rallied in support of their 2nd line, which had protected or covered them; and Major-General Huske, who was in command of that line, detached Wolfe's regiment, to increase the disorder of the Highlanders, by taking them in flank, and raking them there, as they were raked in front, by a vigorous musketry. "We marched," relates the Captain-Lieutenant of that regiment, "up to the enemy, and our left, out-flanking them, wheeled in upon them; the whole then gave them 5 or 6 fires with vast execution, while their front had nothing left to oppose us, but their pistolls and broadswords; and the fire from their center, and rear, (as, by this time, they were 20 or 30 deep,) was vastly more fatal to themselves, than to us. It was," he observes, "surprising they stood so long, at such disadvantage!" They consequently gave ground; Wolfe's corps recovering the 2 cannon lately lost, and making many prisoners.† The Lowlanders, too, farther back on the Prince's right, having presented no adequate or effective opposition to Lieutenant-General Hawley, in defence of some park-walls between him and them, that officer, by the aid of a party of Argyleshire militia, or Campbells, made such openings as enabled him to pass through, and menace that wing still more, or both in flank and rear, with the entire English left of cavalry. All along the Prince's right and centre, the Highlanders being now repulsed—yet having acted, writes a hostile eye-witness, " with that mixture of resolution and dispair that has scarcely been paralell'd," and having left, we are told, in 1 part of the

* On the deaths of Æmilius Paullus and Asdrubal Barca, see Livy and Polybius.

† Another "Letter from Wolfe's Regiment at Inverness, April 18," O. S., published in the newspapers, after mentioning, how "Barrel's regiment was hard wrought by the rebels, who pushed all their strength against them, and *took 2 pieces of cannon from them,*" then adds, "but our regiment, being ordered to flank the rebels, we soon made the place too hot for them, retook the cannon, and took a great number of prisoners," &c.

field, their dead and dying, "in layers 3 and 4 deep!"*—what remained of the Jacobite force generally displayed but 1 feeble and disheartened line, as opposed to the Georgeite army, re-forming and consolidating the several lines of its infantry, for a final and decisive effort; while the right of its cavalry, under Major-General Humphry Bland, advanced to act against the Highland left, as Hawley, and his cavalry, against the Highland right. In these hopeless circumstances, the mass, or all but 2 divisions, of the Prince's troops, one on the right, and the other on the left, broke, and fled. Those of the right, who continued together, retired, with pipes still playing and colours flying, by Balvraid, towards the Nairn, to cross it, in order to reach the mountains of Badenoch, &c.; and displayed such honourable firmness in doing so, that the English dragoons, detached to intercept them, "thought it both safest and best" to let them proceed unmolested, "over the hills and far away!" Those of the left, who continued together, marched for Inverness, in which direction, as on ground most favourable to a pursuit by the enemy's cavalry, the slaughter, among such of the vanquished as did *not* keep in a body, was greatest, and extended over about 4 of the 5 miles from the field of battle to that town. In this action, which lasted, in round numbers, 40 minutes, half occupied in the artillery-firing, and half in the closer conflict,† the Georgeites took 14 of the Jacobite colours, with artillery, &c.; and published their own casualties by the affair as 310 men of all ranks, though 1 of their own officers present says, more, or "about 340." ‡ The Jacobite slain, including so large a proportion of their best officers as to constitute "the soul of the Highland army," have been computed, by native authorities, at above 1000, if not 1200 men. § After remarking, in 1840, "the field *yet* bears witness to the carnage of which it was the scene," as, "in the midst of its dark heath, various little eminences are to be seen, displaying a lively verdure, but too unequivocally expressive of the dreadful tale," and "the way towards Inverness is fringed with many such doleful memorials of the dead," Mr. Chambers adds—"Modern curiosity has, in some cases, violated these sanctuaries, for the purpose of procuring some relic of the ill-fated warriors, to show, as a wonder, in the halls of the Sassenach; ‖ and the

* In the national song, entitled "Culloden Day," the Jacobite author notes,

"There was no lack of bravery there,
No spare of blood or breath;
For *one to two* our foes we dar'd,
For freedom, or for death."

But, concludes the poet,

"The die was risk'd, and foully cast
Upon Culloden day."

† These particulars, as to the portion of time occupied by the engagement, are from the correspondent of the Honourable Colonel Thomas Butler, already referred to.

‡ The Georgeite loss, at Culloden, was officially specified as 50 killed, 259 wounded, 1 missing, total 310. But the Captain-Lieutenant, Thomas Ashe Lee, writes, "our killed and wounded amount to about 340;" and, of Battereau's regiment, in which he had friends, and to which *no* loss is assigned in the Government published return, he informs us, a cannon-ball "kill'd a man or two" belonging to it—so that the accuracy of the return in question *may* be doubted.

§ According to Smollett, "1200 rebels were slain, or wounded, on the field, and in the pursuit;" according to Sir Walter Scott, the Jacobites lost "upwards of 1000 men;" and we *know*, what care was taken, after the action, to *put those wounded, and those slain, upon a level!*

‖ "Everybody who saw the Highlanders lying dead upon the field," alleges a

Gaël, with nobler sentiment, have been, till lately, in the habit of pilgrimising to the spot, in order to translate the bones of their friends to consecrated ground, afar in their own western glens." On those lamented victims of " dark Culloden's fateful day," (the Aughrim of Scotland,*) a native minstrel feelingly exclaims—

> " Shades of the mighty and the brave,
> Who, faithful to your Stuart, fell,
> No trophies mark your common grave,
> Nor dirges to your mem'ry swell!
> But *gen'rous hearts will weep your fate,*
> *When far has roll'd the tide of time;*
> *And bards unborn shall renovate*
> *Your fading fame, in loftiest rhyme!*"—GRIEVE.

As to the Irish from France in this engagement, the Lockhart Papers remark, on the care taken by General O'Sullivan to arrange the Prince's forces for the conflict,—" Mr. O'Sullivan drew up the army in line of battle (he being both Adjutant and Quartermaster-General), and shew'd every batalion their place." The 2nd line of the Jacobites was, according to Home, commanded by the Fontenoy veteran, Brigadier Stapleton. He was at the head of the infantry piquets of the Irish Brigade, making about 400 men. Of the 75 Irish horse of the Regiment of Fitz-James, Captain Shea's troop, with the 2nd or Lord Balmerino's troop of Scotch Life Guards, were retained by Charles about himself, on the small eminence where he stood, behind the right of the 2nd line; and, to the left of that line, detached, or so as to be able to act, if required, with the infantry piquets of the Brigade, was the other troop of Fitz-James's corps. Brigadier Stapleton was duly attentive, to the right and left of the 2nd line, under his command. On the breaking down, by the enemy, of the park wall covering the Jacobite right flank there, the Brigadier despatched a Lowland regiment, under Gordon of Abbachie, to arrest the intruders. On the left, when the opposing cavalry of the English right were the first to advance, in such a confident manner, as if they were to deal with nothing more formidable than a flying foe, the Brigadier and his countrymen interposed, with sufficient effect, to teach the aggressors, that ardour should be tempered by prudence. "The horse, on the right of the King's army," says Home, "were the first that pursued, and they were very near the Macdonalds, when the Irish piquets came down from their place in the 2nd line, and fired upon the dragoons, who halted." This check, to the cavalry of the enemy's right, was given, when, there being no hope of regaining the day, Charles had to leave the field; after " ordering," writes Captain O'Neill, " the Irish piquets, and Fitz-James's horse, to make a stand, and favour the retreat of the Highlanders, which," continues the Captain, " was as gallantly executed." Smollett, too, after noting the final confusion occasioned by the English cavalry among the Prince's force, adds of the latter, " the French piquets, on their left, covered the retreat of the Highlanders, by a close and regular fire." Lord Mahon's injustice in saying no more, with reference to the Irish here, than that "*all* the French auxiliaries *fled* towards Inverness,"

contemporary periodical, "allowed that men of larger size, larger limbs, and better proportioned, could not be found."

* See Moore's lines on Aughrim, in the Melodies, commencing,

"Forget not the field where they perish'd,
The truest, the last of the brave!"

may be best refuted, in the words of Sir Walter Scott. Having premised, how "the 3 regiments of Macdonalds, aware of the rout of their right wing, retreated, in good order, upon the 2nd line," Sir Walter states, how "a body of cavalry, from the right of the King's army, was commanded to attack them on their retreat, but was checked by a fire from the French picquets, who advanced to support the Macdonalds." Sir Walter then asserts of the brave Stapleton, and his covering piquets, "General Stapleton also, and the French auxiliaries, when they saw the day lost, retreated, in a soldier-like manner, to Inverness." Of how much "caution mark'd the guarded way," in which the Brigadier, his countrymen, and such as preserved order like them, were followed by the English horse, we are particularly informed by Sir Walter; who remarks, that those horse, along the road to Inverness, "did *not* charge such of the enemy, whether French, or Highlanders, as kept in a body, but dogged, and watched them closely, on their retreat, moving more or less speedily as they moved, and halting, once or twice, when they halted;" though, he concludes, respecting those mounted *dodgers*, "on the stragglers, they made great havoc!" In other words, like the troops defined by a Chinese Emperor as "good soldiers, when opposed to bad ones, but bad, when opposed to good ones," the conduct of the English cavalry in this pursuit was as vigorous, or *merciless*, against the dispersed, and the unarmed, or numbers who had only come out to see the battle,* as it appears to have been *shirking*, or "willing to wound, and yet afraid to strike," with regard to the retiring regulars, or those maintaining a sufficient formation for self-defence. In fine, so serviceable here at Culloden, as previously at Falkirk, were the few disciplined troops from France to Charles, that, notwithstanding his great disadvantage in point of number, but 1200 of such well-trained auxiliaries would, by the general admission of his army, have turned the scale against the enemy †—Charles himself, in his memorial of November 10th, 1746, to Louis XV., writing, with respect to the little detachment of his Majesty's troops present on that fatal day, "que *douze cent hommes de troupes réglées l'auraient décidé en ma faveur, au vu et au su de toute mon armée.*" According to a surrendered officer of Lord John Drummond's detachment of Royal Scots from France, Captain and Paymaster James Hay, the troops called "French," or the Irish belonging to the infantry of their Brigade and to Fitz-James's horse, and the Scots of the informant's regiment, amounted, in the action, to between 600 and 700 men (of whom, as already shown, the Irish regulars were about 475, and the Scotch comparatively few, as but the remainder,) the loss of the former in the battle being about 100 men, and that of the latter 50. On his approach to Inverness, the Duke of Cumberland was met by a drummer, with a message respecting its surrender, and with a letter in French, as ordered to be written by Brigadier Stapleton; the letter dated from that

* Mr. Jesse, describing that English cavalry pursuit, from the field towards Inverness, as a "frightful scene," states—"Many, who, from motives of curiosity, had approached to witness the battle, fell victims to the indiscriminate vengeance of the victors. The latter, by their *disgraces and discomfitures*, had been provoked to the *most savage thirst for revenge.*

† Had the greater portion of Fitz-James's regiment, intercepted at sea by Commodore Knowles in March, and of Lally's regiment, obliged at the same time to return to port, been able to reach Scotland, Charles, with the little band of regulars, already there, would have had *above* 1200, or more than the number deemed sufficient to give him a victory at Culloden.

place, and directed, "To the Commanding Officer of the Troops of his Royal Highness, the Duke of Cumberland." It had been first received by Major-General Bland, by whom it was forwarded to the Duke, and was as follows: "Sir,—The French officers and soldiers, who are at Inverness, surrender themselves prisoners to his Royal Highness, the Duke of Cumberland, and hope for everything that is to be expected from the English generosity. Signed, Cusack, Murphy, Marquis d'Eguilles, Dehau, O'Brien, Mac Donnell."* In reply to the delivery of this note by the drummer, together with "a message from General Stapleton, offering to surrender, and asking quarter," adds Home, "the Duke made Sir Joseph Yorke alight from his horse, and, with his pencil, write a note to General Stapleton, assuring him of fair quarter, and honourable treatment." The drummer was sent back to Inverness with this courteous answer, and a company of grenadiers, under Captain Campbell, were ordered to take possession of the place, and of the arms of the troops from France there, as prisoners of war.

Next day, 28th, the officers, who had surrendered, were allowed, by the Duke, the liberty of the town of Inverness, on signing a parole of honour, not to leave the place, "without a permission from his Royal Highness." To that document were attached the following names, connected with the Irish in the service of France. BERWICK'S REGIMENT. Stapleton, Brigadier of the Armies of the Most Christian King, and Lieutenant-Colonel—Delahoyde, Captain—Patrick Clery, Captain—Thomas Goold, Lieutenant — Peter O'Reilly, Lieutenant — Eugene O'Keeffe, Lieutenant.—BULKELEY'S REGIMENT. N. Comerford, Captain—O'Donnell, Lieutenant—Thomas Scott, Volunteer.—DILLON'S REGIMENT. Cusack, Captain—Richard Bourke, Captain—Edward Nugent, Captain—John Dillon, Captain—John Mac Donagh, Lieutenant—Michael Burke, Lieutenant—Carbery Fox, Lieutenant.—ROTH'S REGIMENT. Thomas Mac Dermott, Captain—Dudley Mac Dermott, Lieutenant—Peter Taaffe, Lieutenant.—LALLY'S REGIMENT. Robert Stack, Captain †—Richard Murphy, Captain—Alexander Geoghegan, Captain—Miles Swiny, Lieutenant—Patrick Sarsfield, Lieutenant—James Grant, Lieutenant.—FITZ-JAMES'S REGIMENT. John Mac Donnell, Colonel—Francis Nugent, Captain, and Quarter-master to French troops in Scotland—Patrick Nugent, Captain—Robert Shee, Captain—Thomas Bagot, Captain—Mark Bagot, Adjutant—Barnewall, Lieutenant—John Nugent, Lieutenant—Cooke, Cornet — Philip Molloy, Quarter-master. — ROYAL SCOTCH REGIMENT. O'Donoghue, Captain—John St. Leger, Captain.—REGIMENT OF PARIS MILITIA. John O'Brien, Captain. ‡ With these 38 officers, 13 others,

* Printed, in *modern* Scotch fashion, "Macdonald," but should be, as *here* and *subsequently* given, "Mac Donnell." This was the *Irish* officer, who had been 1 of "the 7 men of Moidart."

† Of this officer, it is noted, that, "being wounded, Murphy sign'd for him."

‡ Those names, derived from 4 contemporary lists, have been generally turned from Frenchified into English forms; such evident misprints as "Patrick *Clergue*" and "*O'Danil*" have been altered into "Patrick *Clery*" and "*O'Donnell;*" and the officers of every regiment have been inserted under their respective corps, instead of otherwise. In the London Gazette, under the head of "Whitehall, April 24," O. S., 1746, the Irish, or "French piquets," after the engagement at Culloden, are mentioned, as "amounting to about 300 men," when they "surrendered themselves prisoners at discretion." And a paragraph from "Inverness, April 23," O. S., alleges of those prisoners, that "yesterday 310 of them were shipped off for Newcastle." These and the Irish intercepted *by* Commodore Knowles, and *with* Captain Talbot, would make a considerable number of men and officers.

Scotch, French, or Spanish, signed the same document, making in all 51; among whom was the Marquis d'Eguilles, in poor "Prince Charlie's" late court, known as "the French Ambassador." The gallant commander of the Irish piquets, Walter Stapleton, died at Inverness, in less than a fortnight after the action at Culloden, of the injuries he had received there; or only about a year subsequent to his distinction at Fontenoy, and promotion to the rank of Brigadier. The name of Stapleton—in the 12th century, the period of its Anglo-Norman introduction into Munster, and long after, written De Stapleton—was thus remarkable at the close of the struggle for the Stuarts in Scotland, as, about 55 years before, on a like occasion, in Ireland, when Colonel Stapleton, Deputy-Governor of Limerick for King James II., fell, in October, 1691, heading the sally against the Williamites,* which immediately preceded the truce, that led to the conclusion of the war there, by the famous Treaty. To such honourable associations of the name of Stapleton with Ireland, Flanders, and Scotland, or Limerick, Fontenoy, Falkirk, and Culloden, it may be added, that, as the Colonel was not its only representative among the officers of the Jacobite army in the national war at home, neither was the Brigadier among those of the Brigade abroad. In referring to an alleged proposal (though not acted on) among the Scotch, that their English prisoners should be put to death, Horace Walpole mentions a circumstance creditable to the memory of General Stapleton, who thereupon "urged, that he was come to fight, and *not* to butcher; and that, if they acted any such barbarity, he would leave them, with all his men." It is much to be regretted, that the Duke of Cumberland, in this contest, did not take a leaf out of the Irish officer's book; in showing, that he, too, was above "any such barbarity" as that alluded to, by regulating his conduct on the principle "that he was come to fight, and *not* to butcher."

From the different points of view in which the Irish piquets with Charles's force *might* be regarded—as, on the one hand, born subjects of the reigning dynasty of Great Britain and Ireland, yet fighting against it —and, on the other, as a portion of the troops of the King of France, entitled to the benefit of the Cartel of Frankfort, according to which the regular military, captured on each side, were to be treated as prisoners of war, without any question, as to what country they might be natives of —Major-General Bland would appear to have deemed it most expedient, on *his* part, to devolve the responsibility of a reply to the message and letter from the Irish at Inverness, on his superior officer, the Duke of Cumberland. The Duke, who, however intolerant, and even brutal, to those he designated "rebels," was not incapable of acting with the generosity of a Prince, and the politeness of a gentleman, towards those whom, though enemies, he considered to belong to his own profession as regular soldiers, behaved accordingly, with reference to the message and letter. The remains of the Irish piquets were soon after removed into England; and, owing to an attempt (as might be expected) of *some* members of her Government, to question, or explain away, the right of the *Irish* to be regularly exchanged as *French*, notwithstanding the Cartel of Frankfort, the detention of the prisoners was longer than it ought to have been; so that an official correspondence took place between the

* Plunkett's Light to the Blind. The Deputy Governor of Limerick seems to be the same officer mentioned earlier in the war, or October, 1689, by another Jacobite authority, as "Lieutenant Colonel Stapylton," and defeating a Williamite party "within 6 miles of Carlingford."

French and English on the matter; till it was at last, or in 1747, arranged, irrespective of any political higgling, or according to the terms of the Cartel, and the honest and soldierly view of the case, adopted and advocated by the Duke of Cumberland, from the beginning to the end of the business. "All these prisoners, whilst they were in England," alleges my French authority, "received subsistence money, which the Court of France transmitted to them, and which was paid to their order, without deduction. On the exchange, each officer received the amount of his allowances, during the time he had been absent, at the rate of the English penny, valued as the French sol, and the soldiers and cavalry the same." As, moreover, the treatment of these prisoners in England was good, the majority of the officers being at liberty on their parole, the condition of the piquets there was far superior to that of their campaigning in Scotland; where, in addition to the hardships connected with active service in such a cold climate, severe season, and poor or ravaged country, regular Commissaries and Paymasters from France not having accompanied the hurried landings from the Continent, "these troops," we are told, "had to be satisfied with whatever pay they could get;" and how little reason they "had to be satisfied" on *that* score, may be inferred from what has been previously written.* Their general conduct in aid of Prince Charles, allowing for the smallness of their number, was not less creditable to themselves, than worthy of the famous body of national troops from which they were detached. The volume of light, that blazed from the emerald, as one and indivisible at Fontenoy, was not to be expected from the fragments of it at Falkirk and Culloden; yet the lustre of those fragments there, though necessarily so much less, bore a fair *proportion* to the splendour of the original jewel.

"The gem may be broke
By many a stroke,
But nothing can cloud its native ray;
Each fragment will cast
A light, to the last,—
And thus, Erin, my country, tho' broken thou art,
There's a lustre within thee, that ne'er will decay;
A spirit, which beams through each suffering part,
And now smiles at all pain, on the *Prince's* day." †—MOORE.

To return to Charles. During the engagement at Culloden, he had *his* share of personal danger; 2 pieces of the enemy's well-served artillery having been specially pointed, by its commander, Colonel Belford, against him, and his immediate mounted attendants. He was bespattered, up to his face, with the mud, dashed about by the balls; the 1st horse he rode being so wounded, a couple of inches above the knee, as to become unmanageable,‡ had to be changed for a 2nd; 1 of his servants was killed, who held another horse behind him; and of the little body of Scotch and Irish cavalry around him, consisting of the 2nd, or Lord Balmerino's, troop of Life Guards, and Captain Shea's troop of Fitz-James's Regiment of Horse, each troop seemingly but 37 or 38, or both about 75 in number, the loss appears to have been fully proportioned to

* John O'Connell's French MSS. on Irish Brigade, Appendix to O'Conor's Military Memoirs, and British publications of the time.
† The Stuart Prince, it may be recollected, was *Regent* for his father James III., as the Hanoverian Prince, written of by Moore, was *Regent* for his father George III.!
‡ "Which horse," relates a Highland officer, "is now in the possession of a Scots gentleman."

the skill of the English gunners. A hostile letter from Leith on the battle remarks, with respect to the Life Guards—" The Pretender's Life Guards have suffered greatly. A person, this moment arrived, *saw* 26 of them in a heap, with the lace cut off their vests, and their tartan belts lying beside them!" And, in evidently alluding to such of Fitz-James's horse, as, after being with the Prince at, and accompanying him out of, the fight, were subsequently dismissed, with orders to surrender themselves to the Duke of Cumberland, and next day *did* so, the Duke's account would show, how few of those Irish remained. " As his Royal Highness was at dinner," adds that account, " 3 officers, and about 16 of Fitz-James's regiment, who were mounted, came, and surrendered themselves prisoners." When Napoleon, at Waterloo, though the day was lost beyond recovery, still lingered upon the field, Marshal Soult, and other officers, seized the Emperor's bridle, turned his horse round, and withdrew their Sovereign from useless destruction; the Marshal exclaiming—"Ah, Sire, the enemy is fortunate enough already!" In a similar position with Charles at Culloden, after resorting to entreaties in vain, O'Sullivan, laying hold of the reins of the Prince's horse, and assisted by Sir Thomas Sheridan, and other Irish gentlemen, hurried their unfortunate master from the fatal spectacle, which was a death-blow to the royal claims of his race.* Of Charles's subsequent wanderings, hardships, and perils, between the Highlands and Western Isles of Scotland, for the 5 months he was exposed to the pursuit of his enemies—scenes, amidst which *he displayed a strength of constitution as wonderful, as he did a fortitude, cheerfulness, and presence of mind, entitled to the highest admiration!*—it will only be requisite *here* to touch on *some* circumstances, less as connected with *his* immediate history, than as involving due notices of the principal *Irish* who either served with him, or who finally contributed to effect his return to France.

Among the former, Sir Thomas Sheridan, whose time of life, and infirmities, rendered it peculiarly necessary that he should quit Scotland for the Continent, was so fortunate as to escape, in May, along with his son, the Duke of Perth, Lords John Drummond, Elcho, Nairn, &c., from Arisaig; whence, if not unluckily departed some days before for the Western Isles, Charles himself, O'Sullivan, and Captain O'Neill, might likewise have gotten away, with 2 French privateers, the *Mars* and the *Bellone* from Nantes, that beat off 3 English ships-of-war, the *Greyhound*, the *Baltimore*, and the *Terror;* and, it may be observed, also *brought so large a sum, for the Prince, as* £37,775 ; *which, if landed a few weeks sooner, would most probably, if not certainly, have given a different turn to the contest.*† After various adventures on both elements, " enduring privations of

* On Napoleon at Waterloo, compare the accounts of Generals Gourgaud and Vaudoncourt, and M. Fleury de Chaboulon. Respecting Charles at Culloden, according to Home, "The Cornet, who carried the standard of the 2nd Troop of Horse Guards, has left a paper, signed with his name, in which he says, that the entreaties of Sir Thomas Sheridan, and his other friends," to quit the field, "would have been in vain, if General Sullivan had not laid hold of the bridle of Charles's horse, and turned him about." Sir Walter Scott adds, how Charles "was forced from the field by Sir Thomas Sheridan, and others of the Irish officers, who were about his person."

† " Si j'eusse reçu plutôt," writes Charles to Louis XV., "la moitié seulement de l'argent que votre Majesté m'a envoyé, j'aurais combattu le Duc de Cumberland avec un nombre égal, et *je l'aurais surement battu,*" &c.; since, he goes on to say, so much *was* done, by such a very inferior number as that of the Highland army at Culloden. And they *wearied* and *starving!*

every kind, fleeing from island to island, and from rock to rock, tormented by hunger and thirst, unprotected from the cold, and constantly exposed to every kind of weather," Charles, with "his dear O'Sullivan and his faithful O'Neill," (as I find them designated) and some others, was, towards the end of June, in the island of South Uist, where he, and his companions, were kindly entertained. "For the Mac Donalds in that island," writes a hostile contemporary, "are a generous sort of people, and being all Papists,* they cultivate the old Scots' union with France, both in religion and civil policy. Few, or none of them, though born with a martial genius, enter into the British army, but rather seek their fortunes abroad, and are much assisted toward preferment by the Chevalier and his sons." The enemy, being informed of the quarter in which Charles and those who accompanied him had taken refuge, prepared such a force by sea and land for the apprehension of the party, that all the coasts of Uist, Skye, &c., and the channel towards the mainland, swarmed with armed vessels, or other light craft, on the watch against any attempt to leave Uist, that, moreover, without a passport, was made "high treason;" while the small territory of which Uist consisted, only 20 miles long, and at most 4 broad, was to be searched with detachments of a corps of 2000 men, hoping to gain or share the promised government reward of £30,000, for "the young *Pretender*," by proceeding, in different directions, from the coast, till they should so inclose, as to net or dispatch him, in the interior of the country.

Among the most odious of those "human wolves" who, although Scotchmen by birth, yet, the better to qualify themselves for further preferment, or additional pay, shrank from no inhumanity at the expense of their unhappy Jacobite countrymen, were 3 ruffians, Captains Caroline Scott and John Ferguson, and a Major Lockhart.† Of those 3 sanguinary wretches, the 1st, known as "the ferocious Scott," was within a mile of Charles and his companions, when O'Sullivan, by what he had suffered, found himself so disabled for travelling any more on foot, that it was necessary he should remain, duly disguised, in the care of some faithful boatmen. On the consequent separation between the Prince and his General, my informant, alleges a Georgeite writer, "declared, that the Chevalier's parting with Sullivan was *like tearing his heart from his body* —for *that* was the man's phrase." Charles, then "taking a couple of shirts under his arm," and accompanied only by Captain O'Neill, hastened, as it grew dark, to get from South Uist into Benbecula; which, when the tide was out, was joined with South Uist, but, when the tide was in, formed a separate island. There, "at midnight," relates Captain O'Neill, "we came to a hut, where, by good fortune, we met with Miss Flora Mac Donald," of South Uist, "whom I formerly knew.

---

* Governor Campbell, too, writing from Fort William in August, 1745, to Sir John Cope, refers to the Jacobite landing from France, and sympathy with that movement on the *mainland* of Scotland, as having taken place, "in the country of Moidart—inhabited by the Macdonalds, all Roman Catholics." And Sir Walter Scott, in mentioning the famous Keppoch, (whose death has been noticed at Culloden,) and *his* Mac Donalds, observes, how, though "Keppoch was a Protestant, his clan were Catholics."

† Mr. Jesse, in naming "Captain Caroline Scott, and Major Lockhart," among the vile representatives of official brutality towards the unfortunate Jacobites, remarks—"It is natural, perhaps, as an *Englishman*, to feel some satisfaction, in recording that 2 out of the number were *Scotchmen*." He might have added a 3rd, in Ferguson. But *who* employed and promoted *them?*

I quitted the Prince at some distance from the hut, and went with a design to inform myself," with respect to the enemy, "if the Independent Companies were to pass that way next day, as we had been informed? The young lady answered me, not, and said, that they were not to pass, till the day after. Then I told her, I had brought a *friend* to see her; and she, with some emotion, asked me, if it was *the Prince?* I answered her, it *was;* and instantly *brought him in!* We then consulted on the imminent danger the Prince was in, and could think of no more proper and safe expedient, than to propose to Miss Flora to convey him to the Isle of Sky, where her mother lived." This, as the zealous Captain suggested, Miss Mac Donald might effect, by obtaining from her brother, who commanded 1 of the Independent Companies, a pass, empowering her to return to her mother in that island, accompanied by a female servant, in which character the Prince might be disguised. Miss Mac Donald at first very naturally, though "with the greatest respect and loyalty," declining to act upon the proposal, from the trouble in which it might involve her relatives, "I then," says the noble-hearted O'Neill, " demonstrated to her *the honour and immortality that would redound to her, by such a glorious action;* and she at length acquiesced, after the Prince had told her the sense he would always entertain of so conspicuous a service." * She promised the Prince and the Captain, to acquaint them when the necessary arrangements should be concluded, and they betook themselves to the mountains.

But, though thus far fortunate, it was some time before circumstances admitted of their being relieved from the miseries of their situation. After having been arrested with her servant, as venturing to cross the ford between Benbecula and South Uist without a passport, and been detained longer than was desirable at the adjacent military station, Flora was liberated by her stepfather, Mr. Mac Donald of Armadale, who likewise gave her a passport and letter for Skye, empowering her to proceed thither, with a man to attend her, and " one Betty Burke, an Irish girl," as a good spinner, in which last character the Prince was to be disguised. The means for effecting this disguise were finally attained through the aid of Lady Clanranald, or Clanronald, wife of the proprietor of the island. "Lady Clanronald," alleges the Highland journal, "dress'd up the Prince in his new habit, not without some mirth and railry passing amidst all their distress and perplexity, and a mixture of tears and smiles. The dress was on purpose coarse and homely, suited to the fashion of the wearer, viz., a callico gown, with a light coulered quilted pettycoat, a mantle of dun camelot, made after the Irish fashion, with a hood joined to it." These habiliments were so little adapted to the Prince, that the appearance he made in them subsequently caused 1 of his protectors, the worthy Mac Donald of Kingsburgh, to remark—"Your enemies call you a *pretender;* but, if you be, I can tell you, you are the *worst* of your trade I ever saw." Charles was not ready to depart, with his generous benefactress, for Skye, before it was high time that he should do so, as

* Bishop Forbes alleges of Captain O'Neill's narrative, on this interesting occasion—" In all this, Captain O'Neille is exactly right: for I have heard Miss Mac Donald declare, more than once, that the Captain came to her (bringing the Prince along with him) when she happened to be in a shealing," or cabin, " belonging to her brother; that *the Captain was the contriver of the scheme;* and that she herself was very backward to engage in it: and, indeed, no wonder, (whatever some may say) when one seriously considers the important trust, and the many dangers attending it."

General John Campbell of Mamore (afterwards 4th Duke of Argyle) had not only arrived with a large number of military in Benbecula, but a messenger, with the still more alarming intelligence, that the infamous Captain Ferguson, and an advanced party, were actually at Ormaclade, the residence of Lady Clanranald, reached that lady, while she was still at dinner, in a hut, near the shore, with her friend Flora, the Prince, and O'Neill, previous to the intended embarkation. Lady Clanranald had consequently to hurry home, while Charles and Flora prepared to sail, attended by a trusty Highlander, Neil Mac Echan.*

Charles, who had now to part with the "faithful O'Neill," so long his companion in suffering and danger, could hardly bring himself to agree to such a separation. He requested Flora, and was, for some time, most pressingly joined by the Captain in the request, that *all* should sail together; with which proposal, she, however, very sensibly refused to comply, in as much as such an addition to the number authorized in her pass, while exposing the *supernumerary* party to a risk that could be avoided, might frustrate the entire undertaking. The Prince, nevertheless, was so generous, as to decline going at all unless accompanied by O'Neill, until the latter, on due consideration, perceiving, how imperative it was, that prudence should get the better of attachment, said to Charles— "If you make the least demur, I will instantly go about my business, as I am extremely indifferent what becomes of me, so that your person is safe." Still, it was only with much difficulty, and not until after many entreaties, that Charles would consent to embark, attended only by Flora, and Mac Echan. "Here," exclaims O'Neill, "my hard fate, and the Prince's safety, which was my only object, obliged me to share no longer the fortunes of that *illustrious hero, whose grandeur of soul, with a calmness of spirit particular to himself in such dangers, increased in these moments when the general part of mankind abandon themselves to their fate.*† I now could only recommend him to God and his good fortune, and made my way, amidst the enemy, to South Uist, where we had left Colonel O'Sullivan. Next day I joined O'Sullivan, and found (4 days after the Prince parted) a French cutter, commanded by one Dumont, and who had on board 2 Captains of the Irish Brigade, with a number of Volunteers. Here Colonel O'Sullivan and I concerted what were the properest measures to be taken. We agreed, that he should go on board the cutter, as *he was so reduced by the long fatigues that he had undergone in the mountains, as not to be able to walk;* and that he should bring the cutter to Loch Seaforth, nigh the Isle of Rasay, where the Prince ordered me to join him, by a billet he had sent me, the day before, by one of the boatmen who had rowed him to the Isle of Sky. After having seen my friend on board, and after innumerable difficulties, I got a boat, and went round the Isle of Sky to the Isle of Rasay, place of rendezvous; but, at my landing, had intelligence, that the Prince was returned to the Isle of Sky;

---

* A Mac *Donnell*, (as he himself *wrote* the name,) or Mac Donald. He was father of the celebrated Étienne-Jacques-Joseph-Alexandre Mac Donald, previous to and at the Revolution, an officer of the Irish Brigade, in the Regiment of Dillon; finally Marshal of France, Duke of Tarentum, &c.; and by Napoleon, at Fontainebleau, in 1814, so nobly "faithful found, among the faithless."

† The representations of Charles by his Scotch adherents fully support the warm terms in which he is here spoken of by the Irish officer. Among other circumstances to Charles's credit, we are told, that "he *regretted more the distress of those who suffered for adhering to his interest,* than the hardships and dangers he was hourly exposed to."

whereupon, I hasted to said Isle of Sky again, and there, too, had the grief to learn, that he had departed that island; but, for what place, nobody could inform me in the least. I then repaired to Loch Nammaddy, in North Uist, where, by our agreement, Colonel O'Sullivan was to come to me, in case that, in 8 days, I did not join him at Loch Seaforth." Here also the honest and indefatigable O'Neill was disappointed, yet without his explaining *why*—the reason, however, being, that the French cutter, in which O'Sullivan *was* at the appointed rendezvous, having been heard of by the enemy, and, about 3 hours before O'Neill's return, 2 of their armed wherries, with 30 men in each, having been descried approaching to attack the vessel, advantage was taken of a fair wind to escape, and sail for France.*

"Not finding my friend there," continues O'Neill, with reference to O'Sullivan at Loch Nammaddy, in North Uist, "after a delay of 4 days, I returned to the Isle of Benbecula, where I promised myself greater safety than anywhere else; but I met with a quite different usage, for the very person in whom I had entirely confided, and under whose care I was, betrayed me to Captain Mac Neal, (induced thereto by a great sum of money offered for me,) † who was in that country, under the command of Captain Fergusson of the *Furnace* bomb." The latter, already named as among the most conspicuous of his detestable species in Scotland, was born at Old Meldrum in Aberdeenshire, and having been remarkable, even in his younger years, or among his school-fellows, for a cruel turn of mind, was the fitter instrument for such unscrupulous exercises of power, as would be serviceable to the perpetrator, in proportion to their accordance with the unfeeling policy of a vindictive government.‡ "I was taken," proceeds Captain O'Neill, "by this Captain Mac Neal, in a rock, over a Loch, where I had skulked for 4 days, and brought to Captain Fergusson, who used me with the barbarity of a pirate, stripped me, and had ordered me to be put into a rack, and whipped by his hangman,

---

* In Flora Mac Donald's narrative, I am sorry to see a shameful aspersion sought to be cast upon O'Sullivan, connected with the departure for France of the cutter in which *he* was, without waiting for Captain O'Neill's return. When O'Neill came back "to the place where he had left the cutter," says Flora, "unhappily for him, he found, that the timorous O'Sullivan, having a fair wind, and not having courage to stay till O'Neill's return, being resolved to take care of number 1, obliged the Captain to set sail directly, lest he should be taken, and should lose his precious life." But, as Flora was *not* on board the cutter, how could she *know*, that O'Sullivan, who was *not* its owner, was able to oblige its French Captain to sail away?—moreover, if O'Sullivan were taken, would not his life, as that of an officer in the service of France, or like his friend O'Neill's, be *safe?*—and, is it not evident, that the French Captain of the cutter would naturally, or of his own accord, deem it only prudent to make off, when 2 hostile wherries were actually coming to assail him?—for all he knew, or might reasonably suspect, as precursors of a much greater or completely irresistible force, where the enemy, by the number of their vessels, were masters of the sea. O'Neill, too, in reference to this very circumstance of his having been left behind, styles O'Sullivan "my friend," without attaching any blame to *him*, for the occurrence in question. In a word, the cutter remained at the place appointed, until discovered, and about to be attacked by the enemy; in which case, was it to risk being captured, to *no* purpose? since, *if captured, how was O'Neill to have been taken on board, and brought back to France?*

† It is a pity, that O'Neill has not consigned his betrayer to everlasting historical damnation, by *naming* him.

‡ In a "List of Promotions" for 1746, under October, I meet with "Captain Ferguson, of the *Furnace* bomb," to be "Captain of a newly launch'd 20 gun ship, on the recommendation of the Duke of Cumberland, for his good service during the rebellion."

because I would not confess *where* I thought the Prince was.* As I was just going to be whipped, being already stripped, Lieutenant Mac Caghan of the Scotch Fusileers, who commanded a party under Captain Fergusson, very generously opposed this barbarous usage, and, *coming out with his drawn sword, threatened Captain Fergusson, that he would sacrifice himself and his detachment, rather than see an officer used after such an infamous manner.* I cannot avoid acquainting the public," concludes the Irish Captain, with reference to John Campbell, the future Duke of Argyle, "that 4 days after I was taken, General Campbell sent me word, *upon his parole of honour,* that, if I had money, or other effects, in the country, in sending them to *him,* they should be *safe;* upon which (*always imagining, that the word of honour was as sacredly kept in the English army as in others,*) † I went, with a detachment, for my money, and gold watch, which I had hid in the rock, when I perceived the party searching for me; and sent to General Campbell, by Captain Skipness Campbell, 450 guineas, with my gold watch, broad-sword, and pistols; all which *he has* thought proper (to be sure, consistent with *his* honour,) to *keep from me,* upon divers applications made to him."‡ Captain O'Neill was subsequently transferred, as a prisoner, to the *Eltham* man-of-war, commanded by Commodore Smith, for conveyance to Edinburgh Castle.

Meantime, Flora Mac Donald, having accompanied the Prince through various adventures to Portree, whence he sailed for the Isle of Raasay, was, some days after returning to her home at Armadale in Skye arrested by a party of Captain Ferguson's men, and brought on board the *Furnace,* but consigned, from his unenviable custody, to that of the kind-hearted Captain of the *Eltham.* Thus, observes Mr. Chambers, "it chanced, that she here had, for one of her fellow-prisoners, the worthy Captain O'Neal, who had engaged her to undertake the charge of the Prince—and who, by the way, had made her the offer, on that occasion, of his hand, in marriage, as a protection to her good fame. When she first met him on board, she went playfully up, and slapping him gently on the cheek with the palm of her hand, said, 'To that black face, do I owe all my misfortune!' O'Neal told her, that, *instead of being her misfortune, it was her highest honour;* and that, *if she continued to act up to the character she had already shown, not pretending to repent of what she had done, or to be ashamed of it, it would redound greatly to her happiness.*" Flora, after some detention on board, in Leith Road, off Edinburgh, was conveyed to London; but was only kept there till dismissed, under the Act of Indemnity, in July, 1747. Then about 27, she subsequently married Mr. Mac Donald of Kingsburgh, (son of the generous protector, and sufferer for having protected, Prince Charles,) and, in March, 1790, she died in Skye, aged about 70. "Continuing, to the last, a firm Jacobite," she would resent, with the utmost indignation, the presumption of any one venturing, " in *her* hearing, to call Charles, by his ordinary epithet, the *Pretender*"—and, "at her particular request, her body was wrapped in 1 of the sheets, that had been used by the unfortunate grandson of James II., during the night he rested at Kingsburgh!"

* Such "vigour beyond the law," as this allotted for Captain O'Neill by Ferguson, was, however, not *solely* assumed by him. Scotland under *Cumberlandism* in 1746, was like Ireland under *Orangeism* in 1798.

† Connect this damaging reflection of Captain O'Neill with the quotation respecting the army previously given from Dean Swift, writing to Wogan.

‡ Was it not only natural, that this Duke, as a Whig, should be opposed to a "*restoration?*"

O'Neill was sent from Edinburgh Castle to Berwick-on-Tweed, and remitted to the Continent, according to the cartel, as a French officer— after which, I much regret to know nothing more respecting him. "These," as Dr. Johnson would say, "were *not* Whigs!"—and, as a member of the same ancient Celtic branch of the human family, I may add, in allusion to the older period of our common affinity, *they* were Gaels, of whom their respective Scotias—or Scotia Major and Scotia Minor,* Erin and Alba—may well be proud. If a true-hearted devotion to what appeared the cause of proscribed and distressed right, in opposition to dominant and persecuting might, be worthy of admiration, the Irish officer and the maiden of South Uist, as representatives of *such* devotion, will always be admired in history.

> "While rolling rivers into seas shall run,
> And, round the space of heav'n, the radiant sun;
> While trees the mountain-tops with shades supply,
> Your honour, name, and praise, shall never die."
> DRYDEN'S VIRGIL, Æneis, i., 854-857.

Charles, not many days from his parting with Flora Mac Donald, or about the middle of July, quitted the islands, for the mainland, or western Highlands, of Scotland; by which change of situation, nevertheless, the dangers that menaced him wherever he went, so far from being lessened, became greater than before, and would, indeed, have been altogether insurmountable, but for the undiminished fidelity of the Highlanders to him, as the descendant of "the Bruce of Bannockburn," and, like that illustrious Prince, in the days of his adversity, hunted for his life, by his enemies. Meanwhile, the French cutter, under Captain Dumont, which escaped the armed wherries sent against her by the English, having gotten back to France, General O'Sullivan lost no time in proceeding to Versailles, and representing there, how urgent was the necessity of despatching some vessels, to extricate the Prince, from his equally afflicting and alarming position in Scotland, since the battle of Culloden. When, ere setting out from Rome for France, in 1743, to join the proposed expedition for a "restoration" in England under Marshal Saxe, Charles, *then* high in hope, took leave of his father, he said, "I trust, by the aid of God, that I shall soon be able to lay 3 Crowns at your Majesty's feet"—to which the affectionate and less sanguine reply of his father was, "Be careful of yourself, my dear boy, for I would not lose *you* for all the Crowns in the world!" The effects of O'Sullivan's representations, on behalf of Charles, at the French Court, and of the naturally increased or intense anxiety of James for the safety of his son, caused 2 frigates to be ordered for Scotland, to bring away the Prince. The command of these vessels, the *Heureux* of 30 guns, and the *Princesse de*

---

* According to Archbishop Ussher, there is *no* instance of the territory known, in modern times, as Scotland, having been styled Scotia, previous to the 11th century; in which opinion, the learned Dr. Charles O'Conor follows him; and Mr. Pinkerton, as a Scotch authority, coincides with *both;* alleging, "the truth is, that, from the 4th century, to the 11th, the names Scotia, and Scoti, belonged solely to Ireland and the Irish." Early in the *latter* century, or in 1004, we find the great Brian Borumha, or "Boru," as Ard-Righ of Erin, or Supreme Monarch of Ireland, also designated, "Imperator *Scotorum.*" When the name of Scotia began to be extended to Alba, or Albania, as Scotland had previously been denominated, Erin, Hibernia, or Ireland, as the mother-country of the Scots, was distinguished as "Scotia *Major,*" and her colony in Britain as "Scotia *Minor,*" until, finally, Scotia, or Scotland, became the appellation for the kingdom of North Britain *only.*

Conti of 20 guns, was intrusted to Colonel Warren of the Irish Regiment of Dillon; who, during a portion of the recent contest in Scotland, had corresponded, from Charles's quarters, with the Prince's father, on the Continent; and who, if successful in the important object of this voyage, was promised a Baronetcy by James. The Colonel was accompanied by Charles's late Aide-de-Camp, Sir Thomas Sheridan's son, Captain Sheridan, and a Lieutenant O'Beirne, likewise in the French Service. Sailing, in September, from St. Malo, round Ireland, in order to elude the multitude of the enemy's cruisers, and luckily befriended by a tempest, which cleared the Scotch shore of such unwelcome objects, the 2 French vessels reached Lochnanuagh; and, after having had to remain for several days there, before they could open a correspondence with the Prince, and still longer before he could reach them, they, at last, or by October 1st, took him on board with 23 gentlemen and 107 men of common rank, at the very same spot where he had disembarked about 14 months before. "Though now under the protection of the French flag," adds his Continental biographer, "Charles could hardly be said to have escaped all danger of falling into the hands of his enemies. The English fleet off the coast of Scotland, had, indeed, been dispersed by a storm, a circumstance to which *alone* it had been owing that the 2 French vessels had been able to make so long a stay at Lochnanuagh, and the *Heureux* was now running before a fair wind, along the Irish coast, on her way to France; but the sea was swarming with British cruisers, and it seemed scarcely probable to avoid falling in with *some* of them. The frigate that bore him, however, deserved her name," of *Heureux*, or *Fortunate*, "and, favoured by foggy weather, reached France in safety. A contrary wind prevented her from making Brest; but one French port was as good for her purpose as another; and, on the 10th of October, 1746, a year ever memorable in the annals of the House of Stuart, Charles landed, with his friends, at Roscof, near Morlaix,* in Bretagne." Such was the termination of one of the most remarkable, or chivalrous, enterprises in the records of the human race. It has been a subject of just admiration in ancient and modern times, that, when Dion sailed for Sicily to overthrow the formidable monarchy of Dionysius, he had with him only about 800 men—that, when Timoleon landed in the same island, to rescue it from the great strength of its domestic tyrants and foreign invaders, he had only about 1000 men—that, when Napoleon quitted Elba, to recover the crown of France, he was accompanied by not above 1100 men—that, when Garibaldi disembarked in Sicily, to liberate it from the Bourbon yoke, his force was little more than 1000 men! When Prince Charles Stuart, however, came on shore in Scotland, to reclaim the 3 Crowns of his ancestors from 1 of the most powerful governments in the world, his attendants consisted only of those, so deservedly famous in history and song, as "the 7 men of Moidart"—† *and 4 of the 7 were Irishmen!*

"But, overlabour'd with so long a course,
'Tis time to set at ease the smoking horse,"
(DRYDEN'S VIRGIL, Georgics, iii., 793-794,)

* There was a previous disembarkation, at Morlaix, of Jacobite fugitives, saved by Irish aid. According to Captain Orr, commander of the *Elizabeth* of Glasgow, who left Morlaix, in July, "while *he* was there, an Irish wherry arrived at that port, with about 30 rebel officers."

† "Listen only to the naked truth," observes Charles, in 1 of his Proclama-

PRINCE CHARLES STUART.

or conclude a narrative of that undertaking, which has occupied so much space yet could hardly have been treated of in less, as well, from the share in the several occurrences connected with the names of O'Sullivan, Sheridan, Grant, Brown, Lally, Stapleton, Glascock, Talbot, O'Neill, Warren, and the piquets, in general, of the Irish Brigade, as from the importance of the contest with reference to Great Britain and Ireland; the change of dynasty, commenced by the landing of William of Orange at Torbay, in 1688, not being entirely confirmed, until the success of William of Cumberland at Culloden, in 1746.*

On the Continent, in 1746, the French turned to good account for *themselves*, in the Netherlands, the enterprise of Prince Charles, which, by having caused so many British troops, and Hessians in British pay, to be drawn off to England and Scotland, had proportionably weakened the Allied forces. Bruxelles, or Brussels, invested by the Marshal de Saxe in January, was reduced to surrender in February; from which period, till the conclusion of the campaign in October, Antwerp, Mons, St. Guislan, Charleroy, and Namur, were gained from the Confederates; and their army was defeated at Roucoux, near Liege, with the loss of several thousand men, a number of military ensigns, and many pieces of artillery. But the Irish corps were so incomplete this campaign from such of their fellow-soldiers as had been captured at sea endeavouring to reach Scotland, and such as did land there with Brigadier Stapleton, that the infantry Regiments of Bulkeley, Clare, Roth, Berwick, Dillon, and Lally were generally appointed merely to garrison duty in Flanders and Artois, and to attend to the re-establishment of their respective complements. They were aided in this from Ireland, more especially from the County Clare, or that in which the Lieutenant-General Lord Clare and Earl of Thomond, as *the* O'Brien, had a due local or family interest. Captain Anthony Mac Donough, already mentioned as so distinguished at Fontenoy, was despatched, writes his grandson, "with a Mr. O'Brien, to the County of Clare, to recruit for the Brigade, which they were obliged to do by stealth; and they sent off the recruits by ships that came off the coast of Doolan in Clare with smuggled claret and brandy, and took back the wool of that part of the country, and also the recruits, who were called *wild geese*." The Lord Clare and Earl of Thomond, writing from Paris to his gallant friend, the Captain, remarks, "with your assistance, and O'Brien's, the ranks are near filled up;" and in a subsequent letter, his Lordship adds, "the Brigade being now complete, in a high state of discipline, and as fine a body of fellows as ever

tions, "I, with my own money, hired a vessel, ill provided with money, arms, or friends. I arrived in Scotland, attended by *seven* persons," &c. They are thus referred to in the song—

> "At Moidart our young Prince did land,
> With *seven* men at his right hand,
> And a' to conquer nations *three!*" &c.

In an alleged letter from Frederick of Prussia to Charles, (in Collet's Relics of Literature) it is remarked to the Prince, respecting his Scottish expedition—"All Europe was astonished at the greatness of the enterprise; for, though Alexander, and other heroes, have conquered kingdoms with *inferior* armies, *you* are the only one, who ever engaged in such an attempt *without one*."

* In addition to the leading collections of documents, and historical narratives, that have appeared on the civil war of 1745-6, I have, for *my* abstract of the contest, made due use of the contemporary magazines, and 2 volumes of newspapers for those years, fortunately preserved in Trinity College Library, Dublin.

steped on a parade, I would not give up the command of them, for any honors that could be confered upon me. . . . It would delight you to hear another Irish shout from the Brigade." This state of efficiency is to be understood of the 6 infantry corps, as *a* brigade, more particularly considered *the* Brigade; the Irish horse Regiment of Fitz-James, from the result of its exertions for Prince Charles, having to be entirely renewed, and so *not* ready for active service before April, 1748. At the close of October, 1746, it being apprehended in France, that the English, who had endeavoured, though unsuccessfully, to capture Port L'Orient, in Brittany, might make another landing there, or in Normandy, all the Irish regiments were despatched to winter in those provinces, for their greater security.*

Early in the spring of 1747, the Allied troops, 120,000 in number, or 10,000 more than the French,† were assembled for the approaching campaign in the Netherlands; the Duke of Cumberland as Commander-in-Chief, having his quarters with the British, Hanoverians, and Hessians, about the village of Tilberg; the Prince de Waldeck with the Dutch about Breda; and the Imperial Marshal Bathiani with the Austrians and Bavarians about Venlo. But they were kept encamped in an ill-judged state of inactivity for 6 weeks, at once exposed to bad weather, and so pinched for provisions and forage, as to suffer considerably, through such mismanagement, with respect to their health, and means of subsistence. The French, meanwhile, under the Marshal de Saxe, supported by the celebrated Count de Lowendahl, Count de Claremont, and other experienced General Officers, were kept comfortably cantoned about Brussels, Bruges, and Antwerp; the Marshal, who was remarkable for the care he took of his soldiers, observing—"When the Allied army shall be weakened by sickness and mortality, I will convince the Duke of Cumberland, that the 1st duty of a General is to provide for the health and preservation of his troops." In April, the Marshal's forces were joined by the 6 infantry corps of the Irish Brigade, who, though not employed in the field the preceding summer, had suffered no corresponding diminution of pay, or other allowances, in order that such liberality might render them the fitter for action this year. The French, having to enter early on this campaign, and the distribution of forage occurring proportionably early, or before the country was in a fit condition to be foraged, we find it officially mentioned of the Irish, that here, as on other occasions, they had a larger share of forage allotted to them in every distribution than the French. In the operations which preceded the leading object of the campaign, or that of bringing the Allies to such an engagement, and giving them such a defeat, as might admit of the siege and reduction of Maestricht, the Lord Clare and Earl of Thomond defended Malines, or Mechlin, and the bridge of Valheim, with a corps of 18 battalions and 18 squadrons. Harassed for 6 entire weeks by the enemy, who had collected between Antwerp and him, he baffled the attempts they made against

---

* The account given of the Irish Brigade on the Continent, in 1746, and especially of the time it took to re-establish the Horse Regiment of Fitz-James, after what it had suffered by its connexion with the contest in Scotland, is derived from the *official* "Memoir concerning the Irish Troops," in Mr. O'Conor's Appendix. Yet, at the battle of Roucoux, October 11th, 1746, among "les régiments étrangers qui s'y distinguerent le plus," Fieffé names that of "Dillon." As having lost less, or been recruited sooner, than the other Irish corps, it may have been in that ngagement, and so "distinguished."

† See Smollett and Sismondi.

him; and, in their subsequent march on their left, he observed them so closely, as to be able to give suitable information respecting it to Louis XV., who joined the Marshal de Saxe in June.

After a reduction by the French of several fortified places belonging to the Dutch with garrisons of above 5,000 men, and a baffling by the Marshal de Saxe of an attempt of the Duke of Cumberland at a diversion against Antwerp, the Allies had to retire in the direction of Maestricht, in order to cover and fight for it. The key of their position, or that portion of it, the retention or loss of which would decide the general event of the action in contemplation, was the village of Laffeldt, otherwise Lauberg, Label, or Val, in front of their left wing. This wing was under the immediate command of the Duke of Cumberland, who provided well for the defence of the village with his German and British infantry, aided by artillery, and a reserve of cavalry. In the sanguinary engagement that ensued, July 2nd, the post in question was, for some hours, most gallantly maintained against the French, whose infantry brigades of Monaco, Segur, la Fere, Bourbon, Bettens, Monin, des Vaisseaux, the Irish, Tour-du-pin, du Roi, d'Orleans, supported by artillery and cavalry, were not finally victorious until after several repulses, and, for the most part, such a severe handling, as left the conquerors, so far, little to boast of, compared with the conquered; who had, indeed, to retire altogether towards Maestricht, yet retreated in good order, and then encamped in such a manner about that important place, as to render a siege of it impossible. The necessity for a retreat, on the part of the Allies, arose at a period of the day, when the state of the contest appeared not unlikely to lead to a different result. That unfortunate necessity was owing to the Dutch horse; in this action, as at Fleurus, and Landen, of any thing but "glorious memory." An English officer, made prisoner by the French, writes—"If the left wing of our army had been supported, the battle would have become general, and we should certainly have got a compleat victory. This was prevented by the cowardice and bad behaviour of the Dutch, who turn'd their backs, and, in their flight, put 2 brigades into disorder; on which, the Welsh Fuzileers fired 2 platoons upon the Dutch." Of those "Dutch horse," another English letter, from a gentleman who was present, more fully informs us—"This attack was made upon the infantry of our left wing. Part of this wing was composed of some Dutch horse. These (according to custom) galloped away, full speed, 200 yards *before* they came to their enemy. In their headlong flight, they fell upon a body of Hessians, and 1 squadron of the Scotch Greys, who were borne away in this monstrous tide of Dutch cowardice; and all together fell in confusion upon 2 of our regiments of foot, the Scotch and Welsh Fuzileers, and trampled them to the ground. The Scotch Fuzileers, indeed, fired upon that party of Dutch which were falling upon them, and saved themselves a little; but the Welch were very much hurt. This occasioned such disorder, that the regiments engaged in the village could not be properly supported; so a retreat was necessary." Nor was the event of the action likewise without being influenced by some British cowardice; respecting which, in a Colonel of a battalion of the Guards, &c., the contemporary Dublin Courant, No. 345, reports—"*Col. R—— is since broke, as are several others, who misbehaved that day.*" And Horace Walpole writes—"*Our Guards did shamefully, and many officers.*" Of killed, wounded, and missing, the Allied returns presented, of Continental troops, 3913, among whom the Germans, *viz.,*

2435 Hanoverians, 600 Austrians, and 385 Hessians, formed the greater part, or 3420; the Dutch, as 493, constituting the remainder of those 3913 Continentals; the British amounted to but 2110; the whole thus making 6023. The French estimated their killed and wounded at about the same number, or 6000; while, of prisoners, they lost, according to the Allies, above 60 officers and 700 men. Of colours and standards, some in a more or less imperfect state, or the flag without the staff and *vice versâ*, the Allies claimed to have taken from the French 17. The French allege a capture, on their part, from the Allies, of 16 colours or standards, with 29 pieces of cannon, and 2 pair of drums.*

"We have seen Cumberland before; we will give him another Fontenoy!" was the exclamation among the Highlanders, in reply to Prince Charles, when he addressed them at Inverness, ere they marched thence, to encamp upon Culloden Moor. Providence had *not* willed, that this anticipation of Highland enthusiasm should be realized; but *here* at Laffeldt, the Irish Brigade, who sympathized, as Jacobites, with the Highlanders, were, for the 1st time, since Fontenoy and Culloden, in a position to deal with the Duke of Cumberland in a suitable manner; by renewing, at his expense, the glory of the former engagement, and avenging the disaster of the latter. After the 6 French brigades, or those of Monaco, Segur, la Fere, Bourbon, Bettens, and Monin, had been repelled to the verge of the village in dispute, the Marshal de Saxe caused a battery of heavy artillery to advance with the 2 choice Brigades des Vaisseaux and the Irish. The general inspection of this attack fell to the famous Comte de Clermont; having under him, as Lieutenant-General, the Lord Clare and Earl of Thomond, and as Major-General, the Counts de Fitz-James and Charles Edward Roth and the Duke d'Havré. But, in compliment apparently to Scotland, which had recently acted so gallantly for the Stuarts, at the same time that 1 of her noble Jacobite exiles of the requisite military rank belonged to the Irish Brigade, the immediate leadership of that corps against "the common enemy" was assigned to Lord Dunkeld; who, having entered the service of France as 1 of the Gardes du Corps in 1722, became a Captain in the Regiment of Clare in 1731, and, since 1745, was a Brigadier, in which capacity he was now to act. Through the aid of these 2 fresh brigades, des Vaisseaux and the Irish, the enemy was pushed to the farthest extremity of the village, on his side; yet, by new efforts with his infantry, he forced his way back, and seemed about to recover what he had lost, when the post, so obstinately contended for, was turned by the 3 additional brigades of Tour-du-pin, du Roi, and d'Orleans; which flanking movement on the part of these 3 brigades, with their attendant artillery and cavalry, enabled their fellow-soldiers in the village to become masters of it. A contemporary London periodical remarks—"It is said, in the account of the battle, printed at Liege, that the French King's Brigade march'd up under the command of Marshal Saxe, and *carried the village of Lauberg,*

* I state the losses of the British, Hanoverians, and Hessians, as published by the British government, and, of the Austrians, as given by the English historian Rolt; but correct *his* enumeration of the Dutch, as but 150, into 493, from *their* accounts. The French killed and wounded are set down at about 6000 from Dumortous, in his "Histoire des Conquêtes de Louis XV.;" while, for other particulars on the French and Irish side, I am indebted to the "Rélation de la Victoire remportée à Lawffelt par le Roi sur l'Armée des Alliés le 2 de Juillet, 1747," and to a well-written publication, "Rélation de la Campagne en Brabant et en Flandres en 1747," printed at the Hague, in 1748.

after a repulse of 40 *battalions successively.*" The same periodical then cites a letter from an officer in the Allied army to his friend at York, in which, alluding to the Brigade in question, as that of "Irish, in the French service, who fought like devils," the writer asserts, "that they neither gave nor took quarter; that, observing the Duke of Cumberland to be extremely active in the defence of that post, they were employ'd upon this attack, at their own request; that they, in a manner, cut down all before them, with a full resolution, if possible, to reach his Royal Highness; which they *certainly would have done*, had not Sir John Ligonier come up with a party of horse, and thereby sav'd the Duke, at the loss of his own liberty." The same letter adds, "that it was generally believ'd, that the young Pretender was a volunteer in that action, which animated these rebellious troops to push so desperately; and, *as what advantage the French had at Fontenoy, as well as now, was owing to the desperate behaviour of this Brigade*, it may be said, that *the King of France is indebted, for his success, to the natural-born subjects of the crown of Great Britain.*" * Horace Walpole also informs us—" The Duke was *very near taken*, having, through his short sight, *mistaken a body of French for his own people"*— that so-called "body of French" being evidently the *Irish* in the French service, whom, from their *red* uniform, the Duke would be so likely to mistake, in the smoke and confusion, for some of his *own* British infantry —as, it will be recollected how the French Carabiniers, in the *mêlée* at Fontenoy, were deceived, through a similar cause, at the expense of the Irish. Nor, in reference to the legal disqualifications of the Huguenots in France through the violation of the Edict of Nantes, like those of the Catholics in Ireland through the breach of the Treaty of Limerick, should it pass unnoted, that, while the Irish Catholic exiles of the Brigade were fighting against George II., of whose dominions they were natives, and yet whose son they were *here* endeavouring to kill or make prisoner, the brave General Sir John Ligonier, to whose chivalrous interposition the safety of *that* son is attributed, was a Huguenot or natural subject of Louis XV., against whom, nevertheless, he was fighting, because as disqualified by intolerant legislation to fight on the side of France,† as the Irish Catholic of the Brigade was by similar persecution incapacitated to fight on the side of England. The French official appendix to Mr. O'Conor's work, after observing, how "the Irish Brigade distinguished itself very much, and lost considerably, upon this occasion," says—" M. de Lee was made Brigadier. Pensions of 1200 francs were given to M. Grant, Lieutenant-Colonel of Clare; to Mannery, Lieutenant-Colonel of Dillon's; to Barnwell, Lieutenant-Colonel of Berwick's; and to Hegarty,

---

* In citing this officer's letter, I omit an error, on *his* part, in alleging, "that this Brigade consisted of Scotch and Irish in the French service," &c.; beginning *my* quotation merely with "Irish in the French service." To the conduct of the Irish Brigade, here and at Fontenoy, is the general purport of the letter *alone* applicable —the Scotch regiments, in the French service, *not* having been so connected with the actions referred to—and, as to the comparative proportions of Scotch in the Irish, and of Irish in the Scotch, corps in France, the Lord Clare and Earl of Thomond, writing to the Marshal de Saxe in 1748, affirms—"I am very confident, that there are *not* 40 Scotchmen in the 6 Irish battalions, and there are *many* Irish and English men in the Scotch regiments." The circumstances of Lord Dunkeld, as a Scotchman, having headed the Irish Brigade, and of its spirit having been no less Jacobite than *if* in a great proportion Scotch, apparently caused the writer of the letter to York to fall into the error alluded to.

† Of a noble Protestant family of Languedoc, he had entered the British army at 15, and was finally a Field-Marshal and Earl.

Lieutenant-Colonel of Lally's. M. de Cusack, Lieutenant-Colonel of Rothe's, being already Brigadier, and having a pension of 600 francs given him after the battle of Fontenoy, had but 1000 francs. Commissions of Lieutenant-Colonel were given to MM. Hennesy and Arthur, Captains of the Grenadiers of Bulkeley and Rothe, and to Carroll, Major of Berwick's. A pension of 3000 francs was given to Lord Dunkeld, Brigadier, who commanded the Brigade. Numerous crosses of St. Louis and pensions were given to the Majors and Aides-Majors, and pensions of 600 and 400 francs to the wounded Captains; and of 300 and 200 francs to the Lieutenants." In replying, July 22nd, 1747, to a letter from Lieutenant-General Bulkeley, Colonel of the Regiment so named in the Irish Brigade, the Count d'Argenson, after a reference to the Lieutenant-General having officially complimented him, as Secretary at War, on the recent victory, observes—"It is I, rather, who am more justly indebted to you, for *the distinguished manner in which the Irish Brigade, and your regiment in particular, charged the enemy;* and, although the duties, confided to you at Ostend, did not allow of your being present at this engagement, you do not the less partake of *the glory which your regiment has acquired, by these new proofs of its valour.*" This "glory" appears most conspicuously there in a son of that Captain James Cantillon previously mentioned as so distinguished at Malplaquet in 1709, or the brave and accomplished Captain and Chevalier Thomas de Cantillon, an author as well as a soldier; who signalized himself at the attack of the disputed village here, says my French authority, "in carrying, at the head of his company, the right of the retrenchment, defended by the English Regiment of Pulteney"—that is, the corps known as the 13th, or 1st Somersetshire, Regiment of Foot; on this occasion, the sufferers, it will be noted, by the Regiment of Bulkeley, as the Coldstream Guards had been at Fontenoy.

Lieutenant-General Count Arthur Dillon, in remarking, how, at the battle *here* treated of, "the Irish Brigade fought very valiantly under the eyes of Louis XV.," and how "it was engaged in the attack and 2 recaptures of Lawfeld," adds, that "it met with very rough treatment there, since it lost 1600 men, and 132 officers"—a great number in proportion to the strength of the 6 Irish battalions! even if the original word "perdit," or "lost," should *not* be limited to the sense of "killed," but considered to denote those put "hors de combat" in a general sense, or that of "killed *and* wounded." This, indeed, would seem to be the case, from a contemporary London account of the slain and hurt officers of the Brigade; in making use of which, I correct the usual errors of the foreign spelling and printing with respect to the Irish; insert the mortally wounded under the head of the "killed;" and, for uniformity sake, give only the family names of those included, as the Christian names are in several instances omitted. The document is entitled—"List of the Killed and Wounded of the Irish Regiments in the French Service, at the Battle of Lauffield village, near Maestricht, July 2, 1747." The regiments are thus proceeded with:—BULKELEY'S. Captains, Kennedy, Macgennis, Lee, Mac Carthy, Geraldine, Wollock, and Sweeny, *killed*—Captains, Kearney, Macennery, Mac Mahon; Lieutenants, Bourke (taken prisoner), Mac Mahon, Nagle, Comerford, and Ensign Butler, *wounded.*—CLARE'S. Captains, Grant, Barnwell, O'Brien, Mac Carthy; Lieutenants, Bridgeman, Moore, and Wall, *killed*—Captains, 2 O'Briens, Ryan, Aylmer, Heigher, O'Meara, Sullivan, Plunkett, and Fitz-Gerald, *wounded.*—DILLON'S. The Colonel, captured mortally disabled, or with Captains Prince, Bourke, Lewis; Lieutenants, Nihill, Kennedy, Sheil, and Ensign Moore, *killed*—Captains, 2 Kennedys, O'Connor, Bourke, and Lieutenant Carroll, *wounded.*—ROTH'S. Captain Wivel, *killed*—Captains, Shee, O'Brien, Dalton, and Lieutenant Healy, *wounded.*—BERWICK'S. Captains, Hegarty, Barnwell; and Lieutenants, Laffin and Dwyer, *killed*—Captains, Barnwell, Macgrath, and Mac Carthy, and Lieutenants, Dowdal and Macgrath, *wounded.*—LALLY'S. Lieutenant-Colonel, Lynch, and Captains, Glascock and Geoghegan, *killed* —Lieutenants-Colonel, Hegarty and Dillon, and Lieutenants, Prendergast and Kelly, *wounded.* Then, under the head of "contusions of the same regiment," or that of Lally, are Captain White, Lieutenants Butler, Kearney, and Flaherty, with the observation, that "the contusions of the other regiments are numerous, but slight, which occasioned them not to be mentioned." The officers previously named, (exclusive of those *not* so, as but slightly hurt,) form a total of 69. The 2 principal officers of the Brigade among the victims of this bloody conflict were the Colonel Count Edward Dillon of that noble race, in this instance referred to even by the Anglo-Whiggish, or Anti-Irish, and Anti-Catholic, prejudices of Voltaire, as "le Colonel Dillon, nom célèbre dans les troupes Irlandaises," and another gentleman of noted Galway origin, distinguished as a Jacobite loyalist, or cavalier, in the recent unfortunate expedition to Scotland, Dominick Lynch of the Regiment of Lally; the inscription on whose tomb at Louvain, as copied by Dr. de Burgo in 1769, was as follows:—

D.   O.   M.

Hic, ut voluit, jacet
Prænobilis Dominus
Dominicus Lynch,
Ex Nobili Lynceæorum Galviensi Familia,
Hibernicæ Legionis de Lally
Vice Colonellus,
Qui plurimis in Scotia
Peractis Facinoribus,
Posteà vulneratus in Prælio Laffeltens.,
Die II Julij MDCCXLVII,
Obijt Lovanij,
Die XXVIII Augusti ejusdem Anni.

R.   I.   P.*

The Irish are also *reported* to have lost a "standard;" on no better authority, indeed, than a hostile or English and Anglo-Irish assertion, yet one necessary to be fully refuted *here*, in order to obviate any citation of it *hereafter*, as a supposed proof of such a loss. The London Gentleman's Magazine for September, 1747, alleges, under its "List of Promotions," that "Thomas Davenant, Ensign in Wolfe's Regiment," was appointed, "by the Duke of Cumberland, Ensign in the Coldstream Regiment of Guards;" adding, "he took a standard of the French Irish Brigade in the late battle." In Faulkner's Dublin Journal, No. 2138, (September 8th—12th, O. S., 1747,) it is likewise stated—"His Royal

* This Lieutenant-Colonel of the Regiment of Lally was the officer named "Lynch" elsewhere mentioned among those who accompanied Colonel Warren to Scotland, to bring away the Prince; subsequently noted as employed by Charles "en plusieurs occasions;" and likewise set down, among those officers who came back with him to Bretagne, as receiving a gratification of "1000 livres."

Highness, the Duke, has been pleased to appoint Thomas Davenant,* Ensign in General Wolf's Regiment, and nephew to Thomas Boothby Skrymsher, Esq., to be an Ensign in the Coldstream Regiment of Guards. This young gentleman had the good fortune to take 1 of the standards belonging to the Irish Brigade, in the late battle of Val." But, it was impossible for Ensign Thomas Davenant, or for any other officer of the Allied army in that battle, to take a "standard" from the Irish Brigade *there*. A *standard* is the banner of cavalry, as contrasted with the *colours* for infantry; and the Regiment of Fitz-James, the only regiment of Irish *cavalry* in France, not being in a condition to serve at all this campaign, was not at the engagement in question, and so could not lose a *standard* there. Nor can it be objected, that this asserted capture of an Irish *standard* by the Ensign of Wolfe's Regiment is only a mistake, for a capture of Irish *colours* from some of the infantry corps of the Brigade. In the English announcement from "Whitehall, July 11," of the "Standards and Colours taken from the French in the late Action," with descriptive particulars and mottoes unnecessary to copy *here*, the standards are specified, as, of Belfond's Regiment, 4—of Beauffremont's, 1—of Royal Cravates, 1—or, so far, 6 standards; the colours are specified as, of Diesbach's Swiss Regiment, 2 colour-staffs, flags torn off—of Royal des Vaisseaux, 3 colours, without staffs—of Monaco's, 4 colours—or, so far, 9 colours; and then, after an "N.B.," it is affirmed, another colour was taken by Crauford's Regiment, given in charge to Hussars, but not yet brought in; and a standard was taken by the Hanoverian cavalry, given in charge to Imperialists, but still unreturned. Among those 15, or, including the 2 last, those 17 colours and standards, *none* are noticed, either as having belonged to the Irish Brigade, or as having been captured by Wolfe's Regiment. Of this last corps, too, (otherwise the 8th foot, or King's Own Regiment,) the bravery in the engagement is specially eulogized by an eye-witness. "Let me," he writes, "give you one instance of the resolution of our men, which I *know* to be true. Wolfe's regiment carried into the field 24 rounds a man. This they made use of. Afterwards they had a supply of 8 rounds a man more. After this was spent, they made use of all the ammunition amongst the dead, and wounded, both of their own men, and the enemies. When no farther supply could be had, they formed themselves immediately, to receive their enemy upon their bayonets, and, being ordered to retreat, did it with the utmost regularity." This writer (evidently an officer of the regiment he thus praises) subsequently refers to colours and standards taken from the French, "which," says he, "I have seen," but he is silent as to the capture of *any* from the Irish Brigade. Under such circumstances, then, it is certain, that no cavalry-ensign, or "standard," of the Irish was, or could be, taken at Laffeldt; and it is anything but certain, that any infantry-ensign, or "colours" of theirs, fell into the hands of an officer of Wolfe's regiment. In fine, I am not aware of the existence either of Irish or of French evidence with respect to any loss of the kind by the Irish on this occasion; so that, it was *not* at the expense of the Irish Brigade, Ensign William Davenant acquired his trophy.

As an additional instance of how warmly the feelings of the late civil

* Blundered, as "Drvnent," in the original paragraph of the Dublin paper, but corrected by Colonel Mac Kinnon, giving the paragraph in his "Origin and Services of the Coldstream Guards."

war in Scotland were connected with this battle, we read in the papers of the day, on the authority of a letter from the Allied army in Flanders to a person of distinction, that the Earl of Ancram, son of the Marquis of Lothian, and Lord of the Bedchamber to the Duke of Cumberland, with whom he had fought in Scotland, and by whom he was selected to convey to England the military ensigns taken at Laffeldt, on being recognized there by a Scotch Jacobite officer in the French service who had likewise fought in Scotland, was singled out by the latter exclaiming to his Lordship, "Now I have you, my Lord!"—when an encounter with swords took place, in which his Lordship was wounded in the arm, but ran his antagonist through the body, killing him on the spot. Prince Charles, too, though *not* present, as was commonly supposed, at the battle, was so glad at the defeat given to the Allies, from the tendency of such an event to favour *his* cause, that he wrote from St. Ouen, July 7th, a letter to Louis XV., expressive of the joy he felt, on receiving the news of his Majesty's having gained such a victory over his enemies. In Scotland, the Jacobites, smarting under the triumphant Georgeite government, and wishing proportionably well to France as the friend of "Prince Charlie," gave vent to *their* satisfaction in song at the Duke of Cumberland's defeat, and the hopes they entertained, that it would be productive of still greater humiliation to Hanoverianism. Of the song referred to, entitled "The Battle of Val," I cite the following verses, in the order most conformable to the events of the campaign, from its commencement to the battle.

> " Up, and rin awa, Willie,
> Up, and rin awa, Willie;
> Culloden's laurels you have lost,
> Your puff'd-up looks, and a', Willie.
> This check o' conscience for your sins,
> It stings you to the saul, Willie,
> And breaks your measures this campaign,
> As much as Lowendahl,* Willie.
> Up, and rin awa, &c.

> " The Maese you cross'd just like a thief,
> To feed on turnips raw, Willie,
> In place of our good Highland beef,
> With which you gorg'd your maw, Willie.
> Up, and rin awa, &c.

> " In just reward for their misdeeds,
> Your butchers gat a fa', Willie;
> And a' that liv'd ran aff wi' speed
> To Maëstricht's strang wa', Willie.
> Up, and rin awa, &c.

> " To Hanover, I pray begone,
> Your daddie's dirty sta', Willie,
> And look on *that* as your ain hame,
> And come na here at a', Willie.
> It's best to bide awa, Willie,
> It's best to bide awa, Willie,
> For our brave Prince will soon be back,
> Your loggerhead to claw, Willie."

---

* "During the whole of this campaign," says the annotator of the Scotch Jacobite Minstrelsy, "Count Lowendahl was eminently successful, in defeating the plans of Cumberland."

As Cumberland, when Charles had to retire before him in Scotland, inquired for the residence last occupied by the latter, as "his cousin," in order, by way of bravado, to quarter there, the suffering Jacobite would be gratified on seeing the tables turned, in that respect, as well as others, at "the butcher's" expense, by the success of Louis XV. at Laffeldt. "Le Roi, couvert de la nouvelle gloire qu'il venoit d'acquerir," writes Dumortous, "se rendit, avec le Maréchal de Saxe, à la Commanderie, où le Duc de Cumberland avoit eu son quartier, et ils y passerent la nuit." Or, as the Private Life of Louis XV., after mentioning the victory, more simply states—"His Majesty slept that night where the English Prince had slept the night before."

The French, on finding themselves, notwithstanding their late victory, unable to besiege Maestricht, turned their attention to Bergen-op-Zoom, "the strongest fortification of Dutch Brabant, the favourite work of the famous engineer, Coehorn, never conquered, and generally esteemed invincible." It was amply supplied with artillery, ammunition, and provisions, and the garrison of 3000 men could be increased at will from about 16,000 of the Allied troops occupying military lines, which communicated with the place, and were protected by a chain of forts, surrounded with water. The conducting of this very difficult siege, with a force of 36,000 men, &c., was committed by the Marshal de Saxe to an officer of *Danish*, as the Marshal himself was of *Saxon*, blood royal.* This was the illustrious Waldemar, Count de Lowendahl, a nobleman, not less remarkable for the extent of his intellectual attainments than for the diversity of his military experience; being able to speak 14 languages, and having fought under the most distinguished commanders in Europe; as, in the Austrian service, under Prince Eugene of Savoy, in that of Russia, under Field Marshal Lacy, &c. During above 2 months, from July to September, about Bergen-op-Zoom "nothing was seen but fire and smoke, nothing heard but one continued roar of bombs and cannon. But still the damage fell chiefly on the besiegers, who were slain in heaps; while the garrison suffered very little, and could be occasionally relieved, or reinforced, from the lines." By the diseases alone arising from the unwholesomeness of the situation necessarily occupied by the French as the besiegers, not less than 20,000 of their men were put *hors de service;* and, although the losses which occurred were filled up with proportionable reinforcements from their main army, yet since, by the middle of September, there was no practicable breach in the fortifications, the masonry-work scarcely touched, and, where the parapet *was* injured, 2 men could not march abreast, the place was still in such a condition as, with due vigilance and corresponding measures of defence, to be considered quite beyond being taken by assault, or, according to the general rules of war, impregnable. But as, in writing, genius may, says Pope,

"From vulgar bounds, with brave disorder, part,
And snatch a grace, beyond the reach of art—"

so, in war, on this occasion, it was remarked at the time, the Count de Lowendahl "fit voir qu'il y avait des occasions, où il faut s'élever au-dessus des régles de l'art." An assault being unexpected among the garrison,

* A curious shamrock of Marshals flourished under Louis XV.—the 3 leaves of which, in the persons of Saxe, Lowendahl, and O'Brien, represented the *Saxon*, the *Dane*, and the *Milesian*—and all from a ROYAL stem! But the Milesian alone was of *legitimate* descent.

they did not take precautions against such an attempt; thereby justifying the enterprise, which they might have frustrated.

On September 16th, all being arranged in the dark, for the French *coup-de-main*, the Count, at daybreak, caused a sudden and tremendous discharge of bombs to be poured into the town, followed by his dashing stormers; who, gaining the ramparts in 3 directions, were, with a loss of but 441 killed and wounded, so *surprisingly* successful, that, in 2 hours, the fortress itself, and the adjoining military lines, were captured, the garrison of the former, and the supernumerary force in the latter, consisting between both of above 20 battalions, were slain, taken, or routed; the conquerors obtaining more than 288 pieces of brass or iron cannon, a great many mortars, a quantity of small arms, tents, and ammunition, 17 vessels in the port, loaded with supplies of every kind for "*the invincible garrison of Bergen-op-Zoom!*" as it was confidently styled,* and, in fine, the entire plunder of the place, including the military chests of the Allied regiments, the silver plate and strong boxes of their Princes, and Generals, &c.; the collective mass constituting a prodigious booty, in addition to the uncommon glory of the achievement! The very discouraging effects of this brilliant success of the French upon the Allies and their forces will be best conceived from the following extract of a letter, representing the feelings of the Duke of Cumberland when informed of the occurrence. "The astonishment of the Duke of Cumberland, upon receiving the disagreeable news of the surprise of Bergen-op-Zoom, cannot be described. People must have been present, *as we were*, in order to form a true judgment of the love, which this warlike Prince express'd for the Republick" of the Seven United Provinces, "and the common cause, as well by everything he said on that occasion, as by the *agitation* he was under, upon reading so fatal a relation. This may, with truth, be asserted, that his Royal Highness was scarce ever so much affected before; nay, it's believed, that he would not have been more so, had he received a courier, with the news of the *Pretender's* landing again in Scotland, and of an invasion in England; and the reason was, because his Royal Highness knew perfectly well the situation of affairs at Bergen-op-Zoom, every day receiving advices, that there was but little or no room to fear an assault, unless the French had a mind to sacrifice 10 or 12,000 men, without any prospect of success." Another English writer, in 1761, adds on this point—"The late Mr. Benjamin Robins, the best military mathematician and engineer of his age, who was sent over from hence to assist in defending the place, and who lost his baggage in the lines of that very camp which communicated with the town, declared, that the place was as capable of defence when it was taken, as it was when the French army first sat down before it; and that, if it had been skilfully and faithfully defended, no military force, or skill, however great, could have succeeded against it."

The gallant Count Lally, who, for his remarkable zeal and activity in favour of Prince Charles, was, on the Prince's return from Scotland to France, ennobled, by patent, as "Earl of Moenmoye, Viscount of Bally-

* Such, according to Voltaire, was the inscription or direction on the chests containing the supplies in question; and Allied accounts allege, of the Dutch garrison, that they "abounded with provisions, even to luxury." In addition to the already-noticed authorities on this campaign, I have consulted the "History of Maurice, Count Saxe, Field-Marshal of the French Armies," &c., translated from the French; 2 volumes, London, 1752.

mote, and Baron of Tollendally"—which honours, however, he declined assuming until a "restoration"—and who had signalized himself this campaign in the defence of Antwerp and at the battle of Laffeldt—was attached as Quarter-Master-General to the Count de Lowendahl's army. Previous to the appearance of that force before Bergen-op-Zoom, it having been necessary to dislodge 1700 Dutch from Fort Santlivet, that task was intrusted to Lally, who executed it without loss; and, having reconnoitred Bergen-op-Zoom along with Lowendahl, he was so honoured by him, as to be intrusted with the formation of the plan of attack. Throughout that arduous and destructive siege, Lally, constantly active, sometimes in the trenches, sometimes with detachments, was wounded upon 1 occasion, and almost swallowed up by the explosion of a mine; an English account remarking of him there, how he "was taken such notice of, as to be esteemed one of the best soldiers in all France!" After the fall of Bergen-op-Zoom, Lowendahl, who, in securing the passes of the Scheld, found Lally to have "united the most consummate experience with the most intrepid courage," committed to him the reduction of Forts Frederick-Henry, Lillo, and La Croix. Frederick-Henry being taken, with its garrison, October 2nd, ground was broken, on that day, by Lally before Lillo; when, proposing to attack La Croix at the same time, and going, almost alone, to make a reconnoissance that had not been properly executed, he was made prisoner by a party of the enemy's hussars, but soon exchanged; and, by the 8th, the last of the forts surrendered.

Louis XV., after the fall of Bergen-op-Zoom, having appointed the Marshal de Saxe to be Governor of the conquered Netherlands, and having created Lowendahl, for his late important achievement, a Marshal, set out, September 23rd, for France. His Majesty proceeded to Versailles on the 25th, without entering Paris, although the Parisians, it was observed in England, would have wished "to receive in triumph their successful Monarch, who had done more, in 3 years, than Lewis the Great, in 30!" It was likewise noted in London, how, on the retiring of the French army into quarters, the Irish Brigade were to be cantoned, during the winter, in the menacing position along the coast from Ostend to Calais; with the manifest intention of obliging an English squadron of observation to be kept in the Channel, and, consequently, or so far as concentrated, to be less able to prevent the privateering depredations of the French, on the unprotected vessels of the English merchants.* "Thus," says Rolt, "terminated the campaign of 1747, on the side of the Netherlands; a campaign, truly glorious to the French, prejudicial to all the Confederates, and particularly inglorious to the Dutch; there was not one single town remaining of the Austrian Netherlands unreduced, and only Maestricht to cover the interior barrier of Holland. On the side of Dutch Flanders, the lilies of France were waving triumphant over the head of the Belgian lion; and Bergen-op-Zoom, the maiden fortress, which had never, till now, been violated, was prostituted to the lust of France; notwithstanding the Dutch Governor declared, at the commencement of the siege, that Bergen-op-Zoom was a virgin, and she would die, like the daughter of the brave old Roman, Virginius, before she should be polluted by the faithless Gaul."

In 1748, the Allies, enumerated, on their side, as 110,000 men, united, and encamped about Ruremond, under the Duke of Cumberland,

* As in November and December, 1745, to the number of 160 prizes, estimated at £660,000. See Book VII.

to oppose the French. The Marshal de Saxe—under whom, as connected with the Irish Brigade, were the Lieutenant-General Charles O'Brien, Lord Clare and Earl of Thomond, the Majors-General Count and Duke de Fitz-James, Count Charles Edward Roth, Richard Francis Talbot, 3rd Earl of Tyrconnell, the Count Lally, Brigadier, &c.—had determined on besieging Maestricht, having justly observed, that, *in* it, peace was to be obtained. Outwitting his adversaries so completely by his masterly or mystifying marches, that he succeeded in investing the place, the French Commander opened his trenches before the town on the night of April 15th, and his works were so vigorously pushed on, and his artillery so well served, that everything was to be ready for attacking the covered way on the evening of May 4th; when, about noon, a letter arrived from the Duke of Cumberland, announcing the signature, April 30th, of the preliminaries of peace. By these, and the arrangements consequently made, Maestricht, in deference to the glory of the French arms, was agreed to be given up to the Marshal; at the same time that honourable terms of surrender were to be granted to the garrison. In the operations carried on against the place, the Maréchaux de Camp, or Majors-General de Fitz-James, Lord Tyrconnell, and Count Roth, are duly referred to, as commanding, on several occasions, in the trenches. But the gallant Brigadier Count Lally was most remarkable, as a confidant, and 1 of the chief instruments, of the Marshal de Saxe, in his admirable measures for accomplishing the investment of the town; as exercising, in conjunction with that very able officer, the Marquis de Cremilles, the functions of Quarter-Master-General of the Army; as being severely wounded; and, on the day the place was surrendered, as being, for his signal services there, nominated a Maréchal de Camp, or Major-General, *hors de ligne*, or in the same very honourable way that he had been created a Brigadier!

Peace between France and England, as well as the other belligerent European powers, was not definitively arranged, until the general signature, October 18th, 1748, of the Treaty of Aix-la-Chapelle. In the factious fermentation of a licentious commercial prosperity, united with no less political inconsistency and national conceit, the English, while the basis of their existing legislative system was so rotten that by corruption alone could they be governed, had clamoured against their able Prime Minister, Sir Robert Walpole, for governing by corruption,* and had driven him into war, which (to his credit!) it was a leading object of *his* administration to avoid. "When," writes Lord Macaulay, on the consequent rejoicings in London, "the heralds were attended into the city by the chiefs of the opposition, when the Prince of Wales himself stopped at Temple Bar to drink success to the English arms, the Minister heard all the steeples of the city jingling a merry peal, and muttered, 'They may ring the bells now; they will be wringing their hands before long!'" Sir Robert's sagacity, as a lover of peace, was justified by the event. Of the war generally, Doctor Johnson remarks—" We pleased ourselves with *a victory at Dettingen, where we left our wounded men to the care of our enemies*, but *our army was broken at Fontenoy and Val;* and though, after the *disgrace* which we suffered in the Mediterranean, we had *some* naval success, and an accidental dearth

* "Sir Robert Walpole," according to his son, "used to say, that it was fortunate so few men could be Prime Ministers, as it was best that few should thoroughly know *the shocking wickedness of mankind!*"

made peace necessary for the French, yet *they prescribed the conditions, obliged us to give hostages, and acted as conquerors, though as conquerors of moderation.*" After alluding to the contest in the Netherlands, as one, on the part of England, and her Allies, where "*they never hazarded a battle without sustaining a defeat,*" where "*vast armies, paid by Great Britain, lay inactive, and beheld one fortress reduced after another, until the whole country was subdued,*" &c., "what," more strongly exclaims Smollett, "were the fruits which Britain reaped from this long and desperate war? *A dreadful expense of blood and treasure, disgrace upon disgrace, an additional load of grievous impositions, and the national debt accumulated to the enormous sum of* 80,000,000 *sterling!*" The share which the Irish Brigade had, in bringing about a consummation so injurious to the religious and commercial oppressor of *their* country, appears to have been one of much importance, even from the account in these pages, presented to a reader under the great disadvantage of that corps never having had any Xenophon or Napier among its officers, to do adequate justice to the merits of his countrymen, by recording many circumstances to their honour, necessarily passed over by the writers of other nations, as either altogether unknown, or comparatively uninteresting, to *them,* and so lost to history. But, how high was the opinion in France of the conduct of the Brigade during this war, for the good discipline or union of the several regiments among themselves, as well as for their bravery against the enemy, is emphatically attested by the official Mémoire which states, "*that union has prevailed, to so great a degree, in the Irish Brigade, since all the corps were thus made to serve together, that the most trifling dispute, or altercation, never took place; so that it appeared, as if the different battalions formed but* 1 *single regiment, well united, and unanimous.* It is considered," continues the document, "that *this conduct was as creditable to it, as the exactitude and the willingness with which it served, and as the splendid and transcendent actions by which it distinguished itself!*"* With this war terminates, as has been previously intimated, the more thoroughly national or interesting period of the history of the Brigade. The Penal Code, indeed, was sufficiently active in Ireland, as briefly, yet abundantly, attested by this significant paragraph of the Gentleman's Magazine for April, 1748. "IRELAND—*One George Williams was convicted, at Wexford Assizes, for being perverted from the Protestant to the Popish religion, and sentenc'd to be out of the King's protection, his lands and tenements, goods and chattles, to be forfeited to the King, and his body to remain at the King's pleasure!*" † With reference, likewise, to increased rigour against the Catholics in Ireland, next year, or 1749, a French military writer adds of the Irish—"*Can a noble people be sufficiently allured into this country, whom his Majesty has seen, under his own eyes, serve, and expose*

---

* See Mr. O'Conor's Appendix.

† This punishment was incurred, under the following provision of the "glorious-revolution" Penal Code. "If any person shall seduce a Protestant, to renounce the Protestant, and profess the Popish, religion, the seducer and the seduced shall incur the penalty of Præmunire, mentioned in 16th Rich. II., chap. 5. That is, they shall be put out of the King's protection, their lands and goods forfeited to the King's use, and they shall be attached, by their bodies, to answer to the King and his Council." (Mac Nevin's Pieces of Irish History, p. 130.) In England, under Elizabeth, there was a *worse* statute, which, says Lord Macaulay, "provides that, if any Catholic shall convert a Protestant to the Romish Church, they shall BOTH *suffer* DEATH, *as for* HIGH TREASON."

themselves, so bravely and so usefully?" The vampire, too, of an antinational mercantile tyranny was as blood-sucking, or impoverishing, in Ireland, as ever. Yet the weakening of the popular hope of a "restoration of the Stuarts" from the period of the Peace of Aix-la-Chapelle, the subsequent adverse policy of the Court of France towards that family, and the increased obstacles to the obtaining of recruits, of the rank of soldiers, from Ireland, rendered the Brigade henceforth rather "Irish" as regards officers, than soldiers; * so that, on the whole, what may be styled the *old* Brigade, in its general Irish formation, and Jacobite vigour, may be said to have thrown out its last rays of glory at Laffeldt, in giving Cumberland "another Fontenoy" there, and taking satisfaction, under a Scotch nobleman, for the overthrow and cruel treatment at Culloden, &c., of its brother Jacobites, the Highlanders of Scotland.

* Lieutenant-General, the Honourable Count Arthur Dillon, in his Mémoire to the National Assembly of France, after the breaking out of the Revolution, notes of the *original* and long-maintained *national* formation of the several corps of the Irish Brigade—"Ces régimens étoient entierement composés d'Irlandois à leur arrivée en France, et cette composition subsista, par *les émigrations continuelles qui eurent lieu, tant qu'ils eurent l'espoir de voir la Maison de Stuart remonter sur le trône.* Ils venoient en foule se ranger sous les drapeaux des Rois qu'ils regardoient comme les défenseurs de leur religion, et de leur Souverain légitime. On peut même prouver, qu'outre les Officiers, *la plus grande partie des Sergens étoient nobles.*" That is, in the extended sense of the French word, "*noblesse.*" Then, referring to the *specially* severe legislation, since 1746, against recruiting for the Brigade in Ireland, the Count alleges—"Depuis cette époque, les régimens Irlandois ne purent se procurer, en temps de paix, d'autres soldats de leur nation, que *ceux qui venoient encore en assez grand nombre les joindre.* Mais les émigrations, en Officiers, n'ont jamais été interrompues ; elles subsistent encore avec tant d'activité, que le nombre des sujets nés en Irlande de familles attachées à la réligion Catholique excede, dans ce moment même, les emplois à donner ; qu'il n'y a dans les régimens Irlandois d'autres Officiers, nés en France, que ceux qui sont fils ou descendans d'anciens Officiers de ces régimens qui se sont mariés dans le pays où ils sont citoyens." See, moreover, the *names* of the officers of the several regiments of the Brigade, in the annual volumes of the "Etat Militaire de France," down to the Revolution.

HISTORY OF THE IRISH BRIGADES

IN

THE SERVICE OF FRANCE.

BOOK IX.

IN the period which elapsed from the Peace of 1748 between France and England to the declaration of war between the rival powers in 1756, the annals of the Irish Brigade were illustrated by the deaths of 4 officers of distinction connected with the national force—the 1st, Field-Marshal Count Peter Lacy, or de Lacy, entitled to be noticed in this work, at the period of his decease, as having, for several years, belonged to that force, previous to his entering the service of Russia, although, in the latter, he attained his highest honours—the 2nd, Maréchal de Camp, or Major-General, Richard Francis Talbot, 3rd Earl of Tyrconnell, and Ambassador from France to Prussia—the 3rd, Maréchal de Camp, or Major-General, John Nugent, 5th Earl of Westmeath—the 4th, Daniel O'Connor Sligo, a noble veteran of above 90, deceased a Lieutenant-General in the Austrian service, but, like Lacy, included in this list, as having been originally an officer in the armies of Kings James II. and Louis XIV.

Of the name of Lacy, ennobled, and eminent for its territorial acquisitions among the Norman conquerors of England and Wales, as well as among the early settlers of the same adventurous race in Erin, a Limerick historian observes—"The illustrious and ancient house of Lacy has produced many exalted characters. There were 3 branches of this family, seated at Bruree, Bruff, and Ballingarry, in the County of Limerick. The loss of their possessions did not extinguish the memory of the achievements of their heroic ancestors." The origin of these Limerick Lacys is deduced from William, son of the celebrated Hugue de Lacy, (the 1st great representative of the name in Erin under Henry II.,) by that nobleman's 2nd marriage with the Princess Rose, daughter of the Ex-Ard-Righ, or Monarch of Erin, and King of Connaught, Ruadri or Roderic O'Conor. John Lacy Esquire of Ballingarry was father of Peter, 1 of the offspring of whose union with Maria Courteney, was the future Count and Field-Marshal Peter, born at Killidy or Killeedy, County of Limerick, in 1678.* On the conclusion of the War of the Revolution in Ireland by the Treaty of Limerick in 1691, young Peter, then only entering his 14th year, was an Ensign in the Prince of Wales's Regiment of Infantry, of which his uncle, John Lacy, Quartermaster-General and Brigadier, was Colonel; and quitting Ireland, with the remains of that regiment, as part of King James's army, sailed for France. Landing, in

* The Marshal's mention of his birth-day as "29th September," according to O. S., which in 1678, and until 1752, was that established in Great Britain and Ireland, would place his birth, by N. S., on "October 9th."

January, 1692, at Brest, he proceeded to Nantes, to enter, as a Lieutenant, the Regiment of Athlone.* With that corps, he, in May, joined the Marshal de Catinat's army in Italy; served to the end of the war there, in 1696; in 1697, marched to the Rhine; and, in consequence of the extensive reduction of the Irish Jacobite force in France, subsequent to the Peace of Ryswick, in which reduction his regiment was included, he quitted France, to seek service elsewhere. Disappointed of employment in Hungary, against the Turks, by the Peace of Carlowitz, in January, 1699, between the Porte, Austria, &c., he became 1 of 100 officers at Vienna, engaged for the Czar Peter of Russia, to discipline his troops.

After presentation, with his companions, to Peter, at Narva, he was made Captain of a company, in the infantry Regiment of Colonel Bruce. From this period, 1700, he was involved in the military operations, with various fortune, in Livonia and Ingria, between the Czar, his rival Charles XII. of Sweden, and their subordinate Generals, until 1703, when, after the surrender of Jambourg in Ingria, he was honoured with the command of a company, 100 in number, styled the Grand Musketeers, composed of Russian noblesse, armed and horsed at their own expense. In 1705, with the Czar in Poland, he was made Major of Scheremetoff's Regiment of Infantry, with which, under that Marshal, he fought against the Swedish General Lowenhaupt; and, in 1706, was nominated, by the Czar, Lieutenant-Colonel of the Regiment of Polotzk, and commissioned to instruct 3 newly-raised regiments encamped there. In 1707, sent to join Lieutenant-General Bauer's corps blockading Bucko in Poland, and having to open trenches, in June, at 10 toises from the counterscarp, he repulsed a sally of the enemy with loss; and, the fortress surrendering that month, he was quartered, with his regiment, in Lithuania. In 1708, joining the main Russian army under the Czar, he was appointed Colonel of the Siberian Regiment of Infantry. That army, advancing to Copaisch upon the Borysthenes, intrenched itself there to intercept Charles XII. coming from Saxony, till, Prince Repnin's corps being beaten by the Swedes, it became necessary to retire to Gorigorhi on the other side of the Borysthenes; while Charles marched towards the Ukraine to join the famous Mazeppa, Hetman of the Cossacks; but derived little benefit from the junction, and was still more disappointed at the destruction, or interception, of the greater portion of General Lowenhaupt's force at Lesna, &c., by the Czar. In November, despatched with 2 regiments to Peregova, where the Swedes endeavoured to make a bridge over the Desna, Lacy repulsed them in a smart action with such considerable loss, that they had to relinquish the attempt there. On their subsequently endeavouring to pass the river lower down near Mischin, he again foiled them by a redoubt and battery; but, being ordered to descend a league lower, to guard against a reported design of crossing there, and General Gordon being posted at Mischin, that officer, not so fortunate, was routed,

* The notices of Field-Marshal Count Lacy, in the Continental, London, and Dublin periodicals, at the time of his death, allege, that his father, and 2 brothers, also left Ireland, in 1691, for France. The same notices add, how the father, who was Captain of a company in the Irish Guards of King James II., and the Marshal's elder brother (whose rank is *not* mentioned) both died in the service of France, as well as the younger brother, killed, when Aid-Major in the Regiment of Dorrington, (subsequently Roth's) at Malplaquet. The death of the Marshal's uncle, in the same service, at Marsaglia, has been previously related, under the year 1693.

and the enemy effected their object. In December, detached with 15,000 men, to assault Rumna, where Charles XII. had taken up his quarters, Lacy, with 3 battalions, a company of grenadiers, a regiment of dragoons, and 500 Cossacks, passing the King, possessed himself of, and secured himself in it; a dangerous position, as the Swedish army was cantoned all about the place. In January, 1709, the Czar further rewarded Lacy for his services, by giving him a Regiment of Grenadiers.

At the great battle of Pultowa that summer, where Charles was irretrievably overthrown by the Czar, Lacy, though not yet, or till above 3 years after, nominated a Brigadier, was most highly honoured, in being commissioned to act as such in command, on the right wing of the Russian army, (under Lieutenant-General Bauer) upon which occasion, he was wounded. This uncommon testimony to Lacy's ability, by such a good judge of merit, as the Czar, is perhaps explained by Ferrar. "It was," he says, "Marshal Lacy who taught the Russians to beat the King of Sweden's army, and, from being the worst, to become some of the best, soldiers in Europe. The Russians had been used to fight in a very confused manner, and to discharge their musketry, before they advanced sufficiently near the enemy to do execution. Before the famous battle of Pultowa in 1709, Marshal Lacy advised the Czar, to send orders, that every man should reserve his fire, until he came within a few yards of the enemy. The consequence was, that Charles XII. was totally defeated," and, "in that 1 action, lost the advantage of 9 glorious campaigns." From 1709 to 1721, Lacy, continuing to serve against the Swedes, Turks, &c., was nominated a Brigadier in August, 1712; in the following month, a Major-General; in July, 1720, a Lieutenant-General; distinguishing himself most, in 1720 and 1721, through the successful and destructive descents he made by sea, along the coasts of Sweden, to but 12 miles from Stockholm. At this short distance from that metropolis, he had anchored with 130 gallies, and had encamped his vanguard, when the Swedes were obliged, in September, to conclude the Peace of Nystadt; thereby relinquishing Livonia, Esthonia, Ingria, Carelia, besides a number of islands in the Baltic, to Russia. In July, 1723, Lacy was summoned by the Czar to Petersburgh, to take a seat in the College of War. In June, 1724, at the ceremonies connected with the coronation of the Empress Catherine I., he followed on horseback the Empress's carriage, throwing among the people 1500 gold and 11,000 silver medals. From 1723 to 1725, assisting the College of War at Petersburgh with his opinions and advice, he was, in the latter year, honoured with the insignia of the Order of St. Alexander Newsky, the rank of General-in-Chief of Infantry, and the command of the forces about Petersburgh, as well as those in Ingria and Novogorod; to which, in 1726, were added those in Esthonia and Carelia. In 1727, on the election of the famous Maurice Count de Saxe (subsequently Marshal) as Duke of Courland contrary to the wish of the Court of Petersburgh, Lacy was commissioned to expel the Count from the Duchy, and did so. In 1729, he was named Governor of Livonia, and Commander-in-Chief there, and in Esthonia.

In 1733, being ordered to proceed, in August, with 30,000 men into Poland, to establish Augustus of Saxony as King in opposition to Stanislas, he marched upon Warsaw, which he entered in October. In 1734, pursuing the adherents of Stanislas to Thorn, he drove them from it in January; and, after opening trenches before Dantzick in March, he, in April, 5 miles from that place, at Vizitzina, with only 2000 men, routed 8000 of the Stanislaites, with a loss of 500 of their number, and all their baggage. He besieged Dantzick along with Marshal Munich; the reduction of which, after 135 days' operations from the 1st approaches in February to the surrender in June, cost the Russians above 8000 men, with nearly 200 officers; and Stanislas had to escape from the country in disguise. In acknowledgment of Lacy's services, Augustus this summer presented him with his portrait set in diamonds, valued at 25,000 crowns; at the same time declaring him a Knight of the Order of the White Eagle of Poland. The hostility to King Augustus continuing in 1735, Lacy was detained in Poland, till, by the results of his most remarkable achievement, or the attack and defeat, at Busawitza, with only 1500 dragoons, 80 hussars, and 500 Cossacks, of 20,000 of the Stanislaites under the Palatine of Lublin, and the surrender, in April, of the Castellan Czerski, with the rest of the refractory Poles, the contest was decided in favour of Augustus.* After a suitably honourable reception at Warsaw by that Prince, Lacy, with 15,000, subsequently reduced to about 10,000, infantry, was directed to march to the aid of Austria, then, in consequence of the contest for the crown of Poland, engaged in hostilities with France. Having joined the Imperial army, 6 miles from Manheim, in August, the veteran Prince Eugene of Savoy, its General, on a review of the reinforcement, expressed himself, with the greatest satisfaction, at the fine appearance of the troops; as, in their passage through Germany to the Rhine, says my authority, " every one admired, and was astonished at, the good discipline they observed on their march, and in their quarters." Peace being agreed upon soon after between France and Austria, Lacy, while his forces were quartered for the winter in Bohemia, repaired, early in 1736, to Vienna. " I arrived there," he writes, "the 5th of February. On the 6th, I had a private interview of the Emperor and Empress, both of whom received me in a very gracious manner. On the 7th, I was also admitted to an audience of the Empress-Dowager, Amelia; the 8th with the Duke of Lorrain, and the rest of the Imperial family. On the 10th, I was again admitted to an audience of the Emperor and Empress. The former deigned to present me with his portrait, richly set with diamonds, as also 5000 ducats in money. The 11th, I quitted Vienna. On the road, I met a courier from Petersburgh, who brought me the patent of Field-Marshal."

This promotion, the long-meditated war against Turkey being resolved on, was accompanied by an order, to assume the command of the force, destined for the reduction of the important fortress of Azoph. Travel-

* So considerable, we should observe, had been the progress of administrative improvement in Russia since the time of Peter the Great, while Poland remained in the comparatively wretched or mediæval state of feudal anarchy, which was *already* leading to her ruin as a nation, that Major-General Baron Manstein notes—"During this war, never did 300 Russians go a step out of their way to avoid 3000 Poles. They beat them in every engagement, or rencounter, they had with them. *The Saxons were not so fortunate, having come off by the worst in several occasions of trial with the Poles, who, at length, came to hold them in contempt, whereas they were extremely afraid of the Russians.*" But, according to a certain class of writers, the Saxons ought to have been at least equal, if not superior, in "pluck," or soldiership, to either the Russians, or the Poles, instead of inferior to *both!* As to Poland, her ex-king Stanislas, above referred to, writing against the anarchy there, of which he foresaw the ultimate melancholy result, has, in a work printed so early as 1749, these remarkable words—"Notre tour viendra, sans doute, où nous serons la proie de quelque fameux conquérant; peut-être même *les puissances voisines s'accorderont-elles à partager nos états.*"

ling thither, May 2nd, in his post-carriage, escorted by only 36 dragoons riding some hundred paces before it, the Marshal, at a desert, about 3 leagues in length, which it was necessary to pass, was, with his little party, unexpectedly assailed by about 2000 Tartar marauders. Of the 36 dragoons, 21 were captured, with a domestic, and the carriage; the pillage of the vehicle, however, so luckily engrossing the enemy's attention, that the Marshal himself was able to escape on horseback. During May and June he carried on the siege of Azoph by sap for the greater safety of his men, while his artillery-missiles spread destruction through the interior of the hostile fortress; the Turks, meantime, making constant sallies. At the most important of these, June 14th, the Turks, 3000 strong, attacking the Russian trenches, beating away the guard of 600 men, and filling up part of the works, the Marshal hastened forward with a reserve and picket, rallied his repulsed troops, and after a sharp encounter, costing 856 killed or wounded, drove back the enemy, with a considerable loss, to the town. On this occasion, the Marshal, having advanced too far in order to animate his men, received a gun-shot about the knee, was enveloped by the Turks, and might have been slain or taken by them, but for the uncommon devotion and corresponding exertions of his soldiers; whom, it is remarked, he so "well knew how to spare upon every proper opportunity, to preserve, and to guard from over-fatigue, and the want of subsistence." At last, by the beginning of July, so little provision remained for the besieged, from the destruction of their magazines by the bombardment—the interior of the town being "nothing but a heap of ruins, through the quantity of shells thrown into it"—the Bashaw, in command of the fortress, capitulated; marching out with his garrison, still amounting to 3463 men; and leaving in the place between 200 and 300 pieces of brass or iron artillery, a great quantity of ammunition and military utensils; and 291 Christian captives, who, having been made slaves, were liberated. In August, the Marshal marched, with 7000 of his troops, to support Munich's force, on its return, miserably diminished and harassed, from its invasion, that summer, of the Crimea. Subsequently appointed to command the remains of this force, along with his own army, during the winter, the Marshal established his quarters first at Izoum, and then at Karkow,* in the Ukraine, where he had to be continually on the alert, against the worrying hostilities of the rapacious and ferocious Tartars; ever upon the watch, in numerous and swiftly-mounted detachments, to pass the Russian frontier-lines of defence, and too often successful in plundering and destroying the villages, sweeping away the cattle, and carrying off the unfortunate country people of the interior into a bigoted Mohammedan bondage. The poet Collins, in his picturesque oriental eclogue of "Agib and Secander, or the Fugitives," after remarking,

> "The Turk and Tartar like designs pursue,
> Fix'd to destroy, and steadfast to undo,"

might *well* add of the latter,

> "Yet none so cruel as the Tartar foe,
> To death inur'd, and nurs'd in scenes of woe!"

* The journal of Marshal Lacy, written by himself, ending with the mention of his establishing his head-quarters in October, 1736, at Karkow, for the winter, my remaining authorities respecting the Marshal's military career, are Major-General Baron Manstein, and the Marshal Prince de Ligne.

The Marshal's parties, however, were not without *their* satisfaction against those Scythian banditti; as, in 1 affair, where, of 800, including some Turks, under the brother of the Khaun of the Crimea, 300 were slain, 50 made prisoners, 400 of their horses captured, and 3000 Russian subjects, who had been reduced to slavery, were happily rescued.

In 1737, the Court of St. Petersburgh, having decided upon a 3rd expedition to the Crimea—from the 1st of which, in 1735, Lieutenant-General Leontew, with 28,000 men, had to retire *minus* above 9000 men, and at least as many horses—from the 2nd of which, in 1736, Marshal Munich, with 52,000 men, had likewise to retire *minus* almost 30,000 men, and nearly all his horses—the renewal of the enterprise was intrusted to Lacy, with about 40,000 men, to be supported by a fleet acting under Rear-Admiral Bredal, on the Sea of Azoph. Advancing to, and assembling his entire force at, the river Berda, securing by redoubts at proper intervals his communications with Azoph, and concerting with the Rear-Admiral, anchored at the mouth of the Berda, the operations of the campaign, Lacy proceeded with his army as closely as possible along the shore of the Sea of Azoph, and, on reaching the river Molotschnie-Wodi, established a fort there for his sick men, protected by a good garrison. "June 26," continues the original military narrative, "the army encamped on the shore of that arm of the Sea of Azoph, which joins the lines of Precop; the fleet did not lie there at above a cannon-shot distance from it. Lacy, who wanted to enter, without loss of time, into Crimea, instantly ordered the construction of a bridge, which was finished by the 28th; and some regiments of dragoons, and 3 or 4000 Cossacks, passed over it immediately. By the 30th, the whole army was got over, and continued its march along-shore of the Sea of Azoph. July 2nd, it was joined by 4000 Calmucks. . . . The Khaun of the Tartars of the Crimea, who had never imagined that the Russians would enter his country on that side, was astonished at it, when he received the news. He had posted himself, with all his troops, behind the lines of Precop, which he had taken care to get repaired, and hoped to dispute the pass of them, with the Russians, more successfully than had been done by the old Khaun, the year before. But all this was so much trouble in vain. Lacy was now in full march against Arabat, without having lost a single man. As the Russian army was obliged to continue its march on a narrow enough spit of land, formed by the Sea of Azoph, which stretches as far as Arabat, the Khaun imagined, he might retrieve and rectify everything, at the outlet of that straight. He marched then, with all diligence, in the hope of stopping the Russian army at the lines, which care had been taken to form along the front of that spit of land, so as to compel it, either to a retreat, or even to a battle, if it should obstinately contend for passing.

"But Lacy broke all his measures. As soon as he heard, that the Khaun was arrived at Arabat, and that he was there waiting for him, he caused the depth of that arm of the sea, which separates this spot of land from the rest of Crimea, to be sounded, and, having found a place proper for this purpose, he had rafts made; for the construction of which, all the empty casks of the army, and main timber-pieces of the *chevaux-de-frise*, were employed; and, by this means, crossed this arm of the sea, with the infantry and equipages. The dragoons, Cossacks, or Calmucks, swam, or forded it over. It had not been the Khaun alone who had judged this a rash enterprise of the Marshal Lacy, when he marched on the spit of land towards Arabat; for the Generals of his own army were of the same opinion. All of them, except Spiegel, waited on him one morning, and represented to him, that he was exposing the troops too much, and that they were all running a risk of perishing together. The Marshal answered them, that danger there was in all military enterprises; but that he did not see more, in this one, than in others. However, he desired their counsel, of what they thought was best to be done. They replied, 'To return.' Upon which, Lacy rejoined, that, since the Generals had a mind to return, he would despatch them their passports for it; and actually called for his Secretary, whom he ordered to make them out, and immediately to deliver them to them. He even commanded a party of 200 dragoons to escort them to the Ukrain, there to await his return. It was 3 days before the Generals could prevail on the Marshal to relent, and forgive them the presumption *they* had shown, in proposing to *him* a retreat."

"The Khaun, who had imagined he should beat the Russian army at the outlet near Arabat, was extremely surprised at learning, that it had crossed the arm of the sea, and was now in full march towards him. But he did not think fit to wait for it. He retreated towards the mountains, harassed with the Cossacks and Calmucks close at his heels. Lacy, having advice of the retreat of the enemy, would not continue his march towards Arabat, but wheeled to the right, in order to get among the mountains in quest of the Khaun, and to give him battle, if the thing was practicable. July 23, the Russian army encamped at the distance of 26 wersts, or 7 French leagues, from one of the best towns of Crimea, called Karas-Bazar. There it was attacked by a large choice body of troops, commanded by the Khaun in person. These attacks were, at first, very vigorous; but, after an hour's combat, the Tartars were repulsed, and driven off the field, by the Cossacks and Calmucks, who pursued them 15 wersts, or 4 leagues into the mountains. The army remained in the same camp, but the light troops made an excursion on the side of Karas-Bazar, to ruin the habitations of the Tartars. They returned the same day, with about 600 prisoners, a considerable booty, and a great quantity of cattle. July 25, the Lieutenant-General Douglas commanded the vanguard with 6000 men, dragoons and foot, and the greatest part of the light troops, to march to Karas-Bazar. Marshal Lacy followed them with the rest of the army, having left in camp the equipages and the sick, with 5000 men to guard them," under a Brigadier. "All the advanced guards, that sought to oppose the passage of the troops, were repulsed; and presently there was discovered, on a rising ground, near the town, a retrenched camp, in which there might be about from 12 to 15,000 Turks. Upon this, the Marshal reinforced Douglas with 2 regiments of dragoons; giving him orders to attack the enemy, and to take possession of Karas-Bazar. This was executed, with all imaginable success; the Turks having fled, after about an hour's combat. The inhabitants had entirely abandoned the town; so that there were none remaining in it, but some Greek and Armenian families. The place then was taken without any resistance, pillaged, and reduced to ashes. This town, of which above one half was built of stone, contained about 10,000 houses, 38 mosques and Turkish chapels, 2 Christian churches for the Greeks and Armenians, 50 water-mills, and a number of other public buildings. The booty the troops made was very considerable; the inhabitants not having had time to save their effects. As the town is situate in the avenues to the hills, where the passes are so narrow that scarce 3 men can march abreast, and that, besides, there was no forage, the Marshal measured back his steps, and encamped at a league distance from that place. The Cossacks and Calmucks had orders to penetrate as far as they could into the mountains, and to burn and destroy all the habitations of the Tartars."

"July 26, the army marched back, to occupy the same camp, in which they had left their equipages, and the sick. Scarce had they got into the plain, before they saw the enemies advancing, with the greatest part of their forces, on the other side of the river Karas. Marshal Lacy instantly detached Douglas, with several regiments of foot and dragoons, and a part of the light troops, to attack them. Douglas crossed the river a league above the enemies, and marched strait to them. They cannonaded one another for near an hour; after which the Cossacks came to blows with the enemies. The skirmish was smart on both sides. The Cossacks were thrice repulsed; but the regular troops coming up, in fine order, and with a steady countenance, obliged the enemies to retreat. The army encamped on the field of battle. During the action, Lacy had ordered the Calmucks, to take the enemies in rear and flank. After the affair was over, no Calmucks appeared; at which the Marshal was rather uneasy, apprehending they might have pursued the enemies too far among the mountains; so as to have their retreat to the army cut off, or to have all been put to the sword. But, 2 days afterwards, they returned to the camp, bringing with them above 1000 prisoners; among them were several Mirzas," or Tartar gentlemen, "whom they had taken in an inroad, which they had, of their own heads, made into the mountains, as far as Batchi-Serai. July 27, the army resumed the camp, which it had occupied, before its proceeding to Karas-Bazar. The Marshal then held there a grand Council of War, in which it was resolved, that, since the plan of operations, prescribed to them, had been executed, and that there remained nothing considerable to be undertaken by them, it would be advisable to draw nearer again to the frontiers of the Crimea. It took the army up 5 days to get from this camp to the mouth of Scoungar; in all which time, the light troops had nothing to do, but to reduce to ashes the habitations of the Tartars, that were for 4 or 5 leagues round the army, and of which the number might be equivalent to 1000 villages, or little open towns, the country being extremely populous on that side. They brought also to the camp above 30,000 oxen, and more than 100,000 sheep. The enemies, on their part, did not cease to harass the army on its march, and sometimes found means to carry off some of the officers' servants, who had ventured to go beyond the precinct of the advanced posts, as also some hundreds of horses of the train and equipages. As soon as the army was arrived at the Scoungar, a bridge of boats was ordered to be got ready, and was finished by the next morning, the 2nd of August; when, on the same day, part of the army crossed it, and had scarce the time to form, when the enemies appeared, with their whole force, to oppose the passing. They had been reinforced with some thousands of Turks from the Kaffa. They attacked several times, with great violence, the light troops, but were constantly repulsed. At length, tired with their fruitless attempts, and with losing so many men by the cannon, they retreated, leaving about 100 killed on the spot. August 4th, the Marshal passed the Scoungar, with the rest of the army. There they remained a few days encamped; after which they went on to camp near the river Molotschnie-Wodi, where the Marshal staid out the whole month of August, having found a country abounding in forage. During that time, he detached several parties of light troops towards Precop, and towards the Dnieper, to reconnoitre the motions of the enemies; for he had received advice, that the Khaun, with from 30 to 40,000 men, was come out of Crimea, to attempt some enterprise. August 17, one of the Russian parties fell in with another of Tartars, which they beat, and brought into the camp several prisoners. These said it was true, that the Khaun had come from behind the lines of Precop, immediately after that the Russian army had passed over the Schoungar, and had encamped several days on the *steps;* but that, on learning that the Marshal Lacy had posted himself near Molotzchnie-Wodi, he was afraid of his coming to attack him; which had determined him to re-enter the lines, and retreat to his own country." Meantime, or from the 9th to the 11th of August, the Russian fleet under Rear-Admiral Bredal, and that of the Turks under the Captain-Bashaw, cannonaded each other during 2 days, the Turkish armament withdrawing towards Caffa, on the 3rd. "In the beginning of the month of September, Count Lacy quitted his camp of Molotschnie-Wodi, and resumed the route to Ukrain. The Tartars, very glad at seeing him take his departure, let him alone, without harassing him on his march. In the month of October, he arrived at the frontiers of Russia, and sent his troops into winter-quarters, along the Don and Donetz."

Such was the Marshal's expedition of 1737 into the Crimea, respecting which it has been remarked that, "without knowing why he had been sent into the country, he quitted it with very great glory to himself, and very little sickness to his army"—in the latter most creditable circumstance, showing himself to be very superior, as a commander, to his predecessor, Marshal Munich. For, of Munich's treatment of his army in the course of his invasion of that peninsula, the preceding year, or 1736, we are informed, "that Marshal Munich was too harsh. He unnecessarily fatigued his troops too much. In the burning heat of summer, instead of making them march in the night, or some hours before daybreak, to take the benefit of the freshness of that time, the army never used to begin its march till 2 or 3 hours after sunrise, which greatly contributed to the distempers that got among the troops; and the suffocating heats overcame them so, that some dropped down dead on the march. There were even officers, that, in this campaign, died of hunger, and misery of all kinds."

In 1738, while Marshal Munich commanded one of the Russian armies, against the Infidels, on the side of the Dneister, his brother Marshal, Lacy, was to re-invade the Crimea with the other army, not, at most, including the Cossacks, above from 30 to 35,000 strong. "July 6," proceeds the contemporary account, "he was with his army in sight of Precop. The Khaun, with 40,000 of his troops, was behind the lines, where he hoped to render the entrance into the Crimea more difficult, than it had been the preceding years. He had great confidence in the new lines, which, the year before, the Tartars had made before the Palus Mæotis. But Lacy disconcerted his project, and entered Crimea, without the loss of a single man. For, in summer, the heats dry up a part of the Sea of Azoph, and a west-wind keeps back the flood so, that one may get into the Crimea, almost dryshod. As good luck would have it, this wind began to blow, and the Marshal lost not a moment, for the taking the benefit of it. He instantly drew up his army along the shore, in 1 single line; and happily crossed the sea, before the return of the flood. Some, indeed, of the carriages of the rear-guard, that could not come up quick enough, were lost, by the wind having ceased to blow, and the sea returning, just after the army had passed. They seized on a small fort, called the Czivas-Coula." On "July 8, the Marshal marched towards Precop, and sat down before it. The siege did not last but till the 10th. The continual fire kept up against the place, and the quantity of shells thrown into it, to great effect, obliged the Turkish Commandant to capitulate. Lacy would not hear of his surrender, but as a prisoner of war; which, after several parleys, he accepted. The garrison, consisting of 2000 Janisaries, under a Bashaw of 2 tails, came out of the place, and laid down their arms. Major-General Brigni, the younger, with 2 regiments of foot, entered the place, and took the command of it. He found there to the number of 100 pieces of cannon, most of them brass; but no more than a small quantity of bread. After this expedition, Lacy penetrated farther into Crimea, which he found in a wretched condition, and almost a desert."

"July 20, there was a very smart action between the Tartars, and a part of Lacy's army. A body of near 20,000 men came on with such fury, to attack the Cossacks of the Ukrain, who constituted the rear-guard, that they routed them, and threw into confusion the Azoph Regiment of Dragoons, that had endeavoured to sustain them. Just at that juncture, Lieutenant-General Spiegel came up with 4 regiments of dragoons, and the Cossacks of the Don, to stop the runaways; and, scarce had they had time to recover themselves, before the enemies attacked them afresh, with a great deal of impetuosity. The combat was long and sharp; but the Marshal, having caused some regiments of foot, who had already entered the camp, to advance, the Tartars were obliged to retreat, having left above 1,000 of their slain on the field of battle. On the side of the Russians, there were not above 6 or 700 men killed, including the Cossacks.* General Spiegel was among the wounded; having received a cut of a sabre in the face. Marshal Lacy had it in his instructions, to take Caffa, the strongest place of the Crimea, and a sea-port, in which the Turks often kept their fleet; but he found the country every where so ruined, that it was, with great difficulty, the army could get subsistence. Besides which, the Vice-Admiral Bredal, who was to bring him, in his fleet, provisions from Azoph, had met with a terrible storm, that disabled the greatest part of his vessels, and dispersed the rest; so that the Marshal, after having made some marches onward, thought it best to bring back his army to near Precop; of which he ordered the fortifications to be blown up, and a great part of the lines to be levelled. In his camp here, he remained till towards the end of August, when he resumed his march back to the Ukrain, where his troops went into winter-quarters, in the month of October."

In 1739, the last year of this war against the Turks, hostilities with Sweden being also apprehended by Russia, the army under Marshal Lacy was merely kept quartered along the Ukraine-frontier as a reserve; the more to be relied on, in case of need, from its regiments having, through

* This was evidently a more serious affair, than would appear from a mere estimate of those *killed* on each side; for every 1 of whom, there would not be less than 3 or 4 *wounded*.

their General's good management, "suffered very little loss." On this praiseworthy economy of his soldiers' lives, contrasted with Munich's loss, during his 4 campaigns, of above 90,000 men, exclusive of *any* slain in action, my author, after exclaiming, "What a difference of conduct, between the 2 Marshals, Lacy and Munich, in this war against the Turks!" adds—"It produced at length such an effect at Court, from the complaints, which had been made to it, of the hardships endured by the army, and the little care taken of it, by the leaving it to moulder away, at the precise time that Lacy did not lose a man but by the enemy, that the Empress charged the former, to inspect the conduct of the latter. Lacy's delicacy, however, refused the invidious task; but Munich, having had intelligence of such a commission, reproached the meritorious Lacy, on the occasion. Marshal Lacy, however, did not give himself the pains to inform his accuser, that he had declined the office imputed to him as a crime, (an office, which impugned the frankness and amiableness of his character,) until, after having taken arms in their hands, as antagonists, they were separated by General Lewachef; who, hearing swords clashing in Munich's chamber, ran in, to separate them, declaring he would put them both under an arrest, in the name of the Empress."

In the spring of 1741, Lacy was placed at the head of the Russian force designed to act in Finland against Sweden; where the war-party were so presumptuous, that, with the "pride which goeth before destruction, and a haughty spirit before a fall," we hear they actually expected to recover the provinces formerly possessed on the eastern side of the Baltic, including St. Petersburgh!—generally boasting, that, *as 1 Swede was enough to drive 10 Russians before him, so the Swedish army had only to show itself, in order to be victorious!* But such swaggerers here, like other ridiculous self-glorifiers elsewhere, were to learn, by the event, how much easier it is to bawl for war loudly, than it is to conduct war respectably. When the Athenians, in their decline, would have been persuaded, by their *orators*, to oppose Alexander the Great, and the Senate referred to Phocion, for *his* opinion on the matter—"I am of opinion," said the wise veteran, "that you should either have the sharpest sword, or keep upon good terms with those who have." From a view of the strength of Russia, analogous to that taken by Phocion of the power of Alexander, the King, and the sounder-minded party, in Sweden, were, indeed, for peace; but, being outnumbered, could not control the pernicious clamourers for war.*
The next in command of the Russian army of Finland, under Lacy, was a most illustrious fellow-exile, and brother-Jacobite, Lieutenant-General, the Honourable James Keith, brother of the Earl-Marischal of Scotland, and finally Field-Marshal under Frederick the Great of Prussia, in whose service he fell at Hochkirchen, in 1758. By September, war having been proclaimed between Russia and Sweden, Lacy entered Swedish Finland, proceeding, through a difficult country, towards Wilmanstrand. In this advance, a great alarm took place at 11 at night, which might have been fatal to both the 1st and 2nd in command. The Swedish "Colonel Wilbrand, Commandant of Wilmanstrand, having learned the march of the Russians, had detached 4 men; who, under favour of the night, and of the wood, were to get as near as possible to the enemy's army, and to reconnoitre it. One of the centinels, of the advanced guard in the wood,

* Compare this irrational outcry for bloodshed at Stockholm, with that mentioned in Book VIII. as unfortunately too strong for Sir Robert Walpole at London—and the *bad* results of *both.*

having perceived them, fired upon them. Scarce had the piece gone off, before some regiments of the 2nd line started up all on a sudden, stood to their arms, and, as if they had been all in concert, began to pour a most brisk fire upon the 1st line, without its being possible, for half an hour together, to make them cease. Some cannon were even fired. The regiments, that lay in their way, had an officer and 17 men killed and wounded. The Generals Lacy and Keith ran a great risque of being killed in this false alarm. They had small tents pitched for them to lie in between the lines, which several balls had gone quite through!" Next day, "September 2, about 4 in the afternoon, the army arrived under Wilmanstrand, and took post about a quarter of a mile from the town, near a small village, called Armila. Marshal Lacy and General Keith proceeded directly to reconnoitre the town, under the escort of a battalion of foot, and of 200 grenadiers, on horseback." Wilmanstrand was "a little town at the distance of full 4 German miles from the frontiers of Russia, situate on the side of a great lake. This covered it behind, so that there was no attacking it but in front, which was fortified with a covered-way, a ditch palisadoed, and a fraised rampart; the whole made of earth and fascines. The town, though itself situated on an eminence, had hills all round, which commanded it. The highest was on the right of it, where there was a wind-mill. The Swedes had posted there a main-guard, to hinder the Russians from occupying it. The rest of the situation was extremely broken, and intersected; there was nothing but woods, marshes, and bramble-bushes, rocks, and ravines; so that it was very difficult to approach the town, but by the high road. Here and there, too, one might find little bits of fields, cultivated and enclosed. Whoever considers this description must allow it to be very difficult for troops to act upon such a ground; and that a small body of men, that knew how to defend themselves well, could easily defeat a great one, that should attack them."

Next day, "the 3rd," the Marshal, at first apprehending the Swedish force there to be much greater than it actually was, naturally hesitated on assailing a post, so formidable under those circumstances; till, on learning that its defenders, under Major-General Wrangel, were not more than 5 or 6,000 men, it was decided an attempt should be made to dislodge the Swedes; the Russians, at 2 in the afternoon, advancing accordingly. The Swedes, meantime, " got into order of battle, on the declivity of the Windmill-hill, having a battery of cannon before their center, and their left on a ravine, about a musket-shot from the glacis of the town. Their dragoons, on the right, had posted themselves in a small plain, on the other side of that hill, near a small village. The Russians, being arrived on a rising ground opposite to the Swedish battery, placed there 2 sixpounders, and some three-pounders; and the action began, with a cannonade, on each side. The Swedish artillery made some havock among the grenadiers. Upon this, General Keith, ordered 2 regiments of grenadiers to attack the enemy's battery, and the Regiments of Ingermaland and Astrachan, commanded by Colonel Manstein,[*] to sustain them. But, as the ground was so extremely narrow, that there was no issuing out of the wood which the Russians had before them, but by marching 2 companies in front,—and even then they had to descend a steep ravine, and climb again a hill, in presence of the enemies, and under the fire of their cannon and small arms, which was exceedingly severe,—these 2 regiments

[*] The same, to whose narrative I am so largely indebted.

were thrown into disorder, and gave way. To hinder, then, these beginners of a flight to communicate their confusion to the regiments that were following them, General Keith ordered Manstein to march to the right, to get out of the wood, and to attack the left wing of the enemies, who were quitting the ravine on which they had encamped, and were advancing. This was instantly executed, and so happily, that, after the 1st volley which the Swedes received, at 60 paces distance, they wheeled about, and ran straight towards the town, where the 2 regiments followed them to the glacis, which they began to attack. Whilst this was passing against the left wing of the enemy, the Generals had restored the order of the other troops, and caused the right wing of the Swedes to be attacked; who, having remarked the confusion into which the Russian grenadiers had been thrown, descended from their eminence, and lost, by this means, both the advantage of the ground, and that which they derived from their battery; so that they were soon routed, and the hill carried, by 5 o'clock in the evening. The cannon of the enemy were turned," by the Russians, "against the town, and the Marshal sent a drum to summon it; but the soldiers of the enemy, continuing to fire from the ramparts, killed him. The Russians, extremely provoked at this incident, renewed the assault with fury, and carried the town, towards 7 that evening." In fine, "most of the Swedes, who had been in this action, were killed, or made prisoners. Not 500 men escaped." The Swedish prisoners of every rank amounted to 1351; the other captures from them consisted of 4 standards, 12 colours, 12 cannon, 1 mortar, and the military chest. The Russians killed were 529, and wounded 1837; or, between *both*, 2366 officers and soldiers. The Russians that day were 9900 strong; the Swedes, by their regimental rolls, 5256 in number. Yet, "if the strength of the post which the Swedes occupied, and the disadvantage, to the Russians, of the ground be considered, it was really astonishing, that the former were beaten. It must, however, be owned, that they themselves contributed greatly to it, by their own fault, in quitting the advantageous position they had taken. The resistance they made was extremely obstinate, and served to augment their loss; for there remained, of their dead, on the field of battle, above 3300 men. The fire, which was very fierce, on both sides, lasted above 5 hours." Wilmanstrand, the plunder of which afforded a considerable booty, being soon after demolished, and the inhabitants sent into Russia, the Marshal repassed the Russian frontier; encamping along it, as previous to this invasion.

For the success thus obtained, as so auspicious a commencement of the war, great rejoicings took place at Petersburgh, although "the Court had not been pleased, that Lacy returned with the army. They would have had him gone on to Fredericksham, and have defeated the Swedish troops, one party of them after another; they not being as yet assembled. But these things were not so easy to be executed, as was imagined at Petersburgh. Lacy made it appear, that he could not have undertaken more, without hazarding the loss of all the troops, under his command. The regiments were diminished by the death and wounds of about 2000 men. There were great escorts necessary to bring away the prisoners, which weakened him still more; the other regiments, too, who were on their march to join the army, were not yet arrived, any more than the 3 battalions of Guards, which had been detached from Petersburgh; besides, the troops had not bread left for above 6 days; nor could the horses, employed in carrying the wounded to Wybourg, have well time to return soon enough; so that the Court was obliged to approve of all that had been done." Leaving the command of the army to Lieutenant-General Keith, the Marshal, not long after, returned to Petersburgh; where he extended the benefit of his hospitable residence to his late opponent, the Swedish Major-General Wrangel, who had been wounded by a gunshot in the arm, and made prisoner at Wilmanstrand. In December, the revolution took place at Petersburgh, by which the Princess Elizabeth, youngest daughter of Peter the Great, was made Empress. Of the several secret arrangements for effecting this change in the government, it not having been "thought adviseable previously to consult Marshal Lacy, who never interfered with the intrigues of the Court, he was applied to, at 3 o'clock in the morning, to say, of what party he was?"—that of the Grand Duchess Anne, or the Princess Elizabeth? Perceiving, on the moment, or "although suddenly awakened out of sleep, that there *was*, in fact, an *Empress*, who had the reins, but, not being equally satisfied, if it was the Grand Duchess, or the Princess, who *had* succeeded, he replied, *Of the party of the reigning Empress!* At this answer, which discovered a quickness of conception, and a great presence of mind, address, and judgment,* he was conducted to Court, that he might continue to enjoy his rank and offices, and even receive new marks of gratitude from the new Empress."

On Easter-Sunday, 1742, a mutiny broke out among the Russian Guards, in which the *foreign* officers, especially an Aide-de-Camp of the Marshal, named Sautron, and a Captain Browne, were unmercifully treated. This movement arose from some villains of the corps, who would have consigned every *stranger* to pillage, conflagration, and massacre. The Marshal had those ruffians ironed and punished; and, with "a great courage of body and mind," put down the remainder of the mutineers; by which service, he is stated to have "*saved Petersburgh, and, perhaps, the whole Empire!*" Having noted how "to prevent farther disorders of this kind, Marshal Lacy had piquets of the country regiments posted in all the streets, and ordered frequent patroles by night and by day," my author adds, "notwithstanding which, the whole town of Petersburgh was in great terror; the inhabitants did not think themselves safe in their houses, nor did any one venture out into the streets after dark. Meanwhile, never were greater precautions taken for keeping the gates carefully shut, both night and day, than during that time. Most certain it is, that, if it had not been for the good arrangements made by Marshal Lacy, the disorders would have multiplied, and gone greater lengths."

Towards the close of May, the Marshal reviewed, at Wybourg, the force for his next campaign against the Swedes. It might amount to 35,000 or 36,000 men, of whom 10,000 were to act by sea, in 43 gallies. Among the Generals, under the Marshal, on land, were Keith and Lowendahl—the latter, in connexion with Marshal Saxe's campaigns, already alluded to—among the Major-Generals, a Count Lacy † and

---

* Thus, under similar circumstances, or when suddenly applied to, and roused from his repose at night, it is stated of the warrior-sage, Ulysses—

> "He thought, and answer'd: hardly waking yet,
> Sprung in his mind the momentary wit—
> That wit, which, or in council, or in fight,
> Still met th' emergence, and determin'd right."
>
> POPE'S HOMER, Odyssey, xv., 543-554.

† Besides the Major-General Count Lacy, Mr. Dalton notices, in the Russian service, another General Officer of the name, Maurice Lacy, born at Limerick, in

Browne. Within the last week of June, the Russians entered Swedish Finland, having to traverse a desolated country, by "the worst roads in the universe," and in "some places, of such a nature, that 200 men, behind a good retrenchment, and a barricade of felled trees, might have stopped short a whole army." After repulsing some hostile parties, the Marshal, on "July 5," approached Mendolax, a very strong post by nature, and rendered still stronger by art, with an intention of arresting his progress, but from which, nevertheless, the enemy retired. Had the Swedes rendered an attack necessary, "the Russians must have lost, in the attempt, great part of their infantry, and, probably, have been obliged to abandon the enterprise. Some grenadiers were, for experiment sake, sent to try to clamber up the front of the retrenchment, and employed above an hour, before they could get to the top of the parapet! But, what must it have been, if they had attempted it, under the warm reception of a brisk fire of cannon, and small arms?" By "July 6," the Marshal and his Generals reconnoitred Fredericsham, deciding to open trenches between the 9th and 10th; the eminence for establishing the 1st battery was likewise surveyed by the Count de Lowendahl; and, " in short, all the dispositions were ready for beginning the siege, when the Swedes rendered them useless, by abandoning the town. At 11 at night, it was seen all on fire. . . . The Swedes had, in their retreat, filled several houses with powder, bomb-shells, grenades, and loaded muskets, which went off, one after another, in the air. This hindered the Russians from entering, and putting out the fire. . . . Three-fourths of the houses of Fredericsham were reduced to ashes. There were found, in the place, 10 pieces of brass cannon that were 18 and 24 pounders," with "120 iron cannon of different sizes. Almost all the magazines had been consumed by the flames; so that there was but little found of provisions and ammunition. Only 1 magazine of powder had not been blown up, that contained 400 quintals of powder, and some thousands of barrels of pitch. . . . July 10, on the Festival of St. Peter, the name-day of the Grand-Duke," afterwards the unfortunate Peter III.,* "the *Te Deum* was sung in thanksgiving, that the Russian army had taken Fredericsham, the only fortified town in all Swedish Finland, without losing a single man!" In 2 days after, the Russians reached the river Kymen, from the opposite side of which the Swedish army, with their batteries, upon eminences, galled the Marshal's cuirassiers, till removing them for protection behind a wood, he brought forward his artillery, dismounted, at the 1st fire, 2 of the hostile guns, and soon silenced the rest. Next day, when the greatest portion of his forces had already passed the river, a courier arrived from the Court, with a positive order that, after the enemy were driven beyond the Kymen, it should be made a fortified frontier, and the campaign concluded. Lacy thereupon called a Council of War, in which all the native Russian Generals were for complying with the order from the Court; but the foreign Generals, Keith, Lowendahl, &c., thought it was most desirable, to turn their hitherto uninterrupted tide of success under the Marshal to due account, by penetrating to, and, if possible, reducing Helsingfort.

With this latter opinion, the Marshal himself coinciding, proceeded to

1740. He was invited to Russia by his relative, the Marshal, where he entered the army, when but a boy; and, having fought against the Turks, and, under Suwarrof, in Italy, against the French, he died, unmarried, in 1820.

* Peter III., murdered in 1762, like his unfortunate son, Paul I., in 1801.

near Pernokirk, where the Swedes were very advantageously encamped, and remained so for some days, until, afraid of being turned by the Russian gallies, they fell back to Borgo; thence, after halting some days, with a river before them, retreated to a camp of great strength at Helsingkirk; and then, dreading to be cut off from their magazines, retired to near Helsingfort, where there was a retrenched camp prepared before their arrival; notwithstanding which, they resolved on quitting it, likewise, for Abow. The evening, however, before the Swedes were to march away, as the Russians were drawing near Helsingfort, a Finland peasant requested to see the Marshal, and after acquainting him with the intended departure of the enemy next day for Abow, mentioned, that this might be prevented, by re-opening, through a wood, a road formerly made by Peter the Great, but disused and overrun with bushes for 30 years; which road, when thus rendered passable, would lead, at the other side of the wood, into the highway from Helsingfort to Abow! The Marshal immediately directed 2 of his Engineers, to see if what the peasant alleged was practicable; and they reporting favourably, he despatched, under Lowendahl, 64 companies of grenadiers, and 4 battalions, to make the passage required. Ere the night was over, Lowendahl sent word that the way was cleared, and that he was posted upon the road to Abow! "By 4 in the morning, the whole army was under march, and joined Lowendahl by 6. Scarce was the junction made, when they saw the van of the Swedish army. The Swedes, terribly surprised, at discovering the Russians in a part where they had by no means expected them, returned, as fast as possible, into their camp of Helsingfort, which they continued to fortify, and strengthened with a number of pieces of cannon." Thus intercepted and invested by the Marshal on one element, and soon after blocked up by Admiral Mishakow on the other, the entire Swedish force had, in 15 days, to surrender. "When the Swedish army capitulated, it was near 17,000 strong; and all the Russian forces, that Lacy had, at that time, under his command, did not outnumber the enemy by 500. The garrisons of Frederichsham and Borgo, the various detachments they had been obliged to make, and sickness, had reduced the Russian army to 1 half; so that there were 2 to 1 odds, that if the Swedes had not submitted to those ignominious conditions, and the Marshal had attacked them, the Russians would have been beaten"—taking into account, on the side of the Swedes, "the situation of their camp, which they had had full time to fortify." All Finland being, by this capitulation, subjected to the Russian empire, the Marshal, leaving a due portion of his army to quarter for the winter in the conquered territory, and sending the rest home to Russia, returned himself to the Court, *with whose orders he had twice so judiciously dispensed—in not advancing so far as it had wished last year——and in advancing farther than it wished this year!*

The Russian operations against Sweden, in 1743, were to be conducted from a squadron of gallies and lighter craft, joined by a fleet of larger vessels, or ships of the line and frigates. May 14th, the landforce and provisions to sail in the gallies being embarked from Petersburgh, "the Empress went on board Marshal Lacy's galley, where she assisted at divine service, according to the Greek ritual; after which, she made him a present of a ring of great value, and of a small golden cross, enclosing some relics; and, embracing him, wished him a happy campaign. She went to her Palace, from the windows of which she saw the gallies move off in a line, who gave her a royal salute, as they passed." This squadron under the Marshal steered for, and soon reached, Cronstadt, where the fleet of men-of-war lay; and, between 2 and 3 days after, the wind, which had been so far adverse for sailing, becoming favourable, the combined armament, coming out of the port into the road, formed a line of battle at anchor. "The Empress arrived from Petersburgh, and went on board the Admiral's ship, where she had a long conversation with Marshal Lacy, and the Admiral, Count Gollowin; after which she landed, and dined at Cronstadt, and returned, the same day, to Peterhoff. The fleet of war, which the Russians put to sea this year, consisted of 17 ships of the line, and 6 frigates; it was commanded by the Admiral Count Gollowin, who hoisted his flag on board the *Great Anne*, which carried 110 guns. . . . The fleet of gallies, that went out of Cronstadt, consisted of 34 gallies and 70 *cantschibasses;* a kind of small Turkish vessels, that might each contain as far as a crew of 80 men, and a month's provision for them." In this latter squadron of the gallies and cantschibasses, there were, under Marshal Lacy, 1 General, 2 Lieutenant-Generals, 3 Major-Generals, with "9 regiments of infantry, and 8 companies of grenadiers of the Regiments of Wybourg, Petersburgh, and Cronstadt;" there being also "on board 200 Cossacks of the Don, with their horses, to serve occasionally for incursions into the enemy's country." In proceeding against the Swedes, "the ice, the excessive cold, and strong winds, hindered the Marshal from making way so fast as he wished to do;" until having, by June 6th, followed the hostile fleet as far as Hangouth, he was able to duly reconnoitre it. Then "he who had won so many battles by *land*, eagerly wished to obtain a victory by *sea*. He gave orders to the Admiral Gollowin, to attack, on his part. The Admiral directed for answer, that the Marshal should be informed, that 1 ship more was wanting, to comply with his desire; for that he," the Admiral, "had but 17 against 12, and that Peter I. had left a standing order, that no attack should be made, without the advantageous odds of 3 against 2. The rage of the Marshal may be more easily conceived, than described, at this remark and reply. Several Councils of War were the consequence, several viewing, and reviewings of the 2 fleets; and, in spite of all the Marshal could say, nothing was done." On the 18th, at the requisition of Admiral Gollowin, "the Marshal sent him 14 *kandschibasses* (before described) as a reinforcement. The Swedes, observing this manœuvre, weighed anchor. The Russian squadron took a large offing They brushed each other with a cannonade on both sides; neither had the advantage. The Marshal, as if practised in the nautical profession, manœuvred with considerable address; drove away 2 Swedish ships, which were placed in the Hangouth* passage to stop him; and ultimately obtained an advantage over the enemy, on weathering the cape with his gallies. A thick fog concealed the Swedish fleet, and prevented the Marshal from following up his success." June 23rd, the Marshal was joined by Lieutenant-General Keith, who, with his separate squadron, had acted successfully against the enemy; after this junction, the Swedish gallies made for Stockholm, the combined Russian armaments soon reaching Degerby, an island off Aland; and, by the 29th, the Marshal had signalled to get under weigh for a proposed descent upon the Swedish coast, when this

* Manstein's spelling of this place substituted for the Prince de Ligne's, though in a quotation from the latter.

design, and his long services, were alike terminated, by the announced agreement to preliminaries of peace between Russia and Sweden at Abow. The treaty was concluded there in August ; the river Kymen being appointed the boundary in Finland, by which St. Petersburgh was rendered secure. In September, the Empress Elizabeth despatched her own yacht to bring the Marshal to Court, where great rejoicings were made, in celebration of the peace ; the feasts and entertainments continuing for several days. The Marshal then retiring to his estates in Livonia, of which province he was Governor, resided there, until his decease, in 1751,* in his 73rd year.

He was in person tall, and well-made, in mind distinguished by enlarged views, clearness of perception, and soundness of judgment ; or a due combination of vivacity and vigour, with coolness, secrecy, and the power of varying his conduct, according to the enemies with whom he had to deal,—Swedes, Poles, Turks and Tartars. He was admired and beloved, among his "companions in arms," for the example he gave of intrepidity, endurance of fatigue, and the maintenance of discipline ; accompanied by a conscientious solicitude to acquaint himself with the wants of his troops, and an uncommon attention to their health and preservation. The zeal and ability he had uniformly displayed in subordinate posts elevated him to the chief command of the Russian forces ; and, at their head, his successes proved how worthy he was of that command. Hence, it was noted at the time of his decease, that, if his death was in Russia a subject of regret to the nation at large, it was still more so among all such, as were qualified to be judges of real merit.† Abbé Mac Geoghegan, in the epistolary dedication of his "Histoire de l'Irlande," in 1758, "aux Troupes Irlandoises au Service de la France," thus refers to this illustrious officer, as having long served among them —"La Russie, cet Empire si vaste et si puissant, cet Empire passé tout à coup de tant d'obscurité à tant de gloire, voulut *apprendre de votre corps la discipline militaire.* Pierre le Grand, ce génie si perçant, ce Héros créateur d'une nation aujourd'hui triomphante, ne crut pouvoir mieux confier cette partie si essentielle de l'art de la guerre qu'au Feldt Maréchal de Lacy ; et la digne fille de ce grand Empereur remit toujours à ce guerrier la principale défense du trône auguste, qu'elle remplit avec tant de gloire." According to abstracts from his family papers,—including his will, ordering his body to be "committed to the earth, Christianly and honestly," or "without idle pomp," and referring to his property, as "acquired through long and hard services, with much danger and uneasiness "—he had, by the Countess Martha, his wife, 5 daughters, married, with portions of 10,000 roubles each, to Major-General Boye,

* The Marshal's decease, if, according to Russian or O. S., on "April 30th," would be, by N. S., on "May 11th," 1751. As citing so much from evidence on the Russian side, and of course not interfering with the dates in the extracts made, I have likewise avoided introducing N. S. at all into my biographic sketch, to escape the confusion of 2 modes of dating—and this, with regard to a country, even *still* using O. S. It is sufficient to state here, that the difference between O. S. and N. S., up to 1699, was 10 days ; and, from 1700 to 1800, both inclusive, 11 days.

† Manstein remarking, how "Russia had, in her service, such good Generals, that few powers in Europe could boast the like," adds, "Munich, LACY, Keith, Lowendahl, have illustrated their names, for it to be presumable, that they will descend to the latest posterity. Be this observed, without particularly naming here all the other Generals who commanded under them, among whom there were some, who might have done honor to any service in the world."

the Privy-Councillor Lieven, and Majors-General Browne, Stuart and Von Witten, besides 2 sons. Of these, the elder, in the Polish-Saxon service, was a Royal Chamberlain and Major of Cuirassiers, as well as Count of the Holy Roman Empire. The younger, in the Austrian service, was a Count, Imperial and Royal Chamberlain, Field-Marshal, Grand Cross Knight of the Military Order of Maria Theresa, &c. Their father left landed estates of considerable value, and personal property to the amount of 539,102 florins, or between £50,000 and £60,000, British money. As the survivor of his mother and elder brother, the whole devolved to the Austrian Field-Marshal, born at Petersburgh, in October, 1725, and deceased, at Vienna, in November, 1801.* *His* history, and that of the Lacys in Spain, being unconnected with the annals of the Irish in the service of France, can be merely referred to here, as reflecting, to the present century, much additional military honour upon the name abroad.

The year subsequent to the death of Marshal Lacy in Russia was marked by the decease in Prussia of another distinguished Irish officer, Richard Francis Talbot, 3rd Earl of Tyrconnell—of the name of Talbot. His father, the 2nd Earl, or William Talbot of Haggardstown, County Louth, attainted by the Williamite revolutionists among the Jacobite loyalists who retired to France, has been noticed as Aide-de-Camp to the Duke of Orleans, in Spain, at the capture of Tortosa, in 1708. Richard Francis, successor to the title, born in 1710, and at first, or by commission of August 7th, 1721, a supernumerary or reformed Captain in the Irish Horse Regiment of Nugent, (afterwards Fitz-James) obtained a company in it, February 1st, 1729. He commanded it at the siege of Kehl in 1733, and at the attack of the lines of Etlingen and the siege of Philipsburgh in 1734. Empowered, March 21st, 1735, to hold rank as a Mestre-de-Camp de Cavalerie, he was with the regiment at the affair of Clausen. Employed, with the Army of Westphalia, as Aide-Maréchal-Général des Logis de la Cavalerie, by order of April 21st, 1742, he passed, in August, into Bohemia, with that army. He was present at the captures of Ellenbogen and Caden, at the relief of Braunau, the revictualling of Egra, and several actions in Bavaria. Returning to France with the army in July, 1743, he finished the campaign in Upper Alsace, under the Marshal de Coigny. By order of February 1st, 1744, Maréchal des Logis de la Cavalerie in the Army of Italy, he was at the conquest of the district of Nice, the passage of the Alps, the taking of Château Dauphin, the sieges of Demont and Coni, the battle of Madona-del-Ulmo; was, from May 2nd, Brigadier by brevet, and was declared such, August 1st. Acting as Maréchal Général des Logis de la Cavalerie to the Army of the Lower Rhine by order of April 1st, 1745, he had an opportunity of signalizing himself at the passage of that river, July 19th; and, sailing for Scotland with that portion of his corps, the Regiment of Fitz-James, designed to reinforce Prince Charles there, he was captured at sea by the English, in March, 1746. Exchanged in 1747, and attached to the Army of Flanders, he was at the victory of Laffeldt, in July. Maréchal de Camp, or Major-General, by brevet of January 1st, 1748, he quitted his company; was commissioned, March 19th, as Mestre-de-

* For my information from the Lacy papers, as well as from those of the Mac Donnells in Austria, (in connexion with the affair of Cremona,) I am indebted to my friend, Richard Mac Namara, Esq., Solicitor, 31, North Great George's Street, Dublin.

Camp Reformé à la suite of the Regiment of Fitz-James; was employed as Maréchal de Camp with the Army of the Pays Bas by letters of April 1st; and served at the siege of Maestricht. Soon after the Peace of Aix-la-Chapelle, he left the army, and, not long subsequently, was nominated Ambassador from Louis XV. to Frederick the Great of Prussia. His Lordship's decease is thus mentioned, at Berlin, in March, 1752. "Messire Richard Francis Talbot, Earl of Tirconel, Peer of the Kingdom of Ireland, Marshal of the Camps and of the Armies of the King of France, Chevalier of the Royal and Military Order of St. Louis, and Minister Plenipotentiary of his Most Christian Majesty at this Court, has died, the 12th of this month, in the 42nd year of his age, and after a long sickness, extremely regretted, from the general esteem which he had acquired here."* His Lordship was eminent for his love of good cheer and hospitality; Voltaire, who knew him at Berlin, alluding to him as specially believing that God had made man to eat and to drink, and as keeping a suitable gastronomic establishment, or open table; and in reference to the respective diplomatic positions of his Lordship as an exiled *Irish*, and of the Earl Marischal Keith as an exiled *Scotch* Jacobite, likewise remarks on the strange destiny which made "un Irlandais, Ministre de France à Berlin, et un Ecossais Ministre de Berlin à Paris!" We *now* know, that, from personal dislike and political resentment against his kinsman, George II., Jacobitism, in 1750, was fomented by Frederick of Prussia; who, as a corresponding sign of his ill-will to George, sent the Jacobite Earl Marischal, as Prussian Minister, to Paris. Upon which an English historian, Lord Mahon, not duly allowing for Frederick having been a DEIST, exclaims—"A singular anomaly, at this time, that a *Protestant* Monarch should become the main hope of a *Romish* Pretender!"

In 1754 died a noble and venerable survivor of the War of the Revolution at home, and a distinguished officer of the Irish Brigade abroad, in the person of John Nugent, 5th Earl of Westmeath. At first, or as the Honourable John Nugent, a Cadet in the Horse Guards of King James II., and next engaged in the dragoon service of the Irish army, he fought at the battle of the Boyne, siege of Limerick, &c.; after which, passing into France, he was a Lieutenant in the King's or Sheldon's Regiment of Irish Horse, acting in Flanders, and on the coasts, till the Peace of Ryswick, in 1697. In February, 1698, he was attached, as a supernumerary or reformed Captain, to Sheldon's new Regiment of Irish Horse, formed from his former corps of that description, and Lord Galmoy's, and successively the Regiment of Nugent and Fitz-James. Accompanying it to Italy in 1701, he was at the combat of Chiari; and, in 1702, at the battle of Luzzara. Removed to Flanders in 1704, he obtained a company; and was commissioned as full Captain, April 5th, 1705. He was at the battle of Ramillies in 1706; of Oudenarde in 1708; of Malplaquet in 1709; at the combat of Denain, and sieges of Douay and Quesnoy in 1712; in Germany at those of Landau and Friburgh in 1713; and at the Camp of the Meuse in 1714. Major of his regiment by brevet of January 3rd, 1720, he was commissioned, February 15th, 1721, to hold the rank of a Mestre-de-Camp de Cavalerie. He served at the siege of Kehl in 1733; at the attack of the lines of Etlingen and siege of

* The decease of his Lordship's wife is given as follows, in a Dublin magazine for December, 1759. "Nov. 2. . . . At Paris, Lady Magdaline de Lys, widow of Richard Talbot, who styled himself Earl of Tyrconnel, of Ireland."

Philipsburgh in 1734; and at the affair of Clausen in 1735. Lieutenant-Colonel of his regiment May 23rd, 1736, and Brigadier by brevet January 1st, 1740, he was employed, by letters of August 1st, 1741, in the Army of the Lower Rhine; with which he marched into Westphalia under the Marshal de Maillebois, and passed the winter in the country of Juliers. In August, 1742, proceeding with that army to the frontiers of Bohemia, he was at several actions in Bavaria, and remained there during the winter. Returning to France with that force in July, 1743, he finished the campaign in Lower Alsace, under the orders of the Marshal de Noailles. Maréchal de Camp, or Major-General, by brevet of May 2nd, 1744, he served in Flanders until the Peace; quitting the Lieutenant-Colonelship of the Regiment of Fitz-James, and the army altogether, in June, 1748. On the decease of his elder brother in Ireland, in 1752, aged 96, he became 5th Earl of Westmeath; and died, in his retirement, at Nivelles, in Brabant, July 3rd, 1754, aged 82 or 83. He was the last Catholic representative of that title, being, by his marriage with Margaret, daughter of Count Molza, of the Duchy of Modena in Italy, the father of Thomas, the 6th Earl, and 1st who conformed to the Protestant Established Church of England and Ireland.

A modern Irish tourist in Belgium, &c., observing "everywhere, on the Continent, we met traces of the illustrious and noble families, whom the cruelty and rapacity of conquest had exiled from *our* country," notices, as "a victim to loyalty and patriotism, who, in every change of fortune, had, by his fidelity and bravery, sustained the dignity of his birth and the honour of his name," the gallant soldier, over whose remains a monument was raised by the Empress Maria Theresa of Austria, with the following inscription:—

D. O. M.

Hic jacet
Illmus D. D. Daniel O-Connor Sligoe,
In Exercitu Austriaco Lôcum Tenens Generalis,
Et antiquissimæ apud Hibernos Gentis Caput,
Qui mox apud suos Centurio sub Jacobo II.,
In Gallijs sub Ludovico XIV.,
Dein sub Leopoldo Lotharingiæ Duce,
Ac demum sub invicta Austriâ, eorum Aquilâ
Annis XLVIII
Stipendia emeritus,
Fide ubique, & Virtute patriâ
Suô apud omnes Desideriô relictô,
Decessit planè, ut vixerat,
Christiani Militis Exemplum.
Obijt Bruxellis VII. Februarij MDCCLVI.
Ætatis XCII.
R. I. P.

I am sorry, that an insufficiency of information should oblige me to restrict, to the narrow limits of the above epitaph (given by Dr. de Burgo, and Mr. Matthew O'Conor,) *my* notice, on this occasion, of the distinguished military career of such a worthy representative of the old and long powerful race of O'Connor Sligo.

We now reach that epoch in the annals of the Irish Brigade in France, when, owing to the causes noticed at the end of the preceding book, a decline of the corps, in its composition as a national force, was perceptible; and when its remaining history, as less interesting, may be more compressed, with the exception of that portion of it devoted to the career of the gallant and zealous, yet infamously-victimised, Count Lally. In the disturbed interval, from the Peace of 1748 between England and France, to the declaration of war by those powers in May and June, 1756, such complaints long existed of French encroachments on the English in North America by land, and of English captures at the expense of the French by sea, that the approaching certainty of an open rupture between the 2 nations was evident for a considerable time, previous to the official proclamations on the subject. As the prospect of war increased, the politico-religious hostility of the Cromwello-Williamite or Penal-Code "ascendancy" in Ireland to the mass of the population vented itself in louder outcries against Papists, and in stronger demands for a rigorous enforcement of the existing laws against them. "The French," it was alleged, "are preparing to invade these islands, and the Papists, designing to join them, are secretly organizing themselves for the purpose." The Brigade in France, to which the surviving Catholic nobility and gentry of Ireland sent their younger sons for a provision abroad, since debarred from the sources of a suitable maintenance at home, became the main object of the legislative animosity of the oppressors. This spirit of hostility was, of course, any thing but *lessened* by the circumstance, that, in spite of the more stringent measures adopted *since* 1746 to prevent recruiting for the Irish regiments in France,—and which measures were, indeed, attended, to a great degree, with success,—yet the "flights of the wild geese," or emigrations among the native peasantry to join the Brigade, could not be *entirely* arrested. For instance, among the published affidavits concerning the Whiteboy disturbances in Munster, early in the following reign, (or that of George III.,) we read one, sworn March 30th, 1766, in which the deponent certifies, that he knew " one James Herbert, otherwise Thomas Fitzgerald, who calls himself a French officer," and "that he saw said Herbert, at 4 several times, enlist men in Kilfinnan, and Kilmallock, in the County of Limerick, and ship them off at Bantry, in the County of Cork, for the French service, in the year 1756."* Respecting such obnoxious enlistments, the most remarkable incident, connected with a popular native or Gælic poem known as the "Dirge of O'Sullivan Beare," is thus narrated. "In 1756, one of the O'Sullivans of Bearhaven, who went by the name of Morty Oge, fell under the vengeance of the law. He had long been a very popular character in the wild district which he inhabited, and was particularly obnoxious to the local authorities, who had good reason to suspect him of enlisting men for the Irish Brigade in the French service, in which, it was said, he held a Captain's commission. Information of his raising these 'wild geese,' (the name by which such recruits were known,) was given by a Mr. Puxley; on whom, in consequence, O'Sullivan vowed revenge, which he executed, by shooting him on Sunday, while on his way to church. This called for the interposition of the higher powers; and, accordingly, a party of military was sent round, from Cork, to attack O'Sullivan's house. He was daring, and well-armed; and, the house being fortified, he made an obstinate defence. At last, a confidential servant of his, named Scully, was bribed to wet the powder in the guns and pistols prepared for his defence, which rendered him powerless. He

* We meet with greater risk run, July 1st, 1757, in the case of "Daniel Swiny, committed to Cork gaol, for endeavouring to seduce 2 soldiers of Col. Fitzwilliam's regiment, to enlist them in the French service."

attempted to escape, but, while springing over a high wall in the rear of his house, he received a mortal wound in the back. They tied his body to a boat, and dragged it, in *that* manner, through the sea, from Bearhaven to Cork; where his head was cut off, and fixed on the county jail, where it remained for several years." The following is a translated portion of the "dirge" composed on "Morty Oge" by his faithful nurse, in Irish:—

> "The sun on Ivera
>   No longer shines brightly;
> The voice of her music
>   No longer is sprightly;
> No more, to her maidens,
>   The light dance is dear,
> Since the death of our darling,
>   O Sullivan Beare!
>
> "Had he died calmly,
>   I would not deplore him;
> Or if the wild strife
>   Of the sea-war clos'd o'er him
> But, with ropes round his white limbs,
>   Thro' ocean to trail him,
> Like a fish after slaughter,
>   'Tis therefore I wail him!
>
> "In the hole, which the vile hands
>   Of soldiers had made thee;
> Unhonour'd, unshrouded,
>   And headless, they laid thee!
> No sigh to regret thee,
>   No eye to rain o'er thee,
> No dirge to lament thee,
>   No friend to deplore thee!
>
> "Dear head of my darling,
>   How gory and pale,
> These aged eyes see thee,
>   High spik'd on their jail!
> That cheek, in the summer sun,
>   Ne'er shall grow warm;
> Nor that eye e'er catch light,
>   But the flash of the storm!"

Under these circumstances, a statute was passed in Dublin, through the so-called "*Irish* Parliament" of the anti-national oligarchy there, "inflicting," says my legal authority, "the punishment of DEATH on all natural born subjects in the French service, who should land in Ireland, and on their abettors, and concealers.* This sentence of perpetual banishment deeply affected the Irish-born officers and soldiers of the Brigade. Their hopes and longings were directed to spend the evening of life in their native homes; to enjoy the hospitality of the companions

---

* Fieffé, likewise, having premised, how "le Cabinet de Saint James-rallnma la guerre," remarks—"Comme les blessures que les Irlandais avaient faites à l'armée Anglaise 10 ans auparavant n'étaient pas encore cicatrisées, il jugea prudent de ne pas l'exposer de nouveau aux coups de ces terribles adversaires, et se hâta de publier l'acte suivante;" or that making it "high treason," and punishable by a suitable *death*, for a subject of Great Britain to enter the French service, after May 1st, 1756, without a special written permission from the Crown to do so, &c. Nevertheless, alleges the French historian,—"Les Irlandais repondirent à cette sentence capitale, en s'enrôlant avec plus d'empressement sous les drapeaux de la France," &c.

of their youth ; and, at length, to repose from the toils of exile ! These hopes soothed the hardships of a military life." Thus old Arsetes observes in Tasso,

> ——"Sinking now, as middle life declin'd,
> To hoary age, the winter of mankind;
>
> * * * * *
>
> I loath'd this irksome life, with wandering tir'd,
> And to review my native soil desir'd ;
> There, midst my friends, to pass my latter days,
> And cheer my evenings with a social blaze."
>
> HOOLE'S TASSO, Jerusalem Delivered, xii., 248-9, 252-5.

But such hopes, on the part of the Irish exiles, were destined to be formed in vain. A clause, indeed, was inserted in the act, that any "returning before the 6th of August, 1756, with intent to become dutiful subjects, should be exempt from the penalties of the statute." This clause, however, "sought to deprive men of employments, without giving them the means of subsistence ;" and, as "men of honourable minds prefer death and exile to dependence and beggary," and as "the Brigade officers had no means of support but their commissions," they necessarily continued in the service of France. Daniel O'Conor, younger brother to the venerable Charles O'Conor of Belanagare, writes as an officer of the Brigade, or Captain in the Regiment of Dillon, from St. Omer's, April 28th, 1756, on this point—" Banishment is frightful to every man but a robber, or a murderer, and what man of common sense would submit to the condition of an exile, on account of a post in the French service ? . . . But are we to get any thing for what we are obliged to renounce? or *will there be an act passed to prevent our breathing?*" Indeed, between the flood of demoralization then spreading through France from the court to the camp, &c., and which continued to increase till it swept all before it at the Revolution, and the simultaneous evil working of the penal enactments against any education of Papists in Ireland, &c., as unfortunately manifested in the sufficiently repulsive resemblance which a number of the younger or more recently-appointed officers to the Brigade presented to the illiterate and dissolute scamps in British uniform referred to by Swift, the writer of this letter, as a man of a cultivated mind, and of suitable morality or self-respect, found himself so disagreeably situated at this time in the French service, that he, and others like him, would have quitted it, if possible. Of such a "debauched country" as France, he exclaims to his brother—" I stare, and look round me, as in a wilderness, where nothing like honesty, or sincerity, appears !" It is added, that he then considered "the French service, a service, which, in general, afforded no prospect, but that of growing more and more unhappy, in proportion as one grew old in it;" and where "his days were embittered by the invidious conduct of a number of new officers, ignorant young men, with whom to know the letters of the alphabet was a crime." * Yet, while so naturally " dissatisfied with his situation among them, and that it was not easy for a man of spirit, and information, to be otherwise," it was for *such* a situation this gentleman found himself banned by law from the prospect of any "blest retirement, friend to life's decline," in his native land, where, amidst relatives and friends, he might form that interesting portion

---

* A specimen of the many necessarily sad effects of the penal enactments against any Popish education—i. e., any education for the nation at large !—in Ireland.

in the social circle, so feelingly alluded to, with respect to the veteran Major Mac Dermott of Emlagh, in the County of Roscommon, by the pathetic genius and Jacobite sympathies of Goldsmith, when he notes of the hospitality of the worthy country clergyman—

> "The broken soldier, kindly bade to stay,
> Sate by his fire, and talk'd the night away;
> Wept o'er his wounds, or, tales of sorrow done,
> Shoulder'd his crutch, and shew'd how fields were won." *

By the commencement of 1756, the French Government, having designed to open hostilities in Europe with an expedition for the conquest of Minorca, as such an important stronghold of the enemy in the Mediterranean,† it was likewise resolved, the better to withdraw English attention from this design, that a large force, in 7 camps, should be stationed along the coasts of France, opposite England. In this force, under the Marshal Duke de Belleisle, Count Lally was employed, by letters of December 31st, 1755, as a Maréchal de Camp, or Major-General; and to it were attached, of the Irish corps in the French service, the battalions of Roth, Clare, Berwick, and Lally; and of the Scotch corps, in the same service, those of Royal Ecossais, and Ogilvie. In January, the arrival of Prince Charles at Paris was announced there, with an allusion to the large number of Scots and Irish *still* devoted to him, and prepared to follow his fortune, at all risks; a hope being also expressed, that, since the Prince's disposition was known to be goodness itself, he would overlook the disagreeable necessity that had occasioned his compulsory removal from France, after the Peace of 1748; in which case, there was a promising appearance of so much being done for him, as would only need success, to compensate him for all that was past. Besides the alarm felt in England, with reference to a military visit from the French—against whom aid from Holland being sought and refused,

* O'Conor's History of the Irish Catholics, Memoirs of Charles O'Conor of Belanagare, Musgrave's Memoirs of Rebellions in Ireland, Appendix No. I., 7, Hayes's Ballads of Ireland, &c.

† The French, with a land-force of about 20 battalions, and between 80 and 90 guns, under the Marshal Duke de Richelieu, supported by a fleet from Toulon, became masters of Minorca, early in the summer of 1756, through the reduction of Fort St. Philip, after the naval repulse of the unfortunate Admiral Byng, in attempting to relieve it. Fort St. Philip was defended against Richelieu by the same Irish Protestant veteran, Lieutenant-General William Blakeney, then in his 86th year, who, in his 76th, or in 1746, had defended Stirling Castle, in Scotland, against Prince Charles. Of the defence of Fort St. Philip by the Irish officer, it is set forth, in the 2nd article of the capitulation—"The noble and vigorous defence which the English have made, having deserved all the marks of esteem and veneration that every military person ought to shew to such actions, and Marshal Richelieu, being desirous also to *shew General Blakeney the regard due to the brave defence he has made*, grants to the garrison all the honours of war, they can enjoy under the circumstance," &c. In consequence of this creditable conduct, the Limerick octogenarian, as contrasted with poor Byng, who was condemned to be shot, became the popular hero of the day in England; and was ennobled, or created Baron Blakeney of Castle-Blakeney, and a Knight of the Bath, by George II. In Ireland, he was presented with the freedom of several Corporations, especially those of Dublin and Cork, in gold boxes; his birth-day was observed with the highest marks of respect; and a statue was voted, 1756, and raised to him, 1759, in the Irish metropolis, on Patrick's Day, by the Order of the Friendly Brothers of St. Patrick, at their own expense. His Lordship died, September 20th, 1761, in his 91st year; and was interred, October 2nd, with great funeral pomp, in Westminster Abbey. He was, from 1737 till his decease, Colonel of a distinguished Ulster corps, the 27th, or Enniskillen Regiment of Foot.

a resort was had to the humiliating *protection* of Hessian and Hanoverian mercenaries,*—a due apprehension was evinced, on the part of the Hanoverian representative of royalty there, at the movements of the exiled Stuart heir to the crown, and his friends "over the water." Under the date of "March 1st, 1756," it was proclaimed how " the Master of the Packet-boats at Dover had received orders, to be very circumspect in regard to the persons they should bring over, because information had been received, that many adherents to the Stuart family were then dispersed in different parts of Flanders, and the young *Pretender* himself was actually at St. Amand." † The emerging of Prince Charles from the secluded life he had long led, and his coming again into France, were, no doubt, in a great degree, attributable to representations on the expediency of his doing so, at this juncture, from the zealous Lally; who, of 3 measures which he advised the French Cabinet to adopt with reference to England, mentioned one for a restoration of the Stuarts *first*. When intelligence arrived, in 1755, of the seizure of the French vessels off Newfoundland by the English, Lally being summoned to Versailles, and consulted respecting what measures ought to be adopted, replied—"Three. To make a descent upon England with Prince Charles—to overthrow the power of the English in India—to attack and conquer their settlements in America." But the majority of the assembly deciding, that it was better to endeavour to obtain satisfaction, and prevent a rupture, he exclaimed—"You will not obtain the one—you will not prevent the other—and you will miss the opportunity of destroying your enemy." The result of the Council's deciding, rather on endeavouring to obtain satisfaction and restitution, was, that a definitive reply to their official communication on the subject did not arrive from England till January 13th, 1756, which was one in the negative—250 French ships and 4000 men being, in the interim, captured by the English! As to Lally, a plan

*After relating the ineffectual application, from England, to the Dutch, for 6000 men, and the arrival and encampment of the Hanoverians and Hessians in different parts of the country, Smollett says—"The Ministry was execrated, for having reduced the nation to such a low circumstance of disgrace, as that they should owe their security to German mercenaries."

† Notwithstanding the failure of Prince Charles's attempt in 1745-6 to recover the crowns of his ancestors, the justice of his cause was still considered by numbers in England to be only reserved to a future, and probably not distant, period for success. In 1750, a spirit of dissatisfaction in England with the Government was accompanied by a renewal of Jacobitism there. Among the "signs of disaffection," Lord Mahon mentions the following. "In the neighbourhood of Lichfield, the principal gentlemen clothed their hounds in tartan plaid, with which they hunted a fox, dressed in a red uniform. The romantic adventures of Charles, in his escape from Scotland, were eagerly perused, under the name of 'the young Ascanius.' His busts of plaster were commonly sold in London. The country ladies were proud to sing the ditties in his praise; the country gentlemen to drink his health in deep bumpers." In September, too, that year, George II. being away in Hanover, and the friends of Charles in England having contemplated *some* design in his favour, the Prince came over to London, attended only by a Colonel Brett. After surveying the exterior of the Tower there, 1 gate of which might, they observed, be beaten down by a petard, they went to a rendezvous at Pall Mall, where about 50 of the leading Jacobites, including the Duke of Beaufort and the Earl of Westmoreland, were assembled. Charles said, that, if they could have assembled only 4000 men, he would head them. But, finding that nothing of a *practical* or *fighting* nature had been arranged, he, after a fortnight's stay in London, returned to the Continent. Compare these circumstances, with the favour, already noticed as shown to Jacobitism, by Frederick of Prussia, at this period.

he submitted in outline of an expedition to the East Indies was so much approved of, that he was directed to work at it with 1 of the Ministers, till it should be completed; after which, he applied himself eagerly to Prince Charles's service, meeting the Prince sometimes at the residence of the Duke de Bouillon, sometimes at that of the Ex-King of Poland, Stanislas, and from the coasts of Picardy and the Boulonais, as Commandant in those districts, re-opening a correspondence with the Jacobites in Great Britain and Ireland, until about the middle of July, when he had to abandon any further active concern with Jacobite politics.

The summons he then received, to repair, from his command on the coasts, to Paris, was with reference to India. The French East India Company, founded under Louis XIV., destroyed towards the end of his reign, and re-established early in that of Louis XV., if judged by its directory, the number of its subordinate officials, and even its apparent military strength, might be deemed flourishing; but, in reality, it was *not* so. It was the only European company of the kind, which did not pay a dividend from its trade. It depended, for its subsistence, on secret brigandage, sustained by a royal grant to farm a portion of the tobacco revenue; a grant quite foreign to the purpose of the institution. Whatever else it could realize was retained for its lavish expenditure in India; a great portion of this outlay being absorbed in war, partly against the English there, but still more in pursuit of territorial aggrandizement, and political influence, at the cost of the native powers, generally divided, and weakened, amidst the vast anarchy attendant upon the dissolution of the Mogul empire. The result of such a dissatisfactory state of things was, that the Company required considerable pecuniary, naval, and military aid from France; and that, at the head of the troops to be sent out to India, there should be an officer of well-established reputation, and no common energy, armed with extensive powers for a better regulation of affairs, if the institution was to be upheld at all. When the Deputation from the Secret Committee of the Company applied to the French Minister, the Comte d'Argenson, for 3000 of the King's troops, to be joined with its own, and commanded by M. de Lally, the equally sagacious and well-intentioned Minister, who disapproved of Lally's accepting that post, said to the applicants—"You do not see your way. I am better acquainted than you are with the worth of M. de Lally, and, moreover, he is my friend; but he should be left with us in Europe. He is on fire with activity. He makes no compromise with respect to discipline, has a horror of every proceeding that is not straightforward, is vexed at everything that does not go on rapidly, is silent upon nothing that he knows, and expresses himself in terms not be forgotten. All that is excellent among us; but what is the prospect of it for you, among your factories in Asia? At the first act of negligence that will clash with the service of the King, at the first appearance of insubordination or knavery, M. de Lally will thunder forth, if he does not resort to rough measures. They will cause his operations to fail, in order to be revenged upon him. Pondicherry will have civil war within its walls, as well as foreign war at its gates. I believe the plans of my friend to be excellent; but, in India, a person, different from what he is, ought to be charged with the execution of them. Leave me, in order to deliberate on all that, and come to see me again." But D'Argenson could no more save Lally, than Laocoon could preserve Troy.

———— "Had not Heav'n the fall of Troy design'd,
Or had not men been fated to be blind,
Enough was said and done, t' inspire a better mind!"
          DRYDEN'S VIRGIL, Æneis, ii., 70-72.

The Deputation from the Company came back, only to persist the more earnestly in their previous request. "This prodigious activity, this severity of discipline, this frankness of character are," they exclaimed, "precisely what the Company is in need of, to dispel the opposite vices, of which it has, for such a long time, been the victim." The Minister then replied—"Messieurs, you wish for him. I wash my hands out of it. Regard yourselves as well forewarned, and impress upon your agents the necessity of acting correctly. I am going to propose M. de Lally to the King; who, I have no doubt, will approve of him, with the greatest confidence. It depends on you, not to disappoint it." "As for us," he concluded, addressing himself to 2 of Lally's brother officers of the Brigade, the Duke of Fitz-James, and the Lord Clare and Earl of Thomond, who had come there to support the demand of the Company, "let us preach to our friend moderation even in doing what is good, and patience even at witnessing what is evil." By November 19th, Lally was created Lieutenant-General for the force designed to assist the Company, Commissioner for the King, Syndic of the Company, and Commander-in-Chief of all the French Establishments in the East Indies; by February, 1757, he was granted the honours of a Commander of the Order of St. Louis; and by December 16th, those of a Grand Cross of that Order. Previous to his leaving Paris, the Directory of the Company particularly enjoined him, "to *reform the abuses without number, the extravagant prodigality, and the vast disorder, which swallowed up all its revenues!*" *—an injunction, however, that, in proportion to the very urgency of the necessity which dictated it, would be sure to occasion disobedience, and excite enmity, against *him*, owing to the "vested interests" of so many official vermin in a continuance of the Augean mass of corruption, which *he* would have to denounce and expose. As to Lally's merit, considered *per se*, for this command to which he was raised, his previously high professional character, and especial hatred of the English, naturally recommended him to the heads of the Company. And there was this strong additional reason for calculating on his sparing no pains to render the institution prosperous that, it was only by effecting such a regeneration of its affairs, he could hope to recover what had been the half of his own property, unfortunately for him, (as he tells us) vested in the funds of that body, without *any* return, since 1720.

For this enterprise, Lally, with an annual salary of several thousand pounds while he should be in command, and the guarantee of a subsequent large pension for life, was placed at the head of a brilliant staff, including officers of some of the most illustrious names among the military noblesse of France. He was to have had what would have been a considerable

* The Directors likewise alleged, in their instructions to the General—"As the troubles in India have been the source of fortunes, rapid and vast, to a great number of individuals, the same system always reigns at Pondicherry; where those, who have not yet made their fortune, hope to make it by the same means, and those, who have already dissipated it, hope to make it a second time." Lally, we are elsewhere told, had come to the conclusion, "that his countrymen in India were universally rogues!" And how much *better*, on the whole, did he *find* them to be? "*Experientia docet!*"

force of European troops for India; among whom, the principal corps were his own regiment, raised to 2 battalions, or 1080 men, "tous gens d'élite et de bon volonté," and the regiment of Lorrain, with shipping and money in proportion. The Company, moreover, undertook to pay the whole magnificently. Not only, however, was his departure delayed, for above half a year beyond the period when he thought it would take place, but his military, naval, and financial means were, in the interim, appointed to be much less than had been promised; at which he was naturally so annoyed, that he declined to compromise himself in command with such very diminished resources, till assured the deficiencies complained of should be remedied by the next year. Of the 3000 men, 3,000,000 in cash, and 3 royal men-of-war, besides the vessels of the East India Company originally designed for the Count, a French contemporary notes— "The state of the forces the English had in India, of which an account had been procured, did not require any greater force in 1755. But this nation, ever active, had not remained idle, like her rival; and France, far from diminishing the reinforcements, ought rather to have augmented them, at the distance of 2 years after the time first appointed for sending them." A diminution, on the contrary, by a 3rd, of the troops, money, and men-of-war for the expedition, being announced on the eve of its departure, "the General, exasperated, refused to embark," until "he was ordered not to recede, and promised, that this deficiency should be made up the following year; which was, by no means, the same thing"—even, I may add, *if* that promise were kept. The expedition did not finally sail from Brest and Port l'Orient, until May, 1757; and, between having to put into the Isle of France for a naval reinforcement, alleged mismanagement connected with the Admiral's department, sickness, and adverse weather, it did not appear off the Coromandel coast till towards the latter end of April, 1758. A voyage, that would have been long enough as one of 7 months, thus occupied nearly 12; in consequence of which, the arrival of assistance from Europe for the English in India was not anticipated as it ought to have been, and they had a fleet prepared for action there, under Vice-Admiral Pococke. The 28th, on approaching, in the *Comte de Provence* of 74 guns, to land at Pondicherry, Lally experienced an early proof of the misconduct (or worse) of those in employment there, his vessel being saluted by 5 discharges of cannon loaded with ball, of which 3 pierced the ship through and through, and the 2 others damaged the rigging!—a circumstance, not, I believe, attended with an actual loss of life or limb, yet naturally remarked on as 1 of very bad omen, or augury!* Animated, however, with the hope of obtaining a Marshal's staff, by effecting such a military revolution in India, as would repair the honour of the French arms, and humiliate the English, of whom he was the implacable enemy, Lally, on coming ashore, proceeded at once to business; inquiring what was the state of the Company's affairs?—the account of which was too like what might be expected from the "very bad omen or augury" that had attended his arrival. "Through the capture of Chandernagore by the English, owing to the

---

* "Cette étrange méprise, ou cette *méchanceté* de quelques subalternes," observes Voltaire, "fut d'un très mauvais augure pour les matelots toujours superstitieux, et même pour Lalli, qui ne l'était pas." I italicize "*méchanceté*," as seeming to indicate a suspicion, by Voltaire, of *some* "foul play," on this occasion. Lally's *unwelcome* character, as a disciplinarian and reformer, had, no doubt, preceded him! *Verb. sap.*

long voyage, or delay in the passage, of the armament from France, the Company," he was told, "had suffered a loss, to the amount of 75,000,000; the factory at Pondicherry was in debt 14,000,000, without being able to borrow 1,000,000; and the Governor and Council were consequently after writing to the Company in Europe, that all succour, in men and ships, would be only thrown away, unless accompanied by 10,000,000 in cash!" * This was an extremely discouraging announcement for Lally, who had brought with him but 2,000,000; he had been also disappointed with respect to the number of his men; he could not dispose of a single vessel; while, in the establishments he came to preserve, there did not appear to be adequate magazines, or other available resources. Nevertheless, influenced by the principle of "*forti et fideli nihil difficile,*" or undepressed amidst so much that was calculated to depress him, he was only the more determined, to remedy so many deficiencies, if possible, by the greater energy of spirit, and rapidity of action, on *his* part. "Not finding," it has been observed, "the same means and facilities for military operations as he had been accustomed to in the armies of Europe, he resolved, to create them, as it were, *in spite of nature.*"

By the evening of the day he landed at Pondicherry, or April 28th, he accordingly began to invest Cuddalore, or Gondelour, and reduced it early in May. He next proceeded to besiege Fort St. David, styled, from its great strength, the *Bergen-op-Zoom of India.* Protected, on its only assailable quarter, by several out-forts, that place was furnished with 194 pieces of artillery. Its garrison consisted of 2136 effectives, of whom 1600 were Sepoy or native troops, and 536 Europeans, including 250 sailors from the *Triton* and the *Bridgewater* (that had been run ashore and burned, to avoid capture by the French fleet, at its first appearance off the coast,) besides 83 pensioners, or infirm. To commence his operations against such a formidable strong-hold, he could, he says, draw together, between Europeans and Blacks, only 2200 men, with 28 pieces of artillery; his supplies, even for that force, being by no means what they ought to have been; though, according to English accounts, he was able to assemble, ere the conclusion of the siege, above 2500 Europeans, with about as many Sepoys, and 34 pieces of artillery.† In contending against the various internal annoyances and external obstacles by which he was surrounded and harassed on this occasion,‡ his zeal, activity, and deter-

* "I'm not," like Cassio, "an arithmetician," and so leave the sums of French and Indian money, that generally occur in this narrative, as I have found them, or to be turned into British money by "abler hands."

† Here, as elsewhere, I act on the principle of giving the numbers of the French from French, and of the English from English, accounts, whenever I can get at enumerations on *both* sides. There is "something of rascality," or shameless unfairness, in the *opposite* practice of too many national zealots, mistermed "historians."

‡ On the almost incredible worthlessness (to use no harsher term) of the ruling powers at Pondicherry, as too bitterly experienced by Lally, from the outset of these military operations, Mill justly remarks—"There is no doubt at all, that the neglect of all preparation to enable him to act with promptitude, though they had been expecting him at Pondicherry for 8 months, was extreme, and, to the last degree, culpable." It appears to have been taken for granted at Pondicherry, "that the expected armament was to do every thing, and that those who were there before had no occasion to do any thing!" He likewise shows what good reason Lally had, to complain of the know-nothing and do-nothing Governor and Council there. "They could not tell him the amount of the English forces on the coast; nor whether Cuddalore was surrounded with a dry wall, or a rampart; nor whether there was any river to pass between Pondicherry and Fort St. David. He complains that he lost 48 hours at Cuddalore, because there was not a man at Pondicherry who could

mination were most conspicuous. At the assault upon the hostile outforts and their batteries, which commenced in the evening, continued during the night, and was attended with general success, he reserved the storming of 1 of those posts and its artillery "for himself, at the head of his veteran Irish grenadiers." He then pushed forward his trenches, "without a moment's interruption, even throughout the burning day in the hottest season of the year," and "he was every where present, shrinking from no exposure to the tropical sun, and restricting himself to the smallest portion of rest during the calm sultry night, when the works were carried on by the light of torches and lamps." To the great difficulties with which he had thus to struggle on land, was added a refusal from the navy to aid him by sea, partly owing to the disinclination of the Admiral, partly to that of the men, whose pay was in arrear; till, by appearing in Pondicherry at the head of his grenadiers, to arrest that officer in case of a further refusal to sail as required, and by distributing 60,000 francs, out of his own pocket, to the sailors, the fleet had, between compulsion and shame, to weigh anchor, and show itself before the Fort, thereby excluding all relief from the English.* At last, or June 2nd, after 17 days of open trenches, the fire from the French batteries was so effective against the place, that the greater part of its embrasures were ruined; above 50 of its guns dismounted; the well, that chiefly supplied it with water, was destroyed by a bomb; and this Bergen-op-Zoom of India had to surrender at discretion, under such a retrospect of disadvantages on the side of him to whom it surrendered, that according to his fellow-soldier, the Comte d'Estaing, "nothing but the success of the undertaking could convince one of its possibility!" There were taken in Fort St. David—or exclusive, it would seem, of the previously stormed outworks—180 cannon or mortars, with a quantity of other military *materiel*, provisions of every kind, which were very welcome at Pondicherry, and, what were yet more so, 300,000 livres in specie, with merchandise or effects to the like amount. The captured Fort, which, as mined, countermined, and capable of containing 300 guns upon its ramparts, must have cost a vast sum to build, was destroyed, after the removal of its contents for Pondicherry; the 300,000 livres in coin, and the goods for as much more, being specially forwarded to the Treasurer of the Company.

tell him, that it was open on the side next the sea; that he was unable to find 24 hours' provisions at Pondicherry; and that the Governor, who promised to forward a portion to him upon the road, broke his word; whence the troops were 2 days without food, and some of them died." As to the siege of Fort St. David, Voltaire alleges—" Tout s'opposait dans Pondichéri à l'entreprise du Général. Rien n'était prêt pour le seconder."

* The French author of the Private Life of Lewis XV., who writes in a hostile spirit to Lally, adds of the conduct of the French Admiral, d'Aché, &c., on this occasion—"He had resisted the solicitations that were made to him, to go out of harbour, under pretence of inability. He contented himself with forming *wishes* for the success of Count Lally at Fort St. David, by writing to him, *The only thing I think terrible is, that we cannot assist one another.* Count Lally was obliged to go in person to Pondicherry, and to force the Commodore to weigh anchor, by heading the grenadiers, and by giving orders to arrest him, if he refused to show himself before Fort St. David, in order to deprive the besieged of the hopes of receiving any succours. . . . We do not know, whether M. de Lally had any *right* to act in this manner. He exerted it, however, very *à propos;* for *the Fort capitulated, as soon as M. d'Aché appeared.*" The circumstance of Lally's "distribuant aux matelots 60,000 francs de sa poche" is related by his son. In the naval engagement, which took place shortly before with the English, it may be noted here *en passant*, that, of the Regiment of Lally, 84 fell on board the French fleet.

Such a contribution to the Company's finances was the more acceptable, since their Council, the better (as was *said*) to revive an expiring credit, had already paid away, or disposed of, the whole of the 2,000,000 recently come from France!—and even, in return for 100,000 livres of his own money left with them by the General, were refusing him, he informs us, the support of their credit! As Fort St. David "was expected to have made a better defence, the English historians have not spared the conduct of the commanding officer;" and it is added, that "the French officers, on entering the fort, were surprized at the ease with which they had compelled it to surrender, and the trifling loss to themselves with which its capture had been effected, not amounting to 20 men by the fire from its defences; although many had perished from brain fevers, and strokes of the sun, when working in the trenches, or serving the guns in the torrid and sickening heat." Lally next, or on the 4th, took possession, by a detachment, of Devicottah, whose garrison of 630 men abandoned it with such precipitation, that the artillery, consisting of 80 pieces of cannon, which might have been nailed up or spiked, and the military and commissariat stores, which might have been destroyed or spoiled, were found, on the contrary, in a good condition. Thus, in only about 38 days from his arrival in India and assumption of the command there at a most unfavourable juncture, and notwithstanding that the conduct towards him of those whom he came to assist was anything but what it ought to have been, a considerable territory was acquired or cleared from hostile occupation, between 250 and 300 pieces of artillery were taken with other warlike spoil, as well as some treasure, the prestige of the French arms was restored, and the English, in proportionable alarm, were withdrawing garrisons from various posts to the north, in order to unite them for the defence of Madras, the rival metropolis to Pondicherry.

The return of Lally, on the 7th, from these conquests, to Pondicherry, was celebrated by a grand High Mass, and Te Deum, with sumptuous feasting, and other public rejoicing. The word of the day was "*Madras!*" But the French Admiral would not undertake to assist in attacking that place; preferring a cruise to the south, against such vessels as might be coming from England; and even carrying with him a detachment of the land force, which, to induce him to put to sea again, after the late engagement, had been lent him by the General. *A reference to the accounts of the Council of the Company likewise too strongly countenanced, or confirmed, the very unfavourable impression, which Lally had received, from official authority, in France, of the character and conduct of those connected with the Company's finances.* A further result of such financial mismanagement, (to say no worse,) more unequivocally appeared in the announcement of Leyrit, Governor of Pondicherry, that, beyond 15 days, he would neither be answerable for the payment, nor for the feeding, of the army! The General's extremely natural denunciation of such a discreditable state of things, and its causes, in his own very energetic manner of expressing himself—yet, surely, not more so than was but too glaringly provoked, or merited!—only served, as was foreseen, to create that inveterate hostility towards him from official peculation or delinquency, which would scruple no means, however dishonourable, to ruin him, as an avowed or uncompromising opponent. Under these most untoward circumstances,—rendering it, on the whole, imperative, that since, in spendthrift phraseology, matters could not remain as they were, "something should be done to raise the wind!"—a military expedition was suggested to the General against the Rajah of Tanjore, or Tanjour, to enforce payment of a bond, in the Company's possession, from that Prince, for 5,600,000 rupees. "Lally was, of course, obliged to trust to the information of those acquainted with the country;" and the parties in power, who recommended this Tanjore enterprise to him, diminished, or "extenuated, beyond measure, the difficulties of the undertaking, and made him set out, *upon representations which they knew to be false, and promises which were never intended to be fulfilled.*" In reference to which official knavery, and the other or subordinate ruinous concomitants of such a system, my English authority remarks, how very hard (or rather *impossible*) it was for the General, "to counteract the malignity, to stimulate the indifference, and to supply the enormous deficiencies, by which he was surrounded." The route from Pondicherry to Tanjore was about 50 leagues, or 150 miles, with several rivers to be crossed, &c. Lally, with 2500 men, took the field, the 18th; but, as before, unprovided with the various attendants, considered requisite, in that country, for an army's regular subsistence—*the Munitionaire-Général, moreover, soon absconding, with the whole fund for that purpose!* Hence very great distress, discontent, and disorder among the troops, necessitating a recourse to new and severe measures, on the General's part, in order to "make war support war," and proportionately operating to retard his advance. Proceeding, nevertheless, as soon as possible, in spite of a swarm of active native irregulars, and of 7000 regulars opposed to him, he, by July 18th, approached Tanjore. A negociation ensued with the Rajah. He was menaced, through Lieutenant-Colonel O'Kennedy, with the utmost vengeance, in case of non-compliance with the demands of the French; who, meantime, took possession of the suburbs of Tanjore. The Indian not submitting, Lally commenced battering the place at close range, August 2nd; and, against the evening of the 7th, a breach was effected, which only 24 hours' firing would have rendered practicable. By this time, however, he had no other balls for his artillery than those shot from the town, of which but few suited the calibre of the guns; of powder for them he had but 150 charges; his infantry had not 20 rounds a man; and provisions were running very low in his camp, without the prospect of a further supply, owing to the great number of the Tanjorine horse. Next morning, or the 8th, these misfortunes were aggravated by the purport of the letters he received; 1 from Carical, the only place whence any relief could be expected before Tanjore, mentioning the repulse, on the 3rd, of the French fleet, and the English being in consequence anchored off, and threatening a descent at, Carical; another from Pondicherry, announcing its being menaced by the reported march of 1200 of the English troops from Madras; another from the Mahratta potentate, Gopal Row, denouncing invasion against the territory of the French, unless their army should immediately retire from Tanjore. Lally thereupon summoned a Council of War, at which the great majority of the officers necessarily voted for raising the siege. The wounded were to be removed with a due European escort on the 9th, and to be followed by the army on the 10th; the batteries meantime occasionally firing, to awe the garrison of Tanjore. Information of this resolution reaching the Tanjorine commander, Monacjee, he appointed the morning of the 10th for a general assault on the French camp, to be prefaced with a treacherous attempt on Lally's life; of which assault the better hopes were entertained, from the timely arrival in Tanjore of the last of 2 detachments of select Sepoys, consisting of 1000 men with 50 Europeans, forwarded to the Rajah's aid by the English Governor of Tritchinopoly, Captain (subsequently Brigadier-General) John Caillaud, an able officer of Huguenot origin. The entire force of Monacjee, computed as very superior in number, or 16,000 men, including 4000 cavalry, were drawn out by night, and posted so as to remain undiscovered, until ready to fall most effectively upon the besiegers, before sunrise. The party to assassinate Lally was composed of 50 Black horsemen. At dawn, riding from the city, at a leisurely pace, to the French camp, and being challenged by the outguard, they stated, that they came to offer their services to the French General; and, accordingly, required to be conducted to him. Nothing wrong being suspected, they were conducted towards his quarters, about half a mile in the rear of his camp. Lally, informed of their approach, got out of bed, and merely in his drawers, and luckily with a thorn-stick in his hand, went, accompanied by but 1 attendant, to meet them. At about 100 yards from him, the troop halted, their Captain coming forward on horseback; and being now near enough, to make sure, as it were, of their intended victim, and in order, apparently, to signify to their main force about the town, that the assassination-business was in hand, 1 of the Black troopers galloped to an ammunition-tumbrel, fired his pistol into it, and blew himself up with a suitable explosion, at the same time that the Captain of the troop rode in upon Lally, making a cimetar-cut at his head. Lally, not losing his presence of mind, parried the blow with his wooden life-preserver; his stout and faithful attendant instantly despatching the baffled murderer. The General, nevertheless, was trampled down and stunned by the onset of the rest of the Black troop, till his guard rushing up; he came to himself, and, sabre in hand, at their head, gave the villains, who charged twice, their deserts; 28 of them being shot dead, and the remainder forced to ride into a pond, where they were drowned; his guard losing but 2 men in the encounter. At the noise of the exploded ammunition-tumbrel, and the succeeding musket-shots in the French camp, Monacjee assaulted it, at once so unexpectedly and vigorously, with his whole force, in part directed by English officers, that all seemed lost there for near an hour, or till the French soldiers being rallied, and restored to their usual discipline and efficiency, the assailants were beaten out, with a loss much larger than they inflicted. Of the English Sepoys, more especially, by whom 3 guns within the camp were captured, 75 men were killed or wounded; and the guns were recovered. That night, Lally, spiking his battering-artillery, and lightening his baggage as much as possible, retired from Tanjore.

Between having to keep Monacjee's pursuing troops at bay; in such a hot climate to march 15 or 20 miles a day; sometimes to subsist only on cocoa-nuts, and not enough of them; at other times to suffer cruelly from a want of water; besides the difficulty or trouble of transporting the artillery and carriages across rivers; the retreat of the French was most harassing, and in the privations of it the General fully bore his part. By this expedition to Tanjore, (though unsuccessful, yet not through *his* fault,) the French forces were maintained for about 2 months at the enemy's cost, and nearly 500,000 francs were similarly realized; which, remarked a French officer, was effecting much in a country, the resources of which appeared to be so little. From Carical, where, at his arrival on the 18th, he saw the English squadron still anchored off the mouth of the river, and, along with a fuller account of the French

Admiral's repulse, heard of that officer's approaching intention to leave the Indian coast for the Isle of France, Lally rapidly took horse, with a small cavalry escort, for Pondicherry, to prevent, if possible, such a departure of the navy. He reached Pondicherry the 28th, and immediately summoned the Council there, to support him in remonstrating against such a desertion. And the Council did so. But the French Admiral would have his way; and, merely leaving 500 marines or sailors to serve on shore, he set sail, September 2nd, with the entire fleet, for the Mauritius. An intercepted French letter from Pondicherry to Masulipatam, dated the following day, gives these particulars respecting the recent expedition to Tanjore, or Tanjour, and the naturally depressing departure of the fleet. "We laid siege to Tanjour, and made a breach, but were obliged to retire, for want of provisions and ammunition; leaving behind us 9 pieces of cannon, 8 of which were 24 pounders. The army has suffered greatly from hunger, thirst, watching, and fatigue. We have lost near 200 men, as well by desertion, as by death. This check is very detrimental to us, as well with regard to our reputation, as the real loss we suffered. . . . Poor French, what a situation we are in! What projects we thought ourselves capable of executing, and how greatly are we disappointed in the hopes we conceived, upon taking Fort St. David! I pity our General. He must be extremely embarrassed, *notwithstanding his extensive genius;* without either money or fleet; his troops very discontented; his reputation declining; and the bad season approaching; which will oblige us to subsist at our own expense, being unable to form any enterprize for procuring us other funds. What will become of us? . . . Above 20 officers of different corps have gone on board the fleet; and, if M. Lally had given permission to depart to whoever desired it, the greatest part of them would have embarked; so greatly are these gentlemen disgusted with the service." A paragraph from a French journal, dated "Versailles, December 20th, 1759," and deriving its information concerning this enterprise against Tanjour, from the express forwarded to Europe even by the Admiral d'Aché, after observing, how the ill turn the French affairs in India had taken was "imputed neither to M. Lally, nor to the troops," but entirely to "the Company's Directors on the Coast of Coromandel," then alleges of those Directors, how they "*for the sake of private interests, and personal resentments, injudiciously turned against the King of Tanjour those forces, that should have been employed only against the English settlements;* and, moreover," concludes this Versailles authority, "*had that Prince been properly dealt with by the Company, he would have sided with us against the English.*"

On re-entering the Company's territory from that of Tanjore, Lally had written to the Governor of Pondicherry, how disorder and rapine had attended the march of the army from that city, and would accompany his return there; noting, with reference to the general official corruption and administrative inefficiency which had been the *origin* of his complaints—"In all this, a change must take place, or the Company be overturned." To which the Governor's warning reply was—"He who would wish to establish order, in the financial as well as the commissariat department, will make himself many enemies." *The case, by the way, in a nutshell, of Lally and his enemies!* Meanwhile, it being, after the failure of the Tanjore enterprise, additionally imperative that something else should be done to meet the existing pressure for "more money," attention was directed to an acquisition so desirable as that of Arcot, then under a native ruler, in the English interest. It being requisite previously to reduce the secondary forts of Trivalore, Trinomalee, Carangoly, and Timery, Lally divided his army into 4 parts. The 2 former places were surrendered without opposition; the 2 latter were carried by assault; and, by an agreement with the Governor of Arcot, according to which he was to receive 10,000 rupees, and be taken with his troops into the French service, Lally, amidst the thunder of artillery, entered that metropolis, October 4th; thus insuring the revenues of the nabobship so-called to the French Company. He would next have attacked the fort of Chingleput. But the English, awake to its importance, as covering the country, whence, in case of a siege, Madras should chiefly be provisioned, and, being reinforced, about the middle of September, by a fleet from England with 850 European regulars, to whom were joined all those from Trichinopoly, strongly garrisoned Chingleput, previous to the fall of Arcot. Lally's applications to the Government at Pondicherry for 10,000 rupees, as necessary to put his forces in motion for Chingleput, met with the usual reply of the officials, as to the "exhaustion of their resources;" so that he was "obliged, for want of funds, to place the troops in cantonments," and returned, naturally disappointed and chagrined, to Pondicherry.

After the fall of Cuddalore, Fort St. David, and Devicotah, it having been the intention of Lally next to reduce Madras, and thence march for Bengal to sweep the English from India, he had resolved on consolidating, as far as possible, under his personal command, the French forces throughout the Peninsula; such a consolidation being absolutely requisite if the English were to be expelled, and any partial loss of territory, or diminution of influence in particular districts, that might result from the subordinate removals of troops which he contemplated, being consequently of comparative unimportance; since if the English power was to be crushed, it could not be so but by the French *en masse;* and, when crushed, not only whatever had been relinquished for a time, in order to effect the ruin of that power, would be easily recovered, but the entire Peninsula would be at the feet of France, as the dominant European nation in Hindostan. Nor should such hopes, by Lally, of rooting out the English, be deemed *too* sanguine, had he been but fairly seconded, especially in a financial way, by those he came to defend; of whom so many, as having made fortunes, would not be without a proportionable credit. "The land-forces," says Smollett, "belonging to the" English "East-India Company were so much outnumbered by the reinforcements which arrived with M. Lally, that they *could not pretend to keep the field, but were obliged to remain on the defensive, and provide, as well as they could, for the security of Fort St. George,*" at Madras, "*and the other settlements in that part of India.*" Of the French General's landing on the Coromandel coast, Lord Clive testified in 1772—"Mr. Lally arrived with such a force, as *threatened not only the destruction of all the settlements there*, but OF ALL THE EAST INDIA COMPANY'S POSSESSIONS; and *nothing saved Madras from sharing the fate of Fort St. David at that time, but their,*" the French, "*want of money, which gave time for strengthening and reinforcing the place.*" Even before the fall of Fort St. David, the British historian, Mill, likewise admits, "the English were thrown into the greatest alarm," as, "so much was the power of the enemy now superior to their own, that they *scarcely anticipated any other result, than their expulsion from the country*"—and, had Lally been backed by such a financier as Dupleix, it may consequently be added, in this historian's words respecting the English in India, " it is *more than probable, that their most gloomy apprehensions would have been realized!*" With such grounds, on Lally's part, for the hopes he entertained, strengthened by " a contemptible opinion of the English troops in India," on account of the circumstances under which Fort St. David was taken, he had written to Messieurs de Bussy and Moracin, the former commanding in the Deccan, the latter at Masulipatam, to come and join him. In his letter to Bussy, after the reduction of Fort St. David, he stated—" It is *the whole of British India, which it now remains for us to attack.* I do not conceal from you, that, having taken Madras, it is my resolution to repair immediately, by land, or by sea, to the banks of the Ganges, where your talents and experience will be of the greatest importance to me." In another communication to those gentlemen, he adds—" All my policy is in these 5 words; they are sacramental: *No English in the Peninsula.*" Shortly before his entrance into Arcot, Lally was joined, at Wandewash, by Bussy, from the Deccan. "The characters of the 2 men were very different. Bussy was an excellent soldier, an accomplished gentleman, a polished courtier, and a cool diplomatist; he was anxious for the glory and supremacy of his country in India; but he was not likely to embark his fortune, in any hazardous attempts to forward or secure them. Lally *thought only of the ruin of the English; and, to that 1 end, were sacrificed, at all times, his every interest and emolument!* " Duly attached, as a keen self-seeker, to that separate command in the Deccan, where, by turning to account the discordant politics of the native potentates, he had " feathered his nest," and, if allowed to return, might continue to feather it, far better than he could expect to do, if acting merely in a subordinate position under the scanning eye of Lally, Bussy naturally preferred to be, as the sayingis, "on his own hook," in the more remote and remunerative quarter. He consequently used every effort, even holding out most personally advantageous or lucrative inducements to Lally, in order to be permitted by him, to go back to the Deccan, with a 3rd part of the French troops. Lally, on the other hand, though refusing such a permission, did his utmost to reconcile Bussy to the opposite course of proceeding against Madras; with that view raising him, from the rank of a Lieutenant-Colonel, to that of a Brigadier, as well as granting him a seat in the Council, and a residence in the Palace of the Government, at Pondicherry. For these promotions, Bussy at first expressed himself grateful; but, remaining as bent upon getting back to the Deccan for his own purposes, as Lally was intent upon marching against Madras for the overthrow of the English, the 2 men were irreconcilable. Thus 2 parties were formed, even in the army; the King's troops being for Lally, and those of the Company for Bussy. To strengthen himself still further, Bussy did not neglect to secure powerful friends, or partisans, in Pondicherry, with money, by which, to his equal vexation and surprise, he had found Lally was not to be tempted; at the same time that Lally could not prevail upon this man, with money for *such* purposes, to accommodate the treasury with *any* loan for the *public* service! Bussy was defined, by the late Governor of Pondicherry, to his successor, as a man *to be mistrusted;* Lally had brought a *bad* opinion of him from France; and, from what *since* occurred between them, had Lally any reason to entertain any *better* impression of *such* a character ?*

The worthless administration at Pondicherry having, by November, declared, (as before) its inability to subsist or pay the army, a Council of War was called, at which Comte d'Estaing and the other officers were of opinion, it would be better to die by a bullet at Madras, than perish by hunger at Pondicherry! To reduce Madras, indeed, by a regular siege, *since* Lally first contemplated doing so, had become an undertaking, so much above the resources at his disposal, as to be generally reckoned impracticable. Yet things could not remain *in statu quo;* some movement should be made; and, by an advance against that place, the English might be driven into the Fort, and bombarded there; while the *black town* could be pillaged, and the surrounding country be laid waste —the more easily, as the monsoon season would be an obstacle to a reinforcement, or relief of the enemy, by sea. There being no fund to enable the troops to march except what might be raised by contribution, some Members of the Council at Pondicherry, and other individuals not lost to *all* sense of shame, were induced to advance 34,000 rupees— Lally himself subscribing 60,000 of his own money, and the shabby fox, Bussy, not 1 sous! With this sum of only 94,000 rupees, the General prepared to take the field. The force under his command amounted, by accounts on their side, to 3000 Europeans; of whom 2700 were infantry, and 300 cavalry. They were attended by 5000 Blacks, of whom only about 1500 seem to have been military, or Sepoys; and their train of artillery consisted of 30 pieces, or 20 cannon, and 10 mortars. The rainy season not permitting Lally to advance early in November, as he might otherwise have done, he did not come before Madras, after taking 4 places on his march, until December 12th, when he was without money to subsist his army, even "for a single week!" The main force of the English, under the veteran Colonel Lawrence, having made such movements as might delay the French approaches yet avoid an engagement, in which a defeat would be "the certain loss of Madras," retreated into its citadel, or Fort St. George; a considerable party of Sepoys, under a gentleman of Irish birth or origin, Ensign Crowley,† though then absent, yet subsequently contriving, much to his

---

* Bussy is best "shown up" in the French memoir of Lally, repeatedly cited. Here, as elsewhere, on the subject of Lally, I likewise make use of the histories of Orme and Mill, together with a work, published at Calcutta, in 1855, entitled "European Competition in India, from the Earliest Times, to the Establishment of the Honorable East India Company's Supremacy, by the Fall of Pondicherry, in the year 1761, by Daniel O'Callaghan, Esq., Bengal Medical Service," since Surgeon-Major, Officiating Garrison Surgeon, Fort-William, Calcutta, and Deputy Inspector General of Hospitals, Lucknow. I have also availed myself of British, Irish, and Continental contemporary periodicals, Voltaire, and the Private Life of Lewis XV., previously specified, besides Smollett, Sismondi, Lord Mahon, and the East India Military Calendar. So far, with respect to the *main* authorities, consulted for this Indian portion of my task.

† The O'Crowleys, of Heremonian origin, and at first located in Connaught, afterwards possessed, in the County of Cork, the woody and mountainous territory of Kilshallow, west of the town of Bandon, and on the river so called. They were in peace subject to, and in war among the followers of, Mac Carthy Reagh, Prince or Chieftain of Carbery, in which Barony, the clan-district of Kilshallow lay. The name of O'Crowley has been anglicized into *Croly,* and, as such, is not without note in our modern literature. Whatever may have been the religion of the Ensign above mentioned, I believe it would be *no* objection to his serving the English East India Company, in a *military* way. In France, the name, differently

credit, to join the rest of the garrison, in opposition to a European detachment, under Lieutenant-Colonel Murphy of the Regiment of Lally. When the French were proceeding from a place called "the Mount" towards Madras, writes Orme, "300 Europeans, with 2 twelve-pounders, had been sent off, under the command of Lieutenant-Colonel Murphy, against Pondamalee. They arrived at noon, and Murphy summoned Ensign Crowley, with threats, as resisting in an untenable post, although the fort was of stone, and surrounded by a wet ditch. On Crowley's refusal, the twelve-pounders were employed until night, when 20 of the French detachment had been killed or wounded, and little damage had been done to the wall. But the Sepoys within, expecting neither succour, nor quarter, began to waver. On which, Crowley marched with them out of the fort, in deep silence, at midnight, and passing where he was apprized the enemy kept slight watch, got out of reach before they were ready to pursue; and, knowing the country, came in, the next morning, by the north of the *black town*. The number was 500, in 5 companies, of which 3 were the garrison of Pondimalee, and 2 had retreated hither from the Fort of Tripassore. Their arrival brought in the last of the troops, stationed in distant out-posts, and completed the force with which Madras was to sustain the siege." The garrison of Fort St. George, by their own accounts, amounted, between Europeans and Indian mercenaries, to upwards of 4320 men, the former above 1750 in number.* They were well officered, and were amply supplied with artillery, ammunition, and provisions. The Governor of the Fort for the English East India Company—a gentleman of French, as Lally was of Irish, origin, *both* thus serving on different sides from what they would have done, but for the intolerant legislation so often before alluded to—was Mr. Pigot. He showed himself to be worthy of the high post he held, by a judicious deference, in the more specially military department, to the professional knowledge of Colonel Lawrence, and other experienced officers; by an unremitting attention to the other or more immediate duties of his own station as a civilian; and, not least, by his animating the garrison, to make the best defence in their power, with a promise, should they do so, of 50,000 rupees.† Moreover, from the well-furnished treasury at his disposal—besides, it may be remarked, the great wealth of individuals in the Fort, which was far more than would have defrayed all the expenses of maintaining the place—the Governor remitted 70,000 pagodas for the formation of an additional force, eventually above 5900 horse and foot,‡ with some Europeans and 6 pieces of light artillery; which force, under Captain Preston, Mahomed Issoof, and Major Caillaud, were, in aid of those invested in the Fort, to act against the communications, ravage the territory, and distract the siege operations, of the French.

written O'Crowley, or O'Croly, is to be seen under Louis XIV., XV., and XVI., from the Sous-Lieutenant to the Lieutenant-Colonel, in the Gendarmes Anglois, Gendarmes Ecossois, Régiment d'Aunis, and Regiments of Bulkeley and Walsh, in some instances with the rank of Chevalier of St. Louis.

* Namely, 1605 European military, with 150 European assistants, or attendants, 1755—Sepoys and irregular horse 2420, with 153 select Indians attached to European military, 2573—general total of Europeans as 1755, and of Asiatics as 2573, having consequently been 4328.

† "Celui qui récompense ainsi," notes Voltaire, "est mieux servi que celui qui n'a point d'argent."

‡ The 3 highest amounts of this *varying* force appear as 4680, as 4803, and as 5930. The guns increased from 2 to 6.

Early on the 14th, the French army, crossing the Triplicane river, and dislodging such English and Sepoy outposts as remained to make a show of opposition around the *black town*, entered Madras. While Lally and his staff were engaged reconnoitring Fort St. George, a large proportion of the troops, with some thousands of the inhabitants of Pondicherry who had followed the army, dispersed, on all sides, to avail themselves of such a great booty as the contents of the city presented; and, to that disorder, the quantity of strong liquors found there added intoxication, with its numerous attendant evils. The Regiment of Lorrain was, to its honour! alone uninfected by this brutal indulgence; in which other corps, though distinguished, were, nevertheless, surpassed, to its disgrace! by the Regiment of Lally. Meantime, it was reported to the English on Fort St. George, "that the French troops were all employed in ransacking the houses, and that they had discovered several warehouses filled with arrack, with which most of them had already got drunk ;" while such of them as were perceptible " appeared staggering under their loads, and liquor; on which it was resolved, to make a strong sally, before they could recover themselves." It was undertaken by Lieutenant-Colonel Draper with 500 picked men, supported by 100 more under Major Brereton, with 2 field-pieces. As might be expected under the circumstances, the attack was successful at first, but was finally repulsed; the English having had 212 officers or soldiers, and the French (as taken at a disadvantage) 219 killed, wounded, or captured. In this affray, according to Lally's biographer, the Regiment of Lorrain, mistaking the English for the Regiment of Lally, allowed the enemy to approach on the right, till only undeceived by receiving his fire. D'Estaing, fighting at the head of his corps, was wounded, unhorsed, and made prisoner. Bussy proceeded to the left, where the gallant Chevalier de Crillon, at the head of the Regiment of Lally, was eager to take a decisive part in the contest. Lally, galloping up to the Regiment of Lorrain, which had lost its cannon, and was fallen into disorder, rallied it so effectively, and supported it so well with cavalry, that the cannon which had been lost were regained, and those of the English were seized, and turned against them. The English, then driven from street to street, were compelled to hasten towards the bridge, by which alone they could re-enter their Fort, when Crillon, seeing the opportunity of intercepting them by a dash for the *tête-du-pont*, proposed making it to Bussy; who objected to it, on the plea of their being without cannon. Crillon replied, "This is an affair of bayonets," ordering the regiment to follow him; but was stopped by Bussy, as his superior officer, or a Brigadier, to which he adverted, and his consequent *right* to stop Crillon. But Crillon exclaiming, "No, by God, you shan't stop me!" rushed forward with the comparative few that ventured to accompany him; and though, from the delay to which he had been subjected, he could only come up with the last of the beaten English hastening to the Fort, he was able to kill 50, and take 30!—and, had he been aided with all that he might have been, it is alleged, "*not 1 Englishman would have re-entered the Fort, and the siege would not have lasted 15 days.* Lally remained persuaded," adds his biographer, "*that Bussy, and his party, were unwilling to allow him to take Madras!*" Of his own countrymen, and Bussy's conduct at that *sortie*, Mill states—"They penetrated into the *black town*, before the enemy were collected in sufficient numbers; but were at last opposed by a force, which they could not withstand; and, *had the division of the enemy,* which was under the command of *Bussy*, advanced with sufficient promptitude to cut off their retreat, it is highly probable, that few of them would have made their escape. Lally adduces the testimony of officers, who commanded under Bussy, that *they joined in urging him to intercept the English detachment;* but that he, alleging the want of cannon, absolutely refused. Mr. Orme says, that he justified himself by the delay of Lally's orders; without which, it was contrary to his duty to advance. *To gain, however, a great advantage, at a critical moment,"* concludes Mill, *" a zealous officer will adventure somewhat, under some deficiency both of cannon, and of orders."* We likewise learn from the English on this occasion, that, "notwithstanding the ardour of the onset, it left no advantageous impression of the firmness of the garrison with the French officers ; and Murphy, 1 of the most experience, proposed, that a general assault should be made on the town in the ensuing night in 4 divisions, and offered to lead the principal attack himself. It was lucky for them," affirms the English narrative, "that his advice was not followed."

Next day, the 15th, though there remained in the army-chest but 4000 livres, preparations were made for placing in battery against the Fort the heavier artillery.; which, having been embarked as for a siege, was still far off at sea, except a 13-inch mortar, that, coming by land, with but 150 Sepoys, had its escort intercepted and defeated by a much superior detachment, or 4 companies, of the English Sepoys, under Lieutenant Airey, between Saddrass, and Cobelong. When a captured place becomes the soldier's prey, says the poet,

> " all engage
> In quest of spoil, and, ere the trumpets sound,
> The plunder'd city's scarcely to be found.
> They fell, they bear away, they load the cars ;
> Scarce such a din attends the work of Mars."
>
> LEWIS'S STATIUS, Thebaid, vi., 157–162.

Thus, the unfortunate pillaging of the *black town* absorbed, or diverted to other channels, so much of what might have constituted no small fund for military operations, that the place, continues my English account, "furnished to Lally for the demands of the service only 80,000 livres, lent him by an Armenian merchant, whom he had saved from plunder; and to these were added 12,000 livres, furnished by an Hindu partizan. With these funds, he began to construct his batteries, in the intention, as he repeats, of only bombarding the place, when intelligence was brought, on the 24th of December, that a frigate from the islands had arrived at Pondicherry with 1,000,000 of livres.* It was this circumstance, he says, which now determined him to convert the bombardment into a siege. With only 2 Engineers, and 3 artillery officers, excepting the few who belonged to the Company, all deficient, both in knowledge and

* The Chevalier de l'Eguille, an enterprising and indefatigable naval officer, of an accommodating disposition in the service, having been despatched from Europe for India with 4 ships, 1100 troops, and 3,000,000 of livres, had put in, for a short stay, at the Isle of France, and was about proceeding for Pondicherry, when, as ill luck would have it, the Admiral d'Aché detained him there, with the troops, 2-3rds of the money, and all the vessels but 1, which he permitted to sail, only with 1-3rd of the money, or the 1,000,000 of livres above-mentioned! How very differently matters *might* have turned out at Madras, had L'Eguille been allowed *to join Lally there, with the whole of the vessels, troops, and money, sent from France!*

enterprise; with officers in general dissatisfied and ill-disposed, with only the common men on whom he could depend, and of whose alacrity he never had reason to complain;* he *carried on the siege with a vigour and activity, which commanded the respect even of the besieged, though they were little acquainted with the difficulties under which he toiled.*" For these operations, against an enemy abounding in all the means for making a good defence, and inspired with proportionable determination to do so, the 2 chief batteries of the besiegers in the *black town* were that of the Regiment of Lorrain, on the right, or the more inland, that of the Regiment of Lally on the left, or towards the sea—the *latter* being the quarter from which *the most destructive fire of shot and shell was maintained against the Fort, as well as the approaches most successfully pushed on, to the effecting of a breach.* Of this siege of above 9 weeks, pronounced, by its minutest British chronicler, "without doubt the most strenuous and regular that had ever been carried on in India," and consequently thus detailed by him as "an example and excitement" for posterity, I merely notice such circumstances as may convey a fair *general* conception of its difficulty and importance; anything like a full narrative of it being incompatible with the limits of this work. The consumption of military *materiel* by the Fort was *returned* as 26,554 rounds of cannon-ammunition, 7502 shells, 1990 hand-grenades, 200,000 musket-cartridges, 1768 barrels of gunpowder—the besiegers being *computed* to have expended as many, or more cannon-balls, with 8000 shells—and, while so warmly engaged in front, had likewise to be vigilant and active against the mixed force of several thousand infantry and cavalry, previously mentioned as employed to interrupt the progress of the siege, by harassing hostilities elsewhere. These constantly-annoying enemies were, "like flies," alleges Lally, "no sooner beaten off in one place, than settling in another." The predatory parties of that supernumerary force in English pay were, indeed, extremely detrimental to the French. Thus Mahomed Issoof and his subordinate officer Kistnarow, with 1000 foot and 350 horse, attacking, in December, the Fort of Elvanasore, occupied by 7 French military and 2 companies of Sepoys, with 2 field-pieces, compelled it to surrender, burning a village in sight of Fort St. David; some days after, strengthening their invading corps with 1400 more foot and 250 horse, reduced the fortified Pagoda of Tricalore, held by 3 companies of French Sepoys; and then spread their army, to ravage all the territory tributary to the French, as far as the sea. " On the 15th," asserts the English narrative, "they appeared at Villenore, within sight of Pondicherry, and brought so much terror, that the inhabitants of the adjacent villages took shelter in crowds within the bound hedge," which extended about that metropolis. " On the 18th, they cut the mound of the great tank at Valdoor, and let out the water, to destroy the cultivation it was reserved to fertilize. The sword was little used, but fire every where, and the cattle were driven away to Tricaloor." Again, or January 25th, (1759,) Mahomed Issoof, who, besides his infantry, had

* Orme, also, in noting of Lally's soldiers, at the close of the siege, how long their pay was in arrear, and how very ill-supplied they were in other respects, adds of them—" who, nevertheless, notwithstanding the discontented discourses of their officers, still more dishonourable because they had *all* got plunder, persevered in their duty, with unremitting spirit and alacrity." Yet 200 of the French deserted to Fort St. George, from the ramparts of which, they appeared at intervals, with a bottle of wine in one hand, and a purse in the other; exhorting their countrymen to imitate them.

above 2000 horse, plundered, by a detachment, the country about the Fort of Pondamalee; this party, in addition to other booty, returning "with 3000 sheep and oxen, which had been collected from the country, and were kept, under the protection of the garrison, in the common round the Fort, to supply the French army before Madras." By the 27th, the same active Anglo-Mahommedan partisan, with a body of his horse, approaching Madras, came to the place, but "2 miles north-west of Fort St. George, where most of the oxen belonging to the French army were kept, under the care of a guard of Sepoys and Black horse," whom he "put to flight, and seized most of the cattle." Altogether, it is noted, on the side of the British, "the attention to this army, since their arrival in the neighbourhood, diminished the activity of the enemy's operations against the Fort, by the detachments they were obliged to send, and recall, on different reports, and alarms. Their approach, just as the enemy's works were advanced so near the defences, increased the alacrity of the garrison." On 4 occasions, when more serious demonstrations to relieve the Fort were threatened by the advance of that army, to the number, as was estimated, of 5000 strong, Lally in person, or through his leading officers —among whom was his 1st cousin, Michael Lally, Colonel-Commandant of the 2nd battalion of the family regiment and Brigadier,*—had, according to the French accounts, to make proportionate diversions of force from the siege, by which the enemy, although very superior in number, was always obliged to retire.

At length, or in spite of so much opposition on all sides, a breach in Fort St. George *was* effected, "and the mind of Lally was intensely engaged with preparations for the assault, when he found the officers of his army altogether indisposed to second his ardour." He alleges, "that the most odious intrigues were carried on in the army, and groundless apprehensions were propagated, to shake the resolution of the soldiers, and prevent the execution of the plan;" that his situation as "General was thus rendered critical in the highest degree, and the chances of success exceedingly diminished; yet he still adhered to his design, and only waited for the setting of the moon, which in India sheds a light not much feebler than that of a winter sun." At this decisive juncture, or February 16th, 6 English vessels arrived, for the relief of Madras, with 600 regular troops, and other supplies. "Words," continues Lally, "are inadequate to express the effect which the appearance of them produced. The officer, who commanded in the trenches, deemed it even inexpedient to wait for the landing of the enemy; and, 2 hours before receiving orders, retired from his post." In the existing state of their affairs, any further operations against Fort St. George would be hopeless, and might be ruinous, for the besiegers. "The officers and soldiers had been on no more than half-pay during the first 6 weeks of the expedition, and entirely destitute of pay during the remaining 3. The expenses of the siege, and the half-pay, had consumed, during the 1st month, the 1,000,000 of livres which had arrived from the islands. The officers were on the allowance of the soldiers.

* Michael Lally, son of Michael Lally and a Miss O'Carroll, was born in July, 1714, and entered the Regiment of Dillon, as a Cadet, in January, 1734; in which, he became a supernumerary or reformed Captain by January, 1744. A full Captain in the Regiment of Lally the following October, he attained the grade of Colonel in March, 1747. He was appointed Commandant of the 2nd Battalion of the Regiment and a Brigadier, November 19th, 1756. Reformed, with the Regiment, after his return from India, he died at Rouen, in 1773.

The subsistence of the army, for the last 15 days, had depended almost entirely upon some rice and butter, captured, in 2 small vessels, from Bengal. A very small quantity of gunpowder remained in the camp; and not a larger at Pondicherry. The bombs were wholly consumed 3 weeks before. The Sepoys deserted for want of pay, and the European cavalry threatened, every hour, to go over to the enemy." In fine, even "the defence of Pondicherry rested upon 300 invalids; and, within 12 hours, the English, with their reinforcements, might land, and take possession of the place!" * After a hot fire against the Fort till about 3 in the morning of the 17th, and the blowing up of the enemy's redoubt and powder-mill at Egmore outside the *black town*, which works had cost the English East India Company "£30,000, and could not be restored in a 12-month," Lally consequently raised the siege, having to leave behind him 52 pieces of artillery, besides ammunition; the abandonment of which "he imputed to *the want of serviceable bullocks; and this deficiency to the rapacity of the contractors, leagued with the Council of Pondicherry!*" His entire loss, in this enterprise, is not specified in any account that I have seen. The killed, wounded, and sick, in Fort St. George, during the siege, where "all, in general, did honour, by their behaviour, to the name of Englishmen," were returned as 1378; of whom the European portion deficient was more than filled up by the troops, that came, on the 16th, in the ships.

"General Lally left Madras, in the utmost transports of rage and despair, which a man of honour and ability can feel, who is," says my contemporary English annalist, "neglected by those who ought to support him, and cheated by the villainy of contractors, and of all those who turn war into a low traffic. . . . And certainly, it is worthy of remark, that every where there should appear something more unaccountably wrong and weak in the management of the French, than has been in the conduct of that of almost any other nation, at any time." † In a letter to a friend in the Ministry, Lally had already written from India, on account of the awful want of principle, or probity, there—"*I have not yet beheld the shadow of an honest man. In the name of God, withdraw me from this country, for which I am not made!*" And his still further grounds for indignation and complaint at his situation there are energetically set forth in his correspondence from Madras, during the siege, with the corrupt administration at Pondicherry. December 27th, 1758, he says—"*Hell has vomited me into this country of iniquities, and I wait, like Jonas, for the whale, which will receive me into its belly!*" February 11th, 1759, he states—"If we should fail at Madras, in my opinion, the principal reason to which it should be attributed is, *the pillage of* 15,000,000 *at least*, whereby as much has been lost, in what has been wasted, as in what has been dispersed among the soldiery, and, I am ashamed to say it, among the officers ; *who have not hesitated even to make use of my name, to avail themselves of the Cipays, Chelingues, and others, in order to transfer to Pondicherry a booty, which it was your duty to have detained, on perceiving the enormous quantity of it!*" February 14th, attributing his discouraging situation before Madras

* The easier, too, since we elsewhere learn, that the prisoners there, taken from the English, were so many as 3000!

† In this extract from the Annual Register, I omit, after "who is," the words, "ill seconded by his *troops*," as too general an expression. It has been shown, that "ill seconded by his *officers*" would be more correct.

to the bad conduct of some of the Company's officers, and misapplication, among them and others, of so many of the native forces and camp-attendants for purposes of private rapacity, all more or less associated with the iniquities and treachery of the administration at Pondicherry, he expresses himself to the Governor there, with not less resentment than previously. Of the disreputable behaviour of officers of the Company in command of the *Expedition*, the *Bristol*, &c., he remarks—"A good blow might be struck here. There is a ship in the road, of 20 guns, laden with all the riches of Madras, which, it is said, will remain there till the 20th. The *Expedition* is just arrived, but M. Gorlin is not the man to attack her; for she has made him run away once before. The *Bristol*, on the other hand, did but just make her appearance before St. Thomas; and, on the vague report of 13 ships coming from Porto-Novo, she took fright; and, after landing the provisions with which she was laden, she would not stay long enough, even to take on board 12 of her own guns, which she had lent out for the siege. If I was the judge of the point of honour of the Company's officers, *I would break him like glass, as well as some others of them.* The *Fidelle*, or the *Harlem*, or even the aforesaid *Bristol*, with her 12 guns restored to her, would be sufficient to make themselves masters of the English ship,* if they could manage so as to get to windward of her, in the night." On the scandalous misemployment of the Sepoys and other natives, to transfer the merchandise taken at Madras to Pondicherry, as so much *perquisite* for the misemployers, he observes—"Of 1500 Cipayes which attended our army, I reckon *near 800 are employed upon the road to Pondicherry, laden with sugars, pepper, and other goods; and, as for the Coulis, they are all employed for the same purpose, from the 1st day we came here!*" Finally, mentioning *his* determination to the Governor of Pondicherry, *not* to mix himself up with the officials of the Company in raising money—to keep himself as far as possible apart from their politico-military measures —and announcing his approaching intention of devolving the command of the army on the officer next in rank—he asserts of Pondicherry, that, if it should escape the vengeance it merited of fire from Heaven, nothing could preserve it from destruction by the fire of the English. His remarkable words are—"I had rather go and command the Caffres of Madagascar, than remain in your *Sodom;* which it is impossible but *the fire of the English must destroy, sooner or later, even though that from Heaven should not!*" In fine, can *any* picture of those whom he thus arraigns be rendered at once more disgusting and justifiable, than by adding what he tells us?—"that the retreat of the army from Madras produced at Pondicherry the strongest demonstrations of joy, and was celebrated by his enemies, as an occasion of triumph!"

This disgraceful rejoicing was the infamous satisfaction taken by the unprincipled official clique there, for the keen, indeed, and galling, though certainly not more keen and galling, than abundantly provoked or incontrovertibly merited denunciations, from Lally, of their shameless misconduct, or scandalous corruption and rapacity. Instead, however, of being at all amended, or induced to "turn from their evil ways," as

* The "English ship" had, it has appeared, but "20 guns," and the *Bristol*, with her *full* complement of artillery, would have, as we elsewhere learn, "30 guns," and was "manned with Europeans." Her name of "*Bristol*" would show, that she was originally English, but taken by the French.

they should have been, in consequence of such denunciations from their superior, that impudent clique presumed to make a *grievance* of those denunciations, on account of their sharpness!—just, no doubt, as the 40 thieves of the Arabian tale, if restored to life, after having been so deservedly scalded to death in their jars by honest Morgiana, would have made her boiling oil, in proportion to its disagreeable temperature for their guilty carcasses, a very great source of complaint against her, without at all noticing the *main* point at issue between her and them— or how far she, as a "good and faithful servant," in order to arrest robbery, was excusable in treating them, as practitioners in *that* line, to such an unwelcome, indeed, but amply-earned application of the burning fluid at her disposal. Voltaire, who knew, and was, for some time, a fellow-labourer of, Lally, in 1745-6, with respect to the arrangements for sending a reinforcement of 10,000 men from France to Prince Charles in Britain, notices the "douceur de mœurs," or suavity of manners, by which Lally was then distinguished; the alteration of which the historian naturally attributes to the various causes for irritation in the ill-fated General's subsequent unhappy position. The instructions he had from the Court and from the Directory of the Company in Paris, to have a vigilant eye upon the conduct of the Council at Pondicherry; and those instructions, backed by memoranda on the several abuses connected with the administration of Council, would, it is admitted, have rendered him odious to that body, were he the mildest of mankind; and he had received equally obnoxious directions with respect to the insubordination, want of discipline, and avidity for plunder, among the Company's European troops, or those of the "Bataillon de l'Inde." It was not for the interest—*i. e.*, the private or personal interests—of the Council, the Battalion of India, "et hoc genus omne," that such an uncompromising "homme du Roi," or "King's man," as Lally was invidiously designated, should be *there* from Europe, to discountenance or check that management of affairs, which had been so suited to the taste of those flourishing, or hoping to flourish, by a continuance of the system,

"All in the family way,
All with the strictest propriety!"

or as free as possible from any external interference and economizing control. It was likewise, of course, anything but right in *their* eyes, that this very "homme du Roi," already too distinguished by the reduction of Fort St. David and Arcot, should capture Madras, and should then probably conquer Bengal; in as much as he might thereby become both a reformer too powerful in India, and an accuser too irresistible in France. Such were the grounds for the hostility between Lally and his colonial opponents. That of Lally was warm, frank, too often, perhaps, venting itself in terms more bitter than discreet, yet always ready to "let bygones be bygones," on any manifestation of an amendment, and desire to promote the service of the King. That of his enemies was cold, crafty, underhand, and unscrupulous, not hesitating, for the destruction of an obnoxious individual, to risk the ruin of the public interest. Thus was D'Argenson's too-well-grounded prediction in process of verification!

After retiring from Madras unmolested by the enemy, Lally found his health so impaired by the various harassing toils and numerous vexations he had undergone, that, early in March, he was obliged to quit the camp for Pondicherry,* and devolve the command of the force opposed to the English on M. de Soupire, Maréchal de Camp; leaving it well posted at Conjeveram, with orders not to risk any general action, but remain on the defensive. The troops there were in much distress. From Pondicherry nothing was to be gotten; "what monies could be collected from the country between Conjeveram and Arcot, or borrowed in the camp, scarcely furnished the expenses of the day; and the inhabitants of the neighbouring villages, finding that the English paid punctually, and at better prices, evaded, as much as possible, to carry any provisions to the French camp." In April, the English, in order to entice the French to a suitable distance from Conjeveram, appeared before the Fort of Wandewash, on which Lally proceeded from Pondicherry to join Soupire for the purpose of saving Wandewash; when the English, decamping thence at night, by a forced march, returned to, fell upon, and captured Conjeveram with its garrison, by assault. The following month, the French were so badly off for every kind of supply, pay included, that Lally was deterred "from trusting their good will in action, until he could satisfy their complaints." With this view, "he went to Arcot, and, having detected various frauds in the management of the Amuldar, or renter, who farmed the districts, fined him 40,000 rupees; raising 10,000 more, with the promise of some provisions, from a native potentate of Velore, by agreeing not to molest his country. Satisfying immediate wants with these resources, the General, on the 6th, led the army from Covrepauk to 7 miles west of Conjeveram, where he stationed them advantageously opposite the English, who, under Colonel Monson, from the 12th to the 15th, drew out of their lines to offer battle. But the money and provisions recently obtained being now nearly exhausted, the soldiery renewed their complaints, which, too many, if not most, of their officers, from personal or factious motives, "were little solicitous to repress." Aware of these feelings, says my British authority of Lally, "he would not venture the battle he otherwise wished (for he was *always brave and impetuous*,† and had 2000 Europeans in the field,) before he had tried how far their prejudices might influence their duty, and made several motions, tending to no great consequence, which convinced him, that, in their present mood, they would *not* fight with ardour under his command." He consequently broke up his encampment, on the 15th, to march for Trivatore, dispersed the troops into different quarters, and returned himself to Pondicherry; resolving, in such a very unsatisfactory condition as his army were for money and supplies, and, aided from Europe, as the English had been, *not* to meet them again *en masse* in the field, until he should be better enabled to do so by "the arrival of the French squadron, which was daily expected with reinforcements." The English did not go into cantonments till the 28th, when this spring campaign for 1759, of 100 days, terminated; wherein "the principal object of both sides was to protect their respective territory, and not to risque an engagement without positive advantage, which neither gave."

* "On se déchaîna contre le Général," adds Voltaire of Lally, and his shameless enemies, "on l'accabla de reproches, de lettres anonymes, de satires. Il en tomba malade de chagrin: quelque temps après, la fièvre et de fréquens transports au cerveau le troublèrent pendant 4 mois; et, pour consolation, on lui insultait encore!"

† "To tread the walks of death he stood prepar'd;
And what he greatly thought, he nobly dar'd."
POPE'S HOMER, Odyssey, ii., 311-312.

Lally brought back from the camp to Pondicherry "more resentment than ever against the Governor, the Council, and all who were employed in the civil administration of the Company's affairs; imputing to *their* malversations all the obstacles and impediments, which obstructed the success of *his* arms. *The Council*, he alleged, *received presents from the renters of all the districts, who, emboldened by the knowledge of their peculations, continually evaded the regular payments, or insisted on remissions, in the terms of their leases;* * *and, whilst the Treasury was thus disappointed or defrauded of its incomes, its issues,* he insisted, *were squandered with equal prodigality; because the Council, and their dependants, held shares, in all the supplies for the public service, whether in the camp, or city!*" This was tracking the thefts of Cacus to his den, and letting in light as alarming, as it was unwelcome, to the unkennelled robber, whose "detected fraud appear'd in view," when—

"Expos'd to sight the monster's dungeon lay,
And the huge cave flew open to the day!"
PITT'S VIRGIL, Æneid, viii., 315–316.

The vile faction of peculating civilians, and their interested upholders, or roguish understrappers, at Pondicherry, in proportion to their just or guilty dread of Lally, as disinterring and denouncing their financial malpractices, became additionally exasperated against him, and rallied the more closely about his enemy, Bussy. From illness, (and, doubtless, *other* reasons,) Bussy had retired to Pondicherry since the retreat from Madras, and to him the junta of branded corruptionists, and their subordinate jobbers, paid especial court; constantly expressing regret at what *they* designated the indiscretion of the Ministry in having appointed Lally, rather than Bussy, to the supreme command; a regret, with *their* "auri sacra fames," unquestionably well-founded; Bussy, who had *made* such a fine fortune in India, (and was no less resolved to *keep* it,) being much the more likely man not to interfere with *them* in making *their* fortunes too; and being consequently the character with whom *they* could best sympathize, on the *good* old principle, that

"A fellow-feeling makes us wond'rous kind!"

and that

"Birds of a feather
Flock together!"

During June and July, or since going into cantonments, nothing of more consequence than the detachment of parties to collect preys of cattle occurred between the French and English, with the exception of a bloodless acquisition, July 7th, of the Fort of Covrepauk by Colonel Monson.

* See, in Mr. Mill's work, under the year 1765, the vast extent to which corruption and extortion were carried, under the head of "presents," as received by the *English* East India Company's servants. According to ancient custom, it is stated, "a person in India, who had favours to ask, or evil to deprecate, could not easily believe, till acceptance of his present, that the great man, to whom he addressed himself, was not his foe." On which the same historian subsequently observes—"Besides the oppression of the people of the country, to which the receiving of presents prepared the way, this dangerous practice *laid the foundation of perpetual perfidy in the servants of the Company to the interests of their employers*. Not those plans of policy which were calculated to produce the happiest results to the Company, but those which were calculated to *multiply the occasions for presents*, and render them most effectual, were the plans recommended, by the strongest motives of interest, to the agents and representatives of the Company in India."

"The distresses and discontents of the French continued as urgent as ever, even *after* the expense of the campaign was diminished by their retreat into quarters. In the beginning of August, the whole of Lally's regiment, excepting the Serjeants and Corporals, and 50 of the soldiers, mutinied, and marched out of the Fort of Chittapet; declaring, that they would not return to their colours, until they had received their pay, of which many months was in arrears." However, "their officers, by furnishing their own money, and engaging their honour for more, brought them back, excepting 30, who dispersed about the country." Nevertheless, "this defection, which the cause exempted from rigorous punishment, shook the discipline of the whole army." The dissension, also, between Lally and Bussy was still in full operation, when, on the 20th, a frigate from France "brought orders from the King and Ministry, recalling all the intermediate officers, who had been sent with commissions superior to Bussy's, and appointing him second in command, and to succeed to it after Lally." This caused a more civil intercourse to take place between them, and an *assent* by Lally to a measure proposed by Bussy, although about the most obnoxious that the latter could have proposed—or that he should return to the Deccan. It was not till September 2nd, that D'Aché's fleet from the Mauritius, whose arrival was so long and eagerly looked for by Lally, and the French generally in India, was descried off Ceylon by the English Admiral Pococke; between whom and D'Aché, as soon as the wind admitted, or on the 10th, an engagement ensued. In this action, no ship was lost on either side; the English, who acknowledged a loss of 569 killed or wounded, proved unable to effect their design, of preventing the French reaching Pondicherry; and the latter consequently anchored there, the 15th. On the general result of this and the preceding naval encounters between the French and English in India, "it has been observed," says the Annual Register for 1760, "that history can hardly produce an instance of 2 squadrons fighting 3 pitched battles, under the same commanders, in 18 months, without the loss of a ship, on either side!" Had D'Aché been the bearer of far more assistance than he brought, such assistance would *all* have been needed. The resources of the Government at Pondicherry were too nearly exhausted, as well by the length of the war, as, according to Lally's complaints, "by the *misapplication of the public funds;* a calamity, of which the *violent passion of individuals for private wealth was a copious and perennial fountain.*" He "had, from his first arrival, been struggling on the borders of despair, with wants, which it was altogether out of his power to supply. The English had received, or were about to receive, the most important accession to their power; and nothing but the fleet which had now arrived, and the supplies which it *might* have brought, could enable him, much longer, to contend with the difficulties which environed him."

Under these distressing circumstances, we read, with a mixture of contempt and indignation, how "M. d'Aché had brought, for the use of the colony, £16,000 in dollars, with a quantity of diamonds, valued at £17,000, which had been taken in an English East Indiaman; and, having landed these effects, together with 180 men, he declared his resolution of sailing again for the islands!* Nothing," it may well be

* Was despatching a fleet like D'Aché's to India, with no greater assistance than £16,000, and so few men, anything better than appointing an elephant to carry an infant? Much ado about comparatively nothing! The single *English* East India-

believed, "could exceed the surprise and consternation of the colony upon this unexpected and alarming intelligence. Even those who were the most indifferent to the success of affairs, when the reputation of Lally, and the interest of their country alone, were at stake, now began to tremble, when the very existence of the colony, and their interests along with it, were threatened with inevitable destruction. All the principal inhabitants, civil and military, assembled at the Governor's house, and formed themselves into a National Council. A vehement protest was signed against the departure of the fleet. But the resolution of the Admiral was inflexible; and he could only be induced to leave 400 Caffres, who served in the fleet, and 500 Europeans, partly marines, and partly sailors." Having landed these, he, on the 30th, sailed away, never to return! The value of the African portion of D'Aché's parting present speaks for itself; the European portion of it, or the marines and sailors, were designated merely as "the *scum of the sea*" by Lally; "and, indeed," says my English historian, "most of them, for a while, could be fit for little more than to do duty in the town, whilst the regular troops kept the field." The other contents of the fleet, or the despatches which it brought from Europe, were calculated to render Lally's position *worse* than it previously was. Those documents, indeed, contained, *for the Council at Pondicherry, reprimands, and even menaces, of the severest kind; for Lally, the highest commendations of his achievements, and his principles;* with special instructions, that he should cause an account to be rendered of the administration; the despotism of the government of the Council to be corrected; an inquiry to be instituted into the origin of the existing abuses, in order that they might be cut up by the roots; and, in fine, proceedings to be taken, by the Procureur-Général, with respect to every Member of the Council, and other official, who should be found any way interested in the collection of the revenues of the Company. To intrust *him* with such a commission implied, as he observed in his correspondence, that *he should be an object of general horror in the colony*,—or, in other words, *among such knaves as it was composed of*,—and, accordingly, from this time, is to be dated an offensive and defensive league, or conspiracy, of all the Members of Council and inferior *employés* against him, as receiving such orders—hateful, in proportion to the dishonesty, which had so much to apprehend from *their* enforcement, and from *him* as empowered to enforce them. In short, what situation could now be more unhappy than his?

Long previous to the autumnal season for again taking the field, the English, at Madras, in addition to the European recruits which they received, were encouraged with intelligence of the 84th regiment of 1000 men being at sea to join them, under Lieutenant-Colonel Eyre Coote, famous, as Major, for his services in Bengal, and who was coming, with a commission to command in chief. A further advantage presented itself, in the circumstance of the French force nearest to Madras being weakened by a considerable detachment, which it had been found necessary to despatch elsewhere, or to the south. With such apparently favourable prospects for striking some decisive blow, and proportionably importuned to do so by Major Brereton, who was most eager to distinguish himself before he should be superseded in command by Coote, the Presidency at Madras consented, that an attempt should be made to reduce Wandewash,

man, which the French Admiral captured by chance, *en voyage*, was more valuable than *all* the treasure he had previously on board for Pondicherry!

the head-quarters and principal post of the French between Madras and Pondicherry. Accordingly, on September 26th, or as soon as it was possible to march, after the heavy rains, Major Brereton set out from Conjeveram for Wandewash with 4080 foot and 800 horse; of whom 1600 were Europeans, and the rest, 3280, Sepoy or other mercenaries. At Wandewash, the Fort was held by a native Kellidar, or Governor, and his garrison, that would admit none of the French beyond some gunners; a state of things, in which, under the delicate circumstances they were placed, the latter, in order to avoid worse, had to acquiesce. The French effective force there were quartered mostly under the walls of the Fort, and the rest about the town. They were then but badly off, as well as inferior in number to the English, or only 1100 men, and under the command, *pro tempore*, of a veteran officer of the Irish Brigade, named Mac Geoghegan, a gentleman of very old and illustrious race.

Of the 4 sons of Niall of the Nine Hostages, Ard-Righ or Monarch of Erin from A. D. 379 to 406, known as the progenitors of the Southern Hy-Niall, or offspring of Niall, in Midhe, or Meath, &c., Fiacha, the 3rd, was ancestor of the sept of Mac Geoghegan, hence originally styled Kinel-Fiacha, or kindred of Fiacha,* but taking their subsequent designation of Mac Geoghegans from a Prince, the 6th in descent from the great Niall. The territory of the descendants of Fiacha anciently extended from Bir, in the King's County, to the noted hill of Uisneach, in Westmeath; in later times, or down to the Elizabethean age, the country of Mac Geoghegan was generally limited to the district of Kinaliagh, 12 miles long, and 7 broad, or coextensive with the Barony of Moycashel. Brought comparatively low at first, by the Anglo-Norman obtrusion into Meath of De Lacy and his feudal land-adventurers from Britain in the 12th century, this warlike sept, nevertheless, very soon, or early in the 13th, showed they had only fallen like Antæus, to rise the stronger; "erected, and long maintained the possession of, various castles, the chief being at Castletown-Geoghegan, near Kilbeggan, whose extensive site is marked upon the Ordnance Survey;" and, throughout the middle ages, ranked among the most dreaded neighbours to the *settlers* of the Pale; of whose defeats it might be said—

"Swim at midnight the Shannon, beard wolves in their den,
Ere you ride to Moycashel, on forays again!"

In the Elizabethean war, the heroic Captain Richard Mac Geoghegan of Moycashel, as Constable of the Castle of Dunboy, will *never* be forgotten, from his noble resistance and death there; respecting which, alleges the enemy, "so obstinate and resolved a defence hath not bin seene within this kingdome!" In the Parliamentarian or Cromwellian contest, the gentlemen of this sept upheld its previous reputation for gallantry. The Secretary of the great Owen Roe O'Neill, noting how no family behaved so well as the Geoghegans, states—"Never a one of them was ever killed other then like a brave souldier, and in comaunde in action;" and then naming 10 Geoghegans as officers, from the ranks of Lieutenant-Colonel and Major to those of Captain and Lieutenant, and specifying *where* they were distinguished, he adds—"These 10 Geoghegans comaunders perished to the world, but to future ages left sufficient matter of honorable

* Carn, in the Barony of Moycashel, and County of Westmeath, was formerly called Carn-Fiachach, or the *carn of Fiacha*, from the carn, or sepulchral heap of stones there, to *his* memory.

imitation," &c. In the succeeding unequal struggle against the Anglo-Orange invasion of Ireland, and its numerous Continental and colonial auxiliaries, the members of this old clan duly supported King James II. Brian Mac Geoghegan, Esq. of Donore, and Charles Mac Geoghegan, Esq. of Sionan, sat for the Borough of Kilbeggan, in that Monarch's national Parliament at Dublin, in 1689; and several gentlemen of the name were officers in the royal army, especially among the cavalry. The branch of Sionan, as represented by the above-mentioned Charles, and his 7 sons, fought for the King in Ireland, and afterwards on the Continent. Of these, Conly, the eldest, having, previous to the Williamite revolution, served in France, and acquired the character there of a good officer, was made a Colonel in Ireland; where he fell, greatly regretted, at the battle of Cavan, between the Duke of Berwick, and Colonel Wolseley, in February, 1690. In the course of the same war, 4 of his brothers were also slain. The 2 remaining followed the King to France, where the elder, Anthony, was created, by that Prince, a Baronet. Charles, the younger, died a Captain of Grenadiers in the Regiment of Berwick, leaving 3 sons; of whom, the survivor, Alexander, likewise a Captain of Grenadiers, was the officer in temporary command of the French here at Wandewash. He is first mentioned as in the Regiment of Berwick in 1733; when he served at the siege and reduction of Kehl. A Sous-Lieutenant of the same corps in 1734, he was at the siege of Philipsburgh; and at the affair of Clausen in 1735. He was at the battle of Dettingen, and nominated a Captain en Second in 1743. In 1744, at the siege of Menin, he was subsequently transferred, with the like rank, into the Regiment of Lally. In 1745, having been present at the successful sieges of Tournay, Oudenarde, Dendermonde, and the victory of Fontenoy, he passed into Scotland, to the aid of Prince Charles; commanded a corps of his hussars; and was at the sieges of the town and citadel of Stirling, and battle of Falkirk, in 1746. Between this, and the general termination of the war on the Continent, in 1748, he was made a full Captain or obtained a company, was created a Chevalier of St. Louis, and was present at the reduction of Maestricht that year, by Marshal Saxe. After the breaking out of the war in 1756 between France and England, he sailed for India, as "premier factionnaire" to his regiment, or that of Lally. By the death, on the passage, of his elder brother, a Major and Captain of Grenadiers in that corps, &c., he also became a Captain of Grenadiers. His younger brother was slain in the trenches, at the siege of Fort St. David. Acting under M. de Crillon at the surprise of the camp of Mousaferbeck, Alexander captured 2 pieces of cannon there. Employed, in December, 1758, to clear the way for the entrance of the French army into the *black town* of Madras, previous to the siege of Fort St. George, he did so, in spite of a very great fire from the enemy. At the hostile sortie of the English from the Fort 4 hours after, he vigorously contributed to their repulse, by a flanking attack at the head of 2 companies of his regiment, in which he lost a Lieutenant, a Serjeant, and 14 grenadiers; being wounded himself in both arms, as well as severely in the thigh.

Since September 3rd, Mac Geoghegan had been ordered by Lally, to assemble all the French troops he could, or 800 foot, and 300 horse, for the protection of Wandewash, as the post most likely to be attacked by the enemy from Madras. Major Brereton fixed upon the night between the 29th and 30th for assailing the French in their quarters. His force, for that purpose, was to consist of 1600 picked men; or 920 Europeans and 680 mercenaries, in 3 divisions; each of the 3 supplied with 2 fine brass six-pounders. About 2 in the morning, the 1st or Monson's division of 360 Europeans, the majority grenadiers, besides a company of 100 Sepoys, in all 460 men, reached Wandewash, at a portion of the wall, out of repair, and with neither ditch nor palisade before it; so that the 1st party of grenadiers were able to scramble up, drive away the guard, and open the gate for the rest of the division. In 3 columns, with 2 field-pieces at the head of that in the centre, this division then proceeded through the 3 principal streets; silenced the opposing fire by which they were most annoyed, or that of 2 field-pieces pointed by the French from the esplanade, to sweep the central street; and, having advanced to the openings upon the esplanade where the main body of the French were stationed, then deemed it most prudent to halt, raise a barricade, and wait for daylight; as being disappointed of the co-operation expected from their 2nd, or Gordon's, division. But this minor division of 200 Europeans, 80 Black mercenaries, and 2 field-pieces, at the angle of the rampart where they had approached to enter the town, having been duly discovered, and entirely exposed to view, by blue lights thrown up, were so warmly received by the French fire there, that they were totally defeated; Brereton, to rally the fugitives, having, "in the strong impulse of indignation," vainly "ran the 1st man he met through the body," *pour encourager les autres!* Meantime, as day broke, the fire upon Monson's division from the main body of the French at the esplanade, aided by that from the Fort, became too hot to bear. "The gunners," notes Orme, "whom the Kellidar had admitted into the Fort, plied the cannon on the towers opposite to the 3 streets, to the head of which Monson's division had advanced; and, with the field-pieces on the esplanade, their fire was from 14 guns, all within point blank; from the Fort at 300, from the field-pieces at 100, yards. The return was from the 2 field-pieces at the head of the center-street, and from platoons of musketry in the other 2. The disparity was severe, and could not be long maintained." Under these favourable circumstances, Mac Geoghegan, in order to decide the contest as soon as possible, or before Monson could be effectively reinforced from without, assailed the intruders with such spirit and activity, that he finally drove them out of the place; sending his 300 cavalry to watch their retreat, but not risking his 800 infantry in *any* pursuit beyond the walls of the town, against an enemy, whose reserve of 460 men, under Brereton, was fresh, or untouched, and whose European and Black horse, amounting to 800, were stationed but a mile to the rear of Brereton; besides the still greater force of that officer at his camp, or head-quarters —the whole, compared with the French at Wandewash, making nearer 4 than 3 men to 1. In this affair of about 5 hours' duration (much interrupted, however, by the darkness, &c.,) the English admit a loss of 207 killed, wounded, or missing. The French specify their killed and wounded, at but 114. The English claim a capture of 15 prisoners from the French. The French claim to have captured 5 English officers, 56 soldiers, 4 cannon, and 2 ammunition-waggons from the English. As an off-set to the general depression of mind among the French, so naturally associated with the wretched mockery of assistance brought by, and the sailing away of, D'Aché's fleet for the Mauritius, this repulse, by the Irish officer, of the English at Wandewash, was made the most of at Pondicherry, with a discharge of 100 guns from the ramparts, &c. The advantage obtained by Mac Geoghegan saved, in fact, the French, in India, for the time; though situated as they were, it could only be for a time.*

To the numerous difficulties, with which, as "a sea of troubles," the French in India were left by D'Aché to contend, unaided, and, as there was but too much reason to suppose, in vain, a greater source for alarm, than ever *before* presented itself, was added, October 16th-17th, by the discontent and insubordination which appeared in the army.

> "Nor is this rage the grumbling of a crowd,
> That shun to tell their discontents aloud;
> Where all, with gloomy looks, suspicious go,
> And dread of an informer chokes their woe :
> But, bold in numbers, proudly they appear,
> And scorn the bashful, mean restraints of fear.
> For laws, in great rebellions, lose their end,
> And all go free, when multitudes offend."
>
> ROWE's LUCAN's Pharsalia, v., 357–364.

Other outbreaks, of which there naturally had been several, among the suffering soldiery, were partial; but this mutiny was general, and, all circumstances considered, excusably so. Not less than 10 months' pay was due to the troops; what money they had gotten was instead of provisions, which were by no means regularly furnished; the men were also very badly off for clothing; they were the more indignant at the distress to which they continued to be subjected, even after the bravery lately shown at Wandewash; they conceived that a much larger sum, than that merely *announced* as brought by the fleet, had actually been *remitted* from France; and, worse than all, they were led to believe (evidently from a quarter, whose infamous nature is sufficiently marked by the calumny of the assertion,) that so many evils were greatly owing to the *criminality* of the General, who, at the public cost, had been amassing and secreting a vast amount of wealth! The exasperated soldiery of the Regiments of Lorrain, Lally, and the Battalion of India consequently quitting their quarters, and choosing 2 Serjeants for their Generals, declared, that their arrears of pay should be cleared off in 6 days; after which, if not satisfied, they would go over to the English. By a subscription, however, at Pondicherry, to which Lally himself contributed 50,000 francs, the gallant Crillon 10,000, and others what they could, a sufficient fund was raised to appease this most dangerous commotion; the troops, on condition of receiving what was due them, for half a year, in hand, the rest in a month, and a complete amnesty for the past in writing from the General and the Council, agreeing to return to their duty; which, except 30 deserters, all accordingly did, by the 21st. As the *only* mode for continuing to subsist the army, and for a satisfactory collection of the approaching revenue to be expected from the country, Lally, soon after this reconciliation, decided upon dividing the forces into 2 portions; *that* for the north, to consist of 800 men, stationed at Arcot or Wandewash, and which by moving to the aid of any of his garrisons attacked in those parts might keep the English, for a certain period, in check; *that* for the south, to realize as

---

* Orme, Voltaire, and Mill, *ut sup.*—Mac Geoghegan pedigree, &c., in Miscellany of Irish Archæological Society, vol. i.—Irish and English published annalists *passim* on Mac Geoghegans—O'Neill M.S., in Trinity College, Dublin—Abbé Mac Geoghegan's note, at battle of Cavan, in 1690—French memoir of Captain Alexander Mac Geoghegan in late John O'Connell's M.S. collections at Paris on Irish Brigade —French particulars of contest at Wandewash, in Mercure Historique for 1760.

great a supply as possible from the comparatively untouched or flourishing districts between Outatoor and Tritchinopoly, including the rich and fertile Isle of Seringham, and then be ready, in due time, to march to the assistance of the division holding the English at bay in the north.

The Governor and Council at Pondicherry, we are told, opposed such a "separation of the army as fraught with the most dangerous consequences;" a danger, indeed, "which could not be concealed from Lally himself," as that of "dividing the army in the presence of a superior enemy; but," it is added, "they pointed out *no means by which it was possible to preserve it together.*" Lally imputed the opposition he met with, respecting such a disposition of the army, to a disappointed spirit of peculation on the part of his opposers; since, with reference to the better getting in of the revenue, he likewise announced his intention of having the several collections farmed under his own eye—by which, of course, the usual comfortable perquisites, or snug deductions, "so sweet for the gain" of the jobbing officials, whom he had such abundant reasons for distrusting, would be cut off from those knaves—and hence an outcry, from the hungry spite of *their* frustrated rapacity, that *he* was acting thus, only with a view to personal emolument! But the *real* character of Lally could not be affected by such an accusation from those, whose praise would have proved him as deserving of censure, as their censure would imply that he was worthy of praise. While preparing to draft away, under Crillon, the stronger division intended for the south, the General caused so many parties to be set in motion, as might diffuse an impression of his being altogether bent upon maintaining himself along the northern line of defence, afforded by the stream of the Paliar. In the course of these varied movements, 50 men of his regiment having met with, and ventured to attack, 3 companies of the enemy's Sepoys, or about 300 men, posted at the village of Cherickmalore, on the southern side of the river, opposite Conjeveram, are alleged, by the English, to have been beaten, with a loss of 5 soldiers killed, and 3 taken, besides an officer, mortally wounded.* As to Crillon's march, it was so well planned, and, for a time, concealed or disguised, that, between November 11th and 20th, he was able to anticipate any effective effort, on the part of the English, in the south, to prevent his crossing the river Coleroon into the Isle of Seringham, and, on the 21st, reducing the garrison, in a fortified pagoda there under Captain Smith, to surrender, to the number of 300 Sepoys, 500 Colleries, or long-lance-armed men, and 2 field-pieces, with European gunners. But such success in the south could not compensate for the disparity, in point of numbers, under which Lally, in the north, had, by this time, to confront the English from Madras, strengthened, as they were, by the arrival of the last of the reinforcements they expected from Europe, with the very able Irish officer who was to command against him.

That gentleman, Lieutenant-Colonel Eyre Coote, was the 5th son of the Rev. Dr. Chidley Coote, of Ash-Hill, County of Limerick, by his marriage with Jane, 3rd daughter of the Right Honourable George Evans, of Caharas, or Caras, in the same County, and sister of the 1st

---

* This rare success by Indians, as opposed to Europeans, *may* have been owing to *other* circumstances, as well as numbers, having been much to the advantage of the former, on this occasion. I have thought it but *fair*, in mentioning the matter, to glance at the fact of 100 men having been the general complement of a company of Sepoys.

Lord Carbery.* Young Coote was born in 1726, and appears to have entered the British army early, in which he is stated to have been an Ensign in Scotland, in the civil war of 1745-6. In 1754, he sailed, with his regiment, from Ireland, for the East Indies; and, as Captain, and Major, throughout the subsequent operations in Bengal, or the reductions of Calcutta, Hoogley, Chandernagore, and the battle of Plassey, in conjunction with Admiral Watson, and Colonel (afterwards Lord) Clive, was much distinguished. The victory of Plassey, by which the English East India Company first rose to be a great political, and military, or sovereign power in Hindostan, instead of a corporation of merely tolerated foreign traders, would, in fact, never have been gained, if the irresolution of Clive had not, on second thoughts, been brought to reject its original misgivings, for the superior determination of Coote. "Whatever confidence he might place in his own military talents, and in the valour and discipline of his troops," writes Lord Macaulay of the situation of Clive before the affair of Plassey, "it was no light thing to engage an army 20 times as numerous as his own. Before him lay a river, over which it was easy to advance; but, over which, if things went ill, not one of his little band would ever return. On this occasion, for the first and for the last time, his dauntless spirit, during a few hours, shrank from the fearful responsibility of making a decision. He called a Council of War. The majority declared against fighting, and Clive declared his concurrence with the majority. Long afterwards, he said, that he had never called but 1 Council of War, and that, if he had taken the advice of that Council, the British would never have been masters of Bengal." *Elsewhere*, in connexion with this topic, after designating Coote, as "conspicuous among the founders of the British empire in the east," Lord Macaulay, indeed, admits, of the Irish officer, "at the Council of War, which preceded the battle of Plassey, he earnestly recommended, in opposition to the majority, that daring course, which, after some opposition, was adopted, and which was crowned with such splendid success." But, for a fuller or more satisfactory idea of this memorable consultation, we are indebted to the historians Orme and Malcolm; authorities, unobjectionable in what they admit with respect to Clive, as *both* friendly to him. According to their narratives, Clive, under the alarming circumstances above described, called a Council of War to decide—Whether, in their situation, it would, without further assistance, or merely on their own bottom, be prudent to attack the Nabob of Bengal, or whether they should wait, until joined by some extra native aid? Although it is a proverbial saying, that a Council of War rarely fights, being generally summoned only when a Commander is at his wit's end, such appears to have been Clive's nervousness at the prospect of attacking the Nabob, and his proportionate anxiety to *secure*, as it were, a decision, in correspondence with his feelings, from the Council, that he even went out of the customary course, observed at such assemblies, of taking the opinion of the youngest officer first, and ascending,

* The Rev. Chidley Coote, D.D., was married in 1702, and died in 1730; and his widow survived him till 1763, when she died at Cork. On their gallant and accomplished son Eyre, compare Lodge's Peerage of Ireland, under Coote, Earl of Mountrath, and Evans, Lord Carbery, with the biographical sketches of the General in the East India Military Calendar, Ryan's Worthies of Ireland, &c. Ferrar thus refers to Ash-Hill, in 1787—"The ruins of Kilmallock are well contrasted by Ash-Hill, the seat of Chidley Coote, Esq., which joins the town, and where there is an excellent shrubbery, with a well-improved demesne."

in due gradation, from that to the President's; he himself, on the contrary, giving his own opinion, as against attacking, *first*, or in order to indicate what he wished the votes of *others* to be, and then descending to the opinion of the lowest, according to succession of rank. Of the Council, as might be expected, a majority, or 9, inclusive of, and headed by, himself, decided against proceeding to engage. But the 7 others, inclusive of, and headed by, Major Coote, were of an opposite opinion; the Major, as spokesman of the glorious minority, arguing—that such a delay, to act in presence of the enemy, would abate the existing ardour and confidence of success in the soldiery, which it would be difficult to restore—that, through such a delay, the enemy might be both physically and morally strengthened, by a French reinforcement—that the English force could likewise be surrounded, its communication with Calcutta cut off, and thus as effectually ruined by delay, as by the loss of a battle—and, therefore, that an immediate advance, to decide the contest, should be resolved on, or an immediate return to Calcutta. The consequence was, that, though Clive was necessarily successful in the Council of War, as seconded by the majority of votes, he, after the assembly broke up, reconsidered the matter, and became so convinced of the erroneous course he had advocated, and had led others to advocate—or to remain where they were, instead of pushing forward to fight—that his better sense came round to, and acted upon, the opinion of Coote, in issuing orders to pass the river next morning; by which movement, and its result, in the overthrow of the enemy, he reaped the fruits of superior advice to his own. The conduct of Coote in the council was duly supported by him in the field, or in the part he took at the ensuing discomfiture of the Nabob, which laid the foundation of the British Empire in India. To the comparative merits of Coote and of Clive on this important occasion, the remark of the Roman General in Livy would consequently apply, "that he is the first man, in point of abilities, who of himself forms good counsels; that the next is he, who submits to good advice." And the application of the remark is the more requisite as regards Clive, since he showed himself so unfair, in his subsequent parliamentary evidence on this subject, that he endeavoured to shift from *himself* to *others* every connexion with the very decision, which *he* had done his utmost to procure from *them*. "This," he said, "was the only Council of War that ever I held; and, if I had abided by that Council, it would have been the ruin of the East India Company!" But was it not *he* who had influenced the majority of the Council to come to the decision *they* did?—

"In all you speak, let truth and candour shine."—POPE.

Such, in the person of Coote, was the able adversary whom Lally had now to meet, under most unequal circumstances; or with every advantage on the side of that adversary, in the way of honest political support, and superior military and naval resources, for the campaign upon which he was to enter.

The English Governor and Council at Madras, to profit by the weakness of the French in the north, and thereby prevent them making any further use of their strength in the south, assembled, by November 25th, at Conjeveram, a superior force, of 1700 Europeans, including cavalry, 3000 Blacks, and 15 pieces of artillery, with which Coote, that day, took the field. Having led the French to think he designed attacking Arcot first, although his real object was to reduce Wandewash, he appeared before, and raised his batteries against, the latter, on the 27th, and effected a breach by the 30th; when the native Kellidar, or Governor of the Fort, who had 500 men, being desirous of submitting on terms advantageous to himself, and the French contingent there consisting of but 68 Europeans and 100 Sepoys, a surrender took place. The principal French force at Chittapet being too small to intercept Coote, he next, or on December 3rd, invested Carangoly; by the 6th and 7th, opened fire from 2 batteries, likewise carrying on his approaches; and, on the 10th, being near the crest of the glacis, and having dismounted all the guns of the garrison but 4, the place was given up by the Irish officer in command there, named O'Kennelly,* of the Regiment of Lally; to whom, owing to his gallant defence, as well as a wish to gain time, and the fear of incurring the disgrace of a repulse, almost all that was asked, or favourable terms, were granted. The loss of Arcot, and of such an important territory as would accompany it, being now but too obviously at hand, if Coote's career could not be checked, Lally recalled in due haste the larger portion of his troops from about Seringham in the south; to which, as already observed, he would not have detached them from the rest, could he have maintained the whole together in the north; or if his *only* hope of any relief from his great distress for money had not arisen from the prospect of such an amount of revenue as might be drawn (free of official peculation) from the south. The troops thus recalled, others to arrive under Bussy, at Arcot, and those hitherto obliged to keep on the defensive about Chittapet, would form as many as could be assembled, under the General himself, to deal with Coote; and that officer's further advance was, from the 16th, most effectively diverted, through a cloud of predatory horse, principally Mahrattas, engaged by the French to harass him. Of those mounted ravagers, "which," writes Coote himself, "put me to the greatest distress for want of provisions, as they plundered all the country," another British authority more fully informs us, how every sort of pillage and devastation was extended, even on the north, or British side of the Paliar, to within 20 miles of Madras itself; and how thousands of cattle were swept away, which the enemy "sold to the 1st purchaser at 7 or 8 for a rupee, and then made them the booty of the next excursion. With *this* experience, the inhabitants would no longer redeem them; after which no submissions exempted themselves from the sword; and all abandoned the villages and open country, to seek shelter in the woods, forts, and hills, nearest their reach. Not a man ventured himself, or his bullock, with a bag of rice, to the camp, which, for 3 days, were totally deprived of this staple food." That destructive diversion by the hostile cavalry, the falling of such heavy rains, for a couple of days, as no tents could resist, and a consequent necessity of affording his men some shelter and repose, compelled Coote, on the 19th, to canton his army in the Fort of Covrepauk, and the adjoining villages; and, having also to consult with the Presidency at Madras, he was not able to take the field again before the 26th, when he removed 6 miles from Covrepauk to Chinasimundrum, as presenting the site for "a very advantageous encampment." By that

* The O'Kennellys were of the best old Ulster, or *Irian*, origin. The Lieutenant-Colonel became a Brigadier in 1769, and died previous to 1773. His wife, a Mademoiselle Susan Darcy, is mentioned, as, in consideration of his services, pensioned, in 1789.

time, the increased French force, intended to act under Lally, with Bussy as next in command, was collected about Arcot, where Lally himself arrived on the following day. In this condition, or encamped but 5 miles from each other, though neither, for sufficient reasons, as yet ready to push matters to a decision, the 2 armies remained to the end of the month, and of the year 1759.

On consulting with Bussy respecting the best plan of action to be adopted against Coote, the leading measure advocated by Lally was the recapture of Wandewash. " Bussy, on the other hand, was of opinion, as the French were superior in cavalry, which would render it dangerous for the English to hazard a battle, except in circumstances of advantage, that they should avail themselves of this superiority, by acting upon the communications of the English, which would soon compel them either to fight at a disadvantage, or retire for subsistence to Madras: whereas, if they besieged Wandewash, the English would have 2 important advantages: one, that of fighting with only a part of the French army, while another part was engaged in the siege; the other, that of choosing the advantage of the ground, from the obligation of the French to cover the besiegers. At the same time, the motives of Lally were far from groundless. The mental state of the soldiers required some brilliant exploit, to raise them to the temper of animated action. He was deprived of *all* means of keeping the army for *any* considerable time in the field. By seizing the English magazines, he counted upon retarding, for several days, their march to the relief of Wandewash; and, as the English had breached the Fort, and taken it in 48 hours, he counted, and not unreasonably, upon rendering himself master of the place, before the English could arrive." Accordingly, from January 9th, artfully manœuvring in such a manner as drew Coote from Chinasimundrum, and caused him to resort to other precautions as in apprehension for the immediate safety of Wandewash, Lally, by the 12th, overreached him in arriving at Conjeveram, where, though disappointed in the expectation of finding magazines of rice for the English, the French met with, and carried off, 2000 bullocks, and other booty, on their march for Trivatore; and, the 14th, with a select division of European and Asiatic troops, and 4 field-guns, the General proceeded thence for Wandewash; leaving Bussy with the main body at Trivatore, as the best, or most central point, from which the division to attack Wandewash might be joined, if the English should march after it; or might be opposed and interrupted, should they menace Arcot, as a set-off against, or diversion from, the siege of Wandewash. After reaching that place, the same day, Lally lost no time in his arrangements to carry the pettah, or town, previous to assailing the Fort. The southern quarter, garrisoned with 330 men, (or 30 Europeans and 300 Sepoys,) by the Governor, Captain Sherlock, was to be assaulted, at 3 in the morning, by all the General's infantry, in 2 divisions. Of these, the inferior, or that whose Europeans consisted of the Marines, already mentioned as designated by Lally "the scum of the sea," was to act against the western rampart, merely as a diversion to the real attack in the opposite direction, "where the Europeans were of Lally's regiment," and to be "led by himself." Both divisions, being perceived by the garrison ere they could reach the foot of the wall, were suitably opposed, when the Marines *verified* the bad opinion which had been expressed of them, in breaking, and running round to the General's division; by which, being mistaken, in the darkness and confusion, for enemies, they were not undeservedly treated as such, until the error was detected. This disaster, through the misconduct of the Marines, caused nothing more to be attempted till 8 next morning. The whole of the infantry having then to advance, with 2 field-pieces at their head, against the south side, in 1 column, were exposed to such a fire, that the front of the column halted, without orders. Upon which, Lally rode up, got off his horse, called for volunteers, rushed to the ditch, was himself the 1st man to mount the wall, sword in hand, after 3 of the 7 volunteers who followed him had fallen about him; and his entire column, pouring into the town, obliged the garrison to escape through the streets into the Fort.

Had sufficient expedition been used in forwarding the heavy guns requisite for battering the Fort, and, could the engineers have afterwards been gotten to dispense with professional technicality, or pedantry, by hastening to direct a proper fire against the place, Lally's design of reducing it would seemingly have been accomplished, in *ample* time to anticipate Coote's arrival, for Sherlock's relief. Unfortunately, the siege artillery from Valdore took several days to come up, or until the 20th, when the General ordered the engineers, says Mill, "to batter in breach, with 3 cannon, upon 1 of the towers of the Fort, which was only protected by the fire of a single piece, and which, 5 weeks before, the English, with *inferior* means, *had breached in* 48 *hours.* But the engineers insisted upon erecting a battery, in exact conformity with the rules of the schools;" so that even "the soldiers, in derision, asked, If they were going to attack the fortifications of Luxemburgh?" And well might the soldiers have thus expressed themselves, since, adds Orme of Lally, " he *had* reason to expect greater industry and spirit in the artillery, officers, and engineers, who *might* have breached the place in *half* the time." These circumstances enabled Sherlock to hold the Fort, until Coote could arrive to raise the siege; for which purpose, he appeared, with his army, on the morning of the 22nd, in view of the French camp. His approaches were so skilfully directed, that, after proceeding along the foot of a mountain, until opposite the Fort of Wandewash, and then making a conversion of his lines to the right, his army " would immediately be formed in the strongest of situations; their right protected by the fire of the Fort; their left by the impassable ground under the mountain, and with the certainty of throwing any number of troops, without opposition, into the Fort; who, sallying with the garrison to the other side, might easily drive the *French* from their batteries in the *town;* from whence, the whole of the English army might likewise advance against the French camp, with the choice of attacking it either on the flank, or in the rear; where the main defences, which had been prepared in the front of their encampment, or arose from the usual dispositions on this side, would become entirely useless." * Lally no sooner saw this march commenced along the bottom of the mountain, than equally detecting the drift of Coote's operation, and resolved upon interrupting it, he left 150 of his Europeans and 300 of his Sepoys to man the siege-batteries, and attend to Captain Sherlock in the Fort; drawing off the rest of his troops, disposable for action, to the ground in front of his lines, or the direction in which he designed to engage the enemy.

* In this quotation from Orme, the 2 *italicized* words are adaptive substitutions for "enemy" and "pettah," in the original.

The comparative strength of the French and English, for the ensuing battle of Wandewash, has been computed as follows :—

FRENCH.		ENGLISH.	
	Men.		Men.
Foot,	900 ⎫ 1200	Europeans, of whom 1620	
Marines,	300 ⎭	foot, and 80 horse, . .	1700
Horse,	150	Sepoys, ...	2250 ⎫ 3500
		Black horse, ...	1250 ⎭
Europeans, . .	1350		
Sepoys, ...	1800	Total, ...	5200
Total, ...	3150	Artillery, ...	15 pieces.*
Artillery, ...	16 pieces.		

From about 7 to between 11 and 12 o'clock, there was much preliminary manœuvring and skirmishing. The cannonade then became smarter, as *both* sides advanced to the more serious business of the day. When the English, towards 12 o'clock, were coming forward, Lally, from his right, thought he could perceive such an unsteadiness upon the hostile left, which he attributed to the effect of his artillery, that he proposed, by a wide and dashing sweep over the plain, to get round to, and fall upon, the horse of the English, in the rear, or 3rd line. He accordingly proceeded to his European cavalry, to turn, at their head, the apparently-favourable moment to account. The misconduct, however, which so far justified his subsequent complaint, "that his troops did their duty ill in this action," commenced here. "The cavalry refused to march. The General suspended the commanding officer, and ordered the 2nd Captain to take the command. He, also, disobeyed. Lally addressed himself to the men; and a Cornet crying out, that it was a *shame* to desert their General in the day of battle, the officer, who commanded upon the left, offered to put the troop in motion." Lally was quite correct, as to the wavering which existed in the quarter he hastened to assail; 9-10ths of Coote's cavalry there, or the Black horse, retiring in confusion, on witnessing the French advance; a body of Sepoys, who were to check that advance by a flanking musketry, displaying but too little resolution to do so; and only the 80 European horse of the English, and 2 guns, under Captain Barker,

* I give the French, according to Lally's own enumeration of them, as cited by Mill, with the exception of their artillery in the action, which, in default of any statement on that head by Lally, (as so cited,) I enumerate from Orme. I give the English according to Coote's total of their men and guns; merely adopting the proportions of their European and Black horse from Orme. It was only the Europeans, who were of consequence, on either side, as *soldiers*, in this action; and, without dwelling upon the various causes which existed for Coote's Europeans having been much superior in *morale*, discipline, and condition to Lally's, Coote, as having 1700, had a considerable advantage over Lally, with 1350 Europeans nominally, though, in effect, only his 900 regular infantry, and 150 cavalry, or merely 1050; the 300 Marines having shown themselves not to be relied on as *soldiers*. The comparative numbers of the 3 regular battalions or regiments of infantry in each army, between whom this engagement was fought and decided, would, on an average, be thus :—FRENCH: Lorrain's, Company's, Lally's, each 300, or total 900. ENGLISH: Coote's, Company's, Draper's, each 540, or total 1620. Even should we admit the 300 Marines to have been "all right," Lally would still have only 1200 infantry to Coote's 1620, or the latter still be, by upwards of a 4th, the more numerous. Neither Orme, nor Mill, would appear to have consulted the despatch of *Coote*, to whose alleged totals of his own men and guns, should we not adhere, "*coute* qui *coute ?*"

keeping their ground. But, in less than a minute, upon 10 or 15 of the approaching men and horses being brought down by the fire of Barker's guns, the rest of the French cavalry fell into disorder and panic, wheeled about, and went off at full gallop, followed by the small number of the Anglo-European horse who had stood firm with Barker, as well as by many of the Black horse, who, when they only had to pursue, returned to *distinguish* themselves in that branch of the service;* both following the routed French about a mile, or as far as the rear of their camp.

Lally, necessarily obliged to retire from the English cavalry when thus totally or disgracefully abandoned by his own, joined the nearest portion of his line of infantry, or the Regiment of Lorrain. This corps, as well as the rest, "he found suffering, and with much impatience, from the English cannonade: his own impetuosity concurred with their eagerness to be led to immediate decision, and he gave the order to advance." From the nature of the ground, and corresponding arrangement of the troops on both sides, the hostile lines did not come within musketry-reach till about 1 o'clock. Coote was with his own regiment, opposite that of Lorrain. Coote's "only fired twice, when Lorrain formed in a column 12 in front. The operation is simple, and was expeditious. Colonel Coote made no change in the disposition of his regiment, but ordered the whole to reserve their next fire; which Lorrain, coming on almost at a run, received at the distance of 50 yards in their front, and on both their flanks. It fell heavy, and brought down many, but did not stop the column. In an instant, the 2 regiments were mingled at the push of bayonet. Those of Coote's, opposite the front of the column, were immediately borne down; but the rest, far the greatest part, fell on the flanks, when every man fought only for himself; and, in a minute, the ground was spread with dead and wounded; and Lorrain, having just before suffered from the reserved fire of Coote's, broke, and ran in disorder to regain the camp. Colonel Coote ordered his regiment to be restored to order before they pursued, and rode himself to see the state of the rest of the line."

The 2 centres, consisting of the forces of the 2 East India Companies, meantime keeping up merely a distant though smart fire, as if both equally inclined to leave closer operations to the regular troops elsewhere, and matters now progressing to a more sharp and decisive course between the English right and the French left, in which quarters the Regiment of Draper and the Regiment of Lally were opposed to each other, Coote hastened up to direct the movements of Draper's corps, as Lally, after the defeat of the Regiment of Lorrain, did to join and manœuvre his own regiment. Here, too, however,

"Fortune, that, with malicious joy,
Does man, her slave, oppress,"

and,

"Proud of her office to destroy,
Is seldom pleas'd to bless,"

was still adverse to Lally. His regiment had been well posted, pro-

* As the gallant Spartan Brasidas observes, in Thucydides, of his barbaric opponents—"Such as will give ground, and fly before them, they pursue with eagerness; and are excellently brave, when there is no resistance." Or, as another writer would say of such *soldiership*, it was "yielding to the intrepid, intrepid to the yielding!" See, likewise, the conduct of the English cavalry, at Culloden.

tected by a retrenched tank, in which was another European corps of 300 men, or that of the Marines with 4 field-pieces; at a 2nd tank, to their rear, was a further support of several hundred Sepoys, that had been engaged in the French cause by Bussy; and a still larger reserve of the like native mercenaries were ranged behind a ridge, which extended along the front of the camp in that quarter. But, as Coote and Lally, after their late infantry-contest elsewhere, were coming to take in hand a similar one here, a shot, from 1 of the field-pieces attached to the Regiment of Draper, striking an ammunition-waggon, at the retrenched tank, next to the Regiment of Lally, where the 300 Marines were stationed, caused a disastrous explosion, by which 80 men with their officer, a Knight of Malta, were either killed, or, for the most part, mortally injured. "All who were near, and had escaped the danger, fled, in the 1st impulse of terror, out of the retrenchment, and ran to gain the camp by the rear of Lally's, and were joined, in the way, by the 400 Sepoys at the tank behind, who, although they had suffered nothing, likewise abandoned their post."

Coote thereupon ordered, that, ere the enemy could recover from this confusion, Major Brereton, with the Regiment of Draper, should seize the retrenched tank; from which they might gain the important advantage, of acting, under cover, against the flank of the Regiment of Lally. Bussy, however, who commanded the French on this wing, promptly rallying 50 or 60 fugitives, and adding to them 2 platoons from the Regiment of Lally, so far anticipated the occupation of the tank; returning to bring up the rest of the regiment, for the maintenance of that post. Yet Brereton, advancing so rapidly as to suffer little from the fire of the Regiment of Lally in its divided and distracted condition, assaulted the retrenchment so impetuously on its left, that he carried it, after a volley of much execution from those within, by which he met his own death-wound. "The first of Draper's, who got into the retrenchment, fired down, from the parapet, upon the guns on the left of Lally's, and drove the gunners from them; whilst the rest, being many more than required to maintain the post, formed, and shouldered under it, extending on the plain to the left, to prevent the Regiment of Lally, if attempting to recover the post, from embracing it on this side. Bussy wheeled the Regiment of Lally, and sent off platoons from its left to regain the retrenchment, whilst the rest were opposed to the division of Draper's on the plain." These detached platoons from Lally's, naturally considering themselves *not* strong enough to recover the retrenched tank by an assault, acted with comparative or proportionate faintness, by only maintaining a skirmishing fire against those under cover, or so well protected, in that post. "The action likewise continued only with musketry, but warmly, between the 2 divisions on the plain, until the 2 field-pieces attached to the right of Draper's, which they had left behind when marching to attack the retrenchment, were brought to bear on the flank of Lally's, who had *none* to oppose them, on which their line began to waver, and many were going off. Bussy, as the only chance of restoring this part of the battle, put himself at their head, intending to lead them to the push of bayonet, but had only advanced a little way when his horse was struck with a ball in the head, and, floundering at every step afterwards, he dismounted; during which the fire from Draper's had continued, of which 2 or 3 balls passed through his cloaths, and, when he alighted, only 20 of Lally's had kept near him, the rest had shrunk." He was consequently surrounded and made prisoner. As to Lally, who, "after the rout of Lorrain, rode away to join his own regiment," he, "on the way, saw the explosion of the tumbril at the retrenched tank, the dispersion of the Marines at this post, and the flight of the Sepoys out of the tank behind. He was in this instant near, and intended to speak to, Bussy, but turned suddenly, and ordered the Sepoys, stationed along the ridge in front of the camp, to advance." Since "none obeyed," and, as most of them had been engaged by, and served under, his enemy, Bussy, he, not unnaturally, "suspected treachery, and, unable to controul the impulse of distraction, rode into the camp, to stop the fugitives of Lorrain."

It was about 2 o'clock, when the whole of the French were thus driven from the field, in the direction of their camp. Meantime, however, the French cavalry had recovered from their panic and rout in the beginning of the action, by rallying on the plain to the rear of their camp, keeping the English horse at bay there with various evolutions; and they now endeavoured to compensate, as far as possible, for their recent misconduct, by their repentant gallantry, in covering the retreat. They, on seeing "the flight of Lorrain through the camp, animated with a sense of national honour, resolved to protect them, if, as might be expected, they should endeavour to escape still further, by gaining the plain. In this purpose, they united their squadrons, and drew up in the rear of the camp, and in face of the English cavalry; of whom the Black horse, awed by their resolution, dared not, and the European were too few, to charge them. This unexpected succour probably prevented the utter dispersion of the French army. There were, in the rear of the camp, 2 field-pieces, with their tumbrils of ammunition; at which, the fugitives of Lorrain, encouraged by the appearance of the cavalry, stopped, and yoked them. These protections restored confidence to Lally's and the India battalion, as they arrived, likewise beaten from the field, although *not* in rout, as Lorrain's before.* They set fire to the tents and dangerous stores near them, and the whole filed off into the plain, in much better order than their officers expected. The 3 field-pieces kept in the rear of the line of infantry, and behind them moved the cavalry." Proceeding westward, towards the Fort of Wandewash, they joined the troops who had remained at the batteries there, which were abandoned, with all the stores and heavier baggage; the garrison of the Fort offering no interruption to the retreat. The lighter baggage, and a number of wounded, were saved, or brought away, by Lally. "Coote sent repeated orders to his cavalry, to harass and impede the retreat of the French line. They followed them 5 miles, until 5 in the afternoon, but the Black horse could not be brought up within reach of the carbines of the French cavalry, and much less of their field-pieces. The brunt of the day passed intirely between the Europeans of both armies; the Black troops of neither had any part in it, after the cannonade commenced." The French, with tents, stores, and baggage, as above mentioned, and 11 tumbrils of ammunition, lost, between the field, the camp, and before the Fort of Wandewash, from 22 to 24 pieces of light or heavy artillery, and appear to have certainly had 433 killed, wounded, or captured, exclusive of a further diminution unascertained, but that

* The words, "although *not* in rout, as Lorrain's before," are a requisite addition, from *another* portion of Orme's narrative, to the sentence ending in the original, at the word "field."

would make their entire deficit by the contest, perhaps, 600 men.* Among those taken prisoners, were Lieutenant-Colonel Murphy,† 2 Captains, and 2 Lieutenants of the Regiment of Lally. The English killed and wounded were, of Coote's, 53; the Company's, 49; Draper's, as engaged with Lally's, *most*, or 89; European horse and artillery, 6; Sepoys and Black horse, 70; total, 267.

"Except the battle of Plassey,‡ followed by the revolution in Bengal," remarks the contemporary Annual Register, "this action was the most considerable, in its consequences, of any in which our troops had ever been engaged in India. This was fought in part against European troops, headed by an able General. The dispositions for the battle, and the conduct of Colonel Coote in the engagement, merit every honour." § And Coote's European troops were worthy of *him* as a Commander. "During the whole engagement," he writes, "and ever since I have had the honour of commanding the army, the officers and men have shown the greatest spirit; nor can I say too much for the behaviour of the artillery." Very differently here from Coote was Lally circumstanced, with a force, whose available, or European portion, was the smaller in number, compared with its opponents; in 1 respect, or, at least, as regards the Marines, very inferior in quality; and which was otherwise found too deficient in its conduct, as might be expected from the various bad effects on discipline, or obedience, of long irregularity of pay, accom-

* These details respecting Lally's loss—inclusive of 73 men wounded in the action, and subsequently found at Chittapet—are taken from Orme, as I have not seen any French data on the subject.
† The sept of O'Murchudha, pronounced O'Murraghoo, at first Anglicized O'Murchoe, and finally Murphy, were likewise designated Hy-Felimy, or descendants of Felimy; from their progenitor, a son of the celebrated Enna Kinsellagh, King of Laighin, or Leinster, contemporary of St. Patrick, in the 5th century. The territory of the sept consisted of the Murroos, or Barony of Ballaghkeen, in the County of Wexford; the seat of the Chieftains being in the locality now called Castle-Ellis, where, in 1634, Conall O'Murchudha, the head of the race, died, and was interred; and, till within the present century, a respectable branch still possessed a considerable estate at Oulartleigh. To be a Murphy is to be proverbially associated, at home and abroad, with old Irish or Milesian extraction, even without the prefix of O'; "Don Patricio O'Murphy, the steward of the Duke of Wellington's estate in Spain, being," writes Dr. O'Donovan, in 1861, "the only man living, who retains the O' in this name." During the War of the Revolution in Ireland, the Murphys were represented in the Jacobite army among Hamilton's, Kenmare's, Tyrone's, Bellew's, Kilmallock's, and Hunsdon's infantry, by several officers, from the rank of Major to that of Lieutenant; and 7 of the name, in Wexford alone, besides many more in other Counties, are to be seen in the attainders of the Jacobite loyalists, by the Orange revolutionists. From the sailing of the Irish forces for France, after the Treaty of Limerick, in 1691, to the reign of Louis XVI., there were various Murphys, also, from the rank of Major to that of Lieutenant, in the Irish Regiments of Charlemont, Clancarty, Limerick, Fitz-Gerald, Galmoy, Dillon, and Clare, besides those in *French* regiments; the Lieutenant-Colonel of the Regiment of Lally having been, so far, the highest in rank of his name.
‡ Corrected from the misprint of "Paissy."
§ How inferior in point of *military* merit seems the success of Clive at Plassey over the miserable Surajah Dowla, undermined by treachery, and at the head, rather than in command of, a worthless and distracted Asiatic rabble, to the success of Coote at Wandewash against Lally, with a less numerous, indeed, yet a European force, and in a regular engagement, unattended by any hostile plotting with those about him, to *insure* his defeat! Hence Clive's business at Plassey cost him but 72 men killed or wounded! Besides, even as regards *that* affair of Plassey, was not the advance, to fight there at all, according to *Coote's* original opinion, in opposition to Clive's?

panied with suffering and discontent in proportion; and the latter feeling specially aggravated to *his* prejudice, by the unscrupulous cabals and calumnies of those dishonest and malignant officials, whom *he* would not gratify in their filthy famine for fiscal frauds. Nor can the untoward result of the "chance shot" be forgotten as regards the explosion on Lally's left, where, but for that casualty, and its destructive and disorganizing consequences, there would appear to have been the best prospect of repelling the enemy. Still, amid so many disadvantages as those with which Lally had to contend, he made a good retreat, in which, and the engagement, he behaved in such a manner, that all the officers and soldiers in the King's service, as contrasted with those in the Company's, or the partizan Battalion of India, became indignant at the vile intrigues and falsehoods, that proved so far injurious to the character and authority of their Commander, as not to have been without influence in contributing to the loss of the day. This just indignation these brave men accordingly manifested soon after at Valdore, in flocking around Lally; and exclaiming, with reference to the infamous arts of peculating persecution that marked him out for its victim—" Do not be discouraged, General! *They have caused you to lose the battle*, but you have gained the army. *They have contrived that you should fail*, but *we* will all support you!" On the whole, in this affair of "diamond cut diamond" between Coote and Lally, as each connected with Ireland, it may be fairly observed, that if the one was victorious with honour, the other was unsuccessful without dishonour; and it may be likewise regretted by the country, on which each reflected such a lustre, that either should have been opposed to the other, under a different standard, instead of both, with united invincibility, rather resembling Achilles and Patroclus, in the happier days, when

"Their swords kept time, and conquer'd side by side."
POPE'S HOMER, Iliad, xviii., 401, 402.

The axiom that "knowledge is power" cannot be better exemplified than by a contrast of what Coote did *not* do after his success at Wandewash with what he *might* have done, but for his ignorance of how very badly the French were situated. Had he immediately marched to Pondicherry, he could, as we learn from Lally, have *decided* the contest between the 2 Companies, by making himself master of that metropolis within 8 days! Notwithstanding the repeated letters, entreaties, orders, and menaces, from Lally to the Governor during 2 years, to collect, at all events, a supply of rice there, so far had that functionary been from even commencing the establishment of a single magazine of the kind, that, it is said, "il n'y avoit pas un grain de ris dans la place!" But the English, having had *no* suspicion of the existence of a state of things which would have enabled them to give a wound at once so rapid and so mortal to their enemy, only proceeded to deprive that enemy of his limbs before striking at his head, when, by striking, as they might have struck, immediately and effectively at his head, the limbs would have fallen as a matter of course. Coote's attention was thus directed to a reduction of the subordinate places subject to the French, previous to any attack upon their metropolis. Lally meanwhile withdrew his troops successively by Chittapet and Gingee to Valdore, in order "to prevent the English from taking post between them and Pondicherry, and to protect the districts of the south, from which alone provisions could be obtained. The difficulties of

Lally, which," continues my hostile authority, "had so long been great, were now approaching to extremity. The army was absolutely without equipments, stores, and provisions, and he was destitute of resources to supply them. He repaired to Pondicherry to demand assistance, which he would *not* believe that the Governor and Council were unable to afford." Amply justified, as he considered himself to be, in this impression, and proportionably provoked at their refusal to aid him, "he represented them, as embezzlers, and peculators." In reply, this "knot of rogues," with the audacity of the robber, and the brass of the prostitute, abstained from no imputation of folly, dishonesty, and even "cowardice" (*credite posteri!*) at his expense. The outrageous insubordination of those insolent officials was aggravated by a mutiny of the cavalry, for want of pay; who, when drawn out, in order to retaliate upon the enemy for some devastating and plundering horse-incursions to the country about Pondicherry, whereby 84 villages were burned, and 8,000 head of cattle swept away, not only refused to march with the General, but made dispositions as if they *all* designed to go over, like 27 who actually *did* so, to the English; several of the more violent or ruffianly troopers, on the night of February 11th, being even heard to propose what they termed bringing the General to reason, by turning the guns upon the ramparts of the town against the Government House! On Lally's representation of the depositions to this alarming effect to the Governor and Council, they did nothing better than propose expedients, which, as connected with a preservation of *their* authority in the administration of the revenues, implied, (as might be expected,) that, whatever they or theirs might receive, *he* was to get nothing! To 2 of their agents, European inhabitants of the colony, a large tract of country was let (or rather *under*-let) for a rent of 1,450,000 rupees a year; from whom, on the plea of a diminution of receipts in proportion to recent losses of territory, the answer, like the Council's, was, that "they had *no* money;" whereas a Malabar, to whom Lally had previously rented the districts around Arcot, agreed to advance 50,000 rupees in 10 days, and 80,000 more in 20 days, on condition that what was left of the districts let to the Council's 2 Europeans should be leased to him, with other territory, south of Pondicherry, for 1,750,000 rupees a year. This offer (opposed, of course, by the Council, as keeping *their* finger out of the financial pie,) was necessarily accepted by Lally, since it would furnish him with *some* money, instead of leaving him, at such a critical juncture, without *any;* though it may be added of this pecuniary aid so obtained from the Malabar capitalist, that it, like whatever assistance of the kind had been received in India, could enable the General to do little, if any thing, more, than "stop a gap for the present," or barely keep him afloat, as on a mere temporary plank, amidst the ocean of difficulties which raged around him—*his* position, if any body's *ever* was, being that, in Pope's words, of

"A brave man struggling in the storms of Fate!"

Between the ably-directed superiority of foreign power, and the unscrupulous spirit of domestic disaffection, against which, like Hercules opposed to the 2 serpents, he had at once to contend, the only wonder is, *how* he could so long contrive to resist the former, while in every way crossed and worried by the latter!

Since the victory of the English at Wandewash, the progress of their arms by land, seconded by the presence of a considerable squadron at sea, was so great, that, previous to March 18th, their advanced military outposts approached and skirmished with those of the French around Pondicherry; while the naval armament showed itself off the port, causing the more alarm, from the absence of any force of the kind there. In this emergency, Lally, to impose upon the English, by making them think the French troops to be many more than they really were, issued his orders for a general review, to be held, the 20th, outside the town, along the sea shore, or in view of the hostile squadron; at which display, the regular soldiery were to be apparently augmented by the presence of 1100 Europeans; 600 of whom were invalids only fit for garrison-duty, and the remainder, 500 inhabitants of the place, including the civil servants of the Company, all in uniform, the material for which was supplied. On the day, however, for this well-designed display, 250 of those refractory *employés* of the Company, headed by the Council, and armed with muskets, tumultuously entered the General's apartment; exclaiming, that they would not obey his order, or any command to them, unless from the Governor established by the Company. The Members of the Council were particularly offensive to the General, in claiming an exemption from bearing arms beyond the walls of the town. This behaviour, at such a crisis, was so disreputable, even in the eyes of the very Governor whom they had *professed* themselves ready to obey, that he (to his credit!) offered, if they would march, to place himself at their head; upon which, the seditious quibblers, liars, and dastards "ate dirt," as the honest Turks would say, or shamelessly backed out of what they alleged they would do, by refusing to obey either the Governor, or the General! Lally consequently had the 2 spokesmen of the Council, and 2 others of the most prominent recusants, arrested, and punished those heads of the cabal against him, by banishing them from the town; pronouncing that sentence, as was natural under the circumstances, in terms of cutting severity, not to be forgotten; and, having disarmed and dismissed the rest of the crew, he permitted them, as it were, in the language of the poet, or "with heartless breasts, and unperforming hands," to "leave to men the bus'ness of the war"*—thus granting them the ignominious or feminine exemption *they* claimed, while HE proceeded to hold the review *without* them.

> "As we wax hot in faction,
> In battle we wax cold;
> Wherefore men fight not, as they fought
> In the brave days of old."—LORD MACAULAY.

Judging likewise, and most excusably judging, from this *last* act of opposition, in connexion with the results of his *previous* experience, that the Council's "measure of iniquity was now full to overflowing," as that of an insufferable gang, whose wicked or factious conduct had too generally or plainly emanated from no better principle, than a resolution of opposing him in *every* thing, he prohibited that body to assemble any more, without a special permission, or requisition from himself, to do so. It was surely high time, that a den of the kind should be closed, if the disorder, of which it was so foul a source, was not to reign triumphant, and thus occasion the destruction of the colony much sooner, by the prevalence of a scandalous anarchy within, than it could be accomplished by all the enemy's power from without. During, indeed, but a few days before, 2 other outbreaks of sedition, or mutiny, had been directed against

* See Pitt's version of the scornful speech of Numanus, in Virgil's 9th Æneid.

the General. In 1 of these outbreaks, according to Voltaire, a company of grenadiers armed with sabres, penetrated into the chamber of the General, insolently demanding some money from him. Although alone, his reply was, to charge them sword in hand, and chase them out of the room. Yet *this* was the man, remarks Voltaire, of whom we have subsequently seen it stated in print, that he was a *coward!*

From January to May, the acquisitions, at the expense of the French, by Coote and his subordinate officers, supported by Admirals Cornish and Steevens, continued to draw the fatal circle closer and closer about Pondicherry; as including the reduction of Chittapet, Timery, Arcot, Devicotah, Seringham, Velore, Trinomalee, Permacoil, Alamparvah, Villaporum, Carical, Valdore, Chillambrum, Cuddalore, Verdachelum. In the operations connected with those conquests—which Lally, incapacitated from keeping the field with a proper force, and having no fleet to aid him against an enemy so superior on *both* elements, was unable to interrupt—nothing appears to have occurred with respect to the Irish, but at Arcot and Permacoil. The former place, with a garrison of 247 Europeans, nearly as many Sepoys, 22 pieces of cannon, 4 mortars, plenty of ammunition, and military stores, when not 3 of the defenders had fallen, and 10 days before a storming could have been risked, was given up, February 10th, to Coote by the Governor, designated by Orme as " the French officer, Captain Hussey "—one, I should think, of the *otherwise* respectable Irish family of Anglo-Norman origin,*—who, however, " extenuated the early surrender by the *certainty* of not being relieved," on account of the bad condition to which the French were reduced, by their recent defeat at Wandewash. The defence of the latter place, or Permacoil, was more creditable to a Milesian veteran attached to the Regiment of Lally, Colonel O'Kennedy,† then lame of

* The "Barun Huge de Hosé" was among Henry II.'s earliest Anglo-Normans planted in Midhe, or Meath. There that nobleman obtained "large possessions," or "all the lands of Dies, which Scachlin held," otherwise "the Barony of Deece, the ancient estate of Melaghlin, or Melscachlin." From the locality of Galtrim, Huge de Hosé's successive senior representatives, under the ultimately corrupted or anglicized name of "Hussey," have been known as Palatine "Barons of Galtrim." The titular "Baron of Galtrim," in 1860, was "Edward Horatio Hussey," grandson of John, likewise "Baron," deceased in 1803, a Captain in the Austrian service, in which several Husseys have been officers. During the war of the Revolution in Ireland, 3 Husseys sat as Members in King James's national Parliament of 1689, at Dublin; and, in the Jacobite army, there were Husseys, from the rank of Ensign to that of Colonel, among the infantry Regiments of Sir Maurice Eustace, of Lords Gormanstown and Louth, and of Mac Elligot. Various gentlemen of the name in Leinster and Munster were likewise attainted by the Williamites. M. de la Ponce specifies, among the officers of the Irish Brigade, 6 Husseys of the rank of Captain in the Regiments of Clare, Berwick, and Dillon, 2 of whom were Chevaliers of St. Louis.

† The O'Kennedys were of Dalcassian origin, being descended from the brave Kennedy King of Thomond, or North Munster, deceased in 951, through his son, (and elder brother of the great Brien Boru) Dunchuan. The original country of the O'Kennedys was Glenomra, coextensive with the Parish of Killokennedy, in the County of Clare, whence they were afterwards generally driven in the civil wars of Thomond; though, writes Dr. O'Donovan, in 1860, " some of the race remained behind, and their descendants are still extant in Glenomra, and its vicinity, in the condition of small farmers and cottiers." The clan then settled to the east of the Shannon, in Tipperary, or the district of Ormond, anciently much more extensive than it is in modern times, or as merely comprised in the 2 Baronies of Upper and Lower Ormond. There the sept became subdivided into 3 branches, or those of O'Kennedy Finn the *Fair*, Don, the *Brown*, and Ruadh, the *Red*. Their head, the O'Kennedy sometimes with more,

old wounds, and not long after obliged by his failing sight to return to Europe; who, with a little garrison of only about 145 men, of whom but 15 gunners were Europeans, did not surrender, March 5th, to Coote, until there was neither cannon nor musket ammunition to withstand the final assault about to be given, nor provisions left for more than 2 days; Coote himself, at a previous repulse there, having been wounded in the knee.* An Irish officer, on the other hand, of the Regiment of Lally, merely alluded to as such, or *anonymously*, and as "supposed to be much in his favour," is noticed to have brought censure upon the General from his enemies, as at fault, for *not* having advanced, with a considerable reinforcement of men and stores, to succour Permacoil, in such an expeditious manner, that it *might* have been relieved. But we should know *more* of the circumstances of this "short-coming" attributed to the anonymous Irish officer by the enemies of Lally, before admitting that officer to be censurable, on an imputation from so prejudiced a quarter.

The English, by the commencement of May, had 10 sail of the line at sea, and were encamped under Coote opposite to the partly natural, partly artificial, outwork before Pondicherry, called the bound-hedge. Like that of other towns in India, it was formed of the strong prickly shrubs of the country, as a sufficient barrier against any sudden plundering incursion of irregular cavalry; it was also strengthened at different points by redoubts; and included, besides Pondicherry, an area of nearly 7 square miles about it. To the protection of that metropolis and little territory, with the principal force he still contrived to keep together, the attention of Lally was now directed as well as it could be, amidst the hostility of those whose contributions to the public *defence* were too little known beyond misrepresentations of *him* as the cause of every reverse; while he more justly "retaliated with sarcasms on *their* soreness for the loss of their own peculations, out of the districts which he had been obliged to abandon!" Continual supplies reaching, and more being on the way to, the besiegers, "the early part of May," writes Dr. O'Callaghan, "was occupied in skirmishes and attacks on the French outposts, in which, the British being almost invariably successful, the besieged were driven, by the 20th, within the bound-hedge, and Coote commenced the regular investment of the place; whilst Lally found himself surrounded, and at bay, and shut up in the town with a deficient supply of provisions, and many useless non-combatants to be provided for. In this extremity, deserted by those who ought to have supported him, and thwarted, opposed, and maligned by the Council and Officials within the walls, he had turned his eyes everywhere around, seeking for the aid and alliance of the Indian Princes." Among them he managed to set on foot, with "the famous Hyder Ali, then rising into power in the Mysore country," a treaty for the relief of Pondicherry. "These

---

sometimes with less, power, according to the fortune of war, was known as a Prince, Lord, or Chief of Ormond till the reign of Elizabeth. In the War of the Revolution, the name appears among the infantry, horse, and dragoon officers of King James's army; and the Williamite outlawries exhibit due proscriptions of Kennedy proprietors, as Jacobite loyalists. To the Regiments of Lee, O'Brien, Clare, Bulkeley, Dillon, Berwick, &c., in the Brigade, the O'Kennedys supplied officers, including some Chevaliers of St. Louis.

"Colonel Coote," says Orme, "by constantly exposing his own person with the Sepoys, had brought them to sustain dangerous services, from which the Europeans were preserved."

negociations were conducted with such secrecy and despatch, that they were entirely concealed from the English till the 24th of May, when Coote received intelligence of their success and completion, by a letter from a correspondent within the walls of Pondicherry; informing him, that Lally was about to march, with a strong detachment, to join Hyder Ali at Thiagur; and, although the latter part of the rumour did not prove true, yet, on the 7th of June, he was informed, that the 1st division of the Mysore troops had actually arrived at Thiagur, on their march towards Pondicherry; within sight of which they arrived on the 23rd, when an outpost engagement took place between them and the English, in which both sides claimed the victory. On the 27th, the treaty between Hyder Ali and the French was signed, and, next day, the Mysoreans left the camp, promising soon to return, with augmented forces. Both armies, awaiting their arrival, remained inactive till the 14th of July; on which day, Coote, who had availed himself of the interruption of active operations to visit Madras, and consult with the Council, returned to the British camp. On the 17th, Major Moore was attacked, at Trivadi, by the Mysore forces, and, from their great superiority of numbers, was forced to give way, and retreat; but, towards the end of the month, they received several checks from the British, which, being repeated, on many occasions, in August, and the English troops cutting off their convoys and foraging parties, food began to be very dear and scarce in their camp, and the Sepoys to desert. Lally did everything in his power to persuade them to remain; but they were Orientals, and seeing that his star was on the wane, they withdrew in large bodies, or in small numbers, to escape the English cavalry; and, by the end of August, Lally was abandoned to his fate, and to his own resources, now very much impaired indeed." The English, on the other hand, were preparing to carry on the reduction of Pondicherry with augmented vigour, by forcing their way beyond the bound-hedge and redoubts, on the land side; while, on the sea side, it was determined, that their fleet should "press the dire blockade" even throughout the monsoon season, "a thing never before attempted!" Their army, at the beginning of September, consisted of between 8000 and 9000 men, of whom between 2000 and 3000 were Europeans, and 6000 native foot or horse; and their navy amounted to 17 sail of the line.

"Lally," notes Mill, "had now, and it is no ordinary praise, during almost 8 months since the total discomfiture of his army at Wandewash, imposed upon the English so much respect, as deterred them from the siege of Pondicherry; and, notwithstanding the desperate state of his resources, found means to supply the fort, which had been totally destitute of provisions, with a stock sufficient to maintain the garrison for several months. And he *still* resolved to strike a blow, which might impress them that he was capable of offensive operations of no inconsiderable magnitude." It was of the utmost consequence, that the external line of the bound-hedge and redoubts should be maintained as long as possible against the enemy; since the ground behind that barrier, or between it and Pondicherry, afforded pasture for a number of cattle sufficient to supply the garrison and inhabitants, with the aid of the additions to the existing stock, which might be introduced in small convoys occasionally, or from time to time, so long as the line should remain unforced; whereas, if captured by the English, that capture would be "the beginning of the end" for the besieged, thus reduced to limited, and constantly-decreasing, means of subsistence. The force which Lally could muster, for assailing that of the besiegers, was far inferior in strength to theirs, yet not so much so, that it might not inflict a severe stroke upon them, by stratagem; through which, even though not altogether defeated, they might be so shattered and discouraged, as to be obliged to desist from their immediate design, upon the bound-hedge and redoubts, for some time; if not also compelled, by the autumnal rains, and other circumstances, to defer a renewal of their attempt to a much later period. His consequent plan of action was, on the night of September the 4th, to attack the English camp by surprise, for which undertaking, "dispositions," says the hostile narrative, "were made with much skill and sagacity;" and it adds, that, "although Colonel Coote entertained spies and correspondents in the town, not 1 of them acquired the least surmise of Lally's intentions, or suspected any unusual operation." The entire strength of the French for this *sortie*, (owing to detachments elsewhere) appears to have been but 2400 men, or 1400 European infantry, 100 of the like cavalry, and 900 Sepoys—if the *actual* total were not rather under *that* estimate, when we consider it as an *enemy's*. The English were to be assailed on 3 points in front, or at a retrenchment, and at 2 redoubts, while the Battalion of India and Volunteers of Bourbon, under an experienced officer of the Company's service, were to settle the business, it would seem, by a simultaneous onslaught against the besiegers' rear. "As soon as the firing became general at the entrenchment on the Oulgarry road, the redoubt on the hillock and the tamarind redoubt," or the 3 former posts, "these troops," states Orme, of the Battalion of India, and Volunteers of Bourbon, "were to advance from the village in which they were halting, and proceed along a short road which would bring them to the termination of the Villenore avenue, and exactly in the rear of the right flank of the English encampment; on which they were to fall with the utmost vigour, in full confidence, that the other attacks would have thrown the whole camp into disorder, by the uncertainty and distraction of what and where succours were to be sent." Lally himself, "with a guard of horse, remained at the bridge of Oulgarry. Calculation had been made when all the troops would arrive within equal reach of their respective attacks, where they were to wait in silence for the signal of 2 sky-rockets which were to be thrown up at Oulgarry, when all were to advance to the attacks allotted them. The sky-rockets were shot off a little before midnight, and soon after the firing commenced, nearly at the same time, at the tamarind redoubt, the hillock, and at the retrenchment in the avenue of Oulgarry. The attack at the tamarind redoubt was repulsed; but the redoubt on the hillock was carried; the Lieutenant of the artillery, and 3 gunners, were made prisoners there, and the rest of the guard driven out; nor did they rally." This gave the French "time to carry off a brass three pounder, destroy the carriage of another, spike up a 3rd, and burn down the battery. At the retrenchment in the Oulgarry road, the attack and defence were more fierce. Colonel Coote himself brought down troops to that in the Villenore avenue and Barthelmi's garden, and instead of waiting to be attacked, advanced across to sustain the other redoubt; against which Lorrain's and Lally's persisted, until 8 Serjeants, besides common men, were killed; when the officers, hearing no signs of the *main* attack, on the right and rear of the English camp, drew off. This division, by some *unaccountable* error, instead of advancing to the villages under the Fort of Villenore, halted in another, a mile to the south of it, not far from the river " Ariancopang, "and in a line with the village of Oulgarry. At this erroneous distance, they had not time, after the sky-rockets were fired, to reach the ground of their attack, before the 3 others were either repulsed, or ceased. They were led by D'Harambure, who had always behaved hitherto with gallantry," though, concludes this Anglo-Indian writer,* " Lally, with the usual severity of his prejudices, imputed the failure to a design, as the Commander of the Company's troops, of frustrating the honour which would have redounded on himself, had the hardy effort he was making succeeded to his expectation."

How many reasons there were for this asserted " severity " of Lally's "prejudices," in reference to the Company's officials and partizans, need not be recapitulated here, since " what so tedious as a twice-told tale ! " But, considering that the Company's Battalion of India were so imbued with the hostile feelings of their masters to the General—that their leader, D'Harambure, was a military man of experience and distinction in that service, years before the General's arrival in India—that, after such a long professional career there, he can scarcely, if at all, be supposed anything but very well-informed with respect to the country about Pondicherry—that he, and the Company's troops, or the Battalion of India, with which he was best acquainted, and the *strongest* in the army, would thus seem the fittest to act where appointed, and where a spirited assault would be most likely to render the general operations against the English effective—that, nevertheless, it was *only* the Company's officer and the Company's troops who were *not* up at the time and at the point required—considering all these " ugly-looking circumstances," and the very unscrupulous character of Lally's enemies, *he* cannot, I think, be fairly censured in this instance, any more than in others, for what is termed " the usual severity of his prejudices." The Company's officers and troops were among his special adversaries, and to the absence from, or non-performance of, their task by *them*, through what is unsatisfactorily designated " some *unaccountable* error," though the *rest* of the forces were present to act as had been designed, the frustration of the General's confessedly well-laid plan against the enemy, without a fair trial of it, was unquestionably owing. If even

——————————— " trifles, light as air,
Are, to the jealous, confirmations strong,
As proofs of Holy Writ,"

did not Lally here merely feel, as any body else, in *his* position, must have felt ?—and how much more was *he* acquainted with, than *we* are acquainted with, to justify " the usual severity of his prejudices " in the culpable direction, where that alleged " severity " was made a grievance of ?—as if the provocation for such, and far greater " severity," were not but too abundant, and too intolerable, to admit of any other than the very *worst* opinion being entertained of those, from whom that provocation proceeded ! The necessarily brief duration of this broken-off nocturnal affair, between the French and English, was attended with

* Mr. Orme was a native of India, having been born in the territory of Travancore. To this circumstance, the minuteness of local details in his work is apparently attributable; a minuteness, that makes the book so much more valuable, than generally readable.

little loss to either party, or, apparently, not 50 men a side; the Regiments of Lally and Lorrain being the principal sufferers, on that of the French.

From the 4th to the 13th, the English, under Colonel Monson, (by an unseasonable order from Europe, raised to command, instead of Coote,) having made arrangements by night to break through the bound-hedge and its redoubts, succeeded in doing so; the French forces, except some in the fortified outposts of Ariancopang and Madras, retiring towards the glacis of Pondicherry; yet being joined there by several small escorts, with provisions from the interior of the country, that contrived to elude the English. In carrying the bound-hedge, Monson was so severely wounded by a cannon-shot, and thus disabled from commanding, that Coote, who was about to sail for Bengal, had to take that officer's place, and arrived before Pondicherry, on the 20th. By October 1st, through the construction of several works, and the reduction of the Ariancopang and Madras redoubts, he acquired "the entire possession of the bound-hedge," consequently turning "against the town, with every advantage, the line of circumvallation intended for its defence;" and, soon after, prevented a party with bullocks from entering the place by night. In the night, also, between the 6th and 7th, 2 vessels, the *Baleine* and *Hermione*, were, by 26 armed boats from the English fleet, cut out of the road of Pondicherry; and the decrease of provisions was now so much felt there, that Lally called a council to propose the expulsion of all the Black inhabitants; which proposal, however, through the opposition of Messieurs, the Europeans, who would be thereby deprived of their domestics, was negatived. Nevertheless, several of those recusants requested permission from Coote for their families to retire from the town, as besieged, to the neutral or Danish and Dutch settlements on the coast, and obtained his permission to that effect. On the 7th, when the expulsion of the Blacks was proposed by Lally, (which it would have been the better policy to adopt then, as it had to be executed afterwards,) and on the 8th, the refractory and demoralized crew whom he was making such exertions to defend, acted in such a manner as to justify the worst portion of his subsequent general denunciation of them in France, as "rogues, or villains fit for the rack." Hating him, in proportion to every measure which he was obliged to adopt for the preservation of the place, they, on the former day, threatened to assassinate him, (apparently on account of the *inconvenience* which their "high mightinesses" were unwilling to suffer from the ejection of the Blacks!) and, on the latter day, even proceeded to make that threat good, by an attempt to *poison* him!* Between the 23rd and 25th, the English Admirals, from apprehensions respecting the weather, and in order to refit, having to withdraw for a time, on their unexpected disappearance, the *Compagnie des Indes*, and a sloop in the road of Pondicherry, were directed to turn this lucky absenteeism to account; or be ready to set sail by the 30th, in order to obtain provisions, partly from the Danish settlement at Tranquebar, and partly by intercepting some of the native grain-boats; which, at that season, came down, with wind and tide in their favour, from north to south, mostly keeping in sight of

* Lally's son (most probably from prudential considerations) is rather concise, in merely referring to his father, as "plus haï à chaque mesure que lui imposait le salut de la ville; menacé d'assassinat le 7 Octobre; atteint de poison le 8."

the shore. At sea, towards which, from the prevention, by the great rains, of any land-operations of consequence, the chief attention of both sides continued to be directed, the English armed boats, November 7th, captured 1 boat from Tranquebar, with grain for Pondicherry, and another, freighted thence, with effects of value. Then, learning that the *Compagnie des Indes*, a schooner, and several smaller vessels, were taking in provisions at Tranquebar for Pondicherry, the enemy despatched 2 men-of-war to seize them; which 2, with the *Salisbury* of 50 guns, already at Tranquebar, obliged, on the 8th, the *Compagnie des Indes* to strike; the schooner, laden with 400 bags of wheat, and some barrels of salted meat, running ashore; and the rest having to disperse, and escape, as well as they could. "The news of this loss," we are told, "was received at Pondicherry, with as much concern as a disaster in the field."

The 9th, a ricochet-battery of 4 eighteen-pounders, planted by Coote amidst the ruins of a village, 1400 yards to the north, to harass the garrison of Pondicherry by a plunging fire against the east side of the town, was hotly answered by 12 pieces of cannon from the place; and the battery, proving ineffective, had eventually to be broken up. The 10th, according to the preparations which had been made at Madras for converting the blockade into a regular attack on Pondicherry, the English began to land stores, and otherwise arrange for pressing the siege with vigour. The 12th, information being received, that a convoy of 24 European and 100 Black horse, escorting 100 bullocks laden with salted beef, besides a parcel of the same at the croup of each rider's saddle, designed to enter Pondicherry by night, Coote, in consequence of those horsemen losing time by attempting to augment their stock with 300 bullocks met on the way, had the party intercepted, near the Fort of Ariancopang, on the 13th, at 4 in the morning, by a stronger detachment of 240 horse and foot; but 12 European horsemen of the defeated escort escaping into Pondicherry, by the ferry, under the guns of Fort St. Thomas. On the 16th a vessel, the *Admiral Watson*, of 500 tons, came from Madras, with all kinds of supplies on board, in furtherance of the measures for closer operations, mentioned as commenced by Coote on the 10th; and on the 18th, Mr. Call, the Chief Engineer, reached the besieging camp, to conduct the trenches. To protract the means of subsistence at Pondicherry, too much lessened by the grain which the cavalry-horses consumed there, and turn to better account some of his best troopers, by sending them to join 1 of the 2 divisions of his forces, that, from Thiagar and Gingee, yet in their possession, at once subsisted themselves, and gave employment to the enemies' parties in the interior of the country, Lally, on the 21st, ordered 50 of his horsemen to make a dash through the besiegers' lines; and, at 2 in the morning, protected by the fire of 200 grenadiers, they thus escaped, with the exception of 13, who were captured, from the inability of their horses to keep pace with the others. The heavy rains ceasing by the 26th, Coote, in order to harass the defenders of Pondicherry, by rendering the garrison duty as fatiguing as possible, directed 4 batteries to be raised in such positions, that the shot from them might enfilade the works of the place; at the same time that the men and guns of those batteries might not be exposed to any certain or effective fire from the town. Since the frustrated attempt of the last convoy to enter the place, the blockade was most vigilant, or strict, by land; while, at sea, several armed boats, with arrack and salted provisions for the besieged, were intercepted by the English. On the 27th, the proportionably increasing distress obliging Lally to attend no longer to anything but the stern dictates of necessity, he caused all the Blacks in the town, amounting to about 1400, to be turned out, except a few, who were domestics to the principal inhabitants; and he had to put the soldiery upon an allowance of only a pound of rice a day, with a little meat at intervals.

At the beginning of December, the General was compelled to resort to the stronger measure of ordering every house in the town to be searched for provisions; that whatever should seem superfluous under the circumstances might be brought to the citadel, to be equally divided between the garrison and inhabitants. The search was to include, and commence with, the General's own residence, that others might, if possible, have no grounds for complaining of a regulation, from which *he* did not claim any exemption. It was pretended, however, that those charged with, the execution of this unwelcome task, did not act with sufficient discretion, in reference to officers of distinction. The ill-disposed exclaimed against what they termed the *tyranny* to which they were subjected! M. Dubois, as Intendant of the Army, the leading enforcer of this order, was specially held up to general execration. "When conquering enemies command a search of the kind," remarks Voltaire, "nobody dares to murmur; when the General ordered it, to save the city, all rose up against him." At the head of this impudent clamour were 2 aristocratic Colonels. These military *exquisites*, according to my British authority, "lately arrived from France, men of family, deemed the search in *their* apartments an affront,* and sent word to Mr. Lally, that they would no longer act as officers, but, on every occasion, as Volunteers. But," it is added, "the event justified the severity." As an illustrious ruler writes—

"When tempests rise, and blacken on the view,
To steer the bark is *all* that's left to do:
Tho' Envy hiss, and loud Resentment swell,
Be their's to *rage*, and our's to *govern* well."
FREDERIC THE GREAT.

On the 2nd and 3rd, 2 vessels, a sloop and a pinnace, which remained at Pondicherry, were despatched for Tranquebar. Of these, the pinnace was eventually taken, though not till after she and her companion accomplished their primary task of landing there from Pondicherry 100 infantry, whom Lally sent away, to lessen the consumption of his provisions, and contribute to the accomplishment of another design, he had for some time in contemplation. Relying but little *himself* on the too dubious assurances he had received of a relief by sea, though, from policy, of course, not discouraging the expectation, in *others*, of such aid; and, at any rate, determined upon defending himself so long, that, should a naval relief appear, it would find him, if possible, still holding out to profit by it; he had been for some months in correspondence with a Mahratta potentate, Vizvazypunt, to prevail on him, with his own numerous force, to join the French troops still abroad, or about Gingee and Thiagar, and thus united, compel the English to raise the siege of Pondicherry. Of the French so detached, or not shut up in Pondicherry,

* As if subordinate officers could *ever* be justified in resenting, as an *affront*, what their General might order for the public good, and submit to *himself*, before requiring *them* to do so!

those "assembled at Thiagar," says my English account, "were so much superior to the little posts around, that they became the terror of the country, and their smallest parties brought in provisions in plenty, and without risque." With this force at Thiagar was Major Luke Allen, of the old family of St. Woolstan's, in the County of Kildare. The son of a mother who had 21 children, he passed into France in 1735 to enter the Irish Brigade; rose to be a Major in the Irish Regiment of Bulkeley and a Chevalier of St. Louis; then served with the same rank in the Regiment of Lally; was likewise nominated an Aide-Major-General to the army for India in 1757; and particularly signalized himself there in escalading the Fort of Sarzamalour, by forcing his way into it, accompanied only by 1 officer and 20 soldiers of the Regiment of Lorrain. On the night of December 3rd, taking with him all the cavalry at Thiagar, the Major posted himself in the hills westward of Trinomalee, with the view of joining Vizvazypunt in marching for Pondicherry, should the pending treaty for that purpose be concluded with him; and, a few days after, these cavalry, uniting with the 100 European infantry last landed from Pondicherry at Tranquebar, and acting as a guard to the Envoy from Lally, empowered to conclude the negociation for the relief of Pondicherry, the Envoy, thus doubly protected by horse and foot, succeeded in reaching the Mahratta's camp.

The 4 batteries, which Coote, since November 26th, had ordered to be constructed, were ready for service by December 8th. The 1st, or Prince of Wales's, of 4 guns, was from the beach on the north, to enfilade the great street, running north and south, through what was called the *white town* of Pondicherry; the 2nd, or Duke of Cumberland's, of 4 guns and 2 mortars, was, from the north-west, to enfilade the north face of a large counterguard before the north-west bastion; the 3rd, or Prince Edward's, for 2 guns to the southward, was to enfilade the streets from south to north, so as to cross the fire from the northern battery; the 4th, or Prince William's, of 2 guns and 1 mortar, to the south-west, was to destroy the guns in St. Thomas's redoubt, and any vessel or boat near it. The 4 "opened at midnight, between the 8th and 9th, firing all of them at the same time, and in vollies, on the signal of a shell." On Coote's approaching, with 2 other officers, sufficiently close to the place to perceive the effect of this fire upon the besieged, he found, that dispositions suitable for the occasion had been made by Lally; the garrison on the alert, beating to arms without confusion, and everything being right along the bastions, while blue lights appeared in different parts of the town. This fire of cannon and mortars, with cessations at uncertain periods, was kept up through the rest of the month by Coote, and answered with corresponding vivacity by Lally. The loss of the besiegers, as well as the besieged, in killed or wounded by the artillery, was but small; the former, however, not the less attaining the object " of wasting the garrison with fatigue, which their scanty allowance of provisions little enabled them to endure." For, though some supplies of food were able to run the blockade, or enter the place by sea during the month, yet, by the end of it, the stock in the public magazine, even scanty as the allowance was for each person, would not suffice for above 3 days; it being further ascertained, that no search could procure what would suffice beyond 15 days more. And to such a low scale was the later subsistence of the garrison brought, that, according to Voltaire, "the officer was reduced to a half-pound of rice a day, the soldier to 4 ounces." Lally, as "General, had 2 rations, and 2 little loaves," respecting which it is added, that "a poor woman, burthened with children, having appealed to him for assistance, he ordered that, every day, the half of what was reserved for himself should be given to her." Thus any objection which might be directed against him by the malice of disaffection, on the ground that *he* might well persist in defending the place so long, as having a double portion of food compared with *others*, was forestalled, since he reserved but half for himself; and he acted, at the same time, in a meritorious or charitable manner, by daily allotting the other half, to sustain the poor woman and children. That malice of disaffection, referred to, as but too corruptly anxious for a surrender, is duly admitted, even by a French contemporary writer adverse to Lally; who, in mentioning, how "he had been sent to India by the Company, as much to defend them against their *domestic*, as their *foreign*, enemies," observes, "the first were their most devoted servants, who, *enriched by their spoils, and having nothing more to gain from the distress to which they had reduced them, were inwardly desirous of falling into the hands of the English; in order to cover their particular depredations, under the general system of pillage, which always attends conquest.*" On the 29th, for closer or more decisive operations against the defences than those of the 4 batteries previously specified, which were erected at from 1000 to 1200 yards distance of the town—a new battery, called the Hanover, of 10 guns and 3 mortars, was commenced to the north, at 450 yards from the walls, against the north-west counterguard and curtain of the place. During the remainder of the month, communications reached Lally from his agents with Vizvazypunt, expressing hopes of success in the negociation with that potentate for raising the siege; and it was even reported in the English camp, that a large Mahratta force, with all the French cavalry, were actually on the march to Thiagar, "whence they intended, at all events, to push, with provisions, to Pondicherry."

The year 1760 ended, and the year 1761 commenced, around Pondicherry, amidst a terrible storm of wind and rain, which raged, with corresponding effects on sea and land, from 8 in the evening of December 31st, to between 3 and 4 in the morning of January 1st. The English blockading squadron, then consisting of 8 ships of the line, 2 frigates, a fire-ship, and a store-vessel from Madras, in all 12 sail, were generally dispersed, shattered, or run aground; 3 being sent to the bottom, with 1100 men. Allowing for the difference between the 2 elements, the ravages of the tempest by land were proportioned to the destruction by sea. Having noted how all the temporary barracks of the besiegers' camp and its outposts were swept away, and the ammunition abroad for immediate service ruined, nothing, except under masonry (as the principal store of gunpowder was) being undamaged, my British historian adds—"The soldiers, unable to carry off their muskets, and resist the storm, had left them to the ground, and were driven to seek shelter wherever it was to be found. Many of the Black attendants of the camp, from the natural feebleness of their constitution, perished by the inclemency of the hour. The sea had everywhere broken over the beach, and overflowed the country as far as the bound-hedge; and all the batteries and redoubts which the army had raised were intirely ruined." On the other hand, "the town of Pondicherry beheld the storm, and its effects, as a deliverance sent from Heaven. The sun rose clear, and shewed the havoc spread around. It was proposed by some, to march out immediately, and attack the English army; but this operation was impracticable; because no artillery could move through the inundation, nor could the troops carry their own ammunition dry; otherwise 300 men, properly armed, would not, for 3 hours after day-light, have met with 100 together, in a condition to resist them." Now, or "in the interval before the English ships in the road were repaired, or others joined them from the sea," might a naval relief have securely entered the harbour with supplies, and saved the place, "even in the 11th hour." But no such relief appeared. To profit, nevertheless, to the utmost in *his* power, by such a disaster as this tempest was to the enemy, Lally, on the 2nd, hurried away letters to the French Residents at Tranquebar, Puliacate, and Negapatam; urging them, in the most pressing terms, to avail themselves of the opportunity, afforded by the dispersion of the English fleet, to forward him provisions. To effect this the more readily, he wrote, "offer great rewards. I expect 17,000 Morattoes within these 4 days. In short, risk all, attempt all, force all, and send us some rice, should it be but half a garse at a time."

But the superior resources, and characteristic energy of the English, in naval matters, so soon repaired the damage inflicted by sea, that, "in a week after the storm, which had raised such hopes of deliverance in the garrison of Pondicherry," the blockade of the harbour was resumed, by Rear-Admiral Steevens, with 11 sail of the line, and 2 frigates; whose "boats, continually cruizing, intercepted, or drove away, whatsoever embarkations came towards the road, with provisions." After using every diligence to restore the various works and stations of his lines and encampment to the condition they were in before the hurricane; the more so, as the menacing reports continued with respect to the Mahrattas, who, if such repairs were not made, would have the best opportunity of provisioning the town; Coote resolved, on the 5th, to endeavour to surprise St. Thomas's redoubt, furnished with 4 twenty-four pounders, and the only outpost of consequence still retained by Lally. That redoubt stood in reference to the assailants on the opposite side of a channel connected with the river which supplied water to the ditches of the town. "After it was dark," says my English account, "a French officer, with 3 troops of his nation, who had taken service in the English army, crossed first, whilst Colonel Coote himself, with the rest of the detachment, halted on the nether side of the channel. The officer was challenged, and answered, that he came from the town with a party, which Lally had sent off in haste, on intelligence that the English intended to attack the redoubt this very night. He was believed and admitted; and Colonel Coote, hearing no bustle, or firing, immediately sent over the front of his party, who, as soon as their numbers were sufficient, declared themselves, and threatened to put the whole guard to death, if a single man made the least noise, or attempted to escape. All obeyed, excepting 1 Caffre, who stole away unperceived. They consisted of 1 Serjeant, 5 gunners, 5 Caffres, and some Sepoys." Notwithstanding that the alarm was given at Pondicherry, (no doubt by the Caffre who escaped) upon which blue lights appeared there at 1 in the morning, as if in expectation of an attack, and a well-aimed fire of single shot was also directed thence at the captured post, from 2 to 4 all seeming quiet, the place was secured with suitable works; and left by Coote in the custody of a Lieutenant of Artillery, who, with 40 Europeans, and as many Sepoys as made his party 170 in number, had orders to defend himself to the last. Lally, however, to give the enemy a parting blow there, ordered the veteran Alexander Mac Geoghegan, (who had beaten Brereton at Wandewash) to recapture the surprised post with 2 companies of grenadiers, supported by volunteers from the garrison of Pondicherry. Advancing through water breast-high, the Irish officer and his men reached the fort at 5 o'clock, and assaulting it, according to the English, "on every side at once, few fired, and all pushed, with fixed bayonets, through the ditch, over the parapet. The resistance was not equal, either to the strength of the post, for it was closed on all sides, or to the number of the guard, which were, including the Sepoys, 170 men. Some escaped, by jumping over the parapet; a few were killed; and the greatest part, with the officer, surrendered themselves prisoners.* At noon, Lally sent back all who had been taken to the English camp, for want of provisions to feed them; but on condition, that they should not act again. This discovery of the distress of the garrison could only be required or warranted by the utmost necessity." From the 6th to the 9th, the besiegers worked at a commanding redoubt, on a spit of sand, to mount 16 guns and contain 400 men; and laboured to complete the Hanover battery, which the artillery from the town strove to interrupt, though with little effect; and supplies of siege-cannon, ammunition, and stores, to replace recent losses by the storm, were forwarded by sea from Madras. By the 9th, too, information reached the English, which freed them from any further alarm with respect to Vizvazypunt, and his Mahrattas; that potentate, on being offered so much better terms for agreeing to leave Pondicherry to its fate, than the French could offer to induce him to aid them, having definitively declared, they were to expect nothing from him. Upon this, Major Allen, and his 200 European horse, and 100 foot, quitted the Mahratta camp, and a return to Pondicherry being *then* impossible, marched away to enter the service of Hyder Ali at Bangalore; the Major, with his companions in arms, being thus the only portion of the French force in India enabled by circumstances to act on the principle of "no surrender."† And now, or from the 10th to the 15th, the combined fire of the Hanover and Royal batteries—including 21 cannon, of which 17 were 24, and 4 were 18, pounders, besides 6 mortars—added to the vigour of the besiegers in making their approaches, became as destructive to the defences, as exhausting to the defenders, of the town; where, in order to give the utmost time for the possible appearance of a relieving fleet, the wretchedly inadequate remains of the usual sources for subsistence were eked out by the consumption of camels, elephants, cats, and dogs; the flesh of 1 of the last-mentioned animals selling, in the extreme scarcity, for 16 rupees, or half-crowns, otherwise £2! For a resistance beyond the 15th, even of such food as *did* exist, there would be, in 2 days, NONE!

Meantime, the situation of him, who was charged with the preservation of all, bad as it had been *before* in the atmosphere of that comparative

* Of Alexander Mac Geoghegan, connected with this *last* success on the part of the garrison of Pondicherry, my manuscript memoir merely states, that "le Roi lui accorda, au commencement de l'année 1774, le brevet de Colonel, à Brive-la-Gaillarde."

† Memorandum on Luke Allen in the late John O'Connell's French MSS. on Irish Brigade, compared with Mr. Orme's history. There was a "Luke Allen" to the last, or 1792, an officer of the Irish Brigade, as a Lieutenant in the Regiment of Berwick.

"hell on earth" by which he was surrounded, became, as the siege drew to its termination, or for several weeks, more and more analogous to Milton's idea of the maddening extent of misery, presenting, as it were,

"In the *lowest* deep, a *lower* deep,
Still threat'ning to devour."

While, as regards the vastly-superior besieging force opposed to him, Lally might be deemed but too abundantly occupied in keeping a lion at bay outside the ramparts of Pondicherry, as regards his unprincipled official foes and their partizans, he might be considered to exist amidst so many scorpions within those ramparts. Even *his* naturally-vigorous constitution collapsed, beneath the intolerable amount of increasing trouble and bitter vexation imposed upon him. Confined, from December 4th, to his bed, by convulsions, and receiving there every day the unmanly or heartless annoyance of anonymous letters, threatening him with being despatched by the dagger or poison, and finally believing himself to be actually poisoned—for what, that was most demon-like, might *he* not believe, as worthy of such a Pandemonium?—he fell into epileptic fits. Nevertheless, upon the apprehension of an assault by the besiegers on the night of January 13th, he, although apparently in a dying state, issued a general call to arms, had himself carried out to the ramparts, distributed with his feeble hands whatever wine still remained to the worn-down soldiery there, and took his post at the breach, to meet, as he hoped, a glorious death; in which hope, he was only disappointed by the very sensible resolution of the enemy, not to waste blood in any attempt to storm a place, which, from want alone, should, as they knew, so soon surrender, without fighting.* By this time, writes Mill, he "urged the Council, since a capitulation must regard the civil, as well as the military, affairs of the colony, to concert *general* measures for obtaining the most favourable terms; and procured nothing but chicanery in return. The device of the Council was, to preserve to themselves, if possible, the appearance of having had *no* share in the unpopular transaction of surrender, and the advantage, dear to their resentments, of throwing, with ALL its weight, the blame upon Lally." To his 1st proposal, that they, as representing the civil power, should unite, with him and the military, to obtain the best conditions for the common interest, the answer of the Council was, a refusal to act, under the pretext, that this step, on his part, was premature. With a 2nd proposal from him, to the like effect, they also refused to comply; alleging that, since he had dissolved them as a body, they were then nothing. To which impudent lie the General truly replied, that he had *not* so dissolved them, having only forbidden them to assemble again, without his permission; and adding, that he *therefore* commanded them, in the King's name, to assemble, in order that a mixed council might be formed, with a view to ascertain the means of making the best of existing circumstances for themselves, and the colony at large. To this they rejoined, by casting upon him the *whole* responsibility of arranging matters with Colonel Coote. Lally then called a Council of War, composed of all the leading officers still capable of serving; who agreed upon surrendering, though without being able to agree upon what conditions they should surrender. Consequently, in the evening of the 15th, a Colonel of Artillery, on the part of the military in the place,

* For these and other particulars respecting Lally, I am indebted to Voltaire, and Lally's son.

or the troops of the King of France, and of the French East India Company, was despatched by the General to Coote, with whom it was settled, that the garrison of Pondicherry, as in such want of provisions, should, in the course of the 2 ensuing days, surrender, as prisoners of war, together with the town and citadel, to his Britannic Majesty. The refractory Council necessarily left to negociate *separately* for such terms as more immediately concerned themselves, and those connected with their interests, were deservedly snubbed, through their envoy, by Coote; in being merely referred by him to the substance of his agreement with the military, that surrendered "to be at *his* discretion, which," it was added, "should *not* be deficient in humanity."

Thus the fate of Pondicherry was not decided until 51 weeks after the defeat of Wandewash in the preceding January, though, of the state of affairs, on Lally's side, after *that* defeat, we are told, how "tout fut désespéré alors!"—an assertion sufficiently indicating the merit of the subsequent contest, so long maintained against a coexistence of internal and external hostility, as calculated to discourage hope, as to paralyze exertion. Having premised, how, on the morning of the 16th, pursuant to the arrangements made between the besiegers and the besieged, the grenadiers of Coote's regiment marched from the camp, and took possession of the Valdore gate of Pondicherry, &c., Orme adds—"In the afternoon, the garrison drew up under arms, on the parade before the citadel, and the English troops facing them. Colonel Coote then reviewed the line, which, exclusive of commissioned officers, invalids, and others who had hid themselves, amounted to 1100, all wearing the face of famine, fatigue, or disease.* *The grenadiers of Lorrain and Lally, once the ablest-bodied men in the army, appeared the most impaired, having constantly put themselves forward to every service; and it was recollected, that, from their first landing, throughout all the services of the field, and all the distresses of the blockade, not a man of them had ever deserted to the English army.* The victor soldier gave his sigh (which none but banditti could refuse,) to this solemn contemplation of the fate of war, which *might* have been their own. . . . The next morning," 17th, "the English flag was hoisted in the town, and its display was received by the salute of 1000 pieces of cannon, from every gun of every ship in the road, in all the English posts and batteries, the field-artillery of the line, and on the ramparts and defences of Pondicherry. The surrender," concludes Orme, "was inevitable; for, at the scanty rate of the wretched provisions to which the garrison had, for some time, been reduced, there did not remain sufficient to supply them 2 days more." The artillery in the town amounted to some hundred pieces, with a proportionably large supply of other military *materiel*.

The departure of Lally from Pondicherry for Madras, on the 18th, "was," says an Irish officer in the English service, "accompanied with *scenes and acts more disgraceful to the vanquished, than their conquerors, or worst enemies, could have desired.*" Nor can anything be more just than this statement of the scandalous conduct referred to, "aw'd by no law, by no respect controll'd;" yet merely a sample of that torrent of shameless licentiousness, the general foulness of whose current should

* My French authority, after stating, how Coote "avait une armée de 15,000 hommes, et une flotte qui en renfermait 7000 autres," asserts of Lally, that "700 hommes composaient toutes ses forces," in a most miserable condition, while he "n'avait pas un esquif à opposer à 14 vaisseaux de ligne!"

only be deemed worthy of the deep pollution of its source. Members of the Council, subordinate *employés* of the Company, and officers of its troops, or the partizan "Bataillon de l'Inde"—all combined in animosity against the General on account of his hostility to corruption, to neglect of duty, and the consequent severity of his reproofs, which they resented as insults, whereas, if he had been the man they represented, he would have inflicted not severity of *reproof*, but severity of *punishment*—from an early hour of the day, assembled, along with such as they could delude, or persuade, that *he* was the sole cause of the present calamity; and they resolved to refrain from no outrage at his expense, if not even to make an attempt by open force upon his life, which, though previously menaced with, had escaped destruction by, *poison*. The *employés* "opened the ball" of outrage and sedition by posting up inflammatory placards against him, breaking the windows of his residence, and uproariously designating him traitor and villain. Before noon, a troop of officers, mostly of the factious corps above-mentioned, audaciously ascended the steps of the Government-House in the direction of the General's apartments, and, on meeting his Aide-de-Camp, proceeded to insult him, but were driven away by the guard, who luckily came up in time. The troop, then reassembling, waited below at the gate of the citadel, till 1 o'clock. The great object, however, of their rebellious hatred did not come forth, for his journey to Madras, until late in the day. He then appeared, borne, as he was very ill, in a palanquin, accompanied by 4 faithful troopers of his guard, and followed, at some distance, by 15 trusty English hussars, whom he obtained, and, as the event showed, was but too well justified in having obtained, from Coote, as an escort. There were about the gate, with the worst intentions, 100 villains, generally officers of the battalion before specified, headed by 2 Members of the Council, Moracin and Courtin—1 of whom was afterwards admitted to be a witness against, or accuser of, the General, at Paris! As soon as Lally was seen, a universal outcry, accompanied by the most violent gestures, hisses, and every sort of abusive name, was raised against him; and so alarmingly was even his palanquin approached, with exclamations of insolence, and menaces of death, that the English officer—who, at such a disgusting spectacle, might have congratulated himself on *not* being a Frenchman!—asked permission, from the sick man, to charge the rascals. But Lally, contented with presenting, in each of his feeble hands, a loaded pistol, had the generosity to spare the lives of those desirous of taking his; and, merely directing his escort not to interrupt their march, thus fortunately passed uninjured through the midst of the nefarious gang, letting

"The scattering dogs around at distance bay." *

POPE'S HOMER'S Odyssey, xiv., 40.

Not having murdered their General and Viceroy, or representative of their King, in the person of Lally, those wretches compensated themselves for that failure, by better success against another officer of rank and probity. Their victim was M. Dubois, likewise, as we have seen, obnoxious to them, for fulfilling the duties of his station honestly, or without respect to persons, as regards the search for provisions during

* In addition to the particulars, respecting Lally's departure, from other authority, he himself mentions, in a letter, how he was "attacked, coming out of the Fort of Pondicherry, and should have been murdered, if the English guard, that escorted him, had arrived a minute later!"

the siege; and still more obnoxious, or dreaded, from his having not only expressed his disapprobation in writing upon every questionable act of the corrupt administration at Pondicherry, and its representatives, since he came there, but from his having preserved those numerous writings, or documents; which, if not destroyed, would be productive of very unpleasant consequences in France to the officials thereby criminated, for their various misdeeds in India. Dubois, as long past the period for effective field-service, or, at this time, 70 years of age, had been appointed Intendant, or Commissioner of the King, to Lally's force, and, as short-sighted, always wore spectacles. He quitted the Fort, where he was quartered, on foot, not long after Lally, in order to follow him to Madras; when he was assailed with such noisy and violent demonstrations of mutinous malignity, as those which had been directed against Lally. The veteran Intendant, though unhappily without any escort, or guard, among those villains, yet, with a high spirit, more suited to the boiling vigour of youth, than to the weakness of unprotected age, stopped at this disgraceful uproar, and, facing his insulters, indignantly exclaimed, that, for his conduct *he* was ready to answer to *any* one!—upon which, a ruffian, named Defer, stepped out from the crowd, both drew, and, at the 2nd pass, poor old Dubois was left dead on the spot!

"A generous foe regards, with pitying eye,
The man, whom fate has laid, where all must lie."
DR. JOHNSON.

But such was *not* the case here. The body of the unfortunate "homme du Roi" (in seditious language) was stripped and pillaged; and his death, "violent and iniquitous as it was," being "treated as a meritorious act," there was "no one would assist his servants to remove and bury the corpse," which was at last interred in a garden. Of his writings, which, according to the Satanic maxim of "evil be thou my good," were, for *good* reasons, pounced upon, at his residence, immediately after his fall, "it was known," observes my authority, "that he had, ever since his arrival in Pondicherry, composed protests, on the part of the King, against all the disorders and irregularities which came to his knowledge in any of the departments of the government, and the collection was very voluminous; but," it is added, "none of his papers have ever appeared." Of course not, or what would have been the *use* of first murdering *him*, and then making away with *them?* On this occasion, as elsewhere, it is but too plain, in the expressive language of Scripture, that "men loved darkness rather than light, because their deeds were evil. For every one that doeth evil hateth the light, neither cometh to the light, lest his deeds should be reproved." (John iii. 19-20.) The mutineers next gained access to the chests and trunks of Lally, which, as having *no* object for concealment, he had left behind him at Pondicherry; and they then overhauled them, in order to detect what treasures in gold, diamonds, and bills of exchange, he was *accused* of having amassed, by those who judged of him from themselves; or who would have been so very careful to butter *their* toast on BOTH sides by peculation, or plunder, if in *his* place. Their labours, however, in turning over his baggage, terminated, to their disappointment and vexation, merely in "a mare's nest!" Nothing was gotten beyond a small quantity of plate, clothing, or household stuff, and papers of no consequence; which effects were not obtained by Lally from the English custom-house, till he discharged the debts, contracted in his name, for the defence of Pondicherry.

Pursuant to the directions from Europe to Lally, intercepted at sea, that he should destroy such English settlements as he might capture, the English now resolved to repay the French in their own coin, by demolishing Pondicherry—of which, as a Sodom, it will be recollected, that Lally had predicted the destruction by the English, if not by Heaven! The gentleman appointed Governor of the place until it should be demolished, M. Dupré, a Member of the Council of Madras, appears to have been the grandson of one of those French Protestants whom the intolerant Revocation of the Edict of Nantes obliged to become exiles from their country, and serve foreigners against her. Louis XIV., notes Voltaire, little thought that the metropolis of his East India Company would be destroyed, under *such* superintendence!* After the fall of Pondicherry, the only 2 places of strength still held by the French in India were Thiagar and Gingee; by whose reduction, in February and April following, the ascendancy of England, as a European power, was established in Hindostan.

The causes of this issue of the contest there between England and France, without a general survey of which, the merit of Lally, in supporting such a long though unequal struggle as he *did*, cannot be duly estimated, have been thus stated, and, as compared with French admissions, not unfairly stated, by a gentleman in the late English East India Company's service, and since in that of Great Britain and Ireland. "It was," writes Dr. O'Callaghan, "the patriotism, energy, and disinterestedness of the" English East India "Company at home, and their servants in India, which brought the contest to its triumphant conclusion; supporting, throughout the struggle, our brave commanders and soldiers in the field, at every sacrifice, risk, or loss; and it was the want of these virtues, in our opponents, that mainly conduced to their defeat and ruin. Almost throughout the entire war, the Council Chamber at Pondicherry was distracted by quarrels, mutual hatred, recrimination, and distrust; and, at the time that the French and their cause were becoming odious, from the means to which their armies were obliged to have recourse, to support themselves, and keep the field, *men, in high place and confidence, were dishonestly accumulating great fortunes, by the sacrifice of the public interests and weal.* With the interests of the English committed to their hands, how different was the conduct of the Council at Madras, and the officers of all ranks employed under their command! Firmness, unanimity, harmony, self-devotion, and a desire to sacrifice every personal consideration or emolument for their country's good, animated their councils, and directed their operations; and, at times when every available rupee, either public or private, was being despatched to support the soldiers, and meet the exigencies of the war, the Company's civil servants and functionaries cheerfully and willingly remained in straitened circumstances, and with long arrears of pay due to them from an empty treasury. Hence it was, that the English Commanders were enabled to maintain discipline, and justice towards the natives, procure their willing aid on all occasions, pay for what they wanted, and, even when they had not the means to do so, obtained for promises what the French could not obtain by violence.†

---

* "The fortifications were demolished," alleges another French contemporary respecting Pondicherry, " and the plough was made to pass over this superb city, which hereafter exhibited nothing more than a heap of ruins." Yet, like Carthage and Corinth of old, it has been rebuilt.

† It would be very wrong, however, to consider the English to have been *all* so

. . . The French in India had been obliged, by the force of circumstances, to adopt the system of making war support war; which has so often proved ruinous to their cause, sullied the glory of their arms, and nullified the results of their victories. Neither the Monarchy, nor the French Company, was able, at this time, to meet the expenses and demands of hostilities in India; the former was fully occupied, with its own affairs, in Europe and the Canadas; the latter had never prepared itself, for a long, heavy, and continuous drain on its finances; having always looked upon its possessions in Hisdustan as a certain source of uninterrupted gain, which was to gush forth, and flow in a steady stream, at the stroke of the sword. The English Monarchy sent to the shores of the Coromandel a naval force, worthy of the British nation; and the Company, also strong in that arm, strained, to the highest pitch, their credit at home, and their resources abroad, to carry on their operations in the field, without inflicting, on the country, the losses and horrors, in addition to the unavoidable distresses, of war. These are the features of the contest, which, seconded by the genius and valour of the British Commanders and soldiers, account for its ultimate termination in their favour, after so many vicissitudes, and changes of fortune, on both sides."

The intelligence of the reduction of Pondicherry was received in London with feelings suitable to its importance. The public announcement of it on July 21st, after mentioning the arrival from the East Indies of Captains Hughes and Monckton with the accounts of the event, adds of the reception of such gratifying news by the young King George III., who had only ascended the throne in the preceding October—"The express reached the King, just as he was going to take his morning ride, which, on that account, he declined. At noon, there was a great Court on the occasion; and the Park and Tower guns were fired. At night there were bonfires, &c., and the East India House, in particular, was finely illuminated." What honour Ireland might claim on *both* sides of the contest, in the persons of Coote and Lally, was, of course, unmentioned in England. Yet how considerable was *that* honour! The best Anglo-Indian chronicler of that war notes of the battle of Wandewash in connexion with the merit of Coote, "he fought it with the inexplicit disapprobation of the Presidency in his pocket; but his dispositions had secured resources against mischance. *Before* this important success, the views of no one had extended to the reduction of Pondicherry; but, instantly *after*, all were possessed with the firmest persuasion of this termination of the war. This "fortunate confidence," he continues, "led to the most vigorous counsels,"—with consequences, I may add, corresponding to the poetical axiom, that

"They can conquer, who *believe* they can."
DRYDEN'S VIRGIL, Æneis, v., 300.

On the other hand, to the military energy and ability which so long delayed the accomplishment of *his* labours, Coote bears this high testimuch in the right, and the French *all* so much in the wrong, in India, as might be inferred *here*, if no native view of the English, when they got the upper hand in the Peninsula, were forthcoming, such as the Seer Mutakhareen, in which it is observed, and but too *truly* observed, of the latter—"*The people under their dominion groan everywhere, and are reduced to poverty and distress. O God! come to the assistance of thine afflicted servants, and deliver them from the oppressions they suffer!*" Our countryman Edmund Burke amply confirms this.

mony. "*Nobody has a higher idea than I have of General Lally, who, to my knowledge, has struggled against obstacles, which I believed unconquerable, and has conquered them;* nobody, at the same time, is more his enemy than I, as *seeing him achieve those triumphs to the prejudice of my nation*"—that is, the nation in whose service he was. "*There certainly is not*," concludes Coote, "*a second man, in all India, who could have managed to keep on foot, for so long a period, an army without pay, and without any kind of assistance.*" *

The treatment which Lally, as a prisoner, experienced from his enemies, first with respect to his removal from Pondicherry for Madras, and next with regard to his conveyance thence for England, was anything but in the spirit of *his* conduct towards his wounded and captured English opponents at Fontenoy; anything but indicative of such honourable feelings as would have suggested, that when hostility is carried beyond a certain point, or

"Against a yielded man, 'tis mean, ignoble strife."
DRYDEN'S VIRGIL, Æneis, xii., 1359.

Pigot, the Governor of Madras, whose power, as representing that of the English East India Company after the surrender of Pondicherry, was predominant there, refused the request of the sick General, that, in consideration of the circumstances to which he was reduced, he might be allowed to stay where he was for 4 days; in this refusal apparently

* The handsome and generous tribute of Coote to the merit of his opponent, Lally, is given by Lally's son in French, which I translate into *English*, not having seen *that*, in which, I suppose, Coote wrote. In my preceding account of Lally in India, as an officer of the Irish Brigade, I have necessarily avoided any details respecting naval warfare, operations in the Deccan, &c., where he and his regiment, or the Irish, were *not* immediately engaged; considering such details to be no better than so many "episodes," calculated to interfere with, or divert due attention from, the "main action" of *my* subject, though, of course, circumstances that should be fully described by historians of England, France, and India. In taking leave of Coote here, I may note of him, that, as Lieutenant-General Sir Eyre Coote, he, at his decease, April, 1783, in his 57th year, generally respected and lamented, was considered to have been, "perhaps, the ablest officer in the British army." He was Commander-in-Chief of the East India Company's Forces, Knight of the Bath, and Member of the Supreme Council of Bengal. Nor was he merely a soldier. Dr. Johnson, whom he invited to dinner in Scotland in 1773, mentions himself, and his companion, Mr. Boswell, to have been, on that occasion, "entertained by Sir Eyre Coote with such elegance of conversation, as left them no attention to the delicacies of his table." Having had no issue by his lady, daughter of Charles Hutchinson, Esq., Governor of St. Helena, whom he married in 1769, his property, nearly £200,000—his appointments having amounted to about £16,000 a year—was inherited by his brother, Dr. Charles Coote, Dean of Kilfenora, in Ireland. With reference to Sir Eyre's last victorious campaigns against the formidable Hyder Ali—though under such disadvantages in numbers, &c., opposed to Hyder, as Lucullus opposed to the myriads of Mithridates and Tigranes—Lord Macaulay alleges of the "glorious memory" of the Irish officer, among the Sepoys, even to our own day, or 1842—"Nor is he *yet* forgotten by them. Now and then, a white-bearded old Sepoy may still be found, who loves to talk of Porto-Novo, and Pollilore. It is but a short time since one of those aged men came to present a memorial to an English officer, who holds one of the highest employments in India. A print of Coote hung in the room. The veteran recognised at once that face and figure which he had not seen for more than half a century; and, forgetting his salam to the living, halted, drew himself up, lifted his hand, and, with solemn reverence, paid his obeisance to the dead!" In Anglo-Indian history, indeed, the fame of Coote, as the gainer of the Carnatic from Lally, and the regainer of it from Hyder Ali, will last. What opponent of *Clive*, by the way, could be compared either with Lally, or Hyder Ali?

actuated by the desire of revenge for a previous offence given to him in the General's correspondence, and for the General having paid some visits to Mrs. Pigot, after she absconded from the matrimonial roof. At Madras, the patient, from disease of body, aggravated by chagrin of mind, was barely convalescent on March 10th, in consequence of which, he requested his departure, on a voyage so long as that for England, might be postponed for 6 weeks. But he could no more obtain this favour at Madras, than that of the 4 days, for which he had applied at Pondicherry; and, on the 10th, says Voltaire, " they carried him by force into a merchant-vessel, the Captain of which treated him with inhumanity during the entire passage. He was granted no comfort beyond pork-broth. This English Captain believed," adds Voltaire, "that it was in this manner an Irishman in the service of France ought to be treated!" * As if, even apart from the respect due to the high rank Lally held, he, as having been born in France, and, so far, a Frenchman, was not entitled, by *every* law, to serve the government of the country in which he was born!—and, as if, even though a native of Ireland, he *could* be worthy of such infamous treatment, for being in the service of France, when excluded, by English law, from the service of England! Yet undepressed, it would seem, by such conduct towards him, as merely what was to be expected from a brute, incapable of any better, "it is remarkable," observes an English contemporary notice of Lally, "that, during the whole voyage, he was ever inquisitive, and eager after instructions; enquiring after the uses of every part of the vessel, even from the lowest sailor." Having arrived, September 20th, in the Downs, the General, on the 23rd, reached London. There he was informed of the storm already brewing against him in France; his unprincipled or lying enemies, as the best means of at once deluding the public, and exasperating it against him, having given out, that he had betrayed or sold Pondicherry to the English; while the late administrative body for the East India Company at Paris was changed; Bussy was strengthened by a matrimonial alliance with the family of the Premier, the Duke of Choiseul; and the Admiral D'Aché, who had left Pondicherry unrelieved, was likewise protected by high political influence.

Proportionably anxious to return to France, to bring his maligners to a suitable account there, Lally addressed the following letter to Mr. Pitt, (subsequently Earl of Chatham,) whose ability, as a Minister, in conducting the war of his country against France, had identified the flag of England with victory by sea and land all over the world.

"LONDON, *September 29th*, 1761.

"SIR,—Since my departure, now almost 5 years, from Europe, for the Asiatic climates, I am historically acquainted but with 2 men in this world, the King

* Lally writes, "Mr. Pigot refuses me, with the most unheard of violence, a stay of 6 weeks, which is necessary for the re-establishment of my health; and I am to be conducted on board, like a criminal, by a detachment of soldiers; having positively declared, by the annexed notice, that I will not depart otherwise." Pigot, the Governor of Madras, whose conduct thus appears so reprehensible, ended his life unhappily. Being, in 1776, as Lord Pigot, again Governor at Madras, he was audaciously deposed by a mutinous Council and Commander of the Forces there, and imprisoned upwards of 8 months; the mortification of which, and bad effects on his constitution, at his advanced period of life, caused his death, before an order for his release and restoration could come from Europe. In *this* confinement, did he ever think of NEMESIS, along with his own harshness towards *Lally?*

of Prussia and Mr. Pitt; the one by a series of distress, the other of success; the former snatching at fortune, the latter directing her. But, when I shall have seen and heard here of Mr. Pitt all I have already read of him, I shall always remember I am his prisoner, and liberty to me, though a Frenchman, is of an inestimable value; therefore I earnestly beg your interest, with his Majesty, to grant me leave to repair to my native soil, either upon my parole, or upon the terms of the cartel, in accepting my ransom. Nothing, but my sense of gratitude for this favour, can add to the high regard, with which I am, Sir, your Excellency's

"Most humble and most obedient servant,

"LALLY." *

In reply to this application, he received a permission, through the Admiralty, to return to France, on his parole of honour; and, having first taken care to repay whatever he had borrowed for the public service, he set out for that country, October 5th. On landing there, he, previous to pursuing his route for Paris, paid a visit to his old friend and brother Jacobite, Robert Mac Carthy, Earl of Clancarty, residing at Boulogne. "The Earl," says my account, "received him with great hospitality, and kept him 3 days for the purpose of persuading him to return to England, in order to save himself from the machinations of his enemies. Lally, however, was positive, and would go on; he relied on his services and integrity; and could not bear the imputation of guilt, which would attach to him, by his residence in England. 'Their malice,' said he, 'can but cashier me at the worst.' When the carriage was ordered on the 4th day, in order to proceed on his journey, the Earl followed him to the door of it, and again renewed his entreaties not to go on. He even brought out a bottle of Burgundy, which they drank together at the side of the carriage, to prolong the time, in the hope of some moment of conviviality producing a favourable effect—but in vain. At last they shook hands and parted; with a promise, from Lally, of again visiting him, in the course of the ensuing summer. To this the Earl shook his head, and, in his strong, energetic manner exclaimed— 'Never, my friend; you and I are doomed never to meet again, but in another world'"—and, it is added, "the event justified the Earl's prediction." He but too clearly saw

"Coming events cast their shadows before."—CAMPBELL.

Lally, on reaching Paris, presented himself to the Government, to denounce, as an officer of the Crown, the misdeeds of his subordinates; to offer personal proof of what he alleged on that head; and to abide by the result of what accusations might be directed against himself. The Duke of Choiseul, Minister of War and of Foreign Affairs, answered, that justice should be done him. Yet, as a veteran politician, and as also recently connected by marriage with Bussy, the Duke wished that the existing contest, instead of being permitted to go any further, should be compromised, through a reconciliation of the General with Bussy; and public advances, for a like object, were made, in full court, at Versailles, by the Admiral D'Aché to Lally. But Lally, who believed himself to be as much in the right as his adversaries were in the wrong, was, like Achilles of old, unmoved by any overtures of the kind; the contest had thus to proceed on the terms marked by Bussy when he said, "Either Lally's head must fall or mine;" and things were *then* apparently so

* Chatham Correspondence. Had it been Lally's "better destiny" to serve under Mr. Pitt, they were just the men to have *understood* one another.

settled, or put into such a train by the hand of power, that Bussy's head should be the safer of the 2!* For a year, during which Lally was promised justice by the Government, silence was imposed upon *him;* while, on the other hand, a petition and memorial against him were privately gotten up by the late Governor and Council of Pondicherry, and a multitude of writings from members of the same party were likewise circulated in Paris, to prejudice or poison public opinion the more effectually with respect to him, from whom no reply could proceed, since he was officially muzzled. The hostile petition and memorial having been presented, August 3rd, 1762, in the highest quarter, Lally, on learning, after some time, how injurious were the effects, at court and elsewhere, of those documents to his character, and unable to endure any longer such very unfair or one-sided treatment as he had been subjected to, repaired to Fontainebleau on the subject, when—matters being *now* evidently arranged for duly "turning the tables against him"—he met with no more satisfaction for his pains, than to be told, "It was in agitation to commit him to the Bastille!" He, however, was too firmly convinced of the justice of *his* cause, and had too much of the "gens flecti nescia," about him, to be thus intimidated. Previous to this, 1 of the agents of his enemies had offered to reveal to him all their intrigues, but he refused, with contempt, to avail himself of that offer; and, respecting the last attempt to overawe him by a threat of the Bastille, he addressed the following characteristic or uncompromising letter, November 3rd, to the Duke of Choiseul:—

"MY LORD,—The rumours, which prevail in Paris, have brought me here. My enemies will never be able to terrify me, since I depend on my own innocence, and am sensible of your equity. The King is master of my liberty, but my honour is under the safeguard of the laws, of which he is the protector. I do not ask you, my Lord, who are my slanderers; I know them; but what their slanders are, that I may obviate them; and repel them with such proofs, as will cover the authors of them with shame. I have brought here my head and my innocence, and shall continue here to wait your orders.—I am," &c.

A *lettre-de-cachet* had, in fact, been signed, on November 1st, by the Duke of Choiseul, for committing the General to the Bastille; of which circumstance, he, through the Minister's friends, was informed, in order that he might make use of this information to escape. But, scorning not to "stand his ground" against this political manœuvring, at once to get rid of and ruin him—through first frightening him to fly, and next making flight to be a virtual proof of guilt,—he, by the above letter, manfully defied such double-dealing hostility to do its worst, and then acted in compliance with what he had stated in that letter, by voluntarily giving himself up on the 5th, to be confined in the Bastille.

He claimed, and rightfully claimed, that, as a General Officer, he should be tried by a board composed of those of the like military rank, who, and *not* civilians, would necessarily constitute the fittest tribunal for passing judgment on his conduct in command. But it was perceived, that a concession of this right would too clearly amount to an acquittal for him; while, with that additional advantage on his side, he would *then* be able to direct his attention to a suitable exposure and conviction of those,

* In reference to those overtures for a reconciliation rejected by Lally, his son states of him, "il n'était dans son caractère de fléchir, et il était dans sa destinée d'être victime." Or, as Goldsmith would say, he was "too fond of the right to pursue the expedient." Are not such the characters we *most* admire?

conspiring to destroy him. His demand for such a military trial was consequently evaded, and he remained in the Bastille during this and the ensuing year, (1762-3) ere his enemies could determine upon the plan by which they should begin with effect "to work their wantonness in form of law" against him. To the honour of Louis XV.'s prime mistress, and, to a corresponding extent, prime ministress, of the day, Madame de Pompadour, acting in co-operation with the Minister of Finances, M. Bertin, it seems evident, that, had she lived, the captive would have been "released from prison with glory, or, at least, with impunity"—as he deserved to be. By July, 1763, indeed, the Attorney-General brought forward charges against Lally "of extortions, oppressions, abuses of authority, and even of high treason!" Nevertheless, by subsequent royal letters patent of January, 1764, the fairest mode of proceeding, as that which should be followed with reference to the misfortunes of the East India Company, was intimated to be the institution of a comprehensive judicial inquiry, which, instead of being pointed against any person in particular connected with the Company, should have for its object an examination of *all* the crimes committed in India with regard to the administration and commerce of that body, previous to, as well as since, the sending of the troops there under Lally. Such an equitable inquiry, as singling out no special scape-goat on whose head the sins of others should be visited, but as designed to render any one who might be guilty only accountable for his own misdeeds, would have been ALL that Lally required; but was not, of course, what *they* required, who wanted to save themselves, by making *him* the scape-goat to be condemned for the results of the malpractices of others. And here his enemies, as, in the expressive language of the proverb, "the Devil's children, had the Devil's luck!" For Madame de Pompadour falling sick not long after, and dying in April, the nature of the inquiry to be held was then so unfairly altered or restricted, that it was merely to be directed against Lally,* as, forsooth, *the* great culprit, or others only as *his* accomplices, or adherents!

"This," writes even a hostile contemporary of Lally, "was an essential point gained by his enemies, who, by this contrivance, invalidated the information of abuses made by the General, and, from being accused, became thus the accusers. The reason of this was—that they were at liberty—that, being better acquainted than he with the use that could be made of the enormous sums they had either acquired or purloined, *they had distributed their gold with profusion*—in a word, that, being united in a powerful motive of personal defence, they formed a confederacy, not to be destroyed. It cannot otherwise be accounted for, that, among the *multitude* of dishonest servants of the India Company,—who, *most of them, returned immensely rich, when the Company itself was ruined*—who were, most of them, indicated to Count Lally, at his departure, by the administration in Europe, as prevaricators, in the memorial, containing interesting particulars upon the character and qualifications of the several persons, with this *clause* at the end of each article, *He does not forget himself there*—who were, most of them, acknowledged to be corrupt—who were informed against by the Chief, and denounced to that same Company for depredations, of which the Count pretended he had obtained proofs—it cannot otherwise, let us repeat, be accounted for, that, *among*

* "Till the period of Madame de Pompadour's death," according to Louis XV.'s biographer, "the Duke de Choiseul had only governed the King secondarily; but then he ruled over him entirely." And, consequently, so much the worse for Lally!

this multitude, not 1 man of them should have been punished—and that the *sword of justice should only have fallen upon him, before whose arrival those enormities existed, and who was sent to discover, and chastize them!"* Against this odious cabal for the impunity of guilt, and the punishment of innocence, Lally, who, we are told, "had never once anticipated the possibility of any other sentence than that of an honourable acquittal, defended himself with an ability and vigour of tongue and pen, that, while duly vindicating his own conduct, likewise "stung his foes to wrath," and would have triumphed over them, and their so-called "witnesses, as rogues," if he had been arraigned anywhere else, or before any tribunal bent upon administering justice, instead of *making* a victim for the executioner. From the vague and frivolous nature of the imputations brought against the accused—not 1 of them amounting to a crime, yet, by legal sophistry, argued, on the whole, to constitute him criminal! —he appears, upon a fair allowance for all the trying circumstances of his most unenviable position in India, to have only merited condemnation, by not having contrived to be, in the poet's words,

"A faultless monster, whom the world ne'er saw!"—BUCKINGHAM.

As Mr. Mill, (who cites the French documents of *both* sides on the subject) observes of the persecuted General—" Nothing whatsoever was proved, except that *his conduct did not come up to the very perfection of prudence and wisdom*, and that IT DID DISPLAY THE GREATEST ARDOUR IN THE SERVICE, THE GREATEST DISINTERESTEDNESS, FIDELITY, AND PERSEVERANCE, WITH NO COMMON SHARE OF MILITARY TALENT, AND OF MENTAL RESOURCES!"

His imprisonment of between 3 and 4 years in the Bastille was terminated, in May, 1766, by a sentence, to the effect, that "Thomas Arthur Lally should be decapitated, as duly attainted and convicted of having betrayed the interests of the King, the State, and the Company of the Indies, and of abuses of authority, vexations, and exactions upon the subjects of the King, and strangers resident in Pondicherry." As to the charge of having "betrayed the interests of the King, the State, and the Company," it was in no sense applicable. Within the bounds of fair hostility, Lally had always shown himself to be a most inveterate enemy of the English; he could not, as was mendaciously reported, have obtained money from the English for Pondicherry, a place they were so sure of reducing *gratis*, or merely by famine; and, had he made any bargain of the kind with them, he would as *certainly* have remained in England to enjoy the wages of such perfidy there in safety, instead of returning to France, as the American traitor Arnold afterwards remained in England, rather than return to America. If having "betrayed the interests" be taken in another sense, of pecuniary breach of trust or peculation, it does not appear how such a charge—although too applicable to others—could implicate Lally, since he was not intrusted with the custody of the King's or the Company's money. Under the vague objection of "abuses of authority, vexations," it was impossible, without more precise penal legislation, and corresponding criminatory proofs, than existed to affect him, that he could be capitally condemned, unless by such a system of absurdity, as would have exposed every Commander of an army, or Marshal, on being similarly arraigned before any court in France, to have his head taken off his shoulders! Lally, indeed, among the too numerous and too serious causes for loss of temper, by which he was alternately disgusted and

agonized in India, may have offended too many, even officers, by a severity of remark, and a deficiency of decorum or respect towards them; of which, before his nature was changed, we know, he was incapable elsewhere, or in Europe. Yet such "abuses of authority, vexations," could not be deemed worthy of the headsman's axe, unless by what many were impartial enough, even at the time, to consider a far greater "abuse of authority" on the part of the Parliament of Paris, in passing such a sentence.

> "Some faults must be, that his misfortunes drew,
> But such as may deserve compassion too."—BUCKINGHAM.

It is certain, that the officers, who were his severest accusers, in reference to those causes for personal offence, would have moderated the tone of their evidences against him, had they imagined, that what they stated *could* contribute to consign the unfortunate General to the scaffold! They would rather have made such allowances, for the *very* trying circumstances in which he was placed, as to excuse him. With respect to "exactions," Lally had not only never imposed the contribution even of a single penny at Pondicherry on the Council or inhabitants, but, while he subscribed largely from his own means to forward the public cause, he never troubled the Treasury of the Council for the payment of his appointments as General; postponing his demands on that score till his return to Paris—where his *reward* was calumny, imprisonment, and death!

If any circumstance could place in a specially damning light such at once shameless and cruel ingratitude towards him, it was this, which, more than anything else, eventually served to open the eyes of the public to the abominable injustice of his fate. A hypocritical portion of his nefarious sentence—"lugging in religion," as it were, "by the head and shoulders"—provided that, from his confiscated property, 100,000 crowns should be set apart for the *poor* of Pondicherry! It had been lyingly given out, that the fortune he had managed to amass was one of an enormous amount, and afterwards as lyingly reported, that the returns he had furnished of his means were falsified by the discovery of a large sum, which he had placed where he believed it would have escaped detection by the Government. The actual fortune, however, of the maligned and, murdered veteran was found to be so inconsiderable, that, when his debts were paid out of it, there would not remain 100,000 crowns for the *poor!*—although the infamous Council of Pondicherry had accused him of having realized a treasure of 17,000,000!!!* But, if *he* were not condemned, peculation should account and suffer for its evil gains abroad; ministerial culpability or want of success in the late most disastrous war should be without a victim, against whom to divert public discontent at home; or a sort of Jonas to cast overboard, that the state-vessel, instead of having to encounter a tempest too great for "the pilot to weather the storm," might proceed as required by the political steersman; and such a combination of interests, as so influential, was necessarily aided, to make sure of its prey, by lawyer-sophistry, the

---

* "Ce qui contribua le plus à rétablir sa mémoire dans le public," writes Voltaire, "c'est qu'en effet, après bien des recherches, on trouva qu'il n'avait laissé qu'une fortune médiocre! L'arrêt portait qu'on prendrait sur la confiscation de ses biens 100,000 écus pour les pauvres de Pondichéri. Il ne se trouva pas de quoi payer cette somme, dettes préalables acquittées; *et le Conseil de Pondichéri avait, dans ses requêtes, fait monter ses trésors à 17 millions.*"

too frequent prostitute to power, as presenting prospects of profit or promotion. "By one of those acts of imposture and villainy, of which," notes my well-informed authority, "the history of ministries, in all the countries of Europe, affords no lack of instances, it was resolved, to raise a screen between the Ministry and popular hatred, by the cruel and disgraceful destruction of Lally;" and, as to the co-operation needed from lawyers for the purpose, "the grand tribunal of the nation, the Parliament of Paris, found no difficulty in seconding the wishes of the Ministry, and the artificial cry of the day, by condemning him to an ignominious death."

Over the long and disgusting farce of the politico-legal formalities that were to terminate in such a melancholy tragedy, I pass to the more immediate preliminaries of the final catastrophe, and its heartless perpetration. For the interrogatories that were to precede his sentence, the prisoner was ordered to be removed, in the night between the 4th and 5th of May, 1766, from the Bastille to the prison called the Conciergerie; whence there was, by several flights of stairs, and through different halls, a communication with the great Court of Parliament. Though it was not more than 1 o'clock in the morning when he arrived, he would not go to bed. About 7, he was brought before his Judges, and soon found he might make up his mind for the worst. He was first divested of his honours, or commanded to give up his Grand Cross and Red Riband of the Order of St. Louis. This he did with such power over his feelings, as not to evince any apparent concern. He was next told, to seat himself upon a stool; an indication that the sentence to be passed upon him would at least involve corporal punishment. "He could not," says an enemy, "bear up against this decree of infamy." Covered with 14 scars, how hard was his destiny, to fall into the hands of the executioner!" Accordingly, "then, and not before, he discovered great emotion," uncovered his head, displaying the grey locks of age, bared his breast marked with the wounds of honour, and joining his hands, and looking upwards, as if appealing from earth to heaven, exclaimed— "*Here, then, is the reward of so many years' services!*" * The interrogatories to which he was subjected lasted 6 hours, during which, being greatly fatigued, he was allowed a glass of wine and water. From this examination, he was reconducted to prison. Next day, the 6th, to the surprise and horror of all not interested in such a decision, the sentence of condemnation (already set forth) was pronounced, with a reluctant deferring, by the Parliament, of execution till the 9th. A characteristic deputation from the same iniquitous tribunal to Louis XV. recommended the King to show no mercy, or, as they metaphorically expressed it, " to enchain his clemency!"—that shameless request being made, in order to frustrate the efforts, in Lally's favour, of his connexions and friends, who, in opposition to the meditated murder of the General, loudly demanded what they knew, that, on his behalf, they were so well entitled to demand, "not pardon, but justice!" The Parliament, with their other reasons (such as those *reasons* were!) for thus hounding Lally to death, had, it should be observed, a special motive for being intent on making *him* an example—namely, that, as in their contentions on several occasions with the Crown, a General Officer had been deputed to break up their refractory sittings, they, with proportionable irritation,

* For the "55 years" of one account, and the "45 years" of another, I substitute "*so many* years," as applicable to *either* period passed in the service.

and desire of revenge for such mortifying exercises of authority at their expense, were anxious to have satisfaction against some representative of the like military grade, and more particularly against Lally. Not that he appears to have been such an instrument of the Crown for dissolving them; but that the triumph for which they longed would, they conceived, be the greater, if obtained over him, since he was not only of the rank in the army obnoxious to them, but had also exercised viceregal sway; and thus the offending military and sovereign power would, as it were, be *both* rendered accountable for the past, in his person. In opposition, however, to this corporate spirit of persecution, so strong a feeling was excited in favour of Lally among those of his own profession, that, on the 8th, at the rising of the Council of State, the Marshal de Soubise threw himself upon his knees before the King, beseeching his Majesty to grant, " in the name of the army, at least the pardon of General Lally!" With the treacherous and hypocritical effrontery of a master-politician, the Premier, or Duke of Choiseul, as if *he* had no hand in the abominable treatment of Lally, followed the example of Soubise. Louis raised up the honest Marshal, and fixing his eyes pointedly on the double-dealing Duke, said to him—"It is *you* who have caused him to be arrested. It is too late. They have judged him. They have judged him." And, long after, his Majesty remarked, that such an execution was, indeed, a massacre, though it was *others* who were answerable for it, and not *he*—an attempt of the King to exculpate himself, which, however satisfactory *he* may have deemed it, seems anything but so to *us*.

The evening of this last ineffectual appeal to the Crown for mercy, the unfortunate Count was taken from the Bastille, as too honourable a place of confinement, to a jail for common criminals. Notwithstanding *that* sufficiently ominous removal, and his being aware of the decision against him, he is said to have still clung to the notion, that there would be *some* postponement of his fate. Next day, however, or the 9th, at noon, he was summoned to the chapel of the prison, there to learn, too surely, that he had now only to prepare for DEATH. The officer appointed to read his sentence to him, the attendants to take possession of his person for the executioner after the reading of that sentence, and a confessor, appeared before him. On hearing the unjust doom, he specially denounced, as utterly false, the allegation of his "having betrayed the interests of the King," and naturally devoted, in the strongest terms of indignant despair, the political and legal authors of his unmerited destruction to general execration here, and divine vengeance hereafter. Then, seeming to recover from this vehement outburst of passion, or become more collected in himself, and pacing to and fro for some time, while directing one hand, beneath his dress, towards his heart, and with the other seeking a pair of compasses he had been using for geographical purposes, he affected to kneel down as if to pray, and suddenly attempted to wound himself mortally with the compasses, which penetrated 4 inches, but without effecting his object; a movement he made in lowering himself having preserved the heart. He was, of course, not allowed to repeat the blow, and the blood-stained compasses were handed to the Confessor, the venerable Aubry, Curé of the Parish of St. Louis en l'Ile; who did his utmost to console the unhappy General, and bring him, from this state of distraction, to a different disposition of mind, or feelings of resignation and religion. Nor were those zealous efforts of the Priest without producing such satisfactory results, that, in the generous conflict of sentiment between the principles of his *classical* and *theological* education, the worthy man observed of the Count after his decease—" *He stabbed himself as a hero,* and *repented as a Christian!*" Meanwhile the rage of Lally's enemies against him, instead of being at all mitigated by the approaching certainty of his death, was bent, with a sort of diabolic spirit, or Jewish intensity of vengeance, on adding whatever anguish they could to the closing scene of his existence. The King had intimated to the Parliament, that, so far as might be consistent with the charges for which the prisoner was to suffer, every respect should be shown him, in connexion with his execution. It was consequently understood, and accordingly communicated by the Confessor to the General, that the ceremony was to take place by night; that he was to leave the prison by torch-light in his own carriage, with the Confessor, an officer in a civilian's dress, and a valet-de-chambre; that the carriage might be followed by the coaches of such friends, as desired to pay him that last sad tribute of their regard; and that the executioner should only be in attendance at the scaffold, for the performance of his duty. But the persecutors of Lally could not bear that he should quit life, without draining the gall and wormwood of their inveterate malignity to the very dregs. They contrived to set the above arrangement for the execution aside, as not sufficiently lacerating to the feelings of the dying man.

The principal hand in effecting such a detestable "change for the worse" was the infamous Recorder, Pasquier. This hard-hearted official, whose name is also associated elsewhere with a sentence of most monstrous cruelty,[*] is described as "very expert in the labyrinth and chicanery of the law, very dexterous and subtle, and, at the same time, an old man, subject to prejudices, headstrong, violent, and choleric;" and, having been roughly handled by Lally in the course of his so-called trial, had drawn the final report upon it in such an unfair and sanguinary spirit, as mainly led to his condemnation. Not regarding even this condemnation to be rigorous enough *per se*, the vindictive and remorseless procurer of it now insisted, that an execution of the sentence, merely in the manner above mentioned, was quite inadmissible, as amounting, in *his* opinion, to a mitigation of punishment; death, he argued, being nothing, unless attended by every horror of an infamous apparatus at its infliction! And such accompaniments of an execution, with *extra* forms of brutal insult to the dying, it was accordingly the special object of this revolting specimen of loathsome lawyerism to order—as if to present a sufficiently indignant conception to our minds of the immeasurable contrast between the hero who was to suffer, and the reptile to whom his suffering, and the disgraceful aggravation of it, were to be owing, on this occasion—a lion, as it were, to be destroyed by the paltry poison of a contemptible adder, unappeased at the idea of being merely able to effect that destruction, or spitefully fretting itself until satisfied that every drop of its vile venom should operate most effectually, by agonizing its noble victim, with due intensity, to the very last. It was decided by this rancorous wretch, and his abominable associates, in the unmanly meanness of thus trampling upon the fallen, whose hours were numbered,—that, to render the execu-

[*] That of the poor Chevalier de la Barre, condemned, at Abbeville, although only about 17, to be put to death, by "la torture ordinaire et extraordinaire," and executed accordingly!

tion at once as public and as mortifying as possible to the sufferer, it should be hurried forward by several hours, so as to take place in full day, instead of by night—that the prisoner, before quitting the jail where he was for the scaffold, should have his mouth secured by a gag, which would prevent any passing denunciation from him of the injustice of his sentence, and to the proportionate prejudice of its authors—and that, instead of being conveyed, as previously intended, and as he expected, in his own carriage, succeeded by those of his friends, he should be brought there in a miserable cart, of the kind used for the lowest or worst criminals, in which he should be accompanied by the Confessor, with no better escort than 2 hangmen—the ordinary waggon of the executioner to be the only other vehicle allowed to follow.

The feelings of Lally may be conceived, when, 6 hours sooner than he was led to anticipate, he was summoned to set out for the gallows by an executioner, with the brutal gag, and infamous cart, &c. At the sight of the latter especially, from which he was to be exposed to the public gaze of Paris in full day, Lally looked at the Curé, exclaiming with a natural emotion of disappointment—"I have suffered so much, as to expect any thing from mankind; but *you*, Monsieur, *you* to deceive me!" To which the honest Priest, with suitable energy, replied—"Monsieur le Comte, do not say that I have deceived you. Say that they have deceived *both* of us." Then, or about half-past 4, they set out, in the manner last prescribed, to the site for the execution, on the Place de Grève. The unseemly mud-vehicle, or scavenging-waggon, in which the Count was conveyed, and the large gag which he had to wear, extending beyond his lips in such a way as to disfigure his noble countenance, presented a spectacle so shocking, that the authors of it were very generally censured, even by that considerable proportion of the bystanders, whose superficial sentimentalism was indifferent to the more revolting circumstances of the sufferer's unjust condemnation and death. Among the crowd, naturally drawn together by this scene, were a number of Lally's enemies, who came there to triumph over him, with such an insensibility to all moral decorum, that they were not ashamed to exhibit their vile exultation, as he passed, by *clapping their hands!*—conduct, to which the opposite and indignant feelings of an English gentleman, Horace Walpole, has justly referred, as only worthy of so many Iroquois prisoner-tormentors, or barbarians. At 5, on the arrival of the vehicle in which Lally was at the gallows, he got out, and assisting the clergyman to mount the scaffold, ascended it with the firmness of a soldier, in the presence of an immense assemblage, not merely "of the mob, and of trades-people, but of all the military men, and all the Court." Then, walking round the scaffold, to draw apparently the more attention to the gag which prevented his speaking, and raising his hand to Heaven, as taking it to witness his innocence, the dying veteran submitted his neck to the executioner; by whom his head was severed from his body, with 2 strokes, in his 65th year.

Such was the sad and unmerited end of Lieutenant-General Count Thomas Arthur Lally, by the combined villiany of the peculator, the politician, and the lawyer, in an age, as regards France, of a putrid colonial and a putrefying national morality, too clearly symptomatic of the terrible Revolution, which, in less than 30 years, was to lay the whole of the existing political and social system of that country in ruins. It is very gratifying to be able to state, that this scandalous sacrifice of Lally was not without being resented, as it deserved to be, by a high-minded gentleman of the Irish Brigade. Mr. St. John, in his "Letters from France to a Gentleman in the South of Ireland," published in Dublin in 1788, relates the following anecdote, to that effect, of an Irish officer of the corps, whose family name and title, according to the letters and asterisks employed to indicate them, would correspond, in the Peerage of Ireland, with *Butler* and *Cahir*. "Colonel B * * * * *, who, on the demise of his brother, has since succeeded to the estate and title of Baron C * * * r, was so much affected at the injustice to his gallant countryman, that, appearing at the head of his regiment, he took the cockade from his hat, and spurned it upon the earth; and solemnly swore, he never more would serve a king and people, who, with such ingratitude, so ungenerously sacrificed his friend and countryman, the brave Count Lally. Although, at that time, the family-estate was enjoyed by his elder brother, yet, with a noble and disinterested generosity of soul, he maintained his word, and withdrew from the service of France."

We have seen what a good son the ill-fated Count was to his capricious father, Sir Gerard Lally, whose life he saved in battle; so far entitling himself to rank, for filial heroism, with 2 among the brightest names in the military annals of classic antiquity, with the Macedonian Alexander, and the Roman Scipio, the conqueror of Persia, and the victor of Hannibal. Nor was the Count without being rewarded in *his* turn, by having a son, if not to save his father's life, yet to succeed in vindicating that father's injured honour; by causing every stain, proceeding from the infliction of a capital, though unmerited, sentence, to be erased from his calumniated character. As was observed of Agamemnon, who, though so foully murdered, left an Orestes to obtain satisfaction for his lamented parent's assassination,

"Ev'n to th' unhappy, that unjustly bleed,
Heav'n gives posterity, t' avenge the deed"—

while all who heard of that satisfaction could not but

"admire,
How well the son appeas'd the slaughter'd sire!"
(POPE'S HOMER'S Odyssey, iii., 238-241.)

so, likewise, was it, that the son of Lally acted with reference to *his* deceased father, although through the different course implied by the nature of *his* case. To that son, but a minor at college, as only born in March, 1751, his father, by the last words he wrote previous to his death, committed the vindication of his memory; and this mournful injunction was accepted with such filial piety, and carried out with such a very creditable combination of zeal, perseverance, and ability, that, at length, or in May, 1778, the King (poor Louis XVI.!) in Council, by the unanimous opinions of a large number of Magistrates, and for reasons equally demonstrating the injustice and illegality of the fatal sentence of the Parliament of Paris 12 years before, pronounced that sentence, and whatever resulted from it, to be of no authority, and cancelled accordingly. By this cancelling decision, the memory of the unfortunate Count was cleared from every aspersion cast upon it by law; the fact of his innocence, and of his consequent butchery, merely through the formation of a detestable cabal against him, having, ever since his death, been generally admitted by public opinion. On the promulgation of the royal decree, Voltaire, who, (whatever may have been his errors,) in this and other memorable instances, so honourably lent the aid of his keen and brilliant pen, to defend the right against the wrong, or the weak against the strong; and who, after the fullest consideration, had specially branded the execution of Lally, as "a murder committed with the sword of justice;" from his death-bed, May 26th, or but 4 days previous to his decease, sent the following lines (the last he ever wrote) to the Count's son, to congratulate him on his success. "The dying man revives, on learning this great news. He embraces very tenderly M. de Lally. He sees that the King is the defender of justice. He will die contented." Of the younger Lally, as *not* being an officer of the Irish Brigade, the subsequent distinguished political and literary career can only be referred to here,—by adding that, at his death, in March, 1830, he included among his titles and dignities those of Count and Marquis of Lally Tolendal, Peer of France, Minister of State, Grand Officer of the Legion of Honour, Chevalier Commander and Grand Treasurer of the Order of St. Esprit or the Holy Ghost, Member of the Royal Academy of France. He left by his marriage but 1 daughter, Elizabeth Felicité Claude de Lally Tolendal, through whom the family Peerage was conveyed to her husband, the Count d'Aux.

While the Regiment of Lally was engaged in Asia, the rest of the Irish Brigade had their share in Europe of the great contest between France, England, and so many of the Continental powers, from 1756 to 1763, hence termed the Seven Years' War. But, owing to the extensive demoralization of society, from the palace to the camp, in France * at this degenerate period, the day for military achievements like the past was over. During this unpropitious era of the Seven Years' War, the Irish corps, employed on the Continent, were generally attached to the French forces, appointed to serve in Germany. With the army, that, under the successive commands of the Marshals d'Etrées and Richelieu, penetrated into Hanover in the summer of 1757, and, after dislodging the Duke of Cumberland, in July, from his best position at Hastenbeck, finally reduced him, and his 38,000 Hanoverians, &c., in September, to capitulate at Closter-Seven, and take his departure for England, were the Regiments of Berwick, Fitz-James, and other Irish corps; that of Berwick having been most noticed at Hastenbeck. † The *hero* of Culloden, of whom we here take leave, cuts but a sorry figure in this campaign, according to Frederick the Great of Prussia, who complains of it, as most injurious to *his* affairs.

"At the beginning of April," writes the King, "the French took possession of the towns of Cleves and Wesel, without encountering opposition. The Count de Gisors seized on Cologne, which the French designed to make a place of arms. Marshal d'Etrées, who was to take the command of the army, arrived there in the beginning of May, and advanced, on the 26th, with all his forces, and encamped at Munster. The Duke of Cumberland collected his troops at Bielefeld, whence he had sent a detachment to Paderborn, at the approach of d'Etrées, whose army encamped at Rheda. The Duke retired to Herford, on which the French sent a detachment into Hesse; which meeting with no opposi-

* For sufficiently corroborative details, on this point, compare the Private Life of Lewis XV., so often quoted, with "The History of the French Army," in Colburn's New Monthly Magazine for December, 1862.
† Fieffé and Ponce.

tion, seized on the whole Landgraviate. Cassel itself (the capital) surrendered, after a feeble resistance. The Duke of Cumberland, not intending to maintain his ground till he had passed the Weser, according to the plan of the Hanoverian Ministry, who believed the passage of this river more difficult than that of the Rhine, crossed (July) with his troops, over bridges, that he had prepared in the villages of Rhemun and Vlotho. He gave orders, in the meantime, that the fortifications of the towns of Munden and Hameln should be hastened. *This was thinking tardily.* The French inclined toward Corbie. One of their detachments, having passed the Weser, occasioned the Duke to change his position; and he encamped, with his right at Hameln, and his left at Afferde. The Duke of Orleans, in the interim, threw bridges over the Weser, to cross at Munden. The Duke of Cumberland, who expected soon to be attacked, called in all his detachments, and assembled them at Hastenbeck, the position of which had been described to him as admirable. The right of his army was there well supported, and the centre retreated elbowing. In his front was a wood, and, in this wood, a considerable ravine. The French army approached the Allies, who were reconnoitred by d'Etrées on the 25th, while he was cannonaded by the Duke of Cumberland. On the morrow, the French attacked his left, by gliding through this ravine at the bottom of the wood, and carried the centre battery of the Allies. This the Hereditary Prince of Brunswick recovered, sword in hand; by which first essay, he showed Nature had destined him a hero. Meantime, a Hanoverian Colonel, Breitenbach, took upon himself to collect the first battalions he met, entered the wood, fell upon the French in the rear, expelled them, and seized their cannon and colours. Everybody supposed the battle gained. D'Etrées, who saw his troops routed, had given orders for retreat. These the Duke of Orleans opposed. At length, *to the great astonishment of the whole French army, they learned that the Duke of Cumberland was on the full march, retreating to Hameln. The Hereditary Prince was obliged to abandon the battery, he had, with so much glory, recovered; and the retreat was made with such precipitation, that the brave Colonel Breitenbach even, whose merits were so conspicuous on that day, was forgotten. This worthy officer remained singly the master of the field, and departed by night to join the army, bringing his trophies to the Duke, who wept in despair, to perceive he had been so hasty, to quit a field, which was no longer disputed.** Not all the remonstrances of the Duke of Brunswick (August) and the Generals of his army could dissuade him from continuing to retreat. He marched first to Nienburg, and afterward to Verden; whence, through Rotenburg, and Bremervörde, he took the road for Stade. *By this false manœuvre, he abandoned the whole country to the discretion of the French.* Hameln was immediately occupied by the Duke of Fitz-James." Then mentioning the arrival of the Duke de Richelieu to command the French, and stating, how the Duke "took Hanover, the Duke d'Ayen Brunswick, and M. le Voyer Wolfenbuttle," &c., the King proceeds—" The Duke himself pursued the Allies, passed the Aller, and encamped at Verden. D'Armentieres meantime seized on Bremen, on the 1st of September. The French army advanced toward Rotenburg, with an intent to attack the Duke of Cumberland, but did not find him

* What a general theme, for ridicule and invective, a scene like this, in the life of a *Stuart* Prince, would be, among certain writers! We shall hear of the brave Breitenbach again.

there. He had already retreated to Bremervörde; avoiding, after the battle of Hastenbeck, all engagement with the enemy. No sooner did the King" of Prussia "perceive, by the manœuvres of the Duke of Cumberland, that he confined himself to the defence of the Weser, than he *foresaw what would be the result, and recalled the 6 battalions he had in that army,* to throw them into Magdebourg; which he did very seasonably." Of "the famous Convention, signed, by the Dukes of Cumberland and Richelieu, at Closter-Seven," soon after, or early in September, the King observes—" It was stipulated, that hostilities should cease; that the troops of Hesse, Brunswick, and Gotha, should be sent back into their respective countries; that those of Hanover should remain quiet at Stade, on the other side of the Elbe, within a given district. *Nothing was regulated concerning the Electorate of Hanover, either respecting contributions or restitutions;* so that *this country was abandoned to the discretion of the French.* Scarcely was the Convention concluded, before the Duke of Cumberland, without waiting for its ratification, returned to England. . . . This *disgraceful Convention* completely deranged the affairs of the King" of Prussia.

"The Duke of Cumberland," alleges another contemporary Continental writer, "returned to London, discontented and disgraced, and was turned into ridicule at Paris, where, in a grotesque caricature, he was represented on foot, with a white stick in his hand, going away with his back turned, and in the attitude of shame and despair." An English newspaper announcement, under October 12th, of the Duke's arrival from Hanover at Harwich, adds, "and, in the evening, his Highness pass'd over London Bridge for Kensington," his father's residence, "in a very *private* manner!" The more "private," indeed, the better! For, according to Lord Mahon, "when the Duke first appeared in the royal presence, the King never addressed a word to him, but said aloud, in the course of the evening—'Here is my son, who has *ruined* me, and *disgraced* himself!'" Soon after, "he resigned all his military employments!" A rather unsatisfactory termination, or tail-piece, to the martial career of the vaunted victor of Culloden, and merciless devastator of the Highlands!—reminding us, amidst "grinning Infamy and hissing Scorn," of the ludicrous retirement of the baffled wolf in the poem, as away

"he flies,
And claps his quiv'ring tail between his thighs." *
DRYDEN'S VIRGIL, Æneis, xi., 1185-1186.

On November 5th, 1757, was fought the battle of Rosbach, in Thuringia, between the Prussians under Frederick the Great, and the Imperial forces, or those of Austria and the Circles, under the Prince of Hilderburghausen, and the French acting as auxiliaries, under the Prince of Soubise. The victory of Frederick there, and its results, excited a great sensation at the time, and nowhere more than in England; the

* "I shall not, I trust, be accused of superstition," writes Gibbon, "but, I must remark, that, even in this world, the natural order of events will *sometimes* afford the strong appearances of moral retribution." And could any *glory* (such as it was!) acquired, with the surname of "the butcher," by the Duke in Scotland, compensate for his final *shame* in, and after his return from, Hanover? He died in October, 1765. In our day, or 1866, Hanover, under the line of another Cumberland of unenviable notoriety, has been swept by Prussia from the list of nations. "And so farewell, Hanŏver!" as the Jacobite song says.

effects of which were of corresponding importance, from their influence on the measures of its government for carrying on the war with vigour in Germany, notwithstanding the Duke of Cumberland's recent wretched break-down at Hastenbeck and Closter-Seven. Through disadvantages in point of Generalship, and other prejudicial circumstances, the Austro-Gallic forces, notwithstanding their having been 50,000 strong against some thousands less than half that number of Prussians, were, in about an hour and a half, so outmanœuvred, and beaten, that they lost, in every way, at least 10,000 men, with 63 pieces of cannon, 22 colours or standards, &c.; the Prussians having had comparatively few, or, as *they* said, not 300, killed or wounded! And it was only the shortness of the days, or early setting in of darkness at that season of the year, which saved the vanquished Confederates a diminution in prisoners of perhaps 20,000 men; such was their general dismay, and disarray, at the close of the action! Among the French cavalry, "in that day of desolation," was the Irish Horse Regiment of Fitz-James; whose Colonel-Commandant (for the Colonel-Proprietor of the Fitz-James family) was the Chevalier de Betagh, grandson of the head of the ancient house of Moynalty, County of Meath; previously related to have been so nefariously divested, as a Catholic, of his property, after the Restoration, by sectarian perjury.* "Le Régiment de Fitz-James, cavalerie Irlandoise, dans l'armée du Prince de Soubise," writes Abbé Mac Geoghegan, "s'est distingué à la bataille de Rosback, contre les Prussiens"—leaving us, however, to collect the subjoined details of that distinction from other sources. †

General Seidlitz, with all the Prussian horse as a vanguard, had orders to take such advantage of the numerous hollows of the country, as to turn, or outflank, the Allied right wing of cavalry, and fall upon it, before adequate formations could take place for resisting an attack of the kind, to be made with equal suddenness and vigour. Accordingly, that wing of the Allies, already turned by Seidlitz without being aware of it, only perceived the Prussians for the first time as they came on impetuously, or at full gallop, to the charge in flank. The Prince of Hilderburghausen thereupon endeavoured, as well as he could, to change his flank into a front, in order to receive the Prussians; having, in his 1st line, and leading himself, Bretlack's and Trautmansdorf's 2 Regiments of Imperial Cuirassiers; the Cavalry of the Empire forming a 2nd line. The shock of the 1st line of the Prussians, notwithstanding the advantage under which they attacked, was firmly received, and bravely repelled, especially by the Austrian cuirassiers, who were supported by 10 squadrons from the French reserve of horse, under the Prince of Soubise. The Prussians, being then strengthened by their 2nd line, and with a suitable effect on the contest, Soubise brought up 8 more of his squadrons, including those of the Regiment of Fitz-James; which 8 squadrons re-established the combat for some minutes, but only for some minutes, since the gallant Betagh, and his Irish corps *alone*, of Soubise's cavalry, did *not* forsake Bretlack's and Trautmansdorf's stout cuirassiers.

"Of France, the boasted valour's fled;
The Prussian comes, she 's chill'd with dread;
Ev'n honour frighted quits her breast,
Her lov'd, her long familiar, guest!"—VOLTAIRE.

* See his case, in Book I., under the Regiment of O'Brien, or Clare.

† Official accounts, and officers' letters, in periodicals of the time, and Frederick's own History of the Seven Years' War.

The 2 Austrian regiments were, in consequence, nearly annihilated· and, of the trusty

"companions who stood,
In the day of distress, by their side,"

as Moore would express it, the loss, also, was necessarily considerable; the brave Betagh himself being wounded.* In the knavish and meagre epitome of this discreditable defeat, officially published for Parisian perusal, the circumstance of the Regiment of Fitz-James having been among the 8 squadrons, last brought up to re-establish the combat, is admitted; while any acknowledgment of that regiment *solely* having acted like "true men" by their "brothers in arms, and partners of the war," the heroic cuirassiers, is meanly omitted; and, as an honourable enemy is better than a hollow friend, it is to the great Frederick, that the Irish regiment is *exclusively* indebted for justice, on this occasion. After observing, how his General "Seidlitz had turned the enemy's right, unperceived by themselves, and fell with impetuosity on the cavalry" there, the King states—"The 2 Austrian regiments formed to face him, and sustained the shock; but, being abandoned by the French, *the Regiment of Fitz-James excepted*, they were almost totally destroyed." The author of a poem published but 22 years after this battle, or in Walker's Hibernian Magazine for 1779, and who was acquainted with the Betagh family, adds—

"What in Rosbach's bloody plain befel,
Ambitious Fred'rick's savage troops can tell,
Where one stout legion of Hibernian blood
The fire of all the Prussian arms withstood;
Led by the Betagh twins,† bright twins in fame,
Their goodness, valour, and their skill the same—

* * * * * *

And when, with half his men, one brother fell,
The next, (a tale incredible to tell!)
With the small remnant of his slaughter'd band,
Their way cut thro' the Prussians, sword in hand.
Charm'd with such feats, the King withheld his fire,
And let these heroes unassail'd retire;
Had search made for their leader o'er the field,
That he might to his corpse all honours yield;
To pieces hew'd, his corpse was sought in vain,
Amidst the bleeding heaps of mangled slain."

On this engagement, Mr. O'Conor notes—"At Rosbach, the great Frederick expressed the utmost admiration for the '*wall of red bricks*,' meaning the Swiss and Irish regiments, dressed in scarlet, which neither cavalry, artillery, nor infantry could break, when the rest of the French

* Fieffé, without entering into any details, merely refers to the Regiment of Fitz-James, as suffering considerably here. Courcelles, in noticing Betagh as its Colonel-Commandant, adds, "avec lequel il se trouva à la bataille de Rosbach, où il reçut une blessure," &c.

† On this mention of "the Betagh twins," the author of the poem states in a note—"Betagh of Moynalta was only 9 years old, when outlawed immediately after the late Revolution. . . . I knew the man, at an advanced age; he spoke, of this flagrant act of injustice, with great composure, and forgiveness of his enemies." The just repeal, by the national Parliament, under King James II., in 1689, of the unjust Acts of Settlement and Explanation, would restore, to the Betagh, and other families, the properties of which they had been so shamefully ousted under those Acts; but could only effect such restorations for a time, or while the King was able to maintain his ground in Ireland against William.

army was in utter disorder." M. de la Ponce, likewise, generally refers to the Irish, as having "rendered great services" there.

In 1758, the Irish, after being employed in Germany, are mentioned to have been in Bretagne in September, when part of a British invading force was cut off, in endeavouring to escape, by the Duke d'Aiguillon, Governor of the Province, at the Bay of St. Cass, with a serious proportionable loss to the conquered, in prisoners, killed, wounded, and drowned, including "several officers, men of large fortune and consideration." Early in 1759, the French Government, to compensate itself for the too unsatisfactory aspect of its military affairs in other quarters, commenced preparations, to be made on an extensive scale, at the ports, and along the coast, opposite England, from Dunkirk to Vannes and Nantes, for an invasion, as was announced, of the British Isles. From an enterprise of such "an interesting and domestic nature" for the Irish Brigade, *they*, of course, would not be excluded; whose feelings, in reference to the undertaking corresponded with the purport of Jupiter's gratifying prediction in Virgil, to the effect, that Troy, though ruined, should, through those sprung from her, be avenged on Greece, and *that* just satisfaction be succeeded by a happy era of uninterrupted peace and piety.

> "An age is rip'ning in revolving fate,
> When Troy shall overturn the Grecian state,
> And sweet revenge her conqu'ring sons shall call
> To crush the people that conspir'd her fall.
> * * * * * *
> Then dire debate, and impious war, shall cease,
> And the stern age be soften'd into peace:
> Then banish'd Faith shall once again return,
> And Vestal fires in hallow'd temples burn."
>
> DRYDEN'S VIRGIL, Æneis, i., 386-9, 396-9.

At Dunkirk, a small squadron of 6 ships of war, furnished with a select body of troops, under Brigadier de Flobert, was placed under the command of the most enterprising and successful seaman of his day in France, the celebrated Thurot; that, however, being his name only through the maternal line; his grandfather having been a Captain O'Farrell* of King James II.'s army in Ireland, and subsequently in France. With this squadron, in spite of a superior English one appointed to block him up, Thurot was to get out, and, sailing round Scotland, make such an attempt on some point of the northern coast of Ireland, as would, in the way of a diversion, be serviceable to the main design in hand, or that of landing a

---

* See the account of Thurot in the Annual Register for 1760; and his "Irish extraction" is admitted in the Private Life of Lewis XV. The O'Farrells, or O'Ferralls, "a very celebrated race in all ages," says Charles O'Conor of Belanagare, and of Irian origin, through Fergus Mac Roy, King of Uladh, or Ulster, in the heroic times, were, for centuries, the ruling sept of the territory of Anghaile, or Annaly, in the present County of Longford. This territory was not reduced by the English into a County till the reign of Elizabeth. By the iniquitous plantation system at the expense of the old natives, from the time of James I., the O'Farrells were very great sufferers. During the War of the Revolution from 1688 to 1691, 2 gentlemen of the name sat for the County of Longford, a 3rd for that of Leitrim, and a 4th for Lanesborough, in the national Parliament at Dublin in 1689; more were officers in the army for the support of King James against the invasion of the Prince of Orange; and, in that Prince's consequent attainders of O'Farrells, were included, with others, the 2 Members for the County of Longford. In France, several O'Farrells, or O'Ferralls, were officers of the Brigade, in the Regiments of Fitz-James, Lally, Dillon, Berwick, and Walsh.

large force from France in the southern part of the island. Meantime England, from Normandy, the country of her old Continental conquerors and confiscators, was generally menaced with the disembarkation of a formidable army, at least 53,000 in number, containing some of the choicest corps in the French service; of which large force, the Prince de Conti was announced as Commander-in-Chief, with the Prince de Soubise, and the veteran Charles O'Brien, Lord Viscount Clare and Earl of Thomond, under him, as Field Marshal. Of the Irish and Scotch troops of King Louis, the battalions were stated as 9; those of the former Brigade being the Regiments of Berwick, Bulkeley, Clare, Dillon and Roth. The field and siege artillery was to amount to nearly 90 pieces; and they were to be accompanied by several thousand *extra* stands of arms, and great stores of other military necessaries.

The principal French fleet, or that of Brest, under M. de Conflans, was looked to as specially intended to cover the menaced descent upon England. But the actual object of the French was, a landing from Bretagne in Munster, to be protected by Conflans in autumn, when the chief British blockading squadron, under Sir Edward Hawke, should be driven by the usual winds, at that season of the year, off the French, to the English, coast. The large portion of the French army, and its supplies, designed to sail for Ireland, with the Duke d'Aiguillon, and the Lord Marshal de Thomond, having been drawn towards Vannes, and Hawke's fleet being, as was foreseen, obliged, by the weather, to make for Torbay, Conflans sailed, November 14th, from Brest, with his entire armament, in order that, after sweeping away a small squadron, under Captain Duff at Quiberon Bay, he might protect the conveyance of the French, Irish, and Scotch troops to Munster. And Duff's very inferior force could have been duly disposed of by Conflans, and the rest of the French Admiral's mission, as regards Ireland, would have, most probably, been accomplished, were it not for one of those providential or casual, but, at any rate, most fortunate or opportune, interventions of the elements, by which England, in the course of her history, has been so frequently, or remarkably, befriended.* For, observes a London contemporary with reference to the English admiral at Torbay, "*if Hawke had been wind-bound 48 hours longer than he was, the troops from Vannes, under convoy of Conflans, had certainly sailed for the destined port;*" and, "therefore, *it was a kind of accident that saved us, in the zenith of our power,*" (or even when so strong at sea!) "*from the mischief of an embarkation.*" Conflans, meanwhile, as apparently delivered by the wind from the only opponent of sufficient strength to cope with him, was, on the morning of the 20th, proceeding, with due confidence, to chase away or cut off Duff, when Hawke unexpectedly "turned up" from Torbay, whence he, too, sailed on the 14th, thereby arriving in time to save Duff. The comparative strength of the opposing fleets was then as follows:—French, sail of the line 21, with 1486 guns; frigates 3, with 86 guns; total of vessels 24; of artillery 1572 pieces. English, sail of the line 23, with 1666 guns; frigates 9, with 352 guns; total of

---

* See, on that point, this work, under the years 1692, 1696, 1719, 1744; and, with respect to invasion of Ireland from the Continent being frustrated by the weather more recently, it was observed by Tone, in August, 1797—"Twice within 9 months has England been saved by the wind." As contrasted with England's very expensive foreign confederates, the winds were likewise termed in Parliament, "her only *unsubsidised* allies!"

vessels 32; of artillery 2018 pieces. The English thus had 8 ships and 446 cannon more than the French; the former, nevertheless, having but 15,680 men, while the latter had 16,740, besides those in some of their vessels not enumerated.* On Hawke's reappearance, "Conflans had 2 choices, either to fly, or to stand, and fight it out. But he followed neither perfectly." He "made the signal for a line of battle." Yet, having fewer ships, and being considerably inferior in weight of metal, he sought, he tells us, "to avoid hazarding a general engagement at that time, and rather to train on the enemy through the shoals and rocks in the entrance of the river Vilaine." Unable, however, to carry out this well imagined design for the destruction of the English, the Frenchman, under circumstances of much discredit to French and much honour to English seamanship, was defeated by Hawke, with the loss of 7 ships of the line, and other unfortunate results, which rendered the projected disembarkation of the army from Bretagne in Munster no longer practicable. In a "Loyal Song, viz., Admiral Hawke's Welcome to Old England, on his completing the Ruin of the French Navy, November 20th, 1759"—to "the Tune—*O the Roast Beef*, &c.," the exultation of the English, at that event, is thus expressed—

"With the thanks of the King, this great action was crown'd;
With the thanks of the Commons, their House did resound;
And the voice that pronounc'd them will fly the world round.
        Chorus. { Welcome, brave Hawke! to Old England—
                { To Old England welcome, brave Hawke!

"All hail our bright æra, the fam'd fifty-nine!
All hail Hawke's companions, how greatly they shine!
All hail, George the Second, what glory is thine!
        Chorus. { Welcome, brave Hawke! to Old England—
                { To Old England welcome, brave Hawke!

In Ireland, the English Viceroy, or Duke of Bedford, communicated October 29th, to the Dublin colonial and sectarian legislature, the danger that menaced the existing order of things there, which *they* were so interested in upholding. He announced, how, according to the special despatch of Mr. Secretary Pitt from England, "there was a strong probability, in case the body of troops, consisting of 18,000 men, under the command of the Duc d'Aiguillon, assembled at Vannes, where more than sufficient transports for that number were actually prepared and ready to receive them on board, should, as the season of the year was growing less favourable for cruising, be able to elude his Majesty's squadrons, Ireland would not fail to be one of their objects." The force, however, from France, designed to land in Munster, with the Duke d'Aiguillon, and the Lord Marshal of Clare and Thomond, appears to have been considerably *more* than 18,000. An English private letter, descriptive of the defeat of Conflans, &c., and written from on board the vessel of 1 of Hawke's Captains, Lord Howe, or the "Magnanime, Portsmouth, December 27th, 1759," notes, in connexion with this matter,—"On the 28th, his Lordship went on shore, in a flag of truce, to demand the officers and men of the ship that struck to us, for whom he got credit, and to treat of an exchange of prisoners. He staid 2 days

* These useful details respecting the 2 fleets are derived from Sir Edward Hawke's despatch, dated "Royal George, off Penris Point, November 24th," 1759, and the valuable lists of ships annexed.

on shore, and dined with the Duke d'Aiguillon, 2 Princes of the Blood, and several other General Officers. On the 30th, his Lordship came on board the barge, and brought with him a French General. He is an Irishman, as I am informed, and wore a Blue Ribbon of the Order of St. Louis,* and is Second-in-Command of the expedition destined against Ireland. He had a great deal of respect paid to him, and was received on board with all the honours due to his rank. He dined on board, and, after seeing the Admiral, Lord Howe conducted him on shore again. There are 25,000 men in camp at Quiberon Bay." Another "letter from an officer in Sir Edward Hawke's fleet to a person of distinction at Dublin, and dated at Quiberon Bay," says—"I take this opportunity to congratulate you, and your whole country, on the success of his Majesty's arms, on the 20th of November last; for, had M. Conflans reached this place, and escaped our squadron, the whole strength of the Duke d'Aiguillon's army, consisting in all, here and at Rochefort, of 25,000 effective men, were to be landed on the western parts of Ireland, with at least 20,000 stand of arms; there to be left, to try their skill." Then, alluding to the 5 Regiments of the Irish Brigade previously named, and their Scotch companions, the writer adds, they, "it is said, had, among themselves, divided all the estates of the nobility and gentry of the Counties of Cork, Kerry, Limerick, Clare, and Galway, and such parts where they expected to meet most friends. Conflans was most assuredly ordered to leave them there, and the Duke, and those with him, were to make a conquest of the whole island, or lose their lives in the attempt; it is certainly true, that the Duke d'Aiguillon has now in his pocket a commission from the French King, as Viceroy of Ireland. All this I had from a Lieutenant-Colonel, seemingly a very modest, pretty, well-behaved man, and who (for his behaviour) has been genteelly treated by the Admirals, and all the Captains of the squadron. He commanded the Regiment of Saintonge, who served as Marines on board the *Formidable*"—the captured vessel of the brave French Rear-Admiral, St. André du Verger.

How such a great force from France as 25,000 men, with arms for at least 20,000 more, would have been received on the south and west of Ireland, where the old native and oppressed race, and those sympathizing with them, might be called *the* population of the country, is pretty clear from the contemporary Gaelic song, referring to a "return of the wild geese," or the national Brigade, for emancipation from John Bull's odious, or Penal-Code yoke, as that of Shawn Bui, *i. e.*, yellow or *orange* Jack. After promising, how the Saxon chains should then be shivered for ever, how the nation should be victorious, and from south to north wage a "war to the death" against Shawn Bui, the composer of this spirited effusion exclaims—

"The Wild Geese shall return, and we'll welcome them home—
So active, so arm'd, and so flighty
A flock was ne'er known to this island to come,
Since the years of Prince Fion the mighty— †

* *Not* of the Order of St. Louis, but of St. Esprit, or the Holy Ghost; to the latter of which, it has appeared, in Book I., that the Lord Marshal belonged. The Ribbon of the Order of St. Louis, as mentioned in poor Lally's case, was *red*, not *blue*.

† On the old hero, Fion, or Fin, see Book VII., under state of Ireland in 1745-6.

> They will waste, and destroy, overturn, and o'erthrow—
> They'll accomplish whate'er may in man be;
> Just Heav'n! they will bring desolation and woe
> On the hosts of the tyrannous Shawn Bui."
>
> "And oh! may the God, who hath kept evermore
> This isle in HIS holy protection,
> Bring back to HIS temples HIS priests as before,
> And restore them to Erin's affection!
> To end!—may I sooner be slaughter'd in war,
> Or lie sunk in the waves of the grand Lee,
> Than, with spirit for Freedom, e'er cease to abhor
> The detestable statutes of Shawn Bui." *

The leaders of this powerful army were, indeed, such as, after landing, would have recruited it abundantly,† in proportion to the confidence which would be naturally inspired by their established reputation; that of the Duke d'Aiguillon, as having so recently beaten the English invaders of his country at St. Cass; but that, still *more* of the Second-in-Command, if not virtual General, for this expedition to the "land of his fathers," the veteran Charles O'Brien, Lord Marshal of Clare and Thomond, who, as so distinguished against the Saxon at Fontenoy and Laffeldt, and undoubted descendant, and representative, of the royal hero of Munster that crushed the Danes at Clontarf, would embody the full *popular* conception of a TRUE Liberator for Erin.‡ At all events, the landed "ascendancy" of the Cromwellian and Williamite revolutions in Ireland had, as above hinted, but too good reason to congratulate itself, that so very formidable an invasion did *not* take place. And, what a vast shock to English power, at home and abroad, *must* such an invasion have been, amidst an unprecedentedly extensive and expensive war from Germany to India and America! Certain it is, that never before do we read of so large a force being designed to land from the Continent in Ireland as 25,000 regulars, including a famous body of national veterans like the Brigade, compared, by their admiring countrymen, to the Finian heroes of antiquity, designed to guard Erin against the Roman legions.

The sequel of those great arrangements in France for a landing in Ireland extended beyond 1759 into the following year, as connected with the fate of the lesser expedition, under the brave Thurot. Though his orders had been signed, June 17th, 1759, he was so closely blockaded at Dunkirk by the superior strength of the English, that he was unable to leave that port till October 15th. He had acquired such previous celebrity by his privateering exploits in the *Belleisle*—having, for example, taken within 1 year above 60 vessels from the English—that the intelligence of his departure from Dunkirk, with his small squadron, occasioned much alarm to the enemy. Thus, though several squadrons

---

* O'Daly's Poets and Poetry of Munster.

† A paragraph in Faulkner's Dublin Journal, No. 3416, mentions, on the authority of "a young Irish lad," who left a French vessel in which he was a sailor, how that vessel "carried off great numbers of men from the north-west of Ireland, this year, to Brest."

‡ "Je ne dissimulerai point," a Jew is made to observe, "que, dans nos temps de calamité, nous avons attendu un *libérateur*. C'est la consolation de toutes les nations malheureuses, et surtout des peuples esclaves." The Irish Catholics were among the latter, not, indeed, by conquest, but violation of treaty. Had they been simply conquered, there would not have been any *treaty* with them—to *violate*.

were despatched in quest of him, such was the apprehension entertained of his being at sea, that we are told, "the magistrates of Liverpool assembled on the occasion, and entered into an association for the defence of that opulent town," when " it was proposed to raise 20 companies of 100 men each, to be armed and paid by the inhabitants, and to erect batteries to mount 50 pieces of cannon." Steering so far to the north as to elude the English, yet, at such an unfavourable period of the year in that latitude, and, in such a very tempestuous season, exposed to suffer proportionably, Thurot had to put in first at Gottenberg in Sweden, next at Bergen in Norway; and, for some months, was obliged, by scarcity of food, to ply about among the northern islands of Scotland for such provisions as might be gotten there, before he could sail directly for the coast of Ulster. At last, or January 24th, 1760, being able to do so, in a few days he discovered land, or Tory island,* off the coast of Donegal, and had prepared to disembark the following day, when a most violent storm prevented him. He then steered for Derry, and had made the like arrangements for a descent, when, as he was doubling the point of the harbour, he was blown away by a shifting of the wind, turning to such a tempest, that all had like to be lost! By this time, the 6 ships he had at first were reduced to but 3, extremely shattered; and the men necessarily much diminished and dispirited, as so long subjected to the greatest hardships, on very insufficient sustenance. The day after the storm, the Captains of 2 of the vessels, and the Brigadier in command of the land-force, consequently pressed upon Thurot, that, in consideration of all they had endured, tossed about, and at so short an allowance, he ought to return to France, lest they should perish by famine. Thurot, however, positively refused to return, until he should effect something in reference to the immediate object of the expedition with which he was entrusted; yet, to refresh them, he would steer, he added, for the island of Islay. A letter from that place, in mentioning how 200 soldiers of the French fleet were sent on shore to get provisions, observes—"We may judge of the situation of this squadron from the conduct of these poor creatures, who had no sooner touched dry land, than, with their bayonets, they fell to digging up herbs, and every green thing they met with. At length, they came to a field of potatoes, which they very eagerly dug; and, after shaking off the earth, and wiping them a little on their waistcoats, eat them up, raw as they were, with the greatest keenness!" Here, Thurot met with the further discouragement of learning the defeat of Conflans by Hawke. Nevertheless, " he persisted in his resolution to sail for Ireland. Indeed, he had scarcely any other choice; for he was so poorly victualled, that he could not hope, without some refreshment, to get back to France. And he was further urged on by his love of glory, no small share of which he was certain to add to his character, if he could strike a blow of never so little importance on the coast of Ireland; for, by this, he might make some appearance, of having revenged the many insults which had been offered to the coast of France." After a stay at Islay sufficient to obtain so much, or rather, so little, food, as, at the rate of 6 ounces of oatmeal, with a pint of water, per day, to each man, would support existence to the Bay of Carrickfergus, Thurot sailed thither. He anchored off that place, Feb-

* "This island," says Dr. O'Donovan, "is situated in the sea, about 9 miles from the nearest coast of the Barony of Kilmacrenan, in the County of Donegal." It is, he adds, among the earliest places noticed in the Bardic history of Erin.

ruary 21st, and then, distributing what wine he had aboard to encourage his extremely harassed and enfeebled followers, landed 600 soldiers—or all that remained of his original 1270!—which 600, with so many sailors as might form a body of about 1000, advanced to make themselves masters of the town.

The state of Carrickfergus, at this time, was too indicative of *a government, any thing but duly attentive to the protection of its subjects!* The walls of the town were ruinous in many places; the Castle was untenable, having a breach from 50 to 60 feet in extent, and easily accessible; the gates were so out of order, that they might be soon knocked open; the edifice, moreover, was neither provisioned, nor ammunitioned, for a siege, nor had it a cannon fit for firing; in short, it was, in the words of a local contemporary, "a Castle, which had only the name of one, having nothing therein to offend, or defend, everything being neglected for many years." The officer in command there, Lieutenant-Colonel John Jennings of the 62nd Regiment of Foot, had, at his disposal, only 4 newly-raised companies of Ulster Protestants, mentioned as "all young Irish lads, who had not been inlisted more than 3 or 4 months"—and furnishing, with 4 artillery-men, but 201 officers and soldiers.* Hence, says a writer from Belfast to a correspondent in England—"It is but fit, that the public, on *your* side of the water, should know, *how little care has been taken to put the kingdom into a state of defence, notwithstanding our House of Commons have granted every thing that was asked for that purpose!*" Under those disadvantageous circumstances, Lieutenant-Colonel Jennings had to retire through the town before the French; making as good an opposition as he and his handful of young recruits, deficient of ammunition, could be expected to make, till they got into the Castle. By that time, bullets fell short among them, "from which," says the official letter to the Lord-Lieutenant, "the enemy finding our fire so cool, attacked the gates, sword in hand," when, "from the battering of the shot on both sides, the bolts were knocked back, and the gates opened, and the enemy marched in. But Lieutenant-Colonel Jennings, Lord Wallingford, Captain Bland, Lieutenant Ellis, with some other gentlemen, and about 50 men, repulsed the enemy, and beat them back." Here was seen "great resolution in a few Irish boys, who defended the gate, after it was opened, with their bayonets; and those from the half-moon, after their ammunition was gone, threw stones and bricks." This stout defence so checked the French as to lead to a parley, with respect to a surrender of the Castle as untenable, though a surrender upon honourable terms; 1 of the heads of agreement being, "that the Town and County of Carrickfergus, should not be plundered or burnt, on condition the Mayor and Corporation furnished the French troops with necessary provisions." And could "provisions" be more "necessary" than they *then* were to the long weather-beaten and starving French? like the tempest-tossed followers of Ulysses, when, amidst "famine and meagre want," 1 of them exclaimed,—

>   "A thousand ways frail mortals lead
> To the cold tomb, and dreadful all to tread;
> But dreadful most, when, by a slow decay,
> Pale hunger wastes the manly strength away.
>   *   *   *   *   *   *

* The *exact* amount of the garrison, as derived from the *details* given in the 1st of the "Articles of Capitulation."

> Better to rush at once to shades below,
> Than linger life away, and nourish woe!"
> POPE'S HOMER, Odyssey, xii., 403-406, 415-416.

But the civic functionaries of Carrickfergus, not complying with the stipulation for the provisions which were so much required, and which it *was* in their power to furnish, the French, who, notwithstanding the very great privations under which they were suffering, had, since their landing, observed regular discipline, so that not 1 of the gentlemen's houses along the line of march was entered or molested by them, now very naturally plundered the town; justly alleging, that the Magistrates were to blame for this, since the provisions required were found in the place, and, as *found*, should have been *supplied*, when demanded. Those unaccommodating corporators ought, indeed, to have reflected, that "hunger *will* break through stone walls,"—and to have conducted themselves accordingly, when it was actually in arms within *their* walls. By the pillaging that ensued, considerable damage would appear to have been inflicted upon the inhabitants of Carrickfergus, to the amount, it was estimated, of above £5000; although, on complaints being made to the French officers, redress was given, as far as, they alleged, it was practicable, "by collecting part of the plunder from the men, and returning it to the inhabitants." Orders, too, were issued, "to restore everything to the townspeople;" in consequence of which " some people, who fled from thence, returned to claim what had been taken from them."

Through this successful visit to Ireland at Carrickfergus, although with only *half* the vessels of the little armament that had been confided to him, Thurot, says an English account, " gained as much reputation as could be expected from a fleet, which was no more than a sort of wreck of the grand enterprise," connected with the proposed landing in Munster; so, having victualled, and, by 4 in the morning of February 26th, embarked all his men, he set sail for France. Meantime, however, 3 English ships of war, (*not specially appointed to guard the coast of Ireland, but which merely happened, from stress of weather, to have put in at Kinsale,*) were despatched to intercept him, by the English Viceroy at Dublin. Thurot's 3 vessels, the 1st under his immediate command, were the *Belleisle* rated at 44 guns, the *Blonde* at 32, and the *Terpsicore* at 26. Those of the English officer opposed to him, Captain John Elliott, were the *Æolus* of 32 guns, his own ship, the *Pallas* of 36, and the *Brilliant* of 36. " These frigates," states the Marquis de Bragelonne, Major to the land-force with Thurot, and who writes of him in an unfavourable spirit, " were incomparably stronger and better manned than ours. For, though the *Belleisle* had 44 guns, her strength was not equal to this; and the stormy weather, we had experienced at sea, had obliged us to put some of them under the hatchway, particularly our 18 pounders, and M. Thurot did not heave them up again for the action; so that we had no more than 32 or 34. It was the same thing, in proportion, with our other frigates. Besides, the English had a great many good sailors on board, and we had none, or scarcely any." The French, indeed, if able to avail themselves of *all* the guns on board their 3 vessels, or 102, would have been about equal to the English, who had only 2 more in their 3 vessels, or 104; but the English had a great advantage in artillery, since they *could* employ all theirs, while the French could *not*. If the French, on the other hand, had more men, they were landsmen; whereas, of seamen, the English had the larger number, and in a superior condition. The bad state, too, of the French ships, since "on stormy seas unnumber'd toils they bore," was a circumstance much in favour of the English.

On the 28th, at 4 in the morning, Captain Elliott, having got sight of the French, proceeded to give chase. Thurot, who, after fulfilling the purport of his mission to Ireland, was naturally intent only on getting back to France, and who, besides, with a squadron "so much the worse for the wear" as his, could have no motive for fighting one better prepared for action, endeavoured, if possible, rather to outsail, or escape from, such an enemy; and, amidst his efforts for that purpose, did not, it seems, give the signal from the *Belleisle* for the *Blonde* and the *Terpsicore* to join him, till he was obliged to make the final dispositions for defending himself in the *Belleisle* against the English, who came up with him off the Isle of Man, after a pursuit of 5 hours, or at 9 o'clock. The engagement, in a few minutes, began, at first between Thurot's and Elliott's immediate vessels, the *Belleisle* and the *Æolus*, the latter, however, being joined by the *Pallas* and the *Brilliant*, and thus being 3 against 1; Thurot's 2 other ships, the *Blonde* and the *Terpsicore*, whether from the distance at which they were when signalled, from a want of zeal in their Captains to assist their Commander, or from some other cause, not coming up in due time "to the rescue;" and, when they did come up, making "but a poor fight," or striking so soon, that their presence by no means compensated for their absence.* The *Belleisle*, in this combat which lasted "about an hour and a half," suffering terribly by the enemy's extremely superior fire, lost her bowsprit, mizen-mast, and mainyard; was otherwise so shattered as to be hardly kept from sinking; and had a proportionably large number of her men killed and wounded. Yet such an exceedingly unequal contest was maintained by Thurot under a still further disadvantage. It appears, that between him and his gunners there unfortunately existed such bad feeling, that "most" of them, on this occasion, alleges my French authority, "forsook their posts and hid themselves, without a possibility of bringing them back. . . . . The defection of his gunners rendering the artillery useless, he endeavoured to board; but, having neither grenades nor grappling-irons prepared, he failed in the attempt. The frigate then being in the most deplorable state, and the crew defenceless, exposed to the continual fire of the English, he was solicited to strike, but was determined to receive 1 more broadside; that is to say, to give himself a chance for the last stroke of good fortune which he expected, that of being killed upon the spot, without being exposed to the reproaches of the Ministry, or to the derision of the enemy; and fortune at least granted him *this* last wish. Notwithstanding his disaster, Thurot," concludes this French writer, "was regretted by the Court; they were sensible of the want they were in of

* Captain John Elliott's letter, from "Ramsay Bay, Isle of Man, February 29th, 1760," is *not* calculated to give a correct view of the circumstances of his engagement with Thurot. "On the 28th," he writes, "at 4 in the morning, we got sight of them, and gave chase. About 9, I got up along side their Commodore, (off the Isle of Man,) and, in a few minutes after, the action became general, and lasted about an hour and a half, when they all 3 struck their colours." Yes!—but without the aid of *other* intelligence on the writer's side, including that of his own pilot, as well as information on the side of his opponent, or from a French source, could we, by the above extract, know anything of Thurot's 1 vessel having ever had to contend against the Captain's 3 vessels? To such writing, the line of the song would be applicable—

"'Pon my soul 'tis *true!*—and what will you say 'tis a *lie?*"

such men, for the safety and supply of their colonies." A London narrative of the event, although expressing its natural satisfaction at the occurrence as an English success, yet adds—" The public, indeed, lamented the death of the brave Thurot, who, even whilst he commanded a privateer, fought less for plunder, than for honour; whose behaviour was, on all occasions, full of humanity and generosity; and whose undaunted courage raised him to rank, and merited distinction. His death secured the glory he always sought; he did not live to be brought a prisoner into England; or to hear in France those malignant criticisms, which so often attend unfortunate bravery." Among those of his own profession in France, we are informed, that he was extremely regretted; they who knew him intimately being boundless in their eulogiums of him; affirming that, if he lived some years longer, he would have equalled, or even surpassed, the Barts and Gue-Trouins; having, amidst such a distinguished career, been cut off so early, or when only about 33. His remains did not fall into the hands of the enemy, having been committed, by his own followers, to the waves; or appropriately consigned to that element, on which he acquired a renown that will not fade from the page of history. The successful landing of Thurot in Ireland, as indicative, it was hoped, of a visit from the French, in greater strength, at another time, was regarded with corresponding satisfaction among the mass of the oppressed Catholics there, who, to the close of the century, had a song, in which, alluding, with just pride, to *his* old native or Milesian origin, it was said—

"Blest be the day that *O'Farrell* came here!" *

In 1760, the Irish resuming service with the French in Germany, though without having, it seems, any opportunity for *special* distinction there against the Allies, are merely referred to, as at the affairs of Corbach and Warbourg, with different results, in July, and the victory of Clostercamp, and consequent relief of Wesel, in October. They passed the winter between 1760 and 1761 in quarters between Marbourg and Giessen. "At the commencement of 1761," writes Lieutenant-General Count Arthur Dillon, " 7 piquets were drawn from the Irish regiments, forming a detachment of 350 chosen men. Their destination was to proceed to relieve a portion of the isolated garrison of Gottingen; but, in passing by Fritzlar, M. de Narbonne, who commanded there, retained them, because he knew, that he was about to be attacked, and that he had with him only a battalion of the Royal Grenadiers. M. le Comte de Narbonne, who, after the manner of the ancients, since assumes the name of the locality of his triumph, has always rendered to the Irish detachment the justice which is due to them for the share which they had in this handsome defence, that partly saved the French army. In the meantime General Bredenbach," or rather Breitenbach,†

---

* On the naval enterprises of Conflans and Thurot, I have availed myself of Barbier's Journal Historique et Anecdotique du Regne de Louis XV., Mercure Historique et Politique, Private Life of Lewis XV., Faulkner's Dublin Journal, the Annual Registers, Exshaw's and Gentleman's Magazines, the article Thurot in the Biographie Universelle, and traditional family information (here as elsewhere) from my dear mother, deceased March 28th, 1869, in her 85th year.

† The stout Hanoverian officer, already mentioned, so much to his credit, at Hastenbeck, as contrasted with the *weeping* victor of Culloden, who "left him in the lurch!"

"at the head of 10,000 men, attacked Marbourg, which was defended by all the Irish Brigade. At the report of the march of the enemy, the Regiments of Clare, Rothe, and Berwick set out from Giessen, and got before him to Marbourg, where, reunited with their countrymen, they opposed a resistance that was invincible to an attack of the most vigorous description. General Bredenbach was killed, and his troops retired in disorder; leaving behind them their dead, wounded, and 3 pieces of cannon. The conduct and courage of the defenders of Marbourg and of Fritzlar secured the rallying of the French army."

According to my special French notice of a brave officer of very noble Scotch origin, or the Comte Louis Drummond de Perth, who commenced his military career in France in the Irish Brigade, January 23rd, 1734, as a reformed Captain in the Regiment of Berwick, fought for "Prince Charlie" in 1745-6, was afterwards Lieutenant-Colonel of the Regiment Royal-Ecossois, and finally a Lieutenant-General, this defence of Marbourg—as distinguished from that of Fritzlar—was made by the Irish under his immediate or *personal* conduct there; he being then a Brigadier. "He," it is said, "signalized himself particularly, February 14th, 1761, at the defence of Marbourg, where he commanded the 4 battalions of Bulkeley, Clare, Dillon, and Roth. Attacked 3 times in succession at the barrier of the town, he fought with the greatest valour; repulsed all those hostile attacks; and completely overthrew the enemy in the 3rd. General Brettemback, the commander in these attacks, was killed in the last, along with his Major, his Aide-de-Camp, and 7 other officers of his Etat-Major; the Comte de Drummond making himself master of 3 pieces of cannon, which he presented to the Comte de Rouge, the officer in command there. This brilliant action," it is added, "obliged the enemy to abandon the siege." In advancing to that enterprise, which, unfortunately cost him his life, Lieutenant-General Breitenbach, whose death, remarks an Allied account, "is extremely regretted," had reduced Rosenthal with a magazine of 40,000 rations. Soon after his defeat, however, or February 15th, the Allies proceeding more cautiously, and with such a train of heavy artillery against Fritzlar, as, in a post so weak, and without a single serviceable piece of cannon, rendered the hope of a successful resistance impossible, that place, with a good magazine, had to be surrendered. Yet it was only given up on honourable terms, the garrison consisting of the 7 piquets of the Irish Brigade, 965 of the Grenadiers Royaux, with 105 sick and wounded, having permission to march away, merely on condition of not serving against the Allies for the rest of that campaign. Subsequently, Lord Granby having established himself between Lahne and Omh, we read of his light troops capturing, at Amoeneburgh, "some pickets of the Irish Brigade."

At the combats, July 15th-16th, before Filingshausen and Scheidingen, between the Allies under Prince Ferdinand, Lord Granby, and the Hereditary Prince, under the French under the Marshals de Broglio and de Soubise, the Irish were with the latter Marshal in the direction of Scheidingen, and participated, on the 2nd day, in the early successful operations there, which would have been followed up, but for a despatch from Broglio announcing *his* repulse, with severe loss, from Filingshausen, to Soubise, and consequently directing a retreat to be made from Scheidingen; which accordingly took place, though in a very different style from Broglio's, or in such good order, that the enemy did not attempt to interfere with a movement so well executed. The Irish are also alluded to, as at the affairs of Soest and Unna, and as stationed in the autumn, or October, along the Eder.*

The year 1762, the last of the Seven Years' War, was that of the decease of 2 veteran officers of the Irish Brigade—the 1st in rank "Matthieu de Coock," or Matthew Cooke, Maréchal de Camp, or Major-General, of Horse—a double namesake of, but I cannot say if related to, the Lieutenant-General who died in 1740—the 2nd, Thomas Shortall, Lieutenant-Colonel of Foot. Matthew Cooke commenced his military career July 18th, 1714, as a Mousquetaire; was made, June 22nd, 1717, a reformed, or supernumerary Lieutenant in Nugent's Irish Regiment of Horse; was appointed, on September 3rd, 1727, a full Captain; commanded his company, as such, at the siege of Kehl, in 1733, in which war the regiment became that of Fitz-James; was at the passing of the lines of Etlingen, and the reduction of Philipsburgh, in 1734; and at the affair of Clausen, in 1735. Commissioned to hold rank, March 26th, 1736, as a Mestre-de-Camp-de-Cavalerie, he acted, with his company, from 1741 to 1743, in Westphalia, Bohemia, and Bavaria. Thenceforward to 1748, he was employed between Flanders and Scotland; attaining the grade of Brigadier by brevet, May 1st, 1745; and Maréchal de Camp by brevet, May 10th, 1748. He then quitted his company and the service; and died July 19th, 1762, aged 63 years.

Thomas Shortall was the representative of a name, for centuries, of eminence in the County of Kilkenny; where the memory of the race is yet attested on the map at "Shortallstown," and the remains of several of their castles are still pointed out. In the middle ages, during which the colonial and native aristocracy of Ireland made war on one another, like the feudal nobility in the various kingdoms of the Continent,† the Shortalls were among the confederates of the very distinguished Anglo-Norman family of Grace; descended from one of the most famous chevaliers who settled in the island under Henry II., Raymond, surnamed *le Gras*, more generally written *le Gros;* from which surname of *le Gras* came the native Irish designation of *Grasach*, and the more modern one of GRACE. The heads of the house of Grace were Palatine Barons of Courtstown, where their castle stood; their territory, known as "Grace's country," included 80,000 acres; and their slogan, or war-cry, was "GRASACH-ABÒ!" or "*the Grace for ever!*" The military connexion of the Shortalls with those powerful Barons is thus alluded to, in the old song on Courtstown:—

> "O Courtstown! thou home of the great and renown'd,
> Thy bulwarks, what heroes of battle surround,—
> The Shees, Rooths, and *Shortalls*, whose bosoms still glow
> To join in the conflict with GRASACH-ABÒ!"

The chief of the Graces, at the breaking out of the War of the Revolution in Ireland, was the accomplished and high-minded John Grace, as Baron of Courtstown. In the Parliamentarian or Cromwellian civil war, he had been one of the Council of the Catholic Confederates of Ireland; yet, during that most trying period, acted so unexceptionably, that he was restored to his estate of 32,870 acres in Kilkenny and Tipperary, even by Cromwell himself; or "as," it is said, "a token of

---

* Dillon and Ponce French MSS., Courcelles under Drummond, and publications of the day previously cited.

† See Note 55, to edition of Macariæ Excidium for Irish Archæological Society.

personal admiration for his manly and generous enemy, who never failed to perform the offices of humanity, even to the soldiers who were in arms against him." On the success of the Orange intrigues and invasion in Great Britain, to dethrone the reigning Sovereign there, and the preparations to do the same in Ireland, the old Baron of Courtstown, according to the family historian, "raised and equipped a regiment of foot, and a troop of horse, at his own expense, for the service of King James; whom he farther assisted with money and plate, amounting, it is said, to £14,000 sterling. Possessing a high character, and great local influence, he was early solicited, with splendid promises of favour, to join King William's party; but, yielding to the strong impulse of honourable feelings, he instantly, on perusing the proposal to this effect, from 1 of the Duke of Schomberg's emissaries, seized a card, accidentally lying near him, and returned this indignant answer upon it—'Go, tell your master I despise his offer; tell him that honour and conscience are dearer to a gentleman, than all the wealth and titles a Prince can bestow.' This card, (the 6 of hearts,) which he sent uncovered by the bearer of the rejected offer, is, to this day, very generally known by the name of ' Grace's card,' in the city of Kilkenny." Baron John Grace, dying in 1690, or while the war was going on in Ireland, left as his heir, and Colonel of the family Regiment of Foot, its previous Lieutenant-Colonel, Baron Robert Grace; in which corps, among the Captains and Lieutenants, the name of Shortall is to be found along with that of Grace, "as of old." Of the conduct of this regiment on the fatal day of Aughrim, where its gallant Colonel was so severely wounded that he died the same year, when he would, under other circumstances, have been still "in the vigour of life," we are told,—"The noble enthusiasm of Grace's regiment in this action, evinced a patriotic devotion, that might dignify a Spartan band. Of that fine body, selected from the flower of the youth of Grace's country, not 50 returned to their homes, where they were received with scorn and reproaches, till their chieftain's testimony confirmed their claim to the same heroic intrepidity which had distinguished their fallen comrades. The plaintive strains excited by this event were the aspirations of a whole people. They are still preserved," concludes my authority, Mr. Sheffield Grace, in 1823, "and still elevate the peasant's breast, with sentiments of hereditary pride, and national feeling." Though thus almost annihilated at Aughrim, the Regiment of Grace was recruited so quickly as to serve against the Williamites at the 2nd siege of Limerick, where Thomas Shortall was Captain of a company in it, stronger than usual, or of 100 men. He accompanied the remains of the Irish forces to France; at length, in his 88th year, or June 10th, 1745, attained the rank of Lieutenant-Colonel in the Regiment of Clare; and did not leave the army till in his 90th year, or January 31st, 1747. After quitting the service, he fixed his residence, as a "soldier tir'd of war's alarms," at Landrecy, in French Flanders, living above 14 years longer, apparently with as much happiness as was possible at his very uncommon period of existence; since we are informed, that, "the day before his death, he eat and drank with his friends as usual, and had no ailment but old age." His decease occurred October 25th, 1762, when he was 104 years, 10 months, and 4 days old; having been born at Kilkenny December 21st, 1657. He was believed to be the last survivor of above 30,000 of his countrymen who went to France after the Treaty of Limerick, as well as of many thousands who more recently did so. There was found among the deceased veteran's papers —with reference to the day, when, in the words of the Scotch Jacobite song, each "loyal bonny lad" might "cross the seas, and win his ain"— a due "schedule of his estate, on which were several fine seats."

In Germany, whence the Irish regiments of infantry were withdrawn at the close of 1761, the only occurrence of the campaign of 1762 requisite to be noticed, as connected with the fate of the national cavalry Regiment of Fitz-James, was the action which took place, June 24th, at Graebenstein, where the French, under the Marshals d'Etrées and de Soubise, were so ably surprised by the Allies, under Prince Ferdinand, Lord Granby, and Generals Luckner and Sporken, that they were very roughly handled. "The French army," says the contemporary British annalist, "was most advantageously posted, both for command of the country, and for strength, near a place called Graebenstein, in the frontiers of Hesse; their centre occupied an advantageous eminence; their left wing was almost inaccessible by several deep ravines; and their right was covered by the village of Graebenstein, by several rivulets, and a strong detached body, under one of their best officers. . . . In this situation, they imagined they had nothing to fear from the attempts of Prince Ferdinand; whose army, besides the inferiority of its numbers, was separated in such a manner, and in such distant places, that they judged it impossible it could unite in any attack. But, whilst they enjoyed themselves in full security, the storm was preparing to fall upon them, from all quarters. A considerable corps of the Allied army, under General Luckner, was posted to the eastward of the Weser." Skilfully deluding and eluding Prince Xavier of Saxony appointed to watch him, and "marching in the night, with the utmost speed, he crossed the Weser, turned the right of the French army, and, without being discovered, placed himself upon their rear. General Sporken, at the same time, placed himself so, as to attack the same wing in flank. Prince Ferdinand crossed the Dymel, in order to fall upon their centre. The attack on the enemy's left was commanded by Lord Granby. These preparations were made with so much judgment, celerity, and good order, that the French had not perceived the approach of the Allies, when they found themselves *attacked, with infinite impetuosity, in front, flank, and rear!*" The consequence to the French of such a rousing early in the morning, "*before they had the least apprehension of being attacked,*" was a general scene of alarm and confusion, that would have occasioned a total rout, but for the interposing gallantry of 2 corps, under M. de Castries and M. de Stainville, who made such a vigorous stand, though it cost them dear, that their army was enabled to retire under the cannon of Cassel, and over the Fulda; losing, however, exclusive of slain, military ensigns, guns, and baggage, 2570 prisoners, of whom 162 were officers, while the Allies had not above 897 of all ranks, killed, wounded, or missing.

The severe disadvantage, by which the French suffered so much on this occasion—a disadvantage causing the greatest part of the French officers made prisoners to express themselves so bitterly, "that the Allied army was much scandalized at the manner in which these gentlemen spoke of their Commanders-in-Chief"—proved the ruin of the Regiment of Fitz-James. "M. Reidesel," says an account of the surprise in the London Gazette, "attacked, beat, and totally overthrew the Regiment of Fitz-James, took 300 of their horses, and their 2 standards"—though but 1 standard of that corps, among other captured ensigns, is subsequently specified as brought to St. James's by Captain Sloper, Aide-de-Camp to Prince Ferdinand.* Those of the regiment made prisoners amounted to 70. By another English narrative of this affair of Graebenstein, it would appear, that the annihilated regiment acted, in this last scene of its service, so as to excite a respectful regret on the part of its opponents. "We," it is remarked, "cannot help, in this place, lamenting the fate of Fitz-James's horse, tho' in the service of our enemies; they *proved themselves our brethren,* though misled. Is it not a great misfortune, that, through a false principle of policy, we suffer so many gallant men to enlist in our enemies' service?" A contemporary English letter on this subject also observes—"I am sorry to say, that our nation has found from sad, nay almost fatal, experience, the injury and prejudice we have suffered by it, (if *losing battles* may be so termed) through such unhappy men being employed in the armies of our enemies. . . . To *me* it is very odd, that Britain should, upon several occasions, hire Roman Catholic troops to fight her battles, and yet neglect to employ her own subjects of the same religion, when it is admitted, on all hands, *they are as good soldiers as any in the world.* . . . For my own part, I like a man much better, who openly professes the religion he is really of, than those who pretend to be of the established religion of a country, only to answer sinister purposes; when, in short, upon a close examination, they appear to have none at all." The well-meaning writer consequently asks, whether it would not be the most eligible course for Government, "to publish a Proclamation, offering pardon to all Irish and other officers, soldiers, and seamen, who are subjects of Great Britain, let them be of what religion soever, in case they immediately quitted the Spanish and French services, and embraced that of their own lawful Sovereign and country; and, as an encouragement so to do, promising, at the same time, to provide for them equal to what they enjoy in their present services?" †

The young King George III., too, who ascended the throne, in October, 1760, had, as an advocate for relaxing several of the disabilities imposed upon the great majority of the people of Ireland, commissioned his representative there, the Earl of Halifax, on opening the session of the Dublin "ascendancy" Parliament, in October, 1761, to allude to the adoption of an improved policy towards the Catholics; or one of such toleration, as might not be incompatible with security to the existing political and religious establishment. That "first paternal recommendation of his Majesty in favour of his Irish subjects" eliciting nothing more respectful, or liberal, than "an utter silence" from the sulky Sanhedrim of Cromwello-Williamite or "glorious-revolution" bigots and oppressors to whom it was addressed, the King's government in Ireland, at the latter end of that year, and the beginning of the next, or 1762, (here under consideration) favoured a proposal for raising 6 regiments of Catholics by Lords Kenmare, Kingsland, Sir Patrick Bellew, and others of their religion, to be employed in Portugal, then invaded, as the ally of England, by Spain. This levy, (if it could be *openly* legalized,) was intended to be the com-

* The loss of its standard, (or standards,) on this occasion, by the Regiment of Fitz-James—and that merely under the disadvantage of the force to which it was attached having been so completely *surprised*—is, it will be remarked, the *only* ascertained loss of the kind connected with the annals of the Irish Brigade.

† Pinard, article Coock, Grace's Memoirs of Family of Grace, Gilbert's Historic Literature of Ireland under head of Grace's Annals, Dalton's Irish Army List of James II. at name of Shortall, Irish, English, and Continental contemporary periodicals and newspapers for 1762.

mencement of a different policy from the past towards the suffering Catholics; and, as regards the unfortunate situation of so many of the junior members of the higher families of that faith, then debarred from a profession, the raising of such regiments "would have afforded the means of a decent livelihood to many of the unemployed younger sons of the Catholic nobility and gentry, whom it was *the study of the ascendancy to level to plebeian obscurity.*" But the pernicious position occupied, between the English cabinet and the enslaved people or Catholics of Ireland, by the ruling colonial and sectarian party there, was such, that, as *far* more of what was evil had been inflicted by England upon the country than ever was requisite except for *their* ends, so whatever was good, except for the *same* ends, was opposed; and this measure, among the rest, for levying the Catholic regiments, which accordingly fell to the ground. "The English government," notes Lord Charlemont's biographer, Mr. Hardy, with respect to the proposed organization of those regiments for Portugal, "was resolved to do *something* with regard to the Catholics, and the Irish legislature, at this time, was resolved to do *nothing!*"—which is explained by such a legislature, though termed "Irish," being no better, with but too few exceptions, than the legislature of an odious oligarchy of "Protestant Bashaws," that, in the exercise of their baleful supremacy "lent," it is added, "to a sanguinary code, new terrors of their own!" These "terrors" were connected with the rack-renting oppression, as well as the sectarian persecution, of the enslaved Catholics. "The Popery laws," writes Mr. O'Conor, "had, in the course of half a century, consummated the ruin of the lower orders. Their habitations, visages, dress, and despondency, exhibited the deep distress of a people, ruled with the iron sceptre of conquest. The lot of the negro slave was happiness, compared with that of the then Irish helot; both were subject to the capricious cruelty of mercenary task-masters, and unfeeling proprietors; but the negro slave was well fed, well cloathed, and comfortably lodged. The Irish peasant was half-starved, half-naked, and half-housed. . . . The fewness of negroes gave the West-Indian proprietor an interest in the preservation of his slaves. A superabundance of helots superseded all interest in the comforts or preservation of an Irish cottier; the Code had eradicated every feeling of humanity; and avarice sought to stifle every sense of justice. That avarice was generated by prodigality, the hereditary vice of the Irish gentry, and manifested itself in exorbitant rackrents wrung from their tenantry, and in the lowest wages paid for their labour." Thus, in Ireland, as elsewhere, (or in Ithaca of old, with reference to the rapacious luxury of the intrusive suitors,) it might be observed—

> "No profit springs beneath usurping pow'rs;
> Want feeds not there, where luxury devours,
> Nor harbours charity where riot reigns:
> Proud are the lords, and wretched are the swains."
> POPE'S HOMER, Odyssey, xv., 404-407.

The grinding injustice of such landed oppression, and the proportionable suffering amongst those affected by it, including some of the dominant faith, naturally gave rise to those outbreaks of rural exasperation called the Whiteboy disturbances; for which no better remedies were adopted by "ascendancy" legislation, than enactments of the sanguinary school of Draco; while the outrages of distress and despair were attributed, by those whose exactions had provoked them, to the convenient raw-head and-bloody-bones of "Popery," as the all-sufficient alarm-cry to justify persecution and plunder.

> "Be to the poor like onie whunstane,
> And haud their noses to the grunstane;
> Ply ev'ry art o' legal thieving;
> No matter, stick to sound believing!"—BURNS.

But the Government in England, grown too intelligent to be influenced, on this occasion, by any bamboozling bawl of that bugbear of bigotry from the sectarian and agrarian oppressors of their country, justly testified, with reference to the unfortunate Whiteboys, in the London Gazette of May, 1762, "that the authors of those disturbances consisted of persons of *different* persuasions"—or the common sufferers by a common tyranny in *this* world, whatever might be their creed about *another*. Goldsmith, with his Jacobite sympathies, too clearly alludes, in his "Traveller," to this unnatural state of his own country, under the oligarchical yoke of her so-called "glorious-revolution" ascendancy, "when," he says,

> "I behold a factious band agree,
> To call it freedom, when themselves are free;
> Each wanton judge new penal statutes draw,
> Laws grind the poor, and rich men rule the law." *

But, on the Continent, all the infantry corps of the Irish Brigade, already noticed as removed from Germany, were marched to Flanders, and encamped about Dunkirk, during this campaign of 1762, as part of an army to menace England with an invasion, till the preliminaries of peace were signed in November, which led to the definitive Treaty of Paris, in February, 1763.†

---

* At the close of the session of Parliament previous to his departure from Ireland, Lord Halifax, it is observed, "in the mild language of advice, reproached the aristocracy with their cruelty to the lower orders," by noting how "the mere execution of the laws, without the example of those who execute them, must always be defective." Of the Whiteboys, Arthur Young affirms, that "acts were passed for their punishment, which seemed calculated for the meridian of Barbary;" and, though soon after repealed, as too shameless, yet others remained "the law of the land, that would, if executed, tend more to raise, than quell, an insurrection;" so that, it was too manifest, the landed despots "never thought of a radical cure, from overlooking the real cause of the disease, which, in fact, lay in *themselves*, and not in the wretches they doomed to the gallows."

† Dillon and Ponce MSS., and newspapers of the day.

HISTORY OF THE IRISH BRIGADES

IN

THE SERVICE OF FRANCE.

BOOK X.

ALTHOUGH, from the different circumstances previously noticed, the reputation of the Irish Brigade in the service of France could not be compared, during this last war from 1756 to 1762, with what its celebrity had been down to the Peace of 1748, yet the *still* high character of the corps, as represented by its officers, combined with the eminent distinction of so many Irish in *other* Continental services, continued to reflect more and more discredit on the so-called "glorious-revolution" or "penal-code" system of administration in Ireland, based on the ruin of the proscribed mass of the population. "It is not," writes Dr. Charles O'Conor, "from the hunted remains of a conquered people, thus persecuted, that we are to form an idea of its genius, or its manners. To have a fair view of the native Irish during the reigns of the 2 first Georges, we must follow their nobility and gentry in their exile to those countries, where they were allowed to exercise their abilities. There we find them, whether in an ecclesiastical, military, or mercantile capacity, triumphing over indigence, and rivalling the most illustrious geniuses of France, Spain, Italy, and Germany, without riches to command notice, or patronage to create esteem." * Thus, to the merit of those Irish exiles in a *military* capacity, beyond which the subject of this work does not extend, we have this remarkable testimony from the Emperor Francis I. of Germany, as found among his papers after his death, August 18th, 1765. "The more Irish officers in the Austrian service the better; our troops will always be disciplined; an Irish coward is an uncommon character; and what the natives of Ireland even dislike from

---

* In describing the miserable condition to which the Catholics *in* Ireland were reduced by the results of William's success there, Lord Macaulay, too, says— "There were, indeed, Irish Roman Catholics of great ability, energy, and ambition: but they were to be found every where except in Ireland, at Versailles, and at St. Ildefonso, in the armies of Frederic, and in the armies of Maria Theresa. One exile," Lord Clare, "became a Marshal of France. Another," General Wall, "became Prime Minister of Spain. If he had staid in his native land, he would have been regarded as an inferior, by all the ignorant and worthless squireens, who drank the glorious and immortal memory. In his Palace at Madrid, he had the pleasure of being assiduously courted by the Ambassador of George II., and of bidding defiance, in high terms, to the Ambassador of George III. Scattered over all Europe were to be found brave Irish Generals, dexterous Irish diplomatists, Irish Counts, Irish Barons, Irish Knights of St. Lewis, and of St. Leopold, of the White Eagle, and of the Golden Fleece, who, if they had remained in the house of bondage, could not have been ensigns of marching regiments, or freemen of petty corporations."

principle, they generally perform through a desire of glory." The eulogium of the Emperor is well sustained by the following paragraph from a contemporary London periodical in March, 1766. "On the 17th of this month, his Excellency, Count Mahony,* Ambassador from Spain to the Court of Vienna, gave a grand entertainment in honour of St. Patrick, to which were invited all persons of condition, that were of Irish descent; being himself a descendant of an illustrious family of that kingdom. Among many others, were present Count Lacy, President of the Council of War, the Generals O'Donnel, Mc Guire, O'Kelly, Browne, Plunket, and Mc Eligot, 4 Chiefs of the Grand Cross, 2 Governors, several Knights Military, 6 Staff Officers, 4 Privy-Counsellors, with the principal Officers of State; who, to shew their respect to the Irish nation, wore crosses in honour of the day, *as did the whole Court*." † In connexion, too, with a remarkable anecdote of an Irish officer in the service of Naples, Mr. Boswell, the biographer of Dr. Johnson, in his "Account of Corsica," refers, about the same period, or in 1765, to the generally honourable opinion entertained of the Irish abroad. "During the last war in Italy, at the siege of Tortona, the commander of the army which lay before the town ordered Carew, an Irish officer in the service of Naples, to advance, with a detachment, to a particular post. Having given his orders, he whispered to Carew— 'Sir, I know you to be a gallant man. I have therefore put you upon this duty. I tell you, in confidence, it is certain death for you all. I place you there, to make the enemy spring a mine below you.' Carew made a bow to the General, and led on his men in silence to the dreadful post. He there stood with an undaunted countenance, and having called to one of the soldiers for a draught of wine, 'Here,' said he, 'I drink to all those, who bravely fall in battle!' ‡ Fortunately, at that instant, Tortona capitulated, and Carew escaped. But he had thus a full opportunity of displaying a rare instance of intrepidity. It is with pleasure," concludes Mr. Boswell, alluding to the prejudices of the English, and, in too many instances, of his own countrymen, the Scotch, against Ireland, "it is with pleasure, that I record an anecdote so much to the honour of a gentleman of that nation, on which illiberal reflections are too often thrown, by those of whom it little deserves them. Whatever may be the rough jokes of wealthy insolence, or the envious

* Already noticed, in the account of his gallant father, at the affair of Cremona, in 1702. The 2 quotations respecting the Irish in Austria are from the Annual Registers of 1765 and 1766.

† At the County of Dublin Meeting for Catholic Emancipation, held at Kilmanhain, in September, 1811, a veteran officer, Colonel O'Shea, after stating his having been recently in the Austrian army, at the battle of Wagram, the "Colonel commanding a regiment of upwards of 3000 men," further alleged of the numbers, and high character of his countrymen who had been in that service, and of the opinion of the Austrian Commander-in-Chief, the Arch-Duke Charles, on the subject—" Such is our established reputation, that Arch-Duke Charles said to me 'that never was the House of Austria better officered, than when possessing so many Irish; of whom, at one time, upwards of 30 were Generals.'" Of Irish soldiers, as well as Irish officers, in the Austrian army, it may be mentioned here, that a similarly creditable character has been given. "It is worthy of remark," says Ferrar, the historian of Limerick, "that not one Irishman deserted from the Emperor's service on the frontiers of Holland, although large bribes were offered for recruits, to fill the Dutch levies."

‡ This toast of Carew, under the circumstances in which *he* gave it, reminds us of the alleged remark of Leonidas to his Spartans, before the last struggle at Thermopylæ, that their next repast was to be in another world!

sarcasms of needy jealousy, the Irish have ever been, and will continue to be, highly regarded upon the Continent."

This opinion of the exiled Irish, with a proportionable regret at what a loss their services were to England, and an advantage to France, owing to the unnatural order of things established in Ireland, continued to gain ground, amongst the more intelligent class in England, between the last contest of France and England terminated by the Peace of Paris, and the next arising from the struggle for the independence of the United States of America. During that struggle, the enlightened Arthur Young, arguing, from the bravery of the Protestant Irish in the service of the British Empire, the consequent impolicy of such sectarian legislation, as would not admit that Empire to have also the benefit of the services of their Catholic countrymen, remarks—"Our own service, both by sea and land, as well as that, (unfortunately for us,) of the principal monarchies of Europe, speak their steady and determined courage. . . Think of the loss to Ireland of so many Catholics of small property resorting to the armies of France, Spain, Sardinia, and Austria, for employment! Can it be imagined that they would be so ready to leave their own country, if they could stay in it with any prospect of promotion, successful industry, or even liberal protection? It is known they would not; and that, under a different system, instead of adding strength to the enemies of the Empire, they would be among the foremost to enrich and defend it." Mr. Thicknesse, likewise, an English gentleman, in his "Journey through France, and part of Spain," under the head of "Calais, November 4th, 1776," observes—"I found Berwick's regiment on duty in this town: it is commanded by Mons. le Duc de Fitz-James, and a number of Irish gentlemen, my countrymen, (for so I will call them.) You may easily imagine, that men, who possess the natural hospitality of their own country, with the politeness and good-breeding of this, must be very agreeable acquaintance in general: but I am bound to go farther, and to say, that I am endeared to them by marks of true friendship. The King of France, nor any Prince in Europe, cannot boast of troops better disciplined; nor is the King insensible of their merit, for I have lately seen a letter, written by the King's command, from Comte de St. Germain, addressed to the officers of one of these corps, whereby it appears, that the King is truly sensible of their distinguished merit; for braver men there are not in any service. What an acquisition to France! what a loss to Britain!" When the unfortunate Trojans, from their "sweet homes and ancient realms expell'd," requested, according to the Roman poet, an asylum from Latinus in Italy, their ambassador represented to the King:

> "Nor our admission shall your realm disgrace,
> Nor length of time our gratitude efface—
> Besides, what endless honour you shall gain,
> To save and shelter Troy's unhappy train!"
> DRYDEN'S VIRGIL, Æneis, vii., 317-320.

And the asylum opened by Louis XIV. in France to the expatriated adherents of James II. from Ireland, and to their successors, was attended with no less honour and gratitude. The Duke of Fitz-James has noted of Louis, and his reception of the Irish, how "all France applauded, and the greatest and most powerful Monarch crowned the eulogies of this brave and gallant nation, by his styling them, *ses braves*

Irlandois." And the Duke's contemporary, Lieutenant-General Count Arthur Dillon, stated to the National Assembly of France—"It may be said, without partiality, that there is no example of any nation having done for another what the Irish Catholics have done for France. She had great claims upon their gratitude; but they have acquitted themselves of their debt, in the most noble manner."

On December 30th, 1765, died at Rome, in his 78th year, after 3 years' confinement to his residence, during 2 of which he hardly left his bedchamber, James Francis Edward Stuart, by hereditary right, as contrasted with revolutionary regulation, James III., King of Great Britain and Ireland. He was interred in the Papal capital, January, 1766, with all the pomp and solemnity due to the royalty, of which he, and his son Prince Charles Edward, not merely by the old or Catholic Irish, and especially the Brigade, but by numbers of British Protestants, were regarded as the legitimate representatives, in opposition to the intrusive House of Hanover. Even so far within the reign of George III. as the year 1777, in a conversation "as to the inclinations of the people of England, at that time, towards the Royal Family of Stuart," Dr. Johnson, although in receipt of a pension of £300 a year from the reigning Monarch, observed—"If England were fairly polled, the present King would be sent away to-night, and his adherents hanged to-morrow." And the Doctor further alleged—"Sir, the state of the country is this: the people, knowing it to be agreed, on all hands, that this King has not the hereditary right to the Crown, and there being no hope that he who has it can be restored, have grown cold and indifferent upon the subject of loyalty, and have no warm attachment to any King. They would not, therefore, risk any thing to restore the exiled family. They would not give 20 shillings a-piece to bring it about. But, if a mere vote could do it, there would be 20 to 1; at least, there would be a very great majority of voices for it. For, Sir, you are to consider, that all those who think, a King has a right to his Crown, as a man has to his estate, which is the just opinion, would be for restoring the King, who certainly has the hereditary right, could he be trusted with it; in which there would be no danger now, when laws and everything else are so much advanced: and every King will govern by the laws. And you must also consider, Sir, that there is nothing, on the other side, to oppose this; for it is not alleged by any one, that the present family has any inherent right; so that the Whigs could not have a contest between 2 rights." The ceremonial of the interment of the deceased Prince was as follows. "On Saturday, the 15th of January, 1766, his body, after having lain 5 days in state in his own Palace, was removed, in grand cavalcade, to his parish church, the Church of the Holy Apostles, dressed in royal robes, a crown upon his head, a sceptre in his hand, and, upon his breast, the arms of Great Britain, in gold and jewels. The whole Court, and the members of almost every Order and Fraternity at Rome, as well religious as secular, 16 of them with colours flying, attended the cavalcade; 1000 wax-tapers, besides those borne by other attendants, followed the body; 4 gentlemen, particularly distinguished by the deceased in his life-time, supported the pall. At this church, which was hung with black from one end to the other, and filled with skeletons holding wax-tapers, a solemn *requiem* was performed by Cardinal Albani in his pontificalia, assisted by 20 other Cardinals; the music by the musicians of the Apostolic Palace. The Pope intended to have assisted, but was prevented by the coldness of the weather. The bed of state was illuminated with 1100 wax-tapers; and over it was this inscription, *Jacobus, Magnæ Britanniæ Rex, Anno MDCCLXVI.*, with divers medallions in front, representing the several Orders of Chivalry in Great Britain; the 3 Crowns of England, Scotland, and Ireland, to which were joined the royal insignia, viz., the purple robe lined with ermine, the velvet tunic ornamented with gold, the globe, the sceptre, the crown, and the crosses of St. George and St. Andrew, &c." After lying there during 3 days, the body, on the evening of the 3rd, was removed, in the same bed of state, to St. Peter's; which being done in grand procession, and the obsequies again celebrated there, the corpse was conveyed to the vault appointed for it previous to final interment.* The exclusion of James III. from the sceptre of these islands, as attended with the enslavement of all those of his religion in Ireland, was popularly lamented in the beautifully wild and pathetic air or song of "The Blackbird," which, with Allisdrum's March, the Flowers of Edinburgh, the White Cockade, &c., was a favourite tune among the old Jacobite natives, especially in Munster; and played, with corresponding enthusiasm, on the harp and pipes, when there was no "dastard" by, to "say 'twas forbidden." † After the true, though disinherited King, allegorically termed "the blackbird," being mentioned, in the words, as "all her heart's treasure, her joy, and her pleasure," by "a fair lady" (needless to specify), and she accordingly resolving "in fair or foul weather, to seek out her blackbird wherever he be," she says—

"In Scotland he's lov'd, and dearly approv'd;
In England a stranger he seemeth to be;
But his name I'll advance, in Britain or France;
Good luck to my blackbird, wherever he be!"

And she concludes, by exclaiming of her favourite, though parted from her—

"His right I'll proclaim, and who dares me blame?
Good luck to my blackbird, wherever he be!" ‡

The absence, I may remark, of this fine air from Moore's Melodies is a crying "sin of omission," when some of such very inferior merit have obtained a place, and been "married to immortal verse," in that generally admirable collection.

In 1768 and 1769, France added but too largely to her disgraces under Louis XV., or *the Lewd*, by her most unjust war to subjugate Corsica; § a war, that, by a sort of retribution, commenced the connexion

* Annual Register for 1765, Chronicle and Appendix, pp. 152-3, 205-6, Boswell's Life of Johnson under 1777.
† Family traditional information.
‡ I cite from the "Jacobite Minstrelsy," whose Scotch editor should *not* have omitted to acknowledge that "the Blackbird" is an *Irish* air, "and no mistake"—as, on hearing it, will be manifest to a judge of national music. There were other words to that air in Ireland, in the last century, of which a very aged relative, my dear mother, has merely remembered the following lines—

"'Twas in old England this blackbird was nourish'd—
* * * * * * *
And ladies of honour this blackbird did cherish,
Because that he was the true son of a King.
* * * * * * *
Tho' his fame shall remain in France and in Spain,
Yet I can't see my blackbird wherever I go."

§ See Boswell's and Gregorovius's interesting works on Corsica, Annual Registers for 1768-9, &c.

between the 2 countries, through the results of which the Bourbons were to be superseded, on the French throne, by a Corsican family; and as if to verify the curious observation of Rousseau, in writing of Corsica—" I have some *presentiment, that one day that little island will astonish Europe!"* The very powerful or overwhelming force, despatched from France to effect this conquest, comprised some of the best regiments in her service. Among these corps, were the Regiments of Bulkeley and Roscommon.* The countrymen of Wellington employed to conquer those of Napoleon, the destined Scipio and Hannibal of a future contest greater than that between Rome and Carthage, and *both* then infants, the one as born in May, the other in August, 1769! And the situation of the country of Wellington under the English was unfortunately but too like that of the country of Napoleon under the Genoese; on a transfer from whom, when defeated, of their pretended claims to Corsica, France so infamously assumed a right to attack and subdue the Corsicans. "Their system," writes Mr. Boswell of those detested mercantile oppressors, the Genoese, "was *not* to render the Corsicans happier and better, but, *by keeping them in ignorance, and under the most abject submission, to prevent their endeavouring to get free; while Genoa drained the island of all she could possibly get, choosing rather even to have less advantage by tyranny, than to have a much greater advantage, and risque the consequences of permitting the inhabitants to enjoy the blessings of freedom. . . . What shewed the Genoese policy in the worst light, and could not but be very galling to the Corsicans who remained at home, was, that many of these islanders, who had gone over to the Continent, made a distinguished figure in most of the European states, both in learning, and in arms."* The English Whig Horace Walpole, exclaims of the Genoese, in reference to their oppression of the Corsicans—" I hate the Genoese: they make a commonwealth the most devilish of all tyrannies!" But, what might not a Genoese have *retorted* against England, with respect to Ireland, in *those* days.

In 1770, on apprehension of a rupture with England respecting the Falkland Islands, the Regiment of Clare was sent to India, where it was equally noted for its discipline and bravery. In this year, also, died a distinguished officer of the Irish Brigade, whose entrance into military life dated from the age of Louis XIV.—the Maréchal de Camp and Chevalier Richard Edmond de Cusack. He was descended from an ancient and illustrious family, originally of Guienne, whose progenitor passed into England with her great conqueror Duke William from Normandy, in 1066. In 1211, Geoffroy and André de Cusack came to Ireland with King John, and behaved themselves so well, that John made them large grants of property there. In the reign of Elizabeth, Nicholas Cusack was beheaded for the zeal he evinced in defence of his country and religion. Patrick Cusack and his family having been eminent for bravery in the army of the Confederates of Ireland during the great civil war, or Parliamentarian and Cromwellian rebellion against Charles I. and II., Cromwell seized upon those gentlemen's estates, which, after "the Restoration," instead of being given back to their right owners who had lost them in defence of the Crown, were shamelessly granted, with those of other Irish Catholic loyalists, to James, Duke of York, and other English lords.†

---

* Count Arthur Dillon's Mémoire.

† During the next war in Ireland, or that of the Revolution, the name of Cusack continued to be one of note; 4 of its representatives sitting as Members of the national Parliament, under King James II., in 1689, at Dublin; and several being

Richard Cusack, after the loss of his grandfather fighting against the English or Cromwellian rebels at the fatal battle of Worcester, retired to the Continent, where he entered the service of Spain. He left 3 sons. 1. Girard Alexandre, or Gerald Alexander, de Cusack, Chevalier of St. Louis, Lieutenant-Colonel of the Irish Regiment of Roth, deceased in 1743, after having served 53 years. 2. Charles de Cusack, who having been an officer in the Irish Regiment of Lee, passed into the service of Spain with the rank of Captain of the Walloon Guards, rose to be a Maréchal de Camp, or Major-General, and a Commander of the Order of St. Jago, and, at his death in 1748, in the service of Naples, was Governor of Melazzo in Sicily. 3. Richard Edmond de Cusack, the subject of this notice. Born in Flanders in 1687, he, in his 15th year, or 1702, joined the Regiment of Dorrington, subsequently that of Roth, as a volunteer Cadet. He was at the siege of Kehl, the combat of Munderkingen, and the 1st battle, or victory, of Hochstedt, in 1703; and fought at the 2nd battle, or defeat, of Hochstedt, (otherwise Blenheim) in 1704; in which year, he was made a reformed Lieutenant. He served with the Army of the Rhine in 1705, and for several ensuing campaigns. Nominated a reformed Captain in the same regiment by commission of May 21st, 1709, he was, September 11th, at the great battle of Malplaquet. He was employed in Flanders in 1710; fought at the attack of Arleux in 1711; and was present at the success of Denain, and the sieges of Douay, Quesnoy, and Bouchain in 1712. He was engaged at the reductions of Landau and Friburgh, and the capture of the retrenchments of General Vaubonne in 1713. He became Aide-Major to his regiment (then Roth's) by brevet of August 20th, 1720; had rank in it as a Captain *en second* from June 21st, 1721; and as a Captain *en pied* from June 19th, 1729. He obtained, January 9th, 1731, a company, which he commanded at the siege of Kehl in 1733; at the attack of the lines of Etlingen and the siege of Philipsburgh in 1734; and at the affair of Clausen in 1735. He was created a Chevalier of St. Louis in 1736. Attached to the Army of Flanders in 1742, he became Captain of Grenadiers on January 24th, 1743; Lieutenant-Colonel on April 4th following; and was present, in that grade, at the battle of Dettingen, in June. He served at the sieges of Menin, Ypres, Furnes, and Fort Knock in 1744, conducted under King Louis in person; and finished that campaign, at the Camp of Courtray. He behaved, at the victory of Fontenoy, May 11th, 1745, with such distinction, that he was granted a royal pension of 600 livres; and was at the ensuing reductions of the town and citadel of Tournay, of Oudenarde, of Dendermonde, and Ath. Brigadier of the armies of the King, by brevet of March 20th, 1747, and stationed at the bridge of Walheim, a post among the most important to be guarded during this campaign, he maintained himself there, for 6 weeks, with but 600 men. At the battle of Laffeldt, gained by the King on July 2nd following, he displayed such additional proofs of valour and good conduct, that his previous royal pension of 600 livres was increased to 1600. He served at the capture of Maestricht in 1748; at the Camp of Aimeries in 1754; at that of Calais in 1756; and in Flanders in 1757 and 1758. He

officers of infantry, horse, and dragoons, in the Irish army, or the Regiments of Dorrington, Mountcashel, Slane, Tyrconnell, Galmoy, Maxwell, Clifford; 1 of whom, Colonel Nicholas Cusack, of the branch of Lismullen, was an executing party to the Civil Articles of the Treaty of Limerick. As defenders of their legitimate sovereign and native country in this contest, the Cusacks were also duly marked out for land-spoliation, in the Williamite attainders of 1691.

obtained this last year, October 20th, the government of the towns of Guerande, of Croisick, and Port-du-St.-Nazaire in Bretagne, and was sworn accordingly, March 18th, 1759. Created a Maréchal de Camp by brevet of February 10th, 1759, he gave up his Lieutenant-Colonelcy of the Regiment of Roth, and served no more. He was a Chevalier of the Order of St. Jago, or of the Red Sword, of Spain; and obtained, by a royal brevet of August 1st, 1758, the Commandery of the Hospital of Manceid, in Armagnac, a dependency of that Order. His death, as above-mentioned, in 1770, took place at Corbeil, in his 82nd year, after a life of uninterrupted military service for 56 years. By his 1st wife, Isabella Bridget Fitz-Gerald, he left an only daughter, married to the Marquis l'Espinasse-Langeac, Maréchal de Camp.*

As the quarrel of England and her North American Colonies, which commenced not long after the Peace of 1763, progressed to an extent rendering it every day more evident, that, between the former determined to tax, and the latter not to be taxed, a war should be the result, it was no less evident to the English Government, that the Irish Catholic element, for supplying soldiers to the army, and sailors to the navy, of the Empire, should be more resorted to than ever, whatever might be the Penal-Code or No-Popery prejudice to the contrary. Even in the preceding Seven Years' War, or so soon as the ruling powers in England conceived, that, from the decisive defeat of the last attempt to restore the House of Stuart in 1745-6, and from a further lapse of several years, it might be possible to recruit, though as yet "under the rose," among Irish Papists, without a prospect of such wholesale desertion, as, in the former days of Jacobite fervour, rendered levies of the kind no better than "fairy gifts fading away," it had been resolved, that trials should be made, of how far those Papists could be trusted, in the military and naval line. Thus, in 1757, "the English regiments enlisted Roman Catholic soldiers in Limerick for the 1st time since the Revolution," alleges the Protestant historian Ferrar; adding, "since that time, the narrow, impolitic system has been abandoned of employing only English and Scots' soldiers. Ireland has furnished thousands of brave men to fight the battles of the British Empire, who, before this time, were a bulwark of strength, and a tower of defence, to our natural enemies, the French. Several regiments have been recruited and disciplined in Limerick." In equal ignoring of the existing "ascendancy" law in Ireland, by which no Papist was permitted to bear arms, simultaneous levies were made for the English army from members of the proscribed creed, elsewhere in Munster, as we learn from references to the matter several years after, or in 1774 and 1775, by 2 officers, as Irish Members of Parliament. The former, Major Boyle Roche, said—"He must observe, in the late war, several recruits were raised in Cork and other parts of Munster in the year 1757, *without any scrupulous examination in respect to their religion;* that a greater number of Papists were raised, and went to America; and he called on every military gentleman in the House, who had been in that service, to declare, whether any men had behaved better? And, though they fought against Papists, the French, yet their religion did not influence them to desert; but they did their duty, and were as amenable to discipline, as any men in the army." The latter officer,

* Courcelles, Ponce MSS., personal collections on Irish families.

Colonel Browne, affirmed—"In my opinion, Papists can be, and are, as loyal as any others; of which I will give an instance. In the time of the late war, I recruited the regiment, in which I served, with above 200 Papists raised about Cork. They went to Canada, behaved bravely, and when in garrison in a Popish town, and surrounded with Papists, whilst many Protestants deserted, not 1 of these Papists ran away."* Towards the conclusion of the same war, or in 1762, the liberal Protestant Lord Primate of Ireland, Dr. Stone, also spoke in the Parliament, at Dublin, of "the gallant conduct of the Irish Catholic sailors at Belle-Isle, and at the recent conquest of Martinique."† The *necessity* of having to resort to the same aid is subsequently, or in 1769, alluded to by Sir William Draper, as a military authority, in his 4th letter to Junius. "The troops in the Mediterranean, in the West Indies, in America," writes Sir William, "labour under great difficulties, from the scarcity of men, which is but too visible, all over these kingdoms," or England and Scotland. "Many of our forces are in climates unfavourable to British constitutions; their loss is in proportion. Britain," he concludes, "must recruit all these regiments from her own emaciated bosom, or, more *precariously*, by Catholics from Ireland." And *precarious*, indeed, would England's situation be under such circumstances, or if the intolerant legislation to which the Irish Catholics had been so long subjected should be allowed to continue, while the existence of her empire was to depend more and more upon Irish Catholic soldiers and sailors! Hence, in 1774, the 1st move towards a breach in the ice of the Penal Code was made, even in the "ascendancy" Parliament at Dublin, through an admission of members of the persecuted faith to qualify themselves, in a recognized form, as subjects to the Crown, by a particular Oath of Allegiance for that purpose; dispensing, in their favour, with the merely exclusive, or Protestant terms, upon which alone, a pledge of the kind had hitherto been admissible. By the oath in question, those taking it bound themselves to be loyal to King George III., and his heirs, as Sovereigns of Great Britain and Ireland, in opposition to any claim of the kind, on the part of "Charles III.," (or Prince Charles Edward Stuart, thus regally designated since his father's death,) and the deponents, at the same time, abjured several obnoxious, or intolerant and anti-social, doctrines attributed to their Church.‡

* In a parliamentary debate of May, 1864, when, according to Mr. Macguire, referring to Ireland, "for every single Protestant, or Presbyterian, who enlisted in the Queen's army in that country, there enlisted 5 Catholics," Colonel North said—"During the time he had served in the army, he had, for the most part, been connected with regiments which were composed chiefly of Roman Catholics; one of the very last being the Royal Irish Fusiliers," or 87th, "in which, out of 1000 men, there were not more than 70 or 80 Protestants; and he defied any man to point out an instance, in which the Roman Catholic soldier, in those regiments, had not done his duty most nobly, led by Protestant officers, in the service of a Protestant Queen."

† The extracts of the parliamentary speeches of Major Roche, Colonel Browne, and Primate Stone, are taken from Walker's Hibernian Magazine for 1775, and O'Conor's History of the Irish Catholics, under the year 1762. On the large proportion of Irish soldiers and sailors in the army and navy of Great Britain and Ireland, see the various authorities (suggestive of so many more) in my Green Book, chapters ii.-iii., 2nd edition, Dublin, 1844.

‡ Mr. O'Donoghue, in his learned "Historical Memoir of the O'Briens," having premised, how, until 1774, "no Roman Catholic could take the Oath of Allegiance, without disclaiming the *spiritual* supremacy of the Head of his Church," but that then "this anomalous and dangerous state of things was remedied," writes as

The next year, 1775, when blood was first unfortunately shed between the English and the Americans, is otherwise remarkable for the birth of Daniel O'Connell, by whose exertions the *last* links of the Penal Code were to be broken; a reference to whose origin, in some detail, is allowable here, if only as that *also* of a distinguished officer of the name in the Irish Brigade and *his* relative, to be more particularly noticed farther on. The sept of O'Conghaile, or O'Connell, is deduced in Gaelic genealogy from a very remote royal source, or that of Conary I., Ard-Righ, or Monarch of Erin about the commencement of the Christian era. The O'Connells, and their clan-territory in Kerry, primitively, or down to the 12th century, consisting of the Barony of Magunihy, are mentioned as follows, by the old bardic topographer O'Huidhrin, or O'Heerin—

> " O'Connell, of the slender swords,
> *Is* over the bushy-forted Magunihy;
> A hazel-tree of branching ringlets,
> In the Munster plain of horse-hosts." *

In the disturbed microcosm, or "little world," of Erin, after the Anglo-Norman invasion, there was a similar state of things, in a minor sphere, to that in a greater, upon the Continent, at the fall of the Roman empire; the Goths, who invaded the Romans, having done so, as compelled to retreat from the Huns, who were themselves obliged to retire from other Tartar enemies farther eastwards, or towards China. "The wave behind impels the wave before," as the poet says. Those attacked, and forced to abandon their country, by a stronger race, had to indemnify themselves at the expense of another race, still less powerful. Under such circumstances, the O'Donoghues, driven by "the stranger" from their original territory in Magh-Feimhin, on the plain of Cashel, or the Baronies of Iffa and Offa East, in the County of Tipperary, and having consequently to seek a fresh establishment more to the south, did so in Kerry, where others of the name were previously located.† To this

follows—" The oath, which Roman Catholics were, by this Act, enabled to take before the Judges, or a Justice of the Peace in the country," was—"To bear true allegiance to the Sovereign, and defend him against all attempts and conspiracies against his authority, to disclose all treasons which the party may be informed of against his Majesty, his heirs, and successors, and to support the succession of the Crown in his Majesty's family, renouncing any allegiance, or obedience, to the person assuming the title of Charles III., or any other person claiming a right to the Crown: that the swearer rejects the impious doctrine, that it was lawful to murder persons on pretence of their being heretics, and the doctrine, (equally impious,) that no faith was to be kept with heretics:—renouncing the opinion, that Princes, excommunicated by the Pope, might be murdered by their subjects;—declaring that neither the Pope, nor any other Prince, had, or ought to have, any *temporal* or *civil* jurisdiction within this realm; and that the declaration, thus made and subscribed, was made without any equivocation, mental reservation, or dispensation already had from the Pope, or any authority of the See of Rome. . . . In accordance with this Act, in the next year, 60 of the most eminent of the Roman Catholic merchants and gentry of the city of Dublin, headed by Lord Trimleston, took the Oath of Allegiance in the Court of King's Bench, in presence of the Lord Chief Justice, Lord Annally, and their example was followed *generally* throughout the Kingdom."

* For " O'Conghaile," and " Magh O'g Coinchinn," I substitute the modern equivalents, " O'Connell," and " Magunihy," in this quatrain. The O'Connells were more anciently located in Kerry, than they commonly supposed their sept to have been. Truth makes the race *far* older there than fiction.

† The O'Donoghues were descended from Dubh-da-bhoirean, King of Munster, killed in 957, whose son, Domhnall, commanded the troops of Desmond, or South Munster, at the famous battle of Clontarf, in 1014. In the War of the Revolution,

augmentation of O'Donoghues there, the O'Connells became victims, being attacked, and expelled from the Barony of Magunihy; and they, having to "make up for *their* loss," fell upon their neighbours, the O'Seaghas, or O'Sheas, of the same Conarian origin, and stripped them of their ancient patrimony, the Barony of Iveragh, or Ui-Rathach, from which the O'Seagha, or O'Shea, was, in better days, entitled "King of Ui-Rathach." The chief seat of the O'Connells, in this newly-acquired district, was at Ballycarbery, near Cahirciveen; and, in the capacity of hereditary Castellans, or otherwise, they were followers to Mac Carthy More, till the 17th century. The head branch of the O'Connells was transplanted by Cromwell into the County of Clare; which family, with those of the name in Kerry, supplied distinguished officers to King James II., during the War of the Revolution in Ireland; the principal of the latter being the stout Colonel and Brigadier, Maurice O'Connell of Iveragh, and of Ash-Tower, a property of £600 a year in the County of Dublin, who was killed at the battle of Aughrim.* Of O'Connells, subsequent to this war, several appear to have had good estates; and, among such as saved their property under the Articles of Limerick, was Captain John O'Connell, of Aghgore, and Derrynane, after serving throughout the contest, or from the campaign of Derry in 1689, to that of Aughrim in 1691. This gentleman, by his son Daniel, and grandson Morgan, was the progenitor of the great Emancipator, born at Carhen, near Cahirciveen, August 6th, 1775.

In the interval from the Treaty of Limerick to this period of the 1st move towards a relaxation of the Penal Code in Ireland and the commencement of the war in America, the O'Connells, in Kerry, to whatever remnant of the "good estates" they could contrive to retain, in spite of the "Protestant discoverer,"—or sectarian informer, privileged to rob Catholics by law of such landed property worth having, as he could prove them *guilty* of possessing!—added the profits of a lucrative contraband trade with France; carried on, in *just* or *natural* elusion of the detestable policy of those days, to oppress Ireland commercially, as well as to enslave her religiously. Of the circumstances of this trade, as connected with the "flights of the wild geese," or periodical emigrations to join the Irish Brigade from the different harbours of Kerry, but especially that of Valentia, our late learned Protestant countryman, Dr.

there were only a few O'Donoghues of the ranks of Captain, Lieutenant, and Ensign, in the Irish army; and I also find but few to have been officers in the Irish Brigade. The name was most eminent abroad, in the service of Spain.

* This Maurice, son of Jeffery O'Connell, of Ibrahagh, or Iveragh, was nephew of John O'Connell, a lawyer, noted for his good sense, and agent to the Duke of Ormonde; which John left, by will, his Dublin or Ash-Tower estate, of £600 a year, to Maurice as tenant for life, and to his legitimate male heirs in succession. By his marriage with an English lady, Catherine, daughter of Sir Edward Langton, Maurice left, as his sole heir, Richard, a minor. Through a Williamite outlawry of Maurice *post mortem*—or when he could no longer forfeit, as having been but a tenant for life!—the estate of Ash-Tower was claimed as forfeited to the Crown, sequestered accordingly, and thus, for several years, unjustly withheld from its undoubted heir, the minor. That heir, Richard, was, in the meantime, reared up a Protestant with his English or mother's connexions; having, by the seizure of his property, been, says his printed case, "left a destitute orphan, without support or friends; his relations" in Ireland, it is alleged of the O'Connells, "who are Roman Catholicks, of *good estates*, in the aforesaid kingdom, neglecting him, as being bred up in the Protestant religion." The property of Ash-Tower, however, seems to have been restored; the allegations, in support of the Petition to that effect, being reported as true.

William Cooke Taylor, in his "Reminiscences of Daniel O'Connell" as "by a Munster Farmer," writes—"In consequence of this form of intercourse, what the law called smuggling, and what those engaged in it called *free trade*, was very active between the French ports and this part of Ireland. Morgan O'Connell's store, or shop, at Cahirciveen, received many a cargo of French laces, wines, and silks, which were sold, at an immense profit, in the south and west of Ireland, and enabled him rapidly to accumulate a large fortune. English cruisers avoided the iron-bound coast of Kerry, which then had a reputation even worse than its reality. It was said, that the men of the Kerry coast combined wrecking with smuggling; and that, for both purposes, they had organized a very complete system of posts, and telegraphic signals, along the bluff headlands. When a suspicious sail was announced, nice calculations were made, to ascertain her probable position after nightfall. A horse was then turned out to graze, on the fields near that part of the shore opposite to which she most probably was, and a lantern was tied to the horse's head. Viewed from a distance, this light, rising and falling as the animal fed, produced precisely the same effect as light in the cabin of a distant ship. The crew of the stranger-vessel, thus led to believe that there was open water before them, steered boldly onwards, and could not discover their error, until they had dashed against the rocks.* There is *no* reason to believe, that the O'Connells *ever* engaged in such treacherous transactions; but there is indisputable evidence, that they were largely practised in this part of the country, and that they afforded great protection to smuggling, by deterring the English cruisers from the coast. Daniel O'Connell's infancy was thus passed amid scenes likely to impress his mind with stern hostility to the Protestant ascendancy, and the English government by which it was supported. In the name of that ascendancy, he was taught that his ancestors had been plundered; in the name of that ascendancy, he saw his religion insulted, and his family oppressed; for the Penal Laws opposed serious impediments to his father's investment of the profits of his trade in the acquisition of land.† All around him were engaged in a fiscal war with the English government, and, in the code of Kerry ethics, a seizure by the officers of the Custom-House was regarded as a robbery, and the defrauding of the revenue a simple act of justice to one's self and family." While such was the situation of the O'Connells at home, abroad, in the Regiments of Clare, Berwick, and Walsh, belonging to the Irish Brigade, as well as in other corps of the French army, or the Regiments of Royal Suedois and Salm-Salm, the name was represented, down to the French Revolution, by officers, from the grades of Sous-Lieutenant and Captain to those of Colonel and Maréchal de Camp, including some Chevaliers of St. Louis.‡

---

* With such evil-doings in *Ireland* towards unfortunate vessels and their crews, compare, however, those likewise practised in *England*, as already noticed in Book II., where treating of the exiled Earl of Clancarty; and see the account of the "wreckers" of Bretagne, in Michelet's History of *France*.

† Arthur Young, after alluding to the discouragements, under the Penal Laws, to Catholics engaging in any regular trade, requiring both industry and capital, exclaims—"If they succeed and make a fortune, what are they to do with it? They can neither buy land, nor take a mortgage, nor even fine down the rent of a lease. Where is there a people in the world to be found industrious under such circumstances?"

‡ Under this year, 1775, as the latest to which I have any knowledge of a

It was high time, the year before O'Connell's birth, or in 1774, that the enslaved Catholics in Ireland should have been admitted by statute to qualify themselves as subjects to the Crown, when, in October, 1775, it was acknowledged, in the British House of Lords, how imperative it was for England to avail herself openly of their assistance, if the great strength of the insurrection in North America were to be duly opposed. On seconding the Address to the Throne, from that assembly, Lord Townsend, in dwelling upon the propriety of taking foreigners into the pay of England, added, " and Irish Papists into her service. He said, Papists might be as good soldiers as any others; that it was only by England, that any distinction was made; that France, however rigorous, bigotted, or despotic, made no difference between Protestants and Catholics; that the Hollanders acted in the same manner; that, so men were good soldiers, it was very little matter what might be their creeds." And the recent move, in the right direction, by the English Government in Ireland, with regard to the Catholics, had a corresponding effect upon recruiting there for the service in America, even through such an unprecedented co-operation, as that of a Catholic nobleman, in the person of Lord Kenmare; respecting which, we have this contemporary announcement, under the date of August 20th, 1775. " Major Sir Boyle Roche, Baronet, attended by his Captain, and a grand procession, beat up for recruits in Limerick, and met with great success. This was the 1st man of rank, who, when the war broke out in America, with an honest zeal in his Majesty's service, beat up in person for recruits. Lord Kenmare gave half-a-guinea additional bounty to every recruit." It elsewhere appears, that the Major, " in 1 week, raised 500 recruits, for the King's army." The increasing reasons, from 1775 to 1778, for a further or more substantial relaxation of the Popery Code, suggested by the continued necessity of drawing away troops from Ireland to America, led,

very distinguished officer of the Irish Brigade, I insert the best account I have found of him; which, if extending to the exact date of his decease, would be given in the text at *that* period, instead of in *this* note. The Chevalier Pierre de Nugent, or Sir Peter Nugent, Baronet, was first, or in 1717, a Lieutenant in Nugent's Regiment of Irish Horse, subsequently that of Fitz-James; was a reformed Captain *à la suite*, October 14th, 1718; and, having raised a company by commission of February 2nd, 1727, he commanded it at the reductions of Kehl and Philipsburgh, in 1733 and 1734. He was empowered to rank, March 21st, 1735, as a Mestre-de-Camp de Cavalerie. He served, under the Marshal de Maillebois, with the Army of the Lower Rhine, in September, 1741; passed, with that army, into Westphalia and Bavaria, in 1742; after being at several actions there, returned to France, in July, 1743; and finished the campaign, with his regiment, under the Marshal de Noailles, in Lower Alsace. He did not serve in 1744. Created Brigadier of Horse by brevet of May 1st, 1745, he signalized himself, the 11th, at the battle of Fontenoy; and obtained the same day letters of service to be employed in the rank of Brigadier. After being present at the reductions of Tournay and Oudenarde, he was chosen, in December, to act as Brigadier in the force designed to assist Prince Charles Stuart in Britain; but, being among the select Irish detachment, that attempted, early in March, 1746, to reach Scotland from Ostend by sea, he was captured by Commodore Knowles. Having been exchanged as a prisoner, and returning to France, he was at the reduction of Maestricht in 1748. Maréchal de Camp, or Major-General, by brevet of May 10th, that year, he became Lieutenant-Colonel of his regiment, June 25th, following. Employed with the Army of Germany, under the Prince de Soubise, by letters of June 15th, 1757, he fought valiantly at Rosbach. Engaged, by letters, of November 29th, for the winter, in Germany, he re-entered France with his regiment, in April, 1758. He resigned the Lieutenant-Colonelcy of the corps in 1759; and was created Lieutenant-General of the Armies of the King, by power of July 25th, 1762.

towards the conclusion of that period, to a motion in Parliament, by a Mr. James Fitz-Gerald, that Catholics might be permitted to take leases of lands for 61 years; which proposal, however, though so fair and moderate, was negatived by the usual majority of intolerance in the Dublin "ascendancy" legislature. But, soon after, in 1778, when the ugly intelligence from America arrived, how

"Burgoyne, opposing all the fates,
At Saratoga fought with General Gates,"

and consequently had to surrender, with his entire force, to the mortifying accompaniment of "Yankee Doodle," * the same Parliament, under a pressure from Government—the stronger, as aware that France would join America—passed an act to enable Catholics to take leases for 999 years! The terms, too, in which this measure was expressed, as tending to excite still higher expectations with reference to the future,† occasioned much satisfaction on the part of the Irish Catholics at home and abroad; a satisfaction, at the same time, with which the feelings of French *policy* could not sympathize, inasmuch as the military interest of France in Ireland should be injured, by whatever might be calculated to serve that of England there. A British contemporary writer, justifying "the conduct of the Government in mitigating the Penal Laws against the Papists," after remarking, that, to the harassing legal disabilities, under which the Catholics laboured at home, "France owed some of her bravest Brigades, and Austria her most distinguished Generals," so that the British "Government was not insensible of all this, and, therefore, prudently resolved to give them," the Catholics, "some indulgence," thus proceeds—"Perhaps there never was a period when a step of this kind was more solidly political, or better calculated to promote the common weal. After the surrender of Burgoyne's army, what an alarming prospect appeared to the eyes of the nation! . . . The distresses and dangers of the nation called aloud for the assistance of every source of power which is within us; whilst an application to foreign aids," or German mercenaries procured at an enormous cost, "too forcibly proved a decay in our own vital principle. Nothing, therefore, could be better judged, under such circumstances, than to

---

* Of the name of "Yankee," and the air of "Yankee Doodle," the English translator and annotator of "Travels in North America in 1780, 1781, and 1782, by the Marquis de Chastellux, Member of the French Academy, and Major-General in the French Army, under the Count de Rochambeau," says—"This is a name, given by way of derision, and even simple pleasantry, to the inhabitants of the 4 eastern States. It is thought to come from a savage people, who formerly occupied this country, and dwelt between the Connecticut river, and the State of Massachusetts. . . . The English army serving in America, and England herself, will long have reason to remember the contemptuous use they made of this term in the late unhappy war, and the severe retort they met with on the occasion. The *English* army, at Bunker's Hill, marched to the insulting tune of ' *Yankee Doodle;* ' but, from that period, it became the air of triumph, the Io Pæan of *America*. It was *cuckoo* to the British ear." Our honest countryman, Serjeant Lamb, in his "Journal of the American War," in which he served under Burgoyne, accordingly, mentions how, when the British troops were marching down, from the heights of Saratoga, to the verge of the river, where they were to give up their arms and artillery, "the American drummers and fifers were ordered by General Gates, to play the tune of '*Yankey Doodle.*'"

† On the rejection of Mr. Fitz-Gerald's motion, and the subsequent parliamentary grant of so much *more* than he had moved for, compare Parnell's History of the Penal Laws against the Irish Catholics, from the Treaty of Limerick to the Union, with Plowden's Historical Review.

reunite to the state such a numerous body of faithful subjects. . . . But," continues this writer, "the more Britain rejoiced at this happy event, the more France was confounded! Political France! whose eyes are always open to her own interest, well saw the fatal tendency of such a step to her. No sooner was it seen there, that the act was passed in favour of the Roman Catholics, than an universal damp was seen in every countenance; and the general cry was, ' *Voila! deux cens mille hommes armés contre nous!*'—' See 200,000 men armed against us!' They lamented to think, that their Irish Brigades must now fall to the ground, and that they could no longer expect to be supported by a disaffected party among ourselves, in case they should invade us; and, to show to what length they carried their regret, the students of the English College at Douay wanted to give public thanks to God for the happy event, but they durst not do it! Of all this," he continues, " I am informed by gentlemen of the utmost veracity, who were in France at the time, and who were eye-witnesses and ear-witnesses of what passed." * And "these unquestionable facts," he concludes, "show,

* The Emperor Napoleon, too, alleged to our countryman, Dr. O'Meara, at St. Helena—"When the Catholic question was first seriously agitated, I would have given 50,000,000 to be assured, that it would *not* be granted; for it would have entirely *ruined my projects upon Ireland.*" Napoleon likewise lamented to Las Cases at St. Helena, that, in 1798, he did not go to Ireland, instead of to Egypt; as well he might, from the military strength subsequently derived from Ireland by England, to put him down. On this point, the Duke of Wellington, in 1829, addressing the House of Lords in favour of Catholic Emancipation, observed—"It is already well known to your Lordships, that, of the troops which our gracious Sovereign did me the honour to entrust to my command at various periods during the war—a war undertaken expressly for the purpose of securing the happy institutions and independence of the country—that at least one-half were Roman Catholics. My Lords, when I call your recollection to this fact, I am sure all further eulogy is unnecessary. Your Lordships are well aware for what length of period, and under what difficult circumstances, they maintained the empire buoyant upon the flood, which overwhelmed the thrones and wrecked the institutions of every other people; how they kept alive the only spark of freedom which was left unextinguished in Europe; and how, by unprecedented efforts, they at length placed us, not only far above danger, but at an elevation of prosperity, for which we had hardly dared to hope. These, my Lords, are sacred and imperative titles to a nation's gratitude. My Lords, it is become quite needless for me to assure you, that I have invariably found my Roman Catholic soldiers as patient under privations, as eager for the combat, and as brave and determined in the field, as any other portion of his Majesty's troops; and, in point of loyalty and devotion to their King and country, I am quite certain they have never been surpassed. I claim no merit in admitting, that others might have guided the storm of battle as skilfully as myself. We have only to recur to the annals of our military achievements to be convinced, that few, indeed, of our commanders have not known how to direct the unconquerable spirit of their troops, and to shed fresh glories round the British name. But, my Lords, while we are free to acknowledge this, we must also confess that, without Catholic blood and Catholic valour, no victory could ever have been obtained, and the first military talents in Europe might have been exerted in vain, at the head of an army. My Lords, if on the eve of any of those hard-fought days, on which I had the honour to command them, I had thus addressed my Roman Catholic troops:—'You well know that your country either so suspects your loyalty, or so dislikes your religion, that she has not thought proper to admit you amongst the ranks of her citizens; if on that account you deem it an act of injustice on her part to require you to shed your blood in her defence, you are at liberty to withdraw'—I am quite sure, my Lords, that, however bitter the recollections which it awakened, they would have spurned the alternative with indignation; for the hour of danger and glory is the hour in which the gallant, the generous-hearted Irishman best knows his duty, and is most determined to perform it. But if, my Lords, it had been otherwise;

beyond reply, the propriety of the repeal" in the Penal Laws, "and the advantages that may be expected from it to this country." So much for those measures of English policy, calculated, along with the extinction of any hope of a Stuart "restoration," to be more and more prejudicial to the Irish Brigade from 1757 to 1778, or down to the period which we now approach, when the 3 last corps known as Irish, out of the number that formerly existed in the service of France, were to act with her against England in the American War.

The Court of Versailles, having concluded at Paris a treaty of amity and commerce with the United States of America as an independent power, early in February, 1778, the result was necessarily war between England and France. Like the gallant Lafayette, however, a number of the Irish military in France anticipated its Government, in taking up the cause of America. Among them, there were, so early as 1776, several of the supernumerary or reformed officers of the Brigade. "As this corps," says the announcement of the sailing of those gentlemen for America, "is known to contain some of the best-disciplined officers in Europe, there is no doubt, but that they will meet with all suitable encouragement." The next year, 1777, we find officers of higher rank, or Colonel Conway of the Brigade, and Colonel Roche de Fermoy, in commands of note; the former, after an English allusion to him, as "a Colonel of the Irish Brigade," being further referred to, as "one of that numerous train of officers in the French service, who had taken an active part against Great Britain, in this unhappy civil war." When hostilities broke out between France and England, the Irish regiments in France, who considered themselves entitled to serve *before* other corps against the English—a claim more especially advanced, on this occasion, by the Regiment of Dillon—were not long left unemployed.* In 1779, the Regiment of

---

if they had chosen to desert the cause in which they were embarked, though the remainder of the troops would undoubtedly have maintained the honour of the British arms, yet, as I have just said, no efforts of theirs could ever have crowned us with victory. Yes, my Lords, it is mainly to the Irish Catholics that we all owe our proud pre-eminence in our military career; and that I, personally, am indebted for the laurels with which you have been pleased to decorate my brow —for the honours which you have so bountifully lavished on me, and for the fair fame (I prize it above all other rewards) which my country, in its generous kindness, has bestowed upon me. I cannot but feel, my Lords, that you yourselves have been chiefly instrumental in placing this heavy debt of gratitude upon me— greater, perhaps, than has ever fallen to the lot of any individual; and, however flattering the circumstance, it often places me in a very painful position. Whenever I meet (and it is almost an every-day occurrence) with any of those brave men, who, in common with others, are the object of this bill, and who have so often borne me on the tide of victory; when I see them still branded with the imputation of a divided allegiance, still degraded beneath the lowest menial, and still proclaimed unfit to enter within the pale of the constitution, I feel almost ashamed of the honours which have been lavished upon me. I feel that, though the merit was theirs, what was so freely given to me was unjustly denied to them; that I had reaped, though they had sown; that they had borne the heat and burden of the day, but that the wages and repose were mine alone. My Lords, it is a great additional gratification to me to advocate these principles in conjunction with a distinguished member of my family, so lately at the head of the Government of his native country—a country ever dear to me from the recollections of my infancy, the memory of her wrongs, and the bravery of her people. I glory, my Lords, in the name of Ireland; and it is the highest pleasure I can ambition, to be thus united with the rest of my kindred, in the grateful task of closing the wounds which seven centuries of misgovernment have inflicted upon that unfortunate land."

* Lieutenant-General Count Arthur Dillon thus commences his account of the

Berwick was attached to the squadron of the Count d'Orvilliers. Of the Regiment of Walsh, a considerable portion was likewise appointed to act in detachments as marines; of which detachments, a piquet, with the squadron of the Marquis de Vaudreuil, was present, early that year, at the capture, from the English, of Senegal, in Africa, where it remained in garrison. April 5th, at Brest, in the squadron of M. de la Motte Piquet, the 1st battalion of the Regiment of Dillon, in number 1000 men, subsequently made 1400, embarked for the West Indies under its Colonel-Proprietor, Count Arthur Dillon the younger, grandson and namesake of the 1st Colonel-Proprietor, who brought the regiment from Ireland to France in 1690, and nephew of the 2 other Colonels, slain in command of the corps, at the victories of Fontenoy in 1745, and Laffeldt in 1747. The junction of this squadron from Brest with that of the Count d'Estaing at Martinique strengthening him sufficiently to undertake the long-meditated design of a conquest of the Isle of Grenada from the English, he set sail, June 30th, from Martinique, and, by July 2nd, in the evening, anchoring off Grenada, " immediately landed," says my author, " 2300 men, for the most part Irish, in the service of France, under the conduct of Colonel Dillon."

The Governor of this island for England was an Ulster nobleman, more recently of Scotch descent, but originally of Irish or Milesian blood, George Macartney, 1st Lord Macartney, born in 1737.* Appointed Envoy Extraordinary from George III. to Catherine II., Empress of Russia, in 1764, he, on taking leave at St. James's, was knighted by his Majesty. Thenceforward, to 1767, he acted so satisfactorily in his northern mission, that, besides receiving from Stanislas, King of Poland, the Order of the White Eagle, he was advanced to be Ambassador Extraordinary and Plenipotentiary from the British Court to that of St. Petersburg. In 1768, he was elected a Member of Parliament, both in Great Britain and Ireland; in 1769, was made Chief Secretary for, and Member of the Privy Council in, Ireland, under the administration of Lord Townsend; in 1772, was created a Knight of the Bath; in 1774, sat in the British Parliament for several Scotch boroughs; in 1775, was nominated Captain-General and Governor-in-Chief of the Islands of Grenada, the Grenadines, and Tobago; and, in 1776, was ennobled as Lord Macartney, Baron of Lissanoure, in the County of Antrim. From his connexion with the Isle of Grenada, as attacked by the French, till his death in 1806, his Lordship is most

---

services of his own and the other Irish regiments in this war. "Guerre d'Amérique, 1779. On a vu que les régimens Irlandois ont été constamment employés dans toutes les guerres précédentes; ils ont toujours réclamé le privilège de marcher les *premiers* contre les Anglois dans tous les climats où la France leur feroit la guerre. C'est d'après ce principe que le Régiment de Dillon demanda et obtint de passer en Amérique au commencement de 1779."

* Lord Macartney's origin has been traced from a son of Donogh Mac Carthy, styled "Cairthanach," or *the Friendly*, King of Desmond, in the 14th century. This son, Prince Donal, after having joined the gallant Edward de Brus, or Bruce, as "King of Ireland," in order to drive the English out of Ireland as they had been driven out of Scotland, served Edward's brother, the great Robert, King of Scotland. From him, he received a grant of land in Argyleshire, whence his descendants branched into Galloway, and finally into Ulster, where the name became connected with the Peerage. On this point of his Lordship's Milesian origin, compare M. Lainé's Pedigree of the Mac Carthys in French with Mr. R. F. Cronnelly's Irish Genealogies, under that name. See likewise, Archdall's Lodge's Peerage of Ireland, and Ryan's Worthies of Ireland, under "Lord Macartney."

honourably known as Governor of Madras, in the East Indies, where he *might* have been Governor-General of Bengal, and for his interesting embassy to China; having displayed, throughout life, qualities creditable "to his talents as a statesman, and his feelings as a man."

On the landing of D'Estaing's troops, Lord Macartney retired with what force he had, about 700 men—of whom not 200 were regulars, and the rest militia, sailors, and volunteers—to the eminence entitled Morne de l'Hôpital. This height, which commanded the town of St. George, the fort, and the harbour, besides being very steep by nature, was rendered more difficult of access by rude walls of stone, raised at intervals for that purpose; and the passage upwards was further barred by a strong palisade, behind which were 3 intrenchments, rising one above the other in due gradation. D'Estaing, the day after his landing, or on the 3rd, having reconnoitred the hostile post, and made corresponding dispositions of his troops, summoned Lord Macartney to surrender; whose reply was, that he was ignorant of the strength of the French, but knew his own, and would do his utmost to defend his island. The French commander, anxious to proceed as expeditiously as possible with his enterprise, lest Admiral Byron might arrive with his squadron to relieve Lord Macartney, had brought no artillery with him; and, as to unship and bring up any might take too much time, he could only carry his point by a *coup de main*. He accordingly arranged that the enemy's stronghold should be stormed that night (between the 3rd and 4th,) by 3 columns; Count Dillon and other officers being commissioned, ere it was dark, to examine, as nearly as possible, the approaches by which each column might advance to the palisade and intrenchments. About midnight, the troops were in motion, and, before 2 in the morning, they, at a quarter of a league from the position to be assailed, were arrayed in 3 columns, at the respective directions they were to take. The column on the right, under the Vicomte de Noailles, having with him, among other officers, Lieutenant-Colonel O'Dunn * and Major Mac Donnell, consisted of 300 men of the Regiments of Champagne, Auxerrois, Martinique, and the Artillery. The column in the centre, under the Count Edward Dillon, with a Lieutenant-Colonel, and Major O'Moran, consisted of 300 men of the Regiment of Dillon, and 10 of the Artillery. The column on the left, under Count Arthur Dillon, with M. Browne as Colonel-en-Second, consisted of the grenadiers of the Count's own regiment, the rest of the same corps, and 10 of the Artillery. The direction for this column, in its ascent, exposed it to more danger than the others, from the fire of an English vessel, the *York*. At the head of the grenadiers marched the Count d'Estaing himself; knowing the Irish well, if it were only as having formerly served with poor Lally.

* The O'Duinns, O'Dunns, or Dunnes, of Iregan, the present Barony of Tinnahinch, Queen's County, were descended from Cathair the Great, Ard-Righ or Monarch of Erin, in the 2nd century. From the reign of Louis XIV. to that of Louis XVI., there were O'Dunns in the Irish Brigade, in the Regiments of O'Donnell, Clare, and Walsh, from the rank of Lieutenant to that of Lieutenant-Colonel and Chevalier of St. Louis. James Bernard O'Dunn, born in 1714, having been Envoy from Louis XV. to the Court of Portugal, was pensioned for diplomatic services in 1789; and his son Humphrey, born in 1742, Lieutenant-Colonel of Infantry, and Commandant at Grenada, in the West Indies, was likewise pensioned in 1789. The head of this ancient name in 1866, with an estate from time immemorial in his race, was Major-General Francis Plunkett Dunne of Brittas, in the Queen's County, and its representative in Parliament; whose great-grandfather was killed at the battle of Aughrim.

To this body there was, under the Count de Duras, Colonel-en-Second of the Regiment of Cambresis, and another experienced officer, an advanced guard of 50 Volunteers, with 130 more men from the Regiments of Hainault, Foix, and Martinique; and, to contribute to the success of the 3 real attacks, by making a false one, another party was assigned to the Count de Pondevaux, Lieutenant-Colonel of the Regiment of Auxerrois, a 2nd Lieutenant-Colonel, and 2 Majors, amounting to 200 men of various French corps. At 2 in the morning, the false attack having commenced, and a vessel under the Marquis de Vaudreuil likewise making a useful diversion by its cannonade, as a set-off against the fire of the *York*, the 3 columns marched to scale the Morne by the ascents appointed. The cartridge-shot from the *York* greatly incommoded the column under Count Arthur Dillon. But neither this fire, nor that of the musketry and artillery from the intrenchments, the darkness of the night, nor the other impediments in the way of the assailants, prevented the advanced-guard under the brave Duras, with the grenadiers under the General, from bursting through the palisade, and carrying the intrenchments; D'Estaing himself being among the first who entered them. Count Arthur Dillon is likewise particularized, by the Count de Segur, as greatly distinguished at the head of this column, and wounded; yet, as not withdrawing, on that account, till after the action. In fine, although the defendants claim to have repulsed the assailants at first, and *may* have done so, the post was mastered in less than an hour according to the French, or in about an hour and a half according to the English, by the arrival of all the attacking columns at the summit of the Morne, where they found 11 pieces of cannon and 6 mortars of various calibres. As soon as it was day, a 24-pounder was played from the top of the Morne against the Fort which it commanded, and into which Lord Macartney retired, who had to surrender at discretion, having acted as well as he could, under the circumstances; so that, on his release, and reappearance at Court, he was well received by King George.

By this success, all the plate and most valuable effects of his Lordship and principal officers, as well as those of the wealthy inhabitants of the island, that had been conveyed to his post as the safest depository, became a prey to the French; and they gained a not less considerable booty in the harbour, where there were 30 vessels, of which 20 were merchantmen well-laden, and the remaining 10, privateers. The English prisoners were 700 (of whom 195 regulars of the 48th Regiment and Royal Artillery), the standards taken were 3, the artillery 102 cannon and 16 mortars. The French loss was returned as 106 men, or 35 killed, and 71 wounded. Of Irish names among the officers slain or hurt were those of Mac Sheehy, Duggan, and Morgan; the 1st of these only, or Patrick Mac Sheehy, Lieutenant in the Regiment of Dillon, having been *mortally* wounded by a cannon-shot towards the close of the conflict. In this state, he could merely speak, with much pain, a few words, worthy of the great days of Sparta and Athens. "Is the Morne taken?" he inquired. "Yes," they replied. "Well, then," he rejoined, "I die content!" and expired.* That, in a place thus conquered, there

* The Mac Sheehys, a martial sept, that appear to have been of Ulster origin, and Clan-Colla race, furnished officers to the Irish Brigade while it existed. For the *classic* death of the gallant Patrick, I am indebted to M. de la Ponce. Patrick's nephew, Bernard Mac Sheehy, born in 1774, was Adjutant-General, under the

should be *some* irregularities, affording grounds for complaint against the successful soldiery, may be admitted; though by no means to the degree, that English prejudice, or misinformation, would represent. "Nothing," says the contemporary Annual Register, "could be more unfavourable to D'Estaing's character than the accounts of his conduct in his new acquisition, which were spread about this time. His continuance in the island of Grenada has been represented as a constant scene of severity and oppression. It was said, that his soldiers were indulged in the most unbridled licence; and that, if it had not been for the humanity and tenderness shown by the officers and private men of Dillon's Irish regiment to the inhabitants, their condition would have been too deplorable to be endured, or described." But Botta,* who had more authorities before him than this London periodical, which he also consulted, alleges—" If the French, in this assault, displayed a valour deserving of eternal memory, the moderation and humanity which they manifested, after the victory, merit no inferior encomium. The capital was preserved from pillage, to which it was liable by the ordinary rules of war. The inhabitants were protected in their persons and property. Dillon, in particular, distinguished himself by the generosity of his behaviour." Thus, the good-nature of the Irish is admitted on all hands, and, as to merit of another kind, about 2-3rds of it was theirs; nearly the whole of 2 out of the 3 storming columns having been formed from the Regiment of Dillon, including the column accompanied by D'Estaing, which first carried the intrenchments. The intelligence of the reduction of Grenada, with the standards taken there, was forwarded to France, in the *Diligente* frigate, by Captain Sheldon of that regiment, and a relative of the Count, its Colonel.

It was well that D'Estaing had been so prompt in making himself master of Grenada. On the 6th, Admiral Byron, having 18 sail of the line, and a frigate, with a number of transports conveying troops under General Grant, approached the island, under the impression, that Lord Macartney still held out. D'Estaing, who had 25 sail of the line, accordingly gave battle, with a loss, indeed, of the larger amount of men, but counterbalanced by the greater injury done to the enemy's ships; 1 of which, a transport, was taken. "The British Admiral, in consequence of the disabled condition of his fleet," we are told, "found it necessary to take shelter at St. Christopher's, where he was decided to remain, until the enemy should become weaker, or himself stronger. His retreat spread consternation among the inhabitants of all the British islands," in the West Indies, "who had not for a long time, nor, perhaps, ever before, seen the French masters at sea. A short time after the action, D'Estaing, having repaired his ships, set sail afresh, and

Emperor Napoleon I., at the bloody battle of Eylau, in February, 1807, when he fell by a cannon-shot, greatly regretted, as uniting, with bravery, and military talent of the first order, a vast erudition, and capability of speaking and writing several languages. John Bernard Louis Mac Sheehy, born at Paris, in December, 1783, and attached when a boy, as a gentleman Cadet, to the Regiment of Dillon, attained high honours in the same Imperial service, and subsequently. He served 12 campaigns, received 6 wounds, had 2 horses killed under him, and became a Chevalier of several Military Orders.

The learned Heeren designates the "History of the War of the Independence of the United States of America," by Carlo Botta, (the eminent historian, also, of his own country, Italy,) as "a history of the revolution, compiled, from the best authorities, with care, and well written."

paraded, with his whole force, in sight of St. Christopher's. Byron lay safely moored in the harbour of Basse Terre. The French Admiral sought in vain to draw him out to combat. Finding him obstinate in his immobility, he shaped his course for St. Domingo, where he assembled the merchantmen of the different islands, and dispatched them for Europe, under convoy of 3 ships of the line, and 3 frigates. . . . The news of the battle of Grenada was welcomed in France, with great demonstrations of joy. According to the usage observed on occasion of important victories, the King wrote to the Archbishop of Paris, directing that a *Te Deum* should be sung in the metropolitan Church," or that of *Nôtre Dame*. In this naval combat of July 6th, half of Dillon's corps served on board the French fleet; and, among the officers wounded there, were the Count Edward Dillon, Colonel-en-Second, and M. Plunkett of the Regiment of Walsh.*

The next enterprise of D'Estaing was one to recover Savannah, the capital of Georgia, from the English, who had taken it from the Americans. With 22 sail of the line, 8 frigates, and above 4000 men, including the corps of Dillon, except a portion of it left in Grenada, the French commander reached the Georgian coast, ere the end of August; intercepted 2 English ships of war, with 8 other vessels, containing a quantity of money, clothes, and provisions for the troops in Savannah; and, during September, and the earlier part of October, being joined by 3000 of the Americans, under General Lincoln, pushed on operations against the hostile garrison of 3000 men in that metropolis. By the close, however, of this period, the season had become too dangerous for the French fleet to remain any longer off that coast; the besieging works, meantime, were not advanced enough to promise success in a direct assault upon the place, and yet the French and the Americans should separate; so that, it appeared the only *chance* left them, (unpromising as *that* was,) to effect anything, would be, through a vigorously-combined effort, before parting, to storm the town. Such an attempt was consequently made by D'Estaing and Lincoln in person, October 9th, before daybreak. The French and Americans thus headed, according to Serjeant Lamb in the English service, "resolutely marched up to the lines; but the tremendous and well-directed fire of the batteries, joined to that, in a cross direction, from the gallies, threw their whole columns into confusion; not before, however, they had planted 2 standards on the British redoubts. . . . Meanwhile it was intended, that Count Dillon should secretly pass the edge of the swamps, the redoubts, and batteries, and attack the rear of the British lines. The troops were in motion before day-light; but, a heavy fog arising with the morning, they lost their way in the swamp, and were finally exposed to the view of the garrison, and the fire of the batteries; which was so hot and tremendous, that they in vain attempted to form, and their whole design was defeated." The French had about 700 slain or hurt, of whom above 40 were officers; and, among the latter, the intrepid D'Estaing, who, exposing himself so much here, as elsewhere, had a horse shot under him, and was injured in 3 places. Of Dillon's corps, its Major, Browne, an excellent officer, fell that day; and, of its grenadiers, 63 suffered in life or limb, exclusive of the fusiliers. The Americans are alleged under both heads to have been *minus* "about 400;" while "the loss on the

---

* Besides the authorities that have been mentioned on the conquest of Grenada and defeat of Byron, I make use of French accounts of the day, respecting those events.

British side, as they fought secure, was inconsiderable." Of other reports, or misstatements, from the *same* side, the accounts from Paris, after D'Estaing's return there, assert—" Malgre tout que les Généraux Anglois, ont mandé à leur Cour du peu d'intelligence qui a regné entre les François et les Américains lors de l'expedition de Savannah, jusqu'au point *d'inventer* que M. O-Dune se seroit servi du mot de *lâche* en nommant le Général Lincoln, M. d'Estaing soutient le contraire."

At this siege, according to Ferrar, a "Colonel Browne was Aid-du-Camp to the Count d'Estaing," as previously " in America;" and, on the Count's deciding to attack Savannah, contrary to the opinion of the Colonel and other officers, " the brave Colonel remarked to the Count, though he disapproved his opinion, he should have no cause to complain of his conduct. Accordingly, he marched his regiment immediately to the attack, planted the French colours twice on the walls of Savannah, and in the 3rd attempt was killed." He was " of the family of Moyne," likewise highly represented in the Austrian service. On this occasion, too, the Count de Segur thus refers to his "friend Linch," a distinguished officer of the Brigade, as subsequently Colonel-en-Second of the Regiment of Walsh. " I will relate an anecdote of my friend Linch, that will give an idea of his singular bravery, and of the originality of his disposition. Linch, after being engaged in the campaigns of India, served, before he was employed in the army of Rochambeau, under the orders of the Count d'Estaing, and distinguished himself particularly at the too memorable siege of Savannah. M. d'Estaing, at the most critical moment of that sanguinary affair, being at the head of the right column, directed Linch to carry an urgent order to the 3rd column, which was on the left. These columns were then within grape-shot of the enemy's intrenchments; and, on both sides, a tremendous firing was kept up. Linch, instead of passing through the centre, or in the rear, of the columns, proceeded coolly through the shower of balls and grape-shot, which the French and English were discharging at each other. It was in vain that M. d'Estaing, and those who surrounded him, cried to Linch, to take another direction; he went on, executed his order, and returned by the same way; that is to say, under a vault of flying shot, and where every one expected to witness his instant destruction. ' Zounds!' said the General, on seeing him return unhurt, ' the Devil must be in you, surely! Why did you choose such a road as that, in which you might have expected to perish 1000 times over?' ' Because it was the *shortest*,' answered Linch. Having uttered these few words, he went, with equal coolness, and joined the group that was most ardently engaged in storming the place. He was," adds Segur, "afterwards promoted to the rank of Lieutenant-General, and commanded our infantry, in the 1st engagement we had with the Prussians, on the heights of Valmy," in 1792.

The last event of note in the annals of the Brigade for 1779, was the death of the Count and Chevalier Patrick Darcy. Of the clan-territory of Partraighe, or Partry, in western Connaught, the ancient possessors were the O'Dorchaidhes, otherwise O'Dorcys; in reference to which, the Bard, early in the 15th century, writes—

" Well has O'Dorchaidhe of the lofty mind
Defended that land of heroes,
The country of Partraighe of fine hazel-trees,
With a yellow-knotted spear-shaft in the battle." *

* On this old Milesian name, clan, and territory, see Dr. O'Donovan's learned

From this sept came the founder of the race, subsequently Anglo-Normanized, or colonially metamorphosed, into *D'Arcys*, or *Darcys*, in Galway, where Patrick, born September 27th, 1723, was the son of John Darcy, by his marriage with Jane Lynch. Excluded at home from respectable modes of advancement in life, as of a Catholic family and attached to the Stuarts, he was consigned by his parents, for a due provision, to one of his uncles, settled in France. Having been fortunately placed there under the tuition of the famous Clairaut, he gave proofs of such a progress in mathematics, that, while still but a youth, his reception by the Academie Royale des Sciences at Paris, was most creditable to the precocious ability he displayed, and indicative of the future eminence he was destined to attain in those pursuits, which were to connect him so honourably with that learned body. Unable, however, to devote his life to those abstruse studies, for which nature appeared to have designed him, or obliged by circumstances to take a profession, he adopted that of arms. As Captain by brevet in the Regiment of Condé, he made 3 campaigns, 2 in Germany, and the 3rd in Flanders. Embarked there, in the spring of 1746, with a choice detachment intended to elude the British fleet by night, and join Prince Charles in Scotland, he (as elsewhere duly narrated) was captured at sea by Commodore Knowles; but was released the same year; the winter of which he passed at Paris. Thenceforward, till 1749, notwithstanding the interruptions of a military life, he embodied in several memoirs the results of his application to problems in mechanics and electricity, and prepared an essay, at much greater length, on artillery. Enrolled this year in the Academy of Sciences, he published the essay, and subsequently a memoir on hydraulic machines. The Seven Years' War breaking out, he served as Colonel *à la suite* to the Irish Horse Regiment of Fitz-James, at the battle of Rosbach, in 1757, where it signalized itself so much; and, on its removal from Germany to Flanders, in consequence of having suffered proportionably, he accompanied it there. An invasion of England from that quarter being contemplated, he, as calculated to be so serviceable for such a design, was made a Brigadier. The peace of 1763, however, restored him to his academical labours. In 1770, he was appointed a Maréchal de Camp; and, by this time, having realized a suitable income,* he decided on withdrawing from the uninteresting bustle of the world, into a system of life more adapted to his mature years and elevated tastes. He died October 18th, 1779. He was a good Irishman, and, to the last, a Jacobite loyalist. As the *former*, my French memoir of him, as "Monsieur le Comte Patrice d'Arcy, Maréchal des Camps et Armées du Roi, Chevalier de l'Ordre de St. Louis, Commandeur de l'Ordre de St. Lazare, Pensionnaire Giometre de l'Academie

editions, for the Irish Archæological Society, of Mac Firbis's Genealogies, Tribes, and Customs of Hy-Fiachrach, and O'Dubhagain's and O'Huidhrin's Topographical Poems.

* "Il jouissoit d'une fortune honnête," alleges my manuscript, "formée de la succession d'un oncle établi en France qui l'avoit fait son héritier, des pensions accordées à ses services, et celle de l'Académie, et d'un interêt qu'il avoit dans le produit de quelques mines. . . . Il aima mieux renoncer à une succession très considérable qu'on lui offroit en Irlande, que d'y vivre privé des droits de citoyen, ou forcé de les acheter par un parjure, et par sa soumission aux conditions, sous lesquelles l'Angleterre permettoit à sa patrie de *jouir de la liberté.*" Were these words, which I have *italicized*, written in *irony?* The "penal code" and "commercial restrictions" of England in Ireland were rather an odd kind of *liberty* for the latter to be said to *enjoy!*

Royale des Sciences," states—" Il aima toujours ses compatriotes. Tous les Irlandois qui venoient à Paris s'adressoient à lui. Il n'y en avoit aucun qui n'en reçut ou des sécours dans ses besoins, ou des consolations dans ses peines." As to the *latter*, the same document adds—" En vain la Cour de France, à laquelle le Prétendant tenoit par les liens du sang, en vain la Cour de Rome, qui eût dû soutenir le petit-fils d' un Martyr de la Religion Catholique, embrasserent la cause du vainqueur, le fidele D'Arcy n'abandonna *jamais* celle du vaincu." * In combining the man of the sword with the man of science, the Count may be said to have united the characteristics of 2 classes of warriors, placed under the guidance of opposite divinities by the poet, when he notes—

"These Mars incites, and those Minerva fires."
POPE'S HOMER, Iliad, iv., 499.

The following particulars respecting the remains of this distinguished Irishman are given from the *Ami de la Religion*, as cited in the Dublin *Freeman's Journal* of October 1st, 1845. "A mason, employed at the works at present going forward in the ancient Chapel of the Blessed Virgin, in the Church of St. Philip du Roule, has discovered, at a depth of about a yard and a half below the surface, a leaden coffin, of ancient form. This coffin, considerably damaged by the effects of time, was broken in some parts, so as to expose to view several bones within, particularly the head, in the upper jaw of which the teeth remained almost all perfect. A brass plate, which must have been affixed to the coffin, has been forced off, during the process of exhumation. It bears the following inscription. *Here lieth Messire Patrick Count Darcy, Commandant of the Order of St. Lazarus and of Mount Carmel, Knight of the Royal and Military Order of St. Louis, and General commanding in the Camps and Armies of the King, aged* 54 † *years; deceased in October*, 1779. REQUIESCAT IN PACE. The Curé of St. Philip has given orders, to lower the coffin into the vaults of that Church, where it shall be deposited, and taken care of, for the disposal of the family. The date of 1779 gives reason to presume, very naturally, that members of that family are still in existence." But the Count, though married for some years previous to his decease, is not recorded to have left any offspring; and, since the

---

* This feeling of loyalty to "Prince Charlie," as the representative of *genuine* royalty, was common to many, besides Count Darcy. Thus, in May, 1776, although the Court of Rome, after the death of the Prince's father, had expressly ordered, that no person should give Charles the title of *King*, yet, on his visiting Rome, the ecclesiastics of the English, Scotch, and Irish colleges and convents, *all*, during 4 days, received him with the ceremony used towards crowned heads. "When," it is added, "this procedure became known at Monte Cavallo, (the Pope's palace) orders were issued immediately, for exiling the Superiors of the before-noticed colleges and convents from Rome." And here, it is not altogether irrelevant to mention, that, it was only the same year, a Catholic Bishop was allowed, by the British Government, to proceed to Canada, pursuant to a "secret article" of the Peace of 1763; by which the French Court engaged "not to abet, or assist, in any shape, the son of the Pretender." In Ireland, according to the contemporary authority of the Rev. James White, Parish Priest of St. Mary's, Limerick, with respect to the Catholics, it was only "in January, 1768, they *began* to pray publickly, in all their chapels, for King George III., Queen Charlotte, and all the Royal Family." The renunciation of Charles, as "Charles III.," exacted, on oath, from the Catholics in Ireland, still later, or in 1774, has been related, under that year. So long did the Stuarts render Hanoverianism uneasy!

† An apparent mistake, or misprint; the Count having entered upon the 1st month of 57.

publication of the above paragraph concerning his "mortal remains," no further notice relating to him has appeared till the summary of his life in these pages; where, with reference to him, and so many others of honourable memory, History endeavours to win from Fame the too-long-deferred decision, that

"These *must* not sleep in darkness and in death!"—POPE.

In 1780, the Regiments of Dillon and Walsh were among those represented by detachments serving under the French Admiral, the Count de Guichen, in the West Indies, against the English Admiral, Sir George Rodney, particularly at the 3 engagements fought within 2 months, or in April and May, where each of those 2 great masters of naval tactics found himself opposed to a rival with whom the empire of the sea should be divided, since neither could conquer the other. In 1781, at the combat of April 29th, between the French Admiral, the Comte de Grasse, and the English Admiral, Sir Samuel Hood, before Martinique, 700 of the Regiment of Dillon were present with the former. They afterwards landed in the Isle of Tobago, where the Regiment of Walsh had some days previously arrived; and the 2 corps contributed to the final conquest of the island from the English, by the Marquis de Bouillé, in June. This gallant and high-minded nobleman, who was Governor-General of Martinique, in order to turn to account the absence of the English fleet in November, next resolved upon an attempt to recover the Isle of St. Eustache from the enemy.

That island, the preceding February, when no attack was expected, and no resistance could be made, had been suddenly wrested from Holland, by a considerable English sea and land force, or, so far, with no *honour* attendant upon the achievement; though subsequently with such *dishonour*, through the shameless conduct of Admiral Rodney, General Vaughan, and other officers, as regarded the property of above 3,000,000 found there, that the rapacity and inhumanity displayed by them tended to draw upon England, as was said, "the odium of all Europe." * Since their acquisition of the island, the English had appointed for its defence a select garrison of 723 men and officers, from the 13th and 15th regiments of foot, under Lieutenant-Colonel Cockburne, as Governor; several batteries, also, were raised, mounting 68 pieces of cannon; and, as there was only 1 place, at which it was thought any landing could be

* On this disreputable behaviour at St. Eustache after its bloodless surrender, the opponents of the Government in England were very severe in their censures, as well as on the bad or offensive system of administration, which, they maintained, had added Holland, to America, France, and Spain, as a belligerent enemy to England, while other powers evinced their ill-will to her, in the menacing shape of an armed neutrality. In Parliament, states my London contemporary respecting the opposition, "they denied the necessity of the war with Holland. 'We lost Holland,' said they, 'by our arrogance; by that domineering, insolent spirit, through which we lost America, and which has united half Europe against us, in an armed neutrality. . . . When France,' they continued, 'was considered as the most formidable power in Europe, the nations, on all sides, confederated against her. We ourselves took the lead in that confederacy. We should have derived wisdom from that example, in which we had so great a share; and, when this country rose to an envied and alarming pitch of greatness, a just apprehension of a similar confederacy should have taught us justice, moderation, and wisdom. But, so far were we from adopting such a prudential mode of conduct, that the pride and arrogance of our councils disgusted or alarmed all mankind, and disposed them to any combination, whether for the lessening of our power, or the punishing of our insolence.'"

effected, there was no apprehension entertained of a hostile disembarkation. But a French refugee, who, having been settled in the island when possessed by the Dutch, was well acquainted with the country, informed the Marquis de Bouillé, that at Jenkin's Bay, in the back of the island, notwithstanding the great apparent obstacles there by sea to boats safely reaching the shore, and by land to men getting over the rocks, a descent was practicable, if attempted in the absence of any military opposition, or by surprise; especially since the English engineers, recently directed by the Governor to provide against the possible danger of a hostile disembarkation in that quarter, had pronounced it to be unnecessary, on account of the obstacles referred to, either that any defensive work should be constructed, or that even any guard should be stationed there! Under these circumstances, and the absence of the Count de Grasse's fleet in America, the sense of security on the part of the Governor and garrison of St. Eustache was as complete as could be desired for effecting their downfall. The Marquis de Bouillé, whom his countryman, the plundered refugee, in addition to the useful intelligence he had given, offered to serve as a guide in surprising the English, sailed from St. Pierre's, in Martinique, on November 15th, with 3 frigates, 4 corvettes, and 3 armed boats, accompanied by 300 men of each of the following regiments, Auxerrois, Royal Comtois, Dillon, and Walsh, or 1200 so far, besides 300 grenadiers and chasseurs of different corps, making in all 1500. Lest any alarm should be given to the "stupid peace" of the English at St. Eustache, he caused it to be reported, that he was sailing in a different direction, or going to join the fleet of the Count de Grasse.

From the contrarieties of the winds and currents, the Marquis was not able to sight St. Eustache till the 25th, and that night issued orders to land. But, through a mistake of the pilots, in the 1st place they assigned for the descent, the entire enterprise might have been frustrated. With great difficulty, Count Arthur Dillon, and 30 chasseurs of his regiment, contrived to reach land, in the 1st boat which attempted to do so. The Marquis de Bouillé, and the men he had with him in the 2nd, were as successful, though their boat was lost. This loss, and that of others, made it necessary to look for a less difficult landing-place, at which, in the course of the night, the troops continued to effect their object, by aiding one another with ladders and ropes to ascend a rock. But, about an hour before daybreak, the winds and currents had become so hostile on this perilous coast, that the larger vessels were driven from the shore, and the boats which remained were unserviceable; so that, when but 400 were disembarked, they had to shift for themselves, where they were, as well as they could, since no more could join them. They might then exclaim with the ancient warrior,

"See on what foot we stand! a scanty shore—
The sea behind, our enemies before!"
DRYDEN'S VIRGIL, Æneis, x., 527-8.

Cut off from any retreat, having no artillery, and with only 400 men, out of his 1500, to assail a body of regular troops so considerably superior in number, and provided with artillery and a fort as the English were, the Marquis de Bouillé had no possibility of extricating himself from the predicament in which he was involved, but by advancing, attacking, and vanquishing his opponents; a resolution to which he was the more encouraged, from the excellent spirit he observed in his soldiers.

It was now about half-past 4 in the morning; the distance from the English fort and barracks being about 2 leagues, or 6 miles; and "the way not only extremely difficult, but intersected by a defile in the hills, where a handful of men could have stopped the approach of an army." Count Arthur Dillon was ordered, with the Irish, to proceed directly to the barracks, and to seize the Governor. The Chevalier de Fresne, Major of Royal Comtois, with 100 chasseurs of his regiment and that of Auxerrois, was to rush for the fort, and, if he could not enter by the gate, he was to attempt it by escalade. The Vicomte de Damas, with the rest of the troops, was to support that attack. Dillon's Irish, marching in silence, and with lowered arms, were met by several inhabitants of the island, who took them, by their red uniform, for some of the English. They reached the barracks by 6 o'clock, where a portion of the garrison, "nothing fearing," were on parade, going through their exercise. Dillon and his men, under the advantage of the red uniform, were allowed to approach, when a loud shout, a point-blank volley bringing several to the ground, and a close, with fixed bayonets, had naturally such an effect on men so assailed, as rendered resistance impossible.* The Governor, Lieutenant-Colonel Cockburne, coming up after an early ride, was made prisoner on horseback, by the Chevalier O'Connor, Captain of Chasseurs in the Regiment of Walsh. "I can never forget the day," writes the learned Dr. Charles O'Conor, in 1796, "when Monsieur de Mombre, who travelled in 1787 with Mr. O'Naghton of Lisle, hearing my name mentioned in a long company, went to his port-feuille, and, after exhibiting to every person present a beautiful engraving, in which the Chevalier O'Conor, Captain of Chasseurs in Welch's regiment, is represented in the attitude of making Governor Cockburne prisoner, he politely presented it to me, saying—'Sir, you see the French delight in paying compliments to every brave and faithful nation.'" † The remainder of the enemy were rapidly disposed of, by the Chevalier de Fresne of Royal Comtois reaching the fort as an attempt was made to raise the draw-bridge, which was arrested by M. de la Motte, Captain of Chasseurs in the Regiment of Auxerrois, with a well-timed discharge of musketry; upon which, the entrance being forced, and the bridge drawn up, the considerable portion of the garrison inclosed there laid down their arms, and those dispersed in quarters

* "The troops landed were," notes the contemporary Annual Register, "among the best in France, being principally composed of Count Dillon's regiment, a part of that Irish Brigade, which has been so long and so highly distinguished for its valour, and the excellency of the troops, and which the ill policy both of England and Ireland has driven into the French service. The red uniform of these troops, being the same as the English, contributed greatly to facilitate, and give effect to, the enterprise."

† This capture of Governor Cockburne by O'Connor, and that of Marshal Villeroy by Mac Donnell, would be 2 good subjects for pictures by Irish artists. Of poor O'Connor, a French MS., given to me by the late John O'Connell, adds—"Le Major O'Connor, du Régiment de la Guadeloupe, au commencement de la Révolution, fût fait prisonnier par les Republicains, sur un bâtiment marchand, où il cherchoit à passer dans une île tranquille des Antilles. Il fût inhumainement fusillé avec des circonstances atroces. Il étoit père de 10 jeunes enfants, et avoit servi avec beaucoup de distinction dans le Régiment de Walsh, où il avoit des frères, je crois. Ce fût lui qui se signala lors de la prise chevaleresque de l'Ile de St. Eustache par le Marquis de Bouillé. Il est fait mention de lui dans les Voyages du Capitaine Landolphe, et dans la Revue Maritime de Jules Leconte."

elsewhere came in, and surrendered. The French are said to have lost but 10 men at most, and these by drowning; the English to have had a number killed, besides 677 made prisoners.

One of my English narratives, after observing how a garrison so numerous constituted "a force, which, in less unfortunate times, could not have been safely approached by an *equal*, much less an *inferior*, enemy," alleges, "it has not often happened that *English* troops have met so signal a disgrace." The truth, however, seems to be, that *any* men in the world, if surprised, or taken so completely off their guard, as these troops were, would have been equally disgraced; if such a misfortune, as left no room for a regular display of valour, can be termed "a disgrace." Moreover, a great proportion of these so-called "English troops" consisted of "Irish Catholics," according to Count Arthur Dillon; who, having premised what an advantage it was for France to have Irish regiments, since, the moment such regiments were opposed to the English, the Irish Catholics in the English service would desert in crowds to join their fellow-countrymen in the French army, remarks— "We have seen this in *all* our wars, and again, of late, in that of America, in which, on a single occasion, above 350 Irish Catholics, made prisoners at St. Eustache in the 13th and 15th English regiments, enlisted themselves into those of Dillon and Walsh, in which the greatest part of them exist still"—that is, at the commencement of the French Revolution. "Each soldier thus gained for France," continues the Count, "is worth 3 men to her; she has an enemy the less, a defender the more, and the blood of a citizen saved."

Yet, while making every fair allowance for the defeat and capture of the garrison of St. Eustache under the above-mentioned circumstances, the reduction of the island, in such a dashing and off-hand manner, by the French, was very creditable to the Marquis de Bouillé and his little band of 400 men; nor was the Marquis's subsequent behaviour there less worthy of his noble character. The sum of 1,000,000 in cash, sequestered by the Court of London, and lodged in the Governor's house, was restored to the plundered Dutch, as the Allies of France, on their proving it to be their property; and, to the Governor Cockburne himself, 264,000 livres, claimed by him as his own money, were, with similar liberality, awarded. The remaining sum of 1,600,000 livres, belonging to Admiral Rodney, General Vaughan, &c., as the produce of their unconscionable seizures, and the contents of 6 or 7 hostile vessels in the road, making from 1,800,000 to 2,000,000, was reserved as a fair prize for the conquerors. Of this, the Marquis de Bouillé had 180,000 livres, his cousin the Count de Bouillé, (to *both* of whose accounts I am indebted in this narrative,) had 30,000; and, so on, in proportion, down to the soldiery; *all* of whom got 100 crowns; having consequently no reason to envy their jolly representative in the song—

"How happy the soldier, who lives on his pay,
And spends half-a-crown out of sixpence a day!"

Thus, between 24 English vessels, laden with the spoils of this island to the value of above £700,000, which were intercepted in the spring at sea by the French, and what the Marquis de Bouillé recovered with the island itself in autumn, Messieurs Rodney, Vaughan, & Co. were much more disgraced than enriched by their acquisition of St. Eustache. Nor was that acquisition, to which no opposition could be offered by the Dutch, and the temporary retention of it from February to November, a source of any credit to the English arms, to compensate for a loss, which was looked upon as having occurred in a way but too much to their discredit. The Marquis de Bouillé, in stating his inability to do justice to the very good conduct, and most exact discipline, of his troops, on this occasion, alleges of Count Arthur Dillon, " le Comte de Dillon a donné de nouvelles preuves de son zèle et de son activité extrêmes." The adjacent little islands of Saba and St. Martin, with another English detachment of 63 men and officers,* immediately submitted to the conquerors of St. Eustache; and the Count de Bouillé, Colonel of Infantry, was despatched to France, in the *Aigle* cutter, with the gratifying news, and 4 flags of the 2 English regiments.

Early in 1782, in an expedition to wrest the Isle of St. Christopher from the English, the Regiment of Dillon was employed. It acted there, under the Marquis de Bouillé, at the siege of Brimstone Hill, styled the " Gibraltar of the Antilles;" the capture of which, with 173 pieces of artillery, in February, after 31 days of open trenches, rendered the French masters of the island. Count Arthur Dillon being made its Governor,† his regiment remained there to garrison it in great part, or with the exception of a detachment of 600 men, sent to St. Domingo. Towards the end of the year, the 2nd battalion of the Regiment of Berwick arrived at Martinique; when, however, the prospect of a termination of hostilities caused preparations for further military or naval enterprises to be laid aside. The preliminaries of the expected peace, as regards America, were signed in November, by which England was to acknowledge American independence. In 1783, peace was definitively signed between England and France, as well as America; the English troops altogether evacuated the American territory; and the French forces, having accomplished their honourable mission in America, bade adieu to their liberated allies.

With this war, terminated the strictly military career of the Irish Brigade in the service of France. although the break-up of what remained of a national element in that corps, to such an extent as to disconnect it with the past, was not to occur until the French Revolution. The vast change for the better effected in the condition of Ireland, by the acquisition of Free Trade, and Legislative Independence, through the eloquence of Grattan and the arms of the Volunteers, from 1778 to 1782, attended by further relaxations of the Penal Laws against the Catholics, in the latter year, contributed so much to keep the Irish at home, (instead of reducing them, like the previous system of mis-

* The numbers of this, and the larger English garrison, are given, as specified by Major-General Christie, in his letter from Barbadoes, December 15th, 1781, to Lord George Germaine, sent, by the *Ranger* sloop, with intelligence of the Marquis de Bouillé's success.

† When, after the peace, and restitution of St. Christopher's to the English, Dillon appeared at a levée of George III., the Lord Chancellor, crossing the circle to where the Count was, said to him—" Count Dillon, we knew you to be a brave and able soldier, but we were not aware that you were so good a lawyer. We have investigated, and have confirmed, *all* your judgments, and *all* your decrees, delivered during your government." In connexion with Dillon having been Governor of the Isle of St. Christopher, it may be remarked, that Lieutenant-Colonel Thomas Fitz-Maurice, of the Brigade, was Governor of the Isle of St. Eustache, and Lieutenant-Colonel Humphrey O'Dunn was Commandant in the Isle of Grenada.

government, to emigrate, from want, in large numbers, every year,) that but too few of the *soldiery* of the Brigade were, by this time, IRISH; as distinguished from the *officers*, already noted to have been so, either by birth, or origin, to the last. Of the great domestic revolution referred to, and the extensive prosperity resulting from it, the illustrious orator who did so much to effect that revolution, gives this picture. "The power of the British Parliament, to make law for Ireland, was relinquished. The power of the Irish Parliament, who before could only originate Petitions, not Bills, was restored, in full, complete, and exclusive authority. Nor were these acquisitions a barren liberty. The exports of Ireland increased above one half; her population near a third; and her agriculture, that was not before able to feed a smaller number of inhabitants, (for we were fed by corn from England,) supplied an increased population of 1,000,000, and sent a redundancy to Great Britain. The courtier was astonished. He had contemplated such prospects as the frenzy of the enthusiast. He read that frenzy registered in the public accounts. Nor was all this wealth slow in coming. The nation started into manhood at once. Young Ireland came forth, like a giant, rejoicing in her strength. In less than 10 years, was this increase accomplished. In 1782, we exported £3,300,000; in 1792, what would now be valued at near £11,000,000; in 1784, 24,000,000 of yards of linen; and, in 1792, 45,000,000 of yards of linen. Public prosperity so crowded on the heel of the statute, that the powers of Nature seemed to stand at the right hand of Parliament. The leading causes of this were as evident as the fact. The country became cultivated, because the laws that deprived the Catholic of an interest in the soil were repealed, and an opportunity was given to the operation of her corn laws; her trade increased, because the prohibitions on her trade were removed; and the prohibitions were removed, because she asserted her liberty." Within the period affected by these influential circumstances, or in 1785, we find the 3 Regiments of Dillon, Berwick, and Walsh, to have been each of 2 battalions and 1552 men, or, in all, 4656 strong. The soldiers then, and down to the Revolution, were mostly French, who, having been deserters, but wishing to get back to their own country, represented themselves as strangers, or foreigners, through the languages they had acquired, and attained their object, by engaging to enlist in the Irish regiments; which, as thus comprising so many reformed and experienced men, under excellent officers, ranked high in the army to which they belonged. Of those officers, on the contrary, it appears, that, down to the Revolution, their nationality was unimpaired; the military service in Great Britain and Ireland being still unopened to Irish Catholic gentlemen; and applications for commissions in the 3 regiments of the Brigade having accordingly been much beyond the number required to be filled.*

The years 1787 and 1789—the latter ever memorable as that, in which the great Revolution, destined to be fatal to so many, commenced —were marked by the deaths of 2 brothers of a name, thus distinguished, in the service of France, from the early to the closing days of the history of the Irish Brigade. Jacques-Hyacinthe, first Chevalier, and afterwards Vicomte, de Sarsfield, was descended from a branch of the Sarsfields settled at Limerick, the line running thus: James Sarsfield of Limerick,

* MS. on French Army in 1785, in Royal Irish Academy, Count Arthur Dillon, as already cited, Etats Militaires de France.

father of Paul, father of James, who married, in February, 1716, Marie-Jane Loz de Beaubun. Of this marriage Jacques-Hyacinthe was the eldest son, and began his military career as Gentilhomme à Drapeau in the Regiment of the Gardes Françaises, April 10th, 1740. He raised, and was commissioned as Captain-Proprietor of, a company in the Regiment of Andlau, (subsequently Bourbon-Busset,) January 1st, 1743. He commanded it in Alsace, and with the Army of the Lower Rhine, in 1744; at the camp of Chièvres, and the siege of Ath, in 1745; at the siege of Bruxelles, and the battle of Rocoux, in 1746; at the battle of Laffeldt, and the siege of Bergen-op-Zoom, in 1747; at the siege of Maestricht, in 1748; and at the camp of Sarre-Louis, in 1754. Having parted with his company in October, 1756, he was attached, the 23rd of that month, as a reformed Captain to Fitz-James's Irish Regiment of Horse. He was made Mestre-de-Camp-de-Cavalerie October 21st, 1757, and fought, November 5th, at the battle of Rosbach. Appointed, May 1st, 1760, Aide-Maréchal-Général-des-Logis of the Army of Germany, he was present, that year, at the victories of Corback, of Warburgh, and of Clostercamp. He was created Brigadier of Cavalry, February 20th, 1761; Maréchal-Général-des-Logis-de-Cavalerie to the army of the Prince of Soubise, April 15th following; and took part that campaign at the combats of Soest, of Unna, and of Felinghausen. He was continued in the same post with the Army of Germany by order of April 15th, 1762, and was at the affairs of Graebenstein and Johannesberg. He was declared in May, 1763, Maréchal de Camp, with rank from July 25th, 1762, the date of his brevet. He was nominated Inspector-General of Horse and Dragoons and Lieutenant-General, December 5th, 1781. At his death, in 1787, he was Governor of the Citadel of Lille, and Commander for the King in the province of Hainault and the Cambresis. By his marriage with Marie de Levis, March 26th, 1766, he had an only daughter, Marie Gabrielle, who became the wife of Charles, Baron de Damas. The brother of this Lieutenant-General, Vicomte de Sarsfield, or Guy-Claude, Count de Sarsfield, born in 1718, became Colonel of the Regiment of Provence, and died, without issue, in 1789. I may add here, of the Sarsfields of Cork, that Edmund Sarsfield, born there in 1736, and a gentleman Cadet in the Regiment of Roth in 1752, in 1791, or after the corps had become that of Walsh, and, finally, the 92nd of the Line, was its Lieutenant-Colonel, and a Chevalier of St. Louis.

As if every circumstance tended about the same time to the commencement of a "new order of things" in the political world, on the eve of the great event by which the Irish Brigade in France was to be broken up, the representative of the exiled dynasty, to which they were so loyal, was likewise destined to pass away. In January, 1788, the year previous to that in which the French Revolution began, and about a century from the dethronement of James II. in England by the Prince of Orange, the grandson of James, Prince Charles Edward Stuart, or, as he claimed to be, "Charles III. of Great Britain and Ireland," died in Italy, in his 68th year, the victim of ruined hopes and a ruined constitution—in too great a degree through intemperance, at first brought on by the necessity of resorting to drams, amidst the terrible hardships he had to endure after the battle of Culloden in the Highlands and Western Islands of Scotland—and subsequently welcomed, in order to alleviate the mental misery arising from the disappointment of all the "longings sublime, and aspirations high," which he had been bred up to entertain, as those of his just or natural position.* After the performance of the funeral rites by his brother, Prince Henry, Cardinal of York, at Frascati, the coffin was conveyed to St. Peter's at Rome, where George IV., when Prince Regent, or in 1819, had a stately monument, from the chisel of Canova, erected under the dome; the bas-relief representing, in white marble, the likenesses of the banished Stuart Princes, with this inscription,—

JACOBO III., JACOBI II., MAGN. BRIT. REGIS FILIO
CAROLO EDUARDO ET HENRICO, DECANO
PATRUM CARDINALIUM, JACOBI III. FILIIS,
REGIAE STIRPIS STUARDIAE POSTREMIS.
ANNO MDCCCXIX.
BEATI MORTUI QUI IN DOMINO MORIUNTUR.

Upon the death of Charles, the Cardinal of York, "according to the principles of legitimacy, undoubtedly the rightful King of Great Britain and Ireland," caused a document to be drawn up asserting his claims to that royalty, and a medal to be struck with "*Henricus IX., Magn. Brit. Franciae et Hibern. Rex. Fid. Def. Card. Ep. Tusc.*" on one side; and, on the other, "*Non desideriis hominum, sed voluntate Dei.*" That medal is dated 1788. "In his own house," we are likewise informed, "the Cardinal insisted upon a strict observance of all the etiquette usual in the residence of a reigning Sovereign—a rule, with which even a son of George III. was obliged to comply, when curiosity induced him to seek an interview." The royal Cardinal's income having been much diminished by the earlier results of the French Revolution, was annihilated, in 1798, by the republicans in Italy; so that, after being obliged, by the "infidels in religion," and "zealots in anarchy," (as they are styled) to fly from Rome, he would have been reduced, in old age and ill health, to poverty, but for a pension of £4,000 a year granted him by George III.,† till his decease, aged above 82, at Frascati, in 1807. He was an amiable and pious Prince, and, while his means permitted, generous or charitable; and his taste for literature and the fine arts was evinced by the valuable library and collection of antiquities, of which, in 1798, he was so unfortunately plundered. "By his will," he "expressly required, that his kingly title should be graven on his tomb; and his rights to the

* Dr. Charles O'Conor gives, in connexion with Prince Charles's decease, this affecting anecdote of one of the last of the Protestant Jacobite loyalists, of whom our countryman, the Duke of Ormonde, was the head. "Lord Nairne, with whom I have been acquainted in Rome, adhered to Prince Charles Stuart to the day of his death. He was by principle a rigid Jacobite; he considered the hereditary right of Kings of divine institution; but, at the same time, detested the Roman Catholic religion." He "was in the Palace the day Prince Charles died. I happened to be there also, and, as I knew, that he had forfeited many of the comforts of life, in his native country, for the Stuart cause, and had been the Prince's inseparable companion for a series of years, I watched him with peculiar attention. When he was informed of the Prince's death, he observed deep silence; his countenance spoke the emotions of an honest and faithful, but disappointed and ill-treated, man. He knew, that he was not even mentioned in the Prince's will; but still he advanced to the bed-side, and there, unable any longer to contain himself, on seeing the lifeless remains of him, with whom he had encountered so many dangers, and for whom he had suffered so many calamities, he burst into a flood of tears. Then, lifting up the hand of the deceased, he kissed it, and saying—'*Now, I have done my duty*,' he turned off hastily, and quitted the Palace, never to return." A true blue!

† This act of George III. " .oes equal honour to the King and to the man.

British throne he solemnly bequeathed to Victor Emanuel, King of Sardinia."*

The dissolution of the Irish Brigade in France dates from 1791. By a decree of the National Assembly, July 21st, all regiments, excepting the Swiss, which had hitherto been named, clad, and paid, as foreign corps, were no longer to be distinguished from, but placed in every respect on the footing of, French regiments. In this decree concerning the "troupes étrangères au service de France," the Irish regiments were included; amongst whom, however, such a division of opinions and feelings had already arisen from the turn which the Revolution had taken, that the consequence was a secession of numbers from the service of the new *régime*. Thus, we have, from the dissident refugees of the Regiment of Berwick, assembled at Coblentz, the following address to Louis XVI.'s brother, then Count de Provence, and afterwards Louis XVIII., who, "from the wrath to come," under "madden'd crowds, with fiends to lead them," had retired to that city. "The officers, non-commissioned officers, and soldiers of the Irish Regiment of Berwick, filled with the sentiments of honour and of fidelity, which are hereditary among them, entreat Monseigneur to place at the disposal of the King the devotion which they make of their lives in order to support the royal cause, and to employ their arms with confidence on the most perilous occasions." To which the Count de Provence replied:—" I have received, Gentlemen, with a genuine sensibility, the letter which you have written to me. I will cause to be forwarded to the King, as soon as possible, the expression of your sentiments towards him. I answer you, by anticipation, that it will alleviate his troubles, and that he will receive with pleasure from you the testimony of fidelity, which James II. received 100 years ago from your forefathers. This double epoch should for ever form the device that shall be seen on your colours, and all who shall be faithful subjects will read their duty there, and recognize thence the model they should imitate. As for myself, Gentlemen, be well convinced, that your last act will remain for ever engraven on my soul, and that I shall reckon myself happy, as often as I shall be able to give you proofs of the feelings with which it inspires me towards you." † While one portion of the officers of the Brigade had decided on emigrating, rather than continue to serve under a power so hostile to the throne and the altar as France had become, the other portion preferred to remain in France as *their* country, notwithstanding the change which had occurred in her government. Of the officers, who, on this occasion, shared the exile of the emigrant Bourbon Princes, in order to aid more effectively, as was hoped, the royal cause from abroad, than circumstances would admit of its being aided in France, a modern writer on the subject observes—" The fidelity of these noble *courtisans du malheur* was pure and chivalrous, and they are worthy of our respect and admiration. On the other hand," he adds, "it would be equally unjust and blameable to condemn the brave men, who, considering themselves as the soldiers of France, remained faithful to her destinies, and offered their swords to the service of the Republic and the Empire." Those emigrant officers were taken into her service by

* On the 2 last Stuarts, see Lord Mahon and Klose; and, on the family in general, some good remarks in the letter of honest Robert Burns, No. lxiii., or November 8th, 1788.
† Fieffé.

England, as *also* desirous to restore the Bourbon dynasty in France; and were consequently provided for in a new Irish Brigade, consisting of 6 regiments of infantry.*

After the fall of Napoleon in 1814-15, and the restoration of the Bourbons, in the person of Louis XVIII., that Monarch, as so much attached to the old recollections of his dynasty, was not unmindful of the Irish Brigade. Above all, he could not forget how, in 1792, he himself conveyed the final expression of the gratitude of his family to the representatives of the 3 last regiments of the Brigade, or those of Dillon, Walsh, and Berwick, with a "drapeau d'adieu," or farewell banner, emblematic of their national deserts, and accompanied by these words—

"GENTLEMEN,—We acknowledge the inappreciable services that France has received from the Irish Brigade, in the course of the last 100 years; services that we shall never forget, though under an impossibility of requiting them. Receive this standard, as a pledge of our remembrance, a monument of our admiration, and of our respect; and, in future, generous Irishmen, this shall be the motto of your spotless flag—

'1692—1792,'
'SEMPER ET UBIQUE FIDELIS.'"

The banner for the Brigade represented an Irish harp, and was embroidered with shamrocks and fleurs de lis, or lilies. In 1814, the officers of the old Irish Brigade in France requested the Duke of Fitz-James to present them to the King; which request, the Duke, after thanking them for the honour thereby done him, complied with, in these few words, "which are a summary of the Irish character, in all its chivalrous sublimity," says my French authority—

"SIRE,—I have the honour of presenting to your Majesty the survivors of the old Irish Brigade. These gentlemen only ask for a sword, and the privilege of dying at the foot of the throne."†

Louis, however, was too deeply indebted to England for the recovery of his Crown, to do anything directly opposed to the wishes of her Government, and it particularly pressed upon him, through Lord Castlereagh, that there should be no restoration of an Irish Brigade in France. "This fact is certain," alleges a contemporary in 1814, "and very uncommon exertions must have been used to procure this concession from Louis; because, independent of the general claims of this body on the gratitude of the French monarchy, 1 of these regiments had received a promise from the present King—that, in the event of his restoration, the regiment, for its fidelity, should be promoted to the rank of the *Guards of the King.*"

I have now only to conclude with notices of 2 venerable survivors, for many years, of the gallant corps to which they belonged—the one, an officer of equally high rank and merit—the other, the last who died on the Continent. 1. Of the former survivor of the old Brigade, who was uncle to the celebrated Daniel O'Connell, this memoir, from a member of the family, is given, with some slight alterations and compression. "General Daniel Count O'Connell, Knight Grand Cross of the Order of

---

* The 6 were those of Dillon, Fitz-James, the 2 Walsh-Serrants, Conway, and O'Connell.

† These 2 last incidents respecting Louis and the Brigade, in 1792 and 1814, are taken from 1 of the French MSS., given to me by the late John O'Connell.

the Holy Ghost, and Colonel of the late 6th Regiment of the Irish Brigade in the British service, entered the French army at the age of 14, in the year 1757, as 2nd Lieutenant in the Regiment of the Irish Brigade, commanded by, and called after, the Earl of Clare. He was the youngest of 22 children, of 1 marriage, and was born in August, 1743, at Darrinane, in the County of Kerry, the residence of his father, Daniel O'Connell. His education had, at that early period, been confined to a thorough knowledge of the Greek and Latin languages—a knowledge which he preserved to the latest period of his life—and to a familiar acquaintance with the elements of the mathematics. He served his first campaign during the Seven Years' War in Germany, and became respected by his superior officers, from his strict attention to all his military duties, and beloved by all his companions, from the unaffected grace, gaiety, and generosity of his disposition. At the conclusion of the war, instead of devoting the hours of peace to idleness or pleasure, he dedicated them, with the closest attention, to the study of literature generally, but especially to that of the branches of military engineering. He was attached to the *Corps du Genie* in its early formation, and soon became known to be one of the most scientific of the military engineers of France. He distinguished himself at the siege and capture of Port Mahon, in Minorca, from the English, in the year 1779, being at that time Major in the Regiment of Royal Swedes. He received public thanks for his services on that occasion, and a recommendation, from the Commander-in-Chief to the Minister of War, for promotion. That promotion he immediately obtained, and served at the siege of Gibraltar in the year 1782, as Lieutenant-Colonel of his Regiment, the Royal Swedes, but attached to the corps of engineers. Everybody remembers the attack made by the floating batteries on Gibraltar on the 13th September, 1782, and the glorious and triumphant resistance of the English garrison, under General Elliott. Lieutenant-Colonel O'Connell was 1 of the 3 engineers to whose judgment the plan of attack was submitted, a few days before it was carried into effect. He gave it, as his decided opinion, that the plan would not be successful. The other 2 engineers were of a contrary opinion, and the attack took place accordingly. The event justified his judgment. Upon a point of honour, recognized in the French army, he claimed a right to share the perils of an attack, which was resolved upon against his opinion. When the attempt to storm Gibraltar was resolved on, it became necessary to procure a considerable number of marines, to act on board the floating batteries. For this purpose, the French infantry was drawn up, and being informed of the urgency of the occasion, a call was made for volunteers, amongst the rest, of course, from the Royal Swedes. Lieutenant-Colonel O'Connell's regiment was paraded, and the men having been informed that *he* was to be employed on the service, the battalion stepped forward to one man, declaring their intention to follow their Lieutenant-Colonel. It so happened that the senior Lieutenant-Colonel, the Count De Ferzen, then well known as "le beau Ferzen," and towards whom it was more than suspected that Marie Antoinette entertained feelings of peculiar preference,* had arrived from Paris, but a short time before, to

* In the "Livre Rouge," I find, among the pensions of this Comte de Ferzen of the Royal Swedish Regiment, 1 for "100,000 livres (£4375) upon the recommendation of the Queen, Marie Antoinette." The Count is alluded to by Fieffé, as proportionately grateful, or devoted, to the Royal Family, at the sad period of the Revolution.

join the regiment, which, since his appointment, he had scarcely seen. Attributing the enthusiasm of the men to his appearance, he rode up, and assured them, that he would be proud to lead them. A murmur of disappointment passed along the line; and, at length, some of the older soldiers ventured to declare, that it was *not* with him they volunteered, but with the *other* Lieutenant-Colonel, who had always commanded, and always protected them. With a generosity which does him honour, Ferzen immediately declared, that he would not attempt to deprive Colonel O'Connell of the honour he so well deserved; but that, in making way for him, he would say, that he hoped, when the regiment knew so *much* of *him*, they would be equally ready to follow him. Colonel O'Connell was named 2nd in command of 1 of the floating batteries, and this battery was among the first to come into action. He had, in the early part of the fight, a portion of his ear taken off by a ball; about the period when the batteries began to take fire, a shell from the English mortars burst close to his feet, and severely wounded him in no less than 9 places. Although almost covered with wounds, his recovery was not slow, and, being placed high on the list of those recommended for promotion, he was, in the ensuing year, appointed Colonel commandant of a German regiment of 2 battalions of 1000 men each, then in the French service, but belonging to the Prince of Salm-Salm. The regiment, when Colonel O'Connell got the command, was in the most lamentable state of disorganization and indiscipline; and it was announced to him, by the French Minister of War, that one reason for giving him that regiment was the expectation, that *he* would remedy all its disorders. Nor was that expectation disappointed. There was, in 1787, a grand review of upwards of 50,000 French infantry in Alsace, and it was admitted, that the Regiment of Salm-Salm was the regiment in the highest state of discipline in the whole camp, and its Colonel received public thanks, on that account. He was soon after appointed to the high and responsible office of Inspector-General of all the French Infantry, and he attained also the rank of General Officer. In this capacity he was intrusted with the organization of the general code of military discipline, especially as relating to the interior regimental arrangements; and as his suggestions and book of regulations were adopted into the French armies after the Revolution, and imitated by other nations, the advantages derived from them are still felt by every army in Europe. We have thus traced his career from his entrance in the French service as a 2nd Lieutenant. From that rank, unaided by any interest, without a patron, or a friend, save those he attached to himself by his virtues, he rose to the command of a splendid regiment, and to a rank but little below the highest in the service of France; and he attained that station, at a time when the bigotry of the Penal Code precluded him from holding the most insignificant commission in the British army. Still more brilliant prospects lay before him; but the French Revolution, overturning thrones and altars, obliterated from recollection the fate of private individuals, in the absorbing nature of national interests which that mighty movement involved. He was, it may be well said, stripped of his fame and fortunes by that Revolution; but he might have retained both if he could sacrifice his principles, because both Dumourier and Carnot pressed him, more than once, to accept the command of 1 of the revolutionary armies. He totally declined any such command, feeling it a duty to remain near the person of Louis XVI., and to share, as he did, some of his greatest perils in the days of tumult and anarchy, until that ill-fated, but well-meaning, Monarch was hurled from his throne, and cast into prison. Unable any longer to serve the Bourbon cause in France, General O'Connell joined the French Princes at Coblentz, and made the disastrous campaign of 1792, under the Duke of Brunswick, as Colonel of the Hussars de Berchiny. In 1793, General O'Connell was, on his return to his family, in Kerry, detained in London, with other French officers, by the British Government, to lay and digest plans for the restoration of the Bourbon family. Upon this occasion, he sent in a plan for the campaign of 1794, which attracted so much attention, that Mr. Pitt desired an interview, and received with thanks many elucidations of the plan." Soon after, the Ministry, having determined to form an Irish Brigade of 6 regiments in the British service, " this determination was carried into effect, and 1 of those regiments was placed under the command of General O'Connell. It was stipulated that the Colonels should not be raised to the rank of Generals in the British service, but should receive full pay for life." General O'Connell, during the peace of 1802, returned to France, to look after a large property, to which his lady was entitled; he became a victim of the seizure of British subjects by the then First Consul; and remained a prisoner in France until the downfall of Napoleon, and the restoration of the Bourbons. That event restored him to his military rank in France; and he enjoyed, in the decline of life, amidst the affectionate respect of his relations and friends, the advantage of full pay, as General in the service of France, and Colonel in the service of Great Britain—an advantage which circumstances can, perhaps, never again produce for any man; but which he enjoyed with the full knowledge and approbation of both powers. During the peace of 1814, General O'Connell met Marshal Ney at dinner, at the house of one of the then Ministry. A good deal of conversation passed between them, and at length Ney stated, that he had known General O'Connell before the Revolution, and mentioned in particular having frequently seen him in the year 1787. " My memory," replied the General, " is particularly good; I have seen few officers whom I do not recollect, and I do not think I could have seen a person so likely to be remarkable as Marshal Ney, without recollecting him." "General," returned Ney, " you could not have remarked me; you then commanded the Regiment of Salm-Salm; I was a corporal of hussars; our Colonel and you were fast friends, and frequently exchanged guards; and I have often, as corporal, posted and relieved the hussar sentinel on your tent, while one of your corporals was going through the same duty at my Colonel's." The Revolution of 1830 deprived him, however, of his pay as French General. He refused to take the oath of fidelity to Louis Philippe, and was, of course, destituted. He retired to the country seat of his son-in-law, at Madon, near Blois—a beauteous spot on the Loire, which he had himself ornamented in the most exquisite style of English planting—and there, in his declining health, he waited with resignation the call of his God, which occurred on the 9th of July, 1833, he having then nearly completed his 90th year, and being the oldest Colonel in the English service. " He had never, in the season of his prosperity, forgotten his country, or his God. Loving that country, with the strongest affection, he retained, to the last, the full use of her native language; and, although master of the Spanish, Italian, German, Greek, and Latin, as well as French and English languages, it was, to him, a source of the greatest delight, to find any person, capable of conversing with him in the pure Gaelic of his native mountains, There never lived a more sincere friend—a more generous man. His charities were multiplied and continuous; and it was the surprise of all who knew him, how he could afford to do all the good he did to his kind. He was, all his life, a practical Catholic, and had the comfort of dying, without a pang, amidst all the sacred and sweet consolations of that religion, which he had not forgotten in his youth, and which did not abandon him in the days of darkness and death.—*Requiescat in pace*." 2. Of the latter survivor of the old Brigade, the family announcement of his death to me—exclusive of an additional memorandum as to the deceased having been descended from " Richard Nugent, 8th Baron of Delvin, and the last officer of the Irish Brigade in the French service "—is as follows:—

> *M*
>
> La Ctesse. de Nugent, le Cte. et la Ctesse. Charles de Nugent, Melle. Marie de Nugent, le Cte. et la Ctesse. de Lenzburg, Mrs. Richard, Pierre et Patrice de Nugent, M^{elles.} Jane et Henriette de Nugent, Melle. Marie-Antoinette de Lenzburg, ont l'honneur de vous faire part de la perte douloureuse qu'ils viennent de faire en la personne de Monsieur 𝔏ouis, 𝔉rancois, 𝔅asile, 𝔄ntoine, 𝔄ime, 𝔈^{te} de 𝔑ugent, Ancien Officier de la Brigade Irlandaise au service de France, Ancien Préfet et Ancien Maître des Requêtes, Chevalier des Ordres de la Legion d'Honneur et de St. Maurice et St Lazare de Sardaigne. Leur époux, père, beau père, aïeul et bisaïeul, décédé le 8 Juillet 1859, dans sa 81e année, aux Mesnuls, muni des sacrements de l'Eglise.
>
> 𝔇e 𝔓rofundis.
>
> Château de Mesnuls près Montfort l'Amaury.

With the disappearance of this noble veteran from the stage, the curtain falls on the history of the Irish Brigades in the service of France—not, it is hoped, without *some* honour to the industry, which has raised such a monument to *their* memory, that

> ——"long as valour shineth,
> Or mercy's soul at war repineth,
> So long shall Erin's pride
> Tell how *they* liv'd and died."—Moore.

INDEX.

Abdication, so called, of James II., 2.
Aberdeen, Irish detachment, for Prince Charles, lands at, 435.
Abjuration, oath of, refused by Irish Catholics, 259.
Abow, Swedish army cut off from, obliged by Marshal Lacy to surrender, 496. Peace of, 498.
Acts of Settlement and Explanation justly repealed by Irish Parliament under James II., 4, 45, 157, 158, 582, 583.
Aire, Irish officers distinguished there, 274.
Aix-la-Chapelle, Peace of, an expensive and inglorious war for England terminated by, and decline of Irish Brigade from, 477-479.
Albani, Hippolito, Prince of the Senate, at Rome, eulogizes Irish liberators of Princess Sobieski, 314. Cardinal, celebrates requiem for James III. there, 604. (See, also, Pope Clement XI.)
Albemarle, Henry Fitz-James, Lord Grand Prior, Duke of, and Irish regiment of, 107, 108, 142. Under its Lieutenant-Colonel, distinguished at battle of Luzzara, 218. (See, also, Keppel.)
Alberoni, Cardinal, measures of, from Spain, to restore Stuart dynasty, 316-320.
Albeville, son of Sir Ignatius White, Baronet, and Marquis of, falls nobly at Villaviciosa, 89, 279.
Alcoy, Count O'Mahony baffled before, 250. Finally takes it, 261.
Alcyra, reduced by Count O'Mahony, 249.
Alicant, honourable defence and capitulation of, under Count O'Mahony, 242. Alcoy and Muchemiel relieved from, 250, 251. Recovered from Allies, 262.
Alison, refutation of, respecting Irish Brigade at Blenheim, 228, 229.
Allegiance, oath of, Irish Catholics, in violation of Treaty of Limerick, excluded till 1774 from taking, 159, 609, 610.
Allen, Luke, Aide-Major-General of French in India, distinguished there, 557. Enters service of Hyder Ali, 560.
Allies, force of, under William III., in Ireland, for War of Revolution, 6, 7, 8, 173, 189.
Almanza, battle of, and distinction of Irish at, 245-249.
Altenheim, Irish and English at combat of, 34.
America, England's want of recruits against, leads to 1st relaxation of Penal Code in Ireland, 608, 609, 613-615. Officers from Irish Brigade early join America, 616. Count Dillon's corps with Americans at siege of Savannah, 621, 622.
Anne, Princess, afterwards Queen, joins William of Orange against her father, 2. Her servants rejoice for William's defeat at Steinkirk, 167, 168. Communicates with Sir Patrick Lawless, deputed, by her brother, to arrange for his succession, as James III., 286, 287. Her dying expression respecting James, 294. Her decease, before a due remodelling of the army, *alone* prevents James's accession, 296, 297.
Arabat, Tartars dislodged from, by a bold enterprise of Marshal Lacy, 486, 487.
Arcos, Duke of, dishonourably outmanœuvred by Lord Peterborough, 241, 242.
Arcot occupied by Count Lally, 516. Surrendered by Captain Hussey, 549.
Ariza, rout of Austro-Carlist party there by Irish, 249.
Army, Irish, of James II. in France, 61, 141, 142. British, under George II., very demoralized and brutal, 315, 434, 462.
Arnall, pensioned English newspaper liar, and libeller of the Irish, 229, 309, 335.
Athlone, infantry regiment of, 135-139, 142.
Atterbury, Bishop of Rochester, proposes to proclaim James III., 297. Plots dethronement of George I., 369, 370.
Aughrim, battle of, how lost, 137, 138. Number of Williamite or Allied regiments there, 173, 189.
Augsburg, League of, against Louis XIV., 1, 5, 6, 54, 165, 181, 185. Dissolved by Peace of Ryswick, 188.

Augustus of Saxony established as King of Poland by Marshal Lacy, 483, 484.
Austria, Irish officers of high repute in service of, 601, 602, 614.
Azoph, siege and capture of, from Turks, by Marshal Lacy, 485.

BAGNASCO, MARQUIS DE, his brave defence and honourable surrender of citadel of Montmelian, besieged by French and Irish, 56-57.
Barbets, hostilities between, and Irish, 182-183. (See, also, Vaudois.)
Barcelona, reduction of, by Duke of Vendome, and his creditable notice of the Irish there, 187-188. Reduction of, by Marshal Duke of Berwick, 291-292.
Barnwells, of French origin, amongst the conquerors of England, ennobled in Ireland, and represented by officers in War of Revolution and Irish Brigade, 77, 169, 220, 397, 443, 454, 469-471.
Barrett, family of Norman race, settled in County Cork. Its head, Colonel John, of Castlemore, after serving in Ireland, falls gloriously at Landen, 172-174.
Bart, Jean, celebrated French naval officer, escapes from Plymouth, as Lord Mountcashel from Enniskillen, 23-24.
Bay, Marquis de, General of Philip V. of Spain, defeats, with little loss and inferior numbers, English and Portuguese, at battle of Guadinna, or Gudina, and supports his army at expense of Portugal, 271-272. Beaten, by superior force of Allies, at battle of Saragossa, 275. Decisively repulsed by Major-General Hogan, in Portuguese service, at siege of Campo-Mayor, 288-289.
Bellew, family of Norman blood, among the conquerors of England, of eminence in Ireland, ennobled under James II., and of note in War of Revolution, &c., 79-81.
Bergen-op-Zoom, remarkable siege and capture of by French, at which Count Lally distinguished, 474-476.
Bernex, Count de, routed in Savoy by St. Ruth with the Irish, 54-56.
Berwick, 1st Duke of, and Marshal. His parentage, titles, and military posts, 105-106. Memoir and regiment of, 142-149. Capture of, at Landen, 174-175. Secret Jacobite mission of, to England, 183-184. His son, 2nd Duke of Berwick and Liria, &c., previously Marquis of Tinmouth, 148, 152, 291-292, 303, 339-340. Regiment of Berwick, address from, to Count de Provence, afterwards Louis XVIII., at Coblentz, and his reply, &c., 633-634.
Betagh, ancient family of Moynalty, County Meath, robbed of their estate by Anglo-sectarian perjury, and gallantly represented in Irish Brigade, 45-46, 436, 582-583.
Bethune, excellent defence of, against Allies, by Lieutenant-General Vauban and Major-General Michael Roth, 274.
Blakeney, Lieutenant-General William Lord, of Mount Blakeney, County Limerick, defender of Stirling Castle against Prince Charles, and of Fort St. Philip against Duke de Richelieu, 423-424, 429-432, 505.
Blenheim, battle of, Irish, especially Regiment of Clare, conspicuous there, 224-229.
Boisselot, Major-General, defender of Limerick against Prince of Orange, and Governor of Charleroy, 11-12, 176.
Bolingbroke, Lord, as Minister of Queen Anne, favours succession of James III., instead of George I., 74-75, 296-297.
Bouillé, Marquis de, conquers Island of Tobago, in West Indies, aided by Regiments of Dillon and Walsh, 625. Recovers Island of St. Eustache, accompanied by Regiment of Dillon, and shames the English rapacity there by his honourable conduct, 625-629. Also reduces Island of St. Christopher, 629.
Bourke, otherwise Burke, du Bourg, or de Burgo, family of Norman origin, ennobled, and very powerful in Connaught and Ulster, 136-137. Colonel Walter, granted a 2nd regiment (see Athlone) in France; finally dies a Major-General in Spain; and reference to other officers of the name in Irish Brigade, 151.
Breitenbach, Colonel, discreditably abandoned at Hastenbeck by Duke of Cumberland, 580. As Lieutenant-General, repulsed and slain by Irish, at Marbourg, 593-594.
Briançon, intrenched camp at, for defence of Dauphiné, well maintained against Allies by Lieutenant-General Arthur Dillon, 272-274.
Brigades, Irish, in France, commenced under Lord Mountcashel, 7-9. Number of Irish corps there, why so long kept up, and how recruited, 157-164. Decline of Brigade, from about 1748, 479. Dissolution of, by results of 1st French Revolution, 633. Services of, to France, during a century, pronounced invaluable by Count de Provence, subsequently Louis XVIII.; old officers of, presented

to him after his Restoration; and English opposition to re-establishment of such a force there, 633-634.
Brihuega, Lieutenant-General Stanhope obliged to surrender there, 277.
Brisach, taken by French, and preserved by an Irishman from being retaken by stratagem, 221, 229-231.
Browne, Colonel, *en suite* to Regiment of Lally, with Prince Charles's rear-guard, saves it on march for Penrith, 403-404. Escapes from Carlisle, 442-443. As distinguished at, sent with account of, battle of Falkirk, to Louis XV., and made a Chevalier of St. Louis, 427. With a detachment, conveying money from France for Prince Charles, intercepted by Mac Kays, &c., 440-443. Colonel Browne of Moyne, and Major Browne of Regiment of Dillon, at reduction of Grenada, and slain at Savannah, 617, 618, 621-622.
Bulkeley, ennobled British family of, 35. Francis and Francis Henry, Lieutenants-General in France, and regiment of, there, 36-38. That corps most distinguished against British at Fontenoy and Laffeldt, 359, 470.
Bullock, recruits for Irish Brigade sail from, at night, 160-161.
Bully, Captain of the *Sheerness*, takes a party of the Irish Brigade, &c., at sea to join Prince Charles, 396.
Burgoyne, Lieutenant-General, his surrender in America beneficial to Catholics in Ireland, 614.
Bussy, the enemy of Count Lally in India, and subsequently in France, 517-518, 520-521, 528-529, 538-539, 543-544, 568-570.
Butler, family of Norman origin in Ireland, ennobled, and otherwise eminent, in several branches, 149. Statement of Lafayette respecting that name, 150.
Byron, Admiral, beaten at sea by French in West Indies, 620-621.

CALCINATO, defeat of Imperialists at, by Duke of Vendome, where Irish present, 240.
Camerons, among earliest supporters of Prince Charles, 380. Soonest in Edinburgh, after routing of Cope, with captured flags of his dragoons, 392. Their chief, Lochiel, undeceives English, as to Highlanders being *cannibals*, 392. Jenny Cameron, mistress of Prince Charles, 401. Camerons, in front of Prince's left wing at Falkirk, relieved by piquets of Irish Brigade, &c., 425. At Culloden, break the Regiment of Barrell, and take its colours, and 2 pieces of cannon, 448, 450.
Camisards, or Huguenots of the Cevennes, religious persecution of, and war against, by French government, 219-220.
Campbell, General John, of Mamore, 4th Duke of Argyle, disgraceful charge against, by Captain O'Neill, 462.
Cantillon, Norman family of, settled at Ballyheigh, Co. Kerry, and highly connected in Ireland, till exiled for loyalty to Stuarts; intermarried with Bulkeley family in France, and bear title of Baron of Ballyheigh there, 37-38. Glorious death of Captain James Cantillon at Malplaquet, 268-269. Bravery of his son, Chevalier Thomas de Cantillon, at Laffeldt, 470.
Carabiniers, distinguished French corps of, saved at Luzzara, by Irish Regiment of Albemarle, 218. Kill some of Irish Brigade, by mistake, at Fontenoy, 358-359.
Carangoly, good defence of, by an Irish officer, O'Kennelly, of Regiment of Lally, 538.
Carleton, Captain George, his Memoirs cited, as undoubtedly authentic, 242, 246, 250.
Carlisle, cowardly surrender of, by English militia, to Prince Charles, 388, 389, 414, 419.
Carrickfergus, captured by Thurot, 589-591.
Carthagena, Count O'Mahony made Governor of, by Philip V., 243.
Cassano, battle of, where Irish under Duke of Vendome very distinguished, and proportionably eulogized by him, 233, 234.
Castalla, battle of, gallant act of Captain Waldron of 27th or Enniskillen Foot there, 358.
Castelar, brigade of Irish infantry of, in Spanish service, praised at Saragossa and Villaviciosa, 275, 278.
Castiglione, victory of, greatly owing to General Arthur Dillon, 240.
Catholics of Ireland, well governed by, and corresponding supporters of, James II., against the Revolution, 3-7. Public faith broken with them, under Revolution, by substitution of a persecuting, impoverishing, and enslaving Penal

Code, for a fulfilment of the Treaty of Limerick, 158-160, 216, 217, 220, 246, 257, 258, 308, 341, 344, 355, 367, 368, 375, 376, 412, 413, 478, 502-505, 588, 598-601, 611, 612. A Stuart restoration thus long the *only* hope for Catholic liberation, 157, 158, 161, 163, 164, 193, 194, 216, 258, 259, 281, 282, 294-296, 318-320, 322, 414-418. Their obligations to France great, but fully repaid by their services to her, 608. The gradual relaxation and final removal of the yoke of Anglo-sectarian oppression imposed upon them, chiefly connected with the *necessity* for England's recruiting in Ireland against America and France, 608, 609, 613-616.

Catinat, Lieutenant-General, and afterwards Marshal de, appointed by Louis XIV. to command against Duke of Savoy, 54. Highly extols intrepidity of Irish under him at victory of Marsaglia, 177. Despatches 8 battalions of, against Vaudois, with great effect, 180. Rewards a party of, for its conduct against one of Barbets, 182. In reducing Ath, has the Regiment of Lee of 3 battalions, 186.

Cavalier, the gallant Camisard, or Huguenot, leader in the Cevennes, &c., 248.

Chalandreu, M. de, courage of Irish with, at Guillestre, 171.

Charlemont, infantry regiment of, 120, 131, 132, 142.

Charles of Austria, Archduke, claimant to Crown of Spain, set up by Allies, as Charles III., 145, 234, 235. Gets possession of Catalonia, &c., 240. And, through English naval aid, of Sardinia and Minorca, 262. His army gaining battle of Saragossa, he enters Madrid, but is badly received there, and has to quit it, 275-277. As Charles VI. of Austria, unnecessarily continues war against France, till beaten, and forced to make peace at Rastadt, 289-291. Unjustly imprisons his near relatives, the Princesses Sobieski, to obtain naval protection of George I. against Spain; exhibiting further meanness and tyranny, on the frustration of that imprisonment policy by success of Sir Charles Wogan's enterprise to Inspruck, and its result, in marriage of James III., 308-313. By combining with Russia to force a foreign or Saxon King on Poland, provokes war with France, 327, 328. Death of, occasions War of Austrian Succession, 332.

Charles Edward Stuart, Prince, birth and description of, 313, 339, 340. His 1st design of landing in Great Britain, with French aid, under Count, afterwards Marshal, Saxe, and with best prospects of support there, frustrated by the weather, 341-344. His 2nd enterprise, from his landing in Scotland till his return there from England, 368, 379-406. Sequel of that enterprise to his escape to France, 419-465. Additional allusions to him on the Continent, or in British Isles, 72, 370-374, 376-378, 414-417, 469, 473, 475, 505-507, 609, 610, 624. His death, &c., 631, 632.

Chesterfield, Lord, his review and praise, as Viceroy, of the Georgeite militia in Dublin, 413, 414. His complimentary verses at the Castle to "the dangerous Papist," of due political significance, 418.

Chiari, Irish, at repulse of French there, described as acting most bravely, 195, 196.

Clan or patriarchal system of society, traits of, in Ireland, 127-128, and among Highlanders of Scotland, 390, 449.

Clancarty, Donough Mac Carthy, Earl of, his extensive property, loyalty to James II., capture, imprisonment, and spoliation by Williamites, escape to France, appointment there by James to command of 1 of his Troops of Irish Horse-Guards, return to England, exile thence on a Williamite pension of £300 a year, and death abroad, 10, 11, 64-70. His son and successor, Earl Robert, in British navy, assisted by Duchess of Marlborough to recover his family property, but, illegally prevented doing so by the "ascendancy" legislature in Dublin, joins the Stuart cause in France, 70-72. Curious account of his mode of life and opinions there, 72-75. Remarkable interview with his friend Count Lally, *en route* for Paris, 569. Clancarty, infantry regiment of, 139-142.

Clan-Colla, conquerors of greater portion of Uladh, or Ulster, in 4th century; of whom Mac Donalds of Scotland a leading branch, 330-331, 449.

Clare, O'Briens, Viscounts of Clare and Earls of Thomond, connected with Jacobite cause in Ireland, or Irish Brigade in France, and infantry Regiment of Clare or O'Brien, 26, 27, 38-46.

Clement XI., Pope, (John Francis Albani) sends presents, by Duke of Berwick, for James II., his Queen, and the young Prince of Wales, (or James III.) at St. Germain, as well as a subscription for the exiled Irish Jacobites, 144. God-

father of Princess Sobieski, subsequently Queen of James III.; honours her Irish liberators from her Austro-Hanoverian captivity; and, to the last, a zealous friend and supporter of James, 313, 314.
Clifton, skirmish at, between English and Highlanders, 404, 405.
Clive, Lord, dishonourable, or untruthful, and, as an officer, unworthy to be compared with his Irish contemporary, Sir Eyre Coote, 536, 537, 545, 567.
Cockburne, Lieutenant-Colonel, English Governor of Isle of St. Eustache, or Eustacia, taken prisoner by the Chevalier O'Connor, of the Regiment of Walsh. Treated with noble liberality by the Marquis de Bouillé. That capture, by the Irish officer, the subject of a fine engraving in France, 625-627.
Comerford family, of note in Ireland from reign of King John, and subsequently in French and Spanish services, 275, 427.
Conflans, M. de, French Admiral, through a shifting of the wind, intercepted and defeated by English Admiral Hawke, whereby the landing from France, in Munster, of 25,000 men, including Irish Brigade, prevented, 585-587.
Cooke, Matthew, Lieutenant-General, and Matthew, Major-General, in service of France, memoirs of, 332 and 595.
Coote, Lieutenant-Colonel, afterwards Lieutenant-General, Sir Eyre Coote, son of Rev. Dr. Chidley Coote of Ash-Hill, County Limerick, appointed to command against French in Carnatic, 530, 535. His honourable career, from memorable Council of War before affair of Plassey, to surrender of Pondicherry, with other particulars respecting him, 536-567.
Cope, Lieutenant-General Sir John, Georgeite Commander-in-Chief in Scotland, out-manœuvred, and utterly routed by Jacobites at Preston-Pans, or Gladsmuir, 380-385.
Corsica, Irish serve with French there; most unjust or disgraceful subjugation of, by French; oppression of, by Genoa, like that of Ireland by England, &c., 375-376, 605-606.
Cox, Sir Richard, Judge, and author of *Hibernia Anglicana*, endeavours to subject *all* the Irish Catholics, or Jacobites, with estates, to confiscation, after battle of the Boyne; succeeds in procuring the landed proscription of Earl of Clancarty, of whose property and that of King James, he gets a portion; illegally imprisons for a year an Irish writer, Mac Curtin, for exposing his misrepresentations respecting the old Irish, previous to the Anglo-Norman intrusion; active in trying and hanging Irish engaged as recruits for Irish Brigade; and thus duly interested in Hanoverian succession, 67, 295, 296.
Creagh, family, respectable in Limerick for centuries, a branch of O'Neills of Tradry, County Clare; Sir Michael Creagh and his regiment of infantry in War of Revolution, afterwards that of Dublin, in France, &c., 132-135, 142. Captain (finally Major-General) James Creagh of Irish Brigade, at Fontenoy, 365.
Cremona, famous surprise of, by Prince Eugene, and his expulsion, after a contest of about 11 hours, *most* honourable to Irish there, 197-217.
Crimea, campaigns of Marshal Lacy in, 486-490.
Crofton, Henry, Colonel of Regiment of Irish Dragoons, in service of Philip V. of Spain, made Brigadier, for his bravery at Daroca, and soon after taken prisoner, but released, 242, 243. Distinguished, with his regiment, in routing Portuguese cavalry, at Marquis de Bay's victory over Anglo-Portuguese, for which created Major-General, 271-272. Transfers his regiment to Lord Kilmallock, 277. At Brihuega and Villaviciosa remarkable for his ardour against the English and Germans, 278. Further services of, in district of Cervera, against Carlist miquelet-leader Chover, &c., 283. Dies a Lieutenant-General in Spain, to the last a zealous Jacobite loyalist, 283.
Culloden, battle of, its ruinous antecedents for the Jacobites, 443-447. General account of the action, 447-452. Particulars respecting piquets of Irish Brigade there, 452-455.
Cumberland, Duke of, son of George II., commands Allies in Flanders, and breaks through French centre at Fontenoy, though finally defeated, 350-353, 356-359. Foiled between Shap and Penrith, and before Clifton, in attempting to cut off rear-guard of Highland army, retiring to Scotland, 403-405. In proceeding to recover Carlisle, from its little Jacobite garrison, with an irresistible force, indulges in unbecoming swagger and equivocation; and selects the barbarian Hawley there, to command for him in Scotland, 419-420. After Hawley's defeat at Falkirk, assumes that command, and relieves Stirling Castle, 431. Advances by Perth to Aberdeen, marking his route

644 INDEX.

with plunder and sacrilege, 433-434. Thence proceeds to engage Highland army at Culloden, with every advantage of numbers, condition, &c., on his side, and thus defeats them, 443-451. Acts very commendably towards piquets of Irish Brigade that surrender after the engagement, 453-456. Commanding Allies in Netherlands, is defeated by French at Laffeldt, and most probably saved, only by Sir John Ligonier, from being either killed or made prisoner there by Irish Brigade, 466-469. His defeat rejoiced at by Jacobites in Scotland, 473. His mortification at French capture of Bergen-op-Zoom, 475. Outgeneralled by Marshal Saxe, who consequently invests and takes Maestricht, 476-477. Breaks down most wretchedly in Germany, at Hastenbeck and Closter-Seven; is, on returning to England, received with corresponding displeasure by his father, George II.; and closes his professional career with a resignation of all his military posts, 579-581.

Cusack, family of French origin, established in Ireland under King John, attached to their country and religion, and proportionable sufferers, from reign of Elizabeth to Williamite revolution. Richard Edmond de, of Irish Brigade, Maréchal de Camp, Chevalier of St. Louis in France, and of St. Jago in Spain, &c., 606-608.

DANES aid England against Ireland, in 1690 and 1691, with 11 regiments, 189. Elsewhere mentioned, 218, 224, 226.
Darcy, Patrick, Count, Chevalier, Maréchal de Camp, &c., memoir of, 622-625.
Daroca, Irish distinguished at, 242, 243.
Davenant, English Envoy at Genoa, and Ensign Thomas Davenant, lies about Irish connected with, 314, 471, 472.
Derby, Highland army, under Prince Charles, arrives there, 391. Causes for retreat from, 398, 399.
D'Estaing, Count, in East Indies with Count Lally, 511, 518, 520. In West Indies and America with Irish, 617-622.
Dettingen, battle of, 333-335. George II. and the Black Horse there, 334, 367.
Devils, Irish remarked to fight like, 435, 469.
Dillon, family, and regiment of, in Irish Brigade, with successive Colonel-Proprietors of the name, 27, 28, 46-53. Other Dillons, 94, 212, 213, 215, 245, 618, 621.
Dorrington, William, Lieutenant-General, and his regiment, at first Royal Irish Foot Guards, 89-98.
Dragoons, à pied, or dismounted, 2 Irish regiments of, or King's and Queen's, in France, 61, 142. King's, 77, 84. Queen's, 84-89. Distinguished in Italy and Spain, at Marsaglia, the Ter, &c., 179-181, 185-187.
Drake, Captain Peter of Drakerath, County Meath, in Irish Brigade, Memoirs of cited, 77, 82, 188, 190, 237, 257, 258, 264, 265, 270.
Dromgold, Colonel, exposes Voltaire's gross injustice to Irish Brigade at Fontenoy, 360-361.
Dublin, regiment of, in France. (See Creagh.)
Dudenhoven, in Germany, Irish signalized at, 169-170.
Dunkeld, Lord, Brigadier, leads Irish Brigade at battle of Laffeldt, 468, 470.
Dunkirk, defence of, against Duke of York, by General of Brigade, O'Meara, 333.
Dutch, aid England against Ireland in 1689 with 2, in 1690 with 18, in 1691 with 15, regiments, 189. Large Williamite grants of Irish Jacobite estates to, 40, 67-69, 77, 87. Suffer by Irish at Blenheim and Ramillies, 227-229, 237. Troops, engaged to uphold Hanoverian dynasty in Britain, 302, 342, 388, 419, 420. Driven by England into war, and shamefully plundered at St. Eustache, 625. Honourably treated there by French as Allies, 628.

ENGLAND, in Ireland found so unjust, as to be considered only worthy of distrust, 119. (See further under Catholics of Ireland, and Irish Brigades.)
Enniskillen, unsuccessful expedition of Lord Mountcashel against, 12-21.
Eugene of Savoy, Prince, 170, 171, 195-214, 217-219, 224-234, 240, 244, 245, 259, 260, 263-266, 274, 285, 289-291, 328, 484.

FALKIRK, battle of, and good service of Irish piquets there, 424-427.
Fingal, Robert Plunkett, 6th Earl of, and Captain of Regiment of Berwick, in Irish Brigade, &c., 330-332.
Fitz-Gerald, family, of Continental origin, ennobled and powerful in Ireland, 116-119. Officers named, in Irish Brigade, 44, 45, 107, 108, 119, 120.

Fitz-James, Irish horse regiment of, 155, 333, 350, 352, 365, 396, 397, 425, 435-437, 445, 446, 452, 453, 456, 457, 466, 472, 579, 582, 583, 597, 598.
Fitz-Maurice, family, of Norman race and high rank in Ireland, of whom several officers in Irish Brigade, 38, 629.
Fontenoy, victory of French at, greatly owing to Irish Brigade, 350-367.
Friburgh, siege of, and Irish there, 289, 290.

GALMOY, PIERCE BUTLER, 3rd Lord, Lieutenant-General, and his 2 Irish regiments, of horse and of foot, 149-150, &c.
Gaydon, Chevalier Richard, Major of Regiment of Dillon, 1 of Princess Sobieski's liberators, 310-314. Major-General John, his brother, 322, 323.
Graebenstein, surprise of French at, fatal to Regiment of Fitz-James, 597, 598.
Grant, Irish officer of Regiment of Lally, Engineer, and Colonel of Artillery to Prince Charles, &c., 385, 386, 388, 401, 403, 429, 430.
Grattan, Henry, his description of the great prosperity in Ireland from Free Trade and Legislative Independence, 629, 630.
Guards, Irish Foot, regiment of. (See Dorrington.) Guards, Irish Horse, 2 Troops of, 61-76, 142. Distinguished against Germans in Flanders, 168, 169.

HAMILTONS, of Irish branch of house of Abercorn, brothers, in service of France and James II., 14-17, 33, 34, 183, 256.
Hanover, house of, majority of population of Great Britain and Ireland, long opposed to, 252, 254, 256, 299-300, 307, 317-319, 321-322, 341, 342, 604, 624.
Hanway, Captain, of *Milford*, takes some of Irish Brigade at sea, 396, 397.
Hawley, Lieutenant-General, Henry. (See Cumberland and Falkirk.)
Hochstedt, 1st battle of, or defeat of Imperialists by French, with high honour to Irish Brigade, especially Regiment of Clare, 222. (See, likewise, as 2nd battle of Hochstedt, Blenheim, and 234.)
Hooke, Nathaniel, Baron de, of Hooke Castle, County Waterford, Major-General, Commander of Order of St. Louis, &c., 329-330.

INDEPENDENT Companies, 3, of Jacobite army in France, 141, 142.
India, war between French and English there, 507-567.

JACOBITES, Irish, fidelity of, 28-32, 161, 162, 164, 189, 190, 193, 194. English, conduct of, very inferior to that of Scotch, 385, 393-395, 406, 632.
James II., his reception of Irish forces in France after Treaty of Limerick, 28-31. His restoration twice apparently prevented by weather, 165, 166, 183-185. His good-nature at St. Germain, 190. His death there, 192.
James Francis Edward Stuart, or James III., 2, 3, 157, 192-194, 216, 252-259, 261, 269, 270, 280-284, 286, 287, 293-314, 316-322, 324-327. (See, likewise, his son, Charles Edward, and 604, 605.)

KELLY, REV. GEORGE, Protestant Jacobite, Irish Stuart correspondent from England with Continent, and Secretary to Prince Charles, 369-371, 373, 380, 382, 385.
Keppel, Joost Van, created Earl of Albemarle by William III., granted all Lord Clare's estate, 40.
Kilmallock, Dominick Sarsfield, 4th Lord, Colonel of Infantry and Cavalry in Ireland, 1st Lieutenant of 2nd Troop of Irish Horse Guards, and Colonel of King's Regiment of Dismounted Dragoons in France, 82-84. David, 5th Lord, Governor of Badajos, and Colonel of Irish Regiment of Dragoons, killed at Villaviciosa, 277-279.
Knowles, Commodore, intercepts greater portion of Regiment of Fitz-James, &c., sailing to join Prince Charles in Scotland, 436, 437.

LACY, family, of Norman origin, in County Limerick, 178, 481. Field Marshal Count Peter, of Irish Brigade, and in service of Russia, 481-499.
Laffeldt, battle, defeat of Allies there, and bravery of Irish Brigade, 467-474.
La Hogue, battle, loss of prevents restoration of James II., 165, 166.
Lally, or O'Mullally, family of old Milesian origin, 345-346. Lieutenant-General Count, and regiment of, till Peace of 1748, 346-351, 353, 354, 356, 360, 364, 365, 396, 397, 437, 454, 465, 470, 471, 475-477. Till return from India to France, execution, and vindication of there, 505-579.
Landau, reduction of, and Irish at, 289, 290.
Landen, battle, defeat of William III., and gallantry of Irish there, 171-176.

646   INDEX.

Lawless, Sir Patrick, Lieutenant-General, Ambassador from Spain to England, and Agent to Queen Anne from her brother, 235, 286, 287.
Lee, Andrew, Lieutenant-General, Commander of Order of St. Louis, and his regiment, 33-35, 38, 39. Distinguished in Savoy, Germany, and Flanders, 56, 222, 224, 260, 261.
Lisle, gallant defence of, by Marshal de Boufflers, with Lieutenant-General Andrew Lee and other Irish, &c., 260, 261.
London, panics there, 258, 295, 399, 407, 408.
Lucan, Patrick Sarsfield, 1st Earl of, Major-General, memoir of, &c., 62-64, 165, 168, 174-176. His son, James Francis Edward, 2nd Earl, Knight of the Golden Fleece, and Captain of Body Guard to Philip V. of Spain, reformed Colonel to Irish Horse Regiment of Nugent in France, &c., 291, 292, 318-320.
Luttrell, family, of Norman origin, settled at Luttrell's-town, County Dublin, &c., 98-99. Simon, Privy Counsellor, Lord-Lieutenant, and M.P. for that County, Governor of City, and Colonel of Dragoons under King James in Ireland, and in France, Colonel of Queen's Regiment of Infantry, &c., 100-105.
Luxembourg, Marshal de, defeats William III. at Steinkirk and Landen, &c., 167-168, 171-172.
Luzzara, battle of, and Irish present, 217-219.
Lynch, Captain, at Cremona, 213-215. Dominick, Lieutenant-Colonel of Regiment of Lally, noted in Scotland and at Laffeldt, 471. Colonel en Second of Regiment of Walsh, and Lieutenant-General, 622.

MACARTNEY, GEORGE, Lord, Governor of Isle of Grenada, reduced by French and Irish, 617-619.
Mac Carthy. (See Clancarty, and Mountcashel.)
Mac Donagh, or Mac Donough, Sligo sept, and Clare branch, officers of, in Irish Brigade, 95-97, 210, 215, 357, 361, 366-367.
Mac Donald, clan of Scotland. (See Clan Colla.) Among earliest followers of Prince Charles, 380, 381. Bravery of, at Falkirk, 424, 425. Ruinous misconduct of, at Culloden, yet noble death of Alexander, Chieftain of Keppoch, there, 449, 450. Flora, adventures of, with Captain O'Neill and Prince Charles, 458, 459, 462, 463. Duke of Tarentum and Marshal of France, officer in Irish Brigade, 460.
Mac Donnell, of Mayo race, Francis, son of Henry, in Austrian service, capturer of Marshal de Villeroy at Cremona, &c., 200-202, 207-209.
Mac Elligot, Roger, of County Kerry, Colonel of Foot, in Ireland and France, &c., 139-141.
Macgennis, or Mac Guinness, sept of highest Ulster or Irian blood, represented in Irish Brigade, 330-332.
Mac Geoghegans, of Westmeath, various officers of, especially Chevalier Alexander, distinguished in India, 419, 420, 531-534, 559, 560.
Macguires, Barons of Enniskillen, and others of the name in Irish Brigade, 270.
Mac Sheehys, of Clan Colla origin, in Irish Brigade, 619, 620.
Mac Swiny, or Mac Sweeny, of Ulster race, Knights of St. Jago and St. Louis, 249.
Maestricht, reduction of, and Irish at, 477.
Malplaquet, battle of, and gallantry of Irish Brigade and James III. there, 263-270.
Marlborough, Duke of, 105, 140, 223-229, 235, 236, 243, 244, 259-261, 263-271, 274, 283-285, 289, 305.
Melazzo, in Sicily, defeat of Germans there by Irish, 320, 321.
Mountcashel, Justin Mac Carthy, Lord, commander of 1st Irish Brigade, &c., 7-24. His regiment, and services on Continent, 32, 33, 54-59, 176.

NUGENT, family, of Norman origin, ennobled, and numerous in Ireland. Christopher, of Dardistown, Major-General of Cavalry, and his Regiment of Horse, &c., 153-155. Chevalier, or Sir Peter, Baronet, Lieutenant-Colonel of Regiment of Fitz-James, and Lieutenant-General of Cavalry, 613. Chevalier Louis Francis, last officer, in France, of Irish Brigade, 638. (See, also, Westmeath.)

O'BEIRNE, Connaught sept, members of, distinguished abroad, 230, 243, 464.
O'Briens, 441, 465. (See Clare.)
O'Cahan, O'Kean, or O'Kane, Ulster sept and Clare branch, officers of, noticed in French and English services, 238, 266-268. Rory Dall, and James VI., 129.
O'Callaghans of Munster, in Spanish, French, and English services, 279, 280.

O'Carrolls of Ely, of honourable antiquity, and eminent for bravery at home and abroad, 84-86, 176-178, 217, 232, 234, 239, 242-243, 245, 249, 387, &c.

O'Connells, amongst oldest races in Kerry, officers of the name in France, 610-612. Major-General Count Daniel, &c., of Irish Brigade in French and British services, 634-638.

O'Crowleys, or O'Crolys, from Connaught, subsequently established at Kilshallow, County Cork, officers in France under Louis XIV., XV., and XVI., &c., 518, 519.

O'Donnells of Tir-Connell, celebrity of, &c., 108-113. Brigadier Daniel, in Irish Brigade, 113-115. Less noted clan of County Clare, 114. Hugh, or Ball-dearg, Earl of Tyrconnell, 180, 181, 183.

O'Driscoll, sept of Munster, of Ithian origin. Officers of, Stuart loyalists, plundered as such by Cromwellian and Williamite revolutionists, and distinguished, in Ireland, and on the Continent, 250, 251, 261.

O'Dunnes, of Iregan, Queen's County, chief officer of, in Irish Brigade, Humphrey, Lieutenant-Colonel and Commandant at Grenada, West Indies, &c., 618.

O'Dwyers, of Kilnamanagh, County Tipperary, officers in Jacobite war; in France, including several Chevaliers of St. Louis; in Austria, and in Russia, 248-249.

O'Farrells of Annaly, in War of Revolution, and Irish Brigade, &c., 63, 584.

O'Gara, sept of Connaught, connected with native literature, and Stuart loyalists. Oliver, Colonel of Infantry in Ireland under James II.; on Continent, Lieutenant-Colonel of King's Foot Guards, and Colonel of Queen's Dismounted Dragoons, &c., 86-88, 96, 242.

O'Kennedys, of Dalcassian race, &c., contribute officers and Chevaliers of St. Louis to several corps of the Brigade, 549, 550.

O'Mahony, family of Munster, of doubly royal origin, &c. Chief officer in French and Spanish services, Lieutenant-General Count Daniel, Commander of Order of St. Jago, 204, 205, 207, 208, 210-213, 215-217, 220, 221, 231, 232, 235, 241-243, 245, 247-251, 261, 262, 273, 275-278, 280, 283, 293.

O'Mearas, of Tipperary, in Irish Brigade. (See Dunkirk.)

O'Morans, of Roscommon, represented in Brigade. (See also Dunkirk.)

O'Murphys, of Wexford, officers of name, in Jacobite war, and Irish Brigade, of whom Lieutenant-Colonel of Regiment of Lally most noted, 519, 521, 545.

O'Neills, of Tirone, account of sept of, down to Brigadier Gordon, Colonel of Regiment of Charlemont in France, &c., 120-132, 323, 324. O'Neills, of Tradry, County Clare, of a different race, 132. Captain, the companion of Prince Charles and Flora MacDonald in Scotland, 388, 457-463.

Ormonde, James Butler, 2nd and last Duke of, head of the Jacobite party, 89, 175, 282-285, 299, 302-305, 316-322, 342, 344, 408-412.

O'Rourkes, of Brefny or Leitrim, in France, Spain, and Russia, 201, 250.

Orrery, Earl of, the treacherous Secretary for James III. in England, secret pensioner of Georgeite government, 309.

O'Shaughnessy, Major-General William, of Gort, County Galway, &c., 336, 337.

O'Shea, or Shee, sept of Iveragh in Kerry, till 12th century, &c. Captain, of Fitz-James's Regiment of Horse, with Prince Charles in Scotland, 437, 438, 452, 456, 611.

O'Sullivans, anciently of Tipperary, subsequently of Cork and Kerry, and distinguished abroad. Serjeant Joseph, of Irish Brigade, martyred Jacobite loyalist in 1715, at London, 374, 375. Colonel John, Adjutant-General and Quarter-Master General to Prince Charles in 1745 and 1746, &c., 375-332, 387, 388, 399-403, 426, 427, 432, 433, 439, 440, 446, 447, 452, 457, 458, 460, 461, 463, 465. Morty Ogé, death of, and lamentation for, 502, 503.

Oudenarde, defeat of French there, 259, 260.

PARKER, CAPTAIN, corrected, respecting Dorrington's (or Royal Irish) Regiment, at Malplaquet, &c., 267, 268, 297, 298.

Pego, success of Lieutenant-Colonel O'Driscoll there, 250, 251.

Permacoil, brave defence of, by Colonel O'Kennedy, 549, 550.

Peterborough, Lord, unscrupulous character and conduct of, 241, 242.

Philip V., King of Spain, 195, 234, 235, 241-243, 249, 262, 271, 272, 275-280, 283, 286, 291, 292, 303, 315, 316, 344.

Philipsburgh, reduction of, and Irish at, 328.

Poland. (See Lacy.)

Pondicherry, long resistance of, under Count Lally, 547-562.

Power, family of Norman origin, ennobled in Ireland, and officers named, there, and on Continent, 134, 135.

QUEEN of James II., a favourite of the Irish, &c., 261.

RAMILLIES, defeat of French, and gallantry of Regiment of Clare there, &c., 235-239.
Rosbach, victory of Prussians, and bravery of Regiment of Fitz-James at, &c., 581-584.
Roth, or Rothe, Kilkenny family of, Lieutenants-General Michael, and Charles Edward, and regiment of, 91-94.
Russia. (See Lacy.)

SARAGOSSA, battle of, and distinction of Count O'Mahony and other Irish there, 275, 276.
Sarsfield, Vicomte de, Lieutenant-General, his brother, Colonel of Regiment of Provence, and the Chevalier Edmund, Lieutenant-Colonel in Irish Brigade, 630, 631. (See, also, Kilmallock, and Lucan.)
Schellenberg, battle of, Major-General Andrew Lee distinguished there, &c., 223, 224.
Scotland. (See references under James III., his son, Prince Charles Edward, and Union.)
Seron, castle of, successes of its Irish garrison, 245, 249.
Sheldon, Dominick, Lieutenant-General, his Irish regiments, &c., 76, 152, 153, 620.
Sheridan, or O'Sheridan, family, origin of, Sir Thomas, Governor, &c., to Prince Charles, and Sir Michael, his Aide-de-Camp, &c., 369, 371-374, 382, 386, 388, 401, 427, 432, 457.
Ship, Lieutenant John, his experience of serving with, and character of, the Irish, as soldiers, 435, 436.
Shortall, Lieutenant-Colonel Thomas, of Regiment of Clare, and old Kilkenny family of, 595-597.
Sicily, preserved by Count O'Mahony for Philip V., 262, 273. (See, also, Melazzo.)
Skelton, Major-General Charles, and other Jacobite officers of that loyal name, 328, 329.
Smugglers in Ireland, 162, 465, 611, 612. In England, 402, 407, 421.
Sobieski family, connexion of, with Stuarts, 308-314.
Spire, battle of, defeat of Allies at, and bravery of Irish horse there, 221.
Stapleton, Brigadier Walter, commander of piquets from Irish Brigade with Prince Charles in Scotland, distinguished, and deceased there, 396, 397, 422, 424, 425, 427, 433, 435, 438, 452-455.
St. Christopher and St. Eustache, isles of. (See Bouillé.)
St. David, fort, reduced by Count Lally, 510-512.
St. George, fort, siege of, by Count Lally, 518-524.
St. Ruth, Lieutenant-General, successful campaign of, in Savoy, with French and Irish, 54-56.
Sweden. (See Lacy.)

TALBOT, BRIGADIER RICHARD, Colonel of Regiments of Limerick and Clare, 30, 116. Captain, of *Prince Charles*, with supplies for Scotland, 440-443.
Thurot, his expedition to land in Ulster, reduction of Carrickfergus, and death, 584, 585, 588-593.
Toulon, siege of, and Dillons distinguished at, 244, 245.
Tournay, sieges of, and Irish there, 263, 367, 368.
Trade and industry, *how* circumstanced under Anglo-sectarian legislation in Ireland, 417, 612.
Tyrconnell, William Talbot, 2nd Earl of, Aide-de-Camp to Duke of Orleans in Spain, 262. Richard Francis, 3rd Earl, Major-General and Ambassador from France to Prussia, 436, 499, 500.

UNION, Act of, in Scotland, carried by intimidation and corruption for Anglo-Whig objects, and long detested there, 252-257, 280, 282, 299, 302, 342, 380-382, 386, 422, 434.

VAUDOIS, serve, with Huguenots, against France, 170, 171, 176, 178, 180, 182.
Villaviciosa, decisive defeat of Allies at, and good service of Count O'Mahony, and Irish in general there, to Philip V. of Spain, 277-280.

WALSH-SERRANT, family, in France, origin of *variously* represented, and regiment of, 94-97.
Wandewash, English beaten out of, by French, under Chevalier Alexander Mac Geoghegan, of Irish Brigade, 530-534. Taken by Coote, 537, 538. Town retaken, fort besieged by Lally, and consequent battle there between him and Coote, 539-546.
Warren, Colonel, of Irish Brigade, in Scotland with Prince Charles, and conveys him back to France, 463, 464.
Wauchop, Brigadier John, and Colonel Francis, Scotch Jacobite officers in Ireland and on Continent, 105, 151, 152, 176-178.
Wellington, Duke of, his testimony respecting obligations of England to Irish Catholic recruits, 615, 616. (And see note, [*], 609.)
Westmeath, John Nugent, 5th Earl of, and Major-General, memoir of, 500, 501.
Whiteboys, victims of landlord oppression, 158, 159, 599, 600.
Wild-geese, flights of, or emigrations to join Irish Brigade, 162, 465, 502, 587, 588, 611.
Williams, George, sentence upon, at Wexford Assizes, in 1748, under Penal Code, for being *guilty* of becoming a Catholic, 478.
Winds, favourable to England, 165, 166, 184, 185, 303, 319, 343, 344, 395, 585.
Wogan, old family, of Rathcoffy, County Kildare, &c. Chevalier, or Sir Charles, his romantic career in England and on the Continent, 306-316.
Women, Irish, most prolific known, 85. Women, naked, on horseback, races of, for amusement of Duke of Cumberland's camp, 434.

XERXES and Hawley endeavour to slash courage into their soldiery, 429.

YANKEE and Yankee-Doodle explained, 614.
Ypres, convent of Irish Benedictine nuns at, where British colours, taken by Regiment of Clare at Ramillies, deposited, 237, 238.

ZINZENDORF, regiment of. (See Peterborough.)

www.ingramcontent.com/pod-product-compliance
Lightning Source LLC
Chambersburg PA
CBHW071428300426
44114CB00013B/1357